SAT®

Total Prep

2023

SAT® is a registered trademark of the College Board, which was not involved in the production of, and does not endorse, this product.

Editor-in-Chief

Alexandra Strelka, MA

Contributing Editors

Brandon Deason, MD; M. Dominic Eggert; Katy Haynicz-Smith, MA; J. Scott Mullison; Kathryn Sollenberger, MEd; Glen Stohr, JD

Special thanks to our faculty authors and reviewers:

Michael Cook; Christopher Cosci; Boris Dvorkin; John Evans; Jack Hayes; Rebecca Knauer; Jo L'Abbate; Bird Marathe; Karen McCulloch; Melissa McLaughlin; Gail Rivers; Anne Marie Salloum; Jason Selzer; Gordon Spector; Caroline Sykes; Bob Verini, MFA; Bonnie Wang; and Ethan Weber

Additional special thanks to the following:

Laura Aitcheson; Deborah Becak; Isaac Botier; Brian Carlidge; Paula L. Fleming, MA, MBA; Joanna Graham; Rebekah Hawthorne; Hannah Kelley; Rebecca Knauer; Abnia Loriston, MEd; Camellia Mukherjee; Kristin Murner, PhD; Michael Wolff; Amy Zarkos; and the countless others who made this project possible

SAT® is a registered trademark of the College Board, which was not involved in the production of, and does not endorse, this product.

This publication is designed to provide accurate information in regard to the subject matter covered as of its publication date, with the understanding that knowledge and best practice constantly evolve. The publisher is not engaged in rendering medical, legal, accounting, or other professional service. If medical or legal advice or other expert assistance is required, the services of a competent professional should be sought. This publication is not intended for use in clinical practice or the delivery of medical care. To the fullest extent of the law, neither the publisher nor the editors assume any liability for any injury and/or damage to persons or property arising out of or related to any use of the material contained in this book.

© 2022 by Kaplan, Inc.

Published by Kaplan Publishing, a division of Kaplan, Inc.
750 Third Avenue
New York, NY 10017

All rights reserved. The text of this publication, or any part thereof, may not be reproduced in any manner whatsoever without written permission from the publisher.

10 9 8 7 6 5 4 3 2 1

ISBN-13: 978-1-5062-8219-0

Kaplan Publishing print books are available at special quantity discounts to use for sales promotions, employee premiums, or educational purposes. For more information or to purchase books, please call the Simon & Schuster Special Sales department at 866-506-1949.

TABLE OF CONTENTS

How to Use This Book

This book is designed to help you score high on the SAT. We understand that your time is limited and that this book is hefty, but nobody expects you to read every word. Nor do we expect you to go in order. If you need more work on the Writing and Language section than on Math, for example, then feel free to skip over the math chapters. The most efficient way to use this book is to spend the most time on those areas that give you trouble, starting with those that are tested most often. If you're not sure, use the pretests we provide in each chapter to figure out how much time to spend on that material.

Chapter Organization

Most chapters start with a section called "How Much Do You Know?" that helps you get a sense of how comfortable you already are with the material in the chapter. Answers and explanations follow immediately in the "Check Your Work" section. Each lesson in a chapter starts with a question typical of the way the SAT tests a given topic and ends with a set of practice questions called "Try on Your Own." There is another practice set at the end of each chapter called "How Much Have You Learned?" to reinforce the concepts explained in the chapter. Answers and explanations for the "Try on Your Own" and "How Much Have You Learned?" sections are found at the end of each chapter for easy reference.

Each unit ends with a "Test Yourself" section of additional practice questions. Use these once you have completed an entire unit to gauge your progress.

Practice Tests

Kaplan's Practice Tests are just like the actual SAT. By taking a practice exam you will prepare yourself for the actual test-day experience. Two of your Practice Tests are included in this book and three more can be accessed online. See the "Online Resources" section below to learn how to access your online Practice Tests.

You're Already on Your Way

You already have many of the skills you'll need to excel on the SAT, but you'll need to adapt those skills to the structure of the exam. For example, you already know how to read. You've probably also created outlines for essays you've written in school. This book will teach you to adapt to the SAT by outlining a passage as you read it. It will also teach you to adapt your math skills to solve questions more efficiently, locate grammar issues quickly and confidently, and prioritize the topics that get tested the most.

SmartPoints®

Different topics are worth different numbers of points on the SAT because they show up more or less frequently in questions. By studying the information released by the College Board, Kaplan has been able to determine how often certain topics are likely to appear on the SAT, and therefore how many points these topics are worth on test day. If you master a given topic, you can expect to earn the corresponding number of SmartPoints on test day.

We have used a 600-point scale for SmartPoints because that's the number of points you can earn within the Math and Verbal subscores: the SAT scoring scale is 200–800, so there are $800 - 200 = 600$ points to be earned within each major section of the test. The breakdown of SmartPoints for Math, Reading, and Writing and Language are summarized in the following tables. Keep in mind that these values are approximate because testing administrations differ.

Math		
SmartPoints Category	**# of Points**	**Subcategories**
Linear Equations	110	Linear equations, linear graphs, word problems
Functions	105	Functions, graphs of functions, functions in word problems
Ratios, Proportions, and Percents	70	Setting up a proportion to solve for an unknown, unit conversion, calculating percent and percent change
Geometry	65	Triangles, circles, 3-dimensional figures
Quadratics	60	Quadratic equations, parabolas, modeling data, mixed systems of equations
Statistics and Probability	50	Descriptive statistics, probability, tables and charts, data samples
Systems of Linear Equations	45	Systems of equations, number of possible solutions
Inequalities	35	Inequalities, graphical representations of inequalities
Scatterplots	25	Scatterplots, lines of best fit, modeling data
Exponents, Radicals, Polynomials, and Radical Expressions	25	Exponents, radicals, polynomial operations, graphs of polynomials, modeling growth and decay, rational expressions/equations
Imaginary Numbers	5	Adding, subtracting, multiplying, and dividing complex numbers
Trigonometry	5	Sine, cosine, tangent
TOTAL	**600**	

Reading		
SmartPoints Category	**# of Points**	**Subcategories**
Inference Questions	90	Making deductions
Command of Evidence Questions	60	Citing evidence
Detail Questions	45	Finding details in the text
Vocab-in-Context Questions	45	Determining the meaning of a word as it is used in the passage
Function Questions	40	Explaining *why* the author included a certain detail
Global Questions	20	Determining central ideas and themes, summarizing
TOTAL	**300**	

Writing and Language		
SmartPoints Category	**# of Points**	**Subcategories**
Sentence Structure	85	Correcting run-ons and fragments, using correct conjunctions, punctuation
Development	85	Word choice, relevance, revising text
Agreement	60	Subject-verb agreement, verb tense, pronoun agreement, modifiers, idioms
Organization	40	Transitions, sentence placement
Conciseness	20	Avoiding wordiness and redundancy
Graphs	10	Drawing inferences from a graph included with a passage
TOTAL	**300**	

Online Resources

GO ONLINE

www.kaptest.com/ moreonline

To access the online resources that accompany this book, which include three full-length Practice Tests, 500 extra practice questions, and study planning guidance, follow the steps below:

1. Go to **kaptest.com/moreonline.**

2. Have this book available as you complete the on-screen instructions. Then, whenever you want to use your online resources, go to **kaptest.com/login** and sign in using the email address and password you used to register your book.

Are You Registered for the SAT?

Kaplan cannot register you for the official SAT. If you have not already registered for the upcoming SAT, talk to your high school guidance counselor or visit the College Board's website at www.collegeboard.org to register online and for information on registration deadlines, test sites, accommodations for students with disabilities, and fees.

Don't Forget Your Strengths

As your test date approaches, shift your practice to your strengths. Let's say you're good at geometry. You might not need the instructional text covering geometry in this book, but in the final week before your test date, you should still do a few geometry practice questions. Think about it: your strengths are your most reliable source of points on test day. Build that confidence in the final stretch. And just as if the SAT were an athletic event, get plenty of sleep in the days leading up to it.

Let's Get Started

Want to get a feel for the SAT before you start studying? Take one of the Practice Tests at the back of this book. Otherwise, start by identifying the sections of the test you think will give you the most trouble. Choose a high-yield topic and dig in. On test day, you'll be glad you did!

PART 1

The SAT and You

CHAPTER 1

Inside the SAT

LEARNING OBJECTIVES

After completing this chapter, you will be able to:

- Recall the timing and scope of each section in anticipation of section management
- State what the SAT scoring system means for you the test taker

SAT Structure

The SAT, like any standardized test, is predictable. The more comfortable you are with the test structure, the more confidently you will approach each question type, thus maximizing your score.

The SAT is 3 hours long (or 3 hours and 50 minutes long if you live in a state that requires the essay). The SAT is made up of mostly multiple-choice questions that test two subject areas: Evidence-Based Reading and Writing, and Math. The former is broken into a Reading Test and a Writing and Language Test.

Test	Allotted Time (minutes)	Question Count
Reading	65	52
Writing and Language	35	44
Math	80	58
Essay (only in certain states)	50	1
Total	180 OR 230 (w/Essay)	154 OR 155 (w/Essay)

You may also see an additional 20-minute multiple-choice section, but this is fairly rare.

SAT Scoring

You will receive one score ranging from 200–800 for Evidence-Based Reading and Writing and another for Math. Your overall SAT score will range from 400–1600 and is calculated by adding these two scores together. If your state requires the Essay as part of SAT School Day administrations, you will receive a separate score for it.

In addition to your overall scores, you will receive subscores that provide a deeper analysis of your SAT performance. The SAT also gives you a percentile ranking, which allows you to compare your scores with those of other test takers. For example, a student who scored in the 63rd percentile did better than 63 percent of all others who took that test.

The scores you need depend primarily on which colleges you are planning to apply to. For example, if you want to attend an engineering school, you'll typically need a higher math score than if you want to attend a liberal arts college. Research the colleges you are interested in, find out what scores they require, and structure your SAT studying accordingly.

How to Maximize Your Score

You'll find advice on test-taking strategies below and in the section management chapters at the end of the Math, Reading, and Writing and Language sections of this book. In addition, read the instructional text for those topics you feel weak in and work your way through the practice questions. There are hundreds of them in this book, and they are very similar to those that you will see on test day. Practice will not only improve your skills; it will also raise your confidence, and that's very important to test-day success. Remember, you can use this book in any order you like, and you don't need to use all of it. Prioritize high-yield topics.

Where and When to Take the SAT

The SAT is offered every year on multiple Saturday test dates. Typically, exams are offered in August, October, November, December, March, May, and June. You can take the SAT multiple times. Some states offer special administrations of the SAT on different dates. Sunday tests are available by request for students requiring religious or other exemptions. The SAT is administered at high schools around the country that serve as testing centers. Your high school may or may not be a testing center. Check www.collegeboard.org for a list of testing centers near you. Note that you must register for the SAT approximately one month in advance to avoid paying a late fee. Some SAT test dates also offer SAT Subject Tests. You may not take both the SAT and the Subject Tests in a single sitting.

Digital Testing

Digital testing for the SAT is currently offered at a few testing centers. It will be more widely available in the future, and some testing centers may adopt digital testing while others retain the traditional paper/pencil format. Check the College Board website for updates on computer-based testing. We will also post updates in the online resources for this book as new information becomes available.

The SAT Math Test

The SAT Math Test is broken down into a calculator section and a no-calculator section. Questions across the sections consist of multiple-choice, student-produced response (Grid-in), and more comprehensive multi-part question sets.

	No-Calculator Section	Calculator Section	Total
Duration (minutes)	25	55	80
Multiple-Choice	15	30	45
Grid-in	5	8	13
Total Questions	20	38	58

The SAT Math Test is divided into four content areas: Heart of Algebra, Problem Solving and Data Analysis, Passport to Advanced Math, and Additional Topics in Math.

SAT Math Test Content Area Distribution	
Heart of Algebra (19 questions)	Analyzing and solving equations and systems of equations; creating expressions, equations, and inequalities to represent relationships between quantities and to solve problems; rearranging and interpreting formulas
Problem Solving and Data Analysis (17 questions)	Creating and analyzing relationships using ratios, proportions, percentages, and units; describing relationships shown graphically; summarizing qualitative and quantitative data
Passport to Advanced Math (16 questions)	Using function notation; creating, analyzing, and solving quadratic and higher-order equations; manipulating polynomials to solve problems
Additional Topics in Math (6 questions)	Making area and volume calculations in context; investigating lines, angles, triangles, and circles using theorems; working with trigonometric functions and complex numbers

A few Math questions might look like something you'd expect to see on a science or history test. These "crossover" questions are designed to test your ability to use math in real-world scenarios. There are a total of 18 "crossover" questions that will contribute to subscores that span multiple tests. Nine of the questions will contribute to the Analysis in Science subscore, and nine will contribute to the Analysis in History/Social Studies subscore.

The SAT Reading Test

The SAT Reading Test will focus on your comprehension and reasoning skills when you are presented with challenging extended prose passages taken from a variety of content areas.

SAT Reading Test Overview	
Timing	65 minutes
Questions	52 passage-based, multiple-choice questions
Passages	4 single passages; 1 set of paired passages
Passage Length	500–750 words per passage or passage set

Passages will draw from U.S. and World Literature, History/Social Studies, and Science. One set of History/Social Studies or Science passages will be paired. History/Social Studies and Science passages can also be accompanied by graphical representations of data such as charts, graphs, tables, and so on.

Reading Test Passage Types	
U.S. and World Literature	1 passage with 10 questions
History/Social Studies	2 passages or 1 passage and 1 paired-passage set with 10–11 questions each
Science	2 passages or 1 passage and 1 paired-passage set with 10–11 questions each

The multiple-choice questions for each passage will be arranged with main idea questions at the beginning of the set so that you can consider the entire passage before answering questions about details.

Skills Tested by Reading Test Questions	
Reading for Detail	Finding details in the passage, citing textual evidence
Summarizing	Determining central ideas and themes, understanding how a passage is structured, understanding relationships
Drawing Inferences	Understanding relationships, drawing conclusions from facts stated in a passage, interpreting words and phrases in context
Rhetorical Analysis	Analyzing word choice, analyzing point of view, determining why a fact is included, analyzing arguments
Synthesis	Analyzing multiple texts, analyzing quantitative information

The SAT Writing and Language Test

The SAT Writing and Language Test will focus on your ability to revise and edit text from a range of content areas.

SAT Writing and Language Test Overview	
Timing	35 minutes
Questions	44 passage-based, multiple-choice questions
Passages	4 single passages with 11 questions each
Passage Length	400–450 words per passage

The SAT Writing and Language Test will contain four single passages, one from each of the following subject areas: Careers, Humanities, History/Social Studies, and Science.

Writing and Language Passage Types	
Careers	Hot topics in "major fields of work" such as information technology and health care
Humanities	Texts about literature, art, history, music, and philosophy pertaining to human culture
History/ Social Studies	Discussion of historical or social sciences topics such as anthropology, communication studies, economics, education, human geography, law, linguistics, political science, psychology, and sociology
Science	Exploration of concepts, findings, and discoveries in the natural sciences including Earth science, biology, chemistry, and physics

Passages will also vary in the "type" of text. A passage can be an argument, an informative or explanatory text, or a nonfiction narrative.

Writing and Language Passage Text Type Distribution	
Argument	1–2 passages
Informative/Explanatory Text	1–2 passages
Nonfiction Narrative	1 passage

Some passages and/or questions will refer to one or more data tables or charts. Questions associated with these graphics will ask you to revise and edit the passage based on the data presented in the graphic.

The most prevalent question format on the SAT Writing and Language Test will ask you to choose the best of three alternatives to an underlined portion of the passage or to decide that the current version is the best option. You will be asked to improve the development, organization, and diction in the passages to ensure they conform to conventional standards of English grammar, usage, and style.

Skills Tested by Writing and Language Test Questions	
Expression of Ideas (24 questions)	Organization and development of ideas
Standard English Conventions (20 questions)	Sentence structure, conventions of usage, and conventions of punctuation

The SAT Essay (Required in Certain States)

The College Board has announced that the SAT Essay is being discontinued after the June 5, 2021, test date except in states where it is required as part of SAT School Day administrations. Students testing on a school day should check with their school to learn whether the Essay will be included.

If you do have to write the Essay, see chapter 28 for details.

Test-Taking Strategies

You have already learned about the overall structure of the SAT as well as the structure of the three main areas it entails: Reading, Writing and Language, and Math. The strategies outlined in this section can be applied to any of these tests.

The SAT is different from the tests you are used to taking in school. The good news is that you can use the SAT's particular structure to your advantage.

For example, on a test given in school, you probably go through the questions in order. You spend more time on the harder questions than on the easier ones because harder questions are usually worth more points. You also probably show your work because your teacher tells you that how you approach a question is as important as getting the correct answer.

This approach is not optimal for the SAT. On the SAT, you benefit from moving around within a section if you come across tough questions, because the harder questions are worth the same number of points as the easier questions. Similarly, showing your work is unimportant. It doesn't matter how you arrive at the correct answer—only that you bubble in the correct answer choice.

Strategy #1: Triaging the Test

You do not need to complete questions on the SAT in order. Every student has different strengths and should attack the test with those strengths in mind. Your main objective on the SAT should be to score as many points as you can. While approaching questions out of order may seem counterintuitive, it is a surefire way to achieve your best score.

Just remember, you can skip around within each section, but you cannot work on a section other than the one you've been instructed to work on.

To triage a section effectively, do the following:

- First, work through all the easy questions that you can do quickly. Skip questions that are hard or time-consuming. For the Reading Test, start with the passage you find most manageable and work toward the one you find most challenging. You do not need to go in order.
- Second, work through the questions that are doable but time-consuming.
- Third, work through the hard questions.

A Letter of the Day is an answer choice letter (A, B, C, or D) that you choose before test day to select for questions you guess on.

Strategy #2: Elimination

Even though there is no wrong-answer penalty on the SAT, Elimination is still a crucial strategy. If you can determine that one or more answer choices are definitely incorrect, you can increase your chances of getting the right answer by paring the selection down.

To eliminate answer choices, do the following:

- Read each answer choice.
- Cross out the answer choices that are incorrect.
- There is no wrong-answer penalty, so take your best guess.

Strategy #3: Strategic Guessing

Each multiple-choice question on the SAT has four answer choices and no wrong-answer penalty. That means if you have no idea how to approach a question, you have a 25 percent chance of randomly choosing the correct answer. Even though there's a 75 percent chance of selecting the incorrect answer, you won't lose any points for doing so. The worst that can happen on the SAT is that you'll earn zero points on a question, which means you should *always* at least take a guess, even when you have no idea what to do.

When guessing on a question, do the following:

- Try to strategically eliminate answer choices before guessing.
- If you run out of time, or have no idea what a question is asking, pick a Letter of the Day.
- If a question is taking too long, skip it and guess. Spend your time on those questions that you know how to do; don't allow yourself to get bogged down in fighting it out with a question that is too time-consuming.

PART 2

SAT Math

CHAPTER 2

Prerequisite Skills and Calculator Use

LEARNING OBJECTIVES

After completing this chapter, you will be able to:

- Identify skills necessary to obtain the full benefits of the Math sections of this book
- Use efficiency tips to boost your test-day speed
- Distinguish between questions that need a calculator and questions in which manual calculations are more efficient

Math Fundamentals

LEARNING OBJECTIVES

After this lesson, you will be able to:

- Identify skills necessary to obtain the full benefits of the Math sections of this book
- Use efficiency tips to boost your test-day speed

Prerequisites

This book focuses on the skills that are tested on the SAT. It assumes a working knowledge of arithmetic, algebra, and geometry. Before you dive into the subsequent chapters where you'll try testlike questions, there are a number of concepts—ranging from basic arithmetic to geometry—that you should master. The following sections contain a brief review of these concepts.

Algebra and Arithmetic

Order of operations is one of the most fundamental of all arithmetic rules. A well-known mnemonic device for remembering this order is PEMDAS: Please Excuse My Dear Aunt Sally. This translates to Parentheses, Exponents, Multiplication/Division, Addition/Subtraction. Perform multiplication and division from left to right (even if it means division before multiplication) and treat addition and subtraction the same way:

$$(14 - 4 \div 2)^2 - 3 + (2 - 1)$$
$$= (14 - 2)^2 - 3 + (1)$$
$$= 12^2 - 3 + 1$$
$$= 144 - 3 + 1$$
$$= 141 + 1$$
$$= 142$$

Three basic properties of number (and variable) manipulation—commutative, associative, and distributive—will assist you with algebra on test day:

- **Commutative:** Numbers can swap places and still provide the same mathematical result. This is valid only for addition and multiplication:

$$a + b = b + a \rightarrow 3 + 4 = 4 + 3$$
$$a \times b = b \times a \rightarrow 3 \times 4 = 4 \times 3$$

BUT: $3 - 4 \neq 4 - 3$ and $3 \div 4 \neq 4 \div 3$

- **Associative:** Different number groupings will provide the same mathematical result. This is valid only for addition and multiplication:

$$(a + b) + c = a + (b + c) \rightarrow (4 + 5) + 6 = 4 + (5 + 6)$$
$$(a \times b) \times c = a \times (b \times c) \rightarrow (4 \times 5) \times 6 = 4 \times (5 \times 6)$$

BUT: $(4 - 5) - 6 \neq 4 - (5 - 6)$ and $(4 \div 5) \div 6 \neq 4 \div (5 \div 6)$

- **Distributive:** A number that is multiplied by the sum or difference of two other numbers can be rewritten as the first number multiplied by the two others individually. This does *not* work with division:

$$a(b + c) = ab + ac \rightarrow 6(x + 3) = 6x + 6(3)$$
$$a(b - c) = ab - ac \rightarrow 3(y - 2) = 3y + 3(-2)$$

BUT: $12 \div (6 + 2) \neq 12 \div 6 + 12 \div 2$

Note: When subtracting an expression in parentheses, such as in $4 - (x + 3)$, distribute the negative sign outside the parentheses first: $4 + (-x - 3) \rightarrow 1 - x$.

Subtracting a positive number is the same as adding its negative. Likewise, subtracting a negative number is the same as adding its positive:

$$r - s = r + (-s) \rightarrow 22 - 15 = 7 \text{ and } 22 + (-15) = 7$$
$$r - (-s) = r + s \rightarrow 22 - (-15) = 37 \text{ and } 22 + 15 = 37$$

You should be comfortable manipulating both proper and improper fractions:

- To add and subtract fractions, first find a common denominator, then add the numerators together:

$$\frac{2}{3} + \frac{5}{4} \rightarrow \left(\frac{2}{3} \times \frac{4}{4}\right) + \left(\frac{5}{4} \times \frac{3}{3}\right) = \frac{8}{12} + \frac{15}{12} = \frac{23}{12}$$

- Multiplying fractions is straightforward: multiply the numerators together, then repeat for the denominators. Cancel when possible to simplify the answer:

$$\frac{5}{8} \times \frac{8}{3} = \frac{5}{\cancel{8}_1} \times \frac{\cancel{8}^1}{3} = \frac{5 \times 1}{1 \times 3} = \frac{5}{3}$$

- Dividing by a fraction is the same as multiplying by its reciprocal. Once you've rewritten a division problem as multiplication, follow the rules for fraction multiplication to simplify:

$$\frac{3}{4} \div \frac{3}{2} = \frac{\cancel{3}^1}{\cancel{4}_2} \times \frac{\cancel{2}^1}{\cancel{3}_1} = \frac{1 \times 1}{2 \times 1} = \frac{1}{2}$$

Absolute value means the distance a number is from 0 on a number line. Because absolute value is a distance, it is always positive or 0. Absolute value can *never* be negative:

$$|-17| = 17, |21| = 21, |0| = 0$$

Whatever you do to one side of an equation, you must do to the other. For instance, if you multiply one side by 3, you must multiply the other side by 3 as well.

The ability to solve straightforward one-variable equations is critical on the SAT. For example:

$$\frac{4x}{5} - 2 = 10$$

$$\frac{4x}{5} = 12$$

$$\frac{5}{4} \times \frac{4x}{5} = 12 \times \frac{5}{4}$$

$$x = 15$$

Note: $\frac{4x}{5}$ is the same as $\frac{4}{5}x$. You could see either form on the SAT.

You will encounter **irrational numbers**, such as common radicals and π, on test day. You can carry an irrational number through your calculations as you would a variable (e.g., $4 \times \sqrt{2} = 4\sqrt{2}$). Only convert to a decimal when you have finished any intermediate steps and when the question asks you to provide an *approximate* value.

Mental Math

Even if you're a math whiz, you need to adjust your thought process in terms of the SAT to give yourself the biggest advantage you can. Knowing a few extra things will boost your speed on test day:

- Don't abuse your calculator by using it to determine something as simple as $15 \div 3$ (we've seen it many times). Besides, what if you're in the middle of the no-calculator section? Save time on test day by reviewing multiplication tables. At a bare minimum, work up through the 10s. If you know them through 12 or 15, that's even better!

- You can save a few seconds of number crunching by memorizing **perfect squares**. Knowing perfect squares through 10 is a good start; go for 15 or even 20 if you can.

- **Percent** means "out of a hundred." For example, $27\% = \frac{27}{100}$. You can write percents as decimals, for example, $27\% = 0.27$.

- The ability to recognize a few simple fractions masquerading in decimal or percent form will save you time on test day, as you won't have to turn to your calculator to convert them. Memorize the content of the following table.

Fraction	Decimal	Percent
$\frac{1}{10}$	0.1	10%
$\frac{1}{5}$	0.2	20%
$\frac{1}{4}$	0.25	25%
$\frac{1}{3}$	0.333$\overline{3}$	33.3$\overline{3}$%
$\frac{1}{2}$	0.5	50%
$\frac{3}{4}$	0.75	75%

Tip: If you don't have the decimal (or percent) form of a multiple of one of the fractions shown in the table memorized, such as $\frac{2}{5}$, just take the fraction with the corresponding denominator ($\frac{1}{5}$ in this case), convert to a decimal (0.2), and multiply by the numerator of the desired fraction to get its decimal equivalent:

$$\frac{2}{5} = \frac{1}{5} \times 2 = 0.2 \times 2 = 0.4 = 40\%$$

Graphing

- Basic two-dimensional graphing is performed on a **coordinate plane**. There are two **axes**, *x* and *y*, that meet at a central point called the **origin**. Each axis has both positive and negative values that extend outward from the origin at evenly spaced intervals. The axes divide the space into four sections called **quadrants**, which are labeled I, II, III, and IV. Quadrant I is always the upper-right section and the rest follow counterclockwise, as shown below:

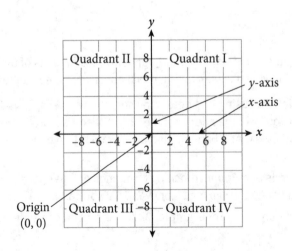

K

- To plot points on the coordinate plane, you need their coordinates. The **x-coordinate** is where the point falls along the x-axis, and the **y-coordinate** is where the point falls along the y-axis. The two coordinates together make an **ordered pair** written as (x, y). When writing ordered pairs, the x-coordinate is always listed first (think alphabetical order). Four points are plotted in the following figure as examples:

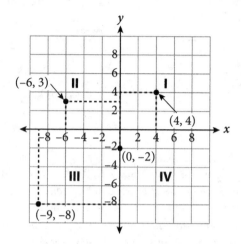

- When two points are vertically or horizontally aligned, calculating the distance between them is easy. For a horizontal distance, only the x-value changes; for a vertical distance, only the y-value changes. Take the positive difference of the x-coordinates (or y-coordinates) to determine the distance—that is, subtract the smaller number from the larger number so that the difference is positive. Two examples are presented here:

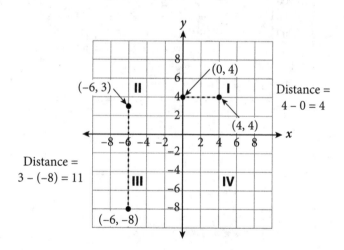

- Two-variable equations have an **independent variable** (input) and a **dependent variable** (output). The dependent variable (often y), depends on the independent variable (often x). For example, in the equation $y = 3x + 4$, x is the independent variable; any y-value depends on what you plug in for x. You can construct a table of values for the equation, which can then be plotted as shown on the next page.

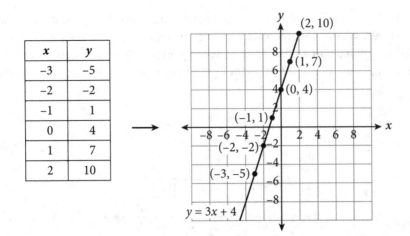

x	y
−3	−5
−2	−2
−1	1
0	4
1	7
2	10

- You may be asked to infer relationships from graphs. In the first of the following graphs, the two variables are year and population. Clearly, the year does not depend on how many people live in the town; rather, the population increases over time and thus depends on the year. In the second graph, you can infer that plant height depends on the amount of rain; thus, rainfall is the independent variable. Note that the independent variable for the second graph is the vertical axis; this can happen with certain nonstandard graphs. On the standard coordinate plane, however, the independent variable is always plotted on the horizontal axis as shown below:

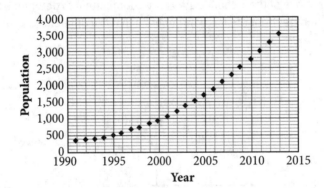

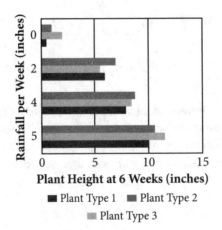

- When two straight lines are graphed simultaneously, one of three possible scenarios will occur:
  - The lines will not intersect at all (no solution).
  - The lines will intersect at one point (one solution).
  - The lines will lie on top of each other (infinitely many solutions).

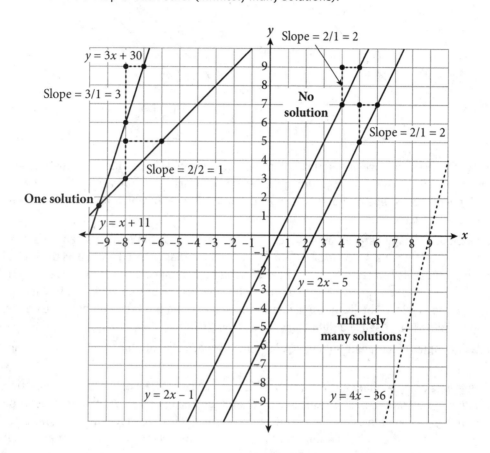

Geometry

- **Adjacent angles** can be added to find the measure of a larger angle. The following diagram demonstrates this:

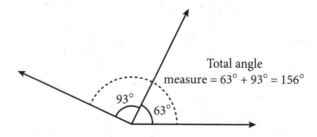

- Two angles that sum to 90° are called **complementary angles**. Two angles that sum to 180° are called **supplementary angles**.

- Two distinct lines in a plane will either intersect at one point or extend indefinitely without intersecting. If two lines intersect at a right angle (90°), they are **perpendicular** and are denoted with ⊥. If the lines never intersect, they are **parallel** and are denoted with ||:

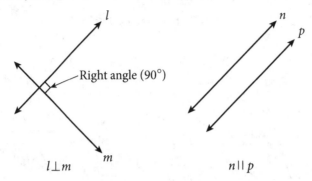

- **Perimeter** and **area** are basic properties that all two-dimensional shapes have. The perimeter of a polygon can easily be calculated by adding the lengths of all its sides. Area is the amount of two-dimensional space a shape occupies. The most common shapes for which you'll need these two properties on test day are triangles, parallelograms, and circles.

- The **area (A) of a triangle** is given by $A = \frac{1}{2}bh$, where b is the base of the triangle and h is its height. The base and height are always perpendicular. Any side of a triangle can be used as the base; just make sure you use its corresponding height (a line segment perpendicular to the base, terminating in the opposite vertex). You can use a right triangle's two legs as the base and height, but in non-right triangles, if the height is not given, you'll need to draw it in (from the vertex of the angle opposite the base down to the base itself at a right angle) and compute it.

- The **interior angles** of a triangle sum to 180°. If you know any two interior angles, you can calculate the third.

- **Parallelograms** are quadrilaterals with two pairs of parallel sides. Rectangles and squares are subsets of parallelograms. You can find the **area of a parallelogram** using $A = bh$. As with triangles, you can use any side of a parallelogram as the base, and again, the height is perpendicular to the base. For a rectangle or square, use the side perpendicular to the base as the height. For any other parallelogram, the height (or enough information to find it) will be given.

- A circle's perimeter is known as its **circumference (C)** and is found using $C = 2\pi r$, where r is the **radius** (distance from the center of the circle to its edge). The **area of a circle** is given by $A = \pi r^2$. The strange symbol is the lowercase Greek letter pi (π, pronounced "pie"), which is approximately 3.14. As mentioned in the algebra section, you should carry π throughout your calculations without rounding unless instructed otherwise.

- A **tangent line**, shown below, touches a circle at exactly one point and is perpendicular to a circle's radius at the point of contact:

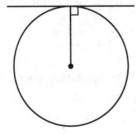

The presence of a right angle opens up the opportunity to draw otherwise hidden shapes, so pay special attention to tangents when they're mentioned.

- A shape is said to have **symmetry** when it can be split by a line (called an **axis of symmetry**) into two identical parts. Consider folding a shape along a line: if all sides and vertices align once the shape is folded in half, the shape is symmetrical about that line. Some shapes have no axis of symmetry, some have one, some have multiple axes, and still others can have infinite axes of symmetry (e.g., a circle):

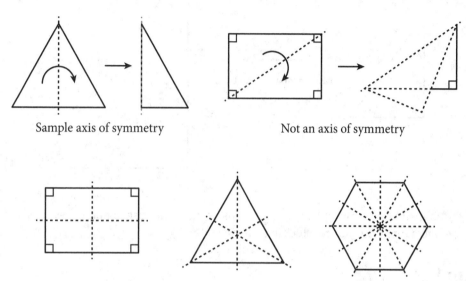

Sample axis of symmetry   Not an axis of symmetry

Sample shapes with corresponding axes of symmetry

- **Congruence** is simply a geometry term that means identical. Angles, lines, and shapes can be congruent. Congruence is indicated by using hash marks: everything with the same number of hash marks is congruent:

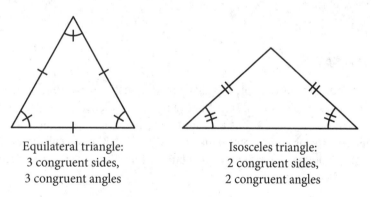

Equilateral triangle: Isosceles triangle:
3 congruent sides,   2 congruent sides,
3 congruent angles   2 congruent angles

- **Similarity** between shapes indicates that they have identical angles and proportional sides. Think of taking a shape and stretching or shrinking each side by the same ratio. The resulting shape will have the same angles as the original. While the sides will not be identical, they will be proportional:

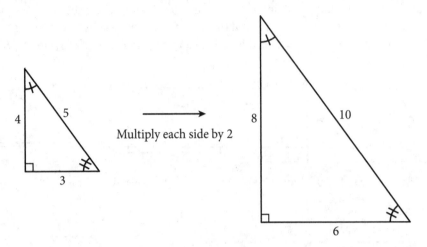

Multiply each side by 2

If you're comfortable with these concepts, read on for tips on calculator use. If not, review this lesson and remember to refer to it for help if you get stuck in a later chapter.

Calculator Use

LEARNING OBJECTIVE

After this lesson, you will be able to:

- Distinguish between questions that need a calculator and questions in which manual calculations are more efficient

Calculators and the SAT

Educators believe that calculators serve a role in solving Math questions, but they are sometimes concerned that students rely too heavily on calculators. They believe this dependence weakens students' overall ability to think mathematically. Therefore, the SAT has a policy on calculator use to promote the idea that students need to be able to analyze and solve math problems both with and without a calculator. The first Math section you see will require you to work without a calculator, while the second Math section will allow you to use one.

Many students never stop to ask whether using a calculator is the most efficient way to solve a problem. This chapter will show you how the strongest test takers use their calculators strategically; that is, they carefully evaluate when to use the calculator and when to skip it in favor of a more streamlined approach. As you will see, even though you can use a calculator, sometimes it's more beneficial to save your energy by approaching a question more strategically. Work smarter, not harder.

Which Calculator Should You Use?

The SAT allows four-function, scientific, and graphing calculators. No matter which calculator you choose, start practicing with it now. You don't want to waste valuable time on test day looking for the exponent button or figuring out how to correctly graph equations. Due to the wide range of math topics you'll encounter on test day, **we recommend using a graphing calculator**, such as the TI-83/84. If you don't already own one, see if you can borrow one from your school's math department or a local library.

A graphing calculator's capabilities extend well beyond what you'll need for the test, so don't worry about memorizing every function. The next few pages will cover which calculator functions you'll want to know how to use for the SAT. If you're not already familiar with your graphing calculator, you'll want to get the user manual; you can find this on the Internet by searching for your calculator's model number. Identify the calculator functions necessary to answer various SAT Math questions, then write down the directions for each to make a handy study sheet.

When Should You Use a Calculator?

Some SAT question types are designed based on the idea that students will do some or all of the work using a calculator. As a master test taker, you want to know what to look for so you can identify when calculator use is advantageous. Questions involving statistics, determining roots of complicated quadratic equations, and other topics are generally designed with calculator use in mind.

Other questions aren't intentionally designed to involve calculator use. Solving some with a calculator can save you time and energy, but you'll waste both if you go for the calculator on others. You will have to decide which method is best when you encounter the following topics:

- Long division and other extensive calculations
- Graphing quadratics
- Simplifying radicals and calculating roots
- Plane and coordinate geometry

Practicing **long computations** by hand and with the calculator will not only boost your focus and mental math prowess, but it will also help you determine whether it's faster to do the work for a given question by hand or reach for the calculator on test day.

Graphing quadratic equations may be a big reason you got that fancy calculator in the first place; it makes answering these questions a snap! This is definitely an area where you need to have an in-depth knowledge of your calculator's functions. The key to making these questions easy with the calculator is being meticulous when entering the equation.

Another stressful area for many students is **radicals**, especially when the answer choices are written as decimals. Those two elements are big red flags that trigger a reach for the calculator. Beware: not all graphing calculators have a built-in radical simplification function, so consider familiarizing yourself with this process.

Geometry can be a gray area for students when it comes to calculator use. Consider working by hand when dealing with angles and lines, specifically when filling in information on complementary, supplementary, and congruent angles. You should be able to work fluidly through those questions without using your calculator.

If you choose to use **trigonometric functions** to get to the answer on triangle questions, make sure you have your calculator set to degrees or radians as required by the question.

To Use or Not to Use?

A calculator is a double-edged sword on the SAT: using one can be an asset for verifying work if you struggle when doing math by hand, but turning to it for the simplest computations will cost you time that you could devote to more complex questions. Practice solving questions with and without a calculator to get a sense of your personal style as well as your strengths and weaknesses. Think critically about when a calculator saves you time and when mental math is faster. Use the exercises in this book to practice your calculations so that by the time test day arrives, you'll be in the habit of using your calculator as effectively as possible.

CHAPTER 3

The Method for SAT Math Questions

LEARNING OBJECTIVE

After completing this chapter, you will be able to:

- Efficiently apply the Math Method to SAT Math questions

How to Do SAT Math

SAT Math questions can seem more difficult than they actually are, especially when you are working under time pressure. The method we are about to describe will help you answer SAT questions, whether you are comfortable with the math content or not. This method is designed to give you the confidence you need to get the right answers on the SAT by helping you think through a question logically, one piece at a time.

Take a look at this question and take a minute to think about how you would attack it if you saw it on test day:

> Building M is an apartment building in city Z. According to data kept by the housing commission in city Z, 24 percent of the 150 apartments in building M have at least 3 bedrooms. There are 1,350 apartment buildings in city Z and the average number of apartments in those buildings is 150. If building M is representative of the apartment buildings in city Z, then which of the following is the best estimate of how many apartments in city Z have fewer than 3 bedrooms?

A) 48,600

B) 67,500

C) 153,900

D) 202,500

Many test takers will see a question like this and panic. Others will waste a great deal of time reading and rereading without a clear goal. You want to avoid both of those outcomes.

Start by defining clearly for yourself **what the question is actually asking**. What do the answer choices represent? In this question, they represent *the number of apartments in city Z that have fewer than 3 bedrooms.*

Next, **examine the information** that you have and organize it logically. The question asks about the number of apartments with fewer than 3 bedrooms. Okay, then what information do you have about number of bedrooms? You know that 24% of the 150 building M apartments have *at least 3* bedrooms. That's the opposite of *fewer than 3*. You can deduce that 100% − 24% = 76% of the 150 apartments in building M have *fewer than 3* bedrooms.

Now **make a strategic decision** about how to proceed. The answer choices are far apart, so you might consider rounding 76% to $\frac{3}{4}$ and estimating. However, this question appears on the calculator section, and it's a quick calculation. Let's say that you decide to use your calculator. Plug the numbers into your calculator and jot down what you know so far:

Fewer than 3 in building M: $0.76 \times 150 = 114$

The question asks for the number of apartments *in city Z* with fewer than 3 bedrooms, so hunt for information tying building M to city Z. You're told that the average number of apartments in city Z buildings is 150, which is identical to the number of apartments in building M, and that building M is "representative" of the apartment buildings in city Z. Translation: what is true for building M is also true for all apartment buildings in city Z. You also know that there are 1,350 apartment buildings in city Z. You can deduce that the number of apartments with fewer than 3 bedrooms in building M (114) times the total number of apartment buildings in city Z (1,350) will give you the number of apartments with fewer than 3 bedrooms in all of city Z. Plug that into your calculator:

$$114 \times 1,350 = 153,900$$

Finally, **confirm** that you answered the right question: you want the number of apartments in city Z with fewer than 3 bedrooms. Great! You're done; the correct answer is **(C)**.

Here are the steps of the method we just used:

The Method for SAT Math Questions	
Step 1.	State what the question is asking
Step 2.	Examine the given information
Step 3.	Choose your approach
Step 4.	Confirm that you answered the right question

You can think of these steps as a series of questions to ask yourself: What do they want? What are they giving me to work with? How should I approach this? Did I answer the right question?

Not all SAT Math questions will require time spent on all the steps. The question above, because it is a word problem, required a fair amount of analysis in steps 1 and 2, but choosing an approach (step 3) was straightforward; the calculations were quick to do on a calculator, so there was no need to estimate. Other questions will require very little thought in steps 1 and 2 but will benefit from a careful strategy decision in step 3. Step 4 is always quick, but you should always do it: just make sure you answered the question that was actually asked before you bubble in your response. Doing so will save you from speed mistakes on questions that you know how to do and should be getting credit for.

There are several approaches you can choose from in step 3: doing the traditional math, as we did in the question above; Picking Numbers; Backsolving; estimating; or taking a strategic guess. In the next two examples, you'll see Picking Numbers and Backsolving in action.

Here's another example. This one is not a word problem, so steps 1 and 2 require negligible mental energy, but pay attention when you get to step 3.

Which of the following is equivalent to the expression $\dfrac{8x-2}{x+1}$?

A) $8 - \dfrac{10}{x+1}$

B) $8 - \dfrac{2}{x+1}$

C) $8 + \dfrac{2}{x+1}$

D) $\dfrac{8-2}{1}$

Step 1: What do they want? An answer choice that is equal to $\dfrac{8x-2}{x+1}$.

Step 2: What do they give you? Only the expression $\dfrac{8x-2}{x+1}$.

Step 3: What approach will you use?

Here's where it gets interesting. The creator of this question may be expecting you to use polynomial long division to solve, and we'll cover that technique in chapter 11 because you may want to have it in your arsenal. But if you don't know how to do polynomial long division, there's no need to panic. You could use an alternate approach called **Picking Numbers** that will work just as well: choose a number to substitute for x in the question, then substitute the same number for x in the choices and see which one matches. Like this:

Pick a small number for x, say 2. When $x = 2$, the original expression becomes:

$$\frac{8x-2}{x+1} = \frac{8(2)-2}{2+1} = \frac{14}{3}$$

Now, plug $x = 2$ into the choices:

(A) $8 - \dfrac{10}{x+1} = 8 - \dfrac{10}{3} = \dfrac{24}{3} - \dfrac{10}{3} = \dfrac{14}{3}$

This is a match. It is always possible that another answer choice can produce the same result, so check the rest to be sure there isn't another match when $x = 2$. (If there is, go back and pick another number to distinguish between the choices that match.)

(B) $8 - \dfrac{2}{x+1} = 8 - \dfrac{2}{3} = \dfrac{24}{3} - \dfrac{2}{3} = \dfrac{22}{3}$

Eliminate (B).

(C) $8 + \dfrac{2}{x+1} = 8 + \dfrac{2}{3} = \dfrac{24}{3} + \dfrac{2}{3} = \dfrac{26}{3}$

Eliminate (C).

(D) $\dfrac{8-2}{1} = 6$

Eliminate (D).

Step 4: Did you solve for the right thing? You found the equivalent expression, so yes. Only **(A)** is a match, so it is the correct answer.

When picking numbers, use numbers that are **permissible** and **manageable**. That is, use numbers that are allowed by the stipulations of the question and that are easy to work with. In this question, you could have picked any real number because x was not defined as positive, negative, odd, even, a fraction, etc. A small positive integer is usually the best choice in this situation. In other questions, other kinds of numbers may be more manageable. For example, in percents questions, 100 is typically a smart number to pick.

Try one more:

Mr. Dvorkin is distributing colored markers to a group of children. If he gives each child 4 markers, he will have 3 markers left over. In order to give each child 5 markers, with no markers left over, he will need 17 additional markers. How many markers does Mr. Dvorkin have?

A) 55

B) 68

C) 83

D) 101

Step 1: What do they want? The number of markers.

Step 2: What do they give you? Two unknowns (the number of children and the number of markers) and sufficient information to set up a system of equations.

Step 3: What approach will you use? You could set up the system of equations, but it might be faster to use a technique called **Backsolving**: plug the choices in for the unknown and see which one works. Here, you need an answer choice that will leave a remainder of 3 when divided by 4. Choices (B) and (D) don't meet this condition, so the answer must be (A) or (C).

(A) If Mr. Dvorkin has 55 markers, and gives each child 4 markers, he will indeed have 3 markers left over, since $55 \div 4 = 13\,R3$. Now, what happens in the other situation? With an extra 17 markers, Mr. Dvorkin should be able to give each child exactly 5 markers. But $55 + 17 = 72$, which is not evenly divisible by 5. Eliminate (A).

You've now eliminated every choice but **(C)**, so it must be correct—you don't even need to test it! For the record:

(C) If Mr. Dvorkin has 83 markers and gives each child 4 markers, he will indeed have 3 left over, since $83 \div 4 = 20\,R3$. With an extra 17 markers, Mr. Dvorkin should be able to give each child exactly 5 markers, and this is in fact what happens: $83 + 17 = 100$, which is evenly divisible by 5.

Step 4: Did you solve for the right thing? The question asked for the number of markers. You found that 83 markers satisfies all conditions of the problem. Choose **(C)** and move on.

Although it wasn't the case in this question, when backsolving, it often makes sense to start with (B) or (C) in case you can tell from the context whether you'll need a larger or smaller answer choice if the one you're testing fails.

Now, it's your turn. Be deliberate with these questions. If there is analysis to do up front, do it. If there is more than one way to do a question, consider carefully before choosing your approach. And be sure to check whether you answered the right question. Forming good habits now, in slow and careful practice, will build your confidence for test day.

Try on Your Own

Directions: Take as much time as you need on these questions. Work carefully and methodically. There will be opportunities for timed practice in future chapters.

1. A cargo airplane has a maximum takeoff weight of 19,000 kilograms. The airplane, crew, and fuel have a combined weight of 14,750 kilograms. The airplane will be loaded with n identical cargo containers, each of which has a weight of 125 kilograms. What is the greatest value of n such that the airplane does not exceed its maximum takeoff weight?

    A) 28

    B) 34

    C) 118

    D) 152

2. A certain model of laptop computer is priced at $550 at a local electronics store. The same model laptop at an online retailer sells for $\frac{9}{10}$ of the electronics store's price. At a luxury department store, the same model laptop sells for $\frac{7}{5}$ of the electronics store's price. How many dollars more is the cost of the laptop at the luxury department store than at the online retailer?

    A) 198

    B) 220

    C) 275

    D) 495

3. A stack of 75 identical plastic plates forms a column approximately $9\frac{7}{8}$ inches tall. At this rate, which of the following is closest to the number of plates that would be needed to form a column 20 inches tall?

    A) 125

    B) 150

    C) 185

    D) 220

4. Last month, Kiera ran 22 more miles than Bianca did. If they ran a combined total of 86 miles, how many miles did Bianca run?

    A) 27

    B) 32

    C) 43

    D) 54

5. If $\frac{4x}{2y} = 4$, what is the value of $\frac{3y}{x}$?

    A) $\frac{3}{4}$

    B) $\frac{4}{3}$

    C) $\frac{3}{2}$

    D) 2

6.

x	2	4	6	8	10
y	$\frac{7}{5}$	$\frac{11}{5}$	$\frac{15}{5}$	$\frac{19}{5}$	$\frac{23}{5}$

Which of the following equations relates y to x according to the values shown in the table above?

A) $y = \left(\frac{2}{5}\right)^x - \frac{7}{5}$

B) $y = \left(\frac{3x}{5}\right)^2 - 2$

C) $y = \frac{5}{2}x - \frac{3}{5}$

D) $y = \frac{2}{5}x + \frac{3}{5}$

7. $n - \sqrt{c + 5} = 1$

    In the equation above, c is a constant. If $n = 5$, what is the value of c ?

    A) -1

    B) 0

    C) 3

    D) 11

8. At a child's lemonade stand, p pitchers of lemonade are made by adding m packets of lemonade mix to cold water. If $m = 2p + 4$, how many more packets of lemonade mix are needed to make each additional pitcher of lemonade?

    A) 0

    B) 1

    C) 2

    D) 4

9. A health club charges a one-time membership fee of $125 plus n dollars for each month. If a member pays $515 dollars for the first six months, including the membership fee, what is the value of n ?

    A) 55

    B) 65

    C) 75

    D) 85

10. If $x > 0$, which of the following is equivalent to $\dfrac{2}{\dfrac{1}{x + 6} + \dfrac{1}{x + 2}}$?

    A) $x^2 + 8x + 12$

    B) $\dfrac{x + 4}{x^2 + 8x + 12}$

    C) $2x + 8$

    D) $\dfrac{x^2 + 8x + 12}{x + 4}$

A Note about Grid-ins

You will see an occasional question without answer choices throughout the Math chapters of this book, starting in the next chapter. On the SAT, several of these Grid-in questions appear at the end of each Math section. Instead of bubbling in a letter, you'll enter your responses to these questions into a grid that looks like this:

If you are gridding a value that doesn't take up the whole grid, such as 50, you can enter it anywhere in the grid as long as the digits are consecutive; it doesn't matter which column you start in. Gridding mixed numbers and decimals requires some care. Anything to the left of the fraction bar will be read as the numerator of a fraction, so you must grid mixed numbers as improper fractions. For instance, say you want to grid the mixed fraction $5\frac{1}{2}$. If you enter 5 1/2 into the grid, your answer will be read as $\frac{51}{2}$. Instead, enter your response as 1 1/2, which will be read (correctly) as $\frac{11}{2}$. Alternatively, you could grid this answer as 5.5.

A repeating decimal can either be rounded or truncated, but it must be entered to as many decimal places as possible. This means it must fill the entire grid. For example, you can grid $\frac{1}{6}$ as .166 or .167 but not as .16 or .17.

Note that you cannot grid a minus sign or any value larger than 9,999, so if you get an answer that is negative or larger than 9,999 to a Grid-in question, you've made a mistake and should check your work.

Reflect

Directions: Take a few minutes to recall what you've learned and what you've been practicing in this chapter. Consider the following questions, jot down your best answer for each one, and then compare your reflections to the expert responses on the following page. Use your level of confidence to determine what to do next.

Think about your current habits when attacking SAT questions. Are you a strategic test taker? Do you take the time to think through what would be the fastest way to the answer?

_____

_____

_____

Do word problems give you trouble?

_____

_____

_____

What are the steps of the Method for SAT Math Questions, and why is each step important?

_____

_____

_____

Expert Responses

Think about your current habits when attacking SAT questions. Are you a strategic test taker? Do you take the time to think through what would be the fastest way to the answer?

If yes, good for you! If not, we recommend doing questions more than one way whenever possible as part of your SAT prep. If you can discover now, while you're still practicing, that Picking Numbers is faster for you on certain types of questions but not on others, you'll be that much more efficient on test day.

Do word problems give you trouble?

If word problems are difficult for you, get into the habit of taking an inventory, before you do any math, of what the question is asking for and what information you have.

What are the steps of the Method for SAT Math Questions, and why is each step important?

Here are the steps:

Step 1. *State what the question is asking*

Step 2. *Examine the given information*

(Taking an inventory is especially important in word problems.)

Step 3. *Choose your approach*

(Taking a moment to decide what approach will be the fastest way to the answer will ultimately save you time.)

Step 4. *Confirm that you answered the right question*

(Making sure you solved for the right thing will save you from losing points to speed mistakes on questions that you know how to do and should be getting credit for.)

Next Steps

If you answered most questions correctly in the "How Much Have You Learned?" section, and if your responses to the Reflect questions were similar to those of the SAT expert, then consider the Method for SAT Math Questions an area of strength and move on to the next chapter. Do keep using the method as you work on the questions in future chapters.

If you don't yet feel confident, review those parts of this chapter that you have not yet mastered and try the questions you missed again. As always, be sure to review the explanations closely.

Math

Answers and Explanations

1. B

Difficulty: Medium

Category: Solving Equations

Strategic Advice: Break apart the question into its mathematical parts; determine what information you have and what value you need to find and then determine how you'll find that value.

Getting to the Answer: You're given the weight of everything on the airplane except the combined weight of the cargo containers, and you're given the maximum takeoff weight of the plane. Therefore, the difference between the maximum takeoff weight and the weight of the plane, crew, and fuel must be the maximum combined weight of the cargo containers.

You're also told that n represents the number of cargo containers that will be loaded on the plane and that each container weighs 125 kilograms. You need to find the number of containers, n, that make up the difference in weights.

The maximum takeoff weight of the plane is 19,000 kilograms, and the weight of the plane, crew, and fuel is 14,750 kilograms. Hence, the maximum number of cargo containers can have a combined weight no greater than $19,000 - 14,750 = 4,250$ kilograms. That means that the maximum number of containers, n, must be 4,250 kilograms $\div$ 125 kilograms = 34 containers. Thus, **(B)** is correct.

2. C

Difficulty: Medium

Category: Solving Equations

Strategic Advice: Think about what you're being asked to find—the difference between the price of the laptop at the luxury department store and at the online retailer—and what information you're given—the actual price at a local electronics store and two fractions of that price that represent the prices at the online retailer and at the luxury department store.

Getting to the Answer: The price of the laptop at the electronics store is $550. You also know that the price at the online retailer is $\frac{9}{10}$ of this, so that price is $\frac{9}{10} \times \$550 = \$495$. The question also states that the price at the luxury store is $\frac{7}{5}$ of the price at the

electronics store, so that's $\frac{7}{5} \times \$550 = \$770$. Therefore, the difference between the price at the luxury department store and the price at the online retailer is $\$770 - \$495 = \$275$. Choice **(C)** is correct.

3. B

Difficulty: Easy

Category: Proportions

Strategic Advice: Because the answer choices are widely spaced apart, and the question asks for the answer that is "closest to the number," estimation will be a better approach than wading into unnecessarily detailed and tedious calculations.

Getting to the Answer: Notice the relationship between the height of the stack of 75 plates and the height of the unknown number of plates: $9\frac{7}{8}$ inches is *about half* of 20 inches. Put another way, a 20-inch stack of plates will be about twice as tall as a stack of 75 plates. Therefore, it's logical to deduce that approximately twice as many plates, or about $2 \times 75 = 150$, will be needed to form a stack 20 inches tall. Hence, **(B)** is correct.

4. B

Difficulty: Medium

Category: Heart of Algebra/Systems of Linear Equations

Strategic Advice: Use the answer choices to your advantage to quickly find Bianca's distance.

Getting to the Answer: The question gives two unknowns and enough information to create a system of equations; therefore, it could be solved with a traditional algebraic approach.

There is, however, a more efficient way: assess the answer choices to see which makes sense for Bianca's distance. Since Kiera ran 22 miles farther than Bianca, and the combined distance they ran is 86 miles, Bianca must have run less than half of 86 miles. Since one-half of 86 is 43, you can quickly eliminate (C) and (D), which are both too big.

Now check (B) against the known information. If Bianca ran 32 miles, then Kiera ran $32 + 22 = 54$ miles. Check if Bianca's distance and Kiera's distance add up to 86: $32 + 54 = 86$; thus, **(B)** is correct.

If you're curious about the algebraic approach, here it is: let b stand for the number of miles Bianca ran and k stand for the number of miles Kiera ran. Then $b + k = 86$, and $k = b + 22$. Now, substitute the value of k in terms of b into the first equation:

$$b + (b + 22) = 86$$
$$2b + 22 = 86$$
$$2b = 64$$
$$b = 32$$

Again, Bianca ran 32 miles, and **(B)** is correct.

5. C

Difficulty: Medium

Category: Solving Equations

Strategic Advice: You have two variables, but only one equation, so solving for each variable will not be possible. Instead, pick numbers for x and y that will make the equation true.

Getting to the Answer: Pick a simple number for x, solve for y, and if y is also easy to work with, plug them into the expression you're trying to find. Say $x = 2$; then you have $\frac{4(2)}{2y} = 4$, which simplifies to $\frac{8}{2y} = 4$. Solving for y, you multiply both sides by $2y$ and get $8 = 8y$, so $y = 1$, another manageable number.

Now, plug these same values of x and y into $\frac{3y}{x}$ to get $\frac{3(1)}{(2)} = \frac{3}{2}$. Thus, **(C)** is correct.

6. D

Difficulty: Medium

Category: Heart of Algebra/Linear Equations

Strategic Advice: The answer choices are split into two types: the first two are exponential and the second two are linear. Therefore, to quickly narrow down the answers, examine the table to determine whether the change in x-values versus y-values is exponential or linear.

Getting to the Answer: Notice that, for every increase of 2 in the x-value, the y-value increases by $\frac{4}{5}$. Therefore, you have a linear relationship, so you can eliminate (A) and (B), which are both exponential functions.

Now, plug values from the table into the remaining answers to see whether the math works out. Try the first column in the table and plug in 2 for x and $\frac{7}{5}$ for y:

(C): $\frac{7}{5} = \frac{5}{2} \times 2 - \frac{3}{5} = 5 - \frac{3}{5} = \frac{25}{5} - \frac{3}{5} = \frac{22}{5}$. This doesn't work out, so **(D)** must be correct. No need to check it. For the record:

(D): $\frac{7}{5} = \frac{2}{5} \times 2 + \frac{3}{5} = \frac{4}{5} + \frac{3}{5} = \frac{7}{5}$

7. D

Difficulty: Medium

Category: Heart of Algebra/Linear Equations

Strategic Advice: Backsolve by plugging the answer choices in for c to determine which one makes the given equation true.

Getting to the Answer: The question provides a linear equation and the value of one of the variables.

Since you're told that $n = 5$, fill this value into the equation, and then simplify to find the root:

$$5 - \sqrt{c + 5} = 1$$
$$4 - \sqrt{c + 5} = 0$$
$$4 = \sqrt{c + 5}$$

Simplifying to this point makes it easier to see if the value of c you plug in works. Now check the answer choices, starting with (B) or (C). If the answer you choose is too large or too small, you'll know which direction to go when testing the next choice.

(B): $4 \neq \sqrt{0 + 5}$. This answer is too small, so try (C) next.

(C): $4 \neq \sqrt{3 + 5}$. This choice is still too small, so the correct choice must be **(D)**. No need to check it. For the record:

(D): $4 = \sqrt{11 + 5} = \sqrt{16} = 4$.

If you prefer the algebraic approach, here it is:

$$5 - \sqrt{c + 5} = 1$$
$$4 - \sqrt{c + 5} = 0$$
$$4 = \sqrt{c + 5}$$
$$4^2 = c + 5$$
$$16 = c + 5$$
$$11 = c$$

Again, **(D)** is correct.

8. C

Difficulty: Medium

Category: Heart of Algebra/Linear Equations

Strategic Advice: Pick a number for p to determine how many packets of mix will be needed, and then pick another number for p to see how the number of packets changes.

Getting to the Answer: Say $p = 2$, then $m = 2(2) + 4 = 8$, so there are 8 packets of mix needed to make 2 pitchers of lemonade. Now try $p = 3$: $m = 2(3) + 4 = 10$. For one additional pitcher, the packets needed increased from 8 to 10, which is a change of 2. Therefore, **(C)** is correct. You can confirm by trying $p = 4$, then $m = 2(4) + 4 = 12$.

9. B

Difficulty: Medium

Category: Heart of Algebra/Linear Equations

Strategic Advice: Backsolve by plugging the answer choices in for n to determine which one matches the given price of six months of membership.

Getting to the Answer: Check the answer choices, starting with (B) or (C). If the answer you choose is too large or too small, you'll know which direction to go when testing the next choice. Multiply the value in the answer choice by the six months and then add the $125 membership fee.

(B): $\$65 \times 6 = \$390$. $\$390 + \$125 = \$515$. This is a match, so **(B)** is correct. Since there can be only one correct answer, you're finished.

Alternatively, you can solve algebraically:

$$\$125 + 6n = \$515$$
$$6n = \$390$$
$$\frac{6n}{6} = \frac{\$390}{6}$$
$$n = \$65$$

(B) is correct.

10. D

Difficulty: Medium

Category: Heart of Algebra/Linear Equations

Strategic Advice: Pick a number for x to determine the numerical value of the given expression, then plug the same number into the answer choices to find the one that matches.

Getting to the Answer: To make calculations easy, say $x = 1$; then the given expression becomes $\dfrac{2}{\dfrac{1}{1+6} + \dfrac{1}{1+2}}$. Now, simplify this expression:

$$= \frac{2}{\dfrac{1}{7} + \dfrac{1}{3}}$$
$$= \frac{2}{\dfrac{3}{21} + \dfrac{7}{21}}$$
$$= \frac{2}{\left(\dfrac{10}{21}\right)}$$
$$= 2 \times \frac{21}{10}$$
$$= \frac{21}{5}$$

Next, plug 1 in for x in the answer choices to see which yields the same value:

(A): $1^2 + 8 \times 1 + 12 = 21$. Eliminate.

(B): $\dfrac{1+4}{1^2 + 8 \times 1 + 12} = \dfrac{5}{21}$. Eliminate.

(C): $2 \times 1 + 8 = 10$. Eliminate. You have eliminated three answer choices so the one left is correct; **(D)** is correct.

For the record: (D): $\dfrac{1^2 + 8 \times 1 + 12}{1 + 4} = \dfrac{21}{5}$. This is a match, which confirms that **(D)** is correct.

You might also have noticed that (B) gave you the reciprocal of the value you were looking for; therefore, the reciprocal of the expression in (B) must give you the correct answer, and that is **(D)**.

The Heart of Algebra

CHAPTER 4

Linear Equations and Graphs

LEARNING OBJECTIVES

After completing this chapter, you will be able to:

- Isolate a variable
- Translate word problems into equations
- Calculate the slope of a line given two points
- Write the equation of a line in slope-intercept form
- Discern whether the slope of a line is positive, negative, zero, or undefined based on its graph
- Describe the slopes of parallel and perpendicular lines

110/600 SmartPoints® (Very High Yield)

Math

How Much Do You Know?

Directions: Try the questions that follow. Show your work so that you can compare your solutions to the ones found in the Check Your Work section immediately after this question set. The "Category" heading in the explanation for each question gives the title of the lesson that covers how to solve it. If you answered the question(s) for a given lesson correctly, and if your scratchwork looks like ours, you may be able to move quickly through that lesson. If you answered incorrectly or used a different approach, you may want to take your time on that lesson.

$$v = \frac{2\pi r}{T}$$

1. Uniform circular motion is used in physics to describe the motion of an object traveling at a constant speed in a circle. The speed of the object is called tangential velocity and it can be calculated using the formula above, where r is the radius of the circle and T is the time is takes for the object to make one complete circle, called a period. Which of the following formulas could be used to find the length of one period if you know the tangential velocity and the radius of the circle?

   A) $T = \dfrac{v}{2\pi r}$

   B) $T = \dfrac{2\pi r}{v}$

   C) $T = 2\pi rv$

   D) $T = \dfrac{1}{2\pi rv}$

$$F = \gamma \frac{m_1 m_2}{r^2}$$

2. The formula above is Newton's law of universal gravitation, where F is the attractive force, γ is the gravitational constant, m_1 and m_2 are the masses of the particles, and r is the distance between their centers of mass. Which of the following gives r in terms of F, γ, m_1, and m_2?

   A) $r = \sqrt{\dfrac{(m_1)(m_2)}{F(\gamma)}}$

   B) $r = \sqrt{\dfrac{F(m_2)}{\gamma(m_1)}}$

   C) $r = \sqrt{\dfrac{\gamma(m_1)}{F(m_2)}}$

   D) $r = \sqrt{\dfrac{\gamma(m_1)(m_2)}{F}}$

3. Andrew works at a travel agency. He gets paid $120 for a day's work, plus a bonus of $25 for each cruise he books. Which of the following equations represents the relationship between the total Andrew earns in a day, d, and the number of cruises he books, c?

   A) $c = 25d + 120$

   B) $c = 120d + 25$

   C) $d = 25c + 120$

   D) $d = 120c + 25$

4. Vera is on her school's track and field team. In a practice long-jump competition against her teammates, she gets 5 points for landing over the nearer line and 10 points for landing over the more distant line. She gets a total of 7 jumps and lands x times over the more distant line and the rest of the times over the nearer line. Which of the following equations represents the relationship between Vera's total score, y, and the number of times she lands over the more distant line, x?

A) $y = 10x$

B) $y = 5x + 35$

C) $y = 10x + 5$

D) $y = 70 - 5x$

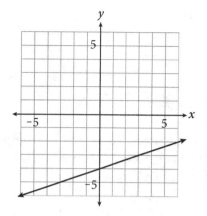

6. The graph shown represents which of the following equations?

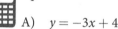

A) $y = -3x + 4$

B) $y = -\frac{1}{3}x + 4$

C) $y = \frac{1}{3}x - 4$

D) $y = 3x - 4$

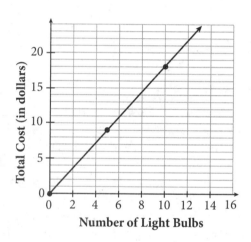

Number of Light Bulbs

5. A hardware store sells light bulbs in different quantities. The graph shows the cost of various quantities. According to the graph, what is the cost of a single light bulb?

A) $0.56

B) $1.80

C) $2.50

D) $3.60

Check Your Work

1. B

Difficulty: Easy

Category: Solving Equations

Getting to the Answer: The goal here is to solve the equation for T. Start by getting T out of the denominator of the fraction. To do this, multiply both sides of the equation by T, and then divide both sides by v:

$$v = \frac{2\pi r}{T}$$

$$T \times v = \left(\frac{2\pi r}{T}\right) \times T$$

$$Tv = 2\pi r$$

$$T = \frac{2\pi r}{v}$$

Choice **(B)** is the correct answer.

2. D

Difficulty: Medium

Category: Solving Equations

Strategic Advice: Even when the equation is entirely made up of variables, the process for isolating one variable is still the same.

Getting to the Answer: This equation needs to be rearranged to solve for r, so start by multiplying both sides by r^2 to get that expression out of the denominator:

$$\left(r^2\right)(F) = \gamma(m_1)(m_2)$$

Next, divide both sides by F:

$$r^2 = \frac{\gamma(m_1)(m_2)}{F}$$

Finally, take the square root of both sides to get r by itself:

$$r = \sqrt{\frac{\gamma(m_1)(m_2)}{F}}$$

(D) is correct.

3. C

Difficulty: Easy

Category: Word Problems

Getting to the Answer: When writing a linear equation to represent a real-world scenario, a flat rate is a constant while a unit rate is always multiplied by the independent variable. You can identify the unit rate by looking for words like *per* or *for each*.

Because the amount Andrew gets paid daily, $120, is a flat rate that doesn't depend on the number of cruises he books, 120 should be the constant in the equation. This means you can eliminate (B) and (D). The question tells you to multiply $25 by the number of cruises he books, c, so the equation is *total pay* $= 25 \times$ *number of cruises* $+ 120$, or $d = 25c + 120$, making **(C)** correct.

4. B

Difficulty: Hard

Category: Word Problems

Getting to the Answer: The key to answering this question is determining how many jumps land across each line. If Vera gets 7 jumps total and x jumps land over the more distant line, then the rest, or $7 - x$, must land over the nearer line. Now, write the expression in words: points per distant line (10) times number of jumps landing over the distant line (x), plus points per near line (5) times number of jumps landing over the near line ($7 - x$). Next, translate the words into numbers, variables, and operations: $10x + 5(7 - x)$. This is not one of the answer choices, so simplify the expression by distributing the 5 and combining like terms: $10x + 5(7 - x) = 10x + 35 - 5x = 5x + 35$, so the equation is $y = 5x + 35$. **(B)** is correct.

5. B

Difficulty: Easy

Category: Linear Graphs

Getting to the Answer: The x-axis represents the number of light bulbs, so find 1 on the x-axis and trace up to where it meets the graph of the line. The y-value is somewhere between $1 and $2, so the only possible correct answer choice is $1.80. **(B)** is correct.

You could also find the unit rate by calculating the slope of the line using two of the points shown on the graph: the graph rises 9 units and runs 5 units from one point to the next, so the slope is $\frac{9}{5}$, or 1.8, which confirms that **(B)** is correct.

6. C

Difficulty: Medium

Category: Linear Graphs

Getting to the Answer: Use the graph to identify the y-intercept and the slope of the line and then write an equation in slope-intercept form, $y = mx + b$. Once you have your equation, look for the answer choice that matches. The line crosses the y-axis at $(0, -4)$ so the y-intercept, b, is -4. The line rises 1 unit for every 3 units that it runs to the right, so the slope, m, is $\frac{1}{3}$. The equation of the line is $y = \frac{1}{3}x - 4$, which matches **(C)**.

You could also graph each of the answer choices in your calculator to see which one matches the given graph, but this is not the most time-efficient strategy. You also have to be very careful when entering fractions—to graph **(C)**, for example, you would enter $(1/3)x - 4$.

Solving Equations

LEARNING OBJECTIVE

After this lesson, you will be able to:

- Isolate a variable

To answer a question like this:

$$\frac{1}{2}(3x + 14) = \frac{1}{6}(7x - 10)$$

Which value of x satisfies the equation above?

A) -26

B) 2

C) 8

D) 16

You need to know this:

Isolating a variable means getting that variable by itself on one side of the equation. To do this, use inverse operations to manipulate the equation, remembering that whatever you do to one side of the equation, you must do to *both* sides.

You need to do this:

It usually makes sense to proceed in this order:

- Eliminate any fractions.
- Collect and combine like terms.
- Divide to leave the desired variable by itself.

Explanation:

Eliminate the fractions by multiplying both sides of the equation by 6:

$$\left(\frac{6}{1}\right)\frac{1}{2}(3x + 14) = \left(\frac{6}{1}\right)\frac{1}{6}(7x - 10)$$
$$3(3x + 14) = (7x - 10)$$

In order to collect all the x terms on one side, you'll first need to distribute the 3 on the left side of the equation:

$$9x + 42 = 7x - 10$$

Next, subtract $7x$ from both sides:

$$2x + 42 = -10$$

Now, subtract 42 from both sides:

$$2x = -52$$

Finally, divide both sides by 2 to leave x by itself:

$$x = -26$$

Choice **(A)** is correct.

If you find isolating a variable to be challenging, try these Drill questions before proceeding to the Try on Your Own set. Isolate the variable in each equation. Turn the page and look at the bottom of the page to see the answers.

Drill

a. $3(x + 2) = 14 - 2(3 - 2x)$

b. $5(6 - 3b) = 3b + 3$

c. $\dfrac{r}{6} - \dfrac{3r}{5} = \dfrac{1}{2}$

d.   Isolate F: $C = \dfrac{5}{9}(F - 32)$

e.   Isolate b: $A = \dfrac{1}{2}(a + b)h$

Math

Try on Your Own

Directions: Take as much time as you need on these questions. Work carefully and methodically. There will be an opportunity for timed practice at the end of the chapter.

HINT: For Q1, what do you need to do before you can collect all the y terms on one side?

$$3y + 2(y - 2) = \frac{3y}{2} + 1$$

1. What value of y satisfies the equation above?

   A) $-\dfrac{10}{7}$

   B) $-\dfrac{6}{13}$

   C) $\dfrac{7}{9}$

   D) $\dfrac{10}{7}$

$$S = \frac{C - \frac{1}{4}I}{C + I}$$

2. A teacher uses the formula above to calculate her students' scores, S, by subtracting $\frac{1}{4}$ of the number of questions the students answered incorrectly, I, from the number of questions they answered correctly, C, and dividing by the total number of questions. Which of the following expresses the number of questions answered incorrectly in terms of the other variables?

   A) $\dfrac{C(1 - 4S)}{4S + 1}$

   B) $\dfrac{C(1 + 4S)}{4S - 1}$

   C) $\dfrac{4C(1 - S)}{4S + 1}$

   D) $\dfrac{4C(1 + S)}{4S - 1}$

Drill answers from previous page:

a. $3x + 6 = 14 - 6 + 4x$
   $3x = 2 + 4x$
   $x = -2$

b. $30 - 15b = 3b + 3$
   $-18b = -27$
   $\dfrac{-18b}{-18} = \dfrac{-27}{-18}$
   $b = \dfrac{3}{2}$

c. $30 \times \left(\dfrac{r}{6} - \dfrac{3r}{5}\right) = \left(\dfrac{1}{2}\right) \times 30$
   $5r - 6(3r) = 15$
   $-13r = 15$
   $r = -\dfrac{15}{13}$

d. $\dfrac{9}{5} \times C = \dfrac{9}{5} \times \dfrac{5}{9}(F - 32)$
   $\dfrac{9}{5}C = F - 32$
   $\dfrac{9}{5}C + 32 = F$

e. $A = \dfrac{1}{2}(a + b)h$
   $2A = (a + b)h$
   $\dfrac{2A}{h} = a + b$
   $\dfrac{2A}{h} - a = b$

3. What value of n satisfies the equation $\frac{7}{8}(n-6) = \frac{21}{2}$?

HINT: For Q5, simplify the numerators before clearing
the equation of fractions.

$$\frac{4 + z - (3 + 2z)}{6} = \frac{-z - 3(5 - 2)}{7}$$

5. What is the value of z in the equation above?

    A) -61

    B) $-\frac{61}{27}$

    C) $\frac{61}{27}$

    D) 61

HINT: For Q4, use $\frac{a}{b}$ as your target and solve for that expression
rather than solving for a and b separately.

4. If $b \neq 0$ and $\frac{3a + b}{b} = \frac{11}{2}$, which of the following
    could be the value of $\frac{a}{b}$?

    A) $\frac{3}{2}$

    B) $\frac{7}{2}$

    C) $\frac{9}{2}$

    D) It is not possible to determine a value of $\frac{a}{b}$.

Word Problems

LEARNING OBJECTIVE

After this lesson, you will be able to:

• Translate word problems into equations

To answer a question like this:

A laser tag arena sells two types of memberships. One package costs $325 for one year of membership with an unlimited number of visits. The second package has a $125 enrollment fee, includes five free visits, and costs an additional $8 per visit after the first five. How many visits over a one-year period would a person who purchases the second package need to use for the cost to equal that of the one-year membership?

A) 20

B) 25

C) 30

D) 40

You need to know this:

The SAT likes to test your understanding of how to describe real-world situations using math equations. For some questions, it will be up to you to extract and solve an equation; for others, you'll have to interpret an equation in a real-life context. The following table shows some of the most common phrases and mathematical equivalents you're likely to see on the SAT.

Word Problems Translation Table	
English	**Math**
equals, is, equivalent to, was, will be, has, costs, adds up to, the same as, as much as	$=$
times, of, multiplied by, product of, twice, double	$\times$
divided by, out of, ratio	$\div$
plus, added to, sum, combined, increased by	$+$
minus, subtracted from, smaller than, less than, fewer, decreased by, difference between	$-$
a number, how much, how many, what	x, n, etc.

You need to do this:

When translating from English to math, *start by defining the variables*, choosing letters that make sense. Then, *break down the question into small pieces*, writing down the translation for one phrase at a time.

Explanation:

The phrase "how many visits" indicates an unknown, so you need a variable. Use an intuitive letter to represent the number of visits; call it v. The question asks when the two memberships will cost the "same amount," so write an equation that sets the total membership costs equal to each other.

The first membership type costs $325 for unlimited visits, so write 325 on one side of the equal sign. The second type costs $8 per visit (not including, or *except*, the first 5 visits), or $8(v - 5)$, plus a flat $125 enrollment fee, so write $8(v - 5) + 125$ on the other side of the equal sign. That's it! Now solve for v:

$$325 = 8(v - 5) + 125$$
$$200 = 8v - 40$$
$$240 = 8v$$
$$30 = v$$

The answer is **(C)**.

Math

Try on Your Own

Directions: Take as much time as you need on these questions. Work carefully and methodically. There will be an opportunity for timed practice at the end of the chapter.

6. A local restaurant is hosting a dance-a-thon for charity. Each couple must dance a minimum of three hours before earning any money for the charity. After the first three hours, couples earn $50 per half-hour of continuous dancing. Which expression represents the total amount earned by a couple who dance h hours, assuming they dance at least three hours?

   A) $25h$

   B) $100h$

   C) $50(h - 3)$

   D) $100h - 300$

HINT: For Q7, start with the most concrete information: 1 is the second value.

---

7. The final value, v, in a four-digit lock code is determined by multiplying the second value by 2, subtracting that expression from the first value, and dividing the resulting expression by half of the third value. The first value is f, the second value is 1, and the third value is t. What is the final value, v, in terms of f and t?

   A) $\dfrac{f - 2}{t}$

   B) $\dfrac{2f - 4}{t}$

   C) $\dfrac{t}{2f - 4}$

   D) $\dfrac{2t - 4}{f}$

HINT: For Q8, profit $=$ sales $-$ expenses

---

8. A pizzeria's top-selling pizzas are The Works and The Hawaiian. The Works sells for $17, and The Hawaiian sells for $13. Ingredient costs for The Works are $450 per week, and ingredient costs for The Hawaiian are $310 per week. If x represents the number of each type of pizza sold in one week, and the weekly profit from the sale of each type of pizza is the same, what is the value of x?

   A) 30

   B) 35

   C) 140

   D) 145

9. A student opens a checking account when she starts a new job so that her paychecks can be directly deposited into the account. Her balance can be computed using the expression $10nw + 50$, where n is the number of hours she works every week and w is the number of weeks that she has worked so far. Assuming she does not withdraw any money from her account, which of the terms in the expression most logically will change if the student gets a raise?

   A) 10

   B) n

   C) w

   D) The expression will not change if the student gets a raise.

10. Malik starts a job at which his starting salary is $25,500 per year. He expects that his salary will increase by a constant dollar amount annually. In 12 years, his salary will be double his starting salary. Assuming salary increases take place only at the end of a full year, how many years must Malik wait until his salary is at least $40,000 annually?

Math

Linear Graphs

LEARNING OBJECTIVES

After this lesson, you will be able to:

- Calculate the slope of a line given two points
- Write the equation of a line in slope-intercept form
- Discern whether the slope of a line is positive, negative, zero, or undefined based on its graph
- Describe the slopes of parallel and perpendicular lines

To answer a question like this:

What is the equation of the line that passes through the points $(-3, -1)$ and $(1, 3)$?

A) $y = -x + 2$

B) $y = -x - 2$

C) $y = x - 2$

D) $y = x + 2$

You need to know this:

The answer choices in this question are written in slope-intercept form: $y = mx + b$. In this form of a linear equation, m represents the **slope** of the line and b represents the **y-intercept**. You can think of the slope of a line as how steep it is. The y-intercept is the point at which the line crosses the y-axis and can be written as the ordered pair $(0, y)$.

You can calculate the slope of a line if you know any two points on the line. The formula is $m = \dfrac{y_2 - y_1}{x_2 - x_1}$, where (x_1, y_1) and (x_2, y_2) are the coordinates of the two points on the line.

A line that moves from the bottom left to the top right has a positive slope. A line that moves from the top left to the bottom right has a negative slope. A horizontal line has a slope of 0 and a vertical line has an undefined slope.

Some SAT questions ask about parallel or perpendicular lines. Parallel lines have the same slope, while perpendicular lines have negative reciprocal slopes.

You need to do this:

- Find the slope of the line.
- Write the equation in slope-intercept form, substituting the value of the slope you found and one of the known points for x and y.
- Solve for the y-intercept.

Explanation:

In this question, $m = \dfrac{3-(-1)}{1-(-3)} = \dfrac{4}{4} = 1$. Of the answer choices, only (C) and (D) have a slope of 1, so rule out (A) and (B), which both have a slope of -1.

To find the y-intercept of the line, write the equation for the line in slope-intercept form and plug in one of the known points for x and y:

$$y = 1x + b$$
$$3 = 1(1) + b$$
$$2 = b$$

The correct answer is **(D)**. For the record, here is the graph of the line. Note that as you would expect from the fact that m is positive, the line moves from the lower left to upper right, and it crosses the y-axis at the y-intercept of $b = 2$.

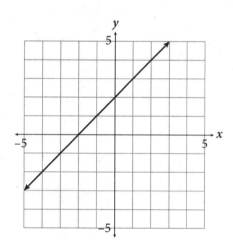

Try on Your Own

Directions: Take as much time as you need on these questions. Work carefully and methodically. There will be an opportunity for timed practice at the end of the chapter.

HINT: For Q11, what do you know about lines that never intersect?

---

11. Line A passes through the coordinate points $(-\frac{2}{5}, 0)$ and $(0, 1)$. Which of the following lines will line A never intersect?

A)

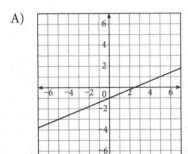

B)

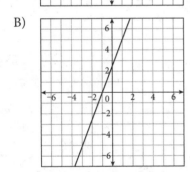

C)

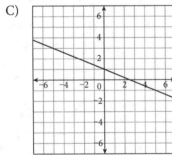

D)

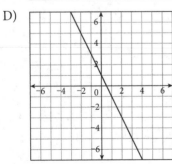

12. In the xy-plane, the point $(4, 7)$ lies on the line t, which is perpendicular to the line $y = -\frac{4}{3}x + 6$. What is the equation of line t?

A) $y = \frac{3}{4}x + 4$

B) $y = -\frac{4}{3}x + 4$

C) $y = \frac{3}{4}x + 7$

D) $y = -\frac{3}{4}x + 4$

HINT: For Q13, remember that at the y-intercept, $x = 0$.

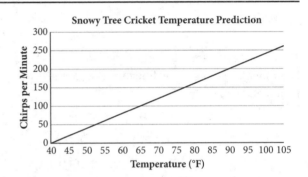

13. The graph shows the correlation between ambient air temperature, t, in degrees Fahrenheit and the number of chirps, c, per minute that a snowy tree cricket makes at that temperature. Which of the following equations represents the line shown in the graph?

A) $c = 4t - 160$

B) $c = \frac{1}{4}t - 160$

C) $c = \frac{1}{2}t - 40$

D) $c = 4t + 160$

Minutes Charging	10	15	30
Percent Charged	34	41.5	64

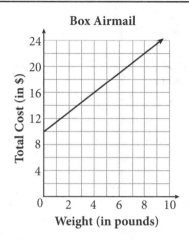

Box Airmail

Total Cost (in $) / Weight (in pounds)

15. Xia is charging her laptop. She records the battery charge for the first 30 minutes after she plugs it in to get an idea of when it will be completely charged. The table above shows the results. If *y* is the percent battery charge on Xia's laptop, which linear equation represents the correct relationship between *y* and *x* ?

A) $y = 1.5x + 19$

B) $y = 2x + 14$

C) $y = 2.5x + 9$

D) $y = 10x + 34$

14. A freight airline charges a flat fee to airmail a box, plus an additional charge for each pound the box weighs. The graph above shows the relationship between the weight of the box and the total cost to airmail it. Based on the graph, how much would it cost in dollars to airmail a 40-pound box?

On Test Day

Remember that the SAT doesn't ask you to show your work. If you find the algebra in a question challenging, there is often another way to get to the answer.

Try this question first using algebra and then using the Picking Numbers strategy you learned in chapter 3. Time yourself. Which approach did you find easier? Which one was faster? Did you get the correct answer both times? Remember your preferred approach and try it first if you see a question like this on test day.

$$\frac{2(a-3)}{b} = \frac{4}{7}$$

16. If the equation above is true, which of the following must NOT be true?

A) $\dfrac{b}{a-3} = \dfrac{7}{2}$

B) $\dfrac{2a}{b} = -\dfrac{10}{7}$

C) $14a - 4b = 42$

D) $\dfrac{a-3}{b} = \dfrac{2}{7}$

The correct answer and both ways of solving can be found at the end of this chapter.

How Much Have You Learned?

Directions: For testlike practice, give yourself 15 minutes to complete this question set. Be sure to study the explanations, even for questions you got right. They can be found at the end of this chapter.

17. Which value of x makes the equation $\frac{8}{5}\left(x + \frac{33}{12}\right) = 16$ true?

    A)   7.25

    B)   8.75

    C)   12.75

    D)   13.25

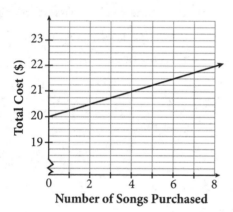

18. The graph above shows the cost of joining and buying music from a music subscription service. What does the y-intercept of the line most likely represent?

    A)   The cost per song

    B)   The cost to join the service

    C)   The cost of buying 20 songs

    D)   The cost of 20 subscriptions to the service

19. If $\frac{3}{4}y = 6 - \frac{1}{3}c$, then what is the value of $2c + \frac{9}{2}y$?

20. Three years ago, Madison High School started charging an admission fee for basketball games to raise money for new bleachers. The initial price was $2 per person; the school raised the price of admission to $2.50 this year. Assuming this trend continues, which of the following equations can be used to describe c, the cost of admission, y years after the school began charging for admission to games?

    A) $c = 6y + 2$

    B) $c = \frac{y}{6} + 2.5$

    C) $c = \frac{y}{6} + 2$

    D) $c = \frac{y}{2} + 2$

Price of One Pound	Projected Number of Pounds Sold
$1.20	15,000
$1.40	12,500
$1.60	10,000
$1.80	7,500
$2.00	5,000
$2.20	2,500

21. Which of the following equations best describes the linear relationship shown in the table, where g represents the number of pounds of grain sold and d represents the price in dollars of one pound of grain?

A) $g = 1.2d + 12,500$

B) $g = 12,500d + 15,000$

C) $g = -12,500d + 17,500$

D) $g = -12,500d + 30,000$

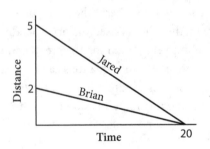

22. Brian and Jared live in the same apartment complex and both bike to and from work every day. The figure above shows a typical commute home for each of them. Based on the figure, which of the following statements is true?

A) It takes Brian longer to bike home because his work is farther away.

B) It takes Jared longer to bike home because his work is farther away.

C) Jared and Brian arrive home at the same time, so they must bike at about the same rate.

D) Jared bikes a longer distance than Brian in the same amount of time, so Jared must bike at a faster rate.

23. When graphing a linear equation that is written in the form $y = mx + b$, the variable m represents the slope of the line and b represents the y-intercept. Assuming that $b > 0$, which of the following best describes how reversing the sign of b will affect the graph?

A) The new line will be shifted down b units.

B) The new line will be shifted down $2b$ units.

C) The new line will be a perfect reflection across the x-axis.

D) The new line will be a perfect reflection across the y-axis.

24. The graph of a line in the xy-plane passes through the points $(5, 4)$ and $\left(3, \frac{1}{2}\right)$. Which of the following equations describes the line?

A) $y = \frac{7}{4}x + \frac{19}{4}$

B) $y = -\frac{7}{4}x - \frac{19}{4}$

C) $y = \frac{7}{4}x - \frac{19}{4}$

D) $y = \frac{4}{7}x + \frac{8}{7}$

25. Line f in the xy-plane passes through the origin and has a slope of $-\frac{2}{5}$. Line z is perpendicular to line f and passes through the point $(6, 2)$. Which of the following is the equation of line z?

   A) $y = -\frac{2}{5}x$

   B) $y = -\frac{2}{5}x - 13$

   C) $y = \frac{5}{2}x$

   D) $y = \frac{5}{2}x - 13$

$$V = \frac{1}{3}\pi\left(\frac{d}{2}\right)^2 h$$

26. A circle of rubber with a constant diameter d is placed on a table; its perimeter is anchored to the table and a string is attached to its center. When the string is pulled upwards, a cone is formed with height h and volume V. The relationship between d, h, and V is represented above. Which of the following statements must be true?

   I.   As the volume of the cone decreases, the height also decreases.
   II. If the diameter of the base of the cone is 6 centimeters, the height can be determined by dividing the volume by 3π.
   III. If the height of the cone triples, the volume must also triple.

   A) I only

   B) I and II only

   C) II and III only

   D) I, II, and III

Reflect

Directions: Take a few minutes to recall what you've learned and what you've been practicing in this chapter. Consider the following questions, jot down your best answer for each one, and then compare your reflections to the expert responses on the following page. Use your level of confidence to determine what to do next.

What should you do to isolate a particular variable in an equation?

_____

_____

_____

What types of keywords should you look for when translating English into math?

_____

_____

_____

What is the most useful equation for a line in the coordinate plane? Why?

_____

_____

_____

When the SAT gives you two points on a line, what can you figure out?

_____

_____

_____

How are parallel and perpendicular lines related to each other?

_____

_____

_____

Expert Responses

What should you do to isolate a particular variable in an equation?

Perform inverse operations until the variable is by itself on one side of the equal sign. If the equation has fractions, make them disappear by multiplying both sides of the equation by the denominator(s). If like terms appear on different sides of the equation, collect them on the same side so that you can combine them.

What types of keywords should you look for when translating English into math?

Look for keywords that signal equality ("is," "has," "was"), variable names ("Marina's age," "the cost of one bathtub"), or one of the four arithmetic operations (addition, subtraction, multiplication, and division).

What is the most useful equation for a line in the coordinate plane? Why?

The best equation is slope-intercept form, $y = mx + b$, because it tells you the slope (m) and the y-intercept (b). Conversely, if you need to derive an equation yourself, you can plug the slope and y-intercept into slope-intercept form and you're done.

When the SAT gives you two points on a line, what can you figure out?

If you know two points, you can figure out the slope of the line with the equation $m = \dfrac{y_2 - y_1}{x_2 - x_1}$. From there, you can plug one of the points and the slope into slope-intercept form and find the y-intercept.

How are parallel and perpendicular lines related to each other?

Parallel lines never intersect and they have equal slopes. Perpendicular lines intersect at a 90° angle and they have negative reciprocal slopes.

Next Steps

If you answered most questions correctly in the "How Much Have You Learned?" section, and if your responses to the Reflect questions were similar to those of the SAT expert, then consider linear equations and graphs an area of strength and move on to the next chapter. Come back to this topic periodically to prevent yourself from getting rusty.

If you don't yet feel confident, review those parts of this chapter that you have not yet mastered. In particular, review the variable isolation drills in the Solving Equations lesson and the definition of slope-intercept form in the Linear Graphs lesson. Then try the questions you missed again. As always, be sure to review the explanations closely. Finally, **go online** (www.kaptest.com/moreonline) for additional practice on the highest yield topics in this chapter.

Answers and Explanations

1.   D

Difficulty: Easy

Getting to the Answer: Distribute the factor of 2, combine like terms, multiply both sides of the equation by 2 to clear the fraction, and then solve for y:

$$3y + 2y - 4 = \frac{3y}{2} + 1$$
$$5y - 4 = \frac{3y}{2} + 1$$
$$10y - 8 = 3y + 2$$
$$7y = 10$$
$$y = \frac{10}{7}$$

Choice **(D)** is correct.

2.   C

Difficulty: Hard

Strategic Advice: Complicated-looking equations appear difficult, but they always succumb to the steps of solving an equation. First, clear the equation of fractions, then collect like terms, and solve for the desired variable.

Getting to the Answer: Clear the equation of the fraction in the numerator by multiplying both sides by 4 to yield:

$$4S = \frac{4C - I}{C + I}$$

Now, multiply both sides by the denominator $C + I$ to clear the equation of fractions:

$$4S(C + I) = 4C - I$$

Distribute the $4S$:

$$4SC + 4SI = 4C - I$$

To solve for I, collect all the terms that include I on one side of the equation:

$$4SI + I = 4C - 4SC$$

Factor out the I:

$$I(4S + 1) = 4C - 4SC$$

Divide to isolate I, and factor out $4C$ from the numerator:

$$I = \frac{4C - 4SC}{4S + 1} = \frac{4C(1 - S)}{4S + 1}$$

(C) is correct.

3.   18

Difficulty: Easy

Getting to the Answer: First, clear the fractions by multiplying both sides of the equation by 8. Then, solve for x using inverse operations:

$$\frac{7}{8}(n - 6) = \frac{21}{2}$$
$$8\left[\frac{7}{8}(n - 6)\right] = 8\left[\frac{21}{2}\right]$$
$$7(n - 6) = 4(21)$$
$$7n - 42 = 84$$
$$7n = 126$$
$$n = 18$$

Grid in **18**.

4.   A

Difficulty: Medium

Strategic Advice: Noticing key information about the answer choices and using that information to pick numbers saves time by eliminating algebra.

Getting to the Answer: Rearranging the terms of the equation such that $\frac{a}{b}$ is on one side and the constants are all on the other will work for this question. First, cross-multiply to get rid of the fractions. Then, use inverse operations to isolate $\frac{a}{b}$:

$$\frac{(3a + b)}{(b)} \bowtie \frac{(11)}{(2)}$$
$$2(3a + b) = 11b$$
$$6a + 2b = 11b$$
$$6a = 9b$$
$$a = \frac{9}{6}b$$
$$\frac{a}{b} = \frac{3}{2}$$

The answer is **(A)**.

There is a faster approach. Notice that 2 shows up in the denominator in most of the choices, indicating that it is likely that *b* equals 2. If $b = 2$, then *a* must be 3 for the numerator to equal 11. Test this by plugging the numbers into the equation:

$$\frac{3(3) + 2}{2} = \frac{11}{2}$$

Thus, $\frac{a}{b} = \frac{3}{2}$, confirming **(A)** as the answer. You can avoid a lot of work by using key information in the answer choices to pick numbers.

5. D

Difficulty: Medium

Getting to the Answer: Simplify the numerators as much as possible, then isolate the variable. Begin by combining like terms on both sides of the equation. Then cross-multiply and solve for *z*:

$$\frac{4 + z - (3 + 2z)}{6} = \frac{-z - 3(5 - 2)}{7}$$
$$\frac{1 - z}{6} = \frac{-z - 9}{7}$$
$$7 - 7z = -6z - 54$$
$$-z = -61$$
$$z = 61$$

Choice **(D)** is correct.

6. D

Difficulty: Medium

Getting to the Answer: Use the information in the question to write your own expression, then look for the answer choice that matches. Simplify your expression only if you don't find a match. If a couple earns $50 *per half-hour* that they dance, then they earn $50 \times 2 =$ $100 *per hour*. Multiply this amount by the number of hours (not including the first 3 hours). This can be expressed as $100(h - 3)$. This is not one of the answer choices, so simplify by distributing the 100 to get $100h - 300$, which is **(D)**.

If you're struggling with the algebra, try picking numbers. Pick a number of hours a couple might dance, such as 5. They don't earn anything for the first 3 hours, but they earn $50 per half-hour for the last 2 hours, which is 50 times 4 half-hours, or $200. Now, find the expression that gives you an answer of $200 when $h = 5$ hours: $100(5) - 300 = 500 - 300 = 200$. If you use Picking Numbers, remember that it is possible that the number

you choose satisfies more than one answer choice, so plug it in to the other three choices. In this case, $h = 5$ does not give a value of 200 in any other equation, which confirms that **(D)** is correct.

7. B

Difficulty: Medium

Getting to the Answer: Translate piece by piece to get a final expression for the final value, *v*. Multiply the second value by 2 to get $2(1) = 2$. Subtract that from the first value to get $f - 2$. Divide this expression by half of the third value to get $\frac{f - 2}{\frac{t}{2}}$, which you can simplify by multiplying by the reciprocal: $\left(\frac{f - 2}{1}\right)\left(\frac{2}{t}\right) = \left(\frac{2f - 4}{t}\right)$. Choice **(B)** matches the final expression. Watch out for (D), the trap answer choice that switches the variables.

8. B

Difficulty: Medium

Getting to the Answer: Write expressions to represent the profit generated by selling each type of pizza. You're told The Works sells for $17 each and that its ingredients cost the pizzeria $450 per week. This means the weekly profit generated by this pizza's sales can be represented by the expression $17x - 450$. Do the same for The Hawaiian: Each one sells for $13, but the pizzeria loses $310 to pay for ingredients each week. Therefore, the weekly profit from this pizza can be represented by $13x - 310$. To determine the value of *x* at which the profit from the sale of each type of pizza is the same, set the two profit expressions equal to each other and solve:

$$17x - 450 = 13x - 310$$
$$4x = 140$$
$$x = 35$$

Thus, **(B)** is correct. Always be sure you're answering the right question; choice (D), 145, is the profit when $x = 35$.

9. A

Difficulty: Easy

Getting to the Answer: When faced with a question that includes abstract expressions, it is helpful to pick concrete numbers to work with. These numbers don't have to be realistic; just choose numbers that are easy to work with. Suppose the student checks her balance after 2 weeks working 3 hours each week. She would have worked a total of 6 hours, which would have to be multiplied by the amount she is paid per hour to get her total pay. In the expression, plugging in $w = 3$ and $n = 2$ demonstrates that the number 10 in the expression must be the amount that she is paid per hour, and thus is the term that would change if the student got a raise. **(A)** is correct. Although 50 is not an answer choice, you can deduce that it must have been her checking account's original balance because it is a constant.

10. 7

Difficulty: Medium

Getting to the Answer: First, notice that the actual dollar amount of the increase each year is unknown, so assign a variable like d. After 12 increases, his salary will rise by $25,500, so write a formula $12d = 25,500$. Solve for d to find that Malik will receive an increase of $2,125 per year.

The question asks how many years must go by until Malik's salary is at least $40,000; the number of years is another unknown, so assign it a variable like n. Multiplying n by the amount of each increase will give you the total increase of dollars over n years, but don't forget to add in the starting salary to reflect his total salary amount:

$$25,500 + 2,125n = 40,000$$
$$2,125n = 14,500$$
$$n \approx 6.8$$

The question asks you to assume that salary increases only take place at the end of a full year. If you are unsure and want to prove that the answer is not 6, check by using $n = 6$ to calculate the total dollar amount: $25,500 + 2,125(6) = 38,250$. Six years is not long enough; grid in **7**.

11. B

Difficulty: Easy

Getting to the Answer: You're asked to identify the line that the one described in the question stem will never intersect. Lines that never intersect are parallel and therefore have identical slopes, so start by finding the slope of the line whose two coordinate pairs are given. You'll find:

$$m = \frac{1 - 0}{0 - \left(-\frac{2}{5}\right)} = \frac{1}{\frac{2}{5}} = \frac{5}{2}$$

Choices (C) and (D) have negative slopes, so eliminate them. Next, find the slopes of (A) and (B). No need to use the slope formula; counting units on the graphs will be faster. The slope of (A) is $\frac{2}{5}$ because for every 2 units the line rises, it runs 5 units to the right. The slope of (B) is $\frac{5}{2}$ because when the line goes up 5 units, it goes 2 units to the right. Therefore, **(B)** is correct.

12. A

Difficulty: Medium

Strategic Advice: Remember that parallel lines have the same slope and perpendicular lines have opposite sign reciprocal slopes.

Getting to the Answer: The first useful piece of information is that the slope of the line perpendicular to line t is $-\frac{4}{3}$. Perpendicular lines have negative reciprocal slopes, so the slope of line t is $\frac{3}{4}$. Eliminate (B) and (D) because they have the incorrect slopes.

Plug the values for the slope and the coordinate point $(4, 7)$ into the slope-intercept equation to solve for b:

$$7 = \frac{3}{4}(4) + b$$
$$7 = 3 + b$$
$$7 - 3 = b$$
$$b = 4$$

Eliminate (C) because it does not have the correct y-intercept. Choice **(A)** is correct.

13. A

Difficulty: Medium

Getting to the Answer: Start by finding the slope of the line by picking a pair of points, such as $(40, 0)$ and $(65, 100)$: $m = \frac{100 - 0}{65 - 40} = \frac{100}{25} = 4$. Choices (B) and (C) have slopes other than 4, so eliminate them. Choices (A) and (D) have y-intercepts of -160 and 40, respectively. Now, read the axis labels carefully: the horizontal axis begins at 40 (not 0). The line is trending downward as x-values get smaller, so the y-intercept (when $x = 0$) must be well below 0 on the vertical axis. Therefore, the answer must be **(A)**.

14. 70

Difficulty: Hard

Getting to the Answer: Because 40 pounds is not shown on the graph, you need more information. In a real-world scenario, the y-intercept of a graph usually represents a flat fee or a starting amount. The slope of the line represents a unit rate, such as the cost per pound to airmail the box.

The y-intercept of the graph is 10, so the flat fee is $10. To find the cost per pound (the unit rate), substitute two points from the graph into the slope formula. Using the points $(0, 10)$ and $(4, 16)$, the cost per pound is $\frac{16 - 10}{4 - 0} = \frac{6}{4} = 1.5$, which means it costs $1.50 per pound to airmail a box. The total cost to airmail a 40-pound box is $\$10 + 1.50(40) = \$10 + \$60 = \$70$. Grid in **70**.

15. A

Difficulty: Hard

Getting to the Answer: The question tells you that the relationship is linear, so start by finding the rate of change (the slope, m) using any two pairs of values from the table and the slope formula. Next, substitute the slope and any pair of values from the table, such as $(10, 34)$, into the equation $y = mx + b$ and solve for b. Finally, use the values of m and b to write the function:

$$m = \frac{y_2 - y_1}{x_2 - x_1} = \frac{64 - 34}{30 - 10} = \frac{30}{20} = 1.5$$

You can stop right there! Only **(A)** has a slope of 1.5, so it must be the correct answer. For the record:

$$34 = 10(1.5) + b$$
$$34 = 15 + b$$
$$19 = b$$

16. B

Difficulty: Hard

Strategic Advice: Watch out for the "NOT" keyword in the question stem. Picking numbers based on clues in the equation is faster than doing the algebra.

Getting to the Answer: To find the answer using Picking Numbers, take advantage of the fact that the equation is a proportion (that is, two fractions equal to each other). If $b = 7$ and $2(a - 3) = 4$, then both fractions will be the same and the numbers you've picked will be valid. Solve for a: $a - 3 = 2$, and $a = 5$. Now plug $b = 7$ and $a = 5$ into the choices, looking for the one that *isn't* true:

(A) $\frac{b}{a - 3} = \frac{7}{5 - 3} = \frac{7}{2}$, eliminate.

(B) $\frac{2a}{b} = \frac{2(5)}{7} = \frac{10}{7} \neq -\frac{10}{7}$

You're done; pick **(B)** and move on. For the record:

(C) $14a - 4b = 14(5) - 4(7) = 70 - 28 = 42$, eliminate.

(D) $\frac{a - 3}{b} = \frac{5 - 3}{7} = \frac{2}{7}$, eliminate.

To solve this question using algebra, first cross-multiply and simplify the original equation:

$$\frac{2(a - 3)}{b} = \frac{4}{7}$$
$$14(a - 3) = 4b$$
$$7(a - 3) = 2b$$
$$7a - 21 = 2b$$
$$7a - 2b = 21$$

Then, repeat this entire process for each answer choice, looking for the one that *doesn't* yield the same equation:

(A) $\frac{b}{a - 3} = \frac{7}{2}$, $2b = 7a - 21$, $21 = 7a - 2b$, eliminate.

(B) $\frac{2a}{b} = -\frac{10}{7}$, $14a = -10b$, $7a = -5b$, $7a + 5b = 0$

This equation is different from the one in the question, so **(B)** is correct. For the record:

(C) $14a - 4b = 42$, $7a - 2b = 21$, eliminate.

(D) $\frac{a - 3}{b} = \frac{2}{7}$, $7a - 21 = 2b$, $7a - 2b = 21$, eliminate.

17. A

Difficulty: Medium

Category: Solving Equations

Getting to the Answer: This question has multiple fractions, so clear the $\frac{8}{5}$ by multiplying both sides of the equation by its reciprocal, $\frac{5}{8}$. Then, because the answers are given in decimal form, change the other fraction to a decimal by dividing the numerator by the denominator:

$$\frac{8}{5}\left(x + \frac{33}{12}\right) = 16$$

$$\frac{5}{8} \times \left[\frac{8}{5}\left(x + \frac{33}{12}\right)\right] = \frac{5}{8} \times 16$$

$$x + 2.75 = 10$$

$$x = 7.25$$

(A) is correct.

18. B

Difficulty: Easy

Category: Linear Graphs

Getting to the Answer: Read the axis labels carefully. The y-intercept is the point at which $x = 0$, which means the number of songs purchased is 0. The y-intercept is $(0, 20)$, so the cost is $20 before buying any songs and therefore most likely represents a flat membership fee for joining the service. **(B)** is correct.

19. 36

Difficulty: Medium

Category: Solving Equations

Getting to the Answer: When you're asked to find an expression rather than a variable value, it means there's likely a shortcut: try to make the expression you have look like the expression you want. Start by eliminating the fractions. A common multiple of 4 and 3 is 12, so multiply both sides of the equation by that. Once the fractions are gone, move both variable terms to the same side:

$$12\left(\frac{3}{4}y = 6 - \frac{1}{3}c\right)$$

$$9y = 72 - 4c$$

$$4c + 9y = 72$$

$$2c + \frac{9}{2}y = 36$$

The expression on the left side is precisely what you're looking for, so grid in **36**.

20. C

Difficulty: Medium

Category: Word Problems

Getting to the Answer: Look closely; buried in the text are two sets of coordinates you can use. The question states that admission was $2 when the admission charge was first implemented and increased to $2.50 after 3 years, making your coordinates $(0, 2)$ and $(3, 2.5)$. The slope of the line passing through these is $m = \frac{2.5 - 2}{3 - 0} = \frac{0.5}{3} = \frac{1}{6}$. Eliminate (A) and (D). Because the admission fee started at $2, 2 is the y-intercept, so the full equation is $c = \frac{y}{6} + 2$. **(C)** is correct.

Because the question says "three years ago," it may be tempting to use $(-3, 2)$ and $(0, 2.5)$ as your coordinates. Think about what that would mean: the first admission charge would be $2.50, as it's impossible to have a negative year. This contradicts the question stem, so (B) is incorrect.

21. D

Difficulty: Medium

Category: Word Problems

Getting to the Answer: Take a quick peek at the answer choices. The equations are given in slope-intercept form, so start by finding the slope. Substitute two pairs of values from the table (try to pick easy ones, if possible) into the slope formula, $m = \frac{y_2 - y_1}{x_2 - x_1}$. Keep in mind that the projected number of pounds sold *depends* on the price, so the price is the independent variable (x) and the projected number is the dependent variable (y). Using the points $(1.2, 15,000)$ and $(2.2, 2,500)$, you can find the slope:

$$m = \frac{2,500 - 15,000}{2.2 - 1.2}$$

$$m = \frac{-12,500}{1}$$

$$m = -12,500$$

This means you can eliminate (A) and (B) because the slope is not correct. Don't let (B) fool you—the projected number of pounds sold goes *down* as the price goes *up*, so there is an inverse relationship, which means the slope must be negative. To choose between (C) and (D), you could find the y-intercept of the line. Pick a point with easy values, such as $(2, 5,000)$, and plug in 5,000 for y and 2 for x:

$$y = mx + b$$
$$5,000 = -12,500(2) + b$$
$$5,000 = -25,000 + b$$
$$30,000 = b$$

(D) is correct. Another option is to substitute $(2, 5,000)$ into (C) and (D) only. Again, **(D)** is correct because $5,000 = -12,500(2) + 30,000$ is a true statement.

22. D

Difficulty: Medium

Category: Word Problems

Getting to the Answer: Consider each choice systematically, using the numbers on the figure to help you evaluate each statement.

It takes Brian and Jared each 20 minutes to bike home, so (A) and (B) are false. Jared bikes 5 miles in 20 minutes, while Brian only bikes 2 miles in 20 minutes; their rates are not the same, so (C) is false. This means **(D)** must be true. Jared starts out farther away than Brian, so Jared must bike at a faster rate to arrive home in the same amount of time.

23. B

Difficulty: Hard

Category: Linear Graphs

Getting to the Answer: You aren't given any numbers in this question, so make some up. Sketch a quick graph of any simple linear equation that has a positive y-intercept (because it is given that $b > 0$). Then, change the sign of the y-intercept and sketch the new graph on the same coordinate plane. Pick a simple equation that you can sketch quickly, such as $y = x + 3$, and then change the sign of b. The new equation is $y = x - 3$. Sketch both graphs. The second line is shifted down 6 units, and because $b = 3$, 6 is $2b$ units. **(B)** is correct. The graph that follows illustrates this. If you're still unsure, try another pair of equations.

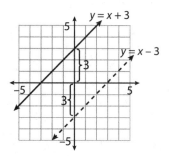

24. C

Difficulty: Medium

Category: Linear Graphs

Strategic Advice: Be careful when the answer choices look very similar to each other. Eliminating incorrect answers during intermediate steps lowers your odds of making a careless mistake.

Getting to the Answer: The question provides two coordinate points, which means that the best approach is to find the slope using the formula $m = \dfrac{y_2 - y_1}{x_2 - x_1}$, then use the slope-intercept equation for a line to find b, the y-intercept. Plugging the results into the slope formula results in:

$$\frac{\frac{1}{2} - 4}{3 - 5} = \frac{\frac{1}{2} - \frac{8}{2}}{-2} = \frac{-\frac{7}{2}}{-2} = -\frac{7}{2} \times -\frac{1}{2} = \frac{7}{4}$$

Eliminate (B) and (D) because they do not have the slope $\frac{7}{4}$. Plug the slope and one of the given points $(5, 4)$ into the slope-intercept equation to solve for b:

$$4 = \frac{7}{4}(5) + b$$
$$4 = \frac{35}{4} + b$$
$$\frac{16}{4} - \frac{35}{4} = b$$
$$b = -\frac{19}{4}$$

Eliminate (A) because it does not have the correct y-intercept; therefore, only **(C)** is left and is correct. Plugging the calculated values for the slope and the y-intercept into the slope-intercept equation indeed gives you choice **(C)**: $y = \frac{7}{4}x - \frac{19}{4}$.

After eliminating (B) and (D), you can save time by noticing that the two possible y-intercepts are $\frac{19}{4}$ and $-\frac{19}{4}$. You really only need to determine if b is positive or negative.

25. D

Difficulty: Easy

Category: Linear Graphs

Getting to the Answer: This question provides an equation for a line perpendicular to line z and a coordinate point for line z, $(6, 2)$. The opposite sign reciprocal of the slope of the perpendicular line, $\frac{5}{2}$, is the slope of line z. Eliminate (A) and (B) because they have the incorrect slope.

Plug the values for the slope and the coordinate point $(6, 2)$ into the slope-intercept equation to solve for b:

$$2 = \frac{5}{2}(6) + b$$
$$2 = 15 + b$$
$$2 - 15 = b$$
$$b = -13$$

Plug the values for the slope and the y-intercept into the slope-intercept equation to get $y = \frac{5}{2}x - 13$. **(D)** is correct.

You can save a little time if you eliminate (C) as soon as you see that $b \neq 0$, which you should be able to tell as soon as you see that $2 = 15 + b$.

26. D

Difficulty: Hard

Category: Word Problems

Strategic Advice: In problems that include verifying statements marked with roman numerals, start with the easiest statement to verify and work to the hardest, eliminating answer choices along the way. This may save you time on test day.

Getting to the Answer: The key to this problem is to see that because the question stem states that d is constant, the cumbersome expression $\frac{1}{3}\pi\left(\frac{d}{2}\right)^2$ is just a constant that is the coefficient of the variable h. The formula is really $V =$ (some constant) $\times h$. In any formula written such that $y = ax$, where a is a constant, as one amount increases (or decreases), the other amount must increase (or decrease) at the same rate. So if V decreases, h must have decreased. Statement I is true; eliminate (C).

Pick the next easiest statement to verify; in this case, statement III. If h increases by tripling, V must also increase by the same rate; it must triple, too. Test this statement if you like by picking a number for h and solving for V, then tripling h and solving for V again. Statement III is true; eliminate (A) and (B). That leaves **(D)** as the correct answer.

On test day, you'd stop here. For the sake of learning, though, you can verify whether statement II is true. Plug $d = 6$ into the formula and solve for h in terms of V:

$$V = \frac{1}{3}\pi\left(\frac{6}{2}\right)^2 h$$
$$V = \frac{(3)^2}{3}\pi h$$
$$\frac{V}{3\pi} = \frac{3\pi h}{3\pi}$$
$$h = \frac{V}{3\pi}$$

Thus, statement II is indeed true.

CHAPTER 5

Systems of Linear Equations

LEARNING OBJECTIVES

After completing this chapter, you will be able to:

- Solve systems of linear equations by substitution
- Solve systems of linear equations by combination
- Determine the number of possible solutions for a system of linear equations, if any

45/600 SmartPoints® (Medium Yield)

How Much Do You Know?

Directions: Try the questions that follow. Show your work so that you can compare your solutions to the ones found in the Check Your Work section immediately after this question set. The "Category" heading in the explanation for each question gives the title of the lesson that covers how to solve it. If you answered the question(s) for a given lesson correctly, and if your scratchwork looks like ours, you may be able to move quickly through that lesson. If you answered incorrectly or used a different approach, you may want to take your time on that lesson.

$$-7x + 2y = 18$$
$$x + y = 0$$

1. In the system of equations above, what is the value of x ?

   A) −2

   B) 0

   C) 2

   D) 4

2. At a certain movie theater, there are 16 rows and each row has either 20 or 24 seats. If the total number of seats in all 16 rows is 348, how many rows have 24 seats?

   A) 7

   B) 9

   C) 11

   D) 13

3. If $17x − 5y = 8$ and $14x − 7y = −7$, what is the value of $3x + 2y$?

   A) −15

   B) −5

   C) 5

   D) 15

4. If $0.2x = 10 − 0.5y$, then $10y + 4x =$

$$\frac{1}{2}x - \frac{2}{3}y = 7$$
$$ax - 8y = -1$$

5. If the system of linear equations above has no solution, and a is a constant, then what is the value of a ?

   A) −2

   B) $-\dfrac{1}{2}$

   C) 2

   D) 6

Answers and explanations are on the next page. ▶ ▶ ▶

Check Your Work

1.   A

Difficulty: Easy

Category: Substitution

Getting to the Answer: Solve the second equation for y in terms of x, then substitute into the first equation and solve:

$$y = -x$$
$$-7x - 2x = 18$$
$$-9x = 18$$
$$x = -2$$

(A) is correct.

2.   A

Difficulty: Hard

Category: Substitution

Getting to the Answer: Create a system of equations in which x represents the number of rows with 20 seats and y represents the number of rows with 24 seats. The first equation should represent the total *number of rows*, each with 20 or 24 seats, or $x + y = 16$. The second equation should represent the total *number of seats*. Because x represents rows with 20 seats and y represents rows with 24 seats, the second equation should be $20x + 24y = 348$. Now solve the system using substitution. Solve the first equation for either variable and substitute the result into the second equation:

$$x + y = 16$$
$$x = 16 - y$$
$$20(16 - y) + 24y = 348$$
$$320 - 20y + 24y = 348$$
$$320 + 4y = 348$$
$$4y = 28$$
$$y = 7$$

So 7 rows have 24 seats, which means **(A)** is correct. This is all the question asks for, so you don't need to find the value of x.

3.   D

Difficulty: Medium

Category: Combination

Getting to the Answer: Subtract the second equation from the first to find that $3x + 2y = 15$, making **(D)** the correct answer.

4.   200

Difficulty: Medium

Category: Number of Possible Solutions

Getting to the Answer: Rearrange the equation so that the y and x terms appear, in that order, on the left side: $0.5y + 0.2x = 10$. What number do you need to multiply $0.5y$ by to get $10y$? Twenty. Notice that $10y + 4x$ is 20 times $0.5y + 0.2x$. Multiply both sides of the equation by 20 to find that $10y + 4x = \mathbf{200}$. Note that both of these equations describe the same line.

5.   D

Difficulty: Hard

Category: Number of Possible Solutions

Getting to the Answer: Graphically, a system of linear equations that has no solution indicates two parallel lines—that is, two lines that have the same slope but different y-intercepts. To have the same slope, the x- and y-coefficients must be the same. To get from $-\frac{2}{3}$ to -8, you multiply by 12, so multiply $-\frac{1}{2}x$ by 12 as well to yield $6x$. Because the other x-coefficient is a, it must be that $a = 6$, and **(D)** is correct. Note that, even though it is more work, you could also write each equation in slope-intercept form and set the slopes equal to each other to solve for a.

Substitution

LEARNING OBJECTIVE

After this lesson, you will be able to:

● Solve systems of linear equations by substitution

To answer a question like this:

If $3x + 2y = 15$ and $x + y = 10$, what is the value of y?

A) -15

B) -5

C) 5

D) 15

You need to know this:

A **system** of two linear equations simply refers to the equations of two lines. "Solving" a system of two linear equations usually means finding the point where the two lines intersect. (However, see the lesson titled "Number of Possible Solutions" later in this chapter for exceptions.)

There are two ways to solve a system of linear equations: substitution and combination. For some SAT questions, substitution is faster; for others, combination is faster. We'll cover combination in the next lesson.

You need to do this:

To solve a system of two linear equations by substitution:

● Isolate a variable (ideally, one whose coefficient is 1) in one of the equations.
● Substitute the result into the other equation.

Explanation:

Isolate x in the second equation, then substitute the result into the first equation:

$$x = 10 - y$$
$$3(10 - y) + 2y = 15$$
$$30 - 3y + 2y = 15$$
$$-y = -15$$
$$y = 15$$

If you needed to know the value of x as well, you could now substitute 15 for y into either equation to find that $x = -5$. The correct answer is **(D)**.

Try on Your Own

Directions: Solve these questions by substitution. Take as much time as you need on these questions. Work carefully and methodically. There will be an opportunity for timed practice at the end of the chapter.

HINT: For Q1, which equation is the easier one to solve for one variable in terms of the other?

---

1. If $7c + 8b = 15$ and $3b - c = 2$, what is the value of b?

HINT: For Q2, the second equation is in a convenient form for substitution. But look at the first equation: what can you learn quickly about x and y?

$$\begin{cases} 3x - 3y = 0 \\ y = 2x + 5 \end{cases}$$

2. Given the system of equations above, what is the sum of x and y?

    A) -10
    B) -5
    C) 0
    D) 5

$$\begin{cases} 4x + 3y = 14 - y \\ x - 5y = 2 \end{cases}$$

3. If (x, y) is a solution to the system of equations above, what is the value of $x - y$?

    A) $\dfrac{1}{4}$
    B) 1
    C) 3
    D) 18

4. If $5a = 6b + 7$ and $a - b = 3$, what is the value of $\dfrac{b}{2}$?

    A) 2
    B) 4
    C) 5.5
    D) 11

5. Marisol is selling snacks at her school's soccer games to raise money for a service project. She buys nuts in cases that contain 24 bags and granola bars in cases that contain 20 packages. She sells the nuts for $1.25 a bag and the granola bars for $1.75 a package. If she raised $160 and sold 112 items, how many cases of granola bars did Marisol buy?

    A) 2
    B) 3
    C) 40
    D) 72

Combination

LEARNING OBJECTIVE

After this lesson, you will be able to:

- Solve systems of linear equations by combination

To answer a question like this:

$$\begin{cases} 4x - 5y = 10 \\ 2x + 3y = -6 \end{cases}$$

If the solution to the system of equations above is (x, y), what is the value of y ?

A) -2

B) -1

C) 1

D) 2

You need to know this:

Combining two equations means adding or subtracting them, usually with the goal of either eliminating one of the variables or solving for a combination of variables (e.g., $5n + 5m$).

You need to do this:

To solve a system of two linear equations by combination:

- Make sure that the coefficients for one variable have the same absolute value. (If they don't, multiply one equation by an appropriate constant. Sometimes, you'll have to multiply both equations by constants.)
- Either add or subtract the equations to eliminate one variable.
- Solve for the remaining variable, then substitute its value into either equation to solve for the variable you eliminated in the preceding step.

Explanation:

Both variables have different coefficients in the two equations, but you can convert the $2x$ in the second equation to $4x$ by multiplying the entire second equation by 2:

$$2(2x + 3y = -6)$$
$$4x + 6y = -12$$

Now that the coefficients for one variable are the same, subtract the second equation from the first to eliminate the x variable. (Note that if the x-coefficients were 4 and -4, you would add the equations instead of subtracting.)

$$4x - 5y = 10$$
$$\underline{-(4x + 6y = -12)}$$
$$0x - 11y = 22$$

Solve this equation for y:

$$-11y = 22$$
$$y = -2$$

(A) is the correct answer. If the question asked for x instead of y, you would now substitute -2 into either of the original equations and solve for x. (For the record, $x = 0$.)

Try on Your Own

Directions: Solve these questions using combination. Take as much time as you need on these questions. Work carefully and methodically. There will be an opportunity for timed practice at the end of the chapter.

HINT: For Q6, there's no need to solve for x and y separately.

$$\begin{cases} 3x + 2y = 15 \\ 2x + 3y = 10 \end{cases}$$

6. Given the system of equations above, what is the value of $5x + 5y$?

HINT: For Q7, should you add or subtract these equations to eliminate a variable?

7. If $2x - 3y = 14$ and $5x + 3y = 21$, what is the value of x?

   A) -1

   B) 0

   C) $\dfrac{7}{3}$

   D) 5

8. If $7c - 2b = 15$ and $3b - 6c = 2$, what is the value of $b + c$?

   A) -27

   B) -3

   C) 8

   D) 17

9. If $y = -x - 15$ and $\dfrac{5y}{2} - 37 = -\dfrac{x}{2}$, what is the value of $2x + 6y$?

10. If $2x + 2y = 22$ and $3x - 4y = 12$, what is the value of $\dfrac{y}{x}$?

Number of Possible Solutions

LEARNING OBJECTIVE

After this lesson, you will be able to:

- Determine the number of possible solutions for a system of linear equations, if any

To answer a question like this:

$$\begin{cases} 5x - 3y = 10 \\ 6y = kx - 42 \end{cases}$$

In the system of linear equations above, k represents a constant. If the system of equations has no solution, what is the value of $2k$?

A) $\dfrac{5}{2}$

B) 5

C) 10

D) 20

You need to know this:

The solution to a system of linear equations consists of the values of the variables that make both equations true.

A system of linear equations may have one solution, infinitely many solutions, or no solution.

If a system of equations represents two lines that intersect, then the system will have exactly **one solution** (in which the x- and y-values correspond to the point of intersection).

If a system of equations has **infinitely many solutions**, the two equations actually represent the same line. For example, $2x + y = 15$ and $4x + 2y = 30$ represent the same line. If you divide the second equation by 2, you arrive at the first equation. Every point along this line is a solution.

If a system of equations has **no solution**, as in the question above, the lines are parallel: there is no point of intersection.

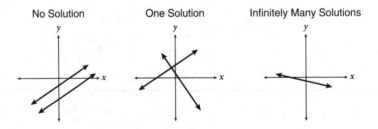

You need to do this:

- If the question states that the system has no solution, manipulate the equations to make the x-coefficients equal to each other and the y-coefficients equal to each other, but be sure that the y-intercepts (or constant terms, if the equations are in $ax + by + c$ form) are different.
- If the question states that the system has infinitely many solutions, make the x-coefficients equal to each other, the y-coefficients equal to each other, and the y-intercepts (or constant terms) equal to each other.
- If the question states that the system has one solution and provides the point of intersection, substitute the values at that point of intersection for x and y in the equations.

Explanation:

Start by recognizing that for two lines to be parallel, the coefficients for x must be identical in the two equations; ditto for the coefficients for y. Manipulate the second equation so that it is in the same format as the first one:

$$kx - 6y = 42$$

The y-coefficient in the first equation, $5x - 3y = 10$, is 3. Divide the second equation by 2 in order to make the y-coefficients in both equations equal:

$$\frac{k}{2}x - 3y = 21$$

Now set the x-coefficient equal to the x-coefficient in the first equation:

$$\frac{k}{2} = 5$$
$$k = 10$$

Note that the question asks for the value of $2k$, so the correct answer is **(D)**, 20.

Try on Your Own

Directions: Take as much time as you need on these questions. Work carefully and methodically. There will be an opportunity for timed practice at the end of the chapter.

$$\begin{cases} 21x - 6y = 54 \\ 9 + y = 3.5x \end{cases}$$

11. The system of equations shown above has how many solutions?

    A) Zero

    B) One

    C) Two

    D) Infinitely many

HINT: For Q12, if a system of equations has infinitely many solutions, what do you know about the two equations?

$$\begin{cases} 6x + 3y = 18 \\ qx - \dfrac{y}{3} = -2 \end{cases}$$

12. In the system of linear equations above, q is a constant. If the system has infinitely many solutions, what is the value of q ?

    A) -9

    B) $-\dfrac{2}{3}$

    C) $\dfrac{2}{3}$

    D) 9

HINT: For Q13, the point of intersection is the solution to the system of equations. Use those concrete x- and y-values.

$$\begin{cases} hx - 4y = -10 \\ kx + 3y = -15 \end{cases}$$

13. If the graphs of the lines in the system of equations above intersect at $(-3, 1)$, what is the value of $\dfrac{k}{h}$?

    A) $\dfrac{1}{3}$

    B) 2

    C) 3

    D) 6

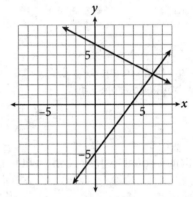

14. What is the y-coordinate of the solution to the system shown above?

    A) -5

    B) 3

    C) 5

    D) 6

$$\begin{cases} 3x - 9y = -6 \\ \dfrac{1}{2}x - \dfrac{3}{2}y = c \end{cases}$$

15. If the system of linear equations above has infinitely many solutions, and c is a constant, what is the value of c ?

    A) -6

    B) -3

    C) -2

    D) -1

On Test Day

Many SAT Math questions can be solved in more than one way. A little efficiency goes a long way in helping you get through the Math sections on time, so it's useful to try solving problems more than one way to learn which way is fastest.

Try this question using two approaches: both substitution and combination. Time yourself on each attempt. Which approach allowed you to get to the answer faster?

16. If $28x - 5y = 36$ and $15x + 5y + 18 = 68$, what is the value of x ?

    A) 1

    B) 2

    C) 3

    D) 4

The answer and both ways of solving can be found at the end of this chapter.

How Much Have You Learned?

Directions: For testlike practice, give yourself 15 minutes to complete this question set. Be sure to study the explanations, even for questions you got right. They can be found at the end of this chapter.

17. If $8x - 2y = 10$ and $3y - 9x = 12$, what is the value of $y - x$?

    A) -8

    B) 2

    C) 12

    D) 22

18. A state college has separate fee rates for resident students and nonresident students. Resident students are charged $421 per semester and nonresident students are charged $879 per semester. The college's sophomore class of 1,980 students paid a total of $1,170,210 in fees for the most recent semester. Which of the following systems of equations represents the number of resident (r) and nonresident (n) sophomores and the amount of fees the two groups paid?

    A) $r + n = 1,170,210$
       $421r + 879n = 1,980$

    B) $r + n = 1,980$
       $879r + 421n = 1,170,210$

    C) $r + n = 1,980$
       $421r + 879n = 1,170,210$

    D) $r + n = 1,170,210$
       $879r + 421n = 1,980$

19. A sofa costs $50 less than three times the cost of a chair. If the sofa and chair together cost $650, how much more does the sofa cost than the chair?

    A) $175

    B) $225

    C) $300

    D) $475

Equation 1	
x	y
-2	6
0	4
2	2
4	0

Equation 2	
x	y
-8	-8
-4	-7
0	-6
4	-5

20. The tables above represent data points for two linear equations. If the two equations form a system, what is the x-coordinate of the solution to that system?

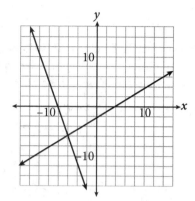

21. If (A, B) is the solution to the system of equations shown above, and A and B are integers, what is the value of $A + B$?

    A) -12

    B) -6

    C) 0

    D) 6

$$\begin{cases} -16 = 7y + 4x \\ k = \dfrac{7}{8}y + \dfrac{1}{2}x \end{cases}$$

22. If the system of linear equations above has infinitely many solutions, and k is a constant, what is the value of k ?

    A) -8

    B) -4

    C) -2

    D) -1

$$\begin{cases} -13 = ay + 24x \\ 9 + 6bx = 5y \end{cases}$$

23. If the system of equations above has no solution, and a and b are constants, then what is the value of $|a + b|$?

    A) 0

    B) 1

    C) 4

    D) 9

24. If $\dfrac{1}{4}x + 2y = \dfrac{11}{4}$ and $-6y - x = 7$, what is half of y ?

	/	/	
.	.	.	.
	0	0	0
1	1	1	1
2	2	2	2
3	3	3	3
4	4	4	4
5	5	5	5
6	6	6	6
7	7	7	7
8	8	8	8
9	9	9	9

25. At a certain toy store, tiny stuffed pandas cost \$3.50 and giant stuffed pandas cost \$14. If the store sold 29 panda toys and made \$217 in revenue in one week, how many tiny stuffed pandas and giant stuffed pandas were sold?

    A) 18 tiny stuffed pandas, 11 giant stuffed pandas

    B) 11 tiny stuffed pandas, 18 giant stuffed pandas

    C) 12 tiny stuffed pandas, 17 giant stuffed pandas

    D) 18 tiny stuffed pandas, 13 giant stuffed pandas

26. A bead shop sells wooden beads for \$0.20 each and crystal beads for \$0.50 each. If a jewelry artist buys 127 beads total and pays \$41 for them, how much more did she spend on crystal beads than wooden beads?

    A) \$11

    B) \$15

    C) \$23

    D) \$26

Reflect

Directions: Take a few minutes to recall what you've learned and what you've been practicing in this chapter. Consider the following questions, jot down your best answer for each one, and then compare your reflections to the expert responses on the following page. Use your level of confidence to determine what to do next.

When is substitution a good choice for solving a system of equations?

_____

_____

_____

When is combination a good choice for solving a system of equations?

_____

_____

_____

What does it mean if a system of equations has no solution? Infinitely many solutions?

_____

_____

_____

Expert Responses

When is substitution a good choice for solving a system of equations?

Substitution works best when at least one of the variables has a coefficient of 1, making the variable easy to isolate. This system, for example, is well suited for substitution:

$$a + 3b = 5$$
$$4a - 6b = 21$$

That's because in the first equation, you can easily isolate a as a = 5 − 3b and plug that in for a in the other equation. By contrast, substitution would not be a great choice for solving this system:

$$2a + 3b = 5$$
$$4a - 6b = 21$$

If you used substitution now, you'd have to work with fractions, which is messy.

When is combination a good choice for solving a system of equations?

Combination is always a good choice. It is at its worst in systems such as this one:

$$2a + 3b = 5$$
$$3a + 5b = 7$$

Neither a coefficient is a multiple of the other, and neither b coefficient is a multiple of the other, so to solve this system with combination you'd have to multiply both equations by a constant (e.g., multiply the first equation by 3 and the second equation by 2 to create a 6a term in both equations). But substitution wouldn't be stellar in this situation, either.

Note that combination may be particularly effective when the SAT asks for a variable expression. For example, if a question based on the previous system of equations asked for the value of 5a + 8b, then you could find the answer instantly by adding the equations together.

What does it mean if a system of equations has no solution? Infinitely many solutions?

A system of equations with no solution represents two parallel lines, which never cross. The coefficient of a variable in one equation will match the coefficient of the same variable in the other equation, but the constants will be different. For example, this system has no solution:

$$2x + 3y = 4$$
$$2x + 3y = 5$$

Subtracting one equation from the other yields the equation 0 = −1, which makes no sense.

If a system of equations has infinitely many solutions, then the two equations represent the same line. For example, this system has infinitely many solutions:

$$2x + 3y = 4$$
$$4x + 6y = 8$$

Dividing the second equation by 2 yields 2x + 3y = 4, so although the two equations look different, they are actually the same.

Next Steps

If you answered most questions correctly in the "How Much Have You Learned?" section, and if your responses to the Reflect questions were similar to those of the SAT expert, then consider Systems of Equations an area of strength and move on to the next chapter. Come back to this topic periodically to prevent yourself from getting rusty.

If you don't yet feel confident, review those parts of this chapter that you have not yet mastered. In particular, review the mechanics for solving a system of equations by substitution and by combination. Then try the questions you missed again. As always, be sure to review the explanations closely. Finally, **go online** (www.kaptest.com/moreonline) for additional practice on the highest yield topics in this chapter.

Answers and Explanations

1. 1

Difficulty: Medium

Getting to the Answer: Start by isolating c in the second equation: $c = 3b - 2$. Then substitute into the first equation and solve:

$$7(3b - 2) + 8b = 15$$
$$21b - 14 + 8b = 15$$
$$29b - 14 = 15$$
$$29b = 29$$
$$b = 1$$

Grid in **1**.

2. A

Difficulty: Easy

Getting to the Answer: The quickest way to solve is to realize that you can rearrange the first equation to find that $x = y$. Then substitute y for x in the second equation: $y = 2y + 5$. Solve to find that $y = -5$. Because $x = y$, x also equals -5, and $x + y = -10$. **(A)** is correct.

3. C

Difficulty: Medium

Getting to the Answer: Because x has a coefficient of 1 in the second equation, solve the system using substitution. Before you select your answer, make sure you found the right quantity (the difference between x and y).

First, solve the second equation for x and substitute:

$$x - 5y = 2$$
$$x = 2 + 5y$$
$$4(2 + 5y) + 3y = 14 - y$$
$$8 + 20y + 3y = 14 - y$$
$$8 + 23y = 14 - y$$
$$24y = 6$$
$$y = \frac{6}{24} = \frac{1}{4}$$

Next, substitute this value back into $x = 2 + 5y$ and simplify:

$$x = 2 + 5\left(\frac{1}{4}\right)$$
$$x = \frac{8}{4} + \frac{5}{4}$$
$$x = \frac{13}{4}$$

Finally, subtract $x - y$ to find the difference:

$$\frac{13}{4} - \frac{1}{4} = \frac{12}{4} = 3$$

(C) is correct.

4. B

Difficulty: Medium

Getting to the Answer: It's equally easy to solve the second equation for either variable. The question asks for $\frac{b}{2}$, so solve for a and substitute to create an equation in only one variable:

$$a = b + 3$$
$$5(b + 3) = 6b + 7$$
$$5b + 15 = 6b + 7$$
$$8 = b$$

So $\frac{b}{2} = 4$, and **(B)** is correct.

5. A

Difficulty: Medium

Getting to the Answer: Set up two equations: one for the number of items sold and one for the money collected. Let $N =$ the number of bags of nuts sold and $G =$ the number of packages of granola bars sold.

The equation for the total items is $N + G = 112$.

The equation for the money collected is $1.25N + 1.75G = 160$.

Even though this is a calculator question, quickly converting the second equation to fractions is an efficient way to save time and prevent an entry mistake: $\frac{5}{4}N + \frac{7}{4}G = 160$.

Multiply by 4 to clear the equation of fractions to get $5N + 7G = 640$.

At this point, you could solve by either combination or substitution. If you use substitution, solve the first equation for N, the number of bags of nuts, because the question asks for G, the number of packages of granola bars. Solving the first equation for N yields $N = 112 - G$.

Substituting that equation into the second equation gives:

$$5(112 - G) + 7G = 640$$
$$560 - 5G + 7G = 640$$
$$560 + 2G = 640$$
$$2G = 80$$
$$G = 40$$

Remember the question asks for the number of *cases* of granola bars Marisol purchased, so divide 40 by 20, the number of packages of granola bars per case. **(A)** is correct.

As an alternative approach, if you read the question carefully and recognized you're solving for the number of *cases*, not packages, the correct answer would have to be either (A) or (B), since (C) and (D) are way too big. You could then test one of those choices, say (A) 2, by multiplying by 20 packages of granola bars per case: $2 \times 20 = 40$. Subtract that number from 112 to get the number of bags of nuts: $112 - 40 = 72$. Multiply each quantity by the price per package: $72 \times 1.25 = 90$ and $40 \times 1.75 = 70$. Then add the sales of the two items together: $90 + 70 = 160$. You've now confirmed the correct answer because $160 is how much Marisol raised. If you had tested (B) instead, then you could have eliminated it and still arrived at the correct answer with no more work because you eliminated all choices except **(A)**.

If you chose any of the other options, you likely answered the wrong question. (B) is the number of cases of nuts Marisol purchased, (C) is the number of packages of granola bars sold, and (D) is the number of bags of nuts sold.

6. 25
Difficulty: Easy

Getting to the Answer: Often, when the SAT asks for a sum or difference of variables, solving by combination yields the answer very quickly. Add the equations:

$$\begin{aligned} 3x + 2y &= 15 \\ + \quad 2x + 3y &= 10 \\ \hline 5x + 5y &= 25 \end{aligned}$$

Grid in **25** and move on.

7. D
Difficulty: Easy

Getting to the Answer: This system is already set up perfectly to solve using combination because the y terms ($-3y$ and $3y$) are opposites. Add the two equations to cancel $-3y$ and $3y$. Then solve the resulting equation for x:

$$\begin{aligned} 2x - 3y &= 14 \\ + \quad 5x + 3y &= 21 \\ \hline 7x \quad\quad &= 35 \\ x \quad\quad &= 5 \end{aligned}$$

Choice **(D)** is correct. The question asks only for the value of x, so you don't need to substitute x back into either equation to find the value of y.

8. D
Difficulty: Easy

Getting to the Answer: If you're not asked to find the value of an individual variable, the question may lend itself to combination. This question asks for $b + c$, so don't waste your time finding the variables individually if you can avoid it. After rearranging the equations so that variables and constants are aligned, you can add the equations together:

$$\begin{aligned} -2b + 7c &= 15 \\ + 3b - 6c &= 2 \\ \hline b + c &= 17 \end{aligned}$$

This matches **(D)**.

9. 59

Difficulty: Hard

Getting to the Answer: You're asked for the value of an expression rather than the value of one of the variables, so try combination. Start by rearranging the two equations so that variables and constants are aligned:

$$x + y = -15$$
$$\frac{x}{2} + \frac{5y}{2} = 37$$

Clear the fractions in the second equation and then add the equations:

$$2\left(\frac{x}{2} + \frac{5y}{2} = 37\right) \rightarrow x + 5y = 74$$

$$\begin{array}{r} x + y = -15 \\ + \quad x + 5y = 74 \\ \hline 2x + 6y = 59 \end{array}$$

This is precisely what the question asks for, so you're done. Grid in **59**.

10. 3/8

Difficulty: Medium

Getting to the Answer: None of the coefficients in either equation is 1, so using combination is a better strategy than substitution here. Examine the coefficients of x: they don't share any factors, so multiply each equation by the coefficient from the other equation:

$$3(2x + 2y = 22) \rightarrow 6x + 6y = 66$$
$$2(3x - 4y = 12) \rightarrow 6x - 8y = 24$$

Subtract the second equation from the first:

$$\begin{array}{r} 6x + 6y = 66 \\ - \ (6x - 8y = 24) \\ \hline 14y = 42 \\ y = 3 \end{array}$$

Next, you need x so you can determine the value of $\frac{y}{x}$. Substitute 3 for y in one of the original equations:

$$2x + 2(3) = 22$$
$$2x + 6 = 22$$
$$2x = 16$$
$$x = 8$$

Plug your x- and y-values into $\frac{y}{x}$ to get $\frac{3}{8}$. Grid in **3/8**.

11. D

Difficulty: Medium

Strategic Advice: Note that (C) is impossible. There are only three possibilities: the lines intersect, in which case there is one solution; the lines are parallel, in which case there are no solutions; or the equations describe the same line, in which case there are infinitely many solutions.

Getting to the Answer: Get the two equations into the same format so that you can distinguish among these possibilities:

$$21x - 6y = 54$$
$$3.5x - y = 9$$

Now it's easier to see that the first equation is equivalent to multiplying every term in the second equation by 6. Both equations describe the same line, so there are infinitely many solutions; **(D)** is correct.

12. B

Difficulty: Hard

Getting to the Answer: A system of equations that has infinitely many solutions describes a single line. Therefore, manipulation of one equation will yield the other. Look at the constant terms: to turn the 18 into a -2, divide the first equation by -9:

$$\frac{(6x + 3y = 18)}{-9} \rightarrow -\frac{6}{9}x - \frac{3}{9}y = -2$$
$$\rightarrow -\frac{2}{3}x - \frac{1}{3}y = -2$$

The y terms and constants in the second equation now match those in the first; all that's left is to set the coefficients of x equal to each other: $q = -\frac{2}{3}$. Choice **(B)** is correct.

Note that you could also write each equation in slope-intercept form and set the slopes equal to each other to solve for q.

13. C

Difficulty: Medium

Getting to the Answer: If the graphs intersect at $(-3, 1)$, then the solution to the system is $x = -3$ and $y = 1$. Substitute these values into both equations and go from there:

$$hx - 4y = -10 \qquad kx + 3y = -15$$
$$h(-3) - 4(1) = -10 \qquad k(-3) + 3(1) = -15$$
$$-3h - 4 = -10 \qquad -3k + 3 = -15$$
$$-3h = -6 \qquad -3k = -18$$
$$h = 2 \qquad k = 6$$

So, $\dfrac{k}{h} = \dfrac{6}{2} = 3$, making **(C)** correct.

14. B

Difficulty: Easy

Getting to the Answer: The solution to a system of linear equations represented graphically is the point of intersection. If the lines do not intersect, the system has no solution.

According to the graph, the lines intersect, or cross each other, at (6, 3). The question asks for the y-coordinate of the solution, which is 3, so **(B)** is correct.

15. D

Difficulty: Hard

Getting to the Answer: A system of linear equations has infinitely many solutions if both lines in the system have the same slope and the same y-intercept (in other words, they are the same line).

To have the same slope, the x- and y-coefficients of the two equations must be the same. Use the x-coefficients here: to turn $\frac{1}{2}$ into 3, multiply by 6. So c becomes $6c$, and $6c = -6$, or $c = -1$, which is **(D)**.

Note that you could also write each equation in slope-intercept form and set the y-intercepts equal to each other to solve for c.

16. B

Difficulty: Medium

Strategic Advice: The numbers here are fairly large, so substitution is not likely to be convenient. Moreover, the y-coefficients have the same absolute value, so combination will probably be the faster way to solve.

Getting to the Answer: Start by writing the second equation in the same form as the first, then use combination to solve for x:

$$\begin{array}{r} 28x - 5y = 36 \\ + 15x + 5y = 50 \\ \hline 43x = 86 \\ x = 2 \end{array}$$

Choice **(B)** is correct.

If you feel more comfortable using substitution, you can maximize efficiency by solving one equation for $5y$ and substituting that value into the other equation:

$$15x + 5y = 50$$
$$5y = 50 - 15x$$
$$28x - (50 - 15x) = 36$$
$$43x - 50 = 36$$
$$43x = 86$$
$$x = 2$$

Note that the arithmetic is fundamentally the same, but the setup using combination is quicker and visually easier to follow.

17. D

Difficulty: Medium

Category: Combination

Strategic Advice: When a question asks for a sum or difference of variables, consider solving by combination.

Getting to the Answer: Rearrange the equations to be in the same form, with the y terms before the x terms, and then add:

$$\begin{array}{r} -2y + 8x = 10 \\ +(3y - 9x = 12) \\ \hline y - x = 22 \end{array}$$

The correct answer is **(D)**.

18. C

Difficulty: Medium

Category: Substitution/Combination

Getting to the Answer: Because you're given the variables (r for resident and n for nonresident), the only thing left for you to do is to break the wording apart into phrases and translate into math. Add together both student types to get the first equation: $r + n = 1,980$. This eliminates (A) and (D). Residents pay \$421 in fees ($421r$), which eliminates (B). Only **(C)** is left, so it has to be the answer.

19. C

Difficulty: Medium

Category: Substitution

Getting to the Answer: Write a system of equations where $c =$ the cost of the chair in dollars and $s =$ the cost of the sofa in dollars. A sofa costs \$50 less than three times the cost of the chair, or $s = 3c - 50$; together, a sofa and a chair cost \$650, so $s + c = 650$.

The system is:

$$\begin{cases} s = 3c - 50 \\ s + c = 650 \end{cases}$$

The top equation is already solved for s, so substitute $3c - 50$ into the bottom equation for s and solve for c:

$$3c - 50 + c = 650$$
$$4c - 50 = 650$$
$$4c = 700$$
$$c = 175$$

Remember to check if you solved for the right thing! The chair costs \$175, so the sofa costs $3(175) - 50 = 525 - 50 = \$475$. This means the sofa costs $\$475 - \$175 = \$300$ more than the chair. Therefore, **(C)** is correct.

20. 8

Difficulty: Medium

Category: Number of Possible Solutions

Strategic Advice: The solution to the system is the point that both tables will have in common, but the tables, as given, do not share any points. You could use the data to write the equation of each line and then solve the system, but this will use up valuable time on test day. Instead, look for patterns that can be extended.

Getting to the Answer: In the table for Equation 1, the x-values increase by 2 each time and the y-values decrease by 2. In the table for Equation 2, the x-values increase by 4 each time and the y-values increase by 1. Use these patterns to continue the tables.

Equation 1	
x	y
-2	6
0	4
2	2
4	0
6	-2
8	**-4**

Equation 2	
x	y
-8	-8
-4	-7
0	-6
4	-5
8	**-4**
12	-3

The point $(8, -4)$ satisfies both equations, so the x-coordinate of the solution to the system is **8**.

21. A

Difficulty: Easy

Category: Number of Possible Solutions

Getting to the Answer: The solution to a system of equations shown graphically is the point of intersection. Read the axis labels carefully. Each grid line represents 2 units. The two lines intersect at the point $(-6, -6)$, so $A + B = -6 + (-6) = -12$, which means **(A)** is correct.

22. C

Difficulty: Hard

Category: Number of Possible Solutions

Getting to the Answer: The system has infinitely many solutions, so both equations must describe the same line. Notice that if you multiply the x- and y-coefficients in the second equation by 8, you arrive at the x- and y-coefficients in the first equation. The constant k times 8 must then equal the constant in the first equation, or -16:

$$8k = -16$$
$$k = -2$$

The correct answer is **(C)**.

23. B

Difficulty: Hard

Category: Number of Possible Solutions

Getting to the Answer: Rearrange the equations and write them on top of each other so that the x and y variables line up:

$$\begin{cases} 24x + ay = -13 \\ 6bx - 5y = -9 \end{cases}$$

In a system of equations that has no solution, the x-coefficients must equal each other and the y-coefficients must equal each other. Thus, for the x-coefficients, $24 = 6b$, which means that $b = 4$. For the y-coefficients, $a = -5$. The question asks for the value of $|a + b|$, which is $|-5 + 4| = |-1| = 1$, choice **(B)**. (Note that if you used the equation $-6bx + 5y = 9$, you would get $a = 5$ and $b = -4$, which would still result in the correct answer.)

24. 9/2 or 4.5

Difficulty: Medium

Category: Substitution/Combination

Getting to the Answer: Start by clearing the fractions from the first equation (by multiplying by 4) to make the numbers easier to work with. Then use combination to solve for y:

$$\begin{array}{r} x + 8y = 11 \\ + \quad -x - 6y = 7 \\ \hline 2y = 18 \\ y = 9 \end{array}$$

Take half of 9 to get $\frac{9}{2}$, then grid in **9/2** or **4.5**.

25. A

Difficulty: Medium

Category: Substitution/Combination

Getting to the Answer: Choose intuitive letters for the variables: t for tiny pandas, g for giant pandas. You're given the cost of each as well as the number of each sold and the total revenue generated. Then write the system of equations that represents the information given:

$$t + g = 29$$
$$3.5t + 14g = 217$$

Multiplying the top equation by -14 allows you to solve for t using combination:

$$\begin{array}{r} -14t - 14g = -406 \\ + \quad 3.5t + 14g = 217 \\ \hline -10.5t \quad\quad = -189 \\ t \quad\quad = 18 \end{array}$$

Solving for t gives 18, which eliminates (B) and (C). Plugging 18 into t in the first equation allows you to find g, which is 11. Choice **(A)** is correct.

26. A

Difficulty: Hard

Category: Substitution/Combination

Getting to the Answer: Choose letters that make sense for the variables: w for wooden and c for crystal. You know the jewelry artist bought 127 beads total. You're also told each wooden bead costs \$0.20 ($0.2w$) and each crystal bead costs \$0.50 ($0.5c$), as well as the fact that she spent \$41 total. You'll have two equations: one relating the number of wooden beads and crystal beads and a second relating the costs associated with each:

$$w + c = 127$$
$$0.2w + 0.5c = 41$$

Either combination or substitution is a good choice for solving this system. Both are shown here:

Combination:

$$2(0.2w + 0.5c = 41) \rightarrow 0.4w + c = 82$$
$$w + \cancel{c} = 127$$
$$\underline{-\quad 0.4w + \cancel{c} = 82}$$
$$0.6w \quad\quad = 45$$
$$w \quad\quad = 75$$

Substitution:

$$w + c = 127 \rightarrow c = 127 - w$$
$$0.2w + 0.5(127 - w) = 41$$
$$0.2w + 63.5 - 0.5w = 41$$
$$-0.3w = -22.5$$
$$w = 75$$
$$75 + c = 127 \rightarrow c = 52$$

The question asks for the difference in the amount spent on each type of bead, not the difference in the quantity of each type. Multiply the bead counts by the correct pricing to get $75 \times \$0.2 = \$15$ for the wooden beads and $52 \times \$0.5 = \$26$ for the crystal beads. Take the difference to get $\$26 - \$15 = \$11$, which is **(A)**.

CHAPTER 6

Inequalities

LEARNING OBJECTIVES

After completing this chapter, you will be able to:

- Solve an inequality for a range of values
- Identify the graph of an inequality or a system of inequalities
- Solve for the point of intersection of the boundary lines of a system of inequalities
- Solve algebraically a system of one inequality with two variables and another inequality with one variable
- Identify one or more inequalities that match a real-life situation

35/600 SmartPoints® (Medium Yield)

How Much Do You Know?

Directions: Try the questions that follow. Show your work so that you can compare your solutions to the ones found in the Check Your Work section immediately after this question set. The "Category" heading in the explanation for each question gives the title of the lesson that covers how to solve it. If you answered the question(s) for a given lesson correctly, and if your scratchwork looks like ours, you may be able to move quickly through that lesson. If you answered incorrectly or used a different approach, you may want to take your time on that lesson.

1. If $\frac{3}{5}p - 2 \geq 5$, what is the least possible value of $\frac{6}{5}p + 2$?

    A)   7

    B)   10

    C)   16

    D)   18

2. If $-3 < \frac{4}{3}h + \frac{1}{6} < 1$, then what is one possible value of $12h - 4$?

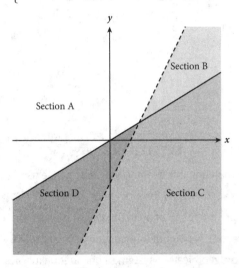

$$\begin{cases} y > 2x - 3 \\ 5y \leq 3x \end{cases}$$

3. The graph above depicts the system of inequalities shown. Which of the labeled section or sections of the graph could represent all of the solutions of the system?

    A)   Sections A and D

    B)   Section B

    C)   Sections C and D

    D)   Section D

4. A bowling alley charges a flat $6.50 fee for shoe and ball rental plus $3.75 per game and 6.325 percent sales tax. If each person in a group of seven people has $20 to spend on a bowling outing, and at least some members of the group must rent shoes and a ball, which inequality best describes this situation, given that the number of shoe and ball rentals is represented by r and the number of games is represented by g ?

    A) $1.06325(6.5r + 3.75g) \leq 140$

    B) $1.06325(6.5r + 3.75g) \leq 20$

    C) $1.06325\left(\dfrac{6.5}{r} + \dfrac{3.75}{g}\right) \leq 140$

    D) $0.06325(6.5r + 3.75g) \leq 20$

5. Marco is paid $80 per day plus $15 per hour for overtime. If he works five days per week and wants to make a minimum of $520 this week, what is the fewest number of hours of overtime he must work?

6. An architect in an arid region determines that a building's current landscaping uses $1,640 worth of water monthly. The architect plans to replace the current landscaping with arid-zone landscaping at a cost of $15,900, which will reduce the monthly watering cost to $770. Which of the following inequalities can be used to find m, the number of months after replacement that the savings in water costs will be at least as much as the cost of replacing the landscaping?

A) $15,900 \geq (1,640 - 770)m$

B) $15,900 > 770m$

C) $15,900 \leq (1,640 - 770)m$

D) $15,900 \leq 770m$

Check Your Work

1. C

Difficulty: Medium

Category: Linear Inequalities

Getting to the Answer: You might be tempted to solve for p, but some critical thinking and algebra make that unnecessary. First, get $\frac{3}{5}p$ by itself by adding 2 to both sides: $\frac{3}{5}p \geq 7$. Next, multiply both sides by 2 to get the value range of $\frac{6}{5}p \geq 14$. Finally, add 2 to both sides to get $\frac{6}{5}p + 2 \geq 14 + 2$. Thus, $\frac{6}{5}p + 2 \geq 16$, so **(C)** is correct.

2. Any value greater than or equal to 0 and less than 3.5

Difficulty: Hard

Category: Linear Inequalities

Getting to the Answer: Don't automatically start solving the two inequalities separately. Instead, look for a series of quick manipulations to convert $\frac{4}{3}h + \frac{1}{6}$ to $12h - 4$. Start by multiplying the entire inequality by 9 to yield $-27 < 12h + \frac{3}{2} < 9$. Next, subtract $\frac{3}{2}$ and then 4 more (to get the desired -4) from all parts of the inequality (converting the fraction component to a decimal will make this step easier), which will become $-32.5 < 12h - 4 < 3.5$. Because Grid-in answers cannot be negative, pick any value that is **greater than or equal to 0 but less than 3.5**.

3. D

Difficulty: Medium

Category: Systems of Inequalities

Getting to the Answer: Sections A and D are all the y values greater than $2x - 3$, so those sections are the solution set for the inequality $y > 2x - 3$. Similarly, Sections C and D are the solution set for $5y \leq 3x$. The solutions for a system of inequalities are all the points that satisfy all (both, in this case) of the inequalities. The points in Section D are in the solution set for both inequalities, so **(D)** is correct.

4. A

Difficulty: Medium

Category: Modeling Real-Life Situations with Inequalities

Getting to the Answer: The question has defined the variables for you (r and g). The bowling alley charges $6.50 for shoe and ball rental and $3.75 per game. Sales tax is 6.325% (0.06325 in decimal form). Rental and game costs are given by $6.5r$ and $3.75g$, respectively. To incorporate sales tax into the total cost, multiply the sum of $6.5r$ and $3.75g$ by 1.06325 (not 0.06325, which gives the cost of sales tax only). The question asks for an inequality that represents the amount that the group can spend, which can be no more than $7 \times 20 = 140$; therefore, the correct inequality is $1.06325(6.5r + 3.75g) \leq 140$. This matches **(A)**.

5. 8

Difficulty: Medium

Category: Modeling Real-Life Situations with Inequalities

Getting to the Answer: Translate from English into math to create an inequality in which h represents the number of hours of overtime Marco must work. Marco gets paid a daily wage plus an hourly rate for overtime, so his weekly pay is his daily rate ($80) times 5 days, plus the number of hours of overtime he works (h) times his overtime rate ($15). If he wants to make *at least* $520, which means that much or more, the inequality is $(80 \times 5) + 15h \geq 520$. Solve for h:

$$400 + 15h \geq 520$$
$$15h \geq 120$$
$$h \geq 8$$

Marco must work at least 8 hours of overtime to make $520 or more this week. Grid in **8**.

6.   C

Difficulty: Medium

Category: Modeling Real-Life Situations with Inequalities

Getting to the Answer: The question asks for the point at which the savings will be *at least as much* as the cost of replacing the landscaping, so the value range could include a value equal to the exact cost of replacement; eliminate the strict inequality in (B). Because you need a value range that is at least as much as the cost of landscaping, you need the cost of landscaping, $15,900, to be *less than* or equal to the value range. Eliminate (A).

The value range will be the value of the monthly savings times the number of months, which will be m times the difference between the old monthly water cost and the new monthly water cost: $(1,640 - 770)m$. Therefore, the entire inequality expression is $15,900 \leq (1,640 - 770)m$, so **(C)** is correct.

Math

Linear Inequalities

LEARNING OBJECTIVES

After this lesson, you will be able to:

- Solve an inequality for a range of values
- Identify the graph of an inequality

To answer a question like this:

Which of the following graphs represents the solution set for $5x - 10y > 6$?

A)
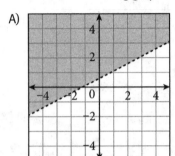

B)
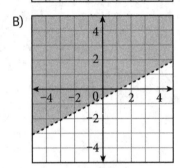

C)
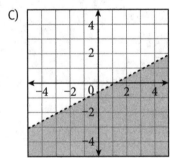

D)
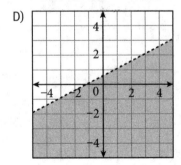

K

You need to know this:

Linear inequalities are similar to linear equations but have two differences:

- You are solving for a **range of values** rather than a single value.
- If you multiply or divide both sides of the inequality by a negative, you must **reverse the inequality sign**.

While linear equations graph as simple lines, inequalities graph as shaded regions. Use solid lines for inequalities with $\leq$ or $\geq$ signs because the line itself is included in the solution set. Use dashed lines for inequalities with $<$ or $>$ signs because, in these cases, the line itself is not included in the solution set. The shaded region represents all points that make up the solution set for the inequality.

You need to do this:

To graph an inequality, start by writing the inequality in slope-intercept form, then graph the solid or dashed line. Finally, add shading:

- For $y > mx + b$ and $y \geq mx + b$, shade the region *above* the line.
- For $y < mx + b$ and $y \leq mx + b$, shade the region *below* the line.

If it's hard to tell which region is above/below the line (which can happen when the line is steep), compare the y-values on both sides of the line.

Explanation:

Rewrite the inequality in slope-intercept form and then identify which half-plane should be shaded. Subtract $5x$ from both sides of the inequality, divide both sides by -10, and flip the inequality symbol to yield $y < \frac{1}{2}x - \frac{3}{5}$. Eliminate (A) and (D) because they have positive y-intercepts. The "less than" symbol indicates that the half-plane below the line should be shaded, making **(C)** the correct answer.

Try on Your Own

Directions: Take as much time as you need on these questions. Work carefully and methodically. There will be an opportunity for timed practice at the end of the chapter.

$$-\frac{a}{6} - a > -\frac{4}{3}$$

1. Which of the following is equivalent to the inequality above?

    A) $a < \frac{7}{8}$

    B) $a > \frac{7}{8}$

    C) $a < \frac{8}{7}$

    D) $a > \frac{8}{7}$

HINT: For Q2, save time by solving for the entire expression, not *c*.

---

2. If $-5c - 7 \leq 8$, what is the least possible value of $15c + 7$?

    A) -38

    B) -4

    C) 15

    D) 22

HINT: For Q3, be careful not to "lose" a negative sign.

$$-\frac{1}{8}(8 - 10x) > 3x - 2$$

3. Which of the following describes all possible values of x?

    A) $x < -\frac{12}{7}$

    B) $x > -\frac{4}{7}$

    C) $x < \frac{4}{7}$

    D) $x > \frac{4}{7}$

$$\frac{1}{4}a - \frac{1}{16}b + 3 < 5$$

4. Which of the following is equivalent to the inequality above?

    A) $4a - b < 8$

    B) $4a - b < 32$

    C) $a - 4b < 32$

    D) $4b - a < 4$

5. If $4c + 20 \geq 31$, what is the least possible value of $12c + 7$?

    A) 18

    B) 40

    C) 51

    D) 58

Systems of Inequalities

LEARNING OBJECTIVES

After this lesson, you will be able to:

- Identify the graph of a system of inequalities
- Solve for the point of intersection of the boundary lines of a system of inequalities
- Solve algebraically a system of one inequality with two variables and another inequality with one variable

To answer a question like this:

If $12x - 4y > 8$ and $\frac{2}{3}x + 6y \geq 14$ form a system of inequalities, which of the following graphs shows the solution set for the system?

A)

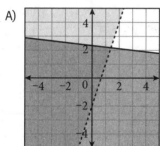

B)

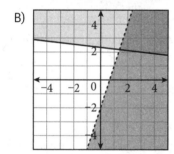

C)

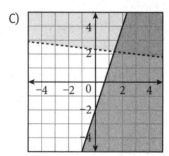

D)

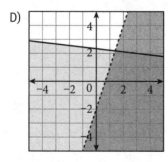

You need to know this:

The solution set for a system of inequalities is not a single point (a single *x*-value and *y*-value) but a region of overlap between the two inequalities: that is, a range of *x*-values and *y*-values. It is easiest to see this graphically.

Systems of inequalities can be presented graphically with multiple boundary lines and multiple shaded regions. Follow the same rules as for graphing single inequalities, but keep in mind that **the solution set is the region where the shading overlaps**.

Note that you generally cannot use substitution or combination to solve a system of two inequalities where both have two variables. That said, the SAT may ask for the maximum or minimum *x*- or *y*-value of a system of inequalities. These questions are actually asking about the intersection of the **boundary lines** of the system. If you see one of these questions, use substitution or combination to solve for the point of intersection, as you learned to do in chapter 5. For an example of this type of question (which is rare on the SAT), see question number 8 in the Try on Your Own set for this lesson.

You may also see an occasional question without a graph asking you to solve a system of one inequality in two variables and another inequality in one variable. As long as both inequalities have the same symbol, you can do this by substitution. Question number 6 in this lesson's Try on Your Own set is an example of this rare question type.

You need to do this:

- To identify the graph of a system of inequalities, follow the same rules as for single inequalities. The solution set is the region where the shading overlaps.
- For a question asking for a maximum or minimum, solve for the intersection point of the boundary lines.
- For a question asking for the range of values that satisfies a system of one inequality in two variables and one inequality in one variable (both with the same sign), solve by substitution.

Explanation:

Rewrite the inequalities in slope-intercept form. Once complete, determine whether each line should be solid or dashed and which half of the plane (above or below the line) should be shaded for each. The correct graph should have a dashed line with a positive slope ($y < 3x - 2$) and a solid line with a negative slope $\left(y \geq -\frac{1}{9}x + \frac{7}{3}\right)$; eliminate (C) because the dashed and solid lines are incorrect. According to the inequality symbols, the half-plane above the solid line and the half-plane below the dashed line should be shaded; the only match is **(B)**.

Try on Your Own

Directions: Take as much time as you need on these questions. Work carefully and methodically. There will be an opportunity for timed practice at the end of the chapter.

$$a < 6b + 4$$
$$3b < 8$$

6. Which of the following consists of all the a-values that satisfy the system of inequalities above?

A) $a < 20$

B) $a < 16$

C) $a < 12$

D) $a < \dfrac{8}{3}$

HINT: For Q7, remember that the solution set is the overlap between both inequalities. Make a sketch or use a graphing calculator.

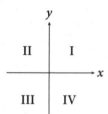

7. If the system of inequalities $y \leq -x + 1$ and $y < \dfrac{1}{2}x$ is graphed on the above plane, which of the quadrants contain(s) no solutions to the system?

A) Quadrant I

B) Quadrant II

C) Quadrant III

D) Quadrants I and II

$$-y \leq 6x - 2{,}200$$
$$3y \geq 9x - 1{,}500$$

8. Given the system of inequalities above, if point (a, b) lies within the solution set, what is the minimum possible value of b ?

$$x < 4 - 2y$$
$$y \leq -2x + 1$$

9. Which of the following ordered pairs satisfies both of the inequalities above?

A) $(-1, 3)$

B) $(1, 1)$

C) $(2, -3)$

D) $(4, 4)$

Math

HINT: For Q10, remember that "solution" means an (x, y) pair
that is true for both inequalities.

$$y > x + r$$
$$y < s - x$$

10. If $x = y = 1$ is a solution to the system of inequalities above, which of the following ordered pairs could correspond to (r, s) ?

    A) $(-1, 1)$

    B) $\left(-\frac{1}{2}, 2\right)$

    C) $\left(-\frac{1}{10}, 3\right)$

    D) $(3, -1)$

Modeling Real-Life Situations with Inequalities

LEARNING OBJECTIVE

After this lesson, you will be able to:

- Identify one or more inequalities that match a real-life situation

To answer a question like this:

To make its sales goals for the month, a toy manufacturer must sell at least $10,400 of toy hoops and basketballs. Toy hoops sell for $8 and basketballs sell for $25. The company hopes to sell more than three times as many basketballs as toy hoops. If h represents the number of toy hoops and b represents the number of basketballs, where h and b are positive integers, which of the following systems of inequalities best describes this situation?

A) $8h + 25b \geq 10,400$

   $b > 3h$

B) $8h + 25b \geq 10,400$

   $h > 3b$

C) $25h + 8b \geq 10,400$

   $b > 3h$

D) $25h + 8b \geq 10,400$

   $h > 3b$

You need to know this:

Word problems involving inequalities require you to do the same sort of translation that you learned in chapter 4. They also require you to get the direction of the inequality sign right. The following table shows which symbols correspond to which words.

English	Symbol
more, greater, longer, heavier	$>$
less, fewer, shorter, lighter	$<$
no less than, no fewer than, at least	$\geq$
no more than, no greater than, at most	$\leq$

You need to do this:

Break down the word problem one inequality at a time. For each one:

- Identify the correct symbol based on the table above.
- Put the value that follows the word "than" or "as" on the right and the other value on the left.
- If the sentence does not use the words "than" or "as," use logic to determine the relationship between the values.

Explanation:

"At least $10,400" means $\geq 10,400$. It's the money from the sales of toy hoops and basketballs that has to be greater than or equal to $10,400, so that's what needs to go on the left of the $\geq$ sign. Each toy hoop costs $8, so the cash generated by sales of toy hoops will be $8h$. Each basketball costs $25, so basketballs will generate $25b$. Add them: $8h + 25b \geq 10,400$. Eliminate (C) and (D).

The company wants to sell "*more than* three times as many basketballs as toy hoops," so write down $>$ and work out what needs to go on each side. The company wants to sell more basketballs than toy hoops, so b should go on the left. Specifically, they want basketball sales to be more than 3 times toy hoop sales, so the final statement is $b > 3h$. **(A)** is correct.

Try on Your Own

Directions: Take as much time as you need on these questions. Work carefully and methodically. There will be an opportunity for timed practice at the end of the chapter.

HINT: For Q11, set up one inequality for the number of ads and a second inequality for the money the ads bring in.

---

11. Ariel enters a contest to sell advertisements in her school's yearbook. To qualify for a prize, she has to sell at least $1,500 worth of advertisements consisting of no fewer than 15 individual ads. Each full-page ad costs $110, each half-page ad costs $70, and each quarter-page ad costs $50. Which of the following systems of inequalities represents this situation, where x is the number of full-page ads she sells, y is the number of half-page ads she sells, and z is the number of quarter-page ads she sells?

    A) $110x + 70y + 50z \geq 1,500$
        $x + y + z \leq 15$

    B) $110x + 70y + 50z \leq 1,500$
        $x + y + z \leq 15$

    C) $110x + 70y + 50z \geq 1,500$
        $x + y + z \geq 15$

    D) $110x + 70y + 50z \leq 1,500$
        $x + y + z \geq 15$

12. A farmer sells watermelons, cantaloupes, and tomatoes from a small cart at a county fair. He needs to sell at least $200 of produce each day. His watermelons are priced at $0.50 per pound, his cantaloupes at $1 per pound, and his tomatoes at $2.50 per pound. His cart can hold no more than 250 pounds. Which of the following inequalities represents this scenario, if w is the number of pounds of watermelons, c is the number of pounds of cantaloupes, and t is the number of pounds of tomatoes?

    A) $0.5w + 1c + 2.5t \geq 200$
        $w + c + t \leq 250$

    B) $0.5w + 1c + 2.5t \leq 200$
        $w + c + t \leq 250$

    C) $0.5w + 1c + 2.5t \geq 200$
        $w + c + t \geq 250$

    D) $0.5w + 1c + 2.5t \leq 200$
        $w + c + t \geq 250$

13. Allison is planting a garden with at least 15 trees. There will be a combination of apple trees, which cost $120 each, and pear trees, which cost $145 each. Allison's budget for purchasing the trees is no more than $2,050. She must plant at least 5 apple trees and at least 3 pear trees. Which of the following systems of inequalities represents the situation described if x is the number of apple trees and y is the number of pear trees?

A) $120x + 145y \geq 2,050$
   $x + y \leq 15$
   $x \geq 5$
   $y \geq 3$

B) $120x + 145y \geq 2,050$
   $x + y \geq 15$
   $x \leq 5$
   $y \leq 3$

C) $120x + 145y \leq 2,050$
   $x + y \geq 15$
   $x \leq 5$
   $y \leq 3$

D) $120x + 145y \leq 2,050$
   $x + y \geq 15$
   $x \geq 5$
   $y \geq 3$

14. A utility shelf in a warehouse is used to store containers of paint and containers of varnish. Containers of paint weigh 50 pounds each and containers of varnish weigh 35 pounds each. The shelf can hold up to 32 containers, the combined weight of which must not exceed 1,450 pounds. Let x be the number of containers of paint and y be the number of containers of varnish. Which of the following systems of inequalities represents this relationship?

A) $50x + 35y \leq 32$
   $x + y \leq 1,450$

B) $50x + 35y \leq 1,450$
   $x + y \leq 32$

C) $85(x + y) \leq 1,450$
   $x + y \leq 32$

D) $50x + 35y \leq 1,450$
   $x + y \leq 85$

HINT: For Q15, read carefully. *At least* is a minimum, so which way should the inequality sign point?

---

15. A bakery is buying flour and sugar from its supplier. The supplier will deliver no more than 750 pounds in a shipment. Each bag of flour weighs 50 pounds and each bag of sugar weighs 20 pounds. The bakery wants to buy at least three times as many bags of sugar as bags of flour. If f represents the number of bags of flour and s represents the number of bags of sugar, where f and s are nonnegative integers, which of the following systems of inequalities represents this situation?

A) $50f + 60s \leq 750$
   $f \leq 3s$

B) $50f + 20s \leq 750$
   $f \leq 3s$

C) $50f + 20s \leq 750$
   $3f \leq s$

D) $150f + 20s \leq 750$
   $3f \leq s$

On Test Day

Modeling real-life situations with inequalities can be tricky, especially when there are multiple inequalities involved or when a question doesn't state the information in the most straightforward way. The good news is that you can often make use of the answer choices to get to the answer quickly.

Try the question below. If you use the choices, you shouldn't have to do any calculations. Just pay close attention to the direction of the inequality signs.

16. A florist is organizing a sale that offers carnations at a price of $4 for 10 and daisies at a price of $7 for 5. The florist plans to order a maximum of 500 flowers for the sale and wants the revenue from the sale to be at least $400. If x is the number of carnations and y is the number of daisies, and the florist sells all the flowers ordered, which system of inequalities best describes this situation?

   A) $0.4x + 1.4y \geq 400$

   $x + y \leq 500$

   B) $0.4x + 1.4y \leq 400$

   $x + y \leq 500$

   C) $0.4x + 1.4y \geq 400$

   $x + y \geq 500$

   D) $0.4x + 1.4y \leq 400$

   $x + y \geq 500$

The answer and explanation can be found at the end of this chapter.

How Much Have You Learned?

Directions: For testlike practice, give yourself 15 minutes to complete this question set. Be sure to study the explanations, even for questions you got right. They can be found at the end of this chapter.

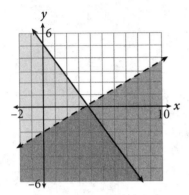

17. The figure above shows the solution set for this system of inequalities:

$$\begin{cases} y < \dfrac{3}{5}x - 2 \\ y \le -\dfrac{4}{3}x + 5 \end{cases}$$

Which of the following is NOT a solution to this system?

A) $(-1, -4)$

B) $(1, -1)$

C) $(4, -1)$

D) $(6, -3)$

18. Ezekiel has $5.00 to spend on snacks. Candy bars cost $0.60 each, gum costs $0.50 per pack, and nuts are priced at $1.29 per small bag. If c represents the number of candy bars, g represents the number of packs of gum, and n represents the number of bags of nuts, which of the following inequalities correctly describes Ezekiel's choices?

A) $\dfrac{c}{0.60} + \dfrac{g}{0.50} + \dfrac{n}{1.29} \le \dfrac{1}{5}$

B) $c + g + n \le 5$

C) $0.60c + 0.50g + 1.29n \le 5.00$

D) $0.60c + 0.50g + 1.29n \ge 5.00$

19. A shipping company employee is in charge of packing cargo containers for shipment. He knows a certain cargo container can hold a maximum of 50 microwaves or a maximum of 15 refrigerators. Each microwave takes up 6 cubic feet of space, and each refrigerator takes up 20 cubic feet. The cargo container can hold a maximum of 300 cubic feet. The employee is trying to figure out how to pack a container containing both microwaves and refrigerators. Which of the following systems of inequalities can the employee use to determine how many of each item (microwaves, m, and refrigerators, r) he can pack into one cargo container?

A) $m \le 6$
   $r \le 20$
   $50m + 15r \le 300$

B) $m \le 50$
   $r \le 15$
   $m + r \le 300$

C) $m \le 50$
   $r \le 15$
   $6m + 20r \le 300$

D) $m \le 50$
   $r \le 15$
   $50m + 15r \le 300$

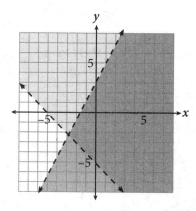

$$\begin{cases} y > -x - 5 \\ y < 2x + 3 \end{cases}$$

20. The figure above shows the solution for the system of inequalities shown. Suppose (a, b) is a solution to the system. If $a = 0$, what is the greatest possible integer value of b?

$3x + 2 > 5$

$-2x + 8 > -10$

21. Which of the following describes the range of x?

A) $x > 1$

B) $x > 9$

C) $-1 < x < 9$

D) $9 > x > 1$

$y \geq -3x + 18$

$y \geq 9x$

22. In the xy plane, the point (a, b) lies in the solution set of the system of inequalities above. What is the minimum possible value of b?

A) $1\frac{1}{2}$

B) 3

C) $7\frac{1}{2}$

D) $13\frac{1}{2}$

23. Francine sells advertising time packages for a local television station. She is able to make up to 15 sales calls per week offering potential advertisers either a prime time package for \$12,000 or a non–prime time package for \$8,000. Her weekly sales goal is to sell more than \$20,000 worth of advertising. Which of the following systems of inequalities represents this situation in terms of p, the number of prime time packages Francine sells in a week, n, the number of non–prime time packages, and u, the number of unsuccessful sales calls for which she sells neither offering?

A) $p + n + u \leq 15$
   $12{,}000p + 8{,}000n > 20{,}000$

B) $p + n + u \geq 15$
   $12{,}000p + 8{,}000n > 20{,}000$

C) $p + n + u \leq 15$
   $12{,}000p + 8{,}000(n + u) > 20{,}000$

D) $p + n + u \leq 15$
   $12{,}000p + 8{,}000n < 20{,}000$

24. Luis has $25 to spend on school supplies. Pencils (p) cost $1.25 per package, notebooks (n) are priced at $2.50 each, and markers ($m$) sell for $4 per pack. He must buy exactly one calendar/planner for $5.75. Which of the following describes how many markers Luis can buy?

   A) $m \leq \dfrac{1.25p + 2.5n + 5.75}{25}$

   B) $m \leq \dfrac{19.25 - 1.25p - 2.5n}{4}$

   C) $m \leq \dfrac{25 - 1.25p - 2.5n}{4} - 5.75$

   D) $m \leq 19.25 - 1.25p - 2.5n$

25. Let a and b be numbers such that $-a < b + 1 < a$. Which of the following must be true?

   I. $a > 0$

   II. $|b| < a$

   III. $b > a + 1$

   A) I only

   B) I and II

   C) II only

   D) I, II, and III

26. The variable x is a positive integer. If $3(x - 1) + 5 > 11$ and $-5x + 18 \geq -12$, how many possible values are there for x?

Reflect

Directions: Take a few minutes to recall what you've learned and what you've been practicing in this chapter. Consider the following questions, jot down your best answer for each one, and then compare your reflections to the expert responses on the following page. Use your level of confidence to determine what to do next.

What is the difference between a linear inequality and a linear equation?

_____

_____

_____

The rules for manipulating an inequality are very similar to those for manipulating an equation. What is the major difference?

_____

_____

_____

When two lines cross in the coordinate plane, they create four regions. How many regions will be shaded if the system of inequalities uses the word "and"? The word "or"?

_____

_____

_____

Expert Responses

What is the difference between a linear inequality and a linear equation?

A linear equation is solved for a single value, whereas a linear inequality is solved for a range of values.

The rules for manipulating an inequality are very similar to those for manipulating an equation. What is the major difference?

When solving an inequality, you can do the same thing to both sides, just as you could for an equation. The big difference is that if you divide or multiply both sides of an inequality by a negative number, you have to flip the inequality sign.

When two lines cross in the coordinate plane, they create four regions. How many regions will be shaded if the system of inequalities uses the word "and"? The word "or"?

Of the four regions, one represents values that satisfy neither inequality. One represents values that satisfy both inequalities. The other two regions represent values that satisfy one inequality but not the other. For an "and" inequality, only the region of values that satisfy both inequalities will be shaded. For an "or" inequality, the only region not shaded will be the one that satisfies neither inequality; the other three regions will be shaded.

Next Steps

If you answered most questions correctly in the "How Much Have You Learned?" section, and if your responses to the Reflect questions were similar to those of the SAT expert, then consider inequalities an area of strength and move on to the next chapter. Come back to this topic periodically to prevent yourself from getting rusty.

If you don't yet feel confident, review those parts of this chapter that you have not yet mastered and try the questions you missed again. As always, be sure to review the explanations closely. Finally, **go online** (www.kaptest.com/moreonline) for additional practice on the highest yield topics in this chapter.

Answers and Explanations

1.   C

Difficulty: Easy

Getting to the Answer: Begin by multiplying all parts of the inequality by 6 to clear the fractions: $-a - 6a > -\frac{24}{3}$, which, when simplified, is $-7a > -8$. Divide both sides by -7, remembering to switch the direction of the sign: $a < \frac{8}{7}$. Therefore, **(C)** is correct.

2.   A

Difficulty: Medium

Getting to the Answer: Don't solve for c on autopilot. Instead, solve for $15c$, then add 7 to both sides. To do this, first multiply both sides of the inequality by -1 to get $5c + 7 \geq -8$. (Notice that the inequality sign had to be flipped due to multiplication by a negative number.) Then subtract 7 from both sides to yield $5c \geq -15$. Multiply both sides by 3: $15c \geq -45$. Finally, add 7 to both sides: $15c + 7 \geq -38$. Choice **(A)** is correct.

3.   C

Difficulty: Medium

Getting to the Answer: First, to clear the fraction, multiply both sides of the inequality by -8, remembering to flip the direction of the inequality sign: $8 - 10x < -24x + 16$.

Next, subtract 8 from both sides, and then add $24x$ to both sides. Divide both sides by 14, and then simplify the fraction:

$$-10x < -24x + 8$$
$$14x < 8$$
$$x < \frac{8}{14}$$
$$x < \frac{4}{7}$$

Thus, **(C)** is correct.

4.   B

Difficulty: Medium

Getting to the Answer: Begin by subtracting 3 from both sides of the inequality to get $\frac{1}{4}a - \frac{1}{16}b < 2$. Next, clear the fractions in that inequality by multiplying all terms by 16: $16 \times \left(\frac{1}{4}a - \frac{1}{16}b < 2\right) = 4a - b < 32$. **(B)** is correct.

5.   B

Difficulty: Medium

Strategic Advice: Because the given inequality contains $4c$ and the value you're solving for has $12c$ (a multiple of $4c$), solve for $4c$ and then multiply by 3 to find $12c$.

Getting to the Answer: Subtract 20 from both sides of the inequality to find that $4c \geq 11$. Multiply by 3: $12c \geq 33$. Finally, add 7 to both sides: $12c + 7 \geq 40$. So the least permissible value for $12c + 7$ is 40. **(B)** is correct.

6.   A

Difficulty: Easy

Getting to the Answer: The question offers a value range of a in terms of $6b$ and a value range for $3b$. Therefore, use the known value range of $3b$ to find the value range of $6b$.

Since $6b$ is two times $3b$, multiply both sides of the second inequality by 2 to find the value range of $6b$: $2 \times 3b < 2 \times 8$, so $6b < 16$.

Because the signs are the same in the two inequalities (both are less-than signs), you can plug 16 in for b in the first inequality: $a < 16 + 4$, or $a < 20$. Hence, **(A)** is correct.

7.   B

Difficulty: Medium

Getting to the Answer: Draw a sketch of the two lines to help visualize the system of inequalities.

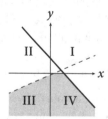

Clearly, quadrants III and IV contain solutions to the system. Eliminate (C). Quadrant II contains no solutions, so you can also eliminate (A). Look closely at quadrant I. The line for $y \leq -x + 1$ intersects both the x and y axes at $+1$. The line for $y < \frac{1}{2}x$ passes through the origin and upward into quadrant I. Thus, there is a very small triangle of solutions to both inequalities that lies in quadrant I. Therefore, **(B)** is correct.

8.   400

Difficulty: Medium

Getting to the Answer: The first task is to express both inequalities in terms of y. Multiply $-y \leq 6x - 2{,}200$ by -1 to get $y \geq -6x + 2{,}200$; don't forget to flip the sign since you are multiplying by a negative number. Divide $3y \geq 9x - 1{,}500$ by 3 to get $y \geq 3x - 500$.

The solution set for these inequalities is the area of the coordinate plane on or above both lines. Thus, the minimum y-value will occur at the intersection of the two lines, whose equations are $y = -6x + 2{,}200$ and $y = 3x - 500$. To find the point of intersection, set these two equations equal to each other: $-6x + 2{,}200 = 3x - 500$. Isolate the x-values on one side to yield $-9x = -2{,}700$ and $x = 300$. Plug this value into one of the equations (it doesn't matter which one because $x = 300$ is where they intersect) to obtain the y-coordinate at the point of intersection: $3(300) - 500 = 400$. The y-coordinate at the point of intersection is the minimum possible value of b that the question was asking for, so grid in **400**.

9.   C

Difficulty: Medium

Getting to the Answer: You could plot the two lines and identify the solution set on a graph, but testing the choices to see if they satisfy both inequalities is a more efficient approach, particularly since one inequality is "less than" and the other is "less than or equal to." If you take this approach, you don't even need to rearrange the inequalities to isolate y on one side.

(A): Substituting these values for x and y in $x < 4 - 2y$ gives you $(-1) < 4 - 2(3)$, which is $-1 < -2$ (not a true statement). You don't need to evaluate the other inequality since this ordered pair is not in the solution set for $x < 4 - 2y$. Eliminate (A).

(B): Substituting these values for x and y in $x < 4 - 2y$ gives you $(1) < 4 - 2(1)$, which is $1 < 2$. The ordered pair is in the solution set for this inequality, so plug the values into $y \leq -2x + 1$ to get $(1) \leq -2(1) + 1$, which simplifies to $1 \leq -1$. Thus, this ordered pair is not in the solution set for the second inequality. Eliminate (B).

(C): Substituting these values for x and y in $x < 4 - 2y$ gives you $(2) < 4 - 2(-3)$, which is $2 < 10$. The ordered pair is in the solution set for this inequality, so plug the values into $y \leq -2x + 1$ to get $(-3) \leq -2(2) + 1$, which

simplifies to $-3 \leq -3$. Since the sign for this inequality is "less than or equal to," this ordered pair is in the solution set. **(C)** is correct.

(D): Since you already identified the correct choice, you do not need to check this pair.

10.   C

Difficulty: Hard

Getting to the Answer: Since the question states that $x = y = 1$ is a solution to the system, plug those values in to get $1 > 1 + r$ and $1 < s - 1$. These inequalities further simplify to $r < 0$ and $s > 2$. Check each pair of values in the answer choices to see which complies with these limitations. Only **(C)** has both $r < 0$ and $s > 2$, and is correct. (B) is incorrect because s must be greater than 2, and (D) reverses r and s.

11.   C

Difficulty: Medium

Getting to the Answer: Translate each part of the word problem into its mathematical equivalent. Because x, y, and z represent the numbers of each of the three ad sizes, the total number of ads will be $x + y + z$. "No fewer than 15 ads" means $x + y + z \geq 15$, so eliminate (A) and (B).

The total cost of the ads Ariel sells will be represented by the number of each size ad sold times the respective cost of each size ad. Thus, $110x + 70y + 50z$ represents the total cost of all of the ads; "at least 1,500" means that $110x + 70y + 50z \geq 1{,}500$. Therefore, **(C)** is correct.

12.   A

Difficulty: Medium

Getting to the Answer: Translate each part of the word problem into its mathematical equivalent. The total weight of produce will be represented by the combined pounds of watermelons, w, cantaloupes, c, and tomatoes, t. This combined weight cannot exceed 250 pounds, so the inequality is $w + c + t \leq 250$. Eliminate (C) and (D).

The total money for the produce sold is represented by the price per pound of each type of produce times the number of pounds of that type. This must be at least (greater than or equal to) \$200, so the inequality is $0.5w + 1c + 2.5t \geq 200$. **(A)** is correct.

13. D

Difficulty: Medium

Getting to the Answer: Translate each part of the word problem into its mathematical equivalent, beginning with the easiest-to-translate components. Allison needs at least 5 apple trees and at least 3 pear trees, so the correct inequalities are $x \geq 5$ and $y \geq 3$. Eliminate (B) and (C). The total number of apple and pear trees combined that Allison purchases must be at least 15, so the correct inequality is $x + y \geq 15$. Eliminate (A). Only **(D)** is left and is correct.

Note that, by being strategic, you never even have to determine the first, most complicated inequality in each of the answer choices. For the record: apple trees cost $120 and pear trees cost $145, so the total amount Allison will spend on trees is $120x + 145y$. This total amount cannot go above $2,050, which means it must be less than or equal to $2,050. Therefore: $120x + 145y \leq 2,050$.

14. B

Difficulty: Medium

Getting to the Answer: First, define the relationship between the weight of each kind of container and the weight the shelf can hold. Since x is the number of 50-pound containers of paint and y is the number of 35-pound containers of varnish, the combined weight of the containers will be represented by $50x + 35y$. This needs to be no more than 1,450 pounds, so the inequality that represents this is $50x + 35y \leq 1,450$. Eliminate (A) and (C).

The question also states that the total number of containers the shelf can hold is no more than 32, so the combined number of containers of paint and containers of varnish must be no more than 32. This is represented by the inequality $x + y \leq 32$. Thus, **(B)** is correct.

15. C

Difficulty: Hard

Getting to the Answer: Begin by translating the weight of the combined bags of flour and sugar. The weight of each bag of flour times the number of bags of flour—plus the weight of each bag of sugar times the number of bags of sugar—will yield the total. Thus, $50f + 20s$ will describe the weight of all of the bags combined. Since

the weight that the supplier can deliver is no more than 750 pounds, the inequality that describes this situation is $50f + 20y \leq 750$. Eliminate (A) and (D).

The question also specifies that the bakery needs to buy at least three times as many bags of sugar as bags of flour. In other words, the number of bags of sugar must be equal to or greater than three times the number of bags of flour. This is represented by $s \geq 3f$, which can be rewritten as $3f \leq s$. **(C)** is correct.

16. A

Difficulty: Hard

Strategic Advice: All the numbers in the answer choices are the same, so you don't actually have to calculate the cost of one carnation or one daisy. The answer choices have done that for you.

Getting to the Answer: Focus on the keywords that tell you the direction of the inequality signs. The florist plans to order a "maximum" of 500 flowers, so that's ≤ 500. Eliminate (C) and (D). The florist wants to earn "at least" $400, or ≥ 400. The correct answer is **(A)**.

17. B

Difficulty: Medium

Category: Systems of Inequalities

Getting to the Answer: The intersection (overlap) of the two shaded regions is the solution to the system of inequalities. Check each point to see whether it lies in the region where the shading overlaps. Be careful—you are looking for the point that is *not* a solution to the system. Choices (A) and (C) lie in the overlap, so you can eliminate them. Choice (D), which is the point $(6, -3)$, lies on a boundary line, and because the line is solid, the point *is* included in the solution region. The only point that does not lie within the overlap must be (B). To check this, plug $(1, -1)$ into the first inequality:

$$y < \frac{3}{5}x - 2$$

$$-1 < \frac{3}{5}(1) - 2$$

$$-1 \not< -\frac{7}{5}$$

Because -1 is not less than $-\frac{7}{5}$, **(B)** is correct.

18. C

Difficulty: Easy

Category: Modeling Real-Life Situations with Inequalities

Getting to the Answer: The fact that Ezekiel has exactly $5.00 means that he can spend up to and including $5.00, so use the less than or equal symbol ($\leq$) for the limit on how much he can spend. For that reason alone, you can eliminate (D). The amount of money Ezekiel spends on each type of snack is the number of units of that snack times its price. So, $0.60c + 0.50g + 1.29n \leq 5.00$. **(C)** is correct.

19. C

Difficulty: Medium

Category: Modeling Real-Life Situations with Inequalities

Getting to the Answer: The clue "hold a maximum" means the container can hold exactly that much or less, so use the less than or equal to symbol ($\leq$) throughout. The cargo container can hold a maximum of 50 microwaves, so the first inequality is $m \leq 50$. Eliminate (A). The container can hold a maximum of 15 refrigerators, so the second inequality is $r \leq 15$. The third inequality deals with the size of each appliance. The cargo container can hold m microwaves multiplied by the size of the microwave, which is 6 cubic feet; it can hold r refrigerators multiplied by the size of the refrigerator, which is 20 cubic feet; and it can hold a maximum of 300 cubic feet total. Put these together to write the final inequality: $6m + 20r \leq 300$, which is **(C)**.

20. 2

Difficulty: Hard

Category: Systems of Inequalities

Getting to the Answer: If (a, b) is a solution to the system, then a is the x-coordinate of any point in the region where the shading overlaps, and b is the corresponding y-coordinate. When $a = 0$ (or $x = 0$), the maximum possible value for b lies on the upper boundary line, $y < 2x + 3$. It looks like the y-coordinate is 3, but to be sure, substitute $x = 0$ into the equation and simplify. You can replace the inequality symbol with an equal sign to make it an equation because you are finding a point on the boundary line, not a range:

$$y = 2(0) + 3$$
$$y = 3$$

The point on the boundary line is $(0, 3)$. The boundary line is dashed (because the inequality is strictly less than), so $(0, 3)$ is *not* a solution to the system. This means 2 is the greatest possible *integer* value for b when $a = 0$. Grid in **2**.

21. D

Difficulty: Medium

Category: Linear Inequalities

Getting to the Answer: Isolate x in each of the given inequalities, then consider the results in combination. For $3x + 2 > 5$, subtract 2 from each side to get $3x > 3$, which means that $x > 1$. For $-2x + 8 > -10$, subtract 8 from each side to get $-2x > -18$. Divide each side by -2, which means that you have to flip the inequality sign to get $x < 9$. Taking the two inequalities together, x must be greater than 1 but less than 9. This can be expressed as $1 < x < 9$ or, alternatively, $9 > x > 1$. **(D)** is correct.

22. D

Difficulty: Medium

Category: Systems of Inequalities

Strategic Advice: If the given inequalities are graphed in the xy-plane, the solution set is the portion of the plane on or above both lines. Since the value of y for both lines increases moving away from the point where they intersect, the minimum value of y will occur at the intersection of these lines, which is the point (a, b).

Getting to the Answer: The boundary lines of this system of inequalities are $y = -3x + 18$ and $y = 9x$. To find their intersection point, set them equal to each other to get $9x = -3x + 18$. So, $12x = 18$ and $x = 1\frac{1}{2}$. That represents a, but the question asks for the value of b. Substitute $1\frac{1}{2}$ for x in either equation, preferably the simpler one: use $y = 9x$ to get $y = 9\left(1\frac{1}{2}\right) = 13\frac{1}{2}$. Therefore, **(D)** is correct.

23. A

Difficulty: Medium

Category: Modeling Real-Life Situations with Inequalities

Strategic Advice: Translating English into math, set up one inequality for Francine's number of sales calls and another for the dollar amount of sales in terms of her goal.

Getting to the Answer: Since Francine can make *up to* 15 sales calls per week and there are three categories of the results of her efforts, you can write the inequality $p + n + u \leq 15$. Eliminate (B). For the monetary goal, that is *more than* $20,000, so this inequality is $12{,}000p + 8{,}000n > 20{,}000$. Note that the unsuccessful sales calls are not included in this inequality since they do not generate any revenue. **(A)** is correct.

24. B

Difficulty: Medium

Category: Modeling Real-Life Situations with Inequalities

Getting to the Answer: The amount Luis spends on each item is that item's price times the quantity he buys. The total amount must be less than or equal to $25. Thus, you can write the inequality $1.25p + 2.50n + 4.00m + 1(5.75) \leq 25.00$. Since the question asks for the number of markers, isolate m on one side of the inequality: $4m \leq 25 - 1.25p - 2.5n - 5.75$. Therefore, $m \leq \dfrac{19.25 - 1.25p - 2.5n}{4}$. **(B)** is correct.

25. A

Difficulty: Hard

Category: Linear Inequalities

Getting to the Answer: Examine each of the roman numeral choices individually, determine which one or ones must be true, then select the correct choice. Subtract 1 from all terms in the given inequality to get $-a - 1 < b < a - 1$, so that b stands alone.

I. Ignoring the middle term, b, the given inequality tells you that $-a < a$. The only way this can be true is if a is a positive number, so statement I must be true. If you have a hard time seeing this, pick a negative number for a. For example, if $a = -1$, then the inequality would say $-(-1) < -1$, which is $1 < -1$, which is false. Note that if $a = 0$, then the inequality becomes $0 < 0$, which is also false. Because statement I must be true, you can eliminate (C).

II. Recall that the absolute value of any number is its distance from 0 on the number line, which is its value without a sign. If b is positive or 0, then, since $b < a - 1$, the value of b, which is the same as $|b|$, must also be less than a. However, if b is negative, the relationship is not directly clear. Pick some numbers that satisfy the original inequality, such as $a = 1$ and $b = -1$. These numbers satisfy the original inequality because $-1 < 0 < 1$. However, $|b| = 1$, so $|b| = a$, and statement II is false. Eliminate (B), (C), and (D). Choice **(A)** is correct.

III. For the record, since a must be positive and any positive value of b is less than $a - 1$, there is no way that $b > a + 1$. Statement III is not true.

26. 3

Difficulty: Medium

Category: Linear Inequalities

Strategic Advice: Isolate x in each of the two inequalities to determine a range for x.

Getting to the Answer: Expand the first inequality to get $3x - 3 + 5 > 11$, so $3x > 9$ and $x > 3$. Multiply the second inequality by -1, so that $5x - 18 \leq 12$. This simplifies to $x \leq 6$. Combine the two results: $3 < x \leq 6$. There are three allowable integer values for x: 4, 5, and 6. Grid in **3**.

Test Yourself: The Heart of Algebra

1. The local farmers market usually sells potatoes for $0.90 per pound. On Fridays, it sells potatoes at a 30 percent discount. The market also sells cantaloupes for $3.50 each. Which of the following represents the total cost, c, if a customer buys 2 cantaloupes and p pounds of potatoes on a Friday?

   A) $c = 0.63p + 7$

   B) $c = 0.9p + 7$

   C) $c = 0.3p + 3.5$

   D) $c = 0.9p + 3.5$

2. If paintbrushes cost $1.50 each and canvases cost 6 times that much, which of the following represents the cost, in dollars, of p paintbrushes and c canvases?

   A) $7.5pc$

   B) $10.5pc$

   C) $9c + 1.5p$

   D) $10.5(p + c)$

3. Mika is purchasing a new car, and her state government charges a tax on car purchases based on the price, p, of the car. If Mika's total expenses for the car are given by the equation $T = 0.04p + p$, then the value 0.04 could represent which of the following?

   A) The purchase price of the car

   B) The dollar amount of tax on the car purchase

   C) The purchase price of the car minus the total tax

   D) The tax rate as a percentage

4. Which value of x makes the equation $\frac{3}{2}(x + 7) = 6$ true?

   A) -5

   B) -3

   C) 9

   D) 11

5. A company is sponsoring a celebrity charity walk. For each celebrity who participates, the company will donate a flat amount to the charity of the celebrity's choice, plus an additional amount for every mile the celebrity walks. If the amount donated to charity on behalf of one celebrity is represented by $y = 100x + 250$, what does the number 250 best represent?

   A) The flat amount donated

   B) The total amount donated

   C) The amount donated per mile

   D) The number of miles the celebrity walked

$$\frac{3(n - 2) + 5}{4} = \frac{11 - (7 - n)}{6}$$

6. In the above equation, what is the value of n?

   A) $-\dfrac{1}{11}$

   B) $\dfrac{5}{11}$

   C) 1

   D) $\dfrac{11}{7}$

7. A store "breaks even" when its sales equal its expenses. Jon has just opened a new surfboard store at the beach. He buys each surfboard wholesale for $80 and has fixed monthly expenses of $3,600. He sells each surfboard for $120. How many surfboards does Jon need to sell in a month to break even?

   A) 18

   B) 30

   C) 45

   D) 90

8. Which of the following scenarios could be supported by the graph above?

   A) As the algae content in a lake increases, the number of fish decreases.

   B) As the algae content in a lake decreases, the number of fish decreases.

   C) As the algae content in a lake increases, the number of fish increases.

   D) As the algae content in a lake increases, the number of fish remains constant.

x	−9	0	3	9
y	11	8	7	?

9. If the values in the table represent a linear relationship, what is the missing value?

   A) 5

   B) 6

   C) 11

   D) 13

10. What was the initial amount of fuel in an airplane's tank, in gallons, if there are now x gallons, if y gallons were used for the last flight, and if 18,000 gallons were added when the plane was refueled?

    A) $y + x - 18{,}000$

    B) $y + x + 18{,}000$

    C) $x - y - 18{,}000$

    D) $y - x + 18{,}000$

11. $\frac{1}{4}(10h) - \frac{3}{2}(h+1) = -\frac{2}{3}\left(\frac{9}{2}h\right) + 6$

    What is the value of h in the equation above?

    A) $\dfrac{9}{8}$

    B) $\dfrac{15}{8}$

    C) There is no value of h for which the equation is true.

    D) There are infinitely many values of h for which the equation is true.

Legislation Impact on Population

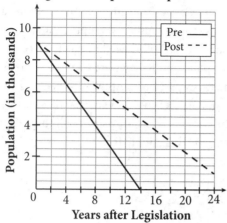

12. The federal government in the United States has the authority to protect species whose populations have reached dangerously low levels. The graph above represents the expected population of a certain endangered species before (Pre) and after (Post) a proposed law aimed at protecting the animal is passed. Based on the graph, which of the following statements is true?

A) The proposed law is expected to accelerate the decline in population.

B) The proposed law is expected to stop and reverse the decline in population.

C) The proposed law is expected to have no effect on the decline in population.

D) The proposed law is expected to slow, but not stop or reverse, the decline in population.

$$0.55x - 1.04 = 0.35x + 0.16$$

13. In the equation above, what is the value of x ?

14. For what value of y does the graph of $\frac{3}{2}y - 2x = 18$ cross the y-axis?

15. The lines created by the equations $y = ax + b$ and $y = cx + d$ intersect at the point (p, q). What is the value of a in terms of the other variables?

   A) $\dfrac{y + d}{b}$

   B) $\dfrac{p + q}{b + d}$

   C) $c - b + \dfrac{d}{p}$

   D) $c + \dfrac{d - b}{p}$

16. $-4x = 3 - 2y$

   $y = -\dfrac{1}{2}x + 3$

   $2y = 10 - x$

   At how many points do the lines defined by the equations above intersect?

   A) 0

   B) 1

   C) 2

   D) 3

17. A family adopted three rescued dogs: Apollo, Bailey, and Cassie. The family adopted Apollo and Bailey 4 years ago and they adopted Cassie 2 years ago. Currently, Apollo's age in years is twice Cassie's. When Apollo and Bailey were adopted, Bailey's age in years was 3 times Apollo's. When Cassie was adopted, Bailey's age was twice that of Apollo. What was the combined age, in years, of all three dogs when Cassie was adopted?

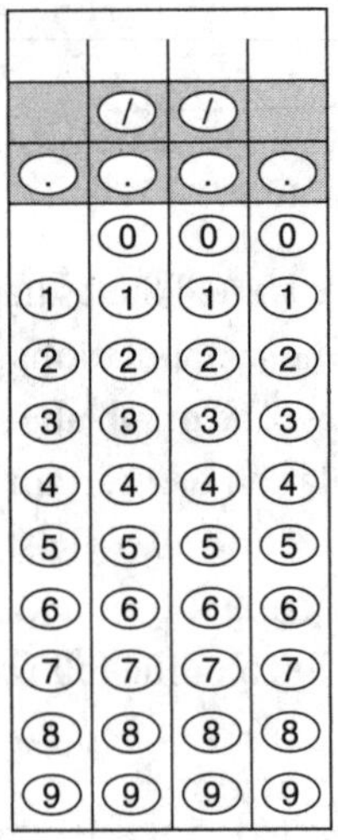

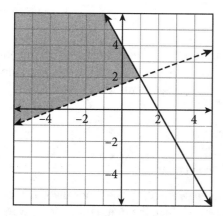

$$4x > y + 8$$
$$8y > 20 + 3y$$

20. Which of the following describes the range of the values of x that satisfy the system of inequalities above?

   A) $x > 3$

   B) $x > 4$

   C) $3 < x < 12$

   D) $x > 12$

18. The shaded region on the graph above shows the solution for a system of inequalities. Which of the following is the system of inequalities depicted on the graph above?

   A) $x + 2y \leq 4$ and $5y - 2x > 8$

   B) $y + 2x \leq 4$ and $5x - 2y \geq 8$

   C) $2x + y \leq 4$ and $5y - 2x > 8$

   D) $2x + y < 4$ and $5y - 2x \geq 8$

$$y - ax \geq -8$$
$$2x + y \leq 6$$

19. The x-coordinate of the point of intersection of the boundary lines of the system of inequalities above is 2. What is the value of a ?

   A) -3

   B) 2

   C) 3

   D) 5

Answers and Explanations

1. A

Difficulty: Easy

Category: Word Problems

Getting to the Answer: Write the equation in words first and then translate from English into math.

The cost of the potatoes is the weight of the potatoes in pounds, p, multiplied by the sale price because the purchase is made on Friday: $\$0.90 \times (100 - 30)\% = 0.9 \times 0.7 = 0.63$. This gives the first part of the expression: $0.63p$. Now, add the cost of two cantaloupes, $3.50 \times 2 = 7$, to get the total cost: $c = 0.63p + 7$, which is **(A)**.

You could also pick numbers to answer this question—pick a number for the weight of the potatoes and calculate how much they would cost (on sale) and add the cost of two cantaloupes. Then find the equation that gives the same amount when you substitute the number you picked.

2. C

Difficulty: Easy

Category: Word Problems

Getting to the Answer: The total cost of the two kinds of items is the cost of the paintbrushes multiplied by the number purchased plus the cost of the canvases multiplied by the number purchased. Because a canvas cost "6 times" the cost of a paintbrush, a canvas costs $6(\$1.50) = \$9$.

Total cost of paintbrushes: $1.50 \times p$, or $1.5p$

Total cost of canvases: $9 \times c$, or $9c$

Sum of both: $9c + 1.5p$

Therefore, **(C)** is correct.

3. D

Difficulty: Easy

Category: Word Problems

Getting to the Answer: Mika's total expenses consist of the amount she pays for the car and some part (or percent) of the purchase price of the car for the tax. The question stem tells you that p is the purchase price, so eliminate (A). The other expression in the equation, $0.04p$, is a small fraction of the purchase price, p,

which is what you would expect the state government's tax charge to be. Therefore, 0.04 would represent the amount of the tax as a percent (4%), which is **(D)**.

4. B

Difficulty: Easy

Category: Solving Equations

Getting to the Answer: When questions involve fractions, find a way to make the numbers easier to work with. In this case, clear the fraction by multiplying both sides of the equation by the denominator, 2:

$$2 \times \left[\frac{3}{2}(x + 7) \right] = 6 \times 2$$
$$3(x + 7) = 12$$
$$3x + 21 = 12$$
$$3x = -9$$
$$x = -3$$

Choice **(B)** is correct.

5. A

Difficulty: Easy

Category: Word Problems

Getting to the Answer: The total amount donated consists of a flat donation and an additional amount per mile. The flat amount is a one-time donation that does not depend on the number of miles walked and therefore should not be multiplied by the number of miles. This means that 250, the constant, is the flat donation. **(A)** is correct. The other expression in the equation, $100x$, represents the amount donated per mile (100) times the number of miles walked (x).

6. D

Difficulty: Medium

Category: Solving Equations

Getting to the Answer: You could start by cross-multiplying, but there are so many terms and parentheses that you are likely to forget to distribute a factor. Instead, simplify the numerators first. Don't forget to distribute the negative to both terms inside the parentheses on the right-hand side of the equation. Don't try to do steps in your head—writing each step down will keep you organized:

$$\frac{3(n-2)+5}{4} = \frac{11-(7-n)}{6}$$

$$\frac{3n-6+5}{4} = \frac{11-7+n}{6}$$

$$\frac{3n-1}{4} = \frac{4+n}{6}$$

$$6(3n-1) = 4(4+n)$$

$$18n-6 = 16+4n$$

$$14n = 22$$

$$n = \frac{22}{14}$$

$$n = \frac{11}{7}$$

Choice **(D)** is correct.

7.   D

Difficulty: Medium

Category: Word Problems

Getting to the Answer: Let x be the number of surfboards Jon sells in a month. Write a linear equation that represents the scenario and then solve for x. Sales must equal expenses for the store to break even. Jon's sales are equal to the selling price ($120) times the number of surfboards he sells (x), so write $120x$ on one side of the equal sign. His monthly expenses are his fixed expenses ($3,600) plus the amount he paid for each surfboard ($80) times the number of surfboards (x), so write $3,600 + 80x$ on the other side of the equal sign. Then, solve for x:

$$120x = 3,600 + 80x$$

$$40x = 3,600$$

$$x = 90$$

Therefore, **(D)** is correct.

8.   A

Difficulty: Medium

Category: Linear Graphs

Getting to the Answer: Regardless of the scenario presented or the missing axis labels on the graph, the slope of the line tells you the answer. The line is decreasing from left to right, so it has a negative slope. This means there is an inverse relationship between the amount of algae and the number of fish. In other words, as one increases, the other must decrease, so **(A)** must be correct.

9.   A

Difficulty: Medium

Category: Linear Graphs

Getting to the Answer: The rate of change (or slope) of a linear relationship is constant, so find the rate and apply it to the missing value. Choose any two points (preferably ones with the most convenient numbers) from the table and substitute them into the slope formula. Using the points $(0, 8)$ and $(3, 7)$, the slope is $\frac{7-8}{3-0} = \frac{-1}{3}$. This means that for every 3 units the x-value increases, the y-value decreases by 1, so to get from $x = 3$ to $x = 9$, decrease the y-value by 1, twice: $7 - 1 - 1 = 5$, making **(A)** correct.

10.   A

Difficulty: Medium

Category: Word Problems

Getting to the Answer: Write an equation in words first and then translate from English into math. Then, rearrange your equation to find what you're interested in, which is the initial amount. Call the initial amount of fuel A. After you've written your equation, solve for A.

Amount now (x) equals initial amount (A) minus fuel used on last flight (y) plus amount added (18,000):

$$x = A - y + 18,000$$

$$x + y - 18,000 = A$$

This is the same as $y + x - 18,000$. Thus, **(A)** is correct.

Note that you could also pick numbers to answer this question.

11. B

Difficulty: Hard

Category: Solving Equations

Getting to the Answer: Do not automatically assume that an equation has *no solution* or *infinite solutions* just because those choices are given as possible answers. This question can be simplified quite a bit by clearing the fractions first. To do this, multiply both sides of the equation by the least common denominator, 12. Next, solve for *h* using inverse operations:

$$\frac{1}{4}(10h) - \frac{3}{2}(h+1) = -\frac{2}{3}\left(\frac{9}{2}h\right) + 6$$

$$12\left[\frac{1}{4}(10h)\right] - 12\left[\frac{3}{2}(h+1)\right] = 12\left[-\frac{2}{3}\left(\frac{9}{2}h\right)\right] + 12(6)$$

$$3(10h) - 18(h+1) = 12(-3h) + 72$$

$$30h - 18h - 18 = -36h + 72$$

$$12h - 18 = -36h + 72$$

$$48h = 90$$

$$h = \frac{90}{48} = \frac{15}{8}$$

Choice **(B)** is correct.

12. D

Difficulty: Hard

Category: Linear Graphs

Getting to the Answer: Compare the differences in the two lines to the statements in the answer choices. The *y*-intercept of both lines is the same. The key difference between the lines is their slopes. The solid line (pre-law) has a steeper slope, while the dashed line has a more gradual slope, so you can eliminate (C). The slope of each line is negative (falling from left to right), so even after the proposed law is implemented, the population is still expected to decline, which means you can eliminate (B). Because the dashed line's slope is more gradual, the decline in the population will be less severe (not accelerating), so you can eliminate (A). This means **(D)** is correct.

13. 6

Difficulty: Easy

Category: Solving Equations

Getting to the Answer: Decimals can be messy, so clear the decimals by multiplying each term by 100—this moves the decimal two places to the right, resulting in an equation with only integer values. Next, solve for *x*:

$$0.55x - 1.04 = 0.35x + 0.16$$

$$100(0.55x - 1.04) = 100(0.35x + 0.16)$$

$$55x - 104 = 35x + 16$$

$$20x = 120$$

$$x = 6$$

Grid in **6**.

14. 12

Difficulty: Medium

Category: Linear Graphs

Getting to the Answer: The place where the line crosses the *y*-axis is the *y*-intercept, or *b* when the equation is written in slope-intercept form ($y = mx + b$), so rewrite the equation in this form. To make the numbers easier to work with, clear the fraction by multiplying each term by 2:

$$\frac{3}{2}y - 2x = 18$$

$$2 \times \left[\frac{3}{2}y - 2x\right] = 18 \times 2$$

$$3y - 4x = 36$$

$$3y = 4x + 36$$

$$y = \frac{4}{3}x + 12$$

The *y*-intercept is **12**.

Because the *y*-intercept of a graph is always of the form (0, *y*), you could also substitute 0 for *x* in the original equation and solve for *y*.

15. D

Difficulty: Medium

Category: Substitution

Getting to the Answer: At their intersection, the two *y*-values will be equal, so you can write $ax + b = cx + d$. The value of *x* at the point of intersection is *p*. Substitute *p* for *x* to get $ap + b = cp + d$. Isolate the term containing *a* on the left side: $ap = cp + d - b$. Divide both sides by *p* to get $a = \dfrac{cp + d - b}{p}$, which simplifies to $a = c + \dfrac{d - b}{p}$, so **(D)** is correct.

16. C

Difficulty: Medium

Category: Number of Possible Solutions

Getting to the Answer: In order to analyze this question, first convert all the equations to standard $y = mx + b$ format. For the first equation, add $4x$ and $2y$ to both sides, which simplifies to $2y = 4x + 3$. Divide this by 2 to get $y = 2x + \frac{3}{2}$. The second equation is already in the desired format, $y = -\frac{1}{2}x + 3$. The third equation merely needs to be divided by 2, which results in the equation $y = -\frac{1}{2}x + 5$.

Look at the slopes of the equations. Two of the lines have the same slope, $-\frac{1}{2}$, so they are parallel. Since parallel lines do not intersect, these two equations by themselves have no intersections. The slope of the other line is 2. Recall that the slopes of perpendicular lines are negative reciprocals, so this line is perpendicular to the other two. Therefore, it has an intersection with each of those two lines. Thus, the lines defined by the three equations have 2 intersections. **(C)** is correct.

17. 13

Difficulty: Hard

Category: Substitution

Getting to the Answer: Set up linear equations based on the information in the question and solve for each dog's current age using substitution, combination, or both. Next, convert those ages to the time when Cassie was adopted and add them up.

Use the first letter of each dog's name as the variable to represent its current age. Since Apollo's age is twice Cassie's, you can write that $A = 2C$. When Apollo and Bailey were adopted 4 years ago, their ages at that time were $(A - 4)$ and $(B - 4)$, respectively. At this time, Bailey's age was three times Apollo's, so $B - 4 = 3(A - 4)$, which simplifies to $B - 4 = 3A - 12$. The final piece of information you can glean from the question is that at the time Cassie was adopted 2 years ago, Bailey was twice as old as Apollo. So, $B - 2 = 2(A - 2)$, which simplifies to $B - 2 = 2A - 4$.

Since there are 2 linear equations in terms of A and B, you can solve for those ages first using combination (elimination):

$$\begin{array}{r} B - 4 = 3A - 12 \\ -(B - 2 = 2A - 4) \\ \hline -2 = A - 8 \end{array}$$

Add 8 to each side to determine that $A = 6$. Plug that value into one of the equations: $B - 4 = 3(6) - 12$. Thus, $B = 18 - 12 + 4 = 10$. You also know that $A = 2C$, so Cassie's age is 3. Thus, the dogs' current ages are 6, 10, and 3, but the question asks for the sum of their ages when Cassie was adopted 2 years ago. This is $4 + 8 + 1 = 13$. Grid in **13**.

18. C

Difficulty: Medium

Category: Systems of Inequalities

Getting to the Answer: Use known points from the graph to determine the equations for the two lines and convert those to inequalities.

The solid line passes through the point $(0, 4)$ and terminates at the point $(1, 2)$. The slope of the line is $\frac{y_2 - y_1}{x_2 - x_1} = \frac{2 - 4}{1 - 0} = -2$ and the y-intercept is 4, so the equation for the line is $y = -2x + 4$. This can be restated as $y + 2x = 4$. Because the shaded region is below this line and the line is solid, the inequality defined by the line is $y + 2x \leq 4$. Eliminate (A).

The dotted line passes through the points $(-4, 0)$ and $(1, 2)$. Thus, the slope of this line is $\frac{2 - 0}{1 - (-4)} = \frac{2}{5}$. Plug in the values for the x-intercept to get $0 = \frac{2}{5}(-4) + b$. So, $b = -\left(\frac{2}{5}\right)(-4) = \frac{8}{5}$. The equation for this line is $y = \frac{2}{5}x + \frac{8}{5}$. Simplify this by multiplying all the terms by 5 to get $5y = 2x + 8$, which converts to $5y - 2x = 8$. Since the line is dotted and the values of the solution are above the line, the inequality is $5y - 2x > 8$. These two inequalities match the ones in **(C)**.

19. D

Difficulty: Medium

Category: Systems of Inequalities

Getting to the Answer: Restate both inequalities as equations that are the boundary lines of the solution to the system of inequalities in terms of y, then set them equal to each other to solve for a.

The boundary line for the inequality $y - ax \geq -8$ is $y = ax - 8$, and the boundary line for the inequality $2x + y \leq 6$ is $y = 6 - 2x$. So, at the intersection of the lines, $ax - 8 = 6 - 2x$. Put the terms with x on the left side to get $ax + 2x = 14$. You know that $x = 2$ at the intersection. Thus, $2a + 2(2) = 14$, so $2a = 10$ and $a = 5$. **(D)** is correct.

20. A

Difficulty: Easy

Category: Systems of Inequalities

Getting to the Answer: Solve the single-variable inequality for y and substitute the result into the other inequality to solve for x. If $8y > 20 + 3y$, then $5y > 20$ and $y > 4$. So, $4x > 4 + 8$, which means that $x > 3$. **(A)** is correct.

Data Analysis

CHAPTER 7

Ratios, Proportions, and Percents

LEARNING OBJECTIVES

After completing this chapter, you will be able to:

- Set up and solve a proportion for a missing value
- Use ratios to perform unit conversions
- Calculate percents and percent change

70/600 SmartPoints® (High Yield)

How Much Do You Know?

Directions: Try the questions that follow. Show your work so that you can compare your solutions to the ones found in the Check Your Work section immediately after this question set. The "Category" heading in the explanation for each question gives the title of the lesson that covers how to solve it. If you answered the question(s) for a given lesson correctly, and if your scratchwork looks like ours, you may be able to move quickly through that lesson. If you answered incorrectly or used a different approach, you may want to take your time on that lesson.

1. Leonardo da Vinci asserted that a person's height is proportional to the length of the person's palm. Don's palm is 5 centimeters in length and he is 120 centimeters tall. Mateo's palm is 7.5 centimeters in length. Assuming that da Vinci's theory is correct, how tall, in centimeters, is Mateo?

   A) 60 centimeters

   B) 80 centimeters

   C) 160 centimeters

   D) 180 centimeters

2. As of 2009, there were about 225 quarters for every 2 fifty-cent coins in circulation. If there were 380 million quarters in circulation that year, approximately how many total quarters and fifty-cent coins, in millions, were there in circulation?

   A) 383

   B) 415

   C) 493

   D) 605

3. If $\dfrac{5}{7a} = \dfrac{1}{b-a}$, which of the following proportions is equivalent?

   A) $\dfrac{a}{b} = \dfrac{5}{12}$

   B) $\dfrac{a}{b} = \dfrac{5}{2}$

   C) $\dfrac{b-a}{a} = \dfrac{5}{7}$

   D) $\dfrac{b-a}{a} = -\dfrac{7}{5}$

4. British Thermal Units (BTUs) and calories are two measures of heat energy. If there are 2,016 calories in 8 British Thermal Units, how many calories are in 3 British Thermal Units?

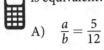

5. Sai's car is leaking engine oil at a rate of 2.5 milliliters per hour. If his car's engine contains 6 liters of oil, what will be the amount of oil, in milliliters, remaining in Sai's engine after 24 hours? (Note: There are 1,000 milliliters in 1 liter.)

Category	Percentage
Completely satisfied	
Somewhat satisfied	
Somewhat dissatisfied	15%
Completely dissatisfied	25%

6. A company conducts a customer satisfaction survey. The results are partly summarized in the table. If 240 customers responded to the survey, how many customers were either completely or somewhat satisfied?

A) 60

B) 96

C) 144

D) 204

7. In a week, a light bulb factory produces 12,500 light bulbs. The ratio of light emitting diodes (LED bulbs) to compact fluorescent lamps (CFL bulbs) is 2:3. Of the LED bulbs produced, 3 percent were defective. If the factory produces no other kind of bulbs, how many LED bulbs were NOT defective?

A) 2,425

B) 4,850

C) 7,275

D) 8,083

8. In 1950, scientists estimated a certain animal population in a particular geographical area to be 6,400. In 2000, the population had risen to 7,200. If this animal population experiences the same percent increase over the next 50 years, what will the approximate population be?

A) 8,000

B) 8,100

C) 8,400

D) 8,600

Check Your Work

1.   D

Difficulty: Easy

Category: Proportions

Getting to the Answer: Since you are given the palm-to-height ratio for Don's as well as Mateo's palm length, set up a proportion using M to represent Mateo's height:

$$\frac{5\text{ cm}}{120\text{ cm}} = \frac{7.5\text{ cm}}{M}$$

Cross-multiply to solve for M:

$$5M = 7.5(120)$$
$$M = \frac{7.5(120)}{5}$$
$$M = 180$$

The correct answer is **(D)**.

2.   A

Difficulty: Easy

Category: Proportions

Getting to the Answer: Notice that the question asks you for the total number of coins in millions, but the ratio given specifies only the parts. Set up a proportion using the given ratio:

$$\frac{225\text{ quarters}}{2\text{ fifty-cent coins}} = \frac{380\text{ million quarters}}{x\text{ fifty-cent coins}}$$

Cross-multiply: $225x = 2 \times 380$ million. Solve for x to find that $x = 3.3\overline{7}$ million fifty-cent coins in circulation. To calculate the total number of fifty-cent coins and quarters in circulation in millions in 2009, add the number of fifty-cent coins to the number of quarters: $3.3\overline{7}$ million $+ 380$ million ≈ 383 million. Choice **(A)** is correct.

3.   A

Difficulty: Medium

Category: Proportions

Getting to the Answer: Since the answer choices are expressed as $\frac{a}{b} =$ and $\frac{b-a}{a} =$, cross-multiply the proportion and rewrite it to get an expression that matches one of the answer choices. Solving for $\frac{b-a}{a}$, you get the following:

$$\frac{5}{7a} = \frac{1}{b-a}$$
$$5(b-a) = 7a$$
$$\frac{b-a}{a} = \frac{7}{5}$$

This does not match (C) or (D), so eliminate them. Now solve for $\frac{a}{b}$:

$$5(b-a) = 7a$$
$$5b - 5a = 7a$$
$$5b = 12a$$
$$\frac{5}{12} = \frac{a}{b}$$

This matches **(A)**.

4.   756

Difficulty: Easy

Category: Unit Conversion

Getting to the Answer: Let x represent the number of calories in 3 BTUs, and set up a proportion equating the ratio of 8 BTUs to 2,016 calories to the ratio of 3 BTUs to x calories: $\frac{8\text{ BTU}}{2,016\text{ CAL}} = \frac{3\text{ BTU}}{x\text{ CAL}}$. Solving for x gives 756 calories. Grid in **756**.

5. 5940

Difficulty: Medium

Category: Unit Conversion

Getting to the Answer: First, determine the amount of oil that will leak out of Sai's engine after 24 hours: $\frac{2.5 \text{ mL}}{1 \text{ hr}} \times 24 \text{ hr} = 60$ mL. Then, use the conversion to determine the amount of oil, in milliliters, initially in the engine: $6 \text{ L} \times \frac{1,000 \text{ mL}}{1 \text{ L}} = 6,000$ mL. Calculate the difference between the two to find the amount of oil remaining in the engine after 24 hours: 6,000 mL − 60 mL = 5,940 mL. Grid in **5940**.

6. C

Difficulty: Easy

Category: Percents

Getting to the Answer: According to the table, 25% of the customers are completely dissatisfied and 15% are somewhat dissatisfied. So, 100% − 25% − 15% = 60% of the customers are completely or somewhat satisfied. Thus, the number of customers who are completely or somewhat satisfied is 60% of 240, or 0.6 × 240 = 144 customers, making **(C)** correct.

7. B

Difficulty: Hard

Category: Percents

Getting to the Answer: Approach the question as a series of steps. Before you bubble in your answer, check that you answered the right question (the number of LED bulbs that were *not* defective).

First, find the total number of LED bulbs produced. Since the ratio of LED to CFL is 2:3 and a total of 12,500 of both kinds of bulbs were produced, two parts LED plus three parts CFL equals 12,500. Let x be the number of LED bulbs produced and use the part-to-whole ratio to set up a proportion:

$$\frac{2}{5} = \frac{x}{12,500}$$

Solve for x by cross-multiplying:

$$2(12,500) = 5x$$
$$25,000 = 5x$$
$$5,000 = x$$

Now find the number of LED bulbs that were not defective: $5,000 \times 97\% = 5,000 \times 0.97 = 4,850$. Choice **(B)** is correct.

8. B

Difficulty: Medium

Category: Percent Change

Getting to the Answer: Find the percent increase in the population from 1950 to 2000 using this formula: $\text{percent increase} = \frac{\text{amount of increase}}{\text{original amount}} \times 100\%$. Then apply the same percent increase to the animal population in 2000.

The amount of increase is 7,200 − 6,400 = 800, so the percent increase is $\frac{800}{6,400} \times 100\% = 0.125 \times 100\% = 12.5\%$ between 1950 and 2000. If the total percent increase over the next 50 years is the same, the animal population should be about

$$7,200 \times (100\% + 12.5\%) = 7,200 \times (112.5\%) =$$
$$7,200 \times 1.125 = 8,100.$$

(B) is correct.

Ratios and Proportions

LEARNING OBJECTIVE

After this lesson, you will be able to:

● Set up and solve a proportion for a missing value

To answer a question like this:

The World War II aircraft carrier *Essex* was 872 feet long with a beam (width) of 147 feet. A museum wishes to build an exact replica scale model of the *Essex* that is 8 feet long. Approximately how many <u>inches</u> wide will the scale model's beam be? (1 foot = 12 inches)

A) 13

B) 16

C) 26

D) 109

You need to know this:

A **ratio** is a comparison of one quantity to another. When writing ratios, you can compare one part of a group to another part of that group or you can compare a part of the group to the whole group. Suppose you have a bowl of apples and oranges: you can write ratios that compare apples to oranges (part to part), apples to total fruit (part to whole), and oranges to total fruit (part to whole).

Keep in mind that ratios convey *relative* amounts, not necessarily actual amounts, and that they are typically expressed in lowest terms. For example, if there are 10 apples and 6 oranges in a bowl, the ratio of apples to oranges would likely be expressed as $\frac{5}{3}$ on the SAT rather than as $\frac{10}{6}$. However, if you know the ratio of apples to oranges and either the actual number of apples or the total number of pieces of fruit, you can find the actual number of oranges by setting up a proportion (see below).

Note that the SAT may occasionally use the word "proportion" to mean "ratio."

A **proportion** is simply two ratios set equal to each other, such as $\frac{a}{b} = \frac{c}{d}$. Proportions are an efficient way to solve certain problems, but you must exercise caution when setting them up. Noting the units of each piece of the proportion will help you put each piece of the proportion in the right place. Sometimes the SAT may ask you to determine whether certain proportions are equivalent—check this by cross-multiplying. You'll get results that are much easier to compare.

$$\text{If } \frac{a}{b} = \frac{c}{d}, \text{ then: } ad = bc, \ \frac{a}{c} = \frac{b}{d}, \ \frac{d}{b} = \frac{c}{a}, \ \frac{b}{a} = \frac{d}{c}, \text{ BUT } \frac{a}{d} \neq \frac{c}{b}$$

Each derived ratio shown except the last one is simply a manipulation of the first, so all except the last are correct. You can verify this via cross-multiplication ($ad = bc$ in each case except the last).

Alternatively, you can pick equivalent fractions $\frac{2}{3}$ and $\frac{6}{9}$ ($a = 2$, $b = 3$, $c = 6$, $d = 9$). Cross-multiplication gives $2 \times 9 = 3 \times 6$, which is a true statement. Dividing 2 and 3 by 6 and 9 gives $\frac{2}{6} = \frac{3}{9}$, which is also true, and so on. However, attempting to equate $\frac{2}{9}$ and $\frac{3}{6}$ will not work.

If you know any three numerical values in a proportion, you can solve for the fourth. For example, say a fruit stand sells 3 peaches for every 5 apricots, and you are supposed to calculate the number of peaches sold on a day when 20 apricots were sold. You would use the given information to set up a proportion and solve for the unknown:

$$\frac{3}{5} = \frac{p}{20}$$

You can now solve for the number of peaches sold, p, by cross-multiplying:

$$60 = 5p$$
$$p = 12$$

Alternatively, you could use the common multiplier to solve for p: the numerator and denominator in the original ratio must be multiplied by the same value to arrive at their respective terms in the new ratio. To get from 5 to 20 in the denominator, you multiply by 4, so you also have to multiply the 3 in the numerator by 4 to arrive at the actual number of peaches sold: $4(3) = 12$.

You need to do this:

Set up a proportion and solve for the unknown, either by cross-multiplying or by using the common multiplier.

Explanation:

The ratio of the length of the real *Essex* to that of the scale model is $\frac{872\,\text{ft}}{8\,\text{ft}}$. You know the actual beam width (147 feet), so set up a proportion and solve for the scale model's beam width:

$$\frac{872\,\text{ft}}{8\,\text{ft}} = \frac{147\,\text{ft}}{x\,\text{ft}}$$
$$872x = 1{,}176\,\text{ft}$$
$$x \approx 1.349\,\text{ft}$$

The question asks for the answer in inches, not feet, so multiply by 12 inches per foot:
$1.349\,\text{ft} \times 12\,\text{in/ft} = 16.188$ inches. The correct answer is **(B)**.

Try on Your Own

Directions: Take as much time as you need on these questions. Work carefully and methodically. There will be an opportunity for timed practice at the end of the chapter.

1. Teachers at a certain school know that, when reviewing for exams, the number of topics they can cover is directly proportional to the length of time they have to review. If teachers can cover 9 topics in a single 45-minute period, how many topics can they cover in a 1-hour period?

   A)   5

   B)   7

   C)   10

   D)   12

2. Objects weigh less on the Moon because the Moon's gravitational pull is less than Earth's. In general, 1 pound on Earth is equal to approximately 0.166 pounds on the Moon. If a person weighs 29 pounds on the Moon, approximately how much, in pounds, does the person weigh on Earth?

   A)   21

   B)   48

   C)   175

   D)   196

3. A machine produces 6 defective parts out of every 3,500 it makes. How many total parts were made during the time the machine produced 27 defective parts?

   A)   14,000

   B)   15,750

   C)   17,500

   D)   21,000

4. The ratio of freshmen to sophomores in an auditorium was 3 to 10. After an additional 270 freshmen and 120 sophomores entered the auditorium, the ratio of freshmen to sophomores was 6 to 5. No other students entered or left the auditorium. How many freshmen were in the auditorium before the additional students entered?

   A)   15

   B)   42

   C)   140

   D)   182

Math

HINT: For Q5, which conversion will be easier? Minutes to hours or hours to minutes?

---

5. Riding her bicycle, Reyna can travel 1 mile in 5.5 minutes. If she rides at a constant rate, which of the following is closest to the distance she will travel in 1.5 hours?

    A)   9 miles

    B)   11 miles

    C)   13 miles

    D)   16 miles

6. If $\dfrac{x + y}{x} = \dfrac{4}{9}$, which of the following proportions is equivalent?

    A) $\dfrac{y}{x} = -\dfrac{5}{9}$

    B) $\dfrac{y}{x} = \dfrac{13}{9}$

    C) $\dfrac{y - x}{x} = -\dfrac{4}{9}$

    D) $\dfrac{y - x}{x} = -\dfrac{9}{4}$

HINT: For Q7, start with the proportion $\dfrac{\text{physicists}}{\text{total}} = \dfrac{2}{5}$, then think about what to substitute for "physicists" and "total."

---

7. All of the attendees at a symposium are either physicists or biologists. If there are 123 physicists and 270 biologists, then how many additional physicists must arrive at the symposium in order for the ratio of physicists to total attendees to become 2 to 5 ?

    A)   25

    B)   50

    C)   57

    D)   114

Unit Conversion

LEARNING OBJECTIVE

After this lesson, you will be able to:

- Use ratios to perform unit conversions

To answer a question like this:

The nearest star to the Sun, Proxima Centauri, is approximately 4.3 light-years away. Another star, Sirius A, is twice that distance from the Sun. If 1 light-year equals 63,000 astronomical units (AU), and 1 AU equals 150 million kilometers, approximately how far is Sirius A from the Sun in trillions of kilometers? (1 trillion = 1,000,000,000,000)

A) 2.2

B) 20

C) 41

D) 81

You need to know this:

You can use ratios to perform unit conversions. This is especially useful when there are multiple conversions or when the units are unfamiliar.

For example, though these units of measurement are no longer commonly used, there are 8 furlongs in a mile and 3 miles in a league. Say you're asked to convert 4 leagues to furlongs. A convenient way to do this is to set up the conversion ratios so that equivalent units cancel:

$$4 \text{ leagues} \times \frac{3 \text{ miles}}{1 \text{ league}} \times \frac{8 \text{ furlongs}}{1 \text{ mile}} = 4 \times 3 \times 8 = 96 \text{ furlongs}$$

Notice that all the units cancel out except the furlongs, which is the one you want.

You need to do this:

Set up a series of ratios to make equivalent units cancel. (Keep track of the units by writing them down next to the numbers in the ratios.) You should be left with the units you're converting into.

Explanation:

Sirius A is twice as far from the Sun as Proxima Centauri, so it is $2(4.3) = 8.6$ light-years away from the Sun. Set up a series of ratios to convert to trillion kilometers:

$$8.6 \text{ light-years} \times \frac{63,000 \text{ AU}}{1 \text{ light-year}} \times \frac{150 \text{ million km}}{1 \text{ AU}} = 8.6 \times 63,000 \times 150 \text{ million km}$$

$$= 81,270,000 \text{ million km}$$

$$= 81.27 \text{ trillion km}$$

Because there are 6 zeros in a million, 81,270,000 million is 81,270,000,000,000. There are 12 zeros in a trillion, so this number equals 81.27 trillion. The correct answer is **(D)**.

Math

Try on Your Own

Directions: Take as much time as you need on these questions. Work carefully and methodically. There will be an opportunity for timed practice at the end of the chapter.

HINT: For Q8, *cubic feet* means ft³ or ft × ft × ft.

---

8. Quinn wants to rent a self-storage unit for her college dorm room furniture for the summer. She estimates that she will need 700 cubic feet of storage space, but the self-storage provider measures its units in cubic meters. If 1 meter is approximately 3.28 feet, about how many cubic meters of space will Quinn need?

   A) 19.84

   B) 25.93

   C) 65.07

   D) 213.41

9. Because court reporters must type every word at a trial or hearing, they must be able to type at a minimum rate of 3.75 words per second in order to be certified. Suppose a trial transcript contains 25 pages with an average of 675 words per page. Assuming the court reporter typed the transcript at the minimum rate, how long was he actively typing?

   A) 1 hour, 15 minutes

   B) 1 hour, 45 minutes

   C) 2 hours, 30 minutes

   D) 3 hours

HINT: For Q10, "how many more" means you're solving for a difference. Subtract, then convert pounds/hour to ounces/minute.

---

10. At 350°F, an oven can cook approximately 3 pounds of turkey per hour. At 450°F, it can cook approximately 4.5 pounds per hour. How many more ounces of turkey can the oven cook at 450°F than at 350°F in 10 minutes? (1 pound = 16 ounces)

    A) 4

    B) 6

    C) 8

    D) 12

11. An emergency room doctor prescribes a certain pain medication to be delivered through an IV drip. She prescribes 800 milliliters of the medication to be delivered over the course of 8 hours. The IV delivers 1 milliliter of medication over the course of 30 drips. How many drips per minute are needed to deliver the prescribed dosage?

12. Botanists studying a particular coastal redwood tree determined that the tree grew 46 meters in the first 50 years of its life. On average, how many centimeters per day did it grow during this period? Assume that there are 365 days in a year, and round your answer to the nearest hundredth of a centimeter. (1 meter = 100 centimeters)

Percents

LEARNING OBJECTIVE

After this lesson, you will be able to:

● Calculate percents

To answer a question like this:

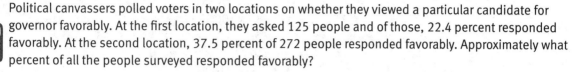

Political canvassers polled voters in two locations on whether they viewed a particular candidate for governor favorably. At the first location, they asked 125 people and of those, 22.4 percent responded favorably. At the second location, 37.5 percent of 272 people responded favorably. Approximately what percent of all the people surveyed responded favorably?

A) 25.7%

B) 30.0%

C) 31.5%

D) 32.7%

You need to know this:

To calculate percents, use this basic equation:

$$\text{Percent} = \frac{\text{part}}{\text{whole}} \times 100\%$$

Alternatively, use this statement: [blank] percent of [blank] is [blank]. Translating from English into math, you get [blank]% × [blank] = [blank].

You need to do this:

- Plug in the values for any two parts of the formula and solve for the third.
- In some calculations, you may find it convenient to express percents as decimals. To do this, use the formula above but stop before you multiply by 100% at the end.

Explanation:

Use a variation of the three-part percent formula to answer this question: whole $\times$ percent = part, where the percent is expressed as a decimal.

First, find the number of people at each location who responded favorably using the formula. Start with the first location: $125 \times 0.224 = 28$. Move on to the second location: $272 \times 0.375 = 102$. Next, find the total number of people who were surveyed at both locations, which is $125 + 272 = 397$, and the total number who responded favorably, $28 + 102 = 130$. Finally, find the percent of people who responded favorably by using the formula one more time:

$$397 \times \text{percent} = 130 \times 100\%$$
$$\text{percent} = \frac{130}{397} \times 100\%$$
$$\approx 0.327 \times 100\%$$
$$= 32.7\%$$

Of all the people surveyed, about 32.7% responded favorably, making **(D)** the correct answer.

Try on Your Own

Directions: Take as much time as you need on these questions. Work carefully and methodically. There will be an opportunity for timed practice at the end of the chapter.

13. A college athletics program found that approximately 3 percent of 308 runners were injured during workouts and that approximately 6 percent of 237 weight lifters were injured during workouts. Which of the following is the closest to the total number of runners and weight lifters who were injured?

    A) 50
    B) 39
    C) 26
    D) 23

HINT: For Q14, what percent of the attendees are teachers?
---

14. At a high school conference, 15 percent of the attendees are sophomores, 30 percent are juniors, 25 percent are seniors, and the remaining 18 attendees are teachers. How many more juniors are there than seniors?

HINT: For Q15, how many gallons of *pigment* is the painter starting with? How many gallons of *pigment* are needed for the final mix? How many gallons of the final paint will it take to provide the needed pigment?
---

15. A painter has 20 gallons of a paint mixture that is 15 percent blue pigment. How many gallons of a mixture that is 40 percent blue pigment would the painter need to add to achieve a mixture that is 20 percent blue pigment?

    A) 4
    B) 5
    C) 8
    D) 12

16. On August 1, the price of one share of a company's stock was $75. On September 1, the price of one share was $10 more than it was on August 1 and 80 percent of the price of one share on October 1. To the nearest dollar, what was the price of one share on October 1?

    A) $68
    B) $99
    C) $102
    D) $106

Percent Change

LEARNING OBJECTIVE

After this lesson, you will be able to:

● Calculate percent change

To answer a question like this:

 On a particular day, a power company makes several changes in the power allocated to a neighborhood. First, it increases the power by 20 percent. Then, it decreases the power by 10 percent. Finally, it increases the power by 30 percent. What is the net percent increase in this neighborhood's power allocation, to the nearest tenth of a percent? (The percent sign is understood after your answer. For example, if the answer is 15.1%, grid in 15.1.)

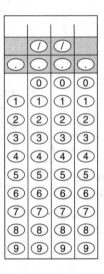

You need to know this:

You can determine the **percent change** in a given situation by applying this formula:

$$\text{Percent increase or decrease} = \frac{\text{amount of increase or decrease}}{\text{original amount}} \times 100\%$$

Sometimes, more than one change will occur. Be careful here, as it can be tempting to take a shortcut by just adding two percent changes together (which will almost always lead to an incorrect answer). Instead, you'll need to find the total amount of the increase or decrease and then apply the formula.

You need to do this:

- Calculate the actual increase or decrease.
- Divide by the *original* amount (not the new amount!).
- Multiply by 100%.

Explanation:

The question does not give an initial value for power allocation, so pick 100 (often the best number to use when picking numbers for questions involving percents) and then calculate the actual change. A 20% increase from 100 is $100 + 100 \times 0.2$ and brings the power allocation to $100 + 20 = 120$. A 10% decrease from 120 is $120 - 120 \times 0.1$ and brings the power allocation to $120 - 12 = 108$. Lastly, an increase of 30% puts the final power allocation at $108 + 0.3 \times 108 = 108 + 32.4 = 140.4$. The actual increase, then, is $140.4 - 100 = 40.4$. (Again, note that simply combining the percents would get you the wrong answer: $10\% - 20\% + 30\% = 40\%$.)

Plugging this increase into the percent change formula yields the following (remember to divide by the *original* amount, 100, rather than by the new amount, 140.4):

$$\text{Percent change} = \frac{40.4}{100} \times 100\% = 40.4\%$$

Grid in **40.4**.

Try on Your Own

Directions: Take as much time as you need on these questions. Work carefully and methodically. There will be an opportunity for timed practice at the end of the chapter.

HINT: For Q17, remember to divide by the *original* value.
---

17. A homeowner's annual property tax payment was $1,494. Due to a property value reassessment, the tax payment was increased to $1,572. To the nearest tenth of a percent, by what percent was the home-owner's property tax payment increased?

    A) 0.1%

    B) 5.0%

    C) 5.2%

    D) 7.9%

18. The price of a single share of a certain corporation's stock was $35. Six months later, the price of a single share of the corporation's stock had risen to $49. To the nearest percent, what was the percent increase in the price per share?

    A) 14%

    B) 29%

    C) 40%

    D) 48%

HINT: For Q19, how does the wording of the question help you determine which container of coins is the original amount?
---

19. The number of coins in jar X is 75. The number of coins in jar Y is 54. By what percent is the number of coins in jar Y less than the number of coins in jar X?

    A) 21%

    B) 28%

    C) 39%

    D) 72%

HINT: For Q20, if you have 75% more senior than juniors, you have all the juniors (100%) plus 75%, or 175%. Adding the percents at the start saves a calculation step.
---

20. At a school rally, there are 50 sophomores, 80 juniors, and 75 percent more seniors than juniors. By what percent is the number of seniors greater than the number of sophomores?

    A) 80%

    B) 140%

    C) 150%

    D) 180%

HINT: For Q21, the final 25% discount is applied to an already reduced price. You *cannot* add the percent discounts together.
---

21. The original price of a newly released smart phone was y dollars. A year later, the original price of the phone was discounted by 36 percent. After another six months, an online retailer was selling the phone at a price that was 25 percent less than the previously discounted price. By what percent was the online retailer's price less than y?

    A) 27%

    B) 48%

    C) 52%

    D) 61%

On Test Day

When a question features multiple percentages, you have to make a key strategic decision: can I do the arithmetic on the percentages themselves and get the answer right away, or do I have to calculate each percentage individually and do the arithmetic on the actual values?

For example, suppose a car traveling 50 miles per hour increases its speed by 20 percent and then decreases its speed by 20 percent. Can you just say that its final speed is 50 miles per hour since $+20\% - 20\% = 0$? No, because after a 20% increase, the car's speed becomes 120% of the original: $1.2(50) = 60$. When the car "decreases its speed by 20 percent," that 20 percent is calculated based on the new speed, 60, not the original speed, and 20 percent of 60 is greater than 20 percent of 50. Thus, the car's final speed is lower than its starting speed: $50(1.2)(0.8) = 48$ miles per hour.

By contrast, suppose you have to find how many more nonsmokers than occasional smokers live in a certain region where there are 13,450 residents, given that 62 percent of them don't smoke and 8 percent of them do smoke occasionally. It may be tempting to find 62 percent of 13,450 ($0.62 \times 13,450 = 8,339$), then find 8 percent of 13,450 ($0.08 \times 13,450 = 1,076$), and finally subtract those two numbers to get the answer ($8,339 - 1,076 = 7,263$). This is a waste of time, though. Instead, you can quickly find the difference between the two percentages ($62 - 8 = 54$) and take 54 percent of the total to get the answer in one step: $13,450 \times 0.54 = 7,263$, the same answer.

If you *can* do arithmetic using the percentages but choose to do arithmetic on the raw numbers instead, you'll waste time doing unnecessary work. But if you *can't* do arithmetic on the percentages (as in the first example) but do anyway, then you'll get the wrong answer. So, being able to tell whether you can or can't do the arithmetic on the percentages is a useful skill.

Luckily, the fundamental principle is simple: you can always do arithmetic on the percentages as long as the percentages are out of the same total. If the totals are different, then you must convert the percentages into actual values. Practice applying this principle on the following question.

22. Flanders Corporation has 250 full-time and 250 part-time employees. If 92 percent of the full-time employees qualify for health insurance benefits, and 74 percent of the part-time employees do not qualify for health insurance benefits, then how many more full-time than part-time employees at Flanders Corporation qualify for health insurance benefits?

   A)   45

   B)   90

   C)   165

   D)   330

The answer and explanation can be found at the end of this chapter.

Math

How Much Have You Learned?

Directions: For testlike practice, give yourself 15 minutes to complete this question set. Be sure to study the explanations, even for questions you got right. They can be found at the end of this chapter.

Undergraduate Costs at a State University

2014–15	2015–16	2016–17	2017–18	2018–19	2019–20
$12,192	$12,804	$13,446	$14,118	$14,820	$15,564

23. The table above summarizes the total cost per undergraduate student per year at a state university for each academic year from 2014–15 to 2019–20.

    If fees account for 8.75 percent of one year's total costs, what is the average fee increase per academic year? Round your answer to the nearest dollar.

24. A gardener planted a 20-inch-tall sapling in his yard. Four months later, the sapling was 27 inches tall. By what percent did the height of the sapling increase over the four months?

    A) 7%

    B) 26%

    C) 35%

    D) 74%

25. From 1997 to 1998, company T's profits increased by 25 percent. From 1998 to 1999, company T's profits rose from $375 million to $483 million. By what percent did company T's profits increase from 1997 to 1999?

    A) 38%

    B) 49%

    C) 54%

    D) 61%

26. At a certain store, the price of a calculator is $150, the price of a radio is $75, and the price of a printer is 16 percent less than the price of a radio. By what percent is the price of a printer less than the price of a calculator?

    A) 39%

    B) 58%

    C) 63%

    D) 87%

27. A car that is traveling at a constant speed of 9 miles per hour is traveling at a constant speed of how many feet per second? (1 mile = 5,280 feet)

    A) 1.5

    B) 6.1

    C) 13.2

    D) 79.2

28. In a certain music store, every guitar is either a dreadnought or a parlor guitar. The ratio of dreadnoughts to parlor guitars in the music store is 4 to 15, and there is a total of 114 guitars in the music store. How many guitars in the music store are dreadnoughts?

    A) 24

    B) 29

    C) 34

    D) 46

29. The population of a town was 84,600 on January 1, 2016, and 74,025 on January 1, 2017. By what percent did the population of the town decrease from January 1, 2016, to January 1, 2017?

    A) 10.5%

    B) 12.5%

    C) 14.5%

    D) 17%

30. The perimeter of regular pentagon *P* is half the perimeter of regular hexagon *H*. What is the ratio of the length of a side of the pentagon to a side of the hexagon?

    A) 1:2

    B) 3:5

    C) 5:6

    D) 5:3

31. A jar contains red, white, and yellow candy pieces in the ratio of 9:5:4, respectively. When 7 pieces of red candy and 5 pieces of white candy are removed from the jar and 3 pieces of yellow candy are added, the ratio of red to white to yellow becomes 4:2:3. If the jar contains only these three colors of candy, how many pieces were originally in the jar?

32. Juan's air mattress deflates at a constant rate of 100 milliliters per minute. If Juan's air mattress contains 300 liters of air, how long will it take, in hours, for the air mattress to completely deflate? (Note: There are 1,000 milliliters in 1 liter.)

Reflect

Directions: Take a few minutes to recall what you've learned and what you've been practicing in this chapter. Consider the following questions, jot down your best answer for each one, and then compare your reflections to the expert responses on the following page. Use your level of confidence to determine what to do next.

What is a ratio and how is it different from a proportion?

_____

_____

_____

If you're given a ratio of one quantity to another, what can you say about the total number of quantities?

_____

_____

_____

When doing unit conversions, how can you make sure you're doing them correctly?

_____

_____

_____

Suppose the value of something increases by 20 percent. How can you calculate the final value in the fewest number of steps? What if the value decreases by 20 percent?

_____

_____

_____

What is the percent change formula and what is the biggest pitfall to avoid when using it?

_____

_____

_____

Expert Responses

What is a ratio and how is it different from a proportion?

A ratio is the relative comparison of one quantity to another. For example, if the ratio of dogs to cats in an animal shelter is 3 to 5, then there are 3 dogs for every 5 cats. A proportion is two ratios set equal to each other.

If you're given a ratio of one quantity to another, what can you say about the total number of quantities?

Given a ratio, you know that the total must be a multiple of the sum of the ratio's parts. For example, if the ratio of dogs to cats is 3 to 5, then the total number of dogs and cats must be a multiple of 3 + 5, or 8. This means that when the SAT gives you one ratio, it's actually giving you several. If you're told that dogs:cats = 3:5, then you also know that dogs:total = 3:8 and cats:total = 5:8. You can use this "hidden" knowledge to your advantage.

When doing unit conversions, how can you make sure you're doing them correctly?

To do unit conversions correctly, set up the conversion in whichever way makes units cancel. For example, to convert 3 feet into inches, you multiply 3 feet by 12 inches per foot, because it cancels out the feet unit. If instead you multiplied 3 feet by 1 foot per 12 inches, then the resulting units would be "feet squared per inch," which makes no sense.

Suppose the value of something increases by 20 percent. How can you calculate the final value in the fewest number of steps? What if the value decreases by 20 percent?

The fastest way to increase a value by 20 percent is to multiply it by 1.2, which is 100% + 20% = 120%. Similarly, to decrease something by 20 percent, you multiply it by 0.8, as that is 100% − 20% = 80%.

What is the percent change formula and what is the biggest pitfall to avoid when using it?

The percent change formula is as follows:

$$\text{Percent change} = \frac{\text{amount of increase or decrease}}{\text{original amount}} \times 100\%$$

A common mistake is to put the new amount on the bottom of the fraction rather than the original amount.

Next Steps

If you answered most questions correctly in the "How Much Have You Learned?" section, and if your responses to the Reflect questions were similar to those of the SAT expert, then consider ratios and the related topics in this chapter to be an area of strength and move on to the next chapter. Come back to this topic periodically to prevent yourself from getting rusty.

If you don't yet feel confident, review those parts of this chapter that you have not yet mastered and try the questions you missed again. As always, be sure to review the explanations closely. Finally, **go online** (www.kaptest.com/moreonline) for additional practice on the highest yield topics in this chapter.

Answers and Explanations

1. D

Difficulty: Easy

Getting to the Answer: To answer a question that says "directly proportional," set two ratios equal to each other and solve for the missing amount. Be sure to match the units in the numerators and in the denominators on both sides of the proportion.

Because the first rate is given in minutes, write 1 hour as 60 minutes. Let t equal the number of topics the teachers can cover in a 60-minute period. Set up a proportion and solve for t:

$$\frac{9 \text{ topics}}{45 \text{ minutes}} = \frac{t \text{ topics}}{60 \text{ minutes}}$$
$$9(60) = 45(t)$$
$$540 = 45t$$
$$12 = t$$

Choice **(D)** is correct.

2. C

Difficulty: Easy

Getting to the Answer: Think about how your answer should look. A person weighs *less* on the Moon, so that person should weigh *more* on Earth. This means your answer must be greater than 29, so you can eliminate (A) right away.

Now, set up a proportion:

$$\frac{0.166 \text{ lb on Moon}}{1 \text{ lb on Earth}} = \frac{29 \text{ lb on Moon}}{p \text{ lb on Earth}}$$
$$0.166p = 29(1)$$
$$p \approx 174.7$$

The person weighs about 175 pounds on Earth. Choice **(C)** is correct.

3. B

Difficulty: Easy

Getting to the Answer: This is a typical proportion question. Use words first to write the proportion. Then translate from English into math. Let n equal the total number of parts made. Set up a proportion and solve for n. Be sure to match the units in the numerators and in the denominators on both sides of the proportion:

$$\frac{\text{defective parts}}{\text{number made}} = \frac{\text{defective parts}}{\text{number made}}$$
$$\frac{6}{3,500} = \frac{27}{n}$$
$$6n = 27(3,500)$$
$$6n = 94,500$$
$$n = 15,750$$

This means **(B)** is correct.

4. B

Difficulty: Hard

Getting to the Answer: This question has two unknowns: you don't know the starting number of either freshmen or sophomores. To solve for two unknowns, you need two equations. Let f represent the original number of freshmen in the auditorium and s represent the original number of sophomores. The starting ratio is $\frac{f}{s} = \frac{3}{10}$. Cross-multiplying yields $10f = 3s$. This is your first equation.

Set up a second equation to represent the adjusted number of freshmen and sophomores:

$$\frac{f + 270}{s + 120} = \frac{6}{5}$$
$$5(f + 270) = 6(s + 120)$$
$$5f + 1,350 = 6s + 720$$

You've determined from the first ratio that $10f = 3s$, and if you multiply this equation by 2, you get $20f = 6s$. Now substitute $20f$ for $6s$ in the above equation:

$$5f + 1,350 = 20f + 720$$
$$630 = 15f$$
$$42 = f$$

There were 42 freshmen in the auditorium to start, so **(B)** is correct.

5.   D

Difficulty: Medium

Getting to the Answer: Use the known time of 5.5 minutes it takes Reyna to travel 1 mile to calculate the distance she can cover in 1.5 hours. So that you're working with the same units, first convert 1.5 hours to minutes: $1.5 \times 60 = 90$ minutes. Let d be the unknown distance and then set up a proportion to solve for d:

$$\frac{1}{5.5} = \frac{d}{90}$$
$$90 = 5.5d$$
$$\frac{90}{5.5} = d$$
$$d \approx 16$$

Therefore, **(D)** is correct.

6.   A

Difficulty: Medium

Getting to the Answer: Since the answer choices are expressed as $\frac{y}{x} =$ and $\frac{y-x}{x} =$, cross-multiply the proportion and rewrite it to get an expression that matches the form of one of the answer choices. Solve for $\frac{y}{x}$:

$$\frac{x+y}{x} = \frac{4}{9}$$
$$9(x+y) = 4x$$
$$9x + 9y = 4x$$
$$9y = -5x$$
$$\frac{y}{x} = -\frac{5}{9}$$

This matches **(A)**.

Alternatively, you could rewrite the proportion as follows:

$$\frac{x}{x} + \frac{y}{x} = \frac{4}{9}$$
$$1 + \frac{y}{x} = \frac{4}{9}$$
$$\frac{y}{x} = \frac{4}{9} - 1$$
$$\frac{y}{x} = -\frac{5}{9}$$

Note that multiplying both sides of the proportion by -1 would give $-\frac{(x+y)}{x} = -\frac{4}{9}$ or $\frac{-x-y}{x} = -\frac{4}{9}$, which does not match (C) or (D).

7.   C

Difficulty: Hard

Getting to the Answer: The ratio of physicists to total attendees is the number of physicists divided by the number of all attendees. Suppose x new physicists arrive at the symposium. The new number of physicists will be $123 + x$, and the new number of all attendees will be the original physicists (123) + biologists (270) + the newcomer physicists (x). The ratio of the first number over the second equals 2 to 5, so set up a proportion and solve for x:

$$\frac{123+x}{123+270+x} = \frac{2}{5}$$
$$\frac{123+x}{393+x} = \frac{2}{5}$$
$$5(123+x) = 2(393+x)$$
$$615 + 5x = 786 + 2x$$
$$3x = 171$$
$$x = 57$$

Therefore, **(C)** is correct.

8.   A

Difficulty: Medium

Getting to the Answer: Map out your route from starting units to ending units, being mindful of the fact that the question deals with units of volume (cubic units). The starting quantity is in ft^3, and the desired quantity is in m^3. The only conversion factor you need is $1 \text{ m} \approx 3.28 \text{ ft}$, but you'll need to use it three times. Setting up your route to m^3, you get:

$$\frac{700 \text{ ft}^3}{1} \times \frac{1 \text{ m}}{3.28 \text{ ft}} \times \frac{1 \text{ m}}{3.28 \text{ ft}} \times \frac{1 \text{ m}}{3.28 \text{ ft}} = \frac{700}{(3.28)^3} \text{m}^3$$
$$\approx 19.84 \text{ m}^3$$

This matches **(A)**.

9.   A

Difficulty: Hard

Getting to the Answer: Whenever multiple rates are given, pay very careful attention to the units. Starting with the number of pages the reporter typed, set up your conversion ratios so that equivalent units cancel. Be sure your units match those in the answer choices:

$$25 \text{ pages} \times \frac{675 \text{ words}}{1 \text{ page}} \times \frac{1 \text{ second}}{3.75 \text{ words}}$$

$$\times \frac{1 \text{ minute}}{60 \text{ seconds}} \times \frac{1 \text{ hour}}{60 \text{ minutes}} = 1.25 \text{ hours}$$

Because 1.25 hours is not an answer choice, convert 0.25 to minutes: 0.25×60 minutes $= 15$ minutes, making **(A)** the correct answer.

10. A

Difficulty: Medium

Getting to the Answer: The 450°F oven cooks $4.5 - 3 = 1.5$ more pounds per hour than the 350°F oven. However, the question asks for the answer in ounces per 10 minutes, so convert from pounds per hour to ounces per minute, then multiply by 10 minutes:

$$\frac{1.5 \text{ lb}}{1 \text{ hr}} \times \frac{16 \text{ oz}}{1 \text{ lb}} \times \frac{1 \text{ hr}}{60 \text{ min}} \times 10 \text{ min} = 4 \text{ oz}$$

In 10 minutes, the oven at 450°F can cook 4 ounces more than the oven at 350°F, making **(A)** the correct answer.

11. 50

Difficulty: Medium

Getting to the Answer: Starting with the prescribed dosage, set up your conversion ratios so that equivalent units cancel and you get drips per minute:

$$\frac{800 \text{ mL}}{8 \text{ hours}} \times \frac{30 \text{ drips}}{1 \text{ mL}} \times \frac{1 \text{ hour}}{60 \text{ minutes}} = 50 \frac{\text{drips}}{\text{minute}}$$

Grid in **50.**

12. 0.25

Difficulty: Easy

Getting to the Answer: The question provides the growth rate, in meters, over a 50-year period. You need to convert this to a rate of centimeters per day. Set up your conversion ratios to make the units cancel:

$$\frac{46 \text{ meters}}{50 \text{ years}} \times \frac{100 \text{ centimeters}}{1 \text{ meter}} \times \frac{1 \text{ year}}{365 \text{ days}}$$

$$\approx 0.252 \frac{\text{centimeters}}{\text{day}}$$

You're told to round to the nearest hundredth of a centimeter, so grid in **0.25**.

13. D

Difficulty: Easy

Getting to the Answer: The question asks for the approximate combined number of runners and weight lifters who were injured. Calculate the approximate number from each group who were injured and then add the numbers together:

$$3\% \times 308 = 0.03 \times 308 \approx 9$$
$$6\% \times 237 = 0.06 \times 237 \approx 14$$
$$9 + 14 = 23$$

Therefore, **(D)** is correct.

14. 3

Difficulty: Medium

Strategic Advice: First find the total number of attendees, then calculate the difference in the actual number of juniors and seniors.

Getting to the Answer: The question gives you the percents of sophomores, juniors, and seniors attending the conference, as well as the actual number of teachers. Add up all of the percents to find the total percent of the attendees who are *not* teachers: $15\% + 25\% + 30\% = 70\%$. Therefore, the 18 teachers account for $100\% - 70\% = 30\%$ of the attendees.

You can solve for the total number of attendees (the whole) by plugging in the corresponding values for percent and part into the equation part = percent × whole. Say the total number of attendees is t:

$$18 = 0.30t$$
$$\frac{18}{0.30} = t$$
$$t = 60$$

So the total number of attendees is 60. Juniors are 30% of this number and seniors are 25%, so the difference between juniors and seniors is 30% − 25% = 5%. Now calculate 5% of the total: $60 \times 0.05 = 3$. Thus, there are 3 more juniors than seniors. Grid in **3**.

15. B

Difficulty: Hard

Getting to the Answer: The question gives you the amount of 15% mixture and the desired concentration (20%) that the painter wants to achieve by adding an unknown quantity of 40% mixture. In effect, the question is asking you to calculate a weighted average where the desired average is known.

Let x represent the unknown number of gallons of the 40% mixture that the painter needs to add. Set up a weighted average equation using the known amount (20 gallons) of the 15% mixture and the unknown amount of the 40% mixture to equal the desired mixture concentration of 20%:

$$\frac{0.15(20) + 0.40(x)}{20 + x} = 0.20$$

Next, multiply both sides of the equation by the denominator and then solve for x:

$$0.15(20) + 0.40x = 0.20(20 + x)$$
$$3 + 0.40x = 4 + 0.20x$$
$$0.20x = 1$$
$$x = 5$$

Thus, the painter needs to add 5 gallons of the 40% mixture to achieve the desired 20% concentration of blue pigment. **(B)** is correct.

16. D

Difficulty: Medium

Getting to the Answer: You need to find the price of a share of the stock on October 1. You know that the price of a share was $75 on August 1 and that on September 1 the price was $10 higher than it was on August 1. Thus, on September 1, it was $75 + $10 = $85.

The question also states that the September 1 price is 80% of the October 1 price. Set up an equation where p represents the October 1 price:

$$0.8p = \$85$$
$$p = \frac{\$85}{0.8}$$
$$p = \$106.25$$

The question asks for the price to the nearest dollar, so **(D)** is correct.

17. C

Difficulty: Easy

Getting to the Answer: The formula for percent increase or decrease is $\frac{\text{actual change}}{\text{original amount}} \times 100\%$. In this case, that's $\frac{1,572 - 1,494}{1,494} \times 100\% \approx 5.2\%$. Therefore, **(C)** is correct.

If you chose (B), you likely divided by the new amount, $1,572, instead of the original amount, $1,494.

18. C

Difficulty: Easy

Getting to the Answer: The formula for percent increase or decrease is $\frac{\text{actual change}}{\text{original amount}} \times 100\%$. Since the price per share of stock started at $35 and ended up at $49, that's $\frac{49 - 35}{35} \times 100\% = 40\%$.

Therefore, **(C)** is correct.

19. B

Difficulty: Medium

Getting to the Answer: The question asks for a percent decrease in the number of coins from the larger jar to the smaller one. The formula for percent decrease is $\frac{\text{actual change}}{\text{original amount}} \times 100\%$. Jar X has 75 coins and jar Y has 54 coins. The phrase "less than" means that you're calculating percent decrease from a starting value of 75 coins (the "original amount"); the calculation is $\frac{75-54}{75} \times 100\% = \frac{21}{75} \times 100\% = 28\%$. Therefore, **(B)** is correct.

20. D

Difficulty: Medium

Strategic Advice: Begin by calculating the number of seniors and then figure out what percent greater this number is than the number of sophomores.

Getting to the Answer: The number of seniors is 75% greater than the number of juniors, so that is $80 + (0.75 \times 80)$, or $1.75 \times 80 = 140$.

The formula for percent increase is $\frac{\text{actual change}}{\text{original amount}} \times 100\%$. In this case, the actual change is the number of seniors minus the number of sophomores, $140 - 50$. The original amount is the number of sophomores because the question asks for a percent "greater than"—greater than the original amount, which is sophomores, or 50: $\frac{140-50}{50} \times 100\% = \frac{90}{50} \times 100\% = 180\%$. Thus, **(D)** is correct.

21. C

Difficulty: Hard

Strategic Advice: When presented with a two-part percent change scenario, you cannot simply add the two percents; you have to calculate the second percent change on the adjusted value that results from the first percent change.

Getting to the Answer: The price of the phone goes through two different changes: an initial discount of 36% and a second reduction of 25% from that discounted price. Because you don't know y, the original price of the phone, you can pick a number to make calculations easier.

Usually, the best number to pick when calculating the percent change of an unknown value is 100, so assume that the initial price of the phone was $100 (the numbers don't have to be realistic, just easy to work with). Now, calculate the resulting price after the first discount: 36% of $100 is $0.36 \times \$100 = \$36$, so the new price of the phone will be $\$100 - \$36 = \$64$.

Next, calculate the change in price after an additional 25% off of the current price of $64: 25% of $64 is $0.25 \times \$64 = \$16$, so the final price will be $\$64 - \$16 = \$48$. (Note you could have also calculated the new price by subtracting the percent discount from 100 percent: $100\% - 25\% = 75\%$, so $0.75 \times \$64 = \$48$.)

The formula for percent change is $\frac{\text{actual change}}{\text{original amount}} \times 100\%$.

Use the starting price of $100 and the final price of $48:

$\frac{100-48}{100} \times 100\% = \frac{52}{100} \times 100\% = 52\%$.

Thus, **(C)** is correct.

22. C

Difficulty: Hard

Getting to the Answer: Although the full-time and part-time employees are separate groups, the total number of employees in each group is the same. Thus, you don't need to calculate the individual number of full- and part-time employees who have benefits. Instead, find the difference as a percent, then find that percent of 250 to get the answer in one step.

Be careful: 74 percent of part-time employees *don't* qualify for benefits. This means that $100\% - 74\% = 26\%$ of them do qualify. Since 92% of full-time employees qualify for benefits, the percent difference is $92 - 26 = 66$. Find 66% of 250: $250 \times 0.66 = 165$. **(C)** is correct.

23. 59

Difficulty: Hard

Category: Percents

Getting to the Answer: Don't switch on autopilot and do five separate cost increase calculations because you can do just one and save time. First, determine the total increase from 2014−15 through 2019−20: $15,564 − $12,192 = $3,372. Dividing $3,372 by 5 (the number of increases) gives $674.40, the average increase per year. To determine what portion of this amount is fees, find 8.75% of $674.40: 0.0875 × $674.40 = $59.01. Rounded to the nearest dollar, the correct answer is 59. Grid in **59**.

24. C

Difficulty: Easy

Category: Percent Change

Getting to the Answer: The formula for percent increase or decrease is $\frac{\text{actual change}}{\text{original amount}} \times 100\%$. In this case, that works out to

$$\frac{27-20}{20} \times 100\% = \frac{7}{20} \times 100\% = 0.35 \times 100\% = 35\%.$$

Hence, **(C)** is correct.

25. D

Difficulty: Hard

Category: Percent Change

Strategic Advice: Begin by determining how much profit company T made in 1997 so that you can calculate the percent increase in profit from 1997 to 1999.

Getting to the Answer: The question indicates that the 1998 profit of $375 million was 25% greater than the 1997 profit. Therefore, you can set up this equation: 125% × 1997 profit = $375 million. This can be written as 1.25p = $375 million, where p represents the 1997 profit. Divide both sides by 1.25 to find that p = $300 million. Thus, the actual change in profit from 1997 to 1999 was $483 million − $300 million = $183 million. The formula for percent increase or decrease is $\frac{\text{actual change}}{\text{original amount}} \times 100\%$. In this scenario, that's $\frac{183}{300} \times 100\% = 61\%$. **(D)** is correct.

26. B

Difficulty: Medium

Category: Percent Change

Strategic Advice: Before you can calculate the percent difference between the price of a printer and the price of a calculator, you need to determine the price of the printer.

Getting to the Answer: The question indicates that the price of the printer is 16% less than the price of the radio, or 16% less than $75. Therefore, the price of the printer is $(100 − 16)\% \times \$75 = 0.84 \times \$75 = \$63$. Thus, the difference in price between the calculator and the printer is $150 − $63 = $87. With this value, you can determine what percent less this is than $150.

The formula for percent increase or decrease is $\frac{\text{actual change}}{\text{original amount}} \times 100\%$. Hence, the price of the printer is $\frac{87}{150} \times 100\% = 58\%$ less than the price of the calculator, so **(B)** is correct.

27. C

Difficulty: Easy

Category: Unit Conversions

Getting to the Answer: The question provides the speed of a car in miles per hour and asks for the speed in feet per second. Set up your conversion ratios so that the units cancel:

$$\frac{9 \text{ miles}}{1 \text{ hour}} \times \frac{5,280 \text{ feet}}{1 \text{ mile}} \times \frac{1 \text{ hour}}{60 \text{ minutes}} \times \frac{1 \text{ minute}}{60 \text{ seconds}}$$

$$= 13.2 \frac{\text{feet}}{\text{second}}$$

Hence, **(C)** is correct.

28. A

Difficulty: Medium

Category: Proportions

Getting to the Answer: This is a Proportions question that requires you to relate the total known number of guitars to the given ratio in order to find the unknown number of dreadnoughts, a type of guitar. First, define the relationship in the proportion with words. Then, translate from English into math. Let d equal the unknown number of dreadnoughts. Set up a proportion and cross-multiply to solve for d:

$$\frac{\text{number of dreadnoughts in the ratio}}{\text{total number of guitars in the ratio}}$$
$$= \frac{\text{actual number of dreadnoughts}}{\text{actual number of guitars}}$$
$$\frac{4}{4+15} = \frac{d}{114}$$
$$4 \times 114 = (4+15)d$$
$$456 = 19d$$
$$24 = d$$

Thus, **(A)** is correct.

Here's another way to approach this question. The total of the two values in the ratio 4:15 is 19. The total number of guitars is 114, which is 6 × 19. Thus, the number of dreadnoughts is 6 × 4 = 24.

29. B

Difficulty: Easy

Category: Percent Change

Getting to the Answer: The formula for percent increase or decrease is $\frac{\text{actual change}}{\text{original amount}} \times 100\%$.

In this case, that works out to

$$\frac{84,600 - 74,025}{84,600} \times 100\% = \frac{10,575}{84,600} \times 100\% = 12.5\%.$$

Choice **(B)** is correct.

30. B

Difficulty: Medium

Category: Proportions

Getting to the Answer: Call the length of each side of the pentagon p and the length of each side of the hexagon h. The perimeter of the pentagon is $5 \times p$ and the perimeter of the hexagon is $6 \times h$, so you can write

the proportion $\frac{5p}{6h} = \frac{1}{2}$. Rather than cross-multiplying, multiply both sides by $\frac{6}{5}$ which is $\frac{6}{5} \times \frac{5p}{6h} = \frac{6}{5} \times \frac{1}{2}$. This simplifies to $\frac{p}{h} = \frac{6}{10} = \frac{3}{5}$. This is another way of expressing 3:5, so **(B)** is correct.

31. 54

Difficulty: Hard

Category: Proportions

Getting to the Answer: Since you are given both the initial values of the different-colored candies and their values after additions and deletions in terms of ratios, you can express these as amounts relative to each other. There are the least amount of yellow candies, so you can write that the initial number of yellow candies is y, the number of white candies is $\frac{5}{4}y$, and the number of red ones is $\frac{9}{4}y$.

Now you can compare the "before and after" quantities of the red or white candies in terms of y. If you choose to look at the red candies, after the deletions and additions, the number of red candies is $\frac{4}{3}(y+3)$ because 3 yellow candies were added. But, 7 reds were removed, so the equation is $\frac{9}{4}y - 7 = \frac{4}{3}(y+3)$. Multiply both sides by 12 to clear the fractions: $27y - 84 = 16y + 48$. So, $11y = 132$, and $y = 12$.

The original number of white candies is $\frac{5}{4}(12) = 15$, and the original number of red is $\frac{9}{4}(12) = 27$. So, the total number of all three colors before the changes is $12 + 15 + 27 = 54$. Grid in **54**.

Another way to solve this question is by picking numbers, making sure they are permissible according to the ratios. You know that the ratio of red to white is 9 to 5, and that after 7 red and 5 white are removed, the ratio will be 4 to 2—in other words, there will be twice as many red as white. Start with 9 red and 5 white candies and work up from there until you find a multiple that works:

9 red, 5 white
2 red, 0 white: doesn't work

18 red, 10 white
11 red, 5 white: doesn't work

27 red, 15 white
20 red, 10 white: this works!

The common multiplier is 3, and there are
$4 \times 3 = 12$ yellow candies. The total is
$27 + 15 + 12 = \textbf{54}$ candies.

32. 50

Difficulty: Medium

Category: Unit Conversion

Getting to the Answer: Since the rate of deflation is
$100 \frac{\text{mL}}{\text{min}}$, convert the initial volume of 300 liters of air to
milliliters: $300 \, \cancel{L} \times \frac{1{,}000 \text{ mL}}{1 \, \cancel{L}} = 300{,}000 \text{ mL}$.
Then, to determine the number of hours it will take
for the air mattress to completely deflate, set up
the calculation so that equivalent units cancel:

$300{,}000 \, \cancel{\text{mL}} \times \frac{1 \, \cancel{\text{min}}}{100 \, \cancel{\text{mL}}} \times \frac{1 \text{ hr}}{60 \, \cancel{\text{min}}} = 50 \text{ hr}$

Grid in **50**.

CHAPTER 8

Tables, Statistics, and Probability

LEARNING OBJECTIVES

After completing this chapter, you will be able to:

- Draw inferences about data presented in a variety of graphical formats
- Find an unknown value given the average
- Calculate mean, median, mode, and range
- Describe standard deviation and margin of error
- Determine whether a survey is valid or biased
- Draw inferences about surveys and data samples
- Calculate probabilities based on data sets

50/600 SmartPoints® (Medium Yield)

How Much Do You Know?

Directions: Try the questions that follow. Show your work so that you can compare your solutions to the ones found in the Check Your Work section immediately after this question set. The "Category" heading in the explanation for each question gives the title of the lesson that covers how to solve it. If you answered the question(s) for a given lesson correctly, and if your scratchwork looks like ours, you may be able to move quickly through that lesson. If you answered incorrectly or used a different approach, you may want to take your time on that lesson.

Questions 1 and 2 refer to the following information.

The amount of glucose, or sugar, in a person's blood is the primary indicator of diabetes. When a person without diabetes fasts (doesn't eat) for eight hours prior to taking a blood sugar test, that person's glucose level will be below 100 milligrams per deciliter. An individual is considered at risk for diabetes, but is not diagnosed as diabetic, when fasting glucose levels are between 100 and 125. If the level is above 125, the person is considered to have diabetes. The following table shows the ages and glucose levels of a group of study participants.

| Age Group | Study Results | | | |
	<100 mg/dL	100–125 mg/dL	>125 mg/dL	Total
18–25	9	22	17	48
26–35	16	48	34	98
36–45	19	35	40	94
Older than 45	12	27	21	60
Total	56	132	112	300

1. According to the data, which age group had the smallest percentage of people with a healthy blood sugar level?

    A) 18–25

    B) 26–35

    C) 36–45

    D) Older than 45

2. Based on the table, if a single participant is selected at random from all the participants, what is the probability that he or she will be at risk for diabetes and be at least 36 years old?

    A) $\dfrac{7}{60}$

    B) $\dfrac{11}{25}$

    C) $\dfrac{31}{77}$

    D) $\dfrac{31}{150}$

History Majors Declared at College X

Year	Number of History Majors
2010	225
2011	287
2012	162
2013	240
2014	s

3. The table above shows the number of history majors declared each year at a certain college from 2010 to 2014. If the median number of history majors declared for the five years was 225, what is the greatest possible value of s ?

A) 161

B) 225

C) 239

D) 288

4. A writers association sponsored a nationwide convention attended by 1,650 nonfiction writers. Before the convention, the association surveyed 150 of the writers who were planning to attend (chosen at random) about their lunch preferences. Thirty-eight said they preferred salads, 23 preferred pizza, 59 preferred sandwiches, and 30 preferred grilled chicken. Based on the results of this survey, how many of the writers attending the convention can be expected to want sandwiches for lunch?

5. A researcher conducted a poll to determine how many people in a city of 100,000 residents enjoy the taste of nondairy milks such as coconut milk or almond milk. The researcher polled 800 city residents who are allergic to dairy. Of those polled, 72 percent responded that they enjoyed the taste of nondairy milks.

Which of the following indicates why the survey results would not allow for a reliable conclusion about the taste preferences of the city's residents?

A) The researcher did not ask people if they prefer the taste of dairy milk to nondairy milks.

B) The survey sample is not representative of the city's residents.

C) The population of the city is too large to get a reliable survey sample.

D) The survey sample likely consisted of only adults and did not consider the opinion of children.

Cookies Baked

	Chocolate Chip	Oatmeal Raisin	Total
With Nuts		40	
Without Nuts			104
Total			186

6. A baker makes 186 cookies. Some are chocolate chip and some are oatmeal raisin, and both kinds are made with and without nuts, as shown in the table above. Because they are more popular, the baker makes $\frac{2}{3}$ of the cookies chocolate chip. If a chocolate chip cookie is chosen at random, what is the probability that it will have nuts?

A) $\frac{21}{93}$

B) $\frac{21}{62}$

C) $\frac{41}{93}$

D) $\frac{21}{41}$

Math

Check Your Work

1. B

Difficulty: Medium

Category: Tables and Graphs

Getting to the Answer: To calculate the percentage of people in each age group with a healthy blood sugar level (<100 mg/dL), divide the number of people in that age group with a healthy blood sugar level by the total number of participants in that same age group and multiply by 100%. Choice **(B)** is correct because $\frac{16}{98} \times 100\% \approx 0.1633 \times 100\% = 16.33\%$, which is a lower percentage than in the other age groups (18.75% for 18–25; 20.21% for 36–45; and 20% for Older than 45).

2. D

Difficulty: Medium

Category: Probability

Getting to the Answer: This question requires careful reading of the table. The first criterion is fairly straight-forward—you're looking for a participant with a blood sugar level in the 100–125 mg/dL range, so focus on that column in the table. The second criterion is a bit trickier— "at least 36 years old" means you'll need to use the values in both the row for 36–45 and the row for Older than 45. Within the 100–125 mg/dL range, there are 35 in the 36–45 age group and 27 in the Older than 45 age group, resulting in a total of $35 + 27 = 62$ out of 300 total participants overall. The probability of randomly selecting one participant who fits the criteria, therefore, is $\frac{62}{300}$, which reduces to $\frac{31}{150}$, or **(D)**.

3. B

Difficulty: Medium

Category: Statistics

Getting to the Answer: The median is the middle number in a series of numbers. Arrange the number of history majors from least to greatest, making sure that 225 is in the middle. Use *s* to balance out the number of history majors on either side of 225. Because there are already two numbers above the median (240 and 287), there must be two numbers below the median, 162 and *s*:

s, 162, 225, 240, 287

or

162, *s*, 225, 240, 287

Because *s* could be on either side of 162, it could be anything less than or equal to 225. Its greatest possible value is therefore 225, which is **(B)**.

4. 649

Difficulty: Medium

Category: Surveys and Data Samples

Getting to the Answer: The question indicates that of the 150 survey respondents, 59 wanted sandwiches. To find the number of the writers attending the convention who can be expected to want sandwiches for lunch, set up a proportion using the number of survey respondents who want sandwiches, the total number of survey respondents, and the total number of writers attending the convention: $\frac{59}{150} = \frac{x}{1,650}$. Cross-multiply to find that $x = 649$. Grid in **649**.

5. B

Difficulty: Medium

Category: Surveys and Data Samples

Getting to the Answer: Determine who is being surveyed and what results are intended. In this question, the intended result is to determine whether people in a large city like nondairy milks. To obtain a representative sample of the population, the survey should randomly select individuals from the population. However, the researcher polled only people who have a dairy allergy. Those people may have acquired tastes and may not be representative of the general population of the city, making **(B)** the correct answer.

6. B

Difficulty: Medium

Category: Probability

Getting to the Answer: The table is not complete, so your first step is to fill in the missing values. Start with what you know and work from there. It may not be necessary to complete the entire table, so stop when you have enough information to answer the question.

There are 186 cookies total and 104 are without nuts, which means $186 - 104 = 82$ have nuts. Because the table already indicates that 40 of those cookies are oatmeal raisin, $82 - 40 = 42$ are chocolate chip. Recall that $\frac{2}{3}$ of the total number of cookies are chocolate chip, which means there are $\frac{2}{3} \times 186 = 124$ chocolate chip cookies, so you can fill this number in the "Total" row of the chocolate chip column. You do not need to fill in any more of the table because the question asks only about chocolate chip cookies with nuts. There are 124 chocolate chip cookies total and 42 of them have nuts, so the probability of randomly choosing one with nuts is $\frac{42}{124}$, or $\frac{21}{62}$, which is **(B)**.

Tables and Graphs

LEARNING OBJECTIVES

After this lesson, you will be able to:

- Draw inferences about data presented in a variety of graphical formats
- Find an unknown value given the average

To solve a question like this:

Appliance Sales

```
              X       X
      X   X       X               X
      X   X   X   X   X   X        X
    ─────────────────────────────────
      1   2   3   4   5   6   7   8   9   10
```

Number Sold

An appliance salesperson sets a goal to sell an average of 6 appliances per day for the first two weeks of his new job. The dot plot shows the number he sold each day during the first 13 days. What is the minimum number of appliances he must sell on the 14th day in order to reach his goal?

A) 5

B) 6

C) 7

D) 8

You need to know this:

The SAT uses some straightforward methods of representing data sets that you are certainly already familiar with. You likely don't need to review, for example, how to look up information in a table or read a bar chart. There are, however, some less common types of plots that show up from time to time that can be confusing at first glance. Graphics you may see on test day include the following:

- **Tables, bar charts, and line graphs** show up all the time in the Math sections (and in the Reading and Writing and Language sections, too). They shouldn't be difficult to interpret, but it's helpful to keep in mind that the test maker often includes more information than you actually need. It's important to consider what the question asks for so that you find only the information that you need.

- **Frequency tables and dot plots** are ways of representing how many times a data point appears within a data set. The sample problem presents its data as a dot plot:

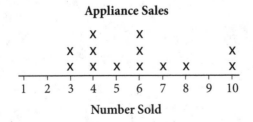

Each "X" represents one instance in the data set of each "number sold." So, for example, there were two different days on which this person sold 3 appliances, three different days on which this person sold 4 appliances, and so on. The data could just as easily be written as a data set: {3, 3, 4, 4, 4, 5, 6, 6, 6, 7, 8, 10, 10}. Or it could be placed in a frequency table:

Number Sold	Frequency
1	0
2	0
3	2
4	3
5	1
6	3
7	1
8	1
9	0
10	2

- **Histograms** look a lot like bar charts and can be read in the same way, but they are similar to frequency tables and dot plots in that they show how many times a certain value shows up in a data set for a variable. The histogram for the appliances data set would look like this:

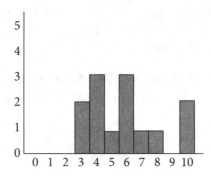

Notice that the histogram is basically the same as the dot plot for this data set. Histograms are better for representing larger data sets for which individual dots would be difficult to count.

You need to do this:

- When presented with a question that uses a graph or table to present information, first inspect the format of the graph or table. What kind of graph or table is it? What information is presented on each axis? What information do you need to find in order to answer the question?

- Find the information you need from the table or graph and then use the information for any calculation the question might require, such as taking the average, finding the median, or thinking about standard deviation.

- Use the average formula, $\text{average} = \dfrac{\text{sum}}{\text{number of items}}$, to find unknowns. For example, if you know that the average of 5 terms is 7, and you know that 4 of the terms are 3, 6, 8, and 9, you can call the last term x and plug into the equation, then solve for x:

$$7 = \frac{3+6+8+9+x}{5}$$
$$35 = 26 + x$$
$$x = 9$$

Explanation:

This question gives you an average and asks for a missing value, which is a kind of calculation that shows up in word problems all the time. First, set up a general equation for the average:

$$\text{Average} = \frac{\text{sum}}{\text{number of items}}$$

The scenario takes place over 14 days, and the average is given as 6 items per day. Let a represent the unknown number of appliances sold on the 14th day and then fill in the number of appliances sold the previous days from the dot plot:

$$6 = \frac{3+3+4+4+4+5+6+6+6+7+8+10+10+a}{14}$$

Multiply both sides by 14 to get rid of the fraction and simplify the addition on the right before isolating a:

$$84 = 3+3+4+4+4+5+6+6+6+7+8+10+10+a$$
$$84 = 76 + a$$
$$a = 8$$

Choice **(D)** is correct.

Try on Your Own

Directions: Take as much time as you need on these questions. Work carefully and methodically. There will be an opportunity for timed practice at the end of the chapter.

Questions 1 and 2 refer to the following information.

	Bob's Bookshop	Clara's Bookshop	Derek's Bookshop	Evelyn's Bookshop	Total
Monday	14	7	15	12	48
Tuesday	8	13	15	13	49
Wednesday	10	13	12	14	49
Thursday	8	15	14	10	47
Friday	13	7	10	9	39
Total	53	55	66	58	232

HINT: For Q1, fraction $= \frac{\text{part}}{\text{whole}}$. Which *part* is the question asking for? Out of which *whole*?

---

1. Which of the four bookshops made the greatest fraction of its total sales on Tuesday?

    A) Bob's Bookshop

    B) Clara's Bookshop

    C) Derek's Bookshop

    D) Evelyn's Bookshop

2. What fraction of all the books sold on Monday, Wednesday, and Friday were sold at Derek's Bookshop and Evelyn's Bookshop?

    A) $\frac{9}{29}$

    B) $\frac{11}{32}$

    C) $\frac{9}{17}$

    D) $\frac{18}{31}$

Questions 3 and 4 refer to the following information.

Numerous health studies have found that people who eat breakfast are generally healthier and weigh less than people who skip this meal. The following table shows the results of a study related to this topic.

Breakfast Study Results

	Breakfast $\leq$1 Time per Week	Breakfast 2–4 Times per Week	Breakfast 5–7 Times per Week	Total
Within Healthy Weight Range	6	15	36	57
Outside Healthy Weight Range	38	27	9	74
Total	44	42	45	131

3. What percent of the participants who were outside a healthy weight range ate breakfast one or fewer times per week?

    A) 29.01%

    B) 51.35%

    C) 56.49%

    D) 86.36%

HINT: For Q4, which group in the study is of interest to this company?

---

4. A large company that provides breakfast for all its employees wants to determine how many of them are likely to be within a healthy weight range, given that all the employees take advantage of the free breakfast all five weekdays. If the company has 3,000 employees, and assuming the participants in the study are a good representative sample, about how many of the employees are likely to be within a healthy weight range?

    A) 825

    B) 1,030

    C) 1,900

    D) 2,400

Questions 5 and 6 refer to the following information.

When people sleep, they experience various types of brain activity. Scientists have classified these types of activity into four sleep stages: 1, 2, 3, and 4 (also known as REM). Stage 3 is the only stage considered to be deep sleep. Suppose a person went to a sleep clinic to have his or her sleeping brainwaves analyzed. A technician monitored the person's brainwaves in 15-minute intervals, for 8 continuous hours, and categorized them into one of the four stages. The bar graph below shows the results of the one-night study.

8-Hour Sleep Study Results

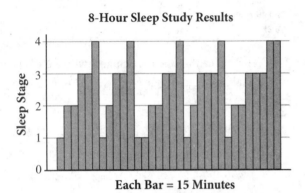

Each Bar = 15 Minutes

5. Based on the graph, how many minutes did the patient spend in non-deep sleep over the course of the entire night?

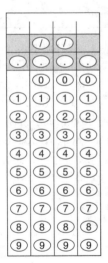

6. After the completion of the one-night study, the patient was monitored an additional four nights. Over the total number of nights that the patient spent at the clinic, he spent an average of 180 minutes in stage 3 sleep per night. If the patient spent an average of 175 minutes in stage 3 sleep on the second, third, and fourth nights, how many minutes did he spend in stage 3 sleep on the last night?

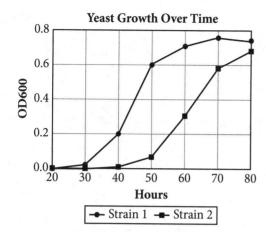

7. A microbiologist is comparing the growth rates of
    two different yeast strains. She indirectly measures
    the number of yeast cells by recording the optical
    density (OD600) of each strain every 10 hours. The
    measurements are presented in the graph above.
    Based on the data, which of the following is NOT a
    true statement?

    A) Between hours 30 and 80, Strain 1 had a
        higher OD600 reading than Strain 2.

    B) The growth rate of Strain 2 was less than the
        growth rate of Strain 1 until hour 50, at which
        point Strain 1's growth rate became the lesser
        one.

    C) Between hours 50 and 70, Strain 2's OD600
        reading increased by approximately 0.03 every
        hour.

    D) The growth rate of Strain 1 was greater than
        the growth rate of Strain 2 throughout the
        monitored period.

Statistics

LEARNING OBJECTIVES

After this lesson, you will be able to:

- Calculate mean, median, mode, and range
- Describe standard deviation and margin of error

To answer a question like this:

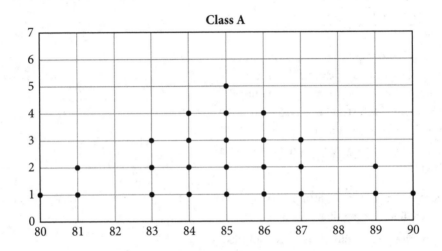

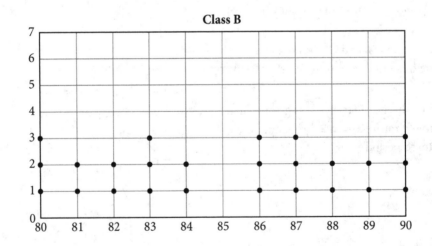

Two classes of 25 students each took an identical exam. Their percent correct scores are shown in the dot plots above. If M_A and S_A are the median and standard deviation, respectively, of class A, and M_B and S_B are the median and standard deviation, respectively, of class B, then which of the following statements is true?

A) $M_A < M_B$ and $S_A < S_B$

B) $M_A > M_B$ and $S_A < S_B$

C) $M_A > M_B$ and $S_A > S_B$

D) $M_A < M_B$ and $S_A > S_B$

You need to know this:

Suppose a nurse took a patient's pulse at different times of day and found it to be 75, 78, 71, 71, and 68. Here are six fundamental statistics figures you can determine for this data set:

- **Mean (also called arithmetic mean or average):** The sum of the values divided by the number of values. For this data set, the mean pulse is $\frac{75+78+71+71+68}{5} = \frac{363}{5} = 72.6$.

- **Median:** The value that is in the middle of the set *when the values are arranged in ascending order*. The pulse values in ascending order are 68, 71, 71, 75, and 78. The middle term is the third term, making the median 71. (If the list consists of an even number of values, the median is the average of the middle two values.)

- **Mode:** The value that occurs most frequently. The value that appears more than any other is 71, which appears twice (while all other numbers appear only once), so it is the mode. If more than one value appears the most often, that's okay; a set of data can have multiple modes. For example, if the nurse took the patient's pulse a sixth time and it was 68, then both 71 and 68 would be modes for this data set.

- **Range:** The difference between the highest and lowest values. In this data set, the lowest and highest values are 68 and 78, respectively, so the range is $78 - 68 = 10$.

- **Standard deviation:** A measure of how far a typical data point is from the mean. A low standard deviation means most values in the set are fairly close to the mean; a high standard deviation means there is much more spread in the data set. On the SAT, *you will need to know what standard deviation is and what it tells you about a set of data, but you won't have to calculate it.*

- **Margin of error:** A description of the maximum expected difference between a true statistics measure (for example, the mean or median) for a data pool and that same statistics measure for a random sample from the data pool. A lower margin of error is achieved by increasing the size of the random sample. As with standard deviation, *you will need to know what a margin of error is on the SAT, but you won't be asked to calculate one.*

You need to do this:

- To compare two standard deviations, look at how spread out the data set is. The more clustered the data, the lower the standard deviation.

- To find the median, arrange *all* values in order. In a dot plot or frequency distribution table, that means finding the group with the middle value.

Explanation:

Start with the standard deviation. The scores in class A are more clustered around the mean, so the standard deviation for class A will be smaller than that for class B, where the scores are more spread out. Eliminate (B) and (C).

To calculate the medians of the two classes, you need to find the middle value in each data set. Each class has 25 students, so the middle score will be the 13th term. Count from the left of each dot plot to find that the 13th score for class A is 85 and for class B is 86. So the median for class B is greater. **(A)** is correct.

Try on Your Own

Directions: Take as much time as you need on these questions. Work carefully and methodically. There will be an opportunity for timed practice at the end of the chapter.

Questions 8 and 9 refer to the following information.

An anthropologist chose 250 citizens at random from each of two European countries and separated them into groups based on how many languages they spoke. The results are shown in the table below.

Number of Languages	Country A	Country B
1	55	70
2	80	30
3	50	20
4	40	70
5	25	60

There are a total of 550,000 citizens in country A and 1.3 million citizens in country B.

8. What is the median number of languages spoken by the sample of citizens from country B?

A) 1

B) 2

C) 3

D) 4

9. Based on the data in the table, which of the following statements most accurately reflects the estimated total number of citizens who speak multiple languages in both countries?

A) Half as many citizens in both countries combined speak exactly five languages as citizens who speak exactly four languages.

B) Twice as many citizens in both countries combined speak exactly five languages as citizens who speak exactly four languages.

C) The number of citizens in both countries combined who speak exactly two languages is less than the number of citizens who speak exactly four languages.

D) The number of citizens in both countries combined who speak exactly two languages is greater than the number of citizens who speak exactly four languages.

HINT: For Q10, when you see the word "consistent," think "standard deviation."

	Charles	Gautam	Brin
Run 1	8.3	8.5	8.4
Run 2	7.7	8.0	8.0
Run 3	7.1	8.5	7.5
Run 4	6.6	7.8	9.0
Run 5	8.0	8.1	7.5
Run 6	6.6	7.5	7.2
Mean Score	7.38	8.07	7.93
Standard Deviation	0.73	0.39	0.67

10. Charles, Gautam, and Brin participated in a snowboarding competition. The scores for each of their six qualifying runs are shown in the table above. According to the data, which of the following is a valid conclusion?

A) Charles had the smallest mean score, so his performance was the least consistent.

B) Gautam had the smallest standard deviation, so his performance was the most consistent.

C) Charles had the largest standard deviation, so his performance was the most consistent.

D) Brin had the highest score on any one run, so her performance was the most consistent.

Ages of Used Cars in Dealer Inventory

Age (Model Years)	Number of Cars
1	3
2	5
3	18
4	17
5	11
6	6
7	2

11. The table above shows the distribution of the ages (in model years) of the cars in a certain dealer's inventory. Which of the following correctly lists the mean, median, and mode of the ages of the cars in ascending order?

A) Mean, Median, Mode

B) Median, Mode, Mean

C) Mode, Mean, Median

D) Mode, Median, Mean

HINT: For Q12, start with the most definite information. What
do you know, given the average of the first 12 days?

12. A company produces an equal number of a certain
product each working day in the month. The daily
reject rates for the first 12 days of this month
ranged from 0.0 percent to 1.5 percent with an
average of 0.4 percent. If there are 22 working
days this month and the company's monthly reject
goal is 0.5 percent or less, what is the maximum
reject rate, as a percent, for the 13th day that would
still enable the company to attain its goal for the
month? (Round your answer to the nearest tenth
and ignore the percent sign when gridding your
response.)

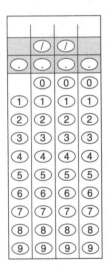

Number of Persons in 65 Households

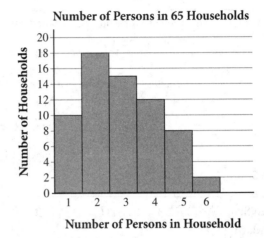

Number of Persons in Household

13. Based on the graph above, how many households
have a number of persons greater than the median
number of persons?

A) 2

B) 10

C) 22

D) 37

Surveys and Data Samples

LEARNING OBJECTIVES

After this lesson, you will be able to:

- Determine whether a survey is valid or biased
- Draw inferences about surveys and data samples

To answer a question like this:

A book club wanted to determine the average number of books read each year by residents of a certain town, so it conducted a survey of 100 patrons of the town's public library. The average number of books read per year by these 100 patrons was 51.5. Which of the following statements must be true based on this information?

A) The survey is biased due to a poor choice of sampling method.

B) The survey is not biased and will likely produce a correct estimate of the number of books read annually by the town's residents.

C) The average number of books read annually by all the town's residents is 51.5.

D) The average number of books read per town resident per year cannot be determined from such a small sample.

You need to know this:

You will see occasional questions on the SAT Math sections that do not test any calculation or even your ability to interpret numerical data. Instead, these questions test your ability to draw logical conclusions about surveys and data sampling methods.

Answering these questions correctly hinges on your ability to tell whether a data sample is **representative** of the larger population. A representative sample is a small group that shares key characteristics with a larger group you are trying to draw conclusions about.

A sample that is selected truly at random is generally representative of the larger group. For example, a scientist who wants to learn the average height of the penguins in a colony of 200 might measure the heights of a random sample of only 20 penguins. As long as the 20 penguins are selected at random, their average height will approximate the average height of the birds in the entire colony.

On the other hand, a sample that is not selected at random may not be representative and may lead to a biased conclusion. For instance, imagine that a small town uses volunteer firefighters and that a stipulation for becoming a volunteer firefighter is living within a mile of the fire station. If you wanted to know what percent of households in the town include at least one volunteer firefighter, you would need to survey a random sample of households from the entire town, not just a sample of households within a mile of the fire station. A sample of households within a mile of the fire station would be a biased sample and would lead to an erroneous conclusion (namely, that the percent of households in the town that include at least one volunteer firefighter is higher than it actually is).

You need to do this:

- Check whether the data sample represents the larger population. If it doesn't, the survey is biased.
- In questions that ask you to draw a conclusion from a random (unbiased) sample, look for the answer choice for which the representative sample accurately reflects the larger population. For example, in a question asking for a conclusion based on a sample of librarians, the correct answer will match the sample to a larger population of librarians, not to a population of, say, accountants.

Explanation:

The sample in this question includes 100 public library patrons. This is not a randomly selected sample. It's a good bet that frequent readers of books will be overrepresented at a public library. Thus, the survey is biased, so **(A)** is correct.

Try on Your Own

Directions: Take as much time as you need on these questions. Work carefully and methodically. There will be an opportunity for timed practice at the end of the chapter.

> HINT: For Q14, who is in the survey group? Who is in the larger population? Are these groups different? If so, the survey is likely biased.

14. A railroad company is planning to build a new station along one of its busiest lines into the downtown area where many commuters work. The company chooses a town where it plans to build the new station. To assess the opinion of the town's residents, the company surveys a sample of 200 residents who commute to the downtown area for work. Over 80 percent of those surveyed are in favor of building the new station.

    Which of the following is true about the survey's reliability?

    A) It is unreliable because the survey sample is not representative of the entire town.

    B) It is unreliable because the survey sample is too small.

    C) It is reliable because nobody in the survey sample works for the railroad company.

    D) It is reliable because the survey sample excludes people who do not ride the train.

15. A bottled water company conducts a survey to find out how many bottles of water people consume per day. If a representative and random sample of 500 people is chosen from a population estimated to be 50,000, which of the following accurately describes how the mean of the sample data relates to the estimated mean of the entire population?

    A) The mean of the sample data is equal to the estimated mean of the population.

    B) The mean of the sample data cannot be used to estimate the mean of the much larger population.

    C) The mean of the sample data should be multiplied by 100 to get the estimated mean of the population.

    D) The mean of the sample data should be multiplied by 1,000 to get the estimated mean of the population.

16. A department store manager wants to determine why customers return the products they buy. The manager surveyed randomly selected customers and asked them to explain why they were returning their products. This sample included 70 customers who were returning dinnerware, of whom 80 percent indicated that at least one piece of dinnerware was chipped or broken.

    Which of the following conclusions is best supported by the sample data?

    A) Most of the products returned to the store contain chipped or broken pieces.

    B) Dinnerware products are more likely to contain chipped or broken pieces than other products.

    C) Most customers returning dinnerware returned products containing chipped or broken pieces.

    D) At least 80 percent of the products sold at the store contain chipped or broken pieces.

17. The owner of a miniature golf course wants to determine what color golf ball is most popular at the course. The owner asked 150 randomly surveyed children what color they prefer. Approximately 60 percent of them said they prefer red, while approximately 30 percent of them said blue.

    This data best supports which of the following conclusions?

    A) Most people prefer a red golf ball when playing miniature golf.

    B) Red golf balls are used twice as often for miniature golf as blue golf balls.

    C) Most children at the miniature golf course prefer a red golf ball.

    D) Approximately 10 percent of miniature golf players prefer a white golf ball.

HINT: For Q18, find the result of the sample in the chart, and then apply that result to the larger group.

A candy company sells jelly beans in five colors: black, green, orange, red, and yellow. The company sells boxes of jelly beans, each of which contains 20 individual bags. Each individual bag contains 75 jelly beans. A customer purchased 5 boxes of jelly beans and selected one bag at random from each box. The customer counted the number of each color in each bag. The results are shown in the chart below.

Color	Bag 1	Bag 2	Bag 3	Bag 4	Bag 5
Black	10	12	8	11	9
Green	13	11	13	12	12
Orange	22	20	21	21	21
Red	20	21	23	21	22
Yellow	10	11	10	10	11

18. Which of the following is the closest approximation of the total number of green jelly beans in the customer's purchase?

    A)   60

    B)   240

    C) 1,200

    D) 4,500

Probability

LEARNING OBJECTIVE

After this lesson, you will be able to:

- Calculate probabilities based on data sets

To answer a question like this:

Number of Cyclists in Regional Race, by Age and Town

Town	Age (years)					Total
	15 to 18	**19 to 25**	**26 to 34**	**35 to 46**	**47 and Older**	**Total**
Pine Falls	9	52	31	26	29	147
Greenville	14	38	42	53	30	177
Salem	5	17	18	13	10	63
Fairview	19	41	32	34	27	153
Total	47	148	123	126	96	540

The table above shows the number of participants in a regional bicycle race, categorized by town and age group. Based on the table, if a cyclist from Fairview is chosen at random, which of the following is closest to the probability that the cyclist was 35 or older at the time of the race?

A) 0.40

B) 0.18

C) 0.11

D) 0.05

You need to know this:

Probability is a fraction or decimal between 0 and 1 comparing the number of desired outcomes to the number of total possible outcomes. A probability of 0 means that an event will not occur; a probability of 1 means that it definitely will occur. The formula is as follows:

$$\text{Probability} = \frac{\text{number of desired outcomes}}{\text{number of total possible outcomes}}$$

For instance, if you roll a six-sided die, each side showing a different number from 1 to 6, the probability of rolling a number higher than 4 is $\frac{2}{6} = \frac{1}{3}$, because there are two numbers higher than 4 (5 and 6) and six numbers total (1, 2, 3, 4, 5, and 6).

To find the probability that an event will *not* happen, subtract the probability that the event will happen from 1. Continuing the previous example, the probability of *not* rolling a number higher than 4 would be:

$$1 - \frac{1}{3} = \frac{2}{3}$$

The SAT tends to test probability in the context of data tables. Using a table, you can find the probability that a randomly selected data value (be it a person, object, etc.) will fit a certain profile. For example, the following table summarizing a survey on water preference might be followed by a question asking for the probability that a person randomly selected for a follow-up survey falls into a given category.

	Tap	Carbonated	Bottled	Total
Female	325	267	295	887
Male	304	210	289	803
Total	629	477	584	1,690

If the question asked for the probability of randomly selecting a female who prefers tap water from all the participants of the original survey, you would calculate it using the same general formula as before:

$$\frac{\text{\# female, tap}}{\text{\# total}} = \frac{325}{1,690} = \frac{5}{26} \approx 0.192.$$

If the question asked for the probability of randomly selecting a female for the follow-up survey, given that the chosen participant prefers tap water, the setup is a little different. This time, the number of possible outcomes is the total participants *who prefer tap water*, which is 629, not the grand total of 1,690. The calculation is now $\frac{\text{\# female, tap}}{\text{\# total, tap}} = \frac{325}{629} \approx 0.517.$

Conversely, if you needed to find the probability of selecting someone who prefers tap water for the follow-up survey, given that the chosen participant is female, the new number of possible outcomes would be the female participant total (887). The calculation becomes $\frac{\text{\# female, tap}}{\text{\# total, females}} = \frac{325}{887} \approx 0.366.$

You need to do this:

- Determine the number of desired and total possible outcomes by looking at the table.
- Read the question carefully when determining the number of possible outcomes: do you need the entire set or a subset?

Explanation:

The number of desired outcomes is the number of cyclists from Fairview who are 35 or older. That means you need to add the "35 to 46" and "47 and Older" categories: $34 + 27 = 61$. The number of possible outcomes is the total number of cyclists from Fairview. The number is given in the totals column: 153. Plug these numbers into the probability formula and divide:

$$\text{Probability} = \frac{\text{\# Fairview, 35 and Older}}{\text{\# Fairview, Total}} = \frac{61}{153} \approx 0.40$$

The correct answer is **(A)**.

Try on Your Own

Directions: Take as much time as you need on these questions. Work carefully and methodically. There will be an opportunity for timed practice at the end of the chapter.

	Marked Defective	Not Marked Defective	Total
Defective Bearing	392	57	449
Non-defective Bearing	168	49,383	49,551
Total	560	49,440	50,000

19. A manufacturing plant produces 50,000 bearings per week. Of these, 449 will be defective. The manager of the plant installs a new quality control device that is designed to detect defective bearings and mark them with a laser. The device is allowed to run for a week and the results are tallied as shown in the table above. According to these results, to the nearest percent, what is the probability that a part that is marked defective will actually be defective?

    A)   30%

    B)   43%

    C)   70%

    D)   87%

HINT: For Q20, what percentage of the fish at the hatchery are salmon? How many salmon are there? How many of those were tested?

The table below shows the distribution of four species of fish at a hatchery that has approximately 6,000 fish.

Species	Percent of Total
Carp	50
Salmon	25
Tilapia	15
Tuna	10

A biologist randomly tests 5 percent of each species of fish for mercury content. Her findings are shown in the following table.

Mercury Content Test Results

Species	Number of Fish with Dangerous Mercury Levels
Carp	11
Salmon	6
Tilapia	5
Tuna	8

20. Based on the biologist's findings, if a single salmon is randomly selected from those that were tested, what is the probability that this particular fish would have a dangerous mercury level?

    A)   0.001

    B)   0.004

    C)   0.02

    D)   0.08

Type of Engineer	Specialization		Total
	Robotics	AV	
Mechanical	198	245	443
Electrical	149	176	325
Total	347	421	768

21. In a research study, a group of mechanical and electrical engineers indicated their specialization preference between robotics and autonomous vehicles (AV). The results are shown in the table above. What is the probability that a randomly selected engineer will be a mechanical engineer specializing in autonomous vehicles?

A) 0.229

B) 0.319

C) 0.553

D) 0.582

HINT: For Q22, how many groups have *at least* 8 days vacation?

Yearly Paid Vacation Days at Excor Manufacturing

	0–7	8–14	14–30	Total
Hourly	79	183	38	300
Salaried	8	27	65	100
Total	87	210	103	400

22. The human resources department at Excor Manufacturing decided to collect data on the paid vacation days accrued by hourly and salaried employees. The table above shows the results of the data collection. If an employee has at least 8 paid vacation days, what is the probability that the person is a salaried employee?

A) $\dfrac{92}{313}$

B) $\dfrac{221}{300}$

C) $\dfrac{313}{400}$

D) $\dfrac{92}{100}$

	Fuel Economy (miles per gallon)	
Engine Type	0–45 mpg	45+ mpg
Hybrid		
Internal Combustion (IC)		
Total	53	258

23. The daily engine production goals of an automobile manufacturer are summarized in the incomplete table above. The factory produced six times as many hybrid engines that achieve 45+ miles per gallon as it did hybrid engines that achieve 0–45 miles per gallon, and the factory produced four times as many internal combustion (IC) engines that achieve 45+ miles per gallon as it did IC engines that achieve 0–45 miles per gallon. If the factory produced 53 engines that achieve 0–45 miles per gallon and 258 engines that achieve 45+ miles per gallon, which of the following is the approximate probability that a 45+ miles per gallon engine selected at random is IC?

A) 0.566

B) 0.535

C) 0.465

D) 0.386

On Test Day

The SAT tests the concept of average fairly heavily. The average formula will serve you well on questions that ask about a sum of values or the average of a set of values, but for questions that give you the average and ask for a missing value in the data set, there is an alternative that can be faster: the balance approach.

The balance approach is based on the the idea that if you know what the average is, you can find the totals on both sides of the average and then add the missing value that makes both sides balance out. This approach is especially helpful if the values are large and closely spaced. Imagine that a question gives you the set $\{976, 980, 964, 987, x\}$ and tells you that the average is 970. You would reason as follows: 976 is 6 over the average, 980 is 10 over, 964 is 6 under, and 987 is 17 over. That's a total of $6 + 10 - 6 + 17 = 27$ over, so x needs to be 27 under the average, or $970 - 27 = 943$.

Try solving the question below both ways, using first the average formula and then the balance approach. If you find the latter to be fast and intuitive, add it to your test-day arsenal.

Height Change in Inches							
Plant Type	Week 3	Week 4	Week 5	Week 6	Week 7	Week 8	Week 9
Zinnia	3	2	1	4	2	1	1
Sunflower	3		8	6	7	2	5
Marigold	1	1	3	2	4	4	3

24. The table above summarizes the height change (inches) over a seven-week period of three different plants grown by Ms. Walker's biology class. If the mean height change for the sunflower plant over the seven-week period is 5 inches, what was the height change in week 4?

The correct answer and both ways of solving can be found at the end of the chapter.

How Much Have You Learned?

Directions: For testlike practice, give yourself 15 minutes to complete this question set. Be sure to study the explanations, even for questions you got correct. They can be found at the end of this chapter.

Question 25 refers to the following information.

The table below summarizes the results of a survey about favorite leisure activities for a group of high school students. Assume that every student has a favorite leisure activity and that each student could select only one favorite.

	Freshmen	Sophomores	Juniors	Seniors	Total
Sports	144	122	134	115	515
Video Games	126	140	152	148	566
Music	120	117	153	148	538
Reading	110	114	63	98	385
Total	500	493	502	509	2,004

25. The research group that conducted the survey wants to select one sophomore at random for a follow-up survey. What is the probability that the student selected will prefer a type of leisure activity other than video games?

A) $\dfrac{140}{493}$

B) $\dfrac{140}{2,004}$

C) $\dfrac{353}{493}$

D) $\dfrac{353}{2,004}$

Questions 26 and 27 refer to the following information.

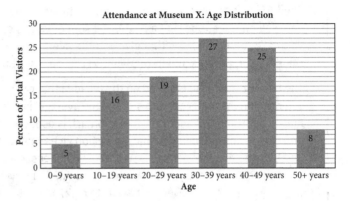

The bar graph above shows the age distribution of visitors to museum X in 2014. Visitors aged 0–9 years get into museum X for free, visitors aged 50 and older pay $5 for admission, and everyone else pays $10.

26. If 553 people aged 20 years and older visited museum X in 2014, then approximately how many people visited museum X in 2014?

27. Assuming, as before, that 553 people aged 20 years and older visited museum X in 2014, how much revenue did museum X collect from tickets sold to people aged 40 and older in 2014? (Ignore the dollar sign when gridding your response.)

28. According to the table, what percent of all the board games sold by the boutique have a "bad" average customer rating? Round to the nearest tenth of a percent and ignore the percent sign when entering your answer.

Questions 28 and 29 refer to the following information.

	1	2	3	4	5	Total
Strategy	5	17	24	10	5	61
Trivia	3	12	28	8	3	54
Role-playing	3	10	30	14	2	59

A small boutique sells board games online. The boutique specializes in strategy, trivia, and role-playing games. Any customer who purchases a game is invited to rate the game on a scale of 1 to 5. A rating of 1 or 2 is considered "bad," a rating of 3 is considered "average," and a rating of 4 or 5 is considered "good." The table above shows the distribution of average customer ratings of the games sold. For example, 24 of the strategy games sold have an average customer rating of 3.

29. The boutique decides to stop selling 50 percent of the games that have a "bad" average customer rating to make room for promising new stock. Assuming no significant changes in ratings in the foreseeable future, what should the difference be between the percentages of games with a "bad" average customer rating before and after the games are removed? Round to the nearest tenth of a percent and ignore the percent sign when entering your answer.

30. Fit and Fab, a membership-only gym, is hoping to open a new branch in a small city in Pennsylvania that currently has no fitness centers. According to the gym management's research, approximately 12,600 residents live within driving distance of the gym. Fit and Fab sends out surveys to a sample of 300 randomly selected residents in this area (all of whom respond) and finds that 40 residents say they would visit a gym if one were located in their area. Based on past survey research, Fit and Fab estimates that approximately 30 percent of these respondents would actually join the gym if one were opened in the area. Based on this information and the results of the sample survey, about how many residents should Fit and Fab expect to join its new branch?

A) 134

B) 504

C) 1,680

D) 3,780

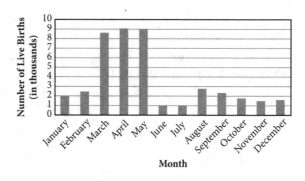

31. Most animals give birth during a general time of year. This is because animals naturally breed so that their young will be born at the time of year when there will be an adequate food supply. The bar graph shows the number of live births in California of a particular jackrabbit species, the black-tailed jackrabbit, over the course of year X. Based on the data, which of the following would be an appropriate conclusion?

A) In general, rabbits give birth during March, April, and May.

B) In general, rabbits give birth during June, July, and August.

C) In general, black-tailed jackrabbits in California give birth during March, April, and May.

D) In general, black-tailed jackrabbits in California give birth during June, July, and August.

32. Soil contains a wide variety of nutrients, including nitrogen, phosphorous, potassium, magnesium, sulfur, and iron. A fertilizer company conducted an experimental study to determine which of five additives is most effective in helping soil retain nutrients. If, after application of the additives, the fertilizer company tested only for the soil nutrients nitrogen and potassium, which of the following is a valid conclusion?

A) The additive that is found to be the most effective will work for all nutrients in the soil.

B) The additive that is found to be the most effective will work only for nitrogen and potassium.

C) The study is biased and therefore not significantly relevant to determining which additive is most effective.

D) The study will be able to produce results concerning only the effects of the additives on nitrogen and potassium.

33. The average (arithmetic mean) of $p + 12t - 5$, $q + 16t + 4$, and $r - 7t + 25$ is $10t + 34$. In terms of t, what is the average of p, q, and r?

A) $3t + 26$

B) $4t + 16$

C) $6t + 16$

D) $8t - 37$

34. As part of its market research, a company sent out a survey to see how much consumers would be willing to pay for a certain product. The survey distinguished between a store brand version of the product and a brand name version, and people participating in the survey received questions about only one of the versions. A summary of the survey results is shown in the following bar graph.

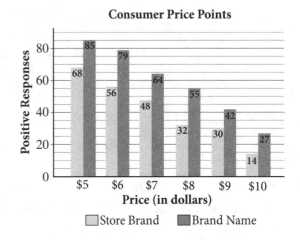

Consumer Price Points

If a consumer is chosen at random from the 600 respondents, what is the probability that the consumer is willing to pay at least $8 for the product?

Reflect

Directions: Take a few minutes to recall what you've learned and what you've been practicing in this chapter. Consider the following questions, jot down your best answer for each one, and then compare your reflections to the expert responses on the following page. Use your level of confidence to determine what to do next.

What are some common ways the SAT may present data?

_____

_____

_____

What is the difference between median, mode, and range?

_____

_____

_____

What does the standard deviation of a data set tell you?

_____

_____

_____

When can you generalize the results of a survey of a small group to a larger group?

_____

_____

_____

What are two ways to calculate the probability of a single event?

_____

_____

_____

Expert Responses

What are some common ways the SAT may present data?

The SAT may present data in tables, bar charts, line graphs, dot plots, and histograms.

What is the difference between median, mode, and range?

The median of a set is the middle value, whereas the mode is the most common value. The range of a set is the distance between the smallest value and the largest one.

What does the standard deviation of a data set tell you?

A data set's standard deviation reflects how far apart the numbers are from each other. The standard deviation of a set whose numbers are all the same—for example, {5, 5, 5, 5}—is 0. The greater the distance between the numbers, the greater the standard deviation.

When can you generalize the results of a survey of a small group to a larger group?

A survey can be generalized to a larger population if the data sample is representative. To be representative, the data sample needs to be drawn at random from the larger population.

What are two ways to calculate the probability of a single event?

One way is to use the basic probability formula:

$$\text{Probability} = \frac{\text{number of desired outcomes}}{\text{number of total outcomes}}$$

Alternatively, the probability that an event happens is 1 minus the probability that it doesn't happen.

Next Steps

If you answered most questions correctly in the "How Much Have You Learned?" section, and if your responses to the Reflect questions were similar to those of the SAT expert, then consider tables, statistics, and probability an area of strength and move on to the next chapter. Come back to this topic periodically to prevent yourself from getting rusty.

If you don't yet feel confident, review those parts of this chapter that you have not yet mastered, then try the questions you missed again. In particular, make sure that you understand the six terms explained in the Statistics lesson and the probability formulas explained in the Probability lesson. As always, be sure to review the explanations closely. Finally, **go online** (www.kaptest.com/moreonline) for additional practice on the highest yield topics in this chapter.

Answers and Explanations

1. B

Difficulty: Easy

Getting to the Answer: The trickiest part of this question is understanding what is being asked. You need to find the shop that had the most Tuesday sales *as a fraction of its total sales*, so focus only on those rows in the table. For each shop, divide the number of books it sold on Tuesday by the number of books it sold all week. Use your calculator to speed up this step.

$$\text{Bob's Bookshop: } \frac{\text{Tuesday total}}{\text{weekly total}} = \frac{8}{53} \approx 0.1509$$

$$\text{Clara's Bookshop: } \frac{\text{Tuesday total}}{\text{weekly total}} = \frac{13}{55} \approx 0.2364$$

$$\text{Derek's Bookshop: } \frac{\text{Tuesday total}}{\text{weekly total}} = \frac{15}{66} \approx 0.2273$$

$$\text{Evelyn's Bookshop: } \frac{\text{Tuesday total}}{\text{weekly total}} = \frac{13}{58} \approx 0.2241$$

The greatest portion of Tuesday sales belongs to Clara's Bookshop, so **(B)** is correct.

2. C

Difficulty: Medium

Getting to the Answer: Add the number of books sold by Derek and Evelyn on Monday, Wednesday, and Friday; then divide the result by the total number of books sold on those days.

Derek's and Evelyn's M/W/F sales:
$(15 + 12) + (12 + 14) + (10 + 9) = 72$

Total M/W/F sales: $48 + 49 + 39 = 136$

Divide Derek's and Evelyn's M/W/F sales by total M/W/F sales to get $\frac{72}{136}$, which simplifies to $\frac{9}{17}$. Choice **(C)** is correct.

3. B

Difficulty: Easy

Getting to the Answer: The question asks only about participants who were outside a healthy weight range, so focus on this row: 38 out of the 74 participants who were outside a healthy weight range ate breakfast one or fewer times per week. This expressed as a percent is $\frac{38}{74} \times 100\% = 0.51351 \times 100\% = 51.35\%$, which matches **(B)**.

4. D

Difficulty: Medium

Getting to the Answer: The question asks about employees who eat breakfast every weekday, so focus on the "5–7 times per week" column in the table. Assuming the participants in the study were a good representative sample, 36 out of 45, or 80%, of the 3,000 employees are likely to be within a healthy weight range. Multiply $0.8 \times 3,000$ to arrive at 2,400, which is **(D)**.

5. 300

Difficulty: Easy

Getting to the Answer: Read the graph carefully, including the key at the bottom indicating that each bar represents 15 minutes. The question states that only stage 3 is considered deep sleep, and the question asks how much time was spent in non-deep sleep. You could count all of the bars that don't represent stage 3, but it would be faster to count the bars that do and then subtract that number from the total. There are 12 bars that represent stage 3, which means the person spent $12 \times 15 = 180$ minutes in deep sleep. The study was for 8 hours, or 480 minutes, so the person spent $480 - 180 = \textbf{300}$ minutes in non-deep sleep.

6. 195

Difficulty: Medium

Strategic Advice: In multi-part Math question sets, the second question often uses information that you had to calculate in the first question. Keep track of your computations and reuse information so that you don't waste time repeating calculations.

Getting to the Answer: Set up the average formula and start filling in the values to find the missing night's stage 3 sleep. You're given two of the three quantities needed for the average formula: the total number of nights is 5 and the average over all the nights is 180 minutes. You know from your work in the previous question that the patient spent 180 minutes in stage 3 sleep on the first night. The following 3 nights, as given in the questions stem, average out to 175 minutes each, so even though you don't know their precise values, you can represent them as 175 three times. Use a variable, *x*, for the unknown number of minutes in stage 3 sleep on the fifth night and solve:

$$180 = \frac{180 + 175 + 175 + 175 + x}{5}$$

$$900 = 705 + x$$

$$x = 195$$

Grid in **195**.

7. D

Difficulty: Medium

Getting to the Answer: Compare each statement to the line graph one at a time, eliminating true statements as you work. Start with (A): at every reading after 20 hours, Strain 1 has a higher OD600 level than Strain 2, so this statement is true. Eliminate (A). Choice (B) states that Strain 2's growth rate (slope) overtook Strain 1's at hour 50, which is consistent with the line graph; eliminate it. It looks as though (C) requires time-consuming calculations, so skip it for now. Choice (D) states that Strain 1's growth rate was greater than Strain 2's over the entire period. This statement contradicts what you already confirmed in (B), which makes **(D)** false and, therefore, correct. There's no need to check (C).

8. D

Difficulty: Medium

Strategic Advice: The median is the middle value when all of the values are in numerical order, so you'll need to find the total number of values in the set and figure out which one is the middle value.

Getting to the Answer: The note above the chart says that the total number of people who were surveyed in country B is 250. Since it is an even set of values, the median will be the average of the 125th and 126th values. To get to those values, add the number of citizens who speak one or two languages: $70 + 30 = 100$. The hundredth value falls within the group that speaks two languages. Keep going because this group does not include the 125th and 126th values. Add the citizens who speak three languages: $100 + 20 = 120$. Still not quite there, so add the citizens who speak four languages: $120 + 70 = 190$. This means that the 125th and 126th values are both 4, so the median is 4. **(D)** is correct.

9. C

Difficulty: Hard

Getting to the Answer: The answer choices compare the number of citizens who speak different numbers of languages. (A) and (B) compare the number of citizens who speak exactly five languages to the number of citizens who speak exactly four languages. Notice that in both countries, the fraction that speaks exactly five languages is smaller than the fraction that speaks exactly four languages, so (B) can be eliminated.

To evaluate (A), you need to calculate the number of citizens who speak five languages and the number of citizens who speak four languages. Take the population in each country and multiply it by the fraction of citizens surveyed who speak the specified number of languages (the denominator of the fraction will be the total number surveyed, 250):

Country A: $(550{,}000)\left(\dfrac{25}{250}\right) = (550{,}000)\left(\dfrac{1}{10}\right) = 55{,}000$

Country B: $(1{,}300{,}000)\left(\dfrac{60}{250}\right) = (1{,}300{,}000)\left(\dfrac{6}{25}\right) = 312{,}000$

This means that $55{,}000 + 312{,}000 = 367{,}000$ citizens speak five languages. Next, calculate how many citizens speak exactly four languages:

Country A: $(550{,}000)\left(\dfrac{40}{250}\right) = (550{,}000)\left(\dfrac{4}{25}\right) = 88{,}000$

Country B: $(1{,}300{,}000)\left(\dfrac{70}{250}\right) = (1{,}300{,}000)\left(\dfrac{7}{25}\right) = 364{,}000$

This means that $88{,}000 + 364{,}000$, or $452{,}000$, citizens speak exactly four languages. Because 312,000 is not half of 364,000, eliminate (A).

Use logic to decide between (C) and (D). Notice that the fraction of citizens who speak four languages in country B, which has a larger population, is more than twice the fraction of citizens in country B who speak two languages—while in country A, which has a smaller population, the fraction of citizens who speak two languages is exactly twice the fraction of citizens who speak four languages. Country B's larger population means that overall, more citizens of both countries combined will speak four languages than two languages. Choice **(C)** is correct.

For the record, here are the calculations for **(C)** and (D):

Country A: $(550{,}000)\left(\dfrac{80}{250}\right) = (550{,}000)\left(\dfrac{8}{25}\right) = 176{,}000$

Country B: $(1{,}300{,}000)\left(\dfrac{30}{250}\right) = (1{,}300{,}000)\left(\dfrac{3}{25}\right) = 156{,}000$

The number of citizens who speak two languages in both countries is $176{,}000 + 156{,}000$, or $332{,}000$, which is fewer than the 452,000 who speak four languages.

10. B

Difficulty: Easy

Getting to the Answer: Consider the definitions of mean and standard deviation: mean is a measure of center, while standard deviation is a measure of spread. The closer the data points for a given snowboarder are to the mean, the more consistent that snowboarder's performance, so the explanation should involve standard deviation. Based on this, you can eliminate (A) and (D). Greater consistency means lower standard deviation (and vice versa); the only choice that reflects this—and correctly represents the data in the table—is **(B)**.

11. C

Difficulty: Medium

Getting to the Answer: You'll have to determine the values of all three measurements so that you can place them in ascending order. The *mode* is 3 because there are 18 cars of that age, which is the most of any age. The total number of cars is $3 + 5 + 18 + 17 + 11 + 6 + 2 = 62$. Since this is an even number, the *median* age will be the average of the 31st and 32nd values. The are $3 + 5 + 18 = 26$ cars that are 1, 2, and 3 years old and 17 that are 4 years old. Thus, the 27th through 43rd $(26 + 17 = 43)$ values are 4, and that is the median.

To find the *mean*, multiply each value by its frequency, total those values, and divide by 62. So, $1 \times 3 = 3$, $2 \times 5 = 10$, $3 \times 18 = 54$, $4 \times 17 = 68$, $5 \times 11 = 55$, $6 \times 6 = 36$, $7 \times 2 = 14$, and $3 + 10 + 54 + 68 + 55 + 36 + 14 = 240$. Divide 240 by 62 to get approximately 3.87. The ascending order of the three values is mode (3), mean (3.87), and median (4), so **(C)** is correct.

12. 6.2

Difficulty: Hard

Getting to the Answer: Read this question carefully, since it is rather unusual. In order to meet a goal of a 0.5% reject rate for the month, use the average formula,

$$0.5\% = \frac{\text{maximum allowable sum of the daily reject rates}}{22}.$$

Thus, the sum of the daily reject rates for a 0.5% average is $22 \times 0.5\% = 11.0\%$. Since 12 days have already passed with an average reject rate of 0.4%, the sum of the daily rates so far is $12 \times 0.4\% = 4.8\%$. So, the sum of the daily rates for the next 10 days cannot exceed

$11.0\% - 4.8\% = 6.2\%$ if the monthly average is to be 0.5% or less.

The question doesn't ask for the total or average of the next 10 days, however. Instead, it asks for the maximum reject rate on the next single day that could still conceivably allow the company to meet its monthly goal. If the other 9 remaining days all had a 0.0% reject rate, then the 10-day total would be the reject rate for that 13th day. This is 6.2%, so grid in **6.2**.

13. C

Difficulty: Medium

Getting to the Answer: There are 65 data points, so the median will be the middle data point, or the 33rd data point once the data are listed in order. Count the number of data points from the end. There are 10 households with 1 person and 18 households with 2 persons, so that adds up to 28 households. Since there are 15 households with 3 persons, the 33rd household will fall in that group, so the median household size is 3 persons. Add the number of households with more than 3 persons: $12 + 8 + 2 = 22$. **(C)** is correct.

14. A

Difficulty: Easy

Getting to the Answer: Any sample used to determine a general opinion needs to be representative and unbiased. The railroad company fails to meet that requirement, surveying only people who commute to work and who would probably benefit from the station. This potentially leaves out a large portion of the population who may not share the commuters' favorable opinion. The use of a biased sample group makes the survey unreliable and not representative, which makes **(A)** the correct answer.

15. A

Difficulty: Medium

Getting to the Answer: As long as a sample is representative, without bias, and relatively large, the mean and median of the sample data will be the same as the expected mean and median of the population from which the sample was taken. The sample here meets all of these requirements. So the mean of the sample equals the estimated mean of the general population, and **(A)** is the correct answer.

16. C

Difficulty: Medium

Getting to the Answer: As the customers were selected at random, it is reasonable to assume that the survey results will be representative of what is true for customers in general. However, the data provided refers only to people who bought dinnerware. So, an inference can be drawn only about dinnerware returns. Based on the 80% of surveyed customers who returned dinnerware items because of damage, it is reasonable to infer that this statistic will be similar for all customers who return dinnerware. That makes **(C)** the correct answer. Choices (A), (B), and (D) are incorrect because they are not confined to dinnerware.

17. C

Difficulty: Medium

Getting to the Answer: To make a reliable inference from a survey, the survey sample needs to be representative, unbiased, and relatively large. In this case, the miniature golf course owner surveyed only children who played at that course. Thus, any inference drawn from the data must be about such children. Since 60% of the surveyed children prefer a red golf ball, it is reasonable to infer that a similar percentage of total children at that golf course would prefer red golf balls. Thus, **(C)** is the correct answer.

18. C

Difficulty: Hard

Getting to the Answer: The customer purchased 5 boxes, each of which contains 20 bags, which means the customer bought a total of $5 \times 20 = 100$ bags. In each bag tested, there were between 11 and 13 green jelly beans. As the bags were chosen at random, it's reasonable to expect that the results will be consistent for all 100 bags. With 11–13 beans per bag, the total number of green jelly beans will likely be between $11 \times 100 = 1,100$ and $13 \times 100 = 1,300$. Right in the middle of that range is 1,200, making **(C)** the correct answer.

Note that if you chose (A) 60, you might have been thinking of the total green jelly beans in just the 5 randomly selected bags. Similarly, if you chose (B) 240, you calculated the approximate number in just one box of 20 bags. Incorrect answer choices often try to anticipate minor mistakes you might make in your calculations. Be sure to confirm that you answered the question being asked.

19. C

Difficulty: Medium

Getting to the Answer: The number of desired outcomes is 392 (marked bearings that are defective). The number of total possible outcomes is 560 (all the bearings that are marked defective). Thus, the probability that a bearing marked defective is in fact defective is $\frac{392}{560} \times 100\% = 0.70 \times 100\% = 70\%$. **(C)** is correct.

20. D

Difficulty: Hard

Getting to the Answer: The probability that one randomly selected salmon from those that were tested would have a dangerous level of mercury is equal to the number of salmon that had dangerous mercury levels divided by the total number of salmon that were tested. This means you need only two numbers to answer this question. One of those numbers is in the second table—6 salmon had dangerous mercury levels. Finding the other number is the tricky part. Use information from the question stem and the first table. The biologist tested 5% of the total number of each species of fish, and 25% of the 6,000 fish are salmon. So, the biologist tested 5% of 25% of 6,000 fish. Multiply to find that $0.05 \times 0.25 \times 6,000 = 75$ salmon were tested. This means the probability is $\frac{6}{75} = 0.08$, which matches **(D)**.

21. B

Difficulty: Medium

Strategic Advice: Recognizing which value goes in the denominator, whether it is the entire total or the total of a subgroup, is essential for probability questions that are based on data in a table.

Getting to the Answer: The question indicates that the random selection is from all the engineers, or the entire total of 768. The specific engineer to be selected is a mechanical engineer who specializes in autonomous vehicles, and the table indicates that there are 245 such engineers. Therefore, the probability of selecting a mechanical engineer specializing in autonomous vehicles from all the engineers is $\frac{245}{768}$, which is ≈ 0.319. **(B)** is correct.

Note that the incorrect answer choices often reflect common misunderstandings and simple table-reading errors. For example, (C) and (D) both use the wrong total and (A) is the probability of choosing an electrical engineer specializing in autonomous vehicles.

22. A

Difficulty: Medium

Strategic Advice: Be on the lookout for "at least" language. It will usually require adding data from multiple rows or columns.

Getting to the Answer: The probability of choosing an employee with "at least" 8 paid vacation days who is salaried is the number of salaried employees with 8 or more paid vacation days divided by the total number of employees with 8 or more paid vacation days. Find the number of salaried employees with 8 or more paid vacation days by adding the salaried employees with 8–14 paid vacation days, 27, and the salaried employees with 15–30 paid vacation days, 65. That means there are $27 + 65$, or 92, salaried employees with 8 or more paid vacation days. The total number of employees with 8 or more paid vacation days is 210 (the total number of employees with 8–14 paid vacation days) plus 103 (the total number of employees with 15–30 paid vacation days), or 313. The probability is $\frac{92}{313}$. **(A)** is correct.

23. C

Difficulty: Hard

Strategic Advice: If totals and the relationships between the data are the only information provided, write out a system of equations.

Getting to the Answer: The question gives the relationships between unknown values in the table, so fill them in accordingly. For hybrid engines, let h be the number that are rated 0–45 miles per gallon. There are 6 times as many hybrid engines that achieve 45+ miles per gallon, so that is $6h$. Similarly, for IC, let c be the number of IC engines that are 0–45 miles per gallon. Because the factory produced four times as many IC engines that achieve 45+ miles per gallon, fill in that blank with $4c$:

	Fuel Economy (miles per gallon)	
Engine Type	**0–45 mpg**	**45+ mpg**
Hybrid	h	$6h$
Internal Combustion (IC)	c	$4c$
Total	53	258

Write a system of equations based on the two miles per gallon columns:

$$h + c = 53$$
$$6h + 4c = 258$$

Solve the first equation for h and substitute the result into the second equation to solve for c:

$$h = 53 - c$$
$$6(53 - c) + 4c = 258$$
$$318 - 6c + 4c = 258$$
$$-2c = -60$$
$$c = 30$$

If c is 30, then there are 4×30, or 120, IC engines that achieve 45+ miles per gallon. The probability of choosing one of those 120 engines out all 258 engines that achieve 45+ miles per gallon is $\frac{120}{258}$, or 0.465. **(C)** is correct. Notice that there is no need to actually calculate h to answer this question.

24. 4

Difficulty: Medium

Category: Statistics

Strategic Advice: When the goal is to find a missing value in a set of data and the average is given, consider using the balance approach. We'll demonstrate both approaches starting with the average formula.

Getting to the Answer: The question is about the height change for the sunflower plant, so ignore the data for the other plants. The given height changes for the other six weeks are: 3, 8, 6, 7, 2, and 5. The average change in height for the sunflower plant is given as 5. If you call the missing value x, plugging the known values into the average formula results in the following:

$$\frac{3 + x + 8 + 6 + 7 + 2 + 5}{7} = 5$$

$$\frac{3 + x + 8 + 6 + 7 + 2 + 5}{7} = 5$$

$$\frac{31 + x}{7} = 5$$

$$31 + x = 35$$

$$x = 4$$

Grid in **4** as the correct answer.

Alternatively, to use the balance approach, write down how much each value is above or below the average of 5. For example, the Week 3 value of 3 is 2 below the average: $3 - 5 = -2$.

Week 3	Week 5	Week 6	Week 7	Week 8	Week 9
3: -2	8: $+3$	6: $+1$	7: $+2$	2: -3	5: $+0$

Now observe that, excluding Week 4, the values are $-2 + 3 + 1 + 2 - 3 = 1$. Without Week 4, the total is 1 more than what you'd expect based on the average. So for the values to balance out to the average, the Week 4 value must be 1 less than the average of 5, or $5 - 1 = 4$. Grid in **4**.

25. C

Difficulty: Medium

Category: Probability

Getting to the Answer: The research firm is choosing one student from among the sophomores, so you need the total number of sophomores, 493, in the denominator of the probability formula, not the total number of students. There are $493 - 140 = 353$ sophomores who prefer activities other than video games, so the probability of choosing a sophomore who doesn't prefer video games is $\frac{353}{493}$. Choice **(C)** is correct.

26. 700

Difficulty: Medium

Category: Tables and Graphs

Getting to the Answer: Identify the pieces of the graph you need and then convert from the percent to the total. You know from the graph that 21% (5% + 16%) of the visitors are *not* aged 20 or older. This means that $100\% - 21\% = 79\%$ were aged 20+. Given that the number of visitors aged 20+ is 553, use the three-part percent formula to calculate the total:

$$\text{total} \times 79\% = 553$$
$$\text{total} = \frac{553}{0.79} = 700$$

Grid in **700**.

27. 2030

Difficulty: Medium

Category: Tables and Graphs

Getting to the Answer: From the previous question, you know that the total number of visitors in 2014 was 700. According to the bar graph, 25% of all the visitors were aged 40–49, and 8% were aged 50+. This means that $0.25 \times 700 = 175$ attendees were aged 40–49, and $0.08 \times 700 = 56$ were aged 50+. The visitors aged 40–49 paid $175 \times \$10 = \$1,750$ for their tickets, and the visitors aged 50+ paid $56 \times \$5 = \$280$ for their tickets. The total revenue for the two groups was therefore $\$1,750 + \$280 = \$2,030$. Grid in **2030**.

28. 28.7

Difficulty: Medium

Category: Tables and Graphs

Getting to the Answer: To be considered "bad," a game must have a rating of 1 or 2. Begin by counting the number of "bad" games. There are $5 + 3 + 3 = 11$ games with a rating of 1 and $17 + 12 + 10 = 39$ games with a rating of 2. That's a total of $11 + 39 = 50$ games. Divide this by the total number of games and multiply by 100%: $\frac{50}{61 + 54 + 59} \times 100\% \approx 28.7\%$. Grid in **28.7**.

29. 12

Difficulty: Medium

Category: Tables and Graphs

Getting to the Answer: You know from the previous question that 50 games are "bad." Reducing this number by 50% is the same as halving it, meaning there will be 25 remaining "bad" games after the removal. Subtract this from the original total game count ($61 + 54 + 59 = 174$) to get the new total, $174 - 25 = 149$. Divide the new "bad" count by this total, and then multiply by 100% as you did before: $\frac{25}{149} \times 100\% \approx 16.7785\%$. Subtracting the new percentage from the old one (rounded to a minimum of four decimal places just to be safe) gives $28.7356\% - 16.7785\% = 11.9571\%$. This rounds to 12.0%. Grid in **12**.

30. B

Difficulty: Medium

Category: Surveys and Data Samples

Getting to the Answer: According to the sample survey, $\frac{40}{300}$ *say* they would join the gym. But the gym estimates that only 30% of these respondents would *actually* join, so multiply 40 by 30% to find that the gym can expect $\frac{12}{300} = 0.04 = 4\%$ of the respondents to join. Multiply this by the total number of residents: $12{,}600 \times 0.04 = 504$ residents, so **(B)** is correct.

31. C

Difficulty: Easy

Category: Tables and Graphs

Getting to the Answer: The question states that the data collected was about black-tailed jackrabbits in California, so any conclusion drawn can be generalized only to that particular species of rabbit in California, not to all rabbits generally. According to the data, the California jackrabbit gives birth mostly during March, April, and May, so **(C)** is correct.

32. D

Difficulty: Medium

Category: Surveys and Data Samples

Getting to the Answer: The question indicates that there are a wide variety of nutrients in the soil, but the study only tests for nitrogen and potassium, so the sample is limited. You can eliminate (A) and (B) because all nutrients were not included in the sample, so you can't say anything about them one way or the other. The additives may or may not help the soil retain other types of nutrients, and you certainly don't know which of the five additives would produce the best results. You can eliminate (C) because the question doesn't tell you anything about the data collection methods, so you can't determine whether the study was biased. This means that the study will only be able to produce results concerning the effects of the additives on soil retention of nitrogen and potassium. Thus, **(D)** is correct.

33. A

Difficulty: Hard

Category: Statistics

Getting to the Answer: The number of variables may look daunting, but the question is just asking you to find an average. The average of a set of terms is equal to the sum of the terms divided by the number of terms; thus, the average of *p*, *q*, and *r* is $\frac{p+q+r}{3}$.

Use the average formula to set up an equation using the rest of the information in the question. Even though you are given expressions with lots of variables, the average formula is still the sum of the terms divided by the number of terms. Notice that the question states that the average of these expressions is $10t + 34$, which translates to "$= 10t + 34$." So you can set up an equation like this:

$$\frac{(p + 12t - 5) + (q + 16t + 4) + (r - 7t + 25)}{3} = 10t + 34$$

Because the question asks for the average of *p*, *q*, and *r* in terms of *t*, solve the equation above for $\frac{p+q+r}{3}$:

$$\frac{p + 12t - 5 + q + 16t + 4 + r - 7t + 25}{3} = 10t + 34$$

$$\frac{p + q + r + 21t + 24}{3} = 10t + 34$$

$$\frac{p + q + r}{3} + \frac{21t}{3} + \frac{24}{3} = 10t + 34$$

$$\frac{p + q + r}{3} = 10t + 34 - 7t - 8$$

$$\frac{p + q + r}{3} = 3t + 26$$

(A) is correct.

34. 1/3 or .333

Difficulty: Medium

Category: Probability

Getting to the Answer: First, find the number of respondents willing to pay at least $8 (which means $8 or more). Be careful—the question doesn't specify store brand or brand name, so use both versions of the product:

$$32 + 55 + 30 + 42 + 14 + 27 = 200$$

Now, find the total number of people in the survey. Again, the question doesn't specify store brand or brand name. The question stem states that there is a total of 600 respondents. This means the probability that a randomly chosen respondent is willing to pay at least $8 is $\frac{200}{600}$, or $\frac{1}{3}$. Grid in **1/3** or **.333**.

CHAPTER 9

Scatterplots

LEARNING OBJECTIVES

After completing this chapter, you will be able to:

- Determine the average rate of change
- Write an equation for a line of best fit
- Extrapolate values from the line of best fit
- Determine whether a linear, a quadratic, or an exponential model describes the data presented in a scatterplot

25/600 SmartPoints® (Medium Yield)

Math

How Much Do You Know?

Directions: Try the questions that follow. Show your work so that you can compare your solutions to the ones found in the Check Your Work section immediately after this question set. The "Category" heading in the explanation for each question gives the title of the lesson that covers how to solve it. If you answered the question(s) for a given lesson correctly, and if your scratchwork looks like ours, you may be able to move quickly through that lesson. If you answered incorrectly or used a different approach, you may want to take your time on that lesson.

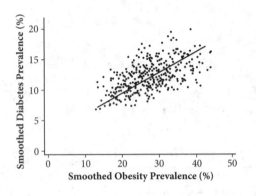

Source: CDC

1. The scatterplot shows the prevalence of obesity plotted against the prevalence of diabetes in various areas of the United States. Which of the following best estimates the average rate of change in the prevalence of diabetes as compared to the prevalence of obesity?

    A)   0.3

    B)   0.9

    C)   1.1

    D)   3

Questions 2 and 3 refer to the following stimulus.

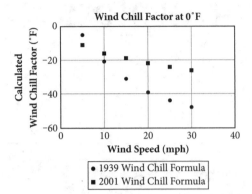

2. Wind chill, a measurement that reflects the temperature that one feels when outside based on the actual temperature and the wind speed, was first introduced in 1939, and the formula was revised in 2001. If the outside temperature is 0°F, what is the approximate wind chill at 40 miles per hour based on the 2001 formula?

    A)   −20°F

    B)   −30°F

    C)   −40°F

    D)   −50°F

3. What wind speed would produce the same wind chill using the 1939 formula as the wind chill produced using the 2001 formula when the outside temperature is 0°F and the wind speed is 40 miles per hour?

    A)   10 miles per hour

    B)   15 miles per hour

    C)   20 miles per hour

    D)   40 miles per hour

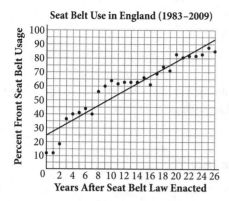

4. The scatterplot above shows data collected each year after the British Parliament enacted a mandatory seat belt law and the line of best fit to the data. Which of the following equations best represents the trend of the data shown in the figure?

A) $y = 0.4x + 25$

B) $y = 1.8x + 15$

C) $y = 2.1x + 35$

D) $y = 2.6x + 25$

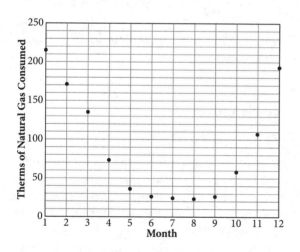

5. The scatterplot above shows the average therms of natural gas used by residential customers over a 12-month period. Of the following equations, which best models the data in the scatterplot?

A) $y = 1.061^x + 312.9$

B) $y = -1.061^x - 312.9$

C) $y = 6.1x^2 - 85.1x + 312.9$

D) $y = -6.1x^2 + 85.1x - 312.9$

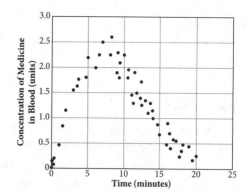

6. Scientists measured the concentration of an experimental medication in blood samples over time. If a quadratic function is used to model the data, which of the following best explains the meaning of the vertex?

A) The average maximum medicine concentration in the blood sample is 7.5 units.

B) The average maximum medicine concentration is more than 20 units.

C) The average maximum medicine concentration in the blood samples occurs around 2.5 minutes.

D) The average maximum medicine concentration in the blood sample occurs between 5 and 10 minutes.

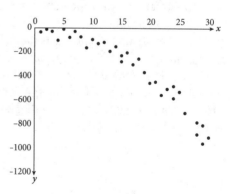

7. For which of the following values of a and b does the equation $y = ax^b$ model the data in the scatterplot above?

A) $a < 0, b < 0$

B) $a < 0, b > 0$

C) $a > 0, b < 0$

D) $a > 0, b > 0$

Check Your Work

1. A

Difficulty: Easy

Category: Line of Best Fit

Getting to the Answer: The scatterplot shows obesity prevalence plotted against diabetes prevalence, and because the line goes up as it moves to the right, there is a positive linear correlation between the two. The phrase "rate of change" is the same as the slope of the line of best fit, so pick two points to plug into the slope formula. Estimating, the endpoints appear to be $(14, 7)$ and $(44, 17)$. (If your estimate is different, that's okay—whenever the SAT requires you to make an estimate, the answer choices will be spread far enough apart that you'll get the correct answer as long as you're looking in the right place and thinking the right way.) Calculate the slope, m:

$$m = \frac{y_2 - y_1}{x_2 - x_1} = \frac{17 - 7}{44 - 14} = \frac{10}{30} = 0.3$$

This matches **(A)**.

2. B

Difficulty: Medium

Category: Line of Best Fit

Getting to the Answer: The 2001 formula plot has a slight curve that straightens as wind speed increases. Extend the line to reflect this trend; once complete, draw a straight line from 40 mph on the x-axis to the extended 2001 formula plot (a straight edge such as an extra pencil will help). Then draw a horizontal line from the intersection of the 2001 formula line and the vertical line to the y-axis; you'll see that the corresponding wind chill is $-30°$F. **(B)** is correct.

3. B

Difficulty: Medium

Category: Line of Best Fit

Getting to the Answer: Since the conditions mentioned are the same as those in the previous question, start with the wind chill calculated using the 2001 formula for that question, $-30°$F.

Draw a horizontal line from $-30°$F on the y-axis until it intersects a data point on the 1939 formula plot.

Draw a vertical line from that point down to the x-axis; you'll find that in 1939, a wind speed of approximately 15 mph would yield a wind chill of $-30°$F. Therefore, the correct answer is **(B)**.

4. D

Difficulty: Medium

Category: Line of Best Fit

Getting to the Answer: A line that "represents the trend of the data" is another way of referring to the line of best fit, which is linear in this diagram. Use the y-intercept and slope of the line of best fit to eliminate the choices.

Start by finding the y-intercept. For this graph, it's about 25, so eliminate (B) and (C). To choose between (A) and (D), find the approximate slope using two points that lie on (or very close to) the line of best fit. Use the y-intercept $(0, 25)$ as one of the points to save time (it's easy to subtract 0) and estimate the second, such as $(21, 80)$. Then, use the slope formula to find the slope:

$$m = \frac{y_2 - y_1}{x_2 - x_1} = \frac{80 - 25}{21 - 0} = \frac{55}{21} = 2.62$$

The result is very close to the slope in **(D)**, making it the correct answer.

5. C

Difficulty: Medium

Category: Scatterplot Modeling

Getting to the Answer: The data in the scatterplot can be modeled by a parabola opening upward. (A) is an exponential growth equation, and (B) is an exponential decay equation. Neither will graph as a parabola, so eliminate both. Recall that a parabola is the graph of a quadratic. For a quadratic equation in the form $ax^2 + bx + c$, a determines whether the parabola opens upward or downward and c is the y-intercept. When $a > 0$, the parabola opens upward, so **(C)** is correct. (D) is a quadratic equation, but $a < 0$, so this equation would graph as a parabola that opens downward.

Math

6. D

Difficulty: Medium

Category: Scatterplot Modeling

Getting to the Answer: The vertex of a parabola opening downward, like this one, is at the maximum. For this scatterplot, the medicine concentration is measured on the y-axis, and the maximum value (the vertex) is about 2.6 units, so the average maximum medicine concentration cannot be above 2.6 units. Eliminate (A) and (B). The x-value of the vertex occurs between 5 and 10 minutes; therefore, **(D)** is correct.

7. B

Difficulty: Hard

Category: Scatterplot Modeling

Getting to the Answer: The shape of the data is concave down with an increasingly negative slope as x increases. The y-values of the data are negative, which indicates $a < 0$. Eliminate (C) and (D). As x increases, the magnitude of the y-values increases. This indicates $b > 0$. Note that if $b < 0$, the y-values would approach 0 as x increases. Thus, **(B)** is correct.

Math

Line of Best Fit

LEARNING OBJECTIVES

After this lesson, you will be able to:

- Determine the average rate of change
- Write an equation for a line of best fit
- Extrapolate values from the line of best fit

To answer a question like this:

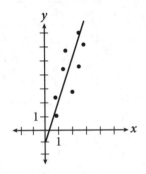

Which of the following equations corresponds to the line of best fit for the data set shown above?

A) $y = 0.4x - 1$

B) $y = 0.4x + 1$

C) $y = 2.5x + 1$

D) $y = 2.5x - 1$

You need to know this:

A **scatterplot** is a visual representation of a set of data points. The data points are plotted on the x- and y-axes such that each axis represents a different characteristic of the data set. For example, in the scatterplot below, each data point represents a dachshund. The x-axis represents the dog's length and the y-axis represents its height.

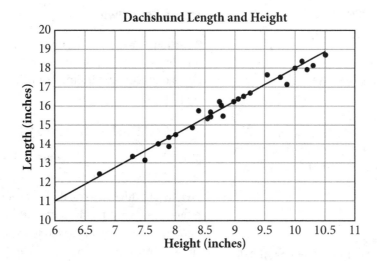

The **line of best fit**, or trend line, is drawn through the **data points** to describe the relationship between the two variables as an equation. This line does not necessarily go through any single data point, but it does accurately reflect the trend shown by the data with about half the points above the line and half below.

The **equation of the line of best fit** is the equation that describes the line of best fit algebraically. On test day, you'll most likely encounter this equation as linear, quadratic, or exponential, though it can also be other types of equations. The next lesson will cover these various forms.

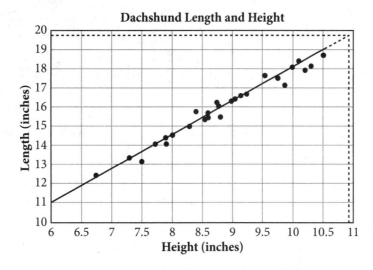

Some SAT questions will require you to extrapolate from the line of best fit. (Question 1 in the Try on Your Own set is an example of this type of question.) For example, you might be asked to predict the length of a dachshund that is 10.9 inches in height. Trace your way up to the line of best fit from the given *x*-value and trace over to find the corresponding *y*-value, in this case about 19.75 inches.

You need to do this:

To determine the equation of the line of best fit for a linear equation, like the one in the dachshund scatterplot, start by finding the slope, also called the **average rate of change**. Watch out for the units when you do this. In the dachshund example, using the points $(6, 11)$ and $(10, 18)$, the slope is

$\dfrac{y_2 - y_1}{x_2 - x_1} = \dfrac{18 - 11}{10 - 6} = \dfrac{7}{4} = 1.75$. Next, find the *y*-intercept. Using the point $(10, 18)$ and plugging

those values into slope-intercept form yields
$18 = 1.75(10) + b$.

Thus, $b = 0.5$ in the dachshund example.
So the equation in slope-intercept form is length =
$(1.75 \times$ height$) + 0.5$.

You can also extrapolate using the equation for the line
of best fit. For a dachshund that is 11 inches tall, the calculation would be length $= 1.75(11) + 0.5 = 19.75$.

Explanation:

Knowing where the *y*-intercept of the line of best fit falls
will help you eliminate answer choices. Because the
line of best fit intersects the *y*-axis below the *x*-axis,
you know that the *y*-intercept is negative, so eliminate
(B) and (C) (the *y*-intercept is +1 for each of those lines).
Now, look at the slope. The line rises along the *y*-axis
much faster than it runs along the *x*-axis, so the slope
must be greater than 1, making **(D)** correct.

Try on Your Own

Directions: Take as much time as you need on these
questions. Work carefully and methodically. There will
be an opportunity for timed practice at the end of the
chapter.

Questions 1 and 2 refer to the following information.

Most chickens reach maturity and begin laying eggs at
around 20 weeks of age. From this point forward, however, as the chicken ages, its egg production decreases.
A farmer was given a flock of 100 chickens (all of which
were the same age) and asked to measure daily egg
output for the entire flock at random intervals starting at
maturity until the chickens were 70 weeks old. The data
are recorded in the scatterplot below and the line of best
fit has been drawn.

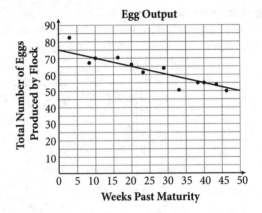

1. Based on the line of best fit, what is the predicted
number of eggs that will be produced by the flock
when it is 33 weeks past maturity?

A) 33

B) 50

C) 58

D) 64

HINT: For Q2, how many tick marks on the *y*-axis represent 5 eggs?

2. How many times did the farmer's data differ by more than 5 eggs from the number of eggs predicted by the line of best fit?

HINT: For Q3, look at the slope. Which two choices can you eliminate immediately?

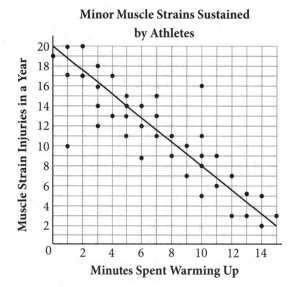

Minor Muscle Strains Sustained by Athletes

3. The scatterplot above shows the number of minor muscle strain injuries sustained in a year by athletes, plotted against their self-reported amount of time spent stretching and doing other warm-up activities before engaging in rigorous physical activity. Which of the following best estimates the average rate of change in the number of injuries compared with the number of minutes spent warming up?

A) −1.2

B) −0.8

C) 2

D) 20

HINT: For Q4, rate of change, increase or decrease, means slope.

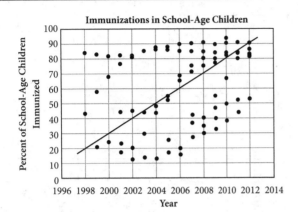

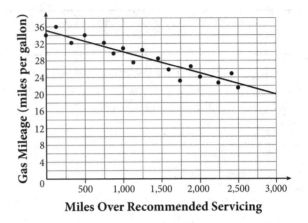

Miles Over Recommended Servicing

4. The graph above shows the percent of school-age children in the United States who received immunizations for various illnesses between 1996 and 2012. What was the average rate of increase in the percent of children immunized per year over the given time period?

    A)   5% per year

    B)   10% per year

    C)   25% per year

    D)   70% per year

5. A car manufacturer compiled data that indicated gas mileage decreased as the number of miles driven between recommended servicing increased. The manufacturer used the equation $y = -\dfrac{1}{200}x + 35$ to model the data. Based on the information, how many miles per gallon could be expected if this particular car is driven 3,400 miles over the recommended miles between servicing?

Scatterplot Modeling

LEARNING OBJECTIVE

After this lesson, you will be able to:

● Determine whether a linear, quadratic, or exponential model describes the data presented in a scatterplot

To solve a question like this:

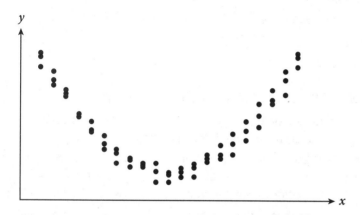

Given that **a, b,** and **c** are constants and that **a** > 0, which of the following is the equation for the line of best fit for the above scatterplot?

A) $y = ax + b$

B) $y = a^{bx}$

C) $y = -ax^2 + bx + c$

D) $y = ax^2 + bx + c$

You need to know this:

There are several patterns that are common forms for the line of best fit. Scatterplots are typically constructed so that the variable on the *x*-axis is the independent variable (input) and the variable on the *y*-axis is the dependent variable (output). The equation for the line of best fit quantifies the relationship between the variables represented by the two axes. The patterns that you are most likely to encounter on the SAT are shown in the table below.

Best Fit Description	Relationship between Variables
Upward-sloping straight line	Linear and positive
Downward-sloping straight line	Linear and negative
Upward-opening parabola	Quadratic with a positive coefficient in front of the squared term
Downward-opening parabola	Quadratic with a negative coefficient in front of the squared term
Upward-sloping curve with an increasing slope	Exponential and positive (e.g., compound interest)
Downward-sloping curve with a flattening slope	Exponential and negative (e.g., radioactive decay)

Here are visual representations of linear, quadratic, and exponential models:

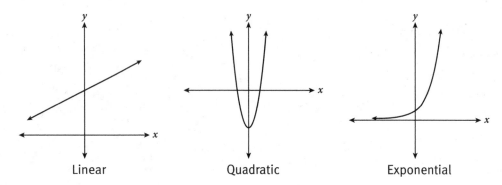

Linear　　　　　Quadratic　　　　　Exponential

You need to do this:

- First, examine the line of best fit (draw it in, if necessary) and determine its curvature.
- If the line of best fit is straight, the scatterplot represents a linear relationship and the correct answer choice will not contain any exponents. It will likely be in slope-intercept form, $y = mx + b$.
- If the line of best fit is a parabola, the correct answer will be in the form of a quadratic equation, $y = ax^2 + bx + c$. If the parabola opens downward, a will be negative; if upward, a will be positive. (Chapter 12 presents more detailed information about parabolas, but this will suffice for now.)
- If the line of best fit starts with a gradual rate of change that steepens over time, the correct answer will represent an exponential relationship in the form $y = ab^x + c$.

Explanation:

The line of best fit for this scatterplot is curved, so it is not a straight line as would be created by the linear equation $y = ax + b$. Eliminate (A).

The exponential equation $y = a^{bx}$ would result in a curve that opens upward in one direction. The line of best fit of the scatterplot opens upward in two directions, so (B) is incorrect.

Quadratic equations create parabolas when graphed, but the negative coefficient of the x^2 term means that (C) would be a downward-opening parabola rather than the upward-opening parabola of the scatterplot. Thus, **(D)** is correct since that equation would be graphed as an upward-opening parabola.

Try on Your Own

Directions: Take as much time as you need on these questions. Work carefully and methodically. There will be an opportunity for timed practice at the end of the chapter.

6. Which of the following is best modeled using a linear regression equation, $y = ax + b$, where $a < 0$?

   A)
   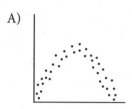

   B)
   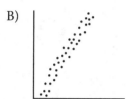

   C)
   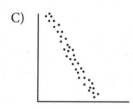

   D)
   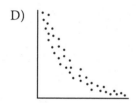

HINT: For Q7, in an exponential equation, you're taking a starting value and multiplying repeatedly by some other value.

7. Adriana used the data from a scatterplot she found on the U.S. Census Bureau's website to determine a regression model showing the relationship between the population in the area where she lived and the number of years, x, after she was born. The result was an exponential growth equation of the form $y = x_0(1 + r)^x$. Which of the following does x_0 most likely represent in the equation?

   A) The population in the year that she was born

   B) The rate of change of the population over time

   C) The maximum population reached during her lifetime

   D) The number of years after her birth when the population reached its maximum

8. Suppose a scatterplot shows a weak negative linear correlation. Which of the following statements is true?

   A) The slope of the line of best fit will be a number less than -1.

   B) The slope of the line of best fit will be a number between -1 and 0.

   C) The data points will follow, but not closely, the line of best fit, which has a negative slope.

   D) The data points will be closely gathered around the line of best fit, which has a negative slope.

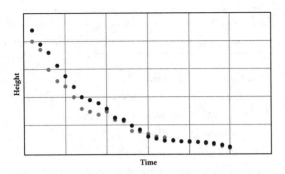

9. A drain at the bottom of a cylindrical water tank
    is opened and the height of the water is meas-
    ured at regular time intervals. The tank is refilled
    and the process is then repeated. The scatterplot
    above shows the measured height on the y-axis
    and time on the x-axis for the two trials. Which of
    the following conclusions can be drawn from the
    observations in the scatterplot?

    A) Water flows out of the drain at a constant rate.

    B) The flow rate from the tank decreases as the
        height of the water in the tank decreases.

    C) The drain is inefficiently designed.

    D) The is no relationship between the height of
        the water in the tank and time.

On Test Day

The SAT often tests your understanding of the real-world implications of the *y*-intercept of the line of best fit. The *y*-intercept indicates the starting value of the item measured on the *y*-axis before any time has passed. Scatterplots will test your ability to recognize the meaning of the *y*-intercept in various ways:

- For linear lines of best fit, common examples include the flat fee for renting an item before the hourly rate begins or the down payment on an item before the monthly payments begin.

- For quadratic lines of best fit, the most common example is the path of a projectile where the *y*-intercept is the starting height of the projectile.

- For exponential lines of best fit, common examples include the principal when calculating compound interest, the starting amount of an isotope with a specific half-life (radioactive decay), or the initial population when calculating population growth over time.

Keep in mind that lines of best fit are only approximate based on the given data, but the logic is straightforward: the *y*-intercept is directly related to the approximate initial amount of what is measured on the *y*-axis. Try the following question to see if you can recognize the real-world implication of the *y*-intercept of the line of best fit.

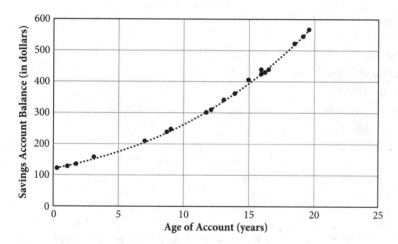

10. Students in a finance class surveyed 20 percent of the account holders at Docen Bank to determine whether the bank's "Stock Market Special" savings account actually paid account holders the promised 10 percent annual interest rate. The scatterplot above shows the data the students collected from account holders about how long ago they opened their accounts and their current balances. The students calculated a line of best fit with the equation $y = 120\left(1 + \dfrac{.08}{12}\right)^{12x}$, which means that the bank was actually paying account holders only an 8 percent annual interest rate. Which of the following best explains how the number 120 in the equation relates to the scatterplot?

A) A "Stock Market Special" account with $120 initially will likely have less than $350 after 15 years.

B) All "Stock Market Special" accounts started with a $120 initial investment.

C) The difference between the promised 10 percent annual interest rate and the actual 8 percent rate is $120 a year.

D) A "Stock Market Special" account with $120 initially will likely have more than $350 after 15 years.

How Much Have You Learned?

Directions: For testlike practice, give yourself 15 minutes to complete this question set. Be sure to study the explanations, even for questions you got right. They can be found at the end of this chapter.

Employee Sick Day Usage

11. The Human Resources department of a company tracks employee sick day usage to see if there are patterns. One of the HR representatives decides to check employee sick day usage against outside temperature. He compiles the information for the employees' sick day usage and temperature in the scatterplot above. Which of the following conclusions can he draw based on this data?

A) There is no relationship between the number of sick days used by employees in general and outside temperature.

B) There is no relationship between the number of sick days used by this company's employees and outside temperature.

C) No conclusions can be drawn about the number of sick days used by this company's employees and outside temperature.

D) There is a relationship, but not a causal link, between the number of sick days used by this company's employees and outside temperature.

12. Scientists plotted data for two animal populations on a scatterplot: population A, which they graphed along the x-axis, and population B, which they graphed along the y-axis. The data showed a strong negative correlation. Which of the following statements is justified?

A) The rise in population A caused the decline in population B.

B) The decline in population B caused the rise in population A.

C) Because the correlation is negative, there cannot be causation between the two populations.

D) The rise in population A is correlated to the decline in population B, but causation is unknown.

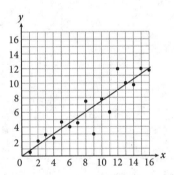

13. By what percent does the y-coordinate of the data point $(12, 12)$ deviate from the y-value predicted by the line of best fit for an x-value of 12 ? (Ignore the percent sign and grid your response to the nearest percent.)

The scatterplot below compares the average gasoline prices in Boston, per gallon, to the average gasoline prices across the United States, per gallon, during a one-year period from 2017 to 2018.

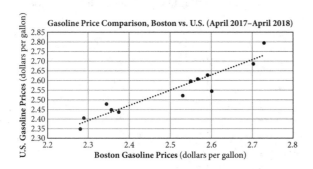

14. Of the following equations, which best models the data in the scatterplot?

    A) $y = -1.7848x + 0.5842$

    B) $y = 1.7848x + 1.5842$

    C) $y = 0.7848x + 0.5842$

    D) $y = -0.7848x + 0.5842$

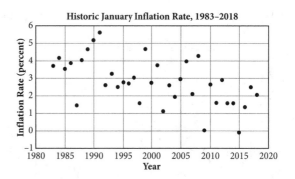

16. Which of the following is the most accurate statement about the scatterplot above?

    A) The data in the scatterplot has a weak positive correlation.

    B) The data in the scatterplot has a strong positive correlation.

    C) The data in the scatterplot has a negative correlation.

    D) There is no correlation in the data set.

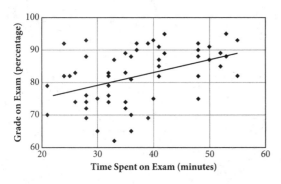

15. A physics professor presented the scatterplot above to her first-year students. What is the significance of the slope of the line of best fit?

    A) The slope represents the rate at which time spent on an exam increases based on a student's exam performance.

    B) The slope represents the average grade on the exam.

    C) The slope represents the rate at which a student's exam grade increases based on time spent on the exam.

    D) The slope has no significance.

Questions 17 and 18 refer to the following information.

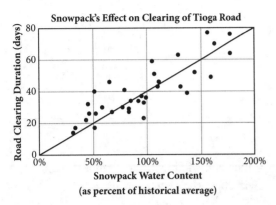

Snowpack's Effect on Clearing of Tioga Road

Source: www.nps.gov/yose/planyourvisit/tiogaopen.htm

Tioga Road is a mountain pass that crosses the Sierra Nevada through northern Yosemite National Park. The road is closed from about November through late May. This time period can change depending on the quantity and nature of the season's snowfall, as well as unforeseen obstacles such as fallen trees or rocks. The scatterplot above compares the snowpack water content on April 1 (for years 1981–2014) as a percent of the historical average to the time it takes the National Park Service to fully clear the road and open it to traffic.

17. For every 5 percent increase in snowpack water content, how many more days does it take the National Park Service to clear Tioga Road?

18. Assuming no unforeseen obstacles or machinery issues, if the road's snowpack water content on April 1 is 248 percent of the historical average, based on the prior experience shown on the graph, how many days will it take to fully clear Tioga Road?

19. Which of the following scatterplots shows a relationship that is appropriately modeled with the equation $y = -ax^2 + bx - c$, where a and c are negative and b is positive?

A)

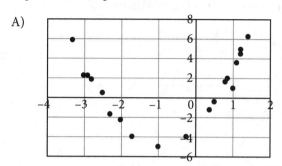

B)

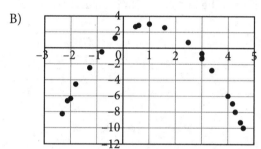

C)

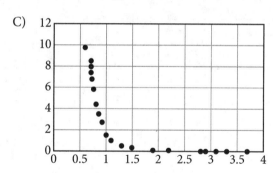

D)

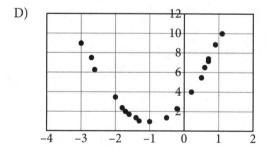

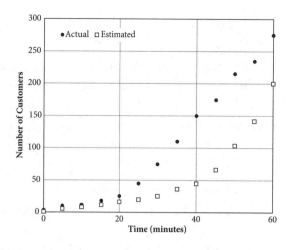

20. The scatterplot above shows the actual and estimated number of customers visiting a new shopping plaza within the first hour of opening. Which of the following statements correctly compares the rates of increase for the actual and estimated numbers of customers?

A) The rate of increase for the actual number of customers is greater than that of the estimated number in every 20-minute interval.

B) The rate of increase for the actual number of customers is less than that of the estimated number in every 20-minute interval.

C) The rate of increase for the actual number of customers is greater than that of the estimated number in the interval from 20 to 40 minutes and less in the interval 40 to 60 minutes.

D) The rate of increase for the actual number of customers is less than that of the estimated number in the interval from 20 to 40 minutes and greater in the interval 40 to 60 minutes.

K 221

Reflect

Directions: Take a few minutes to recall what you've learned and what you've been practicing in this chapter. Consider the following questions, jot down your best answer for each one, and then compare your reflections to the expert responses on the following page. Use your level of confidence to determine what to do next.

What is the significance of a scatterplot's line of best fit?

_____

_____

_____

Given a scatterplot and a line of best fit, how can you tell whether the line of best fit is an accurate one?

_____

_____

_____

What are the three most common patterns for modeling scatterplots that you'll see on test day?

_____

_____

_____

Expert Responses

What is the significance of a scatterplot's line of best fit?

The line of best fit describes the relationship between the two variables of the scatterplot. For example, if the line of best fit is linear and has a positive slope, then the two variables have a linear and positive relationship: as one variable increases, the other one also increases and at a constant rate.

Given a scatterplot and a line of best fit, how can you tell whether the line of best fit is an accurate one?

A line of best fit should be drawn such that approximately half the points are above it and half are below it.

What are the three most common patterns for modeling scatterplots that you'll see on test day?

Most test-day scatterplots can be modeled by a linear ($y = mx + b$), quadratic ($y = ax^2 + bx + c$), or exponential ($y = ab^x + c$) relationship.

Next Steps

If you answered most questions correctly in the "How Much Have You Learned?" section, and if your responses to the Reflect questions were similar to those of the SAT expert, then consider scatterplots an area of strength and move on to the next chapter. Come back to this topic periodically to prevent yourself from getting rusty.

If you don't yet feel confident, review those parts of this chapter that you have not yet mastered, then try the questions you missed again. In particular, make sure that you feel comfortable extrapolating data from a line of best fit. As always, be sure to review the explanations closely.

Answers and Explanations

1.   C

Difficulty: Easy

Getting to the Answer: In this case, you merely need to match the y-value on the line of best fit with the x-value of 33, since the x-axis of the graph represents the number of weeks after maturity. Take care to use the line of best fit rather than an individual point on the graph; (B) is a trap answer. At $x = 33$, the y-value of the line of best fit seems to be just shy of 60. Thus, **(C)** is correct.

2.   2

Difficulty: Easy

Getting to the Answer: Examine the graph, including the axis labels and numbering. Each vertical grid line represents 5 eggs, so look to see how many data points are more than a complete grid space away from the line of best fit. Only 2 data points meet this requirement—the first data point at about 3 weeks and the one between 30 and 35 weeks, making **2** the correct answer.

3.   A

Difficulty: Medium

Getting to the Answer: Examine the graph, paying careful attention to units and labels. The average rate of change is the same as the slope of the line of best fit. The data is decreasing (going down from left to right), so eliminate (C) and (D). To choose between (A) and (B), find the slope of the line of best fit using the slope formula, $m = \dfrac{y_2 - y_1}{x_2 - x_1}$, and any two points that lie on (or very close to) the line. Using the two points $(5, 14)$ and $(10, 8)$, the average rate of change is about $\dfrac{8 - 14}{10 - 5} = \dfrac{-6}{5} = -1.2$, which matches **(A)**.

4.   A

Difficulty: Easy

Getting to the Answer: The question asks for a rate of change, which means you'll need the slope of the line of best fit. Pick a pair of points to use in the slope formula, such as $(1998, 20)$ and $(2012, 90)$:

$$m = \frac{y_2 - y_1}{x_2 - x_1} = \frac{90 - 20}{2012 - 1998} = \frac{70}{14} = 5$$

Choice **(A)** is correct.

5.   18

Difficulty: Medium

Getting to the Answer: Because the y-value of the graph when $x = 3{,}400$ is not shown, this question requires a mathematical solution; extending the line of best fit will not provide an accurate enough answer. The equation of the model is given as $y = -\dfrac{1}{200}x + 35$. Miles over recommended servicing are graphed along the x-axis, so substitute 3,400 for x to find the answer:

$$y = -\frac{1}{200}(3{,}400) + 35 = -17 + 35 = 18$$

Grid in **18**.

6.   C

Difficulty: Easy

Getting to the Answer: A regression equation is the equation of the line (or curve) that best fits the data. A *linear* regression is used to model data that follows the path of a straight line. In the equation given, a represents the slope of the linear regression (the line of best fit), so you are looking for data that is linear and is decreasing, or falling from left to right, which happens when a is negative, or as the question states, when $a < 0$. You can eliminate (A), which is a quadratic curve, and (D), an exponential curve. You can also eliminate (B) because it is increasing (rising from left to right) instead of decreasing (falling from left to right). **(C)** is correct.

7.   A

Difficulty: Easy

Getting to the Answer: When an exponential equation is written in the form $y = x_0(1 + r)^x$, the value of x_0 gives the y-intercept of the equation's graph. To answer this question, you need to think about what the y-intercept would represent in the context described.

Whenever time is involved in a relationship that is modeled by an equation or a graph, it is almost always the independent variable and therefore graphed on the x-axis. Therefore, for this question, population would be graphed on the y-axis, so x_0 most likely represents the population when the time elapsed was zero, or in other words, in the year that Adriana was born, making **(A)** correct.

8. C

Difficulty: Medium

Getting to the Answer: "Correlation" simply means relationship. The word "weak" refers to the strength of the relationship (how close the data lies to the line of best fit), which has no effect on slope. Be careful not to confuse slope and strength. The fact that a data set shows a weak correlation does not give you any information about the magnitude of the slope. This means you can eliminate (A) and (B). Also, keep in mind that the terms "weak" and "negative" are not related, but rather are two independent descriptors of the correlation. So the fact that the rate of change is negative has nothing to do with the strength of the correlation. In a weak correlation, the data points will loosely follow the line of best fit, which makes **(C)** the correct answer.

9. B

Difficulty: Easy

Getting to the Answer: A line of best fit for the scatterplot would show that the measured height of the water decreases over time, but the slope becomes less steep over time, too. The slope, change in height divided by change in time, represents the flow rate of water out of the tank. Since the flow changes as the height of the water changes, (A) is incorrect. Because the slope of the line of best fit becomes less steep as the height of the water decreases, it follows that the flow rate decreases as the height of the water decreases. **(B)** is correct. (D) is incorrect because the height of the water decreases (though at an ever slower rate) as time progresses, so there is a relationship between the height of the water and time. (C) is incorrect because the data presented doesn't imply anything about the efficiency of the drain design.

10. D

Difficulty: Medium

Strategic Advice: Lines of best fit only approximate trends based on a given data set.

Getting to the Answer: In the line of best fit equation that the students calculated, the initial principal is $120, but that does not necessarily mean that **all** of the account holders had that much in the account initially. Eliminate (B).

To test (A) and (D), sketch in the line of best fit:

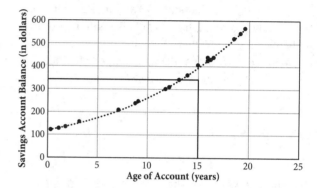

Notice that the line of best fit, which is based on an initial principal of $120, is definitely above $350 at the 15-year mark, so **(D)** is correct. Since the line of best fit is exponential, not linear, there will not be a consistent difference between the 10% annual rate and 8% annual rate, which makes (C) incorrect.

11. B

Difficulty: Medium

Category: Scatterplot Modeling

Getting to the Answer: There are two things to keep in mind for a question like this: correlation does not prove causation, and as a general rule, conclusions can be drawn only about the population studied, not about all populations. The population in the study is only the employees at the company, not all employees in general, so eliminate (A). The data points are scattered and do not form any discernible pattern. This means there is no correlation, which is another way of saying the two variables aren't related, so you can eliminate (D). You can also eliminate (C) because the HR representative **is** able to draw a conclusion—that there is no relationship. Therefore, **(B)** is correct.

12. D

Difficulty: Medium

Category: Scatterplot Modeling

Getting to the Answer: The fact that the two variables are strongly correlated, whether it be negatively or positively, shows only that there is a relationship between the variables. It does not indicate whether the change in one variable caused the change in the other. For example, population A might thrive in wet climates, while population B does not, and in the years studied, rainfall may have increased, which caused the changes in the populations. Eliminate (A) and (B). Conversely, the negative correlation does not discount the possibility of causation; rather, the data does not allow you to draw a conclusion about causation, so eliminate (C). This means **(D)** is the correct answer.

13. 33

Difficulty: Medium

Category: Line of Best Fit

Getting to the Answer: The point $(12, 12)$ is three full grid lines away from the line of best fit, which goes through $(12, 9)$. To find the percent difference between the expected and actual y-values, use the percent change formula. Note that the phrasing of the question indicates that the original value to use is 9, the y-value on the line of best fit: $\frac{12-9}{9} \times 100\% = \frac{3}{9} \times 100\% = 33.3\%$. Grid in **33**.

14. C

Difficulty: Medium

Category: Scatterplot Modeling

Strategic Advice: For scatterplot questions, it is important to determine whether using logic or plugging in values is more efficient.

Getting to the Answer: Notice that the answer choices involve very precise coefficients, which is a good indicator that logic is the best way to get to the correct answer. The slope of the line of best fit is positive, so eliminate (A) and (D), which have negative slopes. It is also important to note that the lower-left corner of the graph is not the origin, which means that the y-intercept needs to be extrapolated. With only two choices left, you can test only one of them. If the equation you test works, then it is correct. If the equation you test does not work, the other is correct. To test (B), choose one of the values

from the scatterplot that is close to the line of best fit, for example $(2.7, 2.7)$. Plugging 2.7 in for x should mean that $y = 2.7$, but with the equation in choice (B) you get:

$$y = 1.7848(2.7) + 1.5842$$
$$y = 4.81896 + 1.5842$$
$$y = 6.40316$$

This does not match the coordinate point, so **(C)** is correct.

15. C

Difficulty: Medium

Category: Line of Best Fit

Getting to the Answer: The slope of a line is always a rate of change of some sort, so you can eliminate (B) and (D). The graph indicates that time spent on the exam is the independent variable, so exam performance depends on it. The choice that correctly describes this relationship is **(C)**.

16. C

Difficulty: Medium

Category: Scatterplot Modeling

Strategic Advice: Correlation refers to how closely the values on the scatterplot match the line of best fit.

Getting to the Answer: Since correlation is related to the best-fit line, it is important to sketch one on the graph. Here's a rough approximation:

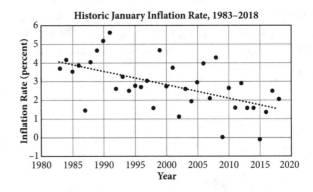

A strong correlation means that the data points are closely gathered around the line of best fit; a weak correlation means that the data points are farther from the line of best fit. The line of best fit has a definite negative slope, so eliminate (A) and (B). When there is no correlation, the data set is distributed evenly over the entire graph, but that is not the case here, so (D) can be eliminated as well. **(C)** is correct.

17. 2

Difficulty: Medium

Category: Line of Best Fit

Getting to the Answer: You're asked for a rate; this means finding the slope of the line of best fit. Start by picking a pair of points, preferably where the line of best fit passes through a gridline intersection to minimize error. The points (0, 0) and (50, 20) are good choices to make the calculation easy. Determine the slope:

$$m = \frac{y_2 - y_1}{x_2 - x_1} = \frac{20 - 0}{50 - 0} = \frac{20}{50} = \frac{2}{5}$$

Don't grid in 2/5, though. Remember what you're being asked: you need the road clearing duration increase for a 5% increase in snowpack water content, not a 1% increase. Therefore, multiply $\frac{2}{5}$ by 5, which yields 2. Grid in **2**.

18. 99.2

Difficulty: Medium

Category: Line of Best Fit

Getting to the Answer: The slope you found in the previous question will save you some time here. The line of best fit on the scatterplot intersects the **y**-axis at (0, 0). Therefore, the equation of the line of best fit is $y = \frac{2}{5}x$. Plug 248 in for **x** and simplify:

$$y = \frac{2}{5}(248) = \frac{496}{5} = 99.2$$

The road clearing time at 248% snowpack water content will take **99.2** days.

19. D

Difficulty: Medium

Category: Line of Best Fit

Strategic Advice: Think about how the graphs of different equations look and eliminate the choices that don't match.

Getting to the Answer: Sketch in the lines of best fit for the answer choices. (A) and (D) are parabolas that open up, (B) is a parabola that opens down, and (C) is an exponential curve. The equation that needs to be modeled is $y = -ax^2 + bx - c$, which is quadratic and graphs as a parabola. Eliminate (C). Pay careful attention to the details "a and c are negative and b is positive." The coefficient in front of the x^2 term determines whether the parabola opens up or down. The negative sign in front of the a multiplies by the negative value for a to create a positive coefficient in front of the x^2 term, which means that the parabola opens up. Eliminate (B). Finally, the c coefficient in the equation determines the y-intercept for the graph. Again, the negative sign in front of c multiplies by the negative value for c to create a positive y-intercept. Eliminate (A) because the best-fit parabola has a negative y-intercept. **(D)** is correct.

20. C

Difficulty: Hard

Category: Scatterplot Modeling

Getting to the Answer: For every 20-minute interval, draw a line of best fit through the data for the actual number of customers and similarly for the estimated number of customers. Then compare the slopes of the lines of best fit for actual and estimated for each 20-minute interval to compare the rates of increase.

In the interval from 0 to 20 minutes, the slope of the line of best fit for the actual number of customers is slightly greater (steeper) than that of the estimated model. In the interval from 20 to 40 minutes, the slope of the line of best fit for the actual data is greater than that of the estimated data. In the interval from 40 to 60 minutes, the slope of the line of best fit for the actual data is less than that of the estimated data. Thus, **(C)** is correct.

Test Yourself: Data Analysis

1. As a car is used or ages, it loses part of its value. This loss in value is called depreciation. A certain car that costs $35,000 new immediately depreciates by $12,000 once it is driven off the lot. After that, for the first 50,000 miles, the car will depreciate approximately $0.15 per mile driven. For every mile after that, it will depreciate by $0.10 per mile driven until the car reaches its scrap value. How much would this car be worth after being driven 92,000 miles?

   A) $11,300
   B) $13,800
   C) $17,000
   D) $27,700

2. A general contractor is building an addition onto a home. He budgets 20 percent for materials, 55 percent for labor, 10 percent for equipment rental, and the rest is his fee. If the estimate the contractor gives to the homeowners says he will spend $5,200 on materials, then how much is his fee?

   A) $2,600
   B) $3,900
   C) $5,200
   D) $6,500

3. In extreme climates, temperatures can vary as much as 20° Celsius in a single day. How many degrees Fahrenheit can these climates vary if the relation between Fahrenheit degrees and Celsius degrees is given by the equation $F = \frac{9}{5}C + 32$?

   A) 20°F
   B) 36°F
   C) 62°F
   D) 68°F

4. An online movie subscription service charges a dollars for the first month of membership and b dollars per month after that. If a customer has paid $108.60 so far for the service, which of the following expressions represents the number of months this customer has subscribed to the service?

   A) $\dfrac{108.60}{a+b}$

   B) $\dfrac{108.60 - a}{b}$

   C) $\dfrac{108.60 - a - b}{b}$

   D) $\dfrac{108.60 - a + b}{b}$

5. A real estate agent uses what she calls a *step-strategy* to sell houses. She puts a house on the market at a higher-than-expected selling price and if it hasn't sold in two weeks, she drops the price by 5 percent. If it still hasn't sold in another 2 weeks, she drops the price by another 3 percent. After that, she continues to drop the price by 3 percent every two weeks until it reaches a cutoff amount assigned by the homeowner, or the house sells, whichever comes first. If a house is originally listed at $200,000 and the homeowner sets a cutoff amount of $184,000, what is the final selling price given that the house sells after being on the market for 5 weeks?

   A) $194,000
   B) $190,000
   C) $184,300
   D) $184,000

6. Mikal has a fish tank in his home with angelfish and catfish in a ratio of 5 to 2. He wants to put a tank in his office with 21 fish total, using the same ratio he has at home. How many catfish does he need for the tank in his office?

   A) 2

   B) 5

   C) 6

   D) 15

7. On a map, the scale is the ratio of the distance shown on the map to the actual distance. A geography teacher has a map on her wall with a scale of 1 inch:100 miles. She uses the school's copier to shrink the large wall map down to the size of a piece of paper to hand out to each of her students. To do this, she makes the map $\frac{1}{4}$ of its original size. Suppose on the students' maps, the distance between two cities is 2.5 inches. How many actual miles apart are those cities?

8. A bank offers a long-term savings account with a 1.0 percent annual interest rate. At the end of each year, the interest is added to the principal. If the initial deposit was $150, how much interest has the account earned at the end of 2 years? Round your answer to the nearest cent and ignore the dollar sign when gridding your answer.

Questions 9 and 10 refer to the following information.

Brian is starting a service project to tutor children in math. He already has five students and decides they can share a single textbook and that each student needs one notebook and four pencils. He records his supply budget in the table shown.

Supply Item	Total Number Needed	Individual Price per Item
Textbook	1	$25.00
Notebook	5	$3.25
Pencil	20	$0.35

9. The textbook makes up what percent of Brian's total supply budget? Round to the nearest tenth of a percent and ignore the percent sign when entering your answer.

10. Brian finds a sponsor who donates $350 for the supplies. Halfway through the year, he has tutored 15 students. If he always purchases the supplies for 5 students at one time, for how many more students can Brian purchase supplies with the remaining donated funds?

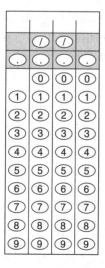

Questions 11 and 12 refer to the following information.

A restaurant offers a 20 percent discount to students and to members of the military. The restaurant is also currently participating in a charity drive. If patrons donate a gently used item of clothing, they get an additional 5 percent off their bill, which is applied before any other discounts, such as student or military discounts.

11. A student brings in an item of clothing and has a total bill, before any discounts, of $13.00. How much does she pay, after all applicable discounts, not including tax? (Ignore the dollar sign when gridding your response.)

12. Sharon is a member of the military. She dines with her friend, Damien. Damien brings an item of clothing, but Sharon forgot to bring one. If Sharon's meal is $16.25 before discounts and Damien's is $12.80 before discounts, how much did the discounts save them altogether? (Ignore the dollar sign when gridding your response.)

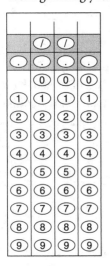

Questions 13 and 14 refer to the following information.

Jordan is beginning a marathon-training program. During his first day of training, he wears a pedometer to get an idea of how far he can currently run. At the end of the run, the pedometer indicates that he took 24,288 steps.

13. Jordan knows from experience that his average stride (step) is 2.5 feet. How many miles did he run on his first day of training? (1 mile = 5,280 feet)

14. If 1 kilometer equals approximately 0.62 miles, how many kilometers did Jordan run? Round your answer to the nearest tenth of a kilometer.

15. A shoe-manufacturing company is thinking about introducing a new product designed to help athletes jump higher. The company conducts a marketing study by asking people outside community gyms and sporting goods stores whether they would purchase such a product. Approximately 40 percent of 3,000 respondents said they would purchase these shoes over regular tennis shoes. Based on the study, the company concludes that 40 percent of shoe customers shopping for tennis shoes would purchase their new product. Which of the following is true about the shoe-manufacturing company's study?

A) The study was too small to draw any conclusions about the larger population.

B) The data from the survey does not represent the whole population because it was not conducted across the whole country.

C) The data from the survey likely underestimates the number of people interested in the new product because it compared the new product only to tennis shoes, not to all types of shoes.

D) The data from the survey likely overestimates the number of people interested in the new product because the survey targeted respondents already interested in athletics.

16. On a used vehicle lot, 50 percent of the vehicles are cars, $\frac{3}{4}$ of which have automatic transmissions. Of the cars with automatic transmissions, $\frac{1}{3}$ have leather interiors. If a vehicle is chosen from the lot at random, what is the probability that it will be a car with an automatic transmission and a leather interior?

A) $\frac{1}{8}$

B) $\frac{1}{6}$

C) $\frac{1}{4}$

D) $\frac{1}{3}$

Reduction of Debt Schedule

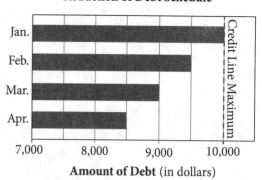

17. The graph above shows the amount of debt Charlize is currently carrying on her credit line each month. If she continues to pay down this debt at the same rate, how many months from when Charlize reached her credit line maximum will it take her to reach $2,500 in debt?

A) 8

B) 15

C) 20

D) 24

Quarterly Profits

	Branch A	Branch B	Branch C	Branch D
Q1	4.1	7.4	8.0	5.4
Q2	3.6	5.2	3.7	6.2
Q3	5.0	4.5	4.9	4.8
Q4	4.9	6.3	5.9	5.6
$\bar{x}$	4.4	5.85	5.625	5.5
s	0.67	1.27	1.82	0.58

18. A company affected by a downturn in the economy decided to close one of its four branches. The table shows each branch's quarterly profits in millions of dollars for 2009, along with the mean ($\bar{x}$) and the standard deviation (s) of the data. The accounting department recommended that the company's board of directors close either the store with the lowest average quarterly profits or the store that performed the least consistently. According to the data in the table, which branches did the accounting department recommend for closure to the board?

A) Branches A or C

B) Branches A or D

C) Branches B or C

D) Branches B or D

Questions 19 and 20 refer to the following information.

At most colleges, students receive letter grades, which correspond to a GPA score, rather than a numerical grade, such as 92. The following figure shows the distribution of grades and corresponding GPA scores among 84 students in a history class.

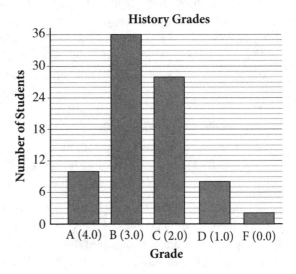

19. What is the approximate mean history GPA for this class of students?

A) 2.0

B) 2.5

C) 2.6

D) 3.0

20. If the professor wants to report that at least half of the grades were a 3.0 or above, which measure of center should she use to describe the results?

A) Mean

B) Range

C) Median

D) Standard deviation

Questions 21 and 22 refer to the following information.

The following table shows the number of houses in a development, categorized by type (single-family or townhouse) and by the number of bedrooms (Br).

Development Houses

	2 Br	3 Br	4 Br	Total
Single-Family	5	19	34	58
Townhouse	24	42	30	96
Total	29	61	64	154

21. In this development, families with children typically reside in single-family homes or townhouses that have 3 or more bedrooms. The local daycare center plans to distribute a flyer advertising its services to only those homes and townhouses. What percent of the houses in the development will receive the flyer? Round to the nearest whole percent and ignore the percent sign when entering your answer.

22. The daycare center decides to offer a free day of services to a family chosen at random from the homes that received a flyer. What is the probability that the family that wins the free day of services lives in a townhouse with 4 bedrooms?

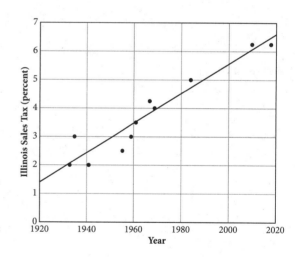

23. The scatterplot above shows the change in Illinois sales tax over the years. According to the line of best fit, which of the following is closest to the estimated yearly increase in sales tax, in percent?

A) 0.05

B) 0.5

C) 5

D) 50

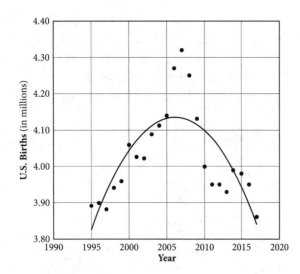

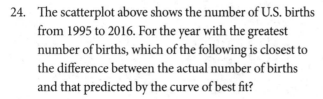

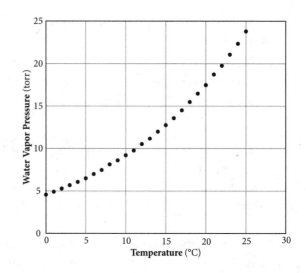

24. The scatterplot above shows the number of U.S. births from 1995 to 2016. For the year with the greatest number of births, which of the following is closest to the difference between the actual number of births and that predicted by the curve of best fit?

A) 0.05

B) 0.10

C) 0.18

D) 0.46

25. The scatterplot above shows the water vapor pressure in torr as a function of temperature in degrees Celsius. Which of the following statements is true about the relationship between water vapor pressure and temperature?

A) The water vapor pressure doubles when the temperature is halved.

B) The water vapor pressure doubles when the temperature is doubled.

C) The rate of increase of water vapor pressure every 5°C is greater at lower temperatures than at higher temperatures.

D) The rate of increase of water vapor pressure every 5°C is greater at higher temperatures than at lower temperatures.

Answers and Explanations

1.   A

Difficulty: Medium

Category: Proportions

Getting to the Answer: When a question involves several rates, break it into separate, manageable pieces and deal with each in turn. When the car is driven off the lot, it immediately loses \$12,000 in value, regardless of how far it is driven, so the after-purchase value is \$35,000 − \$12,000 = \$23,000. The first 50,000 miles reduce the car's value by \$0.15 each, or 50,000(−\$0.15) = −\$7,500. Now the car's value is \$23,000 − \$7,500 = \$15,500. Any miles driven over 50,000 reduce the value by \$0.10 per mile. The number of miles that the car is driven above 50,000 miles is 92,000 − 50,000 = 42,000 miles. This means the car depreciates another 42,000(−0.10) = −\$4,200. The value of the car after being driven 92,000 miles is \$15,500 − \$4,200 = \$11,300, which matches **(A)**.

2.   B

Difficulty: Medium

Category: Percents

Getting to the Answer: The percent of the budget spent on the contractor's fee is 100% − 20% − 55% − 10% = 15%. You're told that the estimate for materials is \$5,200, which represents 20% of the total budget. Let x be the total amount of the budget in dollars. Then 20% of x is \$5,200, or $0.2x = 5,200$. Solve this equation for x:

$$0.2x = 5,200$$
$$x = 26,000$$

The total budget is \$26,000. The contractor's fee represents 15% of this amount, or $0.15 \times \$26,000 = \$3,900$, which means **(B)** is correct. You could also set up the proportion $\frac{15\%}{20\%} = \frac{x}{5,200}$ and solve for x.

3.   B

Difficulty: Medium

Category: Unit Conversion

Getting to the Answer: The question says temperatures can vary by 20°C during a single day. This is not the same as saying the temperature itself is 20°C, so you can't just convert the temperature to Fahrenheit. You aren't given exact numbers, just a range, so you'll need to pick some convenient numbers to work with. You might know (or can tell from the formula) that 0°C is equal to 32°F. So pick 0°C and 20°C. Convert each of these to Fahrenheit and then find the difference:

$$F = \frac{9}{5}(C) + 32$$
$$F_{at\,0} = \frac{9}{5}(0) + 32$$
$$= 0 + 32$$
$$= 32$$
$$F_{at\,20} = \frac{9}{5}(20) + 32$$
$$= 36 + 32$$
$$= 68$$

Therefore, 0°C = 32°F and 20°C = 68°F, which means a change in temperature of 20°C is equivalent to a change of 68° − 32° = 36°F, which is **(B)**.

You could also recognize from the formula that Fahrenheit measurements are exactly $\frac{9}{5}$ of Celsius measurements, so you could multiply 20 by $\frac{9}{5}$ to arrive at 36 as well.

4. D

Difficulty: Hard

Category: Proportions

Getting to the Answer: The key to answering this question is accurate translation from English into math. Start by assigning a variable to what you're looking for. Let m be the number of months the customer has subscribed to the service. The first month costs a dollars and the remaining months $(m - 1)$ are charged at a rate of b dollars per month. So, the total charge for the subscription so far is $a + b(m - 1)$. Set this equal to the amount the customer has paid and solve for m. Note that you're not going to get a nice numerical answer, because the question doesn't give you the actual rates:

$$a + b(m - 1) = 108.60$$
$$a + bm - b = 108.60$$
$$bm = 108.60 - a + b$$
$$m = \frac{108.60 - a + b}{b}$$

The expression for m matches the one in **(D)**.

5. C

Difficulty: Hard

Category: Percents

Getting to the Answer: Draw a chart or diagram detailing the various price reductions for each two-week period.

Length of Time on Market	Percent of Most Recent Price	Resulting Price
List Price (0 weeks)	—	$200,000
After 2 Weeks	100% − 5% = 95%	$190,000
After 4 Weeks	100% − 3% = 97%	$184,300

You can stop here because the house was sold after 5 weeks and the next price reduction would have been at 6 weeks, so the selling price was $184,300, which is **(C)**. For the final calculation, make sure that you take 97% of the reduced price, $190,000, not of the original price.

6. C

Difficulty: Easy

Category: Proportions

Getting to the Answer: You need to find the number of catfish out of a total of 21 that will yield a 5:2 ratio of angelfish to catfish.

Add the parts of the given ratio together to get the total number of parts: $2 + 5 = 7$, so the total number of fish will always be a multiple of 7. Divide the total number of fish Mikal wants by 7 to find the multiple that he'll use for his office tank: $\frac{21}{7} = 3$. Multiply the original ratio by 3 to get the actual numbers of fish. The question asks for catfish, so $2(3) = 6$. **(C)** is correct.

7. 1000

Difficulty: Medium

Category: Proportions

Getting to the Answer: If the student map is $\frac{1}{4}$ the size of the wall map, then 2.5 inches on the student map would be $2.5 \times 4 = 10$ inches on the wall map. Set up a proportion to find the actual distance between the cities using the scale of the wall map:

$$\frac{1}{100} = \frac{10}{x}$$
$$x = 1,000$$

Grid in **1000**.

8.   3.02

Difficulty: Hard

Category: Percents

Getting to the Answer: This question is tricky. The interest is added to the account at the end of each year. The next year, the new, higher amount is the amount that will earn interest.

Start by multiplying the principal by the interest rate: $150 \times 0.01 = 1.50$. Now, add this amount back to the principal: $150 + 1.50 = 151.50$.

This is the amount that will earn interest in the next year. Repeat this process for the second year: $151.50 \times 0.01 = 1.515$, and $151.50 + 1.515 = 153.015$. Subtract the original amount to get the total amount of interest paid: $153.015 - 150.00 = 3.015$. As instructed, round to the nearest cent; **3.02** is correct.

You could also have used your calculator and the exponential growth function $f(5) = 150(1.01)^2$ to arrive at the answer more quickly.

9.   51.8

Difficulty: Medium

Category: Percents

Getting to the Answer: Use the three-part percent formula, $\text{Percent} = \dfrac{\text{part}}{\text{whole}} \times 100\%$. The *part* of the budget represented by the textbook is $25.00. You'll need to do some calculations to find the *whole*. The total cost of all the supplies (or the *whole*) is: 1 textbook ($25.00) + 5 notebooks ($5 \times \$3.25 = \$16.25$) + 20 pencils ($20 \times \$0.35 = \$7.00$) = $48.25. Now use the formula:

$$\text{Percent} = \frac{25}{48.25} \times 100\%$$
$$= 0.51813 \times 100\%$$
$$= 51.81\%$$

Before you grid in your answer, make sure you followed the directions—round to the nearest tenth of a percent and ignore the percent sign; grid in **51.8**.

10.   20

Difficulty: Hard

Category: Tables and Graphs

Getting to the Answer: This question contains several steps. Work carefully and keep your scratchwork neat and clear as you go.

Brian buys one set of materials for every 5 students, and he's had 15 students, so he has purchased $\frac{15}{5} = 3$ sets of materials. From the previous question, you know that a set of materials includes 1 textbook, 5 notebooks, and 20 pencils and costs $48.25, so he has spent $3 \times \$48.25 = \$144.75$. This means Brian has $350.00 - \$144.75 = \$205.25$ left. Divide the remaining money by the cost of each set of materials to find the number of sets he can buy: $\frac{\$205.25}{\$48.25} = 4.254$. Brian can only buy full sets, so ignore the decimal part. Each set can be used for 5 students, so with 4 sets of materials, Brian can tutor $4 \times 5 = 20$ more students. Grid in **20**.

11.   9.88

Difficulty: Easy

Category: Percents

Getting to the Answer: Make sure you read the question carefully. It says the 5% clothing discount is applied before any other discounts, so subtract this discount first.

The student receives a 5% discount for bringing in the item of clothing, which means she pays 95%, so don't waste time multiplying the amount of her check by 0.05 and then subtracting. Instead, just multiply the amount of her check by 0.95 to get $13.00 \times 0.95 = \$12.35$. Then, apply the student discount using the same strategy. The student discount is 20% (which means she paid 80%), so she paid $12.35 \times 0.8 = $**9.88**, not including tax. Grid in **9.88**.

12.   3.89

Difficulty: Medium

Category: Percents

Getting to the Answer: Calculate the discount for each person. Make sure you answer the right question. The question asks about the *savings*, not about what each person pays, so multiply by the discount amounts (either 20% or 5%). With her military discount, Sharon saved $16.25 \times 0.2 = \$3.25$. Damien's discount for participating

Math

in the clothing drive is $12.80 × 0.05 = $0.64. Add the two amounts to find that together they saved a total of $3.25 + $0.64 = **$3.89**. Grid in **3.89**.

13. 11.5

Difficulty: Medium

Category: Unit Conversion

Getting to the Answer: There are a lot of pieces, so use the units to set up a conversion into miles, which is what the question is asking for: the number of miles Jordan ran. Work backward to set up the unit conversion. You want to end up in miles, and you have a conversion between miles and feet. Still working backward, you have a conversion between feet and steps. You know the total number of steps Jordan took, so add the numbers and complete the calculation:

$$24{,}288 \text{ steps} \times \frac{2.5 \text{ ft}}{1 \text{ step}} \times \frac{1 \text{ mi}}{5{,}280 \text{ ft}} = 11.5 \text{ miles}$$

Grid in **11.5**.

14. 18.5

Difficulty: Easy

Category: Unit Conversion

Getting to the Answer: Use the information from your work on the previous question to answer this question quickly. You already know that Jordan ran 11.5 miles. You can use unit conversion again to convert from miles to kilometers, which is the unit you want the answer in:

$$11.5 \text{ miles} \times \frac{1 \text{ kilometer}}{0.62 \text{ miles}} \approx 18.54 \text{ kilometers}$$

The question tells you to round to the nearest tenth of a kilometer, so enter the answer as **18.5**.

15. D

Difficulty: Easy

Category: Surveys and Data Samples

Getting to the Answer: When considering the validity of a study, always look for possible sources of bias. In other words, look for things that might skew the results in either direction. Because the shoe is specifically targeted toward athletes, but is sold in regular shoe stores, conducting the survey outside gyms and sporting goods stores is likely to skew the results. The respondents

are already interested in athletics and so are likely to respond more positively than the average shoe customer. Therefore, the data from the survey likely overestimates the number of people interested in the new product, making **(D)** the correct answer.

16. A

Difficulty: Medium

Category: Probability

Getting to the Answer: Convert 50% to a fraction $\left(\frac{1}{2}\right)$ and then think logically—the final probability is $\frac{1}{3}$ of $\frac{3}{4}$ of $\frac{1}{2}$. When dealing with fractions, "of" means multiply. For example, one-half of 10 is 10 multiplied by the fraction one-half, or 5. So the probability of randomly choosing a vehicle that is a car with an automatic transmission and a leather interior is $\frac{1}{2} \times \frac{\cancel{3}}{4} \times \frac{1}{\cancel{3}} = \frac{1}{8}$.
(A) is correct.

17. B

Difficulty: Medium

Category: Proportions

Getting to the Answer: According to the graph, Charlize has been paying down her debt at a rate of $500 per month. To reach $2,500, she needs to pay off $10,000 − $2,500 = $7,500. The debt owed divided by the monthly payment will give the number of months needed to reach Charlize's goal: $\frac{\$7{,}500}{\$500} = 15$, making **(B)** the correct answer.

18. A

Difficulty: Medium

Category: Statistics

Getting to the Answer: The keywords in the question are *average* and *consistently*. The average is the mean, and consistency relates to how spread out each branch's profits are. First, find the branch with the lowest mean profit. With 4.4 million, branch A had the lowest mean profit, so eliminate choices (C) and (D). Standard deviation is a measure of spread, so now focus on that row only. Think about what standard deviation tells you. A lower standard deviation indicates that profits are less spread out and therefore more consistent. Likewise, a higher standard deviation indicates that profits are more spread out and therefore less consistent. Notice the inverse nature of this relationship: lower standard deviation = more consistent; higher standard deviation = less consistent. Choice **(A)** is correct because at 1.82, the standard deviation of branch C's quarterly profits was the highest, meaning that it performed the least consistently.

19. B

Difficulty: Easy

Category: Statistics

Getting to the Answer: The mean of a set of numbers is the same as the average, which is the sum of the numbers divided by the amount of numbers: $\text{Average} = \frac{\text{sum of values}}{\text{number of values}}$. Use the graph to find the sum of the GPA values, and then calculate the mean. Read the graph carefully—each grid line represents one student. There are 10 students who received a 4.0, 36 who received a 3.0, 28 with a 2.0, and 2 with a 1.0. You can save time by multiplying the frequency in each category by the GPA value. This calculation is called a weighted average. For example, instead of adding ten 4.0s together, just multiply 10 by 4. The sum of all the values, then, is $(10 \times 4) + (36 \times 3) + (28 \times 2) + (8 \times 1) + (2 \times 0) = 212$. Now, divide by the number of values, which is $10 + 36 + 28 + 2 = 84$: $\frac{212}{84} = 2.523$, or about 2.5, which is **(B)**.

20. C

Difficulty: Easy

Category: Statistics

Getting to the Answer: Eliminate (B) and (D) right away because range and standard deviation are measures of spread, not of center. Eliminate (A) because you calculated the mean in the previous question, and it was 2.5, which is less than 3.0. The median is the middle number of a set, so if you want to describe half of the grades above a certain point, the median is perfect since it divides the data into two parts. **(C)** is correct. While you wouldn't spend time to do this during the SAT, you can find the median by counting the number of data points that are either 4.0 and 3.0: $10 + 36 = 46$, which is more than half of 84, so the median is 3.0. **(C)** is indeed correct.

21. 81

Difficulty: Medium

Category: Percents

Getting to the Answer: There are 61 three-bedroom houses and 64 four-bedroom houses, so there are $61 + 64 = 125$ total houses in the development that have 3 or more bedrooms. There are 154 houses in all, which means that $\frac{125}{154} = 0.8117$, or approximately 81%, of all the houses should receive flyers. Grid in **81**.

22. 6/25 or .24

Difficulty: Medium

Category: Probability

Getting to the Answer:
$\text{Probability} = \frac{\text{number of desired outcomes}}{\text{number of possible outcomes}}$. The desired outcomes are the number of townhouses with 4 bedrooms, or 30. Use the information from the previous question that you already calculated: there are 125 houses that received flyers. Therefore, the probability that the winner is from a townhouse with 4 bedrooms is $\frac{30}{125} = \frac{6}{25}$. Grid in **6/25** or **0.24**.

23. A

Difficulty: Medium

Category: Line of Best Fit

Getting to the Answer: The estimated increase in sales tax every year is represented by the slope of the line of best fit. Recall that slope is equal to $\frac{y_2 - y_1}{x_2 - x_1}$. Estimate any two points on the line, for instance $(1920, 1.5)$ and $(1960, 3.5)$, to approximate the slope. The slope is about $\frac{3.5 - 1.5}{1960 - 1920} = \frac{2}{40} = 0.05$. The unit of the sales tax in the graph is percent, so no conversion is needed. **(A)** is correct.

24. C

Difficulty: Medium

Category: Line of Best Fit

Getting to the Answer: The year with the greatest number of births corresponds to the highest point on the scatterplot; this is the point for 2007, with a y-value of about 4.32. The number of births predicted by the curve of best fit for 2007 is approximately 4.14. Thus, the difference is approximately $4.32 - 4.14 = 0.18$. **(C)** is correct.

25. D

Difficulty: Medium

Category: Scatterplot Modeling

Getting to the Answer: The data in the scatterplot can be modeled with a concave up curve (such as quadratic or exponential), which has an increasing positive slope. To visualize this, for every 5°C interval, draw a line of best fit through the data. The slopes of the lines of best fit are steeper at the higher temperatures. Thus, at higher temperatures, the rate of increase of water vapor pressure every 5°C is greater than at lower temperatures. **(D)** is correct.

Passport to Advanced Math

CHAPTER 10

Functions

LEARNING OBJECTIVES

After completing this chapter, you will be able to:

- Apply function notation
- Define the domain and range of a function
- Evaluate the output of a function for a given input
- Interpret the graph of a function
- Write a function to describe a rule or data set

105/600 SmartPoints® (Very High Yield)

How Much Do You Know?

Directions: Try the questions that follow. Show your work so that you can compare your solutions to the ones found in the Check Your Work section immediately after this question set. The "Category" heading in the explanation for each question gives the title of the lesson that covers how to solve it. If you answered the question(s) for a given lesson correctly, and if your scratch-work looks like ours, you may be able to move quickly through that lesson. If you answered incorrectly or used a different approach, you may want to take your time on that lesson.

$$p(x) = 7x + 4$$
$$s(x) = 7 - p(x)$$

1. What is the value of $s(-1)$?

    A) -3

    B)   4

    C)   10

    D)   17

2. A function is defined by the equation 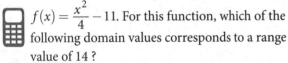 $f(x) = \dfrac{x^2}{4} - 11$. For this function, which of the following domain values corresponds to a range value of 14 ?

    A) -4

    B)   10

    C)   38

    D)   100

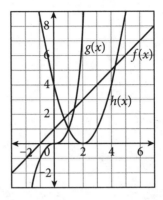

3. In the figure above, what is the value of $h(0) - 3(g(1) - f(2))$?

    A) -2

    B)   5

    C)   10

    D)   12

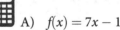

x	2	3	4	5
$f(x)$	7	13	19	25

4. Some values of the function f are shown in the table above. Which of the following defines f ?

    A) $f(x) = 7x - 1$

    B) $f(x) = 6x - 5$

    C) $f(x) = 5x + 1$

    D) $f(x) = 4x + 5$

5. Briana is writing a 60-page paper for a law school class. She estimates that she will average 45 words per minute while typing. If one page contains approximately 500 words, which of the following correctly estimates the number of pages, p, remaining as a function of the number of minutes, m, that Briana types?

A) $p(m) = 60 - \dfrac{9m}{100}$

B) $p(m) = \dfrac{60 - 100}{9m}$

C) $p(m) = 60 - \dfrac{100}{9m}$

D) $p(m) = \dfrac{60 - 9m}{100}$

Check Your Work

1. C

Difficulty: Medium

Category: Function Notation

Getting to the Answer: To evaluate a function at any value, substitute that value for the variable in the function definition. The question asks for the value of $s(-1)$, so replace the x in the s function with -1: $s(-1) = 7 - p(-1)$. To find the value of $p(-1)$, replace the x in the p function with -1: $p(-1) = 7(-1) + 4 = -3$. Replace $p(-1)$ with its value, -3, in the s function: $s(-1) = 7 - (-3) = 10$. **(C)** is correct.

2. B

Difficulty: Medium

Category: Function Notation

Getting to the Answer: In this question, you are given a range value (14), which means $f(x) = 14$, and you are asked for the corresponding domain value (x-value). This means you are solving for x, not substituting for x. Set the function equal to 14 and solve using inverse operations:

$$14 = \frac{x^2}{4} - 11$$
$$25 = \frac{x^2}{4}$$
$$100 = x^2$$
$$\pm 10 = x$$

Because -10 is not one of the answer choices, you know the answer is 10. **(B)** is correct.

3. C

Difficulty: Medium

Category: Graphs of Functions

Getting to the Answer: Start with $h(0)$, which means the y-value when $x = 0$. Based on the graph of the h function, $h(0) = 4$. Repeat with $g(1)$, which is 1, and $f(2)$, which is 3. Manipulate these values as instructed: $4 - 3(1 - 3) = 4 + 6 = 10$. Choice **(C)** is correct.

4. B

Difficulty: Easy

Category: Graphs of Functions

Getting to the Answer: Use one of the given points to test the functions. Choose the point that is easiest for you to test. When $x = 2$, $y = 7$, so plug $x = 2$ into the choices and find the one that yields $y = 7$.

Test (A): $f(2) = 7(2) - 1 = 13$. Eliminate (A).

Test (B): $f(2) = 6(2) - 5 = 7$. Keep (B).

Test (C): $f(2) = 5(2) + 1 = 11$. Eliminate (C).

Test (D): $f(2) = 4(2) + 5 = 13$. Eliminate (D).

Only **(B)** remains, and it is correct.

Since all the choices have different slopes, an alternative approach would be to find the slope of the line by using two points.

Use the formula Slope $= \frac{\text{rise}}{\text{run}}$ to get $\frac{13 - 7}{3 - 2} = 6$. **(B)** is correct.

5. A

Difficulty: Hard

Category: Describing Real-Life Situations with Functions

Getting to the Answer: Use the two given rates to determine Briana's typing rate in pages per minute. She types 45 words per minute, which becomes:

$$\frac{45 \text{ words}}{1 \text{ minute}} \times \frac{1 \text{ page}}{500 \text{ words}} = \frac{45 \text{ pages}}{500 \text{ minutes}} = \frac{9 \text{ pages}}{100 \text{ minutes}}$$

Multiplying this rate by m gets you the number of pages typed after m minutes, which can then be subtracted from the starting page count, 60, to get the number of pages Briana has left to type. The function should read $p(m) = 60 - \frac{9m}{100}$, which matches **(A)**.

Function Notation

LEARNING OBJECTIVES

After this lesson, you will be able to:

- Apply function notation
- Define the domain and range of a function
- Evaluate the output of a function for a given input

To answer a question like this:

$$h(x) = \frac{2x + 7}{x - 4}$$

Which of the following must be true about $h(x)$?

  I. $h(14) = 3.5$

  II. The domain of $h(x)$ is all real numbers

  III. $h(x)$ may be positive or negative

  A) I and II only

  B) I and III only

  C) II and III only

  D) I, II, and III

You need to know this:

A **function** is a rule that generates one unique output for a given input. In function notation, the x-value is the input and the y-value, designated by $f(x)$, is the output. (Note that other letters besides x and f may be used.)

For example, a linear function has the same form as the slope-intercept form of a line; $f(x)$ is equivalent to y:

$$f(x) = mx + b$$

In questions that describe real-life situations, the y-intercept will often be the starting point for the function. You can think of it as $f(0)$, or that value of the function where $x = 0$.

The set of all possible x-values is called the **domain** of the function, while the set of all possible y-values is called the **range**.

You need to do this:

- To find $f(x)$ for some value of x, substitute the concrete value in for the variable and do the arithmetic.
- For questions that ask about the domain of a function, check whether any inputs are not allowed, for example, because they cause division by 0.
- For questions that ask about a function of a function, for example, $g(f(x))$, start on the inside and work your way out.

Explanation:

Check each statement. For the first statement, plug in 14 for x:

$$\frac{2(14)+7}{14-4} = \frac{28+7}{10} = \frac{35}{10} = 3.5$$

So the first statement is true. Eliminate choice (C).

For the second statement, you need to determine the set of all permitted x-values for this function. Note that the function will be undefined at $x = 4$ (because at $x = 4$, the denominator would be 0). Thus, 4 is not a permitted x-value, and the domain is not all real numbers. The second statement is false. Eliminate (A) and (D).

By process of elimination, the answer is **(B)**, and on test day, you would stop here. For the record, here's why the third statement is true: you've already established that $h(x) = 3.5$ is a permitted value. If you plug in a smaller value, such as 0, you get: $h(0) = \dfrac{2(0)+7}{0-4} = \dfrac{7}{-4} = -\dfrac{7}{4}$, so $f(x)$ can be negative as well.

Try on Your Own

Directions: Take as much time as you need on these questions. Work carefully and methodically. There will be an opportunity for timed practice at the end of the chapter.

HINT: For Q1, replace every x in the function definition with -2.

---

1. If $g(x) = -2x^2 + 7x - 3$, what is the value of $g(-2)$?

   A) -25

   B) -9

   C) -1

   D) 3

2. If $k(x) = 5x + 2$, what is the value of $k(4) - k(1)$?

   A)   15

   B)   17

   C)   19

   D)   21

HINT: For Q3, work from the inside parentheses out.

---

x	$g(x)$
-6	-3
-3	-2
0	-1
3	0
6	1

x	$h(x)$
0	6
1	-4
2	2
3	0
4	-2

3. Several values for the functions $g(x)$ and $h(x)$ are shown in the tables above. What is the value of $g(h(3))$?

   A) -1

   B) 0

   C) 3

   D) 6

4. If $p(x) = x^2 - 4x + 8$ and $q(x) = x - 3$, what is the value of $\dfrac{q(p(5))}{p(q(5))}$?

   A)   0

   B)   0.4

   C)   1

   D)   2.5

n	$f(n)$	$g(n)$
2	11.6	1.5
3	13.9	1
4	16.2	0.5

5. The table above shows some values of the linear functions f and g. If $h(n) = 2 \times f(n) - g(n)$, what is the value of $h(6)$?

   A)   21.3

   B)   35.0

   C)   41.1

   D)   42.1

Graphs of Functions

LEARNING OBJECTIVE

After this lesson, you will be able to:

- Interpret the graph of a function

To answer a question like this:

x	$h(x)$
0	−3
1	−2
2	1
3	6
4	13
5	22
6	33

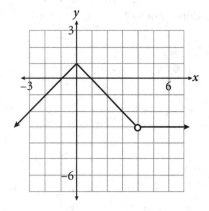

The maximum value of function g, whose graph is shown above, is m. Values for the function h are shown in the table. What is the value of $h(m)$?

A) −3

B) −2

C)   2

D)   4

You need to know this:

Interpreting graphs of functions is similar to interpreting graphs of equations. For example:

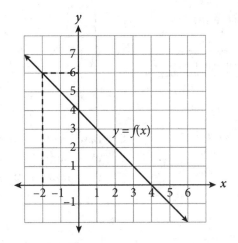

Say the graph above represents the function $f(x)$ and you're asked to find the value of x for which $f(x) = 6$. Because $f(x)$ represents the output value, or range, you can translate this to, "When does the y-value equal 6?" To answer the question, find 6 on the y-axis, then trace over to the function (the line). Read the corresponding x-value: it's -2, so when $f(x) = 6$, x must be -2.

The SAT may sometimes ask about a function's **maximum** or **minimum**. These terms mean the greatest and least value of the function, respectively. This graph of $f(x)$ does not have a maximum or minimum, as the arrows on the line indicate that it continues infinitely in both directions. The question above, however, does show a function with a maximum.

You need to do this:

- Treat $f(x)$ as the y-coordinate on a graph.
- Understand that the maximum and minimum refer to a function's greatest and least y-coordinates, respectively.

Explanation:

Start by identifying m, which occurs at the apex of the function at $(0, 1)$. The "maximum value of function g" means the greatest y-value, so $m = 1$. Next, use the table to find $h(1)$, which is the y-value when $x = 1$. According to the table, when $x = 1$, $h(x) = -2$. **(B)** is correct.

Math

Try on Your Own

Directions: Take as much time as you need on these questions. Work carefully and methodically. There will be an opportunity for timed practice at the end of the chapter.

HINT: For Q6, $p(x)$ means the y-value of the function at x.

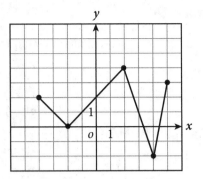

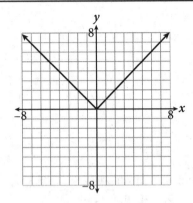

6. The above figure shows the function $p(x) = |x|$. Which statement about the function is NOT true?

   A) $p(0) = 0$

   B) $p(-4) = 4$

   C) $p(4) = -4$

   D) The domain of $p(x)$ is all real numbers.

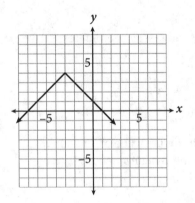

7. The graph of $f(x)$ is shown above. Which of the following represents the domain and range of the function?

   A) Domain: $f(x) \geq 4$; range: all real numbers

   B) Domain: $f(x) \leq 4$; range: all real numbers

   C) Domain: all real numbers; range: $f(x) \geq 4$

   D) Domain: all real numbers; range: $f(x) \leq 4$

8. Based on the above graph, if the coordinates of the maximum of $f(x)$ are (a, b) and the coordinates of the minimum of $f(x)$ are (c, d), what is the value of $a + b + c + d$?

9. The graph of the linear function *f* has intercepts at $(c, 0)$ and $(0, d)$ in the *xy*-plane. If $2c = d$ and $d \neq 0$, which of the following is true about the slope of the graph of *f*?

A) It is positive.

B) It is negative.

C) It equals zero.

D) It is undefined.

HINT: For Q10, which roman numeral statement appears the most often in the answer choices? What advantage would you have if you knew that statement was not part of the correct answer?

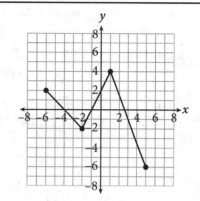

10. The complete graph of the function *f* is shown in the figure above. Which of the following is equal to -1 ?

   I. $f(-4)$

  II. $f(0)$

 III. $f(3)$

A) I and II

B) II only

C) I, II, and III

D) III only

Math

Describing Real-Life Situations with Functions

> **LEARNING OBJECTIVE**
>
> After this lesson, you will be able to:
>
> - Write a function to describe a rule or data set

To answer a question like this:

Type of Ingredient	Number of Cookies per Box	Profit per Box (dollars)
Walnuts	22	1.26
Pecans	20	1.10
Butterscotch	24	1.42
Mint	18	0.94
Macadamias	12	0.46
Hazelnuts	16	0.78

A certain cookie company sells several varieties of chocolate cookies, each with an added ingredient. The company sells the different varieties in differently sized boxes. The number of cookies per box and the profit per box for the different varieties are shown in the table above. The relationship between the number of cookies per box and the profit, in dollars, that the company makes per box can be represented by a linear function. Which of the following functions correctly represents the relationship?

A) $p(n) = 0.11n - 0.25$

B) $p(n) = 0.1n - 0.35$

C) $p(n) = 0.09n - 0.45$

D) $p(n) = 0.08n - 0.5$

You need to know this:

Modeling real-life situations using functions is the same as modeling them using equations; the only difference is the function notation and the rule that each input has only one output.

For example, suppose a homeowner wants to determine the cost of installing a certain amount of carpet in her living room. Say that the carpet costs \$0.86 per square foot, the installer charges a \$29 installation fee, and sales tax on the total cost is 7%. Using your algebra and function knowledge, you can describe this situation in which the cost, c, is a function of square footage, f. The equation would be $c = 1.07(0.86f + 29)$. In function notation, this becomes $c(f) = 1.07(0.86f + 29)$, where $c(f)$ is shorthand for "cost as a function of square footage." The following table summarizes what each piece of the function represents in the scenario.

English	Overall cost	Square footage	Material cost	Installation fee	Sales tax
Math	c	f	$0.86f$	29	1.07

You need to do this:

In word problems involving function notation, translate the math equations exactly as you learned in chapter 4 in the Word Problems lesson, but substitute $f(x)$ for y.

Explanation:

Note that the question asks for the relationship between the number of cookies per box and the profit per box and that the answer choices all start with $p(n)$. Given the context, this translates to the relationship "profit as a function of the number of cookies." All the choices express a linear relationship, so you can't rule out any of them on that basis.

There are several approaches you could take to find the correct answer. One would be to recognize that all the choices are in the form $p(n) = kn + b$ (a variation of the slope-intercept form $y = mx + b$) and that you can set up a system of linear equations using the data from any two rows of the table to solve for k and b. That approach would look like this:

$$1.26 = 22k + b$$
$$\underline{- \quad (1.10 = 20k + b)}$$
$$0.16 = 2k$$
$$0.08 = k$$

$$1.10 = 20(.08) + b$$
$$1.10 = 1.60 + b$$
$$b = -0.5$$

Because $k = 0.08$ and $b = -0.5$, the correct function is $p(n) = 0.08k - 0.5$, so **(D)** is correct.

Another approach would be to use two of the pairs of data points from the table to calculate a slope; for example, using the "pecans" and "macadamias" rows would yield $\frac{1.10 - 0.46}{20 - 12} = \frac{0.64}{8} = 0.08$. Because only one answer has a slope of 0.08, you can pick **(D)**.

Finally, you could backsolve. Plug any one of the rows of data from the table into all four answer choices. The second row has the easiest numbers to work with, so use those. You are checking which equation will produce a profit of $1.10 per box given 20 cookies per box:

A) $0.11(20) - 0.25 = 1.95 \neq 1.10$

B) $0.1(20) - 0.35 = 1.65 \neq 1.10$

C) $0.09(20) - 0.45 = 1.35 \neq 1.10$

D) $0.08(20) - 0.5 = 1.10$

Again, **(D)** is correct.

Try on Your Own

Directions: Take as much time as you need on these questions. Work carefully and methodically. There will be an opportunity for timed practice at the end of the chapter.

HINT: For Q11, pick the easiest number of days from the chart, plug that into the choices, and eliminate any that don't give you the correct vote count. Repeat if necessary until only one choice is left.

Day	Vote Count
3	21
4	35
5	53
6	75
7	101

11. Paulo is one of five contest finalists in the running for a year's worth of college book expenses. The winner is the finalist with the highest number of votes on the contest host's website. Paulo recorded his vote total each day of the contest; data for five days are in the table above. Which of the following represents Paulo's vote count, v, as a function of time, t, in days?

   A) $v(t) = 2t^2 + 3$

   B) $v(t) = \dfrac{t^2}{2} + 3$

   C) $v(t) = 2t^2 + 21$

   D) $v(t) = \dfrac{t^2}{2} + 21$

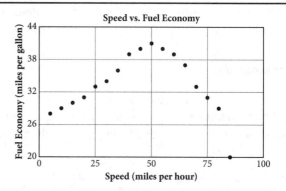

12. The graph above shows a compact car's fuel economy as a function of speed. Which of the following is true?

   A) The rate of increase in fuel economy below 50 miles per hour is greater than the rate of decrease in fuel economy above 50 miles per hour.

   B) The rate of increase in fuel economy below 50 miles per hour is equal to the rate of decrease in fuel economy above 50 miles per hour.

   C) The rate of increase in fuel economy below 50 miles per hour is less than the rate of decrease in fuel economy above 50 miles per hour.

   D) Fuel economy peaks at 50 miles per hour, but nothing can be said about the rates of change in fuel economy above and below 50 miles per hour.

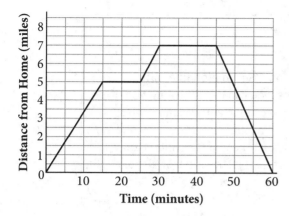

13. The graph above shows Carmel's distance from home over a one-hour period, during which time she first went to the library, then went to the grocery store, and then returned home. Which of the following statements must be true?

A) The grocery store is about 5 miles from Carmel's house.

B) Carmel traveled a total of 7 miles from the time she left home until she returned.

C) The grocery store is 7 miles farther from Carmel's house than the library is.

D) Carmel spent 10 minutes at the library and 15 minutes at the grocery store.

HINT: For Q14, which two readings will be easiest to use to find the number of visitors admitted every 15 minutes?

Time	Total Number of Visitors for the Day
10:10 a.m.	140
12:30 p.m.	420
2:00 p.m.	600
2:50 p.m.	700

14. The entrance gates at a museum allow a constant number of visitors to enter every 15 minutes. A supervisor records the cumulative number of visitors for the day at various times as shown in the table above. The museum does not admit any visitors after 4:45 p.m. What is the projected total number of visitors for the day, assuming that the same number of visitors are granted entrance each 15-minute period throughout the day?

A) 810

B) 895

C) 930

D) 960

Math

On Test Day

The SAT likes to test the modeling of real-life situations. Get comfortable with function notation in these questions. Remember that you can write the equation of a line as $y = mx + b$ or as $f(x) = mx + b$, where m is the slope and b is the y-intercept. Both mean the same thing. In the formula using function notation, the slope indicates rate of change. Often, in questions asking about real-life situations, the x variable indicates time. In that case, the y-intercept (that is, the value of the function at $x = 0$, or $f(0)$) indicates the starting point.

15. An environmental agency is working to reduce the amount of plastic that a community discards in the ocean. Currently, the community discards 6.2 million pounds of plastic annually, and the agency's goal is to eliminate that amount by collecting and recycling the plastic. If the agency increases its collection and recycling capacity at a constant rate, and meets its goal at the end of the eighth year, which of the following linear functions, f, could the agency use to model the amount of plastic being added to the ocean t years into the program?

   A) $f(t) = -\dfrac{62}{40}t + 6.2$

   B) $f(t) = -\dfrac{31}{40}t + 6.2$

   C) $f(t) = \dfrac{31}{40}t + 6.2$

   D) $f(t) = \dfrac{62}{40}t + 6.2$

The correct answer and explanation can be found at the end of the chapter.

How Much Have You Learned?

Directions: For testlike practice, give yourself 15 minutes to complete this question set. Be sure to study the explanations, even for questions you got right. They can be found at the end of this chapter.

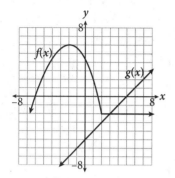

16. Based on the figure above, what is the value of $f(-2) + g(2)$?

    A) −3

    B) 0

    C) 3

    D) 6

17. A company uses the function $P(x) = 150x - x^2$ to determine how much profit the company will make when it sells 150 units of a certain product that sells for x dollars per unit. How much more profit per unit, in dollars, will the company make if it charges $25 for the product than if it charges $20? (Ignore the dollar sign when gridding your response.)

18. The customer service department of a wireless cellular provider has found that on Wednesdays, the polynomial function $C(t) = -0.0815t^4 + t^3 + 12t$ approximates the number of calls received by any given time, where t represents the number of hours that have passed during the workday. Based on this function, how many calls can be expected by the end of one 10-hour workday?

19. A biologist is studying the effect of pollution on the reproduction of a specific plant. She uses the function $n(p)$ to represent these effects, where p is the number of seeds germinated by the test group of the plant over a given period of time. Which of the following lists could represent a portion of the domain for the biologist's function?

    A) $\{\ldots -150, -100, -50, 0, 50, 100, 150 \ldots\}$

    B) $\{-150, -100, -50, 0, 50, 100, 150\}$

    C) $\{0, 0.25, 0.5, 0.75, 1, 1.25, 1.5 \ldots\}$

    D) $\{0, 20, 40, 60, 80 \ldots\}$

20. If $f(x) = 3 - x$ and $g(x) = \dfrac{x^2}{2}$, which of the following is NOT in the range of $f(g(x))$?

A) -3

B) 0

C) 2

D) 4

$$g(x) = -3x - 5$$

21. The function g is defined above. What is the value of $g(-4x)$?

A) 7

B) $-12x - 5$

C) $12x - 5$

D) $12x^2 - 20x$

$$r(x) = 3x - 7$$
$$t(x) = 3x + r(x)$$

22. The functions r and t are defined above. What is the value of $t(2)$?

A) -3

B) -1

C) 0

D) 5

$$f(x) = ax^2 + 3x + 5$$

23. The function f is defined above, and $f(3) = -4$. If a is a constant, what is the value of $f(2)$?

A) -2

B) 3

C) 5

D) 19

24. A function a satisfies $a(-2) = 3$ and $a(3) = 8$. A function b satisfies $b(3) = 4$ and $b(7) = -2$. What is the value of $a(b(7))$?

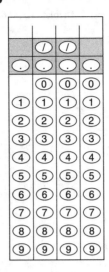

25. The function f, shown in the graph above, is defined for $-7 \le x \le 7$. For which of the following values of x does $f(x) = 4$?

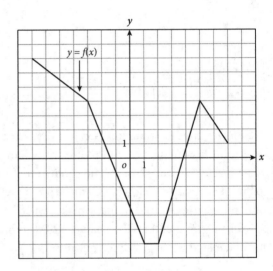

I. -4

II. -3

III. 5

A) III only

B) I and II only

C) II and III only

D) I, II, and III

Reflect

Directions: Take a few minutes to recall what you've learned and what you've been practicing in this chapter. Consider the following questions, jot down your best answer for each one, and then compare your reflections to the expert responses on the following page. Use your level of confidence to determine what to do next.

What are the domain and range of a function?

_____

_____

_____

What is another way to write the function $f(x) = x + 4$?

_____

_____

_____

In the same function, what does x represent? What does $f(x)$ represent?

_____

_____

_____

What will the function look like when graphed?

_____

_____

_____

In a function whose x-value represents time, what does the y-intercept represent?

_____

_____

_____

Expert Responses

What are the domain and range of a function?

The domain of a function indicates the possible x-values and the range of a function indicates the possible y-values. For example, in the function $f(x) = x^2$, *the domain is all real numbers because any number can be squared, and the range is any number greater than or equal to 0, because* x^2 *can't be negative.*

What is another way to write the function $f(x) = x + 4$?

When you graph the function on the xy-coordinate plane, you can replace $f(x)$ *with y. This function is equivalent to* $y = x + 4$.

In the same function, what does x represent? What does $f(x)$ represent?

In this function, x *is the input and* $f(x)$ *is the output.*

What will the function look like when graphed?

The slope of the line is 1 and its y-intercept is 4, so it will move from the lower left to the upper right and cross the y-axis at $y = 4$.

In a function whose *x*-value represents time, what does the *y*-intercept represent?

The y-intercept represents the initial quantity when $t = 0$. *Say a function represents the progress of a machine manufacturing widgets at a rate of 6 widgets per hour. The machine adds the widgets it makes to a growing pile that consisted of 12 widgets when the machine started working. If this function were graphed as a function of time, the y-intercept would be 12—the pile of 12 widgets that were there when the machine started its task.*

Next Steps

If you answered most questions correctly in the "How Much Have You Learned?" section, and if your responses to the Reflect questions were similar to those of the SAT expert, then consider functions an area of strength and move on to the next chapter. Come back to this topic periodically to prevent yourself from getting rusty.

If you don't yet feel confident, review those parts of this chapter that you have not yet mastered. All three lessons in this chapter cover question types that are fairly common on the SAT, and it is to your advantage to have a firm grasp on this material, so go back over it until you feel more confident. Then try the questions you missed again. As always, be sure to review the explanations closely. Finally, **go online** (www.kaptest.com/moreonline) for additional practice on the highest yield topics in this chapter.

Answers and Explanations

1. A

Difficulty: Easy

Getting to the Answer: The notation $g(-2)$ is asking for the value of $g(x)$ when x is -2, so substitute -2 for x and simplify. Don't forget to use the correct order of operations as you work:

$$g(-2) = -2(-2)^2 + 7(-2) - 3$$
$$= -2(4) + (-14) - 3$$
$$= -8 - 14 - 3$$
$$= -25$$

(A) is correct.

2. A

Difficulty: Easy

Getting to the Answer: The notation $k(4)$ is equivalent to the output value of the function when 4 is substituted for the input x, and $k(1)$ is the output value of the function when 1 is substituted for the input x. Substitute 4 and 1 into the function, one at a time, and then subtract the results:

$$k(4) = 5(4) + 2 = 20 + 2 = 22$$
$$k(1) = 5(1) + 2 = 5 + 2 = 7$$
$$k(4) - k(1) = 22 - 7 = 15$$

Choice **(A)** is correct. Caution—subtracting 1 from 4 and then substituting 3 into the function will give a different and incorrect result.

3. A

Difficulty: Medium

Getting to the Answer: The notation $g(h(x))$ can be read "g of h of x." It means that the output when x is substituted in $h(x)$ becomes the input for $g(x)$. First, use the table on the right to find that $h(3)$ is 0. This is your new input. Now, use the table on the left to find $g(0)$, which is -1, making **(A)** the correct answer.

4. D

Difficulty: Medium

Getting to the Answer: Evaluate the numerator and denominator separately:

$$p(5) = 5^2 - 4(5) + 8 = 13$$
$$q(p(5)) = q(13) = 13 - 3 = 10$$
$$q(5) = 5 - 3 = 2$$
$$p(q(5)) = p(2) = 2^2 - 4(2) + 8 = 4$$

Next, combine to get $\dfrac{q(p(5))}{p(q(5))} = \dfrac{10}{4} = 2.5$. The correct answer is **(D)**.

5. D

Difficulty: Hard

Getting to the Answer: Determine the linear change of the functions relative to the change in n, then extrapolate to get the values of $f(6)$ and $g(6)$. You don't need to determine the actual expressions for the functions. As a shortcut, find the changes per 2 unit increase of n and apply that to the values of the functions when $n = 4$. For $f(n)$, the increase from $n = 2$ to $n = 4$ is $16.2 - 11.6 = 4.6$. Thus, the value of $f(6)$ is $f(4) + 4.6 = 16.2 + 4.6 = 20.8$. The change in $g(n)$ for $n = 2$ to $n = 4$ is $0.5 - 1.5 = -1$. So the value of $g(6)$ is $g(4) + (-1) = 0.5 - 1 = -0.5$. Now, calculate $h(6)$: $h(6) = 2 \times f(6) - g(6) = 2(20.8) - (-0.5) = 41.6 + 0.5 = 42.1$. **(D)** is correct.

6. C

Difficulty: Easy

Getting to the Answer: The function graphed is the absolute value function, and all of the values in its range (the y-values) are positive. That makes any negative value as an output impossible. Because you're looking for the statement that is *not* true, **(C)** is correct.

7.   D

Difficulty: Easy

Getting to the Answer: To determine the domain, look at the x-values. To determine the range, look at the y-values. For the domain, the graph is continuous (no holes or gaps in the graph) and has arrows on both sides, so the domain is all real numbers. This means you can eliminate (A) and (B). For the range, the function's maximum (the vertex) is located at $(-3, 4)$, which means that the greatest possible y-value of $f(x)$ is 4. The graph is continuous and opens downward, so the range of the function is $y \leq 4$, which is the same as $f(x) \leq 4$, making **(D)** correct.

8.   8

Difficulty: Medium

Getting to the Answer: The maximum of $f(x)$ occurs at the point where the y-value is the greatest, which in this case is $(2, 4)$. So, $a = 2$ and $b = 4$. The point with the smallest y-value is $(4, -2)$. Thus, $c = 4$ and $d = -2$. The total of the four values is $2 + 4 + 4 + (-2) = 8$. Grid in **8**.

9.   B

Difficulty: Medium

Strategic Advice: Quickly sketching the different possibilities can be helpful.

Getting to the Answer: Because $2c = d$, both the x-intercept, c, and the y-intercept, d, must have the same sign. If both are positive, then d would be greater than c, and the graph of f would look something like this:

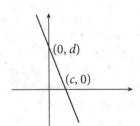

This is all you need to do to solve the question. According to the choices, the slope is always the same regardless of the sign of c and d. In other words, if the slope is negative at one point, then it must be negative all the time. Therefore, **(B)** is correct. On test day, you would move on to the next question without needing to

check what the line looks like when c and d are negative. For the record, if c and d are negative, then d will be less than c, and the graph would look like this:

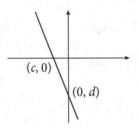

If you're curious to see the algebra, plug $(0, d)$ and $(c, 0)$ into the slope formula:

$$m = \frac{y_2 - y_1}{x_2 - x_1} = \frac{d - 0}{0 - c} = -\frac{d}{c}$$

The question states that $d = 2c$, so sub in $2c$ for d:

$$-\frac{d}{c} = -\frac{(2c)}{c} = -2$$

Therefore, the slope is -2, and the answer is indeed **(B)**.

10.   D

Difficulty: Easy

Strategic Advice: Save time on questions with roman numerals in the choices by testing the roman numeral that appears most often in the choices first. Here, check statement II first because it appears in three of the four choices.

Getting to the Answer: Plug each of the x-values into the function and see which produces a y-value of -1. Statement II is $f(0)$. When $x = 0$, the function's y-value is 2. Statement II is not equal to -1, so any answer choices that include statement II are incorrect. Eliminate (A), (B), and (C). Only **(D)** is left and is correct. On test day, you would stop here and move on to the next question. For the record, statement I is $f(-4) = 0$ and statement III is $f(3) = -1$. Also note that there are two other places where the function's output is -1: $f(-3)$ and $f(-1.5)$, neither of which is an answer choice.

11. A

Difficulty: Medium

Getting to the Answer: Thinking about the *y*-intercept (the starting amount) for the function will reduce the amount of work you need to do. The table indicates that Paulo had 21 votes on day 3, when $t = 3$, not at the start of the contest, when $t = 0$. This means that (C) and (D) are incorrect. To evaluate the remaining answer choices, pick a point, try it in a function, and if it works, then you've found the correct answer. If it doesn't work, then you can confidently select the other answer choice without any further work:

$$(A): 35 = 2(4)^2 + 3$$
$$35 = 2(16) + 3$$
$$35 = 32 + 3$$
$$35 = 35$$

(A) is correct. On test day, you would stop here. For the record, here is the reason (B) is incorrect:

$$(B): 35 = \frac{1}{2}(4)^2 + 3$$
$$35 = \frac{1}{2}(16) + 3$$
$$35 = 8 + 3$$
$$35 \neq 11$$

12. C

Difficulty: Medium

Getting to the Answer: Examine the graph and look for trends in the rate of increase and decrease of fuel economy before and after 50 mph. Note the increase below 50 mph (to the left of 50 on the horizontal axis) and the decrease above 50 mph (to the right of 50): the decreasing part of the graph is steeper than the increasing part. In other words, the rate of increase below 50 mph is less than the rate of increase above 50 mph. Choice **(C)** is correct.

13. D

Difficulty: Medium

Getting to the Answer: Compare each answer choice to the graph, eliminating false statements as you go.

(A): Carmel went to the library first, so the library (not the grocery store) is about 5 miles from her home. Eliminate (A).

(B): Carmel traveled 7 miles away from her home (between $t = 0$ minutes and $t = 30$ minutes), but then also traveled 7 miles back (between $t = 45$ minutes and $t = 60$ minutes), so she traveled a total of 14 miles. Eliminate (B).

(C): When Carmel reached the library, she was 5 miles from home; when she reached the grocery store, she was 7 miles from home. This means the grocery store must be $7 - 5 = 2$ miles farther away. Eliminate (C).

(D) must be correct. Carmel is the same distance from home (5 miles) between $t = 15$ minutes and $t = 25$ minutes, so she spent 10 minutes at the library. She is stopped once again (at the grocery store) between $t = 30$ minutes and $t = 45$ minutes, so she spent 15 minutes at the grocery store.

14. C

Difficulty: Medium

Strategic Advice: The fact that the number of visitors each 15 minutes is constant means that the cumulative number of visitors is a linear function.

Getting to the Answer: Because the time between the numbers of cumulative visitors in the table varies, pick an interval that is easy to work with to determine the number of visitors who enter every 15 minutes. Next, use that value to find how many entered by 4:45 p.m. There are six 15-minute periods between 12:30 p.m. and 2:00 p.m. The number of visitors admitted during that time was $600 - 420 = 180$. So, $\frac{180}{6} = 30$ visitors enter every 15 minutes.

In order to project the cumulative, or total, number of visitors for a specific time, set up a function, $f(v)$. Pick a time that is convenient, such as 2:00 p.m. Since you know that there were 600 visitors by 2:00 p.m. you can write $f(v) = 600 + 30v$, where v is the number of 15-minute periods after 2:00 p.m. The question asks for the cumulative visitors admitted by 4:45 p.m. Thus, v is the number of 15-minute periods between 2:00 and 4:45, which is 11. So, $f(11) = 600 + 30(11) = 930$. **(C)** is correct.

15. B

Difficulty: Medium

Strategic Advice: When modeling a real-life situation with a linear function, the starting point in the description is the y-intercept of the equation and the rate of change is the slope. Eliminate choices as you go; you may find that you are able to answer the question after only one or two steps. Never do more math than necessary to answer the question.

Getting to the Answer: In this question, the agency is reducing the amount of plastic disposed annually, so the slope must be negative. Eliminate (C) and (D) because their positive slopes indicate an *increasing* function.

The starting point, or y-intercept, is the amount of plastic the community is now discarding, or 6.2 million pounds. Unfortunately, this value is the same in (A) and (B), so you will need to find the slope.

The agency wants to eliminate the total amount of plastic in 8 years, so to find the amount of reduction per year, divide 6.2 by 8.

Because $-\dfrac{6.2}{8}$ does not appear in the choices, and the slopes in the choices do not have decimal points, multiply the fraction by 1 in the form of $\dfrac{10}{10}$ to get $-\dfrac{6.2}{8} \times \dfrac{10}{10} = -\dfrac{62}{80} = -\dfrac{31}{40}$. Choice **(B)** is correct.

16. C

Difficulty: Medium

Category: Graphs of Functions

Getting to the Answer: Graphically, the notation $f(-2)$ means the y-value when x is -2. Pay careful attention to which graph is which. It may help to draw dots on the graph. Find $x = -2$ along the horizontal axis, trace up to the graph of $f(x)$, and draw a dot on the graph. Do the same for $g(2)$, as shown here:

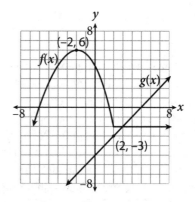

Now, read the y-coordinates from the graph and add: $f(-2)$ is 6 and $g(2)$ is -3, so $f(-2) + g(2) = 6 + (-3) = 3$, which is **(C)**.

17. 3.5 or 3.50

Difficulty: Medium

Category: Describing Real-Life Situations with Functions

Getting to the Answer: Start by evaluating the function at $x = 25$ and at $x = 20$. Make sure you follow the correct order of operations as you simplify:

$$P(25) = 150(25) - (25)^2$$
$$= 3{,}750 - 625$$
$$= 3{,}125$$
$$P(20) = 150(20) - (20)^2$$
$$= 3{,}000 - 400$$
$$= 2{,}600$$

The question asks how much more profit *per unit* the company makes, so find the difference in the amounts of profit and divide by the number of units (150) to get $\dfrac{3{,}125 - 2{,}600}{150} = \dfrac{525}{150} = \$3.50$. Grid in **3.5**.

18. 305

Difficulty: Easy

Category: Describing Real-Life Situations with Functions

Getting to the Answer: At the end of one workday, 10 hours have passed, so evaluate the function at $t = 10$. Make sure you follow the correct order of operations as you simplify:

$$C(t) = -0.0815t^4 + t^3 + 12t$$
$$C(10) = -0.0815(10)^4 + 10^3 + 12(10)$$
$$= -0.0815(10,000) + 1,000 + 120$$
$$= -815 + 1,000 + 120$$
$$= 305$$

Grid in **305**.

19. D

Difficulty: Easy

Category: Describing Real-Life Situations with Functions

Getting to the Answer: The domain of a function includes every possible input value, which is usually represented by x. In this function, instead of x, the input is represented by p, which is the number of seeds germinated by the plants over a given period of time. Because there cannot be a negative number of seeds germinated or a fraction of a seed germinated, the list in **(D)** is the only one that could represent a portion of the function's domain.

20. D

Difficulty: Hard

Category: Graphs of Functions

Getting to the Answer: When working with a composition (also called nested functions), the range of the inner function becomes the domain of the outer function, which in turn produces the range of the composition. In the composition $f(g(x))$, the function $g(x) = \frac{x^2}{2}$ is the inner function. Every value of x, when substituted into this function, will result in a nonnegative value because the result of squaring a number is always a positive number. This means the smallest possible range value of $g(x)$ is 0. If you don't see this relationship, try plugging in various values for x and look for a pattern. Now look at $f(x)$. Substituting large positive values of x in the function will result in

large negative numbers. Consequently, substituting the smallest value from the range of g, which is 0, results in the largest range value for the composition, which is $3 - 0 = 3$. Therefore, 4 is not in the range of $f(g(x))$. **(D)** is correct.

21. C

Difficulty: Medium

Category: Function Notation

Getting to the Answer: To evaluate a function at a particular value, replace the variable in the function with the value. In this question, replace x in the function definition with $-4x$ to get $g(-4x) = -3(-4x) - 5 = 12x - 5$. **(C)** is correct.

Note that you can replace one variable with another. In this question, $-4x$ replaces x. If you chose (A), you likely replaced x in the function definition with -4. If you chose (B), you may have "lost" a negative sign. Finally, (D) results if you multiply each term in the definition by $-4x$ instead of replacing x with $-4x$.

22. D

Difficulty: Medium

Category: Function Notation

Getting to the Answer: To evaluate the value of a function, replace the variable in the definition with the given value. Since the question asks for $t(2)$, and the definition of the t function includes the r function, evaluate $r(2)$ first, then use that result to evaluate $t(2)$:

$$r(2) = 3(2) - 7 = 6 - 7 = -1$$

Because $t(2) = 3(2) + r(2) = 6 - 1 = 5$, **(D)** is correct.

23. B

Difficulty: Medium

Category: Function Notation

Getting to the Answer: To evaluate a function for a particular value, substitute the value for the variable in the function. In this case, substitute 3 for x and then use the given value for $f(3)$ to solve for the value of a:

$$f(3) = a(3)^2 + 3(3) + 5$$
$$-4 = 9a + 9 + 5$$
$$-4 = 9a + 14$$
$$-18 = 9a$$
$$-2 = a$$

Next, use the known value of a to find $f(2)$:

$$f(2) = -2(2)^2 + 3(2) + 5$$
$$f(2) = -2(4) + 6 + 5$$
$$f(2) = -8 + 11$$
$$f(2) = 3$$

(B) is correct.

24. 3

Difficulty: Medium

Category: Function Notation

Getting to the Answer: To evaluate a composite function (a set of nested functions), start with the innermost function and work outward. For this question, begin by evaluating $b(7)$. Because $b(7) = -2$, you know that $a(b(7)) = a(-2)$, so next, evaluate $a(-2)$. The question tells you that $a(-2) = 3$. Grid in **3**.

25. C

Difficulty: Easy

Category: Graphs of Functions

Getting to the Answer: The term $f(x)$ is equivalent to the y-value of the function at x. So this question is asking, "Which values of x produce a y-value of 4?" Draw a horizontal line at the point $y = 4$ and identify where that line intercepts the function. The two points of intersection are -3 and 5. **(C)** is correct.

CHAPTER 11

Exponents, Radicals, Polynomials, and Rational Expressions

LEARNING OBJECTIVES

After completing this chapter, you will be able to:

- Apply exponent rules
- Apply radical rules
- Add, subtract, multiply, and factor polynomials
- Divide polynomials
- Define root, solution, zero, and *x*-intercept and identify them on the graph of a nonlinear function
- Determine whether the growth or decay described in a question is linear or exponential
- Apply the linear and exponential equations to answer growth and decay questions
- Simplify rational expressions
- Isolate a variable in a rational equation

25/600 SmartPoints® (Medium Yield)

Math

How Much Do You Know?

Directions: Try the questions that follow. Show your work so that you can compare your solutions to the ones found in the Check Your Work section immediately after this question set. The "Category" heading in the explanation for each question gives the title of the lesson that covers how to solve it. If you answered the question(s) for a given lesson correctly, and if your scratchwork looks like ours, you may be able to move quickly through that lesson. If you answered incorrectly or used a different approach, you may want to take your time on that lesson.

1. Which expression is equivalent to $2(-4\,j^3k^{-4})^{-3}$?

   A) $-\dfrac{k^{12}}{512\,j^9}$

   B) $-\dfrac{k^{12}}{32\,j^9}$

   C) $-\dfrac{j^9}{32k^{12}}$

   D) $-\dfrac{k^{12}}{128\,j^9}$

$$T = 2\pi\sqrt{\dfrac{L}{g}}$$

2. The formula above was created by Italian scientist Galileo Galilei in the early 1600s to demonstrate that the time it takes for a pendulum to complete a swing—called its period, T—can be found using only the length of the pendulum, L, and the force of gravity, g. He proved that the mass of the pendulum did not affect its period. Based on the equation above, which of the following equations could be used to find the length of the pendulum given its period?

   A) $L = \dfrac{gT}{2\pi}$

   B) $L = \dfrac{gT^2}{4\pi^2}$

   C) $L = \dfrac{T^2}{4\pi^2 g}$

   D) $L = \dfrac{g}{4\pi^2 T^2}$

3. Which of the following represents $\dfrac{\sqrt[6]{x^{10}y^{12}}}{\sqrt[3]{x^5 y^6}}$ written in simplest form, given that $x > 0$ and $y > 0$?

   A) 1

   B) 2

   C) $x^2 y^3 \sqrt{x}$

   D) $xy^2 \sqrt[3]{x^2}$

4. What is the result when $4x^3 - 5x^2 + x - 3$ is divided by $x - 2$?

   A) $4x + 3 + \dfrac{11}{x - 2}$

   B) $4x^2 + 3x - 6$

   C) $4x^2 + 3x + 18$

   D) $4x^2 + 3x + 7 + \dfrac{11}{x - 2}$

5. The function f is a parabolic function that intersects the x-axis. Which of the following statements must be true?

   A) The function has at least one real root.

   B) The function has no real roots.

   C) The function intersects the positive y-axis.

   D) The function has two zeros.

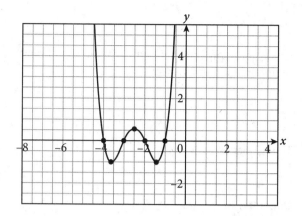

Age (months)	Height (centimeters)
15	80
18	82.5
21	85
24	87.5
27	90

6. The function $f(x) = (x + 1)(x + 2)(x + 3)(x + 4)$ is graphed above. If k is a constant such that $g(x) = k$ and the system of functions f and g have exactly two real solutions, which of the following could be a value of k?

   A) -2

   B) 0

   C) 0.5

   D) 1

7. In the equation $ax^4 + bx^3 + cx^2 - dx = 0$, a, b, c, and d are constants. If the equation crosses the x-axis at 0, -2, 3, and 5, which of the following is a factor of $ax^4 + bx^3 + cx^2 - dx$?

   A) $x - 2$

   B) $x + 3$

   C) $x - 5$

   D) $x + 5$

8. The growth of a young child is given in the chart above. If t represents the number of months after 15 and $f(t)$ represents the child's height, which of the following equations is the best model for the data in the age range shown?

   A) $f(t) = 80t + 3$

   B) $f(t) = \dfrac{5}{6}t + 80$

   C) $f(t) = 80\left(\dfrac{5}{6}\right)^t$

   D) $f(t) = \dfrac{5}{6}(80)^t$

$$\frac{8x}{3(x-5)} + \frac{2x}{3x-15} = \frac{50}{3(x-5)}$$

9. What value(s) of x satisfy the equation above?

   A) 0

   B) 5

   C) No solution

   D) Any value such that $x \neq 5$

10. If $\dfrac{6}{2x-3} + 6a = \dfrac{10}{2x-3} + 4b$ and $3a - 2b = 2$, what is the value of x?

   A) $\dfrac{1}{2}$

   B) 2

   C) No solution

   D) The value cannot be determined from the information given.

Math

Check Your Work

1. B

Difficulty: Easy

Category: Exponents

Getting to the Answer: Move the expression in parentheses to the denominator to make the sign of the exponent outside positive; do not change the signs of the exponents inside the parentheses. Next, distribute the exponent as usual. Divide the 2 into -64, and move k^{-12} back to the numerator and change the sign of its exponent. Work for these steps is shown below:

$$2\left(-4j^3k^{-4}\right)^{-3} = \frac{2}{\left(-4j^3k^{-4}\right)^3}$$

$$= \frac{2}{(-4)^3\left(j^3\right)^3\left(k^{-4}\right)^3}$$

$$= \frac{\cancel{2}}{-\cancel{64}j^9k^{-12}}$$

$$= -\frac{k^{12}}{32j^9}$$

Choice **(B)** is the correct answer.

2. B

Difficulty: Medium

Category: Radicals

Getting to the Answer: The question asks you to solve the equation for L. Use inverse operations to accomplish the task. Divide both sides of the equation by 2π and then square both sides. You'll need to apply the exponent to all the terms on the left side of the equation, including the π:

$$T = 2\pi\sqrt{\frac{L}{g}}$$

$$\frac{T}{2\pi} = \sqrt{\frac{L}{g}}$$

$$\left(\frac{T}{2\pi}\right)^2 = \left(\sqrt{\frac{L}{g}}\right)^2$$

$$\frac{T^2}{4\pi^2} = \frac{L}{g}$$

Finally, multiply both sides by g to remove g from the denominator and isolate L:

$$L = \frac{gT^2}{4\pi^2}$$

The correct answer is **(B)**.

3. A

Difficulty: Hard

Category: Radicals

Getting to the Answer: You can't simplify an expression that has different roots (in this case, sixth and third), so rewrite the expression with fraction exponents first, and then use exponent rules to simplify it. The rule for fraction exponents is "power over root"; use this to rewrite the expression:

$$\frac{\sqrt[6]{x^{10}y^{12}}}{\sqrt[3]{x^5y^6}} = \frac{x^{\frac{10}{6}}y^{\frac{12}{6}}}{x^{\frac{5}{3}}y^{\frac{6}{3}}}$$

When dividing like bases, subtract the exponents. Find common denominators as needed:

$$x^{\frac{10}{6}-\frac{5}{3}}y^{\frac{12}{6}-\frac{6}{3}} = x^{\frac{10}{6}-\frac{10}{6}}y^{\frac{12}{6}-\frac{12}{6}} = x^0y^0$$

Any number raised to the zero power becomes 1, so the expression becomes $1 \times 1 = 1$. Choice **(A)** is correct.

4. D

Difficulty: Medium

Category: Polynomial Division

Getting to the Answer: Since factoring the numerator does not appear to be practical, use polynomial division to find the result:

$$x - 2 \overline{)4x^3 - 5x^2 + x - 3}$$

The first number in this process will be $4x^2$ since $4x^2 \cdot x = 4x^3$:

$$\begin{array}{r} 4x^2 \\ x - 2 \overline{)4x^3 - 5x^2 + x - 3} \\ -\left(4x^3 - 8x^2\right) \\ \hline 3x^2 \end{array}$$

Next, complete the rest of the polynomial division process:

$$\begin{array}{r} 4x^2 + 3x + 7 \\ x - 2 \overline{)4x^3 - 5x^2 + x - 3} \\ -\left(4x^3 - 8x^2\right) \\ \hline 3x^2 + x \\ -\left(3x^2 - 6x\right) \\ \hline 7x - 3 \\ -(7x - 14) \\ \hline 11 \end{array}$$

Remember that you are dividing by $x - 2$, so the remainder of 11 is actually $\frac{11}{x - 2}$. **(D)** is correct.

5. A

Difficulty: Easy

Category: Graphs of Polynomial Functions

Getting to the Answer: The key to this question is knowing that an x-intercept is another word for root, or zero; those three terms are synonyms. Even though the question stem does not say how many roots f has, you know it must have at least one if it intersects the x-axis. **(A)** is correct. Watch out for trap answer (D), which does not consider the case when a parabola touches the x-axis at one point but does not cross it.

6. D

Difficulty: Medium

Category: Graphs of Polynomial Functions

Strategic Advice: Working backward from the answer choices saves time.

Getting to the Answer: The solution or solutions of a system of functions, like a system of equations, can be found at the points of intersection. Because the function $g(x)$ is equal to a constant, all x-values produce the same output—it must represent a horizontal line. A horizontal line and a 4th degree function could intersect 0, 1, 2, 3, or 4 times. Set each of the answer choices equal to k and sketch the resulting functions on the graph. You'll see that only $g(x) = 1$ intersects f exactly twice, so **(D)** is correct. Pay special attention to the scale of the axes to avoid trap answers like (A).

7. C

Difficulty: Medium

Category: Graphs of Polynomial Functions

Getting to the Answer: The question is asking for a factor of the function and tells you where the function crosses the x-axis. The roots are the y-values where the graph crosses the x-axis. To find the factors from the roots, consider what expressions would produce a value of zero. Thus, if the roots are at 0, -2, 3, and 5, then the factored form of this equation must be $x(x + 2)(x - 3)(x - 5)$ because plugging in any one of the four roots will equal zero. The only factor that appears in the answer choices is $x - 5$, so **(C)** is correct.

8. B

Difficulty: Easy

Category: Modeling Growth and Decay

Strategic Advice: Determining the type of growth represented by the data will help to eliminate half of the choices immediately. Look at what happens to the height from each measurement to the next. From 15 to 18 months, the child's height increases by 2.5 centimeters. The same is true for 18 to 21 months, and for 21 to 24 months, and so on. Since 2.5 centimeters are added each equal time interval, the best model for this data would be linear.

Getting to the Answer: Because this growth is linear, eliminate choices (C) and (D) immediately because they represent exponential growth. The remaining two choices differ in both the coefficient of t and the value being added. When linear growth is modeled with the equation $y = mx + b$, m represents the rate of growth and b represents the starting amount. In this case, the starting height is 80 centimeters and the growth rate is 2.5 centimeters every 3 months, or $\frac{5}{6}$ centimeter per month, so choice **(B)** is correct.

9. C

Difficulty: Hard

Category: Rational Expressions and Equations

Getting to the Answer: Because the denominators are the same (just written in different forms), multiplying both sides of the equation by $3x - 15$ will immediately clear all the fractions, the result of which is a much easier equation to solve:

$$8x + 2x = 50$$
$$10x = 50$$
$$x = 5$$

Because there are variables in the denominator, you must check the solution to make sure it is not extraneous. When $x = 5$, each of the denominators is equal to 0, and division by 0 is not possible. Therefore, there is no solution to the equation, making **(C)** the correct answer.

10. B

Difficulty: Hard

Category: Rational Expressions and Equations

Getting to the Answer: Begin by putting the x terms on one side and the a and b terms on the other for the first equation:

$$6a - 4b = \frac{10}{2x - 3} - \frac{6}{2x - 3} = \frac{10 - 6}{2x - 3} = \frac{4}{2x - 3}$$

Now note that the left side of the equation is $6a - 4b$, which is equivalent to $2(3a - 2b)$. The question states that $3a - 2b = 2$. So $6a - 4b = 2(3a - 2b) = 2(2) = 4$. Substitute 4 for $6a - 4b$, multiply both sides by $2x - 3$ to clear the fractions, and solve for x:

$$4 = \frac{4}{2x - 3}$$
$$4(2x - 3) = 4$$
$$2x - 3 = 1$$
$$2x = 4$$
$$x = 2$$

Because "No solution" is an answer choice, make sure that $x = 2$ is not an extraneous solution before selecting choice (B). When $x = 2$, the denominator $2x - 3 \neq 0$. Thus, $x = 2$ is a valid solution, and the answer is **(B)**.

Exponents

LEARNING OBJECTIVE

After this lesson, you will be able to:

- Apply exponent rules

To answer a question like this:

The expression $x\left(x^3y^2\right)^{-4}$ is equivalent to which of the following?

A) $\dfrac{1}{y^2}$

B) $\dfrac{1}{x^4}$

C) $\dfrac{1}{x^{11}y^8}$

D) $\dfrac{1}{x^{16}y^8}$

You need to know this:

Rule	Example
When multiplying two terms with the same base, add the exponents.	$a^b \cdot a^c = a^{(b+c)} \rightarrow 4^2 \cdot 4^3 = 4^{2+3} = 4^5$
When dividing two terms with the same base, subtract the exponents.	$\dfrac{a^b}{a^c} = a^{(b-c)} \rightarrow \dfrac{4^3}{4^2} = 4^{3-2} = 4^1$
When raising a power to another power, multiply the exponents.	$(a^b)^c = a^{(bc)} \rightarrow (4^3)^2 = 4^{3 \cdot 2} = 4^6$; $(2x^2)^3 = 2^3 x^{2 \cdot 3} = 8x^6$
When raising a product to a power, apply the power to all factors in the product.	$(ab)^c = a^c \cdot b^c \rightarrow (2m)^3 = 2^3 \cdot m^3 = 8m^3$
Any nonzero term raised to the zero power equals 1.	$a^0 = 1 \rightarrow 4^0 = 1$
A base raised to a negative exponent can be rewritten as the reciprocal raised to the positive of the original exponent.	$a^{-b} = \dfrac{1}{a^b}$; $\dfrac{1}{a^{-b}} = a^b \rightarrow 4^{-2} = \dfrac{1}{4^2}$; $\dfrac{1}{4^{-2}} = 4^2$
A negative number raised to an even exponent will produce a positive result; a negative number raised to an odd exponent will produce a negative result.	$(-2)^4 = 16$, but $(-2)^3 = -8$

You need to do this:

- Identify the appropriate rule by looking at the operation.
- Apply the rule.
- Repeat as necessary.

SAT exponent questions should be quick points. Make sure you memorize the rules in the table above before test day.

Explanation:

You'll need several exponent rules to answer the question at the beginning of this lesson. The order of operations dictates that you start with the negative exponent. When one power is raised to another, multiply the exponents:

$$x\left(x^3y^2\right)^{-4} = x\left(x^{3(-4)}y^{2(-4)}\right) = x\left(x^{-12}y^{-8}\right)$$

The x out front has no exponent, which means it is raised to the power of 1. To do the multiplication, add the exponents:

$$x^1\left(x^{-12}y^{-8}\right) = x^{-11}y^{-8}$$

Finally, because this expression is not among the choices, you'll need the rule for negative exponents: you can write them as the reciprocal of the positive exponent. Like this:

$$x^{-11}y^{-8} = \frac{1}{x^{11}y^8}$$

The correct answer is **(C)**.

If exponents give you trouble, study the rules in the table above and try these Drill questions before completing the Try on Your Own questions that follow. Simplify each expression (without using a calculator). Turn the page to see the answers.

Drill

a. 3^4

b. $(-5)^3$

c. $4^2 \times 2^{-4}$

d. $\dfrac{2^4}{2^3}$

e. $\left(\dfrac{1}{3}\right)^{-2}$

f. $\left(2^2\right)^3$

g. $(7x)^2$

h. $\left(-\dfrac{1}{2}\right)^{-2}$

i. $\left(a^2\right)^5$

j. $\left(b^3\right)^{-6}$

Try on Your Own

Directions: Take as much time as you need on these questions. Work carefully and methodically. There will be an opportunity for timed practice at the end of the chapter.

HINT: For Q1, how can you get all three bases to have the same value?

---

1. What is the value of $\dfrac{3^5 \times 27^3}{81^3}$?

HINT: For Q2, look for common factors in the numerator and denominator.

$$\frac{18x^4 + 27x^3 - 36x^2}{9x^2}$$

2. If $x \neq 0$, which of the following is equivalent to the expression above?

A) $2x^2 + 3x - 4$

B) $2x^2 + 3x - 6$

C) $2x^4 + 3x^3 - 4x^2$

D) $2x^6 + 3x^5 - 4x^4$

3. Human blood contains three primary cell types: red blood cells (RBC), white blood cells (WBC), and platelets. In an adult male, a single microliter (1×10^{-3} milliliters) of blood contains approximately 5.4×10^6 RBC, 7.5×10^3 WBC, and 3.5×10^5 platelets on average. What percentage of an adult male's total blood cell count is comprised of red blood cells?

A) 1.30%

B) 6.21%

C) 60.79%

D) 93.79%

4. If $n^3 = -8$, what is the value of $\dfrac{\left(n^2\right)^3}{\dfrac{1}{n^2}}$?

HINT: For Q5, how can you get rid of the fraction on the left side?

$$\frac{x^{5r}}{x^{3r-2s}} = x^t$$

5. If $r + s = 6$, what is the value of t in the equation above?

A) 6

B) 12

C) 18

D) 30

Radicals

LEARNING OBJECTIVE

After this lesson, you will be able to:

- Apply radical rules

To answer a question like this:

$$\frac{\sqrt[3]{x} \cdot x^{\frac{5}{2}} \cdot x}{\sqrt{x}}$$

If x^n is the simplified form of the expression above, what is the value of n ?

Drill answers:

a. $3^4 = 3 \times 3 \times 3 \times 3 = 81$

b. $(-5)^3 = (-5) \times (-5) \times (-5) = -125$

c. $4^2 \times 2^{-4} = \frac{16}{16} = 1$

d. $\frac{2^4}{2^3} = 2^1 = 2$

e. $\left(\frac{1}{3}\right)^{-2} = \left(\frac{3}{1}\right)^2 = 9$

f. $\left(2^2\right)^3 = 2^{2 \times 3} = 2^6 = 64$

g. $(7x)^2 = 49x^2$

h. $\left(-\frac{1}{2}\right)^{-2} = (-2)^2 = 4$

i. $\left(a^2\right)^5 = a^{10}$

j. $\left(b^3\right)^{-6} = b^{-18} = \frac{1}{b^{18}}$

You need to know this:

Rule	Example
When a fraction is under a radical, you can rewrite it using two radicals: one containing the numerator and the other containing the denominator.	$\sqrt{\dfrac{a}{b}} = \dfrac{\sqrt{a}}{\sqrt{b}} \rightarrow \sqrt{\dfrac{4}{9}} = \dfrac{\sqrt{4}}{\sqrt{9}} = \dfrac{2}{3}$
Two factors under a single radical can be rewritten as separate radicals multiplied together.	$\sqrt{ab} = \sqrt{a} \times \sqrt{b} \rightarrow \sqrt{75} = \sqrt{25} \times \sqrt{3} = 5\sqrt{3}$
A radical can be written using a fractional exponent.	$\sqrt{a} = a^{\frac{1}{2}} \rightarrow \sqrt{289} = 289^{\frac{1}{2}}$ $\sqrt[3]{a} = a^{\frac{1}{3}} \rightarrow \sqrt[3]{729} = 729^{\frac{1}{3}}$
When you have a fractional exponent, the numerator is the power to which the base is raised, and the denominator is the root to be taken.	$a^{\frac{b}{c}} = \sqrt[c]{a^b} \rightarrow 5^{\frac{2}{3}} = \sqrt[3]{5^2}$
When a number is squared, the original number can be positive or negative, but the square root of a number can only be positive.	If $a^2 = 81$, then $a = \pm 9$, BUT $\sqrt{81} = 9$ only.
Cube roots of negative numbers are negative.	$\sqrt[3]{-27} = -3$

You need to do this:

- Identify the appropriate rule by looking at the answer choices. What form do you need to get the expression into? What rule do you need to apply to get there?
- Apply the rule.
- Repeat as necessary.

SAT Radicals questions should be quick points. Make sure you memorize the rules in the table above before test day.

Explanation:

Write each factor in the expression in exponential form (using fractional exponents for the radicals). Next, use exponent rules to simplify the expression:

$$\frac{\sqrt[3]{x} \cdot x^{\frac{5}{2}} \cdot x}{\sqrt{x}} = \frac{x^{\frac{1}{3}} \cdot x^{\frac{5}{2}} \cdot x^1}{x^{\frac{1}{2}}}$$

Now add the exponents of the factors that are being multiplied and subtract the exponent of the factor that is being divided, find common denominators, and simplify:

$$= x^{\frac{1}{3}+\frac{5}{2}+\frac{1}{1}-\frac{1}{2}} = x^{\frac{2}{6}+\frac{15}{6}+\frac{6}{6}-\frac{3}{6}}$$
$$= x^{\frac{20}{6}} = x^{\frac{10}{3}}$$

The question states that n is the power of x, so the value of n is $\frac{10}{3}$.

If radicals give you trouble, study the rules in the table above and try these Drill questions before completing the following Try on Your Own questions. Simplify each expression (without using a calculator). Turn the page to see the answers.

Drill

a. $\sqrt{\dfrac{121}{9}}$

b. $\sqrt{225}$

c. $\sqrt{\dfrac{16 \times 125}{5}}$

d. $\sqrt{\dfrac{50}{288}}$

e. $\sqrt[3]{-27}$

f. $\dfrac{\sqrt{5}\sqrt{60}}{\sqrt{3}}$

g. $\dfrac{4\sqrt{21} \times 5\sqrt{2}}{10\sqrt{7}}$

h. $9^{\frac{1}{2}} \times \sqrt{4} \times 81^{\frac{1}{4}}$

i. $\dfrac{\sqrt{81x^2}}{\sqrt{64y^4}}$

j. $\sqrt{\dfrac{x^8}{y^{12}}}$

Try on Your Own

Directions: Take as much time as you need on these questions. Work carefully and methodically. There will be an opportunity for timed practice at the end of the chapter.

HINT: For Q6, what do you need to do before squaring both sides?

$$8 + \frac{\sqrt{2x + 29}}{3} = 9$$

6. For what value of x is the equation above true?

- A) -10
- B) -2
- C) 19
- D) No solution

$$3x = x + 14$$
$$\sqrt{3z^2 - 11} + 2x = 22$$

7. If $z > 0$, what is the value of z?

- A) 1
- B) 3
- C) 5
- D) 8

8. Which of the following expressions is equivalent to $-x^{\frac{1}{4}}$?

- A) $-\dfrac{1}{4x}$
- B) $-\dfrac{1}{x^4}$
- C) $-\sqrt[4]{x}$
- D) $\dfrac{1}{\sqrt[4]{-x}}$

For Q9, remember that the denominator of the exponent becomes the root, and the numerator remains the exponent.

---

9. When simplified, $8^{\frac{4}{3}}$ is what number?

	⊘	⊘	
.	.	.	.
0	0	0	0
1	1	1	1
2	2	2	2
3	3	3	3
4	4	4	4
5	5	5	5
6	6	6	6
7	7	7	7
8	8	8	8
9	9	9	9

HINT: For Q10, which approach is faster for you? Algebra or Backsolving?

$$\sqrt{3a + 16} - 3 = a - 1$$

10. In the equation above, if $a > 0$, which of the following is a possible value of a?

- A) 3
- B) 2
- C) 1
- D) -4

Math

Polynomials

> ### LEARNING OBJECTIVE
>
> After this lesson, you will be able to:
>
> - Add, subtract, multiply, and factor polynomials

To answer a question like this:

If $-2x^2 + 5x - 8$ is multiplied by $4x - 9$, what is the coefficient of x in the resulting polynomial?

A) -77

B) -45

C) -32

D) -13

You need to know this:

A **polynomial** is an expression composed of variables, exponents, and coefficients. By definition, a polynomial cannot have a variable in a denominator, and all exponents must be integers. Here are some examples of polynomial and non-polynomial expressions:

Polynomial	$23x^2$	$\frac{x}{5} - 6$	$y^{11} - 2y^6 + \frac{2}{3}xy^3 - 4x^2$	$z + 6$
NOT a Polynomial	$\frac{10}{z} + 13$	$x^3 y^{-6}$	$x^{\frac{1}{2}}$	$\frac{4}{y-3}$

Drill answers:

a. $\dfrac{\sqrt{121}}{\sqrt{9}} = \dfrac{11}{3}$

b. $\sqrt{25} \times \sqrt{9} = 5 \times 3 = 15$

c. $\dfrac{4 \times 5\sqrt{5}}{\sqrt{5}} = 20$

d. $\dfrac{5\sqrt{2}}{12\sqrt{2}} = \dfrac{5}{12}$

e. -3

f. $\dfrac{\sqrt{5} \times 2\sqrt{3}\sqrt{5}}{\sqrt{3}} = 2 \times 5 = 10$

g. $\dfrac{4\sqrt{3}\sqrt{7} \times 5\sqrt{2}}{10\sqrt{7}} = \dfrac{20\sqrt{6}}{10} = 2\sqrt{6}$

h. $3 \times 2 \times 3 = 18$

i. $\dfrac{9|x|}{8y^2}$

j. $\dfrac{x^4}{y^6}$

You need to do this:

To add and subtract polynomials, start by identifying like terms—that is, terms in which the types of variables and their exponents match. For example, x^2 and $3x^2$ are like terms; adding them would give $4x^2$ and subtracting them would give $x^2 - 3x^2 = -2x^2$. Note that you cannot add or subtract unlike terms. For example, there is no way to simplify $x^2 + y$. You can, however, multiply unlike terms: $x^2 \cdot y = x^2y$.

To multiply two polynomials, multiply each term in the first factor by each term in the second factor, then combine like terms.

To factor a polynomial, find a value or variable that divides evenly into each term, for example: $2x^3 + 2x^2 + 2x = 2x\left(x^2 + x + 1\right)$. (Factoring quadratics into binomials is discussed in chapter 12.)

Explanation:

Multiply each term in the first factor by each term in the second factor, then combine like terms:

$$\left(-2x^2 + 5x - 8\right)(4x - 9)$$
$$= -2x^2(4x - 9) + 5x(4x - 9) - 8(4x - 9)$$
$$= -8x^3 + 18x^2 + 20x^2 - 45x - 32x + 72$$
$$= -8x^3 + 38x^2 - 77x + 72$$

The coefficient of x is -77, so **(A)** is correct.

Try on Your Own

Directions: Take as much time as you need on these questions. Work carefully and methodically. There will be an opportunity for timed practice at the end of the chapter.

11. What is the sum of the polynomials $6a^2 - 17a - 9$ and $-5a^2 + 8a - 2$?

    A) $a^2 - 9a - 11$

    B) $a^2 - 25a - 7$

    C) $11a^2 - 9a - 11$

    D) $11a^2 - 25a - 7$

12. What is the difference when $3x^3 + 7x - 5$ is subtracted from $8x^2 + 4x + 10$?

    A) $5x^2 - 3x + 15$

    B) $-3x^3 - 3x + 5$

    C) $3x^3 - 8x^2 + 3x - 15$

    D) $-3x^3 + 8x^2 - 3x + 15$

HINT: For Q13, as you calculate each term, eliminate choices. Stop when there's only one choice left.

---

13. If $A = 4x^2 + 7x - 1$ and $B = -x^2 - 5x + 3$, then what is $\frac{3}{2}A - 2B$?

    A) $4x^2 + \frac{31}{2}x - \frac{9}{2}$

    B) $4x^2 + \frac{41}{2}x - \frac{15}{2}$

    C) $8x^2 + \frac{31}{2}x - \frac{9}{2}$

    D) $8x^2 + \frac{41}{2}x - \frac{15}{2}$

HINT: Which is more efficient for you? Math or backsolving the choices?

---

14. If $x^3 - 9x = 9 - x^2$, which of the following CANNOT be the value of x?

    A) -3

    B) -1

    C) 1

    D) 3

$$(2x^2 + 3x - 4)(3x + 2) = 6x^3 + ax^2 - 6x - 8$$

15. In the above equation, a is a constant. If the equation is true for all values of x, what is the value of a?

    A) 4

    B) 9

    C) 13

    D) 16

Polynomial Division

LEARNING OBJECTIVE

After this lesson, you will be able to:

- Divide polynomials

To answer a question like this:

Which of the following is equivalent to $\dfrac{x^2 + 3x + 7}{x + 4}$?

A) $\dfrac{3 + 7}{4}$

B) $x + \dfrac{3}{4}$

C) $3 + \dfrac{7}{x + 4}$

D) $x - 1 + \dfrac{11}{x + 4}$

You need to know this:

To divide polynomials, you can use an approach called **polynomial long division**. This process is similar to ordinary long division, except that you use polynomials instead of numbers. In the process described below, the *dividend* is the polynomial to be divided, the *divisor* is the polynomial you are dividing the dividend by, and the *quotient* is the result of the division.

You need to do this:

- Start with the dividend arranged so that the powers are in descending order, for example: $x^4 + x^3 + x + 1$. If any terms are missing, put in zeros, like this: $x^4 + x^3 + 0x^2 + x + 1$. Write the problem using a long division sign.
- Divide the first term of the dividend by the first term of the divisor to yield the first term of the quotient.
- Multiply the divisor by the first term of the quotient.
- Subtract the product you got in the last step from the dividend, then bring down the next term, just as you would in ordinary long division. Use the result as the new dividend.
- Repeat the process until you arrive at the remainder.

Math

Explanation:

To divide $x^2 + 3x + 7$ by $x + 4$, set up a long division problem:

$$x + 4 \overline{\smash{\big)}\, x^2 + 3x + 7}$$

Start by dividing the first term of the dividend, x^2, by the first term of the divisor, x. Multiply the entire divisor by x and subtract this product from the dividend:

$$
\begin{array}{r}
x \\
x + 4 \overline{\smash{\big)}\, x^2 + 3x + 7} \\
\underline{-\left(x^2 + 4x\right)} \\
-x + 7
\end{array}
$$

Next, divide the first term of the result of this subtraction, $-x$, by the first term of the divisor, x, to get -1. Repeat the process of multiplying and subtracting:

$$
\begin{array}{r}
x - 1 \\
x + 4 \overline{\smash{\big)}\, x^2 + 3x + 7} \\
\underline{-\left(x^2 + 4x\right)} \\
-x + 7 \\
\underline{-(-x - 4)} \\
+11
\end{array}
$$

You're left with a remainder of 11. Put this over the divisor, $x + 4$, and you're done. The result of the division is $x - 1 + \dfrac{11}{x + 4}$, which is choice **(D)**.

Try on Your Own

Directions: Take as much time as you need on these questions. Work carefully and methodically. There will be an opportunity for timed practice at the end of the chapter.

HINT: For Q16, because $a - 3$ is not a factor of the numerator, you'll have to use polynomial long division.

---

16. Which of the following is equivalent to $\dfrac{2a^2 - 5a - 1}{a - 3}$?

    A) $2a - 2$

    B) $2a + 1 - \dfrac{2}{a - 3}$

    C) $2a + \dfrac{2}{a - 3}$

    D) $2a + 1 + \dfrac{2}{a - 3}$

HINT: For Q17, if the fraction simplifies to $ax + b$, the denominator divides evenly into the numerator. Does that suggest another approach?

$$\dfrac{6x^2 + 19x + 10}{2x + 5}$$

17. If $ax + b$ represents the simplified form of the expression above, then what is the value of $a + b$?

    A) 2

    B) 3

    C) 5

    D) 6

18. Which of the following is equivalent to $\dfrac{4x^2 - 6x}{2x + 2}$?

    A) $2x - \dfrac{10}{2x + 2}$

    B) $2x - 5 + \dfrac{10}{2x + 2}$

    C) $2x - 3$

    D) $2x + 5 - \dfrac{10}{2x + 2}$

HINT: The quotient (result of division) times the divisor (the denominator) equals the dividend (the numerator). For Q19, stop as soon as you have the value of t.

---

19. The equation $\dfrac{36x^2 + 16x - 21}{tx - 4} = -9x + 5 - \dfrac{1}{tx - 4}$ is true for all values of x for which $x \neq \dfrac{4}{t}$, where t is a constant. What is the value of t ?

    A) -20

    B) -4

    C) 4

    D) 12

20. If the polynomial $f(x)$ is evenly divisible by $x - 5$ and the polynomial $g(x) = f(x) + 4$, what is the value of $g(5)$?

    A) -4

    B) 0

    C) 4

    D) 9

Graphs of Polynomial Functions

LEARNING OBJECTIVE

After this lesson, you will be able to:

- Define root, solution, zero, and *x*-intercept and identify them on the graph of a nonlinear function

To answer a question like this:

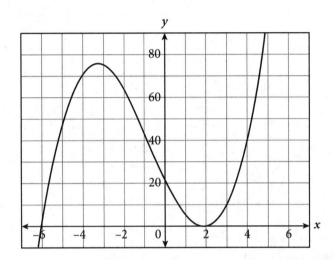

Which of the following could be the function whose graph is shown above?

A) $f(x) = (x - 6)(x + 2)^2$

B) $f(x) = (x + 6)(x - 2)^2$

C) $f(x) = 3x + 23$

D) $f(x) = 6x + 23$

You need to know this:

When applied to polynomial functions, the words **root, solution, zero,** and **_x_-intercept** all mean the same thing: the _x_-values on the function's graph where the function touches or crosses the _x_-axis. You can find the roots of a polynomial function by setting each factor of the polynomial equal to zero. For example, the polynomial function $f(x) = x^2 + x$ factors into $f(x) = x(x + 1)$. Set each factor equal to zero to find that $x = 0$ and $x = -1$. These are the function's solutions, also known as zeros. A solution can be represented using the coordinate pair $(x, 0)$.

Note that if a function crosses the _x_-axis, the factor associated with that _x_-intercept will have an odd exponent. If the function touches but does not cross the _x_-axis, the factor associated with that zero will have an even exponent. For example, the function $f(x) = x(x + 1)$ will cross the _x_-axis at $x = 0$ and $x = -1$, while the function $f(x) = x^2(x + 1)$ will cross the _x_-axis at $x = -1$ but only touch the _x_-axis at $x = 0$.

You need to do this:

- Identify the _x_-values where the function crosses or touches the _x_-axis.
- For each _x_-intercept, change the sign of the _x_-value and add it to the variable _x_ to find the associated factor. For example, if the function crosses the _x_-axis at $x = -1$, then the factor associated with that root must be $x + 1$ (since $x + 1 = 0$ will produce the solution $x = -1$).
- Recognize that if the function only touches the _x_-axis without crossing it, the factor must have an even exponent.

Explanation:

Start by looking at the answer choices. The function is clearly not linear, so rule out (C) and (D). Next, look at the _x_-intercepts on the graph: the function crosses the _x_-axis at $x = -6$ and touches the _x_-axis at $x = 2$. Remember that the _x_-intercepts occur where the factors of the function equal zero. For the _x_-intercepts to be -6 and 2, the factors of the function must be $(x + 6)$ and $(x - 2)$. Because the function touches, but does not cross, the _x_-axis at $x = 2$, the $(x - 2)$ factor must have an even exponent. **(B)** is correct.

Try on Your Own

Directions: Take as much time as you need on these questions. Work carefully and methodically. There will be an opportunity for timed practice at the end of the chapter.

HINT: For Q21, set each factor equal to 0 and solve for x to find the x-intercepts.

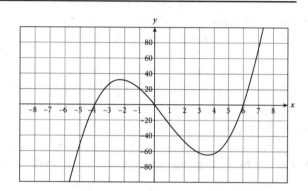

21. Which of the following could be the equation of the graph above?

    A) $y = x^2(x+4)(x-6)$

    B) $y = x(x+4)(x-6)$

    C) $y = x^2(x-4)(x+6)$

    D) $y = x(x-4)(x+6)$

x	$h(x)$
-3	6
-1	0
0	-5
2	-8

22. The function h is defined by a polynomial. The table above gives some of the values of x and $h(x)$. Which of the following must be a factor of $h(x)$?

    A) $x-8$

    B) $x-1$

    C) $x+1$

    D) $x+5$

HINT: In Q23, the definition of the b function has a variable in the denominator. What does this tell you about the value of x?

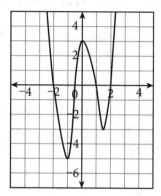

23. The graph of the function $a(x)$ is shown above. If $b(x) = \dfrac{1}{x}$, which of the following is a true statement about $b\big(a(x)\big)$?

    A) $b(a(x))$ is defined for all real numbers.

    B) $b(a(x))$ is undefined for exactly one real value of x.

    C) $b(a(x))$ is undefined for exactly four real values of x.

    D) $b(a(x))$ is undefined for all real numbers.

24. If function *f* has exactly two distinct real zeros, which of the following graphs could be the complete graph of *f(x)* ?

A)

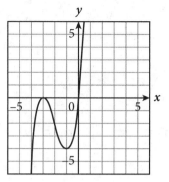

B)

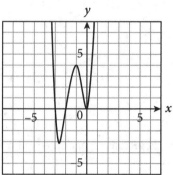

C)

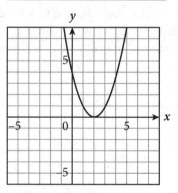

D)

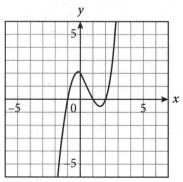

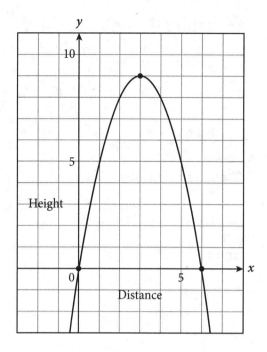

25. The graph of $f(x) = -(x-3)^2 + 9$ above approximates the trajectory of a water balloon shot from a cannon at ground level. In terms of the trajectory, what information is represented by a root of this function?

A) The maximum height achieved by the balloon

B) The total horizontal distance traveled by the balloon

C) The maximum speed of the balloon

D) The initial acceleration of the balloon

Modeling Growth and Decay

LEARNING OBJECTIVES

After this lesson, you will be able to:

• Determine whether the growth or decay described in a question is linear or exponential

• Apply the linear and exponential equations to answer growth and decay questions

To answer a question like this:

A certain car costs $20,000. If the car loses 15 percent of its value each year, approximately how much will the car be worth after 5 years?

A) $5,000

B) $8,900

C) $11,200

D) $15,000

You need to know this:

The terms **growth** and **decay** refer to situations in which some quantity is increased or decreased over time according to a rule:

• If the rule is to add or subtract the same amount each time, then the growth or decay is **linear**. Because the graph of linear growth and decay is a line, you can use the slope-intercept form of a line—$y = mx + b$—to describe it, where b is the starting amount and m is the amount added or subtracted each time x increases by 1.

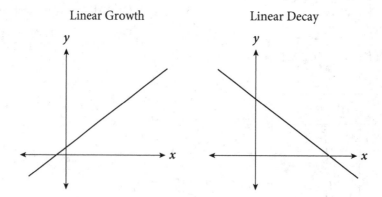

Linear Growth   Linear Decay

- If the rule is to multiply or divide by the same amount each time, then the growth or decay is **exponential**. The general form of an exponential function is $y = ab^x$, where a is the y-intercept and b is the amount multiplied or divided each time x increases by 1. Given that $a > 0$ and $b > 1$, when x is positive, the equation describes exponential growth, and when x is negative, the equation describes exponential decay.

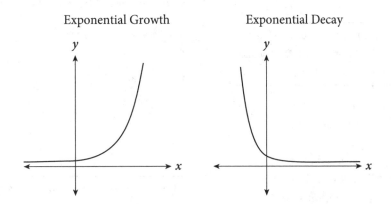

Exponential Growth   Exponential Decay

- When an exponential growth or decay question gives you a growth rate over time, you can use a modified version of the exponential function, $f(x) = f(0)(1 + r)^t$, where $f(0)$ is the amount at time $t = 0$ and r is the growth rate (or decay rate, if negative) expressed as a decimal.

You need to do this:

- First, determine whether the situation described is linear or exponential. If an amount is added or subtracted each time, then the growth is linear; if the original quantity is multiplied or divided by some amount each time, then the growth is exponential.
- Plug the values from the question into the appropriate equation and solve for the missing quantity.
- When the numbers are manageable, you might be able to avoid using the equations by simply carrying out the operations described. For example, if the question says that an amount doubles each day and asks for the amount after three days, then doubling the initial quantity three times will likely be more efficient than plugging the numbers into the exponential growth equation.

Explanation:

The question says that the car loses value at a certain rate per year, which means the question involves exponential decay. The question gives three pieces of important information: the initial value $f(0) = \$20,000$, the rate $r = -0.15$, and the time $t = 5$. The question asks for the approximate value of the car after 5 years, which is $f(5)$. The rate must be expressed as a decimal, and since the value of the car is decreasing, the rate is also negative. Plug these values into the equation $f(t) = f(0)(1 + r)^t$ and use your calculator to solve:

$$f(t) = 20,000(1 - 0.15)^5$$
$$= 20,000(0.85)^5 \approx \$8,900$$

Choice **(B)** is correct.

Math

Try on Your Own

Directions: Take as much time as you need on these questions. Work carefully and methodically. There will be an opportunity for timed practice at the end of the chapter.

HINT: For Q26, keep track of your calculations by making a chart with the number of applicants at the start of the day and the number of applicants eliminated.

---

26. In determining the winner of a speech-writing competition, a panel of judges is able to eliminate one-quarter of the remaining applicants per day of deliberations. If 128 students entered the competition, how many applicants have been eliminated by the end of the third day of deliberations?

27. The manager of a health club determines that the club's membership has increased at a rate of 16 percent per year for the past four years. The club currently has 42 members. If this trend continues, how many years will it take for the club's membership to exceed 100 members?

A) 4 years

B) 5 years

C) 6 years

D) 7 years

HINT: For Q28, no original amount is given. What would be a good number to pick for that amount?

---

28. Radioactive carbon dating can determine how long ago an organism lived by measuring how much of the ^{14}C in the sample has decayed. ^{14}C is an isotope of carbon that has a half-life of 5,600 years. Half-life is the amount of time it takes for half of the original amount to decay. If a sample of a petrified tree contains 6.25 percent of its original ^{14}C, how long ago did the tree die?

A) 22,400 years

B) 28,000 years

C) 35,000 years

D) 89,600 years

HINT: For Q29, is she saving more, the same, or less each month? What does that tell you about the function?

29. Penelope receives the same amount of money each month for her allowance. Each month she spends half of her allowance and puts the rest in a piggy bank. On Penelope's 8th birthday, the piggy bank contains $40. If the piggy bank contains $244 after 2 years, what is her monthly allowance? (Ignore the dollar sign when gridding your response.)

30. At a certain bank, money held in account X earns a monthly interest equal to 2 percent of the original investment, while account Y earns a monthly interest equal to 2 percent of the current value of the account. If $500 is invested into each account, what is the positive difference between the value of account X and account Y after three years? (Round your answer to the nearest dollar and ignore the dollar sign when gridding your response.)

Rational Expressions and Equations

> ### LEARNING OBJECTIVES
>
> After this lesson, you will be able to:
>
> - Simplify rational expressions
> - Isolate a variable in a rational equation

To answer a question like this:

$$\frac{5y + 7}{(y + 4)^2} - \frac{5}{(y + 4)}$$

If the expression above is equal to $\dfrac{-b}{(y + 4)^2}$, where b is a positive constant and $y \neq -4$, what is the value of b ?

A)   4

B)   7

C)   13

D)   27

You need to know this:

A **rational expression** is a ratio expressed as a fraction with a polynomial in the denominator. A **rational equation** is an equation that includes at least one rational expression.

- Factors in a rational expression can be canceled when simplifying, but under no circumstances can you do the same with individual terms. Consider, for instance, the expression $\dfrac{x^2 - x - 6}{x^2 + 5x + 6}$. Some test takers will attempt to cancel the x^2, x, and 6 terms to give $\dfrac{1 - 1 - 1}{1 + 5 + 1} = \dfrac{-1}{7}$, which is *never* correct. Instead, factor the numerator and denominator: $\dfrac{(x + 2)(x - 3)}{(x + 2)(x + 3)}$. Cancel the $x + 2$ factors to get $\dfrac{x - 3}{x + 3}$.

- If a rational expression has a higher-degree numerator than denominator $\left(\text{e.g., } \dfrac{x^2 + 3}{1 - x}\right)$, it can be simplified using polynomial long division. If a rational expression has a lower-degree numerator than denominator $\left(\text{e.g., } \dfrac{1 - x}{x^2 + 3}\right)$, it cannot.

- Because rational expressions have polynomial denominators, they will often be undefined for certain values. For example, the expression $\dfrac{x - 4}{x + 2}$ is defined for all values of x except -2. This is because when $x = -2$, the denominator of the expression is 0, which would make the expression undefined.

- When solving rational equations, beware of undefined expressions. Take the equation $\dfrac{1}{x + 4} + \dfrac{1}{x - 4} = \dfrac{8}{(x + 4)(x - 4)}$, for instance. After multiplying both sides by the common denominator $(x + 4)(x - 4)$, you have $(x - 4) + (x + 4) = 8$. Solving for x yields $2x = 8$, which simplifies to $x = 4$. When 4 is substituted for x, however, you get 0 in the denominator of both the second and third terms of the equation. Therefore, this equation is said to have no solution. (A value that causes a denominator to equal 0 is called an *extraneous solution*.)

You need to do this:

- Find a common denominator.
- Multiply each term by the common denominator and simplify.
- Make sure you haven't found an extraneous solution.

Explanation:

Start by setting the two expressions equal:

$$\frac{5y+7}{(y+4)^2} - \frac{5}{y+4} = \frac{-b}{(y+4)^2}$$

Next, get rid of the fractions. To do this, multiply both sides of the equation by the common denominator, $(y+4)^2$:

$$\left(\frac{5y+7}{(y+4)^2} - \frac{5}{y+4} = \frac{-b}{(y+4)^2} \right)(y+4)^2$$

$$5y+7-5(y+4) = -b$$

Now all that remains is to solve for b:

$$5y+7-5y-20 = -b$$
$$-13 = -b$$
$$b = 13$$

The correct answer is **(C)**.

Try on Your Own

Directions: Take as much time as you need on these questions. Work carefully and methodically. There will be an opportunity for timed practice at the end of the chapter.

HINT: For Q31, multiply both sides by a common denominator or cross-multiply. (They are the same thing.)

---

31. Given the equation $\dfrac{6}{x} = \dfrac{3}{k+2}$ and the constraints $x \neq 0$ and $k \neq -2$, what is x in terms of k?

    A) $x = 2k + 4$

    B) $x = 2k + 12$

    C) $x = 2k - \dfrac{1}{4}$

    D) $x = \dfrac{1}{4}k + 12$

HINT: For Q32, how do you add fractions with different denominators?

$$\dfrac{3a+9}{(a-3)^2} + \dfrac{-9}{3a-9}$$

32. In the expression above, $(a-3)^2 = 6$. What is the value of the expression?

33. If $a > 6$, which of the following is equivalent to
$$\dfrac{\dfrac{2}{a}}{\dfrac{1}{a-2} + \dfrac{1}{a-6}}?$$

    A) $2a^2 - 16a + 24$

    B) $a(2a - 8)$

    C) $\dfrac{a^2 - 8a + 12}{a^2 - 4a}$

    D) $\dfrac{2a - 8}{a^2 - 8a + 12}$

34. If $\dfrac{5}{x+2} = \dfrac{2}{x+1} + \dfrac{1}{2}$ and $x > 1$, what is the value of x?

    A) 2

    B) 3

    C) 6

    D) 9

35. If $\dfrac{16}{7x+4} + A$ is equivalent to $\dfrac{49x^2}{7x+4}$, what is A in terms of x?

    A) $7x + 4$

    B) $7x - 4$

    C) $49x^2$

    D) $49x^2 + 4$

HINT: A common denominator is possible, but messy. Is there another approach to Q36?

$$\dfrac{c+5}{6c} + \dfrac{2}{2c-4} = 0$$

36. The equation above is true for all values of c such that $c \neq -6$ and $c \neq 2$. If $c < 0$, what is the value of c?

    A) -20

    B) -10

    C) 1

    D) 10

On Test Day

Remember that the SAT doesn't ask you to show your work. If you find the algebra in a question challenging, there is often another way to get to the answer.

Try this question first using algebra and then using the Picking Numbers strategy from chapter 3. Which approach do you find easier? There's no right or wrong answer—just remember your preferred approach and try it first if you see a question like this on test day.

37. The expression $\dfrac{3x-1}{x-4}$ is equivalent to which of the following?

A) $\dfrac{1}{2}$

B) $3x - \dfrac{1}{x-4}$

C) $3 - \dfrac{11}{x-4}$

D) $3 + \dfrac{11}{x-4}$

The correct answer and both ways of solving can be found at the end of this chapter.

Math

How Much Have You Learned?

Directions: For testlike practice, give yourself 18 minutes to complete this question set. Be sure to study the explanations, even for questions you got right. They can be found at the end of this chapter.

38. An object launched upwards at an angle has parabolic motion. The height, h, of a projectile at time t is given by the equation $h = \frac{1}{2}at^2 + v_yt + h_0$, where a is the acceleration due to gravity, v_y is the vertical component of the velocity, and h_0 is the initial height. Which of the following equations correctly represents the object's acceleration due to gravity in terms of the other variables?

A) $a = \dfrac{h - v_yt - h_0}{t}$

B) $a = \dfrac{h - v_yt - h_0}{2t^2}$

C) $a = \dfrac{2(h - v_yt - h_0)}{t^2}$

D) $a = t\sqrt{2(h - v_yt - h_0)}$

39. If $\left(16^{3x}\right)\left(32^x\right)\left(8^{3x}\right) = \dfrac{\left(4^{6x}\right)\left(32^{3x}\right)}{4}$, what is the value of x?

A) -2

B) -1

C) 1

D) 2

40. Given that $\dfrac{y}{\sqrt{x - 3}} = \dfrac{\sqrt{x} + 3}{3}$ and $2x + 42 = 9x - 63$, what is the value of y?

		/	/	
	.	.	.	.
		0	0	0
1	1	1	1
2	2	2	2
3	3	3	3
4	4	4	4
5	5	5	5
6	6	6	6
7	7	7	7
8	8	8	8
9	9	9	9

$$y = \frac{3x^2 + 7}{x - 3}$$

41. Which of the following expressions is equivalent to y?

A) $3x + 9 - \dfrac{20}{x - 3}$

B) $3x + 9 + \dfrac{34}{x - 3}$

C) $3x + 43$

D) $3x^2 + \dfrac{9}{x - 3}$

$$z = 15x^2 + 10xy - 6x - 4y$$

42. For which of the ordered pairs, (x, y), below is $z \neq 0$?

A) $(-3, 2)$

B) $(-2, 3)$

C) $\left(\dfrac{2}{5}, 0\right)$

D) $\left(\dfrac{2}{5}, 10\right)$

43. $\sqrt{27^{\frac{2}{3}} + 128^{\frac{4}{7}}} =$

44. Which of the following is equivalent to $\dfrac{4x^2 - 8}{2x + 3}$?

A) $2x - 3 + \dfrac{1}{2x + 3}$

B) $2x - 2$

C) $2x + 3 - \dfrac{1}{2x + 3}$

D) $2x + 4$

$g(x) = \dfrac{2}{2x^3 - 12x^2 - 14x}$

45. For which of the following values of x is the function $g(x)$ defined?

A) -1

B) 0

C) 1

D) 7

$x^3 + 4 = 3x^2 - 7x + 25$

46. For what real value of x is the above equation valid?

A) 0

B) 3

C) 4

D) 7

47. Which of the following equations has a graph for which all roots are greater than 0 ?

A) $y = 4|x|$

B) $y = x^2 - 4$

C) $y = (x - 2)^2$

D) $y = x(x - 2)^2$

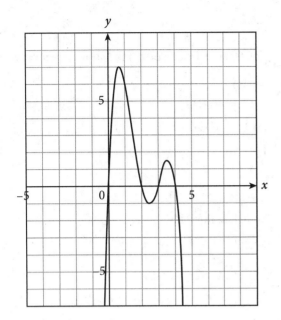

49. A marketing team conducted a study on the use of smartphones. In a certain metropolitan area, there were 1.6 million smartphone users at the end of 2018. The marketing team predicted that the number of smartphone users would increase by 35 percent each year beginning in 2019. If y represents the number of smartphone users in this metropolitan area after x years, then which of the following equations best models the number of smartphone users in this area over time?

A) $y = 1{,}600{,}000(1.35)^x$

B) $y = 1{,}600{,}000(35)^x$

C) $y = 35x + 1{,}600{,}000$

D) $y = 1.35x + 1{,}600{,}000$

48. The graph of the function
$f(x) = -x(x-4)(x-3)(x-2)$ is shown above.
If $f(x) = 0$, how many real solutions exist?

A) 0

B) 2

C) 3

D) 4

Reflect

Directions: Take a few minutes to recall what you've learned and what you've been practicing in this chapter. Consider the following questions, jot down your best answer for each one, and then compare your reflections to the expert responses on the following page. Use your level of confidence to determine what to do next.

How do you multiply two polynomials?

_____

_____

_____

What are the zeros of a polynomial function?

_____

_____

_____

Describe the difference between linear and exponential growth.

_____

_____

_____

Name two ways to simplify rational expressions.

_____

_____

_____

Expert Responses

How do you multiply two polynomials?

Distribute each term in the first set of parentheses to each term in the second set, then combine like terms.

What are the zeros of a polynomial function?

The zeros are the points at which the value of the function (i.e., the y-value) is zero. Think of the zeros as the x-intercepts of the function. The words "roots" and "solutions" mean the same thing.

Describe the difference between linear and exponential growth.

Linear growth is modeled by a linear function, with the equation $y = mx + b$, such that the slope of the line is positive. You're essentially adding the same amount over and over again. (In linear decay, the slope of the line is negative, and you're subtracting the same amount over and over again.)

Exponential growth is modeled by an exponential function in the form $y = ab^x$, where a is the y-intercept and b is the amount multiplied each time, over and over. The slope of an exponential growth function steepens with increasing x-values. (In exponential decay, b is the amount divided by each time, and the slope starts out steeply negative and flattens with increasing x-values.)

Name two ways to simplify rational expressions.

One way is to use polynomial long division, though this will work only if the higher-order polynomial is in the numerator. Another way is to cancel factors that appear in both the numerator and denominator.

Next Steps

If you answered most questions correctly in the "How Much Have You Learned?" section, and if your responses to the Reflect questions were similar to those of the SAT expert, then consider exponents and poly-nomial functions an area of strength and move on to the next chapter. Come back to this topic periodically to prevent yourself from getting rusty.

If you don't yet feel confident, review those parts of this chapter that you have not yet mastered. In particular, review the lessons covering Exponents, Modeling Growth and Decay, and Rational Expressions and Equations as these are high-yield topics on the SAT. Then try the questions you missed again. As always, be sure to review the explanations closely.

Answers and Explanations

1.   9

Difficulty: Medium

Getting to the Answer: You are not allowed to use your calculator on this question, so look for ways to rewrite the larger numbers as the same base. Memorizing the values of small integers up to the fourth or fifth power will help you see these patterns: $27 = 3^3$ and $81 = 3^4$. Now, rewrite the expression as $\dfrac{3^5 \times \left(3^3\right)^3}{\left(3^4\right)^3}$, which becomes $\dfrac{3^5 \times 3^9}{3^{12}} = \dfrac{3^{14}}{3^{12}}$. Subtract the exponents to get 3^2, which equals **9**, the correct answer.

2.   A

Difficulty: Easy

Getting to the Answer: Find the greatest common factor (GCF) of both the numerator and the denominator, which in this question happens to be the denominator. Factor out the GCF, $9x^2$, from the numerator and denominator and then cancel what you can:

$$\frac{18x^4 + 27x^3 - 36x^2}{9x^2} = \frac{\cancel{9x^2}\left(2x^2 + 3x - 4\right)}{\cancel{9x^2}}$$
$$= 2x^2 + 3x - 4$$

This matches **(A)**. As an alternate method, you could split the expression up and reduce each term, one at a time:

$$\frac{18x^4 + 27x^3 - 36x^2}{9x^2} = \frac{18x^4}{9x^2} + \frac{27x^3}{9x^2} - \frac{36x^2}{9x^2}$$
$$= 2x^2 + 3x - 4$$

3.   D

Difficulty: Medium

Getting to the Answer: Start by setting up a ratio that compares RBC count to total blood cell count. Manipulate the quantities to make all the exponents the same (to convert 7.5×10^3 to a product of 10^6 and another number, move the decimal point in 7.5 three places to the left and write "$\times 10^6$" after it), factor out 10^6, and then add the quantities in parentheses together. Once there, you can use exponent rules to simplify your equation. Divide through and multiply by 100 to get the RBC component as a percentage:

$$RBC = \frac{5.4 \times 10^6}{5.4 \times 10^6 + 7.5 \times 10^3 + 3.5 \times 10^5}$$
$$= \frac{5.4 \times \cancel{10^6}}{5.4 \times \cancel{10^6} + 0.0075 \times \cancel{10^6} + 0.35 \times \cancel{10^6}}$$
$$= \frac{5.4 \times \cancel{10^6}}{\cancel{10^6}\,(5.4 + 0.0075 + 0.35)}$$
$$= \frac{5.4}{5.7575}$$

Note that the answer choices are, for the most part, far apart. Because 5.4 is relatively close to 5.7575, you can conclude with confidence that the correct answer is likely close to 100%. Therefore, **(D)** is the correct answer. If this question is in the calculator section, you can plug the numbers into your calculator to check:

$$\%RBC = \frac{5.4}{5.7575} \times 100 \approx 93.79\%$$

Choice **(D)** is still correct.

4.   256

Difficulty: Medium

Getting to the Answer: If $n^3 = -8$, then $n = -2$. Simplify the given expression via exponent rules and then plug -2 in for n:

$$\frac{\left((-2)^2\right)^3}{\dfrac{1}{(-2)^2}} = \frac{4^3}{\dfrac{1}{4}} = 4^3 \times 4 = 4^4 = 256$$

Grid in **256**.

5.   B

Difficulty: Hard

Getting to the Answer: To simplify the division on the left side of the equation, subtract the powers and combine:

$$\frac{x^{5r}}{x^{3r-2s}} = x^{5r-(3r-2s)}$$
$$= x^{5r-3r+2s}$$
$$= x^{2r+2s}$$

Note that in the expression $2r + 2s$, it is possible to factor out a 2. Thus, $x^{2r+2s} = x^{2(r+s)}$. The question indicates that $r + s = 6$, so $x^{2(r+s)} = x^{2(6)} = x^{12}$. This is equal to x^t, so $t = 12$. The answer is **(B)**.

6.   A

Difficulty: Medium

Getting to the Answer: Solve equations containing radical expressions the same way you solve any other equation: isolate the variable using inverse operations. Start by subtracting 8 from both sides of the equation and then multiply by 3. Then, square both sides to remove the radical:

$$8 + \frac{\sqrt{2x + 29}}{3} = 9$$
$$\frac{\sqrt{2x + 29}}{3} = 1$$
$$\sqrt{2x + 29} = 3$$
$$2x + 29 = 9$$

Now you have a simple linear equation that you can solve using more inverse operations: subtract 29 and divide by 2 to find that $x = -10$. Be careful—just because the equation started with a radical and the answer is negative, it does not follow that *No solution* is the correct answer. If you plug -10 into the expression under the radical, the result is a positive number, which means -10 is a perfectly valid solution. Therefore, **(A)** is correct.

7.   C

Difficulty: Medium

Getting to the Answer: First, solve for x and plug that value into the second equation. Subtract x from both sides of the equation to get $2x = 14$, so $x = 7$. Plugging this into the second equation gives you $\sqrt{3z^2 - 11} + 2(7) = 22$. Thus, $\sqrt{3z^2 - 11} = 8$. Square both sides of this equation and solve for z:

$$3z^2 - 11 = 64$$
$$3z^2 = 75$$
$$z^2 = 25$$
$$z = \pm 5$$

Since the question specifies that $z > 0$, **(C)** is correct.

8.   C

Difficulty: Easy

Getting to the Answer: Follow the standard order of operations—deal with the exponent first and then attach the negative sign (because a negative in front of an expression means multiplication by -1). The variable x is being raised to the $\frac{1}{4}$ power, so rewrite the term as a radical expression with 4 as the degree of the root and 1 as the power to which the radicand, x, is being raised:

$$x^{\frac{1}{4}} = \sqrt[4]{x^1} = \sqrt[4]{x}$$

Now attach the negative to arrive at the correct answer, $-\sqrt[4]{x}$, which is **(C)**.

9.   16

Difficulty: Medium

Getting to the Answer: Because this is a no-calculator question, you need to rewrite the exponent in a way that makes it easier to evaluate: use exponent rules to rewrite $\frac{4}{3}$ as a unit fraction raised to a power. Then write the expression in radical form and simplify:

$$8^{\frac{4}{3}} = \left(8^{\frac{1}{3}}\right)^4$$
$$= \left(\sqrt[3]{8}\right)^4$$
$$= 2^4$$
$$= 2 \times 2 \times 2 \times 2$$
$$= 16$$

Grid in **16**.

10.   A

Difficulty: Medium

Getting to the Answer: Start by isolating the radical on the left side of the equation by adding 3 to both sides to get $\sqrt{3a + 16} = a + 2$. Now you can square both sides to get rid of the radical: $3a + 16 = (a + 2)^2 = a^2 + 4a + 4$. Since the right side of this equation is a quadratic, set it equal to 0 in order to determine the solutions: $0 = a^2 + 4a + 4 - (3a + 16) = a^2 + a - 12$. Next, factor the quadratic using reverse FOIL. The two factors of -12 that add up to 1 are -3 and 4, so $(a - 3)(a + 4) = 0$. Thus, a can be either 3 or -4, but the question says $a > 0$, so the only permissible value is 3. **(A)** is correct.

11. A

Difficulty: Easy

Getting to the Answer: Add polynomial expressions by combining like terms. Be careful of the signs of each term. It may help to write the sum vertically, lining up the like terms:

$$6a^2 - 17a - 9$$
$$\underline{+\ -5a^2 + 8a - 2}$$
$$a^2 - 9a - 11$$

The correct choice is **(A)**.

12. D

Difficulty: Medium

Getting to the Answer: First, write the question as a subtraction problem. Pay careful attention to which expression is being subtracted so that you distribute the negative sign correctly:

$$8x^2 + 4x + 10 - \left(3x^3 + 7x - 5\right)$$
$$= -3x^3 + 8x^2 - 3x + 15$$

This expression matches **(D)**.

13. D

Difficulty: Medium

Getting to the Answer: Multiply each term in the first expression by $\frac{3}{2}$ and each term in the second expression by -2. Then add the two polynomials by writing them vertically and combining like terms. You'll have to find a common denominator to combine the x-coefficients and to combine the constant terms:

$$\frac{3}{2}A = \frac{3}{2}\left(4x^2 + 7x - 1\right) = 6x^2 + \frac{21}{2}x - \frac{3}{2}$$
$$-2B = -2\left(-x^2 - 5x + 3\right) = 2x^2 + 10x - 6$$

$$6x^2 + \frac{21}{2}x - \frac{3}{2}$$
$$\underline{+\ 2x^2 + \frac{20}{2}x - \frac{12}{2}}$$
$$8x^2 + \frac{41}{2}x - \frac{15}{2}$$

This means **(D)** is correct. Notice that if you are simplifying the expression from left to right, after you find the x^2-coefficient, you can eliminate (A) and (B). After you find the x-coefficient, you can eliminate (C) and stop your work.

14. C

Difficulty: Hard

Getting to the Answer: In order to solve the equation, move all the terms to one side of the equation and set them equal to 0, then factor the expression. Thus, the given equation becomes $x^3 + x^2 - 9x - 9 = 0$. Think of this as two pairs of terms, $(x^3 + x^2)$ and $(-9x - 9)$. The first pair of terms share a common factor of x^2, so they can be written as $x^2(x + 1)$. The second pair share the common factor of -9, so they are equivalent to $-9(x + 1)$. So, the equation becomes $x^2(x + 1) - 9(x + 1) = 0$. Now, factor out the $(x + 1)$ term: $(x^2 - 9)(x + 1) = 0$.

In order for the product of two terms to be 0, either one or both must be 0. If $x^2 - 9 = 0$, then $x^2 = 9$ and $x = \pm 3$. Eliminate (A) and (D). If $x + 1 = 0$, then $x = -1$. Eliminate (B), so **(C)** is correct. You could also answer the question using Backsolving by plugging in each answer choice until you found the value for x that did *not* satisfy the equation.

15. C

Difficulty: Medium

Strategic Advice: To multiply two polynomials, multiply each term in the first factor by each term in the second factor, then combine like terms.

Getting to the Answer: Multiply each part of the trinomial expression by each part of the binomial one piece at a time and then combine like terms:

$$\left(2x^2 + 3x - 4\right)(3x + 2)$$
$$= 2x^2(3x + 2) + 3x(3x + 2) - 4(3x + 2)$$
$$= 6x^3 + 4x^2 + 9x^2 + 6x - 12x - 8$$
$$= 6x^3 + 13x^2 - 6x - 8$$

Because a represents the coefficient of x^2, $a = 13$. Hence, **(C)** is correct.

16. D

Difficulty: Medium

Getting to the Answer: Use polynomial long division to simplify the expression:

$$\begin{array}{r} 2a + 1 \\ a - 3 \overline{)\, 2a^2 - 5a - 1} \\ -(2a^2 - 6a) \\ \hline a - 1 \\ -(a - 3) \\ \hline 2 \end{array}$$

The quotient is $2a + 1$ and the remainder is 2, which will be divided by the divisor in the final answer: $2a + 1 + \dfrac{2}{a - 3}$. Thus, **(D)** is correct.

17. C

Difficulty: Hard

Getting to the Answer: A fraction is the same as division, so you can use polynomial long division to simplify the expression:

$$\begin{array}{r} 3x + 2 \\ 2x + 5 \overline{)\, 6x^2 + 19x + 10} \\ -(6x^2 + 15x) \\ \hline 4x + 10 \\ -(4x + 10) \\ \hline 0 \end{array}$$

The simplified expression is $3x + 2$, so $a + b = 3 + 2 = 5$, which is **(C)**. As an alternate approach, you could factor the numerator of the expression and cancel common factors:

$$\frac{6x^2 + 19x + 10}{2x + 5} = \frac{(2x + 5)(3x + 2)}{(2x + 5)} = 3x + 2$$

18. B

Difficulty: Medium

Getting to the Answer: Use polynomial long division to simplify the expression:

$$\begin{array}{r} 2x - 5 \\ 2x + 2 \overline{)\, 4x^2 - 6x} \\ -(4x^2 + 4x) \\ \hline -10x \\ -(-10x - 10) \\ \hline +10 \end{array}$$

The quotient is $2x - 5$ and the remainder is 10. Put the remainder over the divisor and add this to the quotient: $2x - 5 + \dfrac{10}{2x + 2}$. **(B)** is correct.

19. B

Difficulty: Hard

Getting to the Answer: The question provides the quotient of $-9x + 5$ of a division problem and asks you to find the coefficient of the first term of the divisor $tx - 4$. Set this up in polynomial long division form to better understand the relationship between t and the other terms:

$$\begin{array}{r} -9x + 5 \\ tx - 4 \overline{)\, 36x^2 + 16x - 21} \end{array}$$

Note that, although the quotient of $-9x + 5$ leaves a remainder of $-\dfrac{1}{tx - 4}$, it's not necessary to consider the remainder when determining the value of t.

Viewed this way, it becomes apparent that $36x^2 \div tx = -9x$. Multiplying both sides by tx gives you $tx(-9x) = 36x^2$; therefore, $t(-9) = 36$, so $t = -4$. **(B)** is correct.

20. C

Difficulty: Hard

Getting to the Answer: Because $f(x)$ is divisible by $x - 5$, the value $x - 5$ must be a factor of $f(x)$. Therefore, you can define $f(x)$ as $(x - 5)(n)$, where n is some unknown polynomial. Since $g(x)$ is $f(x) + 4$, you can say that $g(x)$ must be $(x - 5)(n) + 4$.

Thus, $g(5)$ will be $(5 - 5)(n) + 4 = 0(n) + 4 = 0 + 4 = 4$. Therefore, **(C)** is correct.

21. B

Difficulty: Medium

Getting to the Answer: The solutions, or x-intercepts, of a polynomial are the factors of that polynomial. This polynomial has x-intercepts of -4, 0, and 6. The factors that generate those solutions are $(x + 4)$, x, and $(x - 6)$. Eliminate (C) and (D) because they do not include those three factors. Because the graph *crosses* the x-axis at each x-intercept (rather than merely touching the x-axis), none of the factors can be raised to an even exponent. Therefore, the x^2 term in (A) means it is incorrect. **(B)** is correct.

22. C

Difficulty: Medium

Getting to the Answer: To find the solutions to a polynomial function, factor the polynomial and set each factor equal to 0. The solutions of a function are the x-intercepts, so $h(x)$ or the y-coordinate of the solution must equal 0. From the chart, the only point with $h(x) = 0$ is at $x = -1$. If $x = -1$, the factor that generates that solution is $x + 1 = 0$ because $(-1) + 1 = 0$. **(C)** is correct.

23. C

Difficulty: Hard

Getting to the Answer: Translate the notation: $b(a(x))$ means b of $a(x)$. This tells you to use $a(x)$ as the input for $b(x)$. You can rewrite this as $\dfrac{1}{a(x)}$, which is the reciprocal of $a(x)$. This new function will be undefined anywhere that $a(x) = 0$ because a denominator of 0 is not permitted. Looking at the graph, you can see that $a(x)$ crosses the x-axis four times, at which point the value of $a(x)$ is 0. Since division by 0 is undefined, **(C)** is correct.

24. A

Difficulty: Easy

Getting to the Answer: The phrase "exactly 2 distinct real zeros" means that the graph must have exactly two different x-intercepts on the graph. An x-intercept is indicated any time that the graph either crosses or touches the x-axis. (B) and (D) have three distinct zeros, and (C) has two zeros, but because the graph only touches the x-axis, they are the same, not distinct. The only graph with exactly two distinct zeros is **(A)**.

25. B

Difficulty: Easy

Getting to the Answer: The keyword "root" in the question stem means that you should examine the places at which the graph intersects the x-axis. Thus, this graph has roots at $(0, 0)$ and $(6, 0)$. The x-axis, according to the graph, represents the distance traveled by the balloon. When $x = 0$, the distance the water balloon has traveled is 0, which is the balloon's starting position. The initial location of the balloon is not an answer choice, so the correct answer must be what the other root represents. When $x = 6$, the balloon's height is 0, which is the end point of the balloon's trajectory. This value, 6, is a root that represents the total horizontal distance traveled. **(B)** is correct.

26. 74

Difficulty: Easy

Strategic Advice: The goal is to find the number of applicants *eliminated* after four days, not the number remaining.

Getting to the Answer: The question describes the decay as the result of removing a certain fraction of the remaining applicants each day. The situation involves repeated division, so this is an example of exponential decay. You could use the exponential decay formula for a given rate, but without a calculator, raising a decimal to an exponent might create time-consuming calculations. Instead, determine how many applicants are eliminated each day and tally them up.

After the first day, the judges eliminate one-fourth of 128, or 32, applicants. This leaves $128 - 32 = 96$ applicants. On the second day, one-fourth of 96, or 24, applicants are eliminated, leaving $96 - 24 = 72$. Finally, on the third day, one-fourth are eliminated again; one-fourth of 72 is 18, so there are $72 - 18 = 54$ applicants remaining. If 54 applicants remain, then $128 - 54 = 74$ applicants have been eliminated. Grid in **74**.

27. C
Difficulty: Medium

Strategic Advice: This question gives you a percent increase per year, so use the exponential growth equation to solve for the number of years. Note that the question provides unnecessary information. It doesn't matter that the trend has been happening for the last four years because the question asks only about the number of years after the present.

Getting to the Answer: Use the formula for exponential growth and plug in the values from the question. The rate is 16%, which as a decimal is 0.16. The rate will remain positive because the question asks about increase, or growth; therefore, $r = 0.16$. The current number of members is 42, so this will be $f(0)$. The goal is at least 100 members, so that will be the output, or $f(t)$. Put it all together:

$$f(t) = f(0)(1 + r)^t$$
$$100 = 42(1 + 0.16)^2$$
$$100 = 42(1.16)^t$$

At this point, Backsolving is the best approach. Plug in the number of years for t. Because the answer choices are in ascending order, try one of the middle options first. You might be able to eliminate more than one choice at a time. Choice (B) is $t = 5$:

$$42(1.16)^5 \approx 88$$

Since (B) is too small, (A) must be as well. Eliminate them both. Unfortunately, 88 is not close enough to 100 to be certain that **(C)** is the correct answer, so test it:

$$42(1.16)^6 \approx 102$$

Six years is enough to put the club over 100 members. **(C)** is correct.

28. A
Difficulty: Hard

Strategy Advice: The term "half-life" signals exponential decay because it implies repeated division by 2. Using the exponential decay formula here would be complicated. Instead, you can use the percentage given in the question, along with the Picking Numbers strategy, to figure out how many half-lives have elapsed.

Getting to the Answer: Instead of providing an actual amount of ^{14}C, this question tells you what percent is left. For questions involving percentages of unknown values, it is often a good idea to pick 100. So, assume that the amount of ^{14}C in the sample when the tree died is 100. (Fortunately, there is no need to worry about the units here.) After one half-life, the amount of ^{14}C is halved to 50. A second half-life leaves 25, a third leaves 12.5, and a fourth leaves 6.25, which is 6.25% of 100. So four half-lives have elapsed. Since each half-life is 5,600 years, the tree died $4 \times 5,600$ or 22,400 years ago. Choice **(A)** is correct.

29. 17
Difficulty: Medium

Strategic Advice: The question describes a situation with linear growth since Penelope is adding the same amount of money to her piggy bank each month. Note: the question is asking for her monthly allowance, but she puts in only half that amount each month.

Getting to the Answer: Use the linear growth equation $y = mx + b$. The question gives you the starting amount b ($40), the final amount y ($244), and the amount of time x (2 years, which is 24 months). Plug these values into the equation and solve for m, which is the slope, or the rate of change—or in this case, how much Penelope puts in her piggy bank each month:

$$y = mx + b$$
$$244 = m(24) + 40$$
$$24m = 204$$
$$m = 8.5$$

Remember that what she puts in the piggy bank is only half of her allowance, so her total monthly allowance is twice $8.50. Grid in **17**.

30. 160

Difficulty: Hard

Strategic Advice: This question describes both types of growth. Account X adds a percentage of the original amount, which never changes, so the same amount of money is added each month. Account X grows linearly. Account Y, however, adds a percentage of the current balance, which grows monthly, so account Y grows exponentially.

Getting to the Answer: Account X begins with $500 (the y-intercept, or b) and adds 2% of $500, or $500 \times 0.02 = \$10$ (the rate of change, or m), each month for 3 years, which is 36 months (the input, or x). Plug these values into the linear growth equation to solve for the final value of the account:

$$y = mx + b$$
$$y = 10(36) + 500$$
$$y = 360 + 500 = \$860$$

Account Y begins with $500 ($f(0)$) and adds 2%, or 0.02, (r) each month for 36 months (t). Plug these values into the exponential growth equation to solve for the final value of the account:

$$f(t) = f(0)(1 + r)^t$$
$$f(t) = 500(1 + 0.02)^{36}$$
$$f(t) = 500(1.02)^{36} \approx \$1,019.94$$

The positive difference between the two accounts is therefore $\$1,019.94 - \$860 = \$159.94$. Round up, and grid in **160**.

31. A

Difficulty: Medium

Getting to the Answer: There are two variables and only one equation, but because you're asked to solve for one of the variables *in terms of* the other, you solve the same way you would any other equation, by isolating x on one side of the equation. Cross-multiplying is a quick route to the solution:

$$\frac{6}{x} = \frac{3}{k + 2}$$
$$6(k + 2) = 3x$$
$$6k + 12 = 3x$$
$$\frac{6k}{3} + \frac{12}{3} = \frac{3x}{3}$$
$$2k + 4 = x$$

Switch x to the left side of the equation and the result matches **(A)**.

32. 3

Difficulty: Hard

Getting to the Answer: Because the expression is adding fractions with different denominators, you'll need to establish a common denominator. Note that the second fraction is divisible by 3, so you can simplify the expression and then create the common denominator:

$$\frac{3a + 9}{(a - 3)^2} + \frac{-3}{a - 3}$$
$$= \frac{3a + 9}{(a - 3)^2} + \frac{-3}{a - 3} \times \frac{a - 3}{a - 3}$$
$$= \frac{3a + 9}{(a - 3)^2} + \frac{-3a + 9}{(a - 3)^2}$$
$$= \frac{18}{(a - 3)^2}$$

The question specifies that $(a - 3)^2 = 6$, so $\frac{18}{(a - 3)^2} = \frac{18}{6} = 3$. Therefore, the expression equals 3. Grid in **3**.

33. C

Difficulty: Medium

Getting to the Answer: The denominator of the expression contains the sum of two fractions that themselves have different denominators, so start by finding a common denominator:

$$\frac{\frac{2}{a}}{\frac{a-6}{(a-2)(a-6)}+\frac{a-2}{(a-2)(a-6)}} = \frac{\frac{2}{a}}{\frac{2a-8}{a^2-8a+12}}$$

Next, multiply the numerator of the expression by the reciprocal of the denominator and simplify:

$$\frac{2}{a} \times \frac{a^2-8a+12}{2a-8}$$

$$= \frac{2\left(a^2-8a+12\right)}{2a^2-8a}$$

$$= \frac{a^2-8a+12}{a^2-4a}$$

This expression matches **(C)**.

34. B

Difficulty: Hard

Getting to the Answer: First, subtract $\frac{2}{x+1}$ from both sides to consolidate the two rational expressions on the same side of the equation. Next, multiply the left side of the equation by $\frac{(x+1)(x+2)}{(x+1)(x+2)}$ to establish a common denominator to enable subtraction of fractions. Next, combine like terms and cross-multiply:

$$\frac{5}{x+2} - \frac{2}{x+1} = \frac{1}{2}$$

$$\frac{5x+5}{x^2+3x+2} - \frac{2x+4}{x^2+3x+2} = \frac{1}{2}$$

$$\frac{3x+1}{x^2+3x+2} = \frac{1}{2}$$

$$6x+2 = x^2+3x+2$$

Next, set the equation equal to zero by subtracting $6x+2$ from both sides: $0 = x^2 - 3x$. Now, factor the right side to yield $0 = x(x-3)$.

Therefore, either $x = 0$ or $x = 3$. Since the question specifies that $x > 1$, x must equal 3, and **(B)** is correct.

Note that, if you wanted to avoid the algebra, you could backsolve this question by plugging in the answer choices to find which works in the original equation.

35. B

Difficulty: Hard

Getting to the Answer: Because the question states that the expressions are equivalent, set up the equation $\frac{16}{7x+4} + A = \frac{49x^2}{7x+4}$ and solve for A. Start by subtracting the first term from both sides of the equation to isolate A. Then, simplify if possible (usually by cancelling common factors). The denominators of the rational terms are the same, so they can be combined:

$$\frac{16}{7x+4} + A = \frac{49x^2}{7x+4}$$

$$A = \frac{49x^2}{7x+4} - \frac{16}{7x+4}$$

$$A = \frac{49x^2-16}{7x+4}$$

$$A = \frac{(7x+4)(7x-4)}{7x+4}$$

$$A = 7x - 4$$

The correct choice is **(B)**.

36. B

Difficulty: Medium

Getting to the Answer: While you might be tempted to establish a common denominator in order to add the fractions together, that would be extremely cumbersome. Instead, move the second fraction over to the other side of the equation by subtracting it from both sides. Then cross-multiply to simplify:

$$\frac{c+5}{6c} = \frac{-2}{2c-4}$$

$$(c+5)(2c-4) = -12c$$

$$2c^2+6c-20 = -12c$$

$$2c^2+18c-20 = 0$$

$$c^2+9c-10 = 0$$

$$(c+10)(c-1) = 0$$

Therefore, either $c = -10$ or $c = 1$. The question specifies that $c < 0$, so c must equal -10. **(B)** is correct.

37. D

Difficulty: Medium

Getting to the Answer: The first thought at seeing this question may be to try to break the expression into two separate fractions or see if some expression can be factored out. Unfortunately, that does not help with simplifying the expression. You'll need polynomial long division if you're going to use algebra:

$$x-4 \overline{)\begin{array}{r} 3 \\ 3x - 1 \end{array}}$$
$$\underline{-(3x-12)}$$
$$11$$

That results in the expression $3 + \dfrac{11}{x-4}$, so the correct answer is **(D)**.

Another effective alternative for solving this question is to use Picking Numbers. Choose a small, permissible value like $x = 2$ to find a value for the original expression:

$$\frac{3(2)-1}{(2)-4} = \frac{6-1}{-2} = -\frac{5}{2}$$

Now check each answer choice to see which one is equal to $-\dfrac{5}{2}$ when you plug in $x = 2$:

(A): $\dfrac{3-1}{4} = \dfrac{2}{4} = \dfrac{1}{2}$ ..., eliminate.

(B): $3(2) - \dfrac{1}{(2)-4} = 6 - \dfrac{1}{-2} =$

$6 - \left(-\dfrac{1}{2}\right) = 6 + \dfrac{1}{2} = 6\dfrac{1}{2} = \dfrac{13}{2}$ ..., eliminate.

(C): $3 - \dfrac{11}{(2)-4} = 3 - \dfrac{11}{-2} = 3 - \left(-\dfrac{11}{2}\right) = 3 + \dfrac{11}{2} = \dfrac{17}{2}$ ..., eliminate.

(D): $3 + \dfrac{11}{(2)-4} = 3 + \dfrac{11}{-2} = 3 + \left(-\dfrac{11}{2}\right) = -\dfrac{5}{2}$

38. C

Difficulty: Medium

Category: Rational Expressions and Equations

Getting to the Answer: When solving polynomial equations for one variable, begin by moving all terms that don't contain that variable (in this case a) to one side of the equation. Once there, multiply both sides by 2 to eliminate the fraction, and then divide by t^2 to isolate a:

$$h = \tfrac{1}{2}at^2 + v_0 t + h_0$$
$$h - v_0 t - h_0 = \tfrac{1}{2}at^2$$
$$at^2 = 2(h - v_0 t - h_0)$$
$$a = \frac{2(h - v_0 t - h_0)}{t^2}$$

Choice **(C)** is the correct answer.

39. D

Difficulty: Medium

Category: Exponents

Getting to the Answer: In order to combine terms with exponents by multiplication or division, the terms must all have the same base. All the bases in the given equation are powers of 2, so restate that equation with all the terms in base two: $\left(2^4\right)^{3x} \left(2^5\right)^x \left(2^3\right)^{3x} = \dfrac{\left(2^2\right)^{6x} \left(2^5\right)^{3x}}{2^2}$.
When a base with an exponent is raised to a power, multiply the exponents. An exponent in a denominator is equivalent to the same exponent in the numerator with the sign flipped, so $(2^{12x})(2^{5x})(2^{9x}) = (2^{12x})(2^{15x})(2^{-2})$.

When the numbers with exponents and the same base are multiplied, add the exponents. Thus, the equation further simplifies to $2^{12x+5x+9x} = 2^{12x+15x-2}$. Because the base on each side of the equation is the same, the total of the exponents on both sides must be equal. Therefore, $12x + 5x + 9x = 12x + 15x - 2$. This further simplifies to $26x = 27x - 2$, so $x = 2$. **(D)** is correct.

40. 2

Difficulty: Medium

Category: Radicals

Getting to the Answer: Conveniently, the conjugate of the denominator, $\sqrt{x} - 3$, is the numerator of the other fraction, $\sqrt{x} + 3$, so cross-multiplying will rationalize the fraction.

Cross-multiplying the first equation yields $(y)(3) = \left(\sqrt{x} + 3\right)\left(\sqrt{x} - 3\right)$, which simplifies to $3y = x - 9$. (If this is a difficult simplification for you, study FOIL and the classic quadratics in chapter 12.) In the second equation, you are given that $2x + 42 = 9x - 63$, so $7x = 105$, and $x = 15$. Therefore, $3y = 15 - 9 = 6$, and $y = 2$. Grid in **2**.

You could have chosen to solve the second equation for the value of x, then substituted the result into the proportion and solved for y. Either approach would be equally effective.

41. B

Difficulty: Medium

Category: Polynomial Division

Getting to the Answer: Since there's no common factor in the numerator and denominator, you'll need to resort to using polynomial long division. Notice that the numerator does not have an x term, so include $0x$ in the long division so that the fraction can be shown as $x - 3\overline{)3x^2 + 0x + 7}$. Next, do the long division:

$$
\begin{array}{r}
3x + 9 \\
x - 3 \overline{)3x^2 + 0x + 7} \\
\underline{3x^2 - 9x} \\
9x + 7 \\
\underline{9x - 27} \\
34
\end{array}
$$

The result of the long division is $3x + 9$ with a remainder of 34. The remainder is the "leftover" part that hasn't yet been divided by $x - 3$, so it can be expressed as $\frac{34}{x - 3}$.

Thus, **(B)** is correct.

42. A

Difficulty: Hard

Category: Polynomials

Strategic Advice: You could plug the x- and y-values from each choice into the given equation to see which does not equal zero. However, if you factor the polynomial, you'll save time by avoiding extra calculations.

Getting to the Answer: Look for common factors in the polynomial by groups. The first two terms, $15x^2$ and $10xy$, share the common factor $5x$. The third and fourth terms share a common factor of -2, so you can write the equation as $z = 5x(3x + 2y) - 2(3x + 2y)$. Next, factor out the $(3x + 2y)$ to regroup this as $z = (5x - 2)(3x + 2y)$. Since z is the product of two factors, if either factor equals 0, then $z = 0$.

If $(5x - 2) = 0$, then $x = \frac{2}{5}$. You can immediately eliminate (C) and (D) because, if $x = \frac{2}{5}$, $z = 0$ no matter what the value of y might be. If $(3x + 2y) = 0$, then $x = -\frac{2}{3}y$, as it is in (B). Thus, **(A)** is the only ordered pair for which $z \neq 0$.

43. 5

Difficulty: Hard

Category: Radicals

Getting to the Answer: Remember that the rules for combining terms under a radical are different for addition and multiplication. Although $\sqrt{xy}$ can be written as $\sqrt{x} \times \sqrt{y}$, terms that are added under a radical, such as $\sqrt{x + y}$, must be combined before taking the root. Now, find the value of each term in the radical above, add them, and then take the square root of the sum.

The term, $27^{\frac{2}{3}}$, is the square of the cube root of 27. Since $3 \times 3 \times 3 = 27$, the cube root of 27 is 3, which squared is $3^2 = 9$. The denominator of the exponent in $128^{\frac{4}{7}}$ quite likely means that 128 is some number to the seventh power. A good place to start would be to try 2 because it is small and easy to raise to high powers. Indeed, you'll find that $2 \times 2 \times 2 \times 2 \times 2 \times 2 \times 2 = 128$. So $128^{\frac{4}{7}} = \left(2^7\right)^{\frac{4}{7}} = 2^4 = 16$. Thus, $\sqrt{27^{\frac{2}{3}} + 128^{\frac{4}{7}}} = \sqrt{9 + 16} = \sqrt{25} = 5$. Grid in **5**.

44. A

Difficulty: Medium

Category: Rational Expressions and Equations

Strategic Advice: Since there is no common factor in the numerator and denominator, you might be tempted to dive into polynomial long division. However, if you noticed that the numerator, $4x^2 - 8$, is very close to being the difference of two squares, $4x^2 - 9$, there is a more efficient way to unravel this fraction.

Getting to the Answer: Restate the fraction as $\dfrac{4x^2 - 9}{2x + 3} + \dfrac{1}{2x + 3}$. Now factor the numerator and cancel like terms: $\dfrac{\cancel{(2x + 3)}(2x - 3)}{\cancel{2x + 3}} + \dfrac{1}{2x + 3}$. **(A)** is correct.

45. C

Difficulty: Medium

Category: Rational Expressions and Equations

Strategic Advice: Recall that a denominator equal to zero results in an undefined value for the fraction. To answer this question, determine which of the choices does *not* result in the denominator being equal to zero.

Getting to the Answer: You could plug each of the answer choices into the denominator to see which three equal zero, or you could factor the denominator first to simplify the identification of those values. Start by factoring out $2x$ to show the denominator as $2x(x^2 - 6x - 7)$. The denominator is the product of the two factors, so if either one is 0, the denominator will be 0. If $2x = 0$, $x = 0$, so eliminate (B) because $x = 0$ makes $g(x)$ undefined.

Next, you could either plug the remaining choices into $x^2 - 6x - 7$ to see which choice does not produce a result of zero or you could factor the expression into $(x - 7)(x + 1)$. Thus, either $x = 7$ or $x = -1$ results in the denominator of $g(x)$ equal to zero. Eliminate (A) and (D); **(C)** is correct. For the record, $g(1) = \dfrac{2}{-24}$.

46. B

Difficulty: Medium

Category: Polynomials

Getting to the Answer: In order to solve for possible values of x, first group all the terms on one side of the equation and set the other side to 0. Thus, $x^3 + 4 = 3x^2 - 7x + 25$ can be written as $x^3 - 3x^2 + 7x - 21 = 0$. Factor this by grouping the terms into two pairs. The first pair, $x^3 - 3x^2$, contains the common factor x^2, so it is equivalent to $x^2(x - 3)$. The second pair, $7x - 21$, factors to $7(x - 3)$. Thus, another form of the entire equation is $x^2(x - 3) + 7(x - 3) = 0$. Factor out $(x - 3)$ to get $\left(x^2 + 7\right)(x - 3) = 0$.

If the product of two factors is zero, one or both of the factors must be zero. If $\left(x^2 + 7\right) = 0$, then $x^2 = -7$. Since the square root of a negative number is not a real number, move on to $x - 3 = 0$. In this case, $x = 3$, so **(B)** is correct.

47. C

Difficulty: Medium

Category: Graphs of Polynomial Functions

Strategic Advice: Equations with roots of 0 as well as roots that are less than 0 will be incorrect and can be eliminated. When using elimination, start with the easiest looking choice first, then proceed to the next easiest, and so forth.

Getting to the Answer: Roots on a graph are the points at which $y = 0$. Start by plugging in 0 for y in each choice and solving for x, and then eliminate those choices for which x could be 0 or less. For (A), you would plug in 0 such that $0 = 4|x|$, which is true only for $x = 0$. Eliminate (A). For (B), plug in 0 for y and solve for x:

$$0 = x^2 - 4$$
$$x^2 = 4$$
$$\sqrt{x^2} = \sqrt{4}$$
$$x = \pm 2$$

Since x could equal -2, eliminate (B) as well. Choices (C) and (D) are the products of two factors. If the product of 2 factors is 0, then one of the factors must be 0. In (C), the only value for x that would make the equation equal to 0 is 2, which is greater than 0, so **(C)** is correct. On test day, you would move on, but for the record, in choice (D), $x = 0$ is a root, so (D) is incorrect.

48. D

Difficulty: Medium

Category: Graphs of Polynomial Functions

Getting to the Answer: The notation $f(x) = 0$ is another way of describing the x-axis, so this question is asking how many times the graph intersects or touches the x-axis. This graph crosses the x-axis four times, once each at $x = 0$, $x = 4$, $x = 3$, and $x = 2$, so **(D)** is correct.

49. A

Difficulty: Easy

Category: Modeling Growth and Decay

Getting to the Answer: If the number of smartphone users increases by 35% each year, then the amount of the increase is variable (because it's 35% of a bigger number each time), which means exponential growth. Eliminate (C) and (D). Consider the two remaining equations in terms of the exponential growth function, $f(x) = f(0)(1 + r)^x$. Note that the only difference between the two remaining choices is the r value. Recall that when assembling an exponential growth model, r (the rate) must be in decimal form. Therefore, the number raised to the power of x should be $1 + 0.35$, or 1.35. Choice **(A)** is the only one that fits these criteria.

CHAPTER 12

Quadratics

LEARNING OBJECTIVES

After completing this chapter, you will be able to:

- Solve a quadratic equation by factoring
- Recognize the classic quadratics
- Solve a quadratic equation by completing the square
- Solve a quadratic equation by applying the quadratic formula
- Relate properties of a quadratic function to its graph and vice versa
- Solve a system of one quadratic and one linear equation

60/600 SmartPoints® (High Yield)

How Much Do You Know?

Directions: Try the questions that follow. Show your work so that you can compare your solutions to the ones found in the Check Your Work section immediately after this question set. The "Category" heading in the explanation for each question gives the title of the lesson that covers how to solve it. If you answered the question(s) for a given lesson correctly, and if your scratchwork looks like ours, you may be able to move quickly through that lesson. If you answered incorrectly or used a different approach, you may want to take your time on that lesson.

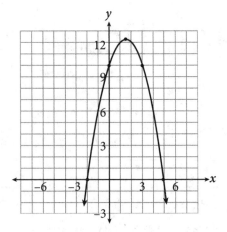

1. Which of the following linear expressions divides evenly into $6x^2 + 7x - 20$?

    A) $3x - 10$

    B) $3x - 5$

    C) $3x - 4$

    D) $3x - 2$

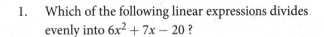
$$x^2 - 10x - 7$$

2. Which of the following expressions is equivalent to the expression above?

    A) $(x - 5)^2 - 32$

    B) $(x - 5)^2 + 32$

    C) $(x + 5)^2 - 32$

    D) $(x + 5)^2 + 32$

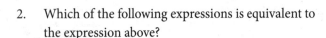
$$3x^2 - 5x = -k$$

3. In the equation above, k is a constant. For which of the following values of k does the equation have at least one real solution?

    A) 2

    B) 3

    C) 4

    D) 5

4. Which of the following could be the equation of the graph shown?

    A) $y = 2x + 10$

    B) $y = -x^2 + \dfrac{3}{2}x + 10$

    C) $y = -(x - 2)(x + 5)$

    D) $y = -(x + 2)(x - 5)$

5. The x-coordinates of the solutions to a system of equations are 3.5 and 6. Which of the following could be the system?

    A) $\begin{cases} y = x + 3.5 \\ y = x^2 + 6 \end{cases}$

    B) $\begin{cases} y = 2x - 7 \\ y = -(x - 6)^2 \end{cases}$

    C) $\begin{cases} y = \dfrac{1}{2}x + 3 \\ y = -(x - 5)^2 + 7 \end{cases}$

    D) $\begin{cases} y = \dfrac{1}{2}x + 7 \\ y = -(x - 6)^2 + 3.5 \end{cases}$

6. The graph of the equation $y = -4x^2 - 3x + 49$ intersects the line $x = -4$ at a point whose y-coordinate is g. The same graph intersects the line $x = 1$ at a point whose y-coordinate is h. What is the value of $g + h$?

   A) -6

   B) 27

   C) 39

   D) 46

7. If $x + y > 0$, $x^2 + 3xy = 90$, and $-xy + y^2 = -9$, what is the value of $x + y$?

Check Your Work

1.   C

Difficulty: Medium

Category: Solving Quadratics by Factoring

Getting to the Answer: Understanding that in algebra "divides evenly" means "is a factor" is the key to answering the question. You could use polynomial long division, but in most cases, factoring is quicker. The leading coefficient of the equation is not 1, so you'll need to use grouping to factor the equation. The general form of a quadratic is $ax^2 + bx + c$. To find the factors, multiply a by c, $6 \times -20 = -120$, and then look for two factors of that product whose sum is equal to b, the coefficient of the middle term. The two factors of -120 that add up to 7 are 15 and -8:

$$6x^2 + 7x - 20 = 6x^2 + 15x - 8x - 20$$
$$= \left(6x^2 + 15x\right) - (8x + 20)$$
$$= 3x(2x + 5) - 4(2x + 5)$$
$$= (2x + 5)(3x - 4)$$

Therefore, $3x - 4$ divides evenly into the expression, so **(C)** correct.

2.   A

Difficulty: Medium

Category: Completing the Square

Getting to the Answer: There are no integer factors of $x^2 - 10x - 7$, since no two integers whose product is -7 add up to -10. Note that the answer choices are stated in vertex format, the same as you would obtain by completing the square of the given expression. Half of the x-coefficient, -10, is -5, so the constant term needed to complete the square is $(-5)^2 = 25$. Thus, you can rewrite and group the given expression as $(x^2 - 10x + 25) - 25 - 7$. This simplifies to $(x - 5)^2 - 32$, which is **(A)**. Noticing that $x^2 - 10x + 25$ is a classic quadratic makes the process of factoring very quick.

3.   A

Difficulty: Medium

Category: The Quadratic Formula

Getting to the Answer: Restate the equation in "standard" quadratic form, $3x^2 - 5x + k = 0$. Recall that a quadratic equation has two real solutions if the discriminant, $b^2 - 4ac$, is positive. The equation has one real solution if the discriminant is 0. For the given equation, $a = 3$, $b = -5$, and $c = k$, so you can set up the inequality $(-5)^2 - 4(3)k \geq 0$. This simplifies to $25 \geq 12k$. The only choice for which this is true is **(A)**.

If you didn't recall the shortcut about the discriminant, consider the quadratic formula, $x = \dfrac{-b \pm \sqrt{b^2 - 4ac}}{2a}$.

If the term inside the radical, $b^2 - 4ac$, is negative, then there are no real solutions.

4.   D

Difficulty: Easy

Category: Graphs of Quadratics

Getting to the Answer: The graph is a parabola, so you can eliminate (A) because its equation is linear. The x-intercepts of the graph are -2 and 5, so the factors of the quadratic are $(x + 2)$ and $(x - 5)$. These factors make $y = 0$ when $x = -2$ and $x = 5$. Eliminate (B) and (C). Only (D) is left, so it must be correct. On test day, you would move on. For the record, the parabola opens downward, so there should be a negative sign in front of the factors. **(D)** is correct.

5. C

Difficulty: Hard

Category: Systems of Quadratic and Linear Equations

Getting to the Answer: You don't actually need to solve each system. Instead, plug 3.5 or 6 into each answer choice and eliminate each one whose y-values don't come out the same. (If the same x-value produces different y-values in two equations, then it is not the x-coordinate of the solution to the system.) Because 3.5 is a decimal, doing arithmetic with it is likely to be messy. So start with 6:

(A): $y = 6 + 3.5 = 9.5$

$y = 6^2 + 6 = 36 + 6 = 42$

Different y-values; eliminate.

(B): $y = 2(6) - 7 = 12 - 7 = 5$

$y = -(6 - 6)^2 = -(0)^2 = 0$

Different y-values; eliminate.

(C): $y = \frac{1}{2}(6) + 3 = 3 + 3 = 6$

$y = -(6 - 5)^2 + 7 = -(1)^2 + 7 = -1 + 7 = 6$

Keep for now. You need to test (D) because it's possible that (D) is the correct answer and (C) just happens to work for $x = 6$ (but not for $x = 3.5$).

(D): $y = \frac{1}{2}(6) + 7 = 3 + 7 = 10$

$y = -(6 - 6)^2 + 3.5 = -(0)^2 + 3.5 = 3.5$

Different y-values; eliminate.

(C) is correct.

6. C

Difficulty: Medium

Category: Graphs of Quadratics

Getting to the Answer: The question is asking for the sum of the y-coordinates of the intersection points of two vertical lines with a parabola. Substitute -4 for x into the equation $y = -4x^2 - 3x + 49$ to find the first intersection point: $y = -4(-4)^2 - 3(-4) + 49 = -4(16) + 12 + 49 = -64 + 12 + 49 = -52 + 49 = -3$. Thus, $g = -3$.

To find the second intersection point, substitute 1 for x into the same equation: $y = -4(1)^2 - 3(1) + 49 = -4(1) - 3 + 49 = -4 - 3 + 49 = -7 + 49 = 42$. Thus, $h = 42$.

Finally, add g and h: $g + h = -3 + 42 = 39$. **(C)** is correct.

7. 9

Difficulty: Medium

Category: Classic Quadratics

Getting to the Answer: Add the two equations.

$$(x^2 + 3xy) + (-xy + y^2) = 90 + (-9)$$
$$x^2 + 3xy - xy + y^2 = 81$$
$$x^2 + 2xy + y^2 = 81$$

Recognizing that $x^2 + 2xy + y^2$ is a classic quadratic makes it easy to rewrite $x^2 + 2xy + y^2 = 81$ as $(x + y)^2 = 81$. Take the square root of both sides to find that $x + y = 9$ or $x + y = -9$. The question says that $x + y > 0$, so discard -9 as a possible solution and grid in **9**.

Math

Solving Quadratics by Factoring

LEARNING OBJECTIVE

After this lesson, you will be able to:

• Solve a quadratic equation by factoring

To answer a question like this:

If $x^2 - 7x = 30$ and $x > 0$, what is the value of $x - 5$?

A)   5

B)   6

C)   10

D)   25

You need to know this:

A quadratic expression is a second-degree polynomial—that is, a polynomial containing a squared variable. You can write a quadratic expression as $ax^2 + bx + c$.

The **FOIL** acronym (which stands for First, Outer, Inner, Last) will help you remember how to multiply two binomials: multiply the first terms together (ac), then the outer terms (ad), then the inner terms (bc), and finally the last terms (bd):

$$(a + b)(c + d) = ac + ad + bc + bd$$

FOIL can also be done in reverse if you need to go from a quadratic to its factors.

To solve a quadratic equation by factoring, the quadratic must be set equal to 0. For example:

$$x^2 + x - 56 = 0$$
$$(x + 8)(x - 7) = 0$$

From the binomial factors, you can find the **solutions**, also called **roots** or **zeros**, of the equation. For two factors to be multiplied together and produce zero as the result, one or both those factors must be zero. In the example above, either $x + 8 = 0$ or $x - 7 = 0$, which means that $x = -8$ or $x = 7$.

You need to do this:

Here are the steps for solving a quadratic equation by factoring:

• Set the quadratic equal to zero.
• Factor the squared term. (For factoring, it's easiest when a, the coefficient in front of x^2, is equal to 1.)
• Make a list of the factors of c. Remember to include negatives.
• Find the factor pair that, when added, equals b, the coefficient in front of x.
• Write the quadratic as the product of two binomials.
• Set each binomial equal to zero and solve.

Explanation:

Set the equation equal to zero and factor the first term:

$$x^2 - 7x = 30$$
$$x^2 - 7x - 30 = 0$$
$$(x \pm ?)(x \pm ?) = 0$$

Next, consider factors of -30, keeping in mind that they must sum to -7, so *the factor with the greater absolute value must be negative*. The possibilities are: -30×1, -15×2, -10×3, and -6×5. The factor pair that sums to -7 is -10×3. Write that factor pair into your binomials:

$$(x - 10)(x + 3) = 0$$

Set each factor equal to zero and solve:

$$(x - 10) = 0 \qquad (x + 3) = 0$$
$$x = 10 \qquad\qquad x = -3$$

The question says that $x > 0$, so $x = 10$. Now that you solved for x, you can answer the question, which asks for $x - 5$: $10 - 5 = 5$. **(A)** is correct.

If factoring quadratics gives you trouble, study the steps in the table above and try these Drill questions before completing the following Try on Your Own questions. Factor each quadratic expression (without using a calculator). Turn the page to see the answers.

Drill

a. $a^2 + 8a + 15$

b. $x^2 + 4x - 21$

c. $b^2 - 7b - 18$

d. $y^2 - 10y + 24$

e. $x^2 + \dfrac{1}{2}x - \dfrac{1}{2}$

f. $5x^2 + 10x + 5$

g. $2x^2 + 12x - 54$

h. $3x^2 - 6x + 3$

i. $x^2 + 3xy + 2y^2$

j. $4a^2 + 4ab - 8b^2$

Try on Your Own

Directions: Take as much time as you need on these questions. Work carefully and methodically. There will be an opportunity for timed practice at the end of the chapter.

1. Which of the following is an equivalent form of the expression $(6 - 5x)(15x - 11)$?

   A) $-75x^2 + 35x - 66$

   B) $-75x^2 + 145x - 66$

   C) $90x^2 - 141x + 55$

   D) $90x^2 + 9x + 55$

HINT: For Q2, what is the easiest way to factor the denominator?

---

2. Which of the following is equivalent to $\dfrac{x^2 - 10x + 25}{3x^2 - 75}$?

   A) $\dfrac{3(x - 5)}{(x + 5)}$

   B) $\dfrac{3(x + 5)}{(x - 5)}$

   C) $\dfrac{(x - 5)}{3(x + 5)}$

   D) $\dfrac{(x + 5)}{3(x - 5)}$

HINT: For Q3, what value in the denominator would make the fraction undefined?

---

3. For what positive value of x is the equation $\dfrac{3}{2x^2 + 4x - 6} = 0$ undefined?

$3x^2 + 9x = 54$

4. What is the sum of the roots of the equation above?

   A) -6

   B) -3

   C) 3

   D) 6

Drill answers from previous page:

a. $a^2 + 8a + 15 = (a + 3)(a + 5)$

b. $x^2 + 4x - 21 = (x - 3)(x + 7)$

c. $b^2 - 7b - 18 = (b + 2)(b - 9)$

d. $y^2 - 10y + 24 = (y - 4)(y - 6)$

e. $x^2 + \frac{1}{2}x - \frac{1}{2} = (x + 1)\left(x - \frac{1}{2}\right)$

f. $5x^2 + 10x + 5 = 5(x + 1)(x + 1)$

g. $2x^2 + 12x - 54 = 2(x - 3)(x + 9)$

h. $3x^2 - 6x + 3 = 3(x - 1)(x - 1)$

i. $x^2 + 3xy + 2y^2 = (x + y)(x + 2y)$

j. $4a^2 + 4ab - 8b^2 = 4(a - b)(a + 2b)$

$$f(x) = (1.3x - 3.9)^2 - \left(0.69x^2 - 0.14x - 9.79\right)$$

5. Which of the following functions is equivalent to the function above?

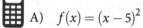

A) $f(x) = (x - 5)^2$

B) $f(x) = x^2 + 10.28x + 5.42$

C) $f(x) = 0.61x^2 + 0.14x + 25$

D) $f(x) = 1.3(x - 3)^2 - 0.69x^2 + 0.14x + 9.79$

Classic Quadratics

LEARNING OBJECTIVE

After this lesson, you will be able to:

- Recognize the classic quadratics

To answer a question like this:

Which of the following expressions is equivalent to $25x^2y^4 - 1$?

A) $5(x^2y^4 - 1)$

B) $-5(xy^2 + 1)$

C) $(5xy - 1)(5xy + 1)$

D) $(5xy^2 - 1)(5xy^2 + 1)$

You need to know this:

Memorizing the following classic quadratics will save you time on test day:

- $x^2 - y^2 = (x + y)(x - y)$
- $x^2 + 2xy + y^2 = (x + y)^2$
- $x^2 - 2xy + y^2 = (x - y)^2$

You need to do this:

When you see a pattern that matches either the left or the right side of one of the above equations, simplify by substituting its equivalent form. For example, say you need to simplify the following:

$$\frac{a^2 - 2ab + b^2}{a - b}$$

You would substitute $(a - b)(a - b)$ for the numerator and cancel to find that the expression simplifies to $a - b$:

$$\frac{a^2 - 2ab + b^2}{a - b} = \frac{(a - b)(a - b)}{a - b} = \frac{a - b}{1} = a - b$$

Explanation:

The expression $25x^2y^4 - 1$ is a difference of perfect squares. It corresponds to the first of the three classic quadratic patterns above. The square root of $25x^2y^4$ is $5xy^2$ and the square root of 1 is 1, so the correct factors are $(5xy^2 - 1)(5xy^2 + 1)$. Choice **(D)** is correct.

Try on Your Own

Directions: Take as much time as you need on these questions. Work carefully and methodically. There will be an opportunity for timed practice at the end of the chapter.

6. For all a and b, what is the sum of $(a-b)^2$ and $(a+b)^2$?

    A) $2a^2$

    B) $2a^2 - 2b^2$

    C) $2a^2 + 2b^2$

    D) $2a^2 + 4ab + 2b^2$

HINT: For Q7, how can you remove the fraction to make factoring easier?

---

7. What is the positive difference between the roots of the equation $y = \frac{1}{3}x^2 - 2x + 3$?

HINT: For Q8, look for a classic quadratic in the denominator.

$$f(x) = \frac{3}{(x-7)^2 + 6(x-7) + 9}$$

8. For which value of x is the function $f(x)$ undefined?

9. Suppose $a^2 + 2ab + b^2 = c^2$ and $c - b = 4$. Assuming $c > 0$, what is the value of a ?

$$2x^2 - 28x + 98 = a(x-b)^2$$

10. In the expression above, $a > 1$ and both a and b are constants. Which of the following could be the value of b ?

    A) -7

    B) 7

    C) 14

    D) 49

Completing the Square

LEARNING OBJECTIVE

After this lesson, you will be able to:

- Solve a quadratic equation by completing the square

To answer a question like this:

Which of the following equations has the same solutions as the equation $40 - 6x = x^2 - y$?

A) $y = (x - 6)^2 - 40$

B) $y = (x - 6)^2 + 40$

C) $y = (x + 3)^2 - 49$

D) $y = (x + 3)^2 + 49$

You need to know this:

For quadratics that do not factor easily, you'll need one of two strategies: completing the square or the quadratic formula (taught in the next lesson). To complete the square, you'll create an equation in the form $(x + h)^2 = k$, where h and k are constants.

As with factoring, completing the square is most convenient when the coefficient in front of the x^2 term is 1.

You need to do this:

Here are the steps for completing the square, demonstrated with a simple example.

Step	Scratchwork
Starting point:	$x^2 + 8x - 8 = 0$
1. Move the constant to the opposite side.	$x^2 + 8x = 8$
2. Divide b, the x-coefficient, by 2 and square the quotient.	$b = 8; \left(\frac{b}{2}\right)^2 = \left(\frac{8}{2}\right)^2 = (4)^2 = 16$
3. Add the number from the previous step to both sides of the equation and factor.	$x^2 + 8x + 16 = 8 + 16$ $(x + 4)(x + 4) = 24$ $(x + 4)^2 = 24$
4. Take the square root of both sides.	$\sqrt{(x + 4)^2} = \pm\sqrt{24} \rightarrow x + 4 = \pm\sqrt{24}$ $= \pm\sqrt{4}\sqrt{6}x + 4 = \pm2\sqrt{6}$
5. Split the result into two equations and solve each one.	$x + 4 = 2\sqrt{6} \rightarrow x = 2\sqrt{6} - 4$ $x + 4 = -2\sqrt{6} \rightarrow x = -2\sqrt{6} - 4$

Explanation:

First, write the equation in standard form: $y = x^2 + 6x - 40$. Add 40 to both sides and complete the square on the right-hand side. Find $\left(\frac{b}{2}\right)^2 = \left(\frac{6}{2}\right)^2 = 3^2 = 9$, and add the result to both sides of the equation:

$$y = x^2 + 6x - 40$$
$$y + 40 = x^2 + 6x$$
$$y + 40 + 9 = x^2 + 6x + 9$$
$$y + 49 = x^2 + 6x + 9$$

Note that all of the answer choices are in factored form. The right side of the equation is a classic quadratic that factors as follows:

$$y + 49 = (x + 3)(x + 3)$$
$$y + 49 = (x + 3)^2$$

Finally, solve for y to get $y = (x + 3)^2 - 49$, which means **(C)** is correct.

If you find completing the square to be challenging, study the steps in the table above and try these Drill questions before completing the following Try on Your Own questions. Turn the page to see the answers.

Drill

a. $x^2 = 10x + 2$

b. $-9 = 2x^2 + 16x + 3$

c. $x^2 - x - 11 = 0$

d. $x^2 + \frac{x}{2} = 4$

e. $-x^2 + 6ax = 2a^2$

Try on Your Own

Directions: Take as much time as you need on these questions. Work carefully and methodically. There will be an opportunity for timed practice at the end of the chapter.

11. Which of the following is a value of x that satisfies the equation $x^2 + 2x - 5 = 0$?

    A) -1

    B) $1 - \sqrt{6}$

    C) $1 + \sqrt{6}$

    D) $-1 - \sqrt{6}$

HINT: For Q12, the algebra will be easier if you substitute another variable for a^2.

$$a^4 - 12a^2 - 72 = 0$$

12. Which of the following is the greatest possible value of a ?

    A) $\sqrt{6 + \sqrt{3}}$

    B) $\sqrt{6\left(1 + \sqrt{3}\right)}$

    C) 12

    D) $6\left(1 + \sqrt{3}\right)$

HINT: For Q13, treat the square root in the b term just like any other: divide it by 2, then square it.

$$x^2 - \left(6\sqrt{5}\right)x = -40$$

13. What is the sum of the possible values of x given the above equation?

    A) 15

    B) $5\sqrt{5}$

    C) $6\sqrt{5}$

    D) 60

$$x^2 + 7x + 1 = 2x^2 - 4x + 3$$

14. Which of the following is a value of x that is valid in the above equation?

    A) $5.5 - \sqrt{28.25}$

    B) $\sqrt{5.5}$

    C) $\sqrt{30.25}$

    D) $5.5 + \sqrt{30.25}$

Drill answers from previous page:

a. $x = 5 \pm 3\sqrt{3}$

b. $x = -4 \pm \sqrt{10}$

c. $x = \dfrac{1 \pm 3\sqrt{5}}{2}$

d. $x = \dfrac{-1 \pm \sqrt{65}}{4}$

e. $x = 3a \pm a\sqrt{7}$

The Quadratic Formula

LEARNING OBJECTIVE

After this lesson, you will be able to:

- Solve a quadratic equation by applying the quadratic formula

To answer a question like this:

Which of the following are the real values of x that satisfy the equation $2x^2 - 5x - 2 = 0$?

A) 1 and 4

B) $-\dfrac{5}{4} + \dfrac{\sqrt{41}}{4}$ and $-\dfrac{5}{4} - \dfrac{\sqrt{41}}{4}$

C) $\dfrac{5}{4} + \dfrac{\sqrt{41}}{4}$ and $\dfrac{5}{4} - \dfrac{\sqrt{41}}{4}$

D) No real solutions

You need to know this:

The quadratic formula can be used to solve any quadratic equation. It yields solutions to a quadratic equation that is written in standard form, $ax^2 + bx + c = 0$:

$$x = \frac{-b \pm \sqrt{b^2 - 4ac}}{2a}$$

The $\pm$ sign that follows $-b$ indicates that you will have two solutions, so remember to find both.

The expression under the radical ($b^2 - 4ac$) is called the **discriminant**, and its value determines the *number* of real solutions. If the discriminant is positive, the equation has two distinct real solutions. If the discriminant is equal to 0, there is only one distinct real solution. If the discriminant is negative, there are no real solutions because you cannot take the square root of a negative number.

The arithmetic can get complicated, so reserve the quadratic formula for equations that cannot be solved by factoring and those in which completing the square is difficult because $a \neq 1$.

You need to do this:

Get the quadratic equation into the form $ax^2 + bx + c = 0$. Then substitute a, b, and c into the quadratic formula and simplify.

Math

Explanation:

In the given equation, $a = 2$, $b = -5$, and $c = -2$. Plug these values into the quadratic formula and simplify:

$$x = \frac{-b \pm \sqrt{b^2 - 4ac}}{2a}$$

$$x = \frac{-(-5) \pm \sqrt{(-5)^2 - 4(2)(-2)}}{2(2)}$$

$$x = \frac{5 \pm \sqrt{25 - (-16)}}{4}$$

$$x = \frac{5 \pm \sqrt{41}}{4}$$

$$x = \frac{5}{4} + \frac{\sqrt{41}}{4} \text{ or } x = \frac{5}{4} - \frac{\sqrt{41}}{4}$$

The correct answer is **(C)**.

If you find the quadratic formula to be challenging, study the formula and try these Drill questions before completing the following Try on Your Own questions. Turn the page to see the answers.

Drill

a. $x^2 - 2x - 20 = 0$

b. $3x^2 - 5x - 2 = 0$

c. $-7x^2 + 14x + 24 = -4$

d. $0.3x^2 + 0.7x - 1 = 0$

e. $\frac{x^2}{2} - x\sqrt{2} - 2 = 0$

Try on Your Own

Directions: Take as much time as you need on these questions. Work carefully and methodically. There will be an opportunity for timed practice at the end of the chapter.

HINT: For Q15, use the discriminant.

---

15. Given the equation $2x^2 + 8x + 4 + 2z = 0$, for what value of z is there exactly one solution for x?

16. The product of all the solutions to the equation $3v^2 + 4v - 2 = 0$ is M. What is the value of M?

    A) -3

    B) $-\dfrac{2}{3}$

    C) $-\dfrac{1}{3}$

    D) $\dfrac{4}{3}$

17. What are the solutions to the equation $4x^2 - 24x + 16 = 0$?

    A) $x = 3 \pm \sqrt{5}$

    B) $x = 4 \pm \sqrt{6}$

    C) $x = 5 \pm \sqrt{3}$

    D) $x = 5 \pm 2\sqrt{2}$

$$3x^2 = m(5x + v)$$

18. What are the values of x that satisfy the equation above, where m and v are constants?

    A) $x = -\dfrac{5m}{6} \pm \dfrac{\sqrt{25m^2 + 12mv}}{6}$

    B) $x = \dfrac{5m}{6} \pm \dfrac{\sqrt{25m^2 + 12mv}}{6}$

    C) $x = -\dfrac{5m}{3} \pm \dfrac{\sqrt{12m^2 + 25mv}}{3}$

    D) $x = \dfrac{5m}{3} \pm \dfrac{\sqrt{25m^2 + 12mv}}{3}$

HINT: For Q19, start with the standard form of a quadratic equation.

$$x(dx + 10) = -3$$

19. The equation above, where d is a constant, has no real solutions. The value of d could be which of the following?

    A) -12

    B) 4

    C) 8

    D) 10

20. Which of the following equations does NOT have any solutions that are real numbers?

    A) $x^2 + 8x - 12 = 0$

    B) $x^2 - 8x + 12 = 0$

    C) $x^2 - 9x + 21 = 0$

    D) $x^2 + 100x - 1 = 0$

Math

Graphs of Quadratics

LEARNING OBJECTIVE

After this lesson, you will be able to:

• Relate properties of a quadratic function to its graph and vice versa

To answer a question like this:

Given the equation $y = -(2x - 4)^2 + 7$, which of the following statements is NOT true?

A) The vertex is $(4, 7)$.

B) The y-intercept is $(0, -9)$.

C) The parabola opens downward.

D) The graph crosses the x-axis at least one time.

You need to know this:

A quadratic function is a quadratic equation set equal to y or $f(x)$ instead of 0. Remember that the solutions (also called "roots" or "zeros") of any polynomial function are the same as the x-intercepts. To solve a quadratic function, substitute 0 for y, or $f(x)$, then solve algebraically. Alternatively, you can plug the equation into your graphing calculator and read the x-intercepts from the graph. Take a look at the examples above to see this graphically.

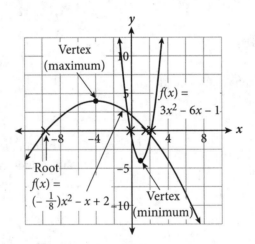

The graph of every quadratic equation (or function) is a **parabola,** which is a symmetric U-shaped graph that opens either upward or downward. To determine which way a parabola will open, examine the value of a in the equation. If a is positive, the parabola will open upward. If a is negative, it will open downward.

Drill answers:

a. $x = 1 \pm \sqrt{21}$

b. $x = 2, x = -\dfrac{1}{3}$

c. $1 \pm \sqrt{5}$

d. $x = -\dfrac{10}{3}, x = 1$

e. $\sqrt{2} \pm \sqrt{6}$

Like quadratic equations, quadratic functions will have zero, one, or two distinct real solutions, corresponding to the number of times the parabola touches or crosses the *x*-axis. Graphing is a powerful way to determine the number of solutions a quadratic function has.

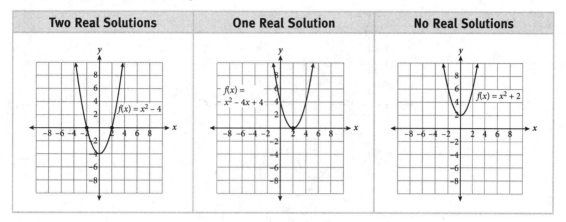

There are three algebraic forms that a quadratic equation can take: standard, factored, and vertex. Each is provided in the following table along with the graphical features that are revealed by writing the equation in that particular form.

Standard	Factored	Vertex
$y = ax^2 + bx + c$	$y = a(x - m)(x - n)$	$y = a(x - h)^2 + k$
y-intercept is *c*	Solutions are *m* and *n*	Vertex is (h, k)
In real-world contexts, starting quantity is *c*	*x*-intercepts are *m* and *n*	Minimum/maximum of function is *k*
Format used to solve via quadratic formula	Vertex is halfway between *m* and *n*	Axis of symmetry is given by $x = h$

You've already seen standard and factored forms earlier in this chapter, but vertex form might be new to you. In vertex form, *a* is the same as the *a* in standard form, and *h* and *k* are the coordinates of the **vertex** (h, k). If a quadratic function is not in vertex form, you can still find the *x*-coordinate of the vertex by plugging the appropriate values into the equation $h = \frac{-b}{2a}$, which is also the equation for the axis of symmetry (see graph that follows). Once you determine *h*, plug this value into the quadratic function and solve for *y* to determine *k*, the *y*-coordinate of the vertex.

The equation of the **axis of symmetry** of a parabola is $x = h$, where h is the x-coordinate of the vertex.

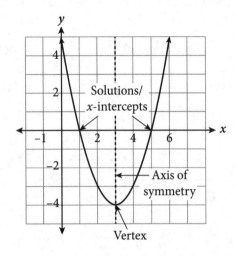

You need to do this:

- To find the vertex of a parabola, get the function into vertex form: $y = a(x - h)^2 + k$ or use the formula $h = \frac{-b}{2a}$.
- To find the y-intercept of a quadratic function, plug in 0 for x.
- To determine whether a parabola opens upward or downward, look at the coefficient of a. If a is positive, the parabola opens upward. If negative, it opens downward.
- To determine the number of x-intercepts, set the quadratic function equal to 0 and solve or examine its graph. (Quadratic function questions show up on both the no-calculator and calculator sections of the SAT.)

Explanation:

Be careful—the equation looks like vertex form, $y = a(x - h)^2 + k$, but it's not quite there because of the 2 inside the parentheses. You could rewrite the equation in vertex form, but this would involve squaring the quantity in parentheses and then completing the square, which would take quite a bit of time. Alternatively, you could notice that the greatest possible value for y in this function is 7, which happens when the squared term, $-(2x - 4)^2$, equals zero. To check (A), find the x-value when $y = 7$:

$$2x - 4 = 0$$
$$2x = 4$$
$$x = 2$$

For the record:

Choice (B): Substitute 0 for x and simplify to find that the y-intercept is indeed $(0, -9)$.

Choice (C): There is a negative in front of the squared term, so the parabola *does* open downward.

Choice (D): Because the parabola opens downward and the vertex is at $y = 7$, above the x-axis, the parabola must cross the x-axis twice. This statement is true as well, which confirms that **(A)** is correct.

Try on Your Own

Directions: Take as much time as you need on these questions. Work carefully and methodically. There will be an opportunity for timed practice at the end of the chapter.

HINT: For Q21, which form of a quadratic equation tells you the *x*-intercepts? Consult the table given earlier if you can't remember.

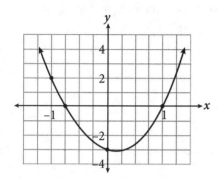

21. The following quadratic equations are all representations of the graph above. Which equation clearly represents the exact values of the *x*-intercepts of the graph?

    A) $y = 4x^2 - x - 3$

    B) $y = (4x + 3)(x - 1)$

    C) $y = 4(x - 0.125)^2 - 3.0625$

    D) $y + 3.0625 = 4(x - 0.125)^2$

HINT: For Q22, through which point on a parabola does the axis of symmetry pass?

---

22. Which equation represents the axis of symmetry for the graph of the quadratic function

    $f(x) = -\dfrac{11}{3}x^2 + 17x - \dfrac{43}{13}$?

    A) $x = -\dfrac{102}{11}$

    B) $x = -\dfrac{51}{22}$

    C) $x = \dfrac{51}{22}$

    D) $x = \dfrac{102}{11}$

23. How many times do the parabolas given by the equations $f(x) = 3x^2 - 24x + 52$ and $g(x) = x^2 + 12x - 110$ intersect?

    A) Never

    B) Once

    C) Twice

    D) More than twice

24. What is the positive difference between the *x*-intercepts of the parabola given by the equation $g(x) = -2.5x^2 + 10x - 7.5$?

HINT: For Q25, what does "maximum height" correspond to on the graph of a quadratic equation?

---

25. A toy rocket is fired from ground level. The height of the rocket with respect to time can be represented by a quadratic function. If the toy rocket reaches a maximum height of 34 feet 3 seconds after it was fired, which of the following functions could represent the height, *h*, of the rocket *t* seconds after it was fired?

    A) $h(t) = -16(t - 3)^2 + 34$

    B) $h(t) = -16(t + 3)^2 + 34$

    C) $h(t) = 16(t - 3)^2 + 34$

    D) $h(t) = 16(t + 3)^2 + 34$

Math

Systems of Quadratic and Linear Equations

LEARNING OBJECTIVE

After this lesson, you will be able to:

- Solve a system of one quadratic and one linear equation

To answer a question like this:

In the xy-plane, the graph of $y + 3x = 5x^2 + 6$ and $y - 6 = 2x$ intersect at points $(0, 6)$ and (a, b). What is the value of b ?

You need to know this:

You can solve a system of one quadratic and one linear equation by substitution, exactly as you would for a system of two linear equations. Alternatively, if the question appears on the calculator section, you can plug the system into your graphing calculator.

You need to do this:

- Isolate y in both equations.
- Set the equations equal to each other.
- Put the resulting equation into the form $ax^2 + bx + c = 0$.
- Solve this quadratic by factoring, completing the square, or using the quadratic formula. (You are solving for the x-values at the points of intersection of the original two equations.)
- Plug the x-values you get as solutions into one of the original equations to generate the y-values at the points of intersection. (Usually, the linear equation is easier to work with than the quadratic.)

Explanation:

Start by isolating y in both equations to get $y = 2x + 6$ and $y = 5x^2 - 3x + 6$. Next, set the right sides of the equations equal and solve for x:

$$2x + 6 = 5x^2 - 3x + 6$$
$$5x^2 - 5x = 0$$
$$5x(x - 1) = 0$$
$$x = 0 \text{ or } x = 1$$

The question says that $(0, 6)$ is one point of intersection for the two equations and asks for the y-value at the other point of intersection, so plug $x = 1$ into either of the original equations and solve for y. Using the linear equation will be faster:

$$y = 2(1) + 6$$
$$y = 8$$

Therefore, the point (a, b) is $(1, 8)$. Grid in **8**.

Try on Your Own

Directions: Take as much time as you need on these questions. Work carefully and methodically. There will be an opportunity for timed practice at the end of the chapter.

HINT: For Q26, note that both equations are equal to a.

$$\begin{cases} a = b^2 + 4b - 12 \\ a = -12 + b \end{cases}$$

26. The ordered pair (a, b) satisfies the system of equations above. What is one possible value of b ?

    A) -6

    B) -3

    C) 2

    D) 3

27. In the xy-coordinate plane, the graph of $y = 5x^2 - 12x$ intersects the graph of $y = -2x$ at points $(0, 0)$ and (a, b). What is the value of a ?

$$\begin{cases} y + 3x = 10 \\ y - x^2 + 7x = 13 \end{cases}$$

28. How many real solutions are there to the system of equations above?

    A)   Exactly 4 real solutions

    B)   Exactly 2 real solutions

    C)   Exactly 1 real solution

    D)   No real solutions

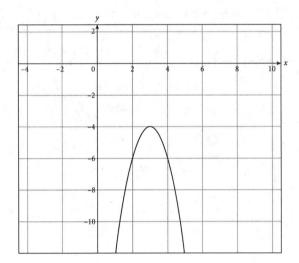

29. The graph of the function f, defined by $f(x) = -2(x - 3)^2 - 4$, is shown in the xy-plane above. The function g (not shown) is defined by $g(x) = 2x - 10$. If $f(c) = g(c)$, what is one possible value of c ?

    A) -6

    B) -4

    C) 2

    D) 4

HINT: For Q30, solve for the points of intersection, then use the formula for distance in the coordinate plane.

30. On the xy-plane, points P and Q are the two points where the parabola with the equation $y = 3x^2 + \frac{14}{3}x - \frac{73}{3}$ and the line with the equation $y = -\frac{4}{3}x - \frac{1}{3}$ meet. What is the distance between point P and point Q?

A) 5

B) 8

C) 10

D) 12

On Test Day

On the SAT, there is often more than one strategy that will get you to the answer. When a question involves a graph of two functions of x intersecting, you can either set the two functions equal to each other and solve for x, or you can use the coordinates of an intersection of the functions and set the values of both functions for that point equal to each other.

Try this question using both approaches. Which approach do you find easier? There's no right or wrong answer—just remember your preferred approach and use it if you see a question like this on test day.

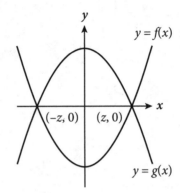

31. The functions $f(x) = 4x^2 - 25$ and $g(x) = -4x^2 + 25$ are graphed in the xy-plane above. The points where the two functions intersect are $(z, 0)$ and $(-z, 0)$. What is the value of z ?

A) 0.5

B) 1.0

C) 2.5

D) 4.0

The correct answer and both ways of solving can be found at the end of this chapter.

How Much Have You Learned?

Directions: For testlike practice, give yourself 18 minutes to complete this question set. Be sure to study the explanations, even for questions you got right. They can be found at the end of this chapter.

32. The equation $\frac{1}{4}\left(4x^2 - 8x - k\right) = 30$ has two solutions: $x = -5$ and $x = 7$. What is the value of $2k$?

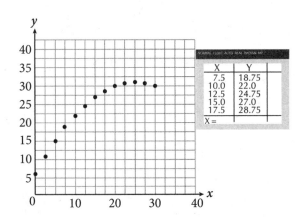

33. The maximum value of the data shown in the scatterplot above occurs at $x = 25$. If the data is modeled using a quadratic regression and the correlation coefficient is 1.0 (the fit is exact), then what is the y-value when $x = 35$?

A)   10

B)   15

C)   22

D)   27

Questions 34 and 35 refer to the following information.

The height of a boulder launched from a Roman catapult can be described as a function of time according to the following quadratic equation: $h(t) = -16t^2 + 224t + 240$.

34. What is the maximum height that the boulder attains?

A)   240

B)   784

C)   1,024

D)   1,696

35. How much time elapses between the moment the boulder is launched and the moment it hits the ground, assuming that the ground is at a height of 0?

A)   7

B)   12

C)   14

D)   15

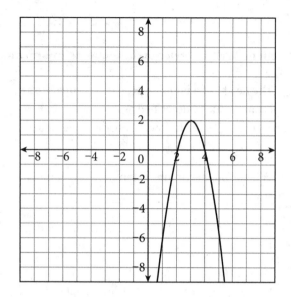

36. If the function shown in the graph is represented by $f(x) = a(x - h)^2 + k$, which of the following statements is NOT true?

A) The value of a is negative.

B) $f(x)$ is symmetrical across the line $y = 3$.

C) The function $g(x) = \frac{2x}{3}$ intersects $f(x)$ at its vertex.

D) The value of h is positive.

$$\begin{cases} y = 2x \\ 2x^2 + 2y^2 = 240 \end{cases}$$

37. If (x, y) is a solution to the system of equations above, what is the value of x^2?

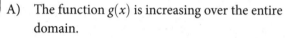

38. What are the x-intercepts of the parabolic function $f(x) = x^2 - 7x + 8\frac{1}{4}$?

A) $-1\frac{1}{2}$ and $3\frac{1}{2}$

B) 1 and $8\frac{1}{4}$

C) $1\frac{1}{4}$ and $5\frac{3}{4}$

D) $1\frac{1}{2}$ and $5\frac{1}{2}$

39. If $g(x) = (x - 2)^2 - 5$, which of the following statements is true?

A) The function $g(x)$ is increasing over the entire domain.

B) The function $g(x)$ is decreasing over the entire domain.

C) The function $g(x)$ is increasing for $x < 2$ and decreasing for $x > 2$.

D) The function $g(x)$ is decreasing for $x < 2$ and increasing for $x > 2$.

40. What is the sum of the solutions of $(6x + 5)^2 - (3x - 2)^2 = 0$?

A) $-\frac{8}{3}$

B) $-\frac{1}{6}$

C) $\frac{7}{3}$

D) 3

$$4x - 12\sqrt{x} + 9 = 16$$

41. If the equation above is true, what is the positive value of the expression $10\sqrt{x} - 15$?

A) 20

B) 25

C) 30

D) 35

42. In the equation $x - 2 = \dfrac{3}{x - 2}$, which of the following is a possible value of $x - 2$?

A) $\sqrt{3}$

B) 2

C) $2 + \sqrt{3}$

D) 3

43. If $\dfrac{z^{x^2+y^2}}{z^{-2xy}} = \left(z^3\right)^3$, x and y are positive integers, and $x > y$, what is the value of $x - y$?

A) 1

B) 2

C) 3

D) 8

Reflect

Directions: Take a few minutes to recall what you've learned and what you've been practicing in this chapter. Consider the following questions, jot down your best answer for each one, and then compare your reflections to the expert responses on the following page. Use your level of confidence to determine what to do next.

What features in a quadratic equation should you look for to decide whether to factor, complete the square, or apply the quadratic formula?

_____

_____

_____

Which constant in the vertex form of a quadratic function gives its maximum or minimum?

_____

_____

_____

Which form of a quadratic equation gives its y-intercept?

_____

_____

_____

Which form of a quadratic equation gives its x-intercepts, assuming the equation has two real roots?

_____

_____

_____

How do you solve a system of one linear and one quadratic equation?

_____

_____

_____

Expert Responses

What features in a quadratic equation should you look for to decide whether to factor, complete the square, or apply the quadratic formula?

Get the equation into standard form. If the coefficient in front of the squared term is 1, try factoring, but don't spend longer than about 15 seconds on the attempt. If you can't get the quadratic factored quickly, look at the coefficient on the middle term: if it is even, completing the square will be an efficient approach. Finally, the quadratic formula will work for any quadratic, no matter what the coefficients are.

Which constant in the vertex form of a quadratic function gives its maximum or minimum?

The vertex form is $y = a(x - h)^2 + k$. The constant k is the y-value at the vertex, which occurs at the maximum or minimum.

Which form of a quadratic equation gives its y-intercept?

The standard form, $y = ax^2 + bx + c$. The y-intercept is given by c.

Which form of a quadratic equation gives its x-intercepts, assuming the equation has two real roots?

The factored form, $y = a(x - m)(x - n)$. The x-intercepts are at $x = m$ and $x = n$.

How do you solve a system of one linear and one quadratic equation?

Put the linear equation in the form $y = mx + b$ and the quadratic in the form $y = ax^2 + bx + c$. Set the right sides of the equations equal to each other and solve.

Next Steps

If you answered most questions correctly in the "How Much Have You Learned?" section, and if your responses to the Reflect questions were similar to those of the SAT expert, then consider quadratics an area of strength and move on to the next chapter. Come back to this topic periodically to prevent yourself from getting rusty.

If you don't yet feel confident, review those parts of this chapter that you have not yet mastered. In particular, study the table describing the different forms of quadratics in the Graphs of Quadratics lesson. Then try the questions you missed again. As always, be sure to review the explanations closely. Finally, **go online** (www.kaptest.com/moreonline) for additional practice on the highest yield topics in this chapter.

Math

Answers and Explanations

1. B

Difficulty: Easy

Getting to the Answer: FOIL the binomials $(6 - 5x)(15x - 11)$: First, Outer, Inner, Last. First: $(6)(15x) = 90x$. Outer: $(6)(-11) = -66$. Inner: $(-5x)(15x) = -75x^2$. Last: $(-5x)(-11) = 55x$. Add all the terms together and combine like terms: $90x - 66 - 75x^2 + 55x = -75x^2 + 145x - 66$. The correct answer is **(B)**.

2. C

Difficulty: Easy

Getting to the Answer: First, factor out a 3 in the denominator to make that quadratic a bit simpler. Next, factor the numerator and denominator using reverse-FOIL to reveal an $x - 5$ term that will cancel out:

$$\frac{x^2 - 10x + 25}{3x^2 - 75} = \frac{x^2 - 10x + 25}{3(x^2 - 25)}$$

$$= \frac{(x - 5)(x - 5)}{3(x - 5)(x + 5)} = \frac{x - 5}{3(x + 5)}$$

The correct answer is **(C)**.

3. 1

Difficulty: Medium

Getting to the Answer: An expression is undefined when it involves division by 0, so the key to the question is to recognize that the denominator will be 0 if either of the factors of the quadratic are 0. Factoring 2 out of the denominator leaves a relatively easy-to-factor quadratic:

$$\frac{3}{2x^2 + 4x - 6} = 0$$

$$\frac{3}{2(x^2 + 2x - 3)} = 0$$

$$\frac{3}{2(x + 3)(x - 1)} = 0$$

The denominator will be 0 if the value of x is either 1 or -3. Because the question asks for a positive value of x, grid in **1**.

4. B

Difficulty: Medium

Getting to the Answer: Set the equation equal to zero, then divide through by 3 on both sides to remove the x^2-coefficient:

$$3x^2 + 9x - 54 = 0$$

$$x^2 + 3x - 18 = 0$$

$$(x - 3)(x + 6) = 0$$

$$x = 3 \text{ or } -6$$

The question asks for the sum of the roots, which is $3 + (-6) = -3$. The correct answer is **(B)**.

5. A

Difficulty: Hard

Strategic Advice: The question asks for an equivalent expression, so ignore the function notation and focus on manipulating the polynomial into standard form so it matches most of the answer choices.

Getting to the Answer: Expand the polynomial and distribute as necessary so that all of the parentheses are eliminated:

$$(1.3x - 3.9)^2 - (0.69x^2 - 0.14x - 9.79)$$

$$(1.3x - 3.9)(1.3x - 3.9) - 0.69x^2 + 0.14x + 9.79$$

$$1.69x^2 - 10.14x + 15.21 - 0.69x^2 + 0.14x + 9.79$$

Decimals are harder to work with than integers, so multiply by 100. Then combine like terms. Factor 100 back out and check to see if the result matches any of the answer choices:

$$169x^2 - 1,014x + 1,521 - 69x^2 + 14x + 979$$

$$100x^2 - 1,000x + 2,500$$

$$\frac{100x^2 - 1,000x + 2,500}{100}$$

$$x^2 - 10x + 25$$

Factor the polynomial: $x^2 - 10x + 25 = (x - 5)^2$. **(A)** is correct.

6. C

Difficulty: Easy

Getting to the Answer: Expand both classic quadratics and combine like terms to find the sum:

$$(a-b)^2 + (a+b)^2$$
$$= \left(a^2 - 2ab + b^2\right) + \left(a^2 + 2ab + b^2\right)$$
$$= 2a^2 + 2b^2$$

This matches **(C)**.

7. 0

Difficulty: Medium

Getting to the Answer: To find the roots, set the equation equal to 0, factor it, and then solve. Clear the fraction the same way you do when solving equations, multiplying both sides of the equation by the denominator of the fraction:

$$0 = \frac{1}{3}x^2 - 2x + 3$$
$$3(0) = 3\left(\frac{1}{3}x^2 - 2x + 3\right)$$
$$0 = x^2 - 6x + 9$$
$$0 = (x-3)(x-3)$$

The equation only has one unique solution $(x = 3)$, so the positive difference between the roots is $3 - 3 = \mathbf{0}$.

8. 4

Difficulty: Hard

Getting to the Answer: A fraction is undefined when the denominator equals 0. To find the value of x where $f(x)$ is undefined, set the denominator to 0 and solve for x.

The equation $(x-7)^2 + 6(x-7) + 9 = 0$ is the expansion of the classic quadratic $a^2 + 2ab + b^2 = (a+b)^2$, where $a = (x-7)$ and $b = 3$, so the denominator will factor as $[(x-7)+3]^2$. That's equivalent to $(x-4)^2$. Set this expression equal to 0 to find that the function is undefined when $x - 4 = 0$, or $x = \mathbf{4}$.

9. 4

Difficulty: Hard

Strategic Advice: Look for classic quadratics so you can avoid reverse-FOIL and save time:
$$x^2 + 2xy + y^2 = (x+y)^2$$

Getting to the Answer: Recognize that $a^2 + 2ab + b^2$ is a classic quadratic that simplifies to $(a+b)^2$. Factor the polynomial and take the square root of both sides to simplify the result:

$$(a+b)^2 = c^2$$
$$\sqrt{(a+b)^2} = \sqrt{c^2}$$
$$a + b = \pm c$$

The question says that c is positive. Subtracting b from both sides gives $a = c - b$. Plugging in 4 for $c - b$ gives $a = \mathbf{4}$.

10. B

Difficulty: Medium

Strategic Advice: Recognizing the classic quadratic $(x-y)^2 = x^2 + 2xy + y^2$ will save you time in factoring.

Getting to the Answer: In this question, the goal is to manipulate the polynomial so that it matches the factored form given. First, recognize that 2, the coefficient of x^2, can be factored out. The resulting expression is then $2\left(x^2 - 14x + 49\right)$. Notice that $\sqrt{49} = 7$ and factor the quadratic to get $2(x-7)(x-7) = 2(x-7)^2$. Now the expression is in the same form as $a(x-b)^2$. Therefore, $b = 7$, so **(B)** is correct.

11. D

Difficulty: Medium

Getting to the Answer: Factoring won't work here because no two factors of -5 sum to 2. However, the coefficient of x^2 is 1, so try completing the square:

$$x^2 + 2x - 5 = 0$$
$$x^2 + 2x = 5$$
$$\left(\frac{b}{2}\right)^2 = \left(\frac{2}{2}\right)^2 = 1^2 = 1$$
$$x^2 + 2x + 1 = 5 + 1$$
$$(x+1)^2 = 6$$
$$x+1 = \pm\sqrt{6}$$
$$x = -1 \pm \sqrt{6}$$

(D) matches one of the two possible values of x, so it's correct.

12. B

Difficulty: Hard

Getting to the Answer: Even though the given equation contains the value a^4, this is a quadratic-style question. You can say that $x = a^2$, so $x^2 - 12x - 72 = 0$. To complete the square, restate this as $x^2 - 12x = 72$. One-half of the x-coefficient is 6, which, when squared, becomes 36. So, $x^2 - 12x + 36 = 108$. Factor to find that $(x - 6)^2 = 108$ and then take the square root of both sides to get $x - 6 = \pm\sqrt{108}$. Since $108 = 36 \times 3$, the radical simplifies to $6\sqrt{3}$.

Now substitute a^2 back in for x: $a^2 - 6 = \pm6\sqrt{3}$ and $a^2 = 6 \pm 6\sqrt{3}$. Since the question asks for the root with the greatest value, you can ignore the root with the minus sign, so $a^2 = 6 + 6\sqrt{3} = 6(1 + \sqrt{3})$. Take the square root of both sides, and ignore the root with the negative sign to get $a = \sqrt{6(1 + \sqrt{3})}$. **(B)** is correct.

13. C

Difficulty: Hard

Getting to the Answer: The radical looks as if it will make the calculation difficult, but it will drop out when you complete the square. The coefficient, b, is $6\sqrt{5}$, so $\left(\frac{6\sqrt{5}}{2}\right)^2 = \left(\frac{36 \times 5}{4}\right) = 45$. Adding 45 to both sides of the equation gives you $x^2 - \left(6\sqrt{5}\right)x + 45 = 5$, so the factored form is $\left(x - 3\sqrt{5}\right)^2 = 5$. Take the square root of both sides to get $x - 3\sqrt{5} = \pm\sqrt{5}$. The two possible values of x are $3\sqrt{5} + \sqrt{5} = 4\sqrt{5}$ and $3\sqrt{5} - \sqrt{5} = 2\sqrt{5}$. The question asks for the sum of these values, which is $4\sqrt{5} + 2\sqrt{5} = 6\sqrt{5}$. **(C)** is correct.

14. A

Difficulty: Hard

Getting to the Answer: Subtract the left side of the equation from the right side:
$0 = 2x^2 - x^2 - 4x - 7x + 3 - 1 = x^2 - 11x + 2$.
Combine like-terms to get $x^2 - 11x = -2$. So, $b = -11$, and $\left(\frac{b}{2}\right)^2 = \left(\frac{11}{2}\right)^2 = 30.25$. Thus, completing the square gives you $x^2 - 11x + 30.25 = 28.25$. (This is a calculator-allowed question, so feel free to use the calculator if you need to do so. You could also have used the calculator to backsolve to find the correct choice.) Factor the left side to get $(x - 5.5)^2 = 28.25$ and $x - 5.5 = \pm\sqrt{28.25}$. Therefore, x can be either $5.5 + \sqrt{28.25}$ or $5.5 - \sqrt{28.25}$. The latter solution matches **(A)**.

15. 2

Difficulty: Hard

Strategic Advice: Recall that when the value of the discriminant, $b^2 - 4ac$, is 0, there is exactly one solution to the quadratic equation.

Getting to the Answer: The given equation is $2x^2 + 8x + 4 + 2z = 0$, but there is a common factor of 2 in all the terms, so this becomes $x^2 + 4x + 2 + z = 0$. So $a = 1$, $b = 4$, and $c = 2 + z$. Set the discriminant $4^2 - 4(1)(2 + z)$ equal to 0 so that there is only one solution. Expand the equation to $16 - 8 - 4z = 0$. Thus, $8 = 4z$, and $z = 2$. Grid in **2**.

16. B

Difficulty: Hard

Getting to the Answer: The question presents a quadratic equation that cannot be easily factored. Therefore, use the quadratic formula to solve. The quadratic formula states that $x = \frac{-b \pm \sqrt{b^2 - 4ac}}{2a}$.

In this case, $a = 3$, $b = 4$, and $c = -2$. Plug in these values to get:

$$x = \frac{-4 \pm \sqrt{4^2 - 4(3)(-2)}}{6}$$
$$= \frac{-4 \pm \sqrt{16 - (-24)}}{6}$$
$$= \frac{-4 \pm \sqrt{40}}{6}$$

Thus, the solutions to the equation are $\frac{-4 + \sqrt{40}}{6}$ and $\frac{-4 - \sqrt{40}}{6}$. The question asks for their product:

$$\left(\frac{-4 + \sqrt{40}}{6}\right)\left(\frac{-4 - \sqrt{40}}{6}\right)$$
$$= \frac{16 + 4\sqrt{40} - 4\sqrt{40} - 40}{36}$$
$$= \frac{-24}{36}$$
$$= -\frac{2}{3}$$

(B) is correct.

17. A

Difficulty: Medium

Strategic Advice: When all of the coefficients in a quadratic equation are divisible by a common factor, simplify the equation by dividing all terms by that factor before solving.

Getting to the Answer: The given equation is $4x^2 - 24x + 16 = 0$, but there is a common factor of 4 in all the terms, so this becomes $x^2 - 6x + 4 = 0$. Therefore, $a = 1$, $b = -6$, and $c = 4$.

The radicals in the answer choices are a strong clue that the quadratic formula is the way to solve this equation.

The quadratic formula is $x = \frac{-b \pm \sqrt{b^2 - 4ac}}{2a}$, and after you plug in the coefficients, you get:

$$x = \frac{6 \pm \sqrt{-6^2 - 4(1)(4)}}{2(1)}$$
$$= \frac{6 \pm \sqrt{36 - 16}}{2}$$
$$= \frac{6 \pm \sqrt{20}}{2}$$

This doesn't resemble any of the answer choices, so continue simplifying:

$$\frac{6 \pm \sqrt{20}}{2}$$
$$= \frac{6 \pm \sqrt{4}\sqrt{5}}{2}$$
$$= \frac{6 \pm 2\sqrt{5}}{2}$$
$$= \frac{6}{2} \pm \frac{2\sqrt{5}}{2}$$
$$= 3 \pm \sqrt{5}$$

Hence, **(A)** is correct.

18. B

Difficulty: Hard

Getting to the Answer: The question presents a variation of a quadratic equation. A glance at the radicals in the answer choices suggests that using the quadratic formula to solve is appropriate. Because there are so many variables, it might help to write down the quadratic formula in your notes as a guide: $x = \frac{-b \pm \sqrt{b^2 - 4ac}}{2a}$.

Begin by reorganizing the quadratic into the standard form $ax^2 + bx + c = 0$:

$$3x^2 = m(5x + v)$$
$$3x^2 = 5mx + mv$$
$$3x^2 - 5mx - mv = 0$$

In this case, $a = 3$, $b = -5m$, and $c = -mv$. Now solve:

$$x = \frac{-(-5m) \pm \sqrt{(-5m)^2 - 4(3)(-mv)}}{6}$$
$$= \frac{5m \pm \sqrt{25m^2 - (-12mv)}}{6}$$
$$= \frac{5m \pm \sqrt{25m^2 + 12mv}}{6}$$
$$= \frac{5m}{6} \pm \frac{\sqrt{25m^2 + 12mv}}{6}$$

Therefore, **(B)** is correct.

19. D

Difficulty: Medium

Getting to the Answer: Get the equation $x(dx + 10) = -3$ into the form $ax^2 + bx + c = 0$. Multiply out the left side of the equation $x(dx + 10) = -3$ to get $dx^2 + 10x = -3$. Add 3 to both sides to yield $dx^2 + 10x + 3 = 0$.

When a, b, and c are all real, the equation $ax^2 + bx + c = 0$ (when $a \neq 0$) does not have real solutions only if the discriminant, which is $b^2 - 4ac$, is negative. In the equation $dx^2 + 10x + 3 = 0$, $a = d$, $b = 10$, and $c = 3$. The discriminant in this question is $10^2 - 4(d)(3) = 100 - 12d$.

Since you're looking for a negative discriminant, that is, $b^2 - 4ac < 0$, you need $100 - 12d < 0$. Solve the inequality $100 - 12d < 0$ for d:

$$100 - 12d < 0$$
$$100 < 12d$$
$$\frac{100}{12} < d$$
$$\frac{25}{3} < d$$
$$8\frac{1}{3} < d$$

Among the answer choices, only 10 is greater than $8\frac{1}{3}$, so **(D)** is correct.

20. C

Difficulty: Medium

Getting to the Answer: Recall that when a quadratic equation has no real solutions, its discriminant, which is $b^2 - 4ac$, will be less than 0. Calculate the discriminant of each answer choice and pick the one that's negative. You don't need to actually solve for x:

(A) $8^2 - 4(1)(-12) = 64 + 48 > 0$. Eliminate.

(B) $(-8)^2 - 4(1)(12) = 64 - 48 > 0$. Eliminate.

(C) $(-9)^2 - 4(1)(21) = 81 - 84 = -3 < 0$. Pick **(C)** and move on. For the record:

(D) $(100)^2 - 4(1)(-1) = 10,000 + 4 > 0$. Eliminate.

21. B

Difficulty: Easy

Getting to the Answer: Quadratic equations can be written in several different forms that tell various pieces of important information about the equation. For example, the constant k in the vertex form of a quadratic equation, $y = a(x - h)^2 + k$, gives the minimum or maximum value of the function. The standard form, $y = ax^2 + bx + c$, gives the y-intercept as c. The factored form of a quadratic equation makes it easy to find the solutions to the equation, which graphically represent the x-intercepts. Choice **(B)** is the only equation written in factored form and therefore is correct. You can set each factor equal to 0 and quickly solve to find that the x-intercepts of the graph are $x = -\frac{3}{4}$ and $x = 1$, which agree with the graph.

22. C

Difficulty: Medium

Getting to the Answer: An axis of symmetry splits a parabola in half and travels through the vertex. Use the formula to find h, plug in the correct values from the equation, and simplify:

$$x = -\frac{b}{2a}$$
$$= -\frac{17}{2\left(\frac{-11}{3}\right)}$$
$$= -\frac{17}{\left(\frac{-22}{3}\right)}$$
$$= -17 \cdot \frac{-3}{22}$$
$$= \frac{51}{22}$$

The correct answer is **(C)**.

23. B

Difficulty: Hard

Getting to the Answer: To find where the two functions intersect, set them equal to each other and solve for x:

$$f(x) = g(x)$$
$$3x^2 - 24x + 52 = x^2 + 12x - 110$$
$$2x^2 - 36x + 162 = 0$$
$$2\left(x^2 - 18x + 81\right) = 0$$
$$x^2 - 18x + 81 = 0$$

Notice that this is a classic quadratic:

$$x^2 - 18x + 81 = 0$$
$$(x - 9)^2 = 0$$
$$x = 9$$

Since there is only one solution for x, there must be only one point of intersection. **(B)** is correct.

24. 2

Difficulty: Medium

Getting to the Answer: An x-intercept of a function is a point at which the y-coordinate equals 0. Set the equation equal to 0, simplify, and factor:

$$g(x) = -2.5x^2 + 10x - 7.5$$
$$0 = -2.5x^2 + 10x - 7.5$$
$$0 = -2.5\left(x^2 - 4x + 3\right)$$
$$0 = x^2 - 4x + 3$$
$$0 = (x - 1)(x - 3)$$
$$x = 1 \text{ or } x = 3$$

The question asks for the *difference* between the x-intercepts, not for the x-intercepts themselves. Thus, $3 - 1 = \mathbf{2}$.

25. A

Difficulty: Hard

Getting to the Answer: The answer choices are all similar, so pay special attention to their differences and see if you can eliminate any choices logically. A rocket goes up and then comes down, which means that the graph will be a parabola opening downward. The equation, therefore, should have a negative sign in front. Eliminate (C) and (D).

To evaluate the two remaining choices, recall the *vertex form* of a quadratic, $y = a(x - h)^2 + k$, and what it tells you: the vertex of the graph is (h, k). The h is the x-coordinate of the maximum (or minimum) and k is the y-coordinate of the maximum (or minimum). In this situation, x has been replaced by t, or time, and y is now $h(t)$, or height. The question says that the maximum height occurs at 3 seconds and is 34 feet, so h is 3 and k is 34. Substitute these values into vertex form to find that the correct equation is $y = -16(x - 3)^2 + 34$. The function that matches is **(A)**.

26. B

Difficulty: Medium

Strategic Advice: Because each of the two expressions containing b is equal to a, the two expressions must be equal to each other.

Getting to the Answer: Set the two expressions equal to each other and then solve for b:

$$b^2 + 4b - 12 = -12 + b$$
$$b^2 + 4b = b$$
$$b^2 + 3b = 0$$
$$b(b + 3) = 0$$

If $b(b + 3) = 0$, then $b = 0$ or $b = -3$. Of these two values, only -3 is among the answer choices, so **(B)** is correct.

27. 2

Difficulty: Medium

Getting to the Answer: The points of intersection of the graphs are the points at which the equations are equal. Since (a, b) is the label for an (x, y) point, set the two equations equal to each other and solve for the value of x to find the value of a:

$$-2x = 5x^2 - 12x$$
$$0 = 5x^2 - 10x$$
$$0 = 5x(x - 2)$$

Thus, $x = 0$ or $x = 2$. The question states that the intersection points are $(0, 0)$ and (a, b), so a must equal 2. Grid in **2**.

28. B

Difficulty: Medium

Getting to the Answer: The solutions to a system of equations are the points at which the equations intersect, which occurs when they are equal. Begin by setting both equations equal to y:

$$\begin{cases} y = -3x + 10 \\ y = x^2 - 7x + 13 \end{cases}$$

Because both equations are equal to y, they are also equal to each other. Set them equal and solve for x:

$$-3x + 10 = x^2 - 7x + 13$$
$$-3x = x^2 - 7x + 3$$
$$0 = x^2 - 4x + 3$$
$$0 = (x - 1)(x - 3)$$

Thus, there are two solutions, $x = 1$ and $x = 3$. **(B)** is correct.

Note that you could also use the discriminant, $b^2 - 4ac$, to determine how many solutions there are. If the discriminant is greater than 0, there are two real solutions; if it's equal to 0, there is one real solution; and if it's less than 0, there are no real solutions. In this case, $b^2 - 4ac = (-4)^2 - 4(1 \times 3) = 16 - 12 = 4$. Because $4 > 0$, there are two real solutions. **(B)** is correct.

29. C

Difficulty: Hard

Getting to the Answer: Because the question states that $f(c) = g(c)$, set the two functions equal to each other and solve for x. To make calculations easier, begin by converting $f(x)$ into standard form:

$$-2(x - 3)^2 - 4$$
$$= -2(x - 3)(x - 3) - 4$$
$$= -2\left(x^2 - 6x + 9\right) - 4$$
$$= -2x^2 + 12x - 18 - 4$$
$$= -2x^2 + 12x - 22$$

Now set the two functions equal:

$$-2x^2 + 12x - 22 = 2x - 10$$

Simplify by dividing all terms by -2:

$$x^2 - 6x + 11 = -x + 5$$

Next, combine like terms and solve for x:

$$x^2 - 6x + 11 = -x + 5$$
$$x^2 - 5x + 6 = 0$$
$$(x - 2)(x - 3) = 0$$

Therefore, $x = 2$ or $x = 3$, which means that c could also be either 2 or 3. Because 3 is not an answer choice, the answer must be 2. **(C)** is correct.

30. C

Difficulty: Hard

Strategic Advice: When you need to find the points of intersection of two equations, set the equations equal to each other.

Getting to the Answer: The question indicates that points P and Q are the points of intersection of the two equations, so set the two equations equal to each other, consolidate terms to get a single quadratic equation equal to 0, and simplify:

$$3x^2 + \frac{14}{3}x - \frac{73}{3} = -\frac{4}{3}x - \frac{1}{3}$$
$$3x^2 + \frac{18}{3}x - \frac{72}{3} = 0$$
$$3x^2 + 6x - 24 = 0$$
$$x^2 + 2x - 8 = 0$$

Factor the equation to find the values of x:

$$x^2 + 2x - 8 = 0$$
$$(x + 4)(x - 2) = 0$$
$$x = -4 \text{ or } 2$$

You can plug each value of x into either of the original equations to find the corresponding values of y. (The linear equation appears easier to work with.) For $x = -4$:

$$y = -\frac{4}{3}(-4) - \frac{1}{3}$$
$$y = \frac{16}{3} - \frac{1}{3}$$
$$y = \frac{15}{3} = 5$$

Therefore, one of the points of intersection is $(-4, 5)$. Find the other point of intersection by plugging in 2 for x into the linear equation:

$$y = -\frac{4}{3}(2) - \frac{1}{3}$$

$$y = -\frac{8}{3} - \frac{1}{3}$$

$$y = -\frac{9}{3} = -3$$

Thus, the other point of intersection is $(2, -3)$.

The question asks for the distance between these two points. The formula for the distance, d, between the points (x_1, y_1) and (x_2, y_2) is $d = \sqrt{(x_2 - x_1)^2 + (y_2 - y_1)^2}$. Thus, find the distance between points P and Q:

$$\sqrt{(-4 - 2)^2 + (5 - (-3))^2}$$

$$= \sqrt{(-6)^2 + 8^2}$$

$$= \sqrt{36 + 64}$$

$$= \sqrt{100}$$

$$= 10$$

Therefore, the distance between points P and Q is 10. **(C)** is correct.

31. C

Difficulty: Medium

Getting to the Answer: The first approach is to set $f(x)$ equal to $g(x)$: $4x^2 - 25 = -4x^2 + 25$. Isolate the x^2 terms on one side to get $8x^2 = 50$, so $4x^2 = 25$. Take the square root of both sides to see that $2x = \pm 5$, which means that the two intersections of the functions occur where $x = -2.5$ and $x = 2.5$. From the graph, you can see that these are the values of $\pm z$, so $z = 2.5$. **(C)** is correct. (Note that even if you had not been given the y-coordinates of the points of intersection, you could have calculated them from knowing their corresponding x-coordinates.)

The second approach is to plug in the coordinates of one of the intersections into either function. Using $f(x)$, the y-coordinate is 0 and the x-coordinate is z. So, $0 = 4z^2 - 25$. The math works out exactly the same as the first method: $4z^2 = 25$, so $z = \pm 2.5$, and, from the graph, you can determine that $z = 2.5$.

32. 40

Difficulty: Medium

Category: Graphs of Quadratics

Getting to the Answer: Since the given equation is valid for both $x = -5$ or $x = 7$, you can plug in either of those values and solve for k. Using 7 as the value of x gives you $\frac{1}{4}\left(4(7)^2 - 8(7) - k\right) = 30$. Multiply both sides by 4 to get $4(49) - 56 - k = 120$. Thus, $-k = 120 - 196 + 56 = -20$, so $k = 20$ and $2k = 40$. Grid in **40**.

33. D

Difficulty: Hard

Category: Graphs of Quadratics

Getting to the Answer: Because the quadratic regression is an exact fit of the data, you can treat the data points as a quadratic function.

The graph of a quadratic function is symmetric with respect to its axis of symmetry, which passes through the x-value of the vertex, or the maximum (or minimum) of the function. The question tells you the maximum occurs at $x = 25$, which makes it the line of symmetry. Because 35 is $35 - 25 = 10$ units to the right of the axis of symmetry, you know that the y-value will be the same as the point that is 10 units to the left of the axis of symmetry, which is $x = 25 - 10 = 15$. Find the corresponding y-value in the table: 27. Therefore, **(D)** is correct.

34. C

Difficulty: Hard

Category: Graphs of Quadratics

Getting to the Answer: Because the height of the boulder is expressed as a quadratic equation with a negative t^2 coefficient, the path of the boulder is a downward-facing parabola. Therefore, the maximum height occurs at the vertex of the parabola. The t-coordinate (generally called the x-coordinate) of the vertex of a parabola is given by $t = \frac{-b}{2a} = \frac{-224}{2(-16)} = 7$. Plug the result into the function to get the h-coordinate: $h(7) = -16(7)^2 + 224(7) + 240 = 1,024$. **(C)** is correct.

35. D

Difficulty: Medium

Category: Graphs of Quadratics

Getting to the Answer: Set the quadratic expression for the height of the boulder equal to 0 and solve for t:

$$-16t^2 + 224t + 240 = 0$$
$$-16\left(t^2 - 14t - 15\right) = 0$$
$$t^2 - 14t - 15 = 0$$
$$(t - 15)(t + 1) = 0$$
$$t = 15 \text{ or } t = -1$$

Because time can't be negative, $t = 15$. **(D)** is correct.

36. B

Difficulty: Medium

Category: Graphs of Quadratics

Getting to the Answer: Keep in mind that the question asks for the statement that's false, so eliminate the true choices as you go. The parabola opens downward, so the a term should be negative. Eliminate (A). The parabola's vertex is in quadrant I, so h and k are both positive. That makes choice (D) true as well; eliminate it. The axis of symmetry is $x = h$, so $x = 3$. According to the graph, the vertex is $(3, 2)$. Choice (B), however, claims that the axis of symmetry is $y = 3$. Choice **(B)** is false and is therefore the correct answer.

For the record, (C) is a true statement because the line $g(x) = \frac{2x}{3}$ passes through the point $(3, 2)$, which is indeed the vertex of $f(x)$.

37. 24

Difficulty: Medium

Category: Systems of Quadratic and Linear Equations

Getting to the Answer: The question tells you that $y = 2x$, so solving the system using substitution is a good option. Divide the second equation by 2 and plug in $2x$ for y:

$$2x^2 + 2y^2 = 240$$
$$x^2 + y^2 = 120$$
$$x^2 + (2x)^2 = 120$$
$$x^2 + 4x^2 = 120$$
$$5x^2 = 120$$
$$x^2 = 24$$

The question asks for the value of x^2, not x, so stop here. Grid in **24**.

38. D

Difficulty: Medium

Category: Completing the Square

Getting to the Answer: The x-intercepts of a function are the values of x that make the function equal to 0. Factoring this function would be cumbersome because you would need to determine two numbers whose product is $8\frac{1}{4}$ and whose sum is -7. This is a good candidate for completing the square.

Start with $x^2 - 7x + 8\frac{1}{4} = 0$, then subtract $8\frac{1}{4}$ from each side to get $x^2 - 7x = -8\frac{1}{4}$. Half of the b-coefficient, -7, is $-3\frac{1}{2}$, which, when squared, is $12\frac{1}{4}$. Add that to both sides to get $x^2 - 7x + 12\frac{1}{4} = 4$. So $\left(x - 3\frac{1}{2}\right)^2 = 4$. Take the square root of both sides to get $x - 3\frac{1}{2} = \pm 2$. Therefore, the x-intercepts are $3\frac{1}{2} \pm 2$, or $1\frac{1}{2}$ and $5\frac{1}{2}$. **(D)** is correct.

39. D

Difficulty: Medium

Category: Graphs of Quadratics

Getting to the Answer: Draw a quick sketch of the equation (or graph it in your graphing calculator):

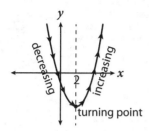

Based on the equation, the graph is a parabola that opens upward with a vertex of $(2, -5)$. A parabola changes direction at the x-coordinate of its vertex. You can immediately eliminate (A) and (B). To the left of 2 on the x-axis (or $x < 2$), the parabola is decreasing, and to the right of 2 on the x-axis (or $x > 2$), it is increasing. **(D)** is correct.

40. A

Difficulty: Medium

Category: Solving Quadratics by Factoring

Getting to the Answer: Rearrange the given equation to read $(6x + 5)^2 = (3x - 2)^2$. Given that the square of a number is the same value as the square of its negative counterpart, you can write that $\pm(6x + 5) = \pm(3x - 2)$. Therefore, either $6x + 5 = 3x - 2$ or $6x + 5 = (-1)(3x - 2) = -3x + 2$.

Solve the first case by subtracting $3x$ and 5 from both sides of the equation: $6x + 5 - 3x - 5 = 3x - 2 - 3x - 5$. Thus, $3x = -7$ and $x = -\frac{7}{3}$. For the alternative equation, add $3x$ to and subtract 5 from both sides: $6x + 5 + 3x - 5 = -3x + 2 + 3x - 5$. Thus, $9x = -3$, so $x = -\frac{1}{3}$.

The question asks for the sum of the two solutions, which is $-\frac{7}{3} + \left(-\frac{1}{3}\right) = -\frac{8}{3}$. **(A)** is correct.

41. A

Difficulty: Hard

Category: Classic Quadratics

Strategic Advice: Technically, this isn't a quadratic equation because the highest power on the variable isn't 2. However, it is a "quadratic-type" equation because the square of the variable part of the middle term is equal to the variable in the leading term. In other words, squaring $\sqrt{x}$ gives you x. You can use factoring techniques you learned for quadratics to answer the question.

Getting to the Answer: The presence of 4, 9, and 16—all perfect squares—is a big clue. Note that $4x - 12\sqrt{x} + 9$ is an instance of the classic quadratic $(a - b)^2 = a^2 - 2ab + b^2$. Use this shortcut to factor the equation and see where that leads you:

$$4x - 12\sqrt{x} + 9 = 16$$
$$\left(2\sqrt{x} - 3\right)^2 = 16$$
$$2\sqrt{x} - 3 = \pm 4$$

The question asks for $10\sqrt{x} - 15$, which happens to be 5 times the quantity on the left side of the last equation above, so multiply the positive result, 4, by 5 to get 20. The correct answer is **(A)**.

42. A

Difficulty: Medium

Category: Solving Quadratics by Factoring

Strategic Advice: When a question asks for a value of an expression, isolate that expression on one side of the equation, if possible, rather than solving for the variable.

Getting to the Answer: Notice that the question asks for a possible value of $x - 2$, not x. Isolate $x - 2$ on one side of the equation by multiplying both sides by $x - 2$ and taking the square root of both sides:

$$(x - 2)(x - 2) = \frac{3}{x - 2} (x - 2)$$
$$(x - 2)^2 = 3$$
$$\sqrt{(x - 2)^2} = \sqrt{3}$$
$$x - 2 = \pm\sqrt{3}$$

Thus, **(A)** is correct.

An alternative strategy is to Backsolve, plugging each choice in for $x - 2$ to see which results in a true statement.

43. A

Difficulty: Hard

Category: Classic Quadratics

Getting to the Answer: Use exponent rules to simplify the fraction. Since the terms in the numerator and denominator have the same base, z, subtract the exponent of the denominator from that of the numerator: $z^{x^2+y^2-(-2xy)} = z^{x^2+2xy+y^2}$. When a value with an exponent is raised to another exponent, multiply the exponents. So, for the term on the right side, $\left(z^3\right)^3 = z^9$. Now the equation is $z^{x^2+2xy+y^2} = z^9$. Since both sides have the common base, z, their exponents must be equal and you can write $x^2 + 2xy + y^2 = 9$.

Factor $x^2 + 2xy + y^2$, a classic quadratic, to get $(x + y)^2 = 9$. Thus, $x + y$ must be either 3 or -3. However, the question limits x and y to positive integers, so they must be 1 and 2. Furthermore, since $x > y$, x must be 2 and y must be 1. Consequently, $x - y = 2 - 1 = 1$. **(A)** is correct.

Test Yourself: Passport to Advanced Math

$$\frac{4x + 8y}{24x - 12}$$

1. Which of the following is the simplified form of the rational expression above?

   A) $\frac{1}{6} - \frac{2y}{3}$

   B) $\frac{x + 2y}{6x - 3}$

   C) $\frac{x + 2y}{2x - 1}$

   D) $\frac{x + 8y}{6x - 12}$

2. What is the resulting coefficient of x when $-x + 6$ is multiplied by $2x - 3$?

   A) -15

   B) -2

   C) 9

   D) 15

3. Which of the following is equivalent to the expression $4\sqrt[3]{ab^9}$?

   A) $4a^{\frac{1}{3}}b^3$

   B) $4a^3 b^{\frac{1}{3}}$

   C) $4a^3 b^{27}$

   D) $\dfrac{4}{a^{\frac{1}{3}}b^3}$

$$\sqrt{0.75} \times \sqrt{0.8}$$

4. Which of the following has the same value as the expression above?

   A) $\frac{3}{5}$

   B) $\frac{\sqrt{15}}{5}$

   C) $\sqrt[4]{0.6}$

   D) $\sqrt{1.55}$

5. Which of the following expressions is equivalent to $\left(27x^6 y^{12}\right)^{\frac{1}{3}}$?

   A) $3x^2 y^4$

   B) $9x^2 y^4$

   C) $\dfrac{27x^6 y^{12}}{3}$

   D) $(27x^6 y^{12})^{-3}$

$$\frac{12x^3 y^2 - 9x^2 y}{6x^4 y + 18x^3 y^3}$$

6. Which of the following is equivalent to the expression above?

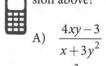

   A) $\dfrac{4xy - 3}{x + 3y^2}$

   B) $\dfrac{3x^2 y - 3xy}{x + 3y^2}$

   C) $\dfrac{4xy - 3}{2x^2 + 6xy^2}$

   D) $\dfrac{4xy - 9}{2x^2 + 18xy^3}$

Math

7. If $30x^3 + 45x^2 - 10x$ is divided by $5x$, what is the resulting coefficient of x?

   A) -2

   B) 6

   C) 9

   D) 10

$$\sqrt{9m^5n^2 - m^4n^2}$$

8. Which of the following is equivalent to the expression above, given that m and n are positive?

   A) $3\sqrt{m}$

   B) $3mn$

   C) $3n\sqrt{m}$

   D) $m^2n\sqrt{9m - 1}$

9. An online business card printer charges a setup fee of \$15 plus \$0.02 per card, based on a minimum order of at least 100 cards. Assuming a customer orders x cards, and $x \geq 100$, which of the following represents the average cost per card, C_{avg}, including the setup fee, before taxes and shipping costs?

   A) $C_{avg} = \dfrac{15 + 0.02}{x}$

   B) $C_{avg} = \dfrac{15}{x} + 0.02$

   C) $C_{avg} = 0.02x + 15$

   D) $C_{avg} = \dfrac{15}{x} + 0.02x$

$$\sqrt{2} \times \sqrt[4]{2}$$

10. Which of the following is equivalent to the product given above?

   A) $\sqrt[4]{8}$

   B) $\sqrt[6]{2}$

   C) $\sqrt[8]{2}$

   D) $\sqrt[8]{4}$

11. Which of the following best describes the solutions to the rational equation $\dfrac{3}{x-2} - \dfrac{12}{x^2-4} = 1$?

   A) No solution

   B) Two valid solutions

   C) Two extraneous solutions

   D) One valid solution and one extraneous solution

12. What is the remainder when $x^3 + 12$ is divided by $x + 2$?

13. If $12 + \dfrac{3\sqrt{x-5}}{2} = 18$, what is the value of x?

14. The factored form of a quadratic equation is $y = (2x - 3)(x + 5)$. What are the solutions to the equation?

A) $x = -5, x = \dfrac{2}{3}$

B) $x = -5, x = \dfrac{3}{2}$

C) $x = 5, x = -\dfrac{2}{3}$

D) $x = 5, x = -\dfrac{3}{2}$

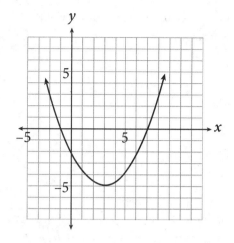

15. If e is half as far from the origin as f in the figure above, which of the following could be the factored form of the graph's equation?

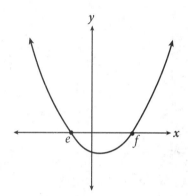

A) $y = \left(x - \dfrac{1}{2}\right)(x + 1)$

B) $y = (x - 1)(x + 2)$

C) $y = (x - 1)(2x + 1)$

D) $y = \left(x + \dfrac{1}{2}\right)(2x + 1)$

16. If $f(x) = ax^2 + bx + c$ represents the quadratic function whose graph is shown in the figure above, which of the following statements is NOT true?

A) $a > 0$

B) $b > 0$

C) $c < 0$

D) $6a = -b$

17. Which of the following equations could represent a parabola that has a minimum value of 5 and whose axis of symmetry is the line $x = -3$?

A) $y = (x - 3)^2 + 5$

B) $y = (x + 3)^2 + 5$

C) $y = (x - 5)^2 + 3$

D) $y = (x + 5)^2 - 3$

$$\begin{cases} x + y = 4 \\ y = x^2 - 2x - 15 \end{cases}$$

18. If (a, b) and (c, d) represent the solutions to the system of equations above, and $a < c$, then which of the following statements is true?

A) $a > 0$ and $c > 0$

B) $a < 0$ and $c < 0$

C) $a > 0$ and $c < 0$

D) $a < 0$ and $c > 0$

19. If the equation of the axis of symmetry of the parabola given by $y = 3x^2 + 12x - 8$ is $x = m$, then what is the value of m?

    A) -8

    B) -4

    X) -2

    D) 0

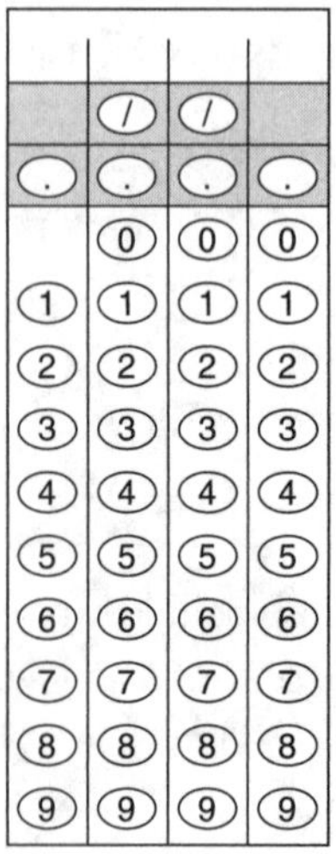

x	$p(x)$
-2	3
0	-3
2	-5
4	-3
6	3
8	13

21. The table above shows several points that lie on the graph of quadratic function $p(x)$. Based on the data in the table, what is $p(-4)$?

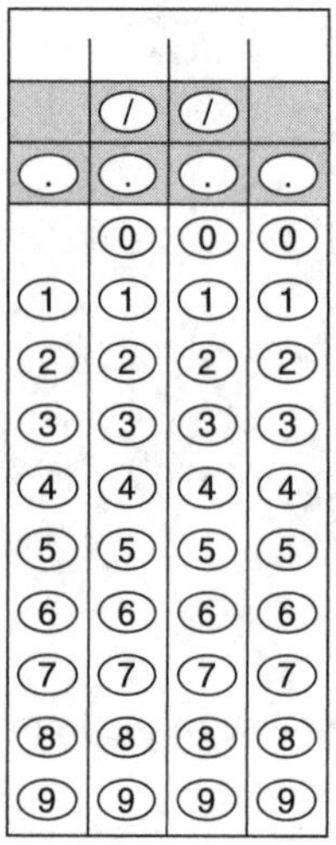

20. If the quadratic equation $y = 3(x + 5)^2 + 12$ is rewritten in standard form, $y = ax^2 + bx + c$, what is the value of c?

22. The rate of temperature decrease of a hot liquid placed in cooler air is directly related to the temperature difference between the liquid and the air at any point in time. Which of the images below shows this relationship if the temperature of the liquid is on the y-axis and time is on the x-axis?

A)

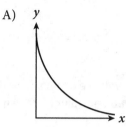

B)

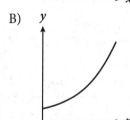

C)

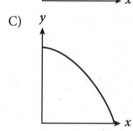

D)

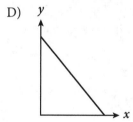

23. Which of the following CANNOT be a function $y = f(x)$?

A) $x = y$

B) $y = 3$

C) $x^2 = y + 3$

D) $y^2 = x + 3$

24. If $f(x) = \dfrac{x^2 - x - 12}{3x - 4}$ and $g(x) = x^2 - 7x + 8$, what is $f(2g(2))$?

A) -2

B) $-\dfrac{1}{2}$

C) 2

D) $\dfrac{7}{2}$

25. If $j(x) = 3x^2 + 6x - 24$, $k(x) = x + 4$, and $x = z - 5$, what is the value of $\dfrac{j(x)}{k(x)}$ when $z = 8$?

A) -3

B) 1

C) 3

D) 7

Answers and Explanations

1. B

Difficulty: Easy

Category: Rational Expressions and Equations

Getting to the Answer: To simplify a rational expression, look for common factors that can be divided out of the numerator and the denominator. If you find any common factors, you can cancel them. Keep in mind that you cannot cancel individual terms. Factor a 4 from the numerator and the denominator and then cancel the $\frac{4}{4}$:

$$\frac{4x + 8y}{24x - 12}$$

$$= \frac{\cancel{4}(1x + 2y)}{\cancel{4}(6x - 3)}$$

$$= \frac{x + 2y}{6x - 3}$$

(B) is correct.

2. D

Difficulty: Easy

Category: Solving Quadratics by Factoring

Getting to the Answer: Distribute each term in the first factor to each term in the second factor (FOIL), being careful with the signs:

$$(-x + 6)(2x - 3) = -x(2x - 3) + 6(2x - 3)$$

$$= -2x^2 + 3x + 12x - 18$$

$$= -2x^2 + 15x - 18$$

The question asks for the coefficient of x, so the answer is 15, which is **(D)**.

3. A

Difficulty: Medium

Category: Radicals

Getting to the Answer: Write each factor in the expression in exponential form and use exponent rules to simplify the expression. The number 4 is being multiplied by the variables. Eliminate (D). The power of a under the radical is 1 and the root is 3, so a is raised to the power of $\frac{1}{3}$. Eliminate (B) and (C). Only **(A)** is left and is correct.

On test day, you would move on, but for the record: the power of b is 9 and the root is 3, so the exponent on b is $\frac{9}{3} = 3$. Therefore, $4\sqrt[3]{ab^9} = 4a^{\frac{1}{3}}b^3$. **(A)** is indeed correct.

4. B

Difficulty: Medium

Category: Radicals

Getting to the Answer: When you see decimals that do not simplify, change them to an equivalent form, such as fractions. Then simplify:

$$\sqrt{0.75} \times \sqrt{0.8} = \sqrt{\frac{3}{4}} \times \sqrt{\frac{4}{5}} = \sqrt{\frac{3}{\cancel{4}} \times \frac{\cancel{4}}{5}} = \sqrt{\frac{3}{5}} = \frac{\sqrt{3}}{\sqrt{5}}$$

A radical is not allowed in the denominator of a fraction, so rationalize it by multiplying the numerator and the denominator by the same radical that you are trying to rationalize: $\frac{\sqrt{3}}{\sqrt{5}} \times \frac{\sqrt{5}}{\sqrt{5}} = \frac{\sqrt{15}}{5}$. **(B)** is correct.

5. A

Difficulty: Medium

Category: Exponents

Getting to the Answer: Write 27 as 3^3 and then use exponent rules to simplify. When you raise an exponent to another exponent, you multiply the exponents:

$$\left(27x^6y^{12}\right)^{\frac{1}{3}}$$

$$= 3^{\left(3 \times \frac{1}{3}\right)}x^{\left(6 \times \frac{1}{3}\right)}y^{\left(12 \times \frac{1}{3}\right)}$$

$$= 3x^2y^4$$

Choice **(A)** is correct.

6.   C

Difficulty: Medium

Category: Rational Expressions and Equations

Getting to the Answer: Find the greatest common factor of both the numerator and the denominator. For this expression, the greatest common factor is $3x^2y$. Factor it out and simplify:

$$\frac{12x^3y^2 - 9x^2y}{6x^4y + 18x^3y^3}$$

$$= \frac{3x^2y\,(4xy - 3)}{3x^2y\,(2x^2 + 6xy^2)}$$

$$= \frac{4xy - 3}{2x^2 + 6xy^2}$$

The correct answer is **(C)**.

7.   C

Difficulty: Medium

Category: Polynomials

Getting to the Answer: Note that each term of the polynomial expression is a multiple of $5x$. This means you don't need to use polynomial long division. Just divide each term by $5x$:

$$\frac{30x^3}{5x} + \frac{45x^2}{5x} - \frac{10x}{5x} = 6x^2 + 9x - 2$$

The question asks for the coefficient of x, so the correct answer is 9, which is **(C)**.

8.   D

Difficulty: Medium

Category: Radicals

Getting to the Answer: The greatest common factor of the terms under the radical is m^4n^2. Factor it out and take the square root of anything that is a perfect square to simplify:

$$\sqrt{9m^5n^2 - m^4n^2} = \sqrt{m^4n^2\,(9m - 1)}$$

$$= m^2n\sqrt{9m - 1}$$

(D) is correct.

9.   B

Difficulty: Easy

Category: Describing Real-Life Situations with Functions

Getting to the Answer: When asked to match an equation to a real-world scenario, Picking Numbers is often the strategy that will get you to the answer the quickest, especially when the answer choices look fairly complicated.

Choose a number of cards to order (at least 100)—say 200 cards. Work the scenario out using your calculator: $15 setup fee $+ 200(0.02) = \$19$. The question asks about the average cost *per card*, so divide this amount by 200 to get $0.095 per card. Now, plug 200 into each of the equations for x, looking for the same result.

Choice (A): $C_{avg} = \dfrac{15 + 0.02}{200} = 0.0751 \rightarrow$ No match.

Choice (B): $C_{avg} = \dfrac{15}{200} + 0.02 = 0.095 \rightarrow$ Match!

Check the remaining answer choices for completeness, but you'll see that only **(B)** is a match for the correct answer.

10.   A

Difficulty: Hard

Category: Radicals

Getting to the Answer: It is not possible to add, subtract, multiply, or divide radicals that represent roots of different degrees (such as a square root and a cube root) when they are written in radical form. Instead, you must write the radicals using fractional exponents and then use exponent rules to combine the terms.

Write each radical using a fractional exponent and then use the rule $a^x \cdot a^y = a^{x+y}$ to answer the question:

$$\sqrt{2} \times \sqrt[4]{2} = 2^{\frac{1}{2}} \times 2^{\frac{1}{4}}$$

$$= 2^{\frac{1}{2} + \frac{1}{4}}$$

$$= 2^{\frac{2}{4} + \frac{1}{4}}$$

$$= 2^{\frac{3}{4}}$$

The answers are written as radicals, so convert back to radicals: $\sqrt[4]{2^3} = \sqrt[4]{8}$. **(A)** is correct.

11. D

Difficulty: Hard

Category: Rational Expressions and Equations

Getting to the Answer: Factor the denominator in the second term to find that the common denominator for all three terms is $(x - 2)(x + 2)$. Multiply each term in the equation by the common denominator (in factored form or the original form, whichever is more convenient) to clear the fractions. Then solve the resulting equation for x:

$$^{(x+2)}\left(x^2 - 4\right)\left(\frac{3}{x - 2}\right) - \left(x^2 - 4\right)\left(\frac{12}{x^2 - 4}\right) = 1\left(x^2 - 4\right)$$

$$3(x + 2) - 12 = x^2 - 4$$

$$3x + 6 - 12 = x^2 - 4$$

$$3x - 6 = x^2 - 4$$

$$0 = x^2 - 3x + 2$$

$$0 = (x - 1)(x - 2)$$

Set each factor equal to 0 to find that the potential solutions are $x = 1$ and $x = 2$. Note that these are only *potential* solutions because the original equation was a rational equation. When $x = 2$, the denominators in both terms on the left side are equal to 0, so 2 is an extraneous solution, which means **(D)** is correct.

12. 4

Difficulty: Medium

Category: Polynomial Division

Getting to the Answer: To find a remainder, use polynomial long division. Add $0x^2$ and $0x$ to the dividend as placeholders for the missing terms:

$$
\begin{array}{r}
x^2 - 2x + 4 \\
x + 2 \overline{\smash{\big)}\, x^3 + 0x^2 + 0x + 12} \\
\underline{-\left(x^3 + 2x^2\right)} \\
-2x^2 + 0x \\
\underline{-\left(-2x^2 - 4x\right)} \\
4x + 12 \\
\underline{-(4x + 8)} \\
4
\end{array}
$$

The remainder is the number left over at the bottom, which is **4**.

13. 21

Difficulty: Medium

Category: Radicals

Getting to the Answer: Solve this radical equation the same way you would solve any other equation: isolate the variable using inverse operations. Like this:

$$12 + \frac{3\sqrt{x - 5}}{2} = 18$$

$$\frac{3\sqrt{x - 5}}{2} = 6$$

$$3\sqrt{x - 5} = 12$$

$$\sqrt{x - 5} = 4$$

$$x - 5 = 16$$

$$x = 21$$

The correct answer is **21**.

14. B

Difficulty: Easy

Category: Solving Quadratics by Factoring

Getting to the Answer: Whenever a quadratic (or any polynomial) equation is given in factored form, you can find the solutions by setting each of the factors equal to 0 and solving for the variable using inverse operations:

$$
\begin{array}{ll}
2x - 3 = 0 & x + 5 = 0 \\
2x = 3 & x = -5 \\
x = \dfrac{3}{2} &
\end{array}
$$

The solutions are $x = -5$ and $x = \frac{3}{2}$, so **(B)** is correct.

15. C

Difficulty: Medium

Category: Graphs of Quadratics

Getting to the Answer: According to the graph, one x-intercept is to the left of the y-axis and the other is to the right. Therefore, one value of x is positive, while the other is negative. Eliminate (D) because both factors have the same sign. To evaluate the remaining equations, find the x-intercepts by setting each factor equal to 0 and solving for x. In (A), the x-intercepts are $\frac{1}{2}$ and -1, but that would mean that e (the negative intercept) is twice as far from the origin as f, not half as

far, so eliminate (A). In (B), the *x*-intercepts are 1 and
-2. Again, *e* is twice as far from the origin as *f*, not half,
so eliminate (B). Only **(C)** is left and must be correct.
The *x*-intercepts are 1 and $-\frac{1}{2}$, which fits the criterion
that *e* is half as far from the origin as *f*.

16. B

Difficulty: Medium

Category: Graphs of Quadratics

Getting to the Answer: A quick glance at the choices
indicates this question is testing the signs of the coefficients of the standard form of the equation of a parabola. The *x*-intercepts of the parabola are -1 and 7, so
the factors that generated those roots are $(x + 1)$ and
$(x - 7)$. In factored form, the equation of the parabola
is $y = a(x + 1)(x - 7)$. Multiplying the binomials yields
$y = a(x^2 - 7x + x - 7) = a(x^2 - 6x - 7)$. Multiplying by
a returns the equation to standard form $ax^2 - 6ax - 7$,
and $b = -6a$. The parabola opens up, so *a* is positive
and thus *b* is negative. Remember that the correct
answer is what is *not* true, so **(B)** is correct.

17. B

Difficulty: Medium

Category: Graphs of Quadratics

Getting to the Answer: When a quadratic equation is
written in the form $y = a(x - h)^2 + k$, the minimum
value (or the maximum value if $a < 0$) is given by *k*, and
the axis of symmetry is given by the equation $x = h$.
The question states that the minimum of the parabola
is 5, so $k = 5$. Eliminate (C) and (D). The question also
states that the axis of symmetry is $x = -3$, so *h* must
be -3. The equation in (A) is not correct because the
vertex form of a parabola has a negative before the *h*,
so $(x - 3)$ would produce an axis of symmetry at $x = 3$,
not -3. **(B)** is correct because $x - (-3) = x + 3$.

You could also graph each equation in your graphing
calculator to see which one matches the criteria given in
the question, but this is likely to take more time.

18. D

Difficulty: Medium

Category: Systems of Quadratic and Linear Equations

Getting to the Answer: The answer choices describe
the sign of the *x*-coordinates of the solutions. This
means you don't need to find exact values for the
solutions. Instead, sketch the system (or graph it in
your calculator) and translate <0 as *negative* and >0
as *positive*.

The top equation is a line and the bottom equation
is a parabola. Write the linear equation in slope-
intercept form and the quadratic equation in factored
form to make them easier to draw: $x + y = 4$ becomes
$y = -x + 4$ and $y = x^2 - 2x - 15$ becomes $(x - 5)(x + 3)$.
Only label the information you need to solve the question. The line has a *y*-intercept of 4 and a negative slope.
The parabola opens upward and crosses the *x*-axis at
5 and -3. The equations look roughly like below:

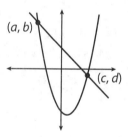

The solutions to the system are the points where the
graphs intersect. The question tells you that $a < c$, so
(a, b) must be the point on the left and (c, d) is the point
on the right. Look at the *x*-values: *a* is to the left of the
y-axis, so it must be negative (or $a < 0$), and *c* is to the
right of the *y*-axis, so it must be positive (or $c > 0$). This
means **(D)** is correct.

19. C

Difficulty: Medium

Category: Graphs of Quadratics

Getting to the Answer: The axis of symmetry of a parabola always passes through the x-coordinate of the parabola's vertex. The trick for finding the x-coordinate of the vertex is to calculate $\frac{-b}{2a}$ (the quadratic formula without the radical part). In the equation, $a = 3$ and $b = 12$, so the equation of the axis of symmetry is $x = \frac{-(12)}{2(3)} = \frac{-12}{6} = -2$. In the question, the equation is $x = m$, so m must be -2, which makes **(C)** correct.

20. 87

Difficulty: Easy

Category: Solving Quadratics by Factoring

Getting to the Answer: Use FOIL to expand the factored form of the quadratic into standard form:

$$y = 3(x + 5)^2 + 12$$
$$= 3(x + 5)(x + 5) + 12$$
$$= 3\left(x^2 + 5x + 5x + 25\right) + 12$$
$$= 3\left(x^2 + 10x + 25\right) + 12$$
$$= 3x^2 + 30x + 75 + 12$$
$$= 3x^2 + 30x + 87$$

The question asks for the value of c, so grid in **87**.

21. 13

Difficulty: Medium

Category: Graphs of Quadratics

Getting to the Answer: The question states that the function is quadratic, so look for symmetry in the table. Notice that the x-values in the table increase by two each time. To find $p(-4)$, you just need to imagine adding one extra row to the top of the table. The points in the table show that $(2, -5)$ is the vertex of the parabola, meaning that the graph is symmetrical around the line $x = 2$. The points $(0, -3)$ and $(4, -3)$ are equidistant from the vertex, as are the points $(-2, 3)$ and $(6, 3)$. This means the point whose x-value is -4 should have the same y-value as the last point in the table $(8, 13)$. So, $f(-4) = $ **13**.

22. A

Difficulty: Hard

Category: Describing Real-Life Situations with Functions

Getting to the Answer: The slope of a graph of temperature versus time is $\frac{\text{change in temperature}}{\text{change in time}}$, which is the rate at which the liquid cools. Since the temperature of the liquid decreases over time, a graph of temperature versus time should slope downward, so you can eliminate (B). As the liquid cools, the temperature difference between the liquid and the air decreases. In other words, the cooling rate decreases, and thus the slope should flatten over time.

Because the slope changes, eliminate (D). A straight line has a constant slope. The graph for (C) has a slope that steepens over time, so eliminate that choice as well. Choice **(A)** has a slope that flattens over time and is the correct answer.

23. D

Difficulty: Medium

Category: Graphs of Functions

Getting to the Answer: The question asks for an equation that *cannot* be represented as a function. Recall that a key characteristic of a function is that every input, x, must have a single output, y. For (A), each value of x produces a single value of y, so it can be written as $y = f(x)$. Eliminate (A). If $y = 3$, then any value of x on an xy-coordinate plane results in a y-value of 3, which is a single value. Eliminate (B). For (C), rearrange the equation to read $y = x^2 - 3$. Again, any value of x results in a single value of y. Eliminate (C). **(D)** is correct because any value of x, except $x = 3$, produces two different values of y. (For instance, if $x = 97$, then $y^2 = 100$, and $y = \pm 10$.)

24. B

Difficulty: Medium

Category: Function Notation

Getting to the Answer: Work from the inside out. Find $g(2)$, multiply it by 2 to find $2g(2)$ and then use the result as the input for $f(x)$: $g(2) = 2^2 - 7(2) + 8 = 4 - 14 + 8 = -2$. Next, $2g(2) = 2(-2) = -4$. Now, find

$$f(-4): \frac{(-4)^2 - (-4) - 12}{3(-4) - 4} = \frac{16 + 4 - 12}{-12 - 4} = \frac{8}{-16} = -\frac{1}{2}.$$

(B) is correct.

25. C

Difficulty: Medium

Category: Function Notation

Getting to the Answer: There are two ways to approach this question. After determining the value of x when $z = 8$, you can either plug that value into both functions or you can write out the equations for $j(x)$ and $k(x)$ and see if there are any common factors that can be canceled out. Both methods begin the same way: $x = 8 - 5 = 3$.

The function $j(x)$ is $3(3)^2 + 6(3) - 24 = 27 + 18 - 24 = 21$ when $x = 3$. Similarly, $k(x) = 3 + 4 = 7$.

So, $\frac{j(x)}{k(x)} = \frac{21}{7} = 3$. **(C)** is correct.

Other Topics in Math

CHAPTER 13

Geometry

LEARNING OBJECTIVES

After completing this chapter, you will be able to:

- Identify similar triangles and apply their properties
- Calculate the length of one side of a right triangle given the lengths of the other two sides
- Recognize the most common Pythagorean triples
- Calculate the other two sides of a 45-45-90 or 30-60-90 triangle, given one side length
- Interpret and manipulate the equation for a circle
- Calculate the length of an arc or the area of a sector defined by a central angle
- Convert degrees to radians
- Calculate the volume of common solids
- Calculate the surface area of common solids

65/600 SmartPoints® (High Yield)

How Much Do You Know?

Directions: Try the questions that follow. Show your work so that you can compare your solutions to the ones found in the Check Your Work section immediately following this question set. The "Category" heading in the explanation for each question gives the title of the lesson that covers how to solve it. If you answered the question(s) for a given lesson correctly, and if your scratchwork looks like ours, you may be able to move quickly through that lesson. If you answered incorrectly or used a different approach, you may want to take your time on that lesson.

Make use of the formula sheet below as needed; you'll have these same formulas available in your test booklet when you take the real SAT.

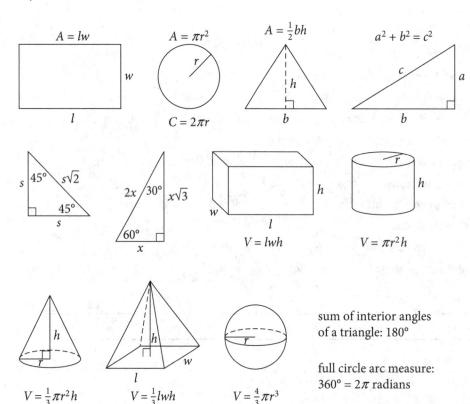

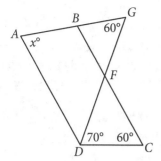

1. In the figure above, line segments AD and BC are parallel. What is the value of x?

    A)   60

    B)   70

    C)   80

    D)   110

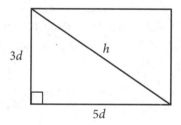

2. In the figure above, the diagonal of the rectangle has length h. What is the value of h in terms of d?

    A) d

    B) $4d$

    C) $\sqrt{34d}$

    D) $d\sqrt{34}$

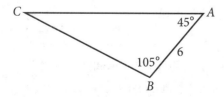

3. What is the area of the triangle shown in the figure?

     A) $18\sqrt{3}$

    B) $9+9\sqrt{3}$

    C) $9+18\sqrt{3}$

    D) $18+18\sqrt{3}$

4. What is the maximum value of y on the circumference of the circle defined by the equation 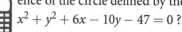 $x^2 + y^2 + 6x - 10y - 47 = 0$?

    A)   9

    B)   14

    C)   16

    D)   19

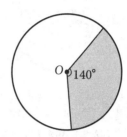

5. If the area of the shaded sector in circle O is 14π square units, what is the radius of the circle?

     A)   6

    B)   8

    C)   9

    D)   12

6. A yogurt factory fills cylindrical containers 80 percent of the way to the top, putting 6 ounces of yogurt in each cup. The containers are 4 inches tall and 2.5 inches wide. What is the approximate volume of 1 ounce of yogurt in cubic inches?

    A)   2.1

    B)   2.6

    C)   3.3

    D)   4.2

Math

Check Your Work

1. B

Difficulty: Medium

Category: Similar Triangles

Getting to the Answer: Notice that $\triangle CDF$ and $\triangle BFG$ are similar: they share a 60° angle, and the vertical angles formed at point F are equal, so their third angles must be equal as well. It follows that $\angle FBG = 70°$. Because line segments AD and BC are parallel, $\angle FBG$ and $\angle BAD$ are corresponding angles (and are therefore equal). You can now conclude that $\angle x = 70°$, so **(B)** is correct.

2. D

Difficulty: Medium

Category: Pythagorean Theorem

Getting to the Answer: The sides $3d$, $5d$, and h form a right triangle, so plug these values into the Pythagorean theorem and then solve for h. When you square $3d$ and $5d$, be sure to square the coefficient and the variable:

$$a^2 + b^2 = c^2$$
$$(3d)^2 + (5d)^2 = h^2$$
$$9d^2 + 25d^2 = h^2$$
$$34d^2 = h^2$$
$$\sqrt{34d^2} = h$$
$$d\sqrt{34} = h$$

Choice **(D)** is correct.

3. B

Difficulty: Hard

Category: Special Right Triangles

Getting to the Answer: First, find the measure of the missing angle in the triangle: $180° - 105° - 45° = 30°$. Next, draw the height of the triangle up from B to a point, D, on side AC to create two right triangles:

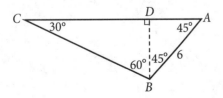

Triangle ABD is a 45-45-90 triangle, so its side lengths are in the ratio $x:x:x\sqrt{2}$. Because side AB is the hypotenuse, set up an equation using the ratio of the sides:

$$6 = x\sqrt{2}$$
$$\frac{6}{\sqrt{2}} = x$$
$$\frac{6}{\sqrt{2}}\left(\frac{\sqrt{2}}{\sqrt{2}}\right) = x$$
$$\frac{6\sqrt{2}}{2} = x$$
$$3\sqrt{2} = x$$

This is the length of both AD and BD. Triangle BDC is a 30-60-90 triangle, so its side lengths are in the ratio of $x:x\sqrt{3}:2x$. You just found that the length of the shorter leg, BD, is $3\sqrt{2}$, so multiply it by $\sqrt{3}$ to find the length of the longer leg $\left(\sqrt{3} \times 3\sqrt{2} = 3\sqrt{6}\right)$. Now, find the length of AC, which is the base of triangle BDC, by adding lengths AD to DC. The result is $3\sqrt{2} + 3\sqrt{6}$. Finally, use the area formula, $A = \frac{1}{2}bh$, to find the area of the whole triangle:

$$A = \frac{1}{2}\left(3\sqrt{2} + 3\sqrt{6}\right)\left(3\sqrt{2}\right)$$
$$= \frac{1}{2}\left(18 + 9\sqrt{12}\right)$$
$$= \frac{1}{2}\left(18 + 9 \cdot 2\sqrt{3}\right)$$
$$= \frac{1}{2}\left(18 + 18\sqrt{3}\right)$$
$$= 9 + 9\sqrt{3}$$

Choice **(B)** is correct.

4. B

Difficulty: Medium

Getting to the Answer: Complete the square of the given equation to arrange it into the standard format for a circle, $(x - h)^2 + (y - k)^2 = r^2$, to determine the center and the radius. The maximum value of y on the circle will be that of a radius drawn vertically up from the center.

The value $6x$ means that one of the terms in the equation for the circle will be $(x + 3)^2$ because that expands to $x^2 + 6x + 9$. Similarly, $10y$ means that the other term on the left side of the circle equation will be $(y - 5)^2 = y^2 + 10y + 25$.

Rewrite the given equation by adding $9 + 25$ to each side: $x^2 + 6x + 9 + y^2 - 10y + 25 - 47 = 9 + 25$. Next, simplify the x and y terms and add 47 to each side to yield $(x + 3)^2 + (y - 5)^2 = 9 + 25 + 47 = 81$. So, the y-coordinate of the center is 5. Since $r^2 = 81$, the radius of the circle is 9. Therefore, the y-coordinate of the point straight above the center is $5 + 9 = 14$. **(B)** is correct.

5. A

Difficulty: Medium

Category: Arc Length and Sectors

Getting to the Answer: The question asks for the radius. If you know the area of the circle, you can find the radius. The question gives enough information to find the area of the circle. Use the relationship $\dfrac{\text{area of sector}}{\text{area of circle}} = \dfrac{\text{central angle}}{360°}$:

$$\frac{14\pi}{A} = \frac{140}{360}$$
$$5{,}040\pi = 140A$$
$$36\pi = A$$

Now, solve for r using $A = \pi r^2$:

$$36\pi = \pi r^2$$
$$36 = r^2$$
$$\pm 6 = r$$

The radius can't be negative, so the correct answer is 6, which is **(A)**.

6. B

Difficulty: Hard

Category: Three-Dimensional Figures

Getting to the Answer: Find the volume of the container using the formula for volume of a cylinder, $V = \pi r^2 h$. The question gives you the width, or the diameter, of the container, so divide by 2 to get the radius: one-half of 2.5 is 1.25. Now, solve:

$$V = \pi (1.25)^2 (4)$$
$$V = \pi (1.5625)(4)$$
$$V = 6.25\pi$$

The factory fills the cup only 80% of the way up, so multiply the container volume by 0.8 to find that the actual volume of the yogurt is $6.25\pi \times 0.8 = 5\pi$, or about 15.708 cubic inches. Divide this by 6 ounces to determine that 1 ounce takes up approximately 2.6 cubic inches of space, which matches **(B)**.

Similar Triangles

LEARNING OBJECTIVE

After this lesson, you will be able to:

- Identify similar triangles and apply their properties

To answer a question like this:

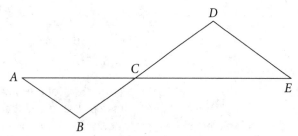

Note: Figure not drawn to scale.

In the figure above, segments *AE* and *BD* intersect at point *C*, and $\angle ABC \cong \angle CDE$. If $BC = DE = 5$ and $AB = 2$, what is the measure of *CD*?

You need to know this:

The corresponding angles and side lengths of **congruent triangles** are equal. **Similar triangles** have the same angle measurements and proportional sides. In the figure that follows, the two triangles have the same angle measurements, so the side lengths can be set up as the following proportion: $\frac{A}{D} = \frac{B}{E} = \frac{C}{F}$.

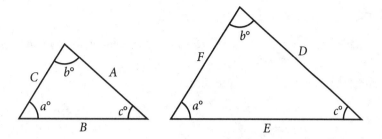

Two triangles are similar if three specific conditions are met:

- Two of their three angles are congruent (**angle-angle**). For example, two triangles that each have one 40° and one 55° angle are similar.

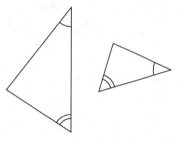

- Two of their three sides are in the same proportion and the intervening angle is congruent (**side-angle-side**). For example, a triangle with sides of 10 and 12 and an intervening angle of 40° and another triangle with sides of 20 and 24 and an intervening angle of 40° are similar.

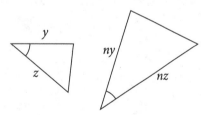

- Their three sides are in the same proportion (**side-side-side**). For example, a triangle with sides of 5, 6, and 8 and a triangle with sides of 15, 18, and 24 are similar.

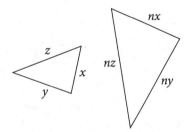

You need to do this:

- Determine whether two triangles are similar by checking for angle-angle, side-angle-side, or side-side-side relationships.
- Find a missing side length by setting up a proportion.

Explanation:

Label the figure with information from the question stem and information you can deduce from geometry principles. These two triangles are similar because they have two sets of congruent angles: one set is the set of vertical angles ($\angle ACB \cong \angle DCE$) and one set is given in the question stem ($\angle ABC \cong \angle CDE$). Corresponding sides in similar triangles are proportional to each other, so set up a proportion to find the missing side length. In this case, CD corresponds to BC and DE corresponds to AB. Let the measure of CD be represented by x and solve:

$$\frac{CD}{BC} = \frac{DE}{AB}$$
$$\frac{x}{5} = \frac{5}{2}$$
$$x = \frac{25}{2}$$

Grid in **25/2** or **12.5**.

Try on Your Own

Directions: Take as much time as you need on these questions. Work carefully and methodically. There will be an opportunity for timed practice at the end of the chapter.

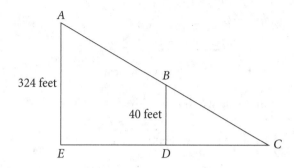

1. The diagram above shows similar triangles *ACE* and *BCD*. If segment *DC* is 50 percent longer than segment *BD*, how long is segment *DE* ?

HINT: Triangles with a shared angle and parallel sides are similar. How can you use this fact in Q2?

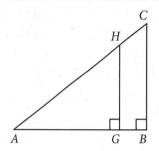

Note: Figure not drawn to scale.

2. Triangle *ABC* above has an area of 150 square units. If lengths $AB = AH = 20$, then what is the length of *HG* ?

    A) 5
    B) 12
    C) 16
    D) 20

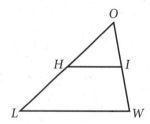

Note: Figure not drawn to scale.

3. Triangle *LOW* is shown in the figure above, where segment *HI* is the bisector of both segments *LO* and *OW*. Given that $LW = 30$ and $HI = 4x - 1$, what is the value of *x* ?

    A) 3.5
    B) 4
    C) 7.75
    D) 8

4. Right triangle *DEF* is similar to right triangle *ABC*, and both are plotted on a coordinate plane (not shown). The vertices of triangle *DEF* are $D(3, 2)$, $E(3, -1)$, and $F(-1, -1)$. The vertices that form triangle *ABC*'s longer leg are $(-8, -3)$ and $(8, -3)$. If vertex *A* is in the same quadrant of the coordinate plane as vertex *D*, what is the *y*-coordinate of vertex *A* ?

HINT: For Q5, translate carefully from English into math and fill in the lengths on the figure.

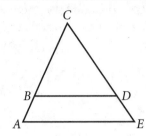

Note: Figure not drawn to scale.

5. In the figure above, $\overline{BD} \| \overline{AE}$ and $AB = 5$. If *BC* is three times *AB*, and if *CD* is 2 more than half *AC*, then what is the length of segment *DE* ?

    A) 3

    B) 4

    C) 5

    D) 6

Pythagorean Theorem

LEARNING OBJECTIVES

After this lesson, you will be able to:

- Calculate the length of one side of a right triangle given the lengths of the other two sides
- Recognize the most common Pythagorean triples

To answer a question like this:

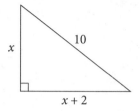

What is the area of the triangle shown?

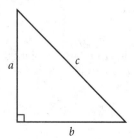

You need to know this:

The **Pythagorean theorem** states that in any right triangle (and *only* in right triangles), the square of the hypotenuse (the longest side) is equal to the sum of the squares of the legs (the shorter sides). If you know the lengths of any two sides of a right triangle, you can use the Pythagorean equation, $a^2 + b^2 = c^2$, to find the length of the third. In this equation, a and b are the legs of the triangle and c is the hypotenuse, the side across from the right angle of the triangle.

Consider an example: a right triangle has a leg of length 9 and a hypotenuse of length 14. To find the missing leg, plug the known values into the Pythagorean equation: $9^2 + b^2 = 14^2$. This simplifies to $81 + b^2 = 196$, which becomes $b^2 = 115$. Take the square root of both sides to find that $b = \sqrt{115}$.

Some right triangles have three side lengths that are all integers. These sets of integer side lengths are called **Pythagorean triples**. The two most common Pythagorean triples on the SAT are 3:4:5 and 5:12:13. Look for multiples of these (e.g., 6:8:10 and 10:24:26) as well. Memorizing these triples now can save you valuable calculation time on test day.

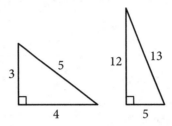

You need to do this:

- Keep in mind that the Pythagorean theorem applies only to right triangles.
- When you need to find a side length of a right triangle, look first for the common Pythagorean triples or their multiples.
- If you cannot identify any Pythagorean triples, substitute any two known side lengths into the equation $a^2 + b^2 = c^2$, where c represents the hypotenuse, to find the third.

Explanation:

You could answer this question by applying the Pythagorean equation, but you would have to do a fair amount of algebra. It's much faster if you recognize that this is a 6:8:10 Pythagorean triple. Then it's just a matter of calculating the area, using the legs as the base and height:

$$A = \tfrac{1}{2}bh = \tfrac{1}{2}(8)(6) = 24$$

For the record, here's the solution using the Pythagorean equation:

$$x^2 + (x+2)^2 = 10^2$$
$$x^2 + x^2 + 4x + 4 = 100$$
$$2x^2 + 4x - 96 = 0$$
$$x^2 + 2x - 48 = 0$$
$$(x+8)(x-6) = 0$$
$$x = -8 \quad \text{or} \quad x = 6$$

At this point, you would throw out the negative root because length must be positive, so you would use 6 and $6 + 2 = 8$ as the legs and calculate the area as shown above.

Grid in **24**.

Try on Your Own

Directions: Take as much time as you need on these questions. Work carefully and methodically. There will be an opportunity for timed practice at the end of the chapter.

HINT: For Q6, draw the direct path and use it as the hypotenuse of a right triangle.

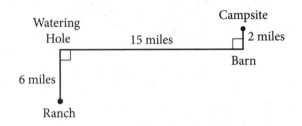

6. A tourist ranch built the horse-riding trail shown in the figure. The trail takes a rider from the ranch to an old watering hole, then to a historic barn, and finally to a campsite where riders can spend the night. If a rider took a horse on a direct path from the ranch to the campsite, how much shorter, in miles, would the trip be?

    A) 6

    B) 8

    C) 17

    D) 23

7. When Ted earned his driver's license, he wanted his first solo drive to be to a friend's house. Previously, Ted had always biked to his friend's house and was able to cut through the yards of neighbors to travel in a straight line. In his car, however, Ted travels a longer distance as he follows the streets. As a result, he travels 6 miles east, 6 miles south, and 2 more miles east by car. How much shorter, in miles, is Ted's bike route than his car route?

8. During a camping trip, Aundria and Annette decide to travel to their campsite using two different routes. Aundria takes the hiking trail that travels 5 miles south, 6 miles east, 7 miles south, and 2 miles west to the campsite; Annette uses the cross-country route that starts at the same point as the hiking trail but goes in a straight line from there to the campsite. About how many miles total will the two travel?

    A) 32.65

    B) 33.42

    C) 34.00

    D) 34.42

Math

9. The lengths of the legs of a right triangle are $3x$ and $x + 1$. The hypotenuse is $3x + 1$. What is the value of x?

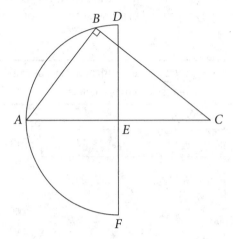

10. In the figure above, E is the center of the semicircle and $AE = EC$. If $AB = 5$ and $BC = 12$, then what is the area of the semicircle?

A) 13π

B) 26π

C) $\dfrac{169}{4}\pi$

D) $\dfrac{169}{8}\pi$

Special Right Triangles

LEARNING OBJECTIVE

After this lesson, you will be able to:

- Calculate the other two sides of a 45-45-90 or 30-60-90 triangle, given one side length

To answer a question like this:

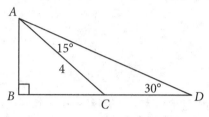

Given triangle *ABC* and triangle *ABD* above, what is the perimeter of triangle *ACD* ?

A) $2\sqrt{6} - 2\sqrt{2}$

B) $4\sqrt{3}$

C) $4 + 2\sqrt{6} + 2\sqrt{2}$

D) $2\sqrt{6} + 6\sqrt{2}$

You need to know this:

The question above requires you to be able to recognize two **special right triangles**. These triangles are defined by their angles. As a result, the ratios of their side lengths are always the same. If you know the length of any one of the three sides of a special right triangle, you can find the lengths of the other two.

The ratio of the sides of a **45-45-90** triangle is $x{:}x{:}x\sqrt{2}$, where x is the length of each leg and $x\sqrt{2}$ is the length of the hypotenuse:

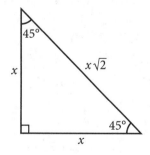

The ratio of the sides of a **30-60-90** triangle is $x:x\sqrt{3}:2x$, where x is the shorter leg, $x\sqrt{3}$ is the longer leg, and $2x$ is the hypotenuse:

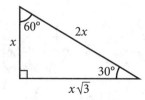

These side length ratios are given on the SAT formula sheet, but for the sake of efficiency on test day, we recommend that you memorize them.

You need to do this:

- Look for hidden special right triangles within other shapes. For example, an equilateral triangle can be bisected (cut in half) to form two congruent 30-60-90 triangles and a square can be divided with a diagonal into two congruent 45-45-90 triangles.

- Use one known side length to deduce the other two. For example, if the shorter leg of a 30-60-90 triangle has a length of 5, then the longer leg has a length of $5\sqrt{3}$, and the hypotenuse has a length of $5(2) = 10$.

Explanation:

Look for hidden special right triangles and add new information to your diagram as you go. Start by finding $\angle ACD$ from the two given angles: $\angle ACD = 180° - 15° - 30° = 135°$. Because $\angle ACB$ is supplementary to $\angle ACD$, $\angle ACB$ measures 45°. $\triangle ABC$ is a right triangle, so its missing angle ($\angle BAC$) is also 45°, making $\triangle ABC$ a 45-45-90 triangle. Since $\angle ADB$ is 30° and $\angle ABC$ is 90°, $\angle BAD$ is 60° and $\triangle ABD$ is a 30-60-90 triangle.

Knowing that you have two special right triangles will allow you to unlock the unknown side lengths. AC is the hypotenuse of the 45-45-90 triangle (side ratio of $x:x:x\sqrt{2}$), so AB and BC (the two legs) must be $2\sqrt{2}$ (solve the equation $4 = x\sqrt{2}$ to find this). AB is also the shorter leg of the 30-60-90 triangle (side ratio of $x:x\sqrt{3}:2x$), so BD (the longer leg) is $2\sqrt{6}$ and AD (the hypotenuse) is $4\sqrt{2}$. To determine CD, take the difference of BD and BC: $2\sqrt{6} - 2\sqrt{2}$. With all sides and angles labeled, the figure looks like this:

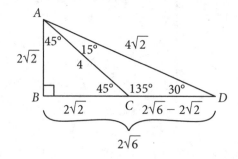

You now have all three sides of triangle ACD, so add them together for the perimeter:

$$4 + \left(2\sqrt{6} - 2\sqrt{2}\right) + 4\sqrt{2}$$

This simplifies to $4 + 2\sqrt{6} + 2\sqrt{2}$, so **(C)** is correct.

Try on Your Own

Directions: Take as much time as you need on these questions. Work carefully and methodically. There will be an opportunity for timed practice at the end of the chapter.

HINT: For Q11, don't rush to use the Pythagorean theorem. Which of the special triangles is triangle *ADB* ?

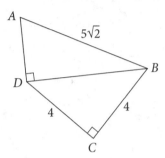

11. What is the area of triangle *DAB* ?

    A) $3\sqrt{2}$

    B) 8

    C) 12

    D) $20\sqrt{2}$

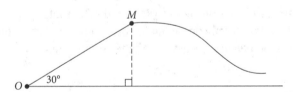

12. The distance from point *O* to point *M* of an amusement ride course shown in the figure above is $200\sqrt{3}$ feet. If the angle of ascent is 30°, what is the height, in feet, of the amusement ride at point *M* ?

    A) $\frac{20}{3}\sqrt{3}$

    B) $100\sqrt{3}$

    C) 200

    D) 300

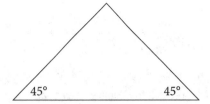

13. Jonas plans to paint the top face of three corner shelves, one of which is shown above. If the longest side of one shelf is 10 inches, what is the total surface area, in square inches, Jonas needs to paint?

    A) 25

    B) 50

    C) 75

    D) 100

14. A tablet screen has a 12-inch diagonal. If the length of the screen is $\sqrt{3}$ times longer than the width, what is the area, in square inches, of the screen?

    A) 12

    B) $12\sqrt{3}$

    C) 36

    D) $36\sqrt{3}$

15. A theater is building a portable ramp to allow equipment and people easy access to the stage, which is 2 meters high. If the ramp is 4 meters long, what is the angle of the incline in degrees?

Circles

LEARNING OBJECTIVE

After this lesson, you will be able to:

● Interpret and manipulate the equation for a circle

To answer a question like this:

Which of the following points in the *xy*-plane represents the center of the circle defined by the equation $x^2 + y^2 - 4x - 8y - 16 = 0$?

A) $(-4, -8)$

B) $(-2, -4)$

C) $(2, 4)$

D) $(4, 8)$

You need to know this:

The equation of a circle in the coordinate plane is as follows:

$$(x - h)^2 + (y - k)^2 = r^2$$

In this equation, called the **standard form**, r is the radius of the circle, and h and k are the *x*- and *y*-coordinates of the circle's center, respectively: (h, k).

You might also see what is referred to as **general form**:

$$x^2 + y^2 + Cx + Dy + E = 0$$

In the general form, the fact that there are x^2 and y^2 terms with coefficients of 1 is an indicator that the equation does indeed graph as a circle. To convert to standard form, complete the square for the *x* terms, then repeat for the *y* terms. Refer to chapter 12 on quadratics for a review of completing the square if needed.

You need to do this:

- Get the circle into standard form.
- Determine the center and radius using the standard form equation.
- Use the center and/or radius to answer the question.

Explanation:

The equation given is in general form rather than in standard form, so complete the square for both x and y. Start by grouping the x terms together and y terms together:

$$x^2 - 4x + y^2 - 8y = 16$$
$$(x - 4x + ?) + (y - 8y + ?) = 16$$
$$(x - 4x + 4) + (y - 8y + 16) = 16 + 4 + 16$$
$$(x - 2)^2 + (y - 4)^2 = 36$$

With the equation in standard form, it is now easy to see that the center is $(2, 4)$. Choice **(C)** is correct.

Try on Your Own

Directions: Take as much time as you need on these questions. Work carefully and methodically. There will be an opportunity for timed practice at the end of the chapter.

HINT: For Q16, which part of the circle's equation would be the easiest to use to eliminate answer choices? The coordinates of the circle's center? The radius?

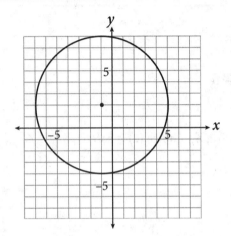

16. Which of the following represents the equation of the circle shown above?

    A) $(x-1)^2 + (y+2)^2 = 6$

    B) $(x+1)^2 + (y-2)^2 = 6$

    C) $(x-1)^2 + (y+2)^2 = 36$

    D) $(x+1)^2 + (y-2)^2 = 36$

HINT: For Q17, complete the square for the *x* and *y* terms.

$$x^2 + 6x + y^2 - 8y = 171$$

17. The equation of a circle in the *xy*-plane is shown above. What is the positive difference between the *x*- and *y*-coordinates of the center of the circle?

$$x^2 + y^2 + 8x - 20y = 28$$

18. What is the diameter of the circle given by the equation above?

    A) 12

    B) 24

    C) 28

    D) 56

19. A circle in the *xy*-plane is defined by the equation $(x-4)^2 + (y+2)^2 = 100$. Which of the following points is located on the circumference of the circle?

    A) $(-3, 5)$

    B) $(0, 9)$

    C) $(4, -2)$

    D) $(4, 8)$

Arc Length and Sectors

LEARNING OBJECTIVES

After this lesson, you will be able to:

- Calculate the length of an arc or the area of a sector defined by a central angle
- Convert degrees to radians

To answer a question like this:

A circle with a diameter of 8 inches is divided into a number of equal sectors such that each sector has an area of $\frac{4\pi}{3}$ square inches. What is the central angle of each sector, in radians?

A) $\frac{\pi}{12}$

B) $\frac{\pi}{6}$

C) $\frac{\pi}{3}$

D) $\frac{2\pi}{3}$

You need to know this:

The SAT may ask you about the following parts of circles: arcs, central angles, and sectors. The ability to set up ratios and proportions correctly is essential for these questions.

- An **arc** is part of a circle's circumference. If the circumference is divided into exactly two arcs, the smaller one is called the **minor arc** and the larger one is called the **major arc**. If a diameter cuts the circle in half, the two arcs formed are called **semicircles**. An arc length can never be greater than the circle's circumference.

- An angle formed by two radii is called a **central angle**. Because a full circle contains 360°, a central angle measure cannot be greater than this.

- The part of a circle's area defined by a central angle is called a **sector**. The area of a sector cannot be greater than the circle's total area.

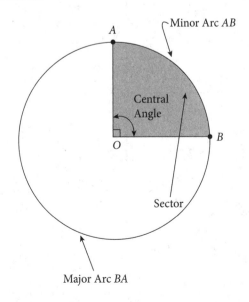

Here's a summary of the ratios formed by these three parts and their whole counterparts:

$$\frac{\text{central angle}}{360°} = \frac{\text{arc length}}{\text{circumference}} = \frac{\text{sector area}}{\text{circle area}}$$

Notice that all of these ratios are equal. Intuitively, this should make sense: when you slice a pizza into four equal slices, each piece should have $\frac{1}{4}$ of the cheese, crust, and sauce. If you slice a circle into four equal pieces, the same principle applies: each piece should have $\frac{1}{4}$ of the degrees, circumference, and area.

An angle whose vertex is on the edge of the circle is called an **inscribed angle**. As this vertex moves along the edge, the measure of the inscribed angle remains constant as long as the minor arc created does not change. When the line segments that create an inscribed angle define the same minor arc that a pair of radii do, a special relationship appears: the central angle measure is twice that of the inscribed angle.

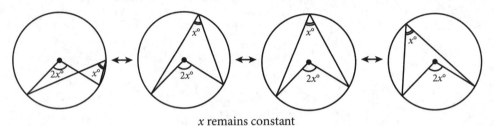

x remains constant

Most Geometry questions present angle measures in degrees, but some may present angle measures in radians. To convert between degrees and radians, use this relationship as a conversion factor: $180° = \pi$ radians. For instance, if you're asked to convert 90° into radians: $90° \times \frac{\pi}{180°} = \frac{\pi}{2}$. Note that there isn't a symbol for radians, so $\frac{\pi}{2}$ is read as "$\frac{\pi}{2}$ radians." This conversion works in the opposite direction as well: to convert radians to degrees, multiply by $\frac{180°}{\pi}$.

Most graphing calculators have both degree and radian modes, so make sure you're in the correct mode for the problem you're working on.

Below is a detailed unit circle diagram with common degree and radian measures (and the coordinates of the ends of their respective radii) that you may see on test day:

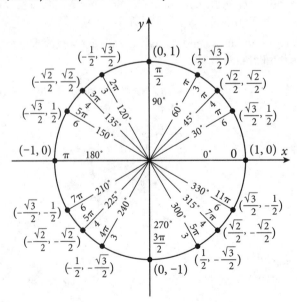

The coordinates at a particular angle measure translate into the leg lengths of the triangle created when a vertical line is drawn from the end of the radius down (or up if you're in quadrant III or IV) to the *x*-axis. For example, at 60°, the horizontal leg has a length of $\frac{1}{2}$ and the vertical leg has a length of $\frac{\sqrt{3}}{2}$.

You need to do this:

- To find the length of an arc or the area of a sector, you need to know the angle that defines the arc or sector as well as the radius of the circle. Questions that are especially tricky might not give you those values directly but will instead give you a way of calculating them.

- When converting between degrees and radians, set up the conversion fraction so that the units cancel:

$$\cancel{\text{degrees}} \times \frac{\pi \, \text{radians}}{180 \, \cancel{\text{degrees}}} \quad \text{and} \quad \cancel{\text{radians}} \times \frac{180 \, \text{degrees}}{\cancel{\text{radians}}}$$

Explanation:

Use the radius to find the area of the circle and divide the total area by the area of one sector to find the number of sectors. Divide the 360° in the whole circle by the number of sectors to find the central angle of each. Finally, convert to radians.

The question says the diameter of the circle is 8 inches, so the radius is 4 inches. A circle with a radius of 4 inches has an area of $\pi r^2 = 16\pi$. The area of each sector multiplied by the number of sectors will be equal to the total area:

$$\text{Area of a sector} \times \text{ number of sectors} = \text{total area}$$

$$\text{Number of sectors} = \frac{\text{total area}}{\text{area of a sector}} = \frac{16\pi}{\frac{4\pi}{3}}$$

$$= 16\pi \times \frac{3}{4\pi} = 4 \times 3 = 12$$

If there are 12 sectors, the central angle defining each sector must be $\frac{1}{12}$ of 360°, or $\frac{1}{12} \times 2\pi = \frac{\pi}{6}$ radians. Choice **(B)** is correct.

Try on Your Own

Directions: Take as much time as you need on these questions. Work carefully and methodically. There will be an opportunity for timed practice at the end of the chapter.

HINT: For Q20, what fraction of the total circumference is arc *AB* ? What does that tell you about central angle *AOB* ?

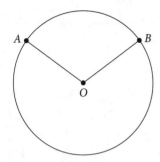

Note: Figure not drawn to scale.

20. In the figure above, circle *O* has a radius of 120 centimeters. If the length of minor arc *AOB* is 200 centimeters, what is the measure of minor angle *AOB*, to the nearest tenth of a degree?

    A)   95.5

    B)   98.2

    C)   102.1

    D)   105.4

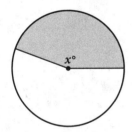

21. In the figure above, the ratio of the shaded area to the non-shaded area is 4 to 5. What is the value of *x*, in degrees?

    A)   135

    B)   145

    C)   160

    D)   170

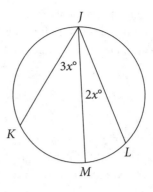

22. In the figure above, points *J*, *K*, *L*, and *M* lie on the circle. If the measure of arc *KML* is 150°, what is the value of *x* ?

    A)   12

    B)   15

    C)   30

    D)   60

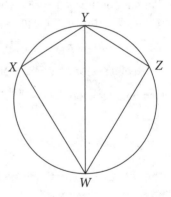

23. In the figure above, points *W*, *X*, *Y*, and *Z* lie on the circle. The measure of arc *YXW* is 180°, and the measure of arcs *XY* and *YZ* each is 60°. If *YZ* = 3, then what is the length of *WX* ?

    A) $\sqrt{3}$

    B)   3

    C) $3\sqrt{3}$

    D)   6

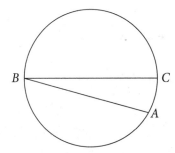

24. In the figure above, *BC* is the diameter of the circle. If the measure of arc *AC* is 30°, then what is the measure of minor arc *BA*, in radians?

A) $\dfrac{\pi}{2}$

B) $\dfrac{2\pi}{3}$

C) $\dfrac{3\pi}{4}$

D) $\dfrac{5\pi}{6}$

Three-Dimensional Figures

LEARNING OBJECTIVES

After this lesson, you will be able to:

- Calculate the volume of common solids
- Calculate the surface area of common solids

To answer a question like this:

Marcus's yard has a large square sandbox serving as a cactus bed. The side lengths of the box are 24 feet, and the box is currently one-third full of sand from the bottom up. Marcus purchases 480 cubic feet of sand, which, when added to the box, will completely fill it. How many inches deep is the cactus bed?

- A) 10
- B) 15
- C) 20
- D) 25

You need to know this:

Over the last several sections, you learned about two-dimensional (2-D) shapes and how to tackle SAT questions involving them. Now you'll learn how to do the same for questions containing three-dimensional (3-D) shapes, also called solids. There are several different types of solids that might appear on the SAT—rectangular solids, cubes, cylinders, prisms, spheres, cones, pyramids—knowing their structures will help you on test day.

The following diagram shows the basic anatomy of a 3-D shape:

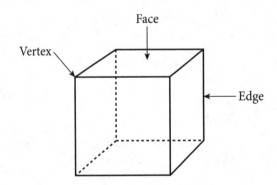

A **face** (or **surface**) is a 2-D shape that acts as one of the sides of the solid. Two faces meet at a line segment called an **edge**, and three faces meet at a single point called a **vertex**.

Volume

Volume is the amount of 3-D space occupied by a solid. Volume is analogous to the area of a 2-D shape. You can find the volume of many 3-D shapes by finding the area of the base and multiplying it by the height. In the table of formulas, the pieces that represent the areas of the bases are enclosed in parentheses.

Rectangular Solid	Cube	Right Cylinder
$(l \times w) \times h$	$(s \times s) \times s = s^3$	$(\pi \times r^2) \times h$

The three 3-D shapes shown above are prisms. Almost all prisms on the SAT are right prisms; that is, all faces are perpendicular to those with which they share edges.

Following are some examples of less commonly seen prisms:

Triangular Prism	Hexagonal Prism	Decagonal Prism

Like the rectangular solids, cubes, and cylinders you saw earlier, these right prisms use the same general volume formula ($V = A_{\text{base}} \times h$).

You might not be told explicitly the area of the base of a prism, in which case you'll need to rely on your two-dimensional geometry knowledge to find it before calculating the volume.

More complicated 3-D shapes include the right pyramid, right cone, and sphere. The vertex of a right pyramid or right cone will always be centered above the middle of the base. Their volume formulas are similar to those of prisms, albeit with different coefficients.

Some of these formulas might look daunting, but you won't have to memorize them for test day. They'll be provided on the reference page at the beginning of each Math section.

Right Rectangular Pyramid	Right Cone	Sphere
$\frac{1}{3} \times (l \times w) \times h$	$\frac{1}{3} \times \left(\pi \times r^2\right) \times h$	$\frac{4}{3} \times \pi \times r^3$

A right pyramid can have any polygon as its base, but the square variety is the one you're most likely to see on the SAT. Also note that the vertex above the base of a right pyramid or cone is not necessarily formed by an intersection of exactly three faces, as in prisms, but it is still a single point and is still called a vertex.

Surface Area

Surface area is the sum of the areas of all faces of a solid. To calculate the surface area of a solid, simply find the area of each face using your 2-D geometry skills, then add them all together.

You won't be expected to know the surface area formulas for right pyramids, right cones, and spheres. They'll be provided at the beginning of each Math section. However, you could be asked to find the surface area of a prism, in which case you'll be given enough information to find the area of each surface of the solid.

You might think that finding the surface area of a solid with many sides, such as a right hexagonal prism, is a tall order. However, you can save time by noticing a vital trait: this prism has two identical hexagonal faces and six identical rectangular faces. Don't waste time finding the area of each of the eight surfaces. Find the area of one hexagonal face and one rectangular face only. Then multiply the area of the hexagonal face by 2 and the area of the rectangular face by 6, add the products together, and you're done. The same is true for other 3-D shapes such as rectangular solids (including cubes), other right prisms, and certain pyramids.

You need to do this:

- To answer questions that involve regular solids, look for ways to find the area of the base and the height.
- To answer questions that involve solids that are not regular, look up and apply the appropriate formula.
- To answer questions that involve surface area, look for surfaces that are the same. Calculate the area of each kind of surface once, and then multiply by the number of identical surfaces in the solid.

Explanation:

One way to approach this question is to find the total volume of the cactus bed first and then use that volume to calculate its depth. If the bed is one-third full, it is two-thirds empty, and according to the question, this empty space is 480 cubic feet. So two-thirds of the total volume is 480:

$$\frac{2}{3} \times V = 480 \text{ ft}^3$$

$$V = 480 \times \frac{3}{2} = 720 \text{ ft}^3$$

The volume of the cactus bed is also equal to the product of its length, width, and height. The question states that the length and width are each 24 feet, so plug these values into the formula and solve for height:

$$V = l \times w \times h$$

$$h = \frac{V}{l \times w}$$

$$= \frac{720}{24 \times 24}$$

$$= \frac{720}{576}$$

$$= 1.25 \text{ feet}$$

The question asks for inches, so do the conversion:

$$1.25 \text{ feet} \times \frac{12 \text{ inches}}{1 \text{ foot}} = 15 \text{ inches}$$

Choice **(B)** is correct.

Try on Your Own

Directions: Take as much time as you need on these questions. Work carefully and methodically. There will be an opportunity for timed practice at the end of the chapter.

HINT: For Q25, refer to the formulas at the beginning of the chapter. On test day, they are included at the beginning of each Math section in your test booklet.

---

25. Two ornamental glass spheres have diameters of 6 inches and 12 inches, respectively. What is the positive difference in their volumes?

    A) 36π

    B) 252π

    C) 288π

    D) $2{,}016\pi$

HINT: For Q26, when the water is poured into a larger glass, what information about the water does not change?

---

26. Alma pours water into a small cylindrical glass with a height of 6 inches and a diameter of 3 inches. The water fills the glass to the very top, so she decides to pour it into a bigger glass that is 8 inches tall and 4 inches in diameter. Assuming Alma doesn't spill any when she pours, how many inches high will the water reach in the bigger glass?

    A)   1.5

    B)   2.25

    C)   3.375

    D)   6.0

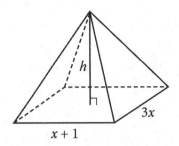

27. If the volume of the pyramid shown in the figure above can be represented by the function $V(x) = x^3 - x$, which of the following expressions represents the pyramid's height?

    A) x

    B) $2x$

    C) $x - 1$

    D) $x - 3$

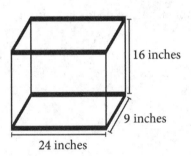

28. A pet store decided to begin selling fish, so the manager purchased 50 of the fish tanks shown above to hold the fish. The staff need to fill the bottom two inches of each tank with sand, which comes only in full-size 40-pound bags. If 1 cubic inch of sand weighs 2 ounces, how many bags of sand does the pet store need to buy? (There are 16 ounces in 1 pound.)

    A)   45

    B)   68

    C)   84

    D)   125

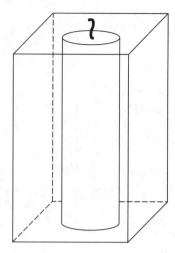

29. In the figure above, a cylindrical candle with a diameter of 2 inches and height of 8 inches sits within a rectangular glass box. The box is the same height as the candle and the area of the base of the box is 15 square inches. If Felipe wants to fill the space between the candle and the box with wax, how many cubic inches of wax does he need?

A) $120 - 8\pi$

B) $120 - 32\pi$

C) $225 - 8\pi$

D) $225 - 32\pi$

On Test Day

What students often find most challenging about questions involving geometry is not the need to remember or apply formulas but rather the fact that the test maker likes to "hide" the path to the solution. The starting information you need will be given, but you'll need to make deductions from that information to assemble all the facts you need to answer the question.

As you consider the question below, ask yourself what information you need to be able to solve. How can you get that information from what you're given?

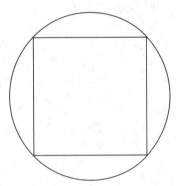

30. In the figure above, a square is inscribed in a circle, and the area of the square is 400 square units. What is the area of the circle in square units?

A) 50π

B) 100π

C) 200π

D) 400π

The explanation appears at the end of this chapter.

How Much Have You Learned?

Directions: For testlike practice, give yourself 22 minutes to complete this question set. Be sure to study the explanations, even for questions you got right. They can be found at the end of this chapter. Note that this question set includes foundational topics in Geometry covered in Math Fundamentals in chapter 2.

Make use of the formula sheet below as needed; you'll have these same formulas available in your test booklet when you take the real SAT.

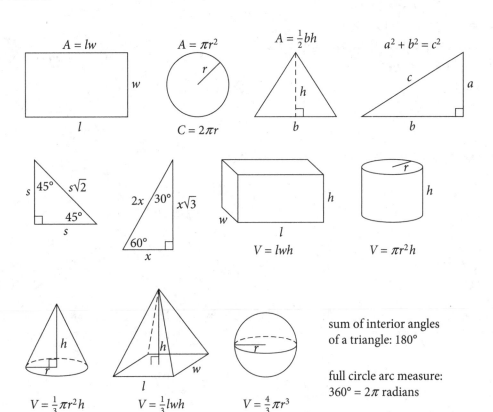

Questions 31 and 32 refer to the following stimulus.

Desiree is making apple juice from concentrate. The cylindrical container of concentrate has a diameter of 7 centimeters and a height of 12 centimeters. To make the juice, the concentrate must be diluted with water so that the mix is 75 percent water and 25 percent concentrate.

31. What is the total volume of juice, rounded to the nearest cubic centimeter, that will be produced if Desiree follows the directions exactly?

32. Desiree is going to serve the apple juice in a cylindrical pitcher with a diameter of 10 centimeters. What is the minimum height of the pitcher, rounded to the nearest centimeter, required for it to hold the apple juice that Desiree made?

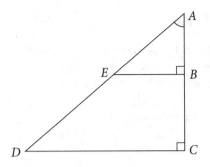

33. Triangles ABE and ACD are shown above. If AB is 3, DC is 12, and AD is 15, which of the following is equal to the ratio 1:3 ?

A) $\dfrac{EB}{AC}$

B) $\dfrac{AE}{DC}$

C) $\dfrac{EB}{DC}$

D) $\dfrac{AE}{AC}$

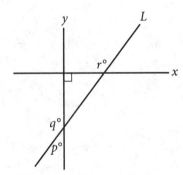

34. In the figure above, if $q = 140$, what is the value of $r - p$?

A) 0

B) 10

C) 90

D) 130

35. The area of a right triangle is 35 square inches. If the longer leg is 3 inches longer than the shorter leg, what is the length of the hypotenuse, in inches?

    A) 10

    B) $\dfrac{\sqrt{35}}{2}$

    C) $7\sqrt{10}$

    D) $\sqrt{149}$

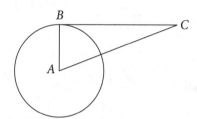

36. Point A is the center of the circle and line segment BC is tangent to the circle. If the measure of $\angle A$ is $(3k + 23)°$ and the measure of $\angle C$ is $(4k - 31)°$, what is the value of k?

37. A sphere with a diameter of 2 inches is resting on a table. If the distance from the center of the sphere to the edge of the table is 10 inches, what is the distance, in inches, between the point where the sphere contacts the table and the table edge?

    A) $4\sqrt{6}$

    B) $3\sqrt{11}$

    C) 10

    D) $\sqrt{101}$

38. At Wesley's Pizzeria, the small pizza is 4 inches smaller in diameter than the large pizza, whose diameter is 16 inches. If each pizza is cut into eight equal slices, one large slice is approximately what percent larger than one small slice?

    A) 44%

    B) 62%

    C) 78%

    D) 84%

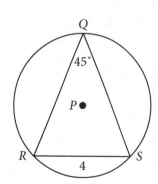

Note: Figure not drawn to scale.

39. In circle P above, $RS = 4$ and $\angle RQS$ measures $45°$. What is the circumference of circle P?

    A) 4π

    B) $4\pi\sqrt{2}$

    C) 8π

    D) $8\pi\sqrt{2}$

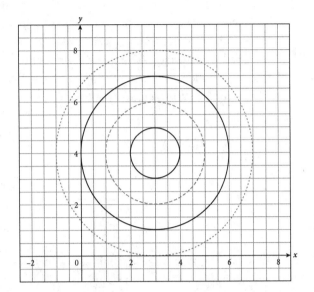

Questions 41 and 42 refer to the following information.

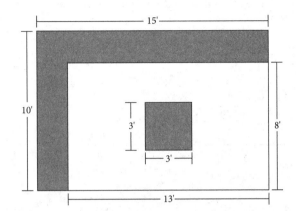

40. An airport instrumentation technician needs to calibrate the air traffic control radar system. An air traffic control radar system display consists of four concentric circles in a coordinate plane. The diameter of the smallest circle is two units, and the diameter of each successive circle is two units larger than that of the previous circle. The diagram above shows the radar system grid before calibration. What is the equation for the smallest dotted circle before the calibration?

A) $(x + 3)^2 + (y + 4)^2 = 4^2$

B) $(x - 3)^2 + (y - 4)^2 = 2^2$

C) $(x - 3)^2 + (y - 4)^2 = 4^2$

D) $(x + 3)^2 + (y + 4)^2 = 8^2$

Material	Price per Square Foot
Quartz	$75
Stainless steel	$67
Granite	$102
Laminate	$71
Wood	$81
Concrete	$55
Soapstone	$97
Travertine	$72

41. An interior designer is trying to determine the best counter material for a kitchen remodel. The designer must cover all of the shaded counter areas in the floor plan above.

What is the area of the counter surface that must be covered, in square feet?

A) 9

B) 46

C) 55

D) 104

42. The family gives the interior designer a $4,500 budget to buy materials for the counter. A list of the available materials and the price per square foot appear in the table above. Which choice provides only options that the interior designer can present to the family that stay within the allotted budget?

    I. Wood

    II. Laminate

    III. Soapstone

    IV. Quartz

    V. Granite

    A) I and III

    B) II, III, IV

    C) I, II, IV

    D) III and V

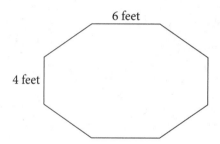

43. A carpenter creates the octagonal dining room table, shown above, by cutting an isosceles right triangle from each corner of the original piece of lumber. If all four isosceles right triangles are congruent and each has an area of $\frac{9}{2}$ square feet, what are the dimensions of the original piece of lumber, in feet?

    A) 8×8

    B) 10×12

    C) 12×14

    D) 14×18

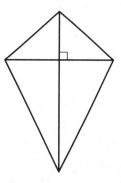

44. Sixty fourth-grade students are making kites that are 18 inches wide and 24 inches tall. Each student uses the vertically symmetrical pattern, shown above, to cut out the kite from an 18- by 24-inch piece of material, such that the height of each kite is parallel to the longer edge of the material. After the students finish making the kites, one of the teachers collects all of the leftover kite material. If all the students successfully make their kites on the first try, how much leftover material will the teacher collect?

    A)   1.5 square feet

    B)   15 square feet

    C)   90 square feet

    D)   12,960 square feet

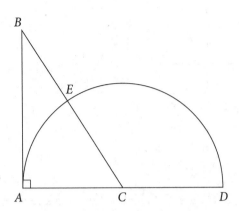

45. In the figure above, C is the center of the semicircle and points A, E, and D are on the semicircle. If CB equals 12 and the measure of angle ABC is 30°, what is the length of CE? (Round your answer to the nearest unit.)

Reflect

Directions: Take a few minutes to recall what you've learned and what you've been practicing in this chapter. Consider the following questions, jot down your best answer for each one, and then compare your reflections to the expert responses on the following page. Use your level of confidence to determine what to do next.

How can you tell whether two triangles are similar?

_____

_____

_____

What are the two Pythagorean triples you are most likely to see on test day?

_____

_____

_____

What are the ratios of the side lengths of a 45-45-90 triangle? Of a 30-60-90 triangle?

_____

_____

_____

What is the standard form for the equation of a circle?

_____

_____

_____

What is the relationship of a circle's central angle to the arc and sector the angle defines?

_____

_____

_____

How would you find the surface area of a right triangular prism with equilateral triangles as its bases?

_____

_____

_____

Expert Responses

How can you tell whether two triangles are similar?

There are three ways to tell:

- *Two of their three angles are congruent (angle-angle).*
- *Two of their three sides are in the same proportion and the intervening angle is congruent (side-angle-side).*
- *Their three sides are in the same proportion (side-side-side).*

What are the two Pythagorean triples you are most likely to see on test day?

The two most common Pythagorean triples on the SAT are 3:4:5 and 5:12:13. You may also see multiples of these, e.g., 6:8:10 or 10:24:26.

What are the ratios of the side lengths of a 45-45-90 triangle? Of a 30-60-90 triangle?

The side lengths of a 45-45-90 triangle are always in the ratio of $x:x:x\sqrt{2}$. The side lengths of a 30-60-90 triangle are always in the ratio of $x:x\sqrt{3}:2x$. Remember that the shortest side of any triangle is across from the smallest angle and the longest side is across from the greatest angle.

What is the standard form for the equation of a circle?

The equation of a circle in the coordinate plane is $(x - h)^2 + (y - k)^2 = r^2$, where r is the radius of the circle and (h, k) is the ordered pair representing its center.

What is the relationship of a circle's central angle to the arc and sector the angle defines?

The central angle, the arc, and the sector are all in proportion to the full circle:

$$\frac{\text{central angle}}{360°} = \frac{\text{arc length}}{\text{circumference}} = \frac{\text{sector area}}{\text{circle area}}$$

How would you find the surface area of a right triangular prism with equilateral triangles as its bases?

Calculate the area of one of the equilateral triangles and multiply by 2. Calculate the area of one of the rectangular faces and multiply by 3. Then add the results.

Next Steps

If you answered most questions correctly in the "How Much Have You Learned?" section, and if your responses to the Reflect questions were similar to those of the SAT expert, then consider Geometry an area of strength and move on to the next chapter. Come back to this topic periodically to prevent yourself from getting rusty.

If you don't yet feel confident, review those parts of this chapter that you have not yet mastered. In particular, review the lessons on similar triangles, the Pythagorean theorem, and special right triangles, as these are high-yield topics on the SAT. Then try the questions you missed again. As always, be sure to review the explanations closely. Finally, **go online** (www.kaptest.com/moreonline) for additional practice on the highest yield topics in this chapter.

Answers and Explanations

1.   426

Difficulty: Medium

Strategic Advice: The figure contains a pair of similar triangles. Use the fact that their sides are in proportion to find the required length.

Getting to the Answer: The question asks for the length of DE. Note that $DC + DE = EC$, which means $DE = EC - DC$. First, find the length of EC by setting up a proportion where BD is related to AC in the same way that DC is related to the unknown EC. AC is 324 and DC is 50% longer than segment BD, or $1.5 \times 40 = 60$ feet:

$$\frac{BD}{AE} = \frac{DC}{EC}$$
$$\frac{40}{324} = \frac{60}{EC}$$
$$\frac{10}{81} = \frac{60}{EC}$$
$$10x = 4{,}860$$
$$EC = 486$$

Subtract the length of DC, 60, from the length of EC, 486, to obtain 426, the length of DE. Grid in **426**.

2.   B

Difficulty: Medium

Getting to the Answer: Given the area of $\triangle ABC$ and the length of the base AB, you can find BC, its height:

$$150 = \tfrac{1}{2}(20)(BC)$$
$$150 = 10(BC)$$
$$15 = BC$$

Because lengths $BC = 15$ and $AB = 20$, $\triangle ABC$ is a 3:4:5 triangle with dimensions scaled up by a factor of 5. The hypotenuse, AC, must be $5 \times 5 = 25$. $\triangle ABC$ and $\triangle AGH$ are similar triangles because they share an angle at

vertex A and they each have a right angle. Therefore, their corresponding sides must be proportional. The question says that the hypotenuse of $\triangle AGH$, AH, is 20, so use this information to create a proportion:

$$\frac{AH}{AC} = \frac{HG}{CB}$$
$$\frac{20}{25} = \frac{HG}{15}$$
$$300 = 25\,HG$$
$$HG = 12$$

Choice **(B)** is the correct answer.

3.   B

Difficulty: Medium

Getting to the Answer: The question says that segment HI is the bisector of segments LO and OW. This tells you two things: 1) HI divides both LO and OW exactly in half and 2) HI is parallel to LW.

Because HI is parallel to LW, angles L and H must be congruent (they are corresponding angles) and angles W and I must be congruent (they are also corresponding angles). Angle O is shared by both triangles. The triangles, therefore, are similar. Side lengths of similar triangles are in proportion to one another. Because I is the midpoint of OW, OI is half as long as OW. (The same is true for the other side: OH is half as long as OL.) So the sides are in the ratio 1:2. The question gives the side lengths of LW and HI. Use this ratio and these side lengths to set up a proportion and solve for x:

$$\frac{1}{2} = \frac{HI}{LW}$$
$$\frac{1}{2} = \frac{4x - 1}{30}$$
$$30 = 2(4x - 1)$$
$$30 = 8x - 2$$
$$32 = 8x$$
$$4 = x$$

The correct answer is **(B)**.

4. 9

Difficulty: Hard

Getting to the Answer: Corresponding sides of similar triangles are proportional. Draw a quick sketch to find as many side lengths as you can, find the ratio of the sides between the two triangles, and use that ratio to find the missing vertex.

Plot all the points given in the question, labeling them as you go so you don't get confused (especially because you won't have graph paper). You know that D and A are in the same quadrant, which means the triangles are both oriented the same way, so make your sketch accordingly:

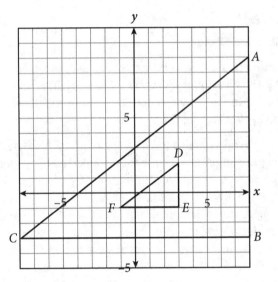

Once you have plotted triangle DEF and the base of triangle ABC, you can determine that the ratio of the triangles is 1:4 (the base of DEF has a length of 4 and the base of ABC has a length of 16). To determine where you should put A, find the length of side DE and then multiply by 4. The length of the vertical side of triangle ABC is $3 \times 4 = 12$. Because one vertex is at $(8, -3)$, vertex A must be 12 vertical units above that point, or $(8, 9)$. The y-coordinate of A is **9**.

5. B

Difficulty: Hard

Getting to the Answer: The figure gives two triangles that look as though they have a lot in common. Analyze them, looking for similarities so you can set up a proportion. Angle C is shared by both triangles. And, because BD is parallel to AE, angles CAE and CBD are congruent—they are corresponding angles. Two pairs of congruent angles means that triangles ACE and BCD are similar by

angle-angle. (You could have analyzed angles CDB and CEA, but you need only two pairs of congruent angles to conclude that two triangles are similar.)

Set up a proportion using the triangles' side lengths. You'll need to translate from English into math as you go: $AB = 5$ and BC is three times that, or 15. This means $AC = 5 + 15 = 20$. CD is 2 more than half AC, $\frac{20}{2} + 2 = 10 + 2 = 12$. Use the three known side lengths to create a proportion and solve for EC:

$$\frac{BC}{AC} = \frac{DC}{EC}$$
$$\frac{15}{20} = \frac{12}{EC}$$
$$15EC = 240$$
$$EC = 16$$

The question asks for the length of segment DE, which is $EC - CD$, or $16 - 12 = 4$. **(B)** is correct.

6. A

Difficulty: Medium

Getting to the Answer: Start by connecting the ranch to the campsite. Then draw in a horizontal line and a vertical line to form a right triangle.

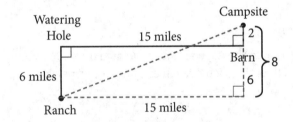

The length of one leg of the triangle is 15 miles, the distance from the watering hole to the barn. The length of the other leg is $6 + 2 = 8$ miles, the distance from the ranch to the watering hole plus the distance from the barn to the campsite. The two legs of the right triangle are 8 and 15. You might recognize the Pythagorean triple 8:15:17, but if you don't, you can always rely on the Pythagorean theorem:

$$8^2 + 15^2 = c^2$$
$$64 + 225 = c^2$$
$$289 = c^2$$
$$\sqrt{289} = \sqrt{c^2}$$
$$17 = c$$

The actual trail is $6 + 15 + 2 = 23$ miles long. The direct route is 17 miles, so the direct route is $23 - 17 = 6$ miles shorter, so **(A)** is the correct answer.

7.   4

Difficulty: Medium

Getting to the Answer: Start by drawing Ted's car and bike routes to his friend's house and labeling your diagram with the distances you know. To find the distance of Ted's bike route, create a right triangle:

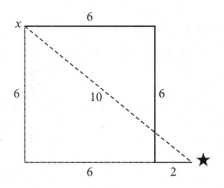

You can use the Pythagorean theorem to find the hypotenuse (bike route), but you'll save time if you recognize that you have a Pythagorean triple (6:8:10, a common multiple of 3:4:5). Thus, Ted's bike route is $6 + 6 + 2 = 14$ miles, and his car route is 10 miles; the difference between the two is **4**.

8.   A

Difficulty: Medium

Getting to the Answer: The question asks for the total distance they traveled. Aundria traveled $5 + 6 + 7 + 2 = 20$ miles. To find the distance Annette traveled, draw and label a diagram of Aundria and Annette's routes and look for a place to sketch in a right triangle so that Annette's direct route is the hypotenuse:

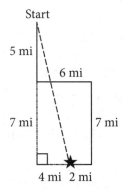

Use the Pythagorean theorem to calculate the distance Annette will travel:

$$c^2 = (5 + 7)^2 + 4^2$$
$$c^2 = 144 + 16$$
$$c^2 = 160$$
$$c = \sqrt{160}$$

Note that the answers are in decimal form, so convert the root value to a decimal: about 12.65 miles. Add this to Aundria's travel distance to find the total distance: $20 + 12.65 = 32.65$ miles. Choice **(A)** is correct.

9.   4

Difficulty: Medium

Getting to the Answer: Use the Pythagorean equation to solve for x:

$$(3x + 1)^2 = (3x)^2 + (x + 1)^2$$
$$9x^2 + 6x + 1 = 9x^2 + x^2 + 2x + 1$$
$$6x = x^2 + 2x$$
$$4x = x^2$$
$$4 = x$$

(Note that x represents a distance and cannot be negative, so -4 is not a viable solution. Moreover, you cannot grid in a negative number.)

Grid in **4**.

10. D

Difficulty: Hard

Getting to the Answer: To calculate the area of the semicircle, you need to find the length of the radius, which is AE. Since $AE = EC$, AE is half of AC. Start by solving for the length of AC, which is the hypotenuse of right triangle ABC. Note that the sides of the triangle are a Pythagorean triple: 5, 12, 13. If you did not recognize the triple, you could have solved for AC using the Pythagorean theorem: $AC = \sqrt{5^2 + 12^2} = 13$. Thus, $AC = 13$ and $AE = \frac{13}{2}$. The area of the semicircle is therefore $\frac{1}{2}\pi r^2 = \frac{1}{2}\pi\left(\frac{13}{2}\right)^2 = \frac{169}{8}$. **(D)** is correct.

11. C

Difficulty: Medium

Getting to the Answer: Triangle DBC is an isosceles right triangle, which means that it is a 45-45-90 right triangle with side length ratios of $x:x:x\sqrt{2}$. Because the two legs are each 4 units long, the hypotenuse DB is $4\sqrt{2}$. DB also acts as one leg of right triangle DAB. Since this leg is $4\sqrt{2}$ and the hypotenuse is $5\sqrt{2}$, triangle DAB is a 3:4:5 right triangle, and the length of AD is $3\sqrt{2}$. The legs of a right triangle are also its base and height, so plug the lengths of the legs into the formula for the area of a triangle, $\frac{1}{2}bh$, to get $\frac{1}{2}\left(4\sqrt{2}\right)\left(3\sqrt{2}\right) = 6 \times 2 = 12$. The correct answer is **(C)**.

12. B

Difficulty: Easy

Getting to the Answer: The height of the amusement ride at point M is perpendicular to the ground, and the roller coaster's angle of ascent is $30°$, which creates a 30-60-90 triangle. Use the ratio of the sides $x:x\sqrt{3}:2x$ to find the height at point M. Because the distance from point O to point M is $200\sqrt{3}$ and corresponds to the hypotenuse of the triangle, then $200\sqrt{3} = 2x$. Solving for x by dividing both sides by 2 gives the length of the side opposite the $30°$ angle, which corresponds to the height of the amusement ride: $x = 100\sqrt{3}$ feet. **(B)** is correct.

13. C

Difficulty: Medium

Getting to the Answer: The top face of the corner shelf is a 45-45-90 triangle. Define the length of the shorter side, say s, and use the ratio of the sides $x:x:x\sqrt{2}$ to solve for it:

$$\frac{1}{\sqrt{2}} = \frac{s}{10}$$
$$s\sqrt{2} = 10$$
$$s = \frac{10}{\sqrt{2}}$$

Next, determine the top face surface area of one corner shelf using $\frac{1}{2}bh$. Note that in a right triangle, the sides that form the $90°$ angle are the base and height. Thus, the surface area of one corner shelf is $\frac{1}{2}\left(\frac{10}{\sqrt{2}}\right)\left(\frac{10}{\sqrt{2}}\right) = \frac{100}{4} = 25$ square inches. The question asks for the total surface area of three corner shelves,

so $3 \times 25 = 75$ square inches. Choice **(C)** is correct.

Alternatively, you could find the altitude perpendicular to the longest side. Note the triangle can be split into two smaller 45-45-90 triangles. Thus, the altitude is the leg of the smaller 45-45-90 triangle, which is half of 10. The top face surface area of one corner shelf is therefore $\frac{1}{2}(10)(5) = 25$ square inches, and the total surface area for the three shelves is $3 \times 25 = 75$ square inches.

14. D

Difficulty: Hard

Getting to the Answer: To find the area of the tablet screen, you need to determine its length and width. Sketch a rectangle with a diagonal of 12. Note the diagonal creates two right triangles and is the hypotenuse. The length and width of the tablet screen correspond to the base and height of the right triangles. The question says that the length is $\sqrt{3}$ times the width, so the ratio of the short leg to the long leg is $1:\sqrt{3}$. This relationship is part of the ratio of the side lengths of a 30-60-90 triangle: $x:x\sqrt{3}:2x$. The hypotenuse is 12, which corresponds to $2x$, so $x = 6$. Therefore, the width is 6, and the length is $\sqrt{3} \times 6 = 6\sqrt{3}$. Use $l \times w$ to calculate the area: $6\sqrt{3} \times 6 = 36\sqrt{3}$ square inches. The correct answer is **(D)**.

15. 30

Difficulty: Medium

Getting to the Answer: Sketch a right triangle with a height of 2 and hypotenuse of 4 to represent the ramp to the stage. The ratio of the short side to the hypotenuse is 2:4, or 1:2. Notice that this matches the ratio of the sides for a 30-60-90 triangle: $x:x\sqrt{3}:2x$. The angle of incline is opposite the short side, which is $30°$. Grid in **30**.

16. D

Difficulty: Easy

Getting to the Answer: The standard form of the equation of a circle is $(x - h)^2 + (y - k)^2 = r^2$, where (h, k) is the center of the circle and r is the length of the radius.

The answer choices have many similarities, which will make them easy to eliminate piece by piece. Use the graph to find the radius. From the center, you can count horizontally or vertically to the edge of the circle to find that its radius is 6. If $r = 6$, then $r^2 = 36$. Eliminate (A) and (B). Now find the x-coordinate of the center of the circle, -1. This means the $(x - h)^2$ part of the equation is $(x - (-1))^2 = (x + 1)^2$. Eliminate (C). Only **(D)** is left and is correct. Note that you do not even need to find the $(y - k)^2$ part of the equation, but for the record: because the y-coordinate of the center of the circle is 2, then $(y - k)^2$ becomes $(y - 2)^2$, and the full equation is $(x + 1)^2 + (y - 2)^2 = 36$. **(D)** is indeed correct.

17. 7

Difficulty: Hard

Getting to the Answer: Rewrite the given equation for the circle in standard form to find the coordinates of the center. Start by completing the square for each of the variables. Take half of the coefficient and then square it. For the x-coefficient, half of 6 is 3, and 3 squared is 9. For the y-coefficient, half of 8 is 4, and 4 squared is 16. Add 9 and 16 to both sides and rewrite as two separate squares of binomials:

$$(x - h)^2 + (y - k)^2 = r^2$$
$$x^2 + 6x + y^2 - 8y = 171$$
$$x^2 + 6x + 9 + y^2 - 8y + 16 = 171 + 9 + 16$$
$$(x + 3)^2 + (y - 4)^2 = 196$$

The coordinates of the center of the circle are $(-3, 4)$. The positive difference is $4 - (-3) = $ **7**. Grid in **7**. If you came up with a negative number, remember that the answer to a Grid-in question cannot be negative.

18. B

Difficulty: Hard

Getting to the Answer: The question asks for the diameter, which is twice the radius. When the equation of a circle is in the form $(x - h)^2 + (y - k)^2 = r^2$, the r represents the length of the radius. The question gives the equation in general form, so you need to complete the square to put the equation into standard form.

You already have an x^2 and a y^2 in the given equation and the coefficients of x and y are even, so completing the square is fairly straightforward—there are just a lot of steps. Start by grouping the x's and y's together. Then, take the coefficient of the x term and divide it by 2, square it, and add it to the two terms with x variables.

Do the same with the y term. Remember to add these amounts to the other side of the equation as well. Then factor the perfect squares and simplify:

$$x^2 + y^2 + 8x - 20y = 28$$
$$x^2 + 8x + y^2 - 20y = 28$$
$$\left(x^2 + 8x + 16\right) + \left(y^2 - 20y + 100\right) = 28 + 16 + 100$$
$$(x + 4)^2 + (y - 10)^2 = 144$$

The equation tells you that r^2 is 144, which means that the radius is 12 and the diameter is twice that, or 24, which is **(B)**.

19. D

Difficulty: Medium

Getting to the Answer: The given equation defines a circle with its center at $(4, -2)$ and a radius of 10. Any point on the circumference of the circle must satisfy that equation. Eliminate (C) because it is the center of the circle. Plug the other choices into the equation to see if they satisfy the given equation:

(A) $(-3 - 4)^2 + (5 + 2)^2 = (-7)^2 + (7)^2 = 49 + 49 = 98$. Since $98 < 100$, this is inside the circle. Eliminate (A).

(B) $(0 - 4)^2 + (9 + 2)^2 = (-4)^2 + (11)^2$. Since the second term alone is greater than 100, this is outside the circle. Eliminate (B).

Only **(D)** is left and is correct. For the record:

(D) $(4 - 4)^2 + (8 + 2)^2 = (0)^2 + (10)^2 = 100$. This point satisfies the equation and is therefore on the circumference. **(D)** is indeed correct.

20. A

Difficulty: Medium

Getting to the Answer: To find a central angle based on a known arc length, use the relationship $\frac{\text{arc length}}{\text{circumference}} = \frac{\text{central angle}}{360°}$. The unknown in the relationship is the central angle, so call it a. Before you can fill in the rest of the equation, you need to find the circumference of the circle: $C = 2\pi r = 2\pi(120) = 240\pi$. Now, you're ready to solve for a:

$$\frac{\text{arc length}}{\text{circumference}} = \frac{\text{central angle}}{360°}$$
$$\frac{200}{240\pi} = \frac{a}{360°}$$
$$\frac{200(360)}{240\pi} = a$$
$$95.5° \approx a$$

(A) is correct. Be careful when you enter this expression into your calculator—you need to put 240π in parentheses so that the calculator doesn't divide by 240 and then multiply by π.

21. C

Difficulty: Medium

Getting to the Answer: Because the ratio of the shaded area to the non-shaded area is 4:5, the ratio of the shaded area to the entire circle is $4:(4+5) = 4:9$. This ratio is the same as the ratio of the interior angle of the shaded sector to 360°, or x:360. Set up a proportion using these ratios:

$$\frac{4}{9} = \frac{x}{360}$$
$$360(4) = 9x$$
$$1,440 = 9x$$
$$160 = x$$

Choice **(C)** is correct.

22. B

Difficulty: Medium

Getting to the Answer: The measure of an arc is directly related to the degree measure of its central angle. The measure of an inscribed angle is half of that of the central angle. Because the measure of arc *KML* is 150°,

the degree measure of the inscribed angle is half of that. The inscribed angle for arc *KML* can be written as $3x + 2x$. Set up an equation to solve for x:

$$3x + 2x = \frac{1}{2}(150)$$
$$5x = 75$$
$$x = 15$$

Choice **(B)** is correct.

23. C

Difficulty: Hard

Getting to the Answer: Note that the figure is composed of two triangles inscribed in a circle. If you have enough information about the triangles, you can find the length of *WX*. Arcs *XY* and *YZ* are each 60°. Because an inscribed angle is half of its corresponding arc, the inscribed angles *XWY* and *ZWY* are each 30°. Similarly, the sum of inscribed angles *XYW* and *ZYW* is half of arc *XWZ*: $\frac{1}{2}(360 - (60 + 60)) = 120$. Thus, angles *XYW* and *XWY* are each 60°. Therefore, both triangles are 30-60-90 special right triangles, so use the ratio of the sides $x : x\sqrt{3} : 2x$ to find the length of *WX*. Given $YZ = 3$, *XY* also equals 3 and $\frac{3}{WX} = \frac{1}{\sqrt{3}}$, so $WX = 3\sqrt{3}$. Choice **(C)** is correct.

24. D

Difficulty: Medium

Getting to the Answer: Since *BC* is the diameter, the measure of arc *BAC* is 180°. Therefore, the measure of arc *BA* is the measure of arc *BAC* minus the measure of arc *AC*: $180° - 30° = 150°$. Use $180° = \pi$ to convert to radians: $150° \times \frac{\pi}{180°} = \frac{5\pi}{6}$. Thus, **(D)** is correct.

25. B

Difficulty: Medium

Getting to the Answer: Begin by finding the volume of each sphere using the volume formula for a sphere, remembering to halve the diameters first:

$$V_1 = \frac{4}{3}\pi r^3 = \frac{4}{3}\pi(3)^3 = \frac{4}{3}\pi(27) = 36\pi$$
$$V_2 = \frac{4}{3}\pi r^3 = \frac{4}{3}\pi(6)^3 = \frac{4}{3}\pi(216) = 288\pi$$

The positive difference is $288\pi - 36\pi = 252\pi$, which is **(B)**.

26. C

Difficulty: Medium

Getting to the Answer: After the water is poured into the larger glass, the volume of the water in the glass will be the same as the volume when it was in the smaller glass. Find the volume of the water in the smaller glass, whose height is 6 inches and radius is 3 inches. Then, substitute this volume into a second equation where the height is unknown and the radius is 4 inches (the radius of the larger glass) and solve for h. The volume of a cylinder equals the area of its base times its height, or $V = \pi r^2 h$:

$$V = \pi r^2 h$$
$$V = \pi (1.5)^2 (6)$$
$$V = \pi (2.25)(6)$$
$$V = 13.5\pi$$

$$13.5\pi = \pi (2)^2 h$$
$$13.5\pi = 4\pi h$$
$$3.375 = h$$

The water will reach 3.375 inches high in the bigger glass. **(C)** is correct.

27. C

Difficulty: Medium

Getting to the Answer: The formula for finding the volume of a pyramid with a rectangular base is $V = \frac{1}{3} lwh$. Start by substituting what you know into the formula. The volume is represented by $x^3 - x$, the length is $x + 1$, and the width is $3x$:

$$V = \frac{1}{3} lwh$$
$$x^3 - x = \frac{1}{3}(x + 1)(3x)h$$
$$x(x^2 - 1) = (x + 1)xh$$

Notice that if you divide both sides of the equation by x, you'll be left with $x^2 - 1$ on the left side and $(x + 1)$ times h on the right side. Note that this is a classic quadratic: the factors of $x^2 - 1$ are $x + 1$ and $x - 1$. So:

$$(x + 1)(x - 1) = (x + 1)h$$
$$x - 1 = h$$

This means the height of the pyramid must be represented by $x - 1$. Therefore, **(C)** is correct.

28. B

Difficulty: Hard

Getting to the Answer: When a question involves many steps, as this one does, plan out the order of your calculations and conversions. In this case, you can go from volume of sand in 1 tank to volume of sand in 50 tanks, to weight of sand in ounces, to weight of sand in pounds, to the number of bags of sand.

The volume of sand in one tank (only 2 inches of the height) will be $V = 24 \times 9 \times 2 = 432$ cubic inches, which means the volume of sand in all 50 tanks will be $50 \times 432 = 21,600$ cubic inches. Each cubic inch of sand weighs 2 ounces, so the weight of all the sand will be $2 \times 21,600 = 43,200$ ounces. There are 16 ounces in 1 pound, so the weight of the sand in pounds is $43,000 \text{ ounces} \times \dfrac{1 \text{ pound}}{16 \text{ ounces}} = 2,700$ pounds. Finally, each bag contains 40 pounds of sand, so the pet store needs to buy $2,700 \text{ pounds} \times \dfrac{1 \text{ bag}}{40 \text{ pounds}} = 67.5$ bags. Because the store cannot buy one-half of one 40-pound bag of sand, it will need to buy 68 bags of sand. **(B)** is the correct answer.

29. A

Difficulty: Medium

Getting to the Answer: Determine the volumes of the rectangular box and of the cylindrical candle. Then calculate the difference between the two to find the volume of space between them. The volume of the box is the area of the base times its height: $15 \times 8 = 120$ cubic inches. Eliminate (C) and (D). Next, use $\pi r^2 h$ to calculate the volume of the cylinder. The diameter is 2 inches, so the radius is 1 inch: $\pi (1)^2 (8) = 8\pi$. The difference of the volumes gives you **(A)**. Felipe needs $120 - 8\pi$ cubic inches of wax.

30. C

Difficulty: Hard

Category: Special Right Triangles

Strategic Advice: The diagonal of the square divides it into two 45-45-90 triangles. Use this information to find the diagonal of the square, which is also the diameter of the circle. From there, you can calculate the area of the circle.

Getting to the Answer: The area of the square is 400, so each side of the square is $\sqrt{400} = 20$. The sides of a 45-45-90 triangle are in the ratio $x:x:x\sqrt{2}$, so the diagonal of the square is $20\sqrt{2}$ and the radius of the circle is half of that, or $10\sqrt{2}$. The area of the circle is then $\pi\left(10\sqrt{2}\right)^2 = \pi(10)^2\left(\sqrt{2}\right)^2 = \pi(100)(2) = 200\pi$.

Choice **(C)** is correct.

31. 1847

Difficulty: Medium

Category: Three-Dimensional Figures

Getting to the Answer: The question asks for the total volume of juice, which is the volume of the cylinder that contains the concentrate plus the amount of water that is added. The height of the can of concentrate is 12 centimeters, and its diameter is 7 centimeters, making the radius 3.5 centimeters. Plug this information into the formula for the volume of a cylinder, $V = \pi r^2 h$:
$$V_{conc} = \pi \times 3.5^2 \times 12 = 147\pi \text{ cm}^3.$$

The ratio of concentrate to total juice is $V_{conc}:(V_{conc} + V_{water})$ or $25:(25 + 75)$, which simplifies to 1:4. Set up the following ratio to calculate the total volume:

$$\frac{147\pi}{V_{Total}} = \frac{1}{4}$$

Cross-multiply to find the total volume of juice:

$$V_{Total} = (147\pi)(4)$$
$$V_{Total} = 588\pi \approx 1{,}847.2$$

The value 1,847.2 rounds to 1,847. Grid in **1847**.

32. 24

Difficulty: Medium

Category: Three-Dimensional Figures

Getting to the Answer: The diameter of the serving pitcher is given as 10 centimeters, so the radius is 5 centimeters. Use the radius and the total volume of apple juice you found in the last question to find the minimum height of the serving pitcher:

$$V_{Total} = 588\pi = \pi\left(5^2\right)(\text{height})$$
$$588\pi = \pi(25)(\text{height})$$
$$588 = 25(\text{height})$$
$$23.52 = \text{height}$$

The height needs to be rounded up to **24**, which is the correct answer.

33. C

Difficulty: Medium

Category: Similar Triangles; Special Right Triangles

Strategic Advice: For questions with right triangles, look for Pythagorean triples and special right triangles.

Getting to the Answer: Begin by transferring all of the information in the question stem to the diagram:

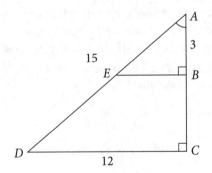

Triangle *ACD* is a right triangle with side length 12 and a hypotenuse of 15, which means its other side length, *AC*, is 9. These side lengths are the 3:4:5 triple multiplied by 3. Because they share angle *A* and both have a right angle, the two triangles are similar by way of angle-angle. Therefore, triangle *ABE* is also a 3:4:5 triangle. Since triangle *ACD* is three times the size of triangle *ABE*, you can easily create a ratio of 1:3. Look for a side of *ABE* in the numerator and the corresponding side of *ACD* in the denominator. Only **(C)** correctly matches up the corresponding sides of *ABE* and *ACD*.

Another option to solve this question is to plug in the values for all of the sides based on the Pythagorean triples and plug those lengths into the answer choices. The diagram below shows the side lengths of the two triangles:

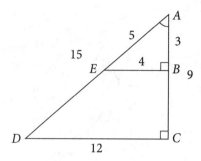

Plugging the lengths into the choices results in:

(A): $\frac{EB}{AC} = \frac{4}{9}$

(B): $\frac{AE}{DC} = \frac{5}{12}$

(C): $\frac{EB}{DC} = \frac{4}{12} = \frac{1}{3}$

There is no need to check (D) because there will be only one set of lengths that work. **(C)** is indeed correct.

34. C

Difficulty: Easy

Category: Lines and Angles

Getting to the Answer: Line L forms a right triangle whose right angle is created by the intersection of the x- and y-axes. The figure shows that q and p are complementary, as they form a straight line, the y-axis, which means $q + p = 180$. The question says that $q = 140$, so $p = 180 - 140 = 40$. One of the interior angles of the triangle, the one created by the y-axis and line L, is vertical to p, so that angle also is 40. Now, find the last angle measure inside the triangle by subtracting: $180 - 90 - 40 = 50$. This angle is supplementary to r, so $r = 180 - 50 = 130$. This means that $r - p = 130 - 40 = 90$. **(C)** is the correct.

35. D

Difficulty: Hard

Category: Pythagorean Theorem

Getting to the Answer: In a right triangle, one leg is the base and the other is the height. Because the question states that one leg is 3 inches longer than the other, use x and $x + 3$ to represent the lengths of these two legs. Use the formula for the area of a triangle to solve for x, the shorter leg:

$$35 = \tfrac{1}{2}(x)(x + 3)$$
$$2(35) = \cancel{2}\left(\frac{1}{\cancel{2}}(x)(x + 3)\right)$$
$$70 = (x)(x + 3)$$
$$70 = x^2 + 3x$$

Next, subtract 70 to make the equation equal 0. Use reverse-FOIL to find that the factors are $(x + 10)$ and $(x - 7)$, which means $x = -10$ and $x = 7$. Lengths cannot be negative, so the shorter leg has a length of 7, and the longer leg has a length of $7 + 3 = 10$. Now, use the Pythagorean theorem to find the length of the hypotenuse:

$$a^2 + b^2 = c^2$$
$$7^2 + 10^2 = c^2$$
$$49 + 100 = c^2$$
$$149 = c^2$$
$$\sqrt{149} = \sqrt{c^2}$$
$$\sqrt{149} = c$$

Choice **(D)** is correct.

36. 14

Difficulty: Medium

Category: Pythagorean Theorem

Getting to the Answer: Since a line tangent to a circle is perpendicular to a radius drawn to meet the tangent line, $\triangle ABC$ must be a right triangle. Therefore, the sum of the measures of $\angle A$ and $\angle C$ is $90°$, and you can write the equation $(3k + 23) + (4k - 31) = 90$. This simplifies to $7k - 8 = 90$ and then to $7k = 98$. Divide both sides by 7 to see that $k = 14$. Grid in **14**.

37. B

Difficulty: Medium

Category: Pythagorean Theorem

Getting to the Answer: Draw a diagram to visualize the situation. A cross section of the sphere resting on the table is shown. Note that the sphere is tangent to the table and that a right triangle is present:

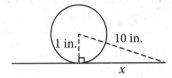

Plug the values from your diagram into the Pythagorean equation: $1^2 + x^2 = 10^2$. Solving for x results in $x = \sqrt{99} = \sqrt{9 \times 11} = 3\sqrt{11}$, so **(B)** is correct.

38. C

Difficulty: Medium

Category: Arc Length and Sectors

Strategic Advice: You can save time solving this question if you recognize that information about 8 slices is unnecessary. The whole large pizza will be the same percent larger than a whole small pizza as a large slice will be compared to a small slice. In other words, if a large slice is 25% larger than a small slice, a large pizza is also 25% larger than a small pizza. That means you need to calculate only the areas of each pizza and plug them into the percent change formula.

Getting to the Answer: The radius of the large pizza is one-half of its diameter of 16 inches, or 8 inches. Use the radius to find the area of the large pizza: $\pi r^2 = \pi(8)^2 = 64\pi$ square inches. The question states that the small pizza is 4 inches smaller in diameter than the large pizza, or $16 - 4 = 12$ inches. The radius of the small pizza is one-half of its diameter of 12 inches, or 6 inches, and the small pizza has an area of $\pi(6)^2 = 36\pi$ square inches.

The question asks by what percent is the large pizza larger than the small pizza, which means that the percent change is in terms of the small pizza. Plug the values in:

$$\frac{64\pi - 36\pi}{36\pi} = \frac{28\pi}{36\pi} = \frac{7}{9} \approx 78\%$$

(C) is correct.

39. B

Difficulty: Medium

Category: Special Right Triangles

Getting to the Answer: Start by drawing in *PR* and *PS* as shown here:

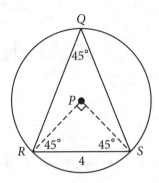

Because the angle formed by *PR* and *PS* defines the same arc as the angle formed by segments *QR* and *QS*, $\angle RPS$ must be twice $\angle RQS$, which is $45° \times 2 = 90°$. In addition to being legs of $\triangle PRS$, *PR* and *PS* are radii, so they are congruent, which makes $\triangle PRS$ a 45-45-90 triangle. Therefore, the radius of circle *P* is $\frac{4}{\sqrt{2}} = 2\sqrt{2}$, and the circumference is $2\pi \times 2\sqrt{2} = 4\pi\sqrt{2}$, so **(B)** is correct.

40. B

Difficulty: Medium

Category: Circles

Getting to the Answer: To find the equation of the smallest dotted circle on the diagram, you need the standard form of the equation of a circle, $(x - h)^2 + (y - k)^2 = r^2$, the coordinates of the center of the circle, and its radius. The center of the circles before calibration is $(3, 4)$. Eliminate (A) and (D). The diameter of the smallest dotted circle is 4 units, which makes its radius 2 units.

Plugging that information into the circle equation results in $(x - 3)^2 + (y - 4)^2 = 2^2$. **(B)** is correct.

41. C

Difficulty: Medium

Category: Quadrilaterals

Getting to the Answer: To find the area of the counter surface that needs to be covered, add the area of the L-shaped portion of the counter and the square portion in the middle. Determine the area of the L-shaped portion of the counter by subtracting the area of the smaller 8 foot by 13 foot rectangle from the larger 10 foot by 15 foot rectangle:

$$\text{Area of L-shaped portion} =$$
$$(10 \times 15) - (8 \times 13) = 150 - 104 = 46 \text{ ft}^2$$

Finally, to find the total area add the area of the 3 foot by 3 foot square in the center, $3 \times 3 = 9$ ft^2, to the 46 ft^2: $9 + 46 = 55$ ft^2. **(C)** is correct.

42. C

Difficulty: Medium

Category: Quadrilaterals

Getting to the Answer: From the answer to the previous question, you already know the area that needs to be covered, 55 square feet. Divide the budget by the area to find the maximum amount that can be spent per square foot:

$$\frac{\$4,500}{55 \text{ square feet}} \approx \$82 \text{ per square foot}$$

Instead of finding the prices for each of the materials, you can take advantage of how the answer choices are set up to speed up the elimination process. Option III, soapstone, appears in three of the four choices, so check it first. Soapstone is $97 per square foot, which is over budget, so eliminate (A), (B), and (D), which all contain option III. **(C)** is correct.

43. B

Difficulty: Medium

Category: Special Right Triangles

Getting to the Answer: Use the area of one isosceles triangle, $\frac{9}{2}$, to solve for the length of the legs of the triangle and add the sum of both legs to the side lengths of the octagonal table given in the diagram. The formula for the area of a triangle is $A = \frac{1}{2}bh$, and since the base and the height are the same for an isosceles right triangle, $b = h$, you can simplify the formula: $A = \frac{b^2}{2}$. Plug in $\frac{9}{2}$ for the area and solve for the length of one of the legs:

$$A = \frac{b^2}{2}$$
$$\frac{9}{2} = \frac{b^2}{2}$$
$$b^2 = 9$$
$$b^2 = \pm 3$$

Lengths cannot be negative, so the length of each leg is 3 feet. Adding the side length to both ends of the 6-foot dimension results in $6 + 3 + 3 = 12$ feet. Adding the side length to both ends of the 4-foot dimension results in $4 + 3 + 3 = 10$ feet. The dimensions of the original piece of lumber are 10 by 12. **(B)** is correct.

Another approach is to recognize that if you use the variable x to represent the leg length of the right isosceles triangle, then the dimensions of the original piece of lumber must be $(6 + 2x)$ feet by $(4 + 2x)$ feet. By extension, since the $2x$ is the same in both, the dimensions of the original piece of lumber must only differ by $6 - 4$, or 2, feet. Eliminate (A) and (D) because the dimensions do not differ by 2 inches. Test (B) by setting $(6 + 2x)$ feet = 12 feet to find a value for the leg length of the triangle:

$$6 + 2x = 12$$
$$2x = 6$$
$$x = 3$$

Plugging $x = 3$ into the area formula results in $\frac{3^2}{2} = \frac{9}{2}$, which confirms **(B)** as the correct answer.

44. C

Difficulty: Medium

Category: Triangles

Getting to the Answer: To calculate the amount of leftover material for all 60 students, first calculate the amount of material that will remain when one student cuts out the pattern. Note that while the dimensions of the material are given in inches, the final answer is in square feet. Do the conversion up front: each student starts out with a 1.5 foot by 2 foot piece of material, the area of which is $1.5 \times 2 = 3$ ft^2.

How do you find the area of the kite? Since it is symmetrical along the vertical axis, if you fold the pattern in half along the vertical axis, you have two equal triangles with a base of 2 feet and a height of $\frac{1.5}{2} = 0.75$ ft. Plugging those values into the area formula results in:

$$\text{Area of both triangles} = 2\left(\frac{1}{2}\right)(2 \text{ ft})(0.75 \text{ ft}) = 1.5 \text{ ft}^2$$

The difference between the area of the original piece of material and area of the kite, $3 - 1.5 = 1.5$ ft^2, is the area of leftover material for one kite. To find the total amount of leftover material, multiply 1.5 ft^2 by 60 to get 90 ft^2. **(C)** is correct. If you noticed that the area of the kite is exactly half the area of the original rectangle, you can save time and simply calculate the area of the kite and multiply it by 60. If you chose (D), be careful and always make sure to check the units.

45. 6

Difficulty: Hard

Category: Special Right Triangles

Getting to the Answer: Since C is the center of the semicircle and points A, E, and D lie on the circumference, CA, CE, and CD are each equal to the radius of the semicircle. Note that CA is also the base of triangle ABC, which is a 30-60-90 triangle given that angle ABC is 30° and that angle BAC is 90°. You know $CB = 12$, so use the ratio of the sides $x:x\sqrt{3}:2x$ to find CA:

$$\frac{CA}{12} = \frac{1}{2}$$
$$CA = \frac{1}{2}(12)$$
$$CA = 6$$

Thus, $CA = 6$ and $CE = $ **6**. Grid in **6**.

CHAPTER 14

Trigonometry

LEARNING OBJECTIVES

After completing this chapter, you will be able to:

- Calculate trigonometric ratios from side lengths of right triangles
- Calculate side lengths of right triangles using trigonometric ratios
- Describe the relationship between the sine and cosine of complementary angles

5/600 SmartPoints® (Low Yield)

How Much Do You Know?

Directions: Try the questions that follow. Show your work so that you can compare your solutions to the ones found in the Check Your Work section immediately after this question set. If you answered most of the questions correctly, and if your scratchwork looks like ours, you may be able to move quickly through this chapter. If you answered incorrectly or used a different approach, you may want to take your time on this chapter.

1. If $\tan x = \dfrac{7}{24}$, what is the value of $\sin x$?

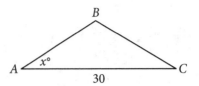

Note: Figure not drawn to scale.

2. If the area of $\triangle ABC$ is 225 and $AB = 17$, what is the value of $\cos x$?

A) $\dfrac{8}{17}$

B) $\dfrac{8}{15}$

C) $\dfrac{17}{30}$

D) $\dfrac{15}{17}$

3. In a right triangle, one of the acute angles is $\cos\left(\dfrac{\pi}{3}\right)$, and $\cos\left(\dfrac{\pi}{3}\right) = \sin x$. What is the measure of x?

A) $\dfrac{\pi}{12}$

B) $\dfrac{\pi}{6}$

C) $\dfrac{\pi}{3}$

D) $\dfrac{2\pi}{3}$

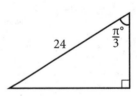

4. If the hypotenuse of the triangle shown above has length 24 units, what is the area in square units of the triangle?

A) $72\sqrt{3}$

B) $144\sqrt{3}$

C) 288

D) $288\sqrt{3}$

Answers and explanations are on the next page. ▶ ▶ ▶

Check Your Work

1. 7/25 or .28

Difficulty: Medium

Getting to the Answer: Recall that $\tan x = \frac{\text{opp}}{\text{adj}}$. This means you know the lengths of the two legs of the triangle, but not its hypotenuse. Draw a picture with the given lengths:

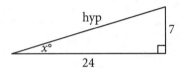

Remember that $\sin x = \frac{\text{opp}}{\text{hyp}}$, so use the Pythagorean theorem to calculate the length of the hypotenuse:

$$7^2 + 24^2 = \text{hyp}^2$$
$$49 + 576 = \text{hyp}^2$$
$$\sqrt{625} = \sqrt{\text{hyp}^2}$$
$$25 = \text{hyp}$$

Plug the length of the hypotenuse into the sine ratio: $\sin x = \frac{7}{25}$. Grid in **7/25** or **.28**.

2. A

Difficulty: Hard

Getting to the Answer: Begin by drawing a height in the triangle:

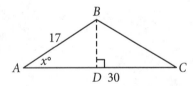

Next, find the length of *BD* using the triangle area formula:

$$A = \frac{1}{2}bh$$
$$225 = \frac{1}{2} \times 30h$$
$$h = \frac{225}{15} = 15 = BD$$

You now have two sides of a right triangle ($\triangle ABD$)—but not necessarily the two sides you need. To find the value of $\cos x$, you need the side adjacent to x and the hypotenuse. Here, you have the opposite side (*BD*) and

the hypotenuse (*AB*), so you need to find the length of the third side (*AD*). You might recognize $\triangle ABD$ as an 8-15-17 Pythagorean triple, but if you don't, you can use the Pythagorean theorem:

$$AD^2 + 15^2 = 17^2$$
$$AD^2 = 17^2 - 15^2$$
$$AD^2 = 289 - 225$$
$$AD = \sqrt{64} = 8$$

You can now find $\cos x$: $\frac{\text{adj}}{\text{hyp}} = \frac{8}{17}$. **(A)** is correct.

3. B

Difficulty: Medium

Getting to the Answer: The sine and cosine of complementary angles are equal, and the sum of the acute angles in a right triangle is $180° - 90° = 90°$. Convert this to radians to find the measure of the missing angle. The sum of the acute angles in a right triangle, in radians, is $90° \times \frac{\pi}{180°} = \frac{90\pi}{180} = \frac{\pi}{2}$. Subtract the known angle to find the other angle: $\frac{\pi}{2} - \frac{\pi}{3} = \frac{3\pi}{6} - \frac{2\pi}{6} = \frac{\pi}{6}$. **(B)** is correct.

4. A

Difficulty: Medium

Getting to the Answer: When the measure of an angle in a triangle is given in radians, you'll usually want to convert it to degrees because you might be able to find a special right triangle. Use the relationship $180° = \pi$ to convert the angle: $\frac{\pi}{3} \times \frac{180°}{\pi} = 60°$.

Now you know the triangle is a 30-60-90 triangle, which has sides that are in the ratio $x : x\sqrt{3} : 2x$. The hypotenuse is $2x = 24$, so $x = 12$ and $x\sqrt{3} = 12\sqrt{3}$. Therefore, the base and height of the triangle are 12 and $12\sqrt{3}$, and the area of the triangle is $\frac{1}{2}(12\sqrt{3})(12) = 72\sqrt{3}$, so **(A)** is correct. Note that because it is a right triangle, it does not matter which leg you call the base and which the height.

Sine, Cosine, and Tangent

LEARNING OBJECTIVES

After this lesson, you will be able to:

- Calculate trigonometric ratios from side lengths of right triangles
- Calculate side lengths of right triangles using trigonometric ratios
- Describe the relationship between the sine and cosine of complementary angles

---

To answer a question like this:

One angle in a right triangle measures $y°$ such that $\cos y° = \frac{24}{25}$. What is the measure of $\sin(90° - y°)$?

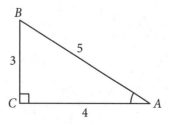

You need to know this:

The SAT tests three trigonometric functions: **sine**, **cosine**, and **tangent**. All three are simply the ratios of side lengths within a right triangle. The notation for sine, cosine, and tangent functions always includes a reference angle; for example, $\cos x$ or $\cos \theta$. That's because you'll need to refer to the given angle within a right triangle to determine the appropriate side ratios.

There is a common mnemonic device for the sine, cosine, and tangent ratios: SOHCAHTOA (commonly pronounced: so-kuh-TOE-uh). Here's what it represents: **S**ine is **O**pposite over **H**ypotenuse, **C**osine is **A**djacent over **H**ypotenuse, and **T**angent is **O**pposite over **A**djacent. See the following triangle and the table for a summary of the ratios and what each equals for angle A in triangle CAB:

Sine (sin)	Cosine (cos)	Tangent (tan)
$\dfrac{\text{opposite}}{\text{hypotenuse}}$	$\dfrac{\text{adjacent}}{\text{hypotenuse}}$	$\dfrac{\text{opposite}}{\text{adjacent}}$
$\dfrac{3}{5}$	$\dfrac{4}{5}$	$\dfrac{3}{4}$

Complementary angles have a special relationship relative to sine and cosine:

- $\sin x° = \cos(90° - x°)$
- $\cos x° = \sin(90° - x°)$

In other words, the sine of an acute angle is equal to the cosine of the angle's complement and vice versa. For example, $\cos 30° = \sin 60°$, $\cos 45° = \sin 45°$, and $\cos 60° = \sin 30°$.

You need to do this:

Apply the appropriate trigonometric ratio to a right triangle or use the relationship between the sine and cosine of complementary angles.

Explanation:

There are two ways to approach this question. You might choose to draw the triangle:

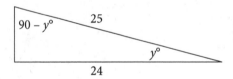

To find $\sin(90° - y°)$, put the side opposite the angle labeled $90° - y°$ over the hypotenuse. You'll get $\dfrac{24}{25}$, exactly the same as $\cos y°$.

Alternatively, you could use the property of complementary angles that says that $\cos x° = \sin(90° - x°)$ to find that $\sin(90° - y°) = \dfrac{24}{25}$.

The fraction can't be gridded in because it takes too many spaces, so divide 24 by 25 and grid in the result, **.96**. Although it doesn't apply here, pay attention to any rounding guidelines in the question stem.

Try on Your Own

Directions: Take as much time as you need on these questions. Work carefully and methodically. There will be an opportunity for timed practice at the end of the chapter.

HINT: Pythagorean triples frequently appear in trig questions. What is the triangle's missing side length in Q1?

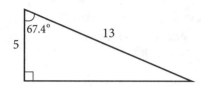

1. Based on the figure above, which of the following is true?

    A) $\sin 22.6° = \dfrac{5}{12}$

    B) $\sin 67.4° = \dfrac{5}{13}$

    C) $\cos 22.6° = \dfrac{5}{13}$

    D) $\cos 67.4° = \dfrac{5}{13}$

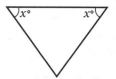

2. The triangle shown above is a cross section of a feeding trough. The triangular cross section is 24 inches deep and 36 inches across the top. If $\cos x = B$, what is the value of B?

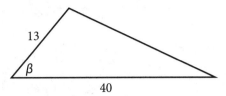

Note: Figure not drawn to scale.

3. If the area of the triangle shown above is 240 square inches, what is tan β ?

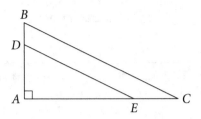

4. In the figure above, DE is parallel to BC and sin $\angle C = 0.6$. Side $AC = 16$ and side $BD = 3$. What is the length of side AE ?

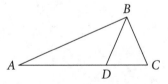

5. If sin $\angle A = \cos \angle C$, what is sin $\angle ABD - \cos \angle DBC$?

A) 0

B) $\frac{1}{2}$

C) 1

D) The result of the subtraction cannot be determined without additional information.

On Test Day

Occasionally, a question will give you more information than you need to determine the correct answer. Think about what information you really need to arrive at the answer before you begin your calculations so that you don't get sidetracked and spend time doing unnecessary work.

As you read through this question, plan your strategy to get the correct value and identify what information you need to carry out that strategy. Note if there is any unnecessary information that you can ignore.

6. Triangle *PQR* is a right triangle with the 90° angle at vertex *Q*. The length of side PQ is 25 and the length of side QR is 60. Triangle *STU* is similar to triangle *PRQ*. The vertices *S*, *T*, and *U* correspond to vertices *P*, *Q*, and *R*, respectively. Each side of triangle *STU* is $\frac{1}{10}$ the length of the corresponding side of triangle *PRQ*. What is the value of cos ∠*U* ?

A) $\frac{5}{13}$

B) $\frac{5}{12}$

C) $\frac{5}{6}$

D) $\frac{12}{13}$

The answer and explanation can be found at the end of this chapter.

Math

How Much Have You Learned?

Directions: For testlike practice, give yourself 7 minutes to complete this question set. Be sure to study the explanations, even for questions you got right. They can be found at the end of this chapter.

7. If $\sin x = \cos\left(\dfrac{13\pi}{6}\right)$, which of the following could be the value of x?

    A) $\dfrac{\pi}{6}$

    B) $\dfrac{\pi}{4}$

    C) $\dfrac{\pi}{3}$

    D) $\dfrac{\pi}{2}$

8. If $\cos x = \sin y$, then which of the following pairs of angle measures could NOT be the values of x and y, respectively?

    A) $\dfrac{\pi}{4}, \dfrac{\pi}{4}$

    B) $\dfrac{\pi}{6}, \dfrac{\pi}{3}$

    C) $\dfrac{\pi}{8}, \dfrac{3\pi}{8}$

    D) $\dfrac{\pi}{2}, \dfrac{\pi}{2}$

9. Angle x is one of the acute angles in a right triangle. If the measure of angle x is $30°$, what is the value of $(\sin x)^2 + (\cos x)^2$?

    A) $\dfrac{1}{4}$

    B) $\dfrac{1}{2}$

    C) 1

    D) 2

10. In a certain triangle, the measures of $\angle A$ and $\angle B$ are $(6k - 8)°$ and $(7k - 45)°$, respectively. If $\dfrac{\sin \angle A}{\cos \angle B} = 1$, what is the value of k?

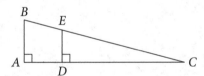

11. In the above triangle, if side $AB = 5$, segment $AD = 3$, and $\tan \angle B = 2.4$, what is the length of segment BE?

    A) 3

    B) $3\dfrac{1}{4}$

    C) $3\dfrac{3}{4}$

    D) $4\dfrac{1}{4}$

Reflect

Directions: Take a few minutes to recall what you've learned and what you've been practicing in this chapter. Consider the following questions, jot down your best answer for each one, and then compare your reflections to the expert responses on the following page. Use your level of confidence to determine what to do next.

What are the definitions of sine, cosine, and tangent?

_____

_____

_____

What is the special relationship of sine to cosine in complementary angles?

_____

_____

_____

Expert Responses

What are the definitions of sine, cosine, and tangent?

Sine is defined as opposite over hypotenuse, cosine as adjacent over hypotenuse, and tangent as opposite over adjacent. The acronym SOHCAHTOA can help you remember these definitions.

What is the special relationship of sine to cosine in complementary angles?

For two complementary angles, sin x° = cos (90° − x°) and cos x° = sin (90° − x°). In other words, if two angles are complementary (add up to 90 degrees), the sine of one equals the cosine of the other.

Next Steps

If you answered most questions correctly in the "How Much Have You Learned?" section, and if your responses to the Reflect questions were similar to those of the SAT expert, then consider trigonometry an area of strength and move on to the next chapter. Come back to this topic in a few days to prevent yourself from getting rusty.

If you don't yet feel confident, review those parts of this chapter that you have not yet mastered, then try the questions you missed again. As always, be sure to review the explanations closely.

Answers and Explanations

1. D

Difficulty: Medium

Getting to the Answer: Find the unknown leg length and angle measure. The triangle is a right triangle with one leg length of 5 and a hypotenuse of 13, so the other leg is length 12. (If you didn't see the Pythagorean triple 5:12:13, you could have used the Pythagorean theorem to find the missing leg length.) Use the measures of the internal angles to find the missing angle:

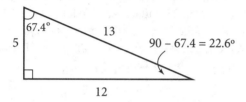

Sine and cosine both involve the hypotenuse, 13, so you can eliminate (A). Compare the remaining answer choices to the trig ratios given by SOHCAHTOA. Sine is opposite over hypotenuse, but the side opposite the 67.4° angle has length 12 (not 5), so eliminate (B). Cosine is adjacent over hypotenuse, but the side adjacent to the 22.6° angle has length 12 (not 5), so eliminate (C). Only **(D)** is left and must be correct. For the record, the side adjacent to the 67.4° angle has length 5 and the hypotenuse has length 13, so $\cos 67.4° = \frac{5}{13}$.

2. 3/5 or .6

Difficulty: Hard

Getting to the Answer: Because trig functions typically apply to right triangles, draw in an altitude and label what you know. You know the trough is 24 inches deep and 36 inches across the top. Because the given angles have equal measures, $x°$, the triangle is isosceles and the altitude bisects the top. Draw a figure:

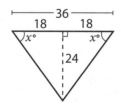

You're given that $B = \cos x$, and the cosine of an angle involves the hypotenuse, so you need to find the length of the hypotenuse using the Pythagorean theorem:

$$18^2 + 24^2 = c^2$$
$$324 + 576 = c^2$$
$$\sqrt{900} = \sqrt{c^2}$$
$$30 = c$$

Finally, $\cos x = \frac{adj}{hyp} = \frac{18}{30} = \frac{3}{5}$. Grid in **3/5** or **.6**.

3. 12/5 or 2.4

Difficulty: Hard

Getting to the Answer: Find the height of the triangle using the information given about the area and add it to the figure:

$$A = \frac{1}{2}bh$$
$$240 = \frac{1}{2}(40)h$$
$$240 = 20h$$
$$12 = h$$

After you find the height, you might recognize the 5-12-13 Pythagorean triple, which gives you another side of the triangle that contains β:

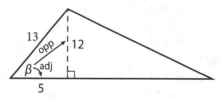

Note: Figure not drawn to scale.

Now use SOHCAHTOA: $\tan \beta = \frac{opp}{adj} = \frac{12}{5}$. Grid in **12/5** or **2.4**.

4.   12

Difficulty: Hard

Getting to the Answer: The fact that DE is parallel to BC means that triangles ABC and ADE are similar. Convert $\sin C$, 0.6, to a fraction, $\frac{3}{5}$. Because sin is $\frac{\text{opposite}}{\text{hypotenuse}}$, both triangles have the side ratio 3:4:5. The question states that $AC = 16$. This is the long leg of a 3:4:5 right triangle, so $AB = 12$ and $BC = 20$.

The other known dimension is $BD = 3$. Since the length of AB is 12, the length of AD is $12 - 3 = 9$. Thus, the ratio of the sides of triangle ADE to those of triangle ABC is $\frac{9}{12} = \frac{3}{4}$. Therefore, AD is $\frac{3}{4}$ of AC, which is $\frac{3}{4} \times 16 = 12$. Grid in **12**.

5.   A

Difficulty: Hard

Getting to the Answer: The sine of an angle is equal to the cosine of its complementary angle, so $\angle A + \angle C = 90°$. Since $\angle B$ is the third interior angle of the triangle ABC, $\angle B = 180° - 90° = 90°$. Therefore, the measures of angles ABD and DBC must total $90°$, which means they are complementary angles. Thus, $\sin \angle ABD = \cos \angle DBC$, and $\sin \angle ABD - \cos \angle DBC = 0$. **(A)** is correct.

6.   D

Difficulty: Medium

Getting to the Answer: The question tells you that triangles PQR and STU are similar. Therefore, their corresponding angles are equal and all sides of STU have the same ratio to their corresponding sides in PQR, in this case, $\frac{1}{10}$. However, since the angles of both triangles are the same, their trig functions are also the same, so there is no need to calculate the lengths of the sides of triangle PQR. Because they are the same ratio, cosine of U will have the same value as the cosine of R, so just calculate the cosine of R value using the side lengths of triangle PQR.

Since $\angle Q = 90°$, sides PQ and QR are legs of the right triangle and PR is the hypotenuse. (If you have trouble visualizing this, you can draw a very quick sketch.) Thus, $\cos R = \frac{QR}{PR}$. You can calculate the value of PR using the Pythagorean theorem:

$$25^2 + 60^2 = PR^2$$
$$625 + 3{,}600 = PR^2$$
$$\sqrt{4{,}225} = \sqrt{PR^2}$$
$$PR = 65$$

You can save a lot of time calculating if you recognize that the two legs, 25 and 60, are the legs of a 5:12:13 triangle multiplied by 5. You can calculate PR as $5 \times 13 = 65$, so look for Pythagorean triples. Either way, $\cos U = \cos R = \frac{60}{65} = \frac{12}{13}$. **(D)** is correct.

7.   C

Difficulty: Hard

Getting to the Answer: Dealing with smaller angles usually makes trig questions easier, so start by subtracting 2π from $\frac{13\pi}{6}$ to get $\frac{13\pi}{6} - 2\pi = \frac{13\pi}{6} - \frac{12\pi}{6} = \frac{\pi}{6}$. (This is permissible because 2π is once around the unit circle; you are not changing the quadrant of the angle.) The equation in the question stem becomes $\sin x = \cos\left(\frac{\pi}{6}\right)$. Complementary angles have a special relationship relative to trig values—the cosine of an acute angle is equal to the sine of the angle's complement and vice versa. The angle measures are given in radians, so you're looking for an angle that, when added to $\frac{\pi}{6}$, gives $\frac{\pi}{2}$ (because $\frac{\pi}{2} = 90°$). Because $\frac{\pi}{6} + \frac{2\pi}{6} = \frac{3\pi}{6} = \frac{\pi}{2}$, the two angles, $\frac{\pi}{6}$ and $\frac{\pi}{3}$, are complementary angles, which means **(C)** is correct.

8. D

Difficulty: Medium

Getting to the Answer: Use the special relationship that complementary angles have in terms of trig functions: the cosine of an acute angle is equal to the sine of the angle's complement and vice versa.

The question asks for the pair of angles that are *not* complementary. In degrees, complementary angles add up to 90, so in radians they add up to $90° \times \frac{\pi}{180°} = \frac{\pi}{2}$.

The only pair of angles that is not complementary is **(D)**, the correct answer, because they add up to $\frac{\pi}{2} + \frac{\pi}{2} = \frac{2\pi}{2} = \pi$.

9. C

Difficulty: Medium

Getting to the Answer: Use the definitions of the common trig functions to put some context to this question. Substitute $\left(\frac{\text{opposite}}{\text{hypotenuse}}\right)^2 + \left(\frac{\text{adjacent}}{\text{hypotenuse}}\right)^2$ for $(\sin x)^2 + (\cos x)^2$. This simplifies to $\frac{\text{opposite}^2 + \text{adjacent}^2}{\text{hypotenuse}^2}$. The Pythagorean theorem states $a^2 + b^2 = c^2$, which is equivalent to $\text{opposite}^2 + \text{adjacent}^2 = \text{hypotenuse}^2$, so this fraction is actually $\frac{\text{hypotenuse}^2}{\text{hypotenuse}^2} = 1$. **(C)** is correct.

If you prefer to work with actual values, recall that the side ratio of a 30-60-90 triangle is $1:\sqrt{3}:2$. So, $\sin x = \frac{1}{2}$ and $\cos x = \frac{\sqrt{3}}{2}$. The question asks for the sum of the squares of those values: $\left(\frac{1}{2}\right)^2 + \left(\frac{\sqrt{3}}{2}\right)^2 = \frac{1}{4} + \frac{3}{4} = 1$. **(C)** is indeed correct.

10. 11

Difficulty: Hard

Getting to the Answer: If $\frac{\sin A}{\cos B} = 1$, then $\sin A = \cos B$, so $\angle A$ and $\angle B$ are complementary. Therefore, the sum of the measures of $\angle A$ and $\angle B$ is $90°$, and you can write the equation $(6k - 8) + (7k - 45) = 90$. This simplifies to $13k - 53 = 90$ and then to $13k = 143$. Divide both sides by 13 to see that $k = 11$. Grid in **11**.

11. B

Difficulty: Hard

Getting to the Answer: Since BA and ED are both perpendicular to AC, they are parallel, and triangles ABC and DEC are similar. If $\tan \angle B = \frac{AC}{AB}$, then $2.4 = \frac{AC}{5}$, and $AC = 12$. Triangle ABC is a 5:12:13 right triangle, and the length of BC is 13. (If you didn't recall Pythagorean triple, you could have calculated the hypotenuse using the Pythagorean theorem.) Given that $AD = 3$ and $AC = 12$, it follows that $DC = 12 - 3 = 9$, and the ratio of the side lengths of $\triangle DEC$ to $\triangle ABC$ is 9:12, which simplifies to 3:4. Because this ratio is the same for all sides, BE is $\frac{1}{4}$ the length of BC, or $\frac{1}{4}(13) = 3\frac{1}{4}$. **(B)** is correct.

CHAPTER 15

Imaginary Numbers

LEARNING OBJECTIVE

After completing this chapter, you will be able to:

- Perform arithmetic operations on imaginary and complex numbers

5/600 SmartPoints® (Low Yield)

How Much Do You Know?

Directions: Try the questions that follow. Show your work so that you can compare your solutions to the ones found in the Check Your Work section immediately after this question set. If you answered most of the questions correctly, and if your scratchwork looks like ours, you may be able to move quickly through this chapter. If you answered incorrectly or used a different approach, you may want to take your time on this chapter.

1. Which of the following is the correct simplification of the expression $(2i - 3) - (6 + 4i)$, where $i = \sqrt{-1}$?

    A) $-9 - 2i$

    B) $-9 + 6i$

    C) $-7 - 4i$

    D) $3 + 6i$

2. Given that $i = \sqrt{-1}$, which of the following is equivalent to $(6i^2 - 7i) + (3 + 6i)$?

    A) $6i^2 + i + 3$

    B) $-3 - i$

    C) $-9 - i$

    D) 10

3. Which of the following is equal to $(17 + 7i)(3 - 5i)$? (Note: $i = \sqrt{-1}$)

    A) 16

    B) 86

    C) $16 - 64i$

    D) $86 - 64i$

4. If the expression $\dfrac{2 - i}{2 + i}$ is written as the complex number $a + bi$, where a and b are real numbers, what is the value of a? (Note: $i = \sqrt{-1}$)

Answers and explanations are on the next page. ▶ ▶ ▶

Check Your Work

1. A

Difficulty: Easy

Getting to the Answer: The real and imaginary components of the two binomials aren't in the same order. Distributing the negative sign inside the second set of parentheses produces $2i - 3 - 6 - 4i$. Combine like terms to obtain $-9 - 2i$, which makes **(A)** correct.

2. B

Difficulty: Easy

Getting to the Answer: Treat i like a variable and simplify the expression by getting rid of the parentheses and combining like terms:

$$\left(6i^2 - 7i\right) + (3 + 6i)$$
$$= 6i^2 - 7i + 3 + 6i$$
$$= 6i^2 - i + 3$$

Notice that the resulting expression almost, but not quite, matches (A), so eliminate (A). Because $i = \sqrt{-1}$, you can square both sides to find that $i^2 = -1$. Plug in -1 for i^2 and combine like terms:

$$6(-1) - i + 3$$
$$= -i - 3$$

Rewrite in $a + bi$ form: $-3 - i$. **(B)** is correct.

3. D

Difficulty: Medium

Getting to the Answer: Use FOIL to multiply the binomials and simplify:

$$(17 + 7i)(3 - 5i)$$
$$= (17 \times 3) + (17 \times (-5i)) + (7i \times 3) + (7i \times (-5i))$$
$$= 51 - 85i + 21i - 35i^2$$
$$= 51 - 64i - (35 \times (-1))$$
$$= 86 - 64i$$

Choice **(D)** is correct.

4. 3/5

Difficulty: Medium

Getting to the Answer: The question is really asking you to manipulate this expression out of its fraction form to match the form $a + bi$ and identify the real component a. To rationalize the denominator, use the conjugate of the denominator, $2 - i$, to multiply the expression by 1:

$$\left(\frac{2-i}{2+i}\right)\left(\frac{2-i}{2-i}\right)$$
$$= \frac{4 - 2i - 2i + i^2}{4 + 2i - 2i - i^2}$$

Since squaring $\sqrt{-1}$ would result in -1, plug in -1 for i^2 and combine like terms:

$$\frac{4 - 2i - 2i + (-1)}{4 + 2i - 2i - (-1)}$$
$$= \frac{3 - 4i}{5}$$

Splitting the terms so that the expression matches the form $a + bi$ results in $\frac{3}{5} - \frac{4}{5}i$. Grid in **3/5**.

Arithmetic Operations with Complex Numbers

LEARNING OBJECTIVE

After this lesson, you will be able to:

- Perform arithmetic operations on imaginary and complex numbers

To answer a question like this:

Which of the following complex numbers is equivalent to $\frac{2+i}{3+5i}$?

A) $\frac{2}{3} + \frac{i}{5}$

B) $\frac{2}{3} - \frac{i}{5}$

C) $\frac{11}{34} + \frac{7i}{34}$

D) $\frac{11}{34} - \frac{7i}{34}$

You need to know this:

The square root of a negative number is not a real number but an **imaginary number**.

To take the square root of a negative number, use *i*, which is defined as $i = \sqrt{-1}$. For example, to simplify $\sqrt{-49}$, rewrite $\sqrt{-49}$ as $\sqrt{-1 \times 49}$, take the square root of -1 (which is by definition *i*), and then take the square root of 49, which is 7. The end result is 7*i*.

The simplification $i^2 = \left(\sqrt{-1}\right)^2 = -1$ is also useful when working with imaginary numbers. For example:

$$\sqrt{-16} \times \sqrt{-25}$$
$$= i\sqrt{16} \times i\sqrt{25}$$
$$= 4i \times 5i$$
$$= 20i^2$$
$$= 20 \times (-1)$$
$$= -20$$

When a number is written in the form $a + bi$, where *a* is the real component and *b* is the imaginary component (and *i* is $\sqrt{-1}$), it is referred to as a **complex number**.

You need to do this:

You can add, subtract, multiply, and divide complex numbers just as you do real numbers:

- To add (or subtract) complex numbers, simply add (or subtract) the real parts and then add (or subtract) the imaginary parts.
- To multiply complex numbers, treat them as binomials and use FOIL. To simplify the product, use the simplification $i^2 = -1$ and combine like terms.
- To divide complex numbers, write them in fraction form and multiply the numerator and denominator by the **conjugate** of the complex number in the denominator. To form the conjugate, change the sign in the complex number. For example, the conjugate of $2 + i$ is $2 - i$.

Explanation:

Use the conjugate to simplify complex numbers in the denominator. The conjugate of $3 + 5i$ is $3 - 5i$, so multiply the expression by 1 in the form $\frac{3 - 5i}{3 - 5i}$ and simplify:

$$\frac{2 + i}{3 + 5i} \times \frac{3 - 5i}{3 - 5i} = \frac{6 - 10i + 3i - 5i^2}{(3 + 5i)(3 - 5i)} = \frac{6 - 7i - 5i^2}{9 - 25i^2}$$

You know $i^2 = -1$, so the expression simplifies to $\frac{6 - 7i - 5(-1)}{9 - 25(-1)} = \frac{11 - 7i}{34}$. To separate the complex expression into its real and imaginary components, write each of the terms in the numerator over the denominator in separate fractions, which produces $\frac{11}{34} - \frac{7i}{34}$. Choice **(D)** is correct.

Try on Your Own

Directions: Take as much time as you need on these questions. Work carefully and methodically. There will be an opportunity for timed practice at the end of the chapter.

HINT: For Q1, what is the value of i^2 ?

---

1. Given that $i = \sqrt{-1}$, what is the sum of the complex numbers $(21i^2 - 12i) + (3 - 5i)$?

   A) 7

   B) $7i$

   C) $-18 - 17i$

   D) $24 - 17i$

2. What is the result of the multiplication $(5 - 6i)(3 + 3i)$? (Note: $i = \sqrt{-1}$)

   A) $33 - 3i$

   B) $23 - 3i$

   C) $11 - i$

   D) -6

HINT: For Q3, multiply the top and bottom of the fraction by the conjugate of the denominator.

---

3. Which of the following is equivalent to $\dfrac{38 + 18i}{4 + 6i}$?
   (Note: $i = \sqrt{-1}$)

   A) $\dfrac{11}{13} - 3i$

   B) $5 - 3i$

   C) $\dfrac{19}{2} + 3i$

   D) $44 + 300i$

$$\frac{7 + i}{8 - i}$$

4. If the expression above is expressed in the form $a + bi$, where $i = \sqrt{-1}$, what is the value of b ?

   A) -1

   B) $\dfrac{3}{13}$

   C) $\dfrac{11}{13}$

   D) $\dfrac{15}{64}$

5. If the expression $\dfrac{-3i^2 + 2i}{2 + i}$ is written in the form $a + bi$, where a and b are real numbers and $i = \sqrt{-1}$, what is the value of a ?

On Test Day

The SAT tests the same patterns over and over again, but they can be presented in a number of different ways. Before you start doing calculations, look closely at this question and see if you recognize a pattern that will help you simplify it. Once you spot the pattern, this question should take you no more than a few seconds to solve.

$$\frac{25i^2 - 9}{5i + 3}$$

6. For $i = \sqrt{-1}$, the expression above is equal to which of the following complex numbers?

A) $5i - 3$

B) $5i + 3$

C) $16i - 9$

D) $80i - 48$

The correct answer and explanation can be found at the end of the chapter.

How Much Have You Learned?

Directions: For testlike practice, give yourself 7 minutes to complete this question set. Be sure to study the explanations, even for questions you got right. They can be found at the end of this chapter.

$$(3 + 4i) - (2 + 3i)$$

7. Given that $i = \sqrt{-1}$, what is the value of the expression above?

   A) $1 - i$

   B) $1 + i$

   C) $1 + 7i$

   D) $5 + 7i$

$$\frac{3i + 2}{-i - 3}$$

8. If the expression above is expressed in the form $a + bi$, where $i = \sqrt{-1}$, what is the value of b?

   A) -0.7

   B) 0.7

   C) -0.9

   D) 0.9

$$\frac{5 + 3i}{7 - 3i}$$

9. Which of the following expressions is equivalent to the expression above, assuming that $i = \sqrt{-1}$?

   A) $\dfrac{1}{5}$

   B) $\dfrac{5}{7}$

   C) $\dfrac{13 + 18i}{20}$

   D) $\dfrac{13 + 18i}{29}$

10. If the expression $\dfrac{1 + 2i}{4 + 2i}$ is rewritten as a complex number in the form of $a + bi$, what is the value of a? (Note: $i = \sqrt{-1}$)

11. Given that $i = \sqrt{-1}$, what is the product of $\dfrac{2 - 4i + 2i^2}{2}$ and $\dfrac{1}{1 - i}$?

    A) $-1 + i$

    B) $-1 - i$

    C) $1 - i$

    D) $1 + i$

Reflect

Directions: Take a few minutes to recall what you've learned and what you've been practicing in this chapter. Consider the following questions, jot down your best answer for each one, and then compare your reflections to the expert responses on the following page. Use your level of confidence to determine what to do next.

In a complex number in the form $a + bi$, what is the definition of i?

_____

_____

_____

What is the procedure for adding, subtracting, or multiplying complex numbers?

_____

_____

_____

What is the procedure for dividing complex numbers?

_____

_____

_____

Expert Responses

In a complex number in the form $a + bi$, what is the definition of i?

In any complex number written as a + bi, i $= \sqrt{-1}$.

What is the procedure for adding, subtracting, or multiplying complex numbers?

To perform arithmetic operations on complex numbers, treat i *as a variable and simplify* i^2 *to* -1.

What is the procedure for dividing complex numbers?

To divide two complex numbers, write the division as a fraction, multiply the numerator and denominator by the conjugate of the denominator, and simplify.

Next Steps

If you answered most questions correctly in the "How Much Have You Learned?" section, and if your responses to the Reflect questions were similar to those of the SAT expert, then consider imaginary numbers an area of strength and move on to the next chapter. Come back to this topic periodically to prevent yourself from getting rusty.

If you don't yet feel confident, review those parts of this chapter that you have not yet mastered, then try the questions you missed again. As always, be sure to review the explanations closely.

Answers and Explanations

1. C

Difficulty: Easy

Getting to the Answer: Plug in -1 for i^2 and combine like terms. Remember to treat i like a variable:

$$\left(21i^2 - 12i\right) + (3 - 5i)$$
$$= 21(-1) - 12i + 3 - 5i$$
$$= -18 - 17i$$

(C) is correct.

2. A

Difficulty: Medium

Getting to the Answer: Treat i as a variable and expand the expression as if it were a binomial. Use FOIL to distribute and then plug in -1 for any i^2 and combine like terms:

$$(5 - 6i)(3 + 3i)$$
$$= 15 + 15i - 18i - 18i^2$$
$$= 15 - 3i - 18(-1)$$
$$= 33 - 3i$$

(A) is correct.

3. B

Difficulty: Hard

Getting to the Answer: Multiply the numerator and denominator by the latter's conjugate and then use FOIL. Combine like terms and reduce fractions as needed:

$$\frac{38 + 18i}{4 + 6i}$$
$$= \frac{38 + 18i}{4 + 6i} \times \frac{4 - 6i}{4 - 6i}$$
$$= \frac{(38 \times 4) + (38 \times -6i) + (18i \times 4) + (18i \times -6i)}{16 - 36i^2}$$
$$= \frac{152 - 228i + 72i - 108i^2}{16 - (-36)}$$
$$= \frac{152 - 156i - (-108)}{52}$$
$$= \frac{260 - 156i}{52}$$
$$= \frac{260}{52} - \frac{156}{52}i$$
$$= 5 - 3i$$

(B) is correct.

4. B

Difficulty: Medium

Getting to the Answer: The question asks for the value of b when a certain complex number is in the form $a + bi$. The given expression has a complex number in the denominator, so start by multiplying the top and bottom by the conjugate of the complex number in the denominator:

$$\left(\frac{7 + i}{8 - i}\right)\left(\frac{8 + i}{8 + i}\right)$$
$$= \frac{56 + 7i + 8i + i^2}{64 + 8i - 8i - i^2}$$

Since squaring $\sqrt{-1}$ results in -1, plug in -1 for i^2 and then combine like terms and reduce:

$$\frac{56 + 7i + 8i + (-1)}{64 + 8i - 8i - (-1)}$$
$$= \frac{55 + 15i}{65}$$
$$= \frac{5(11 + 3i)}{5(13)} = \frac{11 + 3i}{13}$$

Next, write each of the terms in the numerator over the denominator in separate fractions so that the expression matches the form $a + bi$: $\frac{11}{13} + \frac{3i}{13}$. Thus, $b = \frac{3}{13}$, so **(B)** is correct.

5. 8/5 or 1.6

Difficulty: Medium

Getting to the Answer: First, notice that the expression simplifies if you plug in -1 for i^2 in the numerator. Next, rationalize the denominator by multiplying the top and bottom by the conjugate of the denominator:

$$\left(\frac{-3(-1) + 2i}{2 + i}\right)\left(\frac{2 - i}{2 - i}\right)$$
$$= \frac{6 + 4i - 3i - 2i^2}{4 + 2i - 2i - i^2}$$

Notice again that plugging in -1 for i^2 and combining like terms results in more simplification:

$$\frac{6 + 4i - 3i - 2(-1)}{4 + 2i - 2i - (-1)}$$

$$= \frac{8 + i}{5}$$

$$= \frac{8}{5} + \frac{i}{5}$$

Since the question asks for the value of a, grid in **8/5** or **1.6**.

6. A

Difficulty: Medium

Strategic Advice: The expression in the numerator contains a coefficient and a constant that are both perfect squares, with the constant being subtracted. This pattern signals that the numerator is a difference of perfect squares, which can be factored.

Getting to the Answer: While you could rationalize the given fraction with the denominator's conjugate, in this case, the difference of perfect squares in the numerator means you can factor it into binomials and then cancel a factor from the numerator and denominator:

$$\frac{25i^2 - 9}{5i + 3}$$

$$= \frac{(5i + 3)(5i - 3)}{5i + 3}$$

$$= \frac{\cancel{(5i + 3)}(5i - 3)}{\cancel{5i + 3}}$$

$$= 5i - 3$$

Thus, **(A)** is correct.

7. B

Difficulty: Easy

Getting to the Answer: To subtract complex numbers, simply subtract the real parts and then subtract the imaginary parts. Remember to distribute the -1 to both 2 and $3i$ in the second binomial:

$$(3 + 4i) - (2 + 3i)$$

$$= 3 + 4i - 2 - 3i$$

$$= 1 + i$$

(B) is correct.

8. A

Difficulty: Medium

Getting to the Answer: Rewrite the expression so that each complex number is in the standard $a + bi$ form. Then rationalize using the conjugate of the denominator:

$$\left(\frac{3i + 2}{-i - 3}\right) \Rightarrow \left(\frac{2 + 3i}{-3 - i}\right)$$

$$= \left(\frac{2 + 3i}{-3 - i}\right) \times \left(\frac{-3 + i}{-3 + i}\right)$$

$$= \frac{-6 - 9i + 2i + 3i^2}{9 + 3i - 3i - i^2}$$

Combine like terms and plug in -1 for i^2:

$$\frac{-6 - 7i + 3i^2}{9 - i^2}$$

$$= \frac{-6 - 7i + 3(-1)}{9 - (-1)}$$

$$= \frac{-9 - 7i}{10}$$

$$= -\frac{9}{10} - \frac{7i}{10}$$

Since the question asks for the value of b, convert the fraction to a decimal. **(A)** is correct.

9.   D

Difficulty: Medium

Strategic Advice: If part of an answer choice is incorrect, then the whole answer choice is incorrect. Notice that multiplying the numerator by the conjugate of the denominator will result in a complex number in the numerator, so eliminate (A) and (B).

Getting to the Answer: Multiply the expression by the conjugate of the denominator to remove the complex number from the denominator. Note that the two remaining answer choices have the same numerator, $13 + 18i$, which means that you need to simplify the denominator only to decide which is correct. For the record, the simplification of the numerator is included:

$$\frac{5+3i}{7-3i} \times \frac{7+3i}{7+3i}$$

$$= \frac{35 + 21i + 15i + 9i^2}{49 - 21i + 21i - 9i^2}$$

$$= \frac{35 + 36i + 9i^2}{49 - 9i^2}$$

Next, plug in -1 for i^2 and combine like terms. The resulting fraction can be reduced by factoring out 2:

$$\frac{35 + 36i + 9(-1)}{49 - 9(-1)}$$

$$= \frac{26 + 36i}{58} = \frac{\cancel{2}(13 + 18i)}{\cancel{2}(29)} = \frac{13 + 18i}{29}$$

(D) is correct.

10. 8/20 or 4/10 or 2/5 or .4

Difficulty: Medium

Getting to the Answer: The question wants the expression to be in the form $a + bi$. When there is a complex number in the denominator, multiply the top and bottom of the fraction by the conjugate of the the denominator. Plug in -1 for i^2 and combine like terms:

$$\frac{1+2i}{4+2i} \times \frac{4-2i}{4-2i}$$

$$= \frac{4 + 8i - 2i - 4i^2}{16 - 8i + 8i - 4i^2}$$

$$= \frac{4 + 6i - 4(-1)}{16 - 4(-1)}$$

$$= \frac{8 + 6i}{20}$$

$$= \frac{8}{20} + \frac{6i}{20}$$

Grid in **8/20, 4/10, 2/5,** or **.4**. Any of these formats is correct.

11. C

Difficulty: Hard

Strategic Advice: If you factor out the 2, the expression in the numerator of the first fraction is a classic quadratic $x^2 - 2xy + y^2 = (x - y)^2$. Factor the quadratic and and look for terms that cancel.

Getting to the Answer: Multiply the two fractions and factor out a 2. After factoring the classic quadratic, the term $(1 - i)$ cancels out:

$$\left(\frac{2 - 4i + 2i^2}{2}\right)\left(\frac{1}{1-i}\right) = \frac{2\left(1 - 2i + i^2\right)}{2(1-i)}$$

$$= \frac{2(1-i)^2}{2(1-i)} = \frac{\cancel{2}\,\cancel{(1-i)}(1-i)}{\cancel{2}\,\cancel{(1-i)}} = 1 - i$$

(C) is correct.

Test Yourself: Additional Topics in Math

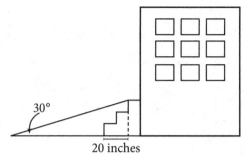

30°

20 inches

Note: Figure not drawn to scale.

1. While a building is being renovated, the property's owners install a temporary ramp, shown in the figure above, to comply with the Americans with Disabilities Act (ADA). The ramp must be placed at a 30° angle, 8 feet from the bottom step. About how long, in inches, is the ramp? (12 inches = 1 foot)

A) 67

B) 116

C) 128

D) 134

2. The longer leg of a right triangle is three times the length of the shorter leg. Given that the length of each leg is a whole number, which of the following could be the length of the hypotenuse?

A) $\sqrt{40}$

B) $\sqrt{47}$

C) $\sqrt{55}$

D) $\sqrt{63}$

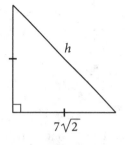

h

$7\sqrt{2}$

3. What is the value of h in the figure above?

A) 3.5

B) 7

C) 12.5

D) 14

4. If the vertices of a right triangle have coordinates $(-6, 4)$, $(1, 4)$, and $(1, -2)$, what is the length of the hypotenuse of the triangle?

A) 7

B) 8

C) $\sqrt{85}$

D) $5\sqrt{17}$

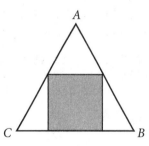

5. In the figure above, the shaded region is a square with an area of 12 square units, inscribed inside equilateral triangle ABC. What is the perimeter of triangle ABC?

A) $18\sqrt{3}$

B) $4 + \sqrt{3}$

C) $4 + 6\sqrt{3}$

D) $12 + 6\sqrt{3}$

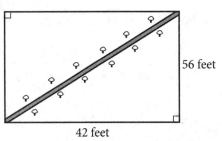

56 feet

42 feet

<u>Note</u>: Figure not drawn to scale.

6. A college has a sidewalk that cuts through a rectangular lawn on the campus. To ensure student safety, the college decides to put lights along both sides of the sidewalk. If the lights are to be placed 5 feet apart, and no lights are placed at either end, as shown in the figure, how many lights does the college need?

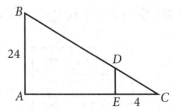

8. In the figure above, $\overline{DE} \parallel \overline{AB}$ and $\overline{DE} \perp \overline{AC}$. If $AE = 28$, what is the length of BD?

9. If the central angles in the circle shown above are in the ratio 4:3:2, what is the measure, in degrees, of the smallest angle?

A) 40

B) 60

C) 72

D) 80

7. Triangle ABC has side lengths of 8, 15, and 17. Which of the following could be the side lengths of a triangle that is similar to ABC?

A) 3, 4, 5

B) 5, 12, 13

C) 10, 17, 19

D) 24, 45, 51

10. What is the length of an arc intercepted by a central angle of 135 degrees in a circle that has a radius of 12 inches?

A) 3π

B) 9π

C) 12π

D) 24π

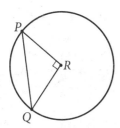

11. What is the length of chord PQ in the figure above if the radius of the circle is 4 centimeters?

A) 4

B) $4\sqrt{2}$

C) 8

D) $8\sqrt{2}$

12. At 2:15, the short hand of an analog clock lines up exactly with the 11-minute tick mark and the long hand lines up with the 15-minute tick mark. What central angle do the hands form at 2:15 ?

A) 18°

B) 20°

C) 24°

D) 28°

13. Which system of equations has no solution?

A)
$$y = x$$
$$x^2 + y^2 = 25$$

B)
$$y = x + 6$$
$$x^2 + y^2 = 9$$

C)
$$y = x - 4$$
$$x^2 + y^2 = 16$$

D)
$$y = x + 8$$
$$x^2 + y^2 = 100$$

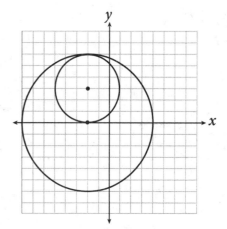

14. If the area of the smaller circle shown above is 144π square units, what is the equation of the larger circle?

A) $(x + 2)^2 + y^2 = 36$

B) $(x + 2)^2 + (y - 3)^2 = 9$

X) $(x + 8)^2 + (y - 12)^2 = 144$

Δ) $(x + 8)^2 + y^2 = 576$

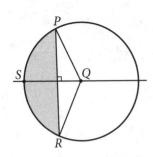

15. If the measure of $\angle PQR$ in the figure above is $120°$, and the radius of the circle is 4 units, what is the area in square units of the shaded portion of the circle?

   A) $\dfrac{4\pi}{3} - 8\sqrt{3}$

   B) $\dfrac{5\pi}{3} - 4\sqrt{3}$

   C) $\dfrac{8\pi}{3} - 4\sqrt{3}$

   D) $\dfrac{16\pi}{3} - 4\sqrt{3}$

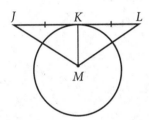

16. In the figure above, $\overline{JL}$ is tangent to circle M at point K. If the area of the circle is 36π, and $JL = 16$, what is the length of $\overline{LM}$?

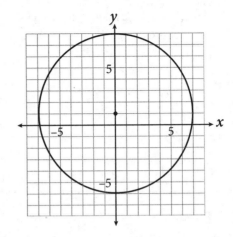

17. If the equation of the circle shown above is written in the form $x^2 + y^2 + ax + by = c$, what is the value of $a + b + c$?

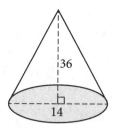

Note: Figure not drawn to scale.

18. What is the volume, in cubic units, of the solid shown above? (The formula for the volume of a cone is provided at the start of the SAT Math section and is $V = \frac{1}{3}\pi r^2 h$.)

    A) 252π

    B) 588π

    C) $1,764\pi$

    D) $2,352\pi$

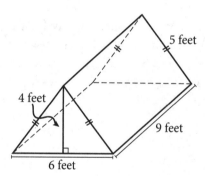

19. The figure above represents a camping tent that will be sprayed using a waterproofing agent. If it takes 1 ounce of the agent to cover 3 square feet, how many ounces will it take to spray the entire tent, inside and outside, including the tent bottom and its front door flaps?

    A)   56

    B)   112

    C)   168

    D)   336

20. What is the volume, in cubic inches, of a cubical cardboard box that has a surface area of 1,176 square inches?

    A)   84

    B)   196

    C)   1,176

    D)   2,744

21. Suppose a cheesemaker produces cheese in rectangular blocks, each with a volume of 576 cubic inches. Customers and restaurants can buy this cheese in increments of $\frac{1}{8}$ blocks. One day, a customer buys $\frac{1}{8}$ of a block and a restaurant buys $\frac{1}{2}$ of a block. If the height of a cheese block is always 8 inches and the width is always 6 inches, what is the difference in the lengths of the two purchases?

    A)   4.5 inches

    B)   6 inches

    C)   7.6 inches

    D)   12 inches

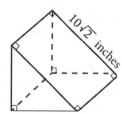

22. A solid wood cube is cut perfectly in half diagonally from corner to corner, as shown above, to be used as chocks, which are wedges placed behind wheels of vehicles to prevent them from rolling. What is the volume in cubic inches of one of these chocks?

    A)   100

    B) $100\sqrt{2}$

    C)   500

    D)   1,000

23. Rupert has a collection of video discs he wants to store in a cubical box with edges of length 10 inches. If each disc is in a container with dimensions of 5 inches by 5 inches by $\frac{1}{4}$ inch, what is the maximum number of discs that can fit into the box?

   A)   60

   B)   80

   C)   120

   D)   160

24. A medical test tube is made up of a cylinder with a half-sphere on the bottom. The volume in square inches of the tube is $\frac{19}{12}\pi$. The diameter of the cylinder and of the half-sphere is 1 inch. If the volume of a sphere is given by the formula $V = \frac{4}{3}\pi r^3$, how tall, in inches, is the test tube? (The formula for the volume of a sphere is provided at the beginning of the SAT Math section.)

   A)   4.75

   B)   5

   C)   6

   D)   6.5

25. The roof of a certain bell tower is in the shape of a square pyramid with a length and width of 20 feet and a slant height of 18 feet. The roof needs new shingles, which are 72 square inches in size. The shingles must overlap so that water doesn't leak between the seams. What is the minimum number of shingles needed to cover the roof, assuming 20 percent extra to account for the overlap?

   A)   432

   B)   518

   C)   1,440

   D)   1,728

26. The opening of a perfectly circular sewer tunnel has a circumference of 8π. The tunnel has a volume of $2,048\pi$ cubic feet. How many feet long is the tunnel?

27. The length, width, and height, respectively, of a rectangular prism are in the ratio 4:2:1. If the volume of the prism is 216 cubic inches, how many inches wide is the prism?

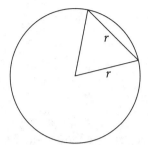

Note: Figure not drawn to scale.

28. What is the sine of the central angle of the circle shown?

A) $\dfrac{1}{2}$

B) $\dfrac{1}{\sqrt{3}}$

C) $\dfrac{\sqrt{2}}{\sqrt{3}}$

D) $\dfrac{\sqrt{3}}{2}$

29. Given that $i = \sqrt{-1}$, what is the value of $(2 + 3i)(4 - 2i)$?

A) $14 + 8i$

B) $14 - 8i$

C) $2 + 8i$

D) $2 - 8i$

30. Which of the following represents a $120°$ angle given in radians?

A) $\dfrac{2\pi}{3}$

B) $\dfrac{3\pi}{4}$

C) $\dfrac{5\pi}{6}$

D) $\dfrac{11\pi}{12}$

Answers and Explanations

1. D

Difficulty: Medium

Category: Special Right Triangles

Getting to the Answer: Two of the angles in the triangle have degree measures 30 and 90, which means the third angle must measure 60 degrees. This means you are dealing with a special right triangle and can use ratio of sides in a 30-60-90 triangle: $x:x\sqrt{3}:2x$ (short leg:long leg:hypotenuse). The only length you know is the long leg—the side represented by the ground and the width of the bottom two steps. The ramp is to be placed $8\text{ feet} \times \dfrac{12\text{ inches}}{1\text{ foot}} = 96\text{ inches}$ from the bottom step, and the steps themselves are an additional 20 inches, which means this leg of the triangle is $96 + 20 = 116$ inches long. Set 116 equal to $x\sqrt{3}$ and use the ratio to determine that you need to divide by $\sqrt{3}$ to find the length of the shorter leg, the ramp's height, and then multiply the result by 2 to find the length of the hypotenuse, which represents the ramp's length:

$$\frac{116}{\sqrt{3}} = 66.97$$
$$66.97 \times 2 = 133.95$$

The result is about 134 inches. **(D)** is correct.

2. A

Difficulty: Medium

Category: Pythagorean Theorem

Getting to the Answer: Start by translating from English into math. Because one leg of the triangle is three times as long as the other, let x and $3x$ represent the lengths. Use the Pythagorean theorem to find the hypotenuse:

$$a^2 + b^2 = c^2$$
$$x^2 + (3x)^2 = c^2$$
$$x^2 + 9x^2 = c^2$$
$$10x^2 = c^2$$
$$\sqrt{10x^2} = c$$

Although you can't find a numerical value for c, you do know that the number under the radical is a multiple of 10, so **(A)** is correct.

3. D

Difficulty: Medium

Category: Special Right Triangles

Getting to the Answer: Because one angle of the triangle measures 90° and the two legs are congruent (notice the tick marks), this is a 45-45-90 triangle. The side lengths of a 45-45-90 triangle are in the ratio $x:x:x\sqrt{2}$, where x represents the length of a leg and $x\sqrt{2}$ represents the length of the hypotenuse. Set up an equation using the ratio and the length of the side, $7\sqrt{2}$, to find h:

$$h = x\sqrt{2}$$
$$= 7\sqrt{2} \times \sqrt{2}$$
$$= 7\sqrt{4}$$
$$= 7(2)$$
$$= 14$$

The length of the hypotenuse is 14, so **(D)** is correct.

4. C

Difficulty: Medium

Category: Pythagorean Theorem

Getting to the Answer: Whenever you're given coordinates in a Geometry question, sketch the figure. You won't have graph paper, so draw carefully and label the coordinates of the points:

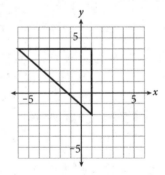

The above sketch shows that the figure is a right triangle. Find the lengths of the legs and then use the Pythagorean theorem to find the length of the hypotenuse. To find the length of the horizontal leg, subtract the x-coordinates: $1 - (-6) = 7$. To find the length of the vertical leg, subtract the y-coordinates: $4 - (-2) = 6$. The leg lengths are 6 and 7. Substitute these values into the Pythagorean theorem to find the length of the hypotenuse:

$$a^2 + b^2 = c^2$$
$$6^2 + 7^2 = c^2$$
$$36 + 49 = c^2$$
$$85 = c^2$$
$$\sqrt{85} = \sqrt{c^2}$$
$$\sqrt{85} = c$$

Choice **(C)** is correct.

5. D

Difficulty: Hard

Category: Special Right Triangles

Getting to the Answer: Start with what you know about the shaded square. Because its area is 12, each side must be $\sqrt{12} = 2\sqrt{3}$.

Triangle ABC is an equilateral triangle, so each of its interior angles measures 60 degrees. The two vertical sides of the square, therefore, each represent the longer leg of a 30-60-90 triangle (the small white triangles on the sides). This leg has a length of $2\sqrt{3}$, which means the length of each short leg is 2. You now have the length of the base of the large equilateral triangle: $2 + 2\sqrt{3} + 2 = 4 + 2\sqrt{3}$. Thus, each side of the large equilateral triangle has length $4 + 2\sqrt{3}$. The perimeter is the sum of all three sides, so multiply by 3 to get $12 + 6\sqrt{3}$, making **(D)** correct.

6. 26

Difficulty: Hard

Category: Pythagorean Theorem

Getting to the Answer: Recognizing the side lengths as part of a 3:4:5 Pythagorean triple saves time: $42 = 3 \times 14$ and $56 = 4 \times 14$, so the hypotenuse must be $5 \times 14 = 70$. A multiple of 14 is difficult to see, so you could use the Pythagorean theorem to find the length of the diagonal shown in the figure:

$$a^2 + b^2 = c^2$$
$$42^2 + 56^2 = c^2$$
$$1{,}764 + 3{,}136 = c^2$$
$$4{,}900 = c^2$$
$$\sqrt{4{,}900} = \sqrt{c^2}$$
$$70 = c$$

The length of the sidewalk is 70 feet. Lights are to be placed every 5 feet, so divide by 5 to get $\frac{70}{5} = 14$. Be careful: the question says that there are no lights at either end of the sidewalk, so subtract 1 from this number to get 13. The college plans to put the lights on *both* sides of the sidewalk, so the total number of lights is $13 \times 2 = $ **26**.

7. D

Difficulty: Easy

Category: Similar Triangles

Getting to the Answer: Corresponding sides of similar triangles are proportional. In other words, the larger triangle is a "scaled-up" version of the smaller triangle. Therefore, you're looking for the same ratio of sides (8:15:17), multiplied by a scale factor. This means **(D)** is correct because each side length of ABC has been scaled up by a factor of 3.

8. 35

Difficulty: Hard

Category: Similar Triangles

Getting to the Answer: Start by determining whether there is a relationship between triangles ABC and EDC. The two triangles share a common angle, C. It is given that $\overline{DE} \perp \overline{AC}$, so angle DEC is a right angle. Because $\overline{DE} \parallel \overline{AB}$, $\overline{BA}$ is also perpendicular to $\overline{AC}$, making angle BAC another right angle. Triangles that have two congruent interior angles are similar, so triangle ABC is similar to triangle EDC.

The length of AE is 28, which means the length of AC is $28 + 4 = 32$. The length of EC is 4, which means that the side lengths of triangle ABC are 8 times the side lengths of triangle EDC. Use this ratio to find DE: $\frac{24}{8} = 3$. A right triangle with side lengths 3 and 4 means a 3:4:5 triangle, but you could also use the Pythagorean theorem to find that $DC = 5$. Multiply DC, 5, by 8 to find BC: $5 \times 8 = 40$. The question asks for the length of BD, which is $40 - 5 = $ **35**.

9. D

Difficulty: Easy

Category: Arc Length and Sectors

Strategic Advice: Whenever you're given a ratio, you can set up an equation. Sometimes the equation takes the form of a proportion and sometimes it takes the form of "the sum of the parts equals the whole." In this question, the *whole* is the total number of degrees in a circle, which is 360.

Getting to the Answer: You know the relative size of each of the parts in this question. You don't know the exact size of one part, so call it *x*. Now, set up an equation:

$$4x + 3x + 2x = 360$$
$$9x = 360$$
$$x = 40$$

Note that the question asks for the measure of the smallest angle, which is represented by 2*x*. The correct answer is 2(40) = 80, which is **(D)**.

10. B

Difficulty: Easy

Category: Arc Length and Sectors

Getting to the Answer: Use the relationship
$$\frac{\text{arc length}}{\text{circumference}} = \frac{\text{central angle}}{360°}$$ to answer this question.
To help you remember this relationship, just think
$$\frac{\text{partial distance}}{\text{whole distance}} = \frac{\text{partial angle}}{\text{whole angle}}.$$

The unknown in this question is the arc length, so call it *a*. You need to find the circumference of the circle before you set up the relationship. The question tells you that the radius is 12 inches, so use the formula $C = 2\pi r$ to find that the circumference is $2\pi(12) = 24\pi$. You also know that the central angle has a measure of 135 degrees, so you're ready to set up and solve the relationship:

$$\frac{\text{arc length}}{\text{circumference}} = \frac{\text{central angle}}{360°}$$
$$\frac{a}{24\pi} = \frac{135}{360}$$
$$360a = 3{,}240\pi$$
$$a = \frac{3{,}240}{360}\pi$$
$$a = 9\pi$$

(B) is the correct answer.

11. B

Difficulty: Easy

Category: Special Right Triangles

Getting to the Answer: Note that each leg of triangle *PQR* also acts as a radius of the circle, which means they are the same length. Because triangle *PQR* is a right triangle with two congruent legs, it is a 45-45-90 triangle. The sides of a 45-45-90 right triangle are always in the ratio $x:x:x\sqrt{2}$. Each leg of the triangle is a radius of the circle, which is given as 4. Side *PQ* is the hypotenuse of the triangle, so it must have length $4\sqrt{2}$, which is **(B)**.

12. C

Difficulty: Medium

Category: Arc Length and Sectors

Getting to the Answer: An analog clock has 12 hours marked off, each of which has 5 tick marks representing minutes, for a total of $12 \times 5 = 60$ tick marks. There are 360° in a circle, so the degree measure between each pair of tick marks is $\frac{360°}{60} = 6°$. At 2:15, the hands of the clock are 4 tick marks apart $(15 - 11)$, so the angle between them is $4 \times 6 = 24°$, which is **(C)**.

13. B

Difficulty: Medium

Category: Circles

Strategic Advice: The SAT would not expect you to algebraically solve four systems of equations on test day for one question—there simply isn't enough time. Therefore, you should look for another way to answer the question. Note that the answer choices are equations in common forms, and consider the graph they would produce.

Getting to the Answer: Each answer choice contains a line that is already written in slope-intercept form and a circle that has its center at the origin. Drawing a quick sketch will get you to the answer more quickly than trying to solve the systems algebraically. If the line and the circle don't intersect, then the system has no solution.

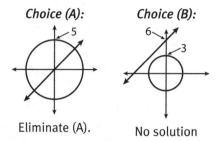

Choice (A):   *Choice (B):*

Eliminate (A).   No solution

You do not need to test (C) and (D). Choice **(B)** is correct because the graphs do not intersect.

14. D

Difficulty: Hard

Category: Circles

Strategic Advice: Note that the graph is not labeled with any units, which means that one square does not necessarily equal one unit.

Getting to the Answer: To find the equation of a circle, you need the radius and the *x*- and *y*-coordinates of the center point. Then, you can use the standard equation: $(x - h)^2 + (y - k)^2 = r^2$, where (h, k) is the center of the circle and *r* is the length of the radius.

Be careful—choice (A) is incorrect, but might appear correct if you assume that one square represents one unit. The graph has no number labels on it, so you'll need to use the information given in the question about the smaller circle to determine the value of each grid line:

$$A = \pi r^2$$
$$144\pi = \pi r^2$$
$$144 = r^2$$
$$\pm 12 = r$$

The radius can't be negative, so it must be 12. There are only three grid lines between the center of the smaller circle and its edge, so each grid line must be equal to $\frac{12}{3} = 4$ units. The center of the larger circle, therefore, is $(-8, 0)$, and its radius is $6 \times 4 = 24$. Thus, the equation must be $(x - (-8))^2 + (y - 0)^2 = 24^2$, or written in simplified form, $(x + 8)^2 + y^2 = 576$. **(D)** is the correct answer.

15. D

Difficulty: Hard

Category: Arc Length and Sectors

Strategic Advice: Find the area of the sector and then *subtract* the area of triangle *PQR* to get the area of the shaded region.

Getting to the Answer: To find the area of the sector, you'll need the area of the whole circle: $A = \pi r^2 = \pi(4)^2 = 16\pi$. Now, use the formula:

$$\frac{\text{area of sector}}{\text{area of circle}} = \frac{\text{central angle}}{360°}$$
$$\frac{A_{\text{sector}}}{16\pi} = \frac{120}{360}$$
$$A_{\text{sector}} = \frac{120 \times 16\pi}{360}$$
$$A_{\text{sector}} = \frac{16\pi}{3}$$

Looking at the answer choices now can save you a lot of time. You can determine the correct answer without finding the area of triangle *PQR*! The first term in each answer choice contains π, which means the first term must represent the area of the sector. The second term does not include π, so it must represent the area of the triangle. Choice **(D)** is the only expression that gives the correct area of the sector, $\frac{16\pi}{3}$.

For the record, here is how to find the area of the triangle. Notice that triangle *PQR* is formed by two radii and a chord. The height of the triangle represents the shorter leg of each of the smaller triangles inside *PQR*. The small triangles are congruent, and because ∠*PQR* has a measure of 120°, each of the small triangles is a 30-60-90 triangle. The radius of the circle, which is the hypotenuse of each small triangle, is 4. The shorter leg (the height of triangle *PQR*), then, is $\frac{4}{2} = 2$. The longer leg (one-half of the base of *PQR*) is $2\sqrt{3}$, which makes the base of triangle *PQR* equal to $4\sqrt{3}$. The area of triangle *PQR*, therefore, is $\frac{1}{2}(4\sqrt{3})(2) = 4\sqrt{3}$. Thus, the area of the shaded region is $\frac{16\pi}{3} - 4\sqrt{3}$, so **(D)** is indeed correct.

16. 10

Difficulty: Medium

Category: Pythagorean Theorem

Strategic Advice: The key to this question is that the radius of a circle is perpendicular to a tangent line—a line that touches a curve at a point without crossing over—at that point. Once you draw the crucial right angle in, just proceed step-by-step until you have enough information to apply the Pythagorean theorem or your knowledge of Pythagorean triplets.

Getting to the Answer: Use the area of the circle to find the radius:

$$A = \pi r^2$$
$$36\pi = \pi r^2$$
$$36 = r^2$$
$$6 = r$$

So, $KM = 6$. You also know that $JL = 16$, and the tick marks on the figure indicate congruence, so KL equals one-half of JL, or 8.

With $KM = 6$ and $KL = 8$, recognize the Pythagorean triple 3:4:5 multiplied by a factor of 2 to get a 6:8:10 triangle. According to the ratio, LM is **10**. You also could have applied the Pythagorean theorem:

$$c^2 = a^2 + b^2$$
$$c^2 = 36 + 64$$
$$c^2 = 100$$
$$c = 10$$

The correct answer is indeed **10**.

17. 46

Difficulty: Hard

Category: Circles

Getting to the Answer: First, find the center and the radius of the circle: Each grid line represents one unit on the graph, so the center is $(0, 1)$ and the radius is 7. Substitute these values into the equation for a circle, $(x - h)^2 + (y - k)^2 = r^2$, and then simplify until the equation looks like the one given in the question:

$$(x - 0)^2 + (y - 1)^2 = 7^2$$
$$x^2 + (y - 1)(y - 1) = 49$$
$$x^2 + y^2 - 2y + 1 = 49$$
$$x^2 + y^2 - 2y = 48$$

There is no x term, so $a = 0$. The coefficient of y is -2 and $c = 48$, so $a + b + c = 0 + (-2) + 48 = $ **46**.

18. B

Difficulty: Easy

Category: Three-Dimensional Figures

Getting to the Answer: If you don't have the formula for the volume of a cone memorized, you can find it on the formula page at the beginning of the test: $V = \frac{1}{3}\pi r^2 h$. The diagram provides you with all of the information that you need. The diameter is 14, which makes the radius $\frac{14}{2} = 7$, and the height is 36. Plug these values into the formula:

$$V = \frac{1}{3}\pi(7)^2(36)$$
$$V = \pi(49)(12)$$
$$V = 588\pi$$

(B) is correct.

19. B

Difficulty: Medium

Category: Three-Dimensional Figures

Strategic Advice: You're looking for surface area because you need to spray all of the faces of the tent. Decompose the figure into 2-D shapes, and add their areas together. Because the tent is sprayed inside and outside, the amount of coverage will be twice the surface area. Lastly, find the number of ounces of waterproofing agent using unit conversion.

Getting to the Answer: The bottom of the tent is a rectangle: $A = lw = (9)(6) = 54$. The two sides of the tent are also rectangles, but one of the dimensions is different from that of the bottom: $2A = 2(lw) = 2(9)(5) = 90$. The front and back of the tent are triangles:

$$2A_{triangle} = 2\left(\frac{1}{2}bh\right) = bh = (6)(4) = 24$$

Thus, the total surface area of the tent is $54 + 90 + 24 = 168$ square feet. Both the inside and outside of the tent need to be sprayed, so double the surface area to get 336 square feet. Use unit conversion to find the number of ounces of waterproofing agent needed:

$$336 \text{ square feet} = \frac{1 \text{ ounce}}{3 \text{ square feet}} = 112 \text{ ounces}$$

(B) is correct.

20. D

Difficulty: Easy

Category: Three-Dimensional Figures

Getting to the Answer: To find the volume of a cubical box, you need to know the length of a side. You can find this value by using the information given about the surface area of the box. The surface area of a cube equals 6 times the area of one face, or $6s^2$, where s is the length of a side. Substitute the given surface area into the formula and solve for s:

$$6s^2 = 1{,}176$$
$$s^2 = 196$$
$$s = 14$$

Thus, the length of a side of the cube is 14 inches. The volume of a cube is given by $V = lwh$ (or $V = s^3$ because the sides are all equal in length), so the volume of the moving box is 14^3, or 2,744 cubic inches. **(D)** is correct.

21. A

Difficulty: Medium

Category: Three-Dimensional Figures

Getting to the Answer: The cheese block purchases have the same height and width, so the block must be cut according to length. Find the original length of the entire block using the formula for volume of a rectangular solid, $V = lwh$, and then solve for length:

$$V = lwh$$
$$576 = (l)(6)(8)$$
$$12 = l$$

The question asks for the difference in the two lengths. The customer bought $\frac{1}{8}$ block, which is equal to $(12)\left(\frac{1}{8}\right) = 1.5$ inches. The restaurant bought $\frac{1}{2}$ block, which is equal to $(12)\left(\frac{1}{2}\right) = 6$ inches. The difference in the lengths is $6 - 1.5 = 4.5$ inches, which is **(A)**.

22. C

Difficulty: Medium

Category: Three-Dimensional Figures

Getting to the Answer: A wedge shape is an unfamiliar solid, so there is no formula that will give you the volume directly. The solid is one-half of a cube, so imagine the other half lying on top of the solid, forming a complete cube:

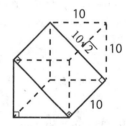

The question tells you that the hypotenuse is $10\sqrt{2}$. Notice that this diagonal with length $10\sqrt{2}$ and two of the cube's edges form an isosceles right triangle, or in other words, a 45-45-90 triangle. In a 45-45-90 triangle, the hypotenuse is $\sqrt{2}$ times the length of a leg, so the legs have length 10. Thus, the volume of the whole cube is $10 \times 10 \times 10 = 1{,}000$ and the volume of the chock is half that, or 500 cubic inches, which is **(C)**.

23. D

Difficulty: Medium

Category: Three-Dimensional Figures

Getting to the Answer: There are two ways to approach this question—but only because both shapes (the storage box and the discs' containers) are rectangular prisms and the dimensions match up nicely (two rows of two discs will exactly fill one layer in the box with no extra space left over). One strategy is to find the volume of the storage box and divide by the volume of each disc. Another strategy is to find how many discs Rupert can fit in length, then in width, then in height, and multiply. The second approach must be used when the shapes are different and when the dimensions don't match up just right.

Strategy 1: The volume of a rectangular prism (or a cube) is given by the formula $V = l \times w \times h$, so the volume of the storage box is $10 \times 10 \times 10 = 1{,}000$ cubic units. The volume of each disc is $5 \times 5 \times \frac{1}{4} = 6.25$. The number of discs that can fit in the box is $1{,}000 \div 6.25 = 160$ discs, which is **(D)**.

Strategy 2: The box has dimensions of 10 inches by 10 inches by 10 inches. Because each disc is 5 inches in length, he can fit $10 \div 5 = 2$ rows of discs along the length of the box. Each disc is 5 inches in width, so he can fit $10 \div 5 = 2$ rows of discs along the width of the box. Finally, each disc is $\frac{1}{4}$ inch tall, so he can fit $10 \div \frac{1}{4} = 10 \times 4 = 40$ rows of discs along the depth of the box. Multiply to find that Rupert can fit $2 \times 2 \times 40 = 160$ video discs in the box.

24. D

Difficulty: Hard

Category: Three-Dimensional Figures

Strategic Advice: Set the question in plain language first and then translate from English into math: the volume of the test tube is equal to the volume of the cylinder plus the volume of the half-sphere. If you don't have the formulas memorized, find them on the formula page to write an equation.

Getting to the Answer: The diameter of the cylinder and the half-sphere is the same, 1 inch, so the radius of each is $\frac{1}{2}$ inch. You also know the total volume, so the the unknown is the height, h, of the cylinder:

$$V_{\text{tube}} = V_{\text{cylinder}} + \frac{1}{2} V_{\text{sphere}}$$

$$\frac{19}{12}\pi = \pi r^2 h + \frac{1}{2}\left(\frac{4}{3}\pi r^3\right)$$

$$\frac{19}{12}\pi = \pi\left(\frac{1}{2}\right)^2 h + \frac{2}{3}\pi\left(\frac{1}{2}\right)^3$$

$$\frac{19}{12}\pi = \frac{1}{4}\pi h + \left(\frac{1}{8}\pi\right)\frac{2}{3}$$

$$\frac{19}{12}\pi - \pi\frac{1}{12} = \frac{1}{4}\pi h$$

$$\frac{3}{2}\pi = \frac{1}{4}\pi h$$

$$6 = h$$

The question asks for the length of the test tube, so you need to add the radius of the half-sphere to the length of the cylinder: $6 + 0.5 = 6.5$ inches. **(D)** is correct.

25. D

Difficulty: Hard

Category: Three-Dimensional Figures

Strategic Advice: Draw the figure and consider the scenario as a real-world question. The roof shingles will go only on the top four triangular faces, not the square base. Calculate the area of one triangle, multiply by 4, convert the units to find the number of shingles required, and add 20% for the extra coverage.

Getting to the Answer: Sketch and label the figure:

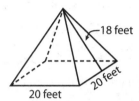

Use the formula for area of a triangle, $A = \frac{1}{2}bh$. The base of each triangular face is 20 feet and the height of the triangle is the slant height of the pyramid, 18 feet. The area of one side of the roof is $\frac{1}{2}(20)(18) = 180$. There are four sides, so the total area to be covered is $4(180) = 720$ square feet. Use unit conversion to change square feet into square inches into the number of shingles:

$$720 \text{ feet}^2 \times \frac{12 \text{ inches}}{1 \text{ foot}} \times \frac{12 \text{ inches}}{1 \text{ foot}} \times \frac{1 \text{ shingle}}{72 \text{ inches}^2}$$

$$= 1{,}440 \text{ shingles}$$

Finally, add 20% to this amount to account for the overlap in the shingles: $1{,}440 \times 1.2 = 1{,}728$ shingles. **(D)** is correct.

26. 128

Difficulty: Medium

Category: Three-Dimensional Figures

Getting to the Answer: The question tells you that the circumference of the opening (which is a circle) is 8π, so substitute this value in the formula for circumference and solve for r:

$$C = 2\pi r$$
$$8\pi = 2\pi r$$
$$4 = r$$

You now have everything you need to find h, which in this case is the length of the tunnel. Use the formula $V = \pi r^2 h$:

$$2{,}048\pi = \pi(4)^2(h)$$
$$2{,}048 = 16h$$
$$128 = h$$

The tunnel is **128** feet long.

27. 6

Difficulty: Medium

Category: Three-Dimensional Figures

Getting to the Answer: Use the formula for volume of a rectangular solid, $V = lwh$, to write an equation. Because the dimensions are given as the ratio 4:2:1, let the length, width, and height be represented by $4x$, $2x$, and $1x$. Substitute the expressions into the formula and solve for $2x$, which is the width:

$$216 = (4x)(2x)(1x)$$
$$216 = 8x^3$$
$$27 = x^3$$
$$3 = x$$
$$2x = 6$$

Grid in **6**.

28. D

Difficulty: Medium

Category: Sine, Cosine, and Tangent

Getting to the Answer: The chord will form a triangle with the two radii of the central angle. Since the chord is the same length as the radii, this is an equilateral triangle. Therefore, each angle, including the central angle, is 60°. Although this triangle does not have a right angle, you can use the side ratios of a 30-60-90 triangle to find sin 60°. That ratio is $1:\sqrt{3}:2$ Since the 60° angle is greater than the 30° angle, it is opposite the longer leg. Because $\sin = \dfrac{\text{opposite}}{\text{hypotenuse}}$, the sine of 60° is $\dfrac{\sqrt{3}}{2}$. **(D)** is correct.

29. A

Difficulty: Medium

Category: Arithmetic Operations with Complex Numbers

Getting to the Answer: Expand the multiplication using FOIL to get $8 - 4i + 12i - 6i^2$. If $i = \sqrt{-1}$, then $i^2 = -1$. Restate the expression as $8 + 8i + 6 = 14 + 8i$. **(A)** is correct.

30. A

Difficulty: Easy

Category: Arc Lengths and Sectors

Getting to the Answer: Use the conversion $180° = \pi$ to convert between degrees and radians. Write the conversion as a ratio, with degrees in the denominator so they cancel. The radian equivalent of 120 degrees is $120° \times \dfrac{\pi}{180°} = \dfrac{120\pi}{180} = \dfrac{2\pi}{3}$. **(A)** is correct.

CHAPTER 16

SAT Math: Timing and Section Management Strategies

LEARNING OBJECTIVES

After completing this chapter, you will be able to:

- Make quick decisions about which questions to spend time on and which to skip
- Attack multi-part questions efficiently

SAT Math Timing and Triage

The non-calculator section has 20 questions to be completed in 25 minutes, which means you'll have 1 minute and 15 seconds per question; the calculator section has 38 questions to be completed in 55 minutes, which means you'll have a little less than a minute and a half per question. This is an average, though. Some questions will be straightforward, meaning that you can get the correct answer in 30 seconds or less. Others will be more difficult and time consuming. Test takers who start at the beginning of the section, attempt the questions in order, and only move on to the next question when the previous one is complete often find that they get bogged down and don't make it to the end of the section, potentially missing questions that they could have answered correctly. Flexibility can earn you more points.

A better approach would be to make your way through the section with a plan to deal with each question. Each time you read a new question, take a moment to gauge your gut reaction:

- Does this question seem quick and easy? Do it immediately.
- Does this question seem time consuming but manageable? Skip it for now. Put a circle around it and try it on a second pass through the section.
- Does this question look confusing or difficult? Skip it. Don't worry about circling or marking questions like this. You'll approach them only after you have worked on the other questions in the section, and only if you have time.

Try to make this decision quickly. The more you practice, the easier it will be to recognize which questions are easier and which are more challenging for you.

When you approach a section this way, you'll end up taking two or three passes through it. This technique ensures that you'll get all of the easy points first and that if you run out of time, you'll know that the questions you didn't attempt were the hardest in the section and that it would have been tougher to get those questions right anyway.

Before the end of the section, make sure you have something bubbled in for every question since there is no penalty for guessing. Also, be very careful when bubbling your answers. It's easy to skip a question but forget to skip a line on the grid and bubble your answer to the next question in the wrong place.

The questions in each Math section will be in approximate order of difficulty, with the easiest questions at the beginning of the section and the most difficult questions at the end of the section. There are two exceptions:

- The difficulty resets with the Grid-in questions. That is, the first Grid-in question is much easier than the last multiple-choice question. If the multiple-choice questions start getting too tough, skip to the Grid-ins.

- The individual questions in a two- or three-part question set might be easier or harder than the questions around them. It's a good idea to attempt them in order, since sometimes the work you did for an earlier question will help you with a later question, but you should still be ready to skip questions within one of these sets if they get too tough.

If you tend to finish the Math sections early but find that you are making speed mistakes, you may consider pausing at the confirmation step to check your logic and calculations before bubbling your response to each question.

If you're still looking for more practice with Math questions after finishing this chapter, **go online** (www.kaptest.com/moreonline) and use the Qbank to generate additional practice sets for yourself.

Try on Your Own

Directions: Use this question set to practice effective question triage. Skip those questions that you feel will take too long; come back to them if you have time. Try to get as many questions correct as you can in 15 minutes. As always, be sure to study the explanations, even for questions you got correct. They can be found at the end of this chapter.

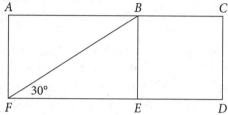

Note: Figure not drawn to scale.

1. Quadrilateral *ABEF* is a rectangle and the length of side *FE* is 9. If quadrilateral *BCDE* is a square, what is its area?

    A) 27

    B) 36

    C) $27\sqrt{3}$

    D) 81

2. If $\frac{7}{9}x - \frac{1}{6}x = \frac{1}{3} + \frac{1}{2}$, what is the value of *x* ?

    A) $\frac{15}{14}$

    B) $\frac{15}{11}$

    C) $\frac{3}{2}$

    D) $\frac{25}{14}$

3. If $f(x) = 2x^2 - 5x + 7$, what is the value of $f(8) - f(3)$?

    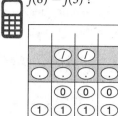

4. Anthony recently completed a trip in 3 hours. If his average speed had been 20 percent faster, how long would the same trip have taken?

    A) 2.2 hours

    B) 2.4 hours

    C) 2.5 hours

    D) 2.8 hours

    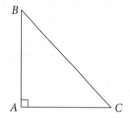

    Note: Figure not drawn to scale.

5. If $\tan \angle B = 1$, and the length of side *BC* is $\frac{6}{\sqrt{2}}$, what is the length of side *AC* ?

    A) $\frac{3}{\sqrt{2}}$

    B) 3

    C) $\frac{6}{\sqrt{2}}$

    D) 6

$$x^2 + 12x = -30$$

6. What is the absolute value of the difference between the two solutions for x in the equation above?

    A) $2\sqrt{6}$

    B) 4

    C) $6\sqrt{2}$

    D) 12

$$3x = 4y - 13$$
$$3y = 31 - 2x$$

7. Given the equations above, what is the value of $x + y$?

Questions 8–10 refer to the following information.

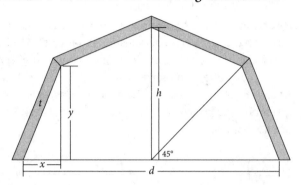

A diagram of a gambrel roof attic is shown above. Gambrel roofs are common on barns because they allow the maximum space for storage while still having a sloped roof. The steepness of the slope of a roof is called its pitch. Gambrel roofs are unique because they have a pitch break where the pitch changes. In a standard plan, the pitch break is calculated so that the four roof trusses all have the same truss length, t. The formula for the length of the base where t is the truss length and n is the number of trusses is as follows:

$$d = \frac{5t}{3 \sin\left(\frac{360}{n}\right)}$$

A cross section of a typical gambrel roof, which is symmetrical about the vertical axis, is shown in the diagram above.

8. Which of the following expresses truss length in terms of the length of the base and the number of trusses?

    A) $t = \dfrac{5 \sin\left(\frac{360}{n}\right)d}{3}$

    B) $t = \dfrac{3 \sin\left(\frac{360}{n}\right)d}{5}$

    C) $t = \dfrac{3d}{5 \sin\left(\frac{360}{n}\right)}$

    D) $t = \dfrac{5d}{3 \sin\left(\frac{360}{n}\right)}$

9. The Greer family is building a new barn and calculating the dimensions based on how much winter hay storage space they need in the gambrel roof attic. If l is the length of the barn from front to back, which one of the following equations can be used to calculate the volume, V, of the attic roof space?

A) $V = l\left(\dfrac{xy + (y + h)(d - 2x)}{2}\right)$

B) $V = \dfrac{\left(xy + \dfrac{(y + h)(d - 2x)}{2}\right)}{l}$

C) $V = l\left(xy + \dfrac{(y + h)(d - 2x)}{2}\right)$

D) $V = l\left(\dfrac{(y + h)(d - 2x)}{2}\right)$

10. After completing the volume calculations, the family decides to use a standard plan for the gambrel roof where the base, d, is 30 feet and the length of the barn from front to back, l, is 40 feet. All four surfaces of the barn roof will need to be shingled at a rate of $3.17 per square foot. Approximately how much will the Greer family spend to have the gambrel roof shingled?

A) $2,300

B) $3,800

C) $9,100

D) $15,200

Answers and Explanations

1.   A

Difficulty: Easy

Category: Geometry (Chapter 13)—Special Right Triangles

Getting to the Answer: The fact that the figures are a rectangle and a square means that all the angles other than those formed by the diagonal are 90°, which means that $\triangle BEF$ is a 30-60-90 triangle. If you don't recall the side ratios of such a triangle, you might consider skipping this question even though you can look up the side ratios on the formula sheet. (It's best to memorize the higher-yield information on the formula sheet so you won't have to spend time looking it up on test day.)

The side ratios of the triangle are $x:x\sqrt{3}:2x$. Since the length of the longer leg, FE, is 9, $x = \dfrac{9}{\sqrt{3}}$ and the lengths are $\dfrac{9}{\sqrt{3}}:9:\dfrac{18}{\sqrt{3}}$. Thus, the side length of the square, BE, is $\dfrac{9}{\sqrt{3}}$, and the area of square $BCDE$ is

$$s^2 = \left(\frac{9}{\sqrt{3}}\right)^2 = \frac{81}{3} = 27.$$ **(A)** is correct.

2.   B

Difficulty: Easy

Category: Linear Equations and Graphs (Chapter 4)—Solving Equations

Getting to the Answer: If you recall that the way to simplify multiple fractions is to clear the denominators by multiplying all terms by a common denominator, then proceed with this question. The numbers appear manageable, so you probably won't even need to use the calculator.

The lowest common denominator (LCD) of the fractions is 18, so multiply all terms by 18. (If you didn't notice that LCD, you could have multiplied by $9 \times 6 = 54$.)

$$18\left(\frac{7}{9}x\right) - 18\left(\frac{1}{6}x\right) = 18\left(\frac{1}{3}\right) + 18\left(\frac{1}{2}\right)$$
$$14x - 3x = 6 + 9$$
$$11x = 15$$
$$x = \frac{15}{11}$$

(B) is correct.

3.   85

Difficulty: Easy

Category: Functions (Chapter 10)—Function Notation

Getting to the Answer: Although this is a Grid-in question, the amount of calculations needed to get the answer are minimal since all that is required is to evaluate a single-variable function twice and make one subtraction. Therefore, you would probably choose to answer this question on a first pass. Even though the question permits the use of the calculator, you are certainly not required to use it. Usually, if you are comfortable making the calculations without the calculator, you will save time and avoid keying errors.

Substitute the two values given into the function. Notice that since you will be subtracting $f(3)$ from $f(8)$, the constant term, 7, will cancel out. Therefore, the calculation is $2(8)^2 - 5(8) - [2(3)^2 - 5(3)]$, which is $2(64) - 5(8) - 2(9) + 5(3)$. This simplifies to $128 - 40 - 18 + 15$, which is 85. Grid in **85** and move on.

4.   C

Difficulty: Medium

Category: Linear Equations and Graphs (Chapter 4)—Word Problems

Getting to the Answer: Your time management decisions often depend on whether you are able to quickly identify the strategy you can use to answer a question. For this question, you will use the formula Distance = rate × time to determine the answer. Since distance is the constant factor and rate and time vary, you'll set rate × time for both scenarios equal to each other. If you don't see this approach fairly quickly, you should move on and mark this question to come back to later.

Set the initial rate to r and the time to make the trip at the new rate to t. The distance for the actual trip is $3r$ and the distance if Anthony increases his average speed is $t(1.2r)$. Set these two equal to each other, $3r = t(1.2r)$. The rs cancel out, so you can write that $t = \dfrac{3}{1.2} = 2.5$. **(C)** is correct.

5. B

Difficulty: Medium

Category: Trigonometry (Chapter 14)—Sine, Cosine, and Tangent

Getting to the Answer: The key to unraveling this question is recognizing that $\angle B = \angle C = 45°$. That fact enables you to set up a side ratio and solve for the length of side AC. If you are unable to make this determination, pass on this question for now and move on. Given that $\tan = \dfrac{\text{opposite}}{\text{adjacent}}$, $\tan \angle B = 1$ means that the sides opposite and adjacent to vertex B are equal.

Triangle ABC is an isosceles right triangle. The side ratio for a 45-45-90 triangle is $s:s:s\sqrt{2}$, so $s\sqrt{2} = \dfrac{6}{\sqrt{2}}$, and $s = \dfrac{6}{\sqrt{2} \times \sqrt{2}} = \dfrac{6}{2} = 3$. **(B)** is correct.

6. A

Difficulty: Medium

Category: Quadratics (Chapter 12)—The Quadratic Formula

Getting to the Answer: Add 30 to each side to get $x^2 + 12x + 30 = 0$. Since there are not any integer factors of 30 that add to 12, you'll have to use either completing the square or the quadratic formula to solve for the possible values of x. If you see a question like this on test day and are not comfortable with those techniques or feel that this question could take too much time to answer, come back to it on a second pass.

If you choose to solve via the quadratic equation, $\dfrac{-b \pm \sqrt{b^2 - 4ac}}{2a}$, substitute 1 for a, 12 for b, and 30 for c, to get $x = \dfrac{-12 \pm \sqrt{12^2 - 4(1)(30)}}{2(1)}$. This simplifies to $x = \dfrac{-12 \pm \sqrt{144 - 120}}{2} = \dfrac{-12 \pm \sqrt{24}}{2}$. Since $\sqrt{24} = \sqrt{4} \times \sqrt{6}$, this further simplifies to $x = -6 \pm \sqrt{6}$.

The question asks for the difference between the two solutions, which is $\left(-6 + \sqrt{6}\right) - \left(-6 - \sqrt{6}\right) = 2\sqrt{6}$. **(A)** is correct.

To complete the square, add the square of half of 12, or 36, to both sides to get $x^2 + 12x + 36 = (x + 6)^2 = 6$. Take the square root of both sides to get $x + 6 = \pm\sqrt{6}$, so $x = -6 \pm \sqrt{6}$. The absolute difference is twice $\sqrt{6}$, or $2\sqrt{6}$, which confirms that **(A)** is correct. Note that the technique of completing the square takes less calculation than using the quadratic formula.

7. 12

Difficulty: Hard

Category: Systems of Equations (Chapter 5)—Combination

Getting to the Answer: Even though you are solving for $x + y$ and you are given equations in terms of $3x$ and $3y$, merely adding the two equations to get $3x + 3y = 4y - 13 + 31 - 2x$ and dividing both sides by 3 does not work. You'll need to solve the system of equations by substitution or combination (elimination) for the values of both variables and add them.

First, put the equations in the same format such as $3x - 4y = -13$ and $2x + 3y = 31$. Using substitution would likely result in working with fractions, so use combination. The x-coefficients are smaller values than the y-coefficients, so the calculations might be a little easier. Create a common x-coefficient of 6 by multiplying the first equation by 2 and the second by 3, then subtracting the second equation from the first:

$$\begin{array}{r} 6x - 8y = -26 \\ -(6x + 9y = 93) \\ \hline -17y = -119 \end{array}$$

So $y = 7$. You can plug $y = 7$ into either of the original equations to find x, but because x is already isolated on one side in the first equation, use it: $3x = 4(7) - 13 = 15$, so $x = 5$. The sum of x and y is thus $7 + 5 = 12$. Grid in **12**.

8. B

Difficulty: Medium

Category: Linear Equations and Graphs (Chapter 4)—Solving Equations

Getting to the Answer: Even when an equation looks complicated, to solve for a specific variable, you only need to move everything else in the equation to the other side of the equal sign. The original equation gives the length of the base, d, in terms of the truss length, t, and the number of trusses, n. To solve for t, multiply both sides of the expression by the $3\sin\left(\frac{360}{n}\right)$ term and divide by 5:

$$d = \frac{5t}{3\sin\left(\frac{360}{n}\right)}$$

$$3\sin\left(\frac{360}{n}\right)d = 5t$$

$$\frac{3\sin\left(\frac{360}{n}\right)d}{5} = t$$

$$t = \frac{3\sin\left(\frac{360}{n}\right)d}{5}$$

(B) is correct. (A), (C), and (D) all contain the incorrect expression in the denominator.

9. C

Difficulty: Hard

Category: Geometry (Chapter 13)—Three-Dimensional Figures

Getting to the Answer: The volume for any 3-D prism can be found by taking the area of the base and multiplying it by the height (or in this case, the length of the barn). You can eliminate (B) immediately because it divides by the length instead of multiplying by it. The cross section of the barn is not a standard shape, but, since it is symmetrical about the vertical axis, it can be broken up into simpler shapes: two equal right triangles and two equal trapezoids.

Start with the area that is easier to calculate: the area of the two right triangles. The base and height of the two triangles are x and y, and plugging those values into the triangle area formula results in $\frac{xy}{2}$. There are *two* equal triangles, so multiply by 2 to get xy as the area of the two triangles. At this point on test day, you could make the strategic leap to eliminate (D) because it does not include the xy term and (A) because it divides the xy term by 2. **(C)** is correct.

If you continue with the calculations, the area formula for a trapezoid is (average of parallel bases) × (height of the trapezoid). Based on the cross-section diagram those values will be:

$$\left(\frac{(y+h)}{2}\right)\left(\frac{(d-2x)}{2}\right)$$

Again, there are two trapezoids, so multiply the expression by 2:

$$\frac{(y+h)(d-2x)}{2}$$

Next, add the area of both triangles and both trapezoids:

$$xy + \left(\frac{(y+h)(d-2x)}{2}\right)$$

(C) is the only choice that multiplies this value by l, which confirms that it is the correct choice. Recognizing that you are building the volume formula from the area of simple shapes allows for powerful strategic elimination (and fewer calculations!).

10. C

Difficulty: Medium

Category: Linear Equations and Graphs (Chapter 4)—
Solving Equations

Getting to the Answer: If the cross section of the roof
shown in the diagram is stretched over the 40-foot
length of the barn, then the four sections of the roof are
four equal rectangles where one dimension is the length
and the other dimension is the truss length. Find the
truss length by plugging the number of trusses, 4, and
the base length, 30 feet, into the truss length formula
that you solved for in question 8:

$$t = \frac{3\sin\left(\frac{360}{4}\right)(30)}{5} = \frac{3\sin(90)(30)}{5} = \frac{3(1)(30)}{5}$$

$$= \frac{90}{5} = 18 \text{ feet}$$

Now that you have the dimension for one section of the
roof, 18 feet by 40 feet, find the area of all four sections:

$$\text{Area of four sections} = 4(18)(40) = 2,880 \text{ ft}^2$$

Finally, the price per square foot needs to be multiplied
by the total area of the roof:

$$\text{Total price} = \left(2,880 \text{ ft}^2\right)\left(\$3.17/\text{ft}^2\right) \approx \$9,100$$

(C) is correct.

PART 3

SAT Reading

CHAPTER 17

The Method for SAT Reading Questions

LEARNING OBJECTIVES

After completing this chapter, you will be able to:

- Read SAT Reading passages strategically
- Apply the Method for SAT Reading Questions efficiently and effectively to SAT Reading questions

How to Do SAT Reading

The SAT Reading section is made up of four passages and one set of paired passages, each approximately 500–750 words long and accompanied by 10–11 questions for a total of 52 questions in the section. To tackle all of this effectively in 65 minutes, the most successful test takers:

- **Read the passages strategically to zero in on the text that leads to points. (See the "Strategic Reading" section of this chapter for a quick overview and chapter 18 for more instruction and practice.)**
- **Approach the questions with a method that minimizes rereading and leads directly to correct answers. (See the "Method for SAT Reading Questions" section of this chapter for an overview and chapters 19 and 20 for more instruction and practice on how to tackle an SAT Reading question set.)**

The key to maximizing correct answers is learning in advance the kinds of questions that the test asks. SAT Reading questions focus more on the author's purpose (*why* she wrote this passage) and the passage's structure (*how* the author makes and supports her points) than on the details or facts of the subject matter (*what* this passage is about).

Knowing that the SAT rewards your attention to *how* and *why* the author wrote the passage or chose to include certain words or examples puts you in the driver's seat. You can read more effectively and answer the questions more quickly and confidently.

In this chapter, we'll give you an overview of how to tackle Reading passages and questions. The other chapters in this unit will help you become a stronger reader and will present the five SAT Reading question types, as well as tips for improving your approach for paired passages and literature passages.

Try the passage and questions that follow on your own. Then, keep reading to compare your approach to ours.

Reading

Questions 1–10 refer to the following passage.

This passage describes the varying and changing scientific theories surrounding sunspots.

Astronomers noted more than 150 years ago that sunspots wax and wane in number in an 11-year cycle. Ever since, people have speculated that the solar cycle might exert some influence on
5 the Earth's weather. In this century, for example, scientists have linked the solar cycle to droughts in the American Midwest. Until recently, however, none of these correlations has held up under close scrutiny.
10 One problem is that sunspots themselves have been poorly understood. Observation revealed that the swirly smudges represent areas of intense magnetic activity where the sun's radiative energy has been blocked and that they are considerably
15 cooler than bright regions of the sun. Scientists had not been able, however, to determine just how sunspots are created or what effect they have on the solar constant (a misnomer that refers to the sun's total radiance at any instant).
20 The latter question, at least, seems to have been resolved by data from the *Solar Maximum Mission* satellite, which has monitored the solar constant since 1980, which was the peak of a solar cycle. As the number of sunspots decreased
25 through 1986, the satellite recorded a gradual dimming of the sun. Over the next year, as sunspots proliferated, the sun brightened. These data suggest that the sun is 0.1 percent more luminous at the peak of the solar cycle, when
30 the number of sunspots is greatest, than at its nadir, according to Richard C. Willson of the Jet Propulsion Laboratory and Hugh S. Hudson of the University of California at San Diego.
The data show that sunspots do not
35 themselves make the sun shine brighter. Quite the contrary. When a sunspot appears, it initially causes the sun to dim slightly, but then after a period of weeks or months islands of brilliance called faculas usually emerge near the sunspot
40 and more than compensate for its dimming effect. Willson says faculas may represent regions where energy that initially was blocked beneath a sunspot has finally breached the surface.

Does the subtle fluctuation in the solar
45 constant manifest itself in the Earth's weather? Meteorological reports offer statistical evidence that it does, albeit rather indirectly. The link seems to be mediated by a phenomenon known as the quasi-biennial oscillation (QBO), a 180-degree
50 shift in the direction of stratospheric winds above the Tropics that occurs about every two years.
Karin Labitzke of the Free University of Berlin and Harry van Loon of the National Center for Atmospheric Research in Boulder, Colorado, were
55 the first to uncover the QBO link. They gathered temperature and air-pressure readings from various latitudes and altitudes over the past three solar cycles. They found no correlation between the solar cycle and their data until they sorted the
60 data into two categories: those gathered during the QBO's west phase (when the stratospheric winds blow west) and those gathered during its east phase. A remarkable correlation appeared: temperatures and pressures coincident with the
65 QBO's west phase rose and fell in accordance with the solar cycle.
Building on this finding, Brian A. Tinsley of the National Science Foundation discovered a statistical correlation between the solar cycle and
70 the position of storms in the North Atlantic. The latitude of storms during the west phase of the QBO, Tinsley found, varied with the solar cycle: storms occurring toward the peak of a solar cycle traveled at latitudes about six degrees nearer the
75 Equator than storms during the cycle's nadir.
Labitzke, van Loon, and Tinsley acknowledge that their findings are still rather mysterious. Why does the solar cycle seem to exert more of an influence during the west phase of the QBO
80 than it does during the east phase? How does the 0.1 percent variance in solar radiation trigger the much larger changes—up to six degrees Celsius in polar regions—observed by Labitzke and van Loon? Van Loon says simply, "We can't explain it."
85 John A. Eddy of the National Center for Atmospheric Research, nonetheless, thinks these QBO findings as well as the *Solar Maximum*

Reading

Mission data "look like breakthroughs" in the search for a link between the solar cycle
90 and weather. With further research into how the oceans damp the effects of solar flux, for example, these findings may lead to models that have some predictive value. The next few years may be particularly rich in solar flux.

1. Which one of the following best describes the main idea of the passage?

   A) The scientific advances provided by the research of Labitzke and van Loon have finally cleared up some of the mysteries that long plagued the study of sunspots.

   B) Recent research combining astronomical and climate data provides a promising foundation for better understanding the relationship between sunspots and Earth's weather.

   C) Despite recent breakthroughs, scientists are unlikely to ever fully explain correlations between sunspot activity and Earth's weather patterns.

   D) Scientists have used data from the *Solar Maximum Mission* satellite to explain how sunspots affect Earth's climate during the quasi-biennial oscillation's west phase.

2. The author's point of view can best be described as that of

   A) a meteorologist voicing optimism that the findings of recent solar research will improve weather forecasting.

   B) an astronomer presenting a digest of current findings to a review board of other astronomers.

   C) a science writer explaining the possible influence of a solar phenomenon on terrestrial weather patterns.

   D) a historian listing the contributions to climate science made by the *Solar Maximum Mission*.

3. The passage indicates which of the following about the sun's luminosity and the solar cycle?

   A) Scientists have found no correlation between the sun's brightness and the solar cycle.

   B) The sun is brightest at the nadir of the solar cycle.

   C) The sun is brightest at the peak and again at the nadir of the solar cycle.

   D) The sun is brightest at the peak of the solar cycle.

Reading

4. Which one of the following provides the best evidence for the answer to the previous question?

    A) Lines 10–11 ("One problem . . . understood")

    B) Lines 15–18 ("Scientists had . . . constant")

    C) Lines 20–24 ("The latter . . . cycle")

    D) Lines 27–31 ("These data . . . nadir")

5. Based on information in the passage, it can most reasonably be inferred that faculas

    A) are directly responsible for increased temperatures on Earth.

    B) have a dimming effect on the sun's luminescence during sunspot activity.

    C) are mostly likely to appear at the peak of the solar cycle.

    D) grow in number as the number of sunspots decreases.

6. Which one of the following provides the best evidence for the answer to the previous question?

    A) Lines 20–24 ("The latter . . . cycle")

    B) Lines 34–35 ("The data . . . brighter")

    C) Lines 36–41 ("When a . . . effect")

    D) Lines 46–47 ("Meteorological . . . indirectly")

7. As used in line 45, "manifest" most nearly means

    A) impact.

    B) disguise.

    C) itemize.

    D) reveal.

8. According to the passage, Labitzke and van Loon's research on the quasi-biennial oscillation (QBO) shows that

    A) the QBO's west phase correlates to the solar cycle.

    B) the QBO's west phase has a longer duration than that of its east phase.

    C) the QBO shows no correlation with the solar cycle.

    D) the reasons for the QBO's correlation to the solar cycle are now well understood.

9. The main purpose of the questions in the second-to-last paragraph (lines 76–84) is to

    A) emphasize how little scientists know about the solar constant.

    B) explain more fully the mysterious nature of the scientists' findings.

    C) question the basis upon which these scientists built their hypotheses.

    D) express doubts about the scientists' interpretations of their findings.

10. The use of the quoted phrase "look like breakthroughs" in line 88 is primarily meant to convey the idea that

    A) information about the solar cycle has allowed scientists to predict changes in Earth's complex climate system.

    B) additional analysis of the link between the solar cycle and Earth's weather may yield useful models.

    C) despite the associated costs, space missions can lead to important discoveries.

    D) an alternative interpretation of the data may contradict the initial findings.

Strategic Reading

The SAT Reading Test is an open-book test; the passage is right there for you to reference. Moreover, the SAT actively tests your skill in looking up details; there are Command of Evidence questions that actually ask you to cite the line numbers for the evidence you used to answer a question. Because of the way the test is constructed, it is in your best interest to read fairly quickly, noting the outline of the passage as you go, marking up the page as you read with margin notes, getting a solid understanding of the main idea, but not taking the time to memorize details. (If you are taking the digital SAT, you will have a tool available to highlight words and phrases in the passage, and you will still be able to take notes.) You can think of this process of outlining the passage as **mapping** it: you are taking note of its major features but letting go of the minor details.

Be sure to read the pre-passage blurb, the short introduction that comes before the passage. Identify any information that helps you to understand the topic of the passage or to anticipate what the author will discuss. For the previous passage, the blurb states the topic (sunspots) and announces that the passage will discuss "varying and changing theories" about them. That's an invitation to keep your eye out for multiple theories as you read.

You'll learn all the skills you need to read strategically in chapter 18, but for now, here's an example of an expert's passage map. Don't worry if yours doesn't look exactly like this (or even anything like this, yet). Follow the expert's thought process in the discussion that follows the passage to see what he was thinking and asking as he read the passage.

Questions 1–10 refer to the following passage.

This passage details the varying and changing scientific theories surrounding sunspots.

Sunspots Passage Map

Astronomers noted more than 150 years ago that sunspots wax and wane in number in an 11-year cycle. Ever since, people have speculated that the solar cycle might exert some influence on
5   the Earth's weather. In this century, for example, scientists have linked the solar cycle to droughts in the American Midwest. Until recently, however, none of these correlations has held up under close scrutiny.

10   One problem is that sunspots themselves have been poorly understood. Observation revealed that the swirly smudges represent areas of intense magnetic activity where the sun's radiative energy has been blocked and that they are considerably
15   cooler than bright regions of the sun. Scientists had not been able, however, to determine just how sunspots are created or what effect they have on the solar constant (a misnomer that refers to the sun's total radiance at any instant).

20   The latter question, at least, seems to have been resolved by data from the *Solar Maximum Mission* satellite, which has monitored the solar constant since 1980, which was the peak of a solar cycle. As the number of sunspots decreased
25   through 1986, the satellite recorded a gradual dimming of the sun. Over the next year, as sunspots proliferated, the sun brightened. These data suggest that the sun is 0.1 percent more luminous at the peak of the solar cycle, when
30   the number of sunspots is greatest, than at its nadir, according to Richard C. Willson of the Jet Propulsion Laboratory and Hugh S. Hudson of the University of California at San Diego.

The data show that sunspots do not
35   themselves make the sun shine brighter. Quite the contrary. When a sunspot appears, it initially causes the sun to dim slightly, but then after a period of weeks or months islands of brilliance called faculas usually emerge near the sunspot
40   and more than compensate for its dimming effect. Willson says faculas may represent regions

Sunspot cycle & earth weather

Sunspots poorly understood

SMM satellite

Sunspot cycle and sun's brightness

Sunspots dim, but faculas even brighter

ANALYSIS

Pre-passage blurb: The passage addresses various and changing theories about sunspots. Keep track of the different ideas and how they've evolved.

¶1: The author introduces the passage's topic—*sunspots*—and zeroes in on a more specific question: *how do they affect Earth's weather?* People have been investigating this for 150 years, but (note the contrast word "however" in line 8) only recently have they gotten some answers. The author will say more about these answers in coming paragraphs.

¶2: The author defines sunspots: areas where magnetic activity blocks some of the sun's energy. However (again, there's a contrast where the author wants to make a point), scientists still have questions: *how are sunspots created and how do they affect the sun's brightness?*

¶3: Here's the first recent discovery. The SMM satellite shows that the sun gets brighter with more sunspots (the solar cycle peak) and dimmer with fewer sunspots (the solar cycle nadir). This sets up a question that the author will have to answer: *If sunspots block and cool the sun's energy, how can the sun be brighter with more sunspots?*

¶4: The author clears up the paradox from the previous paragraph. Sunspots *initially* block the sun's energy, but (this author loves contrasts) then faculas—super bright hot spots—pop up around the sunspots. Faculas are so bright that they "more than compensate" for the sunspots' dimming effect. That's a lot about sunspots, but the author still needs to tie this to Earth's weather.

where energy that initially was blocked beneath a
sunspot has finally breached the surface.

45　　Does the subtle fluctuation in the solar
constant manifest itself in the Earth's weather?
Meteorological reports offer statistical evidence
that it does, albeit rather indirectly. The link
seems to be mediated by a phenomenon known as
the quasi-biennial oscillation (QBO), a 180-degree
50　shift in the direction of stratospheric winds above
the Tropics that occurs about every two years.

Indirect weather effects (QBO)

　　Karin Labitzke of the Free University of Berlin
and Harry van Loon of the National Center for
Atmospheric Research in Boulder, Colorado, were
55　the first to uncover the QBO link. They gathered
temperature and air-pressure readings from
various latitudes and altitudes over the past three
solar cycles. They found no correlation between
the solar cycle and their data until they sorted the
60　data into two categories: those gathered during
the QBO's west phase (when the stratospheric
winds blow west) and those gathered during its
east phase. A remarkable correlation appeared:
temperatures and pressures coincident with the
65　QBO's west phase rose and fell in accordance
with the solar cycle.

Sunspot correlation to temp and air pressure

　　Building on this finding, Brian A. Tinsley of
the National Science Foundation discovered a
statistical correlation between the solar cycle and
70　the position of storms in the North Atlantic. The
latitude of storms during the west phase of the
QBO, Tinsley found varied with the solar cycle:
storms occurring toward the peak of a solar cycle
traveled at latitudes about six degrees nearer the
75　Equator than storms during the cycle's nadir.

Link to storm patterns

　　Labitzke, van Loon, and Tinsley acknowledge
that their findings are still rather mysterious.
Why does the solar cycle seem to exert more of
an influence during the west phase of the QBO
80　than it does during the east phase? How does the
0.1 percent variance in solar radiation trigger the
much larger changes—up to six degrees Celsius
in polar regions—observed by Labitzke and van
Loon? Van Loon says simply, "We can't explain it."

Scientists can't fully explain links

85　　John A. Eddy of the National Center for
Atmospheric Research, nonetheless, thinks these
QBO findings as well as the *Solar Maximum*

¶5: Here, the author starts to connect sunspots to the weather. It introduces something called the QBO that makes winds in the atmosphere change direction every two years. The next paragraph has to tie this to sunspots.

¶6: This paragraph discusses the research of two scientists, Labitzke and van Loon. They found that when the winds are moving westward, temperatures and air pressure correlate to the solar cycle (the cycle of more and fewer sunspots).

¶7: A different scientist—Tinsley—also correlated the sunspot cycle to the position of storms in the Atlantic Ocean. So far, the studies suggest that sunspots do affect the weather, but they don't say how or why.

¶8: This is a little disappointing: the scientists still don't know how or why sunspots seem to affect temperature and air pressure or the location of storms.

¶9: The author ends by citing one more scientist—Eddy—who is optimistic. He calls the research and the SMM satellite data a breakthrough and thinks we can learn a lot more about sunspots and the weather in the next few years.

Reading

Mission data "look like breakthroughs" in the search for a link between the solar cycle

90 and weather. With further research into how the oceans damp the effects of solar flux, for example, these findings may lead to models that have some predictive value. The next few years may be particularly rich in solar flux.

Break-throughs, but more research needed

BIG PICTURE

Main Idea: Scientists have learned quite a bit about sunspots and Earth's weather recently (faculas, the QBO, and storms are all evidence for that) and hope to learn more soon.

Author's Purpose: To outline the recent data and research suggesting that there is a connection between sunspots and the weather (but she doesn't go too far or say that all the mysteries have been solved)

Notice that the SAT expert reads actively, consistently summing up and paraphrasing what the author has said, asking what must come next, and never getting too caught up in details. The expert reader is not thrown off by encountering a new or unfamiliar term. He uses context to understand what it must mean and remembers that he can always consult the passage if he needs to remember a name or a definition. Finally, before turning to the questions, the expert takes a few seconds to summarize the big picture. This will help him answer questions about the passage's main idea and the author's purpose or point of view. To state the main idea, the author's take-home message to the reader, ask yourself what the author would tell the reader if she only had a few seconds to make her point.

The Method for SAT Reading Questions

The best-prepared SAT test takers know that time is one of the SAT Reading section's biggest challenges. They also know that trying to speed up and cut corners can lead to sloppy mistakes, or worse, to reading a paragraph over and over because it just isn't sinking in. So, after setting themselves up for success with helpful passage notes and clear big picture summary, SAT experts use a simple four-step method to tackle each question quickly and confidently.

The Method for SAT Reading Questions	
Step 1.	Unpack the question stem
Step 2.	Research the answer
Step 3.	Predict the answer
Step 4.	Find the one correct answer

For example, take a look at this question from the set above:

The passage indicates which of the following about the sun's luminosity and the solar cycle?

A) Scientists have found no correlation between the sun's brightness and the solar cycle.

B) The sun is brightest at the nadir of the solar cycle.

C) The sun is brightest at the peak and again at the nadir of the solar cycle.

D) The sun is brightest at the peak of the solar cycle.

Because different question types require different strategies, start by *unpacking* the information in the question stem and identifying the question type. You'll learn to name and characterize six SAT Reading question types in chapter 19. The word "indicates" tells you that this is a Detail question, which means that you should be able to find the correct answer in the passage almost verbatim. Also note any research clues. This question asks about the "sun's luminosity," or its brightness.

Next, based on the type of question, *research* the passage or consult your passage map to get the information you need. For this question, you have a margin note for paragraph 3 that says, "SMM sat data: more sunspots = brighter," so direct your research to paragraph 3. Here's the sentence you need: "These data suggest that the sun is 0.1 percent more luminous at the peak of the solar cycle, when the number of sunspots is greatest, than at its nadir."

Now, with the relevant part of the passage in mind, *predict* what the correct answer will say. In this case, you're looking for an answer choice that says that the sun is either brighter at the peak of the solar cycle or dimmer at its nadir.

Finally, check your prediction against the choices and *find* the one correct answer that matches. If you find yourself struggling with two or more answer choices, stop. Rephrase your prediction to establish what the correct answer must say and evaluate the choices against that prediction. Here, only choice **(D)** is a match for the prediction based on the research you did: the sun is indeed brightest at the peak of the solar cycle.

You'll learn the strategies and tactics that experts use for steps 2–4 in chapter 20.

Take a look at our expert's application of the SAT Reading Method to the questions from the Sunspots passage. Look for questions on which your own approach could have been faster and more confident.

Question	Analysis
1. Which one of the following best describes the main idea of the passage? A) The scientific advances provided by researchers such as Labitzke and van Loon have finally cleared up some of the mysteries that long plagued the study of sunspots. B) Recent research combining astronomical and climate data provides a promising foundation for better understanding the relationship between sunspots and Earth's weather. C) Despite recent breakthroughs, scientists are unlikely to ever fully explain correlations between sunspot activity and Earth's weather patterns. D) Scientists have used data from the *Solar Maximum Mission* satellite to explain how sunspots affect Earth's climate during the quasi-biennial oscillation's west phase.	**Step 1: Unpack the question stem.** Questions that ask for the main idea or primary purpose of a passage are Global questions. With a strong big picture summary, these can be answered quickly and confidently. **Step 2: Research the answer.** The main idea of this passage was that scientists have learned quite a bit about sunspots and Earth's weather patterns (e.g., faculas, the QBO, and storms) and are optimistic that they will soon be able to provide more answers. **Step 3: Predict the answer.** The correct answer will match the Main Idea summary. **Step 4: Find the one correct answer.** Choice **(B)** is correct; it matches the scope of the passage without being too broad or too narrow. (A) is too narrow (Labitzke and van Loon were only two of the scientists cited in the passage) and distorts the passage by suggesting that they have "cleared up" the mysteries, when they admit they're still baffled by some of what they've found. (C) presents a pessimistic tone at odds with the optimism that closes the passage. (D) distorts what the passage said about the solar cycle and the QBO; scientists discovered a correlation between the two, but have not yet explained how or why this happens.

Question	Analysis
2. The author's point of view can best be described as that of A) a meteorologist voicing optimism that the findings of recent solar research will improve weather forecasting. B) an astronomer presenting a digest of current findings to a review board of other astronomers. C) a science writer explaining the possible influence of a solar phenomenon on terrestrial weather patterns. D) a historian listing the contributions to climate science made by the *Solar Maximum Mission.*	**Step 1: Unpack the question stem.** Questions that ask about the passage's main idea or the author's overall purpose or point of view are called Global questions. **Step 2: Research the answer.** This question covers the passage as a whole, so the big picture summaries will help predict the answer. **Step 3: Predict the answer.** The author's purpose is to outline recent developments in sunspot research, and the tone and language suggest a general readership. The correct answer will reflect this. **Step 4: Find the one correct answer.** Choice **(C)** matches the prediction. (A) goes outside the scope of the passage; the author focuses on the science behind the discoveries, not on applications like weather forecasting. (B) suggests an expert presentation to an academic peer group; this passage is more journalistic than that. (D) is too narrow; the *Solar Maximum Mission* is mentioned only in the third paragraph.
3. The passage indicates which of the following about the sun's luminosity and the solar cycle? A) Scientists have found no correlation between the sun's brightness and the solar cycle. B) The sun is brightest at the nadir of the solar cycle. C) The sun is brightest at the peak and again at the nadir of the solar cycle. D) The sun is brightest at the peak of the solar cycle.	**Step 1: Unpack the question stem.** A question asking what the passage "indicates" is a Detail question. The correct answer will paraphrase something stated explicitly in the passage. Research paragraph 3 where the author discusses the solar cycle. **Step 2: Research the answer.** Data gathered by the SMM satellite shows that the sun is brightest at the peak of the solar cycle and dimmest at its nadir. **Step 3: Predict the answer.** Your research provides clear-cut criteria for the correct answer: the sun is brightest at the peak of the solar cycle and dimmest at its nadir. **Step 4: Find the one correct answer.** Choice **(D)** matches your prediction and is correct. (A) is contradicted by the passage, though this choice may have been tempting if you stopped after paragraph 2, which says that, until relatively recently, scientists did not know how the two were correlated. (B) says the opposite of what the passage says on this subject. (C) misstates the passage by claiming that the sun brightens again at the nadir of the solar cycle.

Reading

Question	Analysis
4. Which one of the following provides the best evidence for the answer to the previous question? A) Lines 10–11 ("One problem . . . understood") B) Lines 15–18 ("Scientists had . . . constant") C) Lines 20–24 ("The latter . . . cycle") D) Lines 27–31 ("These data . . . nadir")	**Step 1: Unpack the question stem.** This is a Command of Evidence question that asks you to locate a piece of text stated in the passage that supports another statement, most often, as it is in this case, the correct answer to the preceding question. **Step 2: Research the answer.** In Command of Evidence questions, the answer choices all designate specific sentences or statements in the passage and indicate their precise locations by line numbers. Use the choices to conduct your research, keeping in mind that the correct answer here must support the correct answer to the preceding question. **Step 3: Predict the answer.** The answer to the preceding question came directly from the final sentence in paragraph 3, lines 27–33. **Step 4: Find the one correct answer.** Choice **(D)** cites the evidence for the correct answer to the preceding question, making it the correct choice for this Command of Evidence question. (A) summarizes the problems that scientists studying sunspots had in the past. (B) comes from paragraph 2 and describes the questions scientists still had before the SMM satellite data. (C) comes from the beginning of paragraph 3; it describes the source of the data but does not support the answer to the preceding question.

Question	Analysis
5. Based on information in the passage, it can most reasonably be inferred that faculas A) are directly responsible for increased temperatures on Earth. B) have a dimming effect on the sun's luminescence during sunspot activity. C) are mostly likely to appear at the peak of the solar cycle. D) grow in number as the number of sunspots decreases.	**Step 1: Unpack the question stem.** Questions that ask you for a statement that is "based on" the passage are Inference questions. The correct answer may combine two statements to reach a conclusion. **Step 2: Research the answer.** Faculas are discussed in paragraph 4. The passage says they are likely areas where the energy blocked by sunspots breaks through the sun's surface, and that they are probably why the sun is brightest when sunspot activity is high even though sunspots slightly dim the sun. **Step 3: Predict the answer.** In most Inference questions, you won't be able to predict the correct answer word for word, but you can characterize the correct answer as the only one that will follow directly from the relevant text (in this case, paragraph 4). **Step 4: Find the one correct answer.** Choice **(C)** is correct; if faculas are caused by sunspots, there will likely be more of them when there are more sunspots, in other words, at the peak of the solar cycle. (A) is too strong; scientists have found an indirect relationship between sunspot activity and Earth's weather (line 47). (B) is the opposite of what the passage states; faculas are so bright that they "more than compensate" for sunspots' dimming effect. (D) is the direct opposite of the correct answer.

Question	Analysis
6. Which one of the following provides the best evidence for the answer to the previous question? A) Lines 20–24 ("The latter . . . cycle") B) Lines 34–35 ("The data . . . brighter") C) Lines 36–41 ("When a . . . effect") D) Lines 46–47 ("Meteorological . . . indirectly")	**Step 1: Unpack the question stem.** This is a Command of Evidence question that asks you to locate a piece of text stated in the passage that supports another statement, most often, as it is in this case, the correct answer to the preceding question. **Step 2: Research the answer.** Because the previous question was about faculas, the correct answer to this question supports the fact that sunspots are most likely to appear at the peak of the solar cycle. **Step 3: Predict the answer.** For Command of Evidence questions asking for the text that supports the previous answer, use that answer to evaluate the excerpt in each choice. **Step 4: Find the one correct answer.** Choice **(C)** is correct; this is the sentence that explains the relationship between sunspots and faculas, and thus supports the correct answer to the previous question. (A) cites text that provides background information about the SMM. (B) contains a sentence that sets up the introduction of faculas but does not support the correct answer from the previous question. (D) is from the paragraph in which the author begins discussing the relationship between the solar cycle and Earth's weather.
7. As used in line 45, "manifest" most nearly means A) impact. B) disguise. C) itemize. D) reveal.	**Step 1: Unpack the question stem.** This is a Vocabulary-in-Context question. The correct answer will be a word that could take the place of the word in the question stem without changing the meaning of the sentence. **Step 2: Research the answer.** For Vocab-in-Context, read the full sentence containing the word cited in the question stem. **Step 3: Predict the answer.** The scientists in the passage are studying whether the influence of sunspots can be seen in Earth's weather, so "manifest" must mean something like *show* or *display*. **Step 4: Find the one correct answer.** The prediction leads to the correct answer, **(D)**. Choice (A) does not fit the context; the solar cycle might impact the weather, but wouldn't impact itself. (B) means the opposite of the correct answer. (C) suggests another meaning of the word "manifest," which could also refer to a list of items in a shipment.

Question	Analysis
8. According to the passage, Labitzke and van Loon's research on the quasi-biennial oscillation (QBO) shows that A) the QBO's west phase correlates to the solar cycle. B) the QBO's west phase has a longer duration than that of its east phase. C) the QBO shows no correlation with the solar cycle. D) the reasons for the QBO's correlation to the solar cycle are now well understood.	**Step 1: Unpack the question stem.** "According to the passage" signals a Detail question. The answer will be contained in the passage text. **Step 2: Research the answer.** The QBO is introduced in paragraph 5, and Labitzke and van Loon's research is discussed in detail in paragraph 6. **Step 3: Predict the answer.** In a question like this one, it's difficult to predict the exact language of the correct answer choice, but we know it will conform to one of the facts presented in paragraph 6. The researchers tried to correlate temperature and air pressure to the solar cycle. At first, they saw no connection, but when they broke down the QBO into its east and west phases, they found a correlation to the west phase. **Step 4: Find the one correct answer.** Choice **(A)** matches the last sentence of paragraph 6 and is correct. (B) contradicts the passage; the shift from east to west and back occurs roughly every two years. (C) misuses a detail from the passage; the two researchers found no correlation *until* they split the QBO into its east and west phases. (D) contradicts paragraph 8, in which the scientists reveal that they still aren't sure why the QBO's west phase correlates to sunspot activity.

Reading

Question	Analysis
9. The main purpose of the questions in the second-to-last paragraph (lines 76–84) is to A) emphasize how little scientists know about the solar constant. B) explain more fully the mysterious nature of the scientists' findings. C) question the basis upon which these scientists built their hypotheses. D) express doubts about the scientists' interpretations of their findings.	**Step 1: Unpack the question stem.** A question that asks why the author included something in the text is a Function question. The correct answer will explain the author's purpose for including questions in paragraph 8. **Step 2: Research the answer.** This question stem leads you directly to paragraph 8. Determine what the author was trying to achieve by including questions there. **Step 3: Predict the answer.** The author uses the questions in paragraph 8 to illustrate why the scientists consider some of their findings "rather mysterious": despite all that they've learned to date, there are still several questions they can't answer. **Step 4: Find the one correct answer.** The prediction leads to the correct answer, **(B)**; the questions are included to explain why the scientists would consider their finding *mysterious*. (A) doesn't match the context of paragraph 8, which follows several paragraphs about how much scientists have recently learned. (C) runs counter to the author's purpose; the author doesn't try to call the scientist's findings into question. (D) is also out of step with the author's position; the author doesn't say or imply that the scientists have misunderstood the discoveries.

Question	Analysis
10. The use of the quoted phrase "look like break-throughs" in line 88 is primarily meant to convey the idea that A) information about the solar cycle has allowed scientists to predict changes in Earth's complex climate system. B) additional analysis of the link between the solar cycle and Earth's weather may yield useful models. C) despite the associated costs, space missions can lead to important discoveries. D) an alternative interpretation of the data may contradict the initial findings.	**Step 1: Unpack the question stem.** A question that asks how an author supports a point made in the passage, or that asks why the author included something, is a Function question. **Step 2: Research the answer.** This question stem contains a line number. Examine the text immediately before and after the cited line to determine the context of the quote. The quote from the question stem was given by John A. Eddy, who believes that the recent findings will lead to additional exciting discoveries about the relationship between sunspots and Earth's weather patterns. **Step 3: Predict the answer.** The author includes the quote to show optimism about the potential for further research. **Step 4: Find the one correct answer.** The prediction matches correct answer **(B)**. Choice (A) is too strong; scientists may create predictive models in the near future, but they haven't yet. (C) appears to refer to the *Solar Maximum Mission*, but Eddy's quote refers to that *and* the subsequent research; the author doesn't include Eddy's quote to make a point just about space missions. (D) runs contrary to Eddy's optimism.

Putting It All Together

To recap: to do well on SAT Reading, you should:

- Read *actively*, asking what the author's purpose is in writing each paragraph. Anticipate where the passage will go. "Map" the passage by jotting down summaries for each paragraph. You might also circle or underline keywords that indicate the author's opinion, details she wishes to highlight or emphasize, and the comparisons and contrasts she makes in the passage. Note the the passage's main idea and the author's primary purpose in writing it. You will focus on active reading and passage mapping in chapter 18.

- Once you have read and marked up the passage, use the following method to attack the question set:

The Method for SAT Reading Questions	
Step 1.	Unpack the question stem
Step 2.	Research the answer
Step 3.	Predict the answer
Step 4.	Find the one correct answer

By reading strategically and using the Method for SAT Reading Questions every time you practice, you'll internalize the steps. By test day, you'll be attacking this section efficiently and accurately without even thinking about it.

In the next section, you'll see another SAT Reading passage accompanied by 11 questions. Map the passage and apply the Method for SAT Reading Questions presented in this lesson to answer the questions as quickly and confidently as possible.

How Much Have You Learned?

Directions: Take 15 minutes to map this passage and answer the questions. Assess your work by comparing it to the expert responses at the end of the chapter.

Questions 1–11 refer to the following passage.

This passage is adapted from Carrie Chapman Catt's 1917 "Address to the United States Congress." Catt served as president of the National American Woman Suffrage Association, which advocated giving women the right to vote; the closing arguments from her speech are excerpted below.

Your party platforms have pledged woman suffrage. Then why not be honest, frank friends of our cause, adopt it in reality as your own, make it a party program and "fight with us"? As
5 a party measure—a measure of all parties—why not put the amendment through Congress and the Legislatures? We shall all be better friends, we shall have a happier nation, we women will be free to support loyally the party of our choice,
10 and we shall be far prouder of our history.

"There is one thing mightier than kings and armies"—aye, than Congresses and political parties—"the power of an idea when its time has come to move." The time for woman suffrage has
15 come. The woman's hour has struck. If parties prefer to postpone action longer and thus do battle with this idea, they challenge the inevitable. The idea will not perish; the party which opposes it may. Every delay, every trick, every political
20 dishonesty from now on will antagonize the women of the land more and more, and when the party or parties which have so delayed woman suffrage finally let it come, their sincerity will be doubted and their appeal to the new voters will
25 be met with suspicion. This is the psychology of the situation. Can you afford the risk? Think it over.

We know you will meet opposition. There are a few "woman haters" left, a few "old males
30 of the tribe," as Vance Thompson calls them, whose duty they believe it to be to keep women in the places they have carefully picked out for them. Treitschke, made world famous by war literature, said some years ago: "Germany, which
35 knows all about Germany and France, knows

far better what is good for Alsace-Lorraine than that miserable people can possibly know." A few American Treitschkes we have who know better than women what is good for them.
40 There are women, too. . . . But the world does not wait for such as these, nor does Liberty pause to heed the plaint of men and women with a grouch. She does not wait for those who have a special interest to serve, nor a selfish reason for
45 depriving other people of freedom. Holding her torch aloft, Liberty is pointing the way onward and upward and saying to America, "Come."

To you the supporters of our cause, in Senate and House, and the number is large, the
50 suffragists of the nation express their grateful thanks. This address is not meant for you. We are more truly appreciative of all you have done than any words can express. We ask you to make a last, hard fight for the amendment during the
55 present session. Since last we asked for a vote on this amendment your position has been fortified by the addition to suffrage territory of Great Britain, Canada, and New York.

Some of you have been too indifferent to give
60 more than casual attention to this question. It is worthy of your immediate consideration—a question big enough to engage the attention of our Allies in war time, is too big a question for you to neglect. . . .
65 Gentlemen, we hereby petition you, our only designated representatives, to redress our grievances by the immediate passage of the influence to secure its ratification in your own state, in order that the women of our nation
70 may be endowed with political freedom that our nation may resume its world leadership in democracy.

Woman suffrage is coming—you know it. Will you, Honorable Senators and Members of the
75 House of Representatives, help or hinder it?

Reading

1. What was Carrie Chapman Catt's primary purpose in giving this speech?

    A) To assert that women will vote for the party that supports their cause

    B) To demand more women candidates on political party tickets

    C) To persuade lawmakers to pass an amendment ensuring women's right to vote

    D) To rally support for women's equal representation in Congress

2. The stance that Catt takes in her speech is best described as that of

    A) a historian reflecting on historical events.

    B) an official campaigning for political office.

    C) an activist advocating for legislative reform.

    D) a reporter investigating a current controversy.

3. What counterclaim does Catt offer to the argument that some men and women still oppose suffrage?

    A) They are not voicing their opinions in Congress.

    B) They cannot stop the inevitable.

    C) They do have just cause for opposition.

    D) They have no legal basis for their claims.

4. Which choice provides the best evidence for the answer to the previous question?

    A) Lines 7–10 ("We shall all . . . our history")

    B) Lines 48–51 ("To you . . . grateful thanks")

    C) Lines 55–58 ("Since last . . . New York")

    D) Lines 60–64 ("It is worthy . . . to neglect")

5. As used in line 20, "antagonize" most nearly means

    A) dishearten.

    B) embitter.

    C) humiliate.

    D) inhibit.

6. The phrase in lines 21–25 ("when the party . . . with suspicion") implies that

    A) women voters will not support lawmakers who have resisted suffrage.

    B) women will not run for office because they do not trust politicians.

    C) women will vote more women into political office.

    D) women's influence on Congress will be minimal and is not a threat.

7. Catt most likely discusses Treitschke (lines 33–37) for which of the following reasons?

    A) To demonstrate support for women's suffrage in Europe

    B) To remind her audience of what happened to a politician who supported unpopular legislation

    C) To contrast his views on Alsace-Lorraine with the American values of freedom and democracy

    D) To draw an analogy between his views and the views of those who believe they know better than women what is best for women

8. The passage indicates which one of the following about the status of women's suffrage at the time of Catt's speech?

    A) At the time, only a minority of the U.S. population supported women's right to vote.

    B) Women already had the right to vote in at least one state in the United States.

    C) An earlier amendment to grant women the right to vote had been defeated.

    D) The women's suffrage movement was a recent development in American politics.

9. Which choice provides the best evidence for the answer to the previous question?

    A) Lines 14–17 ("The time . . . inevitable")

    B) Lines 28–33 ("There are . . . them")

    C) Lines 55–58 ("Since last . . . New York")

    D) Lines 65–72 ("Gentlemen . . . democracy")

10. As used in line 66, "redress" most nearly means

    A) appeal.

    B) communicate.

    C) implement.

    D) remedy.

11. What can you most reasonably infer from the thoughts expressed in lines 69–72 ("in order that . . . in democracy")?

    A) No citizen in our democracy is free as long as women cannot vote.

    B) Other nations have demanded that our government grant woman suffrage.

    C) A nation needs more women in positions of leadership.

    D) Woman suffrage is essential to true democracy.

Reading

Answers and Explanations

Carrie Chapman Catt Passage Map

This passage is adapted from Carrie Chapman Catt's 1917 "Address to the United States Congress." Catt served as president of the National American Woman Suffrage Association, which advocated giving women the right to vote; the closing arguments from her speech are excerpted below.

Your party platforms have pledged woman suffrage. Then why not be honest, frank friends of our cause, adopt it in reality as your own, make it a party program and "fight with us"? As

5 a party measure—a measure of all parties—why not put the amendment through Congress and the Legislatures? We shall all be better friends, we shall have a happier nation, we women will be free to support loyally the party of our choice,

10 and we shall be far prouder of our history.

"There is one thing mightier than kings and armies"—aye, than Congresses and political parties—"the power of an idea when its time has come to move." The time for woman suffrage has

15 come. The woman's hour has struck. If parties prefer to postpone action longer and thus do battle with this idea, they challenge the inevitable. The idea will not perish; the party which opposes it may. Every delay, every trick, every political

20 dishonesty from now on will antagonize the women of the land more and more, and when the party or parties which have so delayed woman suffrage finally let it come, their sincerity will be doubted and their appeal to the new voters will

25 be met with suspicion. This is the psychology of the situation. Can you afford the risk? Think it over.

We know you will meet opposition. There are a few "woman haters" left, a few "old males

30 of the tribe," as Vance Thompson calls them, whose duty they believe it to be to keep women in the places they have carefully picked out for them. Treitschke, made world famous by war literature, said some years ago: "Germany, which

35 knows all about Germany and France, knows far better what is good for Alsace-Lorraine than

Call for both parties to support women's vote

Time for women's suffrage is NOW

Those who oppose will be suspect in the future

Still have opponents

Examples

ANALYSIS

Pre-passage blurb: You learn a lot here. Catt is speaking to Congress in 1917. She represents an organization pushing for women's suffrage, that is, the right to vote. The passage represents her closing arguments, so you can expect her to offer evidence and reasoning in support of this cause.

¶1: Catt reminds the members of Congress that their parties have supported women's suffrage in their platforms and encourages them, as individuals, to support it as well. It will make the U.S. a happier, prouder nation.

¶2: Catt asserts that women *will* get the right to vote and, as a warning to congressmen opposing suffrage, she argues that women with the vote will most likely not support the congressmen who tried to delay or undermine their right.

¶3: Catt admits that there will still be some who oppose women's suffrage, but argues that their ideas are out-of-date. She is trying to persuade congressmen who might be swayed by a vocal opposition. She uses a moral argument by equating suffrage with liberty.

that miserable people can possibly know." A few American Treitschkes we have who know better than women what is good for them.

40 There are women, too…But the world does not wait for such as these, nor does Liberty pause to heed the plaint of men and women with a grouch. She does not wait for those who have a special interest to serve, nor a selfish reason for

45 depriving other people of freedom. Holding her torch aloft, Liberty is pointing the way onward and upward and saying to America, "Come."

To you the supporters of our cause, in Senate and House, and the number is large, the

50 suffragists of the nation express their grateful thanks. This address is not meant for you. We are more truly appreciative of all you have done than any words can express. We ask you to make a last, hard fight for the amendment during the

55 present session. Since last we asked for a vote on this amendment your position has been fortified by the addition to suffrage territory of Great Britain, Canada, and New York.

Some of you have been too indifferent to give

60 more than casual attention to this question. It is worthy of your immediate consideration—a question big enough to engage the attention of our Allies in war time, is too big a question for you to neglect…

65 Gentlemen, we hereby petition you, our only designated representatives, to redress our grievances by the immediate passage of the influence to secure its ratification in your own state, in order that the women of our nation

70 may be endowed with political freedom that our nation may resume its world leadership in democracy.

Woman suffrage is coming—you know it. Will you, Honorable Senators and Members of the

75 House of Representatives, help or hinder it?

Margin notes:

BUT – liberty will overcome

Thanks to supporters– help us fight

Other countries have suffrage

Suffrage – big/immediate issue

Petition to pass suffrage – then U.S. can again lead in freedom

Final appeal to Congress

¶4: Catt thanks members who already support her cause and encourages them to vote during the present session. She makes this appeal timely by referring to other countries and states that have adopted women's suffrage already.

¶5: Catt chastises those who have ignored the debate over suffrage—it's too big an issue—equating it with war.

¶6: Catt encourages lawmakers to support the suffrage amendment in their various states. She argues that only by granting suffrage can the U.S. once again be a leader of democracy in the world.

¶7: Catt's final appeal is for members of Congress to pick a side: are you with us or against us?

BIG PICTURE

Main Idea: Women's suffrage is inevitable; lawmakers should support it now for reasons both moral (making America freer and more democratic) and practical (better political prospects in the future).

Author's Purpose: To persuade members of Congress to pass a bill sending a proposed amendment to the Constitution (to grant women the right to vote) to the states

1. C

Difficulty: Medium

Category: Global

Strategic Advice: A question asking for an author's or speaker's primary purpose is a Global question. Consult your big picture summary to predict the correct answer.

Getting to the Answer: The pre-passage blurb tells you that Carrie Chapman Catt is speaking to Congress on behalf of the National American Woman Suffrage Association. In the first paragraph, she asks lawmakers to support a constitutional amendment. Additional context provided in the passage makes clear that the amendment would grant women suffrage, making **(C)** correct. While (A) captures a key part of Catt's reasoning, it does not reflect her purpose in giving the speech. (B) distorts the passage; Catt is calling for suffrage, not necessarily for female candidates. Similarly, (D) goes beyond the scope of Catt's speech.

2. C

Difficulty: Easy

Category: Global

Strategic Advice: Some Global questions ask about an author's overall attitude or the perspective from which the passage was written. Use your big picture summary of the main idea and the author's purpose to predict the correct answer.

Getting to the Answer: In the passage, Catt gives a speech in which she appeals to legislators to pass a constitutional amendment, or legislative reform, to grant women suffrage. She is speaking as a political activist. **(C)** is correct. The other three answers all distort Catt's purpose and main point.

3. B

Difficulty: Medium

Category: Detail

Strategic Advice: A question calling for a claim the author or speaker makes explicitly in the text is a Detail question. The research clue in the question stem points to paragraph 3.

Getting to the Answer: In paragraph 3, Catt acknowledges the opposition to woman suffrage, citing "woman haters" (line 29), "old males of the tribe" (lines 29–30), and "women, too" (line 40). She suggests that the

arguments against suffrage are dated and ineffectual, and goes on to state that the world will not slow down and that the cause of liberty will continue. Her underlying message is that suffrage is unavoidable, which echoes her earlier statement in line 17. All of this leads to **(B)** as the correct answer. (A) distorts Catt's response; whether opponents continue to speak out is almost irrelevant in her opinion. (C) is contradicted by Catt's rhetoric; suffrage is just, and it will prevail. (D) distorts Catt's argument; she addresses the moral and sociological reasons for endorsing suffrage.

4. C

Difficulty: Medium

Category: Command of Evidence

Strategic Advice: This is a Command of Evidence question. The correct answer to this question will cite text that provides evidence, either in reasoning or in fact, to support the claim in the answer to the previous question. Each answer choice contains line numbers that help focus your research as you evaluate the choices.

Getting to the Answer: The answer to the previous question asserts that woman suffrage is inevitable. Evidence to support this claim would show that suffrage is advancing, as demonstrated by **(C)**. (A) provides practical reasons to support suffrage but does not support a claim of its inevitability. (B) offers thanks to lawmakers who already support suffrage. (D) is an exhortation to immediate action, not evidence of inevitable victory for the women's suffrage movement.

5. B

Difficulty: Medium

Category: Vocab-in-Context

Strategic Advice: The correct answer to a Vocab-in-Context question like this one will reflect the specific meaning of the word in the context of the surrounding sentence and text.

Getting to the Answer: The text states, "Every delay, every trick, every political dishonesty from now on will antagonize the women of the land more and more" (lines 19–21). The surrounding text suggests that women will become only more resolved to their purpose as a result of delay, as well as more angry—or bitter—with politicians who forestall them, making **(B)** correct. (A) implies that women will give up; Catt clearly argues the opposite. (C) distorts the meaning of the sentence;

tricks and delays will anger women and encourage them to punish deceitful politicians at the polls. (D) sounds plausible (after all, the delays and tricks are meant to impede suffrage), but it doesn't fit the context of the sentence, which predicts a backlash from these tactics.

6. A

Difficulty: Medium

Category: Inference

Strategic Advice: The word "implies" identifies this as an Inference question. The correct answer will reflect the underlying or implied meaning of the excerpted line within the context of the surrounding text. The research clue points to the second half of paragraph 2.

Getting to the Answer: The text cited in the question stem asserts that new voters (the women enfranchised by suffrage) will mistrust political parties whose members have resisted suffrage; this leads to **(A)** as the correct answer. The message of choice (B) runs counter to Catt's argument. (C) goes too far; Catt asserts that women voters will flee the parties who have resisted suffrage, and not that they will vote for female candidates. (D) states the opposite of what Catt implies here.

7. D

Difficulty: Hard

Category: Function

Strategic Advice: A question that asks why an author included a detail or reference in her text is a Function question. Research the referenced detail (in this case, Treitschke) to see the author's purpose for including it in the passage.

Getting to the Answer: For Catt, Treitschke is an example of an outsider who thought he knew better than the residents of an area what was best for them. She analogizes that to male politicians who think they know what's best for women. Choice **(D)** describes Catt's use of the analogy. (A) conflates Treitschke with Catt's later statement that women's suffrage had passed in the United Kingdom. (B) misapplies the Treitschke example to a different argument Catt makes in her speech. (C) distorts Catt's point about Treitschke; she used him as an example of someone whose reasoning was misguided reasoning, not as someone who was anti-democratic.

8. B

Difficulty: Medium

Category: Detail

Strategic Advice: The word "indicates" signals a Detail question. The correct answer will clearly restate or paraphrase something stated in the passage.

Getting to the Answer: The entire speech is, of course, about women's suffrage, but Catt addresses the current status of women's right to vote explicitly near the end of paragraph 4. There, she tells Congress that suffrage laws have recently been passed in Great Britain, Canada, and New York. That directly supports choice **(B)**. (A) is too extreme; in paragraph 3, Catt admits that suffrage still had opponents, but she does not state that only a minority of voters support it. (C) is not supported anywhere in Catt's speech. (D) is a distortion of Catt's claim that momentum for women's suffrage was on the rise.

9. C

Difficulty: Medium

Category: Command of Evidence

Strategic Advice: This is a Command of Evidence question asking you to locate the line in the passage that supports the correct answer to the preceding question. Use the line references in each answer choice to research the passage text.

Getting to the Answer: The correct answer to the preceding question asserted that, at the time of Catt's speech, at least one state in the Union had already granted women the right to vote. That is directly supported by the text cited in choice **(C)**, where Catt encourages suffrage advocates in Congress with the fact that New York recently gave women the right to vote. (A) is Catt's warning to the members of Congress about a potential backlash for their failure to support the suffrage amendment, which is unrelated to the fact that women in New York can vote. (B) cites text in which Catt describes the opponents of women's suffrage; that might have tempted a test taker who chose (A) for the preceding question. (D) contains Catt's call to action in paragraph 6; that does not support the answer to the preceding question.

10. D

Difficulty: Medium

Category: Vocab-in-Context

Strategic Advice: This is a Vocab-in-Context question; the correct answer will correctly replace the original word and retain the meaning of the original sentence.

Getting to the Answer: The text states that Catt and her supporters want congressional lawmakers to "redress our grievances" (lines 66–67), meaning to set right—or to remedy—the ills committed against women. **(D)** reflects this meaning. None of the other choices fits logically into the sentence.

11. D

Difficulty: Medium

Category: Inference

Strategic Advice: The word "implied" signals an Inference question. The correct answer will follow from Catt's statement in the excerpted line. The research clue points you to paragraph 6.

Getting to the Answer: The excerpted line states that once women have the political freedom granted by suffrage, then the nation will resume its leadership in democracy. The implication is that the nation is not a leader in democracy as long as it denies women the right to vote. Therefore, **(D)** is correct. (A) is too extreme for the specific statement cited in the question stem. (B) misuses a detail from paragraph 4; other countries have adopted women's suffrage, but Catt doesn't say they've called on the United States to do the same. (C) is too broad; the quoted statement focuses specifically on the right to vote, not on electing women.

Reflect

Directions: Take a few minutes to recall what you've learned and what you've been practicing in this chapter. Consider the following questions, jot down your best answer for each one, and then compare your reflections to the expert responses on the following page. Use your level of confidence to determine what to do next.

Describe active, or strategic, reading on SAT passages.

_____

_____

_____

What do SAT experts mean by summarizing the big picture of a passage?

_____

_____

_____

How can writing brief "margin notes" help you answer SAT Reading questions more effectively?

_____

_____

_____

What does an SAT expert look for in the question stem of an SAT Reading question?

_____

_____

_____

Why do expert test takers predict or characterize the correct answer to each SAT Reading question before assessing the answer choices?

_____

_____

_____

What will you do differently on future passages and their questions?

_____

_____

_____

Expert Responses

Describe active, or strategic, reading on SAT passages.

Because the SAT asks many questions about why an author has written the passage or about how the author makes a point, expert test takers read for the author's purpose and main idea. Noting keywords that indicate a shift or contrast in points of view or that indicate opinions and emphasis help keep SAT experts on point, as they anticipate where the passage will go.

What do SAT experts mean by summarizing the big picture of a passage?

To read for the big picture means being able to accurately summarize the main idea of a passage and to note the author's purpose for writing it. The big picture summary helps you answer Global questions and questions that ask about the author's opinion or point of view.

How can writing brief "margin notes" help you answer SAT Reading questions more effectively?

Jotting down margin notes provides a reference "map" to the subject or purpose of each paragraph in the passage. It helps locate specific subjects or opinions expressed in the passage when they are called out in the questions.

What does an SAT expert look for in the question stem of an SAT Reading question?

Each question stem indicates the type of question and contains clues as to whether the answer will come from researching the passage text or from the big picture summary. Many question stems have specific clues (for example, line numbers or references to details from the passage) that tell you precisely where to research.

Why do expert test takers predict or characterize the correct answer to each SAT Reading question before assessing the answer choices?

Predicting or characterizing the correct answer allows you to evaluate each answer choice one time and to avoid rereading for every answer choice. Incorrect answers often distort what the passage said or misuse details from the passage, so it's best to research the passage once to know what the correct answer must say before diving into the choices.

What will you do differently on future passages and their questions?

There is no one-size-fits-all answer to this question. Each student has his or her own initial strengths and opportunities in the Reading section. What's important here is that you're honestly self-reflective. Take what you need from the expert's examples and strive to apply it to your own performance. Many test takers convince themselves that they'll never get faster or more confident in SAT Reading, but the truth is, many test takers who now routinely ace the Reading section were much slower and more hesitant before they learned to approach this section systematically and strategically.

Next Steps

If you answered most questions correctly in the "How Much Have You Learned?" section, and if your responses to the Reflect questions were similar to those of the SAT expert, then consider the Method for SAT Reading Questions an area of strength and move on to the next chapter. Come back to this topic periodically to prevent yourself from getting rusty.

If you don't yet feel confident, review the material in this chapter, then try the questions you missed again. As always, be sure to review the explanations closely.

CHAPTER 18

SAT Reading Passage Strategies

After completing this chapter, you will be able to:

- Identify keywords that promote active reading and relate passage text to the questions
- Create short, accurate margin notes that help you research the text efficiently
- Summarize the big picture of the passage

How Much Do You Know?

Directions: In this chapter, you'll learn how SAT experts actively read the passage, take notes, and summarize the main idea to prepare themselves to answer all of the passage's questions quickly and confidently. You saw this kind of reading modeled in the previous chapter. To get ready for the current chapter, take five minutes to actively read the following passage by 1) noting the keywords that indicate the author's point of view and the passage's structure, 2) jotting down a quick description next to each paragraph, and 3) summarizing the big picture (the passage's main idea and the author's purpose for writing it). When you're done, compare your work to the passage notes that follow.

This passage is adapted from a 2018 article summarizing two different proposals for solving problems with maintaining New York City's mass transit system.

The history of the New York City subway system, quickly told: the first stations opened in 1904, and over the next century, it expanded to 472 stations,
5 more than any other subway system in the world, with 850 miles of track. Operating 24 hours a day seven days a week, with an average weekday ridership of approximately 5.7 million, it is the
10 planet's 7th-busiest rapid transit system. While the system is, on many levels, an amazing achievement, it is also beset by a problem that harms both quality of life and economic activity. Such a
15 large system must inevitably suffer from service interruptions and delays; normal wear and tear combined with the sheer age of the system necessitates regular maintenance. However, there
20 is no consensus as to the best way to accomplish the required repairs.

The current maintenance scheme is designed to minimize service interruptions. A subway line in need
25 of repair will be taken out of service during a comparatively less busy time, such as nights or weekends, while another line is re-routed to cover as many as possible of the missing line's
30 stops. The main advantage to this approach is that trains are not taken out of service during rush hour, when

most subway trips occur; subway
35 service generally remains predictable and commuters are, for the most part, able to use the system to get to their destinations on time.

But critics are quick to point out the
40 disadvantages to this approach. Perhaps most obvious is the confusion caused by trains switching lines. The labyrinthine system is hard enough to navigate at the best of times, especially for tourists.
45 A subway rider on the A train naturally expects the train to make stops on the A line. If, instead, it is diverted temporarily to the F line, the rider may find herself miles from her intended
50 destination.

While annoying, the confusion arising from route switching is hardly the most serious problem with the current approach to repairs.
55 Because the system runs 24 hours a day, routine maintenance can generally be done only during the temporary closures on nights and weekends. This means that more serious repair and
60 crucial preventative maintenance is often neglected. Problems that could have been fixed or prevented reasonably expeditiously given a slightly longer closure wind up leading to major
65 breakdowns and service interruptions later on.

On rare occasions, such breakdowns have resulted in entire subway lines being shut down for months or
70 even a year. Beginning in 2019, for

example, the L Train connecting lower
Manhattan to parts of Brooklyn was
scheduled to close for as much as 15
months for long overdue service and
upgrades. In a city fewer than half
75 of whose households own a car, this
can have serious economic impacts.
Residents of the affected area may
face a much longer commute via an
alternate subway line if one is available;
80 or, if there is no alternate subway
service, they may need to take other,
potentially more expensive, modes
of transportation, such as taxis or
ferries. Moreover, studies indicate that
85 increased stress from the commute to
work can lead to lower productivity, and
that businesses near the impacted lines
may see decreased revenue as potential
customers have a harder time getting to
90 them.

One controversial proposal for
reducing breakdowns and the resulting
transit interruptions is to end the
subway's 24-hour service and to shut
95 down for several hours each night.
Proponents of this plan argue that
this would allow time, on a regular
rather than sporadic basis, for more
preventative maintenance. This, they
100 claim, would ultimately lead to more
consistent service; rather than shutting
down entire lines for long periods of
a time, there would merely be shorter
service outages overnight, when fewer
105 people use the subway system. While
this may seem a preferable outcome to
the economic consequences of a total
shutdown resulting from a breakdown,
it has its liabilities as well. While most
110 subway trips may occur during rush
hour, not everyone works during the
daytime. New York is famously known
as the "the city that never sleeps."
Doctors, nurses, bartenders, police
115 officers, and firefighters are just a few

examples of occupations whose workers
need transportation at all hours of
the day and night. Rather than be
120 subjected to a relatively short period
of inconvenience, these workers would
find their commutes irrevocably altered.
One thing, at least, is clear: the city
must carefully consider many economic
125 and social factors in designing a subway
maintenance plan.

Check Your Work

This passage is adapted from a 2018 article summarizing two different proposals for solving problems with maintaining New York City's mass transit system.

The history of the New York City subway system, quickly told: the first stations opened in 1904, and over the next century, it expanded to 472 stations,
5   more than any other subway system in the world, with 850 miles of track. Operating 24 hours a day seven days a week, with an average weekday ridership of approximately 5.7 million, it is the
10 planet's 7th-busiest rapid transit system. While the system is, on many levels, an amazing achievement, it is also beset by a problem that harms both quality of life and economic activity. Such a
15 large system must inevitably suffer from service interruptions and delays; normal wear and tear combined with the sheer age of the system necessitates regular maintenance. However, there
20 is no consensus as to the best way to accomplish the required repairs.

The current maintenance scheme is designed to minimize service interruptions. A subway line in need
25 of repair will be taken out of service during a comparatively less busy time, such as nights or weekends, while another line is re-routed to cover as many as possible of the missing line's
30 stops. The main advantage to this approach is that trains are not taken out of service during rush hour, when most subway trips occur; subway service generally remains predictable
35 and commuters are, for the most part, able to use the system to get to their destinations on time.

But critics are quick to point out the disadvantages to this approach. Perhaps

NYC subway: how to repair? diff. views

Current approach – night and weekend repairs

Critics: line switch confusion

ANALYSIS

Pre-passage blurb: This tells you that the topic of the passage is a debate over the New York City subway system. Expect to see at least two sides in the debate. Note where each different position is discussed.

SAT Reading Strategy: On the SAT, the blurb almost always contains the title of the book or article from which the passage was adapted. Sometimes the test maker will provide additional context as well. Always take advantage of it.

¶1: The author introduces the New York City subway system by highlighting its age and size. Those two factors are the reason maintenance is such a big issue. The scope of the passage comes at the end of the paragraph: there is no agreement on *how* best to perform upkeep on the massive system.

¶2: This paragraph outlines the current maintenance schedule. Repairs happen mostly on nights and weekends. The main advantage is that subway lines are not down during rush hours.

¶3: Here comes the opposing view. One disadvantage of the current system is that trains are rerouted, causing confusion for riders.

40 most obvious is the (confusion caused by)
trains switching lines. The labyrinthine
system is hard enough to navigate at the
best of times, especially for tourists. A
subway rider on the A train naturally
45 expects the train to make stops on
the A line. If, instead, it is diverted
temporarily to the F line, the rider may
find herself miles from her intended
destination.
50   While annoying, the confusion
arising from route switching is
(hardly the most serious) problem
with the current approach to repairs.
(Because) the system runs 24 hours a
55 day, routine maintenance can generally
be done only during the temporary
closures on nights and weekends. This
means that more serious repair and
crucial preventative maintenance is
60 often neglected. Problems that could
have been fixed or prevented reasonably
expeditiously given a slightly longer
closure wind up leading to (major)
breakdowns and service interruptions
65 later on.
    On rare occasions, such breakdowns
have resulted in entire subway lines
being shut down for months or
even a year. Beginning in 2019, (for)
70 (example) the L Train connecting lower
Manhattan to parts of Brooklyn was
scheduled to close for as much as 15
months for long overdue service and
upgrades. In a city fewer than half
75 of whose households own a car, this
can have (serious economic impacts)
Residents of the affected area may
face a much longer commute via an
alternate subway line if one is available;
80 or, if there is no alternate subway
service, they may need to take other,
potentially more expensive, modes
of transportation, such as taxis or
ferries. (Moreover,) studies indicate that
85 increased stress from the commute to

*Even worse
— major
breakdowns*

¶4: A second, worse problem with the current
system is that it doesn't allow enough time for
preventative maintenance. That leads to big
problems down the line.

¶5: These big problems can shut down subway
lines for weeks or months causing grave economic impact to affected riders and businesses.

*Econ. & Soc.
harms of
shutdowns*

K   517

Reading

work can lead to lower productivity, and that businesses near the impacted lines may see decreased revenue as potential customers have a harder time getting to
90 them.

One controversial proposal for reducing breakdowns and the resulting transit interruptions is to end the subway's 24-hour service and to shut
95 down for several hours each night. Proponents of this plan argue that this would allow time, on a regular rather than sporadic basis, for more preventative maintenance. This, they
100 claim, would ultimately lead to more consistent service; rather than shutting down entire lines for long periods of a time, there would merely be shorter service outages overnight, when fewer
105 people use the subway system. While this may seem a preferable outcome to the economic consequences of a total shutdown resulting from a breakdown, it has its liabilities as well. While most
110 subway trips may occur during rush hour, not everyone works during the daytime. New York is famously known as the "the city that never sleeps." Doctors, nurses, bartenders, police
115 officers, and firefighters are just a few examples of occupations whose workers need transportation at all hours of the day and night. Rather than be subjected to a relatively short period
120 of inconvenience, these workers would find their commutes irrevocably altered. One thing, at least, is clear: the city must carefully consider many economic and social factors in designing a subway
125 maintenance plan.

Alt proposal – stop 24-hour service

Pros

Cons

¶6: This paragraph opens with a controversial proposal: stop running the subway 24/7. While this would make more time for preventative maintenance, it too has a big disadvantage: many workers need to commute overnight. The author's conclusion is neutral: New York City has to weigh both sides to make the best decision.

BIG PICTURE

Main Idea: New York City must weigh different economic and social factors to design an effective subway maintenance plan.

Author's Purpose: To explain advantages and disadvantages in opposing views of how best to maintain the New York City subway

---

SAT Reading Strategies—Keywords, Margin Notes, and the Big Picture Summary

LEARNING OBJECTIVES

After this lesson, you will be able to:

- Identify keywords that promote active reading and relate passage text to the questions
- Create short, accurate margin notes that help you research the text efficiently
- Summarize the big picture of the passage

To read and map a passage like this:

This passage was adapted from an article titled "Millennials and the Market," written by a money management expert in 2018.

During the Golden Age of American manufacturing, it was expected that after putting in 30 to 40 years of tedious labor in a factory, workers
5   would be able to retire around age 65 and enjoy the benefits of retirement comforted by the thought that a pension and the Social Security system they had financed for decades would
10 cover their expenses. Unfortunately for millennials (people born between the early 1980s and late 1990s), prospects look increasingly bleak that they will get a return on their investment at
15 retirement age, despite continuing to fund programs like Social Security and Medicare. Fewer than a quarter of all Fortune 500 corporations still offer some form of pension plan to new
20 hires, and the move from company-funded pension plans to 401(k) plans and IRAs that began in the 1970s shows no sign of slackening. In this financial environment, it might be expected
25 that investment in the stock market would be at an all-time high. An analysis of the data, however, indicates a complicated and even fraught relationship between young adults and
30 the stock market.

The trauma associated with the Great Recession (which began in December 2007 and ended in June 2009) left many investors wary of stock
35 market volatility, and that hesitancy was exacerbated among young people, who saw a considerable portion of their families' wealth erased in short order. A study by Pfeffer, Danziger,
40 and Schoeni published in 2014 posited that the average American household

lost a third of its wealth, approximately $28,000, during the Great Recession. This was at the exact moment when a
45 great many millennials were making decisions about attending college, pursuing post-graduate studies, or entering the workforce. For a median-income family, those decisions were
50 all directly correlated to household wealth. The ripple effects of the Great Recession left many millennials ascribing blame directly to the stock market for missed opportunities.
55 Even with a full awareness that the stock market has rebounded and far exceeded the highs seen prior to the Great Recession, many millennials still feel trepidation about investing in the
60 stock market, preferring to save a larger percentage of their salaries than their parents and grandparents did.

Another factor that has directly impacted the willingness of millennials
65 to invest in the stock market is the seismic shift in the job market brought about by the "gig economy," in which short-term contracts and freelance work have replaced permanent
70 employment. To a large degree, the gig economy is still in its nascent phase, with many of the largest purveyors of jobs only incorporated in the last decade. Research has not adequately
75 kept track of the trend, with estimates of participation in the gig economy ranging from 4% to 40% in the United States. The ability to pick up work on a contingency basis allows
80 millennials to feel a greater level of control over their finances, something a significant number of them believe they cannot achieve through stock market investment. The increased
85 diversity of available methods for

building future wealth has caused many millennials to adopt an a la carte approach to preparing for retirement. But is it possible that this approach
90 has been clouded by some common misconceptions about wealth building?

One persistent, albeit erroneous, view is that real estate is a better investment instrument than a stock market
95 portfolio. While it is true that home equity is the stepping-stone from which most individuals begin to build their personal wealth, statistics make it clear that stock market investments are a more
100 stable and lucrative source of long-term wealth. A London Business School study found that over the same 90-year period, the average rate of return on a real estate investment was 1.3% compared to the
105 9.8% annualized total return for the S&P stock 500 index. Investing the $5,500 IRS-imposed annual limit in an IRA for 25 years would result in a return of over $600,000 based on the annualized
110 return rate. Stock investment requires a smaller overhead than real estate investment, and the liquid nature of stocks makes them ideal for retirement: stocks allocated to retirement accounts

115 remain tax-free until they are drawn on. Despite these pieces of tangible evidence, though, the stigma regarding stock market investment persists in the minds of many millennials.

120 Regardless of their feelings about the stock market, one thing is self-evident: without preparation for retirement, millennials will be a generation adrift in a society without the social "safety
125 nets" available to current retirees. The benchmark for the amount of savings the average retiree needs to live comfortably after retirement, which remained at $1 million for many years,
130 now continues to rise, and exacerbating factors, such as the cost of medical care, continue to increase. Armed with that knowledge, millennials need to be proactive about financial planning. By
135 taking full advantage of their penchant for a hands-on approach to finances and leveraging the various financial technologies and services that were not available to the previous generation,
140 millennials can amass the wealth necessary to retire comfortably and on their own terms.

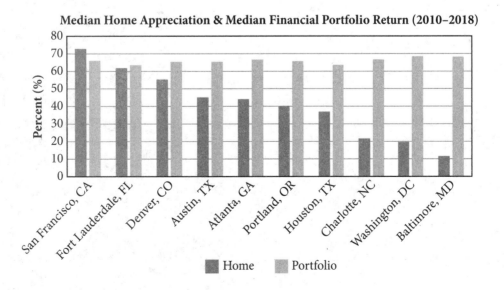

Median Home Appreciation & Median Financial Portfolio Return (2010–2018)

■ Home ■ Portfolio

You need to know this:

- SAT Reading passages are preceded by short blurbs that tell you about the author and source of the passage.
- There are three categories of keywords that reveal an author's purpose and point of view and that unlock the passage's structure:
  - **Opinion and Emphasis**—words that signal that the author finds a detail noteworthy (e.g., *especially, crucial, important, above all*) or has an opinion about it (e.g., *fortunately, disappointing, I suggest, it seems likely*)
  - **Connection and Contrast**—words that suggest that a subsequent detail continues the same point (e.g., *moreover, in addition, also, further*) or that indicate a change in direction or point of difference (e.g., *but, yet, despite, on the other hand*)
    - In some passages, these keywords may show steps in a process or developments over time (e.g., *traditionally, in the past, recently, today, first, second, finally, earlier, since*)
  - **Evidence and Example**—words that indicate an argument (the use of evidence to support a conclusion), either the author's or someone else's (e.g., *thus, therefore, because*), or that introduce an example to clarify or support another point (e.g., *for example, this shows, to illustrate*)

You need to do this:

- Extract everything you can from the pre-passage blurb.
- Read each paragraph actively; outline the passage as you read.
- Summarize the passage's big picture.

Extract everything you can from the pre-passage blurb

- Quickly prepare for the passage by unpacking the pre-passage blurb:
  - What does the title and date of the original book or article tell you about the author and her purpose for writing?
  - What information can you glean from the source (nonfiction book, novel, academic journal, etc.)?
  - Is there any other information that provides context for the passage?

Read each paragraph actively

- Note keywords (circling or underlining them may help) and use them to focus your reading on the following:
  - The author's purpose and point of view
  - The relationships between ideas
  - The illustrations or other support provided for passage claims

---

KEYWORDS

Why pay attention to keywords?

Keywords indicate opinions and signal structure that make the difference between correct and incorrect answers on SAT questions. Consider this question:

With which one of the following statements would the author most likely agree?

1. Coffee beans that grow at high altitudes typically produce dark, mellow coffee when brewed.

2. Coffee beans that grow at high altitudes typically produce light, acidic coffee when brewed.

To answer that based on an SAT passage, you will need to know whether the author said:

Type X coffee beans grow at very high altitudes *and so* produce a dark, mellow coffee when brewed.

That would make choice (1) correct. But if the author instead said:

Type X coffee beans grow at very high altitudes *but* produce a *surprisingly* dark, mellow coffee when brewed.

Then choice (2) would be correct. The facts in the statements did not change at all, but the correct answer to the SAT question would be different in each case because of the keywords the author chose to include.

- As you read, jot down brief, accurate margin notes that will help you research questions about specific details, examples, and paragraphs:
  - Paraphrase the text (put it into your own words) as you go.
  - Ask "What's the author's point and purpose?" for each paragraph.

Summarize the passage's big picture

- At the end of the passage, pause for a few seconds to summarize the passage's big picture. Doing so will help you understand the passage as a whole and will help you prepare for Global questions. Ask yourself:
  - What is the main idea of the entire passage? (If the author had only a few seconds to state what she thinks is most important, what would she say?)
  - Why did the author write it? (State the purpose as a verb, e.g., to *explain*, to *explore*, *to argue, to rebut*, etc.)

Explanation:

This passage was adapted from an article titled "Millennials and the Market," written by a money management expert in 2018.

During the Golden Age of American manufacturing, it was expected that after puttingin 30 to 40 years of tedious labor in a factory, workers
5 would be able to retire around age 65 and enjoy the benefits of retirement comforted by the thought that a pension and the Social Security system they had financed for decades would
10 cover their expenses. Unfortunately for millennials (people born between the early 1980s and late 1990s), prospects look increasingly bleak that they will get a return on their investment at
15 retirement age, despite continuing to fund programs like Social Security and Medicare. Fewer than a quarter of all Fortune 500 corporations still offer some form of pension plan to new
20 hires, and the move from company-funded pension plans to 401(k) plans and IRAs that began in the 1970s shows no sign of slackening. In this financial environment, it might be expected
25 that investment in the stock market would be at an all-time high. An analysis of the data, however, indicates a complicated and even fraught relationship between young adults and
30 the stock market.

Millennials won't have same retirement $

But they don't like stock market

ANALYSIS

Pre-passage blurb: This passage discusses millennials and the stock market. It is written from the perspective of an investment counselor.

SAT Reading Strategy: On the SAT, the pre-passage blurb will always give the author's name, the title of the book or article from which the passage was adapted, and the year it was published. When necessary, the blurb may also include a context-setting sentence with additional information. Train yourself to unpack the blurb to better anticipate what the passage will cover.

¶1: The first opinion keyword is "[u]nfortunately" (line 10). The author explains that, when they retire, millennials will not have the same kinds of pensions and social "safety net" programs that their parents and grandparents had. Then, the author expresses surprise that despite these challenges, millennials are hesitant to invest in the stock market.

SAT Reading Strategy: When an author introduces a surprising or confusing event or condition, expect her to offer some explanation in the following paragraph(s).

Reading

The trauma associated with the Great Recession (which began in December 2007 and ended in June 2009) left many investors (wary) of stock
35 market volatility, and that hesitancy was exacerbated among young people, who saw a considerable portion of their families' wealth erased in short order. A study by Pfeffer, Danziger,
40 and Schoeni published in 2014 posited that the average American household lost a third of its wealth, approximately $28,000, during the Great Recession. This was at the exact moment when a
45 great many millennials were making decisions about attending college, pursuing post-graduate studies, or entering the workforce. For a median-income family, those decisions were
50 all directly correlated to household wealth. The ripple effects of the Great Recession left many millennials (ascribing blame) directly to the stock market for missed opportunities.
55 Even with a full awareness that the stock market has rebounded and far exceeded the highs seen prior to the Great Recession, many millennials still feel (trepidation) about investing in the
60 stock market, preferring to save a larger percentage of their salaries than their parents and grandparents did.
(Another factor) that has directly impacted the willingness of millennials
65 to invest in the stockmarket is the seismic shift in the job market brought about by the "gig economy," in which short-term contracts and freelance work have replaced permanent
70 employment. To a large degree, the gig economy is still in its nascent phase, with many of the largest purveyors of jobs only incorporated in the last decade. Research has not adequately
75 kept track of the trend, with estimates of participation in the gig economy

*Reason:
07–09
recession =
millennials
blame the
market*

*Reason 2:
gig economy
= diff. ways
to make $*

¶2: One reason millennials distrust the stock market is that many came of age during the Great Recession. They saw their families' savings wiped out and, right out of high school, they had to make tough decisions about going to college or getting a job.

¶3: A second reason millennials avoid stock market investing is the rise of the "gig economy," in which many people have short-term, freelance jobs. This makes millennials open to different ways of managing their money, but maybe they have a mistaken viewpoint.

SAT Reading Strategy: When the author poses a question, expect her to answer it in the following sentence or paragraph.

ranging from 4% to 40% in the
United States. The ability to pick up
work on a contingency basis allows
80 millennials to feel a greater level of
control over their finances, something
a significant number of them believe
they cannot achieve through stock
market investment. The increased
85 diversity of available methods for
building future wealth has caused
many millennials to adopt an a la carte
approach to preparing for retirement.
But is it possible that this approach
90 has been clouded by some common
misconceptions about wealth building?
One persistent, albeit erroneous, view
is that real estate is a better investment   *Bad think-*
instrument than a stock market   *ing: house >*
95 portfolio. While it is true that home   *stock mkt*
equity is the stepping-stone from which
most individuals begin to build their
personal wealth, statistics make it clear
that stock market investments are a more
100 stable and lucrative source of long-term
wealth. A London Business School study
found that over the same 90-year period,
the average rate of return on a real estate
investment was 1.3% compared to the
105 9.8% annualized total return for the S&P
stock 500 index. Investing the $5,500
IRS-imposed annual limit in an IRA
for 25 years would result in a return of
over $600,000 based on the annualized
110 return rate. Stock investment requires
a smaller overhead than real estate
investment, and the liquid nature of
stocks makes them ideal for retirement:
stocks allocated to retirement accounts
115 remain tax-free until they are drawn
on. Despite these pieces of tangible
evidence, though, the stigma regarding
stock market investment persists in the
minds of many millennials.
120   Regardless of their feelings about the
stockmarket, one thing is self-evident:
without preparation for retirement,

¶4: One mistake millennials make comes from thinking that owning a home is a better investment than the stock market. Studies show that this isn't true. There are also tax advantages to investing in stocks for retirement.

¶5: Feelings aside, millennials will need investment to have a retirement income. Money for retirement will get tighter, but if millennials use a variety of investments, they can get the wealth they need.

Reading

millennials will be a generation adrift
in a society without the social "safety
125   nets" available to current retirees.
The benchmark for the amount of
savings the average retiree needs to live
comfortably after retirement, which
remained at $1 million for many years,
130   now continues to rise, and exacerbating
factors, such as the cost of medical
care, continue to increase. Armed with
that knowledge, millennials need to be
proactive about financial planning. By
135   taking full advantage of their penchant
for a hands-on approach to finances
and leveraging the various financial
technologies and services that were not
available to the previous generation,
140   millennials can amass the wealth
necessary to retire comfortably and on
their own terms.

Millennials need to adapt their thinking to have retirement $

Graphic: The graph shows return on investment for homes and for stock portfolios in 10 cities during the 2010s. This relates back to paragraph 4. The graph shows that stocks outperformed home ownership (sometimes by a lot) in 9 of the 10 cities.

SAT Reading Strategy: When an SAT Reading passage is accompanied by one or more charts or graphs, ask the following questions as you read them:

- **What information does the graphic contain?**
- **Why has the author included the graphic?**
- **Which paragraph(s) does this information relate to?**
- **Does the graphic display any trends or relationships that support a point made in the passage?**

In the Reading section, you will not be asked to perform calculations from the data in graphs. You will be asked how they relate to the passage and which claims or arguments they support or refute.

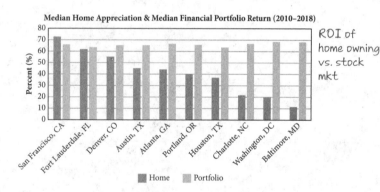

Median Home Appreciation & Median Financial Portfolio Return (2010–2018)

ROI of home owning vs. stock mkt

BIG PICTURE

Main Idea: Millennials are skeptical of investing in the stock market for multiple reasons but will need a variety of investments to be financially secure at retirement.

Author's Purpose: To outline challenges facing millennials in investing for retirement and explain why they are hesitant to invest in the stock market

---

Now, try another passage on your own. Use the SAT Reading strategies and tactics you've been learning to read and map this passage as quickly and accurately as you can.

Try on Your Own

Directions: Actively read and map the following passage by 1) circling or underlining keywords (from the Opinion and Emphasis, Connection and Contrast, or Evidence and Example categories); 2) jotting down brief, accurate margin notes that reflect good paraphrases of each paragraph; and 3) summing up the big picture. When you're done, compare your work to that of an SAT expert in the Expert Responses section.

This passage was adapted from an article titled "Quantum Computing: Where Is It Going?" published in a science magazine in 2018. It discusses the background and potential of quantum computing.

Pharmaceutical companies dream of a time when their research and development process shifts from looking for illnesses whose symptoms
5 can be ameliorated by a specific drug to choosing a disease and creating a drug to eradicate it. Quantum computing may be the key to that goal. The powerful modeling potential
10 unlocked by quantum computing may also someday be employed by autonomous vehicles to create a world free of traffic jams. With plausible applications in so many fields, it is
15 worthwhile to learn a bit about how quantum computing works.

Any understanding of quantum computing begins with its most basic element, the qubit. In classical
20 computing, information is processed by the bit, the binary choice of zero or one. Qubits, on the other hand, allow for infinite superpositions between zero and one and thus can
25 store and process exponentially more complicated values. Imagine showing someone where you live on a globe by pointing only to either the North Pole or the South Pole. While you
30 are likely closer to one pole than the other, you need additional information to represent your specific location. If, however, you could provide your home's latitude and longitude, it could
35 be located without any additional

information. The power of quantum computing lies in the ability to express precise information in a single qubit.

Quantum computing may help
40 scientists and engineers overcome another barrier by reducing energy output while increasing computational speed. The positive correlation between energy output
45 and processing speed often causes classical computers to "run hot" while processing overwhelming amounts of data. Along with their ability to store multiple values simultaneously,
50 qubits are able to process those values in parallel instead of serially. How does processing in parallel conserve energy? Suppose you want to set the time on five separate alarm clocks
55 spaced ten feet apart. You'd have to walk to each clock to change its time. However, if the clocks were connected such that changing the time on one immediately adjusted the other four, you
60 would expend less energy and increase processing speed. Therein lies the benefit of the quantum entanglement of qubits.

While quantum computing has moved beyond the realm of the
65 theoretical, significant barriers still stand in the way of its practical application. One barrier is the difficulty of confirming the results of quantum calculations. If quantum computing
70 is used to solve problems that are impossible to solve with classical computing, is there a way to "check" the results? Scientists hope this paradox may soon be resolved. As a graduate
75 student, Urmila Mahadev devoted

over a decade to creating a verification process for quantum computing. The result is an interactive protocol, based on a type of cryptography called
80 Learning With Errors (LWE), that is similar to "blind computing" used in cloud-computing to mask data while still performing calculations. Given current limitations, Mahadev's protocol
85 remains purely theoretical, but rapid progress in quantum computing combined with further refinement of the protocol will likely result in real-world implementation within the next
90 decade or two.

It is unlikely that early pioneers in the field, including Stephen Wiesner, Richard Feynman, and Paul Benioff, could have foreseen the rapid progress
95 that has been made to date. In 1960, when Wiesner first developed conjugate coding with the goal of improving cryptography, his paper on the subject was rejected for publication
100 because it contained logic far ahead of its time. Feynman proposed a basic quantum computing model at the 1981 First Conference on the Physics of Computation. At that same conference,
105 Benioff spoke on the ability of discrete mechanical processes to erase their own history and their application to Turing machines, a natural extension of Wiesner's earlier work. A year later,
110 Benioff more clearly outlined the theoretical framework of a quantum computer.

The dawn of the 21st century brought advancements at an even
115 more impressive pace. The first 5- and 7-qubit nuclear magnetic resonance (NMR) computers were demonstrated in Munich, Germany, and Santa Fe, New Mexico, respectively. In 2006,
120 researchers at Oxford were able to cage a qubit within a "buckyball," a

buckminsterfullerene molecule, and maintain its state for a short time using precise, repeated microwave pulses. The
125 first company dedicated to quantum computing software, 1QB Information Technologies, was founded in 2012, and in 2018, Google announced the development of the 72-qubit Bristlecone
130 chip designed to prove "quantum supremacy," the ability of quantum computers to solve problems beyond the reach of classical computing.

With progress in quantum
135 computing accelerating, it seems inevitable that within a few decades, the general population will be as familiar with quantum computing as they now are with classical computing. At present,
140 quantum computing is limited by the struggle to build a computer large enough to prove quantum supremacy, and the costs associated with quantum computing are prohibitive to all but
145 the world's largest corporations and governmental institutions. Still, classical computing overcame similar problems, so the future of quantum computing looks bright.

How Much Have You Learned?

Directions: Take five minutes to actively read the following passage by 1) noting the keywords, 2) jotting down margin notes next to each paragraph, and 3) summarizing the big picture. When you're done, compare your work to the Answers and Explanations at the end of the chapter.

This passage was adapted from an article entitled "John Snow Knew Something" published in a popular history magazine in 2018.

Few would deny that doctors use critical thinking to solve problems, but most imagine a difference between the practice of medicine and, say,
5 the methods a police detective might use to solve a case. In fact, medical researchers have long used forensic methods of detection and analysis. The case of John Snow, a
10 19th-century anesthesiologist, is often said to have ushered in the modern era of epidemiology, the branch of medicine that tracks the incidence and distribution of diseases and
15 proposes solutions for their control and prevention.

It would not be until 1861 that Louis Pasteur would propose the link between microorganisms and disease,
20 now known as the germ theory. Before Pasteur's breakthrough, the predominant explanation for the cause of most illnesses was the so-called miasma theory, which held that noxious
25 fumes and pollution—quite literally, as the theory's name implies, "bad air"— were responsible for making people sick. Consequently, during the 1854 outbreak of cholera in Westminster,
30 London, doctors and government officials alike blamed "miasmatic particles" released into the air by decaying organic matter in the soil of the River Thames.
35 Despite the widespread acceptance of the miasma theory, there were those, Snow included, who were skeptical of

this view. Snow would not have known, as doctors do today, that cholera
40 is caused by a bacterial infection, *Vibrio cholerae*. Nevertheless, he was convinced that the spread of the disease was caused by some form of matter passed between individuals, likely
45 through contaminated water.

To demonstrate this, Snow targeted a particularly deadly outbreak in the Soho district of Westminster in London. From August 31 to September
50 3, 1854, 127 people in the area died of cholera. Within a week, that number had risen to over 500. Snow took to the streets. Speaking to residents of the area, he found a commonality among
55 them: most of the victims had used a single public water pump located on Broad Street. Though he was unable to find conclusive proof that the pump was the source of the outbreak, his
60 demonstration of a pattern in the cholera cases prompted authorities to disable the pump by removing its handle. The epidemic quickly subsided.

Soon after the Broad Street pump
65 was shut down, Snow's continued investigation provided additional evidence that contaminated water was the source of the outbreak. Snow created a dot map of the cases of cholera in London
70 and demonstrated that they occurred in areas where water was supplied by two companies that obtained their water from wells near the Thames. Investigation of these wells showed that they had been
75 dug three feet from a cesspit that was leaking sewage into the surrounding soil. Snow also discovered that there were no cases of cholera among workers in a

brewery close to the Broad Street pump.

80 These workers were provided a daily allowance of beer, which they drank instead of water, and although the beer was brewed using the contaminated water, it was boiled during the brewing

85 process. This revelation provided a practical solution for the prevention of future outbreaks.

Snow is now hailed as the "father of modern epidemiology," and the radical

90 nature of his approach—formulating a new theory, substantiating it with verifiable evidence, and proposing preventative action—is fully appreciated. At the time, however, not

95 all were convinced, at least publicly, of Snow's findings. As anxiety over the

outbreak flagged, government officials replaced the handle on the Broad Street pump and publicly denounced Snow's

100 conclusions. It seems they felt that the city's residents would be upset and disgusted to have the unsettling nature of the well's contamination confirmed. It wasn't until 1866, more than a decade

105 after Snow's original investigation and theory—when another cholera outbreak killed more than 5,500 residents of London's East End—that officials working in public health began to

110 accept the link between contaminated water and certain kinds of illness and to take appropriate actions to quell such outbreaks.

Reflect

Directions: Take a few minutes to recall what you've learned and what you've been practicing in this chapter. Consider the following questions, jot down your best answer for each one, and then compare your reflections to the expert responses on the following page. Use your level of confidence to determine what to do next.

Why do SAT experts note keywords as they read?

_____

_____

_____

What are the three categories of keywords? Provide some examples from each category.

- _____

    o Examples: _____

- _____

    o Examples: _____

- _____

    o Examples: _____

Why do SAT experts jot down margin notes next to the text?

_____

_____

_____

What are the elements of a strong big picture summary?

_____

_____

_____

Expert Responses

Why do SAT experts note keywords as they read?

Keywords indicate what the author finds important, express her point of view about the subject and details of the passage, and signal key points in the passage structure. Keywords are the pieces of text that help test takers see which parts of the passage are likely to be mentioned in questions and help test takers to distinguish between correct and incorrect answer choices about those parts of the passage.

What are the three categories of keywords? Provide some examples from each category.

- *Opinion and Emphasis*
  - Examples: *indeed, quite, masterfully, inadequate*
- *Connection and Contrast*
  - Examples: *furthermore, plus, however, on the contrary*
- *Evidence and Example*
  - Examples: *consequently, since, for instance, such as*

Why do SAT experts jot down margin notes next to the text?

Margin notes help the test taker research questions that ask about details, examples, and arguments mentioned in the passage by providing a "map" to their location in the text. Margin notes can also help students answer questions about the passage structure and the purpose of a specific paragraph.

What are the elements of a strong big picture summary?

A strong big picture summary prepares a test taker to answer any question about the main idea of the passage or the author's primary or overall purpose in writing it. After reading the passage, SAT experts pause to ask, "What's the main point of the passage?" and "Why did the author write it?"

Next Steps

If you answered most questions correctly in the "How Much Have You Learned?" section, and if your responses to the Reflect questions were similar to those of the SAT expert, then consider strategic reading and passage mapping an area of strength and move on to the next chapter. Come back to this topic periodically to prevent yourself from getting rusty.

If you don't yet feel confident, review the material in "Reading Passage Strategies," then try mapping the passages you found difficult again. As always, be sure to review the explanations closely. Finally, if keywords give you trouble, **go online** (www.kaptest.com/moreonline) for additional practice with keywords.

Answers and Explanations

Try on Your Own

This passage was adapted from an article titled "Quantum Computing: Where Is It Going?" published in a science magazine in 2018. It discusses the background and potential of quantum computing.

Pharmaceutical companies dream of a time when their research and development process shifts from looking for illnesses whose symptoms
5　can be ameliorated by a specific drug to choosing a disease and creating a drug to eradicate it. Quantum computing maybe the (key) to that goal. The (powerful) modeling (potential)
10　unlocked by quantum computing may also someday be employed by autonomous vehicles to create a world free of traffic jams. With plausible applications in so many fields, it is
15　worthwhile to learn a bit about how quantum computing works.

Any understanding of quantum computing begins with its most basic element, the qubit. In classical
20　computing, information is processed by the bit, the binary choice of zero or one. Qubits, (on the other) hand, allow for infinite superpositions between zero and one and thus can
25　store and process (exponentially) more complicated values. Imagine showing someone where you live on a globe by pointing only to either the North Pole or the South Pole. While you
30　are likely closer to one pole than the other, you need additional information to represent your specific location. If, however, you could provide your home's latitude and longitude, it could
35　be located without any additional information. The power of quantum computing lies in the ability to express precise information in a single qubit.

QC: big potential

QC based on qubits – can store more values

Qubit > bit, much more data

ANALYSIS

Pre-passage blurb: Based on the article's title, you can expect to see a discussion of the past and future of quantum computing.

¶1: The author claims that quantum computing may help solve two big problems—new pharmaceuticals and traffic management. Because of this potential, she says, it's good to learn about quantum computing. Expect some of that background information in paragraph 2.

SAT Reading Strategy: Don't panic when confronted with unfamiliar or scientifically advanced subject matter. Pay attention to the author's purpose for discussing it.

¶2: The basis for quantum computing is the qubit, a much more powerful way to store and process information than the bit (which is what we currently use). The author illustrates this with the "globe" example.

SAT Reading Strategy: When you encounter an example or analogy, always ask, What does this illustrate or explain?

Quantum computing may help scientists and engineers overcome another barrier by reducing energy output while increasing computational speed. The positive correlation between energy output and processing speed often causes classical computers to "run hot" while processing overwhelming amounts of data. Along with their ability to store multiple values simultaneously, qubits are able to process those values in parallel instead of serially. How does processing in parallel conserve energy? Suppose you want to set the time on five separate alarm clocks spaced ten feet apart. You'd have to walk to each clock to change its time. However, if the clocks were connected such that changing the time on one immediately adjusted the other four, you would expend less energy and increase processing speed. Therein lies the benefit of the quantum entanglement of qubits.

While quantum computing has moved beyond the realm of the theoretical, significant barriers still stand in the way of its practical application. One barrier is the difficulty of confirming the results of quantum calculations. If quantum computing is used to solve problems that are impossible to solve with classical computing, is there a way to "check" the results? Scientists hope this paradox may soon be resolved. As a graduate student, Urmila Mahadev devoted over a decade to creating a verification process for quantum computing. The result is an interactive protocol, based on a type of cryptography called Learning With Errors (LWE), that is similar to "blind computing" used in cloud-computing to mask data while still performing calculations. Given current limitations, Mahadev's protocol

[margin note:] Qubits = parallel processing

[margin note:] Faster AND cooler

[margin note:] One barrier to QC – how to check results?

¶3: Another advantage: quantum computing is faster but cooler (current computers overheat). The reason is parallel processing, illustrated by the "five clocks" example.

SAT Reading Strategy: Rhetorical questions help you focus on the author's point in a paragraph and her reason for writing it.

¶4: Here, the passage shifts to obstacles to quantum computing. One problem: when they solve extremely complex problems, regular computers can't check them. One scientist is working on a solution, and the author is optimistic that it will work out in the next 20 years or so.

85 remains purely theoretical, but rapid
progress in quantum computing
combined with further refinement of
the protocol will likely result in real-
world implementation within the next
90 decade or two.

*Probably will
get solved*

It is unlikely that early pioneers in
the field, including Stephen Wiesner,
Richard Feynman, and Paul Benioff,
could have foreseen the rapid progress
95 that has been made to date. In 1960,
when Wiesner first developed conjugate
coding with the goal of improving
cryptography, his paper on the
subject was rejected for publication
100 because it contained logic far ahead
of its time. Feynman proposed a basic
quantum computing model at the 1981
First Conference on the Physics of
Computation. At that same conference,
105 Benioff spoke on the ability of discrete
mechanical processes to erase their
own history and their application to
Turing machines, a natural extension
of Wiesner's earlier work. A year later,
110 Benioff more clearly outlined the
theoretical framework of a quantum
computer.

*QC pioneers
- 1960s –
80s*

¶5: The pre-passage blurb indicated that the
passage would cover quantum computing's
past, and here it is. The point of this paragraph
is that early developers of quantum computing
(the author names three of them) would be
surprised by how quickly it has developed.

The dawn of the 21st century
brought advancements at an even
115 more impressive pace. The first 5- and
7-qubit nuclear magnetic resonance
(NMR) computers were demonstrated
in Munich, Germany, and Santa Fe,
New Mexico, respectively. In 2006,
120 researchers at Oxford were able to
cage a qubit within a "buckyball," a
buckminsterfullerene molecule, and
maintain its state for a short time using
precise, repeated microwave pulses. The
125 first company dedicated to quantum
computing software, 1QB Information
Technologies, was founded in 2012,
and in 2018, Google announced the
development of the 72-qubit Bristlecone
130 chip designed to prove "quantum
supremacy," the ability of quantum

*QC sped up
in 2000s*

¶6: This gives a little more about the past.
Progress in quantum computing really took off
during the 2000s. The author supports that
point with examples of companies that have
created and improved quantum computers.

**SAT Reading Strategy: The SAT doesn't expect
you to know the definitions of technical terms
and phrases. The test will ask you why the
author has included these details or how they
function in the paragraph.**

Reading

computers to solve problems beyond the
reach of classical computing.

    With progress in quantum
135 computing accelerating, it seems
inevitable that within a few decades, the
general population will be as familiar
with quantum computing as they now
are with classical computing. At present,
140 quantum computing is limited by the
struggle to build a computer large
enough to prove quantum supremacy,
and the costs associated with quantum
computing are prohibitive to all but
145 the world's largest corporations and
governmental institutions. Still, classical
computing overcame similar problems,
so the future of quantum computing
looks bright.

QC still difficult, but bright future

¶7: The passage ends on a high note: quantum computing will "inevitably" become popular and its future is "bright." The author acknowledges obstacles, but clearly implies that she expects them to be overcome.

BIG PICTURE

Main Idea: Quantum computing has many potential uses despite current obstacles.

Author's Purpose: To explain some fundamental principles of how quantum computing works to show its enormous potential over classical computing and to give a brief history of its development to anticipate how it can overcome current limitations

---

As with the other passages in this chapter, don't worry about whether you used the exact language found in the expert's map and summary. Instead, focus on how the expert used the skills and strategies outlined here to prepare himself to tackle the question set with speed and confidence.

How Much Have You Learned?

This passage was adapted from an article entitled "John Snow Knew Something" published in a popular history magazine in 2018.

Few would deny that doctors use critical thinking to solve problems, (but) most imagine a difference between the practice of medicine and, say,
5 the methods a police detective might use to solve a case. In fact, medical researchers have long used forensic methods of detection and analysis. The case of John Snow, a
10 19th-century anesthesiologist, is often said to have ushered in the modern era of epidemiology, the branch of medicine that tracks the incidence and distribution of diseases and
15 proposes solutions for their control and prevention.

It would not be until 1861 that Louis Pasteur would propose the link between microorganisms and disease,
20 now known as the germ theory. (Before) Pasteur's breakthrough, the predominant explanation for the cause of most illnesses was the so-called miasma theory, which held that noxious
25 fumes and pollution—quite literally, as the theory's name implies, "bad air"— were responsible for making people sick. (Consequently,) during the 1854 outbreak of cholera in Westminster,
30 London, doctors and government officials alike blamed "miasmatic particles" released into the air by decaying organic matter in the soil of the River Thames.
35 (Despite) the widespread acceptance of the miasma theory, there were those, Snow included, who were skeptical of this view. Snow would not have known, as doctors do today, that cholera

[margin note:] Snow's work used investigation, changed medicine

[margin note:] 1854 – didn't know about germs; miasma theory

ANALYSIS

Pre-passage blurb: The article is about someone named John Snow, who must be a historical figure of some importance. Beyond that, however, there's not too much to go on in this blurb.

¶1: The author provides some background on John Snow. Today, he is known for changing how doctors track and prevent diseases, apparently by using methods often associated with detectives and investigations. The rest of the passage will illustrate why he was so important.

¶2: This paragraph sets the stage. At the time of the cholera outbreak in 1854, people did not know that germs and bacteria caused the disease.

¶3: The author contrasts (note the keywords "Despite" and "Nevertheless") Snow's theories with the popular ideas of his time. He thought cholera might be passed through contaminated water.

40   is caused by a bacterial infection,
     Vibrio cholerae. Nevertheless, he was
     convinced that the spread of the disease
     was caused by some form of matter
     passed between individuals, likely
45   through contaminated water.

Snow: chol-
era from
contam.
H₂O

     To demonstrate this, Snow targeted
     a particularly deadly outbreak in
     the Soho district of Westminster in
     London. From August 31 to September
50   3, 1854, 127 people in the area died of
     cholera. Within a week, that number
     had risen to over 500. Snow took to
     the streets. Speaking to residents of the
     area, he found a commonality among
55   them: most of the victims had used a
     single public water pump located on
     Broad Street. Though he was unable
     to find conclusive proof that the pump
     was the source of the outbreak, his
60   demonstration of a pattern in the
     cholera cases prompted authorities
     to disable the pump by removing its
     handle. The epidemic quickly subsided.

Proof from
interviews
– all used
same pump

¶4: Snow investigated the area and interviewed people. He demonstrated that a
specific water pump was "ground zero" for the
outbreak and got it turned off.

     Soon after the Broad Street pump
65   was shutdown, Snow's continued
     investigation provided additional evidence
     that contaminated water was the source
     of the outbreak. Snow created a dot
     map of the cases of cholera in London
70   and demonstrated that they occurred in
     areas where water was supplied by two
     companies that obtained their water from
     wells near the Thames. Investigation of
     these wells showed that they had been
75   dug three feet from a cesspit that was
     leaking sewage into the surrounding soil.
     Snow also discovered that there were no
     cases of cholera among workers in a
     brewery close to the Broad Street pump.
80   These workers were provided a daily
     allowance of beer, which they drank
     instead of water, and although the beer
     was brewed using the contaminated
     water, it was boiled during the brewing
85   process. This revelation provided a

Water from
contam.
wells

Boiling first
prevented
disease

¶5: Through further investigation, Snow
showed that leaking cesspools were the
source of contamination and used his observations at a nearby brewery to deduce that
boiling water before drinking would prevent
the disease.

practical solution for the prevention of future outbreaks.

Snow is now hailed as the "father of modern epidemiology," and the radical
90 nature of his approach—formulating a new theory, substantiating it with verifiable evidence, and proposing preventative action—is fully appreciated. At the time, however, not
95 all were convinced, at least publicly, of Snow's findings. As anxiety over the outbreak flagged, government officials replaced the handle on the Broad Street pump and publicly denounced Snow's
100 conclusions. It seems they felt that the city's residents would be upset and disgusted to have the unsettling nature of the well's contamination confirmed. It wasn't until 1866, more than a decade
105 after Snow's original investigation and theory—when another cholera outbreak killed more than 5,500 residents of London's East End—that officials working in public health began to
110 accept the link between contaminated water and certain kinds of illness and to take appropriate actions to quell such outbreaks.

Snow not accepted at the time

1866 – another epidemic

¶6: Another contrast: Snow is now seen as a pioneer but wasn't appreciated at the time. It took another epidemic for officials to buy in to his theory.

Reading

BIG PICTURE

Main Idea: John Snow's investigative approach to explaining the cholera epidemic of 1854 ushered in the modern era of epidemiology.

Author's Purpose: To demonstrate how Snow's use of interviews, maps, and data altered the way doctors study the spread and prevention of disease

---

CHAPTER 19

SAT Reading Question Types

LEARNING OBJECTIVES

After completing this chapter, you will be able to:

Unpack SAT Reading question stems by:

- Distinguishing among six SAT Reading question types
- Determining if the correct answer is best found by researching the passage text or by consulting your big picture summary

---

SmartPoints®:

    Inference Questions, 90/300 (Very High Yield)
    Command of Evidence Questions, 60/300 (High Yield)
    Detail Questions, 45/300 (Medium Yield)
    Vocabulary-in-Context Questions, 45/300 (Medium Yield)
    Function Questions, 40/300 (Medium Yield)
    Global Questions, 20/300 (Low Yield)

How Much Do You Know?

Directions: In this chapter, you'll learn to unpack SAT Reading question stems (Step 1 of the Method for SAT Reading Questions). Unpacking a question stem means identifying your task (as identified by the question type) and noting where the answer will be found (a specific reference within the passage text or in your big picture summary). You first saw the question types defined in chapter 17. For your reference as you complete this quiz, here they are again:

- **Global**—asks about the big picture
- **Detail**—asks for explicitly stated facts or details
- **Inference**—asks about points that are unstated but strongly suggested
- **Command of Evidence**—asks for evidence to support the answer to a previous question
- **Function**—asks why the author wrote specific parts of the text
- **Vocabulary-in-Context**—asks for the meaning of a word as it is used in the passage

For each of the following question stems, identify the question type, cite the language in the stem that helped you identify it, and indicate where you would begin to research this question: either your big picture summary or a specific part of the text.

Example

The author of the passage would most likely agree with which one of the following statements concerning hydraulic mining?

Question type: *Inference*

Identifying language: *"would most likely agree"*

Research where? *passage, where author discusses hydraulic mining*

1. The passage indicates that non–rush hour commuters

    Question type:
    Identifying language:
    Research where?

2. As used in line 41, "labyrinthine" most nearly means

    Question type:
    Identifying language:
    Research where?

3. According to the passage, which of the following is true of the New York City subway system?

    Question type:
    Identifying language:
    Research where?

4. The fifth paragraph (lines 66–90) serves mainly to

    Question type:
    Identifying language:
    Research where?

5. Which of the following best expresses the primary purpose of the passage?

    Question type:
    Identifying language:
    Research where?

6. Based on the passage, which choice best describes a claim that critics of the current subway maintenance plan would likely make?

    Question type:
    Identifying language:
    Research where?

7. Which choice provides the best evidence for the answer to the previous question?

    Question type:
    Identifying language:
    Research where?

8. With which one of the following statements would the author of the passage be most likely to agree?

    Question type:
    Identifying language:
    Research where?

9. Based on the passage, advocates of the current New York City subway maintenance plan would most likely agree that

    Question type:
    Identifying language:
    Research where?

10. In the third paragraph, the discussion of two specific subway lines (lines 44–49) primarily serves to

    Question type:
    Identifying language:
    Research where?

Check Your Work

1. The passage indicates that non–rush hour commuters

   Question type: Detail

   Identifying language: "indicates"

   Research where? passage, where author discusses non-rush hour commuters

2. As used in line 41, "labyrinthine" most nearly means

   Question type: Vocab-in-Context

   Identifying language: "most nearly means"

   Research where? passage, line 41

3. According to the passage, which of the following is true of the New York City subway system?

   Question type: Detail

   Identifying language: "According to the passage"

   Research where? passage, where author discusses NYC subway system

4. The fifth paragraph (lines 66–90) serves mainly to

   Question type: Function

   Identifying language: "serves mainly to"

   Research where? passage, fifth paragraph

5. Which of the following best expresses the primary purpose of the passage?

   Question type: Global

   Identifying language: "primary purpose of the passage"

   Research where? big picture summary

6. Based on the passage, which choice best describes a claim that critics of the current subway maintenance plan would likely make?

   Question type: Inference

   Identifying language: "Based on the passage," "would likely make"

   Research where? passage, where author discusses critics' views

7. Which choice provides the best evidence for the answer to the previous question?

   Question type: Command of Evidence

   Identifying language: "provides the best evidence"

   Research where? passage, where you went to answer the previous question

8. With which one of the following statements would the author of the passage be most likely to agree?

   Question type: Inference

   Identifying language: "most likely to agree"

   Research where? big picture summary (no specific clues)

9. Based on the passage, advocates of the current New York City subway maintenance plan would most likely agree that

   Question type: Inference

   Identifying language: "Based on the passage," "would most likely agree"

   Research where? passage, where author discusses advocates' views

10. In the third paragraph, the discussion of two specific subway lines (lines 44–49) primarily serves to

    Question type: Function

    Identifying language: "primarily serves to"

    Research where? passage, third paragraph

How to Unpack SAT Reading Question Stems

LEARNING OBJECTIVES

After this lesson, you will be able to unpack SAT Reading question stems by:

- Distinguishing among six SAT Reading question types
- Determining if the correct answer is best found by researching the passage text or by consulting your big picture summary

To unpack question stems like these:

1. One central idea of the passage is that

2. Which choice best describes the overall structure of the passage?

3. According to the passage, large corporations are

4. As used in line 38, "erased" most nearly means

5. The passage most strongly implies which of the following statements about the Great Recession?

6. Which choice provides the best evidence for the answer to the previous question?

7. In the third paragraph (lines 63–91), the most likely purpose of the author's discussion of the "gig economy" is to

8. In the context of the passage as a whole, the question in lines 89–91 primarily functions to help the author

9. The passage indicates that investing in the stock market

10. Which of the following statements is supported by the graph?

11. Which statement from the passage is most directly reflected by the data presented in the graph?

You'll need to know this:

The six kinds of question types, each of which defines a specific task:

> **1. Global**—asks about the passage's main idea, the author's primary purpose, or the passage's overall organization
>
> Typical Global Question Stems
>
> - The central claim of the passage is that
> - Which choice best summarizes the passage?
> - The main purpose of the passage is to
> - Which choice best describes the developmental pattern of the passage?
> - Which choice best reflects the overall sequence of events in the passage?

2. **Detail**—asks about something explicitly stated in the passage

Typical Detail Question Stems

- According to the passage, which of the following is true of developmental psychology?
- The author indicates that people value solitude because
- In the second paragraph (lines 14–27), what does the author claim are key questions the study must answer?
- The passage identifies which of the following as a factor that influences economic growth?

3. **Inference**—asks for something that follows from the passage without having been stated explicitly in it

Typical Inference Question Stems

- Based on the passage, the author's statement "in response, the Federal Reserve will often lower interest rates" (lines 21–22) implies that
- Which concept is supported by the passage and by the information in the graph?
- Based on information in the passage, it can reasonably be inferred that
- The authors of both passages would most likely agree with which of the following statements?

4. **Command of Evidence**—asks you to cite the support offered in the passage for the correct answer to the previous question or for a given statement

Typical Command of Evidence Question Stems

- Which choice provides the best evidence for the answer to the previous question?
- Which choice best supports the claim that the new policy is unlikely to curtail water pollution?

5. **Function**—asks about the purpose of a piece of text—why the author included it or how the author has used it

Typical Function Question Stems

- The sentence in lines 35–37 serves mainly to
- The main purpose of the fourth paragraph (lines 42–50) is to
- How do the words "must," "necessary," and "imperative" in the third paragraph (lines 35–49) help establish the tone of the paragraph?
- The author uses the image of an explorer overlooking a valley (lines 23–28) most likely to
- The sentence in lines 74–78 ("After ... rest") primarily serves which function in paragraph 7?

6. Vocabulary-in-Context—asks you to define a word as the author used it in the passage

Typical Vocabulary-in-Context Question Stems

- As used in line 55, "platform" most nearly means
- As used in line 29, "substantial" most nearly means

The kinds of research clues found in SAT Reading question stems:

- **Line Numbers**—Mentions of "line 53" or "lines 37–40," often in parentheses, tend to stand out and give you a clear place to start your research. (In Command of Evidence questions, line numbers are found in the answer choices.)
- **Paragraph Numbers**—A reference to "paragraph 5," "the third paragraph," or "the last two paragraphs" is not as precise as a line reference but will still give you an idea of where to look. Start with your margin notes for the paragraph.
- **Quoted Text** (often accompanied by line numbers)—Check the context of the quoted term or phrase to see what the author meant by it in the passage.
- **Proper Nouns**—Names like "Professor James," "World War II," and "Baltimore" will likely stand out in question stems due to the capitalization. If a particular proper noun is discussed in only part of the passage, it narrows the range of text you have to research.
- **Specific Content Clues**—Sometimes a question stem will repeat terminology used in part of the passage like "federalism" or "action potentials." Use your passage map to direct your research to the right part of the passage.
- **Whole Passage Clues**—If a question lacks specific content clues but refers to the passage as a whole, or to the author in general, you are likely dealing with a Global question or an open-ended Inference question, which should lead you to your big picture summary rather than to rereading parts of the text.

You need to do this:

The Method for SAT Reading Questions	
Step 1.	**Unpack the question stem**
Step 2.	Research the answer
Step 3.	Predict the answer
Step 4.	Find the one correct answer

Unpack SAT Reading question stems by:

- Identifying the question type and anticipating how it will need to be answered
- Noting research clues that indicate how best to research the correct answer

---

QUESTION TYPES

Why distinguish question types in SAT Reading?

Unpacking the question stem puts you in control. You'll know exactly what the question is asking, where to find the correct answer, and what form the correct answer will take. Being able to distinguish between the following question types will help you find the correct answer:

- **Global:** The correct answer must take the entire passage into account. A choice that reflects only part of the passage is incorrect.
- **Detail:** The correct answer must be stated in the passage explicitly. A choice that is not directly stated in the passage is incorrect.
- **Inference:** The correct answer will be a conclusion that can be drawn from the passage. A choice that draws too strong a conclusion from the evidence available in the passage is incorrect.
- **Command of Evidence:** The correct answer must directly support the correct answer to the previous question. A choice about the same subject but providing no direct evidence is not good enough.
- **Function:** The correct answer will say *why* a certain detail is included. Look up the detail, then ask yourself what the author was trying to accomplish by putting it there.
- **Vocab-in-Context:** The correct answer will give the meaning of a word as it is used *in the context of the passage*. Choices that give common meanings of the word are often incorrect.

Correct answers to Reading questions are never random or vague. They are tailored to the precise language of the stem, so being able to distinguish the question types will save you time and eliminate confusion during the test.

Answers and Explanations:

1. This is a Global question, as is clear from the phrase "central idea of the passage." Your big picture summary will likely have the answer.

2. The mention of the "overall structure of the passage" indicates that this is also a Global question. In addition to your big picture summary, look for structural trends in your margin notes (particularly for places where the author changes direction or perspective) when answering a Global question about structure.

3. "According to the passage" is a clear sign of a Detail question. Though this question lacks specific line or paragraph clues, the mention of "large corporations" may help to narrow your research.

4. A question stem that begins with a line reference, quotes a term from the passage, and ends in "most nearly means" is always a Vocab-in-Context question. Be sure to go back to the passage to check the context before looking at the answer choices.

5. The word "implies" tells you that this is an Inference question. The proper noun "the Great Recession" gives you something to look for in the passage. The correct answer *must* be true based on the passage but may not be directly stated.

6. The vast majority of Command of Evidence questions have this exact wording: "Which choice provides the best evidence for the answer to the previous question?" All Command of Evidence answer choices feature direct quotes with line numbers, which you should use to guide your research. Start by looking at the lines of text you used to answer the previous question.

7. This is a Function question because it asks for the "most likely purpose" of a specific part of the text. To research it, you should look for mentions of the "gig economy" in the third paragraph. Function questions are *why* questions, so reread the indicated text and ask yourself, "Why did the author include this?"

8. The use of "primarily functions" gives this away as a Function question. The cited lines tell you where to start researching.

9. This is a Detail question, as can be garnered from "indicates." The other clues in the stem suggest that you'll need to search the passage for a discussion of stock market investment.

10. This is an Inference question because it asks for a statement that "is supported" by part of the passage—in this case, the graph. To research such a question, look for major takeaways from the data presented in the graph.

11. This is a less common variation of Command of Evidence, which would be more obvious after looking at the answer choices (quotes from the text with line references). To research, follow the line references until you come upon a quote that describes a major takeaway from the data in the graph.

Try on Your Own

Directions: Analyze each of the following question stems by 1) identifying the word or phrase that describes your task, 2) naming the question type, and 3) noting how best to research the correct answer (research the text or consult the big picture summary). Answers are found at the end of the chapter.

1. According to the passage, which one of the following is true of Urmila Mahadev's graduate work?

   Question type:

   Identifying language:

   Research where?

2. Which choice provides the best evidence for the answer to the previous question?

   Question type:

   Identifying language:

   Research where?

3. The author's attitude toward the potential success of quantum computing can best be described as

   Question type:

   Identifying language:

   Research where?

4. Which statement best describes the technique the author uses to advance the main point of the third paragraph (lines 39–62)?

   Question type:

   Identifying language:

   Research where?

5. The primary purpose of the passage is to

   Question type:

   Identifying language:

   Research where?

6. Based on the passage, the author would most likely criticize classical computing because it

   Question type:

   Identifying language:

   Research where?

7. The passage indicates that which of the following factors slowed early developments in the theory of quantum computing?

   Question type:

   Identifying language:

   Research where?

8. In the second paragraph, the discussion of locating a person's home on a globe (lines 26–36) primarily serves to

   Question type:

   Identifying language:

   Research where?

9. Which one of the following does the passage imply about the development of quantum computing in the 21st century?

   Question type:

   Identifying language:

   Research where?

10. As used in line 123, "maintain" most nearly means

    Question type:

    Identifying language:

    Research where?

For any question types that you misidentified, return to the definitions and question stem examples before you try the final question set in this chapter.

How Much Have You Learned?

Directions: Now, complete a similar assessment under timed conditions. Take a few minutes to analyze each of the following question stems by 1) identifying the word or phrase that describes your task, 2) naming the question type, and 3) noting how best to research the correct answer (research the text or consult the big picture summary).

11. The passage primarily serves to

   Question type:

   Identifying language:

   Research where?

12. Which of the following is most analogous to John Snow's discovery of the source of the cholera outbreak?

   Question type:

   Identifying language:

   Research where?

13. Which choice provides the best evidence for the answer to the previous question?

   Question type:

   Identifying language:

   Research where?

14. The passage indicates that the main reason government officials rejected Snow's hypothesis was

   Question type:

   Identifying language:

   Research where?

15. The second paragraph serves mainly to

   Question type:

   Identifying language:

   Research where?

16. It can reasonably be inferred from the passage that scientists in 1855 would have found which of the following solutions to be most practical in dealing with future outbreaks of cholera?

   Question type:

   Identifying language:

   Research where?

17. The author of this passage writes from the perspective of a

   Question type:

   Identifying language:

   Research where?

18. Which of the following is cited as the primary reason Snow suspected the Broad Street pump as the source of the epidemic?

   Question type:

   Identifying language:

   Research where?

19. As used in line 97, the word "flagged" most nearly means

   Question type:

   Identifying language:

   Research where?

20. The author uses the final sentence of the passage ("It wasn't … outbreaks") at least in part to

   Question type:

   Identifying language:

   Research where?

Reflect

Directions: Take a few minutes to recall what you've learned and what you've been practicing in this chapter. Consider the following questions, jot down your best answer for each one, and then compare your reflections to the expert responses on the following page. Use your level of confidence to determine what to do next.

Why is it important to always unpack the question stem before proceeding?

_____

_____

_____

Can you name the six SAT Reading question types and cite words or phrases that identify each one?

1. _____
   o Identifying language: _____

2. _____
   o Identifying language: _____

3. _____
   o Identifying language: _____

4. _____
   o Identifying language: _____

5. _____
   o Identifying language: _____

6. _____
   o Identifying language: _____

How will you approach SAT Reading question stems differently as you continue to practice and improve your performance in the Reading section? What are the main differences you see between SAT Reading questions and those you're used to from tests in school?

_____

_____

_____

Expert Responses

Why is it important to always unpack the question stem before proceeding?

Knowing the SAT Reading question types makes you a more strategic and efficient reader because the test maker uses the same question types on every test. Fully analyzing each question stem helps you research the text more effectively, predict the correct answer in a way that fits the question stem, and avoid incorrect answers made from misreading the question.

Can you name the six SAT Reading question types and cite words or phrases that identify each one?

1. *Global*
   - Identifying language: *main idea of the passage, author's primary purpose*
2. *Detail*
   - Identifying language: *according to the passage, identifies, claims*
3. *Inference*
   - Identifying language: *implies, can be inferred, based on the passage*
4. *Command of Evidence*
   - Identifying language: *provides the best evidence, best supports, the answer to the previous question*
5. *Function*
   - Identifying language: *is used to, serves mainly to, functions as*
6. *Vocabulary-in-Context*
   - Identifying language: *as used in line [number], most nearly means*

How will you approach SAT Reading question stems differently as you continue to practice and improve your performance in the Reading section? What are the main differences you see between SAT Reading questions and those you're used to from tests in school?

There is no one-size-fits-all answer here. Reflect on your own strengths and weaknesses as you consider how to best improve your performance in the SAT Reading section. Depending on the kinds of classes and teachers you've had in high school, the skills rewarded on SAT Reading questions may be more or less familiar, but almost every test taker needs to be aware of her own instincts as a reader, and needs to break certain reading habits, to master this section of the test. The more you give yourself an honest self-assessment, the better prepared you'll be to handle all of the SAT Reading question types confidently.

Next Steps

If you answered most questions correctly in the "How Much Have You Learned?" section, and if your responses to the Reflect questions were similar to those of the SAT expert, then consider identifying Reading question types an area of strength and move on to the next chapter. Come back to this topic periodically to prevent yourself from getting rusty.

If you don't yet feel confident, review the material in How to Unpack SAT Reading Question Stems, then try the questions you missed again. As always, be sure to review the explanations closely. Finally, **go online** (www.kaptest.com/moreonline) for more practice with full Reading passages and question sets.

Answers and Explanations

1. According to the passage, which one of the following is true of Urmila Mahadev's graduate work?

   Question type: Detail
   Identifying language: "According to the passage"
   Research where? passage, where the author discusses Mahadev's work

2. Which choice provides the best evidence for the answer to the previous question?

   Question type: Command of Evidence
   Identifying language: "provides the best evidence"
   Research where? passage, where you answered the previous question

3. The author's attitude toward the potential success of quantum computing can best be described as

   Question type: Inference
   Identifying language: "can best be described as"
   Research where? passage, where author discusses quantum computing success

4. Which statement best describes the technique the author uses to advance the main point of the third paragraph (lines 39–62)?

   Question type: Function
   Identifying language: "the technique the author uses"
   Research where? passage, third paragraph

5. The primary purpose of the passage is to

   Question type: Global
   Identifying language: "primary purpose of the passage"
   Research where? big picture summary

6. Based on the passage, the author would most
   Question type: Inference

   Identifying language: "Based on the passage"
   Research where? passage, where author discusses classical computing

7. The passage indicates that which of the following factors slowed early developments in the theory of quantum computing?

   Question type: Detail
   Identifying language: "indicates"
   Research where? passage, where author discusses early developments

8. In the second paragraph, the discussion of locating a person's home on a globe (lines 26–36) primarily serves to

   Question type: Function
   Identifying language: "primarily serves to"
   Research where? passage, second paragraph

9. Which one of the following does the passage imply about the development of quantum computing in the 21st century?

   Question type: Inference
   Identifying language: "imply"
   Research where? passage, where author discusses 21st-century development

10. As used in line 123, "maintain" most nearly means

    Question type: Vocab-in-Context
    Identifying language: "most nearly means"
    Research where? passage, line 123

11. The passage primarily serves to

    Question type: Global
    Identifying language: "passage primarily serves to"
    Research where? big picture summary

12. Which of the following is most analogous to John Snow's discovery of the source of the cholera outbreak?

    Question type: Inference
    Identifying language: "most analogous"
    Research where? passage, where author discusses Snow's discovery

13. Which choice provides the best evidence for the answer to the previous question?

    Question type: Command of Evidence
    Identifying language: "provides the best evidence"
    Research where? passage, where you went to answer the previous question

14. The passage indicates that the main reason government officials rejected Snow's hypothesis was

    Question type: Detail
    Identifying language: "indicates"
    Research where? passage, where author discusses officials' rejection of Snow

15. The second paragraph serves mainly to

    Question type: Function
    Identifying language: "serves mainly to"
    Research where? passage, second paragraph

16. It can reasonably be inferred from the passage that scientists in 1855 would have found which of the following solutions to be most practical in dealing with future outbreaks of cholera?

    Question type: Inference
    Identifying language: "reasonably be inferred"
    Research where? passage, where author discusses cholera outbreak solutions

17. The author of this passage writes from the perspective of a

    Question type: Global
    Identifying language: "author ... writes from the perspective of a"
    Research where? big picture summary

18. Which of the following is cited as the primary reason Snow suspected the Broad Street pump as the source of the epidemic?

    Question type: Detail
    Identifying language: "is cited as"
    Research where? passage, where author discusses Broad Street pump

19. As used in line 97, the word "flagged" most nearly means

    Question type: Vocab-in-Context
    Identifying language: "most nearly means"
    Research where? passage, line 97

20. The author uses the final sentence of the passage ("It wasn't ... outbreaks") at least in part to:

    Question type: Function
    Identifying language: "uses ... at least in part to"
    Research where? passage, final sentence

CHAPTER 20

Answering SAT Reading Questions

LEARNING OBJECTIVES

After completing this chapter, you will be able to:

- Research the answer in the passage or your big picture summary
- Predict the correct answer
- Find the one correct answer choice

Reading

How Much Do You Know?

Directions: In this chapter, you'll learn how best to research, predict, and find the correct answers to SAT Reading questions. For this quiz, first take a couple of minutes to refresh your memory of the passage. Then, for each question 1) research the answer in the passage text or from your big picture summary, 2) predict the correct answer in your own words, and 3) identify the one correct answer.

Questions 1–11 refer to the following passage.

This passage is adapted from a 2018 article summarizing two different proposals for solving problems with maintaining New York City's mass transit system.

The history of the New York City subway system, quickly told: the first stations opened in 1904, and over the next century, it expanded to 472 stations,
5   more than any other subway system in the world, with 850 miles of track. Operating 24 hours a day seven days a week, with an average weekday ridership of approximately 5.7 million, it is the
10 planet's 7th-busiest rapid transit system. While the system is, on many levels, an amazing achievement, it is also beset by a problem that harms both quality of life and economic activity. Such a
15 large system must inevitably suffer from service interruptions and delays; normal wear and tear combined with the sheer age of the system necessitates regular maintenance. However, there
20 is no consensus as to the best way to accomplish the required repairs.

NYC subway: how to repair? diff. views

The current maintenance scheme is designed to minimize service interruptions. A subway line in need
25 of repair will be taken out of service during a comparatively less busy time, such as nights or weekends, while another line is re-routed to cover as many as possible of the missing line's
30 stops. The main advantage to this approach is that trains are not taken out of service during rush hour, when most subway trips occur; subway service generally remains predictable
35 and commuters are, for the most part,

Current approach – night and weekend repairs

able to use the system to get to their destinations on time.

But critics are quick to point out the disadvantages to this approach. Perhaps
40 most obvious is the confusion caused by trains switching lines. The labyrinthine system is hard enough to navigate at the best of times, especially for tourists. A subway rider on the A train naturally
45 expects the train to make stops on the A line. If, instead, it is diverted temporarily to the F line, the rider may find herself miles from her intended destination.

Critics: line switch confusion

50 While annoying, the confusion arising from route switching is hardly the most serious problem with the current approach to repairs. Because the system runs 24 hours a
55 day, routine maintenance can generally be done only during the temporary closures on nights and weekends. This means that more serious repair and crucial preventative maintenance is
60 often neglected. Problems that could have been fixed or prevented reasonably expeditiously given a slightly longer closure wind up leading to major breakdowns and service interruptions
65 later on.

Even worse – major breakdowns

On rare occasions, such breakdowns have resulted in entire subway lines being shut down for months or even a year. Beginning in 2019, for
70 example, the L Train connecting lower Manhattan to parts of Brooklyn was scheduled to close for as much as 15 months for long overdue service and upgrades. In a city fewer than
75 half of whose households own a car,

this can have serious economic impacts. Residents of the affected area may face a much longer commute via an alternate subway line if one is available;

80 or, if there is no alternate subway service, they may need to take other, potentially more expensive, modes of transportation, such as taxis or ferries. Moreover, studies indicate that

85 increased stress from the commute to work can lead to lower productivity, and that businesses near the impacted lines may see decreased revenue as potential customers have a harder time getting to

90 them.

Econ. & Soc. harms of shutdowns

One controversial proposal for reducing breakdowns and the resulting transit interruptions is to end the subway's 24-hour service and to shut

95 down for several hours each night. Proponents of this plan argue that this would allow time, on a regular rather than sporadic basis, for more preventative maintenance. This, they

100 claim, would ultimately lead to more consistent service; rather than shutting down entire lines for long periods of a time, there would merely be shorter service outages overnight, when fewer

105 people use the subway system. While this may seem a preferable outcome to the economic consequences of a total shutdown resulting from a breakdown, it has its liabilities as well. While most

110 subway trips may occur during rush hour, not everyone works during the daytime. New York is famously known as the "the city that never sleeps." Doctors, nurses, bartenders, police

115 officers, and firefighters are just a few examples of occupations whose workers need transportation at all hours of the day and night. Rather than be subjected to a relatively short period

120 of inconvenience, these workers would find their commutes irrevocably altered.

Alt proposal – stop 24-hour service

Pros

Cons

One thing, at least, is clear: the city must carefully consider many economic and social factors in designing a subway

125 maintenance plan.

Reading

1. Which of the following best expresses the primary purpose of the passage?

   A) To argue that the New York City subway system maintenance plan should be altered

   B) To explain the effects of the current New York City subway system maintenance plan and a proposed alternative

   C) To discuss the economic and social importance of the New York City subway system

   D) To show how the history of the New York City subway system has resulted in the current maintenance crisis

2. According to the passage, which of the following is true of the New York City subway system?

   A) It is the oldest subway system in the world.

   B) It is the busiest mass transit system in the world.

   C) It has more stations than any other subway system.

   D) A majority of city residents rely on the subway to get to work.

3. Based on the passage, advocates of the current New York City subway maintenance plan would most likely agree that

   A) given its size, the city's subway system is one of the most well maintained in the world.

   B) avoiding service interruptions during rush hour is a paramount consideration when designing a maintenance schedule.

   C) confusion caused by route switching is a minor inconvenience for commuters and tourists.

   D) operating the subway system 24 hours a day seven days a week is untenable given the wear and tear it causes.

4. Which choice provides the best evidence for the answer to the previous question?

   A) Lines 14–19 ("Such a . . . maintenance")

   B) Lines 30–37 ("The main . . . time")

   C) Lines 50–53 ("While . . . repairs")

   D) Lines 96–99 ("Proponents . . . maintenance")

5. Based on the passage, which choice best describes a claim that critics of the current subway maintenance plan would likely make?

   A) The negative impacts that arise from neglecting preventative maintenance outweigh the benefits of minimizing subway service interruptions.

   B) When devising a subway maintenance plan, no factor is more important than avoiding rush hour service interruptions.

   C) The negative impact from subway line closures is greater on commuters than it is on businesses near the affected lines.

   D) Slightly longer periods of scheduled maintenance would help the subway system minimize rush hour service interruptions.

6. Which choice provides the best evidence for the answer to the previous question?

   A) Lines 24–30 ("A subway . . . stops")

   B) Lines 60–65 ("Problems . . . later on")

   C) Lines 69–74 ("Beginning in . . . upgrades")

   D) Lines 84–90 ("Moreover, studies . . . them")

7. As used in line 41, "labyrinthine" most nearly means

   A) subterranean.

   B) mythological.

   C) meandering.

   D) complicated.

8. In the third paragraph, the discussion of two specific subway lines (lines 44–49) primarily serves to

   A) support the contention that line switching has a negative impact on tourism.

   B) illustrate one problem created by the current subway maintenance plan.

   C) underline the importance of minimizing subway service interruptions.

   D) quantify the social costs that arise from extended subway repair schedules.

9. The fifth paragraph (lines 66–90) serves mainly to

   A) illustrate the impact of the current maintenance plan on one subway line.

   B) advocate for increased funding for subway repair and maintenance.

   C) provide support for a proposal to curtail 24-hour subway service.

   D) outline the negative impacts of extended subway line outages.

10. The passage indicates that non–rush hour commuters

    A) would risk losing public transportation options if 24-hour subway service were suspended.

    B) would face only minor inconveniences if 24-hour subway service were suspended.

    C) work primarily in health care and its related fields.

    D) are among the strongest advocates for a change to the current subway maintenance plan.

11. With which one of the following statements would the author of the passage be most likely to agree?

    A) The controversy surrounding New York City's subway system reflects similar issues for mass transit in many American cities.

    B) Without major changes to its subway maintenance plan, New York City will be unable to provide regular service to its 5.7 million weekly riders.

    C) Any plan for maintaining New York City's subway system will entail advantages and disadvantages for commuters.

    D) The social and economic costs resulting from New York City's current subway maintenance schedule justify an end to 24-hour, seven-day subway service.

Check Your Work

1. B

Difficulty: Medium

Category: Global

Strategic Advice: Consult your big picture summary and find the one answer that matches the passage's scope and the author's purpose.

Getting to the Answer: Here, the author does not take a side. He lays out advantages and disadvantages to both the current maintenance plan and one proposal offered by critics of the current plan. That matches **(B)**.

(A) distorts the author's position. He doesn't advocate for the critics of the current plan.

(C) is too narrow. It misses the key subject of subway *maintenance*.

(D) is also too narrow. This answer describes only the first paragraph.

2. C

Difficulty: Medium

Category: Detail

Strategic Advice: The correct answer will be something explicitly stated in the passage.

Getting to the Answer: Start by checking the answers against paragraph 1 where the author provides general facts about the New York City subway. Doing so will lead you to the correct answer, **(C)**.

(A) is unsupported. You're told that the subway opened in 1904, but not whether other subway systems already existed at that time.

(B) is simply incorrect. New York City's subway system is the seventh busiest in the world.

(D) distorts a fact from the passage. The fifth paragraph states that fewer than half of households in the city own a car, but that doesn't mean that everyone in the majority of households that do not own cars takes the subway.

3. B

Difficulty: Hard

Category: Inference

Strategic Advice: The correct answer will follow from the passage text without having been explicitly stated in the text.

Getting to the Answer: The current maintenance plan is outlined in paragraph 2. You're told that its goal is to "minimize service interruptions" and that its main advantage is that trains operate during rush hour. Combining those statements leads to the correct answer, **(B)**.

(A) is too extreme. Everyone seems to agree that maintaining the system is a huge challenge. The debate is over *how* best to implement the necessary repairs.

(C) misuses a detail from the passage. The author says nothing about how serious a problem those who support the current plan consider route switching to be. They might understand that it causes a major inconvenience but still be willing to reroute trains in order to keep the subway open during rush hour.

(D) states a position taken by *critics*, not advocates, of the current plan.

4. B

Difficulty: Medium

Category: Command of Evidence

Strategic Advice: The most common Command of Evidence question stems task you with locating the piece of text that supports the correct answer to the preceding question. Use that answer to direct your research as you evaluate the answer choices.

Getting to the Answer: In this case, the correct answer to the preceding question paraphrased the final sentence in paragraph 3. That sentence covers the lines in **(B)** making that the correct answer here.

(A) cites a sentence from paragraph 1. It contains the phrase "wear and tear," which was part of incorrect answer (D) in the preceding question, but doesn't support the correct answer, **(B)**.

(C) comes from the beginning of paragraph 4. It suggests that there are problems with the current system even bigger than the inconvenience caused by line switching. This choice could be tempting if you chose (C) on the preceding question.

(D) provides evidence for the *critics'* proposal to stop running the subway 24/7. That is not the argument made by advocates of the current system who were the subject of the preceding question.

5. A

Difficulty: Hard

Category: Inference

Strategic Advice: The phrases "[b]ased on the passage" and "would likely" indicate an Inference question. Note that this question asks specifically for the position of the critics of the current plan. The correct answer will be implied by the passage text.

Getting to the Answer: The critics' objections to the current plan are laid out primarily in paragraphs 3 and 4. Quick research shows that they make two arguments. First (paragraph 3), line switching for routine maintenance can be confusing and frustrating for riders. Second (paragraph 4), and worse, the limited time allowed for routine maintenance prevents important preventative maintenance from taking place. That leads to severe service outages that can last for weeks or months. This second criticism accords with the correct answer, **(A)**.

(B) is something that advocates, not opponents, of the current plan might say. See paragraph 2 for this argument.

(C) is an irrelevant comparison. Paragraph 5 lays out the social and economic impacts of extended subway line closures to both riders and businesses, but it doesn't assert that the impacts are worse for one group or the other.

(D) distorts the critics' argument. They contend that slightly longer periods of scheduled maintenance would allow time for preventative maintenance, not that it would reduce rush hour interruptions.

6. B

Difficulty: Medium

Category: Command of Evidence

Getting to the Answer: Here, the correct answer to the preceding question paraphrased the critics' argument in paragraph 4. That paragraph's final sentence, represented by **(B)**, provides the support.

(A) is a sentence from paragraph 2. It explains the rationale behind the current maintenance plan and does not support a criticism of that plan.

(C) contains an example of an extended service outage for one subway line. That's an illustration of the kind of problem the critics hope to avoid, but by itself does not support the claim in the correct answer to the preceding question.

(D) cites a line from the end of paragraph 5. It does not support the correct answer to the preceding question, but might be tempting if you chose (C) there.

7. D

Difficulty: Easy

Category: Vocab-in-Context

Strategic Advice: Check the sentence in which the word was used to determine the author's intended meaning. The correct answer can be substituted for the word without changing the meaning of the sentence.

Getting to the Answer: Here, the author uses "labyrinthine" to describe the New York subway system's complexity. **(D)** fits perfectly.

(A) means *underground*. That is true of the subway system, of course, but it would be redundant for the author to use "labyrinthine" in this way.

(B) plays off the famous labyrinth from Greek mythology, but this definition does not fit the word "labyrinthine" or the context of the sentence.

(C) suggests that the subway system is random or wandering. While the huge system may be difficult to navigate at times, it isn't random.

8. B

Difficulty: Hard

Category: Function

Strategic Advice: The phrase "serves to" tags this as a Function question, asking for the role a specific detail plays in the passage. Research the lines cited in the question stem to see *why* the author has included this example.

Getting to the Answer: The third paragraph introduces the first disadvantage cited by critics of the current subway maintenance schedule. The detail referenced in the question stem provides an example. That purpose is accurately described in the correct answer, **(B)**.

(A) misuses a detail from the passage. You're told that line switching—the problem being discussed—is particularly difficult for tourists, but that's not the reason the author included this example.

(C) refers to the rationale provided by supporters of the current maintenance plan in paragraph 2.

In (D), the word "quantify" suggests that the example provides numbers to show the impact of the current maintenance plan. That's something the author never does in this passage.

9. D

Difficulty: Easy

Category: Function

Strategic Advice: In this case, you're asked for the author's purpose for including an entire paragraph. Consult your margin notes to see the role of paragraph 5 in the passage.

Getting to the Answer: Paragraph 5 details some of the social and economic harms caused by shutting down subway lines. That matches **(D)**.

(A) distorts the purpose of the paragraph. The specific line—the L train—is given as an example of an extended shutdown, but the harms described in the paragraph apply to all similar extended service outages.

(B) is outside the scope of the passage. The author does not discuss the need for increased funding.

(C) refers to a proposal from paragraph 6. The author does not endorse that proposal and does not use paragraph 5 to support it.

10. A

Difficulty: Medium

Category: Detail

Strategic Advice: The phrase "[t]he passage indicates" shows this to be a Detail question. The correct answer will paraphrase a statement made explicitly in the text.

Getting to the Answer: The author discusses non–rush hour commuters in paragraph 5. He lists some examples of these commuters—"doctors, nurses, bartenders, police officers, and firefighters"—and explains that a cessation of 24-hour subway service could permanently alter their commutes. That matches choice **(A)**, the correct answer here.

(B) is the opposite of the what the passage says. The current system creates minor inconveniences for these workers when their subway lines are rerouted or closed for repair, but a suspension of 24-hour service would entail a permanent disruption.

(C) distorts the paragraph. Doctors and nurses are among the non–rush hour commuters, but that doesn't mean they are the majority of them.

(D) is outside the scope of the passage. The author does not discuss which occupations show the strongest support for a change in subway maintenance.

11. C

Difficulty: Hard

Category: Inference

Strategic Advice: For an open-ended Inference question like this one, predict the correct answer based on your big picture summary. Consider also any thesis statement or conclusion that sums up the author's point of view.

Getting to the Answer: This author outlines both sides of a debate and discusses the advantages and disadvantages to both the current subway maintenance plan and proposed alternatives. His conclusion at the end of the passage is neutral, encouraging the city to carefully consider all factors without advocating for a specific outcome. This matches up with the correct answer, **(C)**.

(A) strays beyond the scope of the passage. Be careful not to bring in bigger issues if the author has not discussed them in the passage.

(B) is too extreme. To be sure, the author considers subway maintenance a major issue but stops short of dire predictions like the one stated in this answer choice.

(D) matches the position of one side in the debate, but not that of the author, who remains neutral throughout.

How to Answer SAT Reading Questions

LEARNING OBJECTIVES

After this lesson, you will be able to:

- Research the answer in the passage or your big picture summary
- Predict the correct answer
- Find the one correct answer choice

Reading

To answer questions like these:

Directions: Choose the best answer choice for the following questions.

Questions 1–11 refer to the following passage and supplementary material.

This passage was adapted from an article titled "Millennials and the Market," written by a money management expert in 2018.

During the Golden Age of American manufacturing, it was expected that after putting in 30 to 40 years of tedious labor in a factory, workers
5 would be able to retire around age 65 and enjoy the benefits of retirement comforted by the thought that a pension and the Social Security system they had financed for decades would
10 cover their expenses. Unfortunately for millennials (people born between the early 1980s and late 1990s), prospects look increasingly bleak that they will get a return on their investment at
15 retirement age, despite continuing to fund programs like Social Security and Medicare. Fewer than a quarter of all Fortune 500 corporations still offer some form of pension plan to new
20 hires, and the move from company-funded pension plans to 401(k) plans and IRAs that began in the 1970s shows no sign of slackening. In this financial environment, it might be expected
25 that investment in the stock market would be at an all-time high. An analysis of the data, however, indicates a complicated and even fraught

Millennials won't have same retirement $

relationship between young adults and
30 the stock market.

The trauma associated with the Great Recession (which began in December 2007 and ended in June 2009) left many investors wary of stock
35 market volatility, and that hesitancy was exacerbated among young people, who saw a considerable portion of their families' wealth erased in short order. A study by Pfeffer, Danziger,
40 and Schoeni published in 2014 posited that the average American household lost a third of its wealth, approximately $28,000, during the Great Recession. This was at the exact moment when a
45 great many millennials were making decisions about attending college, pursuing post-graduate studies, or entering the workforce. For a median-income family, those decisions were
50 all directly correlated to household wealth. The ripple effects of the Great Recession left many millennials ascribing blame directly to the stock market for missed opportunities.
55 Even with a full awareness that the stock market has rebounded and far exceeded the highs seen prior to the Great Recession, many millennials still feel trepidation about investing in the
60 stock market, preferring to save a larger percentage of their salaries than their parents and grandparents did.

Reason: 07–09 recession = millennials blame the market

But they don't like stock market

Another factor that has directly impacted the willingness of millennials

65 to invest in the stock market is the seismic shift in the job market brought about by the "gig economy," in which short-term contracts and freelance work have replaced permanent

70 employment. To a large degree, the gig economy is still in its nascent phase, with many of the largest purveyors of jobs only incorporated in the last decade. Research has not adequately

75 kept track of the trend, with estimates of participation in the gig economy ranging from 4% to 40% in the United States. The ability to pick up work on a contingency basis allows

80 millennials to feel a greater level of control over their finances, something a significant number of them believe they cannot achieve through stock market investment. The increased

85 diversity of available methods for building future wealth has caused many millennials to adopt an a la carte approach to preparing for retirement. But is it possible that this approach

90 has been clouded by some common misconceptions about wealth building?

One persistent, albeit erroneous, view is that real estate is a better investment instrument than a stock market

95 portfolio. While it is true that home equity is the stepping-stone from which most individuals begin to build their personal wealth, statistics make it clear that stock market investments are a more

100 stable and lucrative source of long-term wealth. A London Business School study found that over the same 90-year period, the average rate of return on a real estate investment was 1.3% compared to the

105 9.8% annualized total return for the S&P stock 500 index. Investing the $5,500 IRS-imposed annual limit in an IRA for 25 years would result in a return of

Reason 2: gig economy = diff. ways to make $

Bad thinking: house > stock mkt

over $600,000 based on the annualized

110 return rate. Stock investment requires a smaller overhead than real estate investment, and the liquid nature of stocks makes them ideal for retirement: stocks allocated to retirement accounts

115 remain tax-free until they are drawn on. Despite these pieces of tangible evidence, though, the stigma regarding stock market investment persists in the minds of many millennials.

120 Regardless of their feelings about the stock market, one thing is self-evident: without preparation for retirement, millennials will be a generation adrift in a society without the social "safety

125 nets" available to current retirees. The benchmark for the amount of savings the average retiree needs to live comfortably after retirement, which remained at $1 million for many years,

130 now continues to rise, and exacerbating factors, such as the cost of medical care, continue to increase. Armed with that knowledge, millennials need to be proactive about financial planning. By

135 taking full advantage of their penchant for a hands-on approach to finances and leveraging the various financial technologies and services that were not available to the previous generation,

140 millennials can amass the wealth necessary to retire comfortably and on their own terms.

Millennials need to adapt their thinking to have retirement $

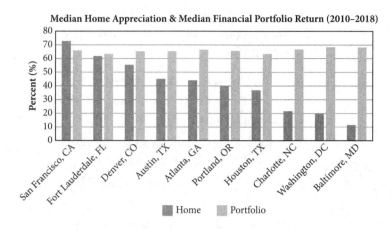

Median Home Appreciation & Median Financial Portfolio Return (2010–2018)

ROI of home owning vs. stock mkt

Reading

1. One central idea of the passage is that

    A) changes to social "safety net" programs such as Social Security and Medicare will force millennials to retire later in life than their parents did.

    B) investing in the stock market is the only money management strategy that will allow millennials to amass savings sufficient to retire comfortably.

    C) leveraging opportunities in the "gig economy" has allowed millennials to avoid the risks associated with investing in the stock market.

    D) despite their distrust of the stock market, millennials will need a variety of investment tools and strategies to build adequate retirement savings.

2. Which choice best describes the overall structure of the passage?

    A) A surprising attitude is introduced, two criticisms of it are offered, an alternative attitude is presented, and data proving the alternative is superior is provided.

    B) A surprising attitude is introduced, two reasons for it are described, a mistaken idea associated with it is revealed through data, and its effect on those holding it is assessed.

    C) A previously held attitude is presented, reasons for its rejection are offered, new data is presented, and those rejecting the old attitude are endorsed.

    D) Two reasons for a previously held attitude are presented, both reasons are rejected, and data is presented to introduce an alternative attitude.

3. According to the passage, large corporations are

    A) less likely to offer their employees pension plans than they were in the past.

    B) more likely to invest in the stock market than millennial individuals are.

    C) opposed to the gig economy because it reduces the number of permanent employees.

    D) skeptical that their current employees will receive their full Social Security benefit.

4. As used in line 38, "erased" most nearly means

    A) canceled.

    B) effaced.

    C) laundered.

    D) eradicated.

5. The passage most strongly implies which of the following statements about the Great Recession?

    A) It could have been avoided by continued funding of Social Security and Medicare.

    B) It impacted families with millennial-age children more severely than any other group.

    C) It resulted from misconceptions about the stability of stock market investments.

    D) It caused at least some millennials to forego their educational and career goals.

6. Which choice provides the best evidence for the answer to the previous question?

    A) Lines 10–17 ("Unfortunately . . . Medicare")

    B) Lines 39–43 ("A study . . . Recession")

    C) Lines 48–54 ("For a . . . opportunities")

    D) Lines 89–91 ("But . . . wealth building")

7. In the third paragraph (lines 63–91), the most likely purpose of the author's discussion of the "gig economy" is to

    A) argue that short-term contracts and freelance work are preferable to permanent employment.

    B) explain why millennials are unable to raise sufficient capital to buy a home.

    C) examine one factor in millennials' hesitancy to invest in the stock market.

    D) cast doubt on claims that up to 40 percent of workers hold short-term and freelance jobs.

8. In the context of the passage as a whole, the question in lines 89–91 ("But is . . . wealth building") primarily functions to help the author

    A) establish that millennials are mismanaging their retirement investments.

    B) show how professional money managers diversify their investments to avoid market volatility.

    C) introduce data that reveals a flaw in the premises that influence millennials' investment choices.

    D) call into question opposing opinions about the effects of the gig economy.

9. The passage indicates that investing in the stock market

    A) is the stepping stone from which most individuals begin to build personal wealth.

    B) remains less stable and lucrative than home ownership as a source of wealth.

    C) has tax implications well suited to retirement planning.

    D) is limited by IRS rules to a $5,500 annual maximum.

10. Which of the following statements about the period from 2010 to 2018 is supported by the graph?

   A) Investment in the stock market generated more wealth than home ownership in every market listed in the graph.

   B) The value of a home appreciated by a greater percentage in Portland, Oregon, than in Charlotte, North Carolina.

   C) The return on a median financial portfolio outperformed the value of home ownership by a greater margin in each subsequent year.

   D) Austin, Texas, saw a greater disparity between home value appreciation and return on financial portfolios than Atlanta, Georgia, saw.

11. Which statement from the passage is most directly reflected by the data presented in the graph?

   A) Lines 48–51 ("For a . . . wealth")

   B) Lines 74–78 ("Research . . . United States")

   C) Lines 98–101 ("statistics . . . wealth")

   D) Lines 110–115 ("Stock . . . drawn on")

You need to know this:

- Use clues to direct your research to a specific part of the passage or to your big picture summary:
  - **Line Numbers**—Reread the indicated text and possibly the lines before and after; look for keywords indicating why the referenced text has been included or how it's used.
  - **Paragraph Numbers**—Consult your margin notes to see the paragraph's purpose and scope before rereading the text. Sometimes your passage map alone is enough to find an answer.
  - **Quoted Text**—Go back to the passage to read the entire quote if the stem or answer choices use ellipses (. . .). Then check the surrounding context of the quoted term or phrase to see what the author meant by it in the passage.
  - **Proper Nouns**—Use your passage map or look for capital letters in the text to find the term, and then check the context to see why the author included it in the passage; note whether the author had a positive, negative, or neutral evaluation of it.
  - **Specific Content Clues**—Use your margin notes to help you search the passage for terms or ideas mentioned in the question stem; these clues will usually refer to something the author offered an opinion about or emphasized.
  - **Whole Passage Clues**—Begin by reviewing your big picture summary, and only go back to the passage if you can't find the information you need. If you do get stuck, the first and last paragraphs are typically the best places to go for global takeaways.
- Predicting what you're looking for in the correct answer saves time and reduces confusion as you read each choice.
- SAT Reading questions always have one correct answer and three incorrect answers:
  - The correct answer will match what the passage says in a way that responds to the task set out in the question stem.
  - Wrong answers often fall into one of five categories. Not every incorrect choice matches one of these types exactly, but learning to spot them can help you eliminate some wrong answers more quickly:
    - **Out of Scope**—contains a statement that is too broad, too narrow, or beyond the purview of the passage
    - **Extreme**—contains language that is too strong (*all*, *never*, *every*, *none*) to be supported by the passage
    - **Distortion**—based on details or ideas from the passage but distorts or misstates what the author says or implies
    - **Opposite**—directly contradicts what the correct answer must say
    - **Misused Detail**—accurately states something from the passage but in a manner that incorrectly answers the question

You need to do this:

The Method for SAT Reading Questions	
Step 1.	Unpack the question stem
Step 2.	**Research the answer**
Step 3.	**Predict the answer**
Step 4.	**Find the one correct answer**

- **Research the answer:**
  - When clues point to a specific part of the passage (line or paragraph numbers, quotations, content discussed only in particular paragraphs), begin by rereading the specified text and immediate context.
    - If the immediate context does not provide enough info to answer the question, gradually expand outward, rereading sentences that come before and after.
  - With whole passage clues or questions that seem to lack clear content clues, begin by reviewing your big picture summary.
  - If you can't figure out where to research the question and your big picture summary doesn't help either, consider using process of elimination, skipping the question and coming back to it later, or just making a guess.

- **Predict or characterize what the correct answer will say or suggest:**
  - Don't worry about phrasing your prediction as a complete sentence or about repeating exactly the language used in the passage. Just try to answer the question posed in your own words based on your research.
  - If you struggle to predict, use your active reading of the passage to characterize the correct answer, setting expectations about characteristics it must possess.
    - For example, if the author has a negative view of a topic in the question, expect a correct answer with negative language and eliminate choices that suggest a positive or neutral view.

- **Find the one correct answer:**
  - Identify the choice that matches your prediction, if possible.
    - Don't expect a word-for-word match, but look for a correspondence of ideas. For example, if you predict that the function of a detail is to "provide support for the main idea," an answer choice that says it "supplies evidence for the author's thesis" would likely be correct.
    - If there is no clear match, use process of elimination:
      - Eliminate any choice that contradicts your prediction or that clearly falls into one of the five wrong answer categories.
      - Choose the only answer remaining or guess among those you were unable to eliminate.

Reading

Answers and Analysis

Question	Analysis
1. One central idea of the passage is that A) changes to social "safety net" programs such as Social Security and Medicare will force millennials to retire later in life than their parents did. B) investing in the stock market is the only money management strategy that will allow millennials to amass savings sufficient to retire comfortably. C) leveraging opportunities in the "gig economy" has allowed millennials to avoid the risks associated with investing in the stock market. D) despite their distrust of the stock market, millennials will need a variety of investment tools and strategies to build adequate retirement savings.	**Answer: D** **Difficulty:** Easy **Category:** Global **Strategic Advice:** Answer Global questions based on your big picture summary. Sometimes, the author has already "boiled down" the central idea and summarized it in a sentence, usually near the beginning of or end of the passage. **Getting to the Answer:** The big picture summary captured the author's main point as it is expressed near the end of the passage: "Millennials are skeptical of investing in the stock market for several reasons, but they'll need a variety of investments to be financially secure at retirement." That matches **(D)** perfectly. (A) distorts the author's point. The author doesn't compare millennials' potential retirement *age* with that of their parents' generation. (B) is extreme. The author thinks millennials are too hesitant to use stock market investments, but concludes that their financial stability will come from a variety of financial technologies and services, not from the stock market alone. (C) is too narrow (the gig economy is discussed only in paragraph 3) and misstates the author's point about the gig economy, which is that it has encouraged millennials to "feel a greater level of control over their finances."

Question	Analysis
2. Which choice best describes the overall structure of the passage?	**Answer: B**

2. Which choice best describes the overall structure of the passage?

A) A surprising attitude is introduced, two criticisms of it are offered, an alternative attitude is presented, and data proving the alternative is superior is provided.

B) A surprising attitude is introduced, two reasons for it are described, a mistaken idea associated with it is revealed through data, and its effect on those holding it is assessed.

C) A previously held attitude is presented, reasons for its rejection are offered, new data is presented, and those rejecting the old attitude are endorsed.

D) Two reasons for a previously held attitude are presented, both reasons are rejected, and data is presented to introduce an alternative attitude.

Answer: B

Difficulty: Medium

Category: Global

Strategic Advice: Occasionally, a Global question will ask you to outline the overall structure of the passage. To answer a question like this, consult your big picture summary and review the notes you've jotted down next to each paragraph.

Getting to the Answer: In this passage, the author introduces a surprising opinion (millennials distrust the stock market), gives two reasons for their opinion (the Great Recession and the "gig economy"), points out an oversight in this opinion (the stock market is usually a better investment than home ownership), and concludes with an assessment of how that opinion needs to balance with other considerations (millennials will need a variety of investment strategies). That outline matches up nicely with the correct answer, **(B)**.

(A) starts off well but runs into trouble with "two criticisms of [the attitude] are offered." Paragraphs 2 and 3 explain *why* millennials distrust the market; those paragraphs don't criticize millennials for their point of view. The end of choice (A) is also problematic. The author offers data to show why millennials' attitudes toward the market are mistaken, not to prove an alternative opinion.

The beginning of choice (C) may be tempting because the author does provide background on older generations' expectations upon retirement, but the remainder of this choice wanders far from the structure of the passage.

(D) goes off course right from the start. This passage does not open with reasons for rejecting an older point of view on investing.

Question	Analysis
3. According to the passage, large corporations are A) less likely to offer their employees pension plans than they were in the past. B) more likely to invest in the stock market than millennial individuals are. C) opposed to the gig economy because it reduces the number of permanent employees. D) skeptical that their current employees will receive their full Social Security benefit.	**Answer: A** **Difficulty:** Easy **Category:** Detail **Strategic Advice:** "According to the passage" at the beginning of a question stem signals a Detail question. The correct answer will paraphrase something stated explicitly in the passage. **Getting to the Answer:** The author discusses large corporations in paragraph 1. She says that two-thirds of large corporations no longer offer pension plans and indicates that this trend is likely to continue. That supports **(A)**, the correct answer. (B) is an irrelevant comparison; the author never discusses how large corporations invest. (C) presents a misused detail; in paragraph 3, the author states that the gig economy has replaced permanent employment with short-term contracts and freelance work, but she does not mention corporate opposition to the gig economy. (D) distorts the passage; the author expresses concern that individuals will not have enough income at retirement despite their investments in Social Security and Medicare, but she does not ascribe this concern to corporations.

Question	Analysis
4. As used in line 38, "erased" most nearly means A) canceled. B) effaced. C) laundered. D) eradicated.	**Answer: D** **Difficulty:** Medium **Category:** Vocab-in-Context **Strategic Advice:** To answer a Vocab-in-Context question, examine the sentence in which the word was used for clues about how the author used the word. You can substitute the correct answer into the sentence without changing the sentence's meaning. **Getting to the Answer:** Here, the author uses "erased" to mean *lost* or *destroyed*. **(D)**, "eradicated," is the best fit for the sentence. (A), "canceled," carries with it the implication that there was a plan or expected event that was deleted from the calendar before it ever took place. The wealth "erased" by the Great Recession already existed; it wasn't canceled before it was created. (B), "effaced," usually refers to removing a sign or indication of something. That doesn't fit the context of money in a savings account or investment. (C), "laundered," may bring to mind the financial crime of "money laundering," but that has no logical connection to the sentence in the passage.

Question	Analysis
5. The passage most strongly implies which of the following statements about the Great Recession?	**Answer: D**

5. The passage most strongly implies which of the following statements about the Great Recession?

A) It could have been avoided by continued funding of Social Security and Medicare.

B) It impacted families with millennial-age children more severely than any other group.

C) It resulted from misconceptions about the stability of stock market investments.

D) It caused at least some millennials to forego their educational and career goals.

Answer: D

Difficulty: Medium

Category: Inference

Strategic Advice: The phrase "most strongly implies" marks this as an Inference question. The correct answer will follow from the passage without having been explicitly stated in the passage. The reference in the question stem to the "Great Recession" points you to paragraph 2.

Getting to the Answer: Paragraph 2 provides one reason that millennials distrust the stock market. Many millennials were considering college and career options when the market crashed in 2007, leading to the Great Recession. As a result, many of these young people blamed the market for "missed opportunities." This directly supports **(D)**.

(A) is outside the scope; the author does not draw a connection between the Great Recession and the two social programs named here.

(B) distorts the passage; while the author cites the damage that the Great Recession did to the "average American family," she doesn't compare the effect on families with millennial-age children to that on other groups of people.

(C) is outside the scope; the author does not discuss any causes of the Great Recession.

Question	Analysis
6. Which choice provides the best evidence for the answer to the previous question? A) Lines 10–17 ("Unfortunately . . . Medicare") B) Lines 39–43 ("A study . . . Recession") C) Lines 48–54 ("For a . . . opportunities") D) Lines 89–91 ("But . . . wealth building")	**Answer: C** **Difficulty:** Medium **Category:** Command of Evidence **Strategic Advice:** Use the answer from the previous question to evaluate the answer choices here. **Getting to the Answer:** The correct answer to the preceding question focused on how the Great Recession curtailed educational and employment opportunities for young people. That is substantiated by the text in **(C)**. (A) comes from paragraph 1 and cannot be used to support the answer to the preceding question. This choice may have been tempting to test takers who thought (A) was the correct answer to the previous question. (B) cites a study that quantified the harm done by the Great Recession, but that does not directly support the correct answer to the preceding question, which focused on missed opportunities for young adults at the time. (D) contains the rhetorical question at the end of paragraph 3; that's outside the scope of the previous question's correct answer.

Reading

Question	Analysis
7. In the third paragraph (lines 63–91), the most likely purpose of the author's discussion of the "gig economy" is to A) argue that short-term contracts and freelance work are preferable to permanent employment. B) explain why millennials are unable to raise sufficient capital to buy a home. C) examine one factor in millennials' hesitancy to invest in the stock market. D) cast doubt on claims that up to 40 percent of workers hold short-term and freelance jobs.	**Answer: C** **Difficulty:** Medium **Category:** Function **Strategic Advice:** Function questions ask you *why* an author included a specific piece of text or *how* she uses it in the passage. In this question stem, the identifying language is "most likely purpose." The research clue sends you back to paragraph 3. **Getting to the Answer:** Paragraph 3 opens with a clear-cut topic sentence: this paragraph will examine "[a]nother factor" that leads millennials to distrust the stock market. That factor is the rise of the gig economy and its effects on millennial attitudes toward money management. That leads right to the correct answer, **(C)**. (A) distorts the passage; the author expresses no preference for one kind of work or another. (B) misuses a detail from paragraph 4; one reason the author gives for considering stock market investment is its lower capital requirements. The author does not explain why millennials would have difficulty raising capital for a down payment on a home. (D) misuses a detail within paragraph 3; the author cites studies showing a range of gig economy participation, but her purpose is not to cast doubt on the high end of those claims.

Question	Analysis
8. In the context of the passage as a whole, the question in lines 89–91 ("But is . . . wealth building") primarily functions to help the author A) establish that millennials are mismanaging their retirement investments. B) show how professional money managers diversify their investments to avoid market volatility. C) introduce data that reveals a flaw in the premises that influence millennials' investment choices. D) call into question opposing opinions about the effects of the gig economy.	**Answer: C** **Difficulty:** Hard **Category:** Function **Strategic Advice:** Most Function questions use "serves to," but occasionally, they'll be as direct as this question stem, asking what a piece of text "functions to" do. The research clue in this stem points to the final sentence in paragraph 3. **Getting to the Answer:** By ending a paragraph with a rhetorical question, the author signals that the following paragraph will provide the answer. Paragraph 4 discusses the flaw in assuming that home ownership is a more stable or profitable investment than the stock market is. The question at the end of paragraph 3 helps the author set up this discussion, so **(C)** is the correct answer. (A) is extreme; the author questions one assumption underlying millennials' "a la carte" investment approach, but she doesn't accuse them of overall mismanagement. (B) is outside the scope. The pre-passage blurb suggests that this author is an investment strategist, but nothing in the passage claims to demonstrate professional approaches to reducing risk. (D) is outside the scope; the author doesn't present or contradict any opposing views in this paragraph.

Question	Analysis
9. The passage indicates that investing in the stock market	**Answer: C**

9. The passage indicates that investing in the stock market

A) is the stepping stone from which most individuals begin to build personal wealth.

B) remains less stable and lucrative than home ownership as a source of wealth.

C) has tax implications well suited to retirement planning.

D) is limited by IRS rules to a $5,500 annual maximum.

Answer: C

Difficulty: Medium

Category: Detail

Strategic Advice: A question asking for something that the "passage indicates" is a Detail question. The correct answer will paraphrase a fact, opinion, or claim made explicitly in the passage. Broadly speaking, the entire passage is about "investing in the stock market," but the author provides her most detailed analysis in paragraph 4, making it the best place to target your research.

Getting to the Answer: The bulk of paragraph 4 compares investment in the market favorably to home ownership. The author demonstrates the large return on a modest investment and then points out other reasons why they are well suited to retirement income. One of those reasons is the investments' tax-free status (lines 112–115); that matches the correct answer, **(C)**.

(A) is a misused detail; this answer choice virtually quotes the passage, but the piece of text it cites refers to home ownership, not to stock market investments.

(B) says the opposite of what's in the passage; the author demonstrates that the stock market is more stable and lucrative than home ownership is.

(D) misuses a detail contained in paragraph 4; the $5,500 annual cap applies to IRA contributions, not to stock market investments in general.

Question	Analysis

10. Which of the following statements about the period from 2010 to 2018 is supported by the graph?

    A) Investment in the stock market generated more wealth than home ownership in every market listed in the graph.

    B) The value of a home appreciated by a greater percentage in Portland, Oregon, than in Charlotte, North Carolina.

    C) The return on a median financial portfolio outperformed the value of home ownership by a greater margin in each subsequent year.

    D) Austin, Texas, saw a greater disparity between home value appreciation and return on financial portfolios than Atlanta, Georgia, saw.

Answer: B

Difficulty: Medium

Category: Inference

Strategic Advice: When a question stem says that the correct answer is "supported by" something in the passage, you're looking at an Inference question. It's no different when the support comes from a graph or chart at the end of the passage. Use the information in the graph to evaluate the answer choices.

Getting to the Answer: To see what is implied by a graph or chart accompanying an SAT Reading passage, make sure you understand what is being represented and look for trends. Here, the x-axis shows 10 different cities. For each one, the percent increase in value of a median-price home and a median-size stock portfolio are given on the y-axis. Only in San Francisco did the value of a home outperform the value of a portfolio of investments. Note that, along the x-axis, the cities are arranged from greatest increase in home value to least. The increases in stock portfolios, while all similar, are not in a particular order. Testing the answers against the graph reveals **(B)** as the correct choice. Charlotte is to the right of Portland on the graph, and you know that means its home values appreciated less than those in Portland.

(A) is contradicted by the case of San Francisco, the one market in which home ownership outperformed stock market investments.

(C) is not supported; the graph does not show year-over-year changes in value. This choice might be tempting to a test taker who glanced at the graph and made the unwarranted assumption that the x-axis represents different years instead of different locations.

(D) can be eliminated by comparing the two named locations. Stock portfolios outperformed home ownership in both cities, but the gap is a little smaller for Austin than it is for Atlanta.

Question	Analysis

11. Which statement from the passage is most directly reflected by the data presented in the graph?

   A)   Lines 48–51 ("For a . . . wealth")

   B)   Lines 74–78 ("Research . . . United States")

   C)   Lines 98–101 ("statistics . . . wealth")

   D)   Lines 110–115 ("Stock . . . drawn on")

Answer: C

Difficulty: Hard

Category: Command of Evidence

Strategic Advice: This question stem is relatively rare. It is a variation on the Command of Evidence question type. Here, instead of asking you to find the text supporting a previous answer choice, the question provides you with the evidence—in this case, it is the graph at the end of the passage—and asks you to find the text it supports.

Getting to the Answer: The graph compares the value of home ownership to stock market investment. The author made the same comparison in paragraph 4. Only **(C)** and (D) contain statements from paragraph 4, and a quick check shows that it is the text in **(C)** that follows from the data shown in the graph.

(A) comes from paragraph 2, which discusses the impact on millennials of the Great Recession. Don't get tripped up by the word "median" here; the sentence from paragraph 2 mentions median-income families, while the graph represents median-value homes and median-size portfolios.

(B) comes from paragraph 3, which discusses the gig economy. Always check the full reference in the answer choice; a hurried or sloppy test taker might see the words "[r]esearch" and "United States" and think that's enough to connect this answer to the graph.

(D) comes from the correct paragraph, but from a point at which the author has moved on from comparing home ownership and is now discussing other advantages of stock market investments as a source of retirement income.

Try on Your Own

Directions: Put the expert question strategies to work on the following passage. First, take a few minutes to refresh your memory of the passage (which you first saw in chapter 18). Then, for each question 1) identify the question type, 2) note where/how you will research the answer, 3) jot down your prediction of the correct answer, and 4) find the one correct answer.

PREDICTIONS

On the real test, you won't have time to write down your full prediction in complete sentences. If you feel the need to write something to help you hold on to your prediction, keep it very brief: a word or two, or even better, a single abbreviation. For example, if you predict that an author is including a detail as support for a broader point, you might just write "suppt" next to the choices.

Directions: Choose the best answer choice for the following questions.

Questions 1–11 refer to the following passage.

This passage was adapted from an article titled "Quantum Computing: Where Is It Going?" published in a science magazine in 2018. It discusses the background and potential of quantum computing.

Pharmaceutical companies dream of a time when their research and development process shifts from looking
5 for illnesses whose symptoms can be ameliorated by a specific drug to choosing a disease and creating a drug to eradicate it. Quantum computing may be the (key) to that goal. The (powerful)
10 modeling (potential) unlocked by quantum computing may also someday be employed by autonomous vehicles to create a world free of traffic jams. With plausible applications in so many fields,
15 it is worthwhile to learn a bit about how quantum computing works.

Any understanding of quantum computing begins with its most basic element, the qubit. In classical
20 computing, information is processed by the bit, the binary choice of zero or one. Qubits, (on the other) hand, allow for infinite superpositions between zero and one and thus can store and process
25 (exponentially) more complicated values.

QC: big potential

QC based on qubits – can store more values

Imagine showing someone where you live on a globe by pointing only to either the North Pole or the South Pole.
30 While you are likely closer to one pole than the other, you need additional information to represent your specific location. If, however, you could provide your home's latitude and longitude, it
35 could be located without any additional information. The power of quantum computing lies in the ability to express precise information in a single qubit.

Quantum computing may help
40 scientists and engineers overcome another barrier by reducing energy output while increasing computational speed. The positive correlation between energy output and processing speed often causes
45 classical computers to "run hot" while processing overwhelming amounts of data. Along with their ability to store multiple values simultaneously, qubits are able to process those values in parallel
50 (instead of) serially. How does processing in parallel conserve energy? Suppose you want to set the time on five separate alarm clocks spaced ten feet apart. You'd have to walk to each clock to change
55 its time. However, if the clocks were connected such that changing the time

Qubit > bit, much more data

Qubits = parallel processing

on one immediately adjusted the other four, you would expend less energy and

60 increase processing speed. Therein lies the (benefit) of the quantum entanglement of qubits.

While quantum computing has moved beyond the realm of the

65 theoretical, (significant barriers) still stand in the way of its practical application. One barrier is the difficulty of confirming the results of quantum calculations. If quantum computing

70 is used to solve problems that are impossible to solve with classical computing, is there a way to "check" the results? Scientists hope this paradox may soon be resolved. As a graduate

75 student, Urmila Mahadev devoted over a decade to creating a verification process for quantum computing. The result is an interactive protocol, based on a type of cryptography called

80 Learning With Errors (LWE), that is similar to "blind computing" used in cloud-computing to mask data while still performing calculations. Given current limitations, Mahadev's protocol

85 remains purely theoretical, but rapid progress in quantum computing combined with further refinement of the protocol will (likely result) in real-world implementation within the next

90 decade or two.

It is (unlikely) that early pioneers in the field, including Stephen Wiesner, Richard Feynman, and Paul Benioff, could have foreseen the (rapid progress)

95 that has been made to date. In 1960, when Wiesner first developed conjugate coding with the goal of improving cryptography, his paper on the subject was rejected for publication

100 because it contained logic far ahead of its time. Feynman proposed a basic quantum computing model at the 1981 First Conference on the Physics of

Faster AND 105 cooler

One barrier 115 to QC – how to check results?

Probably will get solved

QC pioneers – 1960s – 80s

Computation. At that same conference, Benioff spoke on the ability of discrete mechanical processes to erase their own history and their application to Turing machines, a natural extension of Wiesner's earlier work. A year later,

110 Benioff more clearly outlined the theoretical framework of a quantum computer.

The dawn of the 21st century brought advancements at an even

115 (more impressive) pace. The first 5- and 7-qubit nuclear magnetic resonance (NMR) computers were demonstrated in Munich, Germany, and Santa Fe, New Mexico, respectively. In 2006,

120 researchers at Oxford were able to cage a qubit within a "buckyball," a buckminsterfullerene molecule, and maintain its state for a short time using precise, repeated microwave pulses. The

125 first company dedicated to quantum computing software, 1QB Information Technologies, was founded in 2012, and in 2018, Google announced the development of the 72-qubit Bristlecone

130 chip designed to prove "quantum supremacy," the ability of quantum computers to solve problems beyond the reach of classical computing.

With progress in quantum

135 computing accelerating, it seems (inevitable) that within a few decades, the general population will be as familiar with quantum computing as they now are with classical computing. At present,

140 quantum computing is limited by the struggle to build a computer large enough to prove quantum supremacy, and the costs associated with quantum computing are prohibitive to all but

145 the world's largest corporations and governmental institutions. (Still,) classical computing overcame similar problems, so the future of quantum computing (looks bright.)

QC sped up in 2000s

QC still difficult, but bright future

1. The primary purpose of the passage is to

   A) argue that quantum computing will provide the solution to pressing societal problems.

   B) compare the speed and efficiency of quantum computing to that of classical computing.

   C) explain the progress and potential of quantum computing despite current obstacles.

   D) refute those who argue that quantum computing is too impractical and expensive to succeed.

2. According to the passage, which one of the following is true of Urmila Mahadev's graduate work?

   A) It was focused on ways to improve "cloud computing."

   B) Its results cannot be confirmed by classical computing techniques.

   C) It will likely have applications for the pharmaceutical industry.

   D) It may lead to verification of quantum computing calculations.

3. Which choice provides the best evidence for the answer to the previous question?

   A) Lines 1–9 ("Pharmaceutical . . . goal")

   B) Lines 67–73 ("One barrier . . . results")

   C) Lines 78–83 ("The result . . . calculations")

   D) Lines 83–90 ("Given . . . two")

4. In the second paragraph, the discussion of locating a person's home on a globe (lines 26–36) primarily serves to

   A) contrast the processing power of quantum computing to that of classical computing.

   B) illustrate the rapid progress of research in quantum computing.

   C) argue that quantum computing will allow for exponentially more complicated mapping software.

   D) support the claim that quantum computing will enable autonomous vehicles to navigate.

5. Based on the passage, the author would most likely criticize classical computing because it

   A) has developed more slowly than quantum computing in recent years.

   B) lacks any application for autonomous vehicles.

   C) employs serial processing.

   D) cannot verify quantum computing calculations.

6. Which statement best describes the technique the author uses to advance the main point of the third paragraph (lines 39–62)?

   A) She describes research done by leading scientists and engineers.

   B) She proposes a laboratory experiment that would prove a hypothesis.

   C) She offers a hypothetical example to illustrate a complex comparison.

   D) She cites data demonstrating the superior efficiency of one technique.

7. The passage indicates that which of the following factors slowed early developments in the theory of quantum computing?

   A) Feynman and Benioff were discouraged that their computing models were rejected.

   B) At least one academic journal was reluctant to publish papers containing advanced logic.

   C) Quantum computing was too expensive for colleges and universities to support effectively during the 1980s.

   D) A focus on cryptology in the early 1960s drew the most talented researchers away from quantum computing.

8. Which one of the following does the passage imply about the development of quantum computing in the 21st century?

   A) At least some companies anticipate commercial viability for quantum computing in the future.

   B) Recent advancements in hardware have demonstrated "quantum superiority."

   C) Research into quantum computing led to the discovery of the "buckyball."

   D) It has stalled due to reluctance of major corporations and governments to fund such expensive research.

9. Which choice provides the best evidence for the answer to the previous question?

   A) Lines 115–119 ("The first . . . respectively")

   B) Lines 119–124 ("In 2006 . . . pulses")

   C) Lines 124–133 ("The first . . . computing")

   D) Lines 139–142 ("At present . . . supremacy")

10. As used in line 123, "maintain" most nearly means

    A) sustain.

    B) repair.

    C) resupply.

    D) nurture.

11. The author's attitude toward the potential success of quantum computing can best be described as

    A) skeptical.

    B) resigned.

    C) incredulous.

    D) optimistic.

How Much Have You Learned?

Directions: Take 13 minutes to read the passage and answer the associated questions. Try to use the various SAT Reading question strategies you learned in this chapter.

Questions 12–22 refer to the following passage.

This passage was adapted from an article entitled "John Snow Knew Something" published in a popular history magazine in 2018.

Few would deny that doctors use critical thinking to solve problems, but most imagine a difference between the practice of medicine and, say,
5　the methods a police detective might use to solve a case. In fact, medical researchers have long used forensic methods of detection and analysis. The case of John Snow, a
10　19th-century anesthesiologist, is often said to have ushered in the modern era of epidemiology, the branch of medicine that tracks the incidence and distribution of diseases and
15　proposes solutions for their control and prevention.

It would not be until 1861 that Louis Pasteur would propose the link between microorganisms and disease,
20　now known as the germ theory. Before Pasteur's breakthrough, the predominant explanation for the cause of most illnesses was the so-called miasma theory, which held that noxious fumes
25　and pollution—quite literally, as the theory's name implies, "bad air"—were responsible for making people sick. Consequently, during the 1854 outbreak of cholera in Westminster, London,
30　doctors and government officials alike blamed "miasmatic particles" released into the air by decaying organic matter in the soil of the River Thames.

Despite the widespread acceptance
35　of the miasma theory, there were those,

Snow's work used investigation, changed medicine

1854 – didn't know about germs; miasma theory

Snow included, who were skeptical of this view. Snow would not have known, as doctors do today, that cholera is
40　caused by a bacterial infection, *Vibrio cholerae*. Nevertheless, he was convinced that the spread of the disease was caused by some form of matter passed between individuals, likely through contaminated
45　water.

To demonstrate this, Snow targeted a particularly deadly outbreak in the Soho district of Westminster in London. From August 31 to September 3, 1854,
50　127 people in the area died of cholera. Within a week, that number had risen to over 500. Snow took to the streets. Speaking to residents of the area, he found a commonality among them: most
55　of the victims had used a single public water pump located on Broad Street. Though he was unable to find conclusive proof that the pump was the source of the outbreak, his demonstration of a
60　pattern in the cholera cases prompted authorities to disable the pump by removing its handle. The epidemic quickly subsided.

Soon after the Broad Street pump
65　was shut down, Snow's continued investigation provided additional evidence that contaminated water was the source of the outbreak. Snow created a dot map of the cases of cholera in London
70　and demonstrated that they occurred in areas where water was supplied by two companies that obtained their water from wells near the Thames. Investigation of these wells showed that they had been dug
75　three feet from a cesspit that was leaking sewage into the surrounding soil. Snow also discovered that there were no cases of cholera among workers in a brewery close to the Broad Street pump.

Snow: cholera from contam. H_2O

Proof from interviews – all used same pump

Water from contam. wells

80 These workers were provided a daily
allowance of beer, which they drank
instead of water, and although the beer
was brewed using the contaminated
water, it was boiled during the brewing

*Boiling first
prevented
disease*

85 process. This revelation provided a
practical solution for the prevention of
future outbreaks.

   Snow is now hailed as the "father of
modern epidemiology," and the radical

90 nature of his approach—formulating
a new theory, substantiating it with
verifiable evidence, and proposing
preventative action—is fully
appreciated. At the time, however, not

*Snow not
accepted at
the time*

95 all were convinced, at least publicly, of
Snow's findings. As anxiety over the
outbreak flagged, government officials
replaced the handle on the Broad Street
pump and publicly denounced Snow's

100 conclusions. It seems they felt that the
city's residents would be upset and
disgusted to have the unsettling nature
of the well's contamination confirmed.
It wasn't until 1866, more than a decade

105 after Snow's original investigation and
theory—when another cholera outbreak
killed more than 5,500 residents of
London's East End—that officials
working in public health began to

*1866 –
another
epidemic*

110 accept the link between contaminated
water and certain kinds of illness and
to take appropriate actions to quell such
outbreaks.

12. The passage primarily serves to

    A) summarize the history of research into the causes and prevention of cholera.

    B) critique government officials for failing to consider evidence that could have prevented further loss of life.

    C) chronicle an episode in the history of medicine that changed the way in which research is conducted.

    D) demonstrate similarities in the methods used by medical researchers and by police detectives.

13. The author of this passage writes from the perspective of

    A) a public health official advocating for improved disease prevention measures.

    B) a journalist narrating medical history to lay readers.

    C) an editorial opinion writer critiquing the actions of local officials.

    D) a medical school professor explaining the techniques of epidemiological research.

14. The second paragraph serves mainly to

    A) suggest a reasonable alternative to a hypothesis presented later.

    B) outline the scientific and historical context for a problem that required a novel solution.

    C) summarize the conditions that led to a recurring public health issue.

    D) criticize the stubbornness of physicians and politicians against considering new evidence.

15. Which of the following is most analogous to John Snow's theory that contaminated water caused the cholera outbreak?

    A) Gregor Mendel described the principles of biological heredity years before the discovery of genes and DNA.

    B) Robert Koch used Louis Pasteur's experiments to develop the postulates of the germ theory of disease.

    C) Rosalind Franklin produced X-ray diffraction images of DNA, which were used by Watson and Crick to describe its structure.

    D) Galileo Galilei promoted a sun-centered model of the solar system but was put on trial because his views conflicted with those of the Spanish Inquisition.

16. Which choice provides the best evidence for the answer to the previous question?

    A) Lines 17–20 ("It would . . . theory")

    B) Lines 38–45 ("Snow would . . . water")

    C) Lines 57–63 ("Though he . . . subsided")

    D) Lines 85–87 ("This revelation . . . outbreaks")

17. The passage indicates that the main reason government officials rejected Snow's hypothesis was

    A) a lack of concrete scientific proof.

    B) a fear of public backlash.

    C) mistrust of Snow's methods.

    D) financial ties to the city's water suppliers.

18. Which choice provides the best evidence for the answer to the previous question?

    A) Lines 35–38 ("Despite the . . . view")

    B) Lines 57–63 ("Though he . . . subsided")

    C) Lines 68–73 ("Snow created . . . Thames")

    D) Lines 100–103 ("It seems . . . confirmed")

Reading

19. Which of the following is cited as the primary reason Snow suspected the Broad Street pump as the source of the epidemic?

    A) The discovery of decaying organic matter in soil near the Thames releasing gases into the air

    B) The decline of cases of the disease following the removal of the pump handle

    C) A pattern in the geographical location of cases of the disease

    D) A lack of cases of the disease among those working in a brewery near the pump

20. It can be reasonably inferred from the passage that scientists in 1855 would have found which of the following solutions to be most practical in dealing with future outbreaks of cholera?

    A) Using alcoholic beverages in place of water for all applications

    B) Removing the handles from all water pumps in the affected area

    C) Vaccinating the public against the disease using inactive *V. cholerae* bacteria

    D) Advising the public to boil all water from municipal sources before use

21. As used in line 97, the word "flagged" most nearly means

    A) subsided.

    B) indicated.

    C) penalized.

    D) peaked.

22. The author uses the final sentence of the passage ("It wasn't . . . outbreaks") at least in part to

    A) underscore the assertion that Snow's explanation of the cause of the epidemic was ultimately correct.

    B) demonstrate that an explanation of a phenomenon will not be accepted until after the mechanism behind it is fully detailed.

    C) suggest that there is often a significant delay between medical discovery and its application.

    D) lament the loss of life caused by failing to act on medical recommendations that are reasonably supported by evidence.

Reflect

Directions: Take a few minutes to recall what you've learned and what you've been practicing in this chapter. Consider the following questions, jot down your best answer for each one, and then compare your reflections to the expert responses on the following page. Use your level of confidence to determine what to do next.

Why do SAT experts research and predict the correct answer to Reading questions before reading the answer choices?

_____

_____

_____

What are the types of research clues contained in SAT Reading question stems?

_____

_____

_____

What are the five common wrong answer types associated with SAT Reading questions?

- _____
- _____
- _____
- _____
- _____

How will you approach the process of answering SAT Reading questions more strategically going forward? Are there any specific habits you will practice to make your approach to SAT Reading more effective and efficient?

_____

_____

_____

Expert Responses

Why do SAT experts research and predict the correct answer to Reading questions before reading the answer choices?

Expert test takers know that the correct answer to each SAT Reading question is based on the text of the passage. They research to avoid answering based on memory or on a whim. Predicting the correct answer before reading the choices increases accuracy and speed by helping the test taker avoid rereading, confusion, and comparing answer choices to one another.

What are the types of research clues contained in SAT Reading question stems?

Line numbers, paragraph numbers, proper nouns, quoted text, specific content clues, and whole passage clues

What are the five common wrong answer types associated with SAT Reading questions?

- *Out of scope*
- *Opposite*
- *Distortion*
- *Extreme*
- *Misused detail*

How will you approach the process of answering SAT Reading questions more strategically going forward? Are there any specific habits you will practice to make your approach to SAT Reading more effective and efficient?

There is no one-size-fits-all answer here. Reflect on your own habits in answering SAT Reading questions and give yourself an honest assessment of your strengths and weaknesses. Consider the strategies you've seen experts use in this chapter and put them to work in your own practice to increase your accuracy, speed, and confidence.

Next Steps

If you answered most questions correctly in the How Much Have You Learned? section, and if your responses to the Reflect questions were similar to those of the SAT expert, then consider answering Reading questions an area of strength and move on to the next chapter. Come back to this topic periodically to prevent yourself from getting rusty.

If you don't yet feel confident, review the material in How to Answer SAT Reading Questions, and then try the questions you missed again. As always, be sure to review the explanations closely.

Answers and Explanations

1. C

Difficulty: Easy

Category: Global

Strategic Advice: "[P]rimary purpose" indicates a Global question. Consult your big picture summary to predict the correct answer.

Getting to the Answer: The author is convinced that quantum computing has enormous potential despite current obstacles. She explains the basis of quantum computing, outlines its rapid progress, and describes efforts to make it practicable. **(C)** summarizes all of this and is correct.

(A) is too narrow and too strong. The passage opens with examples of problems that quantum computing may *help* solve, but this isn't the author's main point.

(B) is too narrow. The discussion of processing speed and energy output is included in paragraph 3 as one potential advantage of quantum computing.

(D) misstates the author's purpose. The passage was not written to *refute* an opposing point of view, nor does the author contend that anyone else is mistaken in their criticism of quantum computing.

2. D

Difficulty: Medium

Category: Detail

Strategic Advice: "According to the passage" indicates a Detail question. The correct answer is something stated explicitly in the passage. The research clue, Urmila Mahadev, leads you straight to paragraph 4.

Getting to the Answer: Paragraph 4 is about an obstacle to quantum computing: the paradox that arises from the fact that classical computing cannot be used to verify the results of quantum computing. How does Mahadev figure in here? Mahadev dedicated her graduate studies to trying to resolve this paradox. She has come up with a theoretical solution that the author concludes will likely have real-world application in the coming years. That final statement matches **(D)**, making it the correct answer.

(A) is a faulty use of detail. Part of Mahadev's protocol is similar to techniques used in cloud computing, but nothing indicates that she was trying to improve cloud computing.

(B) distorts the paragraph. It is the results of quantum computing that cannot be confirmed by classical computing, not the results of Mahadev's graduate work.

(C) brings in a detail from paragraph 1; pharmaceutical research is irrelevant to Mahadev's graduate studies.

3. D

Difficulty: Medium

Category: Command of Evidence

Strategic Advice: Questions that ask you to locate the evidence for the preceding question's correct answer are Command of Evidence questions. Use your research for the preceding question to put your finger on the relevant support from the passage and match that to the correct answer choice here.

Getting to the Answer: The correct answer to the preceding question said that Mahadev's graduate work would likely lead to verification of quantum computing results. That was from the end of paragraph 4, matching **(D)**.

(A) refers back to paragraph 1; this is irrelevant to Mahadev's work, but matches up with choice (C) in the preceding question.

(B) quotes the statement of the problem that Mahadev's work is trying to solve, but doesn't match the correct answer to the preceding question, which stated that her protocol will likely work.

(C) cites the description of Mahadev's protocol; this answer could be tempting if you incorrectly chose (A) on the preceding question.

4. A

Difficulty: Medium

Category: Function

Strategic Advice: The phrase "serves to" identifies this as a Function question. Check the context of the example cited in the question stem and identify *how* the author uses it.

Reading

Getting to the Answer: The second paragraph outlines why qubits (the basis for quantum computing) are so much more powerful than bits (the building blocks of classical computing). The hypothetical case of pinpointing one's house on a globe illustrates this contrast. Thus, **(A)** is correct.

(B) is off topic. The progress of quantum computing research is discussed in the fifth and sixth paragraphs.

(C) contains a distracting reference to "mapping software," which may remind you of a globe, but the author doesn't discuss software applications at all in this paragraph. Another potentially distracting phrase here is "exponentially more complicated," an exact quote from earlier in the paragraph. When evaluating answer choices in SAT Reading, look for the answer that matches the meaning of your correct-answer prediction, not simply for a choice with familiar words.

(D) inappropriately drags in an example—autonomous vehicles—from the first paragraph. The author does not connect that to the globe analogy in any way.

5. C

Difficulty: Hard

Category: Inference

Strategic advice: "Based on the passage" introduces an Inference question. The correct answer will follow from the passage without having been explicitly stated in the passage. Use the research clues in the question stem to narrow down your search and then consider the implications of what is stated at that point in the passage.

Getting to the Answer: The author compares classical computing unfavorably to quantum computing in paragraphs 2 (quantum computing can handle exponentially more complicated values) and 3 (quantum computing uses parallel processing to run faster with less energy output). Paragraph 3 directly supports the correct answer, **(C)**. Because parallel processing gives quantum computing its advantage, serial processing is the reason classical computing is inferior.

(A) distorts the author's point of view. She describes quantum computing's rapid advancement, but doesn't compare that to classical computing's development.

(B) is extreme. The author doesn't say that classical computing has *no value* for driverless cars, but rather that quantum computing may have great value for this technology in the future.

(D) is a faulty use of detail. This answer choice is true according to paragraph 4, but the author doesn't claim that this is a shortcoming of classical computing.

6. C

Difficulty: Hard

Category: Function

Strategic Advice: On occasion, the SAT will ask you to describe the way in which the author has made or supported a point in the passage. Research a question like this from the clues in the question stem. Be prepared for somewhat abstract language in the answer choices as they will be worded to describe the author's technique, not to recount the details in the paragraph.

Getting to the Answer: In paragraph 3, the author describes a potential advantage of quantum computing by comparing parallel processing in quantum computing to serial processing in classical computing. She illustrates this with the simple thought experiment about the five clocks. That matches the "complex comparison" and "hypothetical example" described in **(C)**.

(A) distorts the paragraph. Quantum computing, you're told, may help scientists and engineers, but doesn't mention any research by people in those occupations.

(B) distorts the author's example. She doesn't suggest that someone set up the five clocks in a laboratory and test them for efficiency.

(D) misses the paragraph entirely; the author doesn't cite any data here.

7. B

Difficulty: Medium

Category: Detail

Strategic Advice: The word "indicates" signals a Detail question. The correct answer will be something explicitly stated in the text. The research clue "early developments" should send you to paragraph 5 to research.

Getting to the Answer: Most of the details in paragraph 5 are positive and speak to a slow but consistent advancement in theorizing and modeling quantum computing. The one setback that is mentioned is the rejection of Wiesner's paper by an academic journal hesitant to publish logic that was "ahead of its time." That's described in the correct answer, **(B)**.

(A) distorts the paragraph, which does not suggest that Feynman's and Benioff's models were rejected.

(C) misapplies a detail from paragraph 7; the expense of quantum computing limits research today. You're told nothing about whether schools funded this research in the 1980s.

(D) contradicts the passage; Wiesner's interest in cryptology appears to have promoted his work leading to early quantum computing models.

8. A

Difficulty: Medium

Category: Inference

Strategic Advice: The word "imply" marks this as an Inference question. The correct answer will be supported by something in the passage's discussion of quantum computing's development in the 21st century.

Getting to the Answer: The passage focuses on the 21st century development of quantum computing in paragraph 6, which contains three main details: the demonstration of MNR computers, the Oxford research that caged a qubit, and the emergence of commercial interest in quantum computing. The last of those, as exemplified in the passage by 1QB Information Technologies and Google, supports choice **(A)** as the correct answer.

(B) distorts the paragraph; Google's Bristlecone chip is intended to prove quantum superiority, but the passage does not say that it has been used successfully.

(C) distorts what the passage says about the Oxford research; there, researchers used a "buckyball," but you're not told who discovered the molecule or when it was discovered.

(D) misuses a claim from paragraph 7; while it's true that quantum computing is very expensive, the last sentence of paragraph 6 contradicts the statement made in this answer choice.

9. C

Difficulty: Medium

Category: Command of Evidence

Strategic Advice: This is a standard Command of Evidence question asking you to locate the text that supports the correct answer to the preceding question. Use that answer to guide your research.

Getting to the Answer: The final sentence of paragraph 6 demonstrates that companies are pursuing quantum computing research. That matches **(C)**.

(A) comes from paragraph 6 but doesn't support the correct answer to the preceding question.

(B) describes the Oxford research; it might be tempting to a test taker who mistakenly chose (C) on the preceding question.

(D) comes from paragraph 7; it cites a hurdle that quantum computing must overcome.

10. A

Difficulty: Medium

Category: Vocab-in-Context

Strategic Advice: For Vocab-in-Context questions, check the sentence in which the word from the question stem is used to paraphrase its meaning in context. The correct answer could be substituted into the sentence without changing the meaning of the sentence at all.

Getting to the Answer: In the sentence at line 123, scientists have been able to maintain the state of qubit using an oddly named molecule. You don't need to understand the details of the process to get the gist of the sentence. The scientists are keeping the qubit in a constant, or stable, state. That matches the correct answer, **(A)**.

(B) doesn't work here because nothing suggests that the qubit was "broken" in the process.

(C) implies that the qubit loses something and needs to be refreshed or made whole; that doesn't fit the context.

(D) means to care for the development of, which would add information not implied by the sentence.

11. D

Difficulty: Medium

Category: Inference

Strategic Advice: A question about the author's attitude is a variety of Inference question. The correct answer follows from the author's opinions and points of view as they are expressed in the passage.

Getting to the Answer: The author concludes the passage on a high note. While acknowledging ongoing difficulties that quantum computing still needs to overcome, she finds it "inevitable" that it will one day be familiar to most people and explicitly states that the field's future "looks bright." Thus, **(D)** is correct.

(A) is too negative to describe this author's point of view.

(B) is also negative; a "resigned" attitude would indicate an author who has accepted an unfortunate result and has stopped fighting against it.

(C) means unbelieving. If the author were incredulous, she would deny that quantum computing could actually happen.

12. C

Difficulty: Easy

Category: Global

Strategic Advice: The phrase "primarily serves to" marks this as a Global question. Consult your big picture summary to predict the correct answer.

Getting to the Answer: For this passage, you can summarize the author's purpose as something like: "Narrate the story of how Snow's cholera research changed doctors' understanding and prevention of disease." That leads to the correct answer, **(C)**. The phrase "chronicle an episode" contains a verb that accurately describes the author's journalistic tone and focuses on the correct scope, a single event.

(A) is too broad; the passage does not attempt to sum up the entire history of cholera research.

(B) is too narrow; officials' rejection of Snow's findings the decade after the 1854 cholera outbreak is an unfortunate coda to the story, not the main point of the passage.

(D) is too narrow; the author mentions forensic evidence and investigation in the introduction to familiarize the reader with techniques that will be discussed.

13. B

Difficulty: Medium

Category: Global

Strategic Advice: This is a relatively rare variation on Global questions that asks you to describe the author's perspective. Consider your big picture summary, especially the author's purpose, to determine the role this author most likely fills.

Getting to the Answer: This passage centers on the story of Snow's cholera research to explain its importance for medical research. The author compares epidemiology to criminal investigation to provide context for the general reader. This leads to **(B)** as the correct answer.

(A) suggests a passage that would likely focus on a current problem and would use language intended to persuade the reader to adopt new policies.

(C) describes an article primarily focused on the mistakes of present-day politicians and bureaucrats.

(D) portrays an expert communicating scientific and technical details to an expert reader.

14. B

Difficulty: Medium

Category: Function

Strategic Advice: When a Function question ("serves . . . to") asks about the role of a paragraph, check your margin notes to see why the author wrote the paragraph and how it fits into the rest of the passage.

Getting to the Answer: Your note for paragraph 2 should indicate that this is where the author laid out the state of medical knowledge in 1854: doctors didn't know about germs; people still believed the miasma theory of disease. The author included this to show how innovative Snow's hypothesis and investigation were. That analysis leads to the correct answer, **(B)**.

(A) states the opposite of what the author intended; the beliefs outlined in paragraph 2 were unreasonable and soon rejected.

(C) distorts the passage; the conditions that led to the outbreak, such as wells dug too near cesspits, are discussed later in the passage.

(D) describes details the author introduces in paragraph 6, not paragraph 2.

15. A

Difficulty: Hard

Category: Inference

Strategic Advice: A question asking you to select a scenario "analogous to" one described in the passage is an Inference question. The correct answer follows from the passage without having been stated explicitly in the passage.

Getting to the Answer: The passage says that Snow hypothesized that cholera was spread by contaminated water even though he and his contemporaries were unaware of germs as the cause of diseases. Among the answer choices, the most appropriate analogy is the one described in **(A)**; Mendel described the workings of heredity even though he didn't know about its underlying structures, genes and DNA.

(B) may be tempting because it mentions Louis Pasteur—a scientist also mentioned in the passage—but it gets the analogy backwards; the situation described in this answer choice involves a scientist building on information already discovered.

(C) describes a situation in which a technological breakthrough (X-ray diffraction images) led to the refinement of a scientific theory; that doesn't match Snow's investigation, performed without the aid of technology.

(D) recounts a case in which social pressure was used in an attempt to silence a scientist; after Snow's discovery, some officials ignored his findings, but the passage does not imply that he was persecuted.

16. B

Difficulty: Medium

Category: Command of Evidence

Strategic Advice: This is a standard Command of Evidence question. Your job is to locate the passage text that directly supports the correct answer to the preceding question.

Getting to the Answer: The correct answer to the question immediately before this one suggested that an important aspect of Snow's theory was that he formulated the theory before scientists had discovered the biological mechanism explaining it. The author said this explicitly in the sentence quoted in choice **(B)**.

The sentence quoted in choice (A) discusses the germ theory of disease but does not directly discuss the fact that Snow would not have known about it.

The sentence quoted in (C) focuses on how Snow pinpointed the physical source of the cholera outbreak, not on how he formulated his initial hypothesis.

The text quoted in (D) explains how Snow's research helped find a way to prevent the spread of cholera; the question preceding this one focused on his theory of its cause, not prevention.

17. B

Difficulty: Medium

Category: Detail

Strategic Advice: The word "indicates" signals a Detail question. The correct answer will paraphrase something explicitly stated in the passage. Target paragraph 6 where the author discussed government officials' rejection of Snow's findings.

Getting to the Answer: The question stem asks for the "reason" officials ignored Snow's hypothesis. This is discussed in lines 94–103. The officials feared public outcry ("upset and disgusted") upon finding out that sewage had leaked into their water supply, a concern that **(B)** sums up succinctly.

(A) misuses a detail from paragraph 4: Snow persuaded officials to remove the pump handle despite a lack of "conclusive proof."

(C) distorts the passage; the author says that officials publicly rejected Snow's findings for political reasons but doesn't say that they doubted his methods.

(D) is outside the scope; nothing in the passage suggests that corruption played a role in the officials' decisions.

18. D

Difficulty: Medium

Category: Command of Evidence

Strategic Advice: This is a standard Command of Evidence question. Your job is to locate the passage text that directly supports the correct answer to the preceding question.

Getting to the Answer: The preceding question focused on why officials rejected Snow's findings. That is directly explained by the sentence quoted in choice **(D)**.

(A) quotes the first sentence of paragraph 3; this addresses Snow's rejection of the miasma theory, not officials' rejection of Snow's theory.

(B) quotes the end of paragraph 4 where the author explained that removal of the pump handle curtailed the cholera outbreak. Because this excerpt contains the phrase "unable to find conclusive proof," it may tempt test takers who mistakenly chose (A) in the preceding question.

(C) quotes a sentence from paragraph 5 that details further steps in Snow's research; it is unrelated to the officials' reactions to his findings.

19. C

Difficulty: Hard

Category: Detail

Strategic Advice: This is a Detail question asking for something "cited" in the passage. Direct your research to paragraph 4, where the author explains how Snow narrowed his search for the cause of the cholera outbreak to the Broad Street pump.

Getting to the Answer: According to the passage, Snow interviewed "residents of the area" and discovered that "most of the victims had used a single pump." That is summed up nicely in the correct answer, **(C)**.

(A) restates what those who still held the miasma theory of disease, not Snow, believed to be the outbreak's source.

(B) gets the order of events backwards; Snow's suspicions about the Broad Street pump *led* to the removal of its handle.

(D) also describes a situation Snow discovered *after* the pump handle was removed.

20. D

Difficulty: Hard

Category: Inference

Strategic Advice: The phrase "reasonably inferred" indicates an Inference question. The correct answer will follow from the passage without having been explicitly stated in the passage.

Getting to the Answer: At the end of paragraph 5, the passage states that Snow's "revelation"—that workers at the brewery near Broad Street pump boiled the water before using it to make beer—provided a way to prevent future outbreaks. Thus, **(D)** is the correct answer.

(A) is extreme; while the brewery employees were fortunate to avoid contamination, the passage does not imply that drinks containing alcohol could be universally substituted for water.

(B) is extreme; the result of this recommendation would be that no one in the city would have water, which would be untenable.

(C) might be a reasonable suggestion today, but the passage tells you that the bacteria was unknown in 1855.

21. A

Difficulty: Medium

Category: Vocab-in-Context

Strategic Advice: To answer a Vocab-in-Context question, check the sentence in which the word was used for clues about its meaning. The correct answer can be substituted for the word in the question stem without changing the meaning of the sentence.

Getting to the Answer: If you know that one meaning of "flag," used as a verb, is *decrease* or *lessen*, this question is straightforward. If you are unfamiliar with this definition, the logic of the sentence still leads to **(A)** as the correct answer. Officials would have replaced the pump handle at the point when public anxiety went down.

(B), "indicated," suggests a use of "flagged" that would be appropriate in a sentence like, "The teacher flagged the error with a sticky note." In the context of the passage, it does not make sense to say that "public anxiety" was flagged in this way.

(C), "penalized," might remind you of the way "flagged" is used to describe a referee's actions in a sporting event, but it is not appropriate for this sentence in the passage.

(D), "peaked," meaning *arriving at the highest point*, is opposite of the correct meaning; officials certainly would not replace the pump handle at the height of public anxiety.

22. A

Difficulty: Hard

Category: Function

Strategic Advice: A question asking how the author uses a piece of text—in this case, a specific sentence—is a Function question. Research the sentence in the context of the paragraph.

Getting to the Answer: The final paragraph of the passage opens with a statement of how Snow is now appreciated as an innovator. The heart of the paragraph then explains how political expediency led to a temporary rejection of his findings. The paragraph's final sentence brings you back to Snow's ultimate vindication, despite an intervening tragedy. **(A)** accurately describes the final sentence's purpose in the paragraph.

(B) distorts the passage; Snow's explanation was accepted because it was effective in preventing cholera, not because he fully explained the bacteria causing the disease.

(C) contradicts the passage; Snow's discovery was applied immediately when officials removed the handle of Broad Street pump.

(D) refers to the 1866 epidemic for the wrong reason; the author mentions this detail to explain what finally motivated acceptance of Snow's ideas, not to criticize the officials' actions.

CHAPTER 21

Paired Passages and Primary Source Passages

LEARNING OBJECTIVES

After completing this chapter, you will be able to:

- Apply unique strategies to effectively read SAT Reading paired passages in preparation for their question sets

- Apply unique strategies to effectively read SAT Reading passages based on primary sources in preparation for their question sets

- Identify the variations on common SAT Reading questions as they are used in paired passages

How Much Do You Know?

Directions: In this chapter, you'll learn to apply the SAT Reading strategies you learned in earlier chapters to paired passages and passages based on primary sources. Take a few minutes to read the following paired passages and answer the five accompanying questions. When you're finished, compare your work to the explanations on the following pages. Identify ways in which the expert reads these paired passages differently than she would a standard science or social studies passage.

Questions 1–5 refer to the following passages.

Passage 1 is adapted from a speech given by Senator Robert Y. Hayne in 1830. Passage 2 is adapted from a speech given in response by Senator Daniel Webster on the following day.

Passage 1

If I could, by a mere act of my will, put at the disposal of the Federal Government any amount of treasure which I might think proper to name, I should limit the amount to the
5 means necessary for the legitimate purpose of Government. Sir, an immense national treasuring would be a fund for corruption. It would enable Congress and the Executive to exercise a control over States, as well as over
10 great interests in the country, nay even over corporations and individuals—utterly destructive of the purity, and fatal to the duration of our institutions. It would be equally fatal to the sovereignty and independence of the States. Sir,
15 I am one of those who believe that the very life of our system is the independence of the States, and there is no evil more to be deprecated than the consolidation of this Government. It is only by a strict adherence to the limitations imposed
20 by the constitution on the Federal Government, that this system works well, and can answer the great ends for which it was instituted. I am opposed, therefore, in any shape, to all unnecessary extension of the powers, or the
25 influence of the Legislature or Executive of the Union over the States, or the people of the States; and, most of all, I am opposed to

those partial distributions of favors, whether by legislation or appropriation, which has a direct
30 and powerful tendency to spread corruption through the land; to create an abject spirit of dependence; to sow the seeds of dissolution; to produce jealousy among the different portions of the Union, and finally to sap the very
35 foundations of the Government itself.

Passage 2

As a reason for wishing to get rid of the public lands as soon as we could, and as we might, the honorable gentleman said, he wanted no permanent sources of income. He wished to
40 see the time when the Government should not possess a shilling of permanent revenue. If he could speak a magical word, and by that word convert the whole capital into gold, the word should not be spoken. The administration of a
45 fixed revenue, [he said] only consolidates the Government, and corrupts the people! Sir, I confess I heard these sentiments uttered on this floor with deep regret and pain.
I am aware that these, and similar opinions,
50 are espoused by certain persons out of the capitol, and out of this Government; but I did not expect so soon to find them here. Consolidation!—that perpetual cry, both of terror and delusion— consolidation! Sir, when gentlemen speak of the
55 effects of a common fund, belonging to all the States, as having a tendency to consolidation, what do they mean? Do they mean, or can they mean, anything more than that the Union of the States will be strengthened, by whatever
60 continues or furnishes inducements to the people of the States to hold together? If they mean merely this, then, no doubt, the public lands as well as everything else in which we have a common interest, tends to consolidation; and to
65 this idea of consolidation every true American ought to be attached; it is neither more nor less than strengthening the Union itself. This is the sense in which the framers of the constitution use

the word consolidation; and in which sense I adopt
70 and cherish it. . . .

This, sir, is General Washington's consolidation. This is the true constitutional consolidation. I wish to see no new powers drawn to the General Government; but I confess I rejoice in whatever
75 tends to strengthen the bond that unites us, and encourages the hope that our Union may be perpetual. And, therefore, I cannot but feel regret at the expression of such opinions as the gentleman has avowed; because I think their obvious tendency
80 is to weaken the bond of our connection.

1. In passage 2, Webster most likely refers to General Washington in order to

   A) make a colorful analogy.

   B) emphasize the precedent for his position.

   C) compare himself to Washington in order to seem more credible.

   D) emphasize the honesty of his position.

2. Which choice best characterizes how Webster responds to Hayne?

   A) He challenges Hayne's understanding of economics.

   B) He cites historical examples to show that Hayne's predictions will not come true.

   C) He finds a neutral path between his position and Hayne's.

   D) He attempts to turn a key word that Hayne uses against him.

3. Based on the ideas expressed in Passage 1, Hayne would most likely rebut Webster's claim in lines 61–67 ("If they mean . . . strengthening the Union itself") by stating that

   A) he (Hayne) does not wish the Union to have more money.

   B) it was a mistake to form a Union.

   C) the Union would weaken if the states were less independent.

   D) the Union will be more corrupt if the Legislative and Executive branches consolidate into one.

4. Which choice provides the best evidence for the answer to the previous question?

   A) Lines 1–6 ("If I could . . . of Government")

   B) Lines 6–7 ("Sir . . . corruption")

   C) Lines 23–24 ("am opposed . . . powers")

   D) Lines 32–35 ("to sow . . . itself")

5. On which of the following points do the writers of the passages express agreement?

   A) The Federal Government should not acquire new powers.

   B) The Constitution alone may not adequately address the current situation.

   C) Money can be a corrupting influence.

   D) The Federal Government is spending more than it can afford.

Check Your Work

Suggested passage notes:

Passage 1

¶1: (lines 1–14): Limit money of gov't

¶1: (lines 15–35): Gov't control of states = bad

Passage 2

¶1: Hayne would not allow gov't perm. income

¶2: Common fund, Consolidation = Strength of Union

¶3: Consolid. goes with Constitution, Washington

1.   B

Difficulty: Easy

Category: Function

Strategic Advice: Function questions ask you why the author included a given detail. Research the detail to help make a prediction, and if necessary, read any surrounding text to help put it in context.

Getting to the Answer: The reference to George Washington comes in the third paragraph. Both before and after the reference, Webster mentions the Constitution and how he wishes to abide by it. Thus, he intends for his ideas to be in the spirit of Washington and the Founders. (Keep in mind that appeals to documents and authorities are common in primary source passages.) Webster is using Washington as a precedent, or established guide, making **(B)** correct.

Washington is neither part of an analogy, nor is he compared to Webster, so eliminate (A) and (C). While you may have a sense of Washington as an "honest" figure, there is nothing in the passage that mentions his honesty, so eliminate (D).

2.   D

Difficulty: Medium

Category: Inference

Strategic Advice: You need to draw an inference about how Webster "responds to Hayne," so this is an Inference question. Expect the answer to relate to Webster's main point and consult your passage map for help.

Getting to the Answer: In the the first paragraph, Webster characterizes Hayne's position, explaining that it makes him feel "deep regret and pain." Primary source passages are explicit about their main ideas, so after reading this, predict that Webster will soon explain *why*

it makes him feel pain. He does so in the second paragraph, focusing on the term "consolidation." He explains that, no matter how much his opponents claim to fear it, it means "strengthening the Union itself." This matches **(D)**.

You could also get to the correct answer by process of elimination. Although Webster notes with humor that Hayne would not "convert the whole capital into gold" given the chance, he does not discuss Hayne's understanding of economics, so (A) is incorrect. While he mentions George Washington, he never uses historical examples to refute any predictions, so (B) is incorrect. Webster states his position quite strongly; this is no "neutral path," so (C) is incorrect as well.

3.   C

Difficulty: Hard

Category: Inference

Strategic Advice: For Inference questions asking how one author would respond to a claim made by the other, start by reading the claim. Then, look for clues in the other passage that indicate how its author would respond. The latter step is especially useful when the next question is a Command of Evidence.

Getting to the Answer: The claim is that consolidation—in this case, indicating a "common fund" for the government—will keep the people of the states together and "[strengthen] the Union." Go back to Hayne's passage for evidence of how he would respond to this. When discussing consolidation, Hayne valorizes "independence of the States," noting that "there is no evil more to be deprecated than the consolidation of this Government." Hayne would contend that consolidation would weaken the States' independence, and he concludes that this in turn would "sow the seeds of dissolution; produce jealousy among the different portions of the Union, and sap the very foundations of the Government itself." This fits **(C)**.

Choice (A) is incorrect because although Hayne wishes to limit the government's permanent revenue, this does not specifically refute Webster's claim about strengthening the Union. (B) is too extreme; while Hayne may wish to limit the federal government's power, he never indicates that the Union should never have existed. (D) distorts the passage. "Consolidation" in this context has nothing to do with the Legislative and Executive branches becoming one.

4. D

Difficulty: Hard

Category: Command of Evidence

Strategic Advice: Look back at your research for the previous question and determine what portion of text you used to support your answer.

Getting to the Answer: Your previous answer was supported with the phrase "sow the seeds of dissolution; produce jealousy among the different portions of the Union, and sap the very foundations of the Government itself." **(D)** is correct.

5. A

Difficulty: Hard

Category: Detail

Getting to the Answer: Hayne's main point is that the federal government should be limited to preserve States' independence. As much as Webster disagrees with Hayne, he actually concedes this point in his final paragraph: "I wish to see no new powers drawn to the General Government." **(A)** is correct.

Both writers would seem to disagree with (B), since they both regard the Constitution as an authority. While Hayne worries about the corrupting influence of money, Webster does not, so (C) is incorrect. You might be tempted by (D), since Hayne wishes to curtail the federal government's activities and Webster believes that it requires permanent income. However, there is not enough information in the passage to determine that the federal government is already spending more than it can afford.

Reading

How to Approach SAT Paired Passages and Primary Sources

Reading

> **LEARNING OBJECTIVES**
>
> After completing this chapter, you will be able to:
>
> - Apply unique strategies to effectively read SAT Reading paired passages in preparation for their question sets
> - Apply unique strategies to effectively read SAT Reading passages based on primary sources in preparation for their question sets
> - Identify the variations on common SAT Reading questions as they are used in paired passages

What are paired passages?

In every SAT Reading section, there is always exactly one pair of shorter passages that takes the place of a single longer passage. The two passages share the same topic (although they'll each have their own take on the subject matter). The combined length of the paired passages is approximately the length of most single passages, so you don't have much, if any, extra reading to do. In this chapter, you'll learn to read paired passages a little differently than you read single passages, and you'll see how the test uses variations of standard SAT Reading questions to test your comprehension of both passages.

What are primary source passages?

In every SAT Reading section, exactly one of the passages (or paired passage sets) is one in which the text is a primary source—a text written or recorded at the time of an event by people with firsthand knowledge of it (for example, laws, speeches, newspaper accounts, and essays). SAT experts expect the language in these passages to reflect an older and more formal style. In many cases, the documents express the strongly articulated position of its author or speaker.

Why learn paired passages and primary sources together?

The one set of paired passages in a Reading section often contain primary sources as their texts. While it is possible that you could see science material in a paired passage set, it's more likely that this is where the primary sources will appear, so it makes sense to practice the skills that apply to both categories of passages together.

To read passages like these and to answer their questions:

Directions: Choose the best answer choice for the following questions.

Questions 1 and 2 refer to the following passages.

Passage 1 is adapted from a speech (1852) by writer, reformer, and ex-slave Frederick Douglass. It was presented at an event commemorating the signing of the Declaration of Independence. Passage 2 is adapted from an essay (1836) by political activist Angelina Emily Grimké. Both writers were active in the abolitionist, or anti-slavery, movement.

Passage 1

O! had I the ability, and could I reach the nation's ear, I would, to-day, pour out a fiery stream of biting ridicule, blasting reproach, withering sarcasm, and stern rebuke. For it is
5 not light that is needed, but fire; it is not the gentle shower, but thunder. We need the storm, the whirlwind, and the earthquake. The feeling of the nation must be quickened; the conscience of the nation must be roused; the propriety of
10 the nation must be startled; the hypocrisy of the nation must be exposed; and its crimes against God and man must be proclaimed and denounced.

What, to the American slave, is your 4th
15 of July? I answer: a day that reveals to him, more than all other days in the year, the gross injustice and cruelty to which he is the constant victim. To him, your celebration is a sham; your boasted liberty, an unholy license;
20 your national greatness, swelling vanity; your sounds of rejoicing are empty and heartless; your denunciations of tyrants, brass fronted impudence; your shouts of liberty and equality, hollow mockery; your prayers and hymns,
25 your sermons and thanksgivings, with all your religious parade, and solemnity, are, to him, mere bombast, fraud, deception, impiety, and hypocrisy—a thin veil to cover up crimes which would disgrace a nation of savages. There is not
30 a nation on the earth guilty of practices, more

shocking and bloody, than are the people of these United States, at this very hour.

Go where you may, search where you will, roam through all the monarchies and despotisms
35 of the old world, travel through South America, search out every abuse, and when you have found the last, lay your facts by the side of the everyday practices of this nation, and you will say with me, that, for revolting barbarity and shameless
40 hypocrisy, America reigns without a rival.

Passage 2

The women of the South can overthrow this horrible system of oppression and cruelty, licentiousness and wrong. Such appeals to your legislatures would be irresistible, for there is
45 something in the heart of man which will bend under moral suasion. There is a swift witness for truth in his bosom, which will respond to truth when it is uttered with calmness and dignity. If you could obtain but six signatures
50 to such a petition in only one state, I would say, send up that petition, and be not in the least discouraged by the scoffs, and jeers of the heartless, or the resolution of the house to lay it on the table. It will be a great thing if the subject
55 can be introduced into your legislatures in any way, even by women, and they will be the most likely to introduce it there in the best possible manner, as a matter of morals and religion, not of expediency or politics. You may petition, too, the
60 different ecclesiastical bodies of the slave states. Slavery must be attacked with the whole power of truth and the sword of the spirit.

1. Which best describes the overall relationship between the two passages?

    A) Passage 2 provides a restatement of Passage 1's central claims.

    B) Passage 2 describes specific steps that could address a problem described in Passage 1.

    C) Passage 2 contests the point of view expressed in Passage 1.

    D) Passage 2 contains additional evidence that could support the claims made in Passage 1.

2. Based on Passage 2, Grimké would most likely offer which of the following responses to Douglass's statement in lines 7–13 ("The feeling . . . denounced")?

    A) Women will be the most effective agents of Douglass's call to action.

    B) The nation's conscience is too hardened to embrace Douglass's rhetoric.

    C) The most effective way to communicate Douglass's message is to highlight the plight of female slaves.

    D) Douglass's critique of the United States is too political to be delivered by women.

You'll need to know this:

About Paired Passages

- Paired passages always address the same topic but will likely have different purposes and may reflect different opinions. Common relationships between the passages include:
  - (Passage 1) One side in a debate over a policy, a moral or ethical issue, or the role of government and (Passage 2) the other side of that debate
  - (Passage 1) A law or a policy proposal and (Passage 2) a commentary on or evaluation of the law or proposal (especially from a person affected by the law or policy)
  - (Passage 1) A report on an event or conflict and (Passage 2) a speech or document from a person involved in the event or conflict
  - (Passage 1) Commentary on an issue as reflected through one social context and (Passage 2) commentary on the same issue reflected through a different context
- The authors of paired passages may disagree with each other but do not have to.
- When paired passages refer to the same detail, each author may have a different reason for including the detail and a different point of view toward it.

About Primary Source Passages

- The SAT always identifies the author(s)/speaker(s) and the date(s) of primary source texts in the blurb introducing the passage(s).
- The main point (thesis or conclusion) of the author/speaker is usually explicitly stated in a primary source text.
- Authors/speakers in primary source texts often support their positions with appeals to broad, abstract concepts (e.g., divine law, natural law, human rights, the common good, dignity, or progress).
- The test never asks if an author's or speaker's opinion is correct (or, in the case of paired passages with primary source texts, which author's position or argument is better).

About Paired Passage Questions

- The question set accompanying paired passages addresses the passages in order: roughly, the first third of the questions are about Passage 1, the next third are about Passage 2, and the final third are about the relationships between the two passages.
- The questions that address single passages are just like those from standard science and social science passages.
- Some questions that address the relationships between the passages are variations on standard SAT Reading question types. For example:
  - **Global**
    - "The primary purpose of each passage is to"
  - **Detail**
    - "Both passages discuss the role of the judiciary in relationship to"

- **Inference**
  - "Based on the passages, both authors would agree with which of the following claims?"
  - "Both authors would most likely agree that the expansion of enfranchisement reflects"
- **Function**
  - "In the context of each passage as a whole, the examples in lines 30–34 of Passage 1 and lines 60–63 of Passage 2 primarily function to help each speaker"
- Other questions are intentionally written to test how accurately you can compare or contrast the two passages or their authors. For example:
  - **Global**
    - "Which choice best states the relationship between the two passages?"
    - "Which choice identifies a central tension between the two passages?"
  - **Inference**
    - "How would the authors of Passage 1 most likely respond to the points made in the final paragraph of Passage 2?"
    - "Madison in Passage 1 would most likely characterize the position taken by Hancock in lines 71–79 in Passage 2 ("Manners, by which . . . memory") as"
    - "Stanton would most likely have reacted to lines 69–72 ("Therefore . . . without fail") of Passage 2 with"

You'll need to do this:

To Actively Read Paired Passages

- Unpack the blurb to discover all that you can about each passage and author; anticipate the possible relationships between the passages.
- Manage your active reading and the question set strategically:
  - Actively read Passage 1 as you would a standard passage—note keywords, jot down the purpose of each paragraph, and summarize the big picture.
  - Answer the questions associated exclusively with Passage 1 (roughly, the first third of the question set).
  - Actively read Passage 2 as you would a standard passage—note keywords, jot down the purpose of each paragraph, and summarize the big picture.
  - Answer the questions associated exclusively with Passage 2 (roughly, the next third in the question set).
  - Answer the questions that ask about both passages in relationship to each other (the final third in the question set).

To Actively Read Primary Source Passages

- Unpack the opening blurb to identify the author(s) and historical time period of the passage(s).
- If you know something about the author(s), issue, or historical period, use that knowledge to anticipate what the passage(s) will say. However:
  - Be careful not to answer questions based on your outside knowledge.
  - The correct answers must be supported by the passage text.

- Actively read the passage as you would a standard social science passage, keeping the following in mind:
  - Don't be discouraged if a primary source text contains antiquated or formal language; define unfamiliar words from context.
  - Locate the author's/speaker's main point (it may be a thesis statement near the beginning of the passage or a concluding summary near the end); if you could boil down the author's position to a single sentence, which one would it be?
  - Note where and how the author/speaker supports the main point.

To Strategically Answer Paired Passages Questions

- Research, predict, and answer questions exclusively addressing one of the passages as you would any standard SAT Reading question.
- To predict and answer Global questions comparing or contrasting both passages, consider your big picture summaries.
- To research, predict, and answer Inference questions comparing or contrasting both passages:
  - Locate the piece of text at issue in the question stem.
  - Consider the other author's likely reaction to or opinion of that piece of text.
  - Especially if the Inference question is followed by a Command of Evidence question, locate the piece of text that supplies the "other author's" likely response. For example, consider this question stem: "Madison in Passage 1 would most likely characterize the position taken by Hancock in lines 71–79 in Passage 2 ("Manners, by which . . . memory") as"
    - First, research the Hancock text from Passage 2 quoted in the question stem. What does it mean? What is Hancock's point?
    - Second, consider what you know about Madison's likely response. Would he agree or disagree with Hancock's point? Why or why not?
    - Third, put your finger on the text in Passage 1 that supports Madison's likely response.

Explanation:

Question 1. This Global question asks you to determine the "overall relationship" between the passages. Consult your passage notes to determine how the passages relate. As you might expect, given the blurb, each writer expresses a strong anti-slavery sentiment. However, while the first passage deals more with the injustices of slavery in the United States, the second focuses more on specific plans to change relevant law ("If you could obtain but six signatures to such a petition . . ."). Therefore, it's accurate to say that Passage 2 "describes specific steps that could address a problem described in Passage 1," **(B)**.

Question 2. This Inference question asks you for the choice that captures Grimké's likely response to Douglass's call to arouse the nation's consciousness in paragraph 1 of Passage 1. The thesis of Grimké's passage is that women can overthrow slavery and, she says, "they will be the most likely to introduce [anti-slavery petitions] in the best possible manner" (lines 56–58). Thus, she seems to believe that women are the most effective messengers for the kinds of critiques Douglass recommends. That matches choice **(A)**.

Choice (B) contradicts Grimké's hopeful attitude toward change. (C) distorts Grimké's suggestion; she thinks women should be the ones to call for an end to slavery, not that focusing on female slaves is the best way to do so. (D) distorts Grimké's point in lines 58–59; she says that, coming from women, the anti-slavery message will be seen as moral and religious rather than political, but her comment does not imply a critique of Douglass's clearly moral message as being political in nature.

Try on Your Own

Directions: Actively read these paired primary source passages and answer their accompanying questions. Try to employ the unique reading strategies experts use for paired passages and primary source texts. Take note of any question stems that are specifically tailored to fit paired passages so that you can research, predict, and answer them strategically.

Questions 1–10 refer to the following passages.

Passage 1 is adapted from Federalist Paper No. 64 (1788), by John Jay, in which he discusses the powers of the president and the Senate to form treaties under Article II of the Constitution. Passage 2 is adapted from Federalist Paper No. 75 (1788), by Alexander Hamilton, on the same subject.

Passage 1

The second section gives power to the President, *"by and with the advice and consent of the Senate, to make treaties, provided two thirds of the Senators present concur . . . "*

5 Some are displeased with it, not on account of any errors or defects in it, but because they say the treaties will have the force of laws, and thus should be made only by the legislature. These gentlemen seem not

10 to consider that the judgement of our courts, and the commissions constitutionally given by our governor, are as valid and as binding on all persons whom they concern as the laws passed by our legislature. All constitutional

15 acts of power, whether in the executive or in the judicial department, have as much legal validity and obligation as if they proceeded from the legislature. It surely does not follow that because the people have given the power

20 of making laws to the legislature, they should therefore likewise give the legislature the power to do every other act of government by which the citizens are to be bound and affected.

Passage 2

The President is to have power, "by and

25 with the advice and consent of the Senate, to make treaties, provided two thirds of the senators present concur." . . .

Though several writers on the subject of government place the power of making

30 treaties in the class of executive authorities, this is evidently an arbitrary classification; for if we attend carefully to its operation, it will be found to partake more of the legislative than of the executive character, though it does

35 not seem strictly to fall within the definition of either of them. The essence of the legislative branch is to enact laws, or, in other words, to prescribe rules for the regulation of the society; while the execution of the laws, and

40 the employment of the common strength, either for this purpose or for the common defense, seem to comprise all the functions of the executive branch. The power of making treaties is, plainly, neither the one nor the

45 other. It relates neither to the execution of the existing laws, nor to the creation of new ones; and still less to an exertion of the common strength. Its objects are CONTRACTS with foreign nations, which have the force of law,

50 but derive it from the obligations of good faith. They are not rules prescribed by the government of the citizen, but agreements between two governments. The power in question seems therefore to form a distinct

55 department, and to belong, properly, neither to the legislative nor to the executive branch. The qualities elsewhere detailed as indispensable in the management of foreign negotiations point to the Executive as the best agent in

60 those transactions; while the vast importance of the trust, and the operation of treaties as laws, plead strongly for the participation of the whole or a portion of the legislative body in the office of making them.

1. Jay includes the reasoning of those who are displeased with the president's treaty-making power (lines 5–9) in order to

   A) provide an opposing conclusion that gives context for his own argument.

   B) acknowledge flaws and defects in Article II of the Constitution.

   C) explain the importance of the legislature in creating laws that impact citizens.

   D) support his own opinions about judicial and executive authority.

2. What does Passage 1 suggest about Jay's opponents' opinion of the second section of Article II of the Constitution?

   A) Jay's opponents' criticisms of the second section would be legitimate if the second section contained errors and defects.

   B) Jay's opponents think anything having the same force as a law is, in effect, a law.

   C) Jay's opponents perceive the legislature as the only branch that should act in ways that legally bind citizens.

   D) Jay's opponents agree with Jay that the legislature should be empowered to enact all duties of government.

3. Which choice provides the best evidence for the answer to the previous question?

   A) Lines 5–9 ("Some are . . . legislature")

   B) Lines 9–14 ("These gentlemen . . . legislature")

   C) Lines 14–18 ("All constitutional . . . legislature")

   D) Lines 18–23 ("It surely . . . affected")

4. Based on Passage 2, it can be inferred that Hamilton would agree with which of the following statements?

   A) Most writers on the subject of government fail to provide evidence sufficient to support their conclusions.

   B) Citizens should not be bound by agreements between one government and another.

   C) Any power that is not properly described as judicial or legislative must be an executive power.

   D) At least some writers on the subject of government reach unsubstantiated conclusions about the scope of executive authority.

5. Which choice provides the best evidence for the answer to the previous question?

   A) Lines 28–31 ("Though several . . . classification")

   B) Lines 36–39 ("The essence . . . society")

   C) Lines 48–51 ("Its objects . . . faith")

   D) Lines 60–64 ("while the . . . them")

6. As used in line 33, "partake" most nearly means

   A) consume.

   B) share.

   C) receive.

   D) savor.

7. As used in line 64, "office" most nearly means

   A) bureaucracy.

   B) workplace.

   C) commission.

   D) situation.

8. Which choice best states the relationship between the two passages?

   A) Both passages refute different points using different evidence but reach the same conclusion.

   B) Passage 2 and Passage 1 examine different but related propositions.

   C) Passage 2 questions assumptions made by the author of Passage 1.

   D) Passages 1 and 2 use different examples to illustrate the same reasoning.

9. Based on Passage 2, how would Hamilton most likely respond to Jay's statement that the decisions of the judicial and executive branches "are as valid and as binding on all persons whom they concern as the laws passed by our legislature" (lines 12–14)?

   A) Hamilton would agree that all non-legislative rules are legitimately binding, and he would agree about the source of that power.

   B) Hamilton would disagree that treaties are as valid as laws passed by the legislature because treaties are contracts.

   C) Hamilton would agree that at least some rules prescribed by the executive branch are just as valid as those issued from the legislature.

   D) Hamilton would disagree with Jay's contention that judicial decisions are as valid as laws passed by the legislature.

10. In Passage 1, Jay's statement at lines 7–9 ("they say . . . legislature") and in Passage 2, Hamilton's statement at lines 36–39 ("The essence . . . society") both serve to help the authors

    A) argue that the power to make treaties should reside exclusively with the legislature.

    B) critique those who place the power to make treaties in the class of executive authorities.

    C) define the widely accepted role of the legislative branch to make laws.

    D) support the contention that treaties carry the same legal authority as laws.

How Much Have You Learned?

Directions: Now, complete a similar assessment under timed conditions. Take 12 minutes to read the passage and answer the accompanying questions

Questions 11–21 refer to the following passages.

Passage 1 is adapted from an 1823 speech by President James Monroe, in which he discusses European colonialism in the Americas. The position expressed in this speech would eventually become known as the Monroe Doctrine. Passage 2 is adapted from a 1905 speech by President Theodore Roosevelt. His position would become known as the Roosevelt Corollary to the Monroe Doctrine.

Passage 1

The American continents, by the free and independent condition which they have assumed and maintain, are hence forth not to be considered as subjects for future
5 colonization by any European powers.

The citizens of the United States cherish friendly sentiments in favor of the liberty and happiness of their fellow men on the European side of the Atlantic. In the wars of
10 the European powers in matters relating to themselves we have never taken any part, nor does it comport with our policy to do so.

It is only when our rights are invaded or seriously menaced that we resent injuries
15 or make preparation for our defense. With the movements in our own hemisphere we are more immediately connected, by causes which must be obvious to all enlightened and impartial observers.
20 We owe it, therefore, to candor and to the amicable relations existing between the United States and European nations to declare that we should consider any attempt on their part to extend their system of government to
25 any portion of this hemisphere as dangerous to our peace and safety. With the existing colonies or dependencies of any European power we have not interfered and shall not interfere. However, we could not view

30 any meddling with those former European colonies who have declared their independence and maintained it, and whose independence we have, on great consideration and on just principles, acknowledged, in any other light
35 than as the manifestation of an unfriendly disposition toward the United States.

Passage 2

It is not true that the United States feels any land hunger or entertains any projects regarding the other nations of the Western
40 Hemisphere except for their welfare. All that this country desires is to see our neighboring countries stable, orderly, and prosperous. Any country whose people conduct themselves well can count upon our hearty friendship.
45 If a nation shows that it knows how to act with reasonable efficiency and decency in social and political matters, if it keeps order and pays its obligations, it need not fear interference from the United States. However,
50 chronic wrongdoing, or an impotence which results in a general loosening of the ties of civilized society, may in America, as elsewhere, ultimately require intervention. . . . In the Western Hemisphere, the adherence of
55 the United States to the Monroe Doctrine may force the United States, however reluctantly, in flagrant cases of such wrongdoing or impotence, to the exercise of an international police power. If every country washed by
60 the Caribbean Sea would show the progress in stable and just civilization which Cuba has shown since our troops left the island, and which so many of the republics in both Americas are constantly and brilliantly
65 showing, all question of interference by this Nation with their affairs would be at an end. Our interests and those of our southern neighbors are in reality identical. They have great natural riches, and if within their
70 borders the reign of law and justice obtains, prosperity is sure to come to them. While

they thus obey the primary laws of civilized society, they may rest assured that they will be treated by us in a spirit of cordial and helpful
75 sympathy. We would interfere with them only in the last resort, and then only if it became evident that their inability or unwillingness to do justice at home and abroad had violated the rights of the United States or had invited foreign
80 aggression to the detriment of the entire body of American nations. Every nation, whether in America or anywhere else, which desires to maintain its freedom and independence must ultimately realize that the right of such
85 independence can not be separated from the responsibility of making good use of it.

11. The primary purpose of the statement in lines 6–9 ("The citizens . . . of the Atlantic") is to

A) respond to critics of the United States.

B) mislead the audience regarding Monroe's intent.

C) recommend that people adopt a certain attitude.

D) balance the overall tone of the message.

12. When discussing his views on foreign policy in Passage 1, Monroe indicates that the United States does not intend to

A) prevent further European colonization in the Americas.

B) intervene in conflicts that exist solely between European powers.

C) maintain a friendly relationship with European powers.

D) allow European powers to keep their existing colonies in the Americas.

13. Which choice provides the best evidence for the answer to the previous question?

A) Lines 9–12 ("In the . . . do so")

B) Lines 15–19 ("With the . . . observers")

C) Lines 20–26 ("We owe . . . safety")

D) Lines 29–36 ("However . . . States")

14. According to Roosevelt in Passage 2, what circumstance must exist before the United States may justifiably interfere with the affairs of another nation in the Western Hemisphere?

A) The other nation must have been invaded by a foreign power.

B) The other nation must have invaded a foreign power.

C) The other nation must have harmed the United States.

D) The other nation must have committed human rights abuses.

15. Which choice provides the best evidence for the answer to the previous question?

    A) Lines 42–44 ("Any country . . . friendship")

    B) Lines 59–67 ("If every . . . end")

    C) Lines 68–71 ("They have . . . them")

    D) Lines 75–81 ("We would . . . nations")

16. As used in line 59, "washed" most nearly means

    A) cleaned.

    B) overwhelmed.

    C) touched.

    D) bathed.

17. As used in line 70, "obtains" most nearly means

    A) gathers.

    B) seizes.

    C) collects.

    D) prevails.

18. Which of the following best describes the relationship between the passages?

    A) Passage 2 expands an idea that was mentioned briefly in Passage 1.

    B) Passage 2 disputes the primary argument advanced in Passage 1.

    C) Passage 2 provides examples to support a central claim made in Passage 1.

    D) Passage 2 offers a justification for the main opinion asserted in Passage 1.

19. Based on the information contained in the passages, it is likely that Monroe and Roosevelt were each motivated at least in part by

    A) a lack of political stability in the Western Hemisphere.

    B) threatened or potential aggression by foreign powers.

    C) ongoing criticism from their political opponents.

    D) a strong commitment to pacifism.

20. Based on the ideas expressed in Passage 1, Monroe would most likely characterize Roosevelt's claim in lines 67–68 ("Our interests . . . identical") as

    A) an appropriate understanding of the relationship between countries in the Americas.

    B) an unfair characterization of an opinion expressed in the Monroe Doctrine.

    C) an unwarranted exaggeration of the actual state of affairs in the Western Hemisphere.

    D) an example of a phenomenon mentioned in the Monroe Doctrine.

21. Which of the following statements can be supported by Passage 2 but not by Passage 1?

    A) The United States intends to maintain friendly relationships with other nations.

    B) European powers should refrain from intervening in matters affecting only North and South America.

    C) At least one nation in the Americas other than the United States has achieved political stability.

    D) The United States should adopt a position of neutrality regarding all conflicts between foreign powers.

Reflect

Directions: Take a few minutes to recall what you've learned and what you've been practicing in this chapter. Consider the following questions, jot down your best answer for each one, and then compare your reflections to the expert responses on the following page. Use your level of confidence to determine what to do next.

What are SAT Reading paired passages? How do expert test takers adjust their active reading to tackle paired passages most effectively?

_____

_____

_____

How are the question sets that accompany paired passages different from those accompanying standard single passages?

_____

_____

_____

What are SAT Reading primary source passages? How do expert test takers adjust their active reading to tackle primary source passages most effectively?

_____

_____

_____

How confident do you feel with paired passages and primary source texts? What can you do in practice to improve your performance and gain even more confidence with these types of passages?

_____

_____

_____

Reading

Expert Responses

What are SAT Reading paired passages? How do expert test takers adjust their active reading to tackle paired passages most effectively?

On each SAT test, one Reading stimulus is a pair of shorter passages instead of a single, long passage. Expert test takers actively read each passage and answer the questions exclusively associated with each. Then, experts compare and contrast the passages' big pictures and details and answer questions associated with both.

How are the question sets that accompany paired passages different from those accompanying standard single passages?

Roughly, the first third of the question set exclusively addresses Passage 1, the next third exclusively addresses Passage 2, and the final third addresses comparisons and contrasts between the passages. The compare/contrast-both-passage question stems are uniquely worded to reward students who accurately summarize the big picture of each passage and who can determine how one author would likely respond to something argued or proposed by the other author.

What are SAT Reading primary source passages? How do expert test takers adjust their active reading to tackle primary source passages most effectively?

On each SAT, one passage (or often, the paired passage set) comes from primary sources, firsthand accounts of historical events or issues. Expert readers use what they know about the authors and events to help anticipate the passages. They actively read for the author's main point and note where and how the author supports that point.

How confident do you feel with paired passages and primary source texts? What can you do in practice to improve your performance and gain even more confidence with these types of passages?

There is no one-size-fits-all answer for this question. Give yourself honest self-assessment. If you feel that paired passages or primary sources are a strength, congratulations! Continue to practice them so that you'll be able to rack up the points associated with these passages on test day. If you feel less confident about either the paired passage format or primary source content, review the strategies in this chapter and try to consistently apply the expert approaches outlined here whenever you practice passages in this format.

Next Steps

If you answered most questions correctly in the "How Much Have You Learned?" section, and if your responses to the Reflect questions were similar to those of the SAT expert, then consider paired and primary source passages an area of strength and move on to the next chapter. Come back to this topic periodically to prevent yourself from getting rusty.

If you don't yet feel confident, review the material in How to Deal with Paired Passages, then try the questions you missed again. As always, be sure to review the explanations closely.

Answers and Explanations

Suggested Passage 1 notes:

> Lines 1–4: president + 2/3 senate can make treaties
> Lines 5–9: objection
> Lines 9–18: Jay's response
> Lines 18–23: Jay's conclusion

Suggested Passage 2 notes:

> Lines 24–36: treaties not purely legislative or executive, but legis. better
> Lines 36–39: responsibilities of legislative
> Lines 39–43: responsibilities of executive
> Lines 43–56: treaties = contracts w/foreign nations, don't fit either branch
> Lines 56–60: reasons to assign to executive
> Lines 61–64: reasons to assign to legislative

1.   A

Difficulty: Medium

Category: Function

Strategic Advice: When a question asks about the purpose of some part of the passage, consider the author's intentions. What is the author trying *to do* with this paragraph, sentence, phrase, word, or in this case, punctuation? Imagine taking away the selected part of the passage and think about how the meaning of the remaining text changes.

Getting to the Answer: Here, if you take away the quotations about what Jay's opponents think (lines 5–9), the beginning of paragraph 2 becomes less clear because there would be no point against which Jay is arguing, so his conclusions would lack context. Thus, your prediction should be that Jay brings up an opposing opinion so he can knock it down to bolster his own conclusion. That matches **(A)**.

Eliminate (B) because it contradicts Jay, who explicitly says that there are no errors or defects in the treaties clause of the Constitution. (C) misuses a detail; the ability of the legislature to create laws that impact citizens' lives is important, but that is not why Jay included the critique of the president's treaty-making authority in the passage. (D) distorts Jay's purpose in mentioning these critics; he goes on to point out what they have overlooked, not to use their criticism to support his own views.

2.   C

Difficulty: Medium

Category: Inference

Strategic Advice: Use the main idea of the passage to make a general prediction. Review what was explicitly said in the passage based on your passage map. Then, evaluate each answer choice.

Getting to the Answer: The first paragraph of Passage 1 addresses Jay's opponents' opinions. These opponents are displeased because they believe that only the legislature should make laws, so this should be the basis of your prediction. **(C)** provides the best match and is correct.

(A) is incorrect because Jay acknowledges that his opponents' arguments are not based on any errors in the Constitution, and there's no way to know whether Jay would agree with them if there were flaws. (B) is incorrect because it misuses a detail; Jay's opponents are not upset about the loose definition of a law, but rather who has the authority to create rules and bind citizens to those rules. (D) contradicts the passage; Jay disagrees with his opponents.

3.   A

Difficulty: Easy

Category: Command of Evidence

Strategic Advice: Look for an answer that cites text supporting the previous answer. Consider keywords in the quotations to spot those that refer to the topic in question.

Getting to the Answer: Look back to your answer for question 2; how did you arrive there? The second and third sentences of Passage 1 provide the only direct references to Jay's opponents' opinions. **(A)** is correct because it suggests the viewpoint of Jay's opponents: that laws should be made exclusively by the legislature.

Eliminate (B) because it explains Jay's response to his opponents, not his opponents' opinion. Eliminate (C) because it is part of the evidence Jay uses in his response to the argument of his opponents. (D) is Jay's clarification of his own point, not the opinion of his opponents.

4. D

Difficulty: Hard

Category: Inference

Strategic Advice: It may be difficult to make a specific prediction for open-ended Inference questions like this one, but the correct answer must follow from the passage. Review your passage map as needed to evaluate each answer choice.

Getting to the Answer: To test the choices for an open-ended Inference question, keep in mind that the correct answer will follow from the passage text. Evaluate each choice by asking: "Is this true based on the passage?" (A) fails this test because it is too broad; Hamilton passes no judgment on "most" writers. (B) falls outside the scope; Hamilton opines on the power to make treaties, but not on their authority over citizens. (C) is extreme; Hamilton does not claim that *any* power that is neither legislative nor judicial is executive. This leaves **(D)**, the correct answer, which is supported in the text by lines 28–31 ("Though several . . . classification"). If Hamilton thinks this classification is arbitrary, then it must not be adequately substantiated.

5. A

Difficulty: Medium

Category: Command of Evidence

Strategic Advice: For a Command of Evidence question, use the line number references in each answer choice to research the passage. If you spotted specific text to support the answer to the preceding question, you can check the answer choices to see if it is cited in one of the Command of Evidence question's choices.

Getting to the Answer: The opening lines of Passage 2 address those who incorrectly think treaty power is strictly executive, so predict that your answer can be found here. The correct answer, **(A)**, directly supports the correct answer to question 6; you may have remembered it from your research on that question.

(B) defines legislative power, (C) defines the object of treaty making, and (D) states an argument for legislative involvement in treaty making. None of these choices is related to the correct answer to the preceding question.

6. B

Difficulty: Medium

Category: Vocab-in-Context

Strategic Advice: On Vocab-in-Context questions, the correct answer can replace the word cited in the question stem without changing the meaning of the sentence. Predict what the correct answer means as well as you can before evaluating the choices.

Getting to the Answer: Historical passages can contain archaic language, so use context clues. The relevant text says that the treaty power "partakes more of the legislative than of the executive character." Hamilton is suggesting that the treaty power *has more in common* with the responsibilities of the legislature than of the executive. **(B)** is correct; *sharing* more characteristics equates to having more in common.

(A) is incorrect; *consume*, or *eat*, doesn't fit into this sentence. (C) would distort the meaning of the sentence. (D) is simply a more evocative form of "consume."

7. C

Difficulty: Hard

Category: Vocab-in-Context

Strategic Advice: On Vocab-in-Context questions, the correct answer can replace the word cited in the question stem without changing the meaning of the sentence. Predict what the correct answer means as well as you can before evaluating the choices.

Getting to the Answer: "[O]ffice" appears in the sentence at the very end of Passage 2, where it is used in a somewhat dated fashion. A good paraphrase of the sentence in which "office" appears would be: "The fact that treaties are in some ways like laws is a reason the legislative branch should have a role in the job/task of making them." The correct answer will be the one that could mean *job* or *task*, making **(C)** the correct answer. "Commission," in this case, means an official assignment or a task for which one is committed or responsible.

(A) distorts the sentence by implying that the legislature should be part of an administrative system. (B) uses a common definition of office (the physical place where people work) that doesn't fit this sentence at all. (D) offers too vague a word to maintain the meaning of the sentence.

8. A

Difficulty: Hard

Category: Global

Strategic Advice: This question is a variation on the Global question type adapted to fit paired passages. To answer a question like this one efficiently, identify the central goal of each passage, and describe them in relation to one another.

Getting to the Answer: Begin by comparing the two passages' main points. Passage 1 supports the way the second section of Article II of the Constitution divides the treaty power between the executive and legislative branches by refuting those who think it should reside solely with the legislature. Passage 2's author also endorses a treaty power shared by the executive and legislative branches, in this case, by refuting those who think treaty powers are an exclusively executive power. **(A)** correctly states that the passages reach the same conclusion through different lines of reasoning.

(B) is incorrect because both passages deal with the same proposition: how treaty power should be allocated between the branches of government. (C) distorts the relationship between passages because Passage 2 does not question any assumptions in Passage 1; the authors generally agree. (D) may sound plausible, but neither passage uses examples to illustrate reasoning.

9. C

Difficulty: Medium

Category: Inference

Strategic Advice: This Inference question asks you to deduce what one author would likely say about the other; the answer will be firmly rooted in the main ideas of both passages.

Getting to the Answer: Make sure you're clear on what the question is asking. While the two authors disagree on some points, such as whether treaty power is primarily an executive or legislative power, they agree that the power to legally bind citizens is not exclusively held by the legislative branch. Jay states that all three branches can issue legally binding rules, and Hamilton argues that treaties created by the executive branch are binding. **(C)** states that at least some executive rules are binding under the powers granted in the Constitution, which makes it the correct answer.

(A) is too broad; the only type of non-legislative rules discussed by Hamilton are treaties, so there's no way to know what he would think of other non-legislative rules. (B) contradicts Hamilton's view that treaties are legally binding. (D) falls outside the scope of Passage 2, as Hamilton does not express any opinion regarding the judiciary.

10. C

Difficulty: Medium

Category: Function

Strategic Advice: The phrase "both serve to" signals a Function question that applies to both passages. Check the quoted text in each passage to identify why each author included the phrase.

Getting to the Answer: In this case, each of the excerpts noted in the question stem offers a definition of typical legislative powers, the authority to make laws. That function is accurately described in choice **(C)**.

(A) does not match either author's conclusion, which is that the power to make treaties is appropriately shared between the executive and legislative branches. (B) applies only to Passage 2. (D) is something both authors do, but not by way of the text quoted in the question stem.

Suggested passage notes:

Passage 1

> ¶1: No more European colonization in Americas
> ¶2: US friends w/Eur; US neutral in Eur conflicts
> ¶3: US will act only if threatened; Eur activities in own hemisphere = threat
> ¶4: US conditions: 1) no new colonies, 2) old colonies OK, 3) no interference w/former colonies

Passage 2

> Lines 37–49: US wants order in W hemisphere
> Lines 49–59: If disorder, US will intervene
> Lines 59–86: R's explanation

11. D

Difficulty: Medium

Category: Function

Strategic Advice: Function questions ask you to determine the purpose of a specific detail or paragraph in the passage. This question wants you to determine the purpose of a statement in the second paragraph, so you should go back to the lines indicated and look for clues that will help you make a prediction. Sometimes, you will need to read before or after the lines indicated to have enough information to answer the question.

Getting to the Answer: In lines 6–9, Monroe states that the people of the United States "cherish" their friendship with Europeans. But why does he mention this, when the primary purpose of the passage is to put European powers on notice that the United States will no longer tolerate their interference in the Americas? Monroe reminds Europeans of their friendship with the United States in order to soften his message. Without this reminder, the overall tone of the passage would be more aggressive and would be less likely to be well-received by a European audience. This prediction matches **(D)** perfectly.

There is no indication that Monroe is responding to critics, so you can eliminate (A). (B) can be eliminated because Monroe's tone is very direct; there is nothing in the passage to indicate that he is trying to trick the European powers into thinking his position is something other than what he says. Finally, (C) is incorrect because Monroe is commenting on an existing attitude, not recommending that people adopt one.

12. B

Difficulty: Easy

Category: Detail

Strategic Advice: The keyword "indicates" signals that this is a Detail question, which means you are looking for a specific fact mentioned in the passage. Refer back to the passage to find what Monroe says the United States does not intend to do. Keep your finger on those lines, since your next task will be a Command of Evidence question that asks you where you found the answer to this question.

Getting to the Answer: In the second paragraph, Monroe states that it is not, and never has been, the policy of the United States to get involved in European matters if they are "relating to themselves" (lines 9–12). In doing so, Monroe indicates that the United States will not intervene in wars that affect only European powers. This prediction matches **(B)**, which is correct.

(A) is the opposite of Monroe's primary message, which is that the United States will not tolerate further European colonization of the Americas (lines 20–26). (C) is also inconsistent with the passage, which states that Americans "cherish" their friendship with Europeans and that the United States enjoys "amicable" relationships with European powers. Finally, (D) contradicts a statement Monroe makes in the final paragraph, where he indicates that the United States will not interfere with existing European colonies.

13. A

Difficulty: Easy

Category: Command of Evidence

Strategic Advice: Command of Evidence questions ask you to identify the support for the previous answer. If you see one of these coming, you can keep your finger on the relevant text when you do your research for the previous question, giving you a quick prediction.

Getting to the Answer: The previous question drew its correct answer from the second paragraph, specifically the second sentence in lines 9–12. Thus, **(A)** is correct.

14. C

Difficulty: Hard

Category: Detail

Strategic Advice: As with other Detail questions, go back to the passage and look up the required information. Keep your finger on the appropriate lines of text so that you can answer the upcoming Command of Evidence question more quickly.

Getting to the Answer: Because the question asks for what circumstance "must" exist, look for forceful language in the passage that indicates a necessary requirement that must be met before the United States may act. You'll find such language in lines 75–81, where Roosevelt says that the United States would intervene "only in the last resort." In this sentence, Roosevelt says that only two circumstances would justify intervention: if a nation were to violate the rights of the United States or if a nation were to put every other country in the Americas at risk by inciting European aggression. Either circumstance would require causing harm to the United States as a prerequisite for intervention, either individually or as part of the collective group of nations in the Americas. Thus, **(C)** is correct.

Regarding the other choices, (A) and (B) are incorrect because Roosevelt does not say that invasion is required to justify intervention. Although invasion may be sufficient to warrant involvement by the United States, there are likely other ways that a country might violate the rights of the United States or invite European aggression. (D) is incorrect because Roosevelt never mentions human rights abuses.

15. D

Difficulty: Medium

Category: Command of Evidence

Strategic Advice: Look back at your research for the previous question and determine what portion of text you used to support your answer.

Getting to the Answer: The answer to the previous question was found in lines 75–81, so **(D)** is correct.

16. C

Difficulty: Easy

Category: Vocab-in-Context

Strategic Advice: For Vocab-in-Context questions, return to the passage, and look for context clues that will reveal something about the meaning of the word in question. To make a prediction, pretend the word is a blank in the sentence and propose a different word to take its place that maintains the original meaning.

Getting to the Answer: In lines 59–60, Roosevelt uses the phrase "washed by the Caribbean Sea" to refer to Cuba and other countries located in and around the Caribbean. The word "washed" in this context means flowed over the shores of. This is a way of saying that these countries are adjacent to, or "touched," by the Caribbean, making **(C)** correct.

Beware the more common and literal meanings of "washed," such as "cleaned" and "bathed." They don't make sense in the context of this passage, so (A) and (D) are incorrect. (B) is incorrect because to be overwhelmed is to be "awash" in something, rather than "washed."

17. D

Difficulty: Hard

Category: Vocab-in-Context

Strategic Advice: For Vocab-in-Context questions, go back to the passage and look for context clues. Make a prediction by pretending that the indicated word is a blank and finding a different word to take its place without changing the meaning of the sentence.

Getting to the Answer: In line 70, Roosevelt says that countries rich in natural resources will prosper if "the reign of law and justice obtains" in them. In other words, countries that achieve political and legal stability will succeed. In this sense, "obtains" is similar to "becomes a reality," or "prevails," making **(D)** correct. Generally, you want to avoid the more common meanings of a word in a Vocab-in-Context question, which means the more familiar uses of "obtains," such as *gathers, seizes,* and *collects,* are likely incorrect. None of them fits the context of this sentence, ruling out (A), (B), and (C).

18. A

Difficulty: Hard

Category: Global

Strategic Advice: This is a Global question asking you to describe the relationship between the passages. Refer back to your passage maps. You should also review the pre-passage blurb for any useful information about the relationship between the passages.

Getting to the Answer: The passages are generally compatible with one another, and the characterization of Passage 2 as a "corollary" to Passage 1 confirms this impression. (A corollary is a claim that follows from another, preexisting claim.) Passage 1 is primarily concerned with informing European powers about a policy decision made by the United States: moving forward, the United States will view European intervention or colonization in the Americas as a form of aggression against the United States. As part of the justification for his stance, Monroe asserts that the United States is "more immediately connected" (line 17) with events in the Americas than are European powers. However, Monroe never expressly indicates what role the United States should play in policing the affairs of other countries within the Americas. In Passage 2, however, Roosevelt fills in the gap by offering a set of criteria to determine when the United States may intervene in the affairs of other nations. Thus, **(A)** is correct because Roosevelt is expanding on the idea mentioned briefly by Monroe in lines 16–17.

(B) can be eliminated because Passage 2 does not "dispute" Passage 1; their relationship is compatible, not contradictory. (C) is incorrect because Passage 2 provides only one example (a reference to Cuba in lines 59–67), and that example does not support any of the claims made by Monroe in Passage 1. (D) is incorrect because the main opinion in Passage 1 is that European powers should not get involved in disputes between countries in the Americas, but Roosevelt is offering a justification for the different (but related) opinion of when the United States should get involved.

19. B

Difficulty: Medium

Category: Inference

Strategic Advice: This question asks you to identify a motivation shared by both authors, so the correct choice must be supported by each passage separately. Because this is an Inference question, the supporting information in one or both of the passages may be implicit rather than explicit.

Getting to the Answer: In Passage 1, Monroe is primarily motivated by concerns about European powers intervening in the Americas, via colonization or some other form of aggression. In Passage 2, Roosevelt's references to the Monroe Doctrine (line 55) and "foreign aggression" (lines 79–80) indicate that he also shares this concern. Thus, **(B)** is correct.

(A) describes a circumstance that motivated Roosevelt's argument in Passage 2, but Passage 1 does not indicate any concerns about political instability in the Americas. (C) is incorrect because there is no indication in either passage that the authors are responding to their political opponents. Finally, (D) is incorrect because neither passage refers to nonviolence or pacifism; additionally, Passage 2 advocates for "policing" other nations and implies that military intervention is appropriate in at least some cases.

20. A

Difficulty: Medium

Category: Inference

Strategic Advice: For Inference questions that ask you how one author would respond to a claim made by the other, start by reading the claim. Then, look for clues in the other passage that indicate how its author would respond.

Getting to the Answer: Roosevelt's claim in lines 67–68 is that the United States and its neighbors in the Americas have the same interests. Looking back at Passage 1, Monroe says in lines 15–17 that the United States is "more connected" with other nations in the Americas. Thus, Monroe would agree with Roosevelt's statement, making **(A)** correct.

(B) and (C) are incorrect because they mischaracterize the relationship between Roosevelt's statement in lines 67–68 and Monroe's opinion; Monroe would generally agree with Roosevelt's statement, so he would not call it an "unfair characterization" or an "unwarranted exaggeration." Lastly, (D) is incorrect because Roosevelt's statement is not an "example" of anything.

Reading

21. C

Difficulty: Medium

Category: Inference

Strategic Advice: Because this is a "which of the following" Inference question, it is most efficient to work through the answer choices by process of elimination.

Getting to the Answer: (A) is incorrect because both Monroe (lines 6–9) and Roosevelt (lines 42–44) mention their intent to maintain friendly relationships with other countries. Likewise, (B) is incorrect because it is a statement that is supported by both passages; the correct choice will be supported only by Passage 2. **(C)** is correct because Passage 2 mentions Cuba (lines 59–67) as an example of another stable country in the Americas, but Passage 1 offers no such examples. (D) is incorrect because it contradicts Passage 2, which advocates for intervention by the United States in at least some circumstances.

CHAPTER 22

Literature Passages

LEARNING OBJECTIVES

After completing this chapter, you will be able to:

- Draw inferences about characters' motivations and relationships
- Identify the tone of a partial or full Literature passage

How Much Do You Know?

Directions: In this chapter, you'll learn to apply the SAT Reading strategies you've learned to Literature passages. Take 10 minutes to actively read this passage and answer the five accompanying questions. Pay close attention to the relationships between characters as you read. When you're finished, compare your work to the explanations on the following pages.

Questions 1–5 refer to the following passage.

This passage is adapted from a short story titled "The Doorman" that takes place in New York City in the early 2000s.

Wallace's grandchildren liked it when his hand shook. They'd grab at it, a twin on each knee. "Me!" Fiona would squeal when she won. "You!" Henry would squeal along with her.

5 Wallace wondered how the submissive boy had come out so unlike his father. Then again, Simon himself was so unlike Wallace. Was there a gene that coded an unfamiliar son?

"You can tell them to stop, Dad," Simon

10 would offer, but why would Wallace do that?

"Dad," Simon would sigh, "just retire," meaning Simon would take care of Wallace's rent and bologna and Listerine. But of course Wallace couldn't abandon the residents of the

15 building where he was doorman. His son didn't think he was of any use anymore, but he was wrong. The new girl in 33A, for example—who would she talk to after midnight, when she got her rumblings? And Simon clearly did not recall

20 the time Wallace helped get that delivery man arrested, the one who swiped Mr. Harrington's wallet straight from his back pocket, and how ever since Mr. Harrington had given Wallace a crisp hundred every Veterans Day.

25 "It has to bother people that you can't carry anything," Simon insisted a few days before the incident.

"They don't mind." Wallace plunged his right hand into the pocket of his slacks to hide

30 its quaking, which just made his whole pant leg tremble from top to bottom.

"Doesn't it bother you, then?"

Wallace didn't answer. He didn't say to his son, *I'm not a dog or a mule. My job isn't about*

35 *how fast I can fetch or how much weight my old back can take. I am respected, too.* Simon didn't get that intangibles mattered. Performance had always been too important to him, even as a kid, but being a lawyer had

40 made him more that way.

The day after Simon had the heart attack, when he was still hospitalized but stable, Wallace headed to work. The 7 train wasn't running from Queens, and the R held a new

45 crowd—two dozen or so teenagers armed with band instruments.

Stiff backpacks pressed in on him as Wallace made his way through flutes and trumpets and clarinets and one tuba. His hearing aid

50 amplified their squeals into shrieks, and he covered his ears as he charted a squiggly path to the open tip of a bench next to a slumbering woman in nurse shoes. How anyone could sleep in such a circus he didn't know. He lowered

55 himself next to her.

Wallace didn't mind the kids on the train. That was another difference between him and Simon—Wallace could appreciate people, generally speaking.

60 Once, Simon had said, "Dad, why have you never said you were proud of me? Not once?"

"That's foolish," Wallace said. "I'm sure I have," though he couldn't remember if he had or not.

65 The boy had started going to see a psychologist because he had anxieties, and the doctor had told his son that the reason he was anxious was because he felt he didn't deserve abundance.

70 "Let me get this straight," Wallace had teased, "I screwed you up because I taught you to be happy with less?" Simon had said no, he wasn't suggesting Wallace had messed up, just that maybe the reason why Simon had a hard

75 time accepting affluence was because he didn't
grow up with it himself.

"I did the best I could," Wallace had said.

"Do you look down on us for the way we live
now?" asked Simon. He had always been a serious
80 person, even as a child, but law had made him
more that way. The gulf between them held more
than just seriousness, though. His wife wore the
kind of jewelry that attracts scamming thieves,
handsome fellows in suits catered Thanksgiving at
85 their condo, and their children, who already had
passports, ate baby food from a farm.

Of course not, Wallace thought, but he said
instead, "I wish I'd been able to afford to buy
you more things," because Simon seemed
90 hungry for him to express some kind of regret.

Simon was a good person and a good son, but
Wallace just hadn't known how to relate to him
lately. He hoped he would have another chance
to try.

1. In the passage, Wallace is mainly presented as someone who

A) feels anger toward his adult son, whose
demeanor and life choices conflict with his own
personality and values.

B) focuses on his commute to his job as a
doorman, which he suspects he will need to
quit soon.

C) identifies as a grandfather whose relationship
with his grandchildren is the most important
part of his life.

D) hopes that his adult son will survive a present
crisis but is conflicted about their ability to
communicate.

2. The main purpose of the sentence in lines 19–24
("And Simon . . . Veterans Day") is to

A) introduce the detail that Wallace served in the
military.

B) provide an example of why Wallace thinks he is
still important at his job.

C) depict a fundamental way in which Simon and
Wallace differ.

D) lead into the description of the impact of
Wallace's physical condition.

3. Which statement best describes a technique the
narrator uses in lines 56–64 to represent the relationship between Wallace and Simon?

A) The narrator demonstrates the hostility in
their relationship by quoting an insult Wallace
directs toward Simon.

B) The narrator hints at the fragility of their
relationship by indicating that Wallace is
starting to become more forgetful.

C) The narrator underscores the disappointment
in their relationship by suggesting that Wallace
is more proud of the teens than of Simon.

D) The narrator highlights the tension in their
relationship by revealing an inconsistency in
Wallace's character.

4. In terms of their material wealth, as compared with
Simon, Wallace is portrayed as

A) unable to afford a car.

B) less well off financially.

C) feeling guilty about how he raised his children.

D) more worried about finances.

5. Which choice provides the best evidence for the
answer to the previous question?

A) Lines 13–15 ("But of course . . . doorman")

B) Lines 41–46 ("The day . . . instruments")

C) Lines 81–86 ("The gulf . . . farm")

D) Lines 91–94 ("Simon . . . try")

Check Your Work

Suggested passage notes:

¶1: W & S = not alike

¶2–3: S wants W to retire; W feels useful as doorman

¶4–7: S focuses on W's hand/performance; W feels respected at work

¶8–10: S heart attack; W likes kids on train

¶11–12: W never expressed pride for S?

¶13–17: S not affluent as child but rich now; S wants W to feel regret

¶18: W wants to relate to S

1.   D

Difficulty: Medium

Category: Global

Strategic Advice: Since the question is asking about the main character of the entire passage, this is a Global question. Review your passage map to make a prediction about the narrator's overall presentation of Wallace.

Getting to the Answer: The passage describes several tense situations between Wallace and his son, Simon. Predict that Wallace is mainly portrayed as having a difficult relationship with his son. Choice **(D)** matches the prediction and is correct: line 41 identifies Simon as having had a heart attack (a "present crisis"), and the final lines of the passage state, "Wallace just hadn't known how to relate to him lately. He hoped he would have another chance to try."

Choice (A) is extreme; although there are many differences between Wallace and Simon, nothing in the text indicates that Wallace is angry. Rather, he hopes to improve their relationship. Choice (B) is incorrect because there is no indication that Wallace plans to quit anytime soon. Choice (C) isn't supported; although the passage opens with Wallace playing with his grandchildren, there isn't anything that suggests they're the most important thing to him.

2.   B

Difficulty: Medium

Category: Function

Strategic Advice: Function questions ask about the purpose of a specific element of the passage. Think about the author's larger purpose for including the cited element; ask yourself, "Why is this here and what does it accomplish?"

Getting to the Answer: The cited sentence describes an incident in which a resident showed appreciation for Wallace's help in his service as a doorman. The paragraph is about why Wallace believes Simon is wrong to think Wallace is not "of any use anymore" at his job. Since the cited sentence supports the main idea of the paragraph by giving a reason why Wallace *is* of use, **(B)** is correct.

Though Wallace's military service is implied by the sentence, this is a minor detail and not the reason the sentence is included in the passage, so (A) is incorrect. Choice (C) is incorrect because, although Simon and Wallace disagree about Wallace retiring, this difference is introduced earlier in the paragraph, and the cited sentence only addresses Wallace's view. Choice (D) is incorrect because the sentence doesn't closely tie into the discussion of Wallace's hand that follows.

3.   D

Difficulty: Hard

Category: Function

Strategic Advice: The reference to "a technique the narrator uses" indicates that this is a Function question. Think about how the author uses the cited lines in the context of the passage.

Getting to the Answer: Getting to the Answer: The lines describe how Wallace may appreciate people "generally speaking," but he doesn't appreciate (or at least has never expressed appreciation for) the specific accomplishments of Simon. This inconsistency in Wallace is one example of the strained relationship between Wallace and Simon that the narrator presents throughout the passage, so **(D)** is correct.

Although Wallace says, "That's foolish," (A) is incorrect because the comment is not meant to insult Simon, but to indicate Wallace's rejection of the idea that he hasn't expressed pride in Simon. Further, the passage doesn't go so far as to indicate hostility between the father and son. Choice (B) is incorrect because Wallace's inability to remember saying he's proud of his son reflects the nature of their relationship, not his aging; his memory is never called into question. Choice (C) distorts details from the passage, which doesn't indicate that Wallace is disappointed in his son; rather, he's sure he has vocalized his pride.

4. B

Difficulty: Medium

Category: Inference

Strategic Advice: Since the question asks about how a character is "portrayed," this is an Inference question. The correct answer will be supported, though not directly stated, in the passage, so you can still make a prediction.

Getting to the Answer: Use your passage notes to help you identify the difference between Simon and Wallace in terms of their wealth. In the middle of the passage, the characters experience tension related to money: a therapist says Simon has difficulty accepting his current wealth since Wallace wasn't affluent when Simon was a child. Simon then asks if Wallace looks down on the affluent way Simon's family lives. Wallace is thus portrayed as having less than Simon, so **(B)** is correct.

Although Wallace rides the train to work, the passage never implies he can't afford a car, so (A) can be eliminated. Wallace says he wishes he'd been able to buy more for Simon because Simon seemed to want him to "express some kind of regret," not because he actually feels guilty, so (C) is incorrect. Wallace never expresses worry about finances; rather, he thinks "intangibles" are important and wants to keep working because it makes him feel helpful, so (D) is incorrect.

5. C

Difficulty: Medium

Category: Command of Evidence

Strategic Advice: The keywords "provides the best evidence for the answer to the previous question" indicate a Command of Evidence question. When you see one of these questions coming, locate the lines you used to answer the preceding question.

Getting to the Answer: The correct answer will provide evidence that Wallace is less wealthy than Simon. The middle portion of the passage contains the discussion of their tensions about money, so check quotes from that section first. Choice **(C)** is correct: it identifies that there is a "gulf" between Wallace and Simon, and it describes that gulf by listing aspects of the more lavish lifestyle of Simon's family (expensive jewelry, catered dinners, and fancy baby food).

None of the other answer choices address the disparity in the characters' wealth. Choice (A) asserts that Wallace does not want to leave the people he helps at his job, (B) includes the details about Simon's heart attack and Wallace riding the bus to work, and (D) reflects Wallace's thoughts about his overall relationship with his son.

How to Read Literature for the SAT

LEARNING OBJECTIVES

After this lesson, you will be able to:

- Draw inferences about characters' motivations and relationships
- Identify the tone of a partial or full Literature passage

Exactly one passage in each SAT Reading section is a Literature passage: an excerpt from a novel or short story. The Literature passage is typically the first passage in the section, but that doesn't mean you have to tackle it first. Some test takers may find fiction engaging and feel comfortable reading dialogue and interpreting an author's descriptions of characters and settings. Others may find their strengths lie in nonfiction passages on science and social studies. Don't make a snap judgment based on how you feel now, though. Practice all of the passage types to give yourself an honest, informed assessment. You'll find more tips and strategies on how best to approach the section in the chapter on SAT Reading section management.

To answer a question like this:

The following passage is an excerpt from English novelist Anne Brontë's *The Tenant of Wildfell Hall*, published in 1848. The excerpt is part of a letter the narrator, Gilbert, has written.

My father, as you know, was a sort of gentleman farmer in —shire; and I, by his express desire, succeeded him in the same quiet occupation, not very willingly, for ambition
5   urged me to higher aims, and self-conceit assured me that, in disregarding its voice, I was burying my talent in the earth, and hiding my light under a bushel. My mother had done her utmost to persuade me that I was capable of
10   great achievements; but my father, who thought ambition was the surest road to ruin, and change but another word for destruction, would listen to no scheme for bettering either my own condition, or that of my fellow mortals. He assured me it
15   was all rubbish, and exhorted me, with his dying breath, to continue in the good old way, to follow his steps, and those of his father before him, and let my highest ambition be, to walk honestly through the world, looking neither to the right
20   hand nor to the left, and to transmit the paternal acres to my children in, at least, as flourishing a condition as he left them to me.
     "Well!—an honest and industrious farmer is one of the most useful members of society; and
25   if I devote my talents to the cultivation of my farm, and the improvement of agriculture in general, I shall thereby benefit, not only my own immediate connections and dependents, but in some degree, mankind at large:—hence I shall
30   not have lived in vain." With such reflections as these, I was endeavouring to console myself, as I plodded home from the fields, one cold, damp, cloudy evening towards the close of October. But the gleam of a bright red fire through the parlour
35   window, had more effect in cheering my spirits, and rebuking my thankless repinings, than all the sage reflections and good resolutions I had

forced my mind to frame;—for I was young then, remember—only four and twenty—and had not
40   acquired half the rule over my own spirit, that I now possess—trifling as that may be.

1.   The narrator's attitude about becoming a farmer, as expressed in lines 23–38 ("Well!—an honest . . . mind to frame"), seems to be one of

A)   bitter resentment.

B)   detached reflection.

C)   forced optimism.

D)   hearty good cheer.

Reading

You need to know this:

The SAT does not generally test symbolism, but it does test your ability to draw inferences about characters' relationships and attitudes and to recognize how the author creates a specific tone or effect.

Unpack the Pre-Passage Blurb Effectively

Be sure to read the little blurb that precedes an SAT Reading passage; this can be especially helpful on Literature passages. The blurb will always give you the author's name, the title of the book or short story from which the passage was adapted, and the original publication date. When necessary, it may provide information about the main characters and setting.

The author. If you happen to know the author, great, but don't expect to. If the name rings a bell that helps you identify the time frame or setting of the passage, take advantage of that, but otherwise, let it go. No questions will ask about the author's identity or biographical information.

Title. A book's title may help you identify its genre—tragedy, romance, coming-of-age story, etc. It may also give you clues about the setting or theme of the passage.

Publication date. The SAT has used Literature passages drawn from various time periods over the last 200 years or so. Obviously, language use and references will be different in passages from the 1850s than those from the 1950s, and you can use that information to provide context about social conditions and historical events, or even about unusual vocabulary.

Characters and setting. When the test adds any information beyond author, title, and date, pay close attention. The people writing the test questions felt this information was essential for test takers to know, and it will always give you a head start in interpreting the passage and anticipating where the story is likely to go. Knowing, for example, that the main character is an adolescent or a mother, or knowing that a story takes place in a coal-mining town or an aristocratic palace, will change your understanding of the passage from the outset.

Tune In to the Narrator's "Voice"

Within the first few lines, you will be able to distinguish a passage written in first person (the narrator as the main character, knowing only what that character knows) from one written in third person (the narrator is separate from the characters and has an omniscient point of view). Keeping this in mind as you read will help you spot the purpose of each paragraph and will help you later with Inference questions ("With which of the following would the narrator/character most likely agree?").

In addition, take note of language that indicates the narrator's or a character's point of view. In a standard science or social studies passage, Opinion and Emphasis keywords help you keep track of an author's ideas about a topic. In Literature passages, the author may put these ideas in the mind or the mouth of a character or in the way a scene or object is described. Take note of the passage's tone (e.g., joyful, nostalgic, anxious, angry, hopeful, ironic, or satirical, etc.), especially if an event or conversation brings about a change in tone. Typically, one or more of the questions will reward your attention to the passage's tone and characters' points of view.

Track What Happens and the Main Character's Reaction or Response

In a standard SAT Reading passage on science or social studies, you can use an author's purpose to anticipate where the passage will go. When the author says there is a debate over a recent theory, you expect the next couple of paragraphs to lay out one side and then the other. If the author introduces a new idea, there will probably be an example to illustrate it. Literature passages unfold a little differently, but if you are reading actively, you can still anticipate and track the development of the story. Use what you know about a character to anticipate the action and to interpret the character's reactions. If an older worker who is concerned about having enough money for retirement has a conversation with her boss, you can understand what she's after, even if she is using language that talks around the subject. If a studious young man absorbed in a book is interrupted by a boisterous group of revelers, you can expect some annoyance or judgment in his reaction, even if he doesn't say anything to the newcomers. Keeping track of these things will help you jot down good paragraph summaries, just as you would in nonfiction passages.

When a character's reaction or response to an event surprises you, consider whether this signals a change in the tone of the passage or indicates that you've glossed over or misunderstood something about the character or situation. In either case, it's always valuable to track not only the plot but also the character's reactions to and interpretations of what is happening.

Use What You Already Know about SAT Reading Strategies and Question Types

While Literature passages have a distinct look and feel, the questions that accompany them are of the same types as those that follow standard science and social studies passages. Thus, while the best test takers apply a few unique reading strategies tailored to Literature, their overall approach remains similar to what they use for all passages. In every case, SAT experts read actively to prepare themselves for the question set. To do that, they read for the big picture, for the author's (or in this case, narrator's or characters') opinions and point of view, and for the passage's structure by noting the purpose and main idea of each paragraph.

For the most part, the questions that accompany Literature passages are worded similarly to those for Science or Social Studies passages. However, in Literature passages, you may also see questions that ask the following:

- For the passage's theme (which corresponds to its main idea)
- About a shift in the narrator's focus
- How the author creates a certain effect
- What is going on in a character's mind

As long as you read actively for tone and characters' motivations, you'll be ready for questions like these.

You need to do this:

- Use the pre-passage blurb to identify all that you can about the following:
  - The author's identity
  - The time frame and location
  - The passage's main character or characters
- Quickly recognize whether the passage is in first person or third person.
- Focus on the main character's defining characteristics: demographics (such as age, social position, occupation, race, and gender) and mental traits (attitudes, opinions, desires, and conflicts).
- Anticipate the character's responses to events or interactions with other characters.
- Note the purpose of each paragraph as you read.

Reading

Explanation:

This is an Inference question: you need to infer the narrator's attitude from clues in the text. The narrator says explicitly in line 4 that he became a farmer "not very willingly" and that he had the "ambition" to pursue "higher aims." This earlier context is important for understanding the tone of lines 23–38; without it, the second paragraph sounds very positive, even cheerful. Against the backdrop of the narrator's unwillingness to become a farmer, however, the second paragraph sounds as if he were trying to talk himself into cheerfully accepting his occupation. Then, in line 31, the narrator states that he is "endeavouring to console [himself]." This is equivalent to "forced optimism." Choice **(C)** is correct.

Try on Your Own

Directions: Actively read this Literature passage and answer the questions that follow. Remember to note the tone of the story as you read and pay close attention to characters' attitudes and relationships.

Questions 1–7 refer to the following passage.

This passage is an excerpt from Sherwood Anderson's short story "Unlighted Lamps." Published 1921. Mary Cochran contemplates how her father's impending death could lead her to leave Huntersburg, the small town where she grew up and now lives.

Pushing her way in among the weeds, many of which were covered with blossoms, Mary found herself a seat on a rock that had been rolled against the trunk of an old apple tree.
5 The weeds half concealed her and from the road only her head was visible. Buried away thus in the weeds she looked like a quail that runs in the tall grass and that on hearing some unusual sound, stops, throws up its head and
10 looks sharply about.

The doctor's daughter had been to the decayed old orchard many times before. At the foot of the hill on which it stood the streets of the town began, and as she sat on the rock she
15 could hear faint shouts and cries coming out of Wilmott Street. A hedge separated the orchard from the fields on the hillside. Mary intended to sit by the tree until darkness came creeping over the land and to try to think out some
20 plan regarding her future. The notion that her father was soon to die seemed both true and untrue, but her mind was unable to take hold of the thought of him as physically dead. For the moment death in relation to her father did
25 not take the form of a cold inanimate body that was to be buried in the ground, instead it seemed to her that her father was not to die but to go away somewhere on a journey. Long ago her mother had done that. There was a
30 strange hesitating sense of relief in the thought.

"Well," she told herself, "when the time comes I also shall be setting out, I shall get out of here and into the world." On several occasions Mary had gone to spend a day with
35 her father in Chicago and she was fascinated by the thought that soon she might be going there to live. Before her mind's eye floated a vision of long streets filled with thousands of people all strangers to herself. To go into such
40 streets and to live her life among strangers would be like coming out of a waterless desert and into a cool forest carpeted with tender young grass.

In Huntersburg she had always lived under
45 a cloud and now she was becoming a woman and the close stuffy atmosphere she had always breathed was becoming constantly more and more oppressive. It was true no direct question had ever been raised touching her own
50 standing in the community life, but she felt that a kind of prejudice against her existed. While she was still a baby there had been a scandal involving her father and mother. The town of Huntersburg had rocked with it and when she
55 was a child people had sometimes looked at her with mocking sympathetic eyes. "Poor child! It's too bad," they said. . . .

For ten or fifteen minutes Mary sat on the stone beneath the tree in the orchard and
60 thought of the attitude of the town toward herself and her father. "It should have drawn us together," she told herself, and wondered if the approach of death would do what the cloud that had for years hung over them had not done. It
65 did not at the moment seem to her cruel that the figure of death was soon to visit her father. In a way Death had become for her and for the time a lovely and gracious figure intent upon good. The hand of death was to open the door
70 out of her father's house and into life. With the cruelty of youth she thought first of the adventurous possibilities of the new life.

Reading

1. Which choice best describes a major theme from the passage?

   A) The bitter grief inevitably produced by death

   B) The difficulty of thinking clearly in nature

   C) A community uprising against an individual

   D) The passage from childhood into adulthood

2. Mary's comment to herself in lines 31–33 ("Well . . . world") most nearly implies that

   A) when her father dies, Mary is going to leave Huntersburg.

   B) Mary is going to leave the decayed orchard and return to the town.

   C) now that her mother has left, Mary is going to move to Chicago.

   D) Mary thinks of her own death as a journey to another world.

3. In line 37, the word "floated" most nearly means

   A) bobbed.

   B) appeared.

   C) glimpsed.

   D) rested.

4. Based on the passage, which answer choice best represents how Mary would describe her father's death?

   A) Unlikely and metaphorical

   B) Appealing and freeing

   C) Vicious but advantageous

   D) Depressing but manageable

5. Which choice provides the best evidence for the answer to the previous question?

   A) Lines 23–28 ("For the moment . . . journey")

   B) Lines 33–37 ("On several . . . to live")

   C) Lines 67–70 ("In a way . . . into life")

   D) Lines 70–72 ("With the cruelty . . . new life")

6. The dialogue in lines 56–57 ("Poor child! It's too bad") mainly serves to

   A) characterize the townspeople's subtle ostracism of Mary.

   B) contradict the previous statement that the townspeople had mocking sympathy for Mary.

   C) reveal the concern that townspeople had about Mary's family's financial situation.

   D) highlight the townspeople's lack of involvement with Mary.

7. Mary indicates that she believes that she and her father should have been brought closer together by

   A) her mother's absence.

   B) her father's approaching death.

   C) their mutual love of Chicago.

   D) the town's shared feelings for them.

How Much Have You Learned?

Directions: Now try a full-length Literature passage and question set under timed conditions. Take 13 minutes to read the passage and answer the accompanying questions.

Questions 8–17 refer to the following passage.

The following passage is adapted from Jules Verne, *Around the World in Eighty Days*, first published in 1873.

Phileas Fogg, having shut the door of his house at half-past eleven, and having put his right foot before his left five hundred and seventy-five times, and his left foot before
5　his right five hundred and seventy-six times, reached the Reform Club. He repaired at once to the dining-room and took his place at the habitual table, the cover of which had already been laid for him. A flunkey handed him
10　an uncut *Times*, which he proceeded to cut with a skill which betrayed familiarity with this delicate operation. The perusal of this paper absorbed Phileas Fogg until a quarter before four, whilst the *Standard*, his next task,
15　occupied him till the dinner hour. Dinner passed as breakfast had done, and Mr. Fogg re-appeared in the reading-room and sat down to the *Pall Mall*[1] at twenty minutes before six. Half an hour later several members of the
20　Reform came in and drew up to the fireplace. They were Mr. Fogg's usual partners at whist:[2] Andrew Stuart, an engineer; John Sullivan and Samuel Fallentin, bankers; Thomas Flanagan, a brewer; and Gauthier Ralph, one of the
25　Directors of the Bank of England.

"Well, Ralph," said Thomas Flanagan, "what about that robbery?"

"Oh," replied Stuart, "the Bank will lose the money."

30　"On the contrary," broke in Ralph, "I hope we may put our hands on the robber. Skillful detectives have been sent to all the principal ports of America and the Continent, and he'll be a clever fellow if he slips through their
35　fingers."

"But have you got the robber's description?" asked Stuart.

"In the first place, he is no robber at all," returned Ralph, positively.

40　"What! a fellow who makes off with fifty-five thousand pounds, no robber?"

"No."

"Perhaps he's a manufacturer, then."

"The *Daily Telegraph* says that he is a
45　gentleman."

It was Phileas Fogg, whose head now emerged from behind his newspapers, who made this remark. A package of banknotes, to the value of fifty-five thousand pounds, had
50　been taken from the principal cashier's table, that functionary being at the moment engaged in registering the receipt of three shillings and sixpence. Let it be observed that the Bank of England reposes a touching confidence in the
55　honesty of the public. There are neither guards nor gratings to protect its treasures; gold, silver, banknotes are freely exposed, at the mercy of the first comer. A keen observer of English customs relates that, being in one of the rooms
60　of the Bank one day, he had the curiosity to examine a gold ingot weighing some seven or eight pounds. He took it up, scrutinized it, passed it to his neighbour, he to the next man, and so on until the ingot, going from hand
65　to hand, was transferred to the end of a dark entry; nor did it return to its place for half an hour. Meanwhile, the cashier had not so much as raised his head. But in the present instance things had not gone so smoothly. The package
70　of notes not being found when five o'clock sounded from the ponderous clock in the "drawing office," the amount was passed to the account of profit and loss.

---

[1] *Pall Mall*: an evening newspaper (the *Pall Mall Gazette*) founded in London in 1865

[2] whist: a trick-taking card game; modern derivatives include hearts and spades

There were real grounds for supposing, as
75 the *Daily Telegraph* said, that the thief did
not belong to a professional band. On the day
of the robbery a well-dressed gentleman of
polished manners, and with a well-to-do air,
had been observed going to and fro in the
80 paying room where the crime was committed.
A description of him was easily procured and
sent to the detectives; and some hopeful spirits,
of whom Ralph was one, did not despair of
his apprehension. The papers and clubs were
85 full of the affair, and everywhere people were
discussing the probabilities of a successful
pursuit; and the Reform Club was especially
agitated, several of its members being Bank
officials.

90   Ralph would not concede that the work of
the detectives was likely to be in vain, for he
thought that the prize offered would greatly
stimulate their zeal and activity. But Stuart
was far from sharing this confidence; and, as
95 they placed themselves at the whist-table, they
continued to argue the matter. "I maintain,"
said Stuart, "that the chances are in favour of
the thief, who must be a shrewd fellow."

"Well, but where can he fly to?" asked
100 Ralph. "No country is safe for him."

"Pshaw!"

"Where could he go, then?"

"Oh, I don't know that. The world is big
enough."

105   "It was once," said Phileas Fogg, in a low
tone.

8. What is the primary purpose of the passage?

   A) To illustrate the problems with theft at the
      Bank of England

   B) To examine the lives of wealthy men in
      England

   C) To introduce Phileas Fogg and his social
      circle at the Reform Club

   D) To parody the social customs of the upper
      class

9. The passage suggests that Phileas Fogg is a man
   who

   A) focuses on cultural activities.

   B) lives beyond his means.

   C) enjoys routine.

   D) keeps to himself.

10. Which choice provides the best evidence for the
    answer to the previous question?

    A) Lines 6–9 ("He repaired . . . for him")

    B) Lines 9–12 ("A flunkey . . . operation")

    C) Lines 15–19 ("Dinner . . . six")

    D) Lines 31–35 ("Skillful . . . fingers")

11. As used in line 6, "repaired" most nearly means

    A) fixed.

    B) returned.

    C) stormed.

    D) proceeded.

12. One impression created by the narrator's descrip-
    tion of Phileas Fogg in the first paragraph is that
    he

    A) keeps abreast of current events.

    B) is a political reformer.

    C) has strong opinions about crime.

    D) makes his living as a banker.

13. Which choice provides the best evidence for the answer to the previous question?

    A) Lines 9–12 ("A flunkey . . . operation")

    B) Lines 19–20 ("Half . . . fireplace")

    C) Lines 31–35 ("Skillful . . . fingers")

    D) Lines 44–48 ("The *Daily* . . . remark")

14. As used in line 51, "functionary" most nearly means

    A) official.

    B) money.

    C) servant.

    D) criminal.

15. According to the passage, which statement about the Bank of England is true?

    A) The public has faith in the integrity of the Bank.

    B) The Bank has taken few precautions to guard against theft.

    C) The Bank has a history of money being stolen.

    D) The Bank has carefully managed public relations.

16. The passage suggests that the thief was not part of a professional crime ring because

    A) the suspect acted alone.

    B) the Bank had never been burglarized before.

    C) the suspect was described as a gentleman.

    D) the Bank carefully screens its customers.

17. The purpose of lines 105–106 ("'It was once,' . . . a low tone") is to

    A) create an ominous atmosphere at the table.

    B) foreshadow Fogg's ideas about the world.

    C) illustrate Fogg's proper demeanor and social skills.

    D) introduce the conflict of the plot.

Reading

Reflect

Directions: Take a few minutes to recall what you've learned and what you've been practicing in this chapter. Consider the following questions, jot down your best answer for each one, and then compare your reflections to the expert responses on the following page. Use your level of confidence to determine what to do next.

What are SAT Reading Literature passages? How do expert test takers adjust their active reading to tackle Literature passages most effectively?

_____

_____

_____

How are the questions that accompany Literature passages different than those accompanying standard Science and Social Studies passages?

_____

_____

_____

How confident do you feel with Literature passages? What can you do in practice to improve your performance and gain even more confidence with these types of passages?

_____

_____

_____

Expert Responses

What are SAT Reading Literature passages? How do expert test takers adjust their active reading to tackle Literature passages most effectively?

On each SAT test, one reading stimulus is taken from a work of fiction such as a novel or short story. Expert test takers actively read Literature passages by paying attention to what happens to the main character and how he or she responds to these events.

How are the questions that accompany Literature passages different than those accompanying standard Science and Social Studies passages?

For the most part, questions accompanying Literature passages are similar to those from standard nonfiction passages, but in literature, you may see 1) Global questions that focus on a change in the passage's tone, 2) Inference questions that ask what the passage's narrator (as opposed to its author) would agree with, or 3) Function questions that ask how or why a character (as opposed to the author) used a detail or reference from the text.

How confident do you feel with Literature passages? What can you do in practice to improve your performance and gain even more confidence with these types of passages?

There is no one-size-fits-all answer for this question. Give yourself honest self-assessment. If you feel that Literature passages are a strength, that's great. Continue to practice them so that you'll be able to rack up the points associated with these passages on test day. If you feel less confident about Literature passages, review the strategies in this chapter and try to consistently apply the expert approaches outlined here whenever you practice passages in this format.

Next Steps

If you answered most questions correctly in the "How Much Have You Learned?" section, and if your responses to the Reflect questions were similar to those of the SAT expert, then consider Literature passages an area of strength and move on to the next chapter. Come back to this topic periodically to prevent yourself from getting rusty.

If you don't yet feel confident, review the instructional text in this chapter, especially the sections on characters' responses and points of view. Then try the questions you missed again. As always, be sure to review the explanations closely.

Answers and Explanations

Suggested passage notes:

¶1: Mary finds a quiet place to think

¶2: M considers her father's death and moving to Chicago

¶3: M never accepted in hometown (Huntersburg)

¶4: father's death will create possibilities for M

1. D

Difficulty: Medium

Category: Global

Getting to the Answer: It is difficult to make a specific prediction for an open-ended question such as this one; however, state the author's purpose in the passage in your own words to help prepare evaluating each answer choice. One purpose of the passage is to describe Mary's thoughts about her future, which she hopes is leaving her small hometown for a big city, where she will seek a new life.

(A) is incorrect because Mary's feelings about death are ambivalent. She cannot conceive of her father's death as a physical reality (lines 20–23), and Death itself is represented as the source of new beginnings (lines 67–72). (B) is the opposite of what is expressed in the first paragraph and the first half of the second paragraph. Mary finds a quiet spot on a rock under an apple tree, away from the noise of Wilmott street, to think about her future. (C) is too extreme. While the town was never kind toward Mary and Mary always felt stifled by the town, "uprising" suggests an intensity that is not present in the passage, which instead describes the town's antagonism toward Mary as a "cloud" (lines 45 and 63). **(D)** is correct because Mary is "becoming a woman" (line 45) and is contemplating a major change in her life, leaving her small hometown after her father's death to seek new possibilities and adventures.

2. A

Difficulty: Medium

Category: Inference

Getting to the Answer: Reread several lines before and after the quoted sentence to focus on the context, and keep the overall purpose of the passage in mind, too. The narrator mentions Mary's thoughts about her father's impending death, Mary's mother's passing, and Mary's desire to move to Chicago. The overall purpose of the passage is to show Mary's father's death as an impetus for Mary to move out of Huntersburg and create a new life for herself.

Evaluate each answer choice. **(A)** is likely correct because "when the time comes" refers to Mary's father's death, and "get out of here" refers to leaving Mary's hometown, Huntersburg. Check the other choices to be sure. (B) is incorrect because Mary wants to leave the town, not return to it. (C) is incorrect because it is the prospect of her father's death that is causing her to consider moving to Chicago, not her mother's absence. (D) is incorrect because Mary thinks of her father's death, not her own, as a journey. **(A)** is confirmed as the correct answer.

3. B

Difficulty: Easy

Category: Vocab-in-Context

Getting to the Answer: Reread the sentence containing "floated" that begins in line 37. Predict another word that could be substituted for "floated" and give the sentence the same meaning as the original one. Mary is imagining a scene in Chicago of long streets filled with lots of people she doesn't know. The image came into her mind, so "arose" or "materialized" would be good predictions. **(B)** matches and is correct.

The vision that "floated" before Mary's mind's eye is not literally floating, so (A) and (D) are incorrect. The term "mind's eye" refers to Mary's imagination, not a literal eye that is seeing the imagined vision; therefore, (C) is also incorrect.

4. B

Difficulty: Hard

Category: Inference

Strategic Advice: Notice that the next question after this one is a Command of Evidence question. When you find the correct answer for this question, keep your finger on the part of the passage where you found it so you'll be able to use it for the Command of Evidence question that follows.

Getting to the Answer: Use your passage map to focus on paragraph 2 and paragraph 4, where the passage mentions Mary's father's death explicitly. While evaluating the answer choices, keep in mind the main idea of the passage, which is how Mary's father's death will enable her to move away from her hometown.

Even though Mary does think of her father's death less as a physical event and more of a journey, (A) is incorrect because her father's death is not unlikely. Rather, Mary is aware that her father's death will come soon. **(B)** is correct because for Mary, death has become "lovely and gracious" and is going to liberate her from Huntersburg (lines 67–70). Although Mary does see an advantage in the prospect of being able to move to Chicago after her father's death, (C) is incorrect because the death itself is not vicious. Instead, it is Mary's youthful focus on her own benefit that is "cruel" (lines 70–72). Finally, (D) is incorrect because the passage does not suggest that Mary feels depressed by the thought of her father's death.

5. C

Difficulty: Hard

Category: Command of Evidence

Getting to the Answer: Keep your finger on the lines where you found the answer to the previous question, lines 67–70, and match that section of the passage to the choices. **(C)** is correct.

(A) is incorrect because it says the only way that Mary can understand her father's death is through metaphor, not that it is appealing and freeing. (B) is incorrect because it does not mention her father's death. (D) is incorrect because it does not express the fact that Mary finds her father's death appealing.

6. A

Difficulty: Medium

Category: Function

Getting to the Answer: Read a little above and a little below lines 56–57 and predict what the author intended in using the phrase. Also, consult your passage map for paragraph 3 to see that its central idea is that the townspeople of Huntersburg did not accept Mary. Predict that the dialogue shows a way that the townspeople expressed their mocking sympathy and made Mary feel oppressed. **(A)** is a good match and is correct.

(B) is incorrect because the dialogue is an example of the townspeople's mocking sympathy, not a contradiction of it. (C) is incorrect because "poor" is not used literally as a marker of poverty. (D) is incorrect because the townspeople do not ignore Mary; instead, they have a negative attitude toward her.

7. D

Difficulty: Hard

Category: Detail

Getting to the Answer: Find the relevant text in the passage. In lines 61–62, Mary says to herself, "It should have drawn us together." The previous sentence states what it is that she believes should have brought her and her father and closer together: "the attitude of the town toward herself and her father" (lines 58–61). Thus, **(D)** is correct.

(A), (B), and (C) are all mentioned in the passage, but Mary never says that any of them should have brought her and her father closer together.

Suggested passage notes:

   ¶1: F's daily routine
   ¶1: cont: F's friends
   ¶2–10: recent robbery
   ¶11: lack of security at bank
   ¶12: thief not a professional robber
   ¶13–19: disagree whether thief will be caught

8. C

Difficulty: Hard

Category: Global

Getting to the Answer: Think about the passage as a whole and use one sentence to predict the purpose of this passage. Make sure the tone of the answer choice matches the tone of the passage. The excerpt provides a brief character sketch of Phileas Fogg and establishes the dynamics of his friendships at the Reform Club. **(C)** is correct; it accurately identifies the purpose of the excerpt.

Choice (A) addresses only a narrow aspect of the passage and ignores the author's careful and extended description of Phileas Fogg. (B) is too broad: the passage describes the life of Fogg, not wealthy English men in general. (D) is extreme. The passage has a neutral tone; there is no evidence of parody.

9. C

Difficulty: Medium

Category: Inference

Getting to the Answer: Review the descriptions of Phileas Fogg and his actions in your passage map. Summarize what the beginning of the passage says about Fogg. Paragraph 1 describes Fogg counting out his steps on his way to the club. Upon arriving at the club, Fogg goes to his "habitual table" (line 8) and performs a routine series of actions. Choice **(C)** is correct, as the details in paragraph 1 depict a man who likes to keep to a set routine.

Choice (A) is incorrect because no cultural activities are described in the passage. (B) is incorrect because although the club, with its servants, fireplace, and dining room, may seem to be luxurious, there is no evidence in the passage that Fogg cannot comfortably pay for these services. (D) is contradicted in the passage starting in line 21, where Fogg's card-playing partners are introduced, and in line 44, where Fogg inserts himself into his friends' conversation. People who keep to themselves do not play cards or enter others' conversations.

10. A

Difficulty: Medium

Category: Command of Evidence

Getting to the Answer: Review your answer to the previous question. Locate the answer choice that directly supports the conclusion you drew. **(A)** is correct. It provides the best support for the idea that Phileas Fogg is a man of habit and routine. The word "habitual" (line 8) and the fact that his table was prepared ahead of time for him suggest that Fogg followed this routine regularly.

None of the incorrect choices addresses Fogg's fondness for routine. Choice (B) supports the idea that Fogg is skilled in cutting open his newspaper, not that he enjoys routine. (C) describes the routine passing of the time but does not mention Fogg. (D) describes the bank robber and does not mention Fogg at all.

11. D

Difficulty: Medium

Category: Vocab-in-Context

Getting to the Answer: Locate context clues to help determine the meaning of the word. Predict a meaning for the word and then match it to the closest answer

choice. The sentence describes Fogg arriving at the club and going to his usual table. A good prediction is simply the word "went." Look for the nearest match in the answers. **(D)** fits the tone and context of the sentence and is correct.

Choice (A) is a common definition for "repaired" but does not make sense in the context. You cannot *fixed* to the dining-room. (B) subtly changes the meaning of the sentence. Although you may think Fogg is returning to his table since it's his "habitual" table, the text is describing events as they occur and not referring to what may have happened earlier. (C) is not supported by the passage; there is no evidence that Fogg is moving with great force or anger.

12. A

Difficulty: Medium

Category: Inference

Getting to the Answer: Review the first paragraph of the passage before choosing an answer. Fogg is very methodical, he walks to the club, reads two newspapers, has dinner, reads another newspaper, and is joined by the men with whom he plays cards. **(A)** is correct because not only does Fogg read three newspapers daily, but he also later chimes in with a comment on the robbery the other men are discussing based on the information he learned in the paper.

There is no mention of politics, so (B) is incorrect. Although Fogg does comment on the bank robbery, his comment is a neutral observation about the description of the perpetrator, not "strong opinions about crime," so (C) is incorrect. (D) is incorrect because Fogg's occupation is not mentioned in the excerpt.

13. D

Difficulty: Easy

Category: Command of Evidence

Getting to the Answer: Review your answer to the previous question. Decide which lines of text show Fogg's knowledge of current events. **(D)** is correct. In these lines, Fogg interjects with additional information from the newspaper about a crime that is a current event.

Choice (A) simply describes Fogg receiving and preparing one of his papers. (B) describes his partners gathering in the reading room and says nothing about Fogg himself. (C) is describing the bank robber, not Fogg.

14. A

Difficulty: Easy

Category: Vocab-in-Context

Getting to the Answer: Find context clues in the target sentence. Predict the meaning of the word and look for a match among the answer choices. "Functionary" (line 51) refers back to the "principal cashier" (line 50) mentioned earlier in the sentence. When you see two related answer choices, such as "official" and "servant," pay attention to the tone and specific context clues to help you choose. **(A)** is correct; if substituted back into the sentence, the meaning of the sentence is unchanged.

Choice (B) is incorrect because you cannot refer to a "cashier" as "money." (C), "servant," is incorrect because it implies a hierarchy that is not present in the passage. Similarly, there is no evidence in the passage that the "cashier" is a "criminal," so (D) is incorrect.

15. B

Difficulty: Medium

Category: Detail

Getting to the Answer: Locate the portion of the text that discusses the bank. Your passage map for paragraph 11 should note a lack of security at the bank. This paragraph describes the lack of security measures at the bank that led to a theft in broad daylight; lines 55–58 note a lack of guards or protective gratings. **(B)** is correct.

Choice (A) is a distortion of information in the excerpt. Lines 53–55 state that the bank had faith in its customers, not that the customers have faith in the bank. (C) and (D) are not mentioned in the passage at all.

16. C

Difficulty: Medium

Category: Inference

Getting to the Answer: Find the part of the passage that describes the thief. Locate sentences that focus on a description of the suspect. Summarize the details in a one-sentence description. Lines 76–80 ("On the day . . . crime was committed") describe the suspect as a gentleman. **(C)** is correct because the passage suggests that the police do not believe the man to be a professional thief due to the description of his appearance and demeanor.

Choice (A) may be true but is not presented as a reason the thief was not professional. (B) and (D) are not mentioned in the passage at all.

17. B

Difficulty: Medium

Category: Function

Getting to the Answer: Reread the cited line. Concentrate on how the sentence affects the text surrounding it. Examining the surrounding text shows that this comment occurs during a discussion about the thief being on the run. Fogg has silently listened to the conversation to this point, but now quietly interjects. This suggests that Fogg will have more to say about the topic; **(B)** is correct.

(A) is extreme. "Ominous" foreshadows a bad or unpleasant event, and the text simply provides Fogg's view without any negative connotations. (C) is a misused detail. The passage does describe Fogg's demeanor, but the statement in the line reference for the question does not. (D) may be tempting if you're familiar with the plot of the book from which this excerpt is drawn, but remember, your answers on the SAT must be based only on the given passage. Since the line reference is the last line in the passage, it cannot be introducing the conflict of the plot of this excerpt.

Reading

CHAPTER 23

SAT Reading: Timing and Section Management Strategies

LEARNING OBJECTIVE

After completing this chapter, you will be able to:

- Recognize at a glance which passages in a section are likely to be easiest for you

---

Timing

You have 65 minutes to read 5 passages and answer 52 questions, so you need to complete each passage and its accompanying questions in an average of 13 minutes to finish on time. (Note that passages are not all the same length or difficulty, so some will take longer than others.) After 32 minutes, you should be about halfway done with the section. When the proctor informs you that there are 5 minutes remaining, you should ideally be working on the last few questions.

Note that this is a brisk pace. Reading for structure can help, as can triaging questions and skipping those that you can see at a glance will be time-consuming. Your real task is not actually to attempt all the questions in 65 minutes but to get as many points from the section as you can.

Section Management

You may want to triage entire passages on the Reading section, not just questions. Some test takers have a hard time with literature, or primary source passages, or science; if you have distinct preferences about subject matter, you might consider leaving a particular passage type for last. For example, the section typically opens with the Literature passage. If that's the passage you feel least confident about, it makes sense to skip it and do it last. (Just be careful with your bubbling.)

Remember that you probably won't spend the same amount of time on each question for a passage. Every question counts for the same number of points, so be sure to complete the questions you find easiest to answer first. Also, be aware that the questions are usually arranged with Globals at the beginning of the set and increasing line number references, and that you will typically see two Command of Evidence questions per passage. Approached correctly, these questions should be quick: when you research the Detail or

Inference question that immediately precedes the Command of Evidence question, leave your finger on the support you find for the correct answer, then look for that support among the answer choices for the Command of Evidence question.

Finally, moving efficiently through this section is important, but that does not mean that you should skip over any text. Reading all of the text in the passage is essential to answering questions efficiently and accurately.

When considering the structure of the entire test, keep in mind that you will have a break after you complete this section. If you start to feel tired, remind yourself that you'll have a break soon. The more focused you can remain, the easier it will be for you to determine each correct answer.

There is a full Reading section in the How Much Have You Learned? section of this chapter. Use it to practice timing: skip questions you find too time-consuming and return to them if you have time. When you are finished, check your work—and reflect on how well you managed the section.

If you're still looking for more practice with Reading question sets after finishing this chapter, **go online** (www.kaptest.com/moreonline) and use the Qbank to generate additional practice sets for yourself.

How Much Have You Learned?

Questions 1–10 refer to the following passage.

The passage is adapted from Wilkie Collins, *The Woman in White*, first published in 1859. It is considered one of the first novels of the mystery genre.

Pesca's face and manner, on the evening when we confronted each other at my mother's gate, were more than sufficient to inform me that something extraordinary had happened.
5 It was quite useless, however, to ask him for an immediate explanation. I could only conjecture, while he was dragging me in by both hands, that, knowing my habits, he had come to the cottage to make sure of meeting
10 me that night and that he had some news to tell of an unusually agreeable kind.

We both bounced into the parlor in a highly abrupt and undignified manner. My mother sat by the open window laughing and
15 fanning herself. Pesca was one of her especial favorites, and his wildest eccentricities were always pardonable in her eyes. From the first moment she found out that the little Professor was deeply and gratefully attached to her son,
20 she opened her heart to him unreservedly and took all his puzzling foreign peculiarities for granted, without so much as attempting to understand any one of them.

My sister Sarah, with all the advantages of
25 youth, was, strangely enough, less pliable. She did full justice to Pesca's excellent qualities of heart, but she could not accept him implicitly, as my mother accepted him, for my sake. Her insular notions of propriety rose in perpetual
30 revolt against Pesca's constitutional contempt for appearances, and she was always more or less undisguisedly astonished at her mother's familiarity with the eccentric little foreigner. I have observed, not only in my sister's case,
35 but in the instances of others, that we of the young generation are nowhere near as hearty and impulsive as some of our elders. I constantly see old people flushed and excited by the prospect of some anticipated pleasure
40 which altogether fails to ruffle the tranquility of their serene grandchildren. Are we, I wonder, quite such genuine boys and girls now as our seniors were in their time? Has the great advance in education taken rather
45 too long a stride, and are we in these modern days just the least trifle in the world too well brought up?

Without attempting to answer those questions decisively, I may at least record that
50 I never saw my mother and my sister together in Pesca's society without finding my mother much the younger woman of the two. On this occasion, for example, while the old lady was laughing heartily over the boyish manner in
55 which we tumbled into the parlor, Sarah was perturbedly picking up the broken pieces of a teacup, which the Professor had knocked off the table in his precipitate advance to meet me at the door.

60 "I don't know what would have happened, Walter," said my mother, "if you had delayed much longer. Pesca has been half mad with impatience, and I have been half mad with curiosity. The Professor has brought some
65 wonderful news with him, in which he says you are concerned, and he has cruelly refused to give us the smallest hint of it till his friend Walter appeared."

"Very provoking: it spoils the set,"
70 murmured Sarah to herself, mournfully absorbed over the ruins of the broken cup.

While these words were being spoken, Pesca, happily and fussily unconscious of the irreparable wrong which the crockery had
75 suffered at his hands, was dragging a large arm-chair to the opposite end of the room, so as to command us all three, in the character of a public speaker addressing an audience. Having turned the chair with its back towards
80 us, he jumped into it on his knees and excitedly addressed his small congregation of three from an impromptu pulpit.

"Now, my good dears," began Pesca, "listen
to me. The time has come—I recite my good
85 news—I speak at last."

"Hear, hear," said my mother, humoring the
joke.

"The next thing he will break, Mamma,"
whispered Sarah, "will be the back of the best
90 arm-chair."

"Among the fine London Houses where I
teach the language of my native country," said
Pesca, "is one, mighty fine, in the big place
called Portland. The golden Papa there, the
95 mighty merchant, says 'I have got a letter from
my friend, and he wants a recommend from
me, of a drawing-master, to go down to his
house in the country. Perhaps you know of a
drawing-master that I can recommend?'

100 "I address myself to the mighty merchant,
and I say, 'Dear sir, I have the man! The first
and foremost drawing-master of the world!'"

1. The narrator's stance is best described as that of

A) a writer learning about a possible teaching
job.

B) a social historian chronicling generational
changes produced by evolving social
conventions.

C) a young man eager to set out on his own,
free of the strictures of his family.

D) a careful observer describing the natures of
three characters he knows well.

2. The central purpose of the first paragraph is to

A) provide insight into the narrator's habits.

B) demonstrate Pesca's disregard for the
narrator's feelings.

C) introduce the tone and setting of the
passage.

D) build suspense regarding the nature of the
news Pesca has brought.

3. The description of Pesca and the narrator in
lines 12–13 ("We both . . . manner") is primarily
meant to

A) illustrate the personalities of the narrator
and Pesca.

B) suggest that their disruptive behavior was
in fact combative.

C) portray Pesca as a bad influence on the
narrator.

D) provide a humorous contrast to the
seriousness of the narrator's mother.

4. The narrator's mother's attitude toward Pesca is
best described as

A) confusion about his enthusiastic manner.

B) disapproving of his unkempt appearance.

C) amusement at his wild schemes.

D) appreciative of his relationship with
her son.

5. Which choice provides the best evidence for the answer to the previous question?

    A) Lines 17–23 ("From . . . them")

    B) Lines 25–27 ("She . . . implicitly")

    C) Lines 28–31 ("Her . . . appearances")

    D) Lines 60–62 ("I don't . . . longer")

6. The questions in lines 41–47 ("Are we . . . brought up?") most nearly imply that

    A) the narrator and his sister received a poor education.

    B) some young people may behave too maturely for their age.

    C) some older people are too childish in their behavior.

    D) some children were raised inappropriately by their parents.

7. According to the passage, the narrator's sister is upset about the broken teacup because

    A) it makes the tea set incomplete.

    B) she does not have the money to replace it.

    C) it was important to her mother.

    D) Pesca deliberately knocked it off the table.

8. The attitude of Pesca toward the narrator's sister is best described as

    A) disrespectful and dismissive of her opinions.

    B) enthusiastic in furthering her education.

    C) unfazed by her concern for his behavior.

    D) disappointed by her disregard for his feelings.

9. Which choice provides the best evidence for the answer to the previous question?

    A) Lines 48–52 ("Without . . . two")

    B) Lines 72–75 ("While . . . his hands")

    C) Lines 79–82 ("Having . . . pulpit")

    D) Lines 91–94 ("Among . . . Portland")

10. As used in line 77, "command" most nearly means

    A) order.

    B) engage.

    C) lead.

    D) bully.

Reading

Reading

Questions 11–20 refer to the following passage.

This is an excerpt from a speech by William Lloyd Garrison, one of the most prominent opponents of slavery in the United States. It was delivered in 1854.

Let me define my positions, and at the same time challenge anyone to show wherein they are untenable.

I am a believer in that portion of the
5 Declaration of American Independence in which it is set forth, as among self-evident truths, "that all men are created equal; that they are endowed by their Creator with certain inalienable rights; that among these
10 are life, liberty, and the pursuit of happiness." Hence, I am an abolitionist. Hence, I cannot but regard oppression in every form—and most of all, that which turns a man into a thing—with indignation and abhorrence. Not
15 to cherish these feelings would be recreancy to principle. They who desire me to be dumb on the subject of slavery, unless I will open my mouth in its defense, ask me to give the lie to my professions, to degrade my manhood,
20 and to stain my soul. I will not be a liar, a poltroon, or a hypocrite, to accommodate any party, to gratify any sect, to escape any odium or peril, to save any interest, or to promote any object. Convince me that one man may
25 rightfully make another man his slave, and I will no longer subscribe to the Declaration of Independence. Convince me that liberty is not the inalienable birthright of every human being, of whatever complexion or clime, and
30 I will give that instrument to the consuming fire. I do not know how to espouse freedom and slavery together. . . .

These are solemn times. It is not a struggle for national salvation; for the nation, as such,
35 seems doomed beyond recovery. The reason why the South rules, and the North falls prostrate in servile terror, is simply this: with the South, the preservation of slavery is paramount to all other considerations—
40 above party success, denominational unity, pecuniary interest, legal integrity, and constitutional obligation. With the North, the preservation of the Union is placed above all other things—above honor, justice, freedom,
45 integrity of soul. . . . All these she is ready to discard for the union. Her devotion to it is the latest and most terrible form of idolatry. . . . If, at any time, she grows restive under the yoke, and shrinks back aghast at the new atrocity
50 contemplated, it is only necessary for that power to crack the whip of disunion over her head, as it has done again and again, and she will cower and obey like a plantation slave— for has she not sworn that she will sacrifice
55 everything in heaven and on earth, rather than the Union?

What then is to be done? Friends of the slave, the question is not whether by our efforts we can abolish slavery . . . but whether
60 we will go with the multitude to do evil, sell our birthright for a mess of pottage, cease to cry aloud and spare not. . . . Let us stand in our lot, "and having done all, to stand." At least, a remnant shall be saved. Living
65 or dying, defeated or victorious, be it ours to exclaim, "No compromise with slavery! Liberty for each, for all, forever! Man above all institutions!"

11. The primary purpose of the passage is to

    A) compare and contrast the justifications for slavery offered by the North and the South.

    B) encourage abolitionists to continue their efforts against slavery.

    C) invite critiques of the author's position.

    D) outline the reasons justifying slavery in order to argue against them.

12. One central idea of the passage is that

    A) the abolition of slavery will save the nation.

    B) the South is primarily responsible for the national tragedy of slavery.

    C) the ideals of the Declaration of Independence and the institution of slavery are mutually exclusive.

    D) the North should uphold the unity of the nation above all other considerations.

13. The main purpose of the second paragraph is to

    A) argue that a practice is inconsistent with a principle.

    B) describe needed changes to a social system.

    C) discuss the underlying ideas in an important document.

    D) suggest a way to resolve a difficult political issue.

14. Based on the passage, Garrison would be most likely to agree with which claim about the relationships of the North and the South to the institution of slavery?

    A) The South will agree to the abolition of slavery only through an amendment to the Constitution.

    B) Slavery will become an issue of ancillary importance as the industry of the South becomes more mechanized.

    C) The North has been complicit in the growth and continuation of slavery.

    D) Because slavery is incompatible with the Declaration of Independence, the North demands abolition.

15. Which choice provides the best evidence for the answer to the previous question?

    A) Lines 4–11 ("I am . . . abolitionist")

    B) Lines 38–42 ("with . . . obligation")

    C) Lines 42–46 ("With . . . union")

    D) Lines 64–68 ("Living . . . institutions")

16. As used in line 30, "instrument" most nearly means

    A) tool.

    B) document.

    C) expedient.

    D) mechanism.

17. The primary function of the third paragraph is to

    A) contrast the South's use of slavery with the North's opposition to slavery.

    B) describe reasons the South opposes, and the North supports, Garrison's view.

    C) identify the reasons both the North and the South oppose Garrison's view.

    D) outline the requirements for the abolition of slavery.

18. Which choice provides the best evidence for the claim that Garrison believes a personal decision to oppose slavery is paramount, whether or not the abolitionist movement is successful?

    A) Lines 31–32 ("I . . . together")

    B) Lines 46–47 ("Her . . . idolatry")

    C) Lines 57–60 ("Friends . . . evil")

    D) Lines 66–68 ("No compromise . . . institutions")

19. In the third paragraph, Garrison implies the most important reason the North tolerates slavery is that

    A) abolition would cause the South to secede from the Union.

    B) goods from the South would become prohibitively expensive without the use of slave labor.

    C) the Declaration of Independence does not prohibit slavery.

    D) the North will not meddle in the social policies of the South.

20. The passage most strongly suggests that the author believes which of the following regarding the abolition of slavery?

    A) Although the abolitionists may fail, they must continue to fight against slavery.

    B) Because the North and the South both have compelling reasons to tolerate slavery, the abolitionists will fail.

    C) With enough Northern support, slavery will eventually be abolished.

    D) Thanks to the efforts of Garrison's followers, the abolition of slavery is imminent.

Questions 21–30 refer to the following passage.

This passage describes some research applications of a bioluminescent jellyfish protein.

Electron excitation is the process by which an electron within an atom is transferred to a higher energy state. Electron excitation is typically followed by the release of a photon
5 when the electron falls back to its normal state. The initial transfer to the higher energy state can be accomplished by absorbing a photon, but it can happen in a variety of other ways as well. For example, the element
10 phosphorus spontaneously combines with oxygen when exposed to air, producing a transfer of energy to the phosphorus electrons. The subsequent release of photons as the electrons fall back to lower energy states is an
15 example of what is termed chemiluminescence, the emission of light as a result of a chemical reaction.

In a related effect called bioluminescence, light is produced by chemical reactions
20 associated with biological activity. Bioluminescence occurs in a variety of life forms and is more common in marine organisms than in terrestrial or freshwater life. Examples of species that exhibit
25 bioluminescence include certain bacteria, jellyfish, clams, fungi, worms, ants, and fireflies. There is considerable diversity in how light is produced, but most processes involve the reaction of a light-emitting
30 molecule with oxygen, catalyzed by an enzyme. The light-emitting molecule varies from one organism to another, but all are grouped under the generic name luciferin. The enzymes catalyzing the reaction fall into
35 two groups: photoproteins and luciferases. As the biochemistry of bioluminescence becomes better understood, researchers are harnessing this biological process in recombinant genetics experiments.
40 In 2008, Osamu Shimomura, Martin Chalfie, and Roger Tsien won the Nobel Prize in chemistry for their work in discovering specific bioluminescent proteins and

employing them to study cellular chemistry.
45 Shimomura laid the foundation through his work on a bioluminescent jellyfish, *Aequorea victoria*. In 1962, he and a colleague isolated three key molecules that produce *A. victoria*'s bioluminescence: coelenterazine, a
50 luciferin; aequorin, a photoprotein; and green fluorescent protein (GFP). The coelenterazine, when combined with aequorin, produces blue light that is then transduced to green light by GFP. Interestingly, GFP does not require any
55 cofactor or substrate besides oxygen; it simply emits a green glow when exposed to blue or ultraviolet light. This means that GFP can be used, by itself, as a marker for the expression of other proteins in a cell. This innovation was
60 Chalfie's contribution, via a paper published in 1992. Roger Tsien's research expanded on this application: he created variants of GFP with stronger fluorescence and in different colors. The result of the collective work of
65 Shimomura, Chalfie, and Tsien is that it is nowadays possible to track a variety of cellular processes using bioluminescent proteins.

One example of this work is the study of cancer using zebrafish that have had
70 the gene for GFP inserted into their DNA immediately next to a gene that codes for certain cancer processes. The result of this genetic manipulation is the ability to see the location of tumor cells. Zebrafish are
75 translucent, so fluorescent tumor cells can be readily identified using a light microscope. A 2003 study of leukemia using this animal model revealed that tumor cells initially arose in the thymus and then spread to muscles and
80 abdominal organs.

Another example is the discovery that bisphenol A (BPA), a common component of plastics, is an endocrine disrupter— specifically, that it has estrogenic activity.
85 In a study conducted in 2002, cells in tissue culture were genetically engineered to express GFP when an estrogen receptor on the cells was stimulated. When exposed to estrogen, the cells glowed fluorescent green. Researchers

90 found that they could cause the cells to exhibit the same fluorescence by exposing them to BPA. However, the concentration of BPA required to induce fluorescence was 100,000 times higher, so it appears that BPA
95 is only weakly estrogenic. Repeating the same experiment with polychlorinated BPA, the researchers found it to have stronger estrogenic activity than ordinary BPA. Because polychlorinated BPA is not easily biodegraded
100 and tends to persist in the environment, they concluded that polychlorinated BPA may function as a worse endocrine disrupter than BPA.

The research applications of GFP are
105 endless, and while a great deal remains to be discovered about bioluminescence in the many species that exhibit it, the discovery of this one jellyfish protein has already produced a variety of useful results.

21. The passage evolves from an explanation of a natural biochemical process to

   A) a description of research made possible through extensions of the natural process.

   B) an explanation of how the natural process developed through evolutionary pressure.

   C) a discussion of efforts by scientists to reverse the effects of the natural process.

   D) an explanation why research based on this process will have no practical results.

22. The function of the first paragraph is to

   A) introduce the main idea of the passage.

   B) identify a point of view with which the author disagrees.

   C) provide evidence for the author's opinion.

   D) discuss a scientific phenomenon similar to the main topic of the passage.

23. According to the passage, bioluminescence is most often found

   A) with oxygen when exposed to the air.

   B) among terrestrial creatures.

   C) in marine life.

   D) in light given off by hot objects.

24. Which of the following provides the best evidence for the answer to the previous question?

   A) Lines 9–12 ("For example . . . electrons")

   B) Lines 18–20 ("In . . . activity")

   C) Lines 21–24 ("Bioluminescence . . . life")

   D) Lines 34–35 ("The enzymes . . . luciferases")

25. The passage suggests that the jellyfish *Aequorea victoria*

    A) would emit green light without the presence of aequorin.

    B) would emit blue light without the presence of aequorin.

    C) would emit no light without the presence of GFP.

    D) would emit blue light without the presence of GFP.

26. Which of the following provides the best evidence for the answer to the previous question?

    A) Lines 24–27 ("Examples . . . fireflies")

    B) Lines 47–51 ("In 1962 . . . (GFP)")

    C) Lines 51–54 ("The coelenterazine . . . GFP")

    D) Lines 61–64 ("Roger . . . colors")

27. Based on the passage, it can be inferred that aequorin, part of *A. victoria*'s bioluminescence machinery, is

    A) a bacterium.

    B) a light-emitting molecule.

    C) a luciferase.

    D) an enzyme.

28. As used in line 45, "foundation" most nearly means

    A) basis.

    B) charity.

    C) organization.

    D) innovation.

29. According to the passage, which of the following has NOT been the subject of GFP-based research?

    A) Leukemia

    B) Electron excitation

    C) Endocrine disrupters

    D) Tumor cells

30. In the experiment in which it was concluded that ordinary BPA is only weakly estrogenic, the researchers are assuming that

    A) whether or not GFP illuminates depends in part on the level of estrogenic activity.

    B) the intensity of the illumination in the GFP is directly correlated with the level of estrogenic activity.

    C) polychlorinated BPA has higher levels of estrogenic activity than does ordinary BPA.

    D) the level of endocrine disruption caused by BPA is correlated with the level of estrogenic activity.

Questions 31–41 refer to the following passage.

The following passage explores the history and impact of public higher education in the United States.

Every year, hundreds of thousands of students graduate from U.S. public universities. Many of the largest and most elite schools in the nation fall into the
5   category of public, or state, institutions. Unlike private universities, which generally operate independently from any government influence, public higher education was established through government legislation
10   and is sustained through state and federal involvement in various ways. A look into the history of U.S. public higher education can shed light on the changing ideals of the American story over the past century and
15   a half.

America's earliest higher-education institutions, like Harvard, were initially developed by and for clergy, or church workers. For 17th-century Puritans in
20   America, church leadership was of utmost importance. At that time, clergy was the main profession for which college degrees were offered. Later, during the 18th and 19th centuries, paralleling the onset of secular
25   (and increasingly scientifically inclined) modern thought, the nation and government acknowledged the need for broader higher education opportunities. Philosophers and politicians alike were aware that well-educated
30   citizens were a vital element of a functional democracy. A better-informed voting population could secure a better political future. Moreover, with aims to advance the fields of technology and agriculture through
35   higher education, legislators anticipated potential economic improvements nationwide as well. It was in the nation's best interest to make college more accessible.

In 1862, President Lincoln signed the Morill
40   Land-Grant Act. This was, in many ways, the force behind the public university system. The Morill Act ensured that public land would be

set aside for the establishment of universities across the country. The coming decades saw a
45   massive increase in the opening of universities in the nation. Hundreds of U.S. public universities began to operate. These schools received federal and state support, offered practical, accessible education, and sought,
50   originally, to advance the fields of agriculture and mechanics. Soon these schools offered wide varieties of subjects and specialties. These universities would be operated by their respective states, but all would adhere to
55   certain broad federal regulations.

At the time, the government was seeking to mend racial injustices through legislation. To this effect, a second land act was passed in 1890 in hopes of inhibiting discrimination
60   in public universities. While at the time this did not accomplish the intended openness and diversity, it paved the way for the culture of diversity the American university system enjoys today. Many public universities are
65   now richly diverse, with regulations in place to accept students of any race, ethnicity, or socioeconomic status. In a similar vein, women, who were once a minority in colleges, increasingly gained a strong presence in U.S.
70   universities over the past 150 years. Women actually surpassed men in overall U.S. college attendance around the turn of the 21st century.

Since the legislation of the 19th century,
75   public universities have undergone momentous growth. The system has evolved to address and accommodate the nuances of 20th- and 21st-century American culture and development. Offering in-state students some
80   of the most affordable degree programs in higher education, these schools have now graduated millions of undergraduate and graduate students. Public universities also manage the majority of the nation's
85   government-funded academic research initiatives. Featuring some of the most competitive athletic programs in the world, as well as elite scholarship and arts programs,

the U.S. public universities's accomplishments
90 seem boundless. With schools in Alaska,
Hawaii, and even U.S. territories like Puerto
Rico and Guam, public university impact
reaches the farthest corners and populations of
the nation. The state school system has been
95 formative for American culture, philosophy,
economics, medicine, politics, and much more.

The eminence of the U.S. public university
network stretches beyond the United States.
Students travel from across the globe to study
100 at top programs. Cutting-edge schools like the
University of Virginia (UVA) and University
of California at Los Angeles (UCLA) receive
continual international attention for their
accomplishments in scholarship and research.
105 Programs, faculty, and students from these
schools participate in the global conversation
in significant ways, working toward a better
future for the planet.

Given those early visions for a more
110 robustly educated voting population, the
enormity of the system that the Morill
Act launched is remarkable. U.S. public
universities have both shaped and employed
many of America's greatest thinkers.
115 Considering their timeline and their
accomplishments, these schools seem to reflect
the post–Civil War history of diversity, liberty,
creativity, and equal opportunity that in many
ways distinguishes the American cultural
120 identity.

31. The passage's primary purpose is to

    A) summarize the accomplishments of U.S.
    public universities since the 19th century.

    B) explain the historical influence of religion
    on the development of the university
    system.

    C) discuss the relationship between U.S.
    higher education and the cultural values of
    the nation.

    D) summarize the historical effect of the
    Morill Land-Grant Act on U.S. public
    universities.

32. Which of the following pieces of evidence would
most strengthen the author's line of reasoning
throughout the passage?

    A) Information about the ways in which
    private and public universities differ in
    paragraph 1

    B) An example of how the 17th-century
    clergy benefited from higher education in
    paragraph 2

    C) Statistics showing increased enrollment
    numbers of minority students in paragraph 4

    D) An example of a competitive public
    university athletic program in paragraph 5

33. In the second paragraph, the author uses the
idea that educated citizens are necessary for a
functioning democracy to

    A) show why an educated workforce increased
    agricultural production.

    B) demonstrate the continued role of the
    clergy in American public life.

    C) explain why the government was playing a
    larger role in public education.

    D) emphasize the importance of technological
    innovation for the economy.

34. Which choice provides the best evidence for the answer to the previous question?

   A) Lines 21–23 ("At that time . . . offered")

   B) Lines 23–28 ("Later . . . opportunities")

   C) Lines 31–33 ("A better-informed . . . future")

   D) Lines 33–37 ("Moreover . . . well")

35. The purpose of the third paragraph is to

   A) highlight an example of the government increasing access to public education.

   B) discuss initial technological advances in agriculture and mechanics.

   C) outline the effects of the Morill Land-Grant Act on the U.S. economy.

   D) explain the relationship between federal and state control of public universities.

36. In line 49, the author's use of the word "accessible" implies that

   A) public universities would expand course offerings to encompass a range of subjects.

   B) the likelihood that people with limited means could attend a university was increasing.

   C) agriculture and mechanics would receive the most federal and state support.

   D) President Lincoln supported passage of the Morill Land-Grant Act to expand education.

37. As used in line 54, "adhere" most nearly means

   A) resist.

   B) notice.

   C) acquiesce.

   D) comply.

38. In the fourth paragraph, the author uses the fact that more women than men now attend college to

   A) contrast the advances of women's rights with racial injustice in public universities.

   B) provide an example of how the land acts initially failed to stop discrimination.

   C) show that public universities have grown increasingly diverse over time.

   D) illustrate the challenges many people still face to attend public universities.

39. Which choice provides the best evidence for the answer to the previous question?

   A) Lines 58–60 ("To this effect . . . universities")

   B) Lines 60–64 ("While . . . today")

   C) Lines 64–67 ("Many . . . status")

   D) Lines 67–70 ("In a similar . . . years")

40. As used in line 77, "nuances" most nearly means

   A) eras.

   B) categories.

   C) circumstances.

   D) variations.

41. The fifth paragraph supports the central idea of the passage by

   A) discussing how public university athletic programs have grown increasingly competitive.

   B) providing evidence of the success of federal legislation meant to invest in public universities.

   C) explaining that in-state tuition rates have increased enrollment in U.S. public universities.

   D) noting that the U.S. public university system has expanded into U.S. territories.

Questions 42–52 refer to the following passages.

Passage 1 discusses the possibility of panspermia, the idea that life on Earth is of extraterrestrial origin. Passage 2 is a response to Passage 1.

Passage 1

Panspermia, the hypothesis that life on Earth originated in outer space, has had a number of supporters since the nineteenth century—some of them quite distinguished—
5   but it has never won general acceptance among biologists. However, recent research has found possible support for panspermia.

Most of the meteorites that strike Earth originated in the lifeless wastes of the asteroid
10 belt. A few, though, have been identified as fragments that were torn from the Moon and Mars by comets and asteroids and eventually drifted to Earth. The Moon and Mars are lifeless, but there is reason to believe that,
15 billions of years ago, Mars was warmer and moister than it is now and capable of supporting life. Indeed, Mars may have been more conducive to the development of life than Earth was during the early history of the
20 solar system. It is feasible that life developed on Mars first and was carried to Earth on space-borne debris.

But could living organisms have survived the journey through space? The effects of cosmic
25 rays on the known Martian meteorites indicate that they took from 700,000 to 15,000,000 years to reach Earth. It seems inconceivable that any life forms could have survived such conditions for so long. However, computer simulations
30 suggest that fragments hurled into space from a collision on Mars would begin reaching Earth in only 16,000 years. Moreover, it is therefore conceivable that an improbable stroke of luck allowed a meteor to carry living things from
35 Mars to Earth—and the Tanpopo experiment has shown that certain bacteria, when clustered together to inhibit damage by ultraviolet rays, can survive in space for at least one year. Panspermia can thus no longer be dismissed
40 as science fiction or the fanciful speculation

of unscientific minds: it is becoming an increasingly viable, even promising, field of research within the field of astrobiology.

Passage 2

While absence of evidence is not evidence
45 of absence, the panspermia hypothesis will remain nothing more than a tantalizing idea until incontrovertible evidence is found that interplanetary transfer of microbes is not only possible, but also historical fact. Finding such
50 evidence is absurdly challenging, the more so because alternative explanations abound for the presence of bacteria on objects in space.

Take the recent discovery of marine and land bacteria similar to species found on Earth
55 (they belong to the genera *Mycobacterium* and *Delftia*) in cosmic dust present on the exterior of the International Space Station (ISS). Even if the discovery is genuine and not the result of cross-contamination of the samples at
60 any stage between their collection and their analysis in a laboratory on Earth, it by no means indicates that the bacteria arrived at the ISS from an extraterrestrial source. It is far more likely that they are ordinary Earth
65 bacteria that were transported to the ISS on the surfaces of supplies or other objects as part of routine restocking, as is known to have occurred in the past. It is also possible, though less likely, that they are ordinary
70 Earth bacteria that were hurled into the outer atmosphere by storm systems. Either way, their discovery on ISS surfaces does not demonstrate their extraterrestrial origin—and the issue of indeterminate origin will hamper
75 any similar type of study. It follows that very carefully designed, novel experiments will be required to conclusively demonstrate or refute the panspermia hypothesis, and while multiple researchers are working on this problem, it
80 will be years, and more probably decades, before we can draw plausible and meaningful inferences.

42. The author of Passage 1 would be most likely to agree with which of the following statements about the solar system?

    A) The Moon used to be more capable of supporting life than it currently is.

    B) It is possible that there was a time when Mars had conditions more suitable to life than Earth did.

    C) It is likely that a fragment from the Moon carried life to Earth.

    D) The life found on Mars billions of years ago could have originated from the asteroid belt.

43. Which choice provides the best evidence for the answer to the previous question?

    A) Lines 8–10 ("Most . . . belt")

    B) Lines 10–13 ("A few . . . Earth")

    C) Lines 17–22 ("Indeed . . . debris")

    D) Lines 29–32 ("However . . . years")

44. As used in line 9, the word "wastes" is closest in meaning to

    A) wilderness.

    B) barren zones.

    C) by-products.

    D) fragments.

45. The main purpose of lines 32–38 ("Moreover . . . year") is to

    A) counter an objection to a hypothesis.

    B) indicate the need for further study.

    C) provide the answer to a question.

    D) describe an event that is likely to have occurred many times.

46. According to the author of Passage 2, which of the following best summarizes the reasons to be skeptical of discoveries of bacteria on extraterrestrial objects as evidence for panspermia?

    A) Scientists cannot avoid bias when examining evidence for hypotheses they believe to be true.

    B) A large number of highly improbable events would need to have occurred at precisely the same time.

    C) It is very unlikely that such bacteria would have survived the lengthy journey from Mars to Earth.

    D) There is high probability that the bacteria came from some terrestrial source.

47. Based on the discussion of the bacteria found on the exterior of the International Space Station, the author of Passage 2 would be most likely to agree with which of the following?

    A) It is easier for bacteria to be carried into Earth's outer atmosphere from its surface than from elsewhere in the solar system.

    B) It is not possible that bacteria from an extraterrestrial source could have survived a journey through space.

    C) The time required to create experiments that will determine the origin of the bacteria makes the process of doing so impractical.

    D) The dust on the ISS that the bacteria are found in likely came from rocks that originated on Earth.

48. Which choice provides the best evidence for the answer to the previous question?

    A) Lines 44–49 ("While . . . fact")

    B) Lines 53–57 ("Take . . . (ISS)")

    C) Lines 63–68 ("It is . . . past")

    D) Lines 75–82 ("It follows . . . inferences")

49. In using the phrase "absence of evidence is not evidence of absence . . ." (lines 44–45), the author is

   A) pointing out a logical flaw in critics' arguments.

   B) condemning the lack of research conducted into the panspermia hypothesis.

   C) laying a logical foundation for an argument made later.

   D) acknowledging that a lack of evidence does not disprove a hypothesis.

50. The author of Passage 2 would be most likely to respond to the evidence presented in lines 14–20 by

   A) dismissing the evidence as completely irrelevant to the topic at hand.

   B) conceding that the evidence does, in fact, lend substantial support to the panspermia hypothesis.

   C) asserting that such evidence is insufficient to support the hypothesis of panspermia and therefore inconclusive.

   D) shifting to a position of provisional acceptance of panspermia dependent upon the results of future experiments.

51. The authors of both passages provide an answer to which of the following questions?

   A) What would be required for the panspermia hypothesis to gain widespread acceptance?

   B) How does the panspermia hypothesis compare to other potential explanations of the origins of terrestrial life?

   C) What conditions would have had to exist to allow microorganisms of extraterrestrial origin to have reached Earth?

   D) Is the panspermia hypothesis currently worth serious consideration as an explanation for the origins of life on Earth?

52. Which choice best states the relationship between the two passages?

   A) Passage 2 directly refutes the evidence presented in Passage 1.

   B) Passage 2 challenges the primary argument of Passage 1.

   C) Passage 2 provides a broader context for the ideas discussed in Passage 1.

   D) Passage 2 considers additional evidence to further the goals of Passage 1.

Answers and Explanations

Suggested passage notes:

¶1: Description of P; good news

¶2: Mom likes P

¶3: Sister doesn't like P b/c too improper; young gen. more stuffy than old

¶4: Mom's reaction to P vs. sister's reaction to P

¶5–6: Mom excited for news; sister upset over cup

¶7–8: P actions

¶9–10: Mom and sister's reactions to P

¶11–12: P's announcement

1. D

Difficulty: Medium

Category: Inference

Strategic Advice: Focus on how the narrator sees the characters and events.

Getting to the Answer: Literature passages tend to focus on the relationships among main characters. Here, the main characters are the narrator, his mother, his sister, and Pesca. The narrator focuses on the reaction that each woman has to Pesca's actions. Predict that the author wants to create a sketch of each woman by using those different responses. **(D)** is correct.

(A) is incorrect because, even though a job is mentioned at the end, it is for a "drawing-master," not a writer. And this is just a small point at the end, which ignores everything else that precedes it in the passage. (B) is incorrect because there's no indication of the narrator being a historian, let alone one who is studying generational changes or social conventions. (C) is incorrect because there is no indication that the narrator is looking to leave his family.

2. C

Difficulty: Medium

Category: Function

Strategic Advice: Consult your passage map to identify the function of the first paragraph.

Getting to the Answer: This paragraph provides context for the rest of the passage. The narrator describes Pesca's expressive nature, his understanding of Pesca, and the reason for the subsequent events in the passage. Predict that this paragraph sets the stage for

understanding how Pesca's character will impact the rest of the story. **(C)** matches that prediction.

(A) is incorrect because the paragraph describes Pesca's behavior, not the narrator's. Even though the narrator's habits are mentioned in one sentence, the paragraph is still about Pesca using that information. (B) is incorrect because Pesca is just excited. He's not said to be dismissive of the narrator's feelings. (D) is incorrect because Pesca's news is not really important to the story. It's more about people's reaction to Pesca's excitement.

3. A

Difficulty: Medium

Category: Function

Strategic Advice: To understand why a narrator chooses a particular phrase, focus on the author's intention in the surrounding text. The cited section will work to accomplish that intention.

Getting to the Answer: Throughout the paragraph, the narrator describes why his mother finds Pesca so pleasing. This introductory wording sets the stage by describing Pesca as undignified. This feature of his personality is a great match for **(A)**.

(B) is incorrect because the word "bouncing" implies good humor, not aggression. (C) is incorrect because the mother appreciates the bond between the narrator and Pesca. There is no suggestion of Pesca being a bad influence. (D) is incorrect because it is the narrator's sister who is more serious, not his mother.

4. D

Difficulty: Medium

Category: Inference

Strategic Advice: Note that the next question is a Command of Evidence question, so make a mark next to any sentences that support the answer to this question. Doing so could come in handy for the next question.

Getting to the Answer: The strongest indication of the mother's attitude comes in the second paragraph. She laughs as Pesca excitedly enters the room. But, more tellingly, she is described as accepting his peculiar behavior because he is "deeply and greatly attached to her son." This is echoed in **(D)**.

(A) is incorrect because, if anything, the mother is said to merely accept any of Pesca's peculiarities without even trying to understand them. That doesn't mean she's confused. Even if she were to find those peculiarities a little confusing, it doesn't follow that she's confused by his enthusiasm. (B) is incorrect because it describes the sister's attitude, not the mother's. (C) is incorrect because there is no indication of any wild schemes.

5.   A

Difficulty: Medium

Category: Command of Evidence

Strategic Advice: Be sure to use any information used in the previous question to save time on this question.

Getting to the Answer: The support for the previous question came primarily from the second paragraph. That includes lines 17–23, which describe how the mother has opened her heart to Pesca because of his attachment to her son. **(A)** is correct.

(B) and (C) are incorrect because they refer to the sister's attitude, not the mother's. (D) is incorrect because, although the mother is speaking, she is not indicating any attitude toward Pesca at that moment.

6.   B

Difficulty: Medium

Category: Inference

Strategic Advice: When given a line reference, consider the context of the surrounding text.

Getting to the Answer: This question refers to some thoughts the narrator presents at the end of the third paragraph. In that paragraph, the narrator is talking about his sister, who is rather serious compared to her mother. The narrator then describes how this is typical of young people, who don't seem as excitable or impulsive as their elders. The narrator's questions at the end hint that younger people are perhaps *too* serious these days. That matches **(B)**.

(A) is incorrect because it misuses the word "education." The author is actually suggesting that young people are so *well* educated that they forget how to have a little fun. (C) is incorrect because the author seems to regret the serious behavior of young people, not the excitable behavior of older people. (D) is incorrect because there is no questioning of how parents are raising their children.

7.   A

Difficulty: Medium

Category: Detail

Strategic Advice: The phrase "According to the passage" means that the correct answer will be spotted directly in the text. Don't rely on memory. Find the detail and literally put your finger on it.

Getting to the Answer: The cause of the sister's disappointment is found in the sixth paragraph, in which she mourns the broken teacup and claims that "it spoils the set." This matches **(A)**.

(B) is incorrect because there's no mention of its cost or how much money the sister has. (C) is incorrect because the mother seems unconcerned with the broken teacup. (D) is incorrect because Pesca is said to have knocked it over upon excitedly entering the room. It's presented as an accident, not a deliberate act.

8.   C

Difficulty: Medium

Category: Inference

Strategic Advice: A quick glance ahead shows that the next question is a Command of Evidence question. It is worth taking note of any lines that support the answer to this question, as those may be useful for the next question.

Getting to the Answer: The passage provides a lot of information about the attitude of the narrator's sister toward Pesca: she has contempt for his appearance and is bothered by his behavior, which resulted in a broken teacup. However, there are few hints about Pesca's attitude. The only clue is in the seventh paragraph, where Pesca is said to be unaware of the broken teacup, suggesting that Pesca is oblivious to the sister's unhappiness. That matches **(C)**.

(A) is incorrect because it's too strong. Pesca is just excited and unaware of the narrator's sister's bad mood; he is not purposely being rude or dismissing her. (B) is incorrect because Pesca's enthusiasm is more about his news, not for any desire to educate the sister. (D) is incorrect because, while the sister is unhappy with Pesca, he does not seem to notice or be disappointed in any way.

9. B

Difficulty: Medium

Category: Command of Evidence

Strategic Advice: Consider the purpose of each given quote to make sure it matches the ideas expressed in the previous question.

Getting to the Answer: The previous question asked about Pesca's attitude toward the narrator's sister. As Pesca never addresses the sister directly, the only suggestion of attitude comes from lines 72–75, in which Pesca is seen as oblivious to the sister's concern about her broken teacup. Those are the lines cited in correct answer **(B)**.

(A) is incorrect because those lines indicate more the sister's attitude toward Pesca, not the other way around. (C) is incorrect because it shows Pesca's excitement in sharing his news with everyone in the room, not his attitude toward the sister in particular. (D) is incorrect because it's Pesca talking about himself, without expressing any attitude toward the sister or anyone else.

10. B

Difficulty: Hard

Category: Vocab-in-Context

Strategic Advice: For Vocab-in-Context questions, read the entire sentence for meaning. Be ready to eliminate choices that give a common definition for the word.

Getting to the Answer: In line 78, the author is describing how Pesca grabbed a chair so that he could be like "a public speaker addressing an audience." In that sense, commanding an audience means seeking their undivided attention, or keeping them engaged. That makes **(B)** the correct answer.

(A), (C), and (D) are incorrect because they all refer to a different concept of commanding that is not consistent with this passage. Pesca is not giving orders or leading or bullying anyone.

Suggested passage notes:

¶1: challenge to find flaw in G's position
¶2: slavery incompatible w/ Dec of Independence
¶3: South's & North's reasons for slavery
¶4: G's opinion—abolitionists can't end slavery, but can oppose it

11. B

Difficulty: Medium

Category: Global

Strategic Advice: Always ask yourself, "Why did the author write this passage?" after you read the passage, and before you start on the questions.

Getting to the Answer: Garrison ends the passage by answering the question in line 57, "What then is to be done?" He goes on to state in the final paragraph that abolitionists should continue their efforts to abolish slavery whether or not they are successful. **(B)** is correct.

(A) and (D) are distortions of information presented in the third paragraph. Garrison outlines the reasons the North and the South use to justify slavery, but dismisses them as erroneous without arguing against them, (D), or comparing them, (A). (C) is too narrow. While, in the first paragraph, Garrison does invite his opponents to criticize his views, this is not mentioned in any of the later parts of the text and is therefore not the central goal of the passage.

12. C

Difficulty: Medium

Category: Global

Strategic Advice: Use your passage map to predict the answer to a Global question.

Getting to the Answer: Review the passage map to refresh your memory of the central ideas. **(C)** is found in the summary of paragraph 2 and is the correct answer.

(A) is a distortion of information in the passage. Although the author believes slavery must be abolished, lines 33–35 state his view that the nation may already be beyond saving. (B) is extreme; Garrison believes that both the North and the South are responsible for the institution of slavery, not that the South is "primarily responsible." (D) is the opposite of what the passage says. As stated in lines 42–46, Garrison believes that the North is putting the Union first, but then he goes on to harshly criticize this view, calling it "the latest and most terrible form of idolatry" in lines 46–47.

13. A

Difficulty: Hard

Category: Function

Strategic Advice: Function questions ask how or why the author used a feature in the passage. Keep the overall purpose of the passage in mind and answer the question, "Why did the author write the second paragraph?"

Getting to the Answer: The passage map notes that slavery is incompatible with the Declaration of Independence, so **(A)** is the correct answer. The practice mentioned in the choice is slavery, and it is inconsistent with the principle that "all men are created equal" in the Declaration of Independence.

(B) is incorrect because although Garrison believes slavery should be abolished, he does not describe what this entails or how it should be done. (C) is incorrect because Garrison states the principle of freedom in the Declaration of Independence and then goes on to discuss how this principle affects his views; he does not discuss the idea of freedom itself. (D) is incorrect because, although Garrison clearly states that slavery should be abolished, he does not propose any way to resolve the conflict that would arise with those who believe slavery should be maintained.

14. C

Difficulty: Medium

Category: Inference

Strategic Advice: Research the answer to an Inference question in the passage. The passage must directly support the answer.

Getting to the Answer: The relationships of the South and the North with slavery are discussed in the third paragraph. Lines 38–39 state that the South considers the continuation of slavery the "paramount" issue; nothing is more important to the South. The North tolerates slavery because that toleration keeps the nation together. Lines 42–44 state that preservation of the union is the North's top priority. Compare these ideas to the choices, and **(C)** is the match. By putting the unity of the nation first, Garrison would argue the North has allowed slavery to continue and to spread.

(A) is incorrect because it is the opposite of what the passage says. Lines 38–42 state that the South will put the preservation of slavery above "constitutional obligation." (B) is incorrect because it is not mentioned in the

passage at all. (D) is incorrect because while the author does believe that slavery is incompatible with the Declaration of Independence, this view is not also attributed to the North. Also, the text never describes the North as demanding abolition.

15. C

Difficulty: Medium

Category: Command of Evidence

Strategic Advice: Put your finger on the lines where you found the answer to the previous question.

Getting to the Answer: If you leave your finger on the line in the passage where you found the previous answer, you can answer Command of Evidence questions quickly. The reason the North tolerated slavery was found in lines 42–44, which matches **(C)**.

(A) and (D) are Garrison's views, not those of either the North or the South. (B) describes the South's view, but the answer to the previous question was the North's toleration of slavery, so the correct evidence will support the North's point of view.

16. B

Difficulty: Medium

Category: Vocabulary-in-Context

Strategic Advice: Look back in the passage and determine how the author used the word given in a Vocab-in-Context question.

Getting to the Answer: Use the line reference to locate the word "instrument," then read above and below that line to determine how the author is using that word. Since "instrument" is preceded by the pronoun "that" in the sentence, determine what "that" is and use the pronoun's antecedent as your prediction. The sentence in line 30 begins in line 27, so "that" must be the noun closest to the start of the sentence—the Declaration of Independence. The Declaration of Independence is a document, so **(B)** is correct.

The remaining answers are incorrect because none of them properly refers to the Declaration of Independence.

17. C

Difficulty: Hard

Category: Function

Strategic Advice: Think of the author's purpose in writing the passage and then ask yourself, "How or why did the author use the third paragraph?"

Getting to the Answer: The correct answer will describe why the author included the third paragraph, or how the third paragraph contributed to the author's point of view. Review the passage map and predict "to describe the reasons both the North and the South accept slavery in the South." **(C)** is correct.

(A) is incorrect because the third paragraph outlines the justifications for slavery offered by both the South and the North. (B) is incorrect because Garrison's view is that slavery should be abolished, and the third paragraph gives the reasons both the South and the North will allow slavery to continue. (D) is incorrect because the author argues for an absolute and immediate end to slavery, and does not list any requirements for this change.

18. C

Difficulty: Hard

Category: Command of Evidence

Strategic Advice: Be sure your choice, on its own, supports the idea in the question.

Getting to the Answer: For Command of Evidence questions, the excerpt from the passage in the choice must answer the question. **(C)** is the only choice that addresses both the effort to abolish slavery ("the question is not whether by our efforts we can abolish slavery") and the personal decision to oppose slavery ("but whether we will go with the multitude to do evil").

(A), (B), and (D) all provide evidence that Garrison opposes slavery, but do not connect that opposition to the success (or lack of success) of the abolitionist movement.

19. A

Difficulty: Easy

Category: Inference

Strategic Advice: Research the answer in the third paragraph, looking for a statement that must be true based on the passage.

Getting to the Answer: The emphasis keywords in the question, "most important," mean the passage must be equally emphatic. In lines 42–44, Garrison states that "above all other things," the North wants "the preservation of the Union." In other words, the North allows slavery to continue because of the fear that, if the North does not, the South will leave the Union. **(A)** is correct.

You may believe (B) to be true if you've studied U.S. history, but this is not mentioned in the text, so it is incorrect. (C) is incorrect because it is the opposite of what the passage says. Garrison argues in the second paragraph that slavery and the Declaration of Independence are incompatible. (D) is incorrect because it is not mentioned in the passage at all.

20. A

Difficulty: Medium

Category: Inference

Getting to the Answer: Use your understanding of the main idea to eliminate choices and then match the remaining choices to the passage. Garrison's main idea is that abolitionists must continue to fight slavery, even though they may not be successful (lines 57–60). **(A)** is correct.

(B) is a distortion of information in the third paragraph. While Garrison did outline the reasons the North and South were both willing to tolerate slavery, Garrison did not consider either view "compelling." Rather, he argued that these were the reasons "the nation . . . seems doomed beyond recovery" (lines 34–35). (C) and (D) similarly distort information in the passage. While Garrison is arguing for the abolition of slavery, he argues, in lines 57–60, that efforts for abolition must continue regardless of their success. Garrison does not state slavery will eventually, (C), or soon, (D), be abolished.

Suggested passage notes:

¶1: chemiluminescence can be caused by electron excitation. ex: phosphorus + oxygen = light

¶2: bioluminescence: light from animals; description of general chemical process

¶3: biolum. in jellyfish; GFP is important molecule

¶4: cancer research based on GFP

¶5: toxic plastics research based on GFP

¶6: GFP research is promising; much is unknown but many results already

21. A

Difficulty: Medium

Category: Global

Getting to the Answer: Use the passage map to see how the passage proceeds. After the discussion of the natural bioluminescence through paragraph 3, the passage moves on to a discussion of research based on this process. Paragraphs 4 and 5 discuss how jellyfish proteins involved in bioluminescence have helped scientists research topics such as cancer and potentially harmful components in plastic. **(A)** describes this part of the passage perfectly and is correct.

Choice (B) is incorrect because there's no discussion in the passage of how bioluminescence evolved. (C) can be eliminated because the research is not intended to reverse the effects of bioluminescence; it's using those effects in an attempt to make new discoveries. (D) is contradicted by the last line of the passage, which says that the research has already produced "useful results."

22. D

Difficulty: Medium

Category: Function

Getting to the Answer: When asked for the function of a paragraph, consider how it relates to the overall purpose of the passage. The purpose of the passage as a whole is to discuss bioluminescence and its research applications. The first paragraph describes chemiluminescence, and the first line of paragraph 2 says that bioluminescence is a "related effect." Therefore, you can predict that the first passage is something that is similar to the main idea but which itself is not the main idea. **(D)** matches this prediction perfectly and is correct.

(A) is incorrect because the first paragraph does not actually discuss the main idea, merely a related topic.

(B) and (C) both imply that the author expresses an opinion; they are both incorrect because the author expresses no opinions in this neutral, explanatory passage.

23. C

Difficulty: Easy

Category: Detail

Strategic Advice: Answer Detail questions by reading around the cited text until you find the information that answers the question.

Getting to the Answer: Paragraph 2 contains general information about bioluminescence. Read around the cited lines to find the detail you need: "Bioluminescence occurs in a variety of life forms and is more common in marine organisms than in terrestrial or freshwater life" (lines 21–24). This matches **(C)**, which is correct.

According to the first paragraph, phosphorus does emit light when combined with oxygen, but this is an example of chemiluminescence, not bioluminescence, so (A) is incorrect. (B) is directly contradicted by the lines you found in your research, so it can be eliminated. (D) is not mentioned anywhere in the passage, so it is also incorrect.

24. C

Difficulty: Easy

Category: Command of Evidence

Getting to the Answer: While researching the previous question, you found that lines 21–24 supported the correct answer. Thus, **(C)** is correct. (A) describes the reaction between phosphorus and oxygen, not bioluminescence. (B) describes bioluminescence in general, but it doesn't establish that it's most common in marine life. (D) merely describes the two types of enzymes that might be involved in a bioluminescent reaction, so it can be eliminated.

25. D

Difficulty: Medium

Category: Inference

Getting to the Answer: Paragraph 3 is where this jelly-fish is discussed, so direct your research there. There are a lot of facts in the paragraph, but what it tells you about the *A. victoria* is fairly straightforward: coelenter-azine and aequorin interact to emit blue light, which is transformed into green light by GFP. Look for an answer that lines up with this information.

(D) is correct. GFP's function is to turn the blue light into green light, so if it wasn't there, the light would be blue. Since aequorin is described as being part of the light-producing process, there would be no biolumines-cence without it, which means (A) and (B) can be elim-inated. (C) is incorrect because the GFP is not directly involved in producing light; it merely changes the color.

26. C

Difficulty: Medium

Category: Command of Evidence

Getting to the Answer: Use your research for the previ-ous question to point you to the correct answer here. The correct answer to the previous question depended on knowing how the *A. victoria* produced light; this is described in lines 51–54, so **(C)** is correct.

(A) cites lines that merely give examples of biolumines-cent creatures, so it can be eliminated. (B) may seem tempting, because lines 47–51 describe the chemicals involved in *A. victoria*'s bioluminescence. However, it doesn't actually provide any information on how they interact to produce light, so it's incorrect. (D) can be eliminated because it describes further research done on GFP, not how GFP works in *A. victoria*.

27. D

Difficulty: Hard

Category: Inference

Getting to the Answer: *A. victoria* is the biolumines-cent jellyfish that, according to the passage map, is discussed in paragraph 3, so start your research there. Aequorin is described as a photoprotein that interacts with a luciferin, which then produces light. However, the passage map indicates that the chemical process of bioluminescence is described in paragraph 2 as

well. Photoproteins are mentioned there as a class of enzymes; therefore, aequorin is an enzyme, so **(D)** is correct.

(A) is incorrect because bacteria are mentioned as an example of an organism that could exhibit biolumines-cence itself. (B) may be tempting since aequorin is part of the light-emitting process. However, according to the passage, it's the luciferin that is the light-emitting molecule; the photoproteins merely start the reaction. According to paragraph 2, luciferase is another class of enzyme, distinct from photoproteins, that could be involved in a bioluminescent reaction, so (C) can be eliminated.

28. A

Difficulty: Easy

Category: Vocab-in-Context

Getting to the Answer: Check out the context in which "foundation" is used. It's used in paragraph 3 in the discussion of how three scientists won a Nobel Prize; the passage says that one of the scientists "laid the foundation" with research on a bioluminescent jellyfish. Thus, you can predict that here, "foundation" is used to mean something like *groundwork*. **(A)**, "basis," matches this prediction and is correct. While (B), "charity," and (C), "organization," can be synonyms for "foundation," they don't fit the context here. (D) can be eliminated because, while the passage does discuss many innova-tions, this isn't one of them.

29. B

Difficulty: Hard

Category: Detail

Strategic Advice: This is a Detail question for which the three incorrect answers will be examples of GFP-based research, while the correct answer will not be. You can't predict something that doesn't appear in the passage, but you can use details from the passage to predict the incorrect answers.

Getting to the Answer: According to the passage map, paragraphs 4 and 5 discuss this research. Paragraph 4 mentions that GFP was used to research tumor cells, with leukemia being given as an example of one type of cancer that was studied. That means (A) and (D) can be eliminated. Paragraph 5 mentions that GFP was used to determine that BPA, a type of plastic, is an endocrine disrupter, so (C) is incorrect. That leaves **(B)**, electron excitation, as the correct answer. This topic is discussed at the beginning of the passage as a process that can sometimes lead to chemiluminescence, not as a subject of GFB research.

30. A

Difficulty: Hard

Category: Inference

Getting to the Answer: This asks for an assumption about estrogen levels in BPA; according to the passage, plastics research is discussed in paragraph 5, so direct your attention there. The researchers concluded that BPA was only weakly estrogenic since more BPA than pure estrogen was needed to trigger the illumination. This means that they must be assuming there's some link between the level of estrogen and whether the GFP illuminates. This is captured perfectly in **(A)**, so it is correct.

(B) is incorrect because there's no indication that the GFP glows more brightly if estrogen levels are higher; the distinction was whether or not the GFP illuminated at all. (C) is a true statement according to the passage, but it's the conclusion of a different study; the question is about ordinary BPA, not polychlorinated BPA, so it is incorrect. (D) can be eliminated since this experiment wasn't intended to test the levels of endocrine disruption; it merely tested whether BPA contained estrogen.

Suggested passage notes:

¶1: 2 types of univ. = pub. & private
¶2: pub univ. goal = ↑ higher ed opportunity
¶3: 1862—gov't gave pub. land for univ.
¶4: history of diversity
¶5: major growth
¶6: US univ. part of global conv.
¶7: univ. reflect diversity, liberty, creativity

31. C

Difficulty: Hard

Category: Global

Strategic Advice: Consider what the passage is about overall and what the author wants the reader to learn, rather than an idea that is mentioned only in passing or in support of the passage's purpose. Reviewing your whole passage map can help you focus on the entirety of the passage.

Getting to the Answer: The author has written a brief history of public higher education in the United States; in both the introduction and conclusion, the author connects the evolution of the public university system with the evolution of generally accepted ideals and cultural values, such as diversity and liberty. Predict that the author is discussing the connection between public higher education and generally accepted ideals. **(C)** is correct.

32. C

Difficulty: Hard

Category: Inference

Strategic Advice: It is difficult to predict the exact answer for this type of question, but concisely stating the author's line of reasoning before reviewing the answer choices will help you eliminate the choices that do not strengthen that theme.

Getting to the Answer: Throughout the passage, the author discusses how the expansion of public universities has impacted American culture. In paragraph 4, the author describes how public universities have gradually become more diverse, offering educational opportunities to many people who would not have otherwise had them in previous years. This has had a significant impact on American culture. Consider which of these pieces of evidence best supports that theme; **(C)** is correct.

33. C

Difficulty: Hard

Category: Function

Getting to the Answer: The correct answer will reflect a specific position supported in both the second paragraph and the passage as a whole. Predict that the author is citing political and economic reasons to explain why the government "acknowledged the need" (line 27) for educated citizens. **(C)** is correct.

34. B

Difficulty: Medium

Category: Command of Evidence

Getting to the Answer: Use your support for the previous question to predict the answer. Consider which choice best shows a clear relationship to your answer. In the previous question, line 27 offered support for your answer; **(B)** is correct because it explicitly states that the government saw the "need for broader higher education opportunities" (lines 27–28).

Reading

35. A

Difficulty: Medium

Category: Function

Getting to the Answer: Summarize the paragraph and think about what the author would want the reader to know after reading it. Be sure to review your passage map, which should already state important information about the paragraph. Your passage map notes that in 1862, the government gave public land for university development; the paragraph states that the Morill Act was an early example of the federal government's desire to increase enrollment at public universities. Predict that the purpose of the paragraph is to explain how the government supported public higher education. **(A)** is correct.

36. B

Difficulty: Medium

Category: Function

Getting to the Answer: The author's choice of words is deliberate. Read the sentence carefully and think about what the author is suggesting when he uses the word "accessible." The passage notes that public universities received federal and state support, which means the universities could then function at a lower cost and could enable more students to attend. Predict that "accessible" was used to describe how higher education was remodeled to be available to more people, especially those with limited means. **(B)** is correct.

37. D

Difficulty: Easy

Category: Vocab-in-Context

Getting to the Answer: Use context clues to help you predict the meaning of the word as it is used in the sentence. The last sentence in paragraph 3 contrasts the fact that although universities would be operated by states, they would still need to follow, or comply with, federal regulations because they received federal support. Predict that "adhere" most nearly means *follow* or *comply with*. **(D)** is correct.

38. C

Difficulty: Medium

Category: Function

Getting to the Answer: Think about why the author would want to include this fact. The paragraph's central idea is that the student populations of public universities have grown increasingly diverse. Predict that the author is describing an example of how public universities have become more diverse. Look for the answer choice that matches this prediction. **(C)** is correct.

39. B

Difficulty: Easy

Category: Command of Evidence

Getting to the Answer: There should be a clear relationship between the correct choice and the previous answer. Since you used the fourth paragraph as a whole to predict the last question, look for the choice that offers support for the specific answer to the previous question. **(B)** clearly states that public universities are diverse today, even though the 1890 land act did not increase diversity when it was passed. This corresponds to the answer to the previous question.

40. D

Difficulty: Easy

Category: Vocab-in-Context

Getting to the Answer: Predict the meaning of the word with context clues from the sentence and paragraph. The second sentence of paragraph 5 states that the public university system "has evolved," which implies it has done so in response to changes or variations in American culture over time. Predict that "nuances" most nearly means *changes* or *variations*. Check your answer choice in the sentence to ensure it makes sense. **(D)** is correct.

41. B

Difficulty: Medium

Category: Inference

Getting to the Answer: Consider the central idea of the passage that you identified in a previous question and the central idea in the fifth paragraph. The passage is primarily about the way in which U.S. higher education has reflected American cultural identity. The fifth paragraph summarizes the major growth public higher education has undergone. Predict that as the American culture has grown to value public higher education, public higher education has undergone major growth; the fifth paragraph gives an example that supports the central idea. **(B)** is correct.

Suggested Passage 1 notes:

¶1: Panspermia not generally accepted but new research may suppt

¶2: Asteroids from Moon/Mars to Earth; Mars may have once had life

¶3: Transfer of life possible

Suggested Passage 2 notes:

¶1: Panspermia just hypothesis—no evidence

¶2: Bacteria on ISS likely from Earth. Special experiments needed to confirm or refute panspermia—concl likely years away.

42. B

Difficulty: Medium

Category: Inference

Strategic Advice: The correct answer will be the one that logically follows from the statements made in the passage.

Getting to the Answer: The keywords in the question, "would be most likely to agree with," identify this as an Inference question. Begin by referring back to the place in the passage where the author discusses elements of the solar system. In paragraph 2, the author states that the Moon and Mars are now lifeless, but that billions of years ago, Mars was warmer and moister and "may have been capable of supporting life." The paragraph further states that Mars may have been more conducive to the development of life than Earth was during the early history of the solar system. **(B)** logically follows from these statements and is the correct answer.

There was no discussion of the Moon being able to support life, so (A) and (C) are incorrect. The author never states that life was actually found on Mars or where such life might have originated, so (D) can be ruled out as well.

43. C

Difficulty: Medium

Category: Command of Evidence

Getting to the Answer: While researching the previous question, you found that lines 17–22 supported the answer. Thus, **(C)** is correct. (A) describes the lifeless area of the asteroid belt but does not discuss whether conditions were favorable for life on either Earth or Mars. (B) indicates that a few asteroids may have come from the Moon and Mars but doesn't mention the conditions of life on Earth or Mars. (D) indicates the relatively short time in which asteroids may have reached Earth from Mars but has nothing to do with the conditions for life on either planet.

44. B

Difficulty: Medium

Category: Vocab-in-Context

Strategic Advice: Look back in the passage and determine how the author used the word given in a Vocab-in-Context question. Imagine that the word is missing and needs to be filled in; predict a synonym.

Getting to the Answer: Use the line reference to locate the word "wastes," then read above and below that line to determine how the author is using that word. Since "wastes" is preceded by the adjective "lifeless" in the sentence, and is being used to describe an area of space, the asteroid belt, you can predict "lifeless area." **(B)** is correct.

The remaining answers are incorrect because, although each of them is an alternative definition of "wastes," none of them makes sense in the context of the sentence.

45. A

Difficulty: Hard

Category: Function

Strategic Advice: Think of the author's purpose in writing this paragraph and then ask yourself: "Why did the author include these lines; how do they help advance the purpose?"

Getting to the Answer: The paragraph begins with a discussion of the problems with the hypothesis of panspermia: the harsh conditions in space and the great amount of time that seems necessary for objects to travel from Mars to Earth. These are reasons that people object to the hypothesis. The cited lines go on to discuss information that might weaken those objections. Therefore, **(A)** is correct.

(B) is incorrect because there is no discussion of further study in this section of the passage. (C) may be tempting, but the information in the cited lines is not there to definitively answer the question of whether panspermia occurs; it is merely there to give evidence that weakens the objections. (D) is incorrect because the author never hints at how often an event might have occurred.

46. D

Difficulty: Medium

Category: Detail

Strategic Advice: Answer Detail questions by reading around the cited text until you find the information that answers the question.

Getting to the Answer: Paragraph 2 of Passage 2 contains information about bacteria found on the exterior of the International Space Station. The author then engages in a lengthy discussion describing the likely terrestrial origins of these bacteria. This matches **(D)**, which is correct.

The author never mentions bias among scientists, so (A) is incorrect. While the author might agree with the statements in (B) and (C), neither of these is the reason given for skepticism about the possibility of extraterrestrial origins for the bacteria found on the ISS, so both are incorrect.

47. A

Difficulty: Hard

Category: Inference

Strategic Advice: The correct answer to an Inference question will be the one that logically follows from the statements made in the passage.

Getting to the Answer: The keywords in the question, "would be most likely to agree with," identifies this as an Inference question. Begin by referring back to the place in the passage where the author discusses the bacteria found on the ISS. The author states that the bacteria are more likely to be from Earth than from an extraterrestrial source—either contamination introduced sometime during the testing process or bacteria that were lofted into the outer atmosphere by storms on Earth. **(A)** logically follows from this information and is the correct answer.

(B) is incorrect because it is too extreme: the author thinks it unlikely that the bacteria have an extraterrestrial origin, but never implies that it is impossible. (C) is incorrect because the author indicates that further "novel experiments" will be needed to make meaningful determinations about the possibility of panspermia and that the process may take decades, but never mentions that such experimentation will take too long to be practical. (D) can be ruled out since the author refers to the dust on the ISS as "cosmic dust," implying that it has a nonterrestrial origin.

48. C

Difficulty: Easy

Category: Command of Evidence

Getting to the Answer: While researching the previous question, you determined that the information in lines 63–71 supported the answer. Thus, **(C)** is correct.

Choice (A) merely says that hard evidence for the panspermia hypothesis is needed, so it can be eliminated. Choice (B) indicates that the bacteria are similar to those found on Earth, but doesn't discuss the likely origins of the bacteria. Choice (D) discusses what kind of experiments will be needed in the future, but this does not support the author's assertion that the bacteria on the ISS likely came from Earth.

49. D

Difficulty: Medium

Category: Function

Strategic Advice: Think of the author's overall purpose in writing the passage and then ask: "Why did the author include this line; in what way does it function?"

Getting to the Answer: Note how the author begins the passage with the cited phrase "While absence of evidence is not evidence of absence" to contrast with what follows: "the panspermia hypothesis will remain nothing more than a tantalizing idea until incontrovertible evidence is found . . ." The author is pointing out that the hypothesis is unsupported by any evidence, but is also conceding that the lack of such evidence is not sufficient to disprove the hypothesis. Therefore, **(D)** is correct.

(A) is incorrect because the cited line is a concession to logic, not a flaw. (B) is incorrect because the author isn't condemning the lack of research, merely stating that there isn't evidence to support the hypothesis. (C) is incorrect because the statement is not a foundation for the author's argument, but an acknowledgment that the lack of evidence is inconclusive.

50. C

Difficulty: Medium

Category: Inference

Strategic Advice: Find the answer that logically follows from the information in the passages.

Getting to the Answer: The keywords in the question, "would be most likely to respond," indicates an Inference question. Begin by referring back to the cited evidence in Passage 1; it provides evidence to support the idea that Mars may have been suitable for life at an earlier time in the history of the solar system. Next, recall the central claim of Passage 2: there is not adequate evidence to consider panspermia as anything more than a "tantalizing hypothesis" until conclusive evidence is found that shows that the interplanetary transfer of microbial life has actually occurred in the past. Since the evidence presented in the cited lines does not accomplish this goal, it follows that the author of Passage 2 would say that such evidence is inadequate; **(C)** logically follows from these statements and is correct.

(A) is too extreme; there is no reason to believe that the author of Passage 2 would consider the cited evidence "completely irrelevant," only insufficient. Because the author's central position is that evidence for the actual transfer of life from Mars to Earth would be needed to conclude that panspermia is a valid hypothesis, (B) and (D) can both be eliminated.

51. D

Difficulty: Medium

Category: Detail

Strategic Advice: You may have a hard time predicting the answer to a "which of the following" question. If so, check each answer choice against information in the passages.

Getting to the Answer: (A) is incorrect because, while Passage 1 states that there is recent research that makes panspermia a more viable hypothesis, it never explains what additional evidence would lead to wider acceptance.

Neither author compares the panspermia hypothesis to other hypotheses regarding the origins of terrestrial life, so (B) is incorrect.

(C) is incorrect because, although Passage 1 hints at some of the factors that might make the transfer of life from Mars to Earth possible, Passage 2 never delves into the conditions necessary for microorganisms to have originated from an extraterrestrial source.

(D) is correct because Passage 1 concludes that the panspermia hypothesis is worthy of scientific consideration while Passage 2 argues that there is insufficient evidence to consider panspermia an explanation for the origins of life on Earth.

52. B

Difficulty: Medium

Category: Function

Strategic Advice: Think about each author's central claim in order to determine the relationship between the two passages.

Getting to the Answer: In simplest terms, the author of Passage 1 argues that the panspermia hypothesis is worthy of serious consideration because there is suggestive evidence that life might have once existed on Mars and evidence that life might be able to survive a voyage through space from Mars to Earth. In contrast, the author of Passage 2 argues that there is insufficient evidence to make the case for panspermia anything more than mere speculation. This matches **(B),** which is the correct choice.

(A) is incorrect because Passage 2 doesn't refute the evidence presented in Passage 1, but rather considers it inadequate. (C) is incorrect because Passage 2 does not provide a broader context for the ideas discussed in Passage 1, but instead refutes them. (D) is incorrect because Passage 2 does not have the purpose of furthering the goals of Passage 1.

Test Yourself: Reading

Directions: For testlike practice, give yourself 65 minutes for this entire section. If you choose to break the section into smaller pieces, give yourself 13 minutes per passage.

Questions 1–11 refer to the following passages and supplementary material.

Passage 1 explains how scientists use radioisotopes to date artifacts and remains. Passage 2 discusses the varying problems with radioactive contaminants.

Passage 1

Archaeologists often rely on measuring the amounts of different atoms present in an item from a site to determine its age. The identity of an atom depends on how many
5 protons it has in its nucleus; for example, all carbon atoms have 6 protons. Each atom of an element, however, can have a different number of neutrons, so there can be several versions, or isotopes, of each element. Scientists name
10 the isotopes by the total number of protons plus neutrons. For example, a carbon atom with 6 neutrons is carbon-12 while a carbon atom with 7 neutrons is carbon-13.

Some combinations of protons and neutrons
15 are not stable and will change over time. For example, carbon-14, which has 6 protons and 8 neutrons, will slowly change into nitrogen-14, with 7 protons and 7 neutrons. Scientists can directly measure the amount of carbon-12
20 and carbon-14 in a sample or they can use radiation measurements to calculate these amounts. Each atom of carbon-14 that changes to nitrogen-14 emits radiation. Scientists can measure the rate of emission and use that
25 to calculate the total amount of carbon-14 present in a sample.

Carbon-14 atoms are formed in the atmosphere at the same rate at which they decay. Therefore, the ratio of carbon-12
30 to carbon-14 atoms in the atmosphere is constant. Living plants and animals have the same ratio of carbon-12 to carbon-14 in their tissues because they are constantly taking in carbon in the form of food or carbon dioxide.
35 After the plant or animal dies, however, it stops taking in carbon and so the amount of carbon-14 atoms in its tissues starts to decrease at a predictable rate.

By measuring the ratio of carbon-12 to
40 carbon-14 in a bone, for example, a scientist can determine how long the animal the bone came from has been dead. To determine an object's age this way is called "carbon-14 dating." Carbon-14 dating can be performed on
45 any material made by a living organism, such as wood or paper from trees or bones and skin from animals. Materials with ages up to about 50,000 years old can be dated. By finding the age of several objects found at different depths
50 at an archeological dig, the archaeologists can then make a timeline for the layers of the site. Objects in the same layer will be about the same age. By using carbon dating for a few objects in a layer, archaeologists know the age
55 of other objects in that layer, even if the layer itself cannot be carbon dated.

Passage 2

Radioactive materials contain unstable atoms that decay, releasing energy in the form of radiation. The radiation can be harmful
60 to living tissue because it can penetrate into cells and damage their DNA. If an explosion or a leak at a nuclear power plant releases large amounts of radioactive materials, the surrounding area could be hazardous until the
65 amount of radioactive material drops back to normal levels. The amount of danger from the radiation and the amount of time until the areas are safe again depends on how fast the materials emit radiation.
70 Scientists use the "half-life" of a material to indicate how quickly it decays. The half-life of a material is the amount of time it takes for half of a sample of that material to decay. A material with a short half-life decays more

75 quickly than a material with a long half-life.
For example, iodine-131 and cesium-137 can
both be released as a result of an accident at a
nuclear power plant. Iodine-131 decays rapidly,
with a half-life of 8 days. Cesium-137, however,
80 decays more slowly, with a half-life of 30 years.
        If an accident releases iodine-131, therefore,
it is a short-term concern. The amount
of radiation emitted will be high but will
drop rapidly. After two months, less than
85 one percent of the original iodine-131 will
remain. An accidental release of cesium-137,
however, is a long-term concern. The amount
of radiation emitted at first will be low but
will drop slowly. It will take about 200 years
90 for the amount of cesium-137 remaining to
drop below one percent. The total amount of
radiation emitted in both cases will be the
same, for the same amount of initial material.
The difference lies in whether the radiation
95 is all released rapidly at high levels in a short
time, or is released slowly at low levels, over a
long time span.

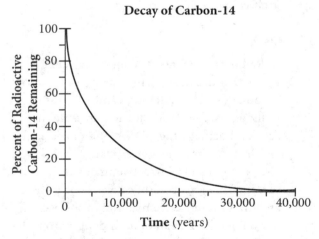

Decay of Carbon-14

This data is from the *Journal of Research of the National Bureau of Standards*, Vol. 46, No. 4, April 1951, pp. 328–333.

1. Based on the information in Passage 1, which of the following could be dated using carbon-14 dating?

    A) An iron pot found in a cave

    B) A rock at the bottom of a quarry

    C) An arrowhead made from bone

    D) The remains of a house made from stone

2. Which choice provides the best evidence for the answer to the previous question?

    A) Lines 11–13 ("For example…carbon-13")

    B) Lines 31–34 ("Living plants…dioxide")

    C) Lines 35–38 ("After the plant…rate")

    D) Lines 44–47 ("Carbon-14 dating…animals")

3. As used in line 29, "decay" most nearly means

    A) yield.

    B) deteriorate.

    C) discharge.

    D) circulate.

4. Which statement best describes the relationship between carbon-12 and carbon-14 in living tissue?

    A) There is more carbon-14 than carbon-12.

    B) There is more carbon-12 than carbon-14.

    C) The ratio of carbon-12 to carbon-14 is constant.

    D) The ratio of carbon-12 to carbon-14 fluctuates greatly.

5. Which choice provides the best evidence for the answer to the previous question?

    A) Lines 14–15 ("Some combinations…time")

    B) Lines 27–29 ("Carbon-14 atoms…decay")

    C) Lines 31–34 ("Living plants…carbon dioxide")

    D) Lines 35–38 ("After the plant…rate")

6. In Passage 2, the author refers to an accident that results in the release of iodine-131 as a "short-term concern" (line 82) because the initial amount of radiation released is

   A) low but will drop slowly.

   B) high but will drop quickly.

   C) low and will drop quickly.

   D) high and will drop slowly.

7. According to the information in Passage 2, living tissue exposed to radioactive material can

   A) be destroyed by high levels of heat caused by the radiation.

   B) become radioactive itself and damage surrounding tissue.

   C) suffer injury when the cells' components are damaged.

   D) be killed by extra protons released by the radioactive material.

8. As used in line 85, "original" most nearly means

   A) earliest.

   B) unique.

   C) unusual.

   D) critical.

9. According to Passage 2, scientists use the half-life of radioactive material to determine the

   A) amount of danger posed by radiation immediately following a nuclear accident.

   B) likelihood of a nuclear accident involving the release of radioactive material at any given location.

   C) amount of radiation contained in a sample of iodine-131 or cesium-137 used in nuclear reactions.

   D) length of time that must pass until an area is safe after the release of radioactive material.

10. Which generalization about the study of physics is supported by both passages?

    A) The study of atomic and nuclear physics can have many applications in a variety of fields.

    B) The study of physics has helped revolutionize how archaeologists study artifacts.

    C) Scientists use physics to keep people and wildlife safe following a nuclear accident.

    D) Scientists use different concepts to date ancient items and assess danger from nuclear accidents.

11. Based on the graph and the information in the passages, which statement is accurate?

    A) Carbon-14 has a half-life of about 5,400 years.

    B) The half-life of carbon-14 is similar to that of cesium-137.

    C) The half-life of iodine-131 is greater than that of cesium-137.

    D) All radioactive materials have a half-life of 30 to 5,400 years.

Questions 12–21 refer to the following passage.

The following passage is adapted from Lucy Maud Montgomery's 1908 novel *Anne of Green Gables*. This excerpt details a conversation between Anne, the young protagonist, and Marilla, Anne's guardian.

"And what are your eyes popping out of your head about now?" asked Marilla, when Anne had just come in from a run to the post office. "Have you discovered another kindred spirit?"

5 Excitement hung around Anne like a garment, shone in her eyes, kindled in every feature. She had come dancing up the lane, like a wind-blown sprite, through the mellow sunshine and lazy shadows of the August evening.

10 "No, Marilla, but oh, what do you think? I am invited to tea at the manse tomorrow afternoon! Mrs. Allan left the letter for me at the post office. Just look at it, Marilla. 'Miss Anne Shirley, Green Gables.' That is the first

15 time I was ever called 'Miss.' Such a thrill as it gave me! I shall cherish it forever among my choicest treasures."

"Mrs. Allan told me she meant to have all the members of her Sunday-school class to tea

20 in turn," said Marilla, regarding the wonderful event very coolly. "You needn't get in such a fever over it. Do learn to take things calmly, child."

For Anne to take things calmly would

25 have been to change her nature. All "spirit and fire and dew," as she was, the pleasures and pains of life came to her with trebled intensity. Marilla felt this and was vaguely troubled over it, realizing that the ups and

30 downs of existence would probably bear hardly on this impulsive soul and not sufficiently understanding that the equally great capacity for delight might more than compensate. Therefore Marilla conceived it

35 to be her duty to drill Anne into a tranquil uniformity of disposition as impossible and alien to her as to a dancing sunbeam in one of the brook shallows. She did not make much headway, as she sorrowfully admitted

40 to herself. The downfall of some dear hope or plan plunged Anne into "deeps of affliction." The fulfillment thereof exalted her to dizzy realms of delight. Marilla had almost begun to despair of ever fashioning this waif of the

45 world into her model little girl of demure manners and prim deportment. Neither would she have believed that she really liked Anne much better as she was.

Anne went to bed that night speechless

50 with misery because Matthew had said the wind was round northeast and he feared it would be a rainy day tomorrow. The rustle of the poplar leaves about the house worried her, it sounded so like pattering raindrops,

55 and the full, faraway roar of the gulf, to which she listened delightedly at other times, loving its strange, sonorous, haunting rhythm, now seemed like a prophecy of storm and disaster to a small maiden who particularly wanted

60 a fine day. Anne thought that the morning would never come.

But all things have an end, even nights before the day on which you are invited to take tea at the manse. The morning, in spite

65 of Matthew's predictions, was fine and Anne's spirits soared to their highest. "Oh, Marilla, there is something in me today that makes me just love everybody I see," she exclaimed as she washed the breakfast dishes. "You don't

70 know how good I feel! Wouldn't it be nice if it could last? I believe I could be a model child if I were just invited out to tea every day. But oh, Marilla, it's a solemn occasion too. I feel so anxious. What if I shouldn't behave properly?

75 You know I never had tea at a manse before, and I'm not sure that I know all the rules of etiquette, although I've been studying the rules given in the Etiquette Department of the Family Herald ever since I came here. I'm

80 so afraid I'll do something silly or forget to do something I should do. Would it be good manners to take a second helping of anything if you wanted to VERY much?"

"The trouble with you, Anne, is that you're
85 thinking too much about yourself. You should
just think of Mrs. Allan and what would be
nicest and most agreeable to her," said Marilla,
hitting for once in her life on a very sound and
pithy piece of advice. Anne instantly realized this.
90   "You are right, Marilla. I'll try not to think
about myself at all."

12. In line 4, what is implied by Marilla's question,
    "'Have you discovered another kindred spirit?'"

    A) Anne is deeply spiritual.

    B) Anne is a sociable person.

    C) Anne seeks out adventures.

    D) Anne has a fear of strangers.

13. The author's use of words such as "dancing" and
    "windblown" in lines 7–8 implies that Anne is

    A) graceful and rhythmic.

    B) messy and disorganized.

    C) energetic and active.

    D) scatterbrained and confused.

14. As used in line 44, "fashioning" most nearly
    means

    A) preparing.

    B) constructing.

    C) styling.

    D) devising.

15. Which choice best describes the relationship
    between Anne and Matthew?

    A) Anne does not trust Matthew's predictions.

    B) Anne is worried about Matthew's safety.

    C) Anne takes Matthew's statements seriously.

    D) Anne is uncertain about Matthew's
        intentions.

16. According to the passage, what does Marilla
    think is Anne's greatest challenge in life?

    A) Anne thinks about herself too much.

    B) Anne must learn to take things calmly.

    C) Anne needs to master the rules of etiquette.

    D) Anne worries too much about things she
        cannot control.

Reading

17. The fourth paragraph is important to the passage's progression of ideas because it

    A) explains the antagonistic relationship between Anne and Marilla.

    B) offers background information about Marilla's concerns about Anne.

    C) explains how Marilla has systematically changed Anne into a model child.

    D) provides a transition from Anne reading the letter to the following morning.

18. As used in line 88, "sound" most nearly means

    A) practical.

    B) clamor.

    C) ethical.

    D) secure.

19. It can be inferred that the author

    A) is an omniscient third-person observer.

    B) allows the reader to know only Anne's inner thoughts.

    C) offers an objective perspective from within the story.

    D) is unaware of actions that take place elsewhere in the story.

20. The passage most strongly suggests that which of the following is true of Marilla?

    A) She hopes Anne will soon learn to admire Mrs. Allan.

    B) She believes Anne's "deeps of affliction" are dangerous.

    C) She has come to dislike Anne's overly excitable nature.

    D) She values calm and even-keeled responses to all situations.

21. Which choice provides the best evidence for the answer to the previous question?

    A) Lines 21–23 ("'You needn't...child'")

    B) Lines 28–34 ("Marilla felt...compensate")

    C) Lines 46–48 ("Neither would...as she was")

    D) Lines 84–89 ("'The trouble...advice'")

Questions 22–32 refer to the following passages.

Passage 1 discusses possible uses of video games in designing educational materials. Passage 2 explores how elements of video games can be used in combating deteriorating cognition in older adults.

Passage 1

Many teenagers have heard from their parents that playing too many video games can negatively affect their learning and socialization. Studies performed in the 1990s
5 supported this claim. Scientists evaluated the content of popular video games and the amount of time children and teenagers were allowed to spend playing them. They eventually connected video games to anger
10 issues, obesity, and addiction.

Studies showed that violent video games played for long periods of time inadvertently mimic the same type of repetition used by teachers to reinforce subject matter. The
15 method of advancement in many violent video games involves winning a contest of some kind. This is also an approach used in the classroom and other settings familiar to children and teenagers. This method makes
20 the content of the video games, including overall aggressive themes, easy to absorb.

Until recently, the only positive effect of playing video games seemed to be an improvement in manual dexterity and
25 computer literacy. These important upsides didn't seem to outweigh the negatives. A 2013 study by the National Academy of Sciences shows that the playing of fast-paced video games can actually improve performance in
30 many areas, such as attention span, spatial navigation, cognition, reasoning, and memory. Researchers tested small pools of gamers and found that those who had a history of playing action-packed video games were
35 better at tasks such as pattern discrimination. They also found that the gamers excelled at conceptualizing 3-D objects.

This new information could change the form that educational materials take. Content
40 developers hope that the new materials may inspire interest in the fields of engineering, math, and technology. Educators can transform this data into classroom experiences that will not only cater to the current interests
45 of students, but also use old patterns of teaching in a new and more modern way.

Passage 2

As adults age, certain brain functions deteriorate. Two of these important functions are cognition and memory. This kind of
50 decline can lead to an associated loss of well-being. The number of adults affected by Alzheimer's disease or dementia is also on the rise. Researchers are racing to find ways for people to maintain brain health while
55 aging. A recent study examined the effects of non-action video-game training on people experiencing cognitive decline.

The study worked with small sample sizes of aging participants. Researchers found
60 that that the use of video games can allow the adult brain to maintain some plasticity. Test subjects trained their memories with games that featured patterned blocks, jigsaw puzzles, facial recognition, and other iterations
65 requiring the recall of patterns. Test subjects who completed as few as twenty training sessions with these video games showed an increase in attention span, alertness, and visual memory. They also showed a decrease
70 in distraction. These results are encouraging, as they suggest that there may be ways to stave off mental decline and to help the elderly maintain functions needed for safe driving and other activities of daily living.

75 More tests need to be done in order to understand the full potential of video games in the anti-aging market. There are several companies currently capitalizing on the success of these studies, and increasingly more games
80 that promise increased cognitive function are sure to find their way to retailers soon.

Reading

22. The central idea of Passage 1 is primarily concerned with

    A) the effects of video games on teenagers who play popular violent video games.

    B) outdated methods used by teachers and content developers to interest students in science and engineering.

    C) how research about the effects of video games on gamers is being used to develop new teaching methods.

    D) how the impact that video games have had on children and teenagers has changed over the past few decades.

23. Which choice provides the best evidence for the answer to the previous question?

    A) Lines 5–8 ("Scientists evaluated . . . them")

    B) Lines 19–21 ("This method . . . absorb")

    C) Lines 22–25 ("Until recently . . . literacy")

    D) Lines 42–46 ("Educators . . . modern way")

24. According to the information in the passage, studies performed in the 1990s support the claim that

    A) excessive video game playing can have a negative effect on teenagers.

    B) children who play video games are more likely to be interested in math and science.

    C) video games can improve performance in many areas related to success in education.

    D) teenagers who spend too much time playing violent video games become violent criminals.

25. As used in line 12, "inadvertently" most nearly means

    A) hastily.

    B) impulsively.

    C) unintentionally.

    D) imprudently.

26. According to the information presented in Passage 1, the content of video games is easily absorbed by teenagers because

    A) games are played for many hours a day on a daily basis.

    B) the games utilize methods used in the classroom to encourage retention.

    C) playing video games improves memory and increases cognitive functions.

    D) teenagers are predisposed to absorb material to which they are repeatedly exposed.

27. Based on the information in Passage 2, the reader can infer that

    A) elderly people who are able to ward off or reverse dementia may be able to live longer independently.

    B) video games could completely cure dementia and other age-related cognitive problems.

    C) playing board games for extended periods of time could have the same effect as playing video games.

    D) too much time spent playing video games would likely have a negative effect on cognition in aging populations.

28. Which choice provides the best evidence for the answer to the previous question?

    A) Lines 51–53 ("The number of . . . rise")

    B) Lines 55–57 ("A recent study . . . decline")

    C) Lines 70–74 ("These results . . . living")

    D) Lines 75–77 ("More tests . . . market")

29. As used in line 48, "deteriorate" most nearly means

    A) adapt.

    B) restrict.

    C) transform.

    D) diminish.

30. The author of Passage 2 supports the central claim of the passage in paragraph 2 by

    A) explaining the results of preliminary research involving the elderly and video games.

    B) describing the physiological causes of memory loss and declining cognitive functions.

    C) listing ways that the elderly can reduce the cognitive effects of aging and Alzheimer's disease.

    D) giving details about the research methods used to study dementia in elderly populations.

31. The purpose of Passage 2 is to

    A) describe the potential of video games to help combat the deterioration of brain function in aging populations.

    B) explain how companies are reaching out to the elderly to increase video game markets.

    C) encourage the reader to play video games as a way to increase memory and attention span.

    D) support research that will increase the quality of life of people as they age and lose brain function.

32. Which generalization about video games does the evidence presented in both passages support?

    A) People who have trouble with memory loss and are easily distracted should avoid video games.

    B) Initial research conducted in the 1990s failed to uncover some of the benefits of playing video games.

    C) Video games could be part of a comprehensive approach to helping people cope with the effects of aging.

    D) Researchers in a diverse range of fields are looking to video games for solutions to problems.

Reading

Questions 33–42 refer to the following passage.

Adapted from "The Red House Mystery" by
A.A. Milne, first published in 1922.

Whether Mark Ablett was a bore or not
depended on the point of view, but it may be
said at once that he never bored his company
on the subject of his early life. However,
5 stories get about. There is always somebody
who knows. It was understood—and this,
anyhow, on Mark's own authority—that
his father had been a country clergyman. It
was said that, as a boy, Mark had attracted
10 the notice, and patronage, of some rich old
spinster of the neighbourhood, who had
paid for his education, both at school and
university. At about the time when he was
coming down from Cambridge, his father
15 had died; leaving behind him a few debts, as
a warning to his family, and a reputation for
short sermons, as an example to his successor.
Neither warning nor example seems to have
been effective. Mark went to London, with an
20 allowance from his patron, and (it is generally
agreed) made acquaintance with the money-
lenders. He was supposed, by his patron and
any others who inquired, to be "writing"; but
what he wrote, other than letters asking for
25 more time to pay, has never been discovered.
However, he attended the theatres and music
halls very regularly—no doubt with a view to
some serious articles in the "Spectator" on the
decadence of the English stage.
30 Fortunately (from Mark's point of view) his
patron died during his third year in London,
and left him all the money he wanted. From
that moment his life loses its legendary
character, and becomes more a matter of
35 history. He settled accounts with the money-
lenders, abandoned his crop of wild oats to
the harvesting of others, and became in his
turn a patron. He patronized the Arts. It was
not only usurers who discovered that Mark
40 Ablett no longer wrote for money; editors were
now offered free contributions as well as free
lunches; publishers were given agreements
for an occasional slender volume, in which
the author paid all expenses and waived all
45 royalties; promising young painters and poets
dined with him; and he even took a theatrical
company on tour, playing host and "lead" with
equal lavishness.

He was not what most people call a snob.
50 A snob has been defined carelessly as a man
who loves a lord; and, more carefully, as a
mean lover of mean things—which would
be a little unkind to the peerage if the first
definition were true. Mark had his vanities
55 undoubtedly, but he would sooner have met
an actor-manager than an earl; he would have
spoken of his friendship with Dante—had
that been possible—more glibly than of his
friendship with the Duke. Call him a snob
60 if you like, but not the worst kind of snob;
a hanger-on, but to the skirts of Art, not
Society; a climber, but in the neighbourhood
of Parnassus, not Hay Hill.

His patronage did not stop at the Arts. It
65 also included Matthew Cayley, a small cousin
of thirteen, whose circumstances were as
limited as had been Mark's own before his
patron had rescued him. He sent the Cayley
cousin to school and Cambridge. His motives,
70 no doubt, were unworldly enough at first; a
mere repaying to his account in the Recording
Angel's book of the generosity which had been
lavished on himself; a laying-up of treasure in
heaven. But it is probable that, as the boy grew
75 up, Mark's designs for his future were based
on his own interests as much as those of his
cousin, and that a suitably educated Matthew
Cayley of twenty-three was felt by him to be
a useful property for a man in his position; a
80 man, that is to say, whose vanities left him so
little time for his affairs.

Cayley, then, at twenty-three, looked after
his cousin's affairs. By this time Mark had
bought the Red House and the considerable
85 amount of land which went with it. Cayley
superintended the necessary staff. His duties,
indeed, were many. He was not quite secretary,

not quite land-agent, not quite business-
adviser, not quite companion, but something
90 of all four. Mark leant upon him and called
him "Cay," objecting quite rightly in the
circumstances to the name of Matthew. Cay,
he felt was, above all, dependable; a big, heavy-
jawed, solid fellow, who didn't bother you with
95 unnecessary talk—a boon to a man who liked
to do most of the talking himself.

33. What is most likely true about Mark's father's
successor?

A) He made more money than Mark's father
had.

B) He was more popular than Mark's father.

C) His sermons were long and boring.

D) He took a great deal of interest in Mark's
life.

34. Which choice provides the best evidence for the
answer to the previous question?

A) Lines 5–8 ("There is...clergyman")

B) Lines 8–13 ("It was...university")

C) Lines 13–17 ("At about the time...
successor")

D) Lines 18–19 ("Neither...been effective")

35. What can be inferred from the author's choice to
place the word "writing" in quotation marks in
line 23?

A) People doubted that Mark was actually
writing.

B) Mark's writing was understood by many to
be terrible.

C) Mark's writing more closely resembled
philosophy than entertainment.

D) Mark was writing in secret but his
acquaintances knew about his talent.

36. Why is the death of Mark's patron fortunate for
him (line 30)?

A) Mark becomes wealthy as a result.

B) Mark and his patron do not like each other.

C) Mark's patron disapproved of his writing.

D) Mark felt pressure from his patron to start
a career.

37. As used in line 39, "usurers" most nearly means

A) employers.

B) lenders.

C) relatives.

D) supporters.

38. As used in line 48, "lavishness" most nearly means

    A) diplomacy.

    B) enthusiasm.

    C) melodrama.

    D) skill.

39. Mark's acquaintances probably consider stories of his later life

    A) less respectable than when he had to work for his money.

    B) more interesting because of the lessons he has learned.

    C) less exciting than those of his earlier life in London.

    D) more scandalous than he is willing to admit.

40. Which choice provides the best evidence for the answer to the previous question?

    A) Lines 22–25 ("He was . . . discovered")

    B) Lines 32–35 ("From that . . . of history")

    C) Lines 54–59 ("Mark had . . . the Duke")

    D) Lines 59–63 ("Call him . . . Hay Hill")

41. "Parnassus" (line 63) is included in the passage to illustrate the idea of

    A) a place where the wealthy gather.

    B) an artistic community.

    C) a myth to which Mark can be compared.

    D) a place that does not really exist.

42. The tone of the last paragraph serves to

    A) suggest parallels between Matthew and Mark.

    B) surprise the reader with Matthew's capabilities.

    C) demonstrate the dramatic changes in Mark's character.

    D) mock Mark for the way he sees Matthew.

Questions 43–52 refer to the following passage.

This passage is adapted from Jane Austen's *Sense and Sensibility*.

Before the house-maid had lit their fire the next day, or the sun gained any power over a cold, gloomy morning in January, Marianne, only half dressed, was kneeling against one
5 of the window-seats for the sake of all the little light she could command from it, and writing as fast as a continual flow of tears would permit her. In this situation, Elinor, roused from sleep by her agitation and sobs,
10 first perceived her; and after observing her for a few moments with silent anxiety, said, in a tone of the most considerate gentleness,

"Marianne, may I ask—?"

"No, Elinor," she replied, "ask nothing; you
15 will soon know all."

The sort of desperate calmness with which this was said, lasted no longer than while she spoke, and was immediately followed by a return of the same excessive affliction. It was
20 some minutes before she could go on with her letter, and the frequent bursts of grief which still obliged her, at intervals, to withhold her pen, were proofs enough of her feeling how more than probable it was that she was writing
25 for the last time to Willoughby.

At breakfast she neither ate, nor attempted to eat any thing; and Elinor's attention was then all employed, not in urging her, not in pitying her, nor in appearing to regard her,
30 but in endeavouring to engage Mrs. Jennings's notice entirely to herself.

As this was a favourite meal with Mrs. Jennings, it lasted a considerable time, and they were just setting themselves, after it,
35 round the common working table, when a letter was delivered to Marianne, which she eagerly caught from the servant, and, turning of a death-like paleness, instantly ran out of the room. Elinor, who saw as plainly by this,
40 as if she had seen the direction, that it must come from Willoughby, felt immediately such a sickness at heart as made her hardly able to hold up her head, and sat in such a general tremour as made her fear it impossible to
45 escape Mrs. Jennings's notice. That good lady, however, saw only that Marianne had received a letter from Willoughby, which appeared to her a very good joke, and which she treated accordingly, by hoping, with a laugh, that she
50 would find it to her liking. Of Elinor's distress, she was too busily employed in measuring lengths of worsted for her rug, to see any thing at all; and calmly continuing her talk, as soon as Marianne disappeared, she said,

55 "Upon my word, I never saw a young woman so desperately in love in my life! MY girls were nothing to her, and yet they used to be foolish enough; but as for Miss Marianne, she is quite an altered creature. I hope, from
60 the bottom of my heart, he won't keep her waiting much longer, for it is quite grievous to see her look so ill and forlorn. Pray, when are they to be married?"

Elinor, though never less disposed to speak
65 than at that moment, obliged herself to answer such an attack as this, and, therefore, trying to smile, replied, "And have you really, Ma'am, talked yourself into a persuasion of my sister's being engaged to Mr. Willoughby? I thought
70 it had been only a joke, but so serious a question seems to imply more; and I must beg, therefore, that you will not deceive yourself any longer. I do assure you that nothing would surprise me more than to hear of their being
75 going to be married."

"For shame, for shame, Miss Dashwood! how can you talk so? Don't we all know that it must be a match, that they were over head and ears in love with each other from the first
80 moment they met? Did not I see them together in Devonshire every day, and all day long; and did not I know that your sister came to town with me on purpose to buy wedding clothes? Come, come, this won't do. Because you are
85 so sly about it yourself, you think nobody else has any senses; but it is no such thing, I can tell you, for it has been known all over town this ever so long. I tell every body of it and so does Charlotte."

90 "Indeed, Ma'am," said Elinor, very seriously, "you are mistaken. Indeed, you are doing a very unkind thing in spreading the report, and you will find that you have though you will not believe me now."

43. As used in line 64, "disposed" most nearly means

A) capable.

B) inclined.

C) shed.

D) permitted.

44. In lines 37–38, the author describes Marianne as "turning of a death-like paleness" in order to emphasize

A) her comical overreaction to an everyday event.

B) the anxiety she feels about the letter's contents.

C) the supernatural elements that surround the house.

D) her knowledge that the letter contains news of illness.

45. The passage most strongly suggests which of the following about Elinor's feelings toward Marianne?

A) Elinor feels protective of Marianne.

B) Elinor is sad that they are not closer.

C) Elinor is jealous of Marianne's success in life.

D) Elinor considers them to be rivals in matters of love.

46. Which choice provides the best evidence for the answer to the previous question?

A) Lines 16–19 ("The sort . . . excessive affliction")

B) Lines 26–31 ("At breakfast . . . to herself")

C) Lines 59–62 ("I hope . . . ill and forlorn")

D) Lines 69–73 ("'I thought . . . any longer'")

47. Which statement does the passage most strongly suggest is true of Mrs. Jennings?

A) She does not have many people with whom to talk.

B) She knows the intimate details of Marianne's feelings.

C) She is not very perceptive about the events around her.

D) She has spoken to Willoughby more recently than Marianne.

48. Which choice provides the best evidence for the answer to the previous question?

    A) Lines 26–31 ("At breakfast...to herself")

    B) Lines 32–39 ("As this was...of the room")

    C) Lines 50–53 ("Of Elinor's...any thing at all")

    D) Lines 55–56 ("'Upon my word...in my life'")

49. As used in line 68, "persuasion" most nearly means

    A) argument.

    B) belief.

    C) excitement.

    D) joke.

50. According to the passage, Mrs. Jennings believes that

    A) Willoughby intends to marry Marianne.

    B) Elinor is overreacting to Willoughby's letter.

    C) Marianne loves someone other than Willoughby.

    D) Elinor is mistaken about why Marianne is upset.

51. Based on the information in the passage, Marianne's situation can most directly be compared to that of

    A) a stray cat who shows affection to strangers in hopes of being fed.

    B) a person who cultivates charm in order to compensate for a lack of physical beauty.

    C) a scientist working on an ambitious project in which only she has faith.

    D) a worker who has not been hired for a job she was certain she would get.

52. What is the author's most likely purpose in providing the last paragraph of dialogue?

    A) To help readers understand why Marianne is so upset

    B) To demonstrate the degree of Elinor's concern about Marianne

    C) To argue that Mrs. Jennings's understanding of the situation may be accurate

    D) To persuade readers that Marianne is not entirely innocent

Reading

Answers and Explanations

Suggested passage notes:

Passage 1

¶1: (central idea): use atoms to date things; isotopes def. & exs.

¶2: isotopes unstable; measure C-14

¶3: C-14 decay = predictable

¶4: C-14 dating; materials; timeline based on layers

Passage 2

¶1: def. radioactive; why dangerous; danger = radiation rate

¶2: half-life def. = decay rate; exs.

¶3: long half-life = long problem

1. C

Difficulty: Hard

Category: Inference

Getting to the Answer: Use your passage map to locate the paragraph that explains carbon-14 dating. This paragraph will contain the description of what materials can be dated using this method. In paragraph 4, the author states that carbon-14 dating can be used on materials made by a living organism. An arrowhead made from a bone is constructed of such material, choice **(C)**.

2. D

Difficulty: Hard

Category: Command of Evidence

Getting to the Answer: Locate each of the answer choices in the passage. The correct answer should provide direct support for the answer to the previous question: the bone arrowhead can be dated using carbon-14 dating. In paragraph 4, the author describes the process for carbon-14 dating. Choice **(D)** is correct because this sentence provides a direct description of the materials that can be dated using carbon-14 dating.

3. B

Difficulty: Medium

Category: Vocab-in-Context

Getting to the Answer: Pretend that the word "decay" is a blank. Reread around the cited word to predict a word that could substitute for "decay" in context. The previous paragraph discusses how scientists measure the rate of emission to calculate the amount of carbon-14 in a sample. "Emission" means release; therefore, the amount of carbon-14 is becoming smaller if the atoms are releasing it. In this sentence, therefore, predict "decay" means to *decrease*, which matches "deteriorate," choice **(B)**.

4. C

Difficulty: Easy

Category: Inference

Getting to the Answer: Look at your notes for paragraph 3. Summarize the ratio of carbon-12 to carbon-14 in living tissue in your own words. Look for the answer choice that most closely matches your prediction. In paragraph 3, the author explains that the ratio of carbon-12 to carbon-14 for living things is the same as the ratio in the atmosphere: constant. Choice **(C)** is correct.

5. C

Difficulty: Medium

Category: Command of Evidence

Getting to the Answer: Review what part of the passage you used to predict an answer for the previous question: the ratio is constant for living things. Of the answer choices, only lines 31–34 explain the ratio of carbon-12 to carbon-14 in living things. Choice **(C)** is correct.

6. B

Difficulty: Medium

Category: Detail

Getting to the Answer: Read around the cited lines. The author directly states why a release of iodine-131 is not cause for long-term concern. In paragraph 3, the author explains that the initial release of radiation from an accident involving iodine-131 will be high, but the level of radiation will drop quickly (lines 82–84). Choice **(B)** is correct.

7. C

Difficulty: Medium

Category: Detail

Getting to the Answer: Use your passage map to find the information about why exposure to radiation is dangerous.

Getting to the Answer: In paragraph 1, lines 59–61, the author explains that radiation is harmful to living tissue because it can cause damage to the cells' DNA, which matches choice **(C)**.

8.   A

Difficulty: Easy

Category: Vocab-in-Context

Getting to the Answer: Pretend that the word "original" is a blank. Reread around the cited word to predict a word that could substitute for "original" in context. The previous paragraph explains how scientists use "half-life" to determine how quickly material decays. If the material is decaying, then predict "original" refers to the *first* material. Choice **(A)** matches your prediction.

9.   D

Difficulty: Medium

Category: Detail

Getting to the Answer: Review your notes for Passage 2. Try to put into your own words how scientists use half-life calculations of radioactive materials. Look for the answer that most closely matches your idea. In paragraph 1, the author explains that the level of danger posed by radiation released during a nuclear accident depends on how quickly radiation is released (lines 66–69). In paragraph 2, the author discusses how the half-life of radioactive material is used to determine how long a material will emit radiation. Paragraph 3 then explains how different half-lives translate into short-term or long-term radiation concerns. Choice **(D)** is correct because it most clearly paraphrases the information in the passage about how scientists use half-life calculations.

10.   A

Difficulty: Hard

Category: Inference

Getting to the Answer: The central idea will be supported by all of the evidence presented in both passages. Review the central idea you identified for each passage in your passage maps. Passage 1 discusses the application of atomic and nuclear physics in archaeology while Passage 2 details how scientists apply atomic and nuclear physics to studies of radioactivity in nuclear power plant accidents. Choice **(A)** is correct.

11.   A

Difficulty: Hard

Category: Inference

Getting to the Answer: Analyze the graph to see that it describes the decay of carbon-14 over time. Think about how this data relates to the texts. The graph portrays the decay of carbon-14 as described in Passage 1. The definition of "half-life" is given in Passage 2. The half-life of a material is the amount of time it takes for half of that material to decay. The graph shows that about 50 percent of carbon-14 remains after 5,400 years. Choice **(A)** is correct.

Suggested passage notes:

> ¶1: A excited
> ¶2: A invited to impt tea
> ¶3: M not excited for A
> ¶4: M wants to make A more calm; unsuccessful
> ¶5: A worried about rain
> ¶6: A very excited even when doing dishes; but also nervous she might misbehave at the tea
> ¶7–8: M gives A advice for being proper at the tea

12.   B

Difficulty: Easy

Category: Inference

Getting to the Answer: Reread the excerpt for clues that reveal Anne's previous behavior and her personality traits. Marilla specifically asks Anne whether she has found "another" kindred spirit, implying that Anne has previously rushed home excited about having made a new friend. This is a clue that Anne is a sociable, friendly person. Choice **(B)** is correct.

13.   C

Difficulty: Medium

Category: Function

Getting to the Answer: Read the sentence and determine how the selected words shape the reader's image of Anne; then, select the answer choice that most accurately reflects this tone and image. The passage states that Anne runs home and implies that she is *excited*. The correct answer, choice **(C)**, supports the image of Anne as energetic.

14. B

Difficulty: Hard

Category: Vocab-in-Context

Getting to the Answer: Predict a word that could replace the word in the question stem, then find its closest match among the answer choices. The passage states that Marilla hopes to *actively change* Anne from her current state and *mold* her into one of her own designs. Thus, of the various uses of the word "fashioning" used in the answer choices, choice **(B)** is correct.

15. C

Difficulty: Medium

Category: Inference

Getting to the Answer: Read the context clues in the passage that relate to Matthew's and Anne's interactions. Examine what these clues suggest about their relationship. Anne goes to bed "speechless with misery" (lines 49–50) because Matthew predicts it will rain the next day. Anne's reaction shows that she takes Matthew's predictions seriously, so choice **(C)** is correct.

16. B

Difficulty: Easy

Category: Detail

Getting to the Answer: Marilla explicitly states that Anne's trouble is that she is "thinking too much about [herself]" (line 85), which matches (A). However, this advice is intended for the specific situation at hand, the tea party, rather than Anne's greater challenge of learning to take things calmly, which will affect her entire life. This challenge is outlined in lines 24–28; thus, choice **(B)** is correct.

17. B

Difficulty: Medium

Category: Function

Getting to the Answer: Reread the paragraph in question and determine what role it plays in the progression of ideas within the passage. Paragraph 4 explains Marilla's feelings about Anne's personality traits, describes how she hoped to temper them, and states that she failed to do so, while also telling the reader that she likes Anne the way she is. Choice **(B)** best represents these ideas.

18. A

Difficulty: Medium

Category: Vocab-in-Context

Getting to the Answer: Read the sentence and paragraph for context clues and determine which usage of the selected word best fits the author's intention. Predict that Marilla's advice is *useful* or *helpful*. Choice **(A)** is correct.

19. A

Difficulty: Medium

Category: Inference

Getting to the Answer: Evaluate the depth of the author's participation in the passage and how many perspectives the author introduces. Use this information to determine the correct answer. The author reveals the inner thinking of both Anne and Marilla while taking no active part in the passage, so choice **(A)** is correct.

20. D

Difficulty: Easy

Category: Inference

Getting to the Answer: Evaluate how Marilla is presented. Throughout the passage, Marilla asks Anne to remain calm, coolly responds to Anne, and hopes to fashion Anne into a demure model child. Predict that Marilla is calm and collected. Choice **(D)** is correct.

21. A

Difficulty: Medium

Category: Command of Evidence

Getting to the Answer: To answer Command of Evidence questions, start by looking at the part of the passage that helped you answer the previous question. Throughout the passage, Marilla asks Anne to remain calm and coolly responds to Anne, and the quotation noted in lines 21–23 shows Marilla doing this; thus, choice **(A)** is correct.

Suggested passage notes:

Passage 1

¶1: neg. effects of video games

¶2: violent games similar to teaching methods

¶3: newer studies show positive effects

¶4: can shape future ed. techniques

Passage 2

¶1: brain deterioration in old age

¶2: studies show video games slow deterioration

¶3: need more research

22. C

Difficulty: Medium

Category: Global

Getting to the Answer: Review your notes about the passage's central ideas. The correct answer will include an idea that is supported by all of the evidence presented in the passage. Avoid answer choices like (A) that refer to only one idea presented in the passage. All of the details presented in the passage are related to the idea that research about the effects of video games on those who play them is being used to develop new educational tools and methods. Choice **(C)** is correct.

23. D

Difficulty: Medium

Category: Command of Evidence

Getting to the Answer: Locate each answer choice in the passage. Consider which lines from the passage most directly support the central idea of the passage, which you identified in the previous question. The central idea of the passage is related to how research about video games is affecting the development of new methods of teaching. Choice **(D)** provides the most direct support for the answer to the previous question.

24. A

Difficulty: Easy

Category: Detail

Getting to the Answer: Use your passage map to find the paragraph that discusses studies performed in the 1990s. The correct answer will be stated explicitly in the passage. In paragraph 1, the author states that studies performed in the 1990s confirmed what parents had long said: too many videos games can have a negative impact on learning and socialization in teenagers. Choice **(A)** is correct.

25. C

Difficulty: Medium

Category: Vocab-in-Context

Getting to the Answer: Treat the tested word as a blank. Replace it with a synonym that makes sense in the context of the sentence, paragraph, and passage. In paragraph 2, the author explains that certain video games simulate a repetition method used in the classroom but indicates that this was *not intentional* on the part of the game developers. Choice **(C)** is correct because "inadvertently" most nearly means "unintentionally" in this context.

26. B

Difficulty: Medium

Category: Detail

Getting to the Answer: Review your passage map notes from paragraph 2. Identify the cause-and-effect relationship the author describes. In paragraph 2, the author explains that when played for extended periods of time, video games mimic methods used in the classroom to teach children information. This is what makes it easier for game players to absorb the content of the games. Choice **(B)** is correct.

27. A

Difficulty: Hard

Category: Inference

Getting to the Answer: The correct answer will not be stated directly in the text but should be supported by the evidence presented. Avoid answers like (B) and (D) that go too far. In paragraph 2, the author asserts that the findings of the research described suggest that those elderly persons who are able to prevent mental decline could better maintain the functions they need to operate independently, such as driving. Choice **(A)** is correct.

28. C

Difficulty: Medium

Category: Command of Evidence

Getting to the Answer: The answer to the previous question will not be directly stated in the answer choice to this question. Rather, the correct answer to this question will provide the strongest support for your answer to the previous question. In the previous question, you inferred from the information in the passage that people who are able to put off the cognitive effects of aging might be able to live longer independently. Choice **(C)** provides the strongest support for this connection.

29. D

Difficulty: Medium

Category: Vocab-in-Context

Getting to the Answer: Reread the target sentence and predict your own definition for the cited word. Then, evaluate the answer choices to find the closest match to your prediction. In this context, "deteriorate" most nearly means *get worse* or *weaken*. Choice **(D)** is correct.

30. A

Difficulty: Medium

Category: Detail

Getting to the Answer: Review your notes from paragraph 2. Consider how the information presented in this paragraph supports the central claim presented by the author in the overall passage. Passage 2 is mostly about how researchers are considering the potential of video games in treating brain deterioration; paragraph 2 focuses on the studies that show video games slow deterioration. Choice **(A)** is correct.

31. A

Difficulty: Medium

Category: Global

Getting to the Answer: Consider the overall message the author is conveying through the information presented in the passage. You determined the central claim to help you solve the previous question: Passage 2 is mostly about how researchers are considering the potential of video games in treating brain deterioration. Use this claim to help you determine the purpose of the passage: to describe how video games can potentially help elderly people who are experiencing brain deterioration. Choice **(A)** is correct.

32. D

Difficulty: Medium

Category: Inference

Getting to the Answer: The correct answer will be supported by the information in both passages. Think generally to predict what both passages agree on; avoid answers like (B) and (C) that refer only to information presented in one of the passages. Both passages discuss how video games are being used by researchers in different fields. Choice **(D)** is correct.

Suggested passage map notes:

¶1: Mark = preacher's son; patron paid for school
¶2: M inherited patron's money & became patron
¶3: interested in art, not nobility
¶4: sent cousin to school
¶5: cousin took care of M

33. C

Difficulty: Medium

Category: Inference

Getting to the Answer: The correct answer will be supported directly by the passage. The passage states that Mark's father left behind "a reputation for short sermons, as an example for his successor" (lines 16–17). However, it then states, "Neither warning nor example seems to have been effective" (lines 18–19). Predict that his successor gave long sermons. Choice **(C)** is correct.

34. D

Difficulty: Medium

Category: Command of Evidence

Getting to the Answer: Carefully review the part of the passage that you used to answer the previous question. The passage discusses Mark's father's successor in the context of his father's death; Mark's father has left an "example" of short sermons for his successor, but "neither warning nor example seems to have been effective" (lines 18–19). This suggests that Mark's father's successor did not follow his example of giving short sermons. Choice **(D)** is correct.

35. A

Difficulty: Hard

Category: Inference

Getting to the Answer: The word "writing" is quoted in order to underscore the fact that it is dialogue. It is Mark who has used the word. The passage goes on to state that "what he wrote . . . has never been discovered" (lines 24–25). Predict that the only reason to believe that writing has taken place is Mark's word; other people have their doubts. Choice **(A)** is correct.

36. A

Difficulty: Easy

Category: Detail

Getting to the Answer: The correct answer is directly stated in the passage. The passage states, "his patron died . . . and left him all the money he wanted" (lines 30–32), which directly supports the idea that he is now wealthy. Predict that Mark's patron's death was fortunate for him because it made him wealthy. Choice **(A)** is correct.

37. B

Difficulty: Medium

Category: Vocab-in-Context

Getting to the Answer: Consider the topic of the paragraph in which the cited word appears. Then, predict a synonym for this word based on the topic and context of the paragraph. Earlier in the paragraph, the passage states, "he settled accounts with the money-lenders" (lines 35–36). The sentence to which the word in question belongs asserts that it was "not only usurers who discovered that Mark Ablett no longer wrote for money" (lines 39–40). "Money-lender," then, seems to be a synonym for "usurer;" predict *money-lenders*. Choice **(B)** is correct.

38. B

Difficulty: Medium

Category: Vocab-in-Context

Getting to the Answer: Consider the usual meaning of "lavish." How might it be applied figuratively here? "Lavish" usually means something like elaborate or sumptuous, depending on the context. Here, it is used to describe how Mark "play[s] host and 'lead'" (line 47).

It seems to be used to describe how Mark enjoys his theater company with enthusiasm and relish. Predict that "lavishness" most nearly means *enthusiasm* or *relish*. Choice **(B)** is correct.

39. C

Difficulty: Medium

Category: Inference

Getting to the Answer: Identify how the passage characterizes Mark's life, then read the answer choices to see how others view it. The passage characterizes Mark's early life in London as an exciting and irresponsible period (lines 1–29). Later, he inherits money, settles his accounts, and becomes financially responsible (lines 30–38). Predict that, compared with his earlier life, his later life (and therefore stories of his later life) was less exciting. Choice **(C)** is correct.

40. B

Difficulty: Medium

Category: Command of Evidence

Getting to the Answer: Identify the paragraph that most directly supports your answer to the previous question about the different periods of Mark's life. Since lines 30–38 discussed Mark's later life, the best evidence to support your previous answer should come from those lines. The lines quoted in choice (B) make a direct distinction between these two periods of Mark's life: when he inherits money, "his life loses its legendary character, and becomes more a matter of history" (lines 32–35). In other words, his earlier life in London is more like a legend, or myth, and his later life is less exciting. Choice **(B)** is correct.

41. B

Difficulty: Hard

Category: Function

Getting to the Answer: Reread the sentence to find the analogy; it will be explicitly stated in the passage. Then, consider why the passage draws the comparison it does. Mark is described as "a hanger-on, but to the skirts of Art, not Society" (lines 61–62). "Art" is being compared with "Parnassus," and "Society" with "Hay Hill." Each appears to be a neighborhood associated with these ideas. Predict that "Parnassus" is an example of Art. Choice **(B)** is correct.

42. D

Difficulty: Hard

Category: Function

Getting to the Answer: Identify the narrator's attitude toward Mark in the last paragraph; your passage map notes remind you that Matthew took care of Mark. The tone of the last paragraph is one of mock-seriousness. On the surface, it appears to take Mark's ideas about himself and his place in the world seriously. But, when read closely, the final sentence characterizes Mark as a pompous and arrogant man who finds Matthew useful because he doesn't steal attention from himself. Matthew "didn't bother you with unnecessary talk—a boon to a man who liked to do most of the talking himself" (lines 94–96). Predict that the last paragraph serves to subtly make fun of Mark; Choice **(D)** is correct.

Suggested passage notes:

> ¶1–3: M very upset, E concerned
> ¶4: M having trouble writing to W
> ¶5: E distracts Mrs. J
> ¶6: M receives letter from W, W concerned, Mrs. J clueless
> ¶7: Mrs. J hopes M marries W
> ¶8: E suggests unlikely
> ¶9–10: Mrs. J saw love, E says Mrs. J will see she is wrong in time

43. B

Difficulty: Medium

Category: Vocab-in-Context

Getting to the Answer: Consider each word carefully. The most common meaning for a word is not necessarily the correct one. Elinor, "though never less disposed to speak" (line 64), nonetheless speaks in this paragraph. The correct answer should be something like *eager*, since Elinor is not eager to speak. Plugging in each of the answer choices will reveal which fits best. Choice **(B)** is similar to *eager*, so it is correct.

44. B

Difficulty: Medium

Category: Function

Getting to the Answer: Read the lines around this phrase. Look for clues that suggest what is making her react as she does. Marianne is clearly expecting bad news in the letter, as she runs out of the room before even opening it. Choice **(B)** is correct: she is driven by her anxiety.

45. A

Difficulty: Easy

Category: Inference

Getting to the Answer: Look for clues about Elinor's behavior toward Marianne. What does this suggest about their relationship? Elinor seems almost as upset by what is upsetting Marianne as Marianne herself is. The sisters are clearly very close, and Elinor's words to Mrs. Jennings make clear that Elinor is trying to prevent Mrs. Jennings from doing further damage to Marianne by spreading rumors. Choice **(A)** is correct, as it reflects the sisters' close relationship.

46. B

Difficulty: Medium

Category: Command of Evidence

Getting to the Answer: Review the answer to the previous question. Consider which of the answer choices provides the clearest sense of Elinor's feelings toward Marianne. Elinor's feelings toward Marianne are protective. This is demonstrated by the lines that show Elinor's trying to distract Mrs. Jennings from noticing Marianne's distress. Choice **(B)** is correct; it is a clear illustration of Elinor's protective feelings.

47. C

Difficulty: Easy

Category: Inference

Getting to the Answer: Determine what Mrs. Jennings thinks is happening. Does it differ in any way from what is actually happening? Mrs. Jennings appears not to have noticed Marianne's distress over Willoughby. She remarks on how much the two of them seem to be in love, despite Marianne's altered behavior. Choice **(C)** is correct because it shows that Mrs. Jennings is not perceptive enough to notice what is happening.

48. C

Difficulty: Medium

Category: Command of Evidence

Getting to the Answer: Review the answer to the previous question. Notice what Mrs. Jennings says or does to support your conclusion about her. Mrs. Jennings is not very perceptive. The passage states that she "was too busily employed . . . to see any thing at all" (lines 51–53) and then observes that Marianne and Willoughby are likely to be married. Choice **(C)** is correct, as it offers an instance of Mrs. Jennings's failure to notice the events around her.

49. B

Difficulty: Medium

Category: Vocab-in-Context

Getting to the Answer: Consider the context of this line. Notice what Elinor is suggesting about Mrs. Jennings. Elinor is surprised that Mrs. Jennings has "talked [herself] into a persuasion" (line 68) that Marianne and Willoughby are to be married. Other context clues make clear that this is what Mrs. Jennings believes will happen, so the correct answer will mean something like *belief*. Choice **(B)**, therefore, is correct.

50. A

Difficulty: Easy

Category: Detail

Getting to the Answer: Read the passage closely to find the answer stated explicitly. Both Elinor and Mrs. Jennings state that Mrs. Jennings believes Willoughby and Marianne are to be married soon. Choice **(A)** is correct.

51. D

Difficulty: Hard

Category: Inference

Getting to the Answer: In your own words, describe Marianne's situation. Marianne is upset because of a letter that has come from a man everybody believes she will marry. Then, read the answer choices to see what situation is analogous. The correct answer should relate to unexpected disappointment. Choice **(D)** is correct: it conveys a sense of disappointment after high expectations have not been met.

52. B

Difficulty: Medium

Category: Function

Getting to the Answer: Consider what would be lost from the passage if this paragraph were not included. Elinor and Mrs. Jennings have argued over the events taking place. The final paragraph shows Elinor trying to convince Mrs. Jennings that she is "doing a very unkind thing" (lines 91–92) by spreading rumors of Marianne's marriage, rumors that will likely humiliate her. Elinor is not simply explaining why she believes Mrs. Jennings is wrong, but trying to stop her from causing Marianne additional pain. Choice **(B)** is correct because it is the only answer choice that conveys this meaning.

PART 4

SAT Writing and Language

CHAPTER 24

The Method for SAT Writing and Language Questions

LEARNING OBJECTIVE

After completing this chapter, you will be able to:

- Efficiently apply the SAT Writing and Language Method

How to Do SAT Writing and Language

The Writing and Language section of the SAT tests a limited number of grammar errors and style or logic issues. You should feel empowered in knowing that you can familiarize yourself with these recurring errors and learn to spot them and address them quickly and efficiently. We'll describe the issues that you're likely to see on test day and how to deal with them in the next two chapters. In this chapter, we'll present a simple series of steps for tackling Writing and Language questions.

Take a look at the passage and questions that follow and think about how you would approach them on test day. Then compare your approach to the recommendations presented.

Questions 1 and 2 refer to the following passage.

Child Expenditures

A report from the United States Department of Agriculture estimates that the average cost of raising a child born in 2015 until age seventeen is over $230,000. This cost includes housing, food, transportation, health care, child care, and education; the overall cost varies considerably from family to family. **1** <u>Therefore,</u> with the average cost of raising a child set at nearly a quarter million dollars, and with additional children in the family raising that financial expenditure accordingly, it becomes clear that parenthood is a major undertaking. When planning a family, **2** <u>financial considerations should be kept in mind by future parents.</u>

1. A) NO CHANGE
   B) However,
   C) Moreover,
   D) Subsequently,

2. A) NO CHANGE
   B) financial considerations should be at the forefront of parents' thinking.
   C) future parents should keep financial considerations in mind.
   D) future parents should consider financial issues to be of paramount importance in the process of their preparations.

There is no need to read the entire passage before you start to answer questions. Instead, answer them as you read. When you see a number, finish the sentence you are reading and then look at the corresponding question. If you can answer the question based on what you've read so far, do so—this will likely be the case if the question is testing grammar. If you need more information—which may happen if the question is testing organization or relevance—keep reading until you have enough context to answer the question.

Sometimes the issue being tested will be obvious to you when you look at the underlined segment. If it isn't, glance at the answer choices to help you determine what the test maker is after. For instance, in question 1, a transition word plus a comma is underlined. Is the question testing the transition or the punctuation? A quick glance at the choices makes it obvious that it's the former, given that they all include the comma but feature different transition words. **Identifying the issue**, using the choices if necessary, is step 1 of the Writing and Language Method.

To find the correct transition, use the surrounding text. The previous sentence addresses the variability of child expenditures, while the sentence that includes the transition word draws a conclusion from the *average* expenditure, not from the variability. The correct transition must highlight this contrast, so the sentence is incorrect as written, and you can eliminate (A). Among the remaining choices, there is only one contrast word: "However." Of the other choices, "Moreover" conveys continuation and "Subsequently" conveys a sequence in time. Neither fixes the error, so eliminate both and choose **(B)** as the correct answer to question 1. **Eliminating answer choices that do not address the issue** is step 2 of the Writing and Language Method.

Sometimes there will be more than one choice that addresses the issue. When that happens, you'll need to base your final response on three considerations: conciseness, relevance, and the potential of a given choice to introduce a new error. Question 2 is an example of a question in which more than one choice addresses the issue. This question features an underlined segment immediately following an introductory phrase—a signal to check for a modification error. Indeed, it is future parents who would be planning a family, so the phrase "future parents" should be right next to the introductory modifying phrase. That eliminates (A) and (B), but you still have to decide between (C) and (D), both of which fix the misplaced modifier. Both of these choices are grammatically correct and relevant to the surrounding context. However, **(C)** is more concise and is therefore the correct answer for question 2. **Choosing the most concise and relevant response from those that are grammatically correct** is step 3 of the Writing and Language Method.

Here are the steps we just illustrated:

The Method for SAT Writing and Language Questions	
Step 1.	Identify the issue (use the choices if need be)
Step 2.	Eliminate answer choices that do not address the issue
Step 3.	Plug in the remaining answer choices and select the most *correct*, *concise*, and *relevant* one

Correct, **concise**, and **relevant** means that the answer choice you select:

- Has no grammatical errors
- Is as short as possible while retaining the writer's intended meaning
- Is relevant to the paragraph and the passage as a whole

Correct answers do *not* change the intended meaning of the original sentence, paragraph, or passage, or introduce new grammatical errors.

Try on Your Own

Directions: Take as much time as you need on these questions. Work carefully and methodically. Practice using the steps that you just learned.

Questions 1–4 refer to the following passage.

Bebop Jazz

For a jazz musician in New York City in the early 1940s, the most interesting place to spend the hours between midnight and dawn was probably a Harlem nightclub called Minton's. After finishing their jobs at other clubs, young musicians like **1** Charlie Parker, Dizzy Gillespie, Kenny Clarke, Thelonious Monk would gather at Minton's and have jam sessions, informal performances featuring lengthy group and solo improvisations. The all-night sessions resulted in the birth of modern jazz as these African American artists together forged a new sound, known as bebop.

Unlike swing, the enormously popular jazz played in the 1930s, bebop was not dance music. It was often blindingly fast, incorporating tricky, irregular rhythms and discordant sounds that jazz audiences had never heard before. Earlier jazz used blue notes but, like much of Western music up to that time, generally stuck to chord tones to create melodies. Bebop, in contrast, relied heavily on chromatic ornamentation and borrowed notes from altered **2** scales. Thereby, it opened up new harmonic opportunities for musicians.

The musicians who pioneered bebop shared two common elements: a vision of the new music's possibilities and astonishing improvisational skill—the

1. A) NO CHANGE

    B) Charlie Parker; Dizzy Gillespie; Kenny Clarke; and Thelonious Monk

    C) Charlie Parker and Dizzy Gillespie, and Kenny Clarke and Thelonious Monk

    D) Charlie Parker, Dizzy Gillespie, Kenny Clarke, and Thelonious Monk

2. Which choice most effectively combines the sentences at the underlined portion?

    A) scales, thereby, it opened up

    B) scales, and thereby opening up

    C) scales, opening up

    D) scales, thereby opening up

ability to play or compose a musical line on the spur of the moment. After all, **3** <u>improvisation, within the context of a group setting, is a hallmark</u> of jazz. Parker, perhaps the greatest instrumental genius jazz has known, was an especially brilliant improviser. He often played double-time, twice as fast as the rest of the band, and his solos were exquisitely shaped, revealing a harmonic imagination that enthralled his listeners.

Like many revolutions, unfortunately, the bebop movement encountered heavy resistance. Opposition came from older jazz musicians initially, but also, later and more lastingly, from a general public alienated by the **4** <u>music's</u> complexity and sophistication. Furthermore, due to the government ban on recording that was in effect during the early years of World War II (records were made of vinyl, a petroleum product that was essential to the war effort), the creative ferment that first produced bebop was poorly documented.

3. A) NO CHANGE
   B) improvisation within the context of a group setting is a hallmark
   C) improvisation within the context of a group setting, is a hallmark
   D) improvisation, within the context of a group setting is a hallmark

4. A) NO CHANGE
   B) musics
   C) musics'
   D) music

Answers and Explanations

1. D

Difficulty: Easy

Category: Sentence Structure: Commas, Dashes, and Colons

Getting to the Answer: Use commas to separate three or more items forming a series or list. This series contains four items. Separate each item with a comma and use a comma with the conjunction "and" to separate the final item from the rest of the series. Choice **(D)** is correct.

2. C

Difficulty: Hard

Category: Conciseness

Getting to the Answer: Consider the relationship between the sentences in order to determine how best to combine them. The second sentence contributes useful information regarding the results of using the "chromatic ornamentation" and "altered scales." Making the second sentence a modifying phrase and connecting it to the first with a comma will eliminate unnecessary words and more clearly and smoothly show the relationship between the ideas. Choice **(C)** is correct. Choice (D) is similar and may be tempting, but since "opening up vast new harmonic opportunities" now directly modifies "altered scales," the word "thereby" is redundant.

3. B

Difficulty: Medium

Category: Sentence Structure: Commas, Dashes, and Colons

Getting to the Answer: When you see a phrase set off by commas, always read the sentence without the phrase to determine if the phrase is nonessential. Although the sentence is still grammatically correct without the information that is set off by the commas, an essential part of the meaning is lost. The author is stating that it is the group setting that characterizes the type of improvisation important to jazz. Choice **(B)** properly removes the commas that set off the phrase.

4. A

Difficulty: Easy

Category: Agreement: Modifiers

Getting to the Answer: When an underlined section features an apostrophe after a noun, check the noun's number. This sentence is correct as written. Although there are many styles of music, the noun "music" is a collective noun and singular. Choice **(A)** correctly uses the singular possessive.

Writing & Lang

CHAPTER 25

Spotting and Fixing Errors: Sentence Structure, Punctuation, and Agreement

LEARNING OBJECTIVES

After completing this chapter, you will be able to:

- Determine the correct punctuation and/or conjunctions to form a complete sentence
- Identify and correct inappropriate uses of semicolons
- Identify and correct inappropriate uses of commas, dashes, and colons
- Use punctuation to set off simple parenthetical elements
- Identify and correct verb agreement issues
- Identify and correct pronoun agreement issues
- Identify and correct modifier agreement issues
- Identify and correct inappropriate uses of apostrophes
- Identify and correct errors in parallel structure
- Identify and correct expressions that deviate from idiomatic English
- Determine the appropriate word in frequently confused pairs

SmartPoints®:

Sentence Structure and Punctuation, 85/300 (Very High Yield)

Agreement, 60/300 (High Yield, especially Verbs and Pronouns)

How Much Do You Know?

Directions: Try the following questions. The "Category" heading in the explanation for each question gives the title of the lesson that covers how to answer it. If you answered the question(s) for a given lesson correctly, you may be able to move quickly through that lesson. If you answered incorrectly, you may want to take your time on that lesson.

Questions 1–6 refer to the following passage.

The Hindenburg

Although they are best known today for their peculiar niche as floating commercials over sports **1** arenas, airships, now more commonly called "blimps," widely used as passenger transportation in the early twentieth century. The most infamous was the *Hindenburg*. When the 804-foot *Hindenburg* was launched in 1936, it was the largest airship in the world. Like most airships, and more specifically zeppelins, of the period, **2** a light gas in the *Hindenburg* filled a simple balloon encased by a solid frame—in this case, hydrogen. In an age when airplanes could carry no more than 10 passengers at a time, **3** they could initially carry 50 passengers, a capacity that was later upgraded to 72. Transatlantic journeys in an airship could cut the travel time in half compared to voyages in ocean liners at the time.

Despite these advantages, the *Hindenburg* was hampered by many of the same drawbacks as other airships. Tickets to fly in the *Hindenburg* were not affordable for most people. The massive amount of fuel needed not only to fill the balloon **4** and to power the propellers made this airship very expensive to operate.

1. A) NO CHANGE
    B) arenas; airships, more commonly called "blimps" today, widely used as
    C) arenas, airships, more commonly called "blimps" today, were widely used as
    D) arenas, airships, more commonly called "blimps" today, widely used to

2. A) NO CHANGE
    B) the *Hindenburg*'s simple balloon was filled with a light gas encased by the solid frame
    C) the solid frame of the *Hindenburg* encased a simple balloon filled with a light gas
    D) the *Hindenburg* was built with a solid frame that encased a simple balloon filled with a light gas

3. A) NO CHANGE
    B) it
    C) the *Hindenburg*
    D) each

4. A) NO CHANGE
    B) but also
    C) and also
    D) nor

Worst of all was the safety concern: hydrogen gas is extremely flammable. Any spark or flame that came near the gas could cause a horrific **5** explosion, which is exactly what happened. On May 6, 1937, in Lakehurst, New Jersey, as the *Hindenburg* **6** landed, it suddenly burst into flames, killing 36 of the 97 passengers and crew on board. By the 1940s, commercial airplanes had advanced in development far beyond the airship's capacity. The airship thus became outdated as a mode of passenger service and acquired its modern-day role as an advertising platform.

5. A) NO CHANGE
    B) explosion; which is
    C) explosion: which is
    D) explosion which—is

6. A) NO CHANGE
    B) had landed
    C) would have landed
    D) was landing

Check Your Work

1.   C

Difficulty: Hard

Category: Sentence Structure: The Basics

Getting to the Answer: The first sentence is long and grammatically complex. Identify the most important pieces and outline the structure. The sentence begins with the word "although," which means that the first clause, "they are best known," is dependent. The following clause, therefore, needs to be independent for the sentence to have a complete, grammatically correct structure. The second clause as written, "airships . . . widely used as passenger transportation," is not an independent clause—it could not stand alone as its own complete sentence. Eliminate (A). Choice (B) is incorrect because the semicolon does not turn the second clause into an independent clause. Similarly, (D) does not make the second clause independent by replacing "as" with "to." Choice **(C)** is correct because "airships . . . were widely used as passenger transportation" is an independent clause: it has a subject "airships" and a predicate verb "were used."

2.   D

Difficulty: Hard

Category: Agreement: Modifiers

Getting to the Answer: The phrases that precede the underlined portion are introductory modifiers. The subject of the sentence needs to immediately follow these modifiers. The introductory phrases talk about something that is like most airships; therefore, the subject must be comparable to most other airships. Neither "a light gas," "the *Hindenburg*'s simple balloon," nor the "solid frame" are comparable to "most airships." The *Hindenburg* itself is a specific airship, which can be logically compared to most airships. Only **(D)** correctly places "the *Hindenburg*" immediately after the introductory phrase as the subject of the sentence. Additionally, the underlined portion must end with "a light gas" because the phrase after the dash specifies which gas: hydrogen.

3.   C

Difficulty: Medium

Category: Agreement: Pronouns

Getting to the Answer: Complex sentences can often benefit from the use of pronouns, reducing wordiness and repetition. That said, make sure that the use of a pronoun will not introduce ambiguity into the sentence. In a complicated sentence including multiple nouns, it is often better to avoid pronouns to preserve the clarity of the author's claims. Choice **(C)** is correct because it avoids any confusion over what the pronoun refers to.

4.   B

Difficulty: Medium

Category: Agreement: Idioms

Getting to the Answer: Check to see if the underlined section is part of an idiomatic expression, such as *either . . . or*. The sentence contains the first half of the idiomatic combination *not only . . . but also*. The use of "and" in this context is incorrect. Choice **(B)**, "but also," is correct.

5.   A

Difficulty: Medium

Category: Sentence Structure: Commas, Dashes, and Colons

Getting to the Answer: Commas set off nonessential information from the main part of the sentence just as parentheses do. The sentence's concluding phrase "which is exactly what happened" is not necessary for understanding the sentence's main clause, which explains how a spark or flame could ignite the hydrogen and cause an explosion. The use of a semicolon or a colon is not appropriate for setting off nonessential information. Eliminate (B) and (C). A dash can replace a comma as a way to emphasize the parenthetical phrase, which would be appropriate here, but (D) misplaces the dash. Choice **(A)** is correct because it uses the necessary punctuation, a comma, in the proper location.

6.   D

Difficulty: Hard

Category: Agreement: Verbs

Getting to the Answer: The sentence expresses a main action that occurs once, "burst," while another action is in process, "landed." An action that occurs once in the past should be in simple past tense. An action that is in process in the past—signaled by the word "as"— should be in past progressive tense, ending in *-ing*. Eliminate (A). Only **(D)** gives the verb in past progressive and is correct.

Sentence Structure: The Basics

LEARNING OBJECTIVES

After this lesson, you will be able to:

- Determine the correct punctuation and/or conjunctions to form a complete sentence
- Identify and correct inappropriate uses of semicolons

To answer a question like this:

In the late spring of 1953, New Zealand mountaineer Sir Edmund Hillary and Nepalese Sherpa Tenzing Norgay became the first people to walk on the top of the world. After a grueling expedition that spanned several **1** months. They had finally reached the summit of Mount Everest.

A) NO CHANGE

B) months, and they

C) months; they

D) months, they

You need to know this:

Fragments and Run-Ons

A complete sentence must have both a subject and a verb and express a complete thought. If any one of these elements is missing, the sentence is a **fragment**. You can recognize a fragment because the sentence will not make sense as written. There are some examples in the table below.

Missing Element	Example	Corrected Sentence
Subject	*Ran a marathon.*	*Lola ran a marathon.*
Verb	*Lola a marathon.*	
Complete thought	*While Lola ran a marathon.*	*While Lola ran a marathon, her friends cheered for her.*

The fragment "While Lola ran a marathon" is an example of a dependent clause: it has a subject (Lola) and a verb (ran), but it does not express a complete thought because it starts with a subordinating conjunction (while). Notice what the word "while" does to the meaning: While Lola ran a marathon, what happened? To fix this type of fragment, eliminate the subordinating conjunction or join the dependent clause to an independent clause using a comma. Subordinating conjunctions are words and phrases such as *since*, *because*, *unless*, *although*, and *due to*.

Unlike a dependent clause, an independent clause can stand on its own as a complete sentence. If a sentence has more than one independent clause, those clauses must be properly joined. If they are not, the sentence is a **run-on**: *Lucas enjoys hiking, he climbs a new mountain every summer.* There are several ways to correct a run-on, as shown in the table below.

To Correct a Run-On	Example
Use a period	*Lucas enjoys hiking. He climbs a new mountain every summer.*
Use a semicolon	*Lucas enjoys hiking; he climbs a new mountain every summer.*
Use a colon	*Lucas enjoys hiking: he climbs a new mountain every summer.*
Use a dash	*Lucas enjoys hiking—he climbs a new mountain every summer.*
Make one clause dependent	*Since Lucas enjoys hiking, he climbs a new mountain every summer.*
Add a FANBOYS conjunction: For, And, Nor, But, Or, Yet, So	*Lucas enjoys hiking, so he climbs a new mountain every summer.*

Semicolons

Semicolons are used in two specific ways:

- A semicolon may join two independent clauses that are not connected by a FANBOYS conjunction (also called a coordinating conjunction), just as you would use a period.
- Semicolons may be used to separate items in a list if those items already include commas.

Use semicolons to . . .	Example
Join two independent clauses that are not connected by a comma and FANBOYS conjunction	*Gaby knew that her term paper would take at least four hours to write; she got started in study hall and then finished it at home.*
Separate sub-lists within a longer list when the sub-lists contain commas	*The team needed to bring uniforms, helmets, and gloves; oranges, almonds, and water; and hockey sticks, pucks, and skates.*

You need to do this:

To recognize and correct errors involving fragments, run-ons, and semicolons, familiarize yourself with the ways in which they are tested:

- Fragments
  - If a sentence is missing a subject, a verb, or a complete thought, it is a fragment.
  - Correct the fragment by adding the missing element.

- Run-ons
  - If a sentence includes two independent clauses, they must be properly joined.
  - Employ one of the following options to properly punctuate independent clauses:
    - Use a period.
    - Insert a semicolon.
    - Use a comma and a FANBOYS (for, and, nor, but, or, yet, so) conjunction.
    - Use a dash.
    - Make one clause dependent by using a subordinating conjunction (since, because, therefore, unless, although, due to, etc.).
- Semicolons
  - A semicolon is used to join two independent clauses that are not connected by a comma and FANBOYS conjunction.
  - Semicolons separate sub-lists within a longer list. (The items inside the sub-lists are separated by commas.)

Explanation:

The sentence before the period in the underlined segment is a fragment; it is a dependent clause that does not express a complete thought. Eliminate (A) because, as written, there is an error. Eliminate (B) because you need only one conjunction to join two clauses, not two. In (B), using both "although" and "and" creates an error. Eliminate (C) because it does not correct the original error: the semicolon serves exactly the same function as the period in the original. Choice **(D)** is correct.

If sentence formation or semicolons give you trouble, study the information above and try these Drill questions before completing the following Try on Your Own questions. Answers can be found on the next page.

Drill

a. Correct the fragment by adding a subject: Brought snacks to the weekend study session.

b. Correct the fragment by completing the thought: After getting to the stadium.

c. Correct the run-on sentence with a punctuation mark: The new arts center just opened it has a crafts room for children under 13.

d. Correct the run-on sentence with a punctuation mark: Herodotus is known as one of the first historians he is even called "The Father of History."

e. Make one clause dependent to correct the run-on sentence: Herodotus is sometimes accused of making up stories for his histories, he claimed he simply recorded what he had been told.

Try on Your Own

Directions: Take as much time as you need on these questions. Work carefully and methodically. There will be an opportunity for timed practice at the end of the chapter.

Questions 2–6 refer to the following passage.

The Sun

It is perhaps impossible to overestimate the impact of the Sun on our planet Earth. **2** The Sun is situated roughly 100 million miles away from the Earth, the Sun provides essentially all of Earth's heat. Functioning like a great thermonuclear reactor, **3** the Sun's core temperature of nearly 30 million degrees Fahrenheit. The energy sources we use daily to fuel our cars and heat our homes, resources like oil and coal harvested from deep within the Earth's crust, were produced by the power of the Sun acting upon living organisms millions of years ago. The radiant energy of the Sun is the reason the Earth has **4** light, warmth, and other forms of electromagnetic waves; plants, animals, and all metabolic life; weather patterns, atmospheric movement, and many more of the Earth's natural phenomena. Yet, while the Sun's ability to provide heat and light can be easily felt by simply lying out on a beach or gazing up into a brilliant blue sky, closer inspection of the Sun's dynamic surface through special telescopes has revealed activity capable of affecting the Earth in less obvious ways.

2. A) NO CHANGE
   B) However, the Sun
   C) Not many know that the Sun
   D) Even though the Sun

3. A) NO CHANGE
   B) the Sun has a core temperature
   C) the core temperature of the Sun
   D) the temperature of the Sun's core

4. A) NO CHANGE
   B) light, warmth, and other forms of electromagnetic waves—plants, animals, and all metabolic life—weather patterns, atmospheric movement, and many more of the Earth's natural phenomena.
   C) light, warmth, other forms of electromagnetic waves, plants, animals, all metabolic life, weather patterns, atmospheric movement, and many more of the Earth's natural phenomena.
   D) light, warmth, and other forms of electromagnetic waves, plants, animals, and all metabolic life, weather patterns, atmospheric movement, and many more of the Earth's natural phenomena.

Drill answers from previous page:

Note: These are not the only ways to correct the sentences; your answers may differ.

a. **My friend** brought snacks to the weekend study session.

b. After getting to the stadium, **we went looking for our seats.**

c. The new arts center just opened. **It** has a crafts room for children under 13.

d. Herodotus is known as one of the first historians; he is even called "The Father of History."

e. **Although** Herodotus is sometimes accused of making up stories for his histories, he claimed he simply recorded what he had been told.

One of the most curious features of the Sun's violent surface is sunspots, which are dark stormy areas half the temperature of the Sun's surface and as large as 19,000 miles across. They were first viewed by telescope as early as **5** 1610 but scientists today know relatively little about them. Scientists have noticed that these spots seem to erupt and fade in 11-year cycles, affecting the Sun's luminosity and, in turn, the Earth's climate. Studies have shown that the charged particles released by solar flares, associated with sunspots, can react with the Earth's magnetic **6** field, the radiation can disrupt satellite communications, radio broadcasts, and even cell phone calls. As scientists continue to carefully observe such occurrences, referred to as "space weather," they gain a greater understanding of the powerful ability of the Sun to impact our lives.

5. A) NO CHANGE
   B) 1610, but scientists
   C) 1610 still scientists
   D) 1610, still scientists

6. A) NO CHANGE
   B) field, however the radiation
   C) field so the radiation
   D) field; the radiation

Sentence Structure: Commas, Dashes, and Colons

> **LEARNING OBJECTIVES**
>
> After this lesson, you will be able to:
>
> - Identify and correct inappropriate uses of commas, dashes, and colons
> - Use punctuation to set off simple parenthetical elements

To answer a question like this:

But climbing Mount Everest may be easier than answering the question posed by decades of non-climbers: Why? Perhaps Mallory said it best in 1923 before his ill-fated ▣7 climb; "Because it is there."

A) NO CHANGE

B) climb: "Because it is there."

C) climb. "Because it is there."

D) climb "Because it is there."

You need to know this:

Answer choices often move punctuation marks around, replace them with other punctuation marks, or remove them altogether. When underlined portions include commas, dashes, or colons, check to make sure the punctuation is used correctly in context.

Commas

There are two ways in which commas are not interchangeable with any other punctuation: a series of items and introductory words or phrases.

Use commas to . . .	Comma(s)
Set off three or more items in a series	*Jeremiah packed a sleeping bag, a raincoat, and a lantern for his upcoming camping trip.*
Separate an introductory word or phrase from the rest of the sentence	*For example, carrots are an excellent source of several vitamins and minerals.*

Commas and Dashes

In many cases, either a comma or a dash may be used to punctuate a sentence. Note that only a comma can be used to set off a leading dependent clause from an independent clause.

Use commas or dashes to . . .	Comma(s)	Dash(es)
Separate independent clauses connected by a FANBOYS conjunction (For, And, Nor, But, Or, Yet, So)	*Jess finished her homework earlier than expected, so she started an assignment that was due the following week.*	*Jess finished her homework earlier than expected—so she started an assignment that was due the following week.*
Separate a dependent clause from an independent clause when the dependent clause is first	*Because Tyson wanted to organize his locker before class, he arrived at school a few minutes early.*	*N/A*
Separate parenthetical elements from the rest of the sentence (use either two commas or two dashes, not one of each; see below for more on parentheticals)	*Professor Mann, who is the head of the English department, is known for assigning extensive projects.*	*Professor Mann—who is the head of the English department—is known for assigning extensive projects.*

Colons and Dashes

Colons and dashes are used to include new ideas by introducing or explaining something or by breaking the flow of the sentence. Note that the clause before the colon or dash must be able to stand on its own as a complete sentence.

Use colons and dashes to . . .	Colon	Dash
Introduce and/or emphasize a short phrase, quotation, explanation, example, or list	*Sanjay had two important tasks to complete: a science experiment and an expository essay.*	*Sanjay had two important tasks to complete—a science experiment and an expository essay.*
Separate two independent clauses when the second clause explains, illustrates, or expands on the first sentence	*Highway 1 in Australia is one of the longest national highways in the world: it circles the entirety of the continent and connects every mainland state capital.*	*Highway 1 in Australia is one of the longest national highways in the world—it circles the entirety of the continent and connects every mainland state capital.*

Unnecessary Punctuation

Knowing when punctuation should not be used is equally important. If an underlined portion includes punctuation, take time to consider if it should be included at all.

Do NOT use punctuation to . . .	Incorrect	Correct
Separate a subject from its verb	*The diligent student council, meets every week.*	*The diligent student council meets every week.*
Separate a verb from its object or a preposition from its object	*The diligent student council meets, every week.*	*The diligent student council meets every week.*
Set off elements that are essential to a sentence's meaning	*The, diligent student, council meets every week.*	*The diligent student council meets every week.*
Separate adjectives that work together to modify a noun	*The diligent, student council meets every week.*	*The diligent student council meets every week.*

Parenthetical Elements

Parenthetical elements may appear at the beginning, in the middle, or at the end of a sentence. They must be properly punctuated with parentheses, commas, or dashes for the sentence to be grammatically correct. A phrase such as *the capital of France* is considered parenthetical if the rest of the sentence is grammatically correct when it is removed. Do not mix and match; a parenthetical element must begin and end with the same type of punctuation.

Parenthetical Element Placement	Parentheses	Comma(s)	Dash(es)
Beginning	*N/A*	*The capital of France, Paris is a popular tourist destination.*	*N/A*
Middle	*Paris (the capital of France) is a popular tourist destination.*	*Paris, the capital of France, is a popular tourist destination.*	*Paris—the capital of France—is a popular tourist destination.*
End	*A popular tourist destination is Paris (the capital of France).*	*A popular tourist destination is Paris, the capital of France.*	*A popular tourist destination is Paris— the capital of France.*

You need to do this:

If the underlined portion includes punctuation, ask yourself:

- Is the punctuation used correctly?

  The punctuation needs to be the correct type (comma, dash, or colon) and in the correct location.

- Is the punctuation is necessary?

  If you cannot identify a reason why the punctuation is included, the punctuation should be removed.

Explanation:

The underlined segment includes a semicolon that is used incorrectly because it neither joins two independent clauses nor separates items containing commas in a series or list. The underlined segment here is intended to emphasize a short quotation, so a colon or dash would be appropriate. **(B)** is correct.

If commas, dashes, and colons give you trouble, study the information above and try these Drill questions before completing the following Try on Your Own questions. Edit each sentence to correct the punctuation issue. Answers can be found on the next page.

Drill

a.   For my birthday, I asked for my favorite dessert chocolate pecan pie.

b.   The story of Emperor Nero playing the fiddle while Rome burned has been debunked by historians but the saying based on it remains popular.

c.   Koalas' fingerprints are nearly indistinguishable from human fingerprints which has occasionally led to mistakes at crime scenes.

d.   Invented by Sir John Harrington in 1596 the flush toilet actually precedes modern indoor plumbing.

e.   Toni Morrison born Chloe Wofford is one of America's most celebrated writers.

Try on Your Own

Directions: Take as much time as you need on these questions. Work carefully and methodically. There will be an opportunity for timed practice at the end of the chapter.

Questions 8–15 refer to the following passage.

Mauritius

[8] Although, most of the products we buy today are made abroad in places well-known to Americans, such as Mexico and China, a quick check of many clothing labels will reveal the name of a country that might not be so [9] familiar. Mauritius. Named in honor of Prince Maurice of Nassau by the Dutch who colonized it in 1638, this small island in the Indian Ocean has a complicated history influenced by several international powers. Since gaining independence in [10] 1968— Mauritius has emerged as a stable democracy with one of Africa's highest per capita incomes. Mauritius is considered a significant [11] player: in the modern global economy one of the few in the Southern Hemisphere.

Yet, before its hard-won economic and political stability, Mauritius underwent several tumultuous phases. After the Portuguese landed on the island in 1511, they hunted a large, slow-moving, native bird known as the dodo into extinction. The Portuguese

8. A) NO CHANGE
    B) Although most
    C) Although; most
    D) Most

9. A) NO CHANGE
    B) familiar and it's Mauritius
    C) familiar: Mauritius
    D) familiar which is Mauritius

10. A) NO CHANGE
    B) 1968; Mauritius
    C) 1968 as Mauritius
    D) 1968, Mauritius

11. A) NO CHANGE
    B) player in the modern global economy, one
    C) player—in the modern global economy—one
    D) player in the modern, global economy one

Drill answers from previous page:

Note: These are not the only ways to correct the sentences; your answers may differ.

a. For my birthday, I asked for my favorite dessert: chocolate pecan pie.

b. The story of Emperor Nero playing the fiddle while Rome burned has been debunked by historians, but the saying based on it remains popular.

c. Koalas' fingerprints are nearly indistinguishable from human fingerprints—which has occasionally led to mistakes at crime scenes.

d. Invented by Sir John Harrington in 1596, the flush toilet actually precedes modern indoor plumbing.

e. Toni Morrison, born Chloe Wofford, is one of America's most celebrated writers. OR Toni Morrison—born Chloe Wofford—is one of America's most celebrated writers.

Writing & Lang

were followed by the Dutch, who brought waves of [12] <u>traders, planters, and slaves; and indentured laborers, merchants, and artisans,</u> whose collective arrival brought international recognition to Mauritius. In 1715, the island again changed hands, this time to the French, and in 1810, with a successful invasion during the Napoleonic Wars, the British became the fourth European power to rule the island. Yet it was during this period of changing [13] <u>colonial powers—Mauritius was traded like a commodity, that</u> the demographics of the island began to experience important changes with great political ramifications.

By the time slavery was abolished in 1835, for example, the growing Indian population, the Creoles who could trace their roots back to island's sugarcane plantations, and the Muslim community originating from present-day Pakistan far outnumbered the remaining Franco-Mauritian elites. And with these demographic changes came political change. The first step toward self-rule came with the legislative elections of [14] <u>1947 and in March</u> of 1968, an official constitution was adopted. Today, Mauritius peacefully balances the diversity of its multicultural society and flourishes in international [15] <u>trade through</u> its advantageous geographic location and large labor force.

12. A) NO CHANGE
    B) traders, planters and slaves, indentured laborers, merchants and artisans,
    C) traders, planters, slaves, indentured laborers, merchants, artisans,
    D) traders, planters, slaves, indentured laborers, merchants, and artisans,

13. A) NO CHANGE
    B) colonial powers—Mauritius was traded like a commodity that
    C) colonial powers—Mauritius was traded like a commodity—that
    D) colonial powers, Mauritius was traded like a commodity that

14. A) NO CHANGE
    B) 1947, and in March
    C) 1947 and, in March
    D) 1947 and in March,

15. A) NO CHANGE
    B) trade, through
    C) trade through,
    D) trade; through

Agreement: Verbs

LEARNING OBJECTIVE

After this lesson, you will be able to:

- Identify and correct verb agreement issues

To answer a question like this:

For example, the editors had their work cut out for them when the part of the book devoted to avalanches and landslides **16** <u>were found</u> to be inaccurate.

A) NO CHANGE

B) was found

C) are found

D) is found

You need to know this:

Verb Tense

Verb tense indicates when an action or state of being took place: in the past, present, or future. The tense of the verb must fit the context of the passage. Each tense can express three different types of action.

Type of Action	Past	Present	Future
Single action occurring only once	Connor **planted** vegetables in the community garden.	Connor **plants** vegetables in the community garden.	Connor **will plant** vegetables in the community garden.
Action that is ongoing at some point in time	Connor **was planting** vegetables in the community garden this morning before noon.	Connor **is planting** vegetables in the community garden this morning before noon.	Connor **will be planting** vegetables in the community garden this morning before noon.
Action that is completed before some other action	Connor **had planted** vegetables in the community garden every year until he gave his job to Jasmine.	Connor **has planted** vegetables in the community garden since it started five years ago.	Connor **will have planted** vegetables in the community garden by the time the growing season starts.

Subject-Verb Agreement

A verb must agree with its subject in person and number:

- Person (first, second, or third)
  - First: *I **ask** a question.*
  - Second: *You **ask** a question.*
  - Third: *She **asks** a question.*
- Number (singular or plural)
  - Singular: *The apple **tastes** delicious.*
  - Plural: *Apples **taste** delicious.*

The noun closest to the verb is not always the subject: *The chair with the lion feet is an antique.* The singular verb in this sentence, *is*, is closest to the plural noun *feet*. However, the verb's actual subject is the singular noun *chair*, so the sentence is correct as written.

When a sentence includes two nouns, only the conjunction *and* forms a compound subject requiring a plural verb form:

- Plural: *Saliyah and Taylor **are** in the running club.*
- Singular: *Either Saliyah or Taylor **is** in the running club.*
- Singular: *Neither Saliyah nor Taylor **is** in the running club.*

Collective nouns are nouns that name entities with more than one member, such as *group*, *team*, and *family*. Even though these nouns represent more than one person, they are grammatically singular and require singular verb forms:

- *The collection of paintings **is** one of the most popular art exhibits in recent years.*
- *The team **looks** promising this year.*

You need to do this:

If the underlined portion includes a verb, check that the verb:

- Reflects the correct tense: does it fit the context?
- Agrees with the subject in person and number

Explanation:

The subject of the verb "were found" is the noun "part," which is singular. The verb is plural, so there is an error. Rule out (A) and (C). (Note that the test makers like to put prepositional phrases or other descriptive phrases, such as the phrase "devoted to avalanches and landslides," between the subject and verb to make the subject-verb agreement error trickier to spot.)

To decide between (B) and (D), look at the context defined by the other verb tense in the sentence. The editors "*had* their work cut out for them," so the sentence describes past events. Choice **(B)** is also in the past tense and is consistent with this context. It is the correct answer.

If verbs give you trouble, study the information above and try these Drill questions before completing the following Try on Your Own questions. Edit each sentence to correct the verb issue. Turn the page to see the answers.

Drill

a. Angel audition for the school play next week.

b. The song, with its upbeat rhythm and catchy lyrics, were wildly popular.

c. Either the governor or the lieutenant governor usually present the award.

d. By the time the last runner completed the marathon, the winner has crossed the finish line hours ago.

e. Few people know that Stephen Hawking both revolutionized physics and co-written children's books with his daughter.

Try on Your Own

Directions: Take as much time as you need on these questions. Work carefully and methodically. There will be an opportunity for timed practice at the end of the chapter.

Questions 17–22 refer to the following passage.

SMOM

At 69 Condotti Street in Rome sits what **17** is believed by many to be the smallest country in the world, a country that few have ever heard of. The Sovereign Military and Hospitaller Order of St. John of Jerusalem of Rhodes and of Malta, or SMOM, **18** were an ancient order of knights well known for its humanitarian activities. The order's headquarters in Rome—a mere 6,000 square meters, or about one acre—is considered an independent state by at least 75 nations. How SMOM got to Rome is a story almost a millennium old, spanning as many places as the order's official name suggests.

SMOM began in 1099, during the First Crusade, a large-scale military conflict pitting Christian armies against the Muslim rulers of what is now Israel. The order's task was to protect and defend Christian pilgrims traveling to Jerusalem as well as **19** providing a hospital for their care. Though it began as a religious order, SMOM developed into a military knighthood as a result of the volatile political situation.

First because of the ongoing conflict between Muslims and Christians and, later, Napoleon Bonaparte's expansionist ambitions, the order was forced to move a number of times. After the Muslims had taken Jerusalem in the 1170s, forcing SMOM to relocate first to the Mediterranean island of Cyprus and

17. A) NO CHANGE
     B) are believed
     C) is to be believed
     D) are to be believed

18. A) NO CHANGE
     B) was
     C) are
     D) is

19. A) NO CHANGE
     B) to provide
     C) providing them
     D) ensuring availability of

then to the nearby island of Rhodes, the Ottoman Turks **20** had seized Rhodes in 1522, forcing SMOM to move again, this time to Malta. Then **21** Napoleon drives the order from Malta in 1798, and the island fell into British hands soon after. SMOM wandered from city to city in Italy, finally establishing its current headquarters in 1834.

Today, SMOM **22** will concentrate on providing humanitarian aid to everyone regardless of creed, establishing hospitals and charities in all corners of the world. Its many activities include vaccination programs, refugee relief, and philanthropic works to combat deadly diseases, such as leprosy and malnutrition.

20. A) NO CHANGE
    B) seized
    C) have seized
    D) would have seized

21. A) NO CHANGE
    B) Napoleon drove
    C) Napoleon had driven
    D) Napoleon was driving

22. A) NO CHANGE
    B) will be concentrating
    C) concentrates
    D) concentrates and is concentrating

Drill answers:

Note: These are not the only ways to correct the sentences; your answers may differ.

a. Angel **will** audition for the school play next week.

b. The song, with its upbeat rhythm and catchy lyrics, **was** wildly popular.

c. Either the governor or the lieutenant governor usually **presents** the award.

d. By the time the last runner completed the marathon, the winner **had** crossed the finish line hours ago.

e. Few people know that Stephen Hawking both revolutionized physics and **co-wrote** children's books with his daughter.

Agreement: Pronouns

LEARNING OBJECTIVE

After this lesson, you will be able to:

• Identify and correct pronoun agreement issues

To answer a question like this:

In their search for Ozark cavefish, the researchers were encouraged by the stability of the caves' ground-water as well as by **23** <u>its</u> length and by the presence of bats.

A) NO CHANGE

B) it's

C) their

D) there

You need to know this:

Pronoun Forms

A pronoun is a word that takes the place of a noun. Pronouns can take three different forms, each of which is used based on the grammatical role it plays in the sentence.

Form	Pronouns	Example
Subjective: The pronoun is used as the subject.	I, you, she, he, it, we, they, who	*Rivka is the student **who** will lead the presentation.*
Objective: The pronoun is used as the object of a verb or a preposition.	me, you, her, him, it, us, them, whom	*With **whom** will Rivka present the scientific findings?*
Possessive: The pronoun expresses ownership.	my, mine, your, yours, his, her, hers, its, our, ours, their, theirs, whose	*Rivka will likely choose a partner **whose** work is excellent.*

Note that a pronoun in subjective form can, logically, be the subject in a complete sentence. Pronouns that are in objective form cannot.

When there are two pronouns or a noun and a pronoun in a compound structure, drop the other noun or pronoun to tell which form to use. For example: *Leo and me walked into town*. If you were talking about yourself only, you would say, "I walked into town," not "Me walked into town." Therefore, the correct form is subjective, and the original sentence should read: *Leo and I walked into town*.

Writing & Lang

Pronoun-Antecedent Agreement

A pronoun's antecedent is the noun it logically represents in a sentence. If the noun is singular, the pronoun must be singular; if the noun is plural, the pronoun must be plural.

Antecedent	Incorrect	Correct
selection	*The selection of books was placed in **their** designated location.*	*The selection of books was placed in **its** designated location.*
A woman	*A woman visiting the zoo fed the giraffes all of the lettuce **they** had purchased.*	*A woman visiting the zoo fed the giraffes all of the lettuce **she** had purchased.*
sapling	*The sapling, along with dozens of flowers, was relocated to where **they** would thrive.*	*The sapling, along with dozens of flowers, was relocated to where **it** would thrive.*
apples	*If apples are unripe, **it** should not be purchased.*	*If apples are unripe, **they** should not be purchased.*

Ambiguous Pronouns

A pronoun is ambiguous if its antecedent is either missing or unclear. When you see an underlined pronoun, make sure you can identify the noun to which it refers.

Ambiguous Pronoun Use	Corrected Sentence
*Anthony walked with Cody to the ice cream shop, and **he** bought a banana split.*	*Anthony walked with Cody to the ice cream shop, and **Cody** bought a banana split.*

You need to do this:

If the underlined portion includes a pronoun, *find the logical antecedent*. If there is no clear antecedent, the pronoun is ambiguous and this error must be corrected. Then, check that the pronoun:

- Uses the correct form
  - If the pronoun is the subject of the sentence, use a subjective pronoun such as I, you, she, he, it, we, they, or who.
  - If the pronoun is an object within the sentence, use an objective pronoun such as me, you, her, him, it, us, they, or whom.
  - If the pronoun indicates possession, use a possessive pronoun such as my, mine, your, yours, his, her, hers, its, our, ours, their, theirs, or whose.
- Agrees with its antecedent
  - A singular antecedent requires a singular pronoun; a plural antecedent requires a plural pronoun.

Explanation:

The phrase "its length" logically refers to the caves, not the groundwater. You need the possessive form, but because the word "caves" is plural, you need the plural "their." Choice **(C)** is correct.

If pronouns give you trouble, study the information above and try these Drill questions before completing the following Try on Your Own questions. Edit each sentence to correct the pronoun issue. Answers can be found on the next page.

Drill

a.   Although the teacher gave the student detention after school, she was not angry.

b.   My uncle likes to go bowling with my sister and I.

c.   The box of nails has been moved from their usual place in the shed.

d.   My favorite singer, who I have wanted to see in person for years, will give a concert a week after my birthday.

e.   The cathedral of Notre Dame, with vast vaulted ceilings and intricate carvings, never fails to amaze their visitors.

Writing & Lang

Try on Your Own

Directions: Take as much time as you need on these questions. Work carefully and methodically. There will be an opportunity for timed practice at the end of the chapter.

Questions 24–29 refer to the following passage.

Akira Kurosawa

What do samurai,[1] cowboys, shogun,[2] gangsters, peasants, and William Shakespeare all have in common? **24** He is just one of the varied influences on the work of Akira Kurosawa (1910–1998), a Japanese film director considered by movie critic Leonard Maltin to be "one of the undisputed giants of cinema." Over his career, Kurosawa's unique blend of Western themes and Eastern settings made **25** them arguably the most important Japanese filmmaker in history.

The most famous example of Kurosawa's style is his 1954 film *Seven Samurai*. Although the setting is medieval Japan, with peasants and samurai, **26** its story is influenced by Western films: a village, terrorized by local bandits, turns to seven down-on-their-

24. A) NO CHANGE
    B) His is just one
    C) They are just some
    D) Theirs are just some

25. A) NO CHANGE
    B) he
    C) him
    D) his

26. A) NO CHANGE
    B) their
    C) the film's
    D) the setting's

Drill answers from previous page:

Note: These are not the only ways to correct the sentences; your answers may differ.

a. Although the teacher gave the student detention after school, **the student** was not angry.

b. My uncle likes to go bowling with my sister and **me**.

c. The box of nails has been moved from **its** usual place in the shed.

d. My favorite singer, **whom** I have wanted to see in person for years, will give a concert a week after my birthday.

e. The cathedral of Notre Dame, with vast vaulted ceilings and intricate carvings, never fails to amaze **its** visitors.

[1] samurai: noble warriors of medieval Japan, similar to European knights
[2] shogun: military dictators of Japan from 1603 to 1868

luck yet good-hearted samurai for the protection **27** they need. Like movie cowboys, these samurai are romantic heroes, sure of their morals and battling clear forces of evil. The traditional Japanese version of a samurai was a noble and often distant symbol of Japan's imperial heritage, but Kurosawa considered the main characters differently. To **28** him, the film's samurai were distinctly human characters, each with a conscience and the will to act to correct the wrongs around them.

Although Kurosawa's films enjoy a lofty reputation in the West, many critics and moviegoers in his home country view his films as neither original nor particularly Japanese. His use of Western ideals and themes—even reinterpreting Western authors such as William Shakespeare and Fyodor Dostoyevsky—leads Japanese cinema lovers, many of **29** who see Kurosawa's use of Japanese culture as mere "window dressing" applied to essentially foreign stories, to regard his work with suspicion. Ironically, it was Kurosawa's success that opened the door for other, more "Japanese" directors, such as Yasujiro Ozu and Kenji Mizoguchi, to gain a wider audience.

27. A) NO CHANGE
    B) it needs.
    C) he needs.
    D) you need.

28. A) NO CHANGE
    B) me
    C) you
    D) us

29. A) NO CHANGE
    B) whose
    C) which
    D) whom

Agreement: Modifiers

LEARNING OBJECTIVES

After this lesson, you will be able to:

- Identify and correct modifier agreement issues
- Identify and correct inappropriate uses of apostrophes

To answer a question like this:

30 Called "Mother of the Universe" by the Tibetan people, the lives of George Mallory and Andrew Irvine had already been claimed by Mount Everest, despite its maternal appellation, before Hillary and Norgay finally conquered its icy peak.

A) NO CHANGE

B) Hillary and Norgay, called "Mother of the Universe" by the Tibetan people, finally conquered the icy peak of Mount Everest, which had already claimed the lives of George Mallory and Andrew Irvine, despite its maternal appellation.

C) The lives of George Mallory and Andrew Irvine, called "Mother of the Universe" by the Tibetan people, had already been claimed by Mount Everest, despite its maternal appellation, before Hillary and Norgay finally conquered its icy peak.

D) Called "Mother of the Universe" by the Tibetan people, Mount Everest had already, despite its maternal appellation, claimed the lives of George Mallory and Andrew Irvine before Hillary and Norgay finally conquered its icy peak.

You need to know this:

A **modifier** is a word or phrase that describes, clarifies, or provides additional information about another part of the sentence. Modifier questions require you to identify the part of a sentence being modified and use the appropriate modifier in the proper place.

In order to be grammatically correct, the modifier must be placed as close to the word it describes as possible. Use context clues in the passage to identify the correct placement of a modifier; a misplaced modifier can cause confusion and is always incorrect on test day.

Note that a common way the SAT tests modifiers is with modifying phrases at the beginning of a sentence. Just like any other modifier, the modifying phrase grammatically modifies whatever is right next to it in the sentence. For example, consider the sentence, "While walking to the bus stop, the rain drenched Bob." The initial phrase, "While walking to the bus stop," grammatically modifies "the rain," creating a nonsense sentence; the rain can't walk to the bus stop. The writer meant that Bob was walking to the bus stop, so the sentence should read, "While walking to the bus stop, Bob was drenched by the rain."

Modifier/Modifying Phrase	Incorrect	Correct
nearly	Andre **nearly** watched the play for four hours.	Andre watched the play for **nearly** four hours.
in individual containers	The art teacher handed out paints to students **in individual containers**.	The art teacher handed out paints **in individual containers** to students.
A scholar athlete	**A scholar athlete**, maintaining high grades in addition to playing soccer were expected of Maya.	**A scholar athlete**, Maya was expected to maintain high grades in addition to playing soccer.

Adjectives and Adverbs

Use adjectives only to modify nouns and pronouns. Use adverbs to modify everything else.

- **Adjectives** are single-word modifiers that describe nouns and pronouns: *Ian conducted an **efficient** lab experiment.*
- **Adverbs** are single-word modifiers that describe verbs, adjectives, or other adverbs: *Ian **efficiently** conducted a lab experiment.*

Note that nouns can sometimes be used as adjectives. For example, in the phrase "the fashion company's autumn line," the word "fashion" functions as an adjective modifying "company," and the word "autumn" functions as an adjective modifying "line."

Comparative/Superlative

When comparing similar things, use adjectives that match the number of items being compared. When comparing two items or people, use the **comparative** form of the adjective. When comparing three or more items or people, use the **superlative** form.

Comparative (two items)	Superlative (three or more items)
better, more, newer, older, shorter, taller, worse, younger	best, most, newest, oldest, shortest, tallest, worst, youngest

Writing & Lang

Possessive Nouns and Pronouns

Possessive nouns and pronouns indicate that something that belongs to someone or something. In general, possessive nouns are written with an apostrophe, while possessive pronouns are not.

To spot errors in possessive noun or pronoun construction, look for . . .	Incorrect	Correct
Two nouns in a row	The **professors lectures** were both informative and entertaining.	The **professor's lectures** were both informative and entertaining.
Pronouns with apostrophes	The book is her's.	The book is **hers**.
Words that sound alike	The three friends decided to ride **there** bicycles to the park over **they're** where **their** going to enjoy a picnic lunch.	The three friends decided to ride **their** bicycles to the park over **there** where **they're** going to enjoy a picnic lunch.

Apostrophes

Use an apostrophe to . . .	Example
Indicate the possessive form of a single noun	My oldest **sister's** soccer game is on Saturday.
Indicate the possessive form of a plural noun	My two older **sisters'** soccer games are on Saturday.
Indicate a contraction (e.g., *don't*, *can't*)	**They've** won every soccer match this season.

Note that plural nouns are formed without an apostrophe.

Incorrect	Correct
Sting **ray's** are cartilaginous fish related to **shark's**.	Sting **rays** are cartilaginous fish related to **sharks**.
There are many **carnival's** in this area every summer.	There are many **carnivals** in this area every summer.

To check whether *it's* is appropriate, replace it in the sentence with *it is* or *it has*. If the sentence no longer makes sense, *it's* is incorrect. The following sentence is correct:

The tree frog blends perfectly into its surroundings. When it holds still, it's nearly invisible.

Note that *its'* and *its's* are never correct.

You need to do this:

If the underlined portion includes a modifier, determine whether the modifier:

- Is placed correctly
  - Is it as near as possible to the word it logically modifies?
  - If it is not in the correct place, where should it be moved?
- Agrees with the word or words it is describing
  - Does the sentence require an adjective or an adverb?
  - Does the noun or pronoun show proper possession?

If the underlined portion includes an apostrophe, make sure it correctly indicates either possession or a contraction. If an apostrophe is missing, select the answer choice that places it in the correct location.

Explanation:

The phrase "despite its maternal appellation" indicates that it was Mount Everest that was known in Tibetan culture as the "Mother of the Universe." That means "Mount Everest" must be placed immediately next to the phrase, "[c]alled 'Mother of the Universe' by the Tibetan people." This is not the case in the current sentence, so there is a modification error. The only choice that corrects the error is **(D)**.

If modifiers give you trouble, study the information above and try these Drill questions before completing the following Try on Your Own questions. Edit each sentence to correct the modifier or apostrophe issue. Answers can be found on the next page.

Drill

a.   Computers have grown exponential more efficient since their invention.

b.   Estella chose to take the route with the most attractively scenery to her destination.

c.   The leaf-tailed gecko's amazing natural camouflage enables it to blend perfectly into it's surroundings.

d.   Between basketball and baseball, basketball is the most popular sport in the United States.

e.   From Edgar Allan Poe to Monty Python, the infamous Spanish Inquisition has provided material for many artists.

Writing & Lang

Try on Your Own

Directions: Take as much time as you need on these questions. Work carefully and methodically. There will be an opportunity for timed practice at the end of the chapter.

Questions 31–37 refer to the following passage.

Sergei Eisenstein

Considered the father of the montage, a popular cinematic technique that involves a rapid succession of shots, often superimposed, **31** the modern movie has as one of its principal architects Russian director Sergei Eisenstein. Although his career was not particularly prolific—he completed only seven feature-length films—Eisenstein's work contains a clarity and sharpness of composition that make the depth of his plots and the **32** powerfully complexity of his juxtaposed images easily accessible to most viewers. In fact, few filmmakers were **33** most instrumental in pushing the envelope of the established, conservative nineteenth-century Victorian theatre than Eisenstein, whose films helped to usher in a new era of abstract thought and expression in art.

Eisenstein's feature debut, a film entitled *Statchka* (*Strike* in English) released in 1925, was many **34** moviegoer's first experience of montage on the big screen. Based on the contemporary theory of biomechanics and criticizing the mechanical and

31. A) NO CHANGE
    B) the modern movie has Russian director Sergei Eisenstein to thank as one of its principal architects.
    C) the Russian director Sergei Eisenstein was one of the principal architects of the modern movie.
    D) critics name the Russian director Sergei Eisenstein as one of the principal architects of the modern movie.

32. A) NO CHANGE
    B) powerful
    C) power
    D) power of

33. A) NO CHANGE
    B) more instrumental
    C) the best at being instrumental
    D) better at instrumentally

34. A) NO CHANGE
    B) movie's goer
    C) moviegoers
    D) moviegoers'

Drill answers from previous page:

Note: These are not the only ways to correct the sentences; your answers may differ.

a. Computers have grown **exponentially** more efficient since their invention.

b. Estella chose to take the route with the most **attractive** scenery to her destination.

c. The leaf-tailed gecko's amazing natural camouflage enables it to blend perfectly into **its** surroundings.

d. Between basketball and baseball, basketball is the **more** popular sport in the United States.

e. The infamous Spanish Inquisition has provided material for many artists, **from Edgar Allan Poe to Monty Python**.

repetitive movements required of exploited factory workers, **35** <u>Eisenstein's montage consisted of a powerful sequence of conflicting images that were</u> able to abbreviate time spans in the film while introducing new metaphors and allusions to the storyline. Essentially, Eisenstein sought to use the montage to create a cumulative emotional effect that was greater than the sum of the individual shots.

    36 <u>Enormously, it was with the successful technique of montage that Eisenstein's work caught the eye of the new Communist Party leaders</u> in Moscow, who saw in his cinematic style a film for the "common man." His next two films, *Battleship Potemkin* and *October: Ten Days That Shook the World*, were commissioned by party officials in an attempt to use Eisenstein's mass appeal to disseminate Soviet propaganda. As a result, these achievements have been frequently criticized **37** <u>for they're</u> lack of artistic integrity. Yet, in the end, regardless of politics, Eisenstein's films continue to have an undeniably significant and lasting impact on filmmakers.

35. A) NO CHANGE
    B) Eisenstein arranged a powerful sequence of conflicting images into a montage that was
    C) Eisenstein used conflicting images in a powerful sequence, composing a montage that was
    D) Eisenstein created a montage consisting of a powerful sequence of conflicting images that were

36. A) NO CHANGE
    B) It was enormously with the successful technique of montage that Eisenstein's work caught the eye of the new Communist Party leaders
    C) It was with the enormously successful technique of montage that Eisenstein's work caught the eye of the new Communist Party leaders
    D) It was with the successful technique of montage that Eisenstein's work caught the eye of the enormously new Communist Party leaders

37. A) NO CHANGE
    B) therefore
    C) for their
    D) for there

Agreement: Parallelism

> **LEARNING OBJECTIVE**
>
> After this lesson, you will be able to:
>
> - Identify and correct errors in parallel structure

To answer a question like this:

Like other ectotherms, Galapagos lava lizards are dependent on their environment for warmth, so they can often be seen basking in the sun to increase their body temperature, which in turn determines their speed of locomotion. The lizards can move very quickly during the day **38** but at night, only slowly.

A) NO CHANGE

B) but at nighttime, that they must move slowly.

C) but at night, they are slower.

D) but only slowly at night.

You need to know this:

Verbs in a list, a compound, or a comparison must be parallel in form.

Feature	Example	Parallel Form
A list	Chloe **formulated** a question, **conducted** background research, and **constructed** a hypothesis before starting the experiment.	3 simple past verb phrases
A compound	**Hunting** and **fishing** were essential to the survival of Midwestern Native American tribes such as the Omaha.	2 -ing verb forms
A comparison	Garrett enjoys **sculpting** as much as **painting**.	2 -ing verb forms

Note that parallelism may be tested using other parts of speech besides verbs. In general, any items in a list, compound, or comparison must be in parallel form. For example, if a list starts with a noun, the other items in the list must also be nouns; if it starts with an adjective, the other items must be adjectives, etc.

Incorrect	Correct
Naomi likes **pumpkin pie and to drink coffee** on chilly weekend afternoons. Which of the dogs is the **most docile and better behaved**?	Naomi likes **pumpkin pie and coffee** on chilly weekend afternoons. or Naomi likes **to eat pumpkin pie and drink coffee** on chilly weekend afternoons. Which of the dogs is the **most docile and best behaved**? or Which of the dogs is the **more docile and better behaved**?

You need to do this:

If the underlined segment contains part or all of a list, compound, or comparison, check that all elements are in parallel form.

Explanation:

The word "but" signals a compound. The elements before and after the word "but" must therefore be parallel. In the sentence as written, in the first half of the compound, the adverbial phrase "very quickly" precedes the prepositional phrase "during the day," but in the second half, the phrase "only slowly" *follows* the phrase "at night." Thus, the structure as written is not parallel, and (A) is incorrect. Choices (B) and (C) do not fix the issue; both place the phrase "at night" (or "at nighttime") in the wrong place. Moreover, (B) introduces the word "that," which creates a dependent clause, turning the sentence into a fragment that does not express a complete thought, and (C) creates a punctuation error: it turns the word "but" into a coordinating conjunction by introducing an independent clause with a subject and verb, "they are," thus creating a need for a comma before the word "but." That leaves **(D)**, which does introduce parallel structure and is correct.

Try on Your Own

Directions: Take as much time as you need on these questions. Work carefully and methodically. There will be an opportunity for timed practice at the end of the chapter.

Questions 39–43 refer to the following passage.

Houses by Mail

Long before the advent of the giant internet retailers like Amazon and Wayfair, and long before there was an internet, there was the Sears Catalog. It was an immense book that **39** exceeded 600 pages in length and there was seemingly every item that a person might buy or dream of buying. Furthermore, it offered a vastly larger selection and lower prices than local stores could do. From pocket watches to patent medicines, **40** women's gowns and water pumps, from hunting rifles to horse-drawn plows, the Sears Catalog offered it all. Whatever you wanted, you simply mailed your order form and payment to the company's Chicago headquarters, and days or weeks later, your order would arrive at your **41** mailbox, local post office, or at the freight depot.

39. A) NO CHANGE
    B) exceeded 600 pages in length and in it was seemingly
    C) exceeded 600 pages in length and seemingly
    D) exceeded 600 pages in length and advertised seemingly

40. A) NO CHANGE
    B) as well as women's gowns and water pumps
    C) from women's gowns to water pumps
    D) and women's gowns to water pumps

41. A) NO CHANGE
    B) mailbox, at the local post office, or freight depot.
    C) mailbox, local post office, or the freight depot.
    D) mailbox, local post office, or freight depot.

Amazingly, there was a period from 1908 to 1940 when you could order an entire house by mail from Sears. In fact, Sears issued a completely separate catalog—*Sears Modern Homes*—specifically to market these homes by mail. Over the 33 years of the program, buyers had the choice of some 370 home designs and floor plans. What's more, the homes offered were not just simple cottages: designs ranged from modest, two-room bungalows to impressive, multi-story mansions that featured 42 intricate decorative elements, servants' quarters, and wrap-around porches.

The homes came in kit form, with all lumber pre-cut and fitted. The kits were delivered by railroad freight cars to the local train depot to be picked up by the buyer and brought to the building site. Each kit could consist of as many as 30,000 pieces, and Sears guaranteed that "a man of average skills" could assemble the home in under 90 days. While many buyers built their own homes, 43 for others, local contractors or builders did the work. It's a tribute to the quality of the Sears homes, and their builders, that some 70 percent of these kit houses are still standing to this day.

42. A) NO CHANGE

B) intricate decorative elements, quarters for servants, and wrap-around porches.

C) intricate decorative elements, servants' quarters, and porches that wrapped around the house.

D) intricate elements of decoration, quarters for servants, and wrap-around porches.

43. A) NO CHANGE

B) others hired local contractors or builders to do the work.

C) local contractors or builders might be hired by others to do the work.

D) the services of local contractors or builders could also be used.

Agreement: Idioms

LEARNING OBJECTIVES

After this lesson, you will be able to:

- Identify and correct expressions that deviate from idiomatic English
- Determine the appropriate word in frequently confused pairs

---

To answer a question like this:

44 The goal of the conference was not only to find ways to reduce carbon emissions but to provide information to communities threatened by sea level rise as well.

A) NO CHANGE

B) Not only was the goal of the conference to find ways to reduce carbon emissions, albeit also to provide information to communities threatened by sea level rise.

C) The goal of the conference was not only to find ways to reduce carbon emissions, and to provide information to communities whom sea level rise threatens.

D) The goal of the conference was not only to find ways to reduce carbon emissions but also to provide information to communities threatened by sea level rise.

You need to know this:

An **idiom** is a combination of words that must be used together to convey either a figurative or literal meaning. Idioms are tested in three ways:

1. Proper preposition use in context: the preposition must reflect the writer's intended meaning.

    *She waits **on** customers.*

    *She waits **for** the bus.*

    *She waits **with** her friends.*

2. Idiomatic expressions: some words or phrases must be used together to be correct.

    *Simone will **either** bike **or** run to the park.*

    ***Neither** the principal **nor** the teachers will tolerate tardiness.*

    *This fall, Shari is playing **not only** soccer **but also** field hockey.*

3. Implicit double negatives: some words imply a negative and therefore cannot be paired with an explicit negative. The words *barely, hardly,* and *scarcely* fall into this category.

    Correct: *Janie **can hardly** wait for vacation.*

    Incorrect: *Janie **can't hardly** wait for vacation.*

Writing & Lang

Frequently Tested Prepositions	Idiomatic Expressions	Words That Can't Pair with Negative Words
at	as . . . as	barely
by	between . . . and	hardly
for	both . . . and	scarcely
from	either . . . or	
of	neither . . . nor	
on	just as . . . so too	
to	not only . . . but also	
with	prefer . . . to	

Commonly Confused Words

English contains many pairs of words that sound alike but are spelled differently and have different meanings, such as *accept* (to take or receive something that is offered) and *except* (with the exclusion of).

Other words, such as *among* (in a group of, or surrounded by, multiple things or people) and *between* (distinguishing one thing from one other thing), do not sound alike but have similar meanings that are often confused.

You'll want to familiarize yourself with the following list of commonly misused words so you can spot them on test day.

Accept: to take or receive something that is offered	*My niece **accepted** her pile of birthday gifts with great enthusiasm.*
Except: with the exclusion of	*All of the presents are toys **except** for a box containing a popular book series.*

Affect: to act on, to have influence on something	*The dreary, rainy weather negatively **affected** Rahul's mood.*
Effect: something that is produced by a cause; a consequence	*A recent study explored the **effects** of weather on mental well-being.*

Lay: to put or place something	*My boss asked me to **lay** the report on her desk before I left for the day.*
Lie: to rest or recline	*After a long day of work, I just want to **lie** down on the couch.*

Writing & Lang

Raise: to build or lift up something; to support the growth of someone	*Many books are dedicated to the topic of **raising** children.*
Rise: to get up	*Ted likes to **rise** early in the morning to exercise before his children wake up.*

Whose: a possessive pronoun	***Whose** uniform shirt is this?*
Who's: a contraction meaning "who is"	***Who's** responsible for ordering new uniforms?*

Their: a possessive pronoun for a plural noun or pronoun	*The college students plan to travel internationally after **their** graduation.*
They're: a contraction for "they are"	***They're** going to visit several countries in East Asia.*
There: at a certain point or place	*The students are excited to experience the foods and cultures **there**.*
There's: a contraction for "there is"	***There's** a tour of an ancient palace that they're looking forward to seeing.*

Among: in a group of, or surrounded by, multiple things or people	*Navya was **among** many doctoral candidates who visited the university.*
Between: distinguishing one thing from one other thing	*Navya had to decide **between** her top two doctoral program choices.*

Amount: sum or quantity of multiple things that cannot be counted	*The **amount** of pollution in the ocean is affecting dolphin populations.*
Number: Sum or quantity of a finite collection that can be counted	*Scientists report that the **number** of dolphins has decreased significantly.*

Less: a smaller extent or amount of things that cannot be counted	*The common supermarket sign "10 items or **less**" is actually incorrect.*
Fewer: of a smaller number, referring to things that can be counted	*Since the items can be counted, the sign should read "10 items or **fewer**."*

Much: great in quantity, referring to things that cannot be counted	*My sister has **much** more patience than I have.*
Many: great in quantity, referring to things that can be counted	***Many** of her friends admire her ability to stay calm in difficult situations.*

Writing & Lang

| **Good:** satisfactory in quality, quantity, or degree; adjective | *Dakota considered both the **good** and bad effects of wind energy before composing her essay.* |
| **Well:** To perform an action in a satisfactory manner; adverb | *Dakota wrote her essay so **well** that her professor used it as an example of excellent persuasive writing.* |

You need to do this:

- If the underlined portion includes a preposition, a conjunction, or *barely/hardly/scarcely*, look for a common idiom error.
- If the underlined segment includes a commonly misused word, check the context to determine whether it is used properly.

Explanation:

A sentence that contains the phrase *not only* must also contain the phrase *but also* (and vice versa). The only choice that includes the phrase *but also* is **(D)**, making it the correct answer.

If idioms give you trouble, study the information above and try these Drill questions before completing the following Try on Your Own questions. Edit each sentence to correct the incorrect idiom. Answers can be found on the next page.

Drill

a.   When Fatima returned home from school, she was unpleasantly surprised to find that her hamster had escaped to its cage again.

b.   The surgeon took great pride of her work, saying she was honored to be able to help when her patients thanked her.

c.   Neither apples or cherries will grow in the Phillipines due to its hot climate.

d.   The day after Kumar tried yoga for the first time, he was so sore he couldn't hardly move.

e.   The attorney wanted to except the case but couldn't because his caseload was already full.

Try on Your Own

Directions: Take as much time as you need on these questions. Work carefully and methodically. There will be an opportunity for timed practice at the end of the chapter.

Questions 45–50 refer to the following passage.

The Intriguing Opossum

Much maligned as a repulsive nuisance, the opossum is actually one of North America's most interesting animals, exhibiting many notable characteristics. For example, opossums boast an incredible array of 50 razor-sharp teeth, the most of any mammal in the world. Also, because opossums are partially or totally immune, <u>**45** neither rabies or snake venom presents much of a danger to them.</u>

While their beady eyes, pointy snouts, and bald tails might make them seem like a cousin of the rat, opossums are actually closely related to the kangaroo and are the only marsupial native to the continent. One of the most primitive animals, existing since the time of the dinosaurs, opossums have survived for millions of years by adapting to diverse habitats—including dense urban areas—and food supplies. <u>**46** There isn't hardly anything that opossums will not eat;</u> included in their possible diet are rodents, birds, frogs, eggs, insects,

45. A) NO CHANGE
    B) neither rabies nor snake venom presents much of a danger to them.
    C) not even rabies nor snake venom presents much of a danger to them.
    D) not much of a danger is presented by even rabies or snake venom.

46. A) NO CHANGE
    B) There is hardly nothing that opossums will not eat;
    C) There is hardly anything that opossums will not eat;
    D) Opossums will not eat hardly anything;

Drill answers from previous page:

Note: These are not the only ways to correct the sentences; your answers may differ.

a. When Fatima returned home from school, she was unpleasantly surprised to find that her hamster had escaped **from** its cage again.

b. The surgeon took great pride **in** her work, saying she was honored to be able to help when her patients thanked her.

c. Neither apples **nor** cherries will grow in the Phillipines due to its hot climate.

d. The day after Kumar tried yoga for the first time, he was so sore he **could hardly** move.

e. The attorney wanted to **accept** the case but couldn't because his caseload was already full.

snails, slugs, earthworms, plants, tree roots, fruits, and grains. Today, many opossums that live in areas densely populated by humans survive on garbage and small mice, even consuming the bones to satisfy their high need for calcium.

Of course, the opossum does have vulnerabilities. Its average three-year life span is not unusual for its size, typically **47** between two or three feet long. What is unusual is that opossums continue growing throughout their lifetimes. Such a state of constant development is linked with metabolic limitations **48** of the amount of food and energy that can be stored within the opossum's body, requiring that ready food sources be available year-round. In addition, opossums are highly susceptible to the cold, making it rather common to see opossums with frostbitten ears and tails.

Nevertheless, opossums have displayed amazing resilience over the years, often surviving attacks from intimidating predators like dogs and even hawks. While the opossum's first reaction when threatened is to begin running to the nearest tree, their primary defense **49** is an affect of the nervous system that, when sensing danger, throws the opossum's body into a catatonic state that dramatically slows its heart rate. The opossum will then **50** lay still, begin to drool, and appear dead, another trait that only adds to the fascinating nature of these animals.

47. A) NO CHANGE
    B) either two or three
    C) at least two or three
    D) between two and three

48. A) NO CHANGE
    B) on
    C) with
    D) for

49. A) NO CHANGE
    B) is an effect of the nervous system
    C) effects the nervous system so
    D) of the nervous system is an affect

50. A) NO CHANGE
    B) have laid
    C) lie
    D) have lain

Writing & Lang

How Much Have You Learned?

Directions: For testlike practice, give yourself 9 minutes to complete this question set. Be sure to study the explanations, even for questions you got right. They can be found at the end of this chapter.

Questions 51–61 refer to the following passage.

The Experts of Visual Communication

When people consider different types of [51] communication often, they think of only verbal or written forms. Few, perhaps, think of art as a [52] mode of communication; however, from early cave paintings and the intricate craftwork of ancient civilizations to contemporary, esoteric, abstract works that challenge traditional notions of aesthetic representation, art has played an essential role in visual communication. In the world of business, the intersection of art and communication is graphic design. [53] The explosion of media brought on by the digital age offered a growing platform for art, through graphic design, to express ideas and messages.

There is almost no detail too small, no space too unimportant to escape the attention of a graphic designer. [54] Their work is nearly ubiquitous in modern commercial life: [55] business logos, billboard advertisements; website layouts, T-shirt designs; and even the decorated cardboard of cereal boxes and coffee cups feature graphic design. In a culture increasingly wired for visual communication, graphic designers wield a powerful influence over the ordinary consumer. They craft the formats, styles, images, and symbols that shape how we perceive products, services, and ideas.

51. A) NO CHANGE
    B) communication often, they think of only verbal
    C) communication, often only they think of verbal
    D) communication, often they think of only verbal

52. A) NO CHANGE
    B) mode of communication; however from early cave paintings
    C) mode of communication, however, from early cave paintings
    D) mode of communication, however from early cave paintings

53. A) NO CHANGE
    B) The explosion of media brings on by the digital age offers
    C) The explosion of media brought on by the digital age offering
    D) The explosion of media brought on by the digital age offers

54. A) NO CHANGE
    B) The work of them
    C) The work of graphic designers
    D) The work of theirs

55. A) NO CHANGE
    B) business logos, billboard advertisements, website layouts, T-shirt designs, and even the decorated cardboard of cereal boxes and coffee cups feature graphic design.
    C) business logos, billboard advertisements, website layouts, T-shirt designs, and, even the decorated cardboard of cereal boxes, and coffee cups feature graphic design.
    D) business logos; billboard advertisements; website layouts; T-shirt designs; and even the decorated cardboard of cereal boxes, and coffee cups feature graphic design.

How do these visual innovators navigate a career path? Most [56] <u>began by studying graphic design and earn</u> a bachelor's degree at a four-year college, where they build skills through interactive class settings to hone expertise. These programs are heavily project-based and provide the sort of experience professional work will require. Students gradually compile design portfolios to showcase their best work. Once students have graduated, these portfolios are essential for the job search because [57] <u>it demonstrates</u> the ability and creative potential of designers.

Competition in the job market for graphic designers is [58] <u>rigorous yet the field offers</u> a variety of professional options. Some work in design studios. There they team with other graphic designers, taking on projects for external clients. Others work "in-house" for businesses that staff their own graphic designers to create media on a more frequent basis. Those with more entrepreneurial inclinations can work as freelance graphic designers, doing their own networking and contracting. Trying to expand their possibilities, [59] <u>many graphic designers are also now applying their knowledge to website and web application design, which</u> continues to be a growing field for tech-minded artists.

[60] <u>Although the demand for graphic designers persists the highly competitive job market</u> gives some prospective artists pause. The trope of the "struggling artist" holds true, it seems, even in our highly visually oriented society. Still, most graphic designers find their [61] <u>careers both satisfying and also invigorating.</u> Perhaps, for the dedicated artists who seek a career in graphic design, the thrill and beauty of the work yields enough motivation and inspiration to persevere and succeed.

56. A) NO CHANGE
   B) have begun by studying graphic design and earning
   C) begin by studying graphic design and earning
   D) will begin by studying graphic design and will earn

57. A) NO CHANGE
   B) you demonstrate
   C) they demonstrate
   D) theirs demonstrate

58. A) NO CHANGE
   B) rigorous, although the field offers
   C) rigorous; even though the field offers
   D) rigorous, but the field offers

59. A) NO CHANGE
   B) much graphic design knowledge also now applies to website and web application design, which
   C) many graphic designers' knowledge also now applies to website and web application design, which
   D) website and web application design allows many graphic designers to apply their knowledge, which

60. A) NO CHANGE
   B) Yet the demand for graphic designers persists; the highly competitive job market
   C) While the demand for graphic designers persists, but the highly competitive job market
   D) Even though the demand for graphic designers persists, the highly competitive job market

61. A) NO CHANGE
   B) careers neither satisfying or invigorating.
   C) careers both satisfying and invigorating.
   D) career not only satisfying but invigorating.

Reflect

Directions: Take a few minutes to recall what you've learned and what you've been practicing in this chapter. Consider the following questions, jot down your best answer for each one, and then compare your reflections to the expert responses on the following page. Use your level of confidence to determine what to do next.

Name at least three ways to correct a run-on sentence.

_____

_____

_____

How does the SAT test subject-verb agreement and parallelism?

_____

_____

_____

What are the three different pronoun forms? When do you use each one?

_____

_____

_____

What is the difference between an adjective and an adverb?

_____

_____

_____

What are the three ways that apostrophes are tested on the SAT?

_____

_____

_____

Which commonly confused words do you need to be especially careful to look out for?

_____

_____

_____

Writing & Lang

Expert Responses

Name at least three ways to correct a run-on sentence.

There are a number of ways to fix a run-on sentence on the SAT. The six ways that you are likely to see are 1) use a period to create two separate sentences, 2) use a semicolon between the two independent clauses, 3) use a colon between the two independent clauses, 4) make one clause dependent, 5) add a FANBOYS conjunction after the comma, or 6) use a dash between the two independent clauses.

How does the SAT test subject-verb agreement and parallelism?

A subject and verb must always agree in person (first, second, or third) and number (singular or plural). You will need to be able to spot subject-verb mismatches and correct them. Parallelism requires that all items in a list, a compound, or a comparison are in parallel form. The SAT may test lists or comparisons in which one item is in the wrong form.

What are the three different pronoun forms? When do you use each one?

The three forms are subjective (when the pronoun is the subject), objective (when the pronoun is the object of a verb or preposition), and possessive (when the pronoun expresses ownership).

What is the difference between an adjective and an adverb?

An adjective is a single word that modifies a noun or a pronoun, while an adverb is a single word that modifies a verb, an adjective, or another adverb.

What are the three ways that apostrophes are tested on the SAT?

Apostrophes on the SAT are used to 1) indicate the possessive form of a singular noun ('s), 2) indicate the possessive form of a plural noun (s'), or 3) indicate a contraction (don't = do not).

Which commonly confused words do you need to be especially careful to look out for?

The answer to this question is specific to you. If you have concerns about more than half of the words out of the list of 24, consider making flash cards to help you practice. The extra effort will ensure that you do not confuse any of the commonly confused words on test day.

Next Steps

If you answered most questions correctly in the "How Much Have You Learned?" section, and if your responses to the Reflect questions were similar to those of the SAT expert, then consider sentence structure, punctuation, and agreement areas of strength and move on to the next chapter. Come back to these topics periodically to prevent yourself from getting rusty.

If you don't yet feel confident, review those parts of this chapter that you have not yet mastered. In particular, review punctuation usage in the Sentence Structure: The Basics and Commas, Dashes, and Colons lessons, as well as how to select the appropriate pronoun or modifier in the Agreement: Pronouns and Agreement: Modifiers lessons. Then try the questions you missed again. As always, be sure to review the explanations closely. Finally, **go online** (www.kaptest.com/moreonline) for additional practice on the highest yield topics in this chapter.

Writing & Lang

Answers and Explanations

1. Review the Explanation portion of the Sentence Structure: The Basics lesson.

2.   D

Difficulty: Medium

Getting to the Answer: The sentence as written is a run-on. Two independent clauses are joined incorrectly by a comma. Eliminate (A). Because the comma is not underlined, you cannot fix the run-on by adding a coordinating conjunction or by replacing the comma with a semicolon. Instead, you need to change one of the independent clauses into a dependent clause. Choice **(D)** is correct because it makes the first clause dependent.

3.   B

Difficulty: Medium

Getting to the Answer: In the passage, the sentence has a subject but is missing a verb. In other words, there is no main action that "the Sun's core temperature" is performing. Eliminate (A). The correct answer will add a verb to the underlined portion. Choice **(B)** is correct because it is the only answer choice that includes a verb, "has."

4.   A

Difficulty: Hard

Getting to the Answer: The underlined portion lists examples of benefits that the Sun provides for the Earth. The list is long, but it is broken up into three main parts: electromagnetic waves, metabolic life, and the Earth's natural phenomena. Each is a category that has two specific items that precede it. When a list has multiple categories, each with its own members, then commas alone are often not sufficient to express the information clearly. Use semicolons to distinguish the main categories, and use commas to separate the items within each category. Choice **(A)** does exactly this and is correct.

5.   B

Difficulty: Easy

Getting to the Answer: When two independent clauses are joined by a coordinating conjunction, such as "but," as is the case in this sentence, the conjunction needs to be preceded by a comma. Eliminate (A) and (C). Also eliminate (D) because "still" is not a FANBOYS conjunction. Choice **(B)** is correct.

6.   D

Difficulty: Medium

Getting to the Answer: Two independent clauses are joined incorrectly by a comma, so you need to combine them according to correct grammar. Eliminate (A). There are several ways to combine two independent clauses, but only one answer choice offers an acceptable method: **(D)** uses a semicolon to join the two independent clauses and is correct. (B) does not use a FANBOYS conjunction and (C) erroneously omits the comma.

7. Review the Explanation portion of the Sentence Structure: Commas, Dashes, and Colons lesson.

8.   B

Difficulty: Medium

Getting to the Answer: When a comma is underlined, check to see if the parts of the sentence before and after the comma need to be separated. In this sentence, the comma separates the subordinating conjunction "although" from the clause it introduces and breaks the link between the dependent clause and the main clause. Choice **(B)** correctly eliminates the unnecessary punctuation.

9.   C

Difficulty: Medium

Getting to the Answer: Technically, "Mauritius" is not a complete sentence; there is no verb. Eliminate (A). You need a choice that will either make "Mauritius" a complete sentence or combine it with the first sentence. Choice **(C)** correctly uses a colon to introduce important information. Both (B) and (D) are missing commas after "familiar," making them grammatically incorrect.

10.   D

Difficulty: Hard

Getting to the Answer: The beginning of the sentence, "Since gaining independence in 1968," is a short introductory phrase that needs to be set off with a comma. Eliminate (A). Neither a dash nor a semicolon is appropriate in this scenario, so eliminate (B) as well. (C) incorrectly makes the independent clause that begins "Mauritius has emerged" dependent. **(D)** correctly uses a comma to separate the introductory phrase from the main clause.

11. B

Difficulty: Hard

Getting to the Answer: When a colon is used to introduce a short phrase, it emphasizes the information in the phrase. A colon that introduces and emphasizes information should be used only if the phrase is not connected to the sentence in another way. In this sentence, the phrase "in the modern global economy" is connected to the main clause with the preposition "in," so the colon is unnecessary. Eliminate (A). Dashes set off unnecessary information, but the phrase "in the modern global economy" is essential to the meaning of the sentence because it describes what kind of player Mauritius is. Eliminate (C). The adjectives "modern" and "global" are cumulative, meaning that their order can change the sense of the phrase. In other words, "modern" describes "global economy," and the phrase "global modern economy" has a different meaning from what is intended. Cumulative adjectives should not have a comma between them, so (D) is incorrect. The sentence's final phrase, "one of the few in the Southern Hemisphere" does need to be set off with a comma because it is a parenthetical phrase that could have been omitted from the sentence. **(B)** is correct.

12. D

Difficulty: Easy

Getting to the Answer: When you have a list of three or more items in a series, separate them with commas, and separate the last two items with a comma and the conjunction "and." This series contains six distinct items. In longer lists, it can be appropriate to use a semicolon to separate the list into logical groups of items. In the underlined portion, however, there is no logical grouping, so a semicolon is unnecessary. Eliminate (A). Choice (B) is incorrect because "and" should appear only between the last and second to last items in the list. (C) is incorrect because it omits "and" altogether. Only **(D)** offers the list correctly.

13. C

Difficulty: Easy

Getting to the Answer: If a dash is used to introduce a break in thought, a second dash must be used to end the parenthetical phrase unless a period ends both the phrase and the sentence. Determine whether the information after the dash is parenthetical by reading the sentence without that information. Although the phrase provides a description of how the "colonial powers" treated Mauritius, the sentence makes logical sense without it. The phrase is therefore parenthetical and must be properly set off. Only choice **(C)** correctly sets off the phrase with both an opening and a closing dash.

14. B

Difficulty: Easy

Getting to the Answer: When two independent clauses are combined with a FANBOYS conjunction, a comma needs to precede the conjunction. Eliminate (A). Only **(B)** places the necessary comma in the appropriate spot.

15. A

Difficulty: Medium

Getting to the Answer: Avoid using unnecessary punctuation. Reread the sentence to determine how its parts are related. This sentence is correct as written because no punctuation is required. The phrase "through its advantageous geographic location and large labor force" completes the thought in the sentence by providing information on how Mauritius "balances" and "flourishes." Choice **(A)** is correct.

16. Review the Explanation portion of the Agreement: Verbs lesson.

17. A

Difficulty: Medium

Getting to the Answer: When a verb is underlined, one of your tasks is to identify its subject to ensure that there is proper subject-verb agreement. The sentence construction is a little unusual, "what is believed," but the vague word "what" is indeed the subject for the verb "is believed." The subject, "what," is singular, so eliminate (B) and (D), which use "are," a verb that goes with a plural subject. The writer is referring to what is believed at the moment, not some time in the future; therefore, eliminate (C). Choice **(A)** is correct because "is" is the correct singular form of the verb and in the correct present tense.

18. D

Difficulty: Medium

Getting to the Answer: Determining whether a subject is singular or plural can be difficult sometimes, especially if the subject refers to many things. Here, "SMOM" is a group of knights, but because it is a single entity, the word functions as a singular. The use of the singular possessive pronoun "its" at the end of the sentence confirms that SMOM is singular. Eliminate (A) and (C). When a verb is underlined, also consider the tense. The entire first paragraph is in present tense and it is clear from the context that SMOM, though an "ancient" order, still exists, so maintain the same tense in this sentence. Choice **(D)** is correct because "is" is a singular verb in present tense.

19. B

Difficulty: Medium

Getting to the Answer: When a subject has multiple verbs, known as compound verbs, they must all be in the same form. The sentence begins with two verbs, both in infinitive form, "to protect" and "to defend." The underlined portion includes a third verb, which needs to be in the infinitive form, as well, to maintain parallelism. **(B)** is correct because it matches the form of the verbs earlier in the sentence.

20. B

Difficulty: Hard

Getting to the Answer: The perfect forms of verbs (i.e., have/has, had, and will have + a past participle) present special challenges in interpretation. It is crucial to determine the order of events. Because the sentence is rather long, focus on the underlined verb, "had seized," and the verb in the opening phrase, "had overrun." The past perfect tense of "had overrun" signals that the action happened in the past and was completed in the past before some other action. The word "After" that begins the sentence and the dates show that the seizing of Rhodes happened after the overrunning of Jerusalem was completed. The only verb tense that expresses that temporal relationship is simple past tense. **(B)** is correct.

21. B

Difficulty: Easy

Getting to the Answer: The paragraph describes actions that occurred in the past and uses the simple past tense to do so, so the underlined portion should follow suit.

Simple past describes a single event that occurred in the past, which is what Napoleon did. **(B)** is correct.

22. C

Difficulty: Easy

Getting to the Answer: The first word of the last paragraph is "Today," which signals a shift from the past tense of the previous paragraphs to present tense. The following sentence's main verb "include" is in present tense and confirms the shift. **(C)** is correct.

23. Review the Explanation portion of the Agreement: Pronouns lesson.

24. C

Difficulty: Medium

Getting to the Answer: When a pronoun is underlined, identify its antecedent. In the passage's first sentence, the writer gives a list, and in the second sentence, you find that these are the varied influences. The pronoun "He" is singular, but it refers to the plural group of "samurai, cowboys, shogun, gangsters, peasants, and William Shakespeare." Eliminate (A). The plural third-person subject pronoun "they" is needed to refer to the list. **(C)** is correct.

25. C

Difficulty: Medium

Getting to the Answer: The underlined portion should refer to "the most important Japanese filmmaker" as stated later in the sentence. "Filmmaker" is singular, but "them" is plural, so eliminate (A). In addition to being singular, the pronoun needs to be in the objective form because it is the "themes" and "settings" that are acting on the filmmaker, the object. The singular objective (and third-person) pronoun is "him." **(C)** is correct.

26. C

Difficulty: Medium

Getting to the Answer: Pronouns can be in the grammatically correct form, but if they lack a clear referent, they need to be replaced with a specific word. The singular pronoun "its" is underlined and several singular nouns precede it, which makes it ambiguous. Eliminate (A). The underlined pronoun "its" is also possessive, so ask yourself whose story the writer is referring to. The logical answer is "the film's story." **(C)** is correct.

27. B

Difficulty: Hard

Getting to the Answer: When a pronoun's antecedent is far away from the pronoun itself, it can be difficult to identify the antecedent. Checking for agreement between a pronoun and its antecedent is also tricky when the noun being replaced is singular in grammar but plural in concept. Both hurdles are present in this question. The entity seeking protection is the "village," which grammatically is singular. The third-person singular pronoun "it" is required. **(B)** is correct.

28. A

Difficulty: Medium

Getting to the Answer: The pronoun "him" is replacing the third-person noun "Kurosawa." The end of the previous sentence raises the topic of what the samurai (in the film *Seven Samurai*) meant to Kurosawa. Any other change in person would cause an undesired shift in the passage. **(A)** is correct.

29. D

Difficulty: Hard

Getting to the Answer: In the passage, the word "of" means that the pronoun that follows should be in the objective form. However, the next word, "who," is in the subjective form; therefore, eliminate (A). Choice (B) is incorrect because "whose" is a possessive pronoun, but an objective pronoun is needed. Choice (C) is incorrect because "many" refers to people and "which" is for inanimate objects. Only **(D)** has the right pronoun in objective form and is correct.

30. Review the Explanation portion of the Agreement: Modifiers lesson.

31. C

Difficulty: Hard

Getting to the Answer: The sentence begins with a modifier, "Considered the father of montage," which means that the subject of the sentence must be the father of montage. Typically, the subject will immediately follow the opening modifying phrase, but in this sentence the next phrase, beginning "a popular cinematic technique," is an additional description, not the main clause. The underlined section is where the main clause begins, and the first words need to be the subject, the father of montage, Sergei Eisentstein. **(C)** is correct.

32. B

Difficulty: Easy

Getting to the Answer: Because the underlined word modifies "complexity," a noun, the underlined word needs to be an adjective. Choice **(B)** is correct.

33. B

Difficulty: Medium

Getting to the Answer: When making a comparison, you should note whether it is between two things or among three or more. In this sentence "few filmmakers" are being compared to Eisenstein. Although "filmmakers" is plural, the logic of the sentence treats them as one thing, so there are two things being compared. The comparative form "more" is needed. Choice **(B)** is correct.

34. D

Difficulty: Medium

Getting to the Answer: The qualifier "many" that precedes the underlined word shows that "moviegoers" is meant to be plural. The plural possessive is constructed by adding an apostrophe after the last "s." Choice **(D)** is correct.

35. A

Difficulty: Hard

Getting to the Answer: The sentence opens with an opening modifying phrase. Whatever that phrase modifies must immediately follow it. Ask yourself what is "[b]ased on the contemporary theory of biomechanics." The answer is Eisenstein's montage, so the underlined segment is correct and no change is needed. Choice **(A)** is correct.

Note that while Eisenstein could be using the montage to make a criticism, it does not make sense to say that Eisenstein is based on the theory of biomechanics. Therefore, the correct answer will not have "Eisenstein" as its subject; eliminate (B), (C), and (D). Choice **(A)** is correct because "Eisenstein's montage" is the subject, and the montage can both criticize and be based on the theory of biomechanics.

36. C

Difficulty: Medium

Getting to the Answer: The only difference among the underlined section and the answer choices is the placement of the word "enormously." The word is an adverb, so it needs to modify a verb, an adjective, or another adverb. Also, modifiers need to be placed near the word or phrase that they modify. Choice **(C)** is correct because it provides the closest placement to "successful," the only word that could be logically modified by "enormously."

37. C

Difficulty: Medium

Getting to the Answer: An apostrophe can signal a contraction, a shortening of two words. The underlined "they're" is a contraction of "they are," which does not make sense in the context of the sentence. Eliminate (A). You need a plural possessive pronoun because it refers back to "achievements." Choice **(C)** is correct.

38. Review the Explanation portion of the Parallelism lesson.

39. D

Difficulty: Medium

Getting to the Answer: "Exceeded 600 pages in length and there was . . ." is not parallel. "Exceeded" is a verb in simple past tense, so it should be followed by another verb in the same tense; "exceeded . . . and advertised . . ." is the correct parallel form, so **(D)** is correct.

40. C

Difficulty: Medium

Getting to the Answer: The sentence contains a list with three phrases: the first is "from pocket watches to patent medicines," and the last is "from hunting rifles to horse-drawn plows." Therefore, the middle phrase must be in the same form—that is, "from (X) to (Y)." Only **(C)** maintains this form and is correct.

41. D

Difficulty: Easy

Getting to the Answer: The three items in the list should all be in the same form; only **(D)** accomplishes this and is the correct answer.

42. A

Difficulty: Medium

Getting to the Answer: The nouns in this three-part list are "elements," "quarters," and "porches." Additionally, there are modifiers attached to each of these nouns. For the sake of parallelism, these modifiers should all appear in the same form. In the original version, all three modifiers appear as adjectives preceding each noun ("intricate decorative elements," "servants' quarters," and "wrap-around porches"). In all of the other choices, the modifiers appear in inconsistent forms. Thus, **(A)** is correct.

43. B

Difficulty: Medium

Getting to the Answer: The portion of the sentence preceding the underlined section contains the subject-predicate phrase "buyers built . . ." The portion that follows should be in the same subject-predicate form to maintain parallelism. Only (B), "others hired . . . ," does so. Therefore, **(B)** is correct.

44. Review the Explanation portion of the Idioms lesson.

45. B

Difficulty: Easy

Getting to the Answer: The construction "neither . . . nor" is idiomatic, so a phrase beginning with "neither" must be followed by "nor." Choice **(B)** is correct.

46. C

Difficulty: Easy

Getting to the Answer: The word "hardly" is a negative like "not." Double negatives, like "not hardly," are grammatical mistakes. Eliminate (A). The word "nothing" is another negative, so eliminate (B). Choice **(C)** is correct because it removes the double negative around "hardly."

47. D

Difficulty: Medium

Getting to the Answer: The construction in the underlined section is not idiomatic: "between . . . or" is incorrect. Eliminate (A). The three answer choices are all correct idiomatically, but only one makes logical sense in the sentence. (B) makes it sound as if an opossum cannot be two and a half feet long, which doesn't make sense. Similarly, (C) does not fit in the context of the passage because the word "typically" means that the opossum length given will be authoritative and precise, not a loose estimation as "at least" suggests. **(D)** is correct because it has the appropriate idiomatic phrase "between . . . and."

48. B

Difficulty: Hard

Getting to the Answer: Make sure that the proper prepositions are being used in the passage. As written, "of" implies that the metabolic limitations belong to the amount of food and energy that can be stored, but the intended meaning is that the metabolic limitations belong to the opossum and put a restriction on the amount of food and energy that can be stored. Eliminate (A). The preposition "on" is correct, given the context because there is a restriction *on* the amount of food that can be stored. Choice **(B)** is correct. If idioms are tricky, think of an analogous situation. A computer's limited warranty has limitations *on* the parts of the computer that are covered if something breaks. It doesn't have limitations *of* or *with* or *for* the parts of the computer.

49. B

Difficulty: Medium

Getting to the Answer: It will help to memorize commonly confused words like "affect" and "effect" and know what they mean and how to use them in various contexts. As written, the underlined portion incorrectly uses "affect," which is almost always a verb, as a noun. Eliminate (A). The intended word is "effect," which means some sort of change brought on by some cause (think *cause and effect*). Choice **(B)** is correct. Choice (C) also uses the word "effect" but incorrectly as a verb. "Effect" is almost always a noun, a thing that happens, but when "effect" is a verb, it means to cause or bring about. The nervous system is not an action that can be caused to happen, so (C) is incorrect.

50. C

Difficulty: Hard

Getting to the Answer: The distinction between "lay" and "lie" is mostly lost in everyday speech, but in formal written English, the difference is important. The word "lay" takes an object; the word "lie" does not. In other words,

you lay down your book, but you lie down. Because the opossum is doing the action (the opossum is not, for example, laying down some food it had just picked up), "lie" is the appropriate verb. **(C)** is correct. The word "laid" is the past participle of "lay," and "lain" is the past participle of "lie." Neither (B) nor (D) offer verb tenses that make sense in the context of the sentence.

51. D

Difficulty: Medium

Category: Agreement: Modifiers

Getting to the Answer: Scan the answer choices to see that the difference is the placement of the words "often" and "only." These two words are modifiers, so they need to be placed as closely as possible to words or phrases that they modify. The word "often" tells the frequency with which people think of verbal or written forms; therefore, it needs to be at the beginning of the phrase. Eliminate (A) and (B), which put "often" before the comma so that it incorrectly modifies the previous phrase. The word "only" describes the limits of which forms of communication people think of, so the word needs to be nearest those forms of communication, "verbal and written." **(D)** is correct. (C) incorrectly places "only" so that it modifies "they."

52. A

Difficulty: Medium

Category: Sentence Structure: The Basics

Getting to the Answer: The underlined section is part of a long sentence that has two independent clauses. To join them you need to use a semicolon, a comma and coordinating (i.e., FANBOYS) conjunction, or a dash. The word "however" is not a coordinating conjunction; eliminate (C) and (D). While "however" does help in connecting the ideas of the first and second clauses, the word is not necessary, and should therefore be set off by a comma. **(A)** is correct.

53. D

Difficulty: Medium

Category: Agreement: Verbs

Getting to the Answer: Verb tense should stay consistent unless a certain thought requires a shift. In the underlined portion, the main verb is "offered," which is past tense, but the rest of the paragraph is in present tense. Eliminate (A). The correct verb form is present tense. Eliminate (C) because the -ing, or progressive, form is not a main verb. The passive voice "brought" is correct because it is the digital age that is bringing on the explosion of media; **(D)** is correct.

54. C

Difficulty: Medium

Category: Agreement: Pronouns

Getting to the Answer: Pronouns need to agree with their antecedents. In the underlined portion, the plural pronoun "their" incorrectly refers to the singular "a graphic designer" at the end of the previous sentence. Eliminate (A). Also, eliminate (B) and (D) because the pronouns they use are also plural and incorrectly refer to a singular antecedent. (B) is also incorrect because "them" is not possessive. **(C)** is correct because it replaces the pronoun with the correct plural referent.

55. B

Difficulty: Medium

Category: Sentence Structure: Commas, Dashes, and Colons

Getting to the Answer: You can treat the underlined portion after the colon as a long list, but also notice that it is a compound subject. All of the underlined items do the same thing: they feature graphic design. Sometimes, it can be helpful to use semicolons to organize complicated and long lists into groups of items, but in this case, the placement of the semicolons is not logical. There is no obvious reason why website layouts and T-shirt designs should be grouped together, nor why they should belong to a group that is separate from business logos and billboard advertisements. Eliminate (A). Both (C) and (D) are incorrect because the last item in the list is decorated cardboard, not cereal boxes and coffee cups. Placing a comma between "the decorated cardboard of cereal boxes" and "and coffee cups" would mean that the coffee cups are not decorated cardboard. **(B)** is correct because it separates each item in the list with a comma.

56. C

Difficulty: Medium

Category: Agreement: Verbs

Getting to the Answer: Verb tense should remain constant unless there is shift in meaning. The second half of the sentence has "they build," which is present tense. The sentence before and the sentence after also have main verbs in present tense, so the main verb of the underlined clause needs to be in present tense, too. **(C)** is correct.

57. C

Difficulty: Medium

Category: Agreement: Pronouns

Getting to the Answer: Pronouns need to match the noun that they are replacing. In the underlined portion, the singular pronoun "it" is supposed to replace the plural "portfolios," so eliminate (A) and (B). The word "portfolios" is not a possessive like "theirs," so (D) is also incorrect. Only **(C)** is left and is correct because "they" correctly replaces "portfolios."

58. D

Difficulty: Medium

Category: Sentence Structure: The Basics

Getting to the Answer: The sentence as constructed has two independent clauses, which need to be joined correctly either with a comma and FANBOYS (coordinating) conjunction, or with a semicolon, or with a dash. As written, there is no comma between "rigorous" and "yet," so eliminate (A). Only **(D)** uses a comma and FANBOYS conjunction, so it is correct.

59. A

Difficulty: Medium

Category: Agreement: Modifiers

Getting to the Answer: When a sentence begins with a modifying phrase, whatever follows must be the thing that is modified and is the subject of the sentence. Logically, the modifying phrase "Trying to expand their possibilities" can refer only to the graphic designers. The pronoun "their" is plural and so is "graphic designers." **(A)** is correct.

Writing & Lang

60. D

Difficulty: Medium

Category: Sentence Structure: The Basics

Getting to the Answer: The word "Although" in the underlined portion signals that the first clause is a dependent clause and the second clause is independent. A comma is required to separate the two, but the sentence as written has no comma. Eliminate (A). A semicolon is not appropriate for subordinating one clause to another, and "yet" is a coordinating (FANBOYS) conjunction, not a subordinating conjunction. Eliminate (B). Choice (C) is incorrect because "while" makes the first clause dependent, and "but" cannot be used to join a dependent and an independent clause. That leaves **(D)**, which is correct because "Even though" subordinates the first clause and uses a comma to separate it from the second clause.

61. C

Difficulty: Medium

Category: Agreement: Idioms

Getting to the Answer: Idiomatic expressions have no logical rules, so they must be memorized. The construction "both . . . and also" is not a valid idiomatic phrase in formal written English. Eliminate (A). The correct construction is "both . . . and," which makes **(C)** correct. (B) is an incorrect form of "neither . . . nor," and it does not make sense in the context of the sentence. The idiom in (D) should be "not only . . . but also," so it is incorrect, too.

Writing & Lang

CHAPTER 26

Spotting and Fixing Issues: Conciseness, Organization, Development, and Graphs

LEARNING OBJECTIVES

After completing this chapter, you will be able to:

- Revise redundant or wordy writing
- Determine the need for transition words or phrases to establish logical relationships within and between paragraphs
- Determine the most logical place for a sentence in a paragraph or passage
- Identify the word that accomplishes the appropriate purpose
- Determine the relevance of a sentence within a passage
- State whether a sentence should be revised, added, or deleted, and provide reasoning
- Provide an introduction or conclusion to a paragraph or passage
- Revise text based on a graph or table

SmartPoints®:

Development, 85/300 (Very High Yield)

Organization, 40/300 (Medium Yield)

Conciseness, 20/300 (Medium Yield)

Graphs, 10/300 (Low Yield)

How Much Do You Know?

Directions: Try the questions below. The "Category" heading in the explanation for each question gives the title of the lesson that covers how to answer it. If you answered the question(s) for a given lesson correctly, you may be able to move quickly through that lesson. If you answered incorrectly, you may want to take your time on that lesson.

Questions 1–11 refer to the following passage.

Genetically Modified Organisms

Although biotechnology companies and the chronically naïve **1** imagine that there is no danger to be feared from genetically modified foods, they overlook a plethora of evidence indicating that they may be gambling with people's lives by continuing to **2** interfere and tamper with nature to create these "Frankenfoods." Potential problems range from the relatively minor—increased possibilities of allergic reactions to certain foods, for instance—to the potentially devastating—the complete skewing of the balance of an ecosystem. All of these factors should be carefully considered before **3** we choose to risk so much for the possibility of a better tomato.

[1] **4** For example, the cultivation of insect-resistant plants could lead to the reduction or even destruction of certain insect species that naturally feed on those plants. [2] A change in the insect population could have a disastrous impact on certain bird species that rely on the affected insects as their food source. [3] **5** Ecosystems are relatively stable, and the ripple created by genetically altering one

1. A) NO CHANGE
    B) insist
    C) hope
    D) think

2. A) NO CHANGE
    B) thoughtlessly interfere and casually tamper
    C) interfere by casually tampering
    D) tamper

3. A) NO CHANGE
    B) we as a society
    C) those of us who comprise society
    D) the citizens making up our population

4. Which choice best connects the sentence with the previous paragraph?

    A) NO CHANGE
    B) On the other hand,
    C) Although unlikely,
    D) DELETE the underlined portion and begin the sentence with a capital letter.

5. Which choice most effectively sets up the information that follows?

    A) NO CHANGE
    B) Humans are tightly connected to ecosystems,
    C) Each ecosystem is an independent entity,
    D) An ecosystem is a delicate thing,

6. A) NO CHANGE
    B) must
    C) would
    D) could

variety of soybean ▐6▌ <u>will</u> translate into a shock wave of unforeseen repercussions in the long term. [4] And alterations in the balance of the bird population could have further-reaching consequences, all the way up the food chain. ▐7▌

Further, it is likely that there are dangerous impacts on the genetically modified organisms themselves and on those who consume foods produced from genetically modified organisms. ▐8▌ Human studies have not been performed, ▐9▌ <u>and</u> the possibility that tampering with an organism's genetic structure could cause far-reaching health consequences for the people who eat genetically modified foods must be prioritized in future scientific research.

Arguments about the potential for genetic engineering to end world hunger by maximizing the quantity and quality of food grown around the world are based on an essential fallacy: people do not starve because there is a lack of food. People starve because it is more profitable for businesses to let food go to waste than to distribute it to the world's impoverished and famine-stricken regions. We have plenty of

7. To make this paragraph most logical, sentence 4 should be

   A) placed where it is now.

   B) placed after sentence 1.

   C) placed after sentence 2.

   D) DELETED from the paragraph.

8. At this point, the writer is considering adding the following sentence.

   > Some studies indicate that certain genetically modified foods have negative effects on the digestive systems and cardiac health of rats that consume those foods in high quantities.

   Should the writer make the addition here?

   A) Yes, because it provides evidence that helps support the main idea of the paragraph.

   B) Yes, because it provides a significant counterargument to the main claim of the paragraph.

   C) No, because it unnecessarily repeats a detail that appears later in the passage.

   D) No, because it shifts the focus of the passage away from the writer's primary topic.

9. A) NO CHANGE

   B) so

   C) or

   D) since

farmland sitting fallow and plenty of food rotting in warehouses. [10] And shockingly, the governments in some countries that struggle with hunger may actually thwart food supplies from reaching their citizens. Many of the agribusinesses arguing that genetically modified foods can solve world hunger are the same companies that accept government subsidies now to limit their production of crops in order to avoid flooding the market. These companies are primarily concerned with profit, and whatever lip service they pay to global well-being, the driving force behind genetically modified organisms and foods is profit, not people. [11] In conclusion, the benefits and risks of any new technology must be carefully considered before implementing that technology.

10. The writer is considering deleting the underlined sentence. Should the sentence be kept or deleted?

A) Kept, because it provides an alternate explanation for the main claim of the paragraph.

B) Kept, because it explains background information about the topic of the paragraph.

C) Deleted, because it contradicts the writer's main claim in the passage.

D) Deleted, because it interrupts the flow of the writer's argument in the paragraph.

11. Which choice most effectively concludes the paragraph and the passage?

A) NO CHANGE

B) It would be nice if we could trust the very companies that could benefit most from the creation of genetically modified organisms.

C) Unfortunately, those companies affect so many aspects of modern life that we have no choice but to trust them.

D) Why would we trust our own well-being and that of the planet to companies recklessly pursuing money at the risk of Mother Earth?

Writing & Lang

Check Your Work

1. B

Difficulty: Medium

Category: Development: Word Choice

Getting to the Answer: Read the sentence to understand the context in which the underlined word, "imagine," is used. The writer uses "imagine" to describe how certain groups portray the risks associated with genetically modified organisms. Because the writer views these groups as the opposition, the word needs to convey a stronger sense of resistance to the truth. As written, this part of the sentence is too benign to match the later references to "gambling with people's lives" and creating "Frankenfoods." Choice **(B)** is correct.

2. D

Difficulty: Easy

Category: Conciseness

Getting to the Answer: "Interfere" and "tamper" have the same meaning and are used to express a single idea about intentionally changing nature. The correct answer will eliminate one of those words. Choice **(D)** is correct.

3. B

Difficulty: Medium

Category: Conciseness

Getting to the Answer: This question tests wordiness, but pure length is not the only consideration in this type of question. The correct answer choice must fully convey the writer's intended meaning. As written, the underlined segment is the shortest answer choice, but it is difficult to determine exactly which group of people the "we" is referring to. Choice **(B)** is correct because it specifies the people included in "we" using the fewest words.

4. A

Difficulty: Medium

Category: Organization: Transitions

Getting to the Answer: In order to determine how best to connect two parts of a passage, identify the relationship between those parts. The previous paragraph discusses the potential for various risks from genetically modified foods, while this sentence identifies one particular risk: danger to insect species. Since it presents a specific instance of a general group, an example transition word is needed; **(A)** is correct. There is no contrast relationship, so (B) is incorrect. Choice (C) is incorrect because the writer is concerned about the risks, so downplaying them would contradict the writer's purpose. Choice (D) would remove the needed connection altogether.

5. D

Difficulty: Medium

Category: Development: Relevance

Getting to the Answer: The rest of the sentence discusses the possible unforeseen dangers of genetically modified organisms, so the correct answer must introduce the potential for harm. Eliminate (A) and (C) because stability and independence do not effectively set up the idea of potential harm. Choice (B) introduces humans, which are off-topic for the paragraph, so it is also incorrect. Choice **(D)** describes ecosystems as "delicate" and therefore easily damaged, so it effectively sets up the information that follows and is the correct answer.

6. D

Difficulty: Medium

Category: Development: Word Choice

Getting to the Answer: Although the word "will" is underlined, neither it nor any of the verbs in the answer choices change the grammatical functions of the sentence or cause an error. In a question like this, check the context to make sure the underlined word suits the meaning the writer wants to convey. Throughout the paragraph, the writer uses the verb "could" to indicate the possibility that certain things are possible but not certain—"could lead" and "could have." Nothing in the paragraph suggests that the writer has shifted from conjecture (indicated by "could") to either certainty ("will" and "would") or necessity ("must"). Choice **(D)** is correct.

7. C

Difficulty: Hard

Category: Organization: Sentence Placement

Getting to the Answer: Sentence 4 discusses how changes to the bird population could have further impacts and begins with the continuation word "And." Logically, it should follow sentence 2, which introduces how changes to the bird population might come about; that way, the paragraph forms a clear logical chain from a change in plants to insects to birds to the larger ecosystem. This also places sentence 3 at the end of the paragraph to sum up with an explanation of the ecology behind the information in the paragraph. The correct answer is **(C)**.

8. A

Difficulty: Medium

Category: Development: Revising Text

Getting to the Answer: When deciding whether to add a sentence, consider what it would contribute to the purpose and main idea of the paragraph. The topic sentence states that harm from eating genetically modified organisms is "likely," but the next sentence says that there have not yet been any human studies. The paragraph's main claim is currently not well supported, and the proposed addition would provide better evidence for it; **(A)** is correct.

9. B

Difficulty: Medium

Category: Organization: Transitions

Getting to the Answer: This question is about choosing the appropriate transition word to connect two clauses of a sentence. The first clause is about the lack of human studies on the effect of eating genetically modified organisms, and the second clause identifies the need for such studies given the potential health risks. The ideas in the second clause are clearly a result of the information in the first, so a cause-and-effect transition is needed. Eliminate (A) and (C). Choice (D) is a cause-and-effect transition, but it would reverse the cause-and-effect relationship of the clauses, so it is incorrect. Only **(B)** correctly conveys the relationship between the ideas in the sentence.

10. D

Difficulty: Medium

Category: Development: Revising text

Getting to the Answer: When a question asks whether to delete a sentence, determine what the main idea of the paragraph is and what the sentence in question contributes to it. In this paragraph, the writer argues that people go hungry not just because of lack of food but because of agribusinesses seeking profit. This sentence offers another reason people go hungry, but that reason is not relevant to the writer's point. In fact, the sentence interrupts the writer's discussion of how agribusiness contributes to hunger. The correct answer is **(D)**.

11. D

Difficulty: Hard

Category: Development: Introductions and Conclusions

Getting to the Answer: To effectively conclude a passage, a sentence must align with the writer's purpose both in the passage as a whole and in the final paragraph. The passage as a whole is a strong argument against GMOs, based primarily on the potential dangers they pose. The final paragraph grows more passionate, criticizing the counterargument raised by advocates for genetically modified organisms. The final sentence must match these arguments. Choice **(D)** is correct because it suggests that the stakes for the planet are enormous and our misplaced trust would have dire consequences. Choice (A) is too objective, and choices (B) and (C) are too submissive, to match the writer's critical tone.

Conciseness

LEARNING OBJECTIVE

After this lesson, you will be able to:

- Revise redundant or wordy writing

To answer a question like this:

As the nineteenth century progressed, nursing became increasingly considered "women's work," until, at the turn of the 20th century, female nurses began to organize, unofficially excluding men. The American Nursing Association was formed in 1917, and men were not officially permitted to join until 1930. One of first goals of the female-dominated nursing community was to have men **1** denied admission to and excluded from military nursing. Traditionally, non-volunteer military nurses had been exclusively male, but in 1901, the United States Army Nurse Corps was formed exclusively for women.

A) NO CHANGE

B) denied to and excluded from

C) excluded from

D) denied and excluded from

You need to know this:

A concise sentence does not include any unnecessary words. Phrasing that is wordy is considered stylistically incorrect on the SAT and needs to be revised. Each word must contribute to the meaning of the sentence; otherwise, it should be eliminated.

A *redundant* sentence says something twice: "The new policy precipitated a crisis situation." A crisis is a type of situation, so there is no need to include both "crisis" and "situation." The sentence should be rephrased as, "The new policy precipitated a crisis." Redundancy is always incorrect on the SAT.

Wordy/Redundant Sentence	Concise Sentence
The superb musical score **added enhancement to the experience of** the play's development.	The superb musical score **enhanced** the play's development.
I did not anticipate the **surprising, unexpected plot twist**.	I did not anticipate the **plot twist.**
The students **increased some of their knowledge of** Tuscan architecture.	The students **learned about** Tuscan architecture.

You need to do this:

Choose the most concise grammatically correct option that conveys the writer's intended meaning. When answering questions about conciseness:

- Consider selecting the "DELETE the underlined portion" answer choice if there is one, according to the following guidelines:
  - If the underlined portion is wordy or redundant, delete it.
  - If the underlined portion does not enhance the intended meaning or clarity of the passage, delete it.
  - Each of the four answer choices is equally likely, so give this option the same weight as the others.
- Identify the shortest answer choice (it will not always be the correct answer, but it is an efficient place to start).
- Identify words and phrases that have the same meaning (e.g., *thoughtful* and *mindful* or *end result* and *final outcome*). Find a choice that deletes one of the redundant expressions.

Explanation:

As written, the underlined segment is redundant: "denied admission to" and "excluded from" have the same meaning. Look for a choice that eliminates one of these phrases. Choice **(C)** is correct.

If conciseness gives you trouble, study the information above and try these Drill questions before completing the following Try on Your Own questions. Eliminate word(s) to make the sentences more concise without losing meaning. Turn the page to see the answers.

Drill

a. It is important to carefully consider and think about what kind of college you wish to attend.

b. Often, a house cat will typically sleep for up to 16 hours per day.

c. The whole team felt a sense of excited anticipation in the seconds before the whistle blew.

d. My sister and I couldn't come to an agreement with each other about what movie we wanted to watch that afternoon.

e. Noctilucent clouds appear approximately 82 kilometers above Earth's surface. This is an altitude more than seven times higher than commercial airlines fly.

Try on Your Own

Directions: Take as much time as you need on these questions. Work carefully and methodically. There will be an opportunity for timed practice at the end of the chapter.

Questions 2–6 refer to the following passage.

Modern Readers

Judging by the types of novels that typically receive the top rankings on contemporary "best seller" lists, one would be wise to conclude that book consumers today do not enjoy reading ancient mythology. Seemingly, such antiquated stories hold little relevance to the concerns of a member of modern society. It is a literature not for the **2** current-day, distracted reader immersed in his "everyday" cares, but for a more imaginative audience with more universal tastes.

To even begin **3** to understand or comprehend this issue, we must understand what it is that most readers seek out in the works they read. What is it in a book—a novel, for example—that causes them to continue turning the pages? The answer can be a bit slippery. Is it the psychological realism of the characters? Is it the drama of the events they encounter? Is it the modern author's consciousness of her position as author and the relationship—distant or intimate, serious or playful—that she develops with her readers?

The obvious answer is that it is all of these things. The defining features of the modern story are its complexity and ambivalence. Narrators are not always reliable. Loyalties are often fleeting, and even a character's central motives may undergo a transformation before the story is done. There is no neat conclusion, no definitive redemption or damnation, and not always even a clear message. In this confusion

2. A) NO CHANGE
    B) modern,
    C) presently current,
    D) DELETE the underlined portion.

3. A) NO CHANGE
    B) to understand or to comprehend
    C) to understand and comprehend
    D) to understand

and dislocation, the modern reader sees his own life reflected, complete with all of its [4] complexity and ambivalence.

In a world where the disparate lives of alienated individuals still manage to affect each other on a daily basis, there is a paradoxical credulity extended toward anything murky and unclear. Far from the cosmopolitan savant he would like us to believe he is (to say nothing of the author who writes for him), the modern reader is only able to take comfort in his own confusion. When, for example, [5] George and Jane suddenly find themselves unable to live together after they come to the completion of their fairy-tale courtship, the contemporary pop intellectual will [6] nod his head sagely. He will think about the relationships in his own life that he didn't understand either.

What escapes the minds of the masses is that, taken past a certain point, realism is not art. Neither unsatisfying conclusions, nor irritating characters, nor obscure motives are indications of the literary talents of

4. A) NO CHANGE
    B) ambivalence
    C) complexity
    D) ambivalent complexity

5. A) NO CHANGE
    B) George and Jane finish their fairy-tale courtship and suddenly find themselves unable to live together,
    C) the fairy-tale courtship of George and Jane is at a finish and they suddenly find themselves unable to live together,
    D) with sudden abruptness George and Jane find themselves unable to live together when they finish their fairy-tale courtship,

6. Which choice most effectively combines the sentences at the underlined portion?

    A) nod his head sagely, and he will think about
    B) nod his head sagely; he will think about
    C) nod his head sagely, thinking about
    D) nod his head sagely, be thinking about

Drill answers:

Note: These are not the only ways to correct the sentences; your answers may differ.

a. It is important to carefully consider ~~and think about~~ what kind of college you wish to attend.

b. ~~Often, a~~ **A** house cat will typically sleep for up to 16 hours per day.

c. The whole team felt ~~a sense of~~ **excited** ~~anticipation~~ in the seconds before the whistle blew.

d. My sister and I couldn't ~~come to an~~ **agree**~~ment with each other~~ about what movie we wanted to watch that afternoon.

e. Noctilucent clouds appear approximately 82 kilometers above Earth's surface~~. This is an altitude~~, more than seven times higher than commercial airlines fly.

the author. The older, mythic characters may be drawn with a broad brush and may possess a simplicity and singularity of purpose that finds no parallel in day-to-day life, but that simplicity is not a sign of an author lacking in subtlety. Rather, a purposeful author will have purposeful characters. Whether the story is meant to illustrate moral principles, explore character types, or simply entertain, a quality work of art must have a purpose.

Organization: Transitions

LEARNING OBJECTIVES

After this lesson, you will be able to:

- Determine the appropriate transition word or phrase to establish logical relationships within and between sentences
- Determine the appropriate transition sentence to establish logical relationships between paragraphs

---

To answer a question like this:

I still remember the magic of walking home under the cold, brittle blue sky, watching the sun strike the glittering blanket laid down by that first snowfall. The world dripped with frosting, and everything was pure and silent. I breathed deeply, enjoying the sting of the icy air in my nostrils, and set off through the trees, listening to the muffled crunch of my footsteps and the chirps of the waking birds. Later, the cars and schoolchildren and mundane lives would turn the wonderland back into dingy slush; the hush would be interrupted by horns and shouts. **7** <u>Indeed,</u> for now, the sparkling, cloistered world was mine alone. I smiled, and for a moment, my mind was still.

A) NO CHANGE

B) But

C) Consequently,

D) In fact,

You need to know this:

Writers use transitions to show relationships such as contrast, cause and effect, continuation, emphasis, and chronology (order of events). Knowing which words indicate which type of transition will help you choose the correct answer on test day.

Contrast Transitions	Cause-and-Effect Transitions	Continuation Transitions	Emphasis Transitions	Chronology Transitions
although, but, despite, even though, however, in contrast, nonetheless, on the other hand, rather than, though, unlike, while, yet	as a result, because, consequently, since, so, therefore, thus	also, furthermore, in addition, moreover	certainly, in fact, indeed, that is	before, after, first (second, etc.), then, finally

You need to do this:

If a transition word is underlined, you must determine the writer's intended meaning and find the transition that best conveys this meaning. Use the surrounding text to pinpoint the appropriate word.

Explanation:

The transition must logically connect the information and ideas in the sentences before and after the underlined portion. In the sentence before the underlined transition, the author acknowledges that the specialness of the day will later wear off. In the sentences following the transition, the author puts aside thoughts of the coming noise and slush to enjoy the first snowfall. So there is a contrast between the idea that the wonder of the day will fade and the perception of that wonder in the present moment. The only contrast transition among the choices is **(B),** which is thus the correct answer.

If transitions give you trouble, study the information above and try these Drill questions before completing the following Try on Your Own questions. Answers can be found on the next page.

Drill

a.   The train was delayed; (<u>therefore/in addition</u>), we arrived at our destination two hours late.

b.   (<u>Since/Although</u>) the critics agreed that the movie was terrible, I went to see it anyway.

c.   We need to finish our project (<u>consequently/before</u>) we leave this afternoon.

d.   The hiking trail was difficult to navigate; (<u>finally/indeed</u>), state park guidelines recommend that only experienced hikers attempt the climb.

e.   The morphology of the amoeba is more complex than you might expect; (<u>furthermore/in contrast</u>), the mechanism underlying amoeboid motion is still not fully understood.

Try on Your Own

Directions: Take as much time as you need on these questions. Work carefully and methodically. There will be an opportunity for timed practice at the end of the chapter.

Questions 8–12 refer to the following passage.

The Internet and Conversation

For as long as I can remember, conversation has always struck me as a strange chimera, something that is half two minds exchanging sophisticated ideas and half two dogs barking at each other. I do not find the banalities of small talk comforting, but boring and idiotic. [8] Now I can dispense with it altogether and proceed right to substantive dialogue, it is almost like flying. I can be talking with the closest of friends or a mere acquaintance with a shared interest. Either way, the kinship is there. I don't feel myself included by smiles, pats on the back, or eye contact so much as by the willingness of a partner to share my ideas or gift me with thoughts of his own. There is nothing more ingratiating than intellectual passion.

In part, this has to do with my habit of observing the world from my bedroom. As a child, I was frequently ill and forced to stay inside. Although my health is much better now, [9] I still go out much less than most people. After all, I have everything I need inside. From my room,

8. A) NO CHANGE
    B) When
    C) Later
    D) Where

9. Which choice provides the best transition within the paragraph?

    A) NO CHANGE
    B) I still remember those long afternoons cooped up inside.
    C) I am still careful to eat well and get plenty of rest.
    D) I regret not being able to play outdoors with other children.

Drill answers from previous page:

a. The train was delayed; **therefore**, we arrived at our destination two hours late.

b. **Although** the critics agreed that the movie was terrible, I went to see it anyway.

c. We need to finish our project **before** we leave this afternoon.

d. The hiking trail was difficult to navigate; **indeed**, state park guidelines recommend that only experienced hikers attempt the climb.

e. The morphology of the amoeba is more complex than you might expect; **furthermore**, the mechanism underlying amoeboid motion is still not fully understood.

I have access to people all over the world through online communities. I can talk about medieval literature with a friend in China and later collaborate on a piece of music with a synthesizer virtuoso in Spain. Everyone can be everywhere they want when they want, **10** and every social interaction feels completely comfortable and natural. There is no need for awkward introductions or a graceful exit—people feel free to launch right into what they want to talk about and, when they are done, just sign off with a "TTYL," or "talk to you later." Every exchange is relaxed and succinct.

11 The Internet facilitates authentic connections among diverse users who share common interests, but empty chatter is far from universal. On certain discussion boards, you can witness opinions stated and arguments debated with an eloquence that people rarely use when speaking, freely sharing knowledge just for the joy of it. I participate in an online Renaissance music discussion group that has a library of original articles that are the product of a master's thesis. The author gained no monetary reward for the information (which he made available for free) and receives little praise for it outside the community that shares his interest. He posts because he is passionate about his **12** subject; nonetheless, his enthusiasm for the music inspires him to share what he knows with anyone who wants to learn.

10. Which choice results in the most effective transition to the information that follows in the paragraph?

A) NO CHANGE

B) and knowledge of useful text acronyms is nearly universal among online conversationalists.

C) and those desiring profound discussion can find one at any time of day or night.

D) DELETE the underlined portion and end the sentence with a period.

11. Which choice best connects the sentence with the previous paragraph?

A) NO CHANGE

B) Though cloistered in a private space, you can now use technology to access virtually any information in the world, but

C) Internet speak is often maligned as vacuous in its reliance on acronyms and abbreviations, but

D) DELETE the underlined portion and begin the sentence with a capital letter.

12. A) NO CHANGE

B) subject; lastly,

C) subject; however,

D) subject; indeed,

Organization: Sentence Placement

LEARNING OBJECTIVE

After this lesson, you will be able to:

● Determine the most logical place for a sentence in a paragraph or passage

To answer a question like this:

[1] It is amazing how little the structure of the American public school system has changed since its inception. [2] Students still change classes according to bells, even though the bell system originated during the days of factories. [3] School is still not in session during the summer, although most students will not use that time to work on farms. [4] Although class and school sizes have varied widely and the curriculum has certainly become varied, the actual system remains surprisingly similar to the way it once was. [5] Despite these idiosyncrasies, however, the American public school system continues to educate the children of this country in a fair and equitable fashion. [6] Without the established structure, the chaotic nature of school would severely inhibit learning. 13

To make this paragraph most logical, sentence 4 should be placed

A) where it is now.

B) before sentence 1.

C) after sentence 1.

D) after sentence 6.

You need to know this:

Some organization questions will ask you to check and potentially fix the placement of a sentence within a paragraph (or a paragraph within a passage, though this is rare). Others will ask you for the best place to insert a new sentence. Your approach in both cases should be the same.

You need to do this:

Look for specific clues that indicate the best organization. Common clues include:

- **Chronology:** If the information is presented in order by the time when it occurred, place the sentence within the correct time frame.

- **Explanation of a term or phrase:** If the passage features a term, such as nuclear fusion, the writer will explain what it is (in this case, the joining of two or more nuclei to form a heavier nucleus) before using the term in other contexts.

- **Introduction of a person:** If the passage introduces someone, such as Grace Hopper, the writer will first refer to the person by first and last name before referring to the person by either first name (Grace) or last name (Hopper) only.

- **Examples:** A general statement is often followed by support in the form of examples.

- **Logic:** Transition words such as "however," "also," "furthermore," and "therefore" may signal the logic of the paragraph. For example, the word "therefore" indicates that a conclusion is being drawn from evidence that should logically come before it.

Explanation:

Sentence 4 argues that the school system has not changed much, so it should precede a sentence that further discusses the unchanged aspects of the school system. If you place sentence 4 after sentence 1, sentences 2 and 3 become examples of specific ways in which the school system has not changed. Moreover, the word "surprising" in sentence 4 echoes the word "amazing" in sentence 1. Sentence 4 also elaborates on sentence 1 by clarifying that the phrase "school system" does not mean only class sizes or curriculum, so sentence 4 fits best after sentence 1 rather than before it. Choice **(C)** is correct.

Try on Your Own

Directions: Take as much time as you need on these questions. Work carefully and methodically. There will be an opportunity for timed practice at the end of the chapter.

Questions 14–18 refer to the following passage.

Earthquakes

[1]

Devastating earthquakes in China, Haiti, Chile, Mexico, and elsewhere have caused many to wonder if earthquake activity so far in 2010 is unusual.

[2]

Still, earthquake activity has obviously disastrous consequences. As USGS Associate Coordinator for Earthquake Hazards, Dr. Michael Blanpied, explains, "While the number of earthquakes is within the normal range, this does not diminish the fact that there has been extreme devastation and loss of life in heavily populated areas."

[3]

[1] Scientists say 2010 is not showing signs of unusually high earthquake activity. [2] Some years have had as few as six such earthquakes, as in 1986 and 1989, while 1943 had 32, with considerable variability from year to year. [3] Since 1900, an average of 16 magnitude 7 or greater earthquakes—the size that seismologists define as major—have occurred worldwide each year. [4] With six major earthquakes striking in the first four months of this year, 2010 is well within the normal range. [5] From April 15, 2009, to April 14, 2010, there have been 18 major earthquakes, a number also well within the expected variation. `14`

14. To make this paragraph most logical, sentence 2 should be placed

A) where it is now.

B) before sentence 1.

C) after sentence 3.

D) after sentence 4.

[4]

[1] What will happen next in recent earthquake locations? [2] It is unlikely that any of these aftershocks will be stronger than the earthquakes experienced so far, but structures damaged in the previous events could be further damaged and should be treated with caution. [3] Beyond the ongoing aftershock sequences, earthquakes in recent months have not raised the likelihood of future major events; that likelihood has not decreased, either. [4] Aftershocks will continue in the regions around each of this year's major earthquakes sites. [5] Large earthquakes will continue to occur just as they have in the past. **15**

[5]

[1] Though the recent earthquakes are not unusual, they are a stark reminder that earthquakes can produce disasters when they strike populated areas, especially areas where the buildings have not been designed to withstand strong shaking. [2] What can be done to prepare? [3] However, families and communities can improve their safety and reduce their losses by taking actions to make their homes, places of work, schools, and businesses as earthquake-safe as possible. **16**

[6]

[1] The Federal Emergency Management Agency (FEMA) recommends specific earthquake preparedness measures, which are especially vital for those who live in earthquake-prone areas. [2] Most importantly, homeowners should check that their homes meet those building codes that are meant to ensure buildings are structurally solid and safe, such as reinforcing masonry walls and securely installing gas appliances. [3] The

15. To make this paragraph most logical, sentence 4 should be placed

A) where it is now.

B) before sentence 1.

C) after sentence 1.

D) after sentence 2.

16. Where is the most logical place in this paragraph to add the following sentence?

> Scientists cannot predict the timing of specific earthquakes.

A) Before sentence 1

B) After sentence 1

C) After sentence 2

D) After sentence 3

house should be assessed for furniture placement that could be potentially hazardous during an earthquake, such as unsecured cabinets, and, based on each room's layout, every family member should learn the safest place to take cover in every part of the house. [4] While we cannot prevent earthquakes, we must take all possible precautions and heed the predictions of scientists. 17

Question 18 asks about the previous passage as a whole.

17. Where is the most logical place in this paragraph to add the following sentence?

> FEMA also advises families to create a plan about what to do if an earthquake were to occur while they were at home.

A) Before sentence 1

B) After sentence 2

C) After sentence 3

D) After sentence 4

Think about the passage as a whole as you answer question 18.

18. To make the passage most logical, paragraph 2 should be placed

A) where it is now.

B) after paragraph 3.

C) after paragraph 5.

D) after paragraph 6.

Development: Word Choice

LEARNING OBJECTIVE

After this lesson, you will be able to:

- Identify the word that accomplishes the appropriate purpose

To answer a question like this:

Incredibly, men could not work as military nurses until after the Korean War. Today, depending on the branch of service, anywhere between 35 percent and 70 percent of military nurses are men; this is in sharp **19** complement to the civilian world, where an average of 9 percent of American nurses are men.

A) NO CHANGE

B) completion

C) contour

D) contrast

You need to know this:

Some questions test your knowledge of the correct word to use in context. You must identify which word(s) best convey the writer's intended meaning.

Incorrect	Correct
The **initial** reason the students gather in the auditorium is that it is the only location large enough for all of them.	The **primary** reason the students gather in the auditorium is that it is the only location large enough for all of them.
It is common for children to **perform** the actions of their parents.	It is common for children to **mimic** the actions of their parents.
Zeke apologized for **overstepping** when he walked into the crowded conference room.	Zeke apologized for **intruding** when he walked into the crowded conference room.

You need to do this:

Read the sentence containing the underlined word but substitute a blank for the word in question. Make your own prediction about what word should go there before looking at the answer choices. Then look for a choice that matches the meaning of your prediction.

Writing & Lang

If one or more of the words among the answer choices are unfamiliar, the process of elimination can still help you get to the correct answer. If you recognize any of the options, decide whether to keep or eliminate them. For the words that remain, use roots, prefixes and suffixes, and word charge to make your decision. If all else fails, trust your instincts and guess; never leave a question blank.

Explanation:

The percentages given are the best clue here: 35–70% of military nurses are men, while only 9% of civilian nurses are men. Those are very different numbers, so the correct word must convey the discrepancy. The only choice that does so is **(D)**.

Try on Your Own

Directions: Take as much time as you need on these questions. Work carefully and methodically. There will be an opportunity for timed practice at the end of the chapter.

Questions 20–25 refer to the following passage.

Batteries Out in the Cold

Many people have trouble starting their cars on a cold winter morning. In a cold car, the engine turns over more slowly or sometimes does not turn over at all. Car owners may [20] credit their cold engines, but the real problem is a cold battery.

A car's electric starter motor is powered by the car's battery. When the motor is [21] united to a battery in a circuit, electrons move through the circuit, creating a current. The more current there is in the circuit, the more power there is to turn the starter motor. Decreasing the number of electrons moving through the circuit decreases the current, resulting in a [22] reduction in the amount of power available to the starter motor. Conversely, increasing the number of electrons moving boosts the current, which then increases the amount of power available to the motor.

Electrons move through a battery as a result of two chemical reactions that occur within the battery, one at each pole. A typical car battery uses lead and sulfuric acid to create these reactions. At the negative pole, lead reacts with sulfate ions in the acid solution around it to form lead sulfate, giving off electrons. At the positive pole, lead oxide reacts with sulfate ions, hydrogen ions, and electrons in the same solution to also form lead sulfate, taking in electrons. The electrons produced at the negative pole flow through the circuit to the positive pole, [23] providing an electric current in the circuit.

20. A) NO CHANGE
    B) critique
    C) accuse
    D) blame

21. A) NO CHANGE
    B) correlated
    C) coupled
    D) assimilated

22. A) NO CHANGE
    B) regression
    C) retraction
    D) constriction

23. A) NO CHANGE
    B) producing
    C) promulgating
    D) asserting

Temperature affects the speed of chemical reactions in two ways. For a chemical reaction to happen, the molecules of the reactants must collide with enough energy to get the reaction going. As the temperature increases, the motion of the molecules increases. The increased motion of the molecules increases the **24** practicality that they will collide and therefore increases the rate of reaction. The amount of energy in the reactants also increases as temperature increases. These factors make it more likely that the molecules in a battery will collide with enough energy to react, thereby increasing the power in the circuit.

Low temperatures have the opposite effect from high temperatures. The chemicals in the battery react more slowly at low temperatures, due to fewer and less energetic collisions, so fewer electrons move through the circuit. Because of this, a cold battery may not provide enough energy to start a car. A cold car that will not start will need either **25** associative power from a connection to another car's battery or a source of heat to warm up the car's own battery and speed up the chemical reactions within it.

24. A) NO CHANGE
    B) process
    C) confirmation
    D) probability

25. A) NO CHANGE
    B) auxiliary
    C) optional
    D) extraordinary

Development: Relevance

> **LEARNING OBJECTIVE**
>
> After this lesson, you will be able to:
>
> - Determine the relevance of a sentence within a passage

To answer a question like this:

For hundreds of years, the medical community and conventional wisdom held that ulcers were caused by stress. Strong gastric juices would sometimes burn sores through the lining of the stomach or intestines causing widely varied symptoms, including internal bleeding, inflammation, and stomach pain. Doctors reasoned that if patients with ulcers changed their daily habits to reduce the level of tension in their lives, altered their diets to avoid foods that would irritate the stomach, and took medicine to moderate the amount of stomach acid, these ulcers would heal. Although the problem often recurred, no one seriously questioned why. This medical advice remained standard for generations, until Dr. Barry Marshall came along.

Beginning in the 1980s, Marshall, an Australian physician, hypothesized that at least some ulcers were caused by bacteria that often lie dormant in the human stomach. **26** The international medical community was fascinated by rare gastric phenomena. It was common knowledge, or so Marshall's colleagues believed, that no microbes could survive for long in the highly acidic environment of the stomach. At medical conferences, the young, unknown Marshall was regarded as at best, a maverick, and at worst, a quack. Over several years, he and his fellow researcher, Dr. J. Robin Warren, attempted to isolate and identify the bacteria that caused ulcers. As is the case with many medical discoveries, their breakthrough came about partly by accident, when they left a culture growing in the lab longer than intended.

Which choice most effectively sets up other physicians' negative opinion of Marshall as described later in the paragraph?

A) NO CHANGE

B) The international medical community scoffed.

C) Marshall had attended the University of Western Australia School of Medicine, graduating in 1974.

D) The stomach produces hydrochloric acid so that the interior of the stomach is highly acidic.

You need to know this:

Some questions will ask you to choose the most relevant information to include at a specific point in a passage. In questions like this, all of the answer choices are grammatically and stylistically correct. Given this fact, your task is to determine which option provides information that is most pertinent to the passage. The correct choice will relate directly to the surrounding text and will provide one or more of the following:

- An example
- Support for a point
- A transition to a new idea

Note that when the question has a question stem, you are not being tested on conciseness, even when asked about deleting information. *When you see a question stem, focus on relevance rather than conciseness.*

You need to do this:

Read a bit of text before and after the underlined portion (at least the entire sentence in which it appears), looking for clues. Eliminate answer choices that

- Mention information that is beyond the scope of the writer's discussion
- Do not relate to the surrounding text
- Do not help express the purpose of the sentence or paragraph

Explanation:

The "negative opinion" referred to in the question stem is the statement, later in the paragraph, that Marshall was regarded as "at best, a maverick, and at worst, a quack." The underlined sentence, as currently written, is irrelevant to the passage, which does not define ulcers as "rare gastric phenomena," so eliminate (A) and examine the other choices for a negative opinion. Both (C) and (D) state neutral facts, but the word "scoffed" in (B) indicates that the medical community was unimpressed with, even disdainful of, Marshall. Choice **(B)** directly relates to the idea that Marshall was perceived as "at worst, a quack" and is correct.

Try on Your Own

Directions: Take as much time as you need on these questions. Work carefully and methodically. There will be an opportunity for timed practice at the end of the chapter.

Questions 27–31 refer to the following passage.

James Polk

For much of his distinguished career, James Knox Polk followed in the footsteps of Andrew Jackson.[1] In fact, "Young Hickory's" policies were very similar to Jackson's: 27 both men favored lower taxes, championed the frontiersmen, farmers, and workers, and neither was afraid to indulge in Tennessee whiskey. Polk, however, did not share Jackson's rather fierce temperament; he was instead known for remaining soft-spoken even as he worked energetically toward his goals. Although history will likely always remember the frontier persona of Andrew Jackson, it was Polk who did much more to shape the course of American history.

The Polk family was poor—James's father had emigrated from Scotland and arrived in the U.S. South penniless. From an early age, Polk suffered ill health that would turn out to be a lifelong affliction. Despite his physical shortcomings, he was an able student and graduated from the University of North Carolina with honors in 1818. Two years later, Polk was admitted to the bar to practice law, and in 1823, 28 he married Sarah Childress, the daughter of a prominent planter and merchant from Murfreesboro. From there, he was elected to the U.S. House of Representatives in 1825, serving until 1839. Polk was also Speaker of the House from 1835 to 1839.

27. A) NO CHANGE

   B) while they agreed on little regarding taxes or the suffrage of frontiersmen, farmers, and workers, both men were known to indulge in Tennessee whiskey.

   C) both men favored lower taxes; championed the frontiersmen, farmers, and workers; and opposed the controversial Bank of the United States.

   D) both men favored lower taxes; championed the frontiersmen, farmers, and workers; and yet they could not agree on the controversial Bank of the United States.

28. Which choice results in a sentence that best supports the point developed in the paragraph and is consistent with the information in the rest of the passage?

   A) NO CHANGE

   B) he married Sarah Childress.

   C) he was elected as governor of Tennessee.

   D) he was elected to the Tennessee House of Representatives.

[1] U.S. president from 1829 to 1837 and War of 1812 hero often referred to as "Old Hickory."

After he left Congress to serve as governor of Tennessee in 1839, it became clear that Polk's political aspirations were high indeed. During the 1844 presidential campaign, [29] a young Abraham Lincoln threw his support behind Whig Henry Clay instead of the Democratic ex-President Martin van Buren. Both men, as part of their platforms, opposed expansionist policies, and neither intended to annex the independent state of Texas or the Oregon Territory. [30] Polk, spurred on by Jackson's advice, recognized that neither candidate had correctly surmised the feelings of the people, so he publicly announced that, as president, he would do his utmost to acquire Texas and Oregon. Polk was the first "dark horse" in American politics, coming out of nowhere to win the Democratic nomination and the election.

As the eleventh President of the United States, Polk pursued an agenda of [31] territorial stability and peace with America's neighbors. First, he reached an agreement with England that divided the Oregon Territory, carving out the present-day states of Washington and Oregon. Polk also quickly annexed Texas and provoked war with Mexico to acquire California and the New Mexico territory. While these achievements were somewhat diminished by controversy from abolitionists who opposed the spread of slavery into new territories, under Polk's leadership the dream of "manifest destiny" became a reality, and the United States fully extended its borders from the Atlantic to the Pacific.

29. Which choice provides the most relevant detail?

A) NO CHANGE

B) the leading Democratic candidate was ex-President Martin van Buren and the Whig candidate was Henry Clay.

C) the issue of slavery's expansion into new territories began its long stint as the most divisive issue to plague national politics.

D) both the leading Democratic candidate, ex-President Martin van Buren, and the Whig candidate, Henry Clay, sought to campaign under the banner of "Manifest Destiny" and territorial expansion.

30. A) NO CHANGE

B) Polk, against Jackson's advice, recognized

C) Polk failed to recognize

D) Polk, against the wishes of his advisors, recognized

31. A) NO CHANGE

B) continued expansion of U.S. territory.

C) an end to slavery in new U.S. territories.

D) pushing the United States into a role on the international stage.

Development: Revising Text

LEARNING OBJECTIVE

After this lesson, you will be able to:

- State whether a sentence should be revised, added, or deleted, and provide reasoning

To answer a question like this:

In an effort to demonstrate that ulcers were caused by bacteria, as he and his colleague Warren believed, Dr. Marshall took a bold step. Although the medical community frowns on such potentially dangerous actions, the doctor experimented on himself by deliberately drinking a flask of the bacteria. Over a two-week period, Marshall developed vague, though not disabling, symptoms, and medical tests showed evidence of ulcers and infection. **32**

In 2005, Marshall's bold move earned him and Warren the Nobel Prize in Medicine. Their important advance, like many other scientific discoveries in history, was a combination of experimentation, persistence, and luck.

At this point, the writer is considering adding the following sentence.

> Other researchers' studies later confirmed that Marshall's and Warren's findings apply to about 90 percent of all ulcers, which can now be cured by a short course of antibiotics instead of being temporarily managed by antacids.

Should the writer make this addition here?

A) Yes, because the new sentence demonstrates that Marshall was not foolish in drinking the flask of bacteria as he could cure himself with antibiotics.

B) Yes, because the new sentence provides conclusive support for Marshall's inference and explains why Marshall and Warren won the Nobel Prize in Medicine.

C) No, because Marshall was a brilliant scientist, and his findings did not need to be confirmed by other researchers.

D) No, because Marshall would not have drunk the flask of bacteria had he believed that doing so would cause ulcers and infection.

You need to know this:

These questions often ask about deleting an underlined portion or adding new text. Consider what information the selection provides and whether that information 1) matches the writer's focus and 2) helps express the purpose of the sentence or paragraph. Consider what the passage might gain or lose if the proposed revision were made. Read the passage both ways—with and without the proposed change—to see which sounds more cohesive. Be sure to read the sentences before and after the proposed revision to best assess the change in context.

The same principle applies if the question asks whether a sentence should be revised: consider what the passage gains or loses as a result of the revision.

Writing & Lang

You need to do this:

- Examine the sentences before and after the proposed revision.
- Think about what is gained or lost, if anything, as a result of the revision. This could be an example, support for an idea, or a better transition.
- Look for the choice that paraphrases your reasoning.

Explanation:

The big clue for this question comes from the final paragraph, which states that Marshall won the Nobel Prize for Medicine for his discovery that bacteria cause ulcers. The new sentence confirms that this conclusion was correct and reveals that his discovery led to a new treatment for ulcers. This is powerful support for his winning the Nobel Prize for Medicine, so it adds relevant context to the passage. This reasoning matches choice **(B)**, which is the correct answer.

Try on Your Own

Directions: Take as much time as you need on these questions. Work carefully and methodically. There will be an opportunity for timed practice at the end of the chapter.

Questions 33–37 refer to the following passage.

Jupiter

As the fifth planet from the Sun **33** in our solar system, Jupiter has inspired fascination and scientific study for centuries. In fact, it was the initial discovery of this colossal, gaseous planet that marked the first time most astronomers seriously considered the possibility that the movement of other planets was not centered around the Earth. More specifically, when Italian astronomer Galileo first viewed Jupiter by telescope, he discovered four large moons in orbit around this enormous planet. **34**

The first close look at Jupiter came in 1973, when the unmanned NASA probe *Pioneer 10* completed a successful flyby and collected important data regarding the planet's chemical composition and interior

33. The writer is considering revising the underlined portion of the sentence to read:

> and by far the most massive in our solar system,

Should the writer make this revision here?

A) Yes, because it establishes an important contrast between Jupiter and the Sun.

B) Yes, because it provides an example for a detail that appears later in the sentence.

C) No, because statistics about Jupiter should be placed in a later paragraph.

D) No, because it contains a fact that contradicts the main claim of the passage.

34. At this point, the writer is considering adding the following sentence:

> Because these moons seemed to revolve around a planet other than Earth, their discovery provided important evidence for Galileo's outspoken support of Copernicus's heliocentric theory of planetary movement.

Should the writer make this addition here?

A) Yes, because it explains a detail that was mentioned earlier in the paragraph.

B) Yes, because it adds to the authority of the passage's claim by identifying famous scientists who studied Jupiter.

C) No, because the subject of planetary movement is outside the scope of the passage.

D) No, because it includes information that is on topic, but irrelevant to the paragraph.

Writing & Lang

structure. **35** <u>After completing its mission to Jupiter, *Pioneer 10* became the first spacecraft to leave the solar system.</u> Designated as one of the gas planets—along with Saturn, Uranus, and Neptune—Jupiter is composed of about 90 percent hydrogen and 10 percent helium and has no solid surface, only varying densities of gas. In fact, very little is known about the interior of Jupiter. When looking at a gas planet like Jupiter, it is really only possible to see the tops of the clouds making up the outermost atmosphere, and probes have been able to penetrate only about 90 miles below this layer. However, after analyzing traces of water and minerals collected from Jupiter's atmosphere, scientists believe that the planet has a core of rocky material amounting to a mass perhaps as much as 15 times that of Earth.

Jupiter's powerful winds are responsible for unique characteristics of the planet. Its high-velocity winds blow in wide bands of latitude, each moving in an alternate direction. Slight chemical and temperature variations result in particular chemical reactions within each band. **36** Measurements taken by a number of probes indicate that the powerful winds moving these bands can reach speeds exceeding 400 miles per hour and likely extend thousands of miles below Jupiter's outer atmosphere. **37** <u>The planet can also rotate on its axis in less than half the time it takes the earth to complete a rotation.</u>

Overall, Jupiter's size and features have intrigued astronomers of the past and continue to invite scientific investigation today.

35. The writer is considering deleting the underlined sentence. Should the writer do this?

A) No, because it adds an interesting detail about the *Pioneer 10* mission.

B) No, because it provides support for the claim that the mission was successful.

C) Yes, because it shifts the focus of the passage from Jupiter to the *Pioneer 10* mission.

D) Yes, because it does not include information about when *Pioneer 10* left the solar system.

36. At this point, the writer is considering adding the following sentence.

These interactions are responsible for creating the array of distinctive, colorful stripes that dominate the planet's appearance.

Should the writer make this addition here?

A) Yes, because it provides support for the claim made in the paragraph's topic sentence.

B) Yes, because it provides a useful transition between ideas in the paragraph.

C) No, because it interrupts the paragraph's discussion of latitude bands on Jupiter's surface.

D) No, because it supplies information that is irrelevant to the main claim of the passage.

37. The writer is considering deleting the underlined sentence. Should the sentence be kept or deleted?

A) Kept, because it provides a relevant detail for the paragraph.

B) Kept, because it effectively links this paragraph with the conclusion paragraph.

C) Deleted, because it does not reflect the topic of the overall passage.

D) Deleted, because it does not support the topic sentence of the paragraph.

Introductions and Conclusions

LEARNING OBJECTIVE

After this lesson, you will be able to:

- Provide an introduction or conclusion to a paragraph or passage

To answer a question like this:

38 As if malpractice suits and unnecessary bankruptcies were not enough of a problem, lawyers have chosen to increase the burden that they place on society by engineering an excess of increasingly ridiculous product warnings. Why else would a box of sleeping pills be marketed with the cautionary note that consumers may experience drowsiness? Or a cup of coffee be emblazoned with a notice that "THIS PRODUCT MAY BE HOT"? Anyone with common sense will not need to be warned about these possibilities, and anyone without common sense is probably not going to be stopped by a warning label from undertaking a foolish course of action anyway. So honestly, in the long run, the only ones who benefit from these warnings are the lawyers who are paid hundreds of dollars an hour to compose them.

Which choice most effectively establishes the main topic of the paragraph?

A) NO CHANGE

B) Each year, effective product warning labels help countless people avoid serious injuries resulting from their use of consumer products.

C) In recent years, a coalition of lawyers and consumer safety advocates has successfully campaigned to require companies to include safety warnings on product labels.

D) Product safety warnings are necessary to protect consumers who thoughtlessly use products without first thinking about the possible risks involved.

You need to know this:

Some questions ask you to improve the beginning or ending of a paragraph or passage.

- An introduction should:
  - Explain the topic and purpose of a paragraph/passage
  - Include information discussed later in the paragraph/passage
  - When applicable, provide an appropriate transition for the previous paragraph
- A conclusion should:
  - Summarize the topic and purpose of a paragraph/passage
  - Include information discussed earlier in the paragraph/passage
  - When applicable, provide an appropriate transition for the next paragraph

You need to do this:

- Determine the writer's intended purpose. This may be stated explicitly in the question stem ("The writer wants to reinforce the earlier claim about mockingbirds...") or may need to be inferred from the passage text.
- Eliminate answer choices that do not reflect this purpose.
- Choose the most relevant option.

Explanation:

The author introduces the central idea that lawyers are responsible for an excess of product warnings. In the remainder of the paragraph, the author argues that many product warnings are unnecessary and ineffective for consumers and beneficial only to the lawyers who write them. There is no discrepancy between the opening statement and the evidence for it, so **(A)** is correct.

Writing & Lang

Try on Your Own

Directions: Take as much time as you need on these questions. Work carefully and methodically. There will be an opportunity for timed practice at the end of the chapter.

Questions 39–42 refer to the following passage.

Human Skin

Although it likely doesn't immediately come to mind when thinking about body organs, **[39]** <u>our skin is the organ that most directly interacts with our environment, communicating messages both to our brains and to those around us.</u> An adult's skin comprises between 15 and 20 percent of the total body weight, even though the outer layer, the epidermis, is only 0.07 to 0.12 millimeters thick (the thickness of a piece of paper). Despite its slimness, the skin serves many essential roles for the human body.

First, the skin serves to regulate and protect the body. One square inch of skin contains up to 4.5 meters of blood vessels, which regulate body temperature. Further, skin forms a protective barrier against the action of physical, chemical, and bacterial agents on the deeper tissues. The skin constitutes the body's first line of defense against external threats including dehydration, infection, injuries, and extreme temperatures, **[40]** <u>and thus the skin requires careful upkeep and care.</u>

[41] <u>The skin serves another essential function in the human body.</u> Whereas our other senses have a definite key organ that can be studied, receptors located at the ends of nerve fibers all over the surface of the body are used to detect external stimuli. These fibers convert tactile stimuli into neural impulses to be sent to the brain through the peripheral and central nervous

39. Which choice provides the most appropriate introduction to the passage?

   A)   NO CHANGE

   B)   the skin is not only the human body's largest organ but also crucial for the body's healthy functioning.

   C)   each square centimeter of human skin has 6 million cells, 5,000 sensory points, and 100 sweat glands.

   D)   the skin is an interesting organ of the human body and thus highly studied by biologists.

40. Which choice most effectively concludes the sentence and paragraph?

   A)   NO CHANGE

   B)   modifying substances that come into contact with the skin's surface.

   C)   although other organs, such as the liver, detoxify harmful substances with special enzymatic processes.

   D)   detoxifying harmful substances with many of the same enzymatic processes the liver uses.

41. Which choice is the best introduction to the paragraph?

   A)   NO CHANGE

   B)   Another important property of the skin is that it provides our sense of touch.

   C)   Although scientists disagree about the total number, we most commonly refer to five human senses.

   D)   The central nervous system communicates messages to our brain about our tactile sensations.

systems. Thus, our skin serves to facilitate our physical interactions with our surroundings.

The most vital function of the skin is to shield the inside of the body; it acts like a "shock absorber." If a body falls, the skin protects all of the internal organs. When the skin is broken, it has its own defense system that immediately goes into repair mode. **42** It is no exaggeration to say that skin is among the most important organs; without it, a body simply cannot continue living.

42. Which choice most effectively concludes the passage?

A) NO CHANGE

B) Since skin covers the body and is easily visible, it is no wonder that its decoration has important cultural meanings.

C) However, more important organs do indeed exist and likely deserve more scientific attention than the skin.

D) Without the skin's properties, most importantly the sense of touch, life would hardly be worth living.

Graphs

LEARNING OBJECTIVE

After this lesson, you will be able to:

● Revise text based on a graph or table

To answer a question like this:

Yet perhaps the most fascinating characteristic of this planet is the rotational speed of the entire globe of gas itself. While Earth takes 24 hours to make a full rotation, Jupiter completes a full rotation **43** in less time, an amazingly short period of time for a planet with a diameter roughly 11 times the diameter of our planet. How Jupiter is able to rotate so fast is just one of many mysteries that scientists continue to explore in their efforts to understand our largest neighbor.

Planets in Our Solar System				
Planet	**Period of Revolution around the Sun (1 planetary year)**	**Period of Rotation (1 planetary day)**	**Mass (kg)**	**Diameter (miles)**
Mercury	87.96 Earth days	58.7 Earth days	3.3×10^{23}	3,031 miles
Venus	224.68 Earth days	243 Earth days	4.87×10^{24}	7,521 miles
Earth	365.26 days	24 hours	5.98×10^{24}	7,926 miles
Mars	686.98 Earth days	24.6 Earth hours	6.42×10^{23}	4,222 miles
Jupiter	11.862 Earth years	9.84 Earth hours	1.90×10^{27}	88,729 miles
Saturn	29.456 Earth years	10.2 Earth hours	5.69×10^{26}	74,600 miles
Uranus	84.07 Earth years	17.9 Earth hours	8.68×10^{25}	32,600 miles
Neptune	164.81 Earth years	19.1 Earth hours	1.02×10^{26}	30,200 miles

Which choice most accurately reflects the data in the table?

A) NO CHANGE

B) in half that time,

C) in fewer than 10 Earth hours,

D) in more time than all the other planets,

You need to know this:

One or more passages on the Writing and Language section may be accompanied by some sort of informational graphic such as a table, bar chart, or pie chart. If a passage is accompanied by a graphic, at least one question will ask you to revise the passage based on the data presented or will ask you to draw an inference based on the data. Search both the question stem and the answer choices for information that will help you pinpoint the specific parts of the table or graph that apply to the question. The correct answer will:

- Be relevant and make sense in context
- Accurately describe data in the table or graph

You need to do this:

- Use the question stem and surrounding context in the passage to determine what data you need from the graphic.
- Eliminate choices that
  - Misrepresent information presented in the graphic
  - Are irrelevant to the surrounding context

Explanation:

The sentence to which the underlined portion belongs is comparing Earth's rotational speed to that of Jupiter's. The relevant information is how much faster Jupiter rotates. Look in the third column of the table for that data to find that Jupiter completes one rotation in 9.84 Earth hours. Compare this information to the answer choices; 9.84 is "fewer than 10," so **(C)** is correct.

Writing & Lang

Try on Your Own

Directions: Take as much time as you need on these questions. Work carefully and methodically. There will be an opportunity for timed practice at the end of the chapter.

Questions 44–47 refer to the following passage.

Child Expenditures

A report from the United States Department of Agriculture estimates that the average cost of raising a child born in 2015 until age seventeen is over $230,000. This total includes **44** housing, food, transportation, health care, child care, and education; the overall cost varies considerably from family to family. However, with the average cost of raising a child set at nearly a quarter million dollars, and with additional children in the family raising that financial expenditure accordingly, it becomes clear that parenthood is a major undertaking. When planning a family, future parents should keep financial considerations in mind.

Even for families that plan for children, costs may be higher than many first-time parents anticipate. For instance, if one parent chooses to spend the first years of the child's life as a full-time caretaker and homemaker, he or she can lose career momentum and end up making a substantially lower salary than someone with the same background who maintains consistent employment. On the other hand, having both parents in the workforce significantly increases what the family must spend on child care, **45** which constituted an average of 18 percent of the overall costs to raise a child in 2012. While these factors should in no way be construed as a recommendation against having children, they speak to the need

44. The writer wants to provide an accurate and specific description of all the components that are included in the cost of raising a child based on the information in the pie charts. Which choice most effectively accomplishes this goal?

A) NO CHANGE

B) basic necessities and other needs;

C) primary needs such as housing, food, clothing, and health care, in addition to child care, transportation, education, and other assorted costs;

D) child care, health care, clothing, transportation, housing, and food;

45. Which choice completes the sentence with accurate data based on the pie charts?

A) NO CHANGE

B) which, combined with education, averaged nearly a fifth of the overall costs to raise a child in 2012.

C) which, combined with education, costs families considerably more in 2012 than in 1960.

D) which made up the largest portion of a family's average expenditures to raise a child in 2012.

for responsible family planning and financial

preparation.

Expenditures on a Child from Birth through Age 17: Average Budgetary Component Shares, 1960 versus 2012

1960

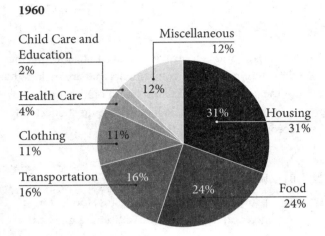

2012

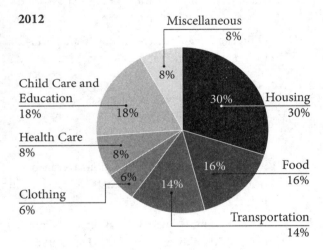

Questions 46 and 47 ask about the pie charts.

46. Which choice offers an accurate interpretation of the data in the pie charts?

   A) In 1960, health care and transportation together accounted for an average of 20 percent of a budget to raise a child.

   B) Households in 1960 spent an average of 31 percent of their total income on housing costs.

   C) The smallest proportion of an average 2012 budget to raise a child was tied between health care and miscellaneous costs.

   D) Households in 2012 spent, on average, less money per child on clothing than did households in 1960.

47. Which claim about the cost of raising children is supported by the two pie charts?

   A) Between 1960 and 2012, the percent of a budget spent on food increased.

   B) Between 1960 and 2012, the percent of a budget spent on health care decreased.

   C) Between 1960 and 2012, the percent of a budget spent on transportation experienced the greatest decrease.

   D) Between 1960 and 2012, the percent of a budget spent on child care and education experienced the greatest increase.

How Much Have You Learned?

Directions: For testlike practice, give yourself 9 minutes to complete this question set. Be sure to study the explanations, even for questions you got right. They can be found at the end of this chapter.

Questions 48–58 refer to the following passage.

Reefs at Risk

Coral reefs are essential to water and coastal ecosystems, yet they are currently at great risk. **48** A coral reef is formed by a community of very small plants and animals. These plants and animals are known as algae and polyps. The algae use sunlight to produce their own food for energy and growth. The polyps eat other small animals that come to feed on the algae. Polyps also make a hard substance, called limestone, which eventually builds up to form a reef. Many people enjoy snorkeling and fishing near these reefs. **49** Coral reefs contain more than one quarter of all marine life and help reduce storm damage to coastal lands.

50 Ultimately, about 10 percent of the world's coral reefs have already been destroyed, and **51** nearly 60 percent of the remaining reefs face at least a medium level of risk.

48. Which choice most effectively combines the underlined sentences?

A) A coral reef is formed by a community of very small plants and animals; these plants and animals are known as algae and polyps.

B) Very small plants and animals, known as algae and polyps, make up the community that forms a coral reef.

C) A coral reef is formed by a community of very small plants and animals.

D) Known as algae and polyps, the community that is called a coral reef is formed by very small plants and animals.

49. The writer is considering deleting the previous sentence. Should the writer make this change?

A) Yes, because it introduces the writer's own opinion and thus does not match the tone of the passage.

B) Yes, because it contains information that is not related to the main ideas of the paragraph.

C) No, because it adds an interesting detail about the topic of the passage.

D) No, because it provides a specific example of why coral reefs are important.

50. A) NO CHANGE
    B) Unfortunately
    C) Consequently
    D) Inevitably

51. Which choice most accurately represents the information in the chart?

A) NO CHANGE

B) 36 percent of the surviving reefs face overexploitation.

C) more than 6 in 10 reefs have faced threats of some kind or another.

D) scientists have classified 36 percent of the remaining reefs as "High Risk."

52 Fishing and boating are popular sports near coral reefs. People who fish for a living often use explosives to catch the many fish that are attracted to coral reefs, causing significant damage. Boats also destroy reefs with their anchors, **53** yet tourists who swim in coral reefs often break coral off to keep as a souvenir.

The health of a coral reef depends on having clean water and sunlight, but industrial activities can threaten these **54** simple resources. Oil or chemical spills in the water near the reefs can harm the polyps, and chemical runoff into streams from mines and farms can also destroy the polyps and algae. Further, development along a coast, such as cutting down trees and building roads or parking lots, increases the amount of dirt and sand that washes into the ocean and settles on the bottom. This debris covers the reef and **55** disrupts sunlight from reaching the coral. Without sufficient sunlight, the algae cannot grow, and in turn, the polyps lack the energy needed to produce limestone and build up the reef.

[1] Marine biologists have found that small crabs living in coral reefs can help prevent the damage caused by coastal development. [2] They remove the particles of dirt and sand that settle on the coral and stop sunlight. [3] The crabs also eat some of the polyps, which **56** would probably suggest that the crabs might also be a threat to the coral. [4] The crabs help the coral survive **57** but benefit from the relationship as well. [5] The crabs living on the coral have a steady source of food, and the reef provides the crabs with shelter from

52. Which choice most effectively establishes the paragraph's central idea?

   A) NO CHANGE
   B) People who participate in activities near coral reefs often cause damage.
   C) Boats are dangerous to the health of coral reefs.
   D) Coral reefs are fragile, and people should be careful around them.

53. A) NO CHANGE
    B) and
    C) but
    D) so

54. A) NO CHANGE
    B) elusive
    C) committed
    D) vital

55. A) NO CHANGE
    B) delays
    C) blocks
    D) covers

56. A) NO CHANGE
    B) suggests
    C) maybe suggests
    D) almost certainly suggests

57. Which choice results in a sentence that best supports the central idea of the paragraph?

   A) NO CHANGE
   B) but are one of millions of animals that live in coral reefs.
   C) and can be very large or very small in size.
   D) and are found on coral reefs all over the world.

predators. [6] However, when the biologists removed crabs from sections of coral, less coral survived than in the sections where the crabs remained. **58**

The destruction of coral reefs does not have to continue. Recognizing the part that local animals, such as crabs, can play to reduce the amount of damage will help to slow the loss of coral reefs and may provide better ways to protect them.

58. To make this paragraph most logical, sentence 6 should be placed

A) where it is now.

B) before sentence 1.

C) after sentence 2.

D) after sentence 3.

The World's Coral Reefs

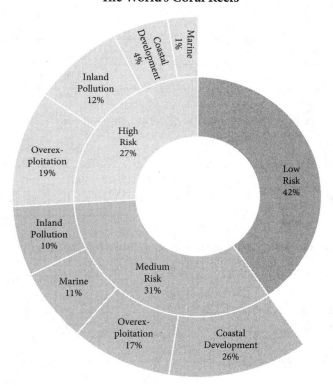

(Citation: Adapted from Wheeling Jesuit University/NASA-supported Classroom of the Future, "Exploring the Environment: Coral Reefs.")

Reflect

Directions: Take a few minutes to recall what you've learned and what you've been practicing in this chapter. Consider the following questions, jot down your best answer for each one, and then compare your reflections to the expert responses on the following page. Use your level of confidence to determine what to do next.

When should you consider selecting "DELETE the underlined portion"?

_____

_____

_____

How can transition words help you determine the most logical placement for a sentence?

_____

_____

_____

Why is relevance important in determining whether a sentence should be revised, added, or deleted?

_____

_____

_____

Name one goal of the introduction of a paragraph/passage. Name one goal of the conclusion of a paragraph/passage.

_____

_____

_____

How can you determine what you need from a graph or table on the SAT Writing and Language section?

_____

_____

_____

Expert Responses

When should you consider selecting "DELETE the underlined portion"?

If the underlined portion is wordy/redundant, does not enhance the meaning of the sentence, or does not provide clarity, select "DELETE the underlined portion." Remember that "DELETE the underlined portion" is just as likely as any of the other three choices.

How can transition words help you determine the most logical placement for a sentence?

The kind of transition word that a sentence begins with (contrast, cause and effect, continuation, emphasis, chronology) determines the purpose the sentence should serve within the context. If the sentence does serve that purpose within the context, it is logically placed.

Why is relevance important in determining whether a sentence should be revised, added, or deleted?

If a sentence is missing relevant information, it needs to be revised. If you are going to add a sentence, it should be relevant to the existing information in the passage. If information is not relevant to the passage, it should be deleted.

Name one goal of the introduction of a paragraph/passage. Name one goal of the conclusion of a paragraph/passage.

A good introduction should explain the topic and purpose and include information that will be discussed later in the paragraph/passage. A good conclusion should summarize the topic and purpose and include information that was discussed earlier in the paragraph/passage.

How can you determine what you need from a graph or table on the SAT Writing and Language section?

The question stem and the context surrounding where the graph or table is mentioned in the passage are the best clues as to what is important. Always read the question stem and take a look at the answer choices before you start to analyze the graph or table.

Next Steps

If you answered most questions correctly in the "How Much Have You Learned?" section, and if your responses to the Reflect questions were similar to those of the SAT expert, then consider organization, development, and graphs areas of strength and move on to the next chapter. Come back to these topics periodically to prevent yourself from getting rusty.

If you don't yet feel confident, review those parts of this chapter that you have not yet mastered. In particular, review common transition words and how they are used in the Organization: Transitions lesson and how to determine if information is relevant in the Development: Relevance lesson. Then try the questions you missed again. As always, be sure to review the explanations closely. Finally, **go online** (www.kaptest.com/moreonline) for additional practice on the highest yield topics in this chapter.

Answers and Explanations

1. **Review the Explanation portion of the Conciseness lesson.**

2. **D**

Difficulty: Medium

Getting to the Answer: Since the previous sentence already identifies that the "distracted reader" is a "member of modern society," repeating a word that means "modern" is redundant. Deleting the underlined phrase is most concise, so choice **(D)** is correct.

3. **D**

Difficulty: Easy

Getting to the Answer: Using two words with essentially the same meaning in the same sentence is redundant. Because "understand" and "comprehend" have the same meaning, the correct answer will eliminate one of those words. Choice **(D)** is the only answer choice that does so and is correct.

4. **A**

Difficulty: Medium

Getting to the Answer: "Complexity" and "ambivalence" are not synonyms, so the inclusion of both is not automatically a conciseness issue. Check the surrounding context to see if both words should be included. The purpose of the paragraph is to suggest that the modern story mirrors modern life. In sentence 2, the writer describes the modern story as having "complexity and ambivalence." It is thus appropriate to repeat the phrase to describe the modern reader's life, making choice **(A)** correct. (B) and (C) are incorrect because using only one of the words changes the meaning of the writer's comparison of the modern story and the modern reader's life. (D) changes the intended meaning by using "ambivalent" to describe "complexity" rather than the reader's "life."

5. **B**

Difficulty: Medium

Getting to the Answer: Choice **(B)** is correct because it most concisely expresses the intended meaning by using "George and Jane" as the subject and "finish . . . and . . . find" as the compound predicate. (A) is incorrect because the phrase "come to the completion" is

unnecessarily wordy. (C) is incorrect because it expresses the intended meaning less concisely than **(B)** by including both "George and Jane" and "they" and using the wordy phrase "at a finish." (D) is incorrect because the words "sudden" and "abruptness" are redundant.

6. **C**

Difficulty: Hard

Getting to the Answer: Questions that require you to combine sentences usually are not testing punctuation, so consider issues such as conciseness. Choice **(C)** most effectively combines the sentences by turning the second sentence into a modifying phrase that provides information about the action in the independent clause. Although (A) and (B) correctly combine the two independent clauses, both are incorrect because repeating the subject ("he") is unnecessary.

7. **Review the Explanation portion of the Organization: Transitions lesson.**

8. **B**

Difficulty: Medium

Getting to the Answer: A transition word must correctly convey the relationship between the information or ideas it connects. In the sentence before the underlined transition, the author describes small talk as boring. In the following sentence, he compares a conversation without small talk to flying. Since the sentence suggests that small talk can be dispensed with only occasionally, choice **(B)** is correct. Choices (A) and (C) are incorrect not only because they use inappropriate transition words, but also because they result in run-on sentences.

9. **A**

Difficulty: Medium

Getting to the Answer: To answer questions about effective transitions within a paragraph, identify the focus of the paragraph both before and after the transition. The first part of the paragraph discusses the reasons the narrator stayed in his room as a child—because he was ill. After the transition, the narrator discusses why he still stays in his room—because he has access to the world through the Internet. The transition needs to show how those ideas are linked. Choice **(A)** provides a logical transition as written.

Writing & Lang

10. A

Difficulty: Medium

Getting to the Answer: This sentence transitions from a discussion of the geographic freedom offered by Internet communication to one about the ease of Internet communication. To complete the transition, the underlined clause needs to relate to ease of communication. The sentence does this effectively as written, so **(A)** is correct. Choice (D) is incorrect because deleting the underlined portion would remove the transition. Choice (C) is incorrect because it references ideas from a different part of the passage. Choice (B) may be tempting because the sentence following the transition does mention text acronyms, but the writer is focused on ease rather than usefulness or frequency, so (B) is not a correct transition.

11. C

Difficulty: Medium

Getting to the Answer: The end of the previous paragraph describes Internet conversations as "relaxed and succinct"; the remainder of this sentence states that "empty chatter" is not everywhere. The change of opinion from "relaxed and succinct" to "empty chatter" is jarring without a transition, so eliminate (D). The remaining answer choices all contain the contrast word "but," so the underlined portion must contrast with the writer's positive opinion about Internet communication. Choice **(C)** is correct.

12. D

Difficulty: Easy

Getting to the Answer: To determine the correct transition word to use in context, first determine the relationship between the ideas it must connect. The first part of this sentence describes a person as "passionate," and the second part says that "his enthusiasm . . . inspires him." The second part elaborates on how his passion motivates him, so a continuation transition is needed to connect the two clauses. The correct answer is **(D)**.

13. Review the Explanation portion of the Organization: Sentence Placement lesson.

14. C

Difficulty: Hard

Getting to the Answer: Sentence 2 includes some unclear references like "some years" and "such earthquakes," while also including very specific information about variations in earthquake frequency in particular

years. Sentence 3 defines "some years" (since 1900) and "such earthquakes" (major ones) and establishes the average number of earthquakes per year. Sentence 2 would thus fit best after sentence 3 so that its references are more clear and it can elaborate on the established baseline with more specific information. Additionally, this placement results in a general-to-specific and chronological structure for the paragraph, improving its overall logic. Choice **(C)** is correct.

15. C

Difficulty: Medium

Getting to the Answer: When reordering a sentence within a paragraph, identify the information in the sentence and locate where in the paragraph that information is discussed. The topic of sentence 4 is aftershocks. Aftershocks are also discussed in sentences 2 and 3. However, in sentence 2, the pronoun "these" indicates that aftershocks have been previously discussed in the paragraph, so a sentence about aftershocks prior to sentence 2 is necessary. Thus, the logical place for sentence 4 is before sentence 2. Choice **(C)** is correct.

16. C

Difficulty: Medium

Getting to the Answer: The transition word "However" at the beginning of sentence 3 indicates that it must contrast with the sentence before it. Sentence 3 is about how to prepare for an earthquake, and sentence 2 asks how to prepare. This does not provide a contrast, but inserting the new sentence before sentence 3 would give a contrast between the inability to precisely predict earthquakes and ways to prepare for them anyway. Placing the new sentence anywhere else in the paragraph would not resolve the logical problem in the paragraph, so **(C)** is the correct answer.

17. B

Difficulty: Medium

Getting to the Answer: The word "also" in this sentence shows that the sentence needs to follow something else that FEMA advises. Additionally, the paragraph will likely elaborate on how to make a home earthquake plan, so this sentence must come before that information. The correct answer is **(B)**. Placing the new sentence anywhere before sentence 2 would make the "also" logically inconsistent, since sentence 2 contains the first recommendation from FEMA, and placing it anywhere after sentence 3 would put it after the explanation of the plan it introduces.

18. B

Difficulty: Hard

Getting to the Answer: An effective body paragraph can provide evidence to support the writer's central idea or introduce a change in the focus of the passage. This paragraph begins with the transition word "still" and establishes a contrast between the number of recent earthquakes and the damage that those earthquakes can cause. The passage also shifts focus from a discussion of earthquake frequency to one of earthquake damage. Therefore, placing this paragraph between the two discussions in paragraph 3 and paragraph 4 makes the most sense. Choice **(B)** is correct.

19. Review the Explanation portion of the Development: Word Choice lesson.

20. D

Difficulty: Medium

Getting to the Answer: Establish how the underlined word is used in the sentence; consider the negative or positive tone of the answer choices. The correct word should reflect a negative tone in relation to the problem with the cold engine. "Credit" is a term with a positive connotation, so it's incorrect. "Critique" means to critically evaluate, which is not the correct meaning in this context. "Accuse" means to charge with a crime, which one wouldn't do with a car's engine. "Blame" has the appropriately negative connotation and the correct meaning in this context, so **(D)** is correct.

21. C

Difficulty: Hard

Getting to the Answer: Establish how the underlined word is used in the sentence based on the surrounding context. The correct word should reflect a connection between the battery and the motor. "United" means made into one entity, so it's incorrect in this context. "Correlated" means associated with, not connected, so it's incorrect. "Coupled" means connected and has the correct meaning in this context. "Assimilated" means to absorb into or to have taken on the customs or characteristics of one's surroundings, so it's not correct here. **(C)** is correct.

22. A

Difficulty: Medium

Getting to the Answer: Use the surrounding context to establish how the underlined word is used in the

sentence; the following sentence points out that the converse situation is when more electrons result in an increase in power, so it makes sense that fewer electrons result in a decrease in power. "Reduction" means decrease, so it is correct. "Regression" means moving backwards. "Retraction" means pulling back or pulling in. "Constriction" means squeezing or putting under inward pressure. Therefore, **(A)** is correct.

23. B

Difficulty: Medium

Getting to the Answer: Establish how the underlined word is used in the sentence; the previous lines describe the process by which the battery "makes" electricity. You can predict a similar meaning for the correct choice. "Providing" means giving, not making. "Producing" means making, so it is correct. "Promulgating" means declaring or making known formally, so it doesn't make sense here, and "asserting" means stating confidently, so it also doesn't make sense. Choice **(B)** is correct.

24. D

Difficulty: Medium

Getting to the Answer: Look at how the word is used in the sentence and analyze its meaning. Use context clues to determine which choice is correct. The last sentence of the paragraph says that the molecules will be "more likely" to collide. "Practicality" is a noun meaning feasibility or usefulness and doesn't make sense here. "Confirmation" means verification, which doesn't make sense in this context; "process" means method or way, but that is not what's being described. "Probability" is a noun meaning likelihood, which does make sense in this context. **(D)** is correct.

25. B

Difficulty: Hard

Getting to the Answer: Use context clues to determine which choice is correct. The sentence says that power will need to be added from another car's battery, so predict something like "additional." "Associative" means resulting from association, which is not logical in this context. "Auxiliary" means additional or supplementary, and is correct. "Optional" means by choice or not required, which doesn't make sense here. "Extraordinary" means exceptional or remarkable, which also doesn't fit the intended meaning. **(B)** is correct.

26. Review the Explanation portion of the Development: Relevance lesson.

27. C

Difficulty: Medium

Getting to the Answer: Pay close attention to long lists of evidence to make sure that each component is in line with the central idea and context of the sentence. Choice **(C)** is correct because it is the only answer choice that both stays focused on matters of policy (as the first part of the sentence mentions) and supports the thesis that Polk and Jackson were in agreement on most points of public policy.

28. D

Difficulty: Medium

Getting to the Answer: Supporting details fit the context of the paragraph and do not contradict details found elsewhere in the passage. They must also logically lead to the information that follows. Select the answer choice that satisfies these guidelines. This paragraph is narrowly concerned with Polk's origins and early political career. Only **(D)** fits the context, does not introduce irrelevant information, and does not contradict later details.

29. B

Difficulty: Medium

Getting to the Answer: Remember that supporting evidence needs to focus on and contribute to the central idea. The author's intent is to introduce the two main candidates in the 1844 election, leading to the following sentence that discusses their opinions of expansionism. Choice **(B)** is correct because it stays focused on the paragraph's topic and contributes to the argument that Polk recognized popular support for expansionism that other candidates overlooked or ignored. All other choices introduce details that are either irrelevant or that contradict information elsewhere in the passage.

30. A

Difficulty: Medium

Getting to the Answer: Examine details and parenthetical asides for relevance to the central idea. The goal is to make sure that no contradictions are being introduced into the narrative. No change is necessary because the underlined section touches on two central themes of the passage: Polk's support for expansionist policies and his close alignment with Jackson's views. All other choices contradict information in other parts of the passage. Choice **(A)** is correct.

31. B

Difficulty: Medium

Getting to the Answer: Examine the paragraph for relevance to the central idea. Be sure that the underlined portion is consistent with the information that follows in the rest of the paragraph. Choice (A) is incorrect because the following sentences describe Polk's expansion of U.S. territory and his provoking a war with Mexico. (B) correctly indicates the idea that Polk's policies expanded U.S. territory. (C) is inconsistent with the information that follows: there's a strong implication that Polk's policies did allow for the expansion of slavery. (D) is incorrect because nothing in the paragraph indicates an expanding international role for the United States. Thus, **(B)** is correct.

32. Review the Explanation portion of the Development: Revising Text lesson.

33. B

Difficulty: Medium

Getting to the Answer: In order to decide whether to revise or add information, consider how the change would contribute to the sentence or paragraph. This sentence states that Jupiter interests scientists but does not provide strong reasoning for why. Making the suggested revision would improve the sentence by offering a detail about what makes Jupiter unique that helps to support the sentence's conclusion. Choice **(B)** is correct.

34. A

Difficulty: Medium

Getting to the Answer: When considering whether to add a sentence, examine the paragraph to determine whether the sentence to be added would contribute useful information or ideas to it. Before the place the writer is thinking of inserting this sentence, the passage states that the discovery of Jupiter prompted scientists to consider that other planets might not orbit Earth. It then notes that moons orbiting Jupiter were discovered at the same time as the planet. However, the passage does not explain the connection between these statements or support the first statement. The sentence to be added would accomplish both, so **(A)** is correct.

35. C

Difficulty: Easy

Getting to the Answer: If you have the option to omit a sentence, think carefully about the author's topic. If the underlined portion strays from the topic, omit it. The author's topic is Jupiter. The underlined portion adds information about *Pioneer 10* that is irrelevant to the topic. Choice **(C)** correctly omits the sentence for this reason.

36. A

Difficulty: High

Getting to the Answer: In order to decide whether a sentence should be added, examine the paragraph to see if the sentence supports its purpose. This paragraph is about the winds of Jupiter causing some of its unique features. The sentence in question might not seem related to Jupiter's winds at first glance, but the sentences before and after it make clear that the "stripes" referred to in the new sentence are the result of bands of wind, since it is these bands that isolate the chemical reactions creating individual colors. Additionally, the colorful, distinctive stripes that the sentence describes are among Jupiter's unique features, so this sentence supports the paragraph's topic; **(A)** is correct.

37. D

Difficulty: Medium

Getting to the Answer: When determining whether to delete a sentence, consider whether it supports the main idea of the passage and the paragraph. This sentence is about Jupiter's rotation speed. While the passage is about Jupiter, this paragraph is specifically about the winds of Jupiter, so its rotation speed is off topic for the paragraph. Choice **(D)** is correct because it deletes the sentence for this reason.

38. Review the Explanation portion of the Introductions and Conclusions lesson.

39. B

Difficulty: Medium

Getting to the Answer: The underlined portion will need to introduce the passage as a whole in addition to fitting well with the rest of its sentence and paragraph. The primary purpose of the passage is to describe the functions of the skin. Choice **(B)** introduces this topic effectively; the detail about the body's largest organ connects to the sentence via a contrast with people not thinking about skin as an organ and to the paragraph via an emphasis on the skin's size. Choice (A) focuses too narrowly on the skin's communication functions. Choice (C) gives details about the skin's composition rather than an introduction to the passage. Choice (D) is vague and the mention of biologists is off topic.

40. D

Difficulty: Medium

Getting to the Answer: Pick the answer choice that is in line with the writer's central idea. In this paragraph, the writer explains how the skin regulates and protects the body. The final sentence is focused on how the skin protects the body, so the underlined portion must be as well. Only **(D)** correctly centers on the protection the skin offers. Choice (A) is about us protecting our skin rather than vice versa; (B) does not discuss protection; (C) does not discuss the skin.

41. B

Difficulty: Hard

Getting to the Answer: When a question asks for a good introduction sentence, first determine the main idea of the paragraph. This paragraph uses a lot of scientific jargon, but the second sentence refers to "other senses," and nerves on the body's surface that receive "tactile stimuli" must refer to the sense of touch. The only answer choice that focuses on the skin and the sense of touch is **(B)**. Choice (A) is too vague to effectively introduce the paragraph. Choice (C) is too broadly focused on all senses and does not mention the skin. Choice (D) does mention touch but discusses the nervous system rather than the skin.

42. A

Difficulty: Medium

Getting to the Answer: Concluding sentences often reassert or summarize the writer's central idea; therefore, they cannot fundamentally conflict with the writer's assertions. In this passage, the writer has made clear that the skin is a very important organ that protects the body from a variety of illnesses and disorders, as well as from physical harm. Choice **(A)** is correct, as it ties preceding points and details together into a coherent conclusion for the writer's argument.

43. Review the Explanation portion of the Graphs lesson.

Writing & Lang

44. C

Difficulty: Medium

Getting to the Answer: The writer wants a specific, comprehensive list of child care costs as presented in the pie graphs. While (A) seems exhaustive, careful reading shows it lacks the categories of clothing and miscellaneous needs; eliminate it. Choice (B) is too general, given that the question asks for "accurate and specific" details. Choice (D) is similarly missing education and miscellaneous expenses. Only **(C)** includes all of the expense categories in the pie charts, with the added bonus of sorting them by importance for easier comprehension.

45. B

Difficulty: Hard

Getting to the Answer: The sentence brings up "what a family must spend on child care," and the underlined portion must elaborate with accurate information from the pie charts. According to the charts, "Child Care and Education" represented 18 percent of expenditures on a child in 2012. Choice **(B)** includes education with child care and correctly describes their combined cost as "nearly a fifth" of total expenses. Choices (A) and (D) omit education, and (D) incorrectly identifies child care as the largest expenditure (rather than housing). Choice (C) may be tempting, since it also includes education, but it inaccurately represents the data: the pie charts show that the *percent* of total expenditures spent on child care and education has increased, but the charts offer no actual dollar amounts, which makes it impossible to compare those amounts.

46. A

Difficulty: Medium

Getting to the Answer: To answer this type of question, carefully check each answer choice against the information in the graphs until you find the one that is correct. In 1960, health care and transportation represented 6 percent and 14 percent, respectively, of the total and 20 percent together. Choice **(A)** is correct. Choice (B) is incorrect because the pie graphs represent budgets spent on children, not total household income. (C) is incorrect because clothing constituted the smallest percent. (D) is incorrect because the graphs do not offer dollar amounts, just proportions of budgets.

47. D

Difficulty: Medium

Getting to the Answer: When a question is very broad and does not offer clues as to what part of the graph to examine, use the answer choices to determine where to look. All of the answer choices for this question require a comparison of percents between the two years. The percent spent on food decreased; eliminate (A). The percent spent on health care increased; eliminate (B). The percent spent on transportation decreased, but not as much as the percent spent on food; eliminate (C). The percent spent on child care and education increased from 2 percent to 16 percent, a greater increase than any other category; **(D)** is correct.

48. B

Difficulty: Medium

Category: Conciseness

Getting to the Answer: As written, the sentences contain redundant language. Look for the answer choice that retains the meaning of the two original sentences but is less wordy and redundant. Choice **(B)** is the correct answer because it contains the same information as the original sentences but in a more concise manner. While (C) is similar, it omits mention of "algae and polyps"; it also uses passive voice, which you should avoid using on the SAT. Choice (D) also includes the necessary information, but it introduces a modifier error, with "Known as algae and polyps" describing "the community" rather than "very small plants and animals."

49. B

Difficulty: Medium

Category: Development: Revising Text

Getting to the Answer: Identify the main idea of the paragraph and then determine whether the sentence supports it. Although sentence 3 is related to the main topic of the paragraph, coral reefs, the information in this sentence does nothing to support the main idea: coral reefs' significance and threatened status. Choice **(B)** is correct.

50. B

Difficulty: Medium

Category: Organization: Transitions

Getting to the Answer: Look for a relationship between the ideas in this sentence and the preceding sentences. The previous sentences describe the importance of coral reefs, and this sentence states that they are in danger of disappearing. "Unfortunately" indicates a shift from positive to negative ideas, so it effectively connects these sentences. Choice **(B)** is the correct answer.

51. A

Difficulty: Medium

Category: Graphs

Getting to the Answer: Evaluate the data presented in the graphic that accompanies the passage. Read each answer choice and eliminate those not supported by the data in the graph. Choice **(A)** is correct. As the chart shows, almost 60 percent of living reefs are in danger: "Medium Risk" 37% + "High Risk" 21% = 58%.

52. B

Difficulty: Easy

Category: Development: Introductions and Conclusions

Getting to the Answer: The correct answer will briefly describe the main idea of the paragraph and will be supported by the details in the paragraph. Be careful of answer choices like (C) that summarize a detail provided in the paragraph rather than the central idea. Choice **(B)** best describes the main idea of the paragraph. All of the details presented in the paragraph are related to how people engaging in activities near coral reefs often cause damage.

53. B

Difficulty: Easy

Category: Organization: Transitions

Getting to the Answer: To determine the best transition word to connect ideas, determine the relationship between the ideas. Boat anchors and people taking souvenirs both damage coral reefs, so the correct answer will show that the ideas are similar. Choice **(B)** is correct.

54. D

Difficulty: Hard

Category: Development: Word Choice

Getting to the Answer: Look for the answer that most clearly conveys the writer's meaning. The writer states that the reef "depends on" the resources of clean water and sunlight. These resources are necessary to the coral reefs, so **(D)**, "vital," is the correct answer. While the resources are "simple," as in (A), that is not the writer's intended meaning in this context. Similarly, it is a distortion of the writer's meaning to say that these resources are "elusive," (B); the writer does not suggest that clean water and sunlight are rare but that the reef's access to what it needs is threatened.

55. C

Difficulty: Medium

Category: Development: Word Choice

Getting to the Answer: Look for the answer that creates the clearest idea within the sentence. The word "blocks" most clearly illustrates how the particles that settle on the coral keep sunlight from reaching the coral. Choice **(C)** is correct.

56. B

Difficulty: Easy

Category: Conciseness

Getting to the Answer: Avoid answers that are grammatically correct but wordy or redundant. Since the word "might" appears later in the sentence, another word that indicates doubt, such as "probably," (A), or "maybe," (C), would result in a redundancy. "Suggests" fits grammatically and is the most concise choice, so **(B)** is the correct answer.

57. A

Difficulty: Medium

Category: Development: Relevance

Getting to the Answer: Avoid answers that are related to the paragraph topic but do not contribute to the paragraph's purpose. The paragraph explains how crabs and coral reefs help each other. Choice **(A)** is the only one that supports this central idea. The other choices offer details about crabs but not about their mutually beneficial relationship with reefs. The correct answer is **(A)**.

58. D

Difficulty: Medium

Category: Organization: Sentence Placement

Getting to the Answer: In order to determine the best place for a sentence, look for clues in the the sentence and the surrounding paragraph. Sentence 6 states that more coral survived with the crabs than without them, implying that the crabs are good for the coral. Additionally, the sentence starts with the contrast word "However," so it must contrast with the sentence before it. Thus, the sentence would effectively follow and refute sentence 3's suggestion that crabs might be damaging the coral; this supports the central idea of the paragraph, that crabs and reefs are good for each other. Choice **(D)** is the correct answer.

Writing & Lang

CHAPTER 27

SAT Writing and Language: Timing and Section Management Strategies

LEARNING OBJECTIVE

After completing this chapter, you will be able to:

- Move quickly and efficiently through the Writing and Language section so that you have a fair chance at every question

Timing

You have 35 minutes to complete 4 passages with 11 questions each. To finish on time, you need to complete each passage and its accompanying questions in an average of 8 minutes and 45 seconds. This means that after 17.5 minutes, you should be halfway done with the section. When the proctor informs you that there are 5 minutes remaining, you should have a little more than half of a passage to finish.

Section Management

While you do want to spend approximately the same amount of time on each passage, you definitely do not need to spend the same amount of time on each question. Every question counts for the same number of points, so be sure to complete the questions you find easiest to answer first. If a particular question is challenging, take a guess and come back to it if you have time. The test rewards students for conciseness, so when you guess, choose the shortest option.

Moving efficiently through this section is important, but that does not mean that you should skip over any text. Even if sections of a passage may not be underlined, you need an understanding of the passage as a whole to answer certain questions. Reading all of the text in the passage is essential to answering questions efficiently and accurately.

There is a full Writing and Language section in the "How Much Have You Learned?" section of this chapter. Use it to practice timing: skip questions you find too time-consuming and return to them if you have time while keeping an eye on the clock. When you are finished, check your work—and reflect on how well you managed the section.

If you're still looking for more practice with Writing and Language question sets after finishing this chapter, **go online** (www.kaptest.com/moreonline) and use the Qbank to generate additional practice sets for yourself.

How Much Have You Learned?

Directions: For testlike practice, give yourself 35 minutes to complete this question set, which is the equivalent of a full Writing and Language section. Be sure to study the explanations, even for questions you got right. They can be found at the end of this chapter.

Questions 1–11 refer to the following passage.

Long History, Short Poem: The Haiku

[1] Of the many forms poetry can take, triolet, ballad, ode, and epigram, to name a few, none is quite as briefly beautiful as the Japanese haiku. With a [2] complex history and a challenging structure, the haiku is as popular as it is difficult to master. Composed of only three lines and 17 or fewer syllables, haiku have been written by some of the world's most prominent poets.

[3] [1] Pre-Buddhist and early Shinto ceremonies included narrative poems called "uta," or songs. [2] These songs were written about common activities like planting and prayer. [3] The most popular "uta" were "waka," or songs featuring 31 syllables broken into five different lines. [4] Later, the "waka" format was distilled into the 5-7-5-7-7 syllables-per-line format that is still used and recognized today. [5] During the same time period, writers played word games. [6] The syllabic 5-7-5-7-7 structure would remain throughout the work, adhering to the guidelines used in ceremonies and royal court proceedings. [7] They would compose lines of poetry, alternating turns, until long strings of text called "renga" were created. [8] It was not until the 15th and 16th centuries that writers of "renga" broke with tradition and shortened the form, writing "hokku," meaning "first verse." [9] [4] This name changed into

1. A) NO CHANGE
    B) Of the many forms poetry can take—triolet, ballad, ode, and epigram, to name a few—none is quite as briefly beautiful as the Japanese haiku.
    C) Of the many forms poetry can take, triolet, ballad, ode and epigram to name a few—none is quite as briefly beautiful as the Japanese haiku.
    D) Of the many forms poetry can take: triolet, ballad, ode, and epigram to name a few, none is quite as briefly beautiful as the Japanese haiku.

2. A) NO CHANGE
    B) composite
    C) compound
    D) variegated

3. Which choice, if added here, would provide the most appropriate introduction to the topic of the paragraph?
    A) Although the format remained unknown to Americans until the 1950s, haiku dates back as early as the seventh century.
    B) The art of haiku includes specific rules about how lines are to be structured, but these rules are difficult to pin down.
    C) Despite its difficult reputation and the years it takes to master, haiku is highly entertaining.
    D) Haiku is a Japanese poetic art form and many poets enjoy the challenge of writing a poem within its rules.

"haiku" over time. **5**

6 Previously, hokku master Matsunaga Teitoku began teaching renga in an attempt to ignite a classical renaissance. He founded a writing school where he taught Matsuo Basho, who is now known as one of Japan's most famous writers. Basho traveled throughout Japan writing about nature and his travels.

It is through Basho's many poems that **7** haiku came to be known as being closely connected with nature and the seasons. **8** Basho influenced many students of verse over the course of his lifetime and was declared the saint of the haiku in the Shinto religion. One of Basho's literary heirs was Fukuda Chiyo-ni, whose popularity during the Edo period, in the eighteenth century, opened opportunities for women poets who followed her.

4. A)   NO CHANGE
    B)   Nobody is quite sure when it became known as "haiku."
    C)   These days, we know this word as "haiku."
    D)   DELETE the underlined portion.

5. To make this paragraph most logical, sentence 7 should be placed
    A)   where it is now.
    B)   after sentence 1.
    C)   after sentence 5.
    D)   after sentence 8.

6. A)   NO CHANGE
    B)   However
    C)   In the next century
    D)   As a result

7. A)   NO CHANGE
    B)   haiku transformed into a mode of artistic expression that was irreversibly intertwined with the themes of
    C)   haiku became popular because it was seen as having something to do with
    D)   haiku developed its common association with

8. Which choice, if added here, would provide the most relevant detail?
    A)   However, haiku can be used to communicate many other ideas as well, from love to humor.
    B)   His words emphasized contentment and solitary contemplation, ideals linked to Japanese religions.
    C)   Basho's poetic influence continues to be felt even now in the work of several modern poets.
    D)   For example, a Basho haiku might focus on a frog or on the coming of spring.

It was not until 1827 that hokku was renamed haiku by Masaoka Shiki. [9] Shiki was a poet, and he most famously shrank the structure of the haiku to its current format of 5-7-5. His work [10] helped Western writers like e. e. cummings and Ezra Pound, but haiku did not become the easily recognizable, popular type of poetry that it is today until writers like Allen Ginsberg and Jack Kerouac popularized it.

These writers were taken by [11] the brevity of the form, but it provided them a new, challenging form of expression while enabling them to share full ideas in such a short form. Both Japanese and American poets continue to use the haiku structure to create snapshots of beauty and calm.

9. A) NO CHANGE
   B) Shiki was a poet who also shrank the structure of the haiku to the current 5-7-5 format.
   C) Shiki was the poet who shrank the structure of the haiku to its current 5-7-5 format.
   D) Shiki was the poet who was also known for shrinking the structure of the haiku to its current format of 5-7-5.

10. A) NO CHANGE
    B) inspired
    C) aided
    D) started

11. A) NO CHANGE
    B) the brevity of the form, it
    C) the brevity of the form, and it
    D) the brevity of the form, as it

Questions 12–22 refer to the following passage.

Physical Therapy Careers: Health Care in Motion

Physical therapy is a health care field that is [12] concurrently rated by the U.S. Bureau of Labor Statistics as one of today's best career choices. Featuring considerable variety in work environments, patient relationships, and job activity levels, the work of a physical therapist has the potential to be both highly motivating and satisfying. [13] Current projections indicate that this particular field of physical therapy should grow significantly over the next decade and continue to be one of the more flexible—not to mention enjoyable and fun—jobs in health care.

[14] A license is required to practice as a physical therapist, whether in the United States or elsewhere. After completing a bachelor's degree (and specific science-related prerequisites), students must obtain a Doctor of Physical Therapy (DPT) degree. This program typically lasts three years. All graduates of DPT programs must then pass the National Physical Therapy Examination. After the exam, they must complete any additional requirements for licensure in the state in which they intend to practice. Once licensed by the state, physical therapists (PTs) are equipped to begin their careers.

[15] PTs work with a broad range of patients in a wide variety of settings, such as hospitals or private clinics. Some clientele, for example, are elderly or ill.

12. A) NO CHANGE
    B) consistently
    C) unusually
    D) finally

13. A) NO CHANGE
    B) And current projections indicate that the field should grow significantly over the next several years and the next decade and remain one of the more flexible—not to mention enjoyable—jobs in health care.
    C) Current projections and predictions by the Bureau of Labor indicate that the field should grow significantly over the next decade and remain one of the more flexible and even enjoyable—jobs in the health care industry.
    D) Current projections indicate that the field should grow significantly over the next decade and remain one of the more flexible and enjoyable jobs in health care.

14. Which choice most effectively establishes the main topic of the second paragraph?
    A) NO CHANGE
    B) Those pursuing careers in physical therapy must undergo the appropriate education and licensure processes.
    C) Requirements vary from state to state to practice physical therapy, just as they do for physicians and physicians' assistants.
    D) Physical therapists must pass a national exam that covers a wide range of material.

15. A) NO CHANGE
    B) PTs work with a broad range of patients, in a wide variety of settings some work in hospitals, while others work in private clinics.
    C) PTs work with a broad range of patients; in a wide variety of settings. Some work in hospitals; others in private clinics.
    D) PTs work with a broad range of patients: the variety of settings, includes hospitals and private clinics.

Other patients include athletes ranging from elite professionals and college sports stars to middle school sports players. **16** Some kinds of PTs have personal, long-term patient **17** relationships, while others focus on research or testing and interact with patients minimally.

[1] **18** A physical therapist primarily works with patients who have suffered motion loss from illness or injury. The goal is to restore mobility while managing and limiting pain.

16. At this point, the writer is considering adding a sentence to support the main topic of the paragraph. Which choice best supports the main topic of paragraph 3?

A) PTs must demonstrate their willingness to spend long hours on the job.

B) Still others include people who have been injured at work.

C) The clientele pay for their physical therapy services according to their ability, so some PTs earn more than others.

D) No special license is required to work with patients who are professional athletes, but some states may require additional courses to work with students.

17. A) NO CHANGE

B) relationships, while others, who focus on research or testing, interact minimally with patients.

C) relationships; others minimal interact with patients and focus on research or testing.

D) relationships. Others focus on research or testing and interact with patients minimally.

18. Which choice most effectively combines the underlined sentences to provide a smooth flow of ideas?

A) NO CHANGE

B) A physical therapist primarily works with patients. They have suffered motion loss from illness or injury. And the therapist's goal is to restore mobility. While managing and limiting pain.

C) A physical therapist, whose goal is to restore mobility and manage pain primarily works with patients who have suffered motion loss or illness or injury.

D) A physical therapist primarily works with patients who have suffered motion loss from illness or injury to restore mobility while managing and limiting pain.

Writing & Lang

[2] <u>[19] This job often involves long-term planning, creatively personalized application, and patience, in addition to highly refined medical knowledge.</u> [3] In many cases, physical therapists invite and rely on patients to participate actively in their own recovery. [4] This interpersonal and [20] <u>collaborative</u> aspect of physical therapy is often essential to the medical work itself. [5] For example, recovering athletes must often commit to long-term conditioning programs before returning to their sports. [6] Surgery or medication alone isn't always enough to restore full mobility; many PT patients must relearn their muscle use and work hard to increase flexibility. [7] PTs determine the course of action and coach their patients through the steps to recovery. [21]

[1] The horizon for employment rates in physical therapy is exceptionally bright. [2] The Bureau of Labor Statistics predicts that the coming decade will see a 36 percent growth in PT jobs. [3] This means that there should be a need for over 70,000 new PTs nationwide. [4] Physical therapist assistants (PTAs) will also be needed. [5] For those willing to commit the time and effort to become experts in physical therapy, the possibilities and quality of the PT work environment are among the most desirable in health care, and considering projected employment rates, such a career seems to be an especially prudent choice. [22]

19. A) NO CHANGE

    B) This job often involves long-term planning, creatively personalized application, patience, and highly refined medical knowledge.

    C) This job often involves long-term planning, creative personalized application and patience, in addition to highly refined medical knowledge.

    D) This job often involves long-term planning, creatively personal application and patience, as well as highly refined medical knowledge.

20. A) NO CHANGE

    B) concentrated

    C) planned

    D) consolidated

21. To make this paragraph most logical, sentence 2 should be placed

    A) before sentence 1.

    B) after sentence 3.

    C) after sentence 5.

    D) after sentence 7.

22. Which sentence should be removed in order to improve the focus of this paragraph?

    A) Sentence 1

    B) Sentence 2

    C) Sentence 3

    D) Sentence 4

Questions 23–33 refer to the following passage.

Feeling the Burn of Lactic Acid

As a person works a muscle excessively or for a long period of time, that person will most likely feel a burning sensation. Coaches and trainers often encourage [23] they're athletes to exercise until they "feel the burn" because that is an indication that the muscle is working hard. Some people [24] bond the burning feeling with "burning" calories, but the burning sensation has nothing to do with the energy released during exercise; [25] first, it is caused by chemicals that form when muscles use more oxygen than they have available.

[26] Blood brings the energy muscles need to move in the form of glucose. The muscles cannot use the glucose directly, however; they can use only adenosine triphosphate (ATP), which is a molecule formed when cells break down glucose. First, the muscle cells break the six-carbon glucose into two three-carbon molecules of pyruvic acid. This makes two ATP molecules available for the muscle cells to use. When enough oxygen is available, the cells [27] then continues to break the pyruvic acid down in a series of steps, each of which produces more ATP. The full cycle releases another 34 ATP molecules, as well as carbon dioxide and water, from one molecule of glucose.

When a cell breaks down glucose without oxygen present, however, it can only accomplish the first step. Even the first step will halt, unless the cell converts the pyruvic acid formed into lactic acid. The longer we exercise without enough oxygen, the more lactic acid we build up in our muscle tissues. You are probably familiar with the discomfort acetic [28] acid found in vinegar, causes when it comes in contact with a cut; lactic acid

23. A) NO CHANGE
    B) their
    C) it's
    D) its

24. A) NO CHANGE
    B) equate
    C) acquaint
    D) observe

25. A) NO CHANGE
    B) instead,
    C) although,
    D) consequently,

26. Which choice most effectively establishes the central idea of this paragraph?
    A) NO CHANGE
    B) Adenosine triphosphate (ATP) is a molecule that is found in all living cells.
    C) Glucose is a carbohydrate that is absorbed into the blood during digestion.
    D) Muscles are made of soft tissue and require an external energy source to move.

27. A) NO CHANGE
    B) did continue
    C) continue
    D) continued

28. A) NO CHANGE
    B) acid, found in vinegar, causes
    C) acid found, in vinegar, causes
    D) acid found in vinegar causes

Writing & Lang

29 annoys muscle tissues in a similar way, causing a burning sensation.

30 [1] Lactic acid does not form during normal daily activities because our muscles have a small store of ATP available, which is easily replenished as it is used. [2] More intense activity, however, quickly uses up that **31** store once the store is used up, and if the level of oxygen needed for the activity is greater than the amount reaching the muscles, lactic acid starts to build up. [3] The buildup of lactic acid occurs most quickly while engaging in so-called power sports, such as sprinting. [4] After we stop exercising, **32** you continue to breathe harder in order to get enough oxygen to convert the lactic acid back to pyruvic acid, to be used in the normal cycle once again. [5] As a result, lactic acid does not return to normal immediately after we stop exercising. **33**

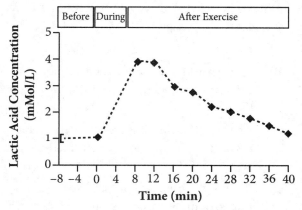

Concentration of Lactic Acid in Blood
Before, During, and After Exercise
(5-minute fast run)

Based on data from Journal of Sport Sciences, 28(9) pp. 975–982.

29. A) NO CHANGE
    B) rubs
    C) hurts
    D) irritates

30. Which choice provides the least support for the central idea of this paragraph?
    A) Sentence 1
    B) Sentence 2
    C) Sentence 3
    D) Sentence 4

31. A) NO CHANGE
    B) store once, the store
    C) store; once the store
    D) store: once the store

32. A) NO CHANGE
    B) we
    C) they
    D) them

33. Based on the information in the graph, which choice, if added here, would provide the most effective conclusion to the passage?
    A) Lactic acid concentration peaks at eight minutes then begins to drop.
    B) At 28 minutes, lactic acid concentration is half of what it is during exercise.
    C) We continue to "feel the burn" for nearly 40 minutes after we stop.
    D) Lactic acid concentration declines steadily when exercise stops.

Writing & Lang

Questions 34–44 refer to the following passage.

Inside Looking Out: Post-Impressionism

Post-Impressionism was an artistic movement that took place between 1886 and 1892 and [34] produces some of the world's foremost artists. Post-Impressionism emerged as one of the many different artistic styles created in response to the Impressionist movement, which focused on creating realistic representations of human perceptions. [35] Next, Impressionists sought to [36] restate nature in their work. They used small, controlled brush strokes in an effort to capture how the human eye sees light. Post-Impressionism was radically different. Artists of this time focused more on self-discovery than anything else. Instead of looking out on a landscape and [37] attempt to paint exactly what they saw, they turned their eyes inward. They interpreted subjects through their own [38] unique vision, which included their personal experiences and emotions. This change influenced the course of all art created since.

[39] Among the Impressionist artists were Claude Monet, Pierre-Auguste Renoir, Edgar Degas, and Mary Cassatt. Paul Cezanne and Georges Seurat used shape and color to describe their worlds rather than mimic them. Their work acted as a bridge between Impressionist art and the more abstract subcategories of Post-Impressionism. Two such subcategories were Cubism and Abstract Expressionism.

34. A) NO CHANGE
     B) produced
     C) was producing
     D) will produce

35. A) NO CHANGE
     B) For example,
     C) Consequently,
     D) However,

36. A) NO CHANGE
     B) clone
     C) counterfeit
     D) replicate

37. A) NO CHANGE
     B) attempting
     C) was attempted
     D) is attempting

38. A) NO CHANGE
     B) single
     C) cautious
     D) acceptable

39. Which choice most effectively establishes the central idea of the paragraph?

     A) NO CHANGE
     B) Modern artists are well versed in many different kinds of styles thanks to the many artists of the past.
     C) Artists in the Post-Impressionist era employed a wide range of methods when creating their art.
     D) Prior to the Impressionist and Post-Impressionist eras, artists painted in a much more realistic style.

[40] Cubism was created by Spanish painter Pablo Picasso and French painter Georges Braque. It featured geometric shapes used to construct conceptual portraits. Both of these artists rejected traditional views on modeling nature and people, as well as classical techniques. Abstract Expressionism used color instead of geometric figures, and artists like Jackson Pollock and Willem de Kooning covered their canvases with color and indistinct forms. Abstract Expressionists aimed to express deep emotional themes. Paul Gauguin and Vincent van Gogh are also considered Abstract Expressionists, as [41] they both prioritized the depiction of their memories and emotions over observations that could be made with the eye. Helen Frankenthaler, whose body of work evolved over the six decades of her career, began painting within this genre as well, before coming to reject its highly personal perspective. [42] Never before had such an emphasis on individualism taken precedence over classical technique, a change that laid the foundation for art in the 20th century and beyond.

40. Which choice most effectively combines the sentences at the underlined portion?

A) NO CHANGE

B) Created by Spanish painter Pablo Picasso and French painter Georges Braque, Cubism featured geometric shapes used to construct conceptual portraits.

C) Cubism was created by Spanish painter Pablo Picasso and French painter Georges Braque, so it featured geometric shapes.

D) Cubism was created by Spanish painter Pablo Picasso and French painter Georges Braque, but it featured geometric shapes.

41. A) NO CHANGE

B) it

C) you

D) we

42. Which choice, if added here, most effectively supports the central idea of the paragraph?

A) Some Impressionist artists, such as Renoir, painted images of children, flowers, and social gatherings.

B) Degas often painted ballet dancers at the barre as well as molding sculptures of them.

C) Art is often viewed as a window into the minds and experiences of artists as they lived their lives.

D) To transfer their emotions to their canvases, Post-Impressionist artists sometimes used violent gestures to apply paint.

[1] These artists worked and created during the same time period and movement. [2] However, they had varying world views and techniques. [3] Today, we can get to know the souls of some of the world's greatest artists by visiting **43** they're Post-Impressionist work in museums around the world. [4] These differences cumulatively succeeded in breaking from the natural guidelines of Impressionism to create something entirely new that dramatically influenced all artists who came after them. [5] In the words of Edvard Munch, another Post-Impressionist painter, "Nature is not only all that is visible to the eye … it also includes the inner pictures of the soul." **44**

43. A) NO CHANGE
    B) their
    C) they are
    D) there

44. To make this paragraph most logical, sentence 3 should be placed
    A) where it is now.
    B) after sentence 1.
    C) before sentence 5.
    D) after sentence 5.

Answers and Explanations

1. B

Difficulty: Medium

Category: Sentence Structure: Commas, Dashes, and Colons

Getting to the Answer: Read the sentence to determine how the list within it should be formatted. If it is more of an aside than a direct part of the sentence's main structure, the list should be set off by punctuation. As the sentence is written, its many commas are confusing. Because there is a list in the sentence, the commas within that list should remain. However, the list of poetic forms is not directly related to the rest of the sentence, so this should be clarified with punctuation. Dashes are the best way to mark this as a separate thought. Choice **(B)** correctly adds dashes to both the beginning and end of the list.

2. A

Difficulty: Medium

Category: Development: Word Choice

Getting to the Answer: This sentence is correct as written. The author wants to convey the idea that the history of the haiku is complicated. Choice **(A)**, "complex," accurately conveys this thought. The words (B), "composite," and (C), "compound," both imply that something is made up of numerous smaller parts and do not describe history. Choice (D), "variegated," can mean either multicolored or various, neither of which makes sense as a way to describe history.

3. A

Difficulty: Hard

Category: Development: Introductions and Conclusions

Getting to the Answer: Consider the purpose of the paragraph, then determine which answer choice makes the most sense as an introduction to the paragraph. The purpose of this paragraph, based on its other sentences, is to explain the history of haiku and how its structure has changed over time. Choice **(A)** is the only answer choice related to these ideas. While the other answer choices may briefly mention the structure of haiku or its history, they all focus on other aspects of haiku—its entertainment value, the difficulty of understanding its rules, or the challenge of writing it.

4. D

Difficulty: Medium

Category: Development: Revising Text

Getting to the Answer: The sentence's placement in the passage is not optimal. The next sentence returns the discussion to the hokku form and readers encounter another explanation of the name "haiku" later, in paragraph 5. Choice **(D)** is correct because the sentence should be omitted from paragraph 2.

5. C

Difficulty: Medium

Category: Organization: Sentence Placement

Getting to the Answer: Consider the information presented by the rest of the paragraph to determine the meaning of the phrase "alternating turns." Sentence 7 describes the specifics of different word games introduced in sentence 5, so it makes sense that it would follow sentence 5. Choice **(C)** is correct.

6. C

Difficulty: Medium

Category: Organization: Transitions

Getting to the Answer: Make sure that this sentence clearly and precisely transitions from the topic of the previous paragraph to the topic of this paragraph. As currently written, the first sentence does not make a clear connection to the preceding paragraph. By making the discussion of time more precise, the beginning of this paragraph flows better from the previous one. The reader understands more clearly how the details in each paragraph connect. Choice **(C)** is correct.

7. D

Difficulty: Medium

Category: Conciseness

Getting to the Answer: The original underlined portion is far wordier than is needed to convey its meaning. Choice **(D)** correctly communicates the information of this sentence without using excess words.

8. D

Difficulty: Hard

Category: Development: Relevance

Getting to the Answer: Find the answer choice that clearly supports the topic sentence of the paragraph. The topic sentence of this paragraph emphasizes the themes in Basho's work and how haiku became associated with nature and the seasons. Only **(D)** provides examples of nature-related subjects of Basho haiku and is therefore correct.

9. C

Difficulty: Hard

Category: Conciseness

Getting to the Answer: This sentence uses more words than needed to communicate its point. Combining ideas by making the second clause dependent creates a more concise sentence. Choice **(C)** is correct because it maintains the sentence's meaning while using fewer words. Choices (B) and (D) also make the second clause dependent, but include extra words such as "also."

10. B

Difficulty: Medium

Category: Development: Word Choice

Getting to the Answer: Consider the precise relationship between Shiki and the other poets mentioned. The correct answer choice will describe his effect on them. It seems clear that Shiki's work influenced cummings and Pound. While "helped" and "aided" both generally suggest that his effect on them was positive, "inspired" is more accurate. Shiki had left his mark, and the other poets learned from him. Choice **(B)** is correct.

11. D

Difficulty: Medium

Category: Organization: Transitions

Getting to the Answer: Read the sentence and determine whether its thoughts are joined logically. The two parts of the sentence are directly related; the writers are "taken with the brevity of the form" because of what it provides them. The sentence does not express this relationship as written, so eliminate (A). Eliminate (B) and (C) because neither choice correctly relates the two parts of the sentence. Choice **(D)** correctly combines the sentence while maintaining the relationship between the two clauses.

12. B

Difficulty: Medium

Category: Development: Word Choice

Getting to the Answer: Read the entire paragraph to determine if a career in physical therapy is rated as a good career choice by the Bureau of Labor Statistics. "Concurrently" means at the same time and "unusually" means not common. "Finally" implies that physical therapy was not a good career choice in the past. Choice **(B)** is correct because it means with regularity.

13. D

Difficulty: Medium

Category: Organization: Conciseness

Getting to the Answer: The sentence as written is unnecessarily wordy and includes a redundancy in the phrase "enjoyable and fun." Eliminate (A). Choices (B) and (C) both correct the redundancy but not the overall wordiness of the sentence, and both introduce new errors. Choice **(D)** is the most concise answer and is therefore correct.

14. B

Difficulty: Medium

Category: Development: Introductions and Conclusions

Getting to the Answer: Read the paragraph to identify its focus. The second paragraph discusses the process of becoming a physical therapist, including education and licensing. Choices (A), (C), and (D) each offer only one component of the paragraph, and (A) and (C) bring up off-topic details like foreign countries and requirements to be a physician. Only choice **(B)** effectively establishes the main topic of the second paragraph.

15. A

Difficulty: Easy

Category: Sentence Structure: The Basics

Getting to the Answer: When an entire sentence is underlined, check that the sentence is structurally sound. Make sure that any independent clauses, dependent clauses, and phrases are correctly joined. Choice (B) forms a run-on with two independent clauses connected without punctuation. (C) includes phrases connected to the sentence with semicolons rather than commas. (D) misuses both colons (not introducing information or ideas) and commas (separating subject from verb). Only the original sentence contains no punctuation errors, so **(A)** is correct.

16. B

Difficulty: Hard

Category: Development: Relevance

Getting to the Answer: Read the paragraph to determine its main topic. The topic sentence describes PTs working with a wide variety of patients, and the following sentences provide examples. Since **(B)** is the only sentence that describes potential patients, it is the correct answer. Choices (C) and (D) may be tempting because they both mention patients, but both discuss patients in the context of other topics—income and licensing, respectively—rather than focusing on the patients themselves.

17. B

Difficulty: Hard

Category: Agreement: Modifiers

Getting to the Answer: This sentence is complex, so spotting the error may be difficult. The modifier "minimally" describes the verb "interact" and so needs to be next to it. Choices (A) and (D) do not correct this error; eliminate them. Choice (C) corrects the error but introduces a different one by changing the adverb "minimally" to the adjective "minimal," which cannot modify a verb. Choice **(B)** correctly moves the modifier next to the word it modifies without introducing new errors.

18. D

Difficulty: Medium

Category: Development: Relevance

Getting to the Answer: As written, the text uses short, choppy sentences. Their topics are related, so combining them by making one no longer an independent clause will both make the paragraph smoother and show the relationship between ideas more clearly. Choice **(D)** is correct. Choice (C) may be tempting because it also makes the second sentence subordinate, but it introduces a comma error so is incorrect.

19. B

Difficulty: Hard

Category: Conciseness

Getting to the Answer: This sentence lists qualities necessary to being a physical therapist. There is no reason that medical knowledge should be set apart from the other qualities; doing so makes the sentence unnecessarily wordy and complex. Choice **(B)** correctly rearranges the sentence so that the four main ideas are combined in a single list, eliminating the unhelpful phrase "in addition to."

20. A

Difficulty: Easy

Category: Development: Word Choice

Getting to the Answer: Read the sentence and any necessary context to determine the meaning of the word. The sentence refers to "This interpersonal ... aspect" of physical therapy; the previous sentence describes how physical therapists "invite" their patients to be active participants. The underlined word must refer to patients and physical therapists working together. Choice **(A)** is correct.

21. D

Difficulty: Hard

Category: Organization: Sentence Placement

Getting to the Answer: When determining where to place a sentence, examine the sentence itself and the paragraph as a whole for clues. Sentence 2 summarizes the qualities a physical therapist needs; the paragraph as a whole describes what a physical therapist does and how those qualities impact their work. This suggests sentence 2 should go at either the beginning or the end of the paragraph. Eliminate (B) and (C). Placing sentence 2 at the beginning of the paragraph would disrupt the transition from the previous paragraph, so (A) is incorrect. Choice **(D)** correctly moves the summative sentence to conclude the paragraph.

Writing & Lang

22. D

Difficulty: Medium

Category: Development: Relevance

Getting to the Answer: Closely read the paragraph to find the central idea. Then, determine which sentence does not match the content. The evidence regarding physical therapy assistants does not connect with the main idea of this paragraph, which centers on the benefits of choosing to become a certified physical therapist. Choice **(D)** is correct.

23. B

Difficulty: Medium

Category: Agreement: Pronouns

Getting to the Answer: Consider the function of the underlined word in the sentence. The underlined word should be a plural possessive pronoun that refers to "coaches and trainers." Choice **(B)** is correct.

24. B

Difficulty: Medium

Category: Development: Word Choice

Getting to the Answer: Think about the overall meaning of the sentence. Consider which answer choice most closely matches the writer's intended meaning. The writer explains that some people connect, or equate, the exercise-prompted burning feeling with burning calories. "Equate" is the most precise word to convey this meaning. Choice **(B)** is correct.

25. B

Difficulty: Medium

Category: Organization: Transitions

Getting to the Answer: Consider the relationship between the thoughts expressed on either side of the semicolon. The writer presents contrasting ideas in this sentence. The relationship between these ideas is best expressed by inserting the transition word "instead" to indicate the contrast between the thoughts. Choice **(B)** is correct.

26. A

Difficulty: Hard

Category: Development: Introductions and Conclusions

Getting to the Answer: The correct answer will include an idea that ties together all the information in the paragraph. Paraphrase the central idea in your own words. This paragraph is primarily about how muscles use glucose to get the energy they need to move. Choice **(A)** is correct because it most effectively states the central idea.

27. C

Difficulty: Medium

Category: Agreement: Verbs

Getting to the Answer: Identify the noun in the clause. Determine whether the noun is singular or plural and what verb tense is used elsewhere in the sentence. The noun "cells" in this clause is plural, and the rest of the sentence is written in present tense. Choice **(C)** is correct because it features the plural present tense form of the verb.

28. B

Difficulty: Medium

Category: Sentence Structure: Commas, Dashes, and Colons

Getting to the Answer: Determine the function of the phrase "found in vinegar" within the sentence. Remember that nonrestrictive elements must be set off from the rest of the sentence with commas before and after. The phrase "found in vinegar" modifies "acetic acid" and is not essential to the understanding of the sentence. Choice **(B)** is correct.

29. D

Difficulty: Medium

Category: Development: Word Choice

Getting to the Answer: Reread the sentence with each of the answer choices in place of the underlined word. All of the answer choices are similar in meaning, so think about the connotation of each one in relation to the overall meaning of the sentence. In this sentence, the connotation of "irritates" most precisely communicates the meaning of what the writer is trying to convey to the reader: bothers. While "annoys" is similar to this meaning, it is mostly used when referring to people, not inanimate or biological objects like lactic acid. Choice **(D)** is correct.

30. C

Difficulty: Medium

Category: Development: Relevance

Getting to the Answer: Identify the central idea of paragraph 4. Think about which sentences are essential to understand the rest of the paragraph. The correct answer could be taken out without changing the meaning or the reader's understanding of the central idea. Although **(C)** is related to the central idea, the details in this sentence provide the least amount of support because they provide an example of a situation in which lactic acid builds up more quickly. The central idea of the paragraph, however, is the buildup and conversion of lactic acid during exercise. Choice **(C)** is correct.

31. C

Difficulty: Medium

Category: Sentence Structure: The Basics

Getting to the Answer: Determine whether two complete thoughts are expressed in this sentence. Two complete sentences, each with a subject and predicate, become a run-on without proper punctuation. As written, this is a run-on sentence. Placing a semicolon between the two complete thoughts makes the sentence grammatically correct. Choice **(C)** is correct.

32. B

Difficulty: Easy

Category: Agreement: Pronouns

Getting to the Answer: Make sure that related pronouns agree in number and person. In this sentence, the writer is referring to all human beings and uses "we" to do so. The underlined pronoun "you" does not match the use of the first-person plural pronoun. Choice **(B)** is correct.

33. C

Difficulty: Hard

Category: Graphs

Getting to the Answer: The correct answer will both reflect the information presented in the graph and be an appropriate conclusion for the passage. Avoid answers like (B) that do not strengthen the central idea of the passage. Choice **(C)** is correct because it contains details presented in the graph that are relevant to the central idea of the passage and because it provides an appropriate conclusion to the passage.

34. B

Difficulty: Easy

Category: Agreement: Verbs

Getting to the Answer: As currently written, this sentence switches verb tense mid-sentence. The other verbs in the sentence, "was" and "took," indicate that the events happened in the past. The tense of the underlined verb should also be in past tense. Eliminate (A) and (D). The underlined verb forms a compound verb with "took," so their forms need to match. Choice **(B)** is correct because it uses the matching past tense.

35. B

Difficulty: Medium

Category: Organization: Transitions

Getting to the Answer: To choose the correct transition, look for the relationship between this sentence and the previous one. The previous sentence states that Impressionists sought to represent human perception. This sentence and the one that follows describe how Impressionists sought to capture how humans saw nature, giving an example of what kind of art the Impressionists were creating. Choice **(B)** shows the correct relationship between the two sentences.

36. D

Difficulty: Medium

Category: Development: Word Choice

Getting to the Answer: The writer wants to convey the idea that the Impressionists tried to paint exactly what they saw in nature. Only **(D)** has the correct connotation and fits within the context of the sentence. To "restate" something, choice (A), means to say it again a second time. Choice (B), "clone," means to make an identical genetic copy of something. Finally, (C), "counterfeit," means to imitate something with the intent to deceive.

37. B

Difficulty: Medium

Category: Agreement: Verbs

Getting to the Answer: When a sentence has paired verbs like these, the verbs have to be parallel. The correct answer must be in the same form as the first verb in the sentence, "looking." That means that the verb "attempting" in choice **(B)** is correct.

38. A

Difficulty: Easy

Category: Development: Word Choice

Getting to the Answer: Check each word for its connotations and pick the answer choice that fits the context of the sentence. This sentence describes how Post-Impressionists focused on self-discovery in art by letting their personal experiences and emotions guide their interpretation of their subjects. Therefore, each artist had his or her own distinct, or "unique," vision. The underlined portion is correct as written, so choice **(A)** is correct.

39. C

Difficulty: Medium

Category: Development: Introductions and Conclusions

Getting to the Answer: Read the entire paragraph and determine the central idea. The paragraph discusses different ways artists in the Post-Impressionism era painted. Choice **(C)** reflects this summary.

40. B

Difficulty: Hard

Category: Conciseness

Getting to the Answer: Choice **(B)** joins the sentences concisely and correctly by changing the verb tense of the first sentence to make it a dependent clause.

41. A

Difficulty: Easy

Category: Agreement: Pronouns

Getting to the Answer: Read the sentence prior to the pronoun to determine whom the pronoun is referencing. The pronoun "they" refers to Paul Gauguin and Vincent van Gogh, so the pronoun needs to be plural and in the third person. Choice **(A)** is correct.

42. D

Difficulty: Hard

Category: Development: Relevance

Getting to the Answer: Read the entire paragraph to identify the central idea. Then find the answer choice that provides evidence about this idea. The paragraph concerns the Post-Impressionist period and what kinds of methods Post-Impressionists used to create their art. Choice **(D)** addresses the central idea by providing additional information about these methods.

43. B

Difficulty: Medium

Category: Agreement: Idioms

Getting to the Answer: "They're" is a contraction meaning "they are," which does not make sense in the context of the sentence. What is needed here is a possessive plural pronoun to match the antecedent "artists." Choice **(B)** is correct.

44. D

Difficulty: Hard

Category: Organization: Sentence Placement

Getting to the Answer: When deciding where to place a sentence, examine both the sentence itself and the surrounding paragraph for clues. Sentence 3 discusses getting to know artists' souls by viewing their artwork. Additionally, it begins with the transition word "Today," which suggests it must come after anything the paragraph discusses from the past. Sentence 4 refers to "these differences." Since sentence 3 does not describe any differences to which this phrase could be referring, the sentence cannot be correct where it is; eliminate (A). Sentence 5 includes a quote about "pictures of the soul" that sentence 3 invokes with its mention of artists' souls. Thus, **(D)** is correct.

Test Yourself: Writing and Language

Directions: For testlike timing, give yourself 9 minutes to answer the questions for each passage.

Questions 1–11 refer to the following passage and supplementary material.

The Brooklyn Bridge: The Eighth Wonder of the World

One of New York City's most iconic landmarks, the Brooklyn Bridge spans 5,989 feet across the East River. Connecting the boroughs of Brooklyn (Kings County) and Manhattan, this bridge was a fantastic marvel of engineering **1** <u>when it was completed in 1883, just years after the Golden Gate Bridge.</u> The Brooklyn Bridge was the longest suspension bridge of **2** <u>its time. It was dubbed</u> the "8th Wonder of the World." Its construction, **3** <u>consequently,</u> was riddled with problems from the very start.

Residents of Brooklyn had **4** <u>watched</u> for a bridge to connect them with Manhattan, as the frozen East River was **5** <u>absolutely so impossible</u> to cross during the winter. The dream would finally come to fruition when New York legislators approved John Augustus Roebling's plan for a suspension bridge over the East River. Roebling had a reputation as an accomplished designer of suspension bridges, and the Brooklyn Bridge

1. Which choice most accurately completes the sentence based on the table?

    A) NO CHANGE

    B) when it was completed in 1883, several years before the Tower Bridge in London, England, was built.

    C) when it was completed in 1883, two years after the Tower Bridge in London, England, was built.

    D) when it was completed in 1883, the same year that the Golden Gate Bridge was built.

2. Which choice most effectively combines the sentences at the underlined portion?

    A) its time, however, it was dubbed

    B) its time, and it was dubbed

    C) its time, was dubbed

    D) its time, it was dubbed

3. A) NO CHANGE

    B) as a result,

    C) for example,

    D) however,

4. A) NO CHANGE

    B) longed

    C) fought

    D) went

5. A) NO CHANGE

    B) absolutely impossible

    C) impossible

    D) so impossible

would be **6** <u>their</u> biggest feat yet, as both the suspension bridge with the longest span (1,600 feet from tower to tower) and as the first steel-cabled suspension bridge.

Roebling would never see his design completed; in fact, he would never even see construction begin. Just before construction was about to start in 1867, Roebling was the victim of **7** <u>a special</u> accident; a boat **8** <u>was smashing</u> into his foot, and he succumbed to tetanus. His son, Washington Roebling, took over the project.

9 <u>Designs for the Brooklyn Bridge included a promenade above the traffic.</u> The first task was for workers to excavate the riverbed in order to anchor the two towers of the bridge to the bedrock below. To accomplish this, bottomless wooden boxes called caissons were sunk into the depths of the river. Once inside, workers would begin the laborious task of removing mud and boulders. To get down into the caissons, workers traveled in airlocks filled with compressed air, which prevented water **10** <u>from entering, if the workers ascended</u> to the surface and left the compressed air too quickly, they would suffer from the debilitating condition known as "caisson disease," or "the bends." Over 100 workers experienced caisson disease, and many others died or were injured from construction-related accidents. The cement-filled caissons remain under the towers of the bridge today.

6. A) NO CHANGE
   B) its
   C) her
   D) his

7. A) NO CHANGE
   B) an exceptional
   C) a common
   D) a freak

8. A) NO CHANGE
   B) smashing
   C) smashed
   D) was smashed

9. Which choice most effectively establishes the central idea of the paragraph?
   A) NO CHANGE
   B) The conditions inside the caissons were so terrible that workmen could stay there only for two hours.
   C) The towers were built of limestone, granite, and cement that came from a village called Rosendale in upstate New York.
   D) The building of the bridge was a monumental and often dangerous undertaking.

10. A) NO CHANGE
    B) from entering. If the workers ascended
    C) from entering if the workers ascended
    D) from entering, since if the workers ascended

Washington Roebling himself suffered from the bends and was partially paralyzed for the rest of his life. Determined to remain part of the project now supervised by his wife, Emily, he watched the construction continue with a telescope. **11** In May, 1883, more than a dozen years after construction began, Emily Roebling was given the first ride over the completed Brooklyn Bridge. She was followed by 150,300 people on that opening day. Despite the setbacks, Manhattan and Brooklyn were finally connected.

11. Which choice provides the clearest, most specific information in the underlined sentence?

A) In 1883, many years after construction began, Emily Roebling was given a ride over the completed Brooklyn Bridge.

B) In May 1883, many years after construction began, Emily Roebling was given the first ride over the completed Brooklyn Bridge.

C) On May 24, 1883, 14 years after construction began, Emily Roebling was given the first ride over the completed Brooklyn Bridge.

D) In 1883, 14 years after construction began, Emily Roebling was given a ride over the completed Brooklyn Bridge.

Bridges of the World			
Bridge Name & Location	**Date Completed**	**Length**	**Largest Single Span**
Akashi Kaikyo Bridge, Japan	1998	12,828 feet	6,527 feet
Brooklyn Bridge, New York	1883	5,989 feet	1,595 feet
Golden Gate Bridge, San Francisco	1937	8,981 feet	4,200 feet
Tower Bridge, London	1894	880 feet	200 feet

Questions 12–22 refer to the following passage and supplementary material.

Pearl Harbor

On December 7, 1941, Japanese fighter planes attacked the American naval base at Pearl Harbor near Honolulu, Hawaii, sinking or damaging 19 ships and destroying 169 planes. More than 2,400 American soldiers, sailors, and marines died in the attack, and another 1,178 were wounded. The next day President Franklin D. Roosevelt **12** hinted the United States's entrance into World War II by asking Congress to declare war on Japan.

Japan and the United States had been in a standoff for years. In 1937, Japan had declared war on China, seeking to expand into Chinese territory and secure its import markets. The United States had responded by placing bans on Japanese exports and imposing other trade embargoes. **13** But Japan had not capitulated; fortunately, it had strengthened its expansionist aims.

Although the conflict with Japan **14** was being understood to be dangerous, the great distance across the Pacific Ocean made it seem unlikely that Japan would attack the United States. American intelligence officials thought that if Japan did attack, it would hit a European colony in the South Pacific, such as Singapore. **15** Nearly the entire Pacific Fleet was moored around Ford Island in the harbor, and hundreds of airplanes were grounded at nearby airfields. Pearl Harbor was a large, vulnerable target.

12. A) NO CHANGE
    B) signaled
    C) mimicked
    D) proved

13. A) NO CHANGE
    B) But Japan had not capitulated; rather,
    C) And Japan had not capitulated; in fact,
    D) However, Japan had not capitulated; furthermore,

14. A) NO CHANGE
    B) was understanding
    C) was understood
    D) was being and understood

15. Which choice best supports the statement made in the previous sentence?
    A) This had been true in multiple previous conflicts with other nations as well.
    B) But Japan had a history of surprising its enemies.
    C) After decades of isolationism, the American navy was impressive.
    D) Therefore, Pearl Harbor was not heavily defended.

The Japanese plan was [16] simple; destroy the Pacific Fleet. That way, the Americans would not be able to fight back as Japan's armed forces spread across the South Pacific. [17] On December 7, after they had been making plans and practicing for months and months, the Japanese launched their attack.

The attack began around [18] 8:00 o'clock a.m., with Japanese planes dropping bombs and raining bullets. Torpedoes and huge [19] bombs, some weighing over a ton and a half, destroyed the battleships USS *Arizona* and USS *Oklahoma*, each of which had hundreds of sailors trapped inside. In all, eight battleships [20] put up with heavy damage. Dry docks and airfields were likewise destroyed.

16. A) NO CHANGE
     B) simple: destroy
     C) simple destroy
     D) simple, destroy

17. Which choice best maintains the writer's tone?
     A) NO CHANGE
     B) On December 7, after months of planning and practice, the Japanese launched their attack.
     C) On December 7, after they had for months and months been practicing, the Japanese launched their attack.
     D) On December 7, after months of planning as well as a voluminous amount of practice, the Japanese launched their attack.

18. A) NO CHANGE
     B) 8:00 o'clock a.m. in the morning
     C) 8:00 a.m. in the morning
     D) 8:00 a.m.

19. A) NO CHANGE
     B) bombs, some weighed
     C) bombs, some were weighing
     D) bombs, some weigh

20. A) NO CHANGE
     B) lost
     C) sustained
     D) tolerated

21 The Pearl Harbor attack united the American people around the long-contentious issue of Japanese aggression: there was widespread determination to go to war. In a December 8 radio address, President Roosevelt said, "I believe I interpret the will of the Congress and of the people when I assert that we will not only defend ourselves to the uttermost, but will make very certain that this form of treachery shall never endanger us again." In a sense, the Japanese plan had backfired. Japanese hopes had been to get trade sanctions lifted; instead, the U.S. entered a war that would **22** end in Japan's defeat by a foreign power.

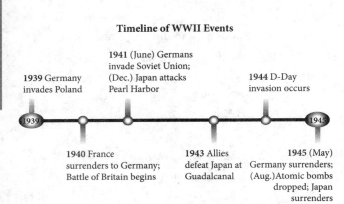

Timeline of WWII Events

1939 Germany invades Poland

1940 France surrenders to Germany; Battle of Britain begins

1941 (June) Germans invade Soviet Union; (Dec.) Japan attacks Pearl Harbor

1943 Allies defeat Japan at Guadalcanal

1944 D-Day invasion occurs

1945 (May) Germany surrenders; (Aug.)Atomic bombs dropped; Japan surrenders

21. Which choice most effectively establishes the main topic of this paragraph?

A) NO CHANGE

B) The United States had been very reluctant to go to war; in fact, it had long been considered an isolationist nation.

C) President Roosevelt had been an extremely popular president so far; he had implemented new programs to pull the United States out of the Great Depression.

D) Japan and the United States might have avoided war if their leaders had managed to come to a diplomatic solution; instead, the conflict had simmered for years.

22. Which choice completes the sentence most accurately, based on the timeline?

A) NO CHANGE

B) end two years later after a long and brutal battle on Guadalcanal.

C) prove to be Japan's last military battle for four long years.

D) cost it millions of lives before Germany's surrender allowed an American victory.

Questions 23–33 refer to the following passage.

Musical Enjoyment: Better in Numbers?

Music is many things to many [23] people: a mode of expression, an escape, or a way to understand life experiences. Although its prominence in global culture has stayed the same, music has changed considerably since its prehistoric invention. [24] Music has evolved from a primarily group-enjoyed art form into one consumed mostly on an individual basis.

Researchers have no way of knowing who first invented music, [25] but educated guesses and surmises can be made about the purposes it served. It is hypothesized that in the Prehistoric Era, early humans used sounds like hand clapping and foot stomping to create rhythmic repetition. [26] For instance, art in both Stone Age cave paintings and later Persian cave paintings shows examples of people using handmade instruments to create music in a group setting. The sounds produced were an early form of communication. The use of music as a tool opened early humans [27] up to one another. Advancing social bonding even in an age before common languages.

23. A) NO CHANGE
    B) people, a mode of expression, an escape, or a way
    C) people; a mode of expression; an escape; or a way
    D) people: a mode of expression or an escape or a way

24. A) NO CHANGE
    B) Music has evolved from an art form that has been primarily enjoyed by groups
    C) Music has evolved from a group art form
    D) Primarily, music as a group art form has evolved

25. A) NO CHANGE
    B) but they can make educated guesses about the purposes it served
    C) but educated guesses and surmises of the purposes it served have been made
    D) but educated guesses or surmises are made about the purposes it served

26. A) NO CHANGE
    B) Similarly
    C) For example
    D) In other words

27. Which choice most effectively combines the sentences at the underlined portion?
    A) up to one another while advancing
    B) up to one another; this advanced
    C) up to one another, advancing
    D) up to one another, a tool advancing

[28] In ancient Egypt, musicians were appointed to play for specific gods. In addition to enhancing religious ceremonies, music was used in the royal court. Gifted musicians were hired to honor the pharaoh and impress guests of the royal family. In American history, music has been used as a vehicle for storytelling. At the time of the Underground Railroad, music was used to deliver messages to groups of people trying to escape slavery. Directions were embedded [29] in lyrics that were well-known to many. Although these examples are very different, they highlight how music was used to encourage social bonding.

[1] With the [30] advent of headphones in 1910, music was changed from an inherently social experience to a personal one. [2] Based on Thomas Edison's discovery of sound created by electrical signals, Nathaniel Baldwin created the first headset that could amplify sound. [3] This invention has been greatly improved upon since. [4] Instead of music being primarily used in group settings, it became a highly individual form of entertainment. [5] While this is seen as a positive departure, studies link the use of headphones to feelings of isolation and decreased personal satisfaction. [6] With music becoming more portable than ever, headphones have enabled people to listen to music in almost any situation, including on their way to work, at the workplace, and at home while their families listen to their own choice of music. [31]

28. Which choice creates the most cohesive transition from the previous paragraph?

A) More recent examples show music primarily becoming a source of entertainment.

B) Music became a notable social bonding tool among wealthy and aristocratic circles.

C) Music from Egypt traveled to America and helped convey the importance of social bonding.

D) Further examples throughout history show the development of music as a social bonding tool.

29. Which choice provides the clearest, most precise information to support the beginning of the sentence?

A) NO CHANGE

B) in lyrics that included references to famous abolitionists

C) in popular lyrics, hiding helpful instructions in plain sight

D) in lyrics that were typically banned by plantation owners

30. A) NO CHANGE

B) enhancement

C) prevalence

D) prohibition

31. To make this paragraph most logical, sentence 5 should be placed

A) where it is now.

B) after sentence 2.

C) before sentence 4.

D) after sentence 6.

[32] <u>Psychologists' and sociologists'</u> hypothesize that the shift in music from a social to an individual enjoyment contributes to a high number of people reporting feelings of loneliness in recent studies. While the long-term psychological effects of this shift will take time to analyze, it is already apparent that humans are less connected in their enjoyment of something we have shared throughout history. [33]

32. A) NO CHANGE
   B) Psychologists and sociologists'
   C) Psychologist's and sociologist's
   D) Psychologists and sociologists

33. Which piece of information, if added to this paragraph, would best support the author's claims?
   A) The number of people reporting feelings of loneliness in recent studies
   B) Which psychologists and sociologists are making these claims
   C) The specific differences in the ways humans have shared music over time
   D) Which long-term psychological effects may be related to using headphones

Questions 34–44 refer to the following passage and supplementary material.

Tesla Lights Up the World

[1] Nikola Tesla, born in 1856, was an Austrian electrical engineer who worked for a telegraph company in Budapest before immigrating to the United States to join Thomas Edison's company in New York. [2] The two engineers did not work well together, and Tesla moved on to work with George Westinghouse, another engineer and inventor, at the Westinghouse Electric & Manufacturing Company in 1885. [3] **34** During his time there, Tesla invented the alternating current system, what we know in our homes as AC power. [4] Several years later, Tesla made the first successful wireless energy transfer. [5] Reportedly, Tesla slept little and often occupied himself with games, such as chess and billiards. **35**

[1] The Westinghouse Electric Company was quick to put Tesla's invention to work. [2] They **36** implemented the use of alternating current during the World Colombian Exposition in **37** 1897, with fantastic results. [3] It was more efficient than Edison's earlier energy transfer system, the direct current (DC) system, as well as more effective. [4] Edison knew that the DC system was difficult to transmit over long distances. [5] He didn't, however, believe that Tesla's AC system was a credible threat to the dominance he and his company held over the electrical market of the time

34. Which sentence has the best flow of ideas?
   A) NO CHANGE
   B) Tesla, while there, invented the AC power system we know in our homes, more formally called the alternating current system.
   C) Tesla invented the alternating current system during his time there, also known in our homes as AC power.
   D) During his time there, the alternating current system, or what we know in our homes as AC power, was invented by him.

35. For the sake of the logic and cohesion of the paragraph, sentence 5 should be
   A) placed where it is now.
   B) placed after sentence 1.
   C) placed before sentence 4.
   D) DELETED from the paragraph.

36. A) NO CHANGE
   B) encouraged
   C) invoked
   D) developed

37. Which choice completes the sentence with accurate data based on the timeline at the end of the passage?
   A) NO CHANGE
   B) 1882,
   C) 1890,
   D) 1893,

because of his invention of the light bulb. [6] **38** <u>But it is Tesla's system that moves power from a main grid across long distances.</u>

[1] Tesla went on to develop the technology that is now used in X-rays, as well as radio and remote controls. [2] Some of his inventions even worked together, expanding his influence on the world and history. [3] Tesla paired his AC system with his understanding of physics to invent an electric motor. [4] Developing the AC system was only the beginning for Tesla, though. [5] To do so, he used his knowledge of magnetism to create a closed system in which a motor could turn without disruption or the use of human labor. [6] The motor generated a stable current that had been lacking in earlier attempts to transition industry to AC power. [7] With Tesla's motor, though, AC power systems could be broadly used in manufacturing and beyond. **39**

Tesla's inventions are not only a part of our daily lives, they continue **40** <u>to be expanded upon to create</u> new advances in science and technology. **41** Tesla's approach to energy transmission, as well as his invention of the radio, including antenna and other recognizable aspects, has allowed leaps and bounds to be made in wireless communications, such as radio broadcasting. Edison may have invented the light bulb,

38. Which choice most effectively concludes the paragraph?

A) NO CHANGE

B) However, bulbs alone do not light our homes; it is Tesla's system that moves power from one grid across long distances to the fixtures we use every day.

C) Later, Tesla developed a system that allows us to use light bulbs every day.

D) We now use Edison's bulbs every day; we can thank Tesla for inventing the system that moves power from one grid across distances to those fixtures.

39. For the sake of the logic and coherence of the paragraph, sentence 4 should be placed

A) where it is now.

B) before sentence 1.

C) after sentence 6.

D) after sentence 7.

40. A) NO CHANGE

B) to be developed into

C) to inspire scientists to make

D) to lead to

41. Which supporting detail is least essential to the following sentence and should be deleted?

A) That Tesla invented the radio

B) That Tesla's invention of the radio included the "antenna and other recognizable aspects"

C) That Tesla's invention of the radio allowed further innovation in wireless communications

D) That radio broadcasting is a kind of wireless communication

[42] but Tesla was an inventor bent on bringing electricity to the people, seeking no fame or fortune. The reach of his technology goes even as far as the mobile phone. Although long gone, Tesla remains [43] a settler on the edge of miraculous invention. [44]

Tesla's Inventions

1882 ➤ Rotating Magnetic Field—A rotating field that enabled alternating current to power a motor.

1883 ➤ AC Motor—The rotating magnetic field was put into practice in this motor, which spun without a mechanical aid.

1890 ➤ Tesla Coil—A coil that enables transformers to produce extremely high voltages.

1893 ➤ Tesla and Westinghouse display their AC current systems at the Columbian Exposition in Chicago.

1897 ➤ Radio—Tesla invented the radio, including antennae, tuners, and other familiar components.

42. A)   NO CHANGE

B)   but Tesla, seeking no fame or fortune, was an inventor bent on bringing electricity to the people.

C)   but seeking no fame or fortune, Tesla was an inventor bent on bringing electricity to the people.

D)   but Tesla was an inventor bent on seeking no fame or fortune, bringing electricity to the people.

43. A)   NO CHANGE

B)   an guide

C)   a champion

D)   a pioneer

44. Based on the timeline, "In 1883," would be most appropriately added to the beginning of which of the following sentences?

A)   Paragraph 1, sentence 2

B)   Paragraph 2, sentence 1

C)   Paragraph 3, sentence 3

D)   Paragraph 4, sentence 3

Questions 45–55 refer to the following passage.

The Power of the PA

[45] Today, physician assistants are vital members of any health care system, but it hasn't always been that way. In 1960s America, there were not enough doctors to meet the primary care needs of patients nationwide. Due to the shortage, and in hopes of improving health care and its accessibility, educators sought to establish alternatives to medical school that would effectively equip other health care workers to share more of the physicians' workload. Their project altered health care history: the physician assistant (PA) was born. In 1967, the first PA program [46] launched at Duke University, notable for its education degrees and sports teams. The coming decades saw the field develop into what is considered today to be one of the most desirable and quickly growing careers in the country.

[1] Becoming a PA is simpler than becoming a physician, which usually takes over nine years of higher education and training. [2] Those seeking acceptance into PA programs typically study science or health as undergraduates. [3] Once practicing, PAs are required to maintain proficiency through continued education and a recertification exam every ten years. [4] They also usually [47] obtain some health-related work experience before applying. [5] [48] Once accepted to a program, most students will be in their programs for about twenty-seven months. [6] Schooling involves both classroom and field study, and students undergo hundreds of hours in clinical training rotations in order to gain a breadth of supervised experience.

[7] Today there are over one hundred and seventy

45. Which choice most effectively introduces the main topic of the paragraph?
  A) NO CHANGE
  B) For many years, doctors and educators struggled to find a role for the high number of incoming medical students.
  C) The difference between physician assistants and nurse practitioners was often hard to quantify, but then came a shift in health care needs.
  D) Physician assistants had long played a vital role in the medical field, but the PA career didn't become popular until the mid-20th century.

46. A) NO CHANGE
  B) launched at Duke University, noted for its education degrees.
  C) launched at the renowned Duke University.
  D) launched at Duke University.

47. A) NO CHANGE
  B) accrue
  C) perceive
  D) formulate

48. A) NO CHANGE
  B) Once accepted
  C) Once they begin
  D) Once programs accept them

accredited PA programs, most of which award masters degrees to graduates. [8] After graduation, **49** graduates must complete one final step: passing the national licensure exam. **50**

While physicians can work **51** anonymously, PAs always work under the supervision of physicians. But like nurse practitioners, another primary care alternative that emerged in the 1960s, PAs can do much of the work commonly expected of a physician. PAs are trained and qualified to meet with, examine, treat, diagnose, and counsel patients. They can prescribe medication, interpret lab data, and help physicians with surgical procedures. **52** In many ways, PAs lighten the workload for physicians on their teams. This enables clinics, hospitals, and other health care systems to run more efficiently and meet patient needs with greater accuracy and timeliness.

Physician assistants enjoy various options in terms of where they can practice. Almost every field of medicine has positions for those PAs who specialize accordingly. Also, depending on the needs of the physicians **53** under which PAs work, as well as the particular limitations that might be imposed by a specific state, the requirements and responsibilities of the job can vary.

49. A) NO CHANGE
    B) physicians
    C) PAs
    D) candidates

50. To make this paragraph most logical, sentence 3 should be placed
    A) where it is now.
    B) after sentence 5.
    C) after sentence 6.
    D) after sentence 8.

51. A) NO CHANGE
    B) defensively
    C) autonomously
    D) fundamentally

52. A) NO CHANGE
    B) On the other hand
    C) For example
    D) First of all

53. A) NO CHANGE
    B) where PAs work
    C) under whom PAs work
    D) who work under PAs

The past half-century saw the career of physician assistant rise from nascence to become a highly sought-after and still rapidly growing addition to American health care. Projections indicate that within the next decade, the number of employed PAs should increase significantly. **54** <u>I believe PAs are an ever-increasing presence</u> in health care and a powerful influence on the medical world for the better. **55**

54. A) NO CHANGE

    B) PAs are an ever-increasing presence

    C) Doctors believe PAs are an ever-increasing presence

    D) You can believe that PAs are an ever-increasing presence

55. Which detail, if added to the paragraph, would best support the writer's claims?

    A) The number of PAs hired over the last half-century

    B) The expected PA-to-patient ratio over the next decade

    C) The number of PA positions compared to the number of nurse practitioner positions

    D) The specific rate at which PAs will be employed over the next decade

Writing & Lang

Questions 56–66 refer to the following passage and supplementary material.

Putting Microbes to Work for Us

[1]

The decline of the world's supply of fossil fuels is a growing concern. With increasingly more countries becoming dependent on fossil fuels for transportation, heating homes, and powering engines, the [56] failing of this finite resource has the potential to cause major disruption around the globe. To combat this issue, scientists are researching alternative energy sources. [57] Used to produce biofuel are living things or the waste of living things, and biofuel is one such alternative.

[2]

[58] Until recently, the primary focus of biofuel development has been ethanol. Ethanol is created from plants such as corn, sugarcane, soybeans, and rice. While ethanol is a viable energy [59] source, its use has been met with several challenges. These have limited its development as a quality alternative to traditional fossil fuels. One roadblock is that ethanol is expensive to produce. The plant must be first broken down into sugars and then fermented by microbes into a final useable product. It cannot be distributed by pipeline because it can pick up impurities along the way, so it must be transported by truck, train, or barge. Additionally, very large areas of cropland must be dedicated to growing these plants in order to produce enough ethanol to be designated for commercial use. This raises ethical questions because it means farmers are growing food sources earmarked solely for fuel when

56. A) NO CHANGE
    B) wilting
    C) depletion
    D) obstruction

57. A) NO CHANGE
    B) Biofuel is produced from living things or the waste of living things, and is one such alternative.
    C) Living things or the waste of living things are used in producing the one such alternative known as biofuel.
    D) One such alternative is biofuel, produced from living things or from the waste of living things.

58. Which choice most effectively introduces the central idea of this paragraph?
    A) NO CHANGE
    B) A variety of food crops can be used to produce ethanol.
    C) Many farmers have begun to grow corn for ethanol rather than food.
    D) Converting corn to ethanol is a complicated and expensive process.

59. A) NO CHANGE
    B) source, its'
    C) source, it's
    D) source, it is

there are many people around the world in [60] <u>horrible</u> need of food. [61] <u>In recent years, the price of corn has increased as the percentage of corn produced for ethanol has stayed the same.</u> In addition, countries such as Brazil are decimating rain forests in order to grow sugarcane for ethanol production.

[3]

Once ethanol is produced, it is limited in its use as a commercial fuel. Therefore, it must be heavily refined and then blended with petroleum-based fuels in order to be used. [62] <u>Standard internal combustion engines, such as those in cars, cannot run on ethanol alone.</u>

[4]

The fossil fuels we rely on today for energy are finite. By researching alternate energy resources, including fuel produced by bacteria and other microbes, we can become less dependent on nonrenewable sources. [63]

60. A) NO CHANGE
    B) dire
    C) grim
    D) grieving

61. Which choice best supports the paragraph with relevant and accurate information based on the graph?
    A) NO CHANGE
    B) In recent years, the price of corn has stayed the same as the percentage of corn produced for ethanol has decreased.
    C) In recent years, the price of corn has increased as the percentage of corn produced for ethanol has increased.
    D) In recent years, the price of corn has decreased as the percentage of corn produced for ethanol has increased.

62. Which choice best supports the central idea of the paragraph?
    A) NO CHANGE
    B) Most fuel sold for automobiles in the United States contains a blend of ethanol and gasoline.
    C) Ethanol has been used as an energy source in the United States for over 200 years.
    D) Although most often used to power automobiles, ethanol can also be used to power other engines.

63. To make the passage most logical, paragraph 4 should be placed
    A) where it is now.
    B) before paragraph 2.
    C) before paragraph 3.
    D) after paragraph 5.

[5]

Researchers in the United Kingdom **64** had been developing a new kind of biofuel that addresses several of the issues hindering ethanol use. They have extracted genes from different species of bacteria and inserted them into *E. coli* bacteria. Once this process is complete, the *E. coli* can then perform the same metabolic functions as the donor **65** bacteria, this enables it to absorb fat molecules, convert these molecules to hydrocarbons, and then excrete the hydrocarbons as a waste product. The hydrocarbons produced by the genetically modified *E. coli* are the same as those found in commercial fossil fuels. **66** Finally, the newly created hydrocarbon molecules are interchangeable with the hydrocarbon molecules found in petroleum-based diesel fuels. This allows them to be used in a typical diesel engine, without any blending or refining.

64. A) NO CHANGE
    B) have developed
    C) had developed
    D) were developing

65. A) NO CHANGE
    B) bacteria; and this enables it
    C) bacteria. This enables it
    D) bacteria this enables it

66. A) NO CHANGE
    B) Therefore,
    C) For example,
    D) Also,

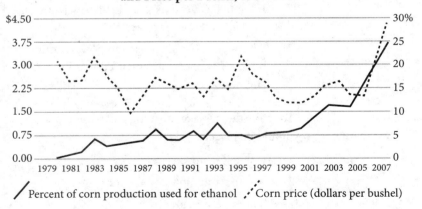

Percentage of U.S. Corn Used to Produce Ethanol and Price per Bushel, 1980–2007

Percent of corn production used for ethanol

Corn price (dollars per bushel)

Adapted from United States Department of Agriculture–Economic Research Service and United States Energy Information Administration, "Percentage of U.S. Corn Used to Produce Ethanol and Price per Bushel, 1980–2007."

Questions 67–77 refer to the following passage and supplementary material.

The Pony Express: Not a Tame Ride

The 19th century saw the Civil War, the California Gold Rush, and the migration of thousands of people to the West along the Oregon Trail. With these events came **67** the really great and strong need for communication between the original colonies and the new state of California. **68** William H. Russell, Alexander Majors, and William B. Waddell brought about the solution to this need by creating Leavenworth & Pike's Peak Express Company, which later became known as the Pony Express.

The Pony Express was a system of riders that ran 2,000 miles from St. Joseph, Missouri, to Sacramento, California. Riders, who carried mail in leather satchels, changed every 75 to 100 miles. They changed horses every 10 to 15 miles. **69** When the Pony Express was at its largest, it had a lot of riders who were paid for their services.

Riders changed horses or took a short break at relay posts, or stations: small, simple cabins, with dirt floors and a few stalls for the horses. Riders could get small meals at the **70** stations, these meals usually consisted of dried fruit, cured meats, pickles, coffee, and cornmeal. At some bigger stations, known as "home stations," riders were able to enjoy a more relaxed meal, perhaps chat with other riders, and get some sleep.

The relay posts were also a source of employment. Each housed a station keeper who was responsible for having horses saddled and ready when a rider arrived,

67. A) NO CHANGE
    B) the very strong and real need
    C) the need
    D) the strong and real need

68. A) NO CHANGE
    B) William H. Russell Alexander Majors and William B. Waddell
    C) William H. Russell Alexander Majors, and William B. Waddell
    D) William H. Russell, Alexander Majors, and, William B. Waddell

69. Which choice provides the most specific information to support the main idea of the paragraph?
    A) When the Pony Express was at its largest, it was a very glamorous job.
    B) At its largest, the Pony Express had over 150 riders of all ages and they were paid.
    C) When the Pony Express peaked, it employed a lot of riders and the youngest one was named Bronco Charlie Miller.
    D) At its peak, the Pony Express employed over 180 riders who ranged in age from 11 to 50 years old and earned $50 a month.

70. A) NO CHANGE
    B) stations these meals usually consisted
    C) stations. These meals usually consisted
    D) stations yet these meals usually consisted

as well as for logging **71** accurate records of arrival and departure times. The job of a station keeper was not an easy one. The **72** stations were located in remote areas, had little access to resources, and were being unprotected from attacks by Native Americans.

73 The riders' routes were fraught with danger of many kinds. In addition to being susceptible to ambush by Native Americans, riders often rode through rough, unfamiliar terrain and were exposed to harsh weather. **74** As a result of these challenges, only one mail delivery was lost during the Pony Express's 19 months of operation.

Shortly after the first riders of the Pony Express set out on April 3, 1860, Congress approved a bill **75** funding the construction of a transcontinental telegraph line on March 5, 1860. The result of this bill was the creation of the Overland Telegraph Company of California and the Pacific Telegraph Company of Nevada. Once it was fully **76** invented on October 24, 1861, the Pony Express was no longer needed. Two days later, the Pony Express announced its closure.

71. A) NO CHANGE
    B) boring
    C) sorrowful
    D) agreeable

72. A) NO CHANGE
    B) stations were located in remote areas, had little access to resources, and were unprotected
    C) stations were being located in remote areas, had little access to resources, and were unprotected
    D) stations were located in remote areas, having little access to resources, and were unprotected

73. Which choice most effectively establishes the main topic of the paragraph?
    A) NO CHANGE
    B) The Pony Express helped tie California with the rest of the country.
    C) The Pony Express was not successful financially.
    D) Some of the riders died while trying to deliver the mail.

74. A) NO CHANGE
    B) Despite
    C) However
    D) For instance

75. Which choice completes the sentence with accurate data based on the timeline?
    A) NO CHANGE
    B) funding the construction of a transcontinental telegraph line on June 8, 1860.
    C) funding the construction of a transcontinental telegraph line on October 24, 1861.
    D) funding the construction of a transcontinental telegraph line on January, 1860.

76. A) NO CHANGE
    B) breached
    C) operational
    D) contrasted

Although its existence was a short one, the Pony Express played an important role in the development of **77** the Pacific Coast. It remains an icon of the Wild West.

History of the Pony Express

January–March 1860 ➤	Russell, Majors, and Waddell establish Pony Express mail service.
April 3, 1860 ➤	First riders leave St. Joseph, Missouri, and Sacramento, California.
June 8, 1860 ➤	Congress authorizes building of transcontinental telegraph line.
October 24, 1861 ➤	East and West coasts connected by telegraph line.
October 26, 1861 ➤	Pony Express discontinued.

77. Which choice most effectively combines the sentences at the underlined portion?

A) the Pacific Coast, since it remains

B) the Pacific Coast, however, it remains

C) the Pacific Coast, that it remains

D) the Pacific Coast and remains

Writing & Lang

K   855

Answers and Explanations

1. B

Difficulty: Medium

Category: Graphs

Getting to the Answer: The table gives specific information about various bridges. Interpret the information to choose the correct answer choice. Choice **(B)** accurately reflects the information in the table since the Tower Bridge was not built until 1894.

2. B

Difficulty: Medium

Category: Sentence Structure: The Basics

Getting to the Answer: Watch out for answer choices that may have incorrect transition words or be incorrect in usage or in punctuation. Choice **(B)** joins the sentences concisely and correctly by using the conjunction "and" to connect the two complete ideas.

3. D

Difficulty: Medium

Category: Organization: Transitions

Getting to the Answer: Study the relationship between this sentence and the previous one to determine which transition word would work logically. The previous sentence states that the bridge was hailed as a wonder. This sentence states that its construction had many problems. These ideas conflict with one another, so a contrast transition is needed. Choice **(D)** is correct.

4. B

Difficulty: Easy

Category: Development: Word Choice

Getting to the Answer: The context of the sentence suggests that the bridge was something that people very much wanted because of the difficulty of crossing the river. Choice **(B)**, "longed," means wanted intensely and is correct.

5. C

Difficulty: Easy

Category: Conciseness

Getting to the Answer: Watch out for answer choices like (A), which are redundant. Be as direct and simple as possible. Additional adjectives do not add more meaning to this content. Choice **(C)** is the most concise and effective way of stating the information in the passage and is therefore correct.

6. D

Difficulty: Easy

Category: Agreement: Pronouns

Getting to the Answer: Reread the sentence to identify the antecedent for the underlined pronoun and determine if the two agree. The antecedent in this sentence is "Roebling," which calls for a singular masculine possessive pronoun. Choice **(D)** is correct.

7. D

Difficulty: Medium

Category: Development: Word Choice

Getting to the Answer: Consider the connotations of each word. Substitute each word choice back into the sentence to see how well it fits the context. Choice **(D)** fits with the context of the sentence, which suggests that such accidents do not happen often. While "special" in (A) and "exceptional" in (B) can indicate uniqueness, they are too positive. Choice **(D)** is correct.

8. C

Difficulty: Medium

Category: Agreement: Verbs

Getting to the Answer: Verb tenses in a sentence should usually match, unless context in the sentence shows that different actions take place in different time periods. However, here all actions are in the past, so the underlined verb should match "succumbed," which appears later in the sentence. Choice **(C)** is correct.

9. D

Difficulty: Hard

Category: Development: Introductions and Conclusions

Getting to the Answer: To find the central idea of a paragraph, identify important details and summarize them. Then, find the choice that is the closest to your summary. The paragraph primarily discusses the hardships faced by workers building the bridge. Choice **(D)** most accurately summarizes the central idea of the paragraph.

10. B

Difficulty: Medium

Category: Sentence Structure: The Basics

Getting to the Answer: The underlined portion includes two complete sentences incorrectly joined with a comma: a run-on. Choice **(B)** divides the two thoughts into two complete sentences by adding a period and capitalizing the first word of the second sentence and is therefore correct. Simply removing the comma, as in (C), does not fix the error. Adding a subordinating conjunction, as in (D), does correct the run-on, but "since" is incorrect because it misrepresents the relationship between the sentences.

11. C

Difficulty: Hard

Category: Development: Relevance

Getting to the Answer: To find the correct answer, look for the sentence that does not exclude any necessary details from the underlined portion. Choice **(C)** correctly maintains the author's inclusion of various details about when the bridge was completed and the significance of Emily's ride.

12. B

Difficulty: Hard

Category: Development: Word Choice

Getting to the Answer: Consider the specific action being described by this word in order to determine which answer choice best conveys the writer's meaning. The paragraph states that President Roosevelt asked Congress to declare war, an action that directly put in motion "the United States' entrance into World War II." Choice **(B)**, "signaled," most effectively conveys this relationship and is therefore correct.

13. B

Difficulty: Medium

Category: Organization: Transitions

Getting to the Answer: Define the relationship between these two clauses, as well as between this and the previous sentence. A semicolon links two complete but separate independent clauses within a sentence. The sentence states two things: "Japan had not capitulated," and "it had strengthened its expansionist aims." The relationship is one of opposites. Both (B) and (C) link the two parts of the sentence in the correct way. Only **(B)**, however, maintains the correct relationship with the previous sentence.

14. C

Difficulty: Medium

Category: Agreement: Verbs

Getting to the Answer: When a verb is underlined, check to make sure it agrees with its subject and with other verbs in the sentence or paragraph. In this case, a past tense verb is needed. The subject of the verb is "the conflict with Japan." The conflict cannot understand anything; people in the United States are understanding it. Therefore, the verb must be in passive voice. Only **(C)** properly constructs the past-tense passive verb form and is correct.

15. D

Difficulty: Hard

Category: Development: Relevance

Getting to the Answer: Before reading the answer choices, think of a sentence that would make sentence 2 more credible if inserted here. Sentence 2 states that "American intelligence officials" had a theory about Japan's behavior. Therefore, the correct sentence will strengthen this idea. Choice **(D)** explains that as a consequence of America's wrong ideas about Japan, it had not bothered to defend Pearl Harbor well. This explanation supports the assertion made in sentence 2.

16. B

Difficulty: Medium

Category: Sentence Structure: Commas, Dashes, and Colons

Getting to the Answer: When punctuation is underlined, make sure that it is used correctly. A semicolon is usually used to join two independent clauses. However, here, the first part of the sentence introduces the second part, which is not a complete thought without it. The correct punctuation to use in this situation is a colon or a dash. Choice **(B)** is correct.

17. B

Difficulty: Medium

Category: Development: Relevance

Getting to the Answer: Identify the overall purpose and tone of the paragraph. The correct answer will convey the information needed to make the sentence effective without being excessively informal. In this sentence, Japan both plans and practices for months. These two ideas can be combined without changing the paragraph's informative tone. Choice **(B)** communicates the ideas of the sentence in the most elegant and neutral way, and it is therefore correct.

18. D

Difficulty: Medium

Category: Conciseness

Getting to the Answer: As written, the underlined text contains redundant information. "8:00" means 8 o'clock, so "o'clock" is unnecessary. Choice **(D)** successfully communicates the time of day without being redundant.

19. A

Difficulty: Medium

Category: Agreement: Modifiers

Getting to the Answer: This sentence is correct as written. The phrase "some weighing over a ton and a half" modifies the word "bombs." A modifying phrase should not be able to stand on its own as a complete sentence to avoid creating a run-on. The *-ing* form "weighing" achieves this goal. Choice **(A)** is correct.

20. C

Difficulty: Hard

Category: Development: Word Choice

Getting to the Answer: Read around the underlined word to find clues to its meaning. Then, pick the answer that offers the clearest meaning. In this context, military equipment is typically described using the expression "sustained damage." While the other choices may make sense grammatically, choice **(C)** most effectively conveys the writer's meaning.

21. A

Difficulty: Hard

Category: Development: Introductions and Conclusions

Getting to the Answer: Describe the purpose of this paragraph in your own words before looking at the answer choices. The rest of the paragraph describes how Japan's attack had not meant to provoke war but resulted in the United States entering the war. Choice **(A)** effectively introduces this topic and sets up the next sentence, in which Roosevelt makes clear that the United States is willing to go to war with Japan.

22. A

Difficulty: Easy

Category: Graphs

Getting to the Answer: Be careful not to bring in outside knowledge. The correct answer choice will be explicitly supported by information in the timeline. The timeline presents a group of historical events, only one of which is reflected in the answer choices. Other choices may or may not be true, but only the sentence as currently written draws its facts from the timeline. Choice **(A)** is correct.

23. A

Difficulty: Easy

Category: Sentence Structure: Commas, Dashes, and Colons

Getting to the Answer: Examine each answer choice, and determine which presents the list in a grammatically correct manner with proper punctuation. The list is presented correctly as is, beginning with a colon and featuring the three items separated with commas with no additional information about the topic presented after the listed items. Choice **(A)** is correct.

24. C

Difficulty: Medium

Category: Conciseness

Getting to the Answer: Reread the sentence and select the answer choice that creates the most concise sentence. Minimize wordiness and awkward word combinations to ensure clarity. Choice **(C)** is correct as it creates the most concise sentence by removing unnecessary and awkward word choices while retaining the meaning of the sentence.

25. B

Difficulty: Hard

Category: Conciseness

Getting to the Answer: The phrase "guesses and surmises" is redundant: surmises are the same thing as guesses. The correct answer will remove one of these words. Choice **(B)** is the only choice that does so.

26. B

Difficulty: Medium

Category: Organization: Transitions

Getting to the Answer: Study the surrounding sentences for context clues to determine which of the answer choices creates a logical flow of ideas. The preceding sentence discusses early humans using hands and feet to create music, and the following sentence discusses humans using tools to create music. The progression of ideas is a comparison of shared intentions and traits, so "Similarly," or choice **(B)**, is correct.

27. C

Difficulty: Medium

Category: Conciseness

Getting to the Answer: When determining how best to combine two sentences, first read them to determine their relationship. The second sentence is currently a fragment, a verb phrase that expands on a phenomenon described in the first sentence. The most effective way to combine the two is to simply connect them with a comma. Choice **(C)** is correct. Although all the choices correct the fragment and combine the sentences, (A), (B), and (D) do so with extra words and sometimes distort the relationship between the ideas.

28. D

Difficulty: Medium

Category: Organization: Transitions

Getting to the Answer: Assess the central idea of both paragraphs and determine which answer choice creates an effective and logical transition from the previous idea while summarizing the next. The passage states music has affected all global cultures, and the noted paragraph explores two more examples showing how music is a social bonding tool. The correct answer, **(D)**, is the only answer that creates a cohesive, logical transition while not limiting the number of cultures affected by music.

29. C

Difficulty: Hard

Category: Development: Revising Text

Getting to the Answer: Reread the sentence and select the answer choice that clearly conveys the author's full meaning. Sometimes adding a detail or two can improve a sentence and strengthen an author's claims. The author claims that directions for escape were embedded in well-known lyrics, implying that some people listening to the music may not have discovered the lyrics' true meaning. Choice **(C)** is correct, as it makes this statement clear and direct for the reader and strengthens the author's claim in a concise manner.

30. A

Difficulty: Medium

Category: Development: Word Choice

Getting to the Answer: Review the rest of the sentence. Look for context clues that can help you determine which answer choice makes the most sense based on the information provided. The sentence states that as of 1910, headphones created a shift in how we listen to music, implying that headphones are a relatively new invention. Since "advent" is the only word meaning the headphones first appeared at a specific point in time, **(A)** is correct.

31. D

Difficulty: Medium

Category: Organization: Sentence Placement

Getting to the Answer: When determining where to place a sentence, read the sentence itself and the surrounding paragraph for clues. Sentence 5 presents a contrast: something viewed as positive leads into negative effects. Thus, this sentence must serve as a transition between ideas. Choice **(D)** is correct because this sentence creates a smooth transition from the positive outcome of greater freedom in listening to music into the negative consequence of isolation discussed in the next paragraph.

32. D

Difficulty: Easy

Category: Agreement: Modifiers

Getting to the Answer: The placement or lack of apostrophes can alter a noun's possessive meaning. Read the entire sentence to understand the author's intention. Which answer choice uses the correct punctuation to convey this idea? The nouns "Psychologists and sociologists" are not in possession of anything in this circumstance. Choice **(D)** correctly reflects this.

33. A

Difficulty: Medium

Category: Development: Relevance

Getting to the Answer: Review the paragraph to assess areas in which the author may have left out facts or may have provided only partial information. Then, determine which answer choice will have the greatest benefit to the reader. The author specifically mentions "recent studies" but does not cite any figures. Doing so will strengthen the importance of these studies, thus **(A)** is correct.

34. A

Difficulty: Hard

Category: Organization: Transitions

Getting to the Answer: The correct answer will flow smoothly from the preceding sentence. Choices (B) and (C) move the opening transition "During his time there" farther back in the sentence, making the progression of ideas less clear. While (D) does maintain the opening

transition phrase, it introduces a modifier error because the introductory phrase "During his time there" no longer properly modifies the subject of the sentence. Choice **(A)** is correct because the sentence begins, "During his time there," smoothly transitioning from the previous sentence and providing context for the rest of the sentence, without introducing any other errors.

35. D

Difficulty: Easy

Category: Development: Revising Text

Getting to the Answer: In order to determine what to do with a sentence, examine the content of the sentence to see how it fits with the content of the paragraph. The paragraph introduces Tesla and his professional activities and accomplishments. Sentence 5 provides accurate, but irrelevant, information regarding Tesla's personal interests and habits; therefore, the correct answer is choice **(D)**.

36. A

Difficulty: Medium

Category: Development: Word Choice

Getting to the Answer: Choose the most contextually appropriate word. Choice **(A)** is correct because "implemented" most accurately conveys the idea that Westinghouse first carried out the use of alternating current, which had already been developed, during the exposition.

37. D

Difficulty: Easy

Category: Graphs

Getting to the Answer: The correct answer will reflect the correct data contained in the timeline. The timeline states that Tesla and Westinghouse displayed the AC system at the Columbian Exposition in 1893, so choice **(D)** is correct.

38. B

Difficulty: Medium

Category: Development: Introductions and Conclusions

Getting to the Answer: Identify the subject of the paragraph and consider what the author wants to convey about it. That is the central idea. Then, select the answer choice that correctly conveys the central idea of the paragraph as supported by the details in the preceding sentences. The paragraph discusses the importance of Tesla's development of alternating current and its impact on daily life. In particular, it distinguishes the legacy of Tesla relative to the contributions of Edison. For this reason, choice **(B)** is correct because it is the only answer choice that emphasizes that Tesla's AC system was crucial (not just incidental) to the success of Edison's bulbs as fixtures in everyday life. "However, bulbs alone do not light our homes" makes clear that Edison's invention would not have done so well without Tesla's.

39. B

Difficulty: Medium

Category: Organization: Sentence Placement

Getting to the Answer: In order to decide where to place a sentence, look for clues in the sentence itself and in the paragraph as a whole. The sentence states that "Developing the AC system was only the beginning," which suggests that the sentence should serve as a transition away from a discussion about the AC system and an introduction to Tesla's other work. The paragraph as a whole discusses some of Tesla's other innovations. Placing sentence 4 at the beginning of the paragraph thus provides a transition from the previous paragraph and an introduction to this one; **(B)** is correct.

40. D

Difficulty: Easy

Category: Conciseness

Getting to the Answer: The correct answer will demonstrate economy of word choice while preserving the meaning of the sentence. The sentence communicates that Tesla's inventions contributed to the development of future technologies. Choice **(D)** is correct because it uses minimal verbiage to express that Tesla's inventions led to later inventions.

41. B

Difficulty: Medium

Category: Development: Revising Text

Getting to the Answer: Consider other information in the passage. The correct answer will identify and remove the least essential supporting information to streamline the rhetoric. The least essential information will not alter the meaning of the sentence and will most likely be irrelevant or redundant. The sentence communicates Tesla's impact on wireless communications. Choice **(B)** is correct because it provides examples that, while somewhat relevant, are nonessential.

42. B

Difficulty: Hard

Category: Agreement: Modifiers

Getting to the Answer: The correct answer will align the modifier with its subject without disrupting the syntax of the remainder of the sentence. The sentence begins "Edison may have invented the light bulb" and proceeds to contrast Edison's achievement with Tesla's. The second part of the sentence is a dependent clause connected with "but" and should lead off with its subject "Tesla," follow with the modifier "seeing no fame or fortune," and then proceed with the rest of the sentence. Choice **(B)** does so and is therefore correct.

43. D

Difficulty: Medium

Category: Development: Word Choice

Getting to the Answer: Examine the surrounding sentence and paragraph to determine what meaning the writer wishes to convey with the underlined word. The paragraph describes Tesla as an early innovator in his field who opened up possibilities for future inventions. Choice **(D)** is correct because "pioneer" most effectively conveys the ideas that Tesla was among the first and that he paved the way for others. The other answer choices convey one or the other of these meanings, but not both.

44. C

Difficulty: Medium

Category: Graphs

Getting to the Answer: Read the information next to 1883 in the timeline and find the answer choice that matches that content. The correct answer will correspond to the same event in the passage and timeline. According to the timeline, in 1883, Tesla used alternating current to power a motor. This date corresponds to the information in sentence 3 of paragraph 3, making choice **(C)** correct.

Writing & Lang

45. A

Difficulty: Medium

Category: Development: Introductions and Conclusions

Getting to the Answer: Reread the paragraph to determine which answer choice best introduces the main point. The correct answer, choice **(A)**, is the only one that accurately explains how the career is now popular and helpful but had to develop over time after a shift in health care needs.

46. D

Difficulty: Easy

Category: Conciseness

Getting to the Answer: Reread the sentence and determine which answer choice creates the most focused sentence. The additional comments about the school's quality and features are unnecessary. Choice **(D)** creates the most focused sentence.

47. B

Difficulty: Medium

Category: Development: Word Choice

Getting to the Answer: Look for nearby context clues and use what you know of each answer choice's definition to determine which word most accurately reflects the intention of the sentence. The intention of the sentence is to state that students should acquire hands-on medical knowledge through work experience. The word with the definition that best describes this acquisition is "accrue," choice **(B)**.

48. B

Difficulty: Easy

Category: Conciseness

Getting to the Answer: Read the entire sentence for context clues and determine which answer choice creates a logical sentence without wordiness or redundancies. Only choice **(B)** correctly eliminates wordiness, as the word "programs" is used later in the same sentence.

49. D

Difficulty: Medium

Category: Conciseness

Getting to the Answer: Find context clues and determine which answer choice creates a logical sentence without wordiness or redundancies. Because there is still an exam to pass before these individuals become PAs, and because the repetition of the words "graduates" and "graduation" is redundant, choice **(D)** is the correct answer.

50. D

Difficulty: Medium

Category: Organization: Sentence Placement

Getting to the Answer: Review the answer choices to determine which creates a paragraph with the best logical progression of ideas. The paragraph discusses the steps a student must take in order to become a PA and should not discuss maintaining one's license until the end, as it is done only after becoming a PA. Choice **(D)** is correct.

51. C

Difficulty: Medium

Category: Development: Word Choice

Getting to the Answer: Use context clues to determine which answer choice best fits the context of the sentence and paragraph while conveying the author's intended meaning. The sentence suggests that doctors work alone while PAs work under supervision. The word with the definition that best describes a doctor's unsupervised work is "autonomously," choice **(C)**.

52. A

Difficulty: Medium

Category: Organization: Transitions

Getting to the Answer: Decide which answer choice offers the best transition for an accurate flow of ideas. Choice **(A)** offers the best transition in order to summarize why the previous information is important and to show the positive effects PAs have on the health care team.

53. C

Difficulty: Hard

Category: Agreement: Pronouns

Getting to the Answer: Evaluate whether the pronoun refers to the subject or object of the sentence, and then determine which answer choice creates a logical and grammatically sound sentence. It is the PA who works under a physician, and because the pronoun refers to the object of the sentence, physicians, the appropriate pronoun to use in this situation is "whom." Therefore, choice **(C)** is correct.

54. B

Difficulty: Medium

Category: Development: Relevance

Getting to the Answer: Reread the paragraph and decide which answer choice maintains the style and tone of the author's voice. The author has not yet referenced him or herself, the reader, or any third party for an opinion in this passage. This makes the consistent tone found in choice **(B)** correct.

55. D

Difficulty: Medium

Category: Development: Relevance

Getting to the Answer: Review the paragraph to determine which claim made by the author is lacking details or supporting evidence that would strengthen the author's case. The second sentence in the paragraph is the only one in which the author makes a claim based on projections, but the author fails to use specific figures. Adding these figures would strengthen this claim, thus choice **(D)** is correct.

56. C

Difficulty: Medium

Category: Development: Word Choice

Getting to the Answer: Think about the overall meaning of the sentence. Select the answer choice that makes the most sense in context. "Depletion" is the reduction of a resource, so choice **(C)** is correct.

57. D

Difficulty: Hard

Category: Organization: Transitions

Getting to the Answer: The example transition "one such" and the introduction of biofuel need to come at the beginning of the sentence in order to provide a clear transition from the previous sentence. Only **(D)** corrects this issue.

58. A

Difficulty: Medium

Category: Development: Introductions and Conclusions

Getting to the Answer: Look for the answer choice that clearly states the main topic of the paragraph and introduces the central idea supported by all of the details presented. Topic sentences or introductory sentences of body paragraphs should generally introduce that paragraph's topic. While other answer choices address details disclosed in the paragraph, choice **(A)** is the most general and also uses the transition "until recently" to tie this paragraph to the one that precedes it.

59. A

Difficulty: Medium

Getting to the Answer: Agreement: Pronouns

Getting to the Answer: "It" refers to ethanol and is possessive. The possessive form of "it" is "its," so the sentence is correct as written. Choice **(A)** is correct.

60. B

Difficulty: Medium

Category: Development: Word Choice

Getting to the Answer: The underlined word, "horrible," is too casual. Be careful of answer choices that are close in meaning to "horrible" but do not fit the established tone. Replace "horrible" with each of the answer choices. In this context, "dire," which means severe or urgent, best fits the tone and style of the sentence. Choice **(B)** is correct.

61. C

Difficulty: Medium

Category: Graphs

Getting to the Answer: Look at the most recent data in the graph. Pay attention to the relationship between the two lines: the solid line represents the percentage of corn production used for ethanol, and the dotted line reflects the price of corn. In the most recent years displayed in the graph, the price of corn and the percentage of corn production used for ethanol have both increased. Choice **(C)** is correct.

62. A

Difficulty: Hard

Category: Development: Relevance

Getting to the Answer: Determine the central idea of the paragraph. In this paragraph, the author explains that ethanol is limited as a commercial fuel. Choice **(A)** describes one way in which ethanol use is limited and is therefore correct.

63. D

Difficulty: Easy

Category: Organization: Sentence Placement

Getting to the Answer: Read this paragraph in the context of the entire passage to determine its proper placement. This paragraph makes general statements about the central idea of the passage and draws a conclusion. Choice **(D)** is correct because paragraph 4 is an appropriate concluding paragraph.

64. B

Difficulty: Easy

Category: Agreement: Verbs

Getting to the Answer: Read the first few sentences of the paragraph to see if the verb tenses match. As written, the underlined portion is in the past perfect tense. The following sentence, however, uses the present perfect verb "have extracted." The underlined portion should also be in the present perfect form; therefore, **(B)** is correct.

65. C

Difficulty: Medium

Category: Sentence Structure: The Basics

Getting to the Answer: Check to see if this sentence contains two independent clauses that create a run-on sentence without proper punctuation. This sentence contains two complete thoughts with two independent main clauses and should therefore be separated into two sentences with a period. Choice **(C)** is correct.

66. B

Difficulty: Medium

Category: Transitions

Getting to the Answer: Read the previous sentence in conjunction with this one. Think about the relationship between the ideas in the two sentences. There is a cause-and-effect relationship between the ideas in the previous sentence and this sentence, but the underlined portion contains a concluding transition. "Therefore" is a cause-and-effect transition, so choice **(B)** is correct.

67. C

Difficulty: Easy

Category: Conciseness

Getting to the Answer: Watch out for choices, like (B), that are extremely wordy. It is better to be as direct and simple as possible. Additional adjectives do not add more meaning to this content. Choice **(C)** is the most concise and effective way of stating the information in the passage.

68. A

Difficulty: Medium

Category: Sentence Structure: Commas, Dashes, and Colons

Getting to the Answer: Study the words in a series and see where a comma might need to be inserted or eliminated. Recall that the SAT requires lists of three to have commas after the first two items in the list, not just after the first item. Choice **(A)** is correct.

69. D

Difficulty: Hard

Category: Development: Relevance

Getting to the Answer: To find the best answer choice, look for the sentence that has the most specific, relevant details. Choice **(D)** has the most relevant details about what the Pony Express was like when it was at its peak.

70. C

Difficulty: Medium

Category: Sentence Structure: The Basics

Getting to the Answer: As written, the underlined portion includes two sentences incorrectly joined by a comma. Choice (B) eliminates the comma, which does not correct the error. Choice (D) adds a coordinating or FANBOYS conjunction (yet), but since it also eliminates the comma and coordinating conjunctions must be used with a comma, it is also incorrect. Choice **(C)** correctly divides the two complete thoughts into two sentences by adding a period and capitalizing the first word of the second sentence.

71. A

Difficulty: Easy

Category: Development: Word Choice

Getting to the Answer: Read the sentence, looking for context clues that identify what meaning the writer intends to convey. The underlined word is describing records of arrival and departure. Records cannot be "sorrowful" or "agreeable," so eliminate (C) and (D). While records could be "boring," that would not fit with the writer's generally positive tone towards the topic. Choice **(A)** effectively describes records in a way that suits the writer's purpose and is correct.

72. B

Difficulty: Medium

Category: Agreement: Verbs

Getting to the Answer: Items in a list should be parallel, that is, in the same form. In this sentence, the list is of verb phrases, so the verbs should be in the same form. The correct answer is **(B)**.

73. A

Difficulty: Hard

Category: Development: Introductions and Conclusions

Getting to the Answer: To find the central idea of a paragraph, identify important details and summarize them in a sentence. Then, find the choice that is the closest to your summary. Do not choose a detail rather than a central idea. The paragraph mostly discusses the challenges riders faced, so choice **(A)** most accurately sums up the central idea of the paragraph.

74. B

Difficulty: Medium

Category: Organization: Transitions

Getting to the Answer: Look for the relationship between this sentence and the previous one to choose the appropriate transition word. Read the word into the sentence to ensure that it makes sense. Choice **(B)** shows the relationship between the two sentences by emphasizing that the riders could overcome these challenges.

75. B

Difficulty: Medium

Category: Graphs

Getting to the Answer: The graphic gives specific information about when events relating to the Pony Express took place. Examine it carefully to choose the correct answer choice. Choice **(B)** is the only one that accurately reflects the information in the timeline.

76. C

Difficulty: Medium

Category: Development: Word Choice

Getting to the Answer: Check the sentence for context clues as to what word must belong in the underlined portion. This sentence states that the Pony Express was no longer needed once a better alternative was ready. The alternative didn't need to be "invented," just built, so eliminate (A). Choice (B), "breached," means to be broken into, so does not make sense in context. Similarly, "contrasted" does not convey that the alternative was in place and working. The only answer that does is "operational," so **(C)** is correct.

77. D

Difficulty: Medium

Category: Conciseness

Getting to the Answer: Consider the relationship between the two sentences when deciding how to combine them. The second sentence is a continuation of the ideas in the first. Choice **(D)** joins the sentences concisely and correctly by eliminating the subject of the second sentence and forming a compound verb with the conjunction "and." The other choices are all wordier, and they misrepresent the relationship between the two sentences.

Writing & Lang

PART 5

SAT Essay

CHAPTER 28

The Method for the SAT Essay

LEARNING OBJECTIVES

After completing this chapter, you will be able to:

- Describe the task the SAT Essay Test requires
- Map the prompt for its big picture and identify three specific features (techniques or types of evidence used)
- Recognize rhetorical features in the prompt to use in your essay
- Organize the features you choose into an essay outline
- State what the graders are looking for

The Essay Task

LEARNING OBJECTIVE

After this lesson, you will be able to:

- Describe the task the SAT Essay Test requires

The College Board has announced that **the SAT Essay is being discontinued** after the June 2021 testing administration, except in states that require it as part of SAT School Day administrations. If you are taking the SAT on a school day, ask your guidance counselor whether the Essay will be included. If you do need to sit for the Essay, read on.

The SAT Essay Test assesses your college and career readiness. The Essay tests your ability to read and analyze a high-quality source document. Your goal is to write a coherent analysis for the source supported with critical reasoning and evidence from the given text. No prior knowledge of the topic is required.

The SAT Essay Test features an argumentative source text of 650–750 words aimed toward a large audience. Passages may examine ideas, debates, and shifts in the arts and sciences as well as civic, cultural, and political life. Rather than having a simple for/against structure, these passages will be nuanced and will relate views on complex subjects. You can expect these passages to be logical in their structure and reasoning.

The SAT Essay prompt will ask you to explain how the presented passage's author builds an argument to convince an audience. In writing your essay, you may analyze elements such as the author's use of evidence, reasoning, style, and persuasion. You will not be limited to those elements listed, however.

Rather than writing about whether you agree or disagree with the presented argument, you will write an essay in which you analyze how the author makes an argument.

The SAT Essay Test will be broken down into three categories for scoring: Reading, Analysis, and Writing. Each of these elements will be scored on a scale of 1–4 by two graders, for a total score of 2–8 for each category.

This chapter will teach you what to look for in the prompt, what kinds of notes are useful, and how to impress the graders favorably.

Essay Essentials

LEARNING OBJECTIVES

After this lesson, you will be able to:

- Map the prompt for its big picture, and identify three specific features (techniques or types of evidence used)

- Organize the points you'll make in an outline. Given the Kaplan Essay Template

The Basics

The **prompt**—the subject of your analysis and writing—is a speech or article by a professional writer or other prominent person. The average length is 700–750 words. That person will be arguing for—that is, trying to persuade readers of—some specific viewpoint. The good news is that the test maker will tell you, flat out, what that viewpoint is; you won't need to deduce it from the article.

Most of the time the writer will be *recommending* a particular social or government policy or a personal behavior. Sometimes the writer will be *recommending against* a policy or behavior. And other times, very occasionally, the argument will be making a *prediction* of what may or may not happen.

Either way, the assignment is the same. In 50 minutes, you need to read the prompt, analyze how it's put together, and write an organized essay explaining how the prompt works. The graders give you scores on each of those tasks—reading, analyzing, and writing.

The Format of the Prompt

It begins with a standard box of text that reads like this:

As you read the passage below, consider how [name of author] uses

- evidence, such as facts or examples, to support claims.

- reasoning to develop ideas and to connect claims and evidence.

- stylistic or persuasive elements, such as word choice or appeals to emotion, to add power to the ideas expressed.

After the introductory text box, there is a note providing the author, date, and origin of the prompt text, and the text itself. The paragraphs are numbered for your convenience, so you can refer the reader to the locations you desire ("In paragraph 3, he says…"). Most prompts are edited down from longer versions, and an ellipsis (…) is used to indicate where text has been removed. You need only consider the text that's present. Don't worry about anything edited out.

Finally, a text box explains the task. It always spells out exactly what the author's point or conclusion is and tells you what they want you to do. For instance:

> Write an essay in which you explain how George W. Bush builds an argument to persuade his audience that his temporary worker program should be adopted by Congress. In your essay, analyze how Bush uses one or more of the features listed in the directions that precede the passage (or features of your own choice) to strengthen the logic and persuasiveness of his argument. Be sure that your analysis focuses on the most relevant features of the passage.
>
> Your essay should not explain whether you agree with Bush's claims, but rather explain how Bush builds an argument to persuade his audience.

You may annotate the prompt, or take notes in the margins, or use the last sheet for scratchwork.

Important note: The graders have to be able to read your writing. They will not read or consider your scratchwork, only the essay itself. You can write in cursive or block letters, whichever is more legible for you. If graders cannot read what you have written in the essay, then they will have to disregard it, which will most likely hurt your score.

Suggested Essay Structure

Here's a structure that is an excellent basis for the SAT Essay assignment. If you understand and practice it, you won't waste time deciding how to arrange the paragraphs of your essay. The details of this structure will be discussed later in this chapter.

Paragraph 1—Restate the prompt's purpose, and then list the evidence types/rhetorical strategies you will discuss. (We recommend listing three.)

Paragraph 2—Mention one evidence type/rhetorical strategy, with examples and analysis.

Paragraph 3—Mention a second evidence type/rhetorical strategy, with examples and analysis.

Paragraph 4—Mention a third evidence type/rhetorical strategy, with examples and analysis.

Paragraph 5—Summarize the entire argument, in your own words.

Memorize this structure and use it on your practice essays. If you know the form of your essay beforehand, you just have to fill in the content on test day.

SAT Essay Timing and Scoring

Timing

You have 50 minutes to complete the Essay. Here are some rough guidelines to get you started:

- Reading: 5 minutes
- Note-taking: 5 minutes
- Analyzing and outlining: 8 minutes
- Writing: 30 minutes
- Quick proofreading: 2 minutes

Don't be concerned if you have trouble executing your first couple of attempts in 50 minutes. In fact, in your first couple of practice essays, don't worry about time constraints at all and concentrate completely on the quality of your essay. Do still time yourself on these early practice essays so you have a benchmark for how close you are to 50 minutes. After you've written a few of these, you'll be able to shave off time, especially from the reading and analyzing tasks.

Scoring

Two different graders will score your essay. Each will award you between 1 and 4 points in the categories of Reading, Analyzing, and Writing, and the two graders' points will be added together in each category. You'll get a Reading score between 2 and 8, an Analyzing score between 2 and 8, and a Writing score between 2 and 8. You'll learn more about what makes for a superior score later in this chapter.

The next lesson will focus on how to get the information you need to write an effective essay from the prompt.

Dissecting the Prompt

LEARNING OBJECTIVES

After this lesson, you will be able to:

- Recognize rhetorical features in the prompt to use in your essay
- Organize the features you choose into an essay outline

The Reading—5 Minutes

Always start with the box of directions *below* the prompt, where they spell out the author's purpose (usually, as we've said, some sort of recommendation). Immediately start thinking of how you'll put that purpose into your own words. Next, jump into the prompt.

You may benefit from an initial quick skim, without note-taking. Try to *read with interest*, noting the general outline of the author's argument.

Get a casual sense of the author's tone and motives. It'll ease you into the prompt gently and lay the groundwork for your more important second pass through the material.

Exercise

Take up to five minutes to read this prompt. Remember to start with the directions box below the passage itself.

As you read the passage below, consider how Barack Obama uses

- evidence, such as facts or examples.
- reasoning to develop ideas and to connect claims and evidence.
- stylistic or persuasive elements, such as word choice or appeals to emotion, to add power to the ideas expressed.

Adapted from U.S. President Barack Obama's address to the first session of Conference of the Parties 21 (COP21), the 2015 Paris Climate Conference, on November 30, 2015.

1 Our understanding of the ways human beings disrupt the climate advances by the day. Fourteen of the fifteen warmest years on record have occurred since the year 2000— and 2015 is on pace to be the warmest year of all. No nation—large or small, wealthy or poor—is immune to what this means.

2 This summer, I saw the effects of climate change firsthand in our northernmost state, Alaska, where the sea is already swallowing villages and eroding shorelines; where permafrost thaws and the tundra burns; where glaciers are melting at a pace unprecedented in modern times. And it was a preview of one possible future—a glimpse of our children's fate if the climate keeps changing faster than our efforts to address it. Submerged countries. Abandoned cities. Fields that no longer grow. . . .

SAT Essay

3   That future is one that we have the power to change. Right here. Right now. But only if we rise to this moment. As one of America's governors has said, "We are the first generation to feel the impact of climate change, and the last generation that can do something about it.". . .

4   Over the last seven years, [the U.S. has] made ambitious investments in clean energy, and ambitious reductions in our carbon emissions. We've multiplied wind power threefold, and solar power more than twentyfold, helping create parts of America where these clean power sources are finally cheaper than dirtier, conventional power. We've invested in energy efficiency in every way imaginable. We've said no to infrastructure that would pull high-carbon fossil fuels from the ground, and we've said yes to the first-ever set of national standards limiting the amount of carbon pollution our power plants can release into the sky. . . .

5   But the good news is this is not an American trend alone. Last year, the global economy grew while global carbon emissions from burning fossil fuels stayed flat. And what this means can't be overstated. We have broken the old arguments for inaction. We have proved that strong economic growth and a safer environment no longer have to conflict with one another; they can work in concert with one another.

6   And that should give us hope. One of the enemies that we'll be fighting at this conference is cynicism, the notion we can't do anything about climate change. Our progress should give us hope during these two weeks—hope that is rooted in collective action. . . .

7   So our task here in Paris is to turn these achievements into an enduring framework for human progress—not a stopgap solution, but a long-term strategy that gives the world confidence in a low-carbon future.

8   Here, in Paris, let's secure an agreement that builds in ambition, where progress paves the way for regularly updated targets—targets that are not set for each of us but by each of us, taking into account the differences that each nation is facing.

9   Here in Paris, let's agree to a strong system of transparency that gives each of us the confidence that all of us are meeting our commitments. . . .

10 Here in Paris, let's reaffirm our commitment that resources will be there for countries willing to do their part to skip the dirty phase of development. . . .

11 And finally, here in Paris, let's show businesses and investors that the global economy is on a firm path towards a low-carbon future. If we put the right rules and incentives in place, we'll unleash the creative power of our best scientists and engineers and entrepreneurs to deploy clean energy technologies and the new jobs and new opportunities that they create all around the world. There are hundreds of billions of dollars ready to deploy to countries around the world if they get the signal that we mean business this time. Let's send that signal. . . .

12   For I believe, in the words of Dr. Martin Luther King, Jr., that there is such a thing
as being too late. And when it comes to climate change, that hour is almost upon us.
But if we act here, if we act now, if we place our own short-term interests behind the
air that our young people will breathe, and the food that they will eat, and the water
that they will drink, and the hopes and dreams that sustain their lives, then we won't
be too late for them. . . .

13   Let's get to work. Thank you very much.

> Write an essay in which you explain how President Obama builds an argument to
> persuade his audience that the Paris conference needs to take timely action on
> the matter of climate change. In your essay, analyze how he uses one or more of
> the features in the directions that precede the passage (or features of your own
> choice) to strengthen the logic and persuasiveness of his argument. Be sure that
> your analysis focuses on the most relevant features of the passage.
>
> Your essay should not explain whether you agree with Obama's claims, but rather
> explain how Obama builds an argument to persuade his audience.

At the very least, your first pass through the prompt should have netted you the following information. The
author's purpose (from the directions box): *to get the Paris conference attendees to take specific and immediate action on climate change.* Author's tone (from the passage itself): *urgently persuasive.* The context (from
the bolded blurb at the beginning): *an opening speech at a 2015 conference.* Your job (from the directions
box): *Explain how he puts together his argument to get them to take action.*

The Note-Taking—5 minutes

Once you have an overall sense of the prompt, you're ready to start thinking it through, taking notes as you go.

Pencil in hand, go paragraph by paragraph, asking yourself what each block of text is doing there. Why has
the author included it? What does it add to the argument? How does it relate to what came before and to what
comes just after? If you can identify some rhetorical devices used, note them.

Here are a couple of things to keep in mind at this stage:

1.   You don't want to think about your essay as a whole. Wait a while. First get a sense of what is happening
in each paragraph block. Then you can look for patterns.

2.   You don't need to incorporate every single paragraph, or every single rhetorical device, into your essay. If
a paragraph strikes you as filler, or unimportant, or secondary, just skip past it and don't worry about it.

Exercise

Take up to five minutes to analyze Obama's speech paragraph by paragraph and note the main points of each paragraph as well as any rhetorical devices you observe. Remember to stay focused on the *why* of the passage rather than the *what*. When you're done, compare your notes to the sample notes below.

Adapted from U.S. President Barack Obama's address to the first session of Conference of the Parties 21 (COP21), the 2015 Paris Climate Conference, on November 30, 2015.

1 Our understanding of the ways human beings disrupt the climate advances by the day. Fourteen of the fifteen warmest years on record have occurred since the year 2000—and 2015 is on pace to be the warmest year of all. No nation—large or small, wealthy or poor—is immune to what this means.

Scary stat!

Affects everyone

2 This summer, I saw the effects of climate change firsthand in our northernmost state, Alaska, where the sea is already swallowing villages and eroding shorelines; where permafrost thaws and the tundra burns; where glaciers are melting at a pace unprecedented in modern times. And it was a preview of one possible future—a glimpse of our children's fate if the climate keeps changing faster than our efforts to address it. Submerged countries. Abandoned cities. Fields that no longer grow. . . .

Personal memory

Eloquent list of changes

3 That future is one that we have the power to change. Right here. Right now. But only if we rise to this moment. As one of America's governors has said, "We are the first generation to feel the impact of climate change, and the last generation that can do something about it. . . ."

Can still prevent disaster: call to action

4 Over the last seven years, [the U.S. has] made ambitious investments in clean energy, and ambitious reductions in our carbon emissions. We've multiplied wind power threefold, and solar power more than twentyfold, helping create parts of America where these clean power sources are finally cheaper than dirtier, conventional power. We've invested in energy efficiency in every way imaginable. We've said no to infrastructure that would pull high-carbon fossil fuels from the ground, and we've said yes to the first-ever set of national standards limiting the amount of carbon pollution our power plants can release into the sky. . . .

How US has been doing the right thing

5 But the good news is this is not an American trend alone. Last year, the global economy grew while global carbon emissions from burning fossil fuels stayed flat. And what this means can't be overstated. We have broken the old arguments for inaction. We have proved that strong economic growth and a safer environment no longer have to conflict with one another; they can work in concert with one another.

How the world has been doing the right thing. Old view: not enough $ to do it

6 And that should give us hope. One of the enemies that we'll be fighting at this conference is cynicism, the notion we can't do anything about climate change. Our progress should give us hope during these two weeks—hope that is rooted in collective action. . . .

Possible objection: nothing to be done Answer: work together

7 So our task here in Paris is to turn these achievements into an enduring framework for human progress—not a stopgap solution, but a long-term strategy that gives the world confidence in a low-carbon future.

Let's go big or go home

8   (Here, in Paris,) let's secure an agreement that builds in ambition, where progress paves the way for regularly updated targets—targets that are not set for each of us but by each of us, taking into account the differences that each nation is facing.   *Go for big targets*

9   (Here, in Paris, let's) agree to a strong system of transparency that gives each of us the confidence that all of us are meeting our commitments. . . .   *Repetition pounds the call to action Transparency*

10   (Here, in Paris, let's) reaffirm our commitment that resources will be there for countries willing to do their part to skip the dirty phase of development. . . .   *Pool resources*

11   (And finally, here in Paris,) let's show businesses and investors that the global economy is on a firm path towards a low-carbon future. If we put the right rules and incentives in place, we'll unleash the creative power of our best scientists and engineers and entrepreneurs to deploy clean energy technologies and the new jobs and new opportunities that they create all around the world. There are <u>hundreds of billions of dollars</u> ready to deploy to countries around the world if they get the signal that we mean business this time. Let's send that signal. . . .   *Must guide global economy*

  We have the means

12   For I believe, in the words of <u>Dr. Martin Luther King, Jr.</u>, that there <u>is such a thing as (being too late.)</u> And when it comes to climate change, that hour is almost upon us. But <u>if we act here, if we act now</u>, if we place our own short-term interests behind the air that our young people will breathe, and the food that they will eat, and the water that they will drink, and the hopes and dreams that sustain their lives, then we (we won't be too late for them. . . .)   *Invoking Dr. King to underscore urgency*

13   <u>Let's get to work. Thank you very much.</u>   *Final, strong call to action*

Expert Assessment of Sample Notes

Here is an assessment of this student's annotations so that you can get the best sense of the process. Italicized numbers refer to paragraphs.

1   The student notes a "scary" statistic, thus noting an effect that the statistic is intended to have on the audience. The student further notes that the purpose of the statistic is to let "everyone" at the conference know that they will be affected by climate change.

2–3   Defines the second paragraph as a personal reminiscence; points out a fancy list of dire outcomes we can look forward to and a shift to the call to action.

4–5   Excellent one-phrase summaries of each of these paragraphs. The student is not stopping to look for patterns. (Finding patterns is part of the next step, analyzing and outlining.)

6   Constantly asking "Why is he saying this?" the student notes a possible objection to the action Obama is recommending—as well as the way to combat that objection, with group commitment.

7   The phrase "go big or go home" encapsulates what the author is implying.

8–11   Notes the repeated phrase and sums up each of the things Obama wants done "here in Paris."

12   "Eloquence plus" is one way to sum up Obama's eloquent phrases ending the speech on a high note. The president is clearly not relying just on wonky statistics and policy recommendations. He's finding poetry in the challenge to fix the global climate and deftly uses Dr. King's words for emphasis.

13   Student notes final call to action. Acting quickly, "here in Paris," is a running theme throughout the passage.

The Analysis and Outline—8 Minutes

Now comes the most important part—and perhaps the trickiest part—for many students just starting to attempt the essay. Now you want to organize your thoughts: to group them together into idea blocks that will demonstrate your command of structure and help you write your essay effectively.

We recommend that you plan on an introduction, a conclusion, and three body paragraphs. Each of those paragraphs should focus on *one* type of evidence or rhetorical appeal that you've located in the prompt. That implies that you should identify three types.

You can make do with only two (and, thus, two body paragraphs). But if you carefully examine the published SAT Essays that the test makers have identified as high-scoring, you will notice that most if not all of them come up with three. And if you practice this a few times, you'll get better and better at it.

The key question to ask yourself is: *As I look at the tactics used and points made, are there three categories I can lump them into?* If you can find two to three items to list under each category, you've got all the evidence you need for a very strong essay.

Here are the various features the student noted in the Obama prompt above:

- Statistics and facts showing the bad news (about climate trends) and the good news (about what the U.S. and world have already done)
- A personal reminiscence—a time when the president saw firsthand the devastation of the Alaska wilderness
- A lot of fancy turns of phrase, designed to whip up emotional responses—almost preacher-like
- Specific goals and plans the delegates can focus on
- A lot of direct thrusts; here's what we have to do; the clock is ticking; no half-measures; get moving
- Past objections (it's too big a job; we can't afford it)
- Counterarguments to those objections (the job's not too big if we pull together; there IS enough money if we play our cards right)
- Expansive visions of the future if we are successful at this Conference

There are probably a few more, or other ways to phrase them, but that's already a fairly extensive list. All you have to do now is pick out three—the three you feel most confident about and interested in—and decide the order in which to mention them. For instance:

Paragraph 2—How Obama paints a grim picture of the current, and possible future, disasters facing the Earth

Paragraph 3—The good news so far: the U.S. has done its job; the world has too, to a degree; we know what needs to be done

Paragraph 4—Obama's employment of emotional, even church-like language to rev up the crowd

That would be one way to go. Here's another:

Paragraph 2—The emotional appeal: all the impassioned language and turns of phrase, which Obama includes from beginning to end

Paragraph 3—The positive reasons he provides for taking action now

Paragraph 4—The objections that have been or could be raised and how Obama's ideas counter them

SAT Essay

Either of those structures would be perfectly fine. (Shortly, we'll share with you a sample essay written to still another paragraph structure.) For now, we would recommend that by the end of that eight minutes of note-taking and analyzing, you will have decided on your three themes and started to assemble the order of the points you want to make in each paragraph.

A Word about the Outline

You should use whatever type of outline makes you feel most comfortable and capable as you practice the essay, but it's unlikely that you'd create a "sentence outline," in which each roman numeral, capitalized, and lowercase point is written as a complete sentence: there just isn't time.

You may find it simpler to create a topic outline. Here, for instance, is a potential outline for a paragraph describing how President Obama paints a grim picture of the situation in 2015:

First body paragraph:

- Starts with scares in ¶1
  - 15 yr. trend
  - all countries
- Alaska
  - strong mental pictures for emotion ¶2
  - children affected
- obstacles to progress
  - cynicism/inaction/lack of will ¶6, ¶11

Alternatively, you may want to skip using an outline and instead label your margin notes. You can number your body paragraphs as I, II, and III (or A, B, and C). Put an A in the margin wherever you have a point to make in your first body paragraph, B for the next one, and so on.

Or you might choose to use an "idea map"—jot down points you want to make and then connect those thoughts with arrows that you can follow as you write.

Experiment with more than one method and go with the one that works best for you on test day.

What the Graders Want

LEARNING OBJECTIVE

After this lesson, you will be able to:

- State what the graders are looking for

Student Response

President Barack Obama's address to the 2015 Climate Conference in Paris comes across as a heartfelt plea for the assembled delegates to turn around what he clearly feels is the number one danger to our planet. He wants to appeal to both the heart and the head, so he employs not just factual evidence, but also personal experience and emotional language to rev up his audience.

The statistical evidence Mr. Obama cites is of two types and serves two different functions. In his very first paragraph he points out what he must feel is a frightening piece of data that will make people sit up, the 15 years since 2000 that show an overwhelming trend toward hotter and hotter temperatures. To make sure every delegate sits up, he reminds them that every country, "large or small, wealthy or poor," will have to live with those consequences. Soon after, however, he takes pains to cite many encouraging statistics. Paragraph 4 lays out some of what the United States has done, including reduce or discourage use of fossil fuel, commit to wind and solar, urge Americans to conserve, and put caps on carbon emissions. The next paragraph emphasizes that the U.S. is far from the only nation that has made positive strides. I sense that he feels that he will energize the crowd better not by harping on the doom and gloom of his opening, but by urging the delegates to stay on the right road that the world is already on. He also anticipates any objection that turning the situation around will be too costly, by directly stating that strong economies and a better environment "can work in concert."

Mr. Obama also wants the delegates to feel the personal pain of what's at stake in climate change, so he describes a trip to Alaska, which many people think of as America's last wilderness. There he witnessed the effects of earth's warming on the population and the geography. He doesn't mention wilderness animals but images of endangered polar bears and seals and such are surely evoked by his "preview" of what could happen if climate change outpaces human efforts to turn it around. Creating unhappy mental images in an audience's mind can make more of an impact than statistics, he seems to realize, especially in the litany of sorry situations with which paragraph 2 ends.

The crisp phrases "Submerged countries" and "Abandoned cities" in paragraph 2 are in line with "Right here. Right now" in paragraph 3. They bring in the kind of rhetorical snap with which Mr. Obama surely wants to hit them between the eyes at the urgency of the situation. "Hundreds of billions of dollars" isn't a statistic, it's a bit of overstatement that implies that if we have the will, we'll have the means. The repeated "Here in Paris" in the calls to four specific actions that the Conference could take, keeps reminding the audience that he is not just interested in making them feel bad, he wants them to act. "Act here…act now" he says in paragraph 12. It comes as no surprise that Dr. Martin Luther King, Jr.'s name is evoked, because Mr. Obama is using the same power of the pulpit Dr. King did, to get the world's sinners, meaning all of us, to mend our ways.

Mr. Obama's speech would probably end with great applause for the soaring list of the long-term issues that are at stake for later generations' air, food, water, and dreams. But he doesn't want applause, he wants results. Probably "Let's get to work" is the snappiest way he could fire up the delegates to get those results.

Graders' Preferences and Analysis

The graders are trained to understand the College Board's stated criteria in particular ways so as to reduce the possibility of personal bias. By studying many graded essays and graders' comments, we have been able to compile the following tables showing what the graders tend to reward and what they tend to downgrade.

Reading

Graders tend to reward . . .	Graders tend to downgrade . . .
Expressing the author's central idea in your own words in the introduction to your essay	Restating the central idea in the author's own words, or presenting the central idea only late in the essay
Summarizing the particulars of the author's argument in your own words	Long quotations from the prompt or restating elements of the argument largely using the author's own words
Identifying relationships between details and the author's claims	Repeating details without considering their connection to the author's claims
Accurately reporting any facts or views that you choose to mention	Factual errors or distortions of authorial views
Sorting out the key individual issues involved	Leaving out key issues or blending several key issues together

Analyzing

Graders tend to reward . . .	Graders tend to downgrade . . .
Clearly identifying rhetorical features/tactics employed (three seems to be the optimum number)	Failing to mention, or misidentifying, rhetorical features/tactics employed; or mentioning too few of them (choosing 3 seems to be very safe)
Identification of specific rhetorical features/tactics (e.g., "contrast," "appeal to . . .," "analogy," "allusions to . . .," "metaphor," "causality," "hypothetical")	Reliance on too-generic rhetorical features/tactics (for instance, "reasoning," "facts," "statistics," "word choice," "imagery")
Explaining those features' intended effect on readers	Omitting consideration of how and why those features were employed
Assessing the strength of the author's use of those features	Omitting consideration of whether the argument's points are effectively presented
Speculation as to the author's views or motives	Treating the author as an objective source of information, rather than as a person engaged in persuasion
A focus on the *why* and *how* of an argument	A focus on the *what* of an argument

Writing

Graders tend to reward . . .	Graders tend to downgrade . . .
Clear, precise assertions	Unclear or vague assertions
Following a logical organizational structure	Meandering structure or stream-of-consciousness organization
Paragraphs organized around a single idea or theme	Paragraphs that take on too many disparate elements that don't fit together
Appropriately qualified statements	Overstatements or hyperbole
Correct grammar	Grammar errors that are noticeable and fixable even within a limited time frame
Interesting turns of phrase	Clichés and boring or obvious phrasing
A variety of sentence structures	Repetitious sentence structure
Complex sentences as appropriate	Run-ons, or overreliance on short, clipped sentences
A conclusion separate from the rest	A conclusion buried within the final paragraph

SAT Essay

Now that you've looked over the criteria, let's go paragraph by paragraph through the student essay, with commentary.

¶1 President Barack Obama's address to the 2015 Climate Conference in Paris comes across as a heartfelt plea for the assembled delegates to turn around what he clearly feels is the number one danger to our planet. He wants to appeal to both the heart and the head, so he employs not just factual evidence, but also personal experience and emotional language to rev up his audience.	*¶1 The first sentence summarizes both the context (the conference) and the purpose (call to action), but in the student's own words. We get the three components that will be discussed, and in that order—facts, personal experience, emotional wording— which tells the reader that the essay will be well organized.*
¶2 The statistical evidence Mr. Obama cites is of two types and serves two different functions. In his very first paragraph he points out what he must feel is a frightening piece of data that will make people sit up, the 15 years since 2000 that show an overwhelming trend toward hotter and hotter temperatures. To make sure every delegate sits up, he reminds them that every country, "large or small, wealthy or poor," will have to live with those consequences. Soon after, however, he takes pains to cite many encouraging statistics. Paragraph 4 lays out some of what the United States has done, including reduce or discourage use of fossil fuel, commit to wind and solar, urge Americans to conserve, and put caps on carbon emissions. The next paragraph emphasizes that the U.S. is far from the only nation that has made positive strides. I sense that he feels that he will energize the crowd better not by harping on the doom and gloom of his opening, but by urging the delegates to stay on the right road that the world is already on. He also anticipates any objection that turning the situation around will be too costly, by directly stating that strong economies and a better environment "can work in concert."	*¶2 Noting the two different types and functions of factual evidence shows that the student has thought through and categorized the text that will be cited in the essay. Overall, this paragraph is an excellent illustration of:* • *Putting the author's ideas into your own words (e.g., the 15-year trend)* • *Explaining why something's been mentioned (e.g., it's frightening)* • *Emphasizing the intended effect on the audience (e.g., to make them pay attention and take action)* *Note the very selective quotations from the speech. That shows care and thought.* *Two side notes about word choice. The repeated "Mr. Obama" shows respect, but simply "Obama" would be acceptable. And it's okay to use the first person pronoun ("I sense that…") when you make a point that you particularly want the reader to realize is your opinion. It would be unfair to say, "He feels that he will energize…," as you can't know that for a fact. If you're uncomfortable with using "I," you could instead say, "He seems to feel that he will energize…" That would have the same effect.*

¶3 Mr. Obama also wants the delegates to feel the personal pain of what's at stake in climate change, so he describes a trip to Alaska, which many people think of as America's last wilderness. There he witnessed the effects of earth's warming on the population and the geography. He doesn't mention wilderness animals but images of endangered polar bears and seals and such are surely evoked by his "preview" of what could happen if climate change outpaces human efforts to turn it around. Creating unhappy mental images in an audience's mind can make more of an impact than statistics, he seems to realize, especially in the litany of sorry situations with which paragraph 2 ends.

¶3 Here is the second of the three argument elements, connected to the previous paragraph with the simple transition, "also wants the delegates to…" Obama's second paragraph is carefully put into the writer's own words. The last sentence here shows the student's understanding that a good essay will consider the why of an author's choices, not just the what.

¶4 The crisp phrases "Submerged countries" and "Abandoned cities" in paragraph 2 are in line with "Right here. Right now" in paragraph 3. They bring in the kind of rhetorical snap with which Mr. Obama surely wants to hit them between the eyes at the urgency of the situation. "Hundreds of billions of dollars" isn't a statistic, it's a bit of overstatement that implies that if we have the will, we'll have the means. The repeated "Here in Paris" in the calls to four specific actions that the Conference could take, keeps reminding the audience that he is not just interested in making them feel bad, he wants them to act. "Act here… act now" he says in paragraph 12. It comes as no surprise that Dr. Martin Luther King, Jr.'s name is evoked, because Mr. Obama is using the same power of the pulpit Dr. King did, to get the world's sinners, meaning all of us, to mend our ways.

¶4 Here is the analysis of the rhetorical devices used by Obama, carefully arranged in a logical order. Notice that the student has not for a moment forgotten the overall purpose of the speech: to get the delegates to act. It's brought up as often as possible.

¶5 Mr. Obama's speech would probably end with great applause for the soaring list of the long-term issues that are at stake for later generations' air, food, water, and dreams. But he doesn't want applause, he wants results. Probably "Let's get to work" is the snappiest way he could fire up the delegates to get those results.

¶5 The conclusion of an SAT Essay should be short. The graders already know what you think of the prompt. Finding a new way to summarize the whole, that doesn't sound redundant or clunky, takes practice and is never easy. This student has noticed that the main theme is encapsulated at the very end in the words "Let's get to work," which fortunately allows for a reminder of the prompt's purpose. Such a reminder is crucial to a good conclusion.

This conclusion is solid. But the good news is that if the rest of the essay is strong, a weak or problematic conclusion will likely not make a big difference to your scores.

Summary of Graders' Analysis

Reading

This student manages to put both the central idea in paragraph 1 (Obama's desire to spur the conference into action), and the summary of the whole argument in paragraph 5, *into the student's own words,* which is crucial to scoring well in this category. There are no inaccuracies in the reporting, and every reported detail relates to some key point Obama is trying to make. (Example: "Hundreds of billions" in paragraph 4, is recognized as more of a booster point than a hard statistic.) Finally, the student wisely minimizes direct quotations. The brief phrases quoted are few in number, but always relevant to a point the student is making. (Example: The four two-word phrases mentioned in paragraph 4 as examples of "rhetorical snap" designed to grab the delegates' attention.)

Analyzing

The student mentions three broad rhetorical features in paragraph 1 and is always aware of how they're meant to affect readers. (Example: The Alaska trip is cited as a way to get the listeners emotionally engaged in the scientific dilemma.) The student speculates plausibly on Obama's motives (example: the reasoning as to why Obama keeps repeating "Here in Paris"). The reader leaves with no doubt that the student thinks Obama has argued strongly, which is not the same thing as the forbidden step of taking a side. (One can admire the strength of an argument whether or not one agrees with it.)

Writing

The overall structure follows the (1. Facts 2. Emotions 3. Rhetoric) structure promised by paragraph 1. Each paragraph properly takes up one of those, in order. The essay contains no notable grammar errors and the sentence structure is pleasingly varied, with a good mix of simple sentences and complex ones. There are some evocative turns of phrase ("appeal to both the heart and the head"; "rev up his audience"; "the doom and gloom of his opening"; "hit them between the eyes"; "get the world's sinners, meaning all of us, to mend our ways"). Finally, the conclusion, which appropriately summarizes the whole speech in new language, is correctly set apart from the rest of the essay.

Next Steps

Try the SAT Essay prompt in the "How Much Have You Learned?" section of this chapter.

SAT Essay

How Much Have You Learned?

We're leaving you with an additional prompt and, to extend your skills, a set of notes and outline that a student prepared from it:

As you read the passage below, consider how George W. Bush uses

- evidence, such as facts or examples.
- reasoning to develop ideas and to connect claims and evidence.
- stylistic or persuasive elements, such as word choice or appeals to emotion, to add power to the ideas expressed.

Adapted from U.S. president George W. Bush's address from the East Room of the White House on January 7, 2004.

1   Many of you here today are Americans by choice, and you have followed in the path of millions. And over the generations we have received energetic, ambitious, optimistic people from every part of the world. By tradition and conviction, our country is a welcoming society. America is a stronger and better nation because of the hard work and the faith and entrepreneurial spirit of immigrants.

2   Every generation of immigrants has reaffirmed the wisdom of remaining open to the talents and dreams of the world. And every generation of immigrants has reaffirmed our ability to assimilate newcomers—which is one of the defining strengths of our country. . . .

3   During one great period of immigration—between 1891 and 1920—our nation received some 18 million men, women and children from other nations. The hard work of these immigrants helped make our economy the largest in the world. The children of immigrants put on the uniform and helped to liberate the lands of their ancestors. One of the primary reasons America became a great power in the 20th century is because we welcomed the talent and the character and the patriotism of immigrant families.

4   The contributions of immigrants to America continue. About 14 percent of our nation's civilian workforce is foreign-born. Most begin their working lives in America by taking hard jobs and clocking long hours in important industries. Many immigrants also start businesses, taking the familiar path from hired labor to ownership.

5   As a nation that values immigration, and depends on immigration, we should have immigration laws that work and make us proud. Yet today we do not. Instead, we see many employers turning to the illegal labor market. We see millions of hard-working men and women condemned to fear and insecurity in a massive, undocumented economy. The system is not working. Our nation needs an immigration system that serves the American economy, and reflects the American Dream. . . .

6   Today, I ask the Congress to join me in passing new immigration laws that reflect these principles, that meet America's economic needs, and live up to our highest ideals.

7   I propose a new temporary worker program that will match willing foreign workers with willing American employers, when no Americans can be found to fill the jobs. This program will offer legal status, as temporary workers, to the millions of undocumented men and women now employed in the United States, and to those in foreign countries who seek to participate in the program and have been offered employment here. This new system should be clear and efficient, so employers are able to find workers quickly and simply.

8   This program expects temporary workers to return permanently to their home countries after their period of work in the United States has expired. And there should be financial incentives for them to do so. I will work with foreign governments on a plan to give temporary workers credit, when they enter their own nation's retirement system, for the time they have worked in America. . . .

9   Some temporary workers will make the decision to pursue American citizenship. Those who make this choice will be allowed to apply in the normal way. . . .

10 The citizenship line, however, is too long, and our current limits on legal immigration are too low. Those willing to take the difficult path of citizenship—the path of work, and patience, and assimilation—should be welcome in America, like generations of immigrants before them. . . .

11 This new system will be more compassionate. Decent, hard-working people will now be protected by labor laws, with the right to change jobs, earn fair wages, and enjoy the same working conditions that the law requires for American workers. Temporary workers will be able to establish their identities by obtaining the legal documents we all take for granted. And they will be able to talk openly to authorities, to report crimes when they are harmed, without the fear of being deported.

12 . . . [O]ur country has always benefited from the dreams that others have brought here. By working hard for a better life, immigrants contribute to the life of our nation. The temporary worker program I am proposing today represents the best tradition of our society, a society that honors the law, and welcomes the newcomer. This plan will help return order and fairness to our immigration system, and in so doing we will honor our values, by showing our respect for those who work hard and share in the ideals of America.

> Write an essay in which you explain how George W. Bush builds an argument to persuade his audience that his temporary worker program should be adopted by Congress. In your essay, analyze how he uses one or more of the features in the directions that precede the passage (or features of your own choice) to strengthen the logic and persuasiveness of his argument. Be sure that your analysis focuses on the most relevant features of the passage.
>
> Your essay should not explain whether you agree with Bush's claims, but rather explain how Bush builds an argument to persuade his audience.

After reading through the President Bush prompt, you may want to consult the following notes and outline before writing your essay.

Student's Three Elements/Devices

1. **Praises past and present contributions to immigrants**

    -   Statistics and generalizations
    -   Paragraph 3: Long tradition, back when 18 mill were welcomed. Grateful for svc in WWI and WWII (immig. kids).
    -   Paragraph 4: Continues today, 14% of workforce. Many start as employees and end up employers.

    Effect: Puts facts behind rhetoric about immigrants—makes their contributions concrete & real

2. **Anticipates and rebuts criticisms**

    -   Critics might say too costly, out of control bureauc. Paragraph 7: he wants "clear and efficient."
    -   Expects temp workers to go back, but critics might worry about their welfare back home. Paragraph 8: we'll help smooth it out.
    -   Critics might say "you're not talking about citizenship." Yes he is: there are provisions for those who want to stay (paragraphs 9–10).

    Effect: Note he gets all of those out of the way before going on to list advantages in paragraph 11. He really wants listeners to accept his plan so polishes off potential objections first.

3. **Uses rhetoric to connect plan to fundamental values**

    -   Early as paragraph 2—U.S. welcomes immigrants
    -   Paragraph 5 details current probs w/system, but a solution, same paragraph, demanded by "Amer economy & Amer dream."
    -   Paragraph 12: conclusion evokes "the best tradition of our society," "honor[ing] the law," & "shar[ing] in the ideals of America."

    Effect: Wants to make his reform plan a moral imperative, not just a practical one. Implies whether you're worried about economy or fairness, this plan speaks to your concerns.

Student's Opening Paragraph

To "sell" his immigration reform plan unveiled in early 2004, President Bush goes beyond the strict, narrow topic of the temporary worker to persuade the audience that immigrants in general need to be congratulated and protected. To do so, he praises their past and present contributions, anticipates and rebuts objections to his plan, and uses rhetoric to connect his plan to fundamental values of the U.S.

PART 6

Countdown to Test Day

CHAPTER 29

Countdown to Test Day

The Week before the Test

- Focus your additional practice on the question types and/or subject areas in which you usually score highest. Now is the time to sharpen your best skills, not cram new information.

- Make sure you are registered for the test. Remember, Kaplan cannot register you. If you missed the registration deadlines, you can request Waitlist Status on the test maker's website, collegeboard.org.

- Confirm the location of your test site. Never been there before? Make a practice run to make sure you know exactly how long it will take to get from your home to your test site. Build in extra time in case you hit traffic or construction on the morning of the test.

- Get a great night's sleep the two days before the test.

The Day before the Test

- Review the methods and strategies you learned in this book.
- Put new batteries in your calculator.
- Pack your backpack or bag for test day with the following items:
  - Photo ID
  - Registration slip or printout
  - Directions to your test site location
  - Five or more sharpened no. 2 pencils (no mechanical pencils)
  - Pencil sharpener
  - Eraser
  - Calculator
  - Extra batteries
  - Non-prohibited timepiece
  - Tissues
  - Prepackaged snacks, like granola bars
  - Bottled water, juice, or sports drink
  - Sweatshirt, sweater, or jacket

The Night before the Test

- No studying!
- Do something relaxing that will take your mind off the test, such as watching a movie or playing video games with friends.
- Set your alarm to wake up early enough so that you won't feel rushed.
- Go to bed early, but not too much earlier than you usually do. You want to fall asleep quickly, not spend hours tossing and turning.

The Morning of the Test

- Dress comfortably and in layers. You need to be prepared for any temperature.
- Eat a filling breakfast, but don't stray too far from your usual routine. If you normally aren't a breakfast eater, don't eat a huge meal, but make sure you have something substantial.
- Read something over breakfast. You need to warm up your brain so you don't go into the test cold. Read a few pages of a newspaper, magazine, or favorite novel.
- Get to your test site early. There is likely to be some confusion about where to go and how to sign in, so allow yourself plenty of time, even if you are taking the test at your own school.
- Leave your cell phone at home. Many test sites do not allow them in the building.
- While you're waiting to sign in or be seated, read more of what you read over breakfast to stay in reading mode.

During the Test

- Be calm and confident. You're ready for this!
- Remember that while the SAT is a three-hour marathon, it is also a series of shorter sections. Focus on the section you're working on at that moment; don't think about previous or upcoming sections.
- Use the methods and strategies you have learned in this book as often as you can. Allow yourself to fall into the good habits you built during your practice.
- Don't linger too long on any one question. Mark it and come back to it later.
- Can't figure out an answer? Try to eliminate some choices and take a strategic guess. Remember, there is no penalty for an incorrect answer, so even if you can't eliminate any choices, you should take a guess.
- There will be plenty of questions you *can* answer, so spend your time on those first.
- Maintain good posture throughout the test. It will help you stay alert.
- If you find yourself losing concentration, getting frustrated, or stressing about the time, stop for 30 seconds. Close your eyes, put your pencil down, take a few deep breaths, and relax your shoulders. You'll be much more productive after taking a few moments to relax.
- Use your breaks effectively. During the five-minute breaks, go to the restroom, eat your snacks, and get your energy up for the next section.

After the Test

- Congratulate yourself! Then, reward yourself by doing something fun. You've earned it!
- If you got sick during the test or if something else happened that might have negatively affected your score, you can cancel your scores by the Wednesday following your test date. Request a score cancellation form from your test proctor or visit the test maker's website for more information.
- Your scores will be available online approximately two to four weeks after your test. The College Board sends scores to colleges 10 days after they are available to you.

PART 7

Practice Tests

How to Score Your Practice Tests

For each subject area in the practice test, convert your raw score, or the number of questions you answered correctly, to a scaled score using the table below. To get your raw score for Evidence-Based Reading and Writing, add the total number of Reading questions you answered correctly to the total number of Writing questions you answered correctly; for Math, add the number of questions you answered correctly for the Math (No Calculator) and Math (Calculator) sections.

Evidence-Based Reading and Writing		Math	
TOTAL Raw Score	Scaled Score	Raw Score	Scaled Score
0	200	0	200
1	200	1	220
2	210	2	240
3	220	3	260
4	240	4	290
5	260	5	310
6	270	6	320
7	270	7	330
8	290	8	340
9	290	9	360
10	300	10	370
11	300	11	380
12	310	12	390
13	320	13	400
14	320	14	410
15	330	15	420
16	330	16	430
17	340	17	430
18	340	18	440
19	350	19	450
20	350	20	450
21	360	21	460
22	360	22	470
23	370	23	480
24	370	24	490
25	370	25	500
26	380	26	510
27	380	27	520
28	380	28	530
29	380	29	540
30	390	30	540
31	390	31	550
32	400	32	560
33	400	33	560
34	410	34	570
35	410	35	580
36	420	36	590
37	430	37	600
38	430	38	600
39	440	39	610
40	440	40	620
41	450	41	630
42	450	42	640
43	460	43	640
44	460	44	660
45	470	45	670
46	480	46	670
47	480	47	680
48	490	48	690

Evidence-Based Reading and Writing		Math	
TOTAL Raw Score	Scaled Score	Raw Score	Scaled Score
49	490	49	700
50	500	50	710
51	500	51	720
52	510	52	740
53	510	53	750
54	520	54	760
55	520	55	770
56	530	56	780
57	530	57	790
58	540	58	800
59	540		
60	550		
61	550		
62	560		
63	560		
64	570		
65	570		
66	580		
67	580		
68	590		
69	590		
70	600		
71	600		
72	610		
73	610		
74	610		
75	620		
76	620		
77	630		
78	630		
79	640		
80	640		
81	660		
82	660		
83	670		
84	680		
85	690		
86	700		
87	700		
88	710		
89	710		
90	730		
91	740		
92	750		
93	760		
94	780		
95	790		
96	800		

SAT Practice Test 1 Answer Sheet

You will see an answer sheet like the one below on test day. Remove (or photocopy) this answer sheet and use it to complete the test. Review the answer key following the test when finished.

When testing, start with number 1 for each section. If a section has fewer questions than answer spaces, leave the extra spaces blank.

SECTION

1

1. Ⓐ Ⓑ Ⓒ Ⓓ	14. Ⓐ Ⓑ Ⓒ Ⓓ	27. Ⓐ Ⓑ Ⓒ Ⓓ	40. Ⓐ Ⓑ Ⓒ Ⓓ
2. Ⓐ Ⓑ Ⓒ Ⓓ	15. Ⓐ Ⓑ Ⓒ Ⓓ	28. Ⓐ Ⓑ Ⓒ Ⓓ	41. Ⓐ Ⓑ Ⓒ Ⓓ
3. Ⓐ Ⓑ Ⓒ Ⓓ	16. Ⓐ Ⓑ Ⓒ Ⓓ	29. Ⓐ Ⓑ Ⓒ Ⓓ	42. Ⓐ Ⓑ Ⓒ Ⓓ
4. Ⓐ Ⓑ Ⓒ Ⓓ	17. Ⓐ Ⓑ Ⓒ Ⓓ	30. Ⓐ Ⓑ Ⓒ Ⓓ	43. Ⓐ Ⓑ Ⓒ Ⓓ
5. Ⓐ Ⓑ Ⓒ Ⓓ	18. Ⓐ Ⓑ Ⓒ Ⓓ	31. Ⓐ Ⓑ Ⓒ Ⓓ	44. Ⓐ Ⓑ Ⓒ Ⓓ
6. Ⓐ Ⓑ Ⓒ Ⓓ	19. Ⓐ Ⓑ Ⓒ Ⓓ	32. Ⓐ Ⓑ Ⓒ Ⓓ	45. Ⓐ Ⓑ Ⓒ Ⓓ
7. Ⓐ Ⓑ Ⓒ Ⓓ	20. Ⓐ Ⓑ Ⓒ Ⓓ	33. Ⓐ Ⓑ Ⓒ Ⓓ	46. Ⓐ Ⓑ Ⓒ Ⓓ
8. Ⓐ Ⓑ Ⓒ Ⓓ	21. Ⓐ Ⓑ Ⓒ Ⓓ	34. Ⓐ Ⓑ Ⓒ Ⓓ	47. Ⓐ Ⓑ Ⓒ Ⓓ
9. Ⓐ Ⓑ Ⓒ Ⓓ	22. Ⓐ Ⓑ Ⓒ Ⓓ	35. Ⓐ Ⓑ Ⓒ Ⓓ	48. Ⓐ Ⓑ Ⓒ Ⓓ
10. Ⓐ Ⓑ Ⓒ Ⓓ	23. Ⓐ Ⓑ Ⓒ Ⓓ	36. Ⓐ Ⓑ Ⓒ Ⓓ	49. Ⓐ Ⓑ Ⓒ Ⓓ
11. Ⓐ Ⓑ Ⓒ Ⓓ	24. Ⓐ Ⓑ Ⓒ Ⓓ	37. Ⓐ Ⓑ Ⓒ Ⓓ	50. Ⓐ Ⓑ Ⓒ Ⓓ
12. Ⓐ Ⓑ Ⓒ Ⓓ	25. Ⓐ Ⓑ Ⓒ Ⓓ	38. Ⓐ Ⓑ Ⓒ Ⓓ	51. Ⓐ Ⓑ Ⓒ Ⓓ
13. Ⓐ Ⓑ Ⓒ Ⓓ	26. Ⓐ Ⓑ Ⓒ Ⓓ	39. Ⓐ Ⓑ Ⓒ Ⓓ	52. Ⓐ Ⓑ Ⓒ Ⓓ

☐ # correct in Section 1

☐ # incorrect in Section 1

SECTION

2

1. Ⓐ Ⓑ Ⓒ Ⓓ	12. Ⓐ Ⓑ Ⓒ Ⓓ	23. Ⓐ Ⓑ Ⓒ Ⓓ	34. Ⓐ Ⓑ Ⓒ Ⓓ
2. Ⓐ Ⓑ Ⓒ Ⓓ	13. Ⓐ Ⓑ Ⓒ Ⓓ	24. Ⓐ Ⓑ Ⓒ Ⓓ	35. Ⓐ Ⓑ Ⓒ Ⓓ
3. Ⓐ Ⓑ Ⓒ Ⓓ	14. Ⓐ Ⓑ Ⓒ Ⓓ	25. Ⓐ Ⓑ Ⓒ Ⓓ	36. Ⓐ Ⓑ Ⓒ Ⓓ
4. Ⓐ Ⓑ Ⓒ Ⓓ	15. Ⓐ Ⓑ Ⓒ Ⓓ	26. Ⓐ Ⓑ Ⓒ Ⓓ	37. Ⓐ Ⓑ Ⓒ Ⓓ
5. Ⓐ Ⓑ Ⓒ Ⓓ	16. Ⓐ Ⓑ Ⓒ Ⓓ	27. Ⓐ Ⓑ Ⓒ Ⓓ	38. Ⓐ Ⓑ Ⓒ Ⓓ
6. Ⓐ Ⓑ Ⓒ Ⓓ	17. Ⓐ Ⓑ Ⓒ Ⓓ	28. Ⓐ Ⓑ Ⓒ Ⓓ	39. Ⓐ Ⓑ Ⓒ Ⓓ
7. Ⓐ Ⓑ Ⓒ Ⓓ	18. Ⓐ Ⓑ Ⓒ Ⓓ	29. Ⓐ Ⓑ Ⓒ Ⓓ	40. Ⓐ Ⓑ Ⓒ Ⓓ
8. Ⓐ Ⓑ Ⓒ Ⓓ	19. Ⓐ Ⓑ Ⓒ Ⓓ	30. Ⓐ Ⓑ Ⓒ Ⓓ	41. Ⓐ Ⓑ Ⓒ Ⓓ
9. Ⓐ Ⓑ Ⓒ Ⓓ	20. Ⓐ Ⓑ Ⓒ Ⓓ	31. Ⓐ Ⓑ Ⓒ Ⓓ	42. Ⓐ Ⓑ Ⓒ Ⓓ
10. Ⓐ Ⓑ Ⓒ Ⓓ	21. Ⓐ Ⓑ Ⓒ Ⓓ	32. Ⓐ Ⓑ Ⓒ Ⓓ	43. Ⓐ Ⓑ Ⓒ Ⓓ
11. Ⓐ Ⓑ Ⓒ Ⓓ	22. Ⓐ Ⓑ Ⓒ Ⓓ	33. Ⓐ Ⓑ Ⓒ Ⓓ	44. Ⓐ Ⓑ Ⓒ Ⓓ

☐ # correct in Section 2

☐ # incorrect in Section 2

Practice Tests

K 899

SECTION

3

1. Ⓐ Ⓑ Ⓒ Ⓓ   5. Ⓐ Ⓑ Ⓒ Ⓓ   9. Ⓐ Ⓑ Ⓒ Ⓓ   13. Ⓐ Ⓑ Ⓒ Ⓓ
2. Ⓐ Ⓑ Ⓒ Ⓓ   6. Ⓐ Ⓑ Ⓒ Ⓓ   10. Ⓐ Ⓑ Ⓒ Ⓓ   14. Ⓐ Ⓑ Ⓒ Ⓓ
3. Ⓐ Ⓑ Ⓒ Ⓓ   7. Ⓐ Ⓑ Ⓒ Ⓓ   11. Ⓐ Ⓑ Ⓒ Ⓓ   15. Ⓐ Ⓑ Ⓒ Ⓓ
4. Ⓐ Ⓑ Ⓒ Ⓓ   8. Ⓐ Ⓑ Ⓒ Ⓓ   12. Ⓐ Ⓑ Ⓒ Ⓓ

correct in Section 3

incorrect in Section 3

16.   17.   18.   19.   20.

SECTION

4

1. Ⓐ Ⓑ Ⓒ Ⓓ   9. Ⓐ Ⓑ Ⓒ Ⓓ   17. Ⓐ Ⓑ Ⓒ Ⓓ   25. Ⓐ Ⓑ Ⓒ Ⓓ
2. Ⓐ Ⓑ Ⓒ Ⓓ   10. Ⓐ Ⓑ Ⓒ Ⓓ   18. Ⓐ Ⓑ Ⓒ Ⓓ   26. Ⓐ Ⓑ Ⓒ Ⓓ
3. Ⓐ Ⓑ Ⓒ Ⓓ   11. Ⓐ Ⓑ Ⓒ Ⓓ   19. Ⓐ Ⓑ Ⓒ Ⓓ   27. Ⓐ Ⓑ Ⓒ Ⓓ
4. Ⓐ Ⓑ Ⓒ Ⓓ   12. Ⓐ Ⓑ Ⓒ Ⓓ   20. Ⓐ Ⓑ Ⓒ Ⓓ   28. Ⓐ Ⓑ Ⓒ Ⓓ
5. Ⓐ Ⓑ Ⓒ Ⓓ   13. Ⓐ Ⓑ Ⓒ Ⓓ   21. Ⓐ Ⓑ Ⓒ Ⓓ   29. Ⓐ Ⓑ Ⓒ Ⓓ
6. Ⓐ Ⓑ Ⓒ Ⓓ   14. Ⓐ Ⓑ Ⓒ Ⓓ   22. Ⓐ Ⓑ Ⓒ Ⓓ   30. Ⓐ Ⓑ Ⓒ Ⓓ
7. Ⓐ Ⓑ Ⓒ Ⓓ   15. Ⓐ Ⓑ Ⓒ Ⓓ   23. Ⓐ Ⓑ Ⓒ Ⓓ
8. Ⓐ Ⓑ Ⓒ Ⓓ   16. Ⓐ Ⓑ Ⓒ Ⓓ   24. Ⓐ Ⓑ Ⓒ Ⓓ

correct in Section 4

incorrect in Section 4

31.   32.   33.   34.

35.   36.   37.   38.

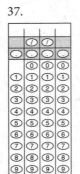

Practice Tests

Reading Test

65 Minutes—52 Questions

This section corresponds to Section 1 of your answer sheet.

Directions: Read each passage or pair of passages, then answer the questions that follow. Choose your answers based on what the passage(s) and any accompanying graphics state or imply.

Questions 1–10 are based on the following passage.

The following passage is adapted from Henry David Thoreau's *Walden*, a mid-19th-century philosophical and personal reflection on the writer's experience living in nature and simplicity. This excerpt is from the chapter titled "Where I Lived, and What I Lived For."

It matters not what the clocks say or the attitudes and labors of men. Morning is when I am awake and there is a dawn in me. Moral reform is the effort to throw off sleep. Why is it
5 that men give so poor an account of their day if they have not been slumbering? They are not such poor calculators. If they had not been overcome with drowsiness, they would have performed something. The millions are awake enough for
10 physical labor; but only one in a million is awake enough for effective intellectual exertion, only one in a hundred millions to a poetic or divine life. To be awake is to be alive. I have never yet met a man who was quite awake. How could I have looked
15 him in the face?

We must learn to reawaken and keep ourselves awake, not by mechanical aids, but by an infinite expectation of the dawn, which does not forsake us in our soundest sleep. I know of no more
20 encouraging fact than the unquestionable ability of man to elevate his life by a conscious endeavor. It is something to be able to paint a particular picture, or to carve a statue, and so to make a few objects beautiful; but it is far more glorious to carve and
25 paint the very atmosphere and medium through which we look, which morally we can do. To affect the quality of the day, that is the highest of arts. Every man is tasked to make his life, even in its

details, worthy of the contemplation of his most
30 elevated and critical hour. If we refused, or rather used up, such paltry information as we get, the oracles would distinctly inform us how this might be done.

I went to the woods because I wished to live
35 deliberately, to front only the essential facts of life, and see if I could not learn what it had to teach, and not, when I came to die, discover that I had not lived. I did not wish to live what was not life, living is so dear; nor did I wish to practice resignation, unless
40 it was quite necessary. I wanted to live deep and suck out all the marrow of life, to live so sturdily and Spartan-like as to put to rout all that was not life, to cut a broad swath and shave close, to drive life into a corner, and reduce it to its lowest terms, and, if it
45 proved to be mean, why then to get the whole and genuine meanness of it, and publish its meanness to the world; or if it were sublime, to know it by experience, and be able to give a true account of it in my next excursion. For most men, it appears to
50 me, are in a strange uncertainty about it, whether it is of the devil or of God, and have somewhat hastily concluded that it is the chief end of man here to "glorify God and enjoy him forever."

Still we live meanly, like ants; though the fable
55 tells us that we were long ago changed into men; like pygmies we fight with cranes; it is error upon error, and clout upon clout, and our best virtue has for its occasion a superfluous and evitable wretchedness. Our life is frittered away by detail.
60 An honest man has hardly need to count more than his ten fingers, or in extreme cases he may add his ten toes, and lump the rest. Simplicity, simplicity,

simplicity! I say, let your affairs be as two or three,
and not a hundred or a thousand; instead of a

65   million count half a dozen, and keep your accounts
on your thumb-nail. In the midst of this chopping
sea of civilized life, such are the clouds and storms
and quicksands and thousand-and-one items to be
allowed for, that a man has to live, if he would not

70   founder and go to the bottom and not make his port
at all, by dead reckoning, and he must be a great
calculator indeed who succeeds. Simplify, simplify.
Instead of three meals a day, if it be necessary eat but
one; instead of a hundred dishes, five; and reduce

75   other things in proportion.

1. The activities described in lines 21–26 ("It is some-
    thing … morally we can do") explain how people
    can

    A) develop a satisfying and morally upright
        career.

    B) give an elevated and proper account of their
        day.

    C) learn to reawaken and live by conscious
        endeavor.

    D) awaken enough for effective intellectual
        exhaustion.

2. As used in line 39, "resignation" most nearly means

    A) complacency.

    B) departure.

    C) quitting.

    D) revival.

3. The first paragraph of the passage most strongly
    suggests that which of the following is true of the
    author?

    A) He believes that to affect the quality of
        the day is the highest form of art.

    B) He feels that people perform poorly at work
        because they sleep too much.

    C) He is determined to spend as many waking
        hours as possible working.

    D) He believes that most people have yet to
        realize their fullest potential in life.

4. Which choice provides the best evidence for the
    answer to the previous question?

    A) Lines 4–6 ("Why is … slumbering")

    B) Lines 9–12 ("The millions … life")

    C) Lines 12–13 ("To be … alive")

    D) Lines 13–14 ("I have … awake")

5. What central claim does the author make about our
    society as a whole?

    A) The few artists in our society do not receive
        the recognition they deserve.

    B) Our society willingly focuses too much on
        drudgery and insignificant details.

    C) Too many people hastily choose to dedicate
        their lives to religion.

    D) People should move to the woods to find
        their own conscious endeavor.

6. What can reasonably be inferred about the author's
    views on religion?

    A) He believes too few people critically examine
        their religious beliefs.

    B) He thinks that his studies in the woods will
        prove that God is sublime.

    C) He thinks that meanness and the sublime are
        the same in nature.

    D) He believes that oracles give us clues about
        how to live a sublime life.

7. Which choice provides the best evidence for the answer to the previous question?

   A) Lines 28–30 ("Every man ... hour")

   B) Lines 34–38 ("I went ... not lived")

   C) Lines 40–49 ("I wanted ... excursion")

   D) Lines 49–53 ("'For most ... forever'")

8. As used in line 42, "Spartan-like" most nearly means

   A) indulgent.

   B) rigid.

   C) pioneering.

   D) austere.

9. The author uses such words as "meanly" and "wretchedness" in lines 54–59 in order to imply that

   A) people are cruel to one another.

   B) society will destroy itself in time.

   C) many people's lives are harsh and mundane.

   D) negative tendencies ruin our intelligence.

10. Which of the following describes an approach to life that is similar to the one Thoreau promotes in this passage?

   A) Taking courses and acquiring books on how to simplify your life

   B) Hiring people to help you do your chores so you can live more simply

   C) Cleaning out your closet so that you are left with only the most essential items of clothing

   D) Traveling to a cabin without cell phone service to get away from life's complications for a weekend

Questions 11–20 are based on the following passage.

This passage is adapted from "The Opening of the Library" by W.E.B. DuBois, professor of Economics and History at Atlanta University, published in the *Atlanta Independent* on April 3, 1902.

"With simple and appropriate exercises the beautiful new Carnegie Library was thrown open to the public yesterday." So says the morning paper of Atlanta, Georgia....

5   The white marble building, the gift of Andrew Carnegie, is indeed fair to look upon. The site was given the city by a private library association, and the City Council appropriates $5,000 annually of the city moneys for its support. If you will climb

10 the hill where the building sits, you may look down upon the rambling city. Northward and southward are 53,905 whites, eastward and westward are 35,912 blacks.

    And so in behalf of these 36,000 people my

15 companions and I called upon the trustees of the Library on this opening day, for we had heard that black folk were to have no part in this "free public library," and we thought it well to go ask why. It was not pleasant going in, for people stared and wondered

20 what business we had there; but the trustees, after some waiting, received us courteously and gave us seats—some eight of us in all. To me, had fallen the lot to begin the talking. I said, briefly:

    "Gentlemen, we are a committee come to ask

25 that you do justice to the black people of Atlanta by giving them the same free library privileges that you propose giving the whites. Every argument which can be adduced to show the need of libraries for whites applies with redoubled force to the blacks.

30 More than any other part of our population, they need instruction, inspiration and proper diversion; they need to be lured from the temptations of the streets and saved from evil influences, and they need a growing acquaintance with what the best of

35 the world's souls have thought and done and said. It seems hardly necessary in the 20th century to argue before men like you on the necessity and propriety

Practice Tests

of placing the best means of human uplifting into the hands of the poorest and lowest and blackest....

40 I then pointed out the illegality of using public money collected from all for the exclusive benefit of a part of the population, or of distributing public utilities in accordance with the amount of taxes paid by any class or individual, and finally I

45 concluded by saying:

"The spirit of this great gift to the city was not the spirit of caste or exclusion, but rather the catholic spirit which recognizes no artificial differences of rank or birth or race, but seeks to give all men equal

50 opportunity to make the most of themselves. It is our sincere hope that this city will prove itself broad enough and just enough to administer this trust in the true spirit in which it was given."

Then I sat down. There was a little pause, and the

55 chairman, leaning forward, said: "I should like to ask you a question: Do you not think that allowing whites and blacks to use this library would be fatal to its usefulness?"

There come at times words linked together which

60 seem to chord in strange recurring resonance with words of other ages and one hears the voice of many centuries and wonders which century is speaking....

I said simply, "I will express no opinion on that

65 point."

Then from among us darker ones another arose. He was an excellent and adroit speaker. He thanked the trustees for the privilege of being there, and reminded them that but a short time ago even this

70 privilege would have been impossible. He said we did not ask to use this library, we did not ask equal privileges, we only wanted some privileges somewhere. And he assured the trustees that he had perfect faith in their justice.

75 The president of the Trustee Board then arose, gray-haired and courteous. He congratulated the last speaker and expressed pleasure at our call. He then gave us to understand four things:

1. Blacks would not be permitted to use the

80 Carnegie Library in Atlanta.

2. That some library facilities would be provided for them in the future.

3. That to this end the City Council would be asked to appropriate a sum proportionate to the

85 amount of taxes paid by blacks in the city.

4. That an effort would be made, and had been made, to induce Northern philanthropists to aid such a library, and he concluded by assuring us that in this way we might

90 eventually have a better library than the whites.

Then he bade us adieu politely and we walked home wondering.

11. Which choice best explains why DuBois wrote this passage?

A) To encourage philanthropists such as Andrew Carnegie to fund new libraries

B) To present the trustees' explanation of why African Americans could not use the library

C) To contrast his position on public access to libraries with that of the trustees

D) To state his support for construction of a new library for just African Americans

12. Which choice provides the best evidence for the answer to the previous question?

A) Lines 14–18 ("And so ... ask why")

B) Lines 40–44 ("I then ... or individual")

C) Lines 67–70 ("He thanked ... impossible")

D) Lines 86–91 ("That an effort ... than the whites")

GO ON TO THE NEXT PAGE

13. As used in line 22, "lot" most nearly means

    A) a predictable result.

    B) a random decision.

    C) an unaccepted consequence.

    D) an agreed-upon responsibility.

14. It can reasonably be inferred from the passage that

    A) the trustees would consider the construction of segregated public library facilities.

    B) the trustees agreed with DuBois's arguments in favor of expanding access to public libraries.

    C) the trustees were open to the idea of integrating Atlanta's public library system.

    D) the trustees proposed concrete plans to provide public library facilities for African Americans.

15. Which choice provides the best evidence for the answer to the previous question?

    A) Lines 54–58 ("There was a little ... to its usefulness")

    B) Lines 75–77 ("The president ... at our call")

    C) Lines 79–80 ("Blacks ... in Atlanta")

    D) Lines 81–82 ("That some ... in the future")

16. As used in line 34, "growing acquaintance" most nearly means

    A) a friendly relationship.

    B) an increasing comprehension.

    C) an active involvement.

    D) a brief initiation.

17. Which claim does DuBois make to the trustees?

    A) Allowing all of Atlanta's residents to use the new library would render it useless.

    B) Blacks will benefit less from access to public libraries than white residents.

    C) Poor blacks have greater need for a public library than other residents.

    D) Atlanta should invest in public libraries and schools for all of its residents.

18. DuBois uses the example of a "catholic spirit" (lines 47–48) to support the argument that

    A) the city's neighborhoods continue to be segregated by race and economic class.

    B) Atlanta has an obligation to provide equal opportunity for all its residents to better themselves.

    C) access to public libraries should be based on the amount of taxes one pays.

    D) Northern philanthropists should provide private money to help pay for a public library.

19. The author's reflections expressed in lines 59–63 most likely indicate that he

    A) wishes he lived in a different century.

    B) is frustrated that people's attitudes have not changed over time.

    C) is thinking about a time when another person said the exact same words to him.

    D) is planning a detailed response to the chairman's question.

20. The four-point list in the passage can be described as

    A) a summary of the author's supporting points.

    B) an acknowledgment of a counterargument.

    C) an introduction to a counterargument.

    D) a response to the author's main argument.

Practice Tests

Questions 21–31 are based on the following passage and supplementary material.

The following passage is adapted from an essay about Denis Diderot, an 18th-century French philosopher.

Over a thirty-year period, Denis Diderot tirelessly undertook a bold endeavor; the philosopher and writer furthered technology education by creating one of the most important
5   books of the 18th century. He documented the Western world's collective knowledge through a massive set of volumes called the *Encyclopédie*. Today, Diderot's *Encyclopédie* remains one of the most accessible primary sources for the
10   study of technology during the Enlightenment, having received exposure in recent times through the Internet.

Since Diderot didn't know all there was to know, he sought contributors, more than 150, and
15   organized their 72,000 articles into entries on politics, economics, technology, and other topics. His goal was to create an intellectual work instructionally useful to all, but soon, his *Encyclopédie* became mired in controversy, and this precursor to the
20   modern encyclopedia was seized after its inception, its publication banned by the French government. The encyclopedia, however, had already sparked mass interest in the secrets of manufacturing and more, and so this "how-to" compendium was widely
25   circulated underground after eventually being published in 1765 by a Swedish printer.

Undoubtedly, the *Encyclopédie* served then as a beacon of free thought, and questions about control of its content caused critics to boil over. For
30   in building a compilation of human knowledge, Diderot made a direct political statement. Essentially, the political statement was: You, the average person, can now know what only kings knew before.

35   In particular, Diderot created an "encyclopedic revolution" by integrating scientific discoveries with the liberal arts. He linked technology to culture when he divided the *Encyclopédie* into three categories: history, philosophy, and poetry. Diderot
40   then assigned subjects to these three groupings such as industry, political theory, theology, agriculture, and the arts and sciences.

The execution was deceptively simple enough because Diderot pursued everyday trade topics
45   such as cloth dying, for example, accompanying his explanations with diagrams and illustrations. Thus, Diderot elevated "unacademic" craft knowledge to a scholarly status, challenging viewpoints about erudition held by the aristocratic ruling class of
50   the time. More important, Diderot suggested that everyone could have access to the rational, down-to-earth truth, since he believed that knowledge about reality could be obtained by reason alone, rather than through authority or other means.

55   Not surprisingly, such rationalist philosophy was considered radical. The new idea of showing in amazing detail how the production techniques used in tanning and metalwork were accomplished displeased those in power. Trade guilds held control
60   of such knowledge, and so Diderot's *Encyclopédie* was viewed as a threat to the establishment. Diderot's ideology of progress by way of better quality materials, technical research, and greater production speed was unprecedented in printed
65   books.

Royal authorities did not want the masses exposed to Diderot's liberal views such as this one: "The good of the people must be the great purpose of government. By the laws of nature and of reason, the
70   governors are invested with power to that end. And the greatest good of the people is liberty."

But the opposition was too late. Despite an official ban, the *Encyclopédie's* beautiful bookplates survived, recording production techniques dating
75   to the Middle Ages. Ironically, with the advent of both the English Industrial Revolution and the French Revolution, the trades shown in Diderot's work changed significantly after the encyclopedia's publication. Therefore, instead of becoming a
80   technical dictionary, the *Encyclopédie* rather serves today as a history of technology, showing us what trades were like before machines swept in to transform industry.

GO ON TO THE NEXT PAGE →

1500–1800 Scientific Revolution

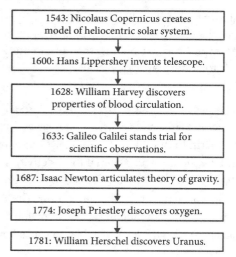

1543: Nicolaus Copernicus creates model of heliocentric solar system.

1600: Hans Lippershey invents telescope.

1628: William Harvey discovers properties of blood circulation.

1633: Galileo Galilei stands trial for scientific observations.

1687: Isaac Newton articulates theory of gravity.

1774: Joseph Priestley discovers oxygen.

1781: William Herschel discovers Uranus.

21. Which choice expresses a central idea of the passage?

   A) Diderot crafted a revolutionary guide for the development of industrial technology.

   B) Diderot provided students with a superb reference for the study of scientific principles.

   C) Diderot's *Encyclopédie* continues to serve as a valuable technical resource.

   D) Diderot's *Encyclopédie* helped promote the liberalization and expansion of knowledge.

22. The passage most clearly reflects the author's

   A) devotion to the study of science.

   B) disdain for intellectualism.

   C) interest in early printing methods.

   D) respect for individual innovation.

23. Which choice provides the best evidence for the answer to the previous question?

   A) Lines 35–37 ("In particular … liberal arts")

   B) Lines 56–59 ("The new idea … in power")

   C) Lines 66–69 ("Royal … of government")

   D) Lines 75–79 ("Ironically … publication")

24. According to the passage, Diderot's main goal in developing the *Encyclopédie* was to

   A) express his views.

   B) challenge political authority.

   C) provide information and instruction.

   D) create a historical record of technology.

25. As used in line 25, "underground" most nearly means

   A) cautiously.

   B) secretly.

   C) perilously.

   D) privately.

26. In line 28, the function of the phrase "a beacon of free thought" is to suggest that Diderot's work

   A) attracted more people to the pursuit of knowledge.

   B) provided information for people most likely to use it.

   C) encouraged revolutionary thinking.

   D) spread scientific theory among intellectual circles.

27. The passage most strongly suggests that during this time period

   A) access to information was limited to select demographics.

   B) advances in printing resulted in comparable advances in other fields.

   C) demands for political and social reform were severely punished.

   D) intellectuals were widely respected and elevated to elite status.

28. Which choice provides the best evidence for the answer to the previous question?

    A) Lines 13–16 ("Since Diderot ... topics")

    B) Lines 43–46 ("The execution ... illustrations")

    C) Lines 59–61 ("Trade guilds ... establishment")

    D) Lines 72–75 ("Despite ... Middle Ages")

29. As used in line 49, "erudition" most nearly means

    A) hierarchy.

    B) sophistication.

    C) skill.

    D) learning.

30. Which choice best describes how the impact of the *Encyclopédie* changed over time?

    A) Advances in science and industry made the *Encyclopédie* obsolete.

    B) Advances in science and industry changed the *Encyclopédie* from a "how-to" source into a history of technology.

    C) Advances in science and industry turned the *Encyclopédie* into an affordable, mass-produced publication used by millions.

    D) Advances in science and industry led to an expansion of the number of *Encyclopédie* volumes in each set.

31. Based on the passage and the graphic, which of the following is most likely to be true?

    A) Diderot would not have included information about Galileo's scientific observations.

    B) Diderot would have included information on the production techniques used to create the first telescope.

    C) Diderot would not have included information about the discovery of Uranus.

    D) Diderot would have included information about Einstein's theory of relativity.

Questions 32–42 are based on the following passages.

The following passages discuss acidity. Passage 1 describes the effect of acid rain on the environment, while Passage 2 focuses on how the human body responds to abnormal acidity levels.

Passage 1

In the past century, due to the burning of fossil fuels in energy plants and cars, acid rain has become a cause of harm to the environment. However, rain would still be slightly acidic even if these activities
5   were to stop. Acid rain would continue to fall, but it would not cause the problems we see now. The environment can handle slightly acidic rain; it just cannot keep up with the level of acid rain caused by burning fossil fuels.
10   A pH of 7 is considered neutral, while pH below 7 is acidic and pH above 7 is alkaline, or basic. Pure rain water can have a pH as low as 5.5. Rain water is acidic because carbon dioxide gas in the air reacts with the water to make carbonic acid. Since it is a
15   weak acid, even a large amount of it will not lower the pH of water much.
     Soil, lakes, and streams can tolerate slightly acidic rain. The water and soil contain alkaline materials that will neutralize acids. These include some types of
20   rocks, plant and animal waste, and ashes from forest fires. Altogether, these materials can easily handle the slightly acidic rain that occurs naturally. The alkaline waste and ashes will slowly be used up, but more will be made to replace it.
25   Anthropomorphic causes of acid rain, such as the burning of fossil fuels, release nitrogen oxide and sulfur oxide gases. These gases react with water to make nitric acid and sulfuric acid. Since these are both strong acids, small amounts can lower the pH of
30   rain water to 3 or less. Such a low pH requires much more alkaline material to neutralize it. Acid rain with a lower pH uses up alkaline materials faster, and more cannot be made quickly enough to replace what is used up. Soil and water become more acidic and
35   remain that way, as they are unable to neutralize the strong acid.

GO ON TO THE NEXT PAGE ⟶

Passage 2

In humans, keeping a constant balance between acidity and alkalinity in the blood is essential. If blood pH drops below 7.35 or rises above 7.45,
40 all of the functions in the body are impaired and life-threatening conditions can soon develop. Many processes in the body produce acid wastes, which would lower the pH of blood below the safe level unless neutralized. Several systems are in place
45 to keep pH constant within the necessary range. Certain conditions, however, can cause acids to be made faster than these systems can react.

Most of the pH control involves three related substances: carbon dioxide, carbonic acid, and
50 bicarbonate ions. Carbonic acid is formed when carbon dioxide reacts with water. Bicarbonate ions are formed when the carbonic acid releases a hydrogen ion. Excess carbonic acid lowers the pH, while excess bicarbonate ions raise it.

55 The kidneys store bicarbonate ions and will release or absorb them to help adjust the pH of the blood. Breathing faster removes more carbon dioxide from the blood, which reduces the amount of carbonic acid; in contrast, breathing more slowly
60 has the opposite effect. In a healthy body, these systems automatically neutralize normal amounts of acid wastes and maintain blood pH within the very small range necessary for the body to function normally.

65 In some cases, these systems can be overwhelmed. This can happen to people with diabetes if their blood sugar drops too low for too long. People with type 1 diabetes do not make enough insulin, which allows the body's cells to
70 absorb sugar from the blood to supply the body with energy. If a person's insulin level gets too low for too long, the body breaks down fats to use for energy. The waste produced from breaking down fats is acidic, so the blood pH drops. If the kidneys
75 exhaust their supply of bicarbonate ions, and the lungs cannot remove carbon dioxide fast enough to raise pH, other functions in the body begin to fail as well. The person will need medical treatment

to support these functions until the pH balancing
80 system can catch up. The system will then keep the blood pH constant, as long as the production of acid wastes does not exceed the body's capacity to neutralize them.

32. Passage 1 most strongly suggests that

    A) the environment will be damaged seriously if people do not reduce the burning of fossil fuels.

    B) scientists must find a way to introduce more alkaline materials into the water supply to combat acid rain.

    C) acid rain will not be a problem in the future as we move away from fossil fuels and toward alternative energy sources.

    D) acidic rain water is more of a problem than acidic soil because soil contains more alkaline materials.

33. Which choice provides the best evidence for the answer to the previous question?

    A) Lines 6–9 ("The environment … fuels")

    B) Lines 12–14 ("Rain water … acid")

    C) Lines 17–18 ("Soil, lakes … rain")

    D) Lines 25–27 ("Anthropomorphic … gases")

34. According to the information in Passage 1, which pH level for rain water would cause the most damage to the environment?

    A) 2.25

    B) 4

    C) 5

    D) 9.1

35. As used in line 17, "tolerate" most nearly means

    A) accept.

    B) endure.

    C) acknowledge.

    D) distribute.

36. Passage 2 most strongly suggests that

    A) a pH of 7.35 is ideal for blood in the human body.

    B) acid wastes in the blood multiply if not neutralized.

    C) the normal range of blood pH narrows as a person ages.

    D) small amounts of acid wastes in the blood are a normal condition.

37. Which choice provides the best evidence for the answer to the previous question?

    A) Lines 38–41 ("If blood pH ... develop")

    B) Lines 46–47 ("Certain conditions ... react")

    C) Lines 60–64 ("In a healthy ... normally")

    D) Lines 68–71 ("People with ... energy")

38. As used in line 75, "exhaust" most nearly means

    A) fatigue.

    B) consume.

    C) deplete.

    D) dissolve.

39. Which of the following plays a role in the environment most similar to the role played by excess bicarbonate ions in the blood?

    A) Acid rain

    B) Ashes from a forest fire

    C) Sulfur oxide gases

    D) Fossil fuels

40. Based on the information in Passage 2, which of the following can cause the body to break down fats to use for energy?

    A) An excess of carbonic acid

    B) Low blood pH

    C) A drop in blood sugar

    D) Not enough insulin

41. Which of the following best describes a shared purpose of the authors of both passages?

    A) To encourage readers to care for delicate systems such as the environment and human body

    B) To explain how the human body neutralizes acid wastes that it produces and deposits in the blood

    C) To describe systems that can neutralize small amounts of acids but become overwhelmed by large amounts

    D) To persuade readers to work toward reducing acid rain by cutting consumption of fossil fuels

42. Both passages support which of the following generalizations?

    A) The human body and environment are delicate systems that require balance to function properly.

    B) There are many similarities between the systems that make up the human body and the water cycle.

    C) Acid rain is an important issue that will continue to impact the environment until we reduce the use of fossil fuels.

    D) Medical treatment is necessary when the pH of a person's blood drops below 7.35 or rises above 7.45.

GO ON TO THE NEXT PAGE ⟹

Questions 43–52 are based on the following passage and supplementary material.

The following passage discusses the benefits of using hydrogen as a renewable energy source.

Scientists worldwide have been working diligently to advance hydrogen as a renewable energy source. Hydrogen, the most abundant element in the universe, is found primarily with
5 oxygen in water. Because it can be safely used as fuel, it is a candidate for gasoline replacement in passenger vehicles.

The potential benefits to moving away from petroleum-based fuel are plentiful. Since hydrogen
10 can be produced within the United States, discovering ways to safely and economically switch to hydrogen fuel would drastically reduce our dependency on other petroleum-producing nations. In addition to making us more
15 independent, hydrogen produces no pollution, including greenhouse gasses, when used as fuel. For this reason alone, forward-thinking scientists have made it a priority to invent new ways to use hydrogen.
20 Until now, there have been several challenges preventing hydrogen from becoming a mainstream form of clean energy. In the United States, engines that run on hydrogen are much more expensive than gasoline. Additionally, it is difficult to store
25 enough hydrogen to get comparable mileage to a gasoline vehicle. However, these factors have not been the biggest drawback in producing hydrogen for use in fuel cells; the biggest drawback has been that fossil fuels were needed to generate
30 large amounts of hydrogen. Relying on fossil fuels to produce this element nearly negates the environmental benefit behind the concept.

Recently, a new method has been discovered, allowing scientists to create large quantities of the
35 element using lower amounts of energy derived from renewable sources. As in traditional methods, scientists employ electrolysis, a process during which electricity is used to break the bonds between the atoms found in water by passing a current
40 through the water via a semiconductor. Once the water molecules are broken into separate hydrogen and oxygen atoms, both are released as individual gasses and the hydrogen can be harvested.

When people think of solar power, huge panels
45 usually come to mind, the type of panels that could not be used to power consumer vehicles in a way equivalent to gasoline. However, scientists have recently been successful at employing solar power as the catalyst in electrolysis, harvesting
50 energy from the sun and using it to break apart water molecules. The same scientists who made this achievement then built a semiconductor out of affordable, oxide-based materials. When these two advances are coupled, they also reduce the
55 economic and environmental cost of generating and processing hydrogen.

Another bonus to this new method of production is that it is significantly more efficient than older production methods. The team of
60 researchers attained the most efficient solar-to-fuel conversion to date, and they did it without using cost-prohibitive materials.

There are still several challenges to be overcome before hydrogen is a viable gasoline replacement.
65 This new method of production, though, is a huge step in the right direction. There are many ongoing research initiatives that aim to make hydrogen extraction even more cost-effective, as well as easy to store. When these issues are solved, hydrogen
70 will become a fuel that works for humanity and the earth at the same time.

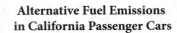

**Alternative Fuel Emissions
in California Passenger Cars**

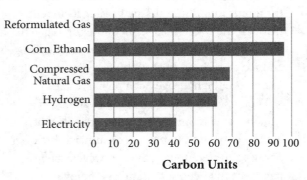

Adapted from U.S. Department of Energy Alternative Fuels Data Center.

43. With which of the following statements would the author most likely agree?

    A) Scientists should consider the final cost to consumers when exploring alternatives to petroleum-based fuels.

    B) The development of hydrogen fuel for automobiles will give a boost to the economy in the United States.

    C) Safety concerns surrounding hydrogen used as fuel pose the biggest problem for scientists studying alternative energy.

    D) Gasoline must be eliminated as a source of fuel for automobiles within the next decade.

44. Which choice provides the best evidence for the answer to the previous question?

    A) Lines 5–7 ("Because it … vehicles")

    B) Lines 9–14 ("Since hydrogen … nations")

    C) Lines 22–24 ("In the United States … gasoline")

    D) Lines 53–71 ("When these … time")

45. According to the passage, which of the following is true of hydrogen?

    A) It exists mostly with oxygen in water molecules in its natural state.

    B) It is more efficient than solar power as an energy source.

    C) It can be used as fuel in most types of engines.

    D) It can be easily harvested from water molecules.

46. As used in line 2, "diligently" most nearly means

    A) impulsively.

    B) persistently.

    C) rapidly.

    D) perpetually.

47. The passage most strongly suggests that which of the following is true of petroleum-based fuel?

    A) Its cost is higher than most alternative fuels.

    B) Its use has a negative effect on the environment.

    C) It cannot be produced in the United States.

    D) It is more efficient than other types of fuel.

48. Which choice provides the best evidence for the answer to the previous question?

    A) Lines 1–3 ("Scientists … source")

    B) Lines 14–16 ("In addition … as fuel")

    C) Lines 57–59 ("Another bonus … methods")

    D) Lines 59–62 ("The team … materials")

GO ON TO THE NEXT PAGE

49. In paragraph 2, why does the author explain that hydrogen energy will reduce our dependency on petroleum-producing nations?

    A) To illustrate why scientists in other countries are not working to develop hydrogen energy

    B) To highlight how hydrogen energy is superior to other forms of alternative energy

    C) To suggest how hydrogen energy can help protect the environment

    D) To clarify why the development of hydrogen as a fuel source is important

50. As used in line 35, "derived" most nearly means

    A) gained.

    B) received.

    C) obtained.

    D) copied.

51. The passage most strongly suggests that which of the following is true about methods of extracting hydrogen from water?

    A) Much additional research is needed to perfect hydrogen extraction.

    B) Scientific breakthroughs will soon make hydrogen extraction unnecessary.

    C) Scientists are on course to develop a safe way to extract hydrogen within one year.

    D) It is unlikely that hydrogen extraction will ever be done in an environmentally friendly way.

52. Information from both the passage and the graphic support the conclusion that

    A) compressed natural gas is the most environmentally friendly form of automobile fuel.

    B) scientists are making great advances in the development of hydrogen as a fuel for automobiles.

    C) electricity produces less air pollution than hydrogen and compressed natural gas.

    D) switching from gasoline to hydrogen to fuel automobiles would significantly reduce air pollution.

IF YOU FINISH BEFORE TIME IS CALLED, YOU MAY CHECK YOUR WORK ON THIS SECTION ONLY. DO NOT TURN TO ANY OTHER SECTION IN THE TEST.

STOP

K 913

Writing and Language Test

35 Minutes—44 Questions

This section corresponds to Section 2 of your answer sheet.

Directions: Each passage in this section is followed by several questions. Some questions will reference an underlined portion in the passage; others will ask you to consider a part of a passage or the passage as a whole. For each question, choose the answer that reflects the best use of grammar, punctuation, and style. If a passage or question is accompanied by a graphic, take the graphic into account in choosing your response(s). Some questions will have "NO CHANGE" as a possible response. Choose that answer if you think the best choice is to leave the sentence as written.

Questions 1–11 are based on the following passage and supplementary material.

Sorting Recyclables for Best Re-Use

From the time a plastic container is thrown into a recycling bin to the time the plastic **1** are actually recycled, it passes through several sorting cycles. In addition to being separated from the non-plastic items, the plastics themselves must be **2** detached, because not all plastics are alike, making some easier to recycle than others.

3 Special machines have been developed to assist in sorting plastics. During manual sorting, people **4** very thoroughly check the numbers on the bottom of each plastic item. The numbers indicate the type of plastic each is made from. Some sorting can be automated by using machines that can detect the composition of the plastic. The detectors in these machines use infrared light to characterize and sort the

1. A) NO CHANGE
   B) is
   C) has been
   D) will be

2. A) NO CHANGE
   B) demolished,
   C) flanked,
   D) categorized,

3. Which choice most effectively sets up the information that follows?
   A) NO CHANGE
   B) Sorting by hand is less efficient than using machines to sort plastics.
   C) Classifying plastics can be done manually or by machines.
   D) Plastics are widely used today, so they need to be recycled.

4. A) NO CHANGE
   B) completely and thoroughly check
   C) thoroughly check
   D) make sure to thoroughly check

GO ON TO THE NEXT PAGE ⟹

plastics, similar to how a human might use visible light to sort materials by their color. By either method, the plastics can eventually be arranged into bins or piles corresponding to the recycling code numbers running from one to seven.

In some cases, plastics are further sorted by the method by which they were manufactured. [5] However, [6] bottles, tubs and, trays are typically [7] made from either PET (polyethylene terephthalate) or HDPE (high density polyethylene), two of the least recovered plastics. Bottles are produced by a process called blow-molding, in which the plastic is heated until soft, then blown up, much like a balloon, while being pushed against a mold. Tubs and trays are usually made by a process called injection molding, in which the plastic is heated until it can be pushed through nozzles into a mold. Different additives are added to the plastics before [8] molding. It depends on the method. Since the additives for injection molding might not be suitable for blow-molding of the recycled plastic, PET and HDPE bottles are often separated out from the other PET and HDPE plastics.

While the numbers 1 through 6 indicate a [9] specific plastic, number 7 indicates that the plastic is either one of many other plastics, or that it is a blend of plastics. These plastics are more difficult to recycle, as different amounts of the various types of number 7 plastics will be sent to recycling each day. They are typically used for products in which the plastic will be mixed with other materials.

5. A) NO CHANGE
   B) For example,
   C) Consequently,
   D) Similarly,

6. A) NO CHANGE
   B) bottles, tubs, and trays
   C) bottles tubs, and trays,
   D) bottles, tubs, and, trays

7. Which choice completes the sentence with accurate data based on the graphic?

   A) NO CHANGE
   B) made from PET (polyethylene terephthalate) or HDPE (high density polyethylene), the two most recovered plastics after the leading type, LDPE.
   C) made from PP (polypropene) or PS (polystyrene), the two most recovered plastics after the leading type, PVC.
   D) made from PP (polypropene) or PS (polystyrene), the two most recovered plastics after the leading type, EPS.

8. Which choice most effectively combines the sentences at the underlined portion?

   A) molding, however, it depends
   B) molding, depending
   C) molding despite depending
   D) molding, it depends

9. A) NO CHANGE
   B) vague
   C) common
   D) pending

Practice Tests

Although there are many types of plastics to be found in a typical recycling bin, each one can play a part in a recycled **10** product, the many cycles of sorting guarantee that each piece can be correctly processed and sent off for re-use. **11**

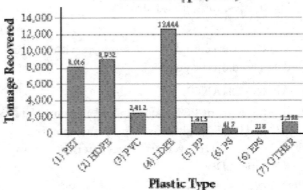

Breakdown of Recovered Plastic by Material Type (2004)

Original graph at http://www.recyclers.co.nz/symbols.php.

10. A) NO CHANGE

    B) product the many

    C) product. The many

    D) product, so the many

11. Which choice most effectively establishes a concluding sentence for the paragraph?

    A) Sorting ensures that plastics will not linger in the landfills, but continue to be of use.

    B) Sorting different types of plastics is done in many ways, either by hand or machine.

    C) Oftentimes, people are required to sort their own plastics by type.

    D) There are many different kinds of plastics, and each one is useful.

GO ON TO THE NEXT PAGE ⟹

Questions 12–22 are based on the following passage.

Interpreter at America's Immigrant Gateway

[12] Among the many diverse and fascinating possibilities for a career, David Kaufman chose language interpretation. Throughout his career as an interpreter at America's largest immigrant-processing station, Kaufman has spent many ferry rides mentally preparing himself for the vivid realities of his job. Although some of his contemporaries might consider his work menial or inconsequential, he cherishes his opportunity to witness and contribute to the unfolding stories of countless immigrants. These immigrant stories, Kaufman knows, hold [13] great significance for his and American history. Most of the brave, sea-worn travelers who disembark at Ellis Island will soon depart as new Americans, [14] lugging all there courage, hope, and worldly possessions into New York City. Many [15] will remain in the city and some other people will disperse across the nation.

12. Which choice provides the most appropriate introduction to the passage?

A) NO CHANGE

B) Many people never consider language interpretation as a job, but David Kaufman knows all about it.

C) All jobs come with difficulties, and David Kaufman believes language interpretation is no different.

D) A pale horizon meets the early-morning sky as David Kaufman's commuter ferry crosses the New York Harbor, bound for Ellis Island.

13. A) NO CHANGE

B) great significance for his—and America's—history.

C) great significance for his: and America's history.

D) great significance for his, and America's, history.

14. A) NO CHANGE

B) lugging all they're courage,

C) lugging all their courage,

D) lugging all there are courage,

15. A) NO CHANGE

B) will remain in the city, but other people will nonetheless disperse across the nation.

C) will remain in the city; many others will disperse across the nation.

D) will remain in the city, though yet others will disperse across the nation.

[1] The year is 1907: the busiest year Kaufman, or Ellis Island, has seen. [2] One and a quarter million immigrants have been admitted to the U.S. this year. [3] Only about 2 percent of Ellis Island's immigrants are denied, typically for perceived potential criminal or public health threats. [4] The rest will establish life in America, although not without difficulty and perseverance. [5] At the immigration station, Kaufman regularly sees the range of raw human emotion, from deep, exhausted grief to powerful hope. [6] He has witnessed it all. **16**

17 Many Ellis Island interpreters were born to European immigrants. **18** His heritage, and surrounding community, enabled him to learn six languages. Fluency in six languages is typical for Ellis Island interpreters, although Kaufman knows some who speak as many as twelve or thirteen. Kaufman knows that in some ways, his ability to listen and translate effectively can impact the course of an immigrant's future. For this reason, he constantly hones his language skills, picking up various **19** shades and dialects in hopes to better help those he serves.

16. Sentence 1 should be placed
    A) where it is now.
    B) after sentence 2.
    C) after sentence 3.
    D) after sentence 4.

17. Which sentence most effectively establishes the central idea of the paragraph?
    A) NO CHANGE
    B) Like many Ellis Island interpreters, Kaufman was born to European immigrants.
    C) Language ability was especially important among Ellis Island interpreters.
    D) Some accused children of European immigrants of having an unfair advantage in getting jobs at Ellis Island.

18. A) NO CHANGE
    B) His heritage, and surrounding community enabled him to learn six languages.
    C) His heritage and surrounding community, enabled him to learn six languages.
    D) His heritage and surrounding community enabled him to learn six languages.

19. A) NO CHANGE
    B) meanings
    C) tricks
    D) nuances

GO ON TO THE NEXT PAGE ⟹

Kaufman assists colleagues at every checkpoint. Ellis Island is equipped with a hospital, dining room, and boarding room, in addition to the more central processing facilities. [20] <u>Kaufman is one of an army of Ellis Island employees spread around the enormous compound.</u> This morning, he helps an Italian family discuss their child's health with nurses. Later, he translates for a Polish woman who expects to meet her brother soon. When Kaufman meets immigrants whose language he cannot speak, he finds another interpreter [21] <u>to help speak to them instead of him doing it.</u>

To some extent, Kaufman sees himself distinctly in the shoes of these immigrants. He intimately knows the reality that almost all Americans, somewhere in their ancestry, were not native to this nation. With every encounter, Kaufman hopes that these immigrants will soon find whatever they crossed oceans to seek. He hopes, as he still does for his own family, that life in America will someday render the [22] <u>advantages</u> of leaving home worthwhile.

20. Which sentence best supports the central idea of the paragraph?

A) NO CHANGE

B) From medical screening to records confirmation to inspection, Kaufman interprets as needs arise.

C) Sometimes, Kaufman feels the stress of being pulled in many different directions, but ultimately he finds his job worthwhile.

D) Kaufman and his colleagues work, eat, and practically live together, making them feel closer than typical coworkers.

21. A) NO CHANGE

B) to help speak instead of him.

C) helping him out with speaking.

D) to help.

22. A) NO CHANGE

B) journeys

C) difficulties

D) penalties

Questions 23–33 are based on the following passage.

Software Sales: A Gratifying Career

Ever since she was a young girl, Stephanie Morales took on the role of family problem solver. [23] She remembers her brother never being able to find his favorite movie when he wanted to watch it: So, she alphabetized the family DVD collection. [24] "They're about efficiency and what makes sense to a user," Morales says, "and putting systems in place so that using something becomes effortless."

Growing up, Morales became notorious among her friends as the one to plan parties and trips, and she was always voted team captain because everyone knew she could see the big picture and enact a plan. [25] After college, she tried a career in interior design, but homes and offices didn't excite her. "I didn't have a passion for furniture or architecture. I knew there must be a field out there that really tapped into my particular skill set," Morales says.

23. A) NO CHANGE
  B) She remembers her brother never being able to find his favorite movie, when he wanted to watch it so she alphabetized the family DVD collection.
  C) She remembers her brother never being able to find his favorite movie; when he wanted to watch it, so she alphabetized the family DVD collection.
  D) She remembers her brother never being able to find his favorite movie when he wanted to watch it, so she alphabetized the family DVD collection.

24. A) NO CHANGE
  B) It's
  C) Their
  D) Its

25. A) NO CHANGE
  B) After college, she tried a career in interior design: but homes and offices, didn't excite her.
  C) After college, she tried a career in interior design—but homes, and offices didn't excite her.
  D) After college she tried a career, in interior design; but homes and offices didn't excite her.

GO ON TO THE NEXT PAGE

Practice Tests

[1] To her surprise, that career turned out to be software consulting. [2] Morales returned from a backpacking trip around Europe to her parents' New Hampshire home, needing income. [3] New Hampshire also has many fine backpacking trails. [4] **26** Although she had no direct experience in the field, Morales convinced a family friend to hire her as a software consultant to work with new clients. **27** **28** She had helped many of her friends with their computers. Knowing her interpersonal skills were strong.

29 Because she was willing to work in a factory, she was able to achieve success as a consultant. For example, Morales worked with a manufacturing company that was growing quickly but had trouble

26. A) NO CHANGE
    B) Although she had no direct experience in the field, Morales convinces
    C) Although she has no direct experience in the field, Morales convinced
    D) Although she will have no direct experience in the field, Morales convinces

27. Which sentence does not support the paragraph's topic and purpose?
    A) Sentence 1
    B) Sentence 2
    C) Sentence 3
    D) Sentence 4

28. A) NO CHANGE
    B) She had helped many of her friends; with their computers and she knew her interpersonal skills were strong.
    C) She had helped many of her friends with their computers; knowing her interpersonal skills were strong.
    D) She had helped many of her friends with their computers, and she knew her interpersonal skills were strong.

29. Which choice most logically introduces the paragraph?
    A) NO CHANGE
    B) Morales's management of data led to the success of the company's advertising campaign.
    C) Where the job really matched up with her strengths was in problem-solving and finding creative solutions.
    D) Morales's advice to the human resources department resulted in higher wages for employees.

30 maintaining employees. The company's human resources department could not keep up with regular payroll and billing, plus running advertisements and interviewing potential replacement employees. Morales used staff management software to gather data about employee satisfaction. Analysis showed that employees found the shift work too challenging for their schedules. The company changed the hours of the morning and evening shifts to meet employees' needs, which led to fewer workers leaving the company.

Nowadays, Morales works with what she calls "big data," such as information about consumer habits gathered through a supermarket membership card. These stores of information are a treasure trove to Morales, because they tell the story of how people interact with the world around them. She uses the data to make changes—just like alphabetizing a DVD collection. Her goal is to **31** vacillate into the health care field, where she wants to bring the benefits of technology to people's physical and mental well-being. **32** For example, Morales is also interested in whether people pay for their medications with credit or debit cards. Morales knows that people's health is extremely important, and every time someone fills a prescription online or has a follow-up visit with their doctor, that information helps medical experts better determine efficacy of the medication. The technological revolution has the power **33** to quicken doctor's visits, improve the care we get, and even save lives.

30. A) NO CHANGE
    B) retaining
    C) containing
    D) detaining

31. A) NO CHANGE
    B) convert
    C) transition
    D) fluctuate

32. Which choice best supports the topic sentence of the paragraph?
    A) NO CHANGE
    B) For example, Morales spends countless hours walking through discount stores surveying the customers.
    C) For example, Morales still gets great satisfaction from organizing her friends' and family's DVD collections.
    D) For example, Morales can use "big data" to determine how many patients from a particular clinic use online automated refills.

33. A) NO CHANGE
    B) to quicken doctor's visits improve the care we get, and even save lives.
    C) to quicken doctor's visits, improve the care we get, and even, save lives.
    D) to quicken doctor's visits; improve the care we get, and even save lives.

GO ON TO THE NEXT PAGE

Questions 34–44 are based on the following passage.

The Art of Collecting

At an art exhibition for artist Henri Matisse, enthusiasts can also view a black-and-white photograph of two siblings. These sisters, wearing Victorian-style dresses and top hats, are the renowned art collectors Claribel and Etta Cone. When Etta passed away in 1949, she **34** bequeathed some 3,000 objects to the Baltimore Museum of Art (BMA). Now, works from the Cone Collection, internationally renowned and consisting of masterpieces by early 20th-century artists, travel on loan from BMA so that people can experience the Cone sisters' visionary passion for and dedication to modern art.

35 Henri Matisse was a well-known supporter of female artists and art patrons, and he revealed these unconventional attitudes in his work. What made the Cone sisters innovative was their recognition of the value of art pieces by virtually unknown avant-garde artists of their time, such as Pablo Picasso. Critics failed to understand the Cones' **36** tastes and such opinions did not squelch the sisters' passion for collecting. According to Katy Rothkopf, senior curator at the

34. A) NO CHANGE
    B) liquidated
    C) delivered
    D) allotted

35. Which choice best establishes the central idea of the paragraph?
    A) NO CHANGE
    B) Together the Cones, supported by the wealth from their family's textile business, gathered one of the finest collections of French art in the United States.
    C) The Cones became great contributors to the Baltimore Museum of Art, and their renowned exhibition was praised by artists around the globe.
    D) During this time period, only the wealthy could afford to purchase original artworks, and the Cones became famous for spending their entire fortune on art.

36. A) NO CHANGE
    B) tastes, so such opinions
    C) tastes therefore such opinions
    D) tastes, but such opinions

BMA, Matisse's use of vibrant color, for example, was initially shocking. "At first the Cones ... really found [the art] quite scary," states Rothkopf. However, the siblings befriended Matisse and other artists, gaining respect for the painters' unorthodox experimentation. As the Cones began buying and collecting art, **37** there selections improved.

"It took a lot of gall—guts—to paint it," Matisse once said about a controversial painting, "but much more to buy it." Claribel and Etta had that kind of gall. **38** Each had took risks by not purchasing traditional landscape paintings and instead amassing works that at the time were considered contemptuous and wild.

[1] A further legacy of the Cone Collection was its documentation of post-World War I Europe. [2] The art the Cones collected **39** suggested changes in Europe, such as the increasing use of machines in contemporary life and the emergence of modern thinking. [3] Traditional limitations in art were overcome by experimental forms and new media, allowing artists to explore their creativity. [4] Today, there are even more experimental forms of art than there were after World War I. **40**

37. A) NO CHANGE
    B) they're
    C) their
    D) her

38. A) NO CHANGE
    B) They took risks
    C) They have taken risks
    D) Each will take risks

39. A) NO CHANGE
    B) depicted
    C) referenced
    D) divulged

40. Which sentence should be deleted to best maintain the theme of the paragraph?
    A) Sentence 1
    B) Sentence 2
    C) Sentence 3
    D) Sentence 4

GO ON TO THE NEXT PAGE

[41] Additionally in visiting Paris, Budapest, Athens, Cairo, and Shanghai, the Cones represented the beginning of the new woman at the turn of the century. [42] Though their unconventional lifestyle, the far-seeing Cone sisters experienced freedom from narrower roles. They avoided the gross inequalities between genders by becoming connoisseurs of radical art. [43]

Public acceptance of the [44] Cone's avant-garde collection testifies to their accomplishments. While the estimated value of their artwork is one billion dollars, their larger contribution is inestimable. As bold patrons, the Cones advanced appreciation for modern art for generations to come.

41. A) NO CHANGE
    B) Additionally, in visiting: Paris,
    C) Additionally, in visiting Paris,
    D) Additionally in visiting Paris

42. A) NO CHANGE
    B) Therefore
    C) Thorough
    D) Through

43. What changes to the paragraph would best strengthen the author's claims?
    A) The author should define the terms "new woman" and "narrower roles."
    B) The author should list more nations and cities visited by the Cone sisters.
    C) The precise centuries referenced by "turn of the century" should be included.
    D) The author should add reactions from contemporary critics to the Cones' travels.

44. A) NO CHANGE
    B) Cones'
    C) Cones
    D) Cones's

IF YOU FINISH BEFORE TIME IS CALLED, YOU MAY CHECK YOUR WORK ON THIS SECTION ONLY. DO NOT TURN TO ANY OTHER SECTION IN THE TEST.

STOP

Math Test

25 Minutes—20 Questions

NO-CALCULATOR SECTION

This section corresponds to Section 3 of your answer sheet.

Directions: For this section, solve each problem and decide which is the best of the choices given. Fill in the corresponding oval on the answer sheet. You may use any available space for scratch work.

Notes:

1. Calculator use is NOT permitted.

2. All numbers used are real numbers, and all variables used represent real numbers, unless otherwise indicated.

3. Figures are drawn to scale and lie in a plane unless otherwise indicated.

4. Unless stated otherwise, the domain of any function f is assumed to be the set of all real numbers x for which $f(x)$ is a real number.

Information:

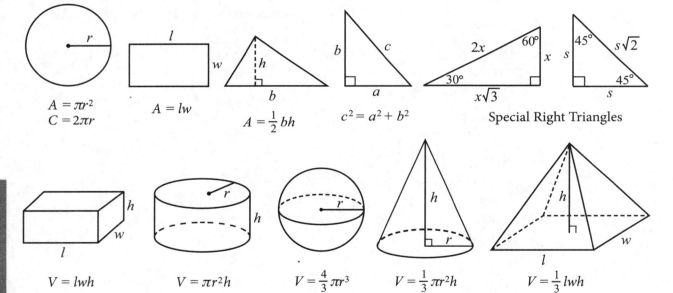

The sum of the degree measures of the angles in a triangle is 180.

The number of degrees of arc in a circle is 360.

The number of radians of arc in a circle is 2π.

GO ON TO THE NEXT PAGE

1. A biologist develops the equation $y = 20.942x + 127$ to predict the regrowth of a certain species of plant x months after a natural disaster occurred. Which of the following describes what the number 20.942 represents in this equation?

   A) The estimated number of the plants after x months

   B) The estimated monthly increase in the number of the plants

   C) The estimated monthly decrease in the number of the plants

   D) The estimated number of the plants that survived the natural disaster

2. Which of the following expressions is equivalent to $25x^2 - \dfrac{4}{9}$?

   A) $\sqrt{5x - \dfrac{2}{3}}$

   B) $x\left(5x - \dfrac{2}{3}\right)$

   C) $\left(5x + \dfrac{2}{3}\right)\left(5x - \dfrac{2}{3}\right)$

   D) $\left(25x + \dfrac{2}{3}\right)\left(25x - \dfrac{2}{3}\right)$

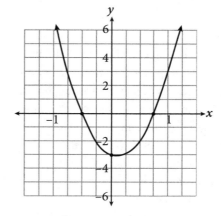

3. Which of the following could be the factored form of the equation graphed in the figure shown?

   A) $y = (2x + 1)(4x - 3)$

   B) $y = (x + 2)(x - 3)$

   C) $y = \left(x - \dfrac{1}{2}\right)\left(x + \dfrac{3}{4}\right)$

   D) $y = \dfrac{1}{2}(x + 1)(x - 3)$

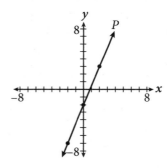

4. Line P is shown in the coordinate plane above. If line Q (not shown) is the result of translating line P left 4 units and down 3 units, what is the slope of line Q?

   A) $-\dfrac{4}{3}$

   B) -1

   C) $\dfrac{4}{3}$

   D) $\dfrac{5}{2}$

Practice Tests

GO ON TO THE NEXT PAGE

$$a = \frac{v_f - v_i}{t}$$

5. Acceleration is the rate at which the velocity of an object changes with respect to time, or in other words, how much an object is speeding up or slowing down. The average acceleration of an object can be found using the formula shown above, where t is the time over which the acceleration is being measured, v_f is the final velocity, and v_i is the initial velocity. Which of the following represents t in terms of the other variables?

A) $t = \dfrac{a}{v_f - v_i}$

B) $t = \dfrac{v_f - v_i}{a}$

C) $t = a(v_f - v_i)$

D) $t = \dfrac{1}{a(v_f - v_i)}$

6. Which of the following equations could represent a parabola that has a minimum value of -5 and whose axis of symmetry is the line $x = 1$?

A) $y = (x - 5)^2 + 1$
B) $y = (x + 5)^2 + 1$
C) $y = (x - 1)^2 - 5$
D) $y = (x + 1)^2 - 5$

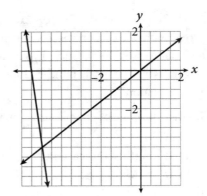

7. If (A, B) is the solution to the system of equations shown in the graph above, what is the value of $A + B$?

A) -18
B) -9
C) 1
D) 5.5

8. If $A = x^2 + 4x + 9$ and $B = x^3 + 6x - 2$, what is $3A + B$?

A) $4x^2 + 18x + 25$
B) $x^3 + x^2 + 10x + 7$
C) $x^3 + 3x^2 + 18x + 25$
D) $3x^3 + 3x^2 + 30x + 29$

9. How many real values of x satisfy the quadratic equation $9x^2 - 12x + 4 = 0$?

A) 0
B) 1
C) 2
D) 4

GO ON TO THE NEXT PAGE

10. Which of the following represents the solution set for the inequality $\frac{3}{5}\left(x + \frac{2}{7}\right) > -6$?

A) $x > -\frac{72}{7}$

B) $x > -\frac{216}{35}$

C) $x > -\frac{136}{35}$

D) $x > -\frac{18}{7}$

11. Acetaminophen is one of the most common drugs given to children and one of the most difficult to give correctly because it's sold in several different forms and different concentrations. For example, the old concentration given by dropper was 80 milligrams of acetaminophen per 1 milliliter of liquid, while the new concentration given by syringe is 160 milligrams per 5 milliliters. Several dosages are shown in the table below.

Infant Acetaminophen Dosages			
Age	0–3 mo	4–11 mo	12–23 mo
Dropper	0.5 ml	1.0 ml	1.5 ml
Syringe	1.25 ml	2.5 ml	3.75 ml

Which linear function represents the relationship between the amount of liquid in the dropper, d, and the amount of liquid in the syringe, s ?

A) $s = 0.4d$

B) $s = 1.25d$

C) $s = 2d$

D) $s = 2.5d$

12. Which of the following equations when graphed on a coordinate plane will not cross the y-axis?

A) $0.5(4x + y) = y - 9$

B) $2(x + 7) - x = 4(y + 3)$

C) $0.25(8y + 4x) - 7 = -2(-y + 1)$

D) $6x - 2(3y + x) = 10 - 3y$

$$\begin{cases} Hx + 2y = -8 \\ Kx - 5y = -13 \end{cases}$$

13. If the solution to the system of equations shown above is $(2, -1)$, what is the value of $\frac{K}{H}$?

A) -3

B) $-\frac{1}{3}$

C) $\frac{1}{3}$

D) 3

14. It is given that $\sin A = k$, where A is an angle measured in radians and $\pi < A < \frac{3\pi}{2}$. If $\sin B = k$, which of the following could be the value of B ?

A) $A - \pi$

B) $\pi + A$

C) $2\pi - A$

D) $3\pi - A$

15. Which of the following is equivalent to the expression $\left(\dfrac{x^{\frac{1}{2}}}{x^{-2}}\right)^2$?

A) x^2

B) $\left(\dfrac{x^2}{x}\right)^{\frac{1}{2}}$

C) $\left(\dfrac{\left(x^2\right)\left(x^{\frac{1}{3}}\right)}{x^4}\right)^3$

D) $\left(\dfrac{\left(x^3\right)\left(x^4\right)}{x^{-3}}\right)^{\frac{1}{2}}$

Practice Tests

Directions: For questions 16–20, enter your responses into the appropriate grid on your answer sheet, in accordance with the following:

1. You will receive credit only if the circles are filled in correctly, but you may write your answers in the boxes above each grid to help you fill in the circles accurately.

2. Don't mark more than one circle per column.

3. None of the questions with Grid-in responses will have a negative solution.

4. Only grid in a single answer, even if there is more than one correct answer to a given question.

5. A **mixed number** must be gridded as a decimal or an improper fraction. For example, you would grid $7\frac{1}{2}$ as 7.5 or 15/2.

   (Were you to grid it as [7 | 1 | / | 2], this response would be read as $\frac{71}{2}$.)

6. A **decimal** that has more digits than there are places on the grid may be either rounded or truncated, but every column in the grid must be filled in to receive credit.

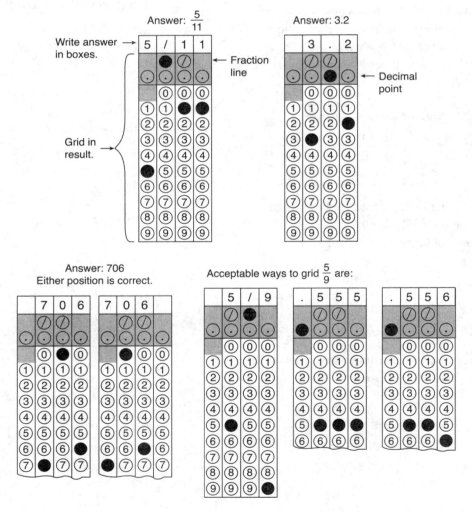

Answer: $\frac{5}{11}$

Answer: 3.2

Write answer in boxes.

Fraction line

Grid in result.

Decimal point

Answer: 706
Either position is correct.

Acceptable ways to grid $\frac{5}{9}$ are:

GO ON TO THE NEXT PAGE ⟶

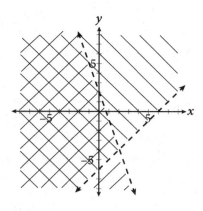

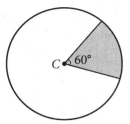

$$\begin{cases} y < -3x + 2 \\ y > x - 6 \end{cases}$$

16. The figure above shows the solution set for the given system of inequalities. Suppose (a, b) is a solution to the system. If $a = 0$, what is the greatest possible integer value of b?

17. Given the function $f(x) = \frac{2}{3}x - 5$, what input value corresponds to an output of 3?

18. If the area of the shaded sector in circle C shown above is 6π square units, what is the diameter of the circle?

19. What is the diameter of the circle given by the equation $x^2 + y^2 + 10x - 4y = 20$?

20. In economics, the law of demand states that as the price of a commodity rises, the demand for that commodity goes down. A company determines that the monthly demand for a certain item that it sells can be modeled by the function $q(p) = -2p + 34$, where q represents the quantity sold in hundreds and p represents the selling price in dollars. It costs \$7 to produce this item. How much more per month in profits can the company expect to earn by selling the item at \$12 instead of \$10? (Profit = sales − costs)

IF YOU FINISH BEFORE TIME IS CALLED, YOU MAY CHECK YOUR WORK ON THIS SECTION ONLY. DO NOT TURN TO ANY OTHER SECTION IN THE TEST.

STOP

Practice Tests

K 931

Math Test

55 Minutes—38 Questions

CALCULATOR SECTION

This section corresponds to Section 4 of your answer sheet.

Directions: For this section, solve each problem and decide which is the best of the choices given. Fill in the corresponding oval on the answer sheet. You may use any available space for scratch work.

Notes:

1. Calculator use is permitted.
2. All numbers used are real numbers, and all variables used represent real numbers, unless otherwise indicated.
3. Figures are drawn to scale and lie in a plane unless otherwise indicated.
4. Unless stated otherwise, the domain of any function f is assumed to be the set of all real numbers x for which $f(x)$ is a real number.

Information:

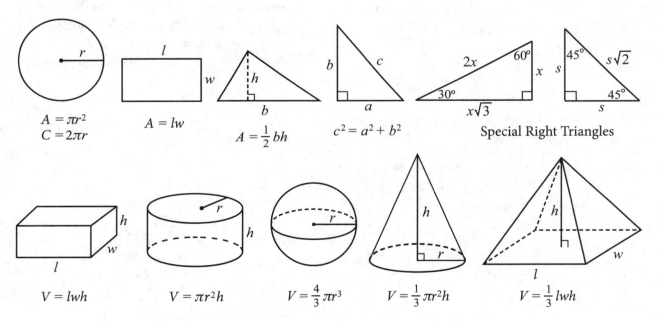

$A = \pi r^2$
$C = 2\pi r$

$A = lw$

$A = \frac{1}{2}bh$

$c^2 = a^2 + b^2$

Special Right Triangles

$V = lwh$

$V = \pi r^2 h$

$V = \frac{4}{3}\pi r^3$

$V = \frac{1}{3}\pi r^2 h$

$V = \frac{1}{3}lwh$

The sum of the degree measures of the angles in a triangle is 180.

The number of degrees of arc in a circle is 360.

The number of radians of arc in a circle is 2π.

GO ON TO THE NEXT PAGE

1. The USDA recommends that adult females consume 75 milligrams of ascorbic acid, also known as vitamin C, each day. Because smoking inhibits vitamin absorption, smokers are encouraged to consume an additional 35 milligrams daily. If one grapefruit contains 40 milligrams of vitamin C and one serving of spinach contains 10 milligrams, which of the following inequalities represents the possible intake of grapefruit, g, and spinach, s, that a smoking female could consume to meet or surpass the USDA's recommended amount of vitamin C?

   A) $40g + 10s \geq 75$

   B) $40g + 10s \geq 110$

   C) $40g + 10s > 110$

   D) $\dfrac{40}{g} + \dfrac{10}{s} \geq 110$

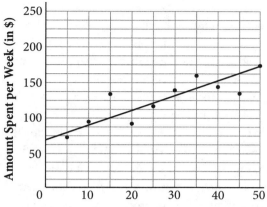

Daily Minutes Watching Commercials

2. The scatterplot above shows the relationship between the amount of time spent watching commercials each day and the amount of money spent each week on brand-name grocery products for 10 consumers. The line of best fit for the data is also shown. Which of the following best represents the meaning of the slope of the line of best fit in the context of this question?

   A) The predicted amount of time spent watching commercials when a person spends 0 dollars on brand-name products

   B) The predicted amount of money spent on brand-name products when a person spends 0 minutes watching commercials

   C) The predicted increase in time spent watching commercials for every dollar increase in money spent on brand-name products

   D) The predicted increase in money spent on brand-name products for every one-minute increase in time spent watching commercials

GO ON TO THE NEXT PAGE

Practice Tests

3. There are very few states in the United States that require public schools to pay sales tax on their purchases. For this reason, many schools pay for student portraits and then the parents reimburse the school. Parents can choose between the basic package for $29.50 and the deluxe package for $44.50. If 182 parents ordered packages and the school's total bill was $6,509, which of the following systems of equations could be used to find the number of parents who ordered a basic package, b, and the number who ordered a deluxe package, d, assuming no parent ordered more than one package?

A)
$$b + d = 6,509$$
$$29.5b + 44.5d = 182$$

B)
$$b + d = 182$$
$$29.5b + 44.5d = 6,509$$

C)
$$2(b + d) = 182$$
$$29.5b + 44.5d = 6,509$$

D)
$$b + d = 182$$
$$29.5b + 44.5d = \frac{6,509}{2}$$

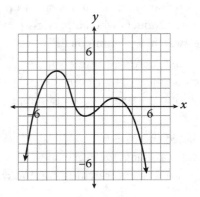

4. The graph of a polynomial function $p(x)$ is shown above. For what value(s) of x does $p(x) = -4$?

A) -1

B) 4

X) -7 and 5

Δ) -7, 4, and 5

5. If $4x + 3 = 19$, what is the value of $4x - 3$?

A) -19

B) 4

C) 13

D) 19

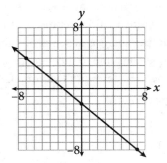

6. What is the slope of the line shown in the above graph?

A) -2

B) $-\dfrac{7}{6}$

C) $-\dfrac{6}{7}$

D) 2

GO ON TO THE NEXT PAGE

Legislation Impact

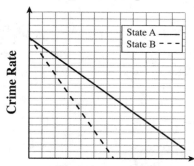

State A ———
State B - - - -

Crime Rate

Years after Legislation

7. Most crimes in the United States are governed by state law rather than federal. Suppose two states passed laws that raised the penalty for committing armed robbery. The figure above represents the crime rate for armed robbery in both states after the laws were passed. Based on the graph, which of the following statements is true?

   A) State A's law had a more positive impact on the crime rate for armed robbery.

   B) State B's law had a more positive impact on the crime rate for armed robbery.

   C) The laws in both states had the same impact on the crime rate for armed robbery.

   D) Without axis labels, it is not possible to determine which state's law had a bigger impact.

8. On average, for every 2,500 cans of colored paint a home improvement chain mixes, exactly 40 are the wrong color (defective). At this rate, how many cans of paint were mixed during a period in which exactly 128 were defective?

   A) 5,200

   B) 7,500

   C) 8,000

   D) 10,200

9. According to the American Association of University Women, the mean age of men who have a college degree at their first marriage is 29.9 years. The mean age of women with a college degree at their first marriage is 28.4 years. Which of the following must be true about the combined mean age, m, of men and women with college degrees at their first marriage?

   A) $m = 29.15$

   B) $m > 29.15$

   C) $m < 29.15$

   D) $28.4 < m < 29.9$

10. When scuba divers ascend from deep water, they must either rise slowly or take safety breaks to avoid nitrogen buildup in their lungs. The length of time a diver should take to ascend is directly proportional to how many feet she needs to ascend. If a scuba diver can safely ascend 165 feet in 5.5 minutes, then how many feet can she ascend in 90 seconds?

   A) 45

   B) 60

   C) 75

   D) 90

11. The chief financial officer of a shoe company calculates that the cost, C, of producing p pairs of a certain shoe is $C = 17p + 1,890$. The marketing department wants to sell the shoe for $35 per pair. The shoe company will make a profit only if the total revenue from selling p pairs is greater than the total cost of producing p pairs. Which of the following inequalities gives the number of pairs of shoes, p, that the company needs to sell in order to make a profit?

   A) $p < 54$

   B) $p > 54$

   C) $p < 105$

   D) $p > 105$

12. The human body has a very limited ability to store carbohydrates, which is why it is important for athletes to consume them during long training sessions or competitions. It is recommended that athletes consume approximately 3 calories per minute in situations like these. How many calories would an athlete biking a 74-mile race need to consume, assuming he bikes at an average speed of 9.25 miles per hour during the race?

A)   480

B)   1,440

C)   1,665

D)   2,053.5

x	3	−1	−5	−7
y	0	14	28	?

13. If the values in the table above represent a linear relationship, what is the missing value?

A)   21

B)   30

C)   35

D)   42

Questions 14 and 15 refer to the following information.

The figure shows the age distribution of homebuyers and the percent of the market each age range makes up in a particular geographic region.

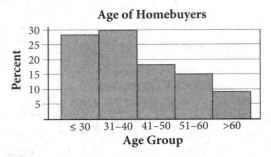

14. A new real estate agent is deciding which age group she should market toward in order to get the most clients. Which of the following measures of the data would be best for her to use when making this decision?

A)   Mean

B)   Mode

C)   Range

D)   Median

15. Based on the information in the figure, which of the following statements is true?

A)   The shape of the data is skewed to the right, so the mean age of homebuyers is greater than the median.

B)   The shape of the data is skewed to the left, so the median age of homebuyers is greater than the mean.

C)   The shape of the data is fairly symmetric, so the mean age of homebuyers is approximately equal to the median.

D)   The data has no clear shape, so it is impossible to make a reliable statement comparing the mean and the median.

GO ON TO THE NEXT PAGE

16. A railway company normally charges \$35 round trip from the suburbs of a city into downtown. The company also offers a deal for commuters who use the train frequently to commute from their homes in the suburbs to their jobs in the city. Commuters can purchase a discount card for \$900, after which they only have to pay \$12.50 per round trip. How many round trips, t, must a commuter make in order for the discount card to be a better deal?

A) $t < 40$

B) $t > 40$

C) $t < 72$

D) $t > 72$

17. Most people save money before going on vacation. Suppose Etienne saved \$800 to spend during vacation, 20 percent of which he uses to pay for gas. If he budgets 25 percent of the remaining money for food, allots \$300 for the hotel, and spends the rest of the money on entertainment, what percentage of the original \$800 did he spend on entertainment?

A) 14.5%

B) 17.5%

C) 22.5%

D) 28.5%

18. A microbiologist placed a bacteria sample containing approximately 2,000 microbes in a petri dish. For the first 7 days, the number of microbes in the dish tripled every 24 hours. If n represents the number of microbes after h hours, then which of the following equations is the best model for the data during the 7-day period?

A) $n = 2{,}000(3)^{\frac{h}{24}}$

B) $n = 2{,}000(3)^{24h}$

C) $n = \dfrac{h}{24} \times 2{,}000$

D) $n = 24h \times 2{,}000$

	For	Against	Undecided	Total
1L	32	16	10	58
2L	24	12	28	64
3L	17	25	13	55
Total	73	53	51	177

19. A survey is conducted regarding a proposed change in the attendance policy at a law school. The table above categorizes the results of the survey by year of the student (1L, 2L, or 3L) and whether they are for, against, or undecided about the new policy. What fraction of all 1Ls and 2Ls are against the new policy?

A) $\dfrac{14}{61}$

B) $\dfrac{24}{61}$

C) $\dfrac{28}{53}$

D) $\dfrac{28}{177}$

20. Which of the following expressions is equivalent to $(6 + 5i)^3$? (Note: $i = \sqrt{-1}$.)

A) $11 + 60i$

B) $216 - 125i$

X) $-234 + 415i$

Δ) $-3{,}479 + 1{,}320i$

GO ON TO THE NEXT PAGE

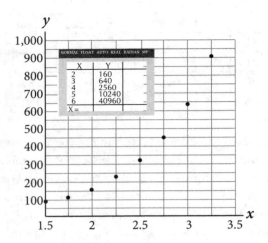

21. If an exponential function is used to model the data shown in the figure above, and it is written in the form $f(x) = f(0)(1 + r)^x$, what would be the value of r?

A) 2

B) 3

C) 4

D) 5

22. The Great Pyramid of Giza, built in the 26th century BCE just outside of Cairo, Egypt, had an original height of 480 feet, 8 inches, before some of the stones in which it was encased fell away. Inside the pyramid is a 53.75-foot passage, called the Dead End Shaft, which archeologists have yet to discover the purpose of. Suppose a museum is building a scale model of the pyramid for patrons to explore. Because of the museum's ceiling height, they can only make the pyramid 71 feet, 6 inches tall. About how many feet long should the museum's Dead End Shaft be? (1 foot = 12 inches)

A) 8

B) 12

C) 30

D) 96

$$\frac{-x^2 - 10x + 24}{2 - x}$$

23. Which of the following is equivalent to the expression above, given that $x \neq 2$?

A) $-x - 12$

B) $x - 12$

C) $12 - x$

D) $x + 12$

24. Ethanol is an alcohol commonly added to gasoline to reduce the use of fossil fuels. A commonly used ratio of ethanol to gasoline is 1:4. Another less common and more experimental additive is methanol, with a typical ratio of methanol to gasoline being 1:9. A fuel producer wants to see what happens to cost and fuel efficiency when a combination of ethanol and methanol are used. In order to keep the ratio of gasoline to total additive the same, what ratio of ethanol to methanol should the company use?

A) 1:1

B) 4:9

C) 9:4

D) 36:9

GO ON TO THE NEXT PAGE

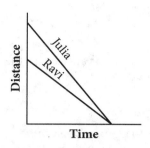

25. Julia and Ravi are meeting at a museum. The figure above represents the drives from their homes to the museum. Based on the figure, which of the following statements is true?

    A) Julia drove to the museum at a faster speed than Ravi.

    B) Julia and Ravi drove to the museum at about the same speed.

    C) It took Ravi longer to arrive at the museum because his home is farther away.

    D) It took Julia longer to arrive at the museum because her home is farther away.

26. If the graph of the function $g(x)$ passes through the point $(8, -3)$, then through which point does the graph of $-g(x - 4) - 6$ pass?

    A) $(-12, -9)$

    B) $(-12, -3)$

    X) $(4, -3)$

    Δ) $(12, -3)$

27. If $f(x) = x - 1$, $g(x) = x^3$, and $x \leq 0$, which of the following could NOT be in the range of $f(g(x))$?

    A) -27

    B) -3

    C) -1

    D) 1

28. Given the equation $y = -3(x - 5)^2 + 8$, which of the following statements is NOT true?

    A) The y-intercept is $(0, 8)$.

    B) The axis of symmetry is $x = 5$.

    C) The vertex is $(5, 8)$.

    D) The parabola opens downward.

29. Every weekend for 48 hours, a law firm backs up all client files by scanning and uploading them to a secure remote server. On average, the size of each client file is 2.5 gigabytes. The law firm's computer can upload the scans at a rate of 5.25 megabytes per second. What is the maximum number of client files the law firm can back up each weekend? (1 gigabyte = 1,000 megabytes)

    A)   362

    B)   363

    C)   476

    D)   477

30. Main Street and 2nd Street run parallel to each other. Both are one-way streets. Main Street runs south and 2nd Street runs north. The city is planning to build a new road, also one-way, that runs toward the southeast and cuts through both streets at an angle. Traffic turning off of Main Street would have to make a 125° turn onto the new road. What angle would traffic turning off of 2nd Street have to make turning onto the new road?

    A)   55°

    B)   65°

    C)   125°

    D)   235°

Practice Tests

Directions: For questions 31–38, enter your responses into the appropriate grid on your answer sheet, in accordance with the following:

1. You will receive credit only if the circles are filled in correctly, but you may write your answers in the boxes above each grid to help you fill in the circles accurately.

2. Don't mark more than one circle per column.

3. None of the questions with Grid-in responses will have a negative solution.

4. Only grid in a single answer, even if there is more than one correct answer to a given question.

5. A **mixed number** must be gridded as a decimal or an improper fraction. For example, you would grid $7\frac{1}{2}$ as 7.5 or 15/2.

(Were you to grid it as [7][1][/][2], this response would be read as $\frac{71}{2}$.)

6. A **decimal** that has more digits than there are places on the grid may be either rounded or truncated, but every column in the grid must be filled in to receive credit.

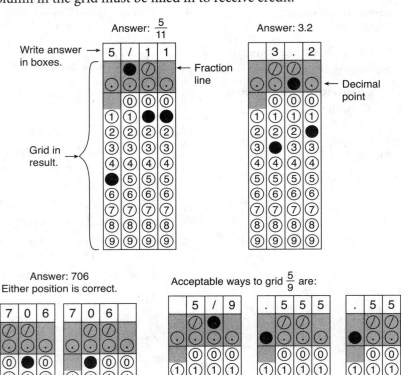

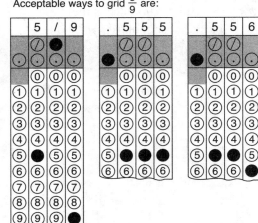

GO ON TO THE NEXT PAGE ⇨

$$\frac{4h - (21 - 8h)}{3} = \frac{15 + 6(h - 1)}{2}$$

31. What is the value of h in the equation above?

32. A company is buying two warehouses near its production plants in two states, New York and Georgia. As is always the case in the real estate market, the geographic location plays a major role in the price of the property. Consequently, the warehouse in New York costs $30,000 less than four times the Georgia warehouse. Together, the two warehouses cost the company $445,000. How many more thousand dollars does the New York property cost than the Georgia property?

Fuel Efficiency Ratings

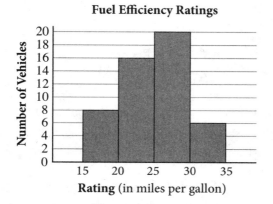

33. The histogram above shows the number of vehicles that a car rental agency currently has available to rent, categorized by fuel efficiency ratings. If a customer randomly selects one of the available cars, what is the probability that he will get a car that has a fuel efficiency rating of at least 25 miles per gallon? Enter your answer as a decimal number.

34. The volume of a rectangular shipping crate being loaded onto a barge for international shipment across the Panama Canal is 10,290 cubic feet. If the length to width to height ratio of the crate is 3:5:2 (in that order), what is the length of the crate in feet?

Regional Manager Job Performance

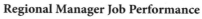
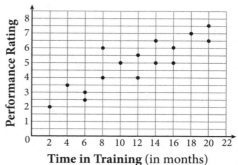

35. A company conducted a study comparing the overall job performance of its regional managers with the length of time each one spent in the company's management training program. The scatterplot above shows the results of the study. What is the length of the time spent in training, in months, of the manager represented by the data point that is the greatest distance from the line of best fit (not shown)?

36. If $(2^{32})(2^{32}) = 2^{(2^x)}$, what is the value of x?

Questions 37 and 38 refer to the following information.

Three cars all arrive at the same destination at 4:00 p.m. The first car traveled 144 miles mostly by highway. The second car traveled 85 miles mainly on rural two-lane roads. The third car traveled 25 miles primarily on busy city streets.

37. The first car traveled at an average speed of 64 miles per hour. The second car started its drive at 2:18 p.m. How many minutes had the first car already been traveling before the second car started its drive?

38. The third car encountered heavy traffic for the first 60 percent of its trip and only averaged 15 miles per hour. Then traffic stopped due to an accident and the car did not move for 20 minutes. After the accident was cleared, the car averaged 30 miles per hour for the remainder of the trip. At what time in the afternoon did the third car start its trip? Use only digits for your answer. (For example, enter 1:25 p.m. as 125.)

IF YOU FINISH BEFORE TIME IS CALLED, YOU MAY CHECK YOUR WORK ON THIS SECTION ONLY. DO NOT TURN TO ANY OTHER SECTION IN THE TEST.

STOP

Practice Tests

Essay Test

50 Minutes

You will be given a passage to read and asked to write an essay analyzing it. As you write, be sure to show that you have read the passage closely. You will be graded on how well you have understood the passage, how clear your analysis is, and how well you express your ideas.

Your essay must be written on the lines in your answer booklet. Anything you write outside the lined space in your answer booklet will not be read by the essay graders. Be sure to write or print in such a way that it will be legible to readers not familiar with your handwriting. Additionally, be sure to address the passage directly. An off-topic essay will not be graded.

As you read the passage, think about the author's use of

- evidence, such as statistics or other facts.

- logic to connect evidence to conclusions and to develop lines of reasoning.

- style, word choice, and appeals to emotion to make the argument more persuasive.

Adapted from William Faulkner's Nobel Prize Acceptance Speech, delivered in Stockholm on December 10, 1950.

1 I feel that this award was not made to me as a man, but to my work—a life's work in the agony and sweat of the human spirit, not for glory and least of all for profit, but to create out of the materials of the human spirit something which did not exist before. So this award is only mine in trust. It will not be difficult to find a dedication for the money part of it commensurate with the purpose and significance of its origin. But I would like to do the same with the acclaim too, by using this moment as a pinnacle from which I might be listened to by the young men and women already dedicated to the same anguish and travail, among whom is already that one who will some day stand where I am standing.

2 Our tragedy today is a general and universal physical fear so long sustained by now that we can even bear it. There are no longer problems of the spirit. There is only the question: When will I be blown up? Because of this, the young man or woman writing today has forgotten the problems of the human heart in conflict with it-self which alone can make good writing because only that is worth writing about, worth the agony and the sweat.

3 He must learn them again. He must teach himself that the basest of all things is to be afraid: and, teaching himself that, forget it forever, leaving no room in his workshop for anything but the old verities and truths of the heart, the universal truths lacking which any story is ephemeral and doomed—love and honor and pity and pride and compassion and sacrifice. Until he does so, he labors under a curse. He writes not of love but of . . . defeats in which nobody loses anything of value, of victories without hope, and, worst of all, without pity or compassion. His griefs grieve on no universal bones, leaving no scars. . . .

4 Until he learns these things, he will write as though he stood among and watched the end of man. I decline to accept the end of man. It is easy enough to say that man is immortal because he will endure: that when the last ding-dong of doom has clanged and faded from the last worthless rock hanging tideless in the last red and dying evening, that

even then there will still be one more sound: that of his puny inexhaustible voice, still talking. I refuse to accept this. I believe that man will not merely endure: he will prevail. He is immortal, not because he alone among creatures has an inexhaustible voice, but because he has a soul, a spirit capable of compassion and sacrifice and endurance. The poet's, the writer's, duty is to write about these things. It is his privilege to help man endure by lifting his heart, by reminding him of the courage and honor and hope and pride and compassion and pity and sacrifice which have been the glory of his past. The poet's voice need not merely be the record of man, it can be one of the props, the pillars to help him endure and prevail.

> Write an essay that analyzes the author's approach in persuading his readers that authors must write from the heart to ensure that mankind prevails. Focus on specific features, such as the ones listed in the box above the passage, and explain how these features strengthen the author's argument. Your essay should discuss the most important rhetorical features of the passage.
>
> Your essay should not focus on your own opinion of the author's conclusion, but rather on how the author persuades his readers.

IF YOU FINISH BEFORE TIME IS CALLED, YOU MAY CHECK YOUR WORK ON THIS SECTION ONLY. DO NOT TURN TO ANY OTHER SECTION IN THE TEST.

STOP

K   943

Answer Key
Reading Test

1. C	14. A	27. A	40. D
2. A	15. D	28. C	41. C
3. D	16. B	29. D	42. A
4. B	17. C	30. B	43. A
5. B	18. B	31. C	44. C
6. A	19. B	32. A	45. A
7. D	20. D	33. A	46. B
8. D	21. D	34. A	47. B
9. C	22. D	35. B	48. B
10. C	23. A	36. D	49. D
11. C	24. C	37. C	50. C
12. A	25. B	38. C	51. A
13. D	26. A	39. B	52. D

Writing and Language Test

1. B	12. D	23. D	34. A
2. D	13. B	24. B	35. C
3. C	14. C	25. A	36. D
4. C	15. C	26. A	37. C
5. B	16. A	27. C	38. B
6. B	17. B	28. D	39. B
7. B	18. D	29. C	40. D
8. B	19. D	30. B	41. C
9. A	20. B	31. C	42. D
10. C	21. D	32. D	43. A
11. A	22. C	33. A	44. B

Practice Tests

Math Test—No Calculator

1. B	6. C	11. D	16. 1
2. C	7. B	12. C	17. 12
3. A	8. C	13. D	18. 12
4. D	9. B	14. D	19. 14
5. B	10. A	15. D	20. 800

Math Test—Calculator

1. B	11. D	21. B	31. 11.5 or 23/2 or 69/6
2. D	12. B	22. A	32. 255
3. B	13. C	23. D	33. .52
4. C	14. B	24. C	34. 21
5. C	15. A	25. A	35. 8
6. C	16. B	26. D	36. 37
7. B	17. C	27. D	37. 33
8. C	18. A	28. A	38. 220
9. D	19. A	29. A	
10. A	20. C	30. A	

Answers and Explanations

Reading Test

Suggested passage map notes:

¶1: sleep more do better
¶2: man is responsible for being present in life
¶3: HDT wanted to live fully, used nature to achieve it
¶4: let go of small things
¶5: keep life simple

1. C

Difficulty: Medium

Category: Detail

Getting to the Answer: Reread the entire paragraph to assess the intention of the sentence in question and determine which answer choice best shows the author's reason for including this sentence. The author's previous statements in the paragraph directly relate to the idea that the conscious endeavors described are the very activities that will reawaken people. Thus, **(C)** is correct.

2. A

Difficulty: Hard

Category: Vocab-in-Context

Getting to the Answer: Read the complete sentence for context clues and determine which answer choice's definition best serves the idea presented. The sentence suggests the author wants to live actively and "suck out all the marrow of life" (line 41) rather than live in a resigned, accepting manner. Thus, **(A)** is correct because it best describes how the author does not wish to live.

3. D

Difficulty: Medium

Category: Inference

Getting to the Answer: Read the first paragraph expressly for the purpose of determining the author's views. The author suggests that most people are only awake enough for physical labor, some for intellectual discussions, and very few for a higher calling. This implies that he feels most people are not working toward their fullest potential, so **(D)** is correct.

4. B

Difficulty: Hard

Category: Command of Evidence

Getting to the Answer: Choose the quote from the passage that best supports the correct answer to the previous question. Choice **(B)** is the correct answer not just because it shows the author's belief that most people are not truly awake, but also because it shows that the author thinks most people spend their lives pursuing goals beneath their human potential.

5. B

Difficulty: Easy

Category: Global

Getting to the Answer: Consider the entire passage to determine the author's central claim about society. Then choose the answer choice that correctly reflects this. Throughout the passage, the author frequently mentions that our society focuses on mundane labor and details and that we shun a life of conscious endeavors. Thus, **(B)** is the correct answer.

6. A

Difficulty: Medium

Category: Inference

Getting to the Answer: Because the author's views on religion are not explicitly stated, you must make inferences by examining details in the entire passage. Throughout the third paragraph, the author explains that he is going to the woods to determine the sublime or mean qualities of nature and God, and he states that far too many people hastily agree to preconceived ideas on these topics. Choice **(A)** is correct.

7. D

Difficulty: Easy

Category: Command of Evidence

Getting to the Answer: Choose the quote from the passage that best supports the correct answer to the previous question. Choice **(D)** is the correct answer because it offers the most direct evidence that the author believes a person should critically examine his or her religious beliefs before dedicating a life to them.

8. D

Difficulty: Medium

Category: Vocab-in-Context

Getting to the Answer: Read the sentence for context clues and determine which answer choice comes closest to reflecting the author's intent. The sentence and paragraph as a whole describe the author's indifference to the harshness of life for the sake of accomplishing a goal. Thus, **(D)**, "austere," is correct.

9. C

Difficulty: Medium

Category: Function

Getting to the Answer: Carefully read the paragraph and ask yourself how these particular words help Thoreau convey his message. The author touches on many broad, negative aspects of human nature and existence in the paragraph, and the use of "meanly" and "wretchedness" strengthen the negative tone of the message. Choice **(C)** is correct.

10. C

Difficulty: Medium

Category: Inference

Getting to the Answer: Think about the author's intention in this passage when he discusses his views on how life should be lived. Identify the types of actions he promotes and review the answer choices to find the one that is most similar. The author urges readers to "simplify," and as an example he urges them to eat one meal a day instead of three and to reduce the number of dishes from 100 to 5. You can infer from this that Thoreau would advocate paring down one's clothing to the bare essentials. Choice **(C)** is correct.

Suggested passage map notes:

¶1: new library
¶2: library still segregated
¶3: African Am excluded from using library
¶4: WEB wants African Am to be allowed to use it; education will keep them off the streets
¶5–6: public money means it should be used by all
¶7: chairman says integration will kill library
¶8: segregation should be in the past
¶9–10: African Am in crowd spoke, thanked the trustees for listening
¶11–12: trustees gave response: said no

11. C

Difficulty: Medium

Category: Global

Getting to the Answer: Consider which answer choice describes an idea that is supported throughout the text. The passage begins with DuBois's arguments in favor of expanding access to public libraries and ends with the trustees' response to his arguments, highlighting the difference between the two positions. Therefore, **(C)** is correct.

12. A

Difficulty: Medium

Category: Command of Evidence

Getting to the Answer: The correct answer will support your response to the previous question. Choice **(A)** indicates that DuBois would present an argument "in behalf" (line 14) of others while asking the trustees to explain their side.

13. D

Difficulty: Medium

Category: Vocab-in-Context

Getting to the Answer: Make sure that your answer choice does not alter the meaning of the sentence in the passage. The paragraph in which the word appears indicates that speaking on behalf of so many others was not a responsibility DuBois took lightly, and the decision about who would speak had been previously decided. Choice **(D)** is correct.

14. A

Difficulty: Medium

Category: Inference

Getting to the Answer: Eliminate answer choices that are not suggested in the passage. Choice **(A)** is correct. The president of the Trustee Board did not make assurances, but he detailed a course of action that would potentially result in a new library for African Americans if the city council approved funding.

15. D

Difficulty: Hard

Category: Command of Evidence

Getting to the Answer: Review your answer to the previous question. Read each choice and figure out which one provides specific support for that answer. Choice **(D)** indicates the trustees' support for separate library facilities with approved funding. It best supports the idea that segregated library facilities would at least be considered.

16. B

Difficulty: Medium

Category: Vocab-in-Context

Getting to the Answer: Look for context clues in the sentence to help you determine the correct meaning. Choice **(B)** reflects the meaning of the phrase in the sentence; DuBois was arguing for the necessity of literacy and a strong comprehension of the books that a library offers.

17. C

Difficulty: Hard

Category: Detail

Getting to the Answer: Pay close attention to the reasons DuBois presents that support his argument for expanding access to public libraries. Avoid choices that sound plausible but take the ideas too far. Choice **(C)** is correct. DuBois specifically argues that the reason whites need public libraries "applies with redoubled force" (line 29) to poor African Americans.

18. B

Difficulty: Medium

Category: Function

Getting to the Answer: Look for the argument in the passage that this particular example supports. Choice **(B)** is correct. Note that DuBois's mention of the "catholic spirit" (lines 47–48) is used to remind the trustees that we create differences between us, and what we have in common should inspire us to ensure that everyone has equal opportunity to improve themselves.

19. B

Difficulty: Medium

Category: Inference

Getting to the Answer: Read the cited lines, and then read them in the context of the paragraphs that come before and after. Think about how the chairman's words are affecting the author at this point in the passage. The chairman has just suggested that integrating the library "would be fatal to its usefulness" (lines 57–58), implying that African Americans and whites would be unable to use the library alongside each other without violence or chaos. Because DuBois's aim is to integrate the library, he is frustrated by the chairman's words, which echo the assumptions of past centuries. Choice **(B)** is correct.

20. D

Difficulty: Medium

Category: Function

Getting to the Answer: Keep in mind that the question is asking how this portion of the passage functions in relation to the passage as a whole. DuBois argued in favor of expanding access to public libraries for all citizens. The Trustee Board's president then responded to DuBois's persuasive argument. Therefore, **(D)** is correct.

Suggested passage map notes:

¶1: DD created volumes of documented tech advances during his time

¶2: DD found people to contribute, volumes were controversial

¶3: *Encyclopédie* was progressive

¶4: science merged with liberal arts

¶5: made mundane crafts scholarly

¶6: angered people who protected trade secrets

¶7: upper society was angry

¶8: opposition too late, encyclo eventually became historical book

21. D

Difficulty: Medium

Category: Function

Getting to the Answer: Keep in mind that the correct answer will reflect the central purpose and opinion of the author as expressed in the passage. The passage explores the impact and influence of Diderot's *Encyclopédie*. The author states that the value of the work is not in its merit as a lasting technical reference or dictionary, but as a repository of historical knowledge and as an early attempt to extend the knowledge of the day to the masses. Choice **(D)** is correct.

22. D

Difficulty: Medium

Category: Function

Getting to the Answer: Choose the answer that reflects that author's overall point of view, or perspective, suggested by the passage. The passage examines the individual achievements of Diderot, specifically his efforts to extend the access to knowledge to a greater segment of European society. Choice **(D)** is correct, because it speaks to the author's obvious respect for Diderot as an innovator.

23. A

Difficulty: Medium

Category: Command of Evidence

Getting to the Answer: Reread each quote in the context of the passage. This will help you decide the correct answer. The correct answer to the previous question asserts that the author admires the individual

accomplishments of innovators such as Diderot. Choice **(A)** is correct, because it calls attention to Diderot's contributions as revolutionizing encyclopedic thought.

24. C

Difficulty: Medium

Category: Detail

Getting to the Answer: Scan the passage for statements about Diderot's intentions and goals. Be sure not to confuse the results of his efforts with his goals. The passage states that Diderot's goal "was to create an intellectual work instructionally useful to all" (lines 17–18). While the work did create political controversy and also became part of the historical record, neither of these was his main goal. Choice **(C)** is correct.

25. B

Difficulty: Easy

Category: Vocab-in-Context

Getting to the Answer: Decide which answer choice could be substituted for the word without changing the meaning of the sentence. The paragraph states that Diderot's work was banned by the French government; therefore, the work's circulation, once published, was done secretly. Choice **(B)** is correct.

26. A

Difficulty: Medium

Category: Function

Getting to the Answer: The correct answer will reflect the meaning and intention behind the excerpted phrase as well as the surrounding text. The term "beacon" means a light that can be seen far away, usually with the purpose of guiding or attracting people to it. The phrase "free thought" in this context refers to the right of people to pursue knowledge. The surrounding text describes Diderot's work as having political purpose in expanding access to knowledge beyond the established elite to the masses. Therefore, **(A)** is correct.

27. A

Difficulty: Medium

Category: Inference

Getting to the Answer: Eliminate answer choices that don't represent the author's ideas. The passage refers repeatedly to the impact of Diderot's work in making information accessible to more people. The author states that political, economic, and intellectual elites opposed the publication of his encyclopedia because it lessened their control on trades and other valuable information. Choice **(A)** is correct.

28. C

Difficulty: Medium

Category: Command of Evidence

Getting to the Answer: Avoid answers that provide evidence for incorrect answers to the previous question. The correct answer to the previous question asserts that information was limited to a specific demographic, or segment of the population, at that time. Choice **(C)** is correct because it states clearly that the trade guilds, a select demographic, controlled certain knowledge and opposed the expansion of access to such knowledge.

29. D

Difficulty: Medium

Category: Vocab-in-Context

Getting to the Answer: Remember that you're looking for the answer that will make the most sense when substituted for the original word. The sentence discusses the way in which Diderot changed the perception and exploration of knowledge, making **(D)** correct. The word "erudition" refers to learning acquired by reading and study.

30. B

Difficulty: Medium

Category: Inference

Getting to the Answer: Remember that the correct answer must be based on information in the passage, not on speculation. Based on the last sentence of the passage and the information in paragraph 4, **(B)** is correct. It's the only answer choice directly supported by information in the passage.

31. C

Difficulty: Medium

Category: Inference

Getting to the Answer: Eliminate answer choices that cannot be inferred from the information in the passage and graphic. Choice **(C)** is the correct answer; Uranus was discovered after Diderot's *Encyclopédie* was published. Other answer choices are either impossible, as in the case of (D), or cannot be inferred from the information provided.

Suggested passage map notes:

Passage 1

 ¶1: acid rain is a problem
 ¶2: explain pH scale
 ¶3: slightly acidic rain ok
 ¶4: human-made problems make bad acid rain

Passage 2

 ¶1: human blood needs controlled pH
 ¶2: pH controlled in body
 ¶3: kidneys aid in maintaining pH
 ¶4: uncontrolled pH causes problems—ex: diabetes

32. A

Difficulty: Medium

Category: Inference

Getting to the Answer: Consider what the author of Passage 1 is saying in the first paragraph about the causes and consequences of acid rain. Avoid answers like (C) that go too far and are not directly supported by the evidence in the passage. The author clearly states that acid rain, largely caused by the burning of fossil fuels, is bad for the environment. It is reasonable to conclude that if the burning of fossil fuels is not reduced, the environment will be damaged. Therefore, **(A)** is correct.

33. A

Difficulty: Medium

Category: Command of Evidence

Getting to the Answer: Look back at your answer to the previous question. Think about the information you found in the passage that helped you choose this answer. The last sentence in the first paragraph provides the strongest evidence for the idea that burning fossil fuels will seriously damage the environment. Therefore, **(A)** is correct.

34. A

Difficulty: Easy

Category: Detail

Getting to the Answer: Find where Passage 1 discusses the pH of rain water. Determine whether lower or higher pH levels indicate that rain water is dangerously acidic. The passage states that the pH of pure rain water can be as low as 5.5, and a pH level of 3 can cause soil and water to become too acidic. A pH level of 2.25 is less than 3, meaning it is even more dangerously acidic; therefore, the correct answer is **(A)**.

35. B

Difficulty: Easy

Category: Vocab-in-Context

Getting to the Answer: Remember that some answer choices might be synonyms for "tolerate" but do not reflect the meaning of the word in this context. In this context, "tolerate" most nearly means "endure." Choice **(B)** is the correct answer.

36. D

Difficulty: Hard

Category: Inference

Getting to the Answer: Reread the text, looking for evidence to support each of the answer choices. The first paragraph of Passage 2 states: "Many processes in the body produce acid wastes" (lines 41–42), from which you can infer that it's normal to have acid wastes in the blood. Choice **(D)**, therefore, is the correct answer.

37. C

Difficulty: Medium

Category: Command of Evidence

Getting to the Answer: Look for evidence that supports the inference you made in the previous question. In lines 60–64, the author explains how normal amounts of acid are neutralized in the blood. Choice **(C)** is correct.

38. C

Difficulty: Medium

Category: Vocab-in-Context

Getting to the Answer: Eliminate any answer choices that don't make sense in the context of the sentence. In this context, "exhaust" means "to use up" or "deplete." Therefore, **(C)** is the correct answer.

39. B

Difficulty: Hard

Category: Inference

Getting to the Answer: Read paragraph 2 of Passage 2 again and determine the role of excess bicarbonate ions in the blood. Each answer choice is mentioned in Passage 1. Determine how each acts in the environment. Choice **(B)** is the correct answer. In Passage 2, the author explains that excess bicarbonate ions raise the pH of the blood, neutralizing acid wastes. In paragraph 3 of Passage 1, the author explains that alkaline materials in the environment, such as ashes from a forest fire, neutralize acid in the water supply.

40. D

Difficulty: Medium

Category: Inference

Getting to the Answer: You are looking for a cause-and-effect relationship to answer this question. Skim Passage 2, looking for an explanation of what causes the body to break down fats for energy. In paragraph 4 of Passage 2, the author explains that low insulin will cause the body to break down fats for energy. Therefore, **(D)** is the correct answer.

Practice Tests

41. C

Difficulty: Medium

Category: Global

Getting to the Answer: Consider the main topic and purpose of each passage. Decide what the passages have in common. Each passage describes a different system, the environment and the human body, respectively, and how each system deals with acid. In each passage, the author describes how acid can be introduced into the system and neutralized in small amounts but also describes the ways in which large amounts of acid can damage or overwhelm each system, making **(C)** the correct answer.

42. A

Difficulty: Easy

Category: Inference

Getting to the Answer: The question is asking you about both passages. Eliminate answers that only address the information found in one of the passages. Although Passage 1 is about the environment and Passage 2 is about the human body, both passages are about delicate systems that need balance to remain healthy, so **(A)** is correct.

Suggested passage map notes:

¶1: hydrogen next renewable resource
¶2: looking for safe, low-cost hydrogen fuel
¶3: challenges to hydrogen fuel production
¶4: new method for harvesting hydrogen
¶5: using solar power to harvest hydrogen, reduces cost of harvesting
¶6: more efficient way to harvest
¶7: more research to be done

43. A

Difficulty: Medium

Category: Inference

Getting to the Answer: Avoid answers like (B), which are related to details presented but take the ideas too far. Think about the arguments presented by the author throughout the passage. In paragraph 3, the author lists drawbacks to hydrogen fuel as a replacement for gasoline. In this paragraph, the author notes that

engines that run on hydrogen are more expensive than those that use gasoline. Choice **(A)** is the correct answer.

44. C

Difficulty: Medium

Category: Command of Evidence

Getting to the Answer: Read the previous question again. Look at each quote from the passage and decide which provides the strongest evidence. Choice **(C)** is the correct answer as it provides the strongest evidence that the author is concerned with the cost to consumers of using hydrogen fuel.

45. A

Difficulty: Medium

Category: Detail

Getting to the Answer: Eliminate answer choices that contain details that are not stated directly in the text. In paragraph 1, the author states that hydrogen is found primarily with oxygen in water; therefore, **(A)** is correct.

46. B

Difficulty: Easy

Category: Vocab-in-Context

Getting to the Answer: Read the sentence again and replace "diligently" with each of the answer choices. Look for the answer that does not change the meaning of the sentence. When you consider the overall meaning of the sentence, **(B)** is the best choice. In this context, "persistently" means nearly the same thing as "diligently."

47. B

Difficulty: Medium

Category: Inference

Getting to the Answer: Pay attention to the parts of the passage that refer to petroleum-based fuels and the reasons scientists are seeking alternatives. Though the author does not explicitly state that petroleum-based fuels are bad for the environment, he or she does give the fact that hydrogen produces no pollution as a reason to look toward hydrogen and away from petroleum products. You can infer, then, that **(B)** is the correct answer.

48. B

Difficulty: Medium

Category: Command of Evidence

Getting to the Answer: Read the previous question again. Look at each quote from the passage and decide which most clearly supports the idea stated in the correct answer for that question. In paragraph 2, the author lists potential benefits for using hydrogen energy over petroleum-based energy sources. No pollution is one of the potential benefits, which leads to the conclusion that petroleum products are bad for the environment. Choice **(B)** is therefore the correct answer.

49. D

Difficulty: Medium

Category: Function

Getting to the Answer: Think about the purpose that paragraph 2 serves in creating the author's overall argument. In paragraph 2, the author asserts that decreasing dependence on other petroleum-producing countries is a potential benefit to the development of hydrogen as a fuel. The inclusion of this point helps clarify why hydrogen fuel is important. Choice **(D)** is correct.

50. C

Difficulty: Medium

Category: Vocab-in-Context

Getting to the Answer: Keep in mind that although all answer choices might be synonyms of "derived," only one fits the context of the sentence in which the word appears. In this context, "derived" most nearly means **(C)**, "obtained."

51. A

Difficulty: Medium

Category: Inference

Getting to the Answer: Locate the parts of the passage that discuss advances in extracting hydrogen molecules from water. Then, find the answer choice that makes the most sense in the context of the passage. In lines 66–71, the author discusses research initiatives that focus on hydrogen extraction. You can infer from the fact that there are "many ongoing research initiatives" (lines 66–67) that much more research will be needed before hydrogen extraction is perfected. Choice **(A)** is correct.

52. D

Difficulty: Medium

Category: Inference

Getting to the Answer: Avoid answer choices that are supported only by the information in one of the sources. Look for the answer that is supported by both the passage and the graphic. The data presented in the graphic supports the author's argument that hydrogen fuel produces less greenhouse gas than gasoline. Choice **(D)** is correct.

Writing and Language Test

1. B

Difficulty: Easy

Category: Agreement: Verbs

Getting to the Answer: Read the sentence and check to see whether the verb agrees with the subject. The verb "are" is in a plural form, but the subject is singular. Choice **(B)** is correct because it is the singular form of the verb "to be."

2. D

Difficulty: Medium

Category: Development: Word Choice

Getting to the Answer: Read the sentences surrounding the word to better understand the context in which the word appears. Then, substitute each answer choice into the sentence to see which fits into the context best. The passage states that the plastics are sorted by types. Only **(D)** has the correct connotation and fits within the context of the sentence.

3. C

Difficulty: Hard

Category: Development: Introductions and Conclusions

Getting to the Answer: Read the entire paragraph and write down the central idea. Then, review the answer choices and look for a close match with your prediction. The paragraph discusses the two methods used to sort plastics. Choice **(C)** is closest to this summation.

4. C

Difficulty: Easy

Category: Conciseness

Getting to the Answer: Watch out for choices like (A) and (B), which use extra words that do not add meaning to the sentence. It is better to be as direct and simple as possible. The word "thoroughly" indicates that the people doing the job are paying attention to every detail. Additional words such as "very" or "completely" do not add more meaning to this sentence. Choice **(C)** is the most concise and effective way of stating the information.

5. B

Difficulty: Medium

Category: Organization: Transitions

Getting to the Answer: Look for the relationship between this sentence and the previous one. This will help you choose the appropriate transition word. Read the sentence using the word you chose to ensure that it makes sense. Choice **(B)** shows the relationship between the two sentences by giving an example of how the products are manufactured.

6. B

Difficulty: Medium

Category: Sentence Structure: Commas, Dashes, and Colons

Getting to the Answer: Study the words in a series to see where a comma might need to be placed or eliminated. Only one answer choice will include the correct punctuation. Choice **(B)** is correct.

7. B

Difficulty: Hard

Category: Graphs

Getting to the Answer: The graphic gives specific information about how much of each type of plastic was recovered. Study the graphic in order to select the correct answer choice. Choice **(B)** accurately reflects the information in the graphic.

8. B

Difficulty: Medium

Category: Conciseness

Getting to the Answer: Watch out for choices that may include incorrect transition words. Choice **(B)** uses the present participle "depending" to join the sentences concisely and correctly.

9. A

Difficulty: Easy

Category: Development: Word Choice

Getting to the Answer: Check each answer choice for its connotations, and be sure to pick one that fits with the context of the sentence. Substitute each answer choice for the word to see which works best. Notice that the sentence sets up a contrast between plastics numbered 1 through 6 and plastics with the number 7, which may consist of one of many other plastics or a blend of plastics. Choice **(A)** is correct because the word "specific" indicates that each of the numbers 1 through 6 is used for only one type of plastic.

10. C

Difficulty: Medium

Category: Sentence Structure: The Basics

Getting to the Answer: Two complete thoughts should be two separate sentences. Be careful of inappropriate transition words. Choice **(C)** divides the two thoughts into two complete sentences by adding a period and capitalizing the first word of the second sentence.

11. A

Difficulty: Medium

Category: Development: Introductions and Conclusions

Getting to the Answer: Read the entire paragraph and then read each of the choices. Decide which one sums up the paragraph best by stating the overall central idea. Choice **(A)** is the correct answer. It concludes the paragraph by stating the overall central idea of the paragraph and passage.

12. D

Difficulty: Hard

Category: Development: Introductions and Conclusions

Getting to the Answer: Read the entire first paragraph. The correct answer should offer descriptive details and introduce David Kaufman as a character. The first paragraph discusses David Kaufman specifically and his relationship to his job. While (A), (B), and (C) are informative, they do not add beauty or descriptive interest to the paragraph. Only **(D)** sparks the reader's interest with descriptive language and relates directly to the following sentences, so it is the correct answer.

13. B

Difficulty: Medium

Category: Sentence Structure: Commas, Dashes, and Colons

Getting to the Answer: Determine whether the information is all one thought or whether the sentence suggests that some part of it is an aside. The sentence is mainly discussing Kaufman, but it also introduces the idea of America's history almost as an afterthought. By setting this aside within dashes, the sentence will draw attention to its parenthetical relationship to the rest of the sentence. Choice **(B)** is correct.

14. C

Difficulty: Easy

Category: Agreement: Pronouns

Getting to the Answer: Determine whether the underlined word is being used as a place or a possessive. Then consider which answer choice would be most appropriate here. In this sentence, "there" is describing "baggage" belonging to these new Americans. It should therefore be changed to the correct possessive form "their," making **(C)** correct.

15. C

Difficulty: Medium

Category: Conciseness

Getting to the Answer: Eliminate unnecessary words. Then reorder the nouns and verbs to achieve the most concise language possible. Choice **(C)** contains no unnecessary words. It concisely explains the actions taken by the two different groups of people and is the correct answer.

16. A

Difficulty: Medium

Category: Organization: Sentence Placement

Getting to the Answer: Consider the function of this sentence. At what point in the paragraph should this function be employed? The sentence is setting a scene, so it should be placed where it is now, at the beginning of the paragraph. To place it later would cause confusion in the following sentences, as the reader does not have all the information he or she needs. Choice **(A)**, leaving it in its current position, is the correct answer.

17. B

Difficulty: Medium

Category: Development: Introductions and Conclusions

Getting to the Answer: The correct answer should introduce an idea that is supported by the sentences that follow. Consider whether the current sentence should be revised to do this. The rest of the paragraph discusses the relationship between immigrant communities and language ability, as well as information about Kaufman's position. Therefore, the introductory sentence to this paragraph should tie together these thoughts. Choice **(B)** is the correct answer, as it ties Kaufman to his background in an immigrant community.

18. D

Difficulty: Easy

Category: Sentence Structure: Commas, Dashes, and Colons

Getting to the Answer: Determine whether the information enclosed in commas is separate or should be integrated into the rest of the sentence. The subject of the sentence is a compound noun: "his heritage and surrounding community." Therefore, the nouns making up this compound noun should not be separated by commas. Choice **(D)** punctuates this sentence correctly.

19. D

Difficulty: Hard

Category: Development: Word Choice

Getting to the Answer: Consider the tone of this sentence as well as its meaning. Then review the answer choices to determine which one best matches both the tone and the meaning. The sentence suggests that Kaufman is trying to make his language abilities more refined and precise in order to help the immigrants. While (C), "tricks," is tempting, it does not match the more formal tone of the passage. Choice **(D)**, "nuances," conveys the fact that Kaufman is trying to understand the subtleties of language; this answer maintains the passage's formal tone.

20. B

Difficulty: Medium

Category: Development: Relevance

Getting to the Answer: Reread the rest of the paragraph to determine which answer choice would most effectively add specific, relevant detail to this section of the passage. The paragraph notes that Kaufman helps "at every checkpoint," then mentions the variety of facilities Ellis Island possesses. Choice **(B)** adds detail about the variety of ways Kaufman helps at Ellis Island and is therefore the correct answer.

21. D

Difficulty: Medium

Category: Conciseness

Getting to the Answer: Consider whether the sentence's intended meaning can be conveyed in fewer words. All that is really needed in this sentence is "to help." The reader will still understand what is happening. The other options are wordy and awkward. Choice **(D)** is the correct answer.

22. C

Difficulty: Medium

Category: Development: Word Choice

Getting to the Answer: Before looking at the answer choices, identify a word on your own that will convey the correct meaning for the context. The context of the sentence makes clear that the correct word is something that is "rendered … worthwhile." In other words, it is a challenging situation that will be made worthwhile by living in America. While both (C) and (D) are negative words, **(C)**, "difficulties," specifically connotes something hard or troubling, so it is the correct answer.

23. D

Difficulty: Medium

Category: Sentence Structure: The Basics

Getting to the Answer: Determine the relationship between the two different parts of the sentence. Then, choose the punctuation that fits best. In this sentence, two independent clauses are joined by the coordinating conjunction "so." When two independent clauses are joined in this manner, a comma is needed before the conjunction. Only **(D)** combines the two independent clauses correctly.

24. B

Difficulty: Easy

Category: Agreement: Pronouns

Getting to the Answer: Substitute the phrases for their contractions, such as "It is," for "It's" to determine the correct usage. "They're" and "Their" are inappropriate because when the subject is not clear (such as "It is raining"), it is grammatically correct to use "it" instead of "they." Choice **(B)** is correct.

25. A

Difficulty: Medium

Category: Sentence Structure: Commas, Dashes, and Colons

Getting to the Answer: Commas should be used sparingly to help the reader understand the passage. Only one comma is needed to successfully combine two independent clauses with a conjunction. Choice **(A)** is the correct answer.

26. A

Difficulty: Hard

Category: Agreement: Verbs

Getting to the Answer: Read the entire paragraph to establish the verb tense. Identify the key verbs in the paragraph and their tenses. Both "turned" and "returned" are past tense, making **(A)** the correct choice.

27. C

Difficulty: Medium

Category: Development: Relevance

Getting to the Answer: Determine the focus of the paragraph by identifying its topic and purpose. Then, read the answer choices, looking for the choice that is least relevant. The paragraph has an informational purpose and is about the unusual route Morales took to a career in software sales. The opinion that "New Hampshire also has many fine backpacking trails" is extraneous to this topic and purpose. Choice **(C)** is correct.

28. D

Difficulty: Medium

Category: Sentence Structure: The Basics

Getting to the Answer: Identify whether the underlined portion contains sentences or fragments, or a combination of both. Then, determine the best way to join them. The underlined portion contains a sentence and a fragment. Only **(D)** correctly rewords the fragment to make it an independent clause and then uses a conjunction to join the two parts of the sentence.

29. C

Difficulty: Medium

Category: Development: Introductions and Conclusions

Getting to the Answer: Read the entire paragraph and summarize the supporting details to help you determine the appropriate topic sentence. The supporting details of the paragraph all relate to Morales's ability to come up with a creative solution to a company's problem. Choice **(C)** is the correct topic sentence of the paragraph.

30. B

Difficulty: Medium

Category: Development: Word Choice

Getting to the Answer: Notice the prefixes used in the answer choices and think about what they mean. Then choose the word that best fits into the context of the sentence. The prefix "re-" means *back*, as in *return* or *replace*. "Retaining" means to keep or hold back. This fits into the context of the sentence, so **(B)** is correct.

31. C

Difficulty: Medium

Category: Development: Word Choice

Getting to the Answer: Read the sentence to determine which word provides the correct meaning in context. "Vacillate" means to be indecisive, "convert" means to change into a different form, and "fluctuate" means to change continually. Choice (C), "transition," means to move from one thing to another. Morales's goal is to move from one field to another, so **(C)** is the correct answer.

32. D

Difficulty: Medium

Category: Development: Relevance

Getting to the Answer: Identify the topic sentence in the paragraph. Then, review the answer choices to find the one that best supports it. The topic sentence of the paragraph is about "big data." Morales's use of "big data" to gather information regarding health care supports the topic sentence. The other choices do not involve capturing data from outside sources. Choice **(D)** is correct.

33. A

Difficulty: Medium

Category: Agreement: Verbs

Getting to the Answer: When a sentence contains a series of actions, make sure the elements are parallel and punctuated correctly. Then, determine whether you should eliminate or insert any commas. Choice **(A)** is correct, because there are three identifiable actions in the series: "quicken," "improve," and "save."

34. A

Difficulty: Medium

Category: Development: Word Choice

Getting to the Answer: Read for context clues and determine which answer offers the most appropriate word choice. The sentence states that Etta "passed away" before her art was given to the BMA. Because this was a gift after death, "bequeathed" is the most appropriate word choice in this sentence. Choice **(A)** is correct.

35. C

Difficulty: Hard

Category: Development: Introductions and Conclusions

Getting to the Answer: After reading the paragraph, reread each sentence to determine which one summarizes the overall message of the paragraph. Aside from (C), all other sentences offer details and ideas that are not supported by the rest of the paragraph. Only **(C)** encapsulates the central idea that the Cones contributed their art to the BMA.

36. D

Difficulty: Medium

Category: Organization: Transitions

Getting to the Answer: Reread the sentence to figure out what is meant. Then, choose the coordinating conjunction that creates the most logical and grammatically correct sentence. Choice **(D)** is correct. Because the second independent clause discusses what the sisters did despite the statement in the first independent clause, the coordinating conjunction "but" is most appropriate here.

37. C

Difficulty: Easy

Category: Agreement: Pronouns

Getting to the Answer: Read for context clues and determine which answer choice is most logical and grammatically correct. The possessive determiner "their" is grammatically correct and correctly explains the sisters' ownership of the selections, so **(C)** is the correct answer.

38. B

Difficulty: Medium

Category: Agreement: Verbs

Getting to the Answer: Read the surrounding sentences for context clues to determine which pronoun and verb combination creates the clearest and most effective sentence. The pronoun must be "they," as it refers to both Etta and Claribel. The rest of the paragraph is written in the past tense, making "took" the correct verb. Choice **(B)** is correct.

39. B

Difficulty: Medium

Category: Development: Word Choice

Getting to the Answer: Read the sentence for context clues, and determine which answer offers the most appropriate word choice. The sentence describes what the art collected by the Cones showed, or "depicted." The other answer choices are less precise, making **(B)** the correct answer.

40. D

Difficulty: Hard

Category: Development: Relevance

Getting to the Answer: Read the entire paragraph and determine the central idea. Then read the answer choices, looking for the choice that distracts from the paragraph's focus. The central idea of the paragraph is that the Cone collection documented the changes in post–World War I Europe. The statement "Today, there are more experimental forms of art than there were after World War I" may be accurate, but it does not relate to the central idea. Choice **(D)** is the correct answer.

41. C

Difficulty: Medium

Category: Sentence Structure: Commas, Dashes, and Colons

Getting to the Answer: Reread the sentence to determine which set of punctuation marks creates a grammatically correct sentence. Introductory words such as "additionally" are followed by a comma when they begin a sentence. The word "Paris" is the beginning of a list and also should be followed by a comma. No other punctuation is required in this portion of the sentence, so **(C)** is correct.

42. D

Difficulty: Medium

Category: Agreement: Idioms

Getting to the Answer: Reread the sentence for context clues to determine which answer choice provides the correct meaning. The current underlined word, "though," means *despite*, creating an illogical contrast between the two parts of the sentence. The definitions for (B), "therefore" (*for that reason*), and (C), "thorough" (*completed with exacting detail*), likewise do not create logical sentences. The definition of "through" best expresses the idea that the sisters experienced freedom *by means of* their lifestyle. Choice **(D)** is the correct answer.

43. A

Difficulty: Hard

Category: Development: Relevance

Getting to the Answer: Determine the central idea of the paragraph, and decide which additional facts noted in the answer choices would have the greatest benefit to the reader. Because the paragraph is about how the Cones challenged traditional views of women, and because the author uses several undefined but important terms, **(A)** is the correct answer.

44. B

Difficulty: Medium

Category: Agreement: Modifiers

Getting to the Answer: Review the sentence to assess which answer choice offers the correct use of plural punctuation to convey the proper sense of possession. The possessive plural of "Cones" refers to both sisters owning something and requires an apostrophe after the "s" with no additional letters or punctuation. Choice **(B)** is correct.

Math Test—No Calculator

1. B

Difficulty: Easy

Category: Heart of Algebra/Linear Equations

Getting to the Answer: Look at the structure of the equation. It is written in the form $y = mx + b$. The question is asking about 20.942, which is m in the

equation, and therefore represents a rate of change. The variable x represents number of months. The value of m is positive, so it represents the estimated monthly increase in the number of the plants after the natural disaster occurred. **(B)** is correct.

2. C

Difficulty: Easy

Category: Passport to Advanced Math/Quadratics

Getting to the Answer: The expression is a difference of two squares, so write each term as a quantity squared and then use the difference of squares rule $a^2 - b^2 = (a + b)(a - b)$:

$$25x^2 - \frac{4}{9}$$

$$= (5x)^2 - \left(\frac{2}{3}\right)^2$$

$$= \left(5x + \frac{2}{3}\right)\left(5x - \frac{2}{3}\right)$$

Choice **(C)** is correct.

3. A

Difficulty: Medium

Category: Passport to Advanced Math/Quadratics

Getting to the Answer: Factored form of a quadratic equation reveals the roots, or x-intercepts, of the equation, so start by identifying the x-intercepts on the graph. An x-intercept is an x-value that corresponds to a y-value of 0. Read the axis labels carefully—each grid line represents $\frac{1}{4}$, so the x-intercepts of the graph, and therefore the roots of the equation, are $x = -\frac{1}{2}$ and $x = \frac{3}{4}$. This means you are looking for factors that when solved result in these values of x. Choice **(A)** is correct because $2x + 1$ gives you $x = -\frac{1}{2}$ and $4x - 3$ gives you $x = \frac{3}{4}$.

4. D

Difficulty: Easy

Category: Heart of Algebra/Linear Equations

Getting to the Answer: Don't jump right into translating the line. Think about how the translation would affect the slope—it wouldn't. Translating the line moves all the points by the same amount, so the slope doesn't change. Find the slope of line P by counting the rise and the run from one point to the next, and you'll have your answer. From the y-intercept $(0, -2)$, the line rises 5 units and runs 2 units to the point $(2, 3)$, so the slope is $\frac{5}{2}$. **(D)** is correct.

5. B

Difficulty: Easy

Category: Passport to Advanced Math/Rational Equations

Getting to the Answer: Solve the equation for t. Multiply both sides of the equation by t to get it out of the denominator, and then divide both sides by a:

$$a = \frac{v_f - v_i}{t}$$

$$t\left(a = \frac{v_f - v_i}{t}\right)t$$

$$ta = v_f - v_i$$

$$t = \frac{v_f - v_i}{a}$$

This matches **(B)**.

6. C

Difficulty: Medium

Category: Passport to Advanced Math/Quadratics

Getting to the Answer: Imagine the graph of a parabola. The minimum value is the y-coordinate of its vertex and the axis of symmetry also passes through the vertex. Use these properties to identify the vertex, and then use it to write the equation of the parabola in vertex form, $y = a(x - h)^2 + k$, where (h, k) is the vertex. If the minimum of the parabola is -5, then the vertex of the parabola looks like $(x, -5)$. The axis of symmetry, $x = 1$, tells you the x-coordinate—it's 1. That means (h, k) is $(1, -5)$, and the equation of the parabola looks like $y = a(x - 1)^2 - 5$. The value of a in each of the answer choices is 1, so **(C)** is correct.

7. B

Difficulty: Medium

Category: Heart of Algebra/Systems of Linear Equations

Getting to the Answer: The solution to a system of linear equations shown graphically is the point where the lines intersect. Read the axis labels carefully. Each grid line represents $\frac{1}{2}$. The two lines intersect at $(-5, -4)$, so $A + B = -5 + (-4) = -9$. **(B)** is correct.

8. C

Difficulty: Easy

Category: Passport to Advanced Math/Polynomials

Getting to the Answer: When adding or subtracting polynomial expressions, simply combine like terms (terms that have the same variable part). Pay careful attention to the exponents. To keep things organized, arrange the terms in descending order before you combine them. Substitute the given expressions for A and B into $3A + B$. Distribute the 3 to each term of A and then combine like terms. Be careful—the first term of B is x^3, not x^2, so these cannot be combined:

$$3\left(x^2 + 4x + 9\right) + \left(x^3 + 6x - 2\right)$$

$$= 3x^2 + 12x + 27 + x^3 + 6x - 2$$

$$= x^3 + 3x^2 + 12x + 6x + 27 - 2$$

$$= x^3 + 3x^2 + 18x + 25$$

This matches **(C)**.

9. B

Difficulty: Medium

Category: Passport to Advanced Math/Quadratics

Getting to the Answer: A quadratic equation can have zero, one, or two real solutions. There are several ways to determine exactly how many. You could graph the equation and see how many times it crosses the x-axis, you could calculate the discriminant (the value under the square root in the quadratic formula), or you could try to factor the equation. Use whichever method gets you to the answer the quickest. Notice that the first and last terms in the equation are perfect squares—this is a hint that it could be a perfect square trinomial, which it is. The factored form of the equation is $(3x - 2)(3x - 2)$. Both factors are the same, so there is only one real value, $x = \frac{2}{3}$, that satisfies the equation, so **(B)** is correct.

10. A

Difficulty: Medium

Category: Heart of Algebra/Inequalities

Getting to the Answer: When an equation or an inequality involves fractions, there are a number of ways to approach it. You could distribute the fractions or you could clear the fractions by multiplying both sides by the lowest common denominator. In this question, clearing one fraction at a time will prevent having to work with messy fractions and large numbers. First, multiply everything by 5, and then divide by 3—this will clear the first fraction:

$$5 \times \left[\frac{3}{5}\left(x + \frac{2}{7}\right) \right] > [-6] \times 5$$

$$3\left(x + \frac{2}{7}\right) > -30$$

$$\frac{3\left(x + \frac{2}{7}\right)}{3} > \frac{-30}{3}$$

$$x + \frac{2}{7} > -10$$

Now, multiply everything by 7 and go from there:

$$7 \times \left[x + \frac{2}{7} \right] > [-10] \times 7$$

$$7x + 2 > -70$$

$$7x > -72$$

$$x > -\frac{72}{7}$$

Choice **(A)** is correct.

11. D

Difficulty: Medium

Category: Heart of Algebra/Linear Equations

Getting to the Answer: Don't let all the contextual information confuse you. The question at the end tells you that you are looking for the linear relationship between the pairs of numbers in the last two rows of the table. This amounts to writing an equation in the form $y = mx + b$. Take a peek at the answers—none of the equations have a y-intercept, so all you need to do is write the equation $y = mx$, or here, $s = md$. To find m, use any two ordered pairs from the table and the slope formula. Be careful—d represents x in the equation,

so the dropper amounts should be written first in the ordered pairs. Using $(0.5, 1.25)$ and $(1.0, 2.5)$, the slope is:

$$m = \frac{y_2 - y_1}{x_2 - x_1}$$

$$= \frac{2.5 - 1.25}{1.0 - 0.5}$$

$$= \frac{1.25}{0.5}$$

$$= 2.5$$

This means the equation is $s = 2.5d$, which matches **(D)**.

12. C

Difficulty: Medium

Category: Heart of Algebra/Linear Equations

Getting to the Answer: Think conceptually before you start simplifying the equations. The only type of line that does not cross the y-axis is a vertical line (because it runs parallel to the axis). All vertical lines take the form $x = a$. In other words, a vertical line does not have a y term. Eliminate equations that will clearly have a y term once simplified. You don't need to worry about the x terms or the constants.

(A): Although it may appear that the y terms will cancel, you must first distribute 0.5. The result is $0.5y$ on the left side of the equation and y on the right, which do not cancel, eliminate.

(B): No y terms on the left, but $4y$ on the right, eliminate.

(C): $0.25(8y) = 2y$ on the left, and $-2(-y) = 2y$ on the right, which do indeed cancel, so **(C)** is correct.

You don't need to waste time checking (D)—just move on to the next question. (Choice (D): $-6y$ on the left and $-3y$ on the right, which do not cancel.)

13. D

Difficulty: Medium

Category: Heart of Algebra/Systems of Linear Equations

Getting to the Answer: Typically, solving a system of equations means finding the values of x and y that satisfy both equations simultaneously. Because the solution to the system satisfies both equations, you can substitute 2 and -1, for x and y, respectively, and then solve for H and K. Before selecting your answer, check that you found what the question was asking for (the value of $\frac{K}{H}$):

$$Hx + 2y = -8$$
$$H(2) + 2(-1) = -8$$
$$2H - 2 = -8$$
$$2H = -6$$
$$H = -3$$

$$Kx - 5y = -13$$
$$K(2) - 5(-1) = -13$$
$$2K + 5 = -13$$
$$2K = -18$$
$$K = -9$$

So, $\frac{K}{H} = \frac{-9}{-3} = 3$, **(D)**.

14. D

Difficulty: Hard

Category: Additional Topics in Math/Trigonometry

Getting to the Answer: If an angle with measure A such that $\pi < A < \frac{3\pi}{2}$ is drawn on a unit circle, its terminal side will fall in quadrant III, and $\sin A = k$ will be a negative value (because sine represents the y-value of the point that intersects the unit circle). If $\sin B = k$ also (and k is negative), then the terminal side of B must land in either of quadrants III or IV (because sine is negative in those quadrants). Choose an easy radian measure (in quadrant III) for angle A, such as $\frac{5\pi}{4}$. Try each answer choice to see which one results in an angle that lies in the third or fourth quadrant:

(A): $\frac{5\pi}{4} - \pi = \frac{5\pi}{4} - \frac{4\pi}{4} = \frac{\pi}{4}$, which is in quadrant I; eliminate.

(B): $\pi + \frac{5\pi}{4} = \frac{4\pi}{4} + \frac{5\pi}{4} = \frac{9\pi}{4}$, which is in Quadrant I (because it is the same as $\frac{\pi}{4}$ rotated one full circle); eliminate.

(C): $2\pi - \frac{5\pi}{4} = \frac{8\pi}{4} - \frac{5\pi}{4} = \frac{3\pi}{4}$, which is in Quadrant II; eliminate.

(D): $3\pi - \frac{5\pi}{4} = \frac{12\pi}{4} - \frac{5\pi}{4} = \frac{7\pi}{4}$, which is in Quadrant IV, so **(D)** is correct.

15. D

Difficulty: Hard

Category: Passport to Advanced Math/Exponents

Getting to the Answer: For this question, use the following rules of exponents: when you raise a power to a power, you multiply the exponents, and when you divide with exponents, you subtract them. Distribute the 2 outside the parentheses to the exponent in the numerator and in the denominator:

$$\left(\frac{x^{\frac{1}{2}}}{x^{-2}}\right)^2 = \frac{x^{\frac{1}{2} \times 2}}{x^{-2 \times 2}} = \frac{x^1}{x^{-4}}$$

Now, subtract the exponents:

$$\frac{x}{x^{-4}} = x^{1-(-4)} = x^{1+4} = x^5$$

Unfortunately, x^5 is not one of the answer choices, so look for an answer choice that is also equivalent to x^5. You can eliminate (A) right away, and the exponents in (B) look too small, so start with (C), which simplifies to $\frac{x^7}{x^{12}} = \frac{1}{x^5}$ and is therefore not correct. Choice **(D)** is correct:

$$\left(\frac{\left(x^3\right)\left(x^4\right)}{x^{-3}}\right)^{\frac{1}{2}} = \left(\frac{x^7}{x^{-3}}\right)^{\frac{1}{2}}$$
$$= \left(x^{7-(-3)}\right)^{\frac{1}{2}}$$
$$= \left(x^{10}\right)^{\frac{1}{2}}$$
$$= x^5$$

Practice Tests

16. 1

Difficulty: Medium

Category: Heart of Algebra/Inequalities

Getting to the Answer: If (a, b) is a solution to the system, then a is the x-coordinate of any point in the region where the shading overlaps, and b is the corresponding y-coordinate. When $a = 0$ (or $x = 0$), the maximum possible value for b lies on the upper boundary line, $y < -3x + 2$. (You can tell which boundary line is the upper line by looking at the y-intercept.) The point on the boundary line is (0, 2), but the boundary line is dashed (because the inequality is strictly less than), so you cannot include (0, 2) in the solution set. This means **1** is the greatest possible integer value for b when $a = 0$.

17. 12

Difficulty: Medium

Category: Passport to Advanced Math/Functions

Getting to the Answer: For any function $f(x)$, the x is the input value and the output is the result after plugging in the input and simplifying. The question tells you that the *output* is 3 (not the input), so set the equation equal to 3 and solve for x:

$$3 = \frac{2}{3}x - 5$$
$$8 = \frac{2}{3}x$$
$$3 \times 8 = \cancel{3} \times \frac{2}{\cancel{3}}x$$
$$24 = 2x$$
$$12 = x$$

Grid in **12**.

18. 12

Difficulty: Medium

Category: Additional Topics in Math/Geometry

Getting to the Answer: Use the relationship $\frac{\text{area of sector}}{\text{area of circle}} = \frac{\text{central angle}}{360°}$. To help you remember this relationship, just think $\frac{\text{partial area}}{\text{whole area}} = \frac{\text{partial angle}}{\text{whole angle}}$. The unknown in this question is the diameter of the circle, which is twice the radius. You can find the radius of the circle by first finding the area of the whole circle,

and then by using the area equation, $A = \pi r^2$. You have everything you need to find the area of the circle. Because this is a no-calculator question, you can bet that numbers will simplify nicely:

$$\frac{\text{area of sector}}{\text{area of circle}} = \frac{\text{central angle}}{360°}$$
$$\frac{6\pi}{A} = \frac{60}{360}$$
$$\frac{6\pi}{A} = \frac{1}{6}$$
$$A = 36\pi$$

Now, solve for r using $A = \pi r^2$:

$$36\pi = \pi r^2$$
$$36 = r^2$$
$$\pm 6 = r$$

The radius can't be negative, so it must be 6, which means the diameter of the circle is twice that, or **12**.

19. 14

Difficulty: Hard

Category: Additional Topics in Math/Geometry

Getting to the Answer: When the equation of a circle is in the form $(x - h)^2 + (y - k)^2 = r^2$, the r represents the length of the radius. To get the equation into this form, complete the squares. You already have an x^2 and a y^2 in the given equation and the coefficients of x and y are even, so completing the square is fairly straightforward—there are just a lot of steps. Start by grouping the xs and ys together. Then, take the coefficient of the x term and divide it by 2, square it, and add it to the two terms with x variables. Do the same with the y term. Don't forget to add these amounts to the other side of the equation as well. This creates a perfect square of x terms and y terms, so take the square root of each:

$$x^2 + y^2 + 10x - 4y = 20$$
$$x^2 + 10x + y^2 - 4y = 20$$
$$\left(x^2 + 10x + 25\right) + \left(y^2 - 4y + 4\right) = 20 + 25 + 4$$
$$(x + 5)^2 + (y - 2)^2 = 49$$

The equation tells you that $r^2 = 49$, which means that the radius is 7 and the diameter is twice that, or **14**.

20. 800

Difficulty: Hard

Domain: Passport to Advanced Math/Functions

Getting to the Answer: Think about this question logically and in terms of function notation. Find the quantity that the company can expect to sell at each price using the demand function. Don't forget that the quantity is given in hundreds. Then, find the total sales, the total costs, and the total profits using multiplication. Set up a table like the following:

Price	$12	$10
Quantity	$q(12) = -2(12) + 34$ $= -24 + 34$ $= 10$	$q(10) = -2(10) + 34$ $= -20 + 34$ $= 14$
In hundreds	$10(100) = 1,000$	$14(100) = 1,400$
Sales	$1,000(12) = \$12,000$	$1,400(10) = \$14,000$
Costs	$1,000(7) = \$7,000$	$1,400(7) = \$9,800$
Profits	$\$5,000$	$\$4,200$

The company will earn $\$5,000 - \$4,200 = \textbf{\$800}$ more per month.

Math Test—Calculator

1. B

Difficulty: Easy

Category: Heart of Algebra/Inequalities

Getting to the Answer: When trying to match an inequality to a real-world scenario, you need to examine the numbers, the variables, and the inequality symbol. The question asks how much is needed to "meet or surpass" the recommended amount, which is another way of saying *greater than or equal to*, so you can eliminate (C). Adult females should consume 75 milligrams of vitamin C and smokers should consume an additional 35 milligrams, so the total amount that a smoking female should consume is $75 + 35 = 110$ milligrams. This means the right-hand side of the equation should be ≥ 110, and you can eliminate (A). To choose between (B) and (D), think in concrete terms. *Multiplying* (not dividing) the number of milligrams in each grapefruit or serving of spinach yields the total amount of vitamin C in each, so **(B)** is correct.

2. D

Difficulty: Easy

Category: Problem Solving and Data Analysis/ Scatterplots

Getting to the Answer: You don't need to know the slope of the line of best fit to answer the question, so don't waste valuable time trying to find it. Instead, use the labels on the axes to determine the meaning of the slope. On a graph, slope means the change in the *y*-values (rise) compared to the change in the *x*-values (run). In a real-world scenario, this is the same as the unit rate. In this context, the rise is the amount of money spent and the run is the number of minutes watching commercials. Thus, the unit rate, or slope, represents the predicted increase in money spent on brand-name products for every one-minute increase in time spent watching commercials, so **(D)** is correct.

3. B

Difficulty: Easy

Category: Heart of Algebra/Systems of Linear Equations

Getting to the Answer: Whenever a question gives you information about a total number of items and a total cost of those items, you should write one equation that represents the total number (here, the number of packages) and a second equation that represents the total cost (here, the cost of the portraits). The number of parents who ordered basic packages plus the number who ordered deluxe packages equals the total number of parents (182), so one equation is $b + d = 182$. This means you can eliminate (A) and (C). Now, write the cost equation: cost per basic package (29.5) times number ordered (b) plus cost per deluxe package (44.5) times number ordered (d) equals the total bill ($\$6,509$). The cost equation is $29.5b + 44.5d = 6,509$. Together, these two equations form the system in correct answer **(B)**. Don't let (D) fool you—there are two choices of packages, but this does not impact the total amount of the school's bill.

4.　C

Difficulty: Easy

Category: Passport to Advanced Math/Functions

Getting to the Answer: Understanding the language of functions will make answering this question very simple. Another way of saying "For what values of x does $f(x) = -4$?" is "What is the x-value when $y = -4$?" Draw a horizontal line across the graph at $y = -4$ and find the x-coordinates of any points that hit your line.

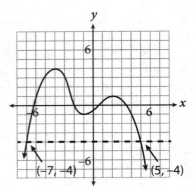

The line hits the graph at $x = -7$ and at $x = 5$, so **(C)** is correct.

5.　C

Difficulty: Easy

Category: Heart of Algebra/Linear Equations

Getting to the Answer: Don't let this fairly simple question fool you. Just because 3 and −3 are opposites, this does not mean the value on the right-hand side of the equal sign will be the opposite of 19. Solve for x, then substitute that value into the second equation for x and simplify:

$$4x + 3 = 19$$
$$4x = 16$$
$$x = 4$$

Thus, $4x - 3 = 4(4) - 3 = 16 - 3 = 13$. **(C)** is correct.

You might also recognize that $4x - 3$ is 6 less than $4x + 3$, so you can simply subtract 6 from 19 to arrive at 13. This is a great shortcut, but only works when the variable terms are identical.

6.　C

Difficulty: Easy

Category: Heart of Algebra/Linear Equations

Getting to the Answer: To find the slope of a line from its graph, either count the rise and the run from one point to the next or choose two points that lie on the line and substitute them into the slope formula, $m = \dfrac{y_2 - y_1}{x_2 - x_1}$. Use whichever method gets you to the answer the quickest. Pay careful attention to negative signs. Using the points $(0, -2)$ and $(7, -8)$, the slope is:

$$m = \frac{-8 - (-2)}{7 - 0}$$
$$= \frac{-6}{7}$$
$$= -\frac{6}{7}$$

Choice **(C)** is correct.

7.　B

Difficulty: Easy

Category: Heart of Algebra/Linear Equations

Getting to the Answer: Compare the differences in the two lines to the statements in the answer choices. Pay attention to which line represents each state. Be careful—this is a real-world scenario, and the word "positive" does not refer to the slope of the lines. The key difference between the lines in the graph is their slopes. The dashed line (State B) has a steeper negative slope, while the solid line (State A) has a more gradual slope. This means that the crime rate for armed robbery in State B decreased at a faster rate than in State A. Because, in the real world, a positive impact means fewer crimes, State B's law had a more positive impact on the crime rate for armed robbery. This matches **(B)**.

8.　C

Difficulty: Easy

Category: Problem Solving and Data Analysis/Rates, Ratios, Proportions, and Percentages

Getting to the Answer: When ratios involve large numbers, simplify if possible to make the calculations easier. Let p equal the number of cans of paint mixed. Set up a proportion and solve for p. Try writing the proportion in words first:

$$\frac{4\cancel{0} \text{ defective}}{2,50\cancel{0} \text{ mixed}} = \frac{128 \text{ defective}}{p \text{ mixed}}$$

$$\frac{4}{250} = \frac{128}{p}$$

$$4p = 32,000$$

$$p = 8,000$$

Choice **(C)** is correct.

9. D

Difficulty: Medium

Category: Problem Solving and Data Analysis/Statistics and Probability

Getting to the Answer: Because the mean ages are different and you do not know how many men or women have college degrees and get married, you need to reason logically to arrive at the correct answer. The mean age of the women is lower than that of the men, so the combined mean cannot be greater than or equal to that of the men. Similarly, the mean age of the men is greater than that of the women, so the combined mean cannot be less than or equal to the mean age of the women. In other words, the combined mean age must fall somewhere between the two means, making **(D)** correct.

10. A

Difficulty: Easy

Category: Problem Solving and Data Analysis/Rates, Ratios, Proportions, and Percentages

Getting to the Answer: To answer a question that says "directly proportional," set two ratios equal to each other and solve for the missing amount. Don't forget—match the units in the numerators and in the denominators on both sides. Let f equal the number of feet that the diver can safely ascend in 90 seconds. Set up a proportion and solve for f. Because the first rate is given in terms of minutes, write 90 seconds as 1.5 minutes:

$$\frac{165 \text{ feet}}{5.5 \text{ minutes}} = \frac{f \text{ feet}}{1.5 \text{ minutes}}$$

$$1.5(165) = 5.5(f)$$

$$247.5 = 5.5f$$

$$45 = f$$

Choice **(A)** is correct.

11. D

Difficulty: Medium

Category: Heart of Algebra/Inequalities

Getting to the Answer: You could graph the cost function ($y = 17p + 1,890$) and the revenue function ($y = 35p$) and try to determine where the revenue function is greater (higher on the graph). However, the numbers are quite large and this may prove to be very time-consuming. Instead, create and solve an inequality comparing revenue and cost. If the revenue from a single pair of shoes is $35, then the total revenue from p pairs is $35p$. If revenue must be greater than cost, then the inequality should be $35p > 17p + 1,890$. Now, solve for p using inverse operations:

$$35p > 17p + 1,890$$

$$18p > 1,890$$

$$p > 105$$

This matches **(D)**.

12. B

Difficulty: Easy

Category: Problem Solving and Data Analysis/Rates, Ratios, Proportions, and Percentages

Getting to the Answer: This is a question about rates, so pay careful attention to the units. As you read the question, decide how and when you will need to convert units. First, determine how long it will take the athlete to complete the race. Set up a proportion:

$$\frac{9.25 \text{ miles}}{1 \text{ hour}} = \frac{74 \text{ miles}}{x \text{ hours}}$$

$$9.25x = 74$$

$$x = 8$$

The question asks for the total number of calories needed. The recommended rate of consumption is given in calories per minute and you now know the number of hours that it will take the athlete to complete the race. You could convert the number of hours to minutes ($8 \times 60 \text{ minutes} = 480 \text{ minutes}$) and then multiply this by 3 (the calorie per minute rate given) to find that the athlete should consume $480 \times 3 = 1,440$ calories, which matches **(B)**. Or, you could also convert the given rate (3 calories per minute) to a per-hour rate ($3 \times 60 = 180$ calories per hour) and then multiply this by the number of hours it will take the athlete to finish the race ($180 \times 8 = 1,440$ calories).

13. C

Difficulty: Medium

Category: Heart of Algebra/Linear Equations

Getting to the Answer: The rate of change (or slope) of a linear relationship is constant, so find the rate and apply it to the missing value. You could also look for a pattern in the table. Choose any two points (preferably ones with the nicest numbers) from the table and substitute them into the slope formula. Using the points $(3, 0)$ and $(-1, 14)$, the slope is $\frac{14 - 0}{-1 - 3} = \frac{14}{-4} = \frac{7}{-2}$. This means that for every 2 units the x-value decreases, the y-value increases by 7, and the decrease from $x = -5$ to $x = -7$ happens to be -2. So, increase the y-value by 7: $28 + 7 = 35$. **(C)** is correct.

14. B

Difficulty: Medium

Category: Problem Solving and Data Analysis/Statistics and Probability

Getting to the Answer: Think about what the question is asking. The real estate agent wants to figure out which measure of the data (mean, mode, range, or median) is going to be most useful. The *mode* of a data set tells you the data point, or in this case the age range, that occurs most often. If the real estate agent markets to the age range that represents the mode, **(B)**, she will be marketing to the largest group of clients possible.

15. A

Difficulty: Hard

Category: Problem Solving and Data Analysis/Statistics and Probability

Getting to the Answer: Some data sets have a *head*, where many data points are clustered in one area, and one or two *tails*, where the number of data points slowly decreases to 0. Examining the tail will help you describe the shape of the data set. A data set is *skewed* in the direction of its longest tail. The graph in this question has its tail on the right side, so the data is skewed to the right. When data is skewed to the right, the mean is greater than the median because the mean is more sensitive to the higher data values in the tail than is the median, so **(A)** is correct. If you're not sure about the mean/median part, read the rest of the answer choices—none of them describes the data as skewed to the right, so you can eliminate all of them.

16. B

Difficulty: Medium

Category: Heart of Algebra/Inequalities

Getting to the Answer: The question states that t represents the number of round trips. The cost of one round trip without the discount card is $35 per trip, or $35t$. If a commuter purchases the discount card, round trips would equal the cost of the card plus $12.50 per trip, or $900 + 12.5t$. Combine these into an inequality, remembering which way the inequality symbol should be oriented. You want the cost with the discount card to be less than ($<$) the cost without the card, so the inequality should be $900 + 12.5t < 35t$. Now, solve for t:

$$900 + 12.5t < 35t$$
$$900 < 22.5t$$
$$40 < t$$

Turn the inequality around to find that $t > 40$, which means a commuter must make more than 40 trips for the discount card to be a better deal, which is **(B)**.

17. C

Difficulty: Medium

Category: Problem Solving and Data Analysis/Rates, Ratios, Proportions, and Percentages

Getting to the Answer: Etienne starts with $800. He spends 20% of $800, or $0.2(\$800) = \$160$, on gas. He has $\$800 - \$160 = \$640$ left over. He budgets 25% of $640, or $0.25(\$640) = \$160$, for food and allots $300 for the hotel. He spends all the remaining money on entertainment, which is $\$640 - \$160 - \$300 = \$180$. Divide this amount by the original amount to find the percent he spent on entertainment: $\frac{180}{800} = 0.225 = 22.5\%$. **(C)** is correct.

18. A

Difficulty: Medium

Category: Passport to Advanced Math/Scatterplots

Getting to the Answer: When the dependent variable in a relationship increases by a scale factor, like doubling, tripling, etc., there is an exponential relationship between the variables that can be written in the form $y = a(b)^x$, where a is the initial amount, b is the scale factor, and x is time. The question states that the number of microbes tripled every 24 hours, so the relationship is exponential. This means you can eliminate (C) and (D) right away. Choices (A) and (B) are written in the form $y = a(b)^x$, with the initial amount equal to 2,000 and the scale factor equal to 3, so you can't eliminate either one at first glance. To choose between them, try an easy number for h (like 24) in each equation to see which one matches the information given in the question. In the first equation, $n = 2,000(3)^{\frac{24}{24}} = 2,000 \times (3)^1 = 6,000$, which is 2,000 tripled, so **(A)** is correct.

19. A
Difficulty: Medium

Category: Problem Solving and Data Analysis/Statistics and Probability

Getting to the Answer: When working with two-way tables, always read the question carefully, identifying which pieces of information you need. Here, you need to focus on the "Against" column and the "1L" and "2L" rows. To stay organized, it may help to circle these pieces of information in the table. There are 58 1Ls and 64 2Ls in the survey sample, for a total of $58 + 64 = 122$ 1Ls and 2Ls. There are 16 1Ls and 12 2Ls against the policy, for a total of $16 + 12 = 28$. This means that 28 out of the 122 1Ls and 2Ls are against the new policy. Written as a fraction, this is $\frac{28}{122}$, which reduces to $\frac{14}{61}$. **(A)** is correct.

20. C
Difficulty: Medium

Category: Additional Topics in Math/Imaginary Numbers

Getting to the Answer: You will not be expected to raise a complex number like the one in this question to the third power by hand. That's a clue that you should be able to use your calculator. The definition of i has been programmed into all graphing calculators, so you can perform basic operations on complex numbers using the calculator (in the Calculator Section of the test). Enter the expression as follows: $(6 + 5i)^3$. On the TI83/84 calculators, you can find i on the button with the decimal point. After entering the expression and pressing Enter, the calculator should return $-234 + 415i$, which is **(C)**.

You could, however, expand the number by hand by writing it as $(6 + 5i)(6 + 5i)(6 + 5i)$ and carefully multiply it out.

21. B
Difficulty: Hard

Category: Problem Solving and Data Analysis/Scatterplots

Getting to the Answer: When an exponential function is written in the form $f(x) = f(0)(1 + r)^x$, the quantity $(1 + r)$ represents the growth rate or the decay rate depending on whether the y-values are increasing or decreasing. The y-values are increasing in this graph, so r represents a growth rate. Because the data is modeled using an exponential function (not a linear function), the rate is not the same as the slope. Look at the y-values in the calculator screenshot—they are quadrupling as the x-values increase by 1. In the equation, this means that $(1 + r) = 4$. Solve this equation to find that $r = 3$. **(B)** is correct.

22. A
Difficulty: Medium

Category: Problem Solving and Data Analysis/Rates, Ratios, Proportions, and Percentages

Getting to the Answer: Pay careful attention to the units. You need to convert all of the dimensions to inches and then set up and solve a proportion. There are 12 inches in 1 foot, so the real pyramid's height was $(480 \times 12) + 8 = 5,760 + 8 = 5,768$ inches; the length of the passage in the real pyramid was $53.75 \times 12 = 645$ inches; the museum's pyramid height will be 71 feet, 6 inches, or 858 inches; and the length of the museum's passage is unknown. Set up a proportion and solve for the unknown. Use words first to help you keep the measurements in the right places:

$$\frac{\text{real passage length}}{\text{real height}} = \frac{\text{museum passage length}}{\text{museum height}}$$

$$\frac{645}{5,768} = \frac{x}{858}$$

$$553,410 = 5,768x$$

$$95.94 = x$$

The museum should make the length of its passage about 96 inches, or $96 \div 12 = 8$ feet. **(A)** is correct.

Practice Tests

23. D

Difficulty: Medium

Category: Passport to Advanced Math/Rational Equations

Getting to the Answer: You could use polynomial long division to answer this question or you could try to factor the numerator and see if any terms cancel. It is very tricky to factor a quadratic equation with a negative coefficient on x^2, so start by factoring -1 out of both the numerator and the denominator. To factor the resulting quadratic in the numerator, you need to find two numbers whose product is -24 and whose sum is 10. The numbers are -2 and $+12$:

$$\frac{-x^2 - 10x + 24}{2 - x} = \frac{-1(x^2 + 10x - 24)}{-1(x - 2)}$$
$$= \frac{(x - 2)(x + 12)}{x - 2}$$
$$= x + 12$$

This matches **(D)**.

24. C

Difficulty: Hard

Category: Problem Solving and Data Analysis/Rates, Ratios, Proportions, and Percentages

Getting to the Answer: You're given two ratios: ethanol to gasoline and methanol to gasoline. Your job is to "merge" them so you can directly compare ethanol to methanol. Both of the given ratios contain gasoline, but the gasoline amounts (4 and 9) are not identical. To directly compare them, find a common multiple (36). Multiply each ratio by the factor that will make the number of parts of gasoline equal to 36 in each:

Ethanol to Gasoline: $(1:4) \times (9:9) = 9:36$

Methanol to Gasoline: $(1:9) \times (4:4) = 4:36$

Now that the number of parts of gasoline needed is the same in both ratios, you can merge the two ratios to compare ethanol to methanol directly: 9:36:4. So the proper ratio of ethanol to methanol is 9:4, which is **(C)**.

25. A

Difficulty: Medium

Category: Heart of Algebra/Linear Equations

Getting to the Answer: Add reasonable numbers to the graph such as the ones shown in the following example:

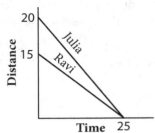

Use the numbers to help you evaluate each statement. It took Julia and Ravi each 25 minutes to drive to the museum, so you can eliminate (C) and (D). Julia drove 20 miles in 25 minutes, while Ravi only drove 15 miles in 25 minutes; their rates are not the same, so (B) is not correct. This means **(A)** must be correct. Julia starts out farther away than Ravi, so Julia must have driven at a faster speed than Ravi to arrive at the museum in the same amount of time.

26. D

Difficulty: Hard

Category: Passport to Advanced Math/Functions

Getting to the Answer: Transformations that are grouped with the x in a function shift the graph horizontally and therefore affect the x-coordinates of points on the graph. Transformations that are not grouped with the x shift the graph vertically and therefore affect the y-coordinates of points on the graph. Remember, horizontal shifts are always backward of what they look like.

Perform each transformation on the coordinates of the point, one at a time, following the same order of operations that you use when simplifying arithmetic expressions. Start with $(x - 4)$. This shifts the graph right 4 units, so add 4 to the x-coordinate of the given point: $(8, -3) \rightarrow (8 + 4, -3) = (12, -3)$. Next, apply the negative in front of g, which is not grouped with the x, so it makes the y-coordinate the opposite of what it was: $(12, -3) \rightarrow (12, 3)$. Finally, the -6 is not grouped with x, so subtract 6 from the y-coordinate: $(12, 3) \rightarrow (12, 3 - 6) = (12, -3)$. Therefore, **(D)** is correct. You could also plot the point on a coordinate plane, perform the transformations (right 4, reflect vertically over the *x*-axis, and then down 6), and find the resulting point.

27. D

Difficulty: Medium

Category: Passport to Advanced Math/Functions

Getting to the Answer: Sometimes, a question requires thought rather than brute force. Here, you need to understand that when dealing with compositions, the range of the inner function becomes the domain of the outer function, which in turn produces the range of the composition. In the composition $f(g(x))$, the function $g(x) = x^3$ is the inner function. Because the question states that *x* is either zero or a negative number ($x \leq 0$), every value of *x*, when substituted into this function, will result in zero or a negative number (because a negative number raised to an odd power is always negative). This means that the largest possible range value for $g(x)$ is 0, and consequently that the largest possible domain value for $f(x)$ is also 0. Substituting 0 for *x* in $f(x)$ results in −1, which is the largest possible range value for the composition. Because $1 > -1$, it is not in the range of $f(g(x))$, so **(D)** is correct.

28. A

Difficulty: Hard

Category: Passport to Advanced Math/Quadratics

Getting to the Answer: To answer this question, you need to recall nearly everything you've learned about quadratic graphs. The equation is given in vertex form $(y = a(x - h)^2 + k)$, which reveals the vertex (h, k), the direction in which the parabola opens (upward when $a > 0$ and downward when $a < 0$), the axis of symmetry $(x = h)$, and the minimum/maximum value of the function (k).

Start by comparing each answer choice to the equation, $y = -3(x - 5)^2 + 8$. The only choice that you cannot immediately compare is (A), because vertex form does not readily reveal the *y*-intercept, so start with (B). Don't forget, you are looking for the statement that is not true.

(B): The axis of symmetry is given by $x = h$, and *h* is 5, so this statement is true and therefore not correct; eliminate.

(C): The vertex is given by (h, k), so the vertex is indeed (5, 8) and this choice is not correct; eliminate.

(D): The value of *a* is −3, which indicates that the parabola opens downward, so this choice is also incorrect, eliminate. That means **(A)** must be the correct answer. To confirm, you could substitute 0 for *x* in the equation to find the *y*-intercept:

$$y = -3(x - 5)^2 + 8$$
$$= -3(0 - 5)^2 + 8$$
$$= -3(-5)^2 + 8$$
$$= -3(25) + 8$$
$$= -75 + 8$$
$$= -67$$

The *y*-intercept is (0, −67), not (0, 8), so the statement is not true and therefore the correct answer.

29. A

Difficulty: Hard

Category: Problem Solving and Data Analysis/Rates, Ratios, Proportions, and Percentages

Getting to the Answer: Don't let all the technical words in this question overwhelm you. Solve it step-by-step, examining the units as you go. Notice that some of the numbers in the answer choices are just 1 apart, so think carefully before selecting your answer. Start by determining the number of megabytes the computer can upload in 1 weekend (48 hours):

$$\frac{5.25 \text{ megabytes}}{1 \text{ second}} \times \frac{60 \text{ seconds}}{1 \text{ minute}} \times \frac{60 \text{ minutes}}{1 \text{ hour}} \times 48 \text{ hours}$$
$$= 907{,}200 \text{ megabytes}$$

Convert this amount to gigabytes (because the information about the scans is given in gigabytes, not megabytes):

$$907{,}200 \text{ megabytes} \times \frac{1 \text{ gigabyte}}{1{,}000 \text{ megabytes}}$$
$$= 907.2 \text{ gigabytes}$$

Each client file is about 2.5 gigabytes in size, so divide this number by 2.5 to determine how many client files the computer can upload to the remote server: $907.2 \div 2.5 = 362.88$ files. Remember, you should round this number down to 362, because the question asks for the maximum number the computer can upload, and it cannot complete the 363rd scan in the time allowed. Choice **(A)** is correct.

30. A

Difficulty: Medium

Category: Additional Topics in Math/Geometry

Getting to the Answer: This question does not provide a graphic, so sketch a quick diagram of the information presented. Be sure to show the direction of traffic for each street. The question describes two parallel streets, cut by a transversal. Start with that, and then add all the details:

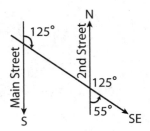

Traffic traveling south on Main Street must make a 125° turn onto the new road. This is the angle between where the traffic was originally headed and where it is headed after it makes the turn. Traffic on 2nd Street is traveling north, the opposite direction. As shown in the diagram, the angle that the northbound traffic would make is supplementary to the corresponding angle made by the southbound traffic. When two parallel lines are cut by a transversal, corresponding angles are congruent, which means that cars turning off of 2nd Street will make a $180 - 125 = 55$ degree turn onto the new road. Choice **(A)** is correct.

31. 11.5 or 23/2 or 69/6

Difficulty: Easy

Category: Heart of Algebra/Linear Equations

Getting to the Answer: Simplify each numerator. Then, cross-multiply. Finally, isolate the variable using inverse operations:

$$\frac{4h - (21 - 8h)}{3} = \frac{15 + 6(h - 1)}{2}$$

$$\frac{4h - 21 + 8h}{3} = \frac{15 + 6h - 6}{2}$$

$$\frac{12h - 21}{3} = \frac{6h + 9}{2}$$

$$2(12h - 21) = 3(6h + 9)$$

$$24h - 42 = 18h + 27$$

$$6h = 69$$

$$h = \frac{69}{6} = \frac{23}{2} = 11.5$$

32. 255

Difficulty: Medium

Category: Heart of Algebra/Systems of Linear Equations

Getting to the Answer: Translate English into math to write the two equations: The New York property costs 30 thousand dollars less than four times the cost of the Georgia property, so $N = 4G - 30$; together, the two properties cost 445 thousand dollars, so $N + G = 445$.

The system of equations is:

$$\begin{cases} N = 4G - 30 \\ N + G = 445 \end{cases}$$

The top equation is already solved for N, so substitute $4G - 30$ into the second equation for N and solve for G:

$$4G - 30 + G = 445$$

$$5G - 30 = 445$$

$$5G = 475$$

$$G = 95$$

The Georgia property costs 95 thousand dollars, so the New York property costs $4(95) - 30 = 350$ thousand dollars. This means the New York property costs $350 - 95 = $ **255** thousand more dollars than the Georgia property.

33. .52

Difficulty: Medium

Category: Problem Solving and Data Analysis/Statistics and Probability

Getting to the Answer: The probability that an event will occur is the number of desired outcomes (number of available cars that have a rating of at least 25 miles per gallon) divided by the number of total possible outcomes (total number of cars). "At least" means that much or greater, so find the number of cars represented by the two bars to the right of 25 in the histogram: $20 + 6 = 26$ cars. Now, find the total number of available cars: $8 + 16 + 20 + 6 = 50$. Finally, divide to find the indicated probability: $\frac{26}{50} = $ **.52**.

34. 21

Difficulty: Medium

Category: Additional Topics in Math/Geometry

Getting to the Answer: Use the formula for finding the volume of a rectangular solid, $V = lwh$, to write an equation. Because the dimensions are given as the ratio 3:5:2, let the length, width, and height be represented by $3x$, $5x$, and $2x$. Substitute the expressions into the formula and solve for x:

$$10{,}290 = (3x)(5x)(2x)$$
$$10{,}290 = 30x^3$$
$$343 = x^3$$
$$7 = x$$

The length was represented by $3x$, so multiply to find that the length is $3(7) = $ **21** feet.

35. 8

Difficulty: Medium

Category: Problem Solving and Data Analysis/ Scatterplots

Getting to the Answer: Draw the line of best fit so that approximately half of the data points fall above the line and half fall below it:

Regional Manager Job Performance

Look for the point that is farthest from the line you drew, which is (8, 6). Because time is plotted along the horizontal axis, this point represents a manager who spent **8** months in the training program.

36. 37

Difficulty: Hard

Category: Passport to Advanced Math/Exponents

Getting to the Answer: Although this question is in the calculator portion of the test, you get an overflow error if you try to use your calculator. This is because the numbers are simply too large. You'll need to rely on the rules of exponents to answer this question. When a power is raised to a power, multiply the exponents. You want to be able to add the exponents later, so the bases need to be the same, and you'll need to recognize that 32 is the same as 2 raised to the 5th power:

$$\left(2^{32}\right)^{\left(2^{32}\right)}$$
$$= 2^{\left(32 \times 2^{32}\right)}$$
$$= 2^{\left(2^5 \times 2^{32}\right)}$$

Now that the two bases in the exponent are the same, you can add their exponents:

$$= 2^{\left(2^{5+32}\right)}$$
$$= 2^{\left(2^{37}\right)}$$

Therefore, $x = $ **37**.

37. 33

Difficulty: Medium

Category: Problem Solving and Data Analysis/Rates, Ratios, Proportions, and Percentages

Getting to the Answer: Questions that involve distance, rate, and time can almost always be solved using the formula Distance = rate × time. Use the speed, or rate, of the first car (64 miles per hour) and its distance from the destination (144 miles) to determine how long it traveled. You don't know the time, so call it t:

$$\text{Distance} = \text{rate} \times \text{time}$$
$$144 = 64t$$
$$2.25 = t$$

This means it took 2.25 hours for the first car to arrive. You need the number of minutes, so multiply 2.25 by 60 to get $60 \times 2.25 = 135$ minutes. Now determine how long it took the second car. It started its drive at 2:18 p.m. and arrived at 4:00 p.m., so it took 1 hour and 42 minutes, or 102 minutes. This means that the first car had been traveling for $135 - 102 = $ **33** minutes before the second car started its drive.

Practice Tests

38. 220

Difficulty: Hard

Category: Problem Solving and Data Analysis/Rates, Ratios, Proportions, and Percentages

Getting to the Answer: To get started, you'll need to find the distance for each part of the third car's trip— the question only tells you the total distance (25 miles). Then, use the formula Distance = rate × time to find how long the car traveled at 15 miles per hour and then how long it traveled at 30 miles per hour.

First part of trip (60% of the drive):

$$0.6 \times 25 \text{ miles} = 15 \text{ miles}$$
$$15 = 15t$$
$$1 = t$$

So the first part of the trip took 1 hour. Then the car did not move for 20 minutes due to the accident.

Last part of trip (40% of the drive remained):

$$0.4 \times 25 \text{ miles} = 10 \text{ miles}$$
$$10 = 30t$$
$$\frac{10}{30} = t$$
$$t = \frac{1}{3}$$

So the last part of the trip took one-third of an hour, or 20 minutes. This means it took the third car a total of 1 hour and 40 minutes to arrive at the destination. Because the car arrived at 4:00 p.m., it must have left at 2:20 p.m. Enter the answer as **220**.

Essay Test Rubric

The Essay Demonstrates . . .

4—Advanced	• **(Reading)** A strong ability to comprehend the source text, including its central ideas and important details and how they interrelate, and effectively use evidence (quotations, paraphrases, or both) from the source text. • **(Analysis)** A strong ability to evaluate the author's use of evidence, reasoning, and/or stylistic and persuasive elements and/or other features of the student's own choosing; make good use of relevant, sufficient, and strategically chosen support for the claims or points made in the student's essay; and focus consistently on features of the source text that are most relevant to addressing the task. • **(Writing)** A strong ability to provide a precise central claim; create an effective organization that includes an introduction and conclusion, as well as a clear progression of ideas; successfully employ a variety of sentence structures; use precise word choice; maintain a formal style and objective tone; and show command of the conventions of standard written English so that the essay is free of errors.
3—Proficient	• **(Reading)** Satisfactory ability to comprehend the source text, including its central ideas and important details and how they interrelate, and use evidence (quotations, paraphrases, or both) from the source text. • **(Analysis)** Satisfactory ability to evaluate the author's use of evidence, reasoning, and/or stylistic and persuasive elements and/or other features of the student's own choosing; make use of relevant and sufficient support for the claims or points made in the student's essay; and focus primarily on features of the source text that are most relevant to addressing the task. • **(Writing)** Satisfactory ability to provide a central claim; create an organization that includes an introduction and conclusion, as well as a clear progression of ideas; employ a variety of sentence structures; use precise word choice; maintain an appropriate formal style and objective tone; and show control of the conventions of standard written English so that the essay is free of significant errors.
2—Partial	• **(Reading)** Limited ability to comprehend the source text, including its central ideas and important details and how they interrelate, and use evidence (quotations, paraphrases, or both) from the source text. • **(Analysis)** Limited ability to evaluate the author's use of evidence, reasoning, and/or stylistic and persuasive elements and/or other features of the student's own choosing; make use of support for the claims or points made in the student's essay; and focus on relevant features of the source text. • **(Writing)** Limited ability to provide a central claim, create an effective organization for ideas, employ a variety of sentence structures, use precise word choice, maintain an appropriate style and tone, or show control of the conventions of standard written English, resulting in certain errors that detract from the quality of the writing.

1—Inadequate	• (Reading) Little or no ability to comprehend the source text or use evidence from the source text.
	• (Analysis) Little or no ability to evaluate the author's use of evidence, reasoning, and/or stylistic and persuasive elements; choose support for claims or points; or focus on relevant features of the source text.
	• (Writing) Little or no ability to provide a central claim, organization, or progression of ideas; employ a variety of sentence structures; use precise word choice; maintain an appropriate style and tone; or show control of the conventions of standard written English, resulting in numerous errors that undermine the quality of the writing.

Sample Essay Response #1 (Advanced Score)

When William Faulkner made his Nobel Prize Acceptance Speech in 1950, he was speaking at the height of the Cold War. The memory of the devastation of the atomic bombs dropped on Japan was still fresh in people's minds, and it's clear from Faulkner's speech that people were afraid more destruction was to come. Faulkner felt strongly that in order for mankind to prevail, writers must write from the heart, rather than writing from fear. In this speech, he uses several techniques to persuade his audience of his claim: he establishes his authority, uses vivid language and imagery, and appeals to his audience's sense of duty.

At the ceremony, Faulkner was speaking from a position of strength and expertise, having just been awarded the Nobel Prize for Literature. In a subtle way, he reminds his audience of this expertise throughout the speech, lending credibility to his claims. In the first paragraph, he redefines the award as an honor for his life's work in mining the human spirit to create great literature. He then reminds the audience of his position as an elder statesman by directing his speech to the "young men and women" who are also engaged in this great work, and goes on to tell them what they must "learn" and "teach themselves" about life and writing. By framing the speech as a lesson for younger writers based on his career-long exploration of the human spirit, Faulkner establishes his authority and commands respect for his ideas.

Faulkner also uses vivid language and imagery to create a vision of a higher purpose to which he would like his audience to aspire. In paragraphs 2 and 3, he paints a picture of the writer as an artist involved in a great struggle, which he characterizes with words like "agony" and "sweat." According to Faulkner, a writer will never succeed if he avoids universal truths, and until the writer realizes this, "he labors under a curse." To Faulkner, a writer who writes from a place of fear instead of compassion creates meaningless work that touches upon "no universal bones, leaving no scars." On the other hand, a writer who writes with pity and compassion lifts the reader's heart and reminds him of his "immortal" nature. This type of vivid language, which is clearly written from Faulkner's heart, helps to support his argument that writing from the heart is the way to create great literature that inspires mankind to prevail.

Finally, in speaking to his audience of younger writers, he calls upon their sense of duty. It's clear earlier in the speech that Faulkner is concerned that younger writers are being defeated by fear, and are failing to explore the rich material of the human heart. He asserts that rather than writing about defeat, they should elevate humans by reminding them of their great capacity for courage, compassion, sacrifice, and other noble qualities. These characteristics are unique to humans and are the "glory" of their past, which Faulkner exhorts them to carry into the future. In the final line, Faulkner calls upon writers to be more than just record-keepers—rather, they should actively inspire humankind to prevail.

In a time of great fear, William Faulkner used his Nobel Prize acceptance speech to express his belief that writers must write from the heart in order to ensure the success of mankind. To convince his audience that they should accept his claim, he first establishes his authority, then uses vivid language and imagery to illustrate the value of writing from the heart, and finally calls upon his audience's sense of duty to elevate the human race. Through skillful use of these features, he constructs a persuasive argument.

Sample Essay Response #2 (Proficient Score)

William Faulkner believed that authors must write from their hearts to make sure that humans prevail on Earth. In his Nobel Prize Acceptance Speech, Faulkner uses his expertise, vivid language, and calls to his audience's sense of responsibility to make his case.

In this speech, Faulkner speaks as both a writer and a teacher. He acknowledges that young writers are listening to him; and he has lessons to give to them. Since he just won the Nobel Prize his listeners believe him to be an expert and this makes them more willing to accept his message. He tells his young listeners that they have lost their way, and they must relearn the "problems of the human heart," which are what make good writing. Faulkner tells his listeners that being afraid is the lowest of human feelings, and they need to put their fears aside and instead explore the higher truths of the human heart. Faulkner knows that his young audience is looking up to him, and so he uses his position of authority to guide them to strive for something greater than their fear.

Faulkner also uses vivid language to enhance his argument. Twice he uses the phrase "agony and sweat" to describe the struggle of the writer who writes from the heart. This type of vivid language makes the writer's struggle seem like a goal worth fighting for. Faulkner describes writing that avoids the problems of the human heart as having no "bones" or "scars." By using words that evoke the human body, Faulkner implies that this type of writing has no weight or depth. Faulkner uses very vivid language to paint a picture of a world after a nuclear apacalypse, which is what his audience fears. In this picture, the evening is "red and dying," the rocks are "worthless" and man's voice is "puny" but still talking. Faulkner then tells his audience he refuses to accept this bleak image—that man will do more than just exist, he will prevail. By using vivid language to describe the defeatist view of mankind, Faulkner makes his audience feel revulsion at this image, and makes the alternative seem much more appealing.

Faulkner wanted writers to write about courage, hope, love, compassion, and pity because these things uplift the human spirit. Faulkner calls upon his listeners' sense of responsibility by telling them that they have a duty to write about these subjects. His implication is that if they don't, mankind will fall back into the bleakness he described previously. He also says that the writer has a responsibility to be a "pillar" holding up mankind. By making his audience feel that they have a responsibility to help mankind, Faulkner strengthens his position.

In this speech, Faulkner makes an effective argument that writers must write from the heart to save mankind and help it prevail. To strengthen his argument, he uses the features of expertise, vivid language, and calls to responsibility.

SAT Practice Test 2 Answer Sheet

You will see an answer sheet like the one below on test day. Remove (or photocopy) this answer sheet and use it to complete the test. Review the answer key following the test when finished.

When testing, start with number 1 for each section. If a section has fewer questions than answer spaces, leave the extra spaces blank.

SECTION 1

1. (A) (B) (C) (D)   14. (A) (B) (C) (D)   27. (A) (B) (C) (D)   40. (A) (B) (C) (D)
2. (A) (B) (C) (D)   15. (A) (B) (C) (D)   28. (A) (B) (C) (D)   41. (A) (B) (C) (D)
3. (A) (B) (C) (D)   16. (A) (B) (C) (D)   29. (A) (B) (C) (D)   42. (A) (B) (C) (D)
4. (A) (B) (C) (D)   17. (A) (B) (C) (D)   30. (A) (B) (C) (D)   43. (A) (B) (C) (D)
5. (A) (B) (C) (D)   18. (A) (B) (C) (D)   31. (A) (B) (C) (D)   44. (A) (B) (C) (D)
6. (A) (B) (C) (D)   19. (A) (B) (C) (D)   32. (A) (B) (C) (D)   45. (A) (B) (C) (D)
7. (A) (B) (C) (D)   20. (A) (B) (C) (D)   33. (A) (B) (C) (D)   46. (A) (B) (C) (D)
8. (A) (B) (C) (D)   21. (A) (B) (C) (D)   34. (A) (B) (C) (D)   47. (A) (B) (C) (D)
9. (A) (B) (C) (D)   22. (A) (B) (C) (D)   35. (A) (B) (C) (D)   48. (A) (B) (C) (D)
10. (A) (B) (C) (D)   23. (A) (B) (C) (D)   36. (A) (B) (C) (D)   49. (A) (B) (C) (D)
11. (A) (B) (C) (D)   24. (A) (B) (C) (D)   37. (A) (B) (C) (D)   50. (A) (B) (C) (D)
12. (A) (B) (C) (D)   25. (A) (B) (C) (D)   38. (A) (B) (C) (D)   51. (A) (B) (C) (D)
13. (A) (B) (C) (D)   26. (A) (B) (C) (D)   39. (A) (B) (C) (D)   52. (A) (B) (C) (D)

correct in Section 1

incorrect in Section 1

SECTION 2

1. (A) (B) (C) (D)   12. (A) (B) (C) (D)   23. (A) (B) (C) (D)   34. (A) (B) (C) (D)
2. (A) (B) (C) (D)   13. (A) (B) (C) (D)   24. (A) (B) (C) (D)   35. (A) (B) (C) (D)
3. (A) (B) (C) (D)   14. (A) (B) (C) (D)   25. (A) (B) (C) (D)   36. (A) (B) (C) (D)
4. (A) (B) (C) (D)   15. (A) (B) (C) (D)   26. (A) (B) (C) (D)   37. (A) (B) (C) (D)
5. (A) (B) (C) (D)   16. (A) (B) (C) (D)   27. (A) (B) (C) (D)   38. (A) (B) (C) (D)
6. (A) (B) (C) (D)   17. (A) (B) (C) (D)   28. (A) (B) (C) (D)   39. (A) (B) (C) (D)
7. (A) (B) (C) (D)   18. (A) (B) (C) (D)   29. (A) (B) (C) (D)   40. (A) (B) (C) (D)
8. (A) (B) (C) (D)   19. (A) (B) (C) (D)   30. (A) (B) (C) (D)   41. (A) (B) (C) (D)
9. (A) (B) (C) (D)   20. (A) (B) (C) (D)   31. (A) (B) (C) (D)   42. (A) (B) (C) (D)
10. (A) (B) (C) (D)   21. (A) (B) (C) (D)   32. (A) (B) (C) (D)   43. (A) (B) (C) (D)
11. (A) (B) (C) (D)   22. (A) (B) (C) (D)   33. (A) (B) (C) (D)   44. (A) (B) (C) (D)

correct in Section 2

incorrect in Section 2

Practice Tests

SECTION

3

1. Ⓐ Ⓑ Ⓒ Ⓓ
2. Ⓐ Ⓑ Ⓒ Ⓓ
3. Ⓐ Ⓑ Ⓒ Ⓓ
4. Ⓐ Ⓑ Ⓒ Ⓓ

5. Ⓐ Ⓑ Ⓒ Ⓓ
6. Ⓐ Ⓑ Ⓒ Ⓓ
7. Ⓐ Ⓑ Ⓒ Ⓓ
8. Ⓐ Ⓑ Ⓒ Ⓓ

9. Ⓐ Ⓑ Ⓒ Ⓓ
10. Ⓐ Ⓑ Ⓒ Ⓓ
11. Ⓐ Ⓑ Ⓒ Ⓓ
12. Ⓐ Ⓑ Ⓒ Ⓓ

13. Ⓐ Ⓑ Ⓒ Ⓓ
14. Ⓐ Ⓑ Ⓒ Ⓓ
15. Ⓐ Ⓑ Ⓒ Ⓓ

correct in
Section 3

incorrect in
Section 3

16. 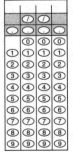 17. 18. 19. 20.

SECTION

4

1. Ⓐ Ⓑ Ⓒ Ⓓ
2. Ⓐ Ⓑ Ⓒ Ⓓ
3. Ⓐ Ⓑ Ⓒ Ⓓ
4. Ⓐ Ⓑ Ⓒ Ⓓ
5. Ⓐ Ⓑ Ⓒ Ⓓ
6. Ⓐ Ⓑ Ⓒ Ⓓ
7. Ⓐ Ⓑ Ⓒ Ⓓ
8. Ⓐ Ⓑ Ⓒ Ⓓ

9. Ⓐ Ⓑ Ⓒ Ⓓ
10. Ⓐ Ⓑ Ⓒ Ⓓ
11. Ⓐ Ⓑ Ⓒ Ⓓ
12. Ⓐ Ⓑ Ⓒ Ⓓ
13. Ⓐ Ⓑ Ⓒ Ⓓ
14. Ⓐ Ⓑ Ⓒ Ⓓ
15. Ⓐ Ⓑ Ⓒ Ⓓ
16. Ⓐ Ⓑ Ⓒ Ⓓ

17. Ⓐ Ⓑ Ⓒ Ⓓ
18. Ⓐ Ⓑ Ⓒ Ⓓ
19. Ⓐ Ⓑ Ⓒ Ⓓ
20. Ⓐ Ⓑ Ⓒ Ⓓ
21. Ⓐ Ⓑ Ⓒ Ⓓ
22. Ⓐ Ⓑ Ⓒ Ⓓ
23. Ⓐ Ⓑ Ⓒ Ⓓ
24. Ⓐ Ⓑ Ⓒ Ⓓ

25. Ⓐ Ⓑ Ⓒ Ⓓ
26. Ⓐ Ⓑ Ⓒ Ⓓ
27. Ⓐ Ⓑ Ⓒ Ⓓ
28. Ⓐ Ⓑ Ⓒ Ⓓ
29. Ⓐ Ⓑ Ⓒ Ⓓ
30. Ⓐ Ⓑ Ⓒ Ⓓ

correct in
Section 4

incorrect in
Section 4

31. 32. 33. 34.

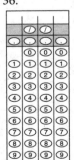

35. 36. 37. 38.

Reading Test

65 Minutes—52 Questions

This section corresponds to Section 1 of your answer sheet.

Directions: Read each passage or pair of passages, then answer the questions that follow. Choose your answers based on what the passage(s) and any accompanying graphics state or imply.

Questions 1–10 are based on the following passage.

The following passage is adapted from Charles Dickens's 1860 novel *Great Expectations*. In this scene, the narrator, a boy named Pip, eats breakfast with his older sister's acquaintance, Mr. Pumblechook. Pumblechook has agreed to take Pip to see Miss Havisham, a wealthy woman who has requested this visit, although Pip has never met her.

Mr. Pumblechook and I breakfasted at eight o'clock in the parlor behind the shop, while the shopman took his mug of tea and hunch of bread and butter on a sack of peas in the front premises.
5 I considered Mr. Pumblechook wretched company. Besides being possessed by my sister's idea that a mortifying and penitential character ought to be imparted to my diet,[1]—besides giving me as much crumb as possible in combination with as
10 little butter, and putting such a quantity of warm water into my milk that it would have been more candid to have left the milk out altogether,—his conversation consisted of nothing but arithmetic. On my politely bidding him Good morning, he
15 said, pompously, "Seven times nine, boy?" And how should I be able to answer, dodged in that way, in a strange place, on an empty stomach! I was hungry, but before I had swallowed a morsel, he began a running sum that lasted all through the
20 breakfast. "Seven?" "And four?" "And eight?" . . . And so on. And after each figure was disposed of, it was as much as I could do to get a bite or a sup, before the next came; while he sat at his ease

guessing nothing, and eating bacon and hot roll, in
25 (if I may be allowed the expression) a gorging and gormandizing manner.

For such reasons, I was very glad when ten o'clock came and we started for Miss Havisham's; though I was not at all at my ease regarding the
30 manner in which I should acquit myself under that lady's roof. Within a quarter of an hour we came to Miss Havisham's house, which was of old brick, and dismal, and had a great many iron bars to it. Some of the windows had been walled
35 up; of those that remained, all the lower were rustily barred. There was a courtyard in front, and that was barred; so we had to wait, after ringing the bell, until some one should come to open it. While we waited at the gate, I peeped in (even
40 then Mr. Pumblechook said, "And fourteen?" but I pretended not to hear him), and saw that at the side of the house there was a large brewery. No brewing was going on in it, and none seemed to have gone on for a long long time.
45 A window was raised, and a clear voice demanded "What name?" To which my conductor replied, "Pumblechook." The voice returned, "Quite right," and the window was shut again, and a young lady came across the court-yard, with keys in her
50 hand.

"This," said Mr. Pumblechook, "is Pip."

"This is Pip, is it?" returned the young lady, who was very pretty and seemed very proud; "come in, Pip."

---

[1]Pip's sister indicated to Pumblechook that Pip should be grateful, even penitent (unreasonably so) for his help.

55   Mr. Pumblechook was coming in also, when she stopped him with the gate.

   "Oh!" she said. "Did you wish to see Miss Havisham?"

   "If Miss Havisham wished to see me," returned
60 Mr. Pumblechook, discomfited.

   "Ah!" said the girl; "but you see she don't."

   She said it so finally, and in such an undiscussible way, that Mr. Pumblechook, though in a condition of ruffled dignity, could not protest. But he eyed me
65 severely,—as if I had done anything to him!—and departed with the words reproachfully delivered: "Boy! Let your behavior here be a credit unto them which brought you up by hand!"[2] I was not free from apprehension that he would come back to
70 propound through the gate, "And sixteen?" But he didn't.

   [2]Pumblechook is speaking of Pip's sister, who often boasts that she raised him "by hand."

1. According to the first paragraph, Pip's breakfast with Mr. Pumblechook is

   A) eaten on the run.

   B) small and of poor quality.

   C) better than Pip usually receives.

   D) carefully cooked and served.

2. As used in line 5, "wretched" most nearly means

   A) shameful.

   B) deprived.

   C) distressing.

   D) heartbroken.

3. Based on the passage, it can be inferred that Mr. Pumblechook

   A) has looked forward to his morning with Pip.

   B) is as uncomfortable as Pip is during breakfast.

   C) has known Pip and his sister for a very long time.

   D) is indifferent to Pip's discomfort during breakfast.

4. Which choice provides the best support for the answer to the previous question?

   A) Lines 1–4 ("Mr. Pumblechook and I . . . premises")

   B) Lines 6–13 ("Besides . . . arithmetic")

   C) Lines 46–47 ("To which my . . . 'Pumblechook'")

   D) Lines 62–64 ("She said . . . not protest")

5. What theme is communicated through the experiences of Pip, the narrator?

   A) The world can be a puzzling and sometimes cruel place.

   B) Young people are misunderstood by their elders.

   C) Mean-spirited people deserve to be treated harshly.

   D) The favors one receives in life should be reciprocated.

6. Which word best describes the young lady's demeanor when she approaches Pip and Mr. Pumblechook?

   A) Rude

   B) Timid

   C) Self-centered

   D) Authoritative

7. Which of the following is true when Mr. Pumblechook leaves Pip at Miss Havisham's house?

   A) Pip is excited to finally meet Miss Havisham.

   B) Pip is nervous about being away from his sister for so long.

   C) Pip is relieved to be away from Mr. Pumblechook.

   D) Pip is anxious about spending time with the young lady who greets them.

8. Which choice provides the best support for the answer to the previous question?

   A) Lines 1–4 ("Mr. Pumblechook . . . premises")

   B) Lines 45–46 ("A window . . . name")

   C) Lines 62–64 ("She said . . . not protest")

   D) Lines 68–71 ("I was not . . . he didn't")

9. As used in line 63, "condition" most nearly means

   A) illness.

   B) prerequisite.

   C) state.

   D) limitation.

10. The function of the parenthetical comment in line 25 is to reveal that

   A) Pip is usually more polite in his references to others.

   B) Mr. Pumblechook appreciates gourmet food.

   C) Pip is very angered that his own breakfast is so meager.

   D) Mr. Pumblechook has no qualms about over-eating in public.

Questions 11–20 are based on the following passage.

This passage is adapted from Martin Luther King Jr.'s "Letter from Birmingham Jail."

. . . I think I should give the reason for my being in Birmingham, since you have been influenced by the argument of "outsiders coming in." I have the honor of serving as president of the Southern
5 Christian Leadership Conference, an organization operating in every Southern state with headquarters in Atlanta, Georgia. We have some eighty-five affiliate organizations all across the South, one being the Alabama Christian Movement for Human
10 Rights. Whenever necessary and possible we share staff, educational, and financial resources with our affiliates. Several months ago our local affiliate here in Birmingham invited us to be on call to engage in a nonviolent direct action program if such were
15 deemed necessary. We readily consented and when the hour came we lived up to our promises. So I am here, along with several members of my staff, because we were invited here. I am here because I have basic organizational ties here. Beyond this, I
20 am in Birmingham because injustice is here. . . .

   Moreover, I am cognizant of the interrelatedness of all communities and states. I cannot sit idly by in Atlanta and not be concerned about what happens in Birmingham. Injustice anywhere is a threat to
25 justice everywhere. We are caught in an inescapable network of mutuality, tied in a single garment of destiny. Whatever affects one directly affects all indirectly. Never again can we afford to live with the narrow, provincial "outside agitator" idea. Anyone
30 who lives inside the United States can never be considered an outsider anywhere in this country. . . .

   You may well ask, "Why direct action? Why sit-ins, marches, etc.? Isn't negotiation a better
35 path?" You are exactly right in your call for negotiation. Indeed, this is the purpose of direct action. Nonviolent direct action seeks to create such a crisis and establish such creative tension that a community that has constantly refused to
40 negotiate is forced to confront the issue. It seeks

GO ON TO THE NEXT PAGE

so to dramatize the issue that it can no longer be ignored. I just referred to the creation of tension as a part of the work of the nonviolent resister. This may sound rather shocking. But I must confess that
45 I am not afraid of the word tension. I have earnestly worked and preached against violent tension, but there is a type of constructive nonviolent tension that is necessary for growth. Just as Socrates felt that it was necessary to create a tension in the mind
50 so that individuals could rise from the bondage of myths and half-truths to the unfettered realm of creative analysis and objective appraisal, we must see the need of having nonviolent gadflies to create the kind of tension in society that will help men rise
55 from the dark depths of prejudice and racism to the majestic heights of understanding and brotherhood. So the purpose of the direct action is to create a situation so crisis-packed that it will inevitably open the door to negotiation. We, therefore, concur
60 with you in your call for negotiation. Too long has our beloved Southland been bogged down in the tragic attempt to live in monologue rather than dialogue. . . .

My friends, I must say to you that we have
65 not made a single gain in civil rights without determined legal and nonviolent pressure. History is the long and tragic story of the fact that privileged groups seldom give up their privileges voluntarily. Individuals may see the moral light
70 and voluntarily give up their unjust posture; but as Reinhold Niebuhr has reminded us, groups are more immoral than individuals.

We know through painful experience that freedom is never voluntarily given by the oppressor;
75 it must be demanded by the oppressed. . . . For years now I have heard the word "Wait!" It rings in the ear of every African American with a piercing familiarity. This "wait" has almost always meant "never." It has been a tranquilizing thalidomide,
80 relieving the emotional stress for a moment, only

to give birth to an ill-formed infant of frustration. We must come to see with the distinguished jurist of yesterday that "justice too long delayed is justice denied." We have waited for more than three
85 hundred and forty years for our constitutional and God-given rights. The nations of Asia and Africa are moving with jet-like speed toward the goal of political independence, and we still creep at horse and buggy pace toward the gaining of a cup of
90 coffee at a lunch counter. . . .

11. King's purpose for writing this letter is

A) to explain why he came to Birmingham to protest.

B) to launch a nonviolent protest movement in Birmingham.

C) to open an affiliate of the Southern Christian Leadership Conference in Birmingham.

D) to support fellow civil rights activists in Birmingham.

12. Which choice provides the best evidence for the answer to the previous question?

A) Lines 1–2 ("I think . . . in Birmingham")

B) Lines 3–7 ("I have . . . Atlanta, Georgia")

C) Lines 7–10 ("We have some . . . Rights")

D) Lines 24–25 ("Injustice anywhere . . . everywhere")

13. The passage most strongly suggests that which of the following statements is true?

A) King was warmly welcomed when he arrived in Birmingham.

B) King received criticism for his decision to come to Birmingham.

C) King did not want to cause a disruption by coming to Birmingham.

D) King was abandoned by his supporters when he arrived in Birmingham.

GO ON TO THE NEXT PAGE

14. As used in lines 21–22, "interrelatedness of all communities and states" most nearly means that

    A) King has personal connections to people in the town.

    B) the Southern Christian Leadership Conference needs national support.

    C) events in one part of the country affect everyone in the nation.

    D) local civil rights groups operate independently of one another.

15. Based on paragraph 2, it can be reasonably inferred that King believed circumstances in Birmingham at the time

    A) were unfair and wrong.

    B) constituted an isolated event.

    C) justified his arrest.

    D) required federal intervention.

16. Which choice provides the best evidence for the answer to the previous question?

    A) Lines 21–22 ("Moreover, . . . states")

    B) Lines 24–25 ("Injustice anywhere . . . everywhere")

    C) Lines 25–27 ("We are caught . . . destiny")

    D) Lines 28–29 ("Never again . . . idea")

17. As used in line 41, "dramatize" most nearly means

    A) cast events in an appealing light.

    B) draw attention to significant events.

    C) exaggerate events to seem more important.

    D) turn events into a popular performance.

18. Which choice most clearly paraphrases a claim made by King in paragraph 3?

    A) A failure to negotiate in the South has provoked secret action by civil rights activists

    B) A focus on dialogue blinds reformers to the necessity for direct action to promote change

    C) Direct action is necessary to motivate people to talk about prejudice and racism

    D) Nonviolent protest encourages a sense of brotherhood and understanding among citizens

19. Paragraph 4 best supports the claims made in paragraph 3 by

    A) arguing that nonviolent pressure is most likely to spur just action by individuals.

    B) clarifying that throughout history, privileged classes have been reluctant to let go of privilege.

    C) drawing a distinction between the morality of individuals and of groups.

    D) pointing out that few gains in civil rights have been made without nonviolent pressure.

20. King refers to "the gaining of a cup of coffee at a lunch counter" (lines 89–90) primarily to

    A) call attention to the sedative effect of delaying civil rights reform in the United States.

    B) emphasize that white Americans will not willingly end oppression against black Americans.

    C) describe the progress made toward the winning of equal rights in other countries.

    D) underscore the contrast between progress made in other countries and the United States.

Practice Tests

Questions 21–31 are based on the following passages and supplementary material.

The idea of a World Bank became a reality in 1944 when delegates to the Bretton Woods Conference pledged to "outlaw practices which are agreed to be harmful to world prosperity." Passage 1 discusses the benefits of the World Bank, while Passage 2 focuses on the limited life span of the Bretton Woods system.

Passage 1

In 1944, 730 delegates from forty-four Allied nations met in Bretton Woods, New Hampshire, just as World War II was ending. They were attending an important conference. This mostly
5   forgotten event shaped our modern world because delegates at the Bretton Woods Conference agreed on the establishment of an international banking system.

To ensure that all nations would prosper,
10 the United States and other allied nations set rules for a postwar international economy. The Bretton Woods system created the International Monetary Fund (IMF). The IMF was founded as a kind of global central bank from which member
15 countries could borrow money. The countries needed money to pay for their war costs. Today, the IMF facilitates international trade by ensuring the stability of the international monetary and financial system.
20 The Bretton Woods system also established the World Bank. Although the World Bank shares similarities with the IMF, the two institutions remain distinct. While the IMF maintains an orderly system of payments and receipts between
25 nations, the World Bank is mainly a development institution. The World Bank initially gave loans to European countries devastated by World War II, and today it lends money and technical assistance specifically to economic projects in developing
30 countries. For example, the World Bank might provide a low-interest loan to a country attempting to improve education or health. The goal of the World Bank is to "bridge the economic divide between poor and rich countries." In short, the
35 organizations differ in their purposes. The Bank

promotes economic and social progress so people can live better lives, while the IMF represents the entire world in its goal to foster global monetary cooperation and financial stability.
40 These two specific accomplishments of the Bretton Woods Conference were major. However, the Bretton Woods system particularly benefited the United States. It effectively established the U.S. dollar as a global currency. A global
45 currency is one that countries worldwide accept for all trade, or international transactions of buying and selling. Because only the U.S. could print dollars, the United States became the primary power behind both the IMF and the
50 World Bank. Today, global currencies include the U.S. dollar, the euro (European Union countries), and the yen (Japan).

The years after Bretton Woods have been considered the golden age of the U.S. dollar. More
55 importantly, the conference profoundly shaped foreign trade for decades to come.

Passage 2

The financial system established at the 1944 Bretton Woods Conference endured for many years. Even after the United States abrogated
60 agreements made at the conference, the nation continued to experience a powerful position in international trade by having other countries tie their currencies to the U.S. dollar. The world, however, is changing.
65 In reality, the Bretton Woods system lasted only three decades. Then, in 1971, President Richard Nixon introduced a new economic policy by ending the convertibility of the dollar to gold. It marked the end of the Bretton Woods
70 international monetary framework, and the action resulted in worldwide financial crisis. Two cornerstones of Bretton Woods, however, endured: the International Monetary Fund (IMF) and the World Bank.
75 Since the collapse of the Bretton Woods system, IMF members have been trading using a

GO ON TO THE NEXT PAGE ⟶

flexible exchange system. Namely, countries allow their exchange rates to fluctuate in response to changing conditions. The exchange rate between
80 two currencies, such as the Japanese yen and the U.S. dollar, for example, specifies how much one currency is worth in terms of the other. An exchange rate of 120 yen to dollars means that 120 yen are worth the same as one dollar.

85 Even so, the U.S. dollar has remained the most widely used money for international trade, and having one currency for all trade may be better than using a flexible exchange system.

This seems to be the thinking of a powerful
90 group of countries. The Group of Twenty (G20), which has called for a new Bretton Woods, consists of governments and leaders from 20 of the world's largest economies including China, the United States, and the European Union. In 2009, for
95 example, the G20 announced plans to create a new global currency to replace the U.S. dollar's role as the anchor currency. Many believe that China's yuan, quickly climbing the financial ranks, is well on its way to becoming a major world reserve
100 currency.

In fact, an earlier 1988 article in *The Economist* stated, "30 years from now, Americans, Japanese, Europeans, and people in many other rich countries and some relatively poor ones will probably be
105 paying for their shopping with the same currency."

The article predicted that the world supply of currency would be set by a new central bank of the IMF. This prediction seems to be coming to fruition since the G20 indicated that a "world currency is
110 in waiting." For an international construct such as the original Bretton Woods to last some 26 years is nothing less than amazing. But move over Bretton Woods; a new world order in finance could be on the fast track.

Top 10 International Currencies						
(Percent Shares of Average Daily Currency Trading)						
	2007		2010		2013	
	Share	*Rank*	*Share*	*Rank*	*Share*	*Rank*
U.S. Dollar (USD)	85.6%	1	84.9%	1	87.0%	1
Euro (EUR)	37.0%	2	39.1%	2	33.4%	2
Japanese Yen (JPY)	17.2%	3	19.0%	3	23.0%	3
UK Pound (GBP)	14.9%	4	12.9%	4	11.8%	4
Australian Dollar (AUD)	6.6%	6	7.6%	5	8.6%	5
Swiss Franc (CHF)	6.8%	5	6.3%	6	5.2%	6
Canadian Dollar (CAD)	4.3%	7	5.3%	7	4.6%	7
Mexican Peso (MXN)	1.3%	12	1.3%	14	2.5%	8
Chinese Yuan (CNY)	0.5%	20	0.9%	17	2.2%	9
New Zealand Dollar	1.9%	11	1.6%	10	2.0%	10

Adapted from Mauldin Economics; Bank for International Settlements, September 2013 Triennial Central Bank Survey.

21. Based on Passage 1, it can reasonably be inferred that

    A) world leaders recognized the need for markets to function independently.

    B) Bretton Woods increased U.S. economic influence around the world.

    C) the IMF and the World Bank work closely together to ensure prosperity.

    D) the conclusion of World War II had little influence on events at Bretton Woods.

22. Which choice provides the best evidence for the answer to the previous question?

    A) Lines 9–11 ("To ensure . . . economy")

    B) Lines 11–13 ("The Bretton . . . Fund")

    C) Lines 47–50 ("Because only . . . World Bank")

    D) Lines 54–56 ("More importantly . . . to come")

23. As used in line 38, "foster" most nearly means

    A) publicize.

    B) rear.

    C) stabilize.

    D) encourage.

24. Which statement best explains the difference between the purposes of the IMF and the World Bank?

    A) The IMF provides money to pay for war costs, while the World Bank offers assistance to rebuild countries recovering from war across the globe.

    B) The IMF encourages stability in the global financial system, while the World Bank promotes economic development in relatively poor nations.

    C) The IMF supports the U.S. dollar in international markets, while the World Bank provides low-interest loans to many nations around the world.

    D) The IMF offers governments advice about participation in global markets, while the World Bank encourages monetary cooperation between nations.

25. Based on the second paragraph in Passage 2, it can be reasonably inferred that

    A) the United States did not support the goals of the IMF and the World Bank.

    B) Bretton Woods was originally intended to last for three decades.

    C) President Nixon acted to reinforce the decisions made at Bretton Woods.

    D) some U.S. policy decisions differed from international consensus over Bretton Woods.

26. Which choice provides the best evidence for the answer to the previous question?

    A) Lines 65–66 ("In reality . . . three decades")

    B) Lines 66–69 ("Then, in 1971 . . . to gold")

    C) Lines 71–74 ("Two cornerstones . . . World Bank")

    D) Lines 75–77 ("Since the collapse . . . exchange system")

27. As used in line 97, "anchor" most nearly means

    A) key.

    B) fastening.

    C) rigid.

    D) supporting.

28. It can reasonably be inferred from both Passage 2 and the graphic that

    A) international markets are increasingly comfortable using the yuan as trade currency.

    B) the United States favors using the yuan as one of the world's reserve currencies.

    C) the G20 wants to replace the yuan and other currencies with a new global currency.

    D) the IMF continues to support the yuan and other currencies in a flexible exchange system.

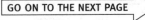

29. The last paragraph of Passage 2 can be described as

    A) a refutation of opponents' criticisms.

    B) an indication of the author's opinion.

    C) a summary of the author's main points.

    D) an introduction of a contradictory position.

30. Which statement most effectively compares the authors' purposes in both passages?

    A) Passage 1's purpose is to contrast the functions of the IMF and World Bank, while Passage 2's purpose is to outline the benefits of a flexible trade system to the United States.

    B) Passage 1's purpose is to describe the history of international trade in the 20th century, while Passage 2's purpose is to explain why the Bretton Woods system collapsed.

    C) Passage 1's purpose is to describe Bretton Woods's effect on the global economy, while Passage 2's purpose is to suggest that a new currency for global trade may soon be implemented.

    D) Passage 1's purpose is to promote the economic benefits of the IMF and World Bank, while Passage 2's purpose is to encourage the reestablishment of the Bretton Woods system.

31. Both passages support which generalization about the global economy?

    A) U.S. influence on global trade has continued under a flexible exchange system.

    B) The purposes of the International Monetary Fund and the World Bank are indirectly related.

    C) The Group of Twenty represents the financial interests of the world's largest economies.

    D) International institutions such as the IMF continue to influence economic trade and development.

Questions 32–42 are based on the following passage.

This passage is adapted from an article about treating paralysis.

According to a study conducted by the Christopher and Dana Reeve Foundation, more than six million people in the United States suffer from debilitating paralysis. That's close to
5 one person in every fifty who suffers from a loss of the ability to move or feel in areas of his or her body. Paralysis is often caused by illnesses, such as stroke or multiple sclerosis, or injuries to the spinal cord. Research scientists have made
10 advances in the treatment of paralysis, which means retraining affected individuals to become as independent as possible. Patients learn how to use wheelchairs and prevent complications that are caused by restricted movement. This
15 retraining is key in maintaining paralytics' quality of life; however, an actual cure for paralysis has remained elusive—until now.

In 2014, surgeons in Poland collaborated with the University College London's Institute of Neurology
20 to treat a Polish man who was paralyzed from the chest down as a result of a spinal cord injury. The scientists chose this patient for their study because of the countless hours of physical therapy he had undergone with no signs of progress. Twenty-one
25 months after their test subject's initial spinal cord injury, his condition was considered complete as defined by the American Spinal Injury Association (ASIA)'s Impairment Scale. This meant that he experienced no sensory or motor function in the
30 segments of his spinal cord nearest to his injury.

The doctors used a technique refined during forty years of spinal cord research on rats. They removed one of two of the patient's olfactory bulbs, which are structures found at the top of the human
35 nose. From this structure, samples of olfactory ensheathing cells, responsible for a portion of the sense of smell, were harvested. These cells allow the olfactory system to renew its cells over the course of a human life. It is because of this constant

40 regeneration that scientists chose these particular
cells to implant into the patient's spinal cord.
After being harvested, the cells were reproduced
in a culture. Then, the cells were injected into the
patient's spinal cord in 100 mini-injections above

45 and below the location of his injury. Four strips of
nerve tissue were then placed across a small gap in
the spinal cord.

After surgery, the patient underwent a
tailormade neurorehabilitation program. In the

50 nineteen months following the operation, not only
did the patient experience no adverse effects, but
his condition improved from ASIA's class A to class
C. Class C is considered an incomplete spinal cord
injury, meaning that motor function is preserved to

55 a certain extent and there is some muscle activity.
The patient experienced increased stability in the
trunk of his body, as well as partial recovery of
voluntary movements in his lower extremities. As
a result, he was able to increase the muscle mass in

60 his thighs and regain sensation in those areas. In
late 2014, he took his first steps with the support of
only a walker.

These exciting improvements suggest that the
nerve grafts doctors placed in the patient's spinal

65 cord bridged the injured area and prompted the
regeneration of fibers. This was the first-ever
clinical study that showed beneficial effects of cells
transplanted into the spinal cord. The same team
of scientists plans to treat ten more patients using

70 this "smell cell" transplant technique. If they have
continued success, patients around the world can
have both their mobility and their hope restored.

32. The passage is primarily concerned with

A) how various diseases and injuries can cause permanent paralysis.

B) ways in which doctors and therapists work to improve patients' quality of life.

C) one treatment being developed to return mobility to patients suffering paralysis.

D) methods of physical therapy that can help patients with spinal cord injuries.

33. The author includes a description of retraining paralytics in lines 9–14 primarily to

A) describe how people with paralysis cope with everyday tasks.

B) appeal to the reader's sympathies for people with paralysis.

C) show that most research scientists do not believe a cure can be found.

D) help readers appreciate the significance of research that may lead to a cure.

34. Based on the information in the passage, it can be inferred that the author

A) believes more research should be done before patients with paralysis are subjected to the treatment described in the passage.

B) feels that increased mobility will have a positive impact on patients suffering from all levels of paralysis.

C) thinks that more scientists should study paralysis and ways to improve the quality of life for patients with limited mobility.

D) was part of the research team that developed the new method of treating paralysis described in the passage.

GO ON TO THE NEXT PAGE →

35. Which choice provides the best support for the answer to the previous question?

    A) Lines 7–9 ("Paralysis is . . . spinal cord")

    B) Lines 18–21 ("In 2014 . . . injury")

    C) Lines 56–58 ("The patient . . . extremities")

    D) Lines 70–72 ("If they . . . restored")

36. As used in line 14, "restricted" most nearly means

    A) confidential.

    B) dependent.

    C) increased.

    D) limited.

37. In line 49, the author's use of the word "tailor-made" helps reinforce the idea that

    A) the injected cells were from the patient and were therefore well-suited to work in his own body.

    B) spinal cord cells were replaced during the transplant portion of the individualized treatment.

    C) olfactory bulbs were removed from rats and placed in the patient's spinal cord during surgery.

    D) the method used by doctors to locate the damaged area required expertise and precision.

38. It reasonably can be inferred from the passage that

    A) the patient's treatment would have been more successful if scientists had used cells from another area of his body instead of from his olfactory bulbs.

    B) cells from olfactory bulbs will be used to cure diseases that affect areas of the body other than the spinal cord.

    C) the patient who received the experimental treatment using cells from olfactory bulbs would not have regained mobility without this treatment.

    D) soon doctors will be able to treat spinal injuries without time-consuming and demanding physical therapy.

39. Which choice provides the best evidence for the answer to the previous question?

    A) Lines 9–12 ("Research scientists . . . possible")

    B) Lines 21–24 ("The scientists . . . progress")

    C) Lines 32–35 ("They removed . . . nose")

    D) Lines 63–66 ("These exciting . . . fibers")

40. As used in line 31, "refined" most nearly means

    A) advanced.

    B) improved.

    C) experienced.

    D) treated.

41. The success of the patient's treatment was due in large part to

    A) studies done on other patients.

    B) research conducted by other doctors in Poland.

    C) many experiments performed on rats.

    D) multiple attempts on various types of animals.

42. The procedure described in which cells from olfactory bulbs are injected into a damaged area of the spinal cord is most analogous to which of the following?

    A) Replacing a diseased organ in a patient with an organ from a donor who has the same tissue type

    B) Giving a patient with a high fever an injection of medication to bring the core body temperature down

    C) Placing a cast on a limb to hold the bone in place to encourage healing after suffering a break

    D) Grafting skin from a healthy area of the body and transplanting it to an area that has suffered severe burns

Questions 43–52 are based on the following passage and supplementary material.

The following passage is adapted from an essay about mercury in fish.

Mercury is an unusual element; it is a metal but is liquid at room temperature. It is also a neurotoxin and a teratogen, as it causes nerve damage and birth defects. Mercury can be found just about
5 everywhere; it is in soil, in air, in household items, and even in our food. Everyday objects, such as thermometers, light switches, and fluorescent light bulbs, contain mercury in its elemental form. Batteries can also contain mercury, but they
10 contain it in the form of the inorganic compound mercury chloride. Mercury can also exist as an organic compound, the most common of which is methylmercury. While we can take steps to avoid both elemental and inorganic mercury, it is much
15 harder to avoid methylmercury.

Most of the mercury in the environment comes from the emissions of coal-burning power plants; coal contains small amounts of mercury, which are released into the air when coal burns.
20 The concentration of mercury in the air from power plants is very low, so it is not immediately dangerous. However, the mercury is then washed out of the air by rainstorms and eventually ends up in lakes and oceans.

25 The mercury deposited in the water does not instantaneously get absorbed by fish, as elemental mercury does not easily diffuse through cell membranes. However, methylmercury diffuses into cells easily, and certain anaerobic bacteria
30 in the water convert the elemental mercury to methylmercury as a byproduct of their metabolic processes. Methylmercury released into the water by the bacteria diffuses into small single-celled organisms called plankton. Small shrimp and other
35 small animals eat the plankton and absorb the methylmercury in the plankton during digestion. Small fish eat the shrimp and then larger fish eat the smaller fish; each time an animal preys on another animal, the predator absorbs the
40 methylmercury. Because each animal excretes the methylmercury much more slowly than it absorbs it, methylmercury builds up in the animal over

time and is passed on to whatever animal eats it, resulting in a process called bioaccumulation.

45 As people became aware of the bioaccumulation of mercury in fish, many reacted by eliminating seafood from their diet. However, seafood contains certain omega-3 fatty acids that are important for good health. People who do not eat enough
50 of these fatty acids, especially eicosapentaenoic acid (EPA) and docosahexaenoic acid (DHA), are more likely to have heart attacks than people who have enough EPA and DHA in their diet. Because fish and shellfish, along with some algae, are the
55 only sources of these fatty acids, eliminating them from our diet might have worse health effects than consuming small amounts of mercury.

Scientists have studied the effects of mercury by conducting tests on animals and by studying
60 various human populations and recording the amount of mercury in their blood. By determining the levels of mercury consumption that cause any of the known symptoms of mercury poisoning, they were able to identify a safe level of mercury
65 consumption. The current recommendation is for humans to take in less than 0.1 microgram of mercury for every kilogram of weight per day. This means that a 70-kilogram person (about 155 pounds) could safely consume 7 micrograms of
70 mercury per day. Because haddock averages about 0.055 micrograms of mercury per gram, that person could safely eat 127 grams (about 4.5 ounces) of haddock per day. On the other hand, swordfish averages about 0.995 micrograms of mercury per
75 gram of fish, so the 70-kilogram person could safely eat only about 7 grams (about one-quarter of an ounce) of swordfish per day.

Nutritionists recommend that, rather than eliminate fish from our diet, we try to eat more of
80 the low-mercury fish and less of the high-mercury fish. Low-mercury species tend to be smaller omnivorous fish while high-mercury species tend to be the largest carnivorous fish. Awareness of the particulars of this problem, accompanied by
85 mindful eating habits, will keep us on the best course for healthy eating.

GO ON TO THE NEXT PAGE ⇒

Species	Average Weight Range (grams)	Average Mercury Concentration (parts per billion)
Alaskan Pollock	227–1,000	31
Atlantic Haddock	900–1,800	55
Atlantic Herring	100–600	84
Chub Mackerel	100–750	88
Cod	800–4,000	111
Skipjack Tuna	2,000–10,000	144
Black-Striped Bass	6,820–15,900	152
Albacore Tuna	4,540–21,364	358
Marlin	180,000	485

43. The author of the passage would most likely agree with which of the following statements?

   A) Mercury poisoning is only one of many concerns that should be considered when choosing which fish to add to one's diet.

   B) More should be done by scientists and nutritionists to inform people about the dangers of mercury poisoning.

   C) Fish is an essential part of a healthy diet and can be eaten safely if recommendations for mercury consumption are kept in mind.

   D) The mercury present in the air is more dangerous to people than the mercury consumed by eating fish with high mercury levels.

44. Which choice provides the best evidence for the answer to the previous question?

   A) Lines 16–18 ("Most of . . . plants")

   B) Lines 32–34 ("Methylmercury released . . . plankton")

   C) Lines 58–61 ("Scientists . . . their blood")

   D) Lines 83–86 ("Awareness . . . eating")

45. In addition to the levels of mercury in a specific species of fish, people should also consider which of the following when determining a safe level of consumption?

   A) Their own body weight

   B) Where the fish was caught

   C) The other meats they are eating

   D) What they ate the day before

46. As used in line 20, "concentration" most nearly means

   A) focus.

   B) application.

   C) density.

   D) awareness.

47. The passage most strongly suggests which of the following statements is accurate?

   A) It is not possible to completely avoid environmental exposure to mercury.

   B) Inorganic mercury is more dangerous to humans than organic mercury.

   C) Most of the exposure to mercury experienced by humans comes from fish consumption.

   D) Mercury is one of the most abundant elements found in nature.

48. Which choice provides the best evidence for the answer to the previous question?

   A) Lines 1–2 ("Mercury is an unusual . . . temperature")

   B) Lines 4–6 ("Mercury . . . our food")

   C) Lines 20–22 ("The concentration . . . dangerous")

   D) Lines 28–32 ("However, methylmercury . . . processes")

Practice Tests

49. The main purpose of paragraph 3 is to explain

    A) the reasons why mercury deposited in water is not harmful to fish.

    B) the relationships between predators and prey in aquatic animals.

    C) how the largest fish accumulate the greatest amounts of mercury.

    D) the difference between methylmercury and other types of mercury.

50. Which of the following pieces of evidence would most strengthen the author's line of reasoning?

    A) More examples in paragraph 1 of places mercury is found

    B) Details in paragraph 2 about the levels of mercury found in the air

    C) An explanation in paragraph 4 of how to treat mercury poisoning

    D) More examples in paragraph 5 of how many micrograms of mercury people of different weights could eat

51. As used in line 84, "particulars" most nearly means

    A) data.

    B) specifics.

    C) points.

    D) evidence.

52. Based on the information in the passage and the graphic, which of the following statements is true?

    A) The fish with the lowest average weight is the safest to eat.

    B) A person can safely eat more marlin than albacore tuna in one day.

    C) Eating large fish carries a lower risk of mercury poisoning than eating small fish.

    D) A person can safely eat more Alaskan pollock than black-striped bass in one day.

IF YOU FINISH BEFORE TIME IS CALLED, YOU MAY CHECK YOUR WORK ON THIS SECTION ONLY. DO NOT TURN TO ANY OTHER SECTION IN THE TEST. STOP

Writing and Language Test

35 Minutes—44 Questions

This section corresponds to Section 2 of your answer sheet.

Directions: Each passage in this section is followed by several questions. Some questions will reference an underlined portion in the passage; others will ask you to consider a part of a passage or the passage as a whole. For each question, choose the answer that reflects the best use of grammar, punctuation, and style. If a passage or question is accompanied by a graphic, take the graphic into account in choosing your response(s). Some questions will have "NO CHANGE" as a possible response. Choose that answer if you think the best choice is to leave the sentence as written.

Questions 1–11 are based on the following passage and supplementary material.

The UN: Promoting World Peace

The United Nations (UN) is perhaps the most important political contribution of the 20th century. Some may argue that the work of the UN **1** : an international peacekeeping organization—has proven futile, given persisting global conflict. But the UN's worldwide influence demands a closer look. This organization's global impact is undeniable. The UN is a strong political organization determined to create opportunities for its member nations to enjoy a peaceful and productive world. **2**

1. A) NO CHANGE
    B) —an international peacekeeping organization;
    C) —an international peacekeeping organization—
    D) ; an international peacekeeping organization,

2. Which choice would most clearly end the paragraph with a restatement of the author's claim?

    A) The UN is an organization dedicated to advancing social and political justice around the world.
    B) Those who argue otherwise are not well educated about geopolitical issues in the 20th century or today.
    C) The UN has had its share of corruption over the years, but it has a well-earned reputation of effectively settling international disputes.
    D) A better understanding of the UN suggests that the UN enables far greater peace in today's world than could have been possible otherwise.

Practice Tests

[3] <u>Decades ago,</u> provoked by the events of World Wars I and II, world leaders began imagining a politically neutral force for international peace. The UN was born in 1945 with 51 participating nations. It was to be a collective political authority for global peace and security. Today, 193 nations are UN members. **[4]** <u>In keeping with the original hope, the UN still strives toward peaceful international relations.</u>

Understandably, no single organization can perfectly solve the world's countless, complex problems. But the UN has offered consistent relief for many of the past half-century's most difficult disasters and conflicts. It also provides a safe space for international conversation. Moreover, it advocates for issues such as justice, trade, hunger relief, human rights, health, and gender **[5]** <u>equality, the UN</u> also coordinates care for those displaced by disaster and conflict, **[6]** <u>dictates</u> environmental protection, and works toward conflict reconciliation.

3. A) NO CHANGE
   B) Recently,
   C) Consequently,
   D) In other words,

4. A) NO CHANGE
   B) In having kept with the original hope, the UN still strives toward peaceful international relations.
   C) In keeping with the original hope, the UN still strived toward peaceful international relations.
   D) In keeping with the original hope, the UN still strove toward peaceful international relations.

5. A) NO CHANGE
   B) equality. The UN
   C) equality: the UN
   D) equality, The UN

6. A) NO CHANGE
   B) prefers
   C) promotes
   D) celebrates

GO ON TO THE NEXT PAGE →

[7] The UN's budget, goals, and personnel count have significantly expanded with time to meet more needs. [8] The year 2014 witnessed the UN peacekeeping force grow to over 100,000 strong. These uniformed, volunteer, civilian personnel represent 128 nations. The UN's budget has also grown over the years to support an international court system, as well as countless agencies, committees, and centers addressing sociopolitical topics. Today's UN undertakes important work, and it functions with remarkable organization and efficiency. Critics highlight shortcomings to discount the UN's effectiveness. But considering the countless disasters to which the UN has responded over its six decades of existence, today's world might enjoy [9] far less peace, freedom, and safety without the UN.

7. Which choice provides the most logical introduction to the paragraph?

A) NO CHANGE

B) The UN has developed over the years, but critics charge it has met with limited success.

C) The responsibilities of the UN have expanded in recent years in response to challenging events.

D) The UN has maintained a quiet but effective voice on the world stage in spite of criticism.

8. Which choice best completes the sentence with accurate data based on the graphic?

A) NO CHANGE

B) The year 2010 led to an increase of approximately 100,000 in the UN peacekeeping force.

C) The year 2010 saw the UN peacekeeping force grow to approximately 100,000 strong.

D) The year 2010 saw the UN peacekeeping force decrease to just over 100,000 strong.

9. A) NO CHANGE

B) considerably less peace, less freedom, and less safety

C) much less peace, less freedom, and less safety

D) significantly less peace and freedom, and less safety

[1] From promoting overarching sociopolitical change to offering food and care for displaced groups, the UN serves to protect human rights. [2] Equally **10** quotable are its initiatives to foster international collaboration, justice, and peace. [3] The UN provided aid to the Philippines after the disastrous 2013 typhoon. [4] Certainly, this work is not finished. [5] But no other organization's scope of work compares with the influence of the UN. [6] This brave endeavor to insist on and strive for peace, whatever the obstacles, has indeed united hundreds of once-divided nations. [7] Today, with eleven Nobel Peace Prizes to its name, the UN is undoubtedly an irreplaceable and profoundly successful force for peace. **11**

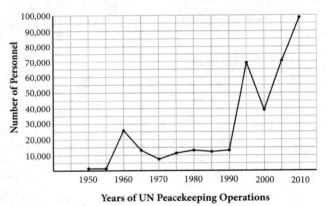

UN Peacekeeping Personnel Numbers Since 1950

Years of UN Peacekeeping Operations

10. A) NO CHANGE
    B) luminous
    C) noteworthy
    D) repeatable

11. Which sentence should be removed to improve the focus of the concluding paragraph?
    A) Sentence 1
    B) Sentence 3
    C) Sentence 5
    D) Sentence 6

GO ON TO THE NEXT PAGE

Questions 12–22 are based on the following passage.

DNA Analysis in a Day

Jane Saunders, a forensic DNA specialist, arrives at work and finds a request waiting for her: She needs to determine if the DNA of a fingernail with a few skin cells on it [12] match any records in the criminal database.

"Human DNA is a long, double-stranded [13] molecule; each strand consists of a complementary set of nucleotides," she explains. "DNA has four nucleotides: [14] adenine (A), thymine (T), guanine (G), and, cytosine (C). On each strand is a sequence of nucleotides that 'match,' or pair up with the nucleotides on the other, or complementary, strand. [15] On the other hand, when there is an adenine on one strand, there is a thymine on the complementary strand, and where there is guanine on one strand, there is cytosine on the complementary strand."

She begins by [16] moving the DNA from the rest of the sample, transferring it to a [17] reaction tube. She adds a solution of primers, DNA polymerase, and nucleotides. Her goal is to separate the two strands of the DNA molecules and then make complementary copies of each strand.

12. A) NO CHANGE
    B) matches
    C) has matched
    D) will be matching

13. A) NO CHANGE
    B) molecule, each strand consists
    C) molecule each strand consists
    D) molecule but each strand consists

14. A) NO CHANGE
    B) adenine (A), thymine (T), guanine (G), and cytosine (C).
    C) adenine (A), thymine (T) guanine (G) and cytosine (C).
    D) adenine (A) thymine (T), guanine (G) and cytosine (C).

15. A) NO CHANGE
    B) Specifically,
    C) However,
    D) Similarly,

16. A) NO CHANGE
    B) reviewing
    C) changing
    D) detaching

17. Which choice most effectively combines the sentences at the underlined portion?
    A) reaction tube since she adds
    B) reaction tube, however, she adds
    C) reaction tube, and adding
    D) reaction tube, she adds

GO ON TO THE NEXT PAGE

[18] The process of testing the DNA includes several steps and many changes in temperature. After mixing the primers, DNA polymerase, and nucleotides with the evidence DNA, Saunders closes the reaction tube and puts it in a thermocycler. It is programmed to raise the temperature to 94°C to separate the double strands into single strands, and then lower the temperature to 59°C to attach the primers to the single strands. Finally, it raises the temperature to 72°C for the DNA polymerase to build the complementary strands. The thermocycler holds each temperature for one minute and repeats the cycle of three temperatures for at least 30 cycles. At the end of each cycle, the number of DNA segments containing the sequence marked by the primers doubles. If the original sample contains only 100 DNA strands, [19] the absolute final sample will have billions of segments.

[1] After a short lunch break, Saunders needs to separate and identify the copied DNA segments. [2] She had used primers that bind to 13 specific sites in human DNA called short tandem repeats, or STRs. [3] The 13 STRs are segments of four nucleotides that repeat, such as GATAGATAGATA. [4] "Now here's where the real magic happens!" Saunders says excitedly. [5] "Most DNA is identical for all humans. [6] But STRs vary greatly. [7] The chances of any two humans—other than identical twins—having the same set of 13 STRs is less than one in one trillion." [20]

18. Which sentence most effectively establishes the central idea?

   A) NO CHANGE
   B) The object of testing the DNA is to re-create many strands of the DNA in question.
   C) Saunders uses a variety of machines in order to analyze the DNA.
   D) Saunders would be unable to identify the DNA without the thermocycler.

19. A) NO CHANGE
    B) absolutely the final sample
    C) the final sample
    D) the most final sample

20. Where should sentence 1 be placed to make the paragraph feel cohesive?

   A) Where it is now
   B) After sentence 2
   C) After sentence 3
   D) After sentence 4

GO ON TO THE NEXT PAGE

Saunders knows that the detectives will be [21] prepared to hear her findings, so she sits down at her desk to compare her results with the criminal database in the hopes of finding a match. [22] Is it possible that too much time is spent identifying DNA in cases that are relatively easy to solve?

21. A) NO CHANGE
    B) eager
    C) impatient
    D) conditioned

22. At this point, the writer wants to add a conclusion that best reflects Jane's feelings conveyed in the passage. Which choice accomplishes that?

    A) NO CHANGE
    B) It takes a good deal of work and expense to identify DNA in the world of modern forensics.
    C) She takes pride in the fact that her scientific expertise plays such a key role in bringing criminals to justice.
    D) She marvels at how far science has come in DNA analysis.

Questions 23–33 are based on the following passage.

Will Your Start-Up Succeed?

According to research from Harvard Business School, the majority of small businesses **23** fail in fact the success rate for a first-time company owner is a meager 18 percent. With odds so dismal, why would anyone become a business entrepreneur?

24 Veteran entrepreneurs achieve a higher 30 percent success rate, so the most predictive factor for success appears to be the number of innovations that a person has "pushed out." More specifically, the people who succeed at building a robust start-up are the ones who have previously tried. Finally, many entrepreneurs **25** grab the idea for their business by solving practical problems, and it's more than luck; 320 new entrepreneurs out of 100,000 *do* succeed by starting a company at the right time in the right industry.

Mitch Gomez is evidence of this data. He **26** did graduate from college with a degree in accounting. "I quickly realized that I have too big of a personality to be content practicing accounting," he laughs. He first built a successful insurance claims **27** service, and next founded his own independent insurance agency. "I continually employ my accounting skills, but I've ascertained that I'm an even more effective salesperson."

23. A) NO CHANGE
B) fail, in fact,
C) fail; in fact,
D) fail: in fact

24. Which sentence most effectively establishes the central idea?
A) NO CHANGE
B) The Small Business Administration defines a small business as one with fewer than 500 employees and less than $7 million in sales annually.
C) Many small businesses fail because company founders are not realistic about the amount of time it takes for a company to become profitable.
D) Running a small business can take up a lot more time than punching a clock for someone else and might not be enjoyable for everyone.

25. A) NO CHANGE
B) derive
C) achieve
D) grasp

26. A) NO CHANGE
B) has graduated
C) graduated
D) would have graduated

27. A) NO CHANGE
B) service. And next
C) service and next
D) service; and next

GO ON TO THE NEXT PAGE

Similarly, Barbara Vital, the woman behind Vital Studio, explains, "I love spending as much time with my family as possible." Vital saw an opportunity to **28** launch a monogramming business when her two young sons started school, so she founded a company that offers monogrammed backpacks and water bottles for kids, as well as **29** totes, rain boots; and baseball caps for college students. What is the secret to Vital's success? "I'm always learning how to incorporate social media and add functionality to my product website to keep customers happy," she says.

Finally, Chris Roth is an entrepreneur who can step out of his comfort zone. Always seeking a new **30** challenge his company designed and manufactured technology to keep the nozzles of water misting systems clean. Roth has also established a corporate travel agency and a truck customization company, most recently claiming he has become an innovator who beat the odds by "striving to serve customers better than my competition." **31** Large companies often employ corporate travel agencies to arrange travel for their employees and clients.

Gomez, Vital, and Roth **32** agrees that although being an entrepreneur can be a formidable challenge, exceptionally skillful entrepreneurs have important strategies for success, including stretching **33** his personal boundaries and recovering from failures. "And nothing beats being your own boss," adds Gomez.

28. A) NO CHANGE
    B) present
    C) propel
    D) impact

29. A) NO CHANGE
    B) totes; rain boots; and
    C) totes, rain boots, and,
    D) totes, rain boots, and

30. A) NO CHANGE
    B) challenge: his company
    C) challenge; his company
    D) challenge, his company

31. Which sentence would best support the central idea?
    A) NO CHANGE
    B) Savvy entrepreneurs know which risks are worth taking and which risks can tank their business before their doors open.
    C) Now Roth's small business installs water misters on restaurant patios and even sets up misting stations at outdoor music festivals.
    D) Many new small businesses fail because company founders fail to do market research and identify the needs of their community.

32. A) NO CHANGE
    B) agree
    C) should agree
    D) had agreed

33. A) NO CHANGE
    B) their
    C) our
    D) her

Questions 34–44 are based on the following passage and supplementary material.

Edgard Varèse's Influence

Today's music, from rock to jazz, has many **[34]** influences. And perhaps none is as unique as the ideas from French composer Edgard Varèse. Called "the father of electronic music," he approached compositions from a different theoretical perspective than classical composers such as Bartók and Debussy. He called his **[35]** works "organized sound"; they did not **[36]** endear melodies but waged assaults of percussion, piano, and human voices. He thought of sounds as having intelligence and treated music spatially, as "sound objects floating in space."

His unique vision can be credited to his education in science. Born in 1883 in France, Varèse was raised by a great-uncle and grandfather in the Burgundy region. He was interested in classical music and composed his first opera as a teenager. While the family lived **[37]** in Italy he studied engineering in Turin, where he learned math and science and was inspired by the work of the artist Leonardo da Vinci.

In 1903, he returned to France to study music at the Paris Conservatory. There, he composed the radical percussion performance piece *Ionisation*, which featured cymbals, snares, bass drum, xylophone, and sirens wailing. Later compositions were scored for the theremin, a new electronic instrument controlled by **[38]** the player's hands waving over its antennae, which sense their position. No composer had ever scored music for the theremin before.

34. A) NO CHANGE
    B) influences, and perhaps none is as
    C) influences, but perhaps none is as
    D) influences. Or perhaps none is as

35. A) NO CHANGE
    B) works "organized sound": They
    C) works "organized sound", they
    D) works—"organized sound"—they

36. A) NO CHANGE
    B) amplify
    C) deprive
    D) employ

37. A) NO CHANGE
    B) in Italy, he studied engineering in Turin, where he
    C) in Italy he studied engineering in Turin where he
    D) in Italy, he studied engineering in Turin; where he

38. A) NO CHANGE
    B) the players' hands
    C) the players hands
    D) the player's hands'

GO ON TO THE NEXT PAGE

In his thirties, Varèse moved to New York City, where he played piano in a café and conducted other composers' works until his own compositions gained success. His piece *Amériques* was performed in Philadelphia in 1926. Varèse went on to travel to the western United States, where he recorded, lectured, and collaborated with other musicians. By the 1950s, he was using tape recordings in **39** <u>contention</u> with symphonic performance. His piece *Déserts* was aired on a radio program amid selections by Mozart and Tchaikovsky but was received by listeners with hostility. **40**

Varèse's ideas were more forward-thinking than could be realized. One of his most ambitious scores, called *Espace*, was a choral symphony with multilingual lyrics, which was to be sung simultaneously by choirs in Paris, Moscow, Peking, and New York. He wanted the timing to be orchestrated by radio, but radio technology did not support worldwide transmission. If only Varèse **41** <u>had had</u> the Internet!

Although many of **42** <u>their</u> written compositions were lost in a fire in 1918, many modern musicians and composers have been influenced by Varèse, including Frank Zappa, John Luther Adams, and John Cage, who

39. A) NO CHANGE
    B) conjunction
    C) appropriation
    D) supplication

40. If added to the paragraph, which fact would best support the author's claims?
    A) The critical response to his 1926 performance in Philadelphia
    B) The selections by Mozart and Tchaikovsky that were played on the radio
    C) Which specific states he traveled to in the western United States
    D) The cities in which the radio program was aired

41. A) NO CHANGE
    B) would have had
    C) would have
    D) have had

42. A) NO CHANGE
    B) its
    C) our
    D) his

wrote that Varèse is "more relevant to present musical necessity than even the Viennese masters." **43** <u>Despite being less famous than Stravinsky or Shostakovich, his impact is undeniable.</u> **44** <u>Varèse's love of science and mathematics is shown in his later compositions, but less so in his early works.</u>

Composer	Number of Surviving Works
Edgard Varèse	14
Benjamin Britten	84
Charles Ives	106
Igor Stravinsky	129
Arnold Schoenberg	290
Dmitri Shostakovich	320

43. Which choice most accurately and effectively represents the information in the graph?

A) NO CHANGE

B) Despite having fewer surviving works than his contemporaries, his impact is undeniable.

C) Even though he wrote pieces using a wider range of instruments than other composers, his impact is undeniable.

D) Even though far fewer of his works are now performed compared with those of his contemporaries, his impact is undeniable.

44. Which sentence best summarizes the central idea?

A) NO CHANGE

B) In contrast with his newfound popularity, Varèse's early works have long been ignored due to increasing critical hostility.

C) Varèse and his innovative compositions became an inspiration for artists seeking to challenge traditional musical beliefs.

D) Though Varèse's contemporary critics failed to call him a "Viennese master," this distinction is changing.

IF YOU FINISH BEFORE TIME IS CALLED, YOU MAY CHECK YOUR WORK ON THIS SECTION ONLY.
DO NOT TURN TO ANY OTHER SECTION IN THE TEST. **STOP**

1006 K

Math Test

25 Minutes—20 Questions

NO-CALCULATOR SECTION

This section corresponds to Section 3 of your answer sheet.

Directions: For this section, solve each problem and decide which is the best of the choices given. Fill in the corresponding oval on the answer sheet. You may use any available space for scratch work.

Notes:

1. Calculator use is NOT permitted.
2. All numbers used are real numbers, and all variables used represent real numbers, unless otherwise indicated.
3. Figures are drawn to scale and lie in a plane unless otherwise indicated.
4. Unless stated otherwise, the domain of any function f is assumed to be the set of all real numbers x for which $f(x)$ is a real number.

Information:

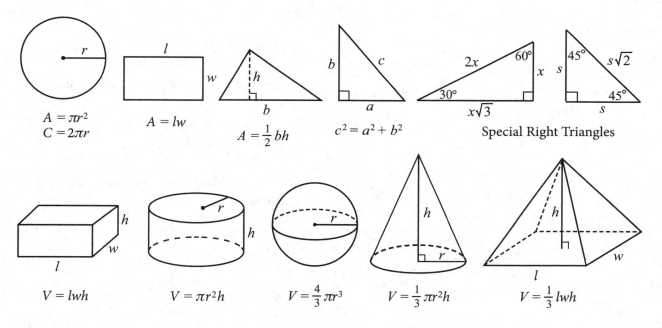

$A = \pi r^2$
$C = 2\pi r$

$A = lw$

$A = \frac{1}{2}bh$

$c^2 = a^2 + b^2$

Special Right Triangles

$V = lwh$

$V = \pi r^2 h$

$V = \frac{4}{3}\pi r^3$

$V = \frac{1}{3}\pi r^2 h$

$V = \frac{1}{3}lwh$

The sum of the degree measures of the angles in a triangle is 180.

The number of degrees of arc in a circle is 360.

The number of radians of arc in a circle is 2π.

Practice Tests

$$\frac{4(n-2)+5}{2} = \frac{13-(9+4n)}{4}$$

1. In the equation above, what is the value of n?

   A) $\frac{5}{6}$

   B) $\frac{5}{2}$

   C) There is no value of n that satisfies the equation.

   D) There are infinitely many values of n that satisfy the equation.

$$\frac{18x^3 + 9x^2 - 36x}{9x^2}$$

2. Which of the following is equivalent to the expression above?

   A) $2x - \frac{4}{x}$

   B) $18x^3 - 36x$

   C) $2x + 1 - \frac{4}{x}$

   D) $18x^3 - 36x + 1$

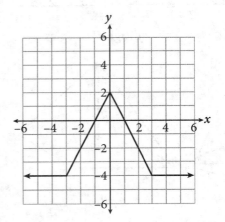

3. The figure above shows the graph of $f(x)$. For which value(s) of x does $f(x)$ equal 0?

   A) -3 and 3

   B) -1 and 1

   X) -1, 1, and 2

   D) 2 only

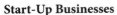

Start-Up Businesses

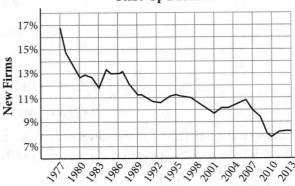

4. A start-up business is typically one that offers a "new" type of service or produces a "new" product. Start-ups are designed to search for a sustainable business model. The function shown in the graph above represents new business start-up rates in the United States from 1977 to 2013 as reported by the U.S. Census Bureau. If t represents the year, then which of the following statements correctly describes the function?

   A) The function is increasing overall.

   B) The function is decreasing overall.

   C) The function is increasing for all t such that $1977 < t < 2013$.

   D) The function is decreasing for all t such that $1977 < t < 2013$.

5. Which of the following systems of inequalities has no solution?

   A) $\begin{cases} y \geq x \\ y \leq 2x \end{cases}$

   B) $\begin{cases} y \geq x \\ y \leq -x \end{cases}$

   C) $\begin{cases} y \geq x+1 \\ y \leq x-1 \end{cases}$

   D) $\begin{cases} y \geq -x+1 \\ y \leq x-1 \end{cases}$

GO ON TO THE NEXT PAGE ⟹

6. At what value(s) of x do the graphs of $y = -2x + 1$ and $y = 2x^2 + 5x + 4$ intersect?

   A) -8 and $\dfrac{1}{2}$

   B) -3 and $-\dfrac{1}{2}$

   C) -3 and 3

   D) $-\dfrac{1}{2}$ and 3

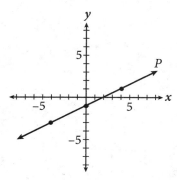

7. If line P shown in the graph above is reflected over the x-axis and shifted up 3 units, what is the new y-intercept?

   A) $(0, -4)$

   B) $(0, -2)$

   X) $(0, 2)$

   Δ) $(0, 4)$

8. Which of the following are roots of the equation $3x^2 - 6x - 5 = 0$?

   A) $1 \pm 2\sqrt{6}$

   B) $\dfrac{1 \pm 2\sqrt{2}}{3}$

   C) $\dfrac{3 \pm 2\sqrt{2}}{3}$

   D) $\dfrac{3 \pm 2\sqrt{6}}{3}$

9. If $m = \dfrac{1}{n^{-\frac{1}{4}}}$, where both $m > 0$ and $n > 0$, which of the following gives n in terms of m?

   A) $n = m^4$

   B) $n = \dfrac{1}{m^4}$

   C) $n = \dfrac{1}{\sqrt[4]{m}}$

   D) $n = m^{\frac{1}{4}}$

$$\begin{cases} y = 3x - 1 \\ y = \dfrac{5x + 8}{2} \end{cases}$$

10. If (x, y) represents the solution to the system of equations shown above, what is the value of y?

    A) 10

    B) 19

    C) 29

    D) 31

11. If $0 < \dfrac{d}{2} + 1 \le \dfrac{8}{5}$, which of the following is not a possible value of d?

    A) -2

    B) $-\dfrac{6}{5}$

    C) 0

    D) $\dfrac{6}{5}$

12. The value of $\cos 40°$ is the same as which of the following?

    A) $\sin 50°$

    B) $\sin (-40°)$

    C) $\cos (-50°)$

    D) $\cos 140°$

13. A business's "break-even point" is the point at which revenue (sales) equals expenses. When a company breaks even, no profit is being made, but the company is not losing any money either. Suppose a manufacturer buys materials for producing a particular item at a cost of $4.85 per unit and has fixed monthly expenses of $11,625 related to this item. The manufacturer sells this particular item to several retailers for $9.50 per unit. How many units must the manufacturer sell per month to reach the break-even point for this item?

A)   810

B)   1,225

C)   2,100

D)   2,500

14. If $\frac{1}{2}y - \frac{3}{5}x = -16$, what is the value of $6x - 5y$?

A)   32

B)   80

C)   96

D)   160

15. If $f(g(2)) = -1$ and $f(x) = x + 1$, then which of the following could define $g(x)$?

A) $g(x) = x - 6$

B) $g(x) = x - 4$

C) $g(x) = x - 2$

D) $g(x) = x - 1$

GO ON TO THE NEXT PAGE

Directions: For questions 16–20, enter your responses into the appropriate grid on your answer sheet, in accordance with the following:

1. You will receive credit only if the circles are filled in correctly, but you may write your answers in the boxes above each grid to help you fill in the circles accurately.

2. Don't mark more than one circle per column.

3. None of the questions with Grid-in responses will have a negative solution.

4. Only grid in a single answer, even if there is more than one correct answer to a given question.

5. A **mixed number** must be gridded as a decimal or an improper fraction. For example, you would grid $7\frac{1}{2}$ as 7.5 or 15/2.

   (Were you to grid it as [7 | 1 | / | 2], this response would be read as $\frac{71}{2}$.)

6. A **decimal** that has more digits than there are places on the grid may be either rounded or truncated, but every column in the grid must be filled in to receive credit.

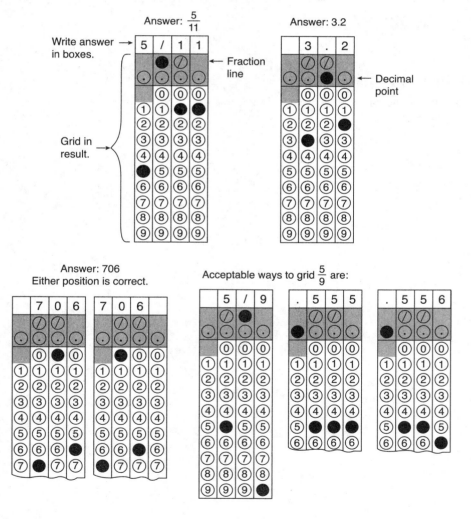

Practice Tests

$$k(10x - 5) = 2(3 + x) - 7$$

16. If the equation above has infinitely many solutions and k is a constant, what is the value of k ?

17. A right triangle has leg lengths of 18 and 24 and a hypotenuse of $15n$. What is the value of n ?

$$\frac{\sqrt{x} \cdot x^{\frac{5}{4}} \cdot x^2}{\sqrt[4]{x^3}}$$

18. If the expression above is combined into a single power of x with a positive exponent, what is that exponent?

19. If the product of $\left(3 + \sqrt{-16}\right)\left(1 - \sqrt{-36}\right)$ is written as a complex number in the form $a + bi$, what is the value of a ? $(\sqrt{-1} = i.)$

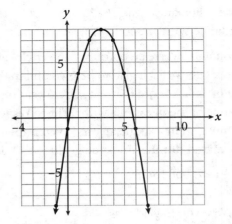

20. If the equation of the parabola shown in the graph is written in standard quadratic form, $y = ax^2 + bx + c$, and $a = -1$, then what is the value of b ?

IF YOU FINISH BEFORE TIME IS CALLED, YOU MAY CHECK YOUR WORK ON THIS SECTION ONLY. **STOP**
DO NOT TURN TO ANY OTHER SECTION IN THE TEST.

1012 K

Math Test

55 Minutes—38 Questions

CALCULATOR SECTION

This section corresponds to Section 4 of your answer sheet.

Directions: For this section, solve each problem and decide which is the best of the choices given. Fill in the corresponding oval on the answer sheet. You may use any available space for scratch work.

Notes:

1. Calculator use is permitted.
2. All numbers used are real numbers, and all variables used represent real numbers, unless otherwise indicated.
3. Figures are drawn to scale and lie in a plane unless otherwise indicated.
4. Unless stated otherwise, the domain of any function f is assumed to be the set of all real numbers x for which $f(x)$ is a real number.

Information:

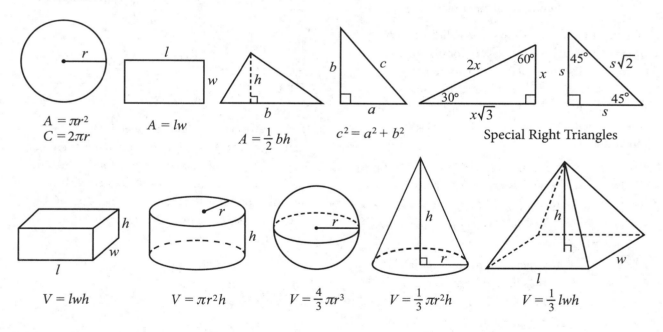

$$A = \pi r^2$$
$$C = 2\pi r$$

$$A = lw$$

$$A = \frac{1}{2} bh$$

$$c^2 = a^2 + b^2$$

Special Right Triangles

$$V = lwh$$

$$V = \pi r^2 h$$

$$V = \frac{4}{3} \pi r^3$$

$$V = \frac{1}{3} \pi r^2 h$$

$$V = \frac{1}{3} lwh$$

The sum of the degree measures of the angles in a triangle is 180.

The number of degrees of arc in a circle is 360.

The number of radians of arc in a circle is 2π.

GO ON TO THE NEXT PAGE

$$\begin{cases} 4x + y = -5 \\ -4x - 2y = -2 \end{cases}$$

1. What is the y-coordinate of the solution to the system of equations shown above?

   A) -7

   B) -3

   C) 0

   D) 7

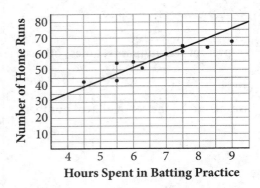

Hours Spent in Batting Practice

2. The scatterplot above shows data collected from 10 major league baseball players comparing the average weekly time each one spent in batting practice and the number of home runs he hit in a single season. The line of best fit for the data is also shown. What does the slope of the line represent in this context?

   A) The estimated time spent in batting practice by a player who hits zero home runs

   B) The estimated number of single-season home runs hit by a player who spends zero hours in batting practice

   C) The estimated increase in time that a player spends in batting practice for each home run that he hits in a single season

   D) The estimated increase in the number of single-season home runs hit by a player for each hour he spends in batting practice

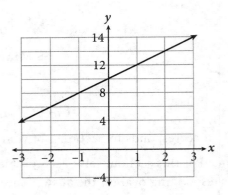

3. Where will the line shown in the graph above intersect the x-axis?

   A) -5.5

   B) -5

   X) -4.5

   Δ) -4

4. The function $f(x)$ is defined as $f(x) = -3g(x)$, where $g(x) = x + 2$. What is the value of $f(5)$?

   A) -21

   B) -1

   C) 4

   D) 7

5. Sara is grocery shopping. She needs laundry detergent, which is on sale for 30 percent off its regular price of $8.00. She also needs dog food, which she can buy at three cans for $4.00. Which of the following represents the total cost, before tax, if Sara buys x bottles of laundry detergent and 12 cans of dog food?

   A) $C = 2.4x + 48$

   B) $C = 5.6x + 16$

   C) $C = 5.6x + 48$

   D) $C = 8.4x + 16$

GO ON TO THE NEXT PAGE

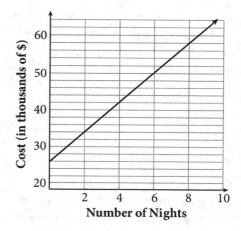

Number of Nights

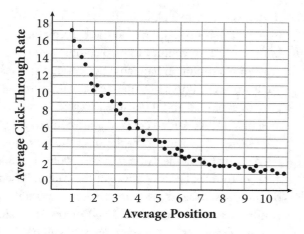

Average Position

6. The graph above shows the average cost of back surgery followed by a hospital stay in the United States. The hospital charges for the surgery itself plus all the costs associated with recovery care for each night the patient remains in the hospital. Based on the graph, what is the average cost per night spent in the hospital?

   A) $2,600
   B) $4,000
   C) $6,600
   D) $8,000

7. The figure above represents a click-through rate curve, which shows the relationship between a search result position in a list of Internet search results and the number of people who clicked on advertisements on that result's page. Which of the following regression types would be the best model for this data?

   A) A linear function
   B) A quadratic function
   C) A polynomial function
   D) An exponential function

8. Kudzu is a vine-like plant that grows indigenously in Asia. It was brought over to the United States in the early 20th century to help combat soil erosion. As can often happen when foreign species are introduced into a non-native habitat, kudzu growth exploded and it became invasive. In one area of Virginia, kudzu covered approximately 3,200 acres of a farmer's cropland, so the farmer tried a new herbicide. After two weeks of use, 2,800 acres of the cropland were free of the kudzu. Based on these results, and assuming the same general conditions, how many of the 30,000 acres of kudzu-infested cropland in that region would still be covered if all the farmers in the entire region had used the herbicide?

   A) 3,750
   B) 4,000
   C) 26,000
   D) 26,250

x	-2	-1	0	1	2	3
$g(x)$	5	3	1	-1	-3	-5
$h(x)$	-3	-2	-1	0	1	2

9. Several values for the functions $g(x)$ and $h(x)$ are shown in the table above. What is the value of $g(h(3))$?

   A) -5
   B) -3
   X) -1
   D)   2

10. Mae-Ling made 15 shots during a basketball game. Some were 3-pointers and others were worth 2 points each. If s shots were 3-pointers, which expression represents her total score?

    A) $3s$
    B) $s + 30$
    C) $3s + 2$
    D) $5s + 30$

11. Crude oil is sold by the barrel, which refers to both the physical container and a unit of measure, abbreviated as bbl. One barrel holds 42 gallons and, consequently, 1 bbl = 42 gallons. An oil company is filling an order for 2,500 barrels. The machine the company uses to fill the barrels pumps at a rate of 37.5 gallons per minute. If the oil company has 8 machines working simultaneously, how long will it take to fill all the barrels in the order?

    A) 5 hours and 50 minutes
    B) 12 hours and 45 minutes
    C) 28 hours and 30 minutes
    D) 46 hours and 40 minutes

GO ON TO THE NEXT PAGE

Practice Tests

	Jan	Feb	Mar	Apr
Company A	54	146	238	330
Company B	15	30	60	120

12. Company A and company B are selling two similar toys. The sales figures for each toy are recorded in the table above. The marketing department at company A predicts that its monthly sales for this particular toy will continue to be higher than company B's through the end of the year. Based on the data in the table, and assuming that each company sustains the pattern of growth the data suggests, which company will sell more of this toy in December of that year and how much more?

A) Company A; 182

B) Company A; 978

C) Company B; 29,654

D) Company B; 60,282

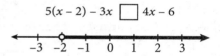

13. Which symbol correctly completes the inequality whose solution is shown above?

A) $<$

B) $>$

X) $\leq$

Δ) $\geq$

Questions 14 and 15 refer to the following information.

A student is drawing the human skeleton to scale for a school assignment. The assignment permits the student to omit all bones under a certain size because they would be too small to draw. The longest bone in the human body is the femur, or thighbone, with an average length of 19.9 inches. The tenth longest bone is the sternum, or breastbone, with an average length of 6.7 inches.

14. If the scale factor of the drawing is one-eighth, about how long in inches should the student draw the femur?

A) 2

B) 2.5

C) 2.8

D) 3

15. The student draws the femur, but then realizes she drew it too long, at 3.5 inches. She doesn't want to erase and start over, so she decides she will adjust the scale factor to match her current drawing instead. Based on the new scale factor, about how long in inches should she draw the sternum?

A) 0.8

B) 1

C) 1.2

D) 1.5

GO ON TO THE NEXT PAGE

Practice Tests

16. If a line that passes through the ordered pairs $(4 - c, 2c)$ and $(-c, -8)$ has a slope of $\frac{1}{2}$, what is the value of c?

    A) -5

    B) -3

    X) -2

    D) 2

From	Distance to LHR
DCA	3,718
MIA	4,470

17. Two airplanes departed from different airports at 5:30 a.m., both traveling nonstop to London Heathrow Airport (LHR). The distances the planes traveled are recorded in the table. The Washington, D.C. (DCA) flight flew through moderate cloud cover and as a result only averaged 338 miles per hour. The flight from Miami (MIA) had good weather conditions for the first two-thirds of the trip and averaged 596 miles per hour, but then encountered some turbulence and only averaged 447 miles per hour for the last part of the trip. Which plane arrived first and how long was it at the London airport before the other plane arrived?

    A) MIA; 2 hours, 40 minutes

    B) MIA; 3 hours, 30 minutes

    C) DCA; 1 hour, 20 minutes

    D) DCA; 3 hours, 40 minutes

18. Which of the following quadratic equations has no real solution?

    A) $0 = -3(x + 1)(x - 8)$

    B) $0 = 3(x + 1)(x - 8)$

    C) $0 = -3(x + 1)^2 + 8$

    D) $0 = 3(x + 1)^2 + 8$

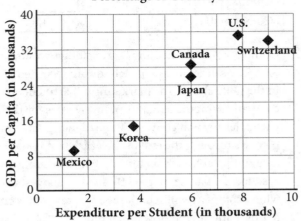

Annual Expenditures per Student as a Percentage of Country's GDP

Adapted from the Organization for Economic Cooperation and Development (OECD), 2003.

19. A student looked at the graph above and determined based on the data that spending more money per student causes the gross domestic product (GDP) to increase. Which of the following statements is true?

    A) The student is correct; the data shows that increased spending on students causes an increase in the GDP.

    B) The student is incorrect; the data shows that having a higher GDP causes an increase in the amount of money a country spends on students.

    C) The student is incorrect; there is no correlation and, therefore, no causation between GDP and expenditures on students.

    D) The student is incorrect; the two variables are correlated, but changes in one do not necessarily cause changes in the other.

GO ON TO THE NEXT PAGE ⟹

20. In chemistry, the combined gas law formula $\frac{p_1 V_1}{T_1} = \frac{p_2 V_2}{T_2}$ gives the relationship between the volumes, temperatures, and pressures for two fixed amounts of gas. Which of the following gives p_2 in terms of the other variables?

    A) $p_1 = p_2$

    B) $\frac{p_1 T}{V} = p_2$

    C) $\frac{p_1 V_1 T_2}{T_1 V_2} = p_2$

    D) $\frac{p_1 V_1 V_2}{T_1 T_2} = p_2$

21. An object's weight is dependent upon the gravitational force being exerted upon the object. This is why objects in space are weightless. If 1 pound on Earth is equal to 0.377 pounds on Mars and 2.364 pounds on Jupiter, how many more pounds does an object weighing 1.5 tons on Earth weigh on Jupiter than on Mars? (1 ton = 2,000 pounds)

    A) 1,131

    B) 4,092

    C) 5,961

    D) 7,092

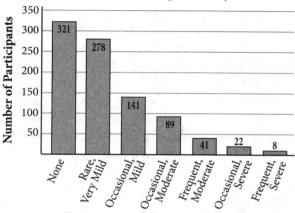

**Clinical Trial: Headache Side Effect
900-Participant Study**

Number of Participants (y-axis): None 321, Rare, Very Mild 278, Occasional, Mild 141, Occasional, Moderate 89, Frequent, Moderate 41, Occasional, Severe 22, Frequent, Severe 8

Frequency and Severity of Headaches

22. When a drug company wants to introduce a new drug, it must subject the drug to rigorous testing. The final stage of this testing is human clinical trials, in which progressively larger groups of volunteers are given the drug and carefully monitored. One aspect of this monitoring is keeping track of the frequency and severity of side effects. The figure above shows the results for the side effect of headaches for a certain drug. According to the trial guidelines, all moderate and severe headaches are considered to be adverse reactions. Which of the following best describes the data?

    A) The data is symmetric with more than 50 percent of participants having adverse reactions.

    B) The data is skewed to the right with more than 50 percent of participants having adverse reactions.

    C) The data is skewed to the right with more than 75 percent of participants failing to have adverse reactions.

    D) The data is skewed to the right with approximately 50 percent of participants having no reaction at all.

23. In the legal field, "reciprocity" means that an attorney can take and pass a bar exam in one state and be allowed to practice law in a different state that permits such reciprocity. Each state bar association decides with which other states it will allow reciprocity. For example, Pennsylvania allows reciprocity with the District of Columbia. It costs $25 less than 3 times as much to take the bar in Pennsylvania than in D.C. If both bar exams together cost $775, how much less expensive is it to take the bar exam in D.C. than in Pennsylvania?

A) $200

B) $275

C) $375

D) $575

24. A grain producer is filling a cylindrical silo 20-feet wide and 60-feet tall with wheat. Based on past experience, the producer has established a protocol for leaving the top 5 percent of the silo empty to allow for air circulation. Assuming the producer follows standard protocol, what is the maximum number of cubic feet of wheat that should be put in the silo?

A) $5,144\pi$

B) $5,700\pi$

C) $20,577\pi$

D) $22,800\pi$

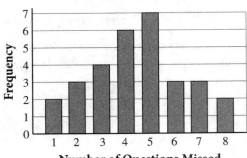

Driver's Education Test Results

25. Mr. Juno took his driver's education class to the Department of Motor Vehicles to take their driver's license test. The number of questions missed by each student in the class is recorded in the bar graph above. Which of the following statements is true?

A) More than half of the students missed 5 or more questions.

B) The mean number of questions missed was between 4 and 5.

C) More students missed 3 questions than any other number of questions.

D) Thirty-six students from Mr. Juno's class took the driver's license test that day.

26. If the graph of the equation $y = ax^2 + bx + c$ passes through the points $(0, 2)$, $(-6, -7)$, and $(8, -14)$, what is the value of $a + b + c$?

A) -19

B) -2

C) 1.75

D) 2.25

GO ON TO THE NEXT PAGE

27. A bakery sells three sizes of muffins—mini, regular, and jumbo. The baker plans daily muffin counts based on the size of his pans and how they fit in the oven, which result in the following ratios: mini to regular equals 5 to 2 and regular to jumbo equals 5 to 4. When the bakery caters events, it usually offers only the regular size, but it recently decided to offer a mix of mini and jumbo instead of regular. If the baker wants to keep the sizes in the same ratio as his daily counts, what ratio of mini to jumbo should he use?

    A) 1:1

    B) 4:2

    C) 5:2

    D) 25:8

$$\frac{1}{3}x + \frac{1}{2}y = 5$$
$$kx - 4y = 16$$

28. If the system of linear equations shown above has no solution, and k is a constant, what is the value of k?

    A) $-\dfrac{8}{3}$

    B) -2

    C) $\dfrac{1}{3}$

    D) 3

29. What is the value of $3^{90} \times 27^{90} \div \left(\dfrac{1}{9}\right)^{30}$?

    A) 9^{60}

    B) 9^{120}

    C) 9^{150}

    D) 9^{210}

30. If a right cone is three times as wide at its base as it is tall, and the volume of the cone is 384π cubic inches, what is the diameter in inches of the base of the cone?

    A) 8

    B) 12

    C) 16

    D) 24

GO ON TO THE NEXT PAGE

Directions: For questions 31–38, enter your responses into the appropriate grid on your answer sheet, in accordance with the following:

1. You will receive credit only if the circles are filled in correctly, but you may write your answers in the boxes above each grid to help you fill in the circles accurately.
2. Don't mark more than one circle per column.
3. None of the questions with Grid-in responses will have a negative solution.
4. Only grid in a single answer, even if there is more than one correct answer to a given question.
5. A **mixed number** must be gridded as a decimal or an improper fraction. For example, you would grid $7\frac{1}{2}$ as 7.5 or 15/2.

   (Were you to grid it as [7 1 / 2], this response would be read as $\frac{71}{2}$.)
6. A **decimal** that has more digits than there are places on the grid may be either rounded or truncated, but every column in the grid must be filled in to receive credit.

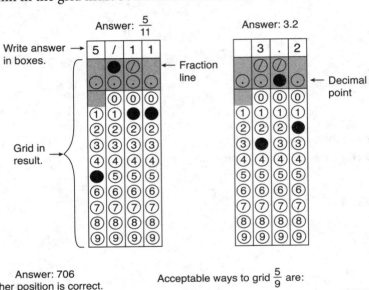

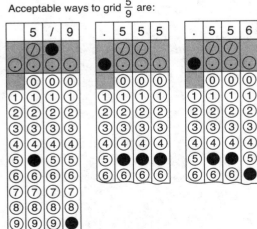

GO ON TO THE NEXT PAGE

31. If $0.004 \leq m \leq 0.4$ and $1.6 \leq n \leq 16$, what is the maximum value of $\frac{m}{n}$?

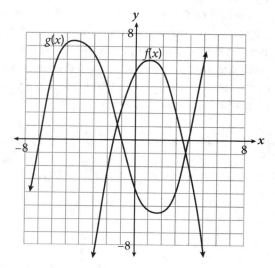

32. The graph above shows a quadratic function $f(x)$ and a cubic function $g(x)$. Based on the graph, what is the value of $(f - g)(3)$, assuming all integer values?

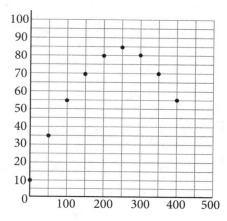

33. Nine data points were used to generate the scatterplot shown above. Assuming all whole number values for the data points, what is the maximum value in the range of the data?

Years at Company	Technicians	Sales Workers
$y < 1$	38	30
$1 \leq y \leq 3$	15	19
$y > 3$	54	48

34. A company conducts a survey among its employees and categorizes the results based on job category and longevity (the number of years the employee has been working for the company). The Director of Human Resources wants to conduct a small follow-up focus group meeting with a few employees to discuss the overall survey results. If the Human Resources Director randomly chooses four employees who participated in the initial survey, what is the probability that all of them will have been with the company for longer than three years? Enter your answer as a decimal and round to the nearest hundredth.

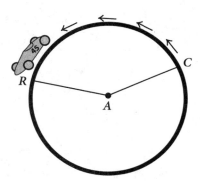

35. Most racetracks are in the shape of an ellipse (an elongated circle similar to an oval), but Langhorne Speedway in Pennsylvania was originally a circular track. If a race car is traveling around this track, starting at point C and traveling 1,500 feet to point R, and the radius of the track is 840 feet, what is the measure to the nearest degree of minor angle CAR ?

36. If $Ax + By = C$ is the standard form of the line that passes through the points $(-4, 1)$ and $(3, -2)$, where A is an integer greater than 1, what is the value of B?

Practice Tests

Questions 37 and 38 refer to the following information.

The Great Depression began in 1929 and lasted until 1939. It was a period of extreme poverty, marked by low prices and high unemployment. The main catalytic event to the Great Depression was the Wall Street Crash (stock market crash). The Dow, which measures the health of the stock market, started Black Thursday (October 24, 1929) at approximately 306 points.

37. The stock market had been in steady decline since its record high the month before. If the market had declined by 19.5 percent between its record high and opening on Black Thursday, what was the approximate value of the Dow at its record high? Round your answer to the nearest whole point.

38. By the end of business on Black Thursday, the Dow had dropped by 2 percent. Over the course of Friday and the half-day Saturday session, there was no significant change. Unfortunately, the market lost 13 percent on Black Monday, followed by another 12 percent on Black Tuesday. What was the total percent decrease from opening on Black Thursday to closing on Black Tuesday? Round your answer to the nearest whole percent and ignore the percent sign when entering your answer.

IF YOU FINISH BEFORE TIME IS CALLED, YOU MAY CHECK YOUR WORK ON THIS SECTION ONLY. DO NOT TURN TO ANY OTHER SECTION IN THE TEST. **STOP**

1024 K

Practice Tests

Essay Test

50 Minutes

You will be given a passage to read and asked to write an essay analyzing it. As you write, be sure to show that you have read the passage closely. You will be graded on how well you have understood the passage, how clear your analysis is, and how well you express your ideas.

Your essay must be written on the lines in your answer booklet. Anything you write outside the lined space in your answer booklet will not be read by the essay graders. Be sure to write or print in such a way that it will be legible to readers not familiar with your handwriting. Additionally, be sure to address the passage directly. An off-topic essay will not be graded.

As you read the passage, think about the author's use of

- evidence, such as statistics or other facts.

- logic to connect evidence to conclusions and to develop lines of reasoning.

- style, word choice, and appeals to emotion to make the argument more persuasive.

Adapted from Robert F. Kennedy's address to the National Union of South African Students' Day of Affirmation, delivered June 6, 1966.

1   We stand here in the name of freedom.

2   At the heart of that Western freedom and democracy is the belief that the individual man, the child of God, is the touchstone of value, and all society, groups, the state, exist for his benefit. Therefore the enlargement of liberty for individual human beings must be the supreme goal and the abiding practice of any Western society.

3   The first element of this individual liberty is the freedom of speech.

4   The right to express and communicate ideas, to set oneself apart from the dumb beasts of field and forest; to recall governments to their duties and obligations; above all, the right to affirm one's membership and allegiance to the body politic—to society—to the men with whom we share our land, our heritage and our children's future.

5   Hands in hand with freedom of speech goes the power to be heard—to share the decisions of government which shape men's lives. Everything that makes life worthwhile—family, work, education, a place to rear one's children and a place to rest one's head—all this rests on decisions of government; all can be swept away by a government which does not heed the demands of its people. Therefore, the essential humanity of men can be protected and preserved only where government must answer—not just to those of a particular religion, or a particular race; but to all its people.

6   These are the sacred rights of Western society. These are the essential differences between us and Nazi Germany, as they were between Athens and Persia. . . .

7   For two centuries, my own country has struggled to overcome the self-imposed handicap of prejudice and discrimination based on nationality, social class or race—discrimination profoundly repugnant to the theory and command of our Constitution. Even as my father grew up in Boston, signs told him that "No Irish need apply."

GO ON TO THE NEXT PAGE

8   Two generations later President Kennedy became the first Catholic to head the nation; but how many men of ability had, before 1961, been denied the opportunity to contribute to the nation's progress because they were Catholic, or of Irish extraction.

9   In the last five years, the winds of change have blown as fiercely in the United States as anywhere in the world. But they will not—they cannot—abate.

10   For there are millions of African Americans untrained for the simplest jobs, and thousands every day denied their full equal rights under the law; and the violence of the disinherited, the insulated, the injured, looms over the streets of Harlem and Watts and South Chicago.

11   But an African American trains as an astronaut, one of mankind's first explorers into outer space; another is the chief barrister of the United States Government, and dozens sit on the benches of court; and another, Dr. Martin Luther King, is the second man of African descent to win the Nobel Peace Prize for his nonviolent efforts for social justice between the races.

12   We must recognize the full human equality of all our people before God, before the law, and in the councils of government. We must do this not because it is economically advantageous, although it is; not because the laws of God and man command it, although they do command it; not because people in other lands wish it so. We must do it for the single and fundamental reason that it is the right thing to do.

13   And this must be our commitment outside our borders as well as within.

14   It is your job, the task of the young people of this world, to strip the last remnants of that ancient, cruel belief from the civilization of man.

15   Each nation has different obstacles and different goals, shadowed by the vagaries of history and experience. Yet as I talk to young people around the world I am impressed not by the diversity but by the closeness of their goals, their desires and concerns and hopes for the future. There is discrimination in New York, apartheid in South Africa and serfdom in the mountains of Peru. People stagnate in the streets of India; intellectuals go to jail in Russia; thousands are slaughtered in Indonesia; wealth is lavished on armaments everywhere. These are differing evils. But they are common works of man.

16   And therefore they call upon common qualities of conscience and of indignation, a shared determination to wipe away the unnecessary sufferings of our fellow human beings at home and particularly around the world.

> Write an essay that analyzes the author's approach in persuading his readers that the expansion of liberty for all must be the guiding principle of any Western society. Focus on specific features such as the ones listed in the box above the passage and explain how these features strengthen the author's argument. Your essay should discuss the most important rhetorical features of the passage.
>
> Your essay should not focus on your own opinion of the author's conclusion, but rather on how the author persuades his readers.

IF YOU FINISH BEFORE TIME IS CALLED, YOU MAY CHECK YOUR WORK ON THIS SECTION ONLY. DO NOT TURN TO ANY OTHER SECTION IN THE TEST.   STOP

Answer Key
Reading Test

1. B	14. C	27. A	40. B
2. C	15. A	28. A	41. C
3. D	16. B	29. B	42. D
4. B	17. B	30. C	43. C
5. A	18. C	31. D	44. D
6. D	19. D	32. C	45. A
7. C	20. D	33. D	46. C
8. D	21. B	34. B	47. A
9. C	22. C	35. D	48. B
10. A	23. D	36. D	49. C
11. A	24. B	37. A	50. D
12. A	25. D	38. C	51. B
13. B	26. B	39. B	52. D

Writing and Language Test

1. C	12. B	23. C	34. C
2. D	13. A	24. A	35. A
3. A	14. B	25. B	36. D
4. A	15. B	26. C	37. B
5. B	16. D	27. C	38. A
6. C	17. C	28. A	39. B
7. A	18. A	29. D	40. A
8. C	19. C	30. D	41. A
9. A	20. A	31. C	42. D
10. C	21. B	32. B	43. B
11. B	22. C	33. B	44. C

Math Test—No-Calculator

1. A	6. B	11. A	16. 1/5 or .2
2. C	7. D	12. A	17. 2
3. B	8. D	13. D	18. 3
4. B	9. A	14. D	19. 27
5. C	10. C	15. B	20. 6

MATH TEST—CALCULATOR

1. D	11. A	21. C	31. 1/4 or .25
2. D	12. C	22. C	32. 6
3. B	13. A	23. C	33. 85
4. A	14. B	24. B	34. .06
5. B	15. C	25. B	35. 102
6. B	16. B	26. C	36. 7
7. D	17. A	27. D	37. 380
8. A	18. D	28. A	38. 25
9. B	19. D	29. D	
10. B	20. C	30. D	

ANSWERS AND EXPLANATIONS

Reading Test

Suggested passage map notes:

¶1: Pip eating paltry breakfast, Mr. P making him do math while he eats, Pip does not like Mr. P
¶2: Pip visiting Miss H, Miss H's house in disrepair
¶3–9: lady lets in Pip, makes Mr. P go away
¶10: Pip happy to be rid of Mr. P for now

1. B

Difficulty: Easy

Category: Detail

Getting to the Answer: Examine the description of breakfast in the first paragraph before choosing the correct answer. In lines 9–10, Pip uses "crumb" and "little butter" to describe what he ate, and he also says that "a quantity of warm water" had been added to his milk. Therefore, it's clear that Pip's breakfast with Mr. Pumblechook is **(B)**, "small and of poor quality."

2. C

Difficulty: Medium

Category: Vocab-in-Context

Getting to the Answer: Eliminate answer choices that might be synonyms of "wretched" but don't make sense in the context of the passage. When Pip describes Mr. Pumblechook's company to be "wretched," he means "distressing" or *causing misery*. Choice **(C)** is the correct answer.

3. D

Difficulty: Medium

Category: Inference

Getting to the Answer: Review the passage for details that reveal Mr. Pumblechook's attitude. By his actions, you can infer that Mr. Pumblechook is indifferent to Pip's discomfort. Choice **(D)** is the correct answer.

4. B

Difficulty: Medium

Category: Command of Evidence

Getting to the Answer: Find each answer choice in the passage. Think about your answer for the previous question, and determine which lines provide the strongest support for that answer. In the first paragraph, Pip describes how Mr. Pumblechook offers him a meager breakfast and quizzes him on arithmetic during their meal rather than making conversation. Choice **(B)** is the correct answer.

5. A

Difficulty: Hard

Category: Global

Getting to the Answer: Study the answer choices. Eliminate any that go too far in their interpretation of characters and events in the passage. Though (B) seems to reflect what might be true of Pip and Mr. Pumblechook's relationship, and one might believe that (C) and (D) are true, the correct answer is **(A)**. This theme most clearly reflects the message conveyed through Pip's experiences in this passage.

6. D

Difficulty: Medium

Category: Inference

Getting to the Answer: Review the section of the passage that describes the young lady's appearance and actions. Select the answer choice that describes her entire demeanor, not just part of it. In line 53, the young lady is described as seeming "very proud." When she tells Mr. Pumblechook that he may not enter, she speaks "finally" (line 62) and in an "undiscussible way" (lines 62–63). This indicates that she is being authoritative. The correct answer is **(D)**.

7. C

Difficulty: Medium

Category: Inference

Getting to the Answer: Think about details in the passage that relate to the characters' relationships. What do they reveal about how Pip probably feels at the end of the passage? It is reasonable to infer that Pip is relieved when he is no longer in Mr. Pumblechook's company. Therefore, **(C)** is the correct answer.

8. D

Difficulty: Hard

Category: Command of Evidence

Getting to the Answer: Locate each answer in the passage and decide which one provides the best support for the answer to the previous question. At the end of the passage, Pip "was not free from apprehension" (lines 68–69) that Mr. Pumblechook would return but then tells the reader that no return took place. Choice **(D)** best supports the idea that Pip is relieved to be away from Mr. Pumblechook.

9. C

Difficulty: Easy

Category: Vocab-in-Context

Getting to the Answer: Substitute each answer choice for "condition." The correct answer will not change the meaning of the sentence. Choice **(C)** is the correct answer. The narrator says that Mr. Pumblechook is "in a condition of ruffled dignity." In this context, "state" means the same as "condition."

10. A

Difficulty: Medium

Category: Function

Getting to the Answer: Think of what the parenthetical comment by Pip tells you about his personality. In a sense, Pip is apologizing for what he is about to say of Mr. Pumblechook. The parenthetical comment reveals that Pip is usually more polite in his references to others. Choice **(A)** is the correct answer.

Suggested passage map notes:

> ¶1: MLK states why he is Birmingham, history of SCLC, in Birmingham due to injustice
> ¶2: MLK cannot let injustice continue, we are one people
> ¶3: MLK explains why peaceful protests are needed, benefits of tension to open negotiations
> ¶4: nonviolent pressure only way to enact change
> ¶5: justice must be demanded by the oppressed

11. A

Difficulty: Medium

Category: Global

Getting to the Answer: Avoid answer choices that deal with related issues but do not address the main purpose of the letter. The passage as a whole addresses why King came to Birmingham, and then builds on his explanation for being in Birmingham to explore his cause. Choice **(A)** is correct.

12. A

Difficulty: Easy

Category: Command of Evidence

Getting to the Answer: Choose the answer that relates directly to the purpose you identified in the previous question. King begins the letter by stating, "I think I should give the reason for my being in Birmingham," which clearly explains his purpose for writing the letter from the jail. Choice **(A)** is correct.

13. B

Difficulty: Medium

Category: Inference

Getting to the Answer: Determine whether the details in the passage and its title, which relate to how King was treated when he arrived in Birmingham, indicate a positive or negative reception. The title of the passage, "Letter from Birmingham Jail," indicates that King was incarcerated after his arrival in Birmingham. Furthermore, he is writing to an audience that considered him an "'[outsider] coming in'" (line 3). It is reasonable to infer from these details that King received criticism for his decision to come to Birmingham; therefore, **(B)** is correct.

Practice Tests

14. C

Difficulty: Easy

Category: Vocab-in-Context

Getting to the Answer: Read the complete sentence and the surrounding paragraph to best understand the meaning of the phrase within its greater context. In the paragraph, King goes on to explain that events in Birmingham must necessarily concern him. He states that an injustice in one place threatens justice everywhere and even writes, "Whatever affects one directly affects all indirectly" (lines 27–28). This suggests that events in Birmingham affect people throughout the nation. Choice **(C)** is correct as it explains that the "interrelatedness of all communities and states" refers to the idea that events in one part of the country affect the entire nation.

15. A

Difficulty: Easy

Category: Inference

Getting to the Answer: Predict King's opinions before reviewing the answer choices. The correct answer can be inferred directly from King's views as expressed in the paragraph. In this paragraph, King refers specifically to injustice and how it affects people everywhere. From this, you can most clearly infer that King considered circumstances in Birmingham to be unfair and wrong. Choice **(A)** is correct.

16. B

Difficulty: Easy

Category: Command of Evidence

Getting to the Answer: Review the answer to the previous question. Read the answer choices to identify the one whose rhetoric provides clear support for the inference. Although the entire paragraph provides general support and context for the inference, only **(B)** suggests that circumstances in Birmingham were unjust, that is, unfair and wrong.

17. B

Difficulty: Medium

Category: Vocab-in-Context

Getting to the Answer: Before viewing the answer choices, think about the purpose of the word in the sentence and form an alternate explanation of the word. Then, identify the answer choice that best reflects that meaning and

intent. King says that direct action in Birmingham aims to "dramatize the issue that it can no longer be ignored." This suggests that the issue, or events, in Birmingham are of great significance and demand attention that they have not received. Therefore, **(B)** is correct.

18. C

Difficulty: Hard

Category: Detail

Getting to the Answer: Consider the overall thrust of King's argument in this paragraph. Choose the answer that encapsulates this idea. In paragraph 3, King responds to charges that activists should focus on negotiation, not direct action. He argues that direct action is needed to spur negotiations. King reasons that nonviolent protests create the tension between forces in society needed to bring people to the table to discuss the relevant issues of prejudice and racism. His claim in the paragraph is that direct action is needed to spur negotiation, making choice **(C)** correct.

19. D

Difficulty: Hard

Category: Inference

Getting to the Answer: Identify an idea in paragraph 4 that provides clear support to the claim made in the previous paragraph. In paragraph 3, King claims that nonviolent direct action is needed to prompt negotiations on civil rights. In paragraph 4, he supports that argument by explaining that no gains have been made in civil rights without such nonviolent action, as choice **(D)** states.

20. D

Difficulty: Medium

Category: Function

Getting to the Answer: Read the complete paragraph to best understand the context and purpose of the cited line. The correct answer will identify what the phrase helps achieve in the paragraph. At the start of the paragraph, King argues that oppressors do not willingly give more freedom to the people whom they oppress. He goes on to explain the delay tactics that have kept African Americans from winning equal rights, and concludes that oppressed peoples in other nations are winning independence while African Americans still cannot get a cup of coffee at a lunch counter. The phrase helps King underscore the contrast between these two scenarios, so **(D)** is the correct answer.

Suggested passage map notes:

Passage 1

¶1: background of Bretton Woods

¶2: created IMF to facilitate international trade

¶3: created World Bank to give loans to war affected countries, bridge rich and poor countries

¶4: BW made U.S. dollar global currency

¶5: shaped foreign trade

¶6: BW made U.S. powerful

Passage 2:

¶1: BW only lasted 3 decades, Nixon changed economic policy

¶2: BW collapsed, IMF began flexible exchange system for currency

¶3: U.S. dollar still widely used

¶4: G20 wants to create global currency

¶5–6: predicts worldwide currency, new world order in finance coming

21. B

Difficulty: Medium

Category: Inference

Getting to the Answer: Remember that you are being asked to choose an inference suggested by Passage 1, not a statement of fact. The passage notes that the U.S. dollar became a global currency that nations around the world accept for trade, leaving the United States in a stronger position to influence international markets. Choice **(B)** is the correct answer.

22. C

Difficulty: Medium

Category: Command of Evidence

Getting to the Answer: The correct choice should support your answer to the previous question. Consider which choice best shows a clear relationship with your answer to the item above. Choice **(C)** explicitly states the United States became the "primary power" behind the institutions established at Bretton Woods.

23. D

Difficulty: Medium

Category: Vocab-in-Context

Getting to the Answer: Predict an answer based on the context of the passage. The correct answer should not alter the meaning of the sentence in the passage. Then, choose the option that best fits your prediction. The passage states that the IMF gives loans to member countries to ensure their continued stability. Choice **(D)** is correct because it most closely reflects the IMF's goals of proactively promoting global economic growth and stability.

24. B

Difficulty: Medium

Category: Inference

Getting to the Answer: Locate information in the passage that accurately summarizes the purposes of both institutions. Then, ask yourself how these purposes differ. Both institutions encourage economic growth. However, Passage 1 notes that the IMF maintains payments and receipts between nations. The World Bank, on the other hand, focuses on "economic and social progress" (line 36) in individual countries. Choice **(B)** is the correct answer.

25. D

Difficulty: Hard

Category: Inference

Getting to the Answer: Eliminate any answer choices that are not suggested in the passage. Choice **(D)** is correct. The paragraph states that President Nixon's decision broke with the Bretton Woods framework. It can be reasonably inferred that the decision differed from the consensus of other nations, given the fact that many nations had agreed to Bretton Woods.

26. B

Difficulty: Medium

Category: Command of Evidence

Getting to the Answer: The answer choice should support your answer to the previous question. The paragraph states that President Nixon's decision "marked the end" of the Bretton Woods framework, which best supports the inference that the United States did not have the support of other nations. The correct answer is **(B)**.

27. A

Difficulty: Medium

Category: Vocab-in-Context

Getting to the Answer: Reread the sentence in which the word appears and decide which meaning makes the most sense in context. The sentence is referring to a new global currency that might take the place of the U.S. dollar as the major, or key, currency. Therefore, **(A)** is the correct definition of "anchor" in this context.

28. A

Difficulty: Hard

Category: Inference

Getting to the Answer: Study the yuan's percent share of use in daily trading relative to other currencies in the graphic over time. What does this suggest about global views of the yuan? Passage 2 explicitly states that the yuan is "becoming a major world reserve currency" (lines 99–100). This is supported by the data in the chart, which shows the yuan's percent share of use in daily trading climbing from 0.5 percent in 2007 to 2.2 percent in 2013. Choice **(A)** is correct.

29. B

Difficulty: Medium

Category: Inference

Getting to the Answer: Determine what purpose the final paragraph of Passage 2 serves in relation to the rest of the passage. Passage 2 is mostly about the changes to the world's financial system since the 1944 Bretton Woods Conference. The last paragraph of Passage 2 discusses a prediction about that system with which the author appears to agree. This is an opinion rather than a fact; therefore, **(B)** is correct.

30. C

Difficulty: Medium

Category: Global

Getting to the Answer: Identify the overall purpose of each passage. Then, consider which answer choice accurately describes these purposes. Choice **(C)** is the correct answer. Passage 1 focuses on the effects of Bretton Woods, while Passage 2 focuses on the reasons why the international economy may transition to a new global currency.

31. D

Difficulty: Medium

Category: Inference

Getting to the Answer: Keep in mind that the correct answer will be a statement that is evident in both passages. The role of the IMF is mentioned prominently in both passages. Therefore, **(D)** is the correct answer.

Suggested passage map notes:

> ¶1: 6 million U.S. people paralyzed; causes of paralysis
> ¶2: patient in Poland became subject of study
> ¶3: spinal cord research on rats, now used to develop treatment
> ¶4: patient responded well to treatment
> ¶5: future benefits of treatment

32. C

Difficulty: Easy

Category: Global

Getting to the Answer: Keep in mind that the correct answer will be supported by all of the information in the text rather than just a few details. The passage is concerned with one experimental treatment that doctors are exploring to help patients regain mobility. Choice **(C)** is the correct answer.

33. D

Difficulty: Medium

Category: Function

Getting to the Answer: Review the cited lines to determine how the information they present affects the reader's perception of the information that follows in the passage. Just after describing how the treatment of people with paralysis consists of retraining, the author informs the reader that a cure may be in sight. The description of retraining helps the reader understand that finding a cure is a significant leap forward. Choice **(D)** is correct.

34. B

Difficulty: Medium

Category: Inference

Getting to the Answer: Consider the main points the author makes throughout the passage. The correct answer will be directly related to these points, even if it is not directly stated in the passage. Choice **(B)** is the correct answer. It can be inferred that the author feels that increased mobility will have a positive impact on patients suffering from all levels of paralysis.

35. D

Difficulty: Easy

Category: Command of Evidence

Getting to the Answer: Locate each answer choice in the passage. Decide which one provides the best support for the answer to the previous question. In the last line of the passage, the author says that patients with paralysis "can have both their mobility and their hope restored" (lines 71–72). Thus, **(D)** offers the strongest support for the answer to the previous question.

36. D

Difficulty: Easy

Category: Vocab-in-Context

Getting to the Answer: The correct answer will not only be a synonym for "restricted" but will also make sense in the context of the sentence in the passage. Eliminate answers, such as (A), that are synonyms for "restricted" but do not make sense in context. Here, the author is explaining that patients in wheelchairs must learn to prevent complications from restricted movement. In this context, "restricted" most nearly means "limited," answer choice **(D)**.

37. A

Difficulty: Hard

Category: Function

Getting to the Answer: Locate lines 46–47 in the passage and then read the paragraph that comes before them. This will help you identify why the author chose "tailor-made" to describe the patient's treatment. The patient received his own cells during the treatment, meaning that the treatment was tailored to his own body. Choice **(A)** fits this situation and is therefore the correct answer.

38. C

Difficulty: Hard

Category: Inference

Getting to the Answer: Remember that when a question is asking you to infer something, the answer is not stated explicitly in the passage. In paragraph 2, the author explains that the patient who received the experimental treatment had not seen an increase in mobility despite "countless hours" (line 23) of physical therapy. Therefore, it is logical to infer that the patient would not have regained mobility without this experimental treatment. Choice **(C)** is the correct answer.

39. B

Difficulty: Medium

Category: Command of Evidence

Getting to the Answer: Think about how you selected the correct answer for the previous question. Use that information to help you choose the correct answer to this question. In paragraph 2, the author explains that the patient selected for the experimental treatment had not regained mobility despite intensive physical therapy. This provides the strongest support for the answer to the previous question, so **(B)** is correct.

40. B

Difficulty: Easy

Category: Vocab-in-Context

Getting to the Answer: Substitute each of the answer choices for "refined." Select the one that makes the most sense in context and does not change the meaning of the sentence. In this context, "refined" most nearly means "improved." Choice **(B)** is the correct answer.

41. C

Difficulty: Easy

Category: Inference

Getting to the Answer: Skim the passage and look for details about how doctors came to use the treatment described. In paragraph 3, the author explains that the doctors used a technique that was developed during years of research on rats. Therefore, **(C)** is the correct answer.

Practice Tests

42. D

Difficulty: Medium

Category: Inference

Getting to the Answer: Compare and contrast each answer choice with the procedure described in the passage. As in the procedure described in the passage, skin transplants for burn victims involve taking tissue containing healthy cells from one area of the body and using it to repair damage done to another area. Choice **(D)** is the correct answer.

Suggested passage map notes:

¶1: what mercury is, uses for mercury

¶2: causes of mercury pollution

¶3: water affected by mercury, issue for many organisms

¶4: consumption of mercury-laden seafood, risks and benefits

¶5: explanation of safe levels of mercury based on bodyweight and fish type

¶6: nutritionists' recommendations

43. C

Difficulty: Medium

Category: Inference

Getting to the Answer: The correct answer will be directly supported by the evidence in the passage. Avoid answers like (A) and (B) that go beyond what can logically be inferred about the author. The author explains how mercury gets into the fish that humans eat and goes on to say that it is possible to eat fish that contain mercury without getting mercury poisoning. Choice **(C)** is the correct answer because it is directly supported by the evidence in the passage.

44. D

Difficulty: Medium

Category: Command of Evidence

Getting to the Answer: The correct answer will provide direct support for the answer to the previous question. Avoid answers like (B) that include relevant details but do not provide direct support. In the last paragraph, the author says that nutritionists recommend eating low-mercury fish instead of eliminating fish altogether,

adding that an awareness of the issues with mercury can help us make healthy eating choices. This statement supports the answer to the previous question, so **(D)** is the correct answer.

45. A

Difficulty: Easy

Category: Detail

Getting to the Answer: Review the details provided in the passage about how to determine a safe level of mercury consumption. In paragraph 5, the author explains that humans should consume less than 0.1 microgram of mercury for every kilogram of their own weight. Therefore, **(A)** is the correct answer.

46. C

Difficulty: Easy

Category: Vocab-in-Context

Getting to the Answer: Eliminate answer choices that are synonyms for "concentration" but do not make sense in context. In this sentence, the author is describing the amount of mercury in the air from power plants. "Concentration" most nearly means "density" in this context, so **(C)** is the correct answer.

47. A

Difficulty: Medium

Category: Inference

Getting to the Answer: Eliminate any answer choices that are not directly supported by information in the passage. The passage strongly suggests that it is impossible to avoid exposure to mercury. Therefore, **(A)** is the correct answer.

48. B

Difficulty: Easy

Category: Command of Evidence

Getting to the Answer: Locate each of the answer choices in the passage. The correct answer should provide support for the answer to the previous question. In paragraph 1, the author explains that mercury can be found in many places. This supports the conclusion that it is impossible to avoid mercury completely. Choice **(B)** is the correct answer.

49. C

Difficulty: Hard

Category: Function

Getting to the Answer: Think about how the process paragraph 3 describes relates to the rest of the passage. Paragraph 3 describes the process by which larger organisms absorb mercury by eating smaller organisms. This information is necessary to understanding why larger fish have the highest mercury levels. Choice **(C)** is correct.

50. D

Difficulty: Hard

Category: Inference

Getting to the Answer: Consider one of the central ideas of the passage. The correct answer would help provide additional support for this idea. One central idea in the passage is that people can eat fish if they know what mercury levels are safe for human consumption. The author states that scientists have determined safe mercury levels by studying at what point symptoms of mercury poisoning occur. However, the author only provides one example weight of how many micrograms of mercury a person could eat. Therefore, **(D)** is the correct answer.

51. B

Difficulty: Easy

Category: Vocab-in-Context

Getting to the Answer: Reread the sentence and replace "particulars" with each answer choice. Though the answer choices are similar in meaning to a certain degree, one of them makes the most sense when substituted for "particulars." In this context, "particulars" most nearly means "specifics"; therefore, **(B)** is the correct answer.

52. D

Difficulty: Hard

Category: Inference

Getting to the Answer: Remember that the correct answer will be supported by information in both the passage and the graphic. Refer to the passage to draw conclusions about the information in the graphic. The passage states that it is safe to eat fish that contain mercury as long as certain guidelines are followed regarding daily consumption. The graphic shows that Alaskan pollock has the lowest concentration of mercury of the fish listed. Therefore, **(D)** is the correct answer; a person can safely eat more Alaskan pollock than black-striped bass in one day.

Writing and Language Test

1. C

Difficulty: Medium

Category: Sentence Structure: Commas, Dashes, and Colons

Getting to the Answer: Examine the passage to determine whether the current punctuation is incorrect. Then consider which set of punctuation marks correctly emphasizes the selected part of the sentence. The dashes provide emphasis for the idea that the UN is a peacekeeping organization; the dashes help set off this part of the sentence from the remaining content. The correct answer is **(C)**.

2. D

Difficulty: Hard

Category: Development: Introductions and Conclusions

Getting to the Answer: Review the main points made so far. The correct answer should touch on or summarize previous ideas in the paragraph. Choice **(D)** is correct. This concluding sentence effectively summarizes the ideas that compose the paragraph's main claim.

3. A

Difficulty: Medium

Category: Organization: Transitions

Getting to the Answer: Read the previous paragraph and identify the word or phrase that is the best transition between the two paragraphs. The previous paragraph describes the UN today, and the paragraph beginning with the phrase in question explains the origins of the UN in the 1940s. Choice **(A)** indicates the correct shift in time period and provides the most effective transition between paragraphs.

4. A

Difficulty: Medium

Category: Agreement: Verbs

Getting to the Answer: Pay close attention to the context of the previous sentence to help you establish the correct verb tense for this particular sentence. The correct answer is **(A)**. It uses the present tense to logically follow the previous sentence that refers to the UN in the present tense as well.

5. B

Difficulty: Easy

Category: Sentence Structure: The Basics

Getting to the Answer: Watch out for choices that may create a run-on sentence. The correct choice is **(B)**, which provides a clear separation between one complete sentence and the next.

6. C

Difficulty: Easy

Category: Development: Word Choice

Getting to the Answer: Substitute each choice in the complete paragraph. The correct answer will most appropriately fit within the context of the sentence and the paragraph. The correct answer is **(C)**. The UN encourages, or promotes, environmental protection.

7. A

Difficulty: Medium

Category: Development: Introductions and Conclusions

Getting to the Answer: The correct choice should introduce a central idea that is supported by subsequent sentences in the paragraph. The correct answer is **(A)**. The expansion of the UN's budget, goals, and personnel number connects to specific evidence in the rest of the paragraph.

8. C

Difficulty: Medium

Category: Graphs

Getting to the Answer: Notice that the graphic gives specific information about the increases and decreases in the UN peacekeeping force over a period of time. Study the answer choices to find the one that best relates to the paragraph while using accurate

information from the graphic. The graphic shows data through the year 2010 and does not indicate that personnel levels rose above 100,000. Choice **(C)** is the correct answer.

9. A

Difficulty: Medium

Category: Conciseness

Getting to the Answer: Watch out for unnecessarily wordy choices like (B). The correct answer is **(A)** because it effectively communicates an idea without additional words that distract from the content.

10. C

Difficulty: Easy

Category: Development: Word Choice

Getting to the Answer: Look at the context of the sentence in which the word appears as well as the paragraph itself to choose the answer that works best. Choice **(C)**, "noteworthy," is synonymous with *worth mentioning*, which clearly fits within the context of the paragraph and the author's intent to highlight the accomplishments of the UN.

11. B

Difficulty: Medium

Category: Development: Revising Text

Getting to the Answer: Read the entire paragraph. Identify the sentence that is least relevant to the paragraph's topic and purpose. The purpose of this paragraph is to sum up the central ideas of the passage. Choice **(B)** introduces a detail that, while important, does not summarize the central ideas of the passage and therefore detracts from the paragraph's focus.

12. B

Difficulty: Easy

Category: Agreement: Verbs

Getting to the Answer: Read the sentence and notice that the verb in question is in a clause with intervening prepositional phrases that come between the subject and the verb. Check to see what the subject is and whether the verb agrees with the subject. The verb "match" is in a plural form, but the subject is "DNA," not one of the other nouns in the prepositional phrases. "DNA" is singular. Choice **(B)** is the correct answer

Practice Tests

because it is the singular form of the verb *to match*.

13. A

Difficulty: Medium

Category: Sentence Structure: The Basics

Getting to the Answer: Read the sentence to determine whether the two clauses separated by the semicolon are independent or not. If they are both independent, a semicolon is the appropriate punctuation. Be careful of answer choices with inappropriate transition words. A semicolon is the correct way to separate two independent but related clauses, so **(A)** is the correct answer.

14. B

Difficulty: Easy

Category: Sentence Structure: Commas, Dashes, and Colons

Getting to the Answer: Study the words in a series and see where a comma might need to be inserted or eliminated. Choice **(B)** is correct.

15. B

Difficulty: Hard

Category: Organization: Transitions

Getting to the Answer: When you see an underlined transition, identify how the sentence relates to the previous one to determine what kind of transition is appropriate. Choice **(B)** is correct because the sentence to which the transition belongs provides more detail about a general statement that preceded it.

16. D

Difficulty: Easy

Category: Development: Word Choice

Getting to the Answer: Imagine that the sentence has a blank where the word in question is. Read the entire paragraph for context and predict what word could complete the blank. Review the answer choices to find the word closest in meaning to your prediction. The paragraph later states that Jane Saunders's goal is to separate the two strands of DNA. Only answer choice **(D)** has the correct connotation and fits within the context of the sentence.

17. C

Difficulty: Medium

Category: Conciseness

Getting to the Answer: It is important to combine sentences in order to vary sentence structures. But the correct choice should not only be the most effective way to combine the two sentences, it must also be in parallel construction with the first sentence. Watch out for choices that may have incorrect transition words as well. Choice **(C)** is the correct answer. It joins the sentences concisely and correctly because the verb "adding" is in parallel construction with the earlier verbs "detaching" and "transferring." The subject in both sentences is the same, "she," so it can be dropped when combining the two sentences.

18. A

Difficulty: Medium

Category: Development: Introductions and Conclusions

Getting to the Answer: Read the entire paragraph and then put each answer choice at the beginning. Choose the one that makes the most sense and is further explained by subsequent details in the paragraph. The paragraph discusses the process of identifying DNA, which is lengthy and involves changing the temperature of the DNA several times. Choice **(A)** is closest to this summation of what is to follow and is the correct answer.

19. C

Difficulty: Easy

Category: Conciseness

Getting to the Answer: Watch out for choices that are wordy or redundant. Choice **(C)** is the most concise and effective way of stating the information in the passage.

20. A

Difficulty: Medium

Category: Organization: Sentence Placement

Getting to the Answer: Consider the function of this sentence. At what point in the paragraph should this function be employed? The sentence is setting the scene, so it should be placed where it is now, at the beginning of the paragraph. To place it later would make the meaning of the paragraph unclear. Choice **(A)** is the correct answer.

Practice Tests

21. B

Difficulty: Easy

Category: Development: Word Choice

Getting to the Answer: Think about the connotations of each answer choice and be sure to pick the one that fits with the context of the sentence. Substitute each answer choice for the word to see which word works best. "Eager" best reflects how the detectives would be feeling while waiting for important test results. They would be eagerly anticipating this important information and would want it as quickly as possible. Choice **(B)** is the correct answer.

22. C

Difficulty: Hard

Category: Development: Introductions and Conclusions

Getting to the Answer: Decide which sentence sounds like the most appropriate way to conclude the passage. The rhetorical question currently in the passage, choice (A), introduces an opinion that the passage never reveals; there is no sign that Jane Saunders would feel this way. Likewise, there is no indication in the passage of how expensive modern DNA analysis is, choice (B) nor that Saunders marvels about how far science has come in DNA analysis, choice (D). Choice **(C)** is the correct answer; it presents a fairly natural way for Saunders to feel given her accomplishments for the day.

23. C

Difficulty: Medium

Category: Sentence Structure: The Basics

Getting to the Answer: Check to see whether there are two independent clauses within this sentence. Two independent clauses without punctuation indicate a run-on sentence. As written, this is a run-on sentence. Choice **(C)** is the correct answer because it separates the two complete but related thoughts with a semicolon.

24. A

Difficulty: Medium

Category: Development: Introductions and Conclusions

Getting to the Answer: Eliminate answers that might contain details related to the central idea but do not properly express the central idea. This paragraph is mostly about the characteristics of people who are successful entrepreneurs. Choice **(A)** is the correct

answer because it introduces the main idea by summarizing the traits people must have to achieve success as a business owner.

25. B

Difficulty: Hard

Category: Development: Word Choice

Getting to the Answer: Eliminate answers such as (D) that mean nearly the same thing as "grab" but do not clarify the meaning of the sentence. In this context, "derive" best clarifies the meaning of the sentence, which explains how entrepreneurs get ideas for their businesses. Choice **(B)** is the correct answer.

26. C

Difficulty: Easy

Category: Agreement: Verbs

Getting to the Answer: Read the rest of the paragraph and pay attention to the verb tense used. The verbs in the rest of this paragraph are in past tense. "Graduated" is the past tense of the verb *to graduate*, so **(C)** is the correct answer.

27. C

Difficulty: Medium

Category: Sentence Structure: Commas, Dashes, and Colons

Getting to the Answer: Examine the structure of the whole sentence. Consider whether the punctuation is correct or even necessary. The subject of this sentence is "he," and it is followed by a compound predicate containing the verbs "built" and "founded." When a compound predicate contains only two items, a comma should not separate either verb from the subject. No punctuation is necessary, so **(C)** is the correct answer.

28. A

Difficulty: Medium

Category: Development: Word Choice

Getting to the Answer: Replace the underlined word with each answer choice. Consider which word makes the most sense in context and conveys the clearest meaning. The sentence discusses how Vital began her own business. In this context, "launch" conveys the most precise meaning because it connotes the start of a major endeavor. Choice **(A)** is the correct answer because no change is needed.

29. D

Difficulty: Easy

Category: Sentence Structure: Commas, Dashes, and Colons

Getting to the Answer: This sentence contains a list of items in a series. Think about the rules of punctuation for items in a series. Items in a series should be separated by commas, with a comma following each word except the last item in the series. The word "and" is not an item in the series and, therefore, should not be followed by a comma. Therefore, **(D)** is the correct answer.

30. D

Difficulty: Easy

Category: Sentence Structure: Commas, Dashes, and Colons

Getting to the Answer: Identify the main elements of this sentence, such as the subject, predicate, and any restrictive or nonrestrictive clauses. Remember that a nonrestrictive clause should be set off with a comma. The clause "always seeking a new challenge" is nonrestrictive and should be set off from the rest of the sentence with a comma. Choice **(D)** is the correct answer.

31. C

Difficulty: Hard

Category: Development: Relevance

Getting to the Answer: Identify the central idea of the paragraph. Read each answer choice and consider which sentence could be added to the paragraph to provide support for the central idea you identified. This paragraph is mostly about Chris Roth, an entrepreneur who now has several companies. **(C)** is the correct answer because it provides specific details about one of the companies Roth owns.

32. B

Difficulty: Easy

Category: Agreement: Verbs

Getting to the Answer: Read the entire sentence. Identify the subject and determine whether it is plural or singular. Determine the correct verb tense for the sentence. The subject of this sentence is plural (Gomez, Vital, and Roth), so the verb must be plural as well. **(B)** is the correct answer because "agree" is the plural present tense of the verb "to agree."

33. B

Difficulty: Easy

Category: Agreement: Pronouns

Getting to the Answer: Read the entire sentence and identify the antecedent for the underlined pronoun. The correct answer will be the pronoun that is in agreement with the antecedent. In this sentence, the antecedent is "entrepreneurs," which requires a third-person plural pronoun. Therefore, **(B)** is the correct answer.

34. C

Difficulty: Medium

Category: Organization: Transitions

Getting to the Answer: Read the two sentences connected by the underlined portion and decide which answer choice creates a grammatically correct and logical sentence. Choice **(C)** is correct. Using the coordinating conjunction "but" with a comma to combine the sentences shows that the second portion, which mentions Varèse as being unique, stands in contrast to the first portion, which mentions many influential artists. The other options, featuring "and" and "or," do not show this necessary contrast.

35. A

Difficulty: Hard

Category: Sentence Structure: The Basics

Getting to the Answer: Reread the entire sentence to assess how the punctuation in the answer choices affects how each portion of the sentence relates to one another. The correct answer is **(A)**. The semicolon correctly links the two independent clauses that have a direct relationship with one another.

36. D

Difficulty: Medium

Category: Development: Word Choice

Getting to the Answer: Read the sentence for context clues and think about the author's intention. Then, determine which answer provides the most appropriate word choice. "Employ" is the only word that matches the meaning of the sentence, which states that Varèse did not use traditional melodies. Thus, choice **(D)** is correct.

37. B

Difficulty: Medium

Category: Sentence Structure: Commas, Dashes, and Colons

Getting to the Answer: Reread the sentence to determine how each portion relates to the others. Then, examine how the punctuation in the answer choices affects these relationships. The portion of the sentence discussing the family's move to Italy is an introductory element and needs a comma to offset it from the rest of the sentence. The portion discussing what Varèse learned in Turin is a parenthetical element and also requires a comma. Therefore, choice **(B)** is correct.

38. A

Difficulty: Medium

Category: Agreement: Modifiers

Getting to the Answer: Review the sentence for context clues and to assess the subject's ownership of the objects in the sentence. Then, determine which form of the possessive noun correctly reflects this ownership. The hands in the sentence belong to a single player using a single theremin; therefore, the correct answer will use the singular possessive noun "player's." Choice **(A)** is correct.

39. B

Difficulty: Medium

Category: Development: Word Choice

Getting to the Answer: Read the sentence for context clues. Decide on the answer choice that makes the sentence's meaning precise and clear. "Conjunction" is the only word that relates to two things occurring at the same time to create a single outcome, which is the intended meaning of the sentence. Choice **(B)** is correct.

40. A

Difficulty: Hard

Category: Development: Relevance

Getting to the Answer: Assess the central idea of the introductory sentence in the paragraph and determine which additional fact noted in the answer choices would have the greatest benefit to the reader. The introductory sentence states that Varèse worked in New York until he secured his first success. Describing the critical reaction to the next event mentioned would help strengthen the idea that the Philadelphia performance was a successful event in Varèse's career. Choice **(A)** is the correct answer.

41. A

Difficulty: Hard

Category: Agreement: Verbs

Getting to the Answer: Consider what kind of situation the author is presenting here and decide which tense of the verb "has" creates a grammatically correct sentence that reflects this meaning. Keep in mind the time of the events in the sentence. The sentence imagines a situation in which Varèse had been able to use the Internet, an unrealistic action. The double "had had" is correct; it describes past-tense actions that might have occurred in the past but didn't. Choice **(A)** is correct.

42. D

Difficulty: Easy

Category: Agreement: Pronouns

Getting to the Answer: Read the entire sentence to figure out who is the owner of the burned compositions. Then, select the proper personal pronoun for this antecedent. Choice **(D)** is the correct singular possessive pronoun because the burned compositions belonged to Varèse, one person, and not a group of artists.

43. B

Difficulty: Medium

Category: Graphs

Getting to the Answer: Study the information in the graphic to determine which answer choice most accurately finishes the sentence. Choice **(B)** is correct because it accurately reflects information included in the graphic.

44. C

Difficulty: Medium

Category: Development: Introductions and Conclusions

Getting to the Answer: After reading the final paragraph, examine each answer choice to determine which best summarizes the paragraph's overall message. Choice **(C)** is correct. It is the one sentence that sets up the idea that Varèse's challenging work has been an inspiration to many later artists, an idea supported by the rest of the paragraph.

Math Test—No Calculator

1. A

Difficulty: Easy

Category: Heart of Algebra/Linear Equations

Getting to the Answer: You could start by cross-multiplying to get rid of the denominators, but simplifying the numerators first will make the calculations easier. Don't forget to distribute the negative to both terms in the parentheses on the right-hand side of the equation:

$$\frac{4(n-2)+5}{2} = \frac{13-(9+4n)}{4}$$
$$\frac{4n-8+5}{2} = \frac{13-9-4n}{4}$$
$$\frac{4n-3}{2} = \frac{4-4n}{4}$$
$$4(4n-3) = 2(4-4n)$$
$$16n-12 = 8-8n$$
$$16n = 20-8n$$
$$24n = 20$$
$$n = \frac{20}{24} = \frac{5}{6}$$

Choice **(A)** is correct.

2. C

Difficulty: Easy

Category: Passport to Advanced Math/Rational Expressions

Getting to the Answer: Don't be tempted—you can't simply cancel one term when a polynomial is divided by a monomial. You can, however, split the expression into three terms, each with a denominator of $9x^2$, and simplify. You could also use polynomial long division to answer the question. Use whichever method gets you to the answer more quickly on test day. For example:

$$\frac{18x^3+9x^2-36x}{9x^2} = \frac{18x^3}{9x^2} + \frac{9x^2}{9x^2} - \frac{36x}{9x^2}$$
$$= 2x+1-\frac{4}{x}$$

Choice **(C)** is correct.

3. B

Difficulty: Easy

Category: Passport to Advanced Math/Functions

Getting to the Answer: When using function notation, $f(x)$ is simply another way of saying y, so this question is asking you to find the value(s) of x for which $y = 0$, or in other words, where the graph crosses the x-axis. Don't be tempted by the flat parts of the graph—they have a slope of 0, but the function itself does not equal 0 here (it equals -4). The graph crosses the x-axis at the points $(-1, 0)$ and $(1, 0)$, so the values of x for which $f(x) = 0$ are -1 and 1. **(B)** is correct.

4. B

Difficulty: Easy

Category: Passport to Advanced Math/Functions

Getting to the Answer: Your only choice for this question is to compare each statement to the graph. Cross out false statements as you go. A function is decreasing when the slope is negative; it is increasing when the slope is positive. You can see from the graph that the trend is decreasing (going down from left to right), so eliminate (A) and (C). Now, take a closer look to see that there are some time intervals over which the function increases (goes up), so you can't say that the function in decreasing for *all t* such that $1977 < t < 2013$. You can only make a general statement about the nature of the function, like the one in **(B)**. The right-hand side of the graph is lower than the left side, so the function is decreasing overall.

5. C

Difficulty: Medium

Category: Heart of Algebra/Inequalities

Getting to the Answer: You don't need to use algebra to answer this question, and you also don't need to graph each system. Instead, think about how the graphs would look. The only time a system of linear inequalities has no solution is when it consists of two parallel lines shaded in opposite directions. All the inequalities are written in slope-intercept form, so look for parallel lines (two lines that have the same slope but different y-intercepts). The slopes in (A) are different ($m = 1$ and $m = 2$), so eliminate this choice. The same is true for (B) ($m = 1$ and $m = -1$) and (D) ($m = -1$ and $m = 1$). This means **(C)** must be correct ($m = 1$ and $m = 1$, $b = 1$ and $b = -1$).

The graph of the system is shown here:

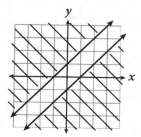

Because the shading never overlaps, the system has no solution.

6.　B

Difficulty: Medium

Category: Passport to Advanced Math/Quadratics

Getting to the Answer: Although this question asks where the graphs intersect, it is not necessary to actually graph them. The point(s) at which the two graphs intersect are the points where the two equations are equal to each other. Therefore, set the equations equal and use algebra to solve for x. Because the question only asks for the x-values, you don't need to substitute the results back into the equations to solve for y:

$$-2x + 1 = 2x^2 + 5x + 4$$
$$-2x = 2x^2 + 5x + 3$$
$$0 = 2x^2 + 7x + 3$$
$$0 = (2x + 1)(x + 3)$$

Now that the equation is factored, solve for x:

$$2x + 1 = 0 \quad \text{and} \quad x + 3 = 0$$
$$2x = -1 \qquad\qquad x = -3$$
$$x = -\frac{1}{2}$$

Choice **(B)** is correct.

7.　D

Difficulty: Medium

Category: Heart of Algebra/Linear Equations

Getting to the Answer: You can approach this question conceptually or concretely. When dealing with simple transformations, drawing a quick sketch is most likely the safest approach. You are only concerned about the y-intercept, so keep your focus there. When the graph is

reflected over the x-axis, the y-intercept will go from $(0, -1)$ to $(0, 1)$. Next, the line is shifted up 3 units, which adds 3 to the y-coordinates of all the points on the line, making the new y-intercept $(0, 4)$. Choice **(D)** is correct, as shown in the sketch below:

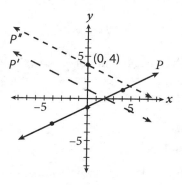

8.　D

Difficulty: Medium

Category: Passport to Advanced Math/Quadratics

Getting to the Answer: The roots of an equation are the same as its solutions. Take a peek at the answer choices—they contain radicals, which tells you that the equation can't be factored. Instead, either complete the square or solve the equation using the quadratic formula, whichever you are most comfortable with. The equation is already written in the form $y = ax^2 + bx + c$, and the coefficients are fairly small, so using the quadratic formula is probably the quickest method. Jot down the values that you'll need: $a = 3$, $b = -6$, and $c = -5$. Then, substitute these values into the quadratic formula and simplify:

$$x = \frac{-b \pm \sqrt{b^2 - 4ac}}{2a}$$
$$= \frac{-(-6) \pm \sqrt{(-6)^2 - 4(3)(-5)}}{2(3)}$$
$$= \frac{6 \pm \sqrt{36 + 60}}{6}$$
$$= \frac{6 \pm \sqrt{96}}{6}$$

This is not one of the answer choices, so simplify the radical. To do this, look for a perfect square that divides into 96 and take its square root. Then, if possible, cancel any factors that are common to the numerator and the denominator:

Practice Tests

$$x = \frac{6 \pm \sqrt{16 \times 6}}{6}$$

$$= \frac{6 \pm 4\sqrt{6}}{6}$$

$$= \frac{\cancel{2}(3 \pm 2\sqrt{6})}{\cancel{2}(3)}$$

$$= \frac{3 \pm 2\sqrt{6}}{3}$$

Choice **(D)** is correct. Be careful—you can't simplify the answer any further because you cannot divide the square root of 6 by 3.

9. A

Difficulty: Medium

Category: Passport to Advanced Math/Exponents

Getting to the Answer: When you write an equation in terms of a specific variable, you are simply solving the equation for that variable. To do this, you'll need to use the property that raising a quantity to the one-fourth power is the same as taking its fourth root and that applying a negative exponent to a quantity is the same as writing its reciprocal. Rewrite the equation using these properties and then solve for n using inverse operations. Note that the inverse of taking a fourth root of a quantity is raising the quantity to the fourth power:

$$m = \frac{1}{n^{-\frac{1}{4}}}$$

$$m = \frac{\sqrt[4]{n}}{1}$$

$$(m)^4 = \left(\sqrt[4]{n}\right)^4$$

$$m^4 = n$$

Choice **(A)** is correct.

10. C

Difficulty: Medium

Category: Heart of Algebra/Systems of Linear Equations

Getting to the Answer: When a system consists of two equations already written in terms of y, the quickest way to solve the system is to set the equations equal to each other and then use inverse operations. Don't let the fraction intimidate you—you can write the first equation as a fraction over 1 and use cross-multiplication:

$$\frac{3x - 1}{1} = \frac{5x + 8}{2}$$

$$2(3x - 1) = 5x + 8$$

$$6x - 2 = 5x + 8$$

$$6x = 5x + 10$$

$$x = 10$$

Don't let (A) fool you—the question is asking for the value of y, not the value of x. To find y, substitute 10 for x in either equation and simplify:

$$y = 3(10) - 1$$

$$= 30 - 1$$

$$= 29$$

Choice **(C)** is correct.

11. A

Difficulty: Medium

Category: Heart of Algebra/Inequalities

Getting to the Answer: You don't need to separate this compound inequality into pieces. Just remember, whatever you do to one piece, you must do to all three pieces. The fractions in this question make it look more complicated than it really is, so start by clearing them. To do this, multiply everything by the least common denominator, 10:

$$0 < \frac{d}{2} + 1 \le \frac{8}{5}$$

$$10(0) < 10\left(\frac{d}{2} + 1\right) \le \left(\frac{8}{5}\right)10$$

$$0 < 5d + 10 \le 16$$

$$-10 < 5d \le 6$$

$$-2 < d \le \frac{6}{5}$$

Now, read the inequality symbols carefully. The value of d is between -2 and $\frac{6}{5}$, not including -2 because of the $<$ symbol, so **(A)** is the correct answer. Don't let (C) fool you—you can't have a 0 *denominator* in a rational expression, but in this expression, the variable is in the numerator, so it *can* equal 0.

12. A

Difficulty: Medium

Category: Additional Topics in Math/Trigonometry

Getting to the Answer: The measure of 40° does not appear on the unit circle, which should give you a clue that there must be a property or relationship on which you can rely to help you answer the question. Complementary angles have a special relationship relative to trig values: the cosine of an acute angle is equal to the sine of the angle's complement and vice versa. Because only one of the answers can be correct, look for the simplest relationship (complementary angles): $50°$ is complementary to $40°$, so $\cos 40° = \sin 50°$, which means **(A)** is correct.

13. D

Difficulty: Medium

Category: Heart of Algebra/Linear Equations

Getting to the Answer: Assign a variable to the unknown and then create an equation that represents the scenario. Let n be the number of units the manufacturer sells in a month. Sales must equal expenses for the manufacturer to break even (sales $=$ expenses). The sales are equal to the selling price ($\$9.50$) times the number of units sold (n), so write $9.5n$ on one side of the equal sign. The monthly expenses are the fixed expenses ($\$11,625$) plus the amount paid for the materials needed to produce one unit ($\$4.85$) times the number of units (n), so write $11,625 + 4.85n$ on the other side of the equal sign. Then, solve for n:

$$9.5n = 11,625 + 4.85n$$
$$4.65n = 11,625$$
$$n = 2,500$$

Choice **(D)** is correct.

14. D

Difficulty: Medium

Category: Heart of Algebra/Linear Equations

Getting to the Answer: There is only one equation given and it has two variables. This means that you don't have enough information to solve for either variable. Instead, look for the relationship between the left side of the equation and the other expression that you are trying to find. The expression you are trying to find ($6x - 5y$) has the x-term first and then the y-term, so start by reversing the order of the terms on the left side of the given equation. Also, notice that the x term in $6x - 5y$ is not negative, so multiply the equation by -1:

$$\frac{1}{2}y - \frac{3}{5}x = -16 \quad \rightarrow \quad -\frac{3}{5}x + \frac{1}{2}y = -16$$
$$-1\left(-\frac{3}{5}x + \frac{1}{2}y = -16\right) \quad \rightarrow \quad \frac{3}{5}x - \frac{1}{2}y = 16$$

Finally, there are no fractions in the desired expression, so clear the fractions by multiplying both sides of the equation by 10. This yields the expression that you are looking for, so no further work is required—just read the value on the right-hand side of the equation, which is 160:

$$10\left(\frac{3}{5}x - \frac{1}{2}y\right) = 16(10)$$
$$6x - 5y = 160$$

Choice **(D)** is correct.

15. B

Difficulty: Medium

Category: Passport to Advanced Math/Functions

Getting to the Answer: Understanding the language of functions will make questions that seem complicated much more doable. When you know the output of a function (or in this question, a composition of two functions), you can work backward to find the input. Because $g(x)$ is the inside function for this composition, its output becomes the input for $f(x)$. Unfortunately, you don't have any information about g yet. You do know, however, that f of some number, $g(2)$, is -1, so set $f(x)$ equal to -1 and solve for x:

$$-1 = x + 1$$
$$-2 = x$$

You now know that $f(-2) = -1$. In the equation for the composition, $g(2)$ represents x, so you also know that $g(2)$ must be -2. Your only option now is to use brute force to determine which equation for g, when evaluated at 2, results in -2.

(A): $g(2) = 2 - 6 = -4$ (not -2), eliminate.

(B): $g(2) = 2 - 4 = -2$

You don't need to go any further; **(B)** is correct.

You could check your answer by working forward, starting with $g(2)$:

$$g(2) = 2 - 4 = -2$$
$$f(g(2)) = f(-2) = -2 + 1 = -1$$

Practice Tests

16. 1/5 or .2

Difficulty: Medium

Category: Heart of Algebra/Linear Equations

Getting to the Answer: There are two variables but only one equation, so you can't actually solve the equation for k. Instead, recall that an equation has infinitely many solutions when the left side is identical to the right side. When this happens, everything cancels out and you get $0 = 0$, which is always true. Start by simplifying the right-hand side of the equation. Don't simplify the left side because k is already in a good position:

$$k(10x-5) = 2(3+x)-7$$
$$k(10x-5) = 6+2x-7$$
$$k(10x-5) = 2x-1$$

Next, compare the left side of the equation to the right side. Rather than distributing the k, notice that $2x$ is a fifth of $10x$ and -1 is a fifth of -5, so if k were $\frac{1}{5}$ (or 0.2), then both sides of the equation would equal $2x - 1$, and it would therefore have infinitely many solutions. Thus, k is **1/5 or .2**. Grid in either of these responses.

17. 2

Difficulty: Medium

Category: Additional Topics in Math/Geometry

Getting to the Answer: You could use the Pythagorean theorem to solve this, but it will save valuable time on test day if you recognize that this question is testing your knowledge of Pythagorean triples. The triangle is a right triangle with leg lengths of 18 and 24, which, when divided by 6, are in the proportion 3:4. This means that the triangle is a scaled up 3:4:5 right triangle with a scale factor of 6. To keep the same proportion, the hypotenuse must be $5 \times 6 = 30$. For $15n$ to equal 30, n must be **2**.

18. 3

Difficulty: Hard

Category: Passport to Advanced Math/Exponents

Getting to the Answer: You need to use rules of exponents to simplify the expression. Before you can do that, you must rewrite the radicals as fraction exponents. Use the phrase "power over root" to help you convert the radicals: $\sqrt{x} = \sqrt[\text{root}\rightarrow 2]{x^{1\leftarrow\text{power}}} = x^{\frac{1}{2}}$ and $\sqrt[\text{root}\rightarrow 4]{x^{3\leftarrow\text{power}}} = x^{\frac{3}{4}}$. Then, use rules of exponents to simplify the expression. Add the exponents of the factors that are being multiplied and subtract the exponent of the factor that is being divided:

$$\frac{\sqrt{x}\cdot x^{\frac{5}{4}}\cdot x^2}{\sqrt[4]{x^3}} = \frac{x^{\frac{1}{2}}\cdot x^{\frac{5}{4}}\cdot x^{\frac{2}{1}}}{x^{\frac{3}{4}}}$$
$$= x^{\frac{1}{2}+\frac{5}{4}+\frac{2}{1}-\frac{3}{4}} = x^{\frac{2}{4}+\frac{5}{4}+\frac{8}{4}-\frac{3}{4}} = x^{\frac{12}{4}} = x^3$$

The exponent of the simplified expression is **3**.

19. 27

Difficulty: Hard

Category: Additional Topics in Math/Imaginary Numbers

Getting to the Answer: Each of the factors in this product has two terms, so they behave like binomials. This means you can use FOIL to find the product. To avoid messy numbers, simplify the two radicals first using the definition of i. Write each of the numbers under the radicals as a product of -1 and the number, take the square roots, and then FOIL the resulting expressions:

$$\left(3+\sqrt{-16}\right)\left(1-\sqrt{-36}\right) = \left(3+\sqrt{16\times(-1)}\right)\left(1-\sqrt{36\times(-1)}\right)$$
$$= (3+4i)(1-6i)$$
$$= 3-18i+4i-24i^2$$
$$= 3-14i-24(-1)$$
$$= 3-14i+24$$
$$= 27-14i$$

The question asks for the value of a (the real part of the expression), so the correct answer is **27**.

Practice Tests

20. 6

Difficulty: Hard

Category: Passport to Advanced Math/Quadratics

Getting to the Answer: When you are given the graph of a parabola, try to use what you know about intercepts, the vertex, and the axis of symmetry to answer the question. Here, you could try to use points from the graph to find its equation, but this is not necessary because the question only asks for the value of b. As a shortcut, recall that you can find the vertex of a parabola using the formula $x = -\dfrac{b}{2a}$ (the quadratic formula without the radical part). You are given that $a = -1$. Now, look at the graph—the vertex of the parabola is $(3, 8)$, so substitute 3 for x, -1 for a, and solve for b:

$$3 = -\frac{b}{2(-1)}$$

$$3 = -\left(\frac{b}{-2}\right)$$

$$3 = \frac{b}{2}$$

$$3(2) = b$$

$$6 = b$$

As an alternate method, you could plug the value of a and the vertex (from the graph) into vertex form of a quadratic equation and simplify:

$$y = a(x - h)^2 + k$$
$$= -1(x - 3)^2 + 8$$
$$= -1\left(x^2 - 6x + 9\right) + 8$$
$$= -x^2 + 6x - 9 + 8$$
$$= -x^2 + 6x - 1$$

The coefficient of x is b, so $b = \mathbf{6}$.

Math Test—Calculator

1. D

Difficulty: Easy

Category: Heart of Algebra/Systems of Linear Equations

Getting to the Answer: A quick examination of the equations in the system will tell you which strategy to use to solve it. Because $4x$ and $-4x$ are opposites of one another, the system is already perfectly set up to solve

by elimination (combining the two equations by adding them):

$$\begin{array}{r} \cancel{4x} + y = -5 \\ \underline{-\cancel{4x} - 2y = -2} \\ -y = -7 \\ y = 7 \end{array}$$

Choice **(D)** is correct.

2. D

Difficulty: Easy

Category: Problem Solving and Data Analysis/Scatterplots

Getting to the Answer: Graphically, slope is the ratio of the change in the y-values (rise) to the change in the x-values (run). In a real-world scenario, this is the same as the unit rate. In this context, the rise describes the change in the number of home runs hit in a single season, and the run describes the change in the number of hours a player spends in batting practice. Thus, the unit rate, or slope, represents the estimated increase (since the data trends upward) in the number of single-season home runs hit by a player for each hour he spends in batting practice. **(D)** is correct.

3. B

Difficulty: Easy

Category: Heart of Algebra/Linear Equations

Getting to the Answer: Finding an x-intercept is easy when you know the equation of the line—it's the value of x when y is 0. Notice that the answer choices are very close together. This means you shouldn't just estimate visually. Take the time to do the math. Everything you need to write the equation is shown on the graph—just pay careful attention to how the grid lines are labeled. The y-intercept is 10 and the line rises 2 units and runs 1 unit from one point to the next, so the slope is $\dfrac{2}{1} = 2$. This means the equation of the line, in slope-intercept form, is $y = 2x + 10$. Now, set the equation equal to zero and solve for x:

$$0 = 2x + 10$$
$$-10 = 2x$$
$$-5 = x$$

The line will intersect the x-axis at -5, which is **(B)**.

4. A

Difficulty: Easy

Category: Passport to Advanced Math/Functions

Getting to the Answer: When you see an expression like $f(x)$, it means to substitute the given value for x in the function's equation. When there is more than one function involved, pay careful attention to which function should be evaluated first. You are looking for the value of $f(x)$ at $x = 5$. Because $f(x)$ is defined in terms of $g(x)$, evaluate $g(5)$ first by substituting 5 for x in the expression $x + 2$:

$$g(5) = 5 + 2 = 7$$
$$f(5) = -3g(5) = -3(7) = -21$$

Therefore, **(A)** is correct.

5. B

Difficulty: Medium

Category: Heart of Algebra/Linear Equations

Getting to the Answer: Write an equation in words first, and then translate from English into math. Keep in mind that the laundry detergent is on sale, but the dog food is not. The detergent is 30% off, which means Sara only pays $100 - 30 = 70\%$ of the price, or $0.7(\$8) = \$5.60$. The dog food is 3 cans for \$4 and she buys 12 cans, which means she buys 4 sets of 3, so she pays $4 \times \$4 = \$16$ for the dog food. The total cost equals the detergent price (\$5.60) times how many she buys (x) plus the total dog food price (\$16). This translates as $C = 5.6x + 16$, which matches **(B)**. Note that there are variables in the answer choices, so you could also use the Picking Numbers strategy to answer this question.

6. B

Difficulty: Medium

Category: Heart of Algebra/Linear Equations

Getting to the Answer: The cost per night in the hospital is the same as the unit rate, which is represented by the slope of the line. Use the grid lines and the axis labels to count the rise and the run from the y-intercept of the line $(0, 26,000)$ to the next point that hits an intersection of two grid lines, $(2, 34,000)$. Pay careful attention to how the grid lines are marked (by 2s on the x-axis and by 2,000s on the y-axis). The line rises 8,000 units and runs

2 units, so the slope is $\dfrac{8,000}{2}$, which means it costs an average of \$4,000 per night to stay in the hospital. Note that you could also use the slope formula and the two points to find the slope:

$$\frac{34,000 - 26,000}{2 - 0} = \frac{8,000}{2} = 4,000$$

Choice **(B)** is correct.

7. D

Difficulty: Medium

Category: Problem Solving and Data Analysis/ Scatterplots

Getting to the Answer: You aren't given much information to go on except the shape of the graph, so you'll need to think about what the shape means. Remember, linear functions increase at a constant rate, exponential functions increase at either an increasing or decreasing rate, gradually at first and then more quickly or vice versa, and quadratics and polynomials reverse direction one or more times. The graph begins by decreasing extremely quickly, but then it almost (but not quite) levels off. Therefore, it can't be linear, and because it doesn't change direction, an exponential function, **(D)**, would be the best model for the data.

8. A

Difficulty: Medium

Category: Problem Solving and Data Analysis/Statistics and Probability

Getting to the Answer: This is a science crossover question. Read the first three sentences quickly—they are simply describing the context. The second half of the paragraph poses the question, so read that more carefully. In the sample, 2,800 out of 3,200 acres were free of kudzu after applying the herbicide. This is $\dfrac{2,800}{3,200} = 0.875 = 87.5\%$ of the area. For the whole region, assuming the same general conditions, $0.875(30,000) = 26,250$ acres should be free of the kudzu. Be careful—this is not the answer. The question asks how much of the cropland would *still be covered* by kudzu, so subtract to get $30,000 - 26,250 = 3,750$ acres. **(A)** is correct.

Practice Tests

9. B

Difficulty: Medium

Category: Passport to Advanced Math/Functions

Getting to the Answer: The notation $g(h(x))$ indicates a composition of two functions, which can be read "g of h of x." It means that the output when x is substituted in $h(x)$ becomes the input for $g(x)$. First, use the top and bottom rows of the table to find that $h(3)$ is 2. This is your new input. Now, use the top and middle rows of the table to find $g(2)$, which is -3, so **(B)** is correct.

10. B

Difficulty: Medium

Category: Heart of Algebra/Linear Equations

Getting to the Answer: The key to answering this type of question is determining how many results fit in each category. Here, you need to know how many shots were 3-pointers and how many were 2-pointers. Mae-Ling successfully made 15 shots total and s were 3-pointers, so the rest, or $15 - s$, must have been 2-pointers. Write the expression in words first: points per 3-pointers (3) times number of shots that were 3-pointers (s), plus points per regular goal (2) times number of regular goals ($15 - s$). Now, translate from English into math: $3s + 2(15 - s)$. This is not one of the answer choices, so simplify the expression by distributing the 2 and then combining like terms: $3s + 2(15 - s) = 3s + 30 - 2s = s + 30$. This matches **(B)**.

11. A

Difficulty: Medium

Category: Problem Solving and Data Analysis/Rates, Ratios, Proportions, and Percentages

Getting to the Answer: Let the units in this question guide you to the answer. You can do one conversion at a time or all of them at once. Just be sure to line up the units so they'll cancel correctly. The company uses 8 machines, each of which pumps at a rate of 37.5 gallons per minute, so the rate is actually $8 \times 37.5 = 300$ gallons per minute. Find the total number of gallons needed and then use the rate to find the time:

$$2{,}500 \; \cancel{bbl} \times \frac{42 \; \cancel{gallons}}{1 \; \cancel{bbl}} \times \frac{1 \; \text{minute}}{300 \; \cancel{gallons}} = 350 \; \text{minutes}$$

The answers are given in hours and minutes, so change 350 minutes to $350 \div 60 = 5.833$ hours, which is 5 hours and 50 minutes. **(A)** is correct.

12. C

Difficulty: Medium

Category: Problem Solving and Data Analysis/Functions

Getting to the Answer: Look for a pattern for the sales of each company. Then, apply that pattern to see which one will sell more in the last month of the year. Writing a function that represents each pattern will also help, but you have to be careful that you evaluate the function at the correct input value. Company A's sales can be represented by a linear function because each month the company sells 92 more of the toy than the month before, which is a constant difference. The sales can be represented by the function $f(t) = 92t + 54$, where t is the number of months *after January*. December is 11 months (not 12) after January, so during the last month of the year company A should sell $f(11) = 92(11) + 54 = 1{,}066$ of the toy. Company B's sales can be represented by an exponential function because the sales are doubling each month, which is a constant ratio (2 for doubling). The function is $g(t) = 15(2)^t$, where t is again the number of months *after January*. In December, company B should sell $g(11) = 15(2)^{11} = 30{,}720$. This means that in December, company B should sell $30{,}720 - 1{,}066 = 29{,}654$ more of the toy than company A. Choice **(C)** is correct.

13. A

Difficulty: Medium

Category: Heart of Algebra/Inequalities

Getting to the Answer: Apply logic to this question first and then algebra. The dot at the beginning of the shaded portion is an open dot, so -2 is not included in the solution set of the inequality. This means you can eliminate (C) and (D) because those symbols *would* include the endpoint. Don't immediately choose (B) just because the arrow is pointing to the right, which typically indicates *greater than*. When dealing with an inequality, if you multiply or divide by a negative number, you must flip the symbol, so the answer is not necessarily what you might think. Because you were able to eliminate two of the choices, the quickest approach is to pick one of the remaining symbols, plug it in, and see if it works. If it does, choose that answer. If it doesn't, then it must be the other symbol. Try (A):

$$5(x-2) - 3x < 4x - 6$$
$$5x - 10 - 3x < 4x - 6$$
$$2x - 10 < 4x - 6$$
$$-2x < 4$$
$$x > -2$$

The resulting inequality, $x > -2$, means all the values on the number line greater than (or to the right of) -2, so the initial inequality symbol must have been $<$. Choice **(A)** is correct.

14. B

Difficulty: Easy

Category: Problem Solving and Data Analysis/Rates, Ratios, Proportions, and Percents

Getting to the Answer: When a question involves scale factors, set up a proportion and solve for the missing value:

$$\frac{1}{8} = \frac{x}{19.9}$$
$$8x = 19.9$$
$$x = 2.4875 \approx 2.5$$

Choice **(B)** is correct.

15. C

Difficulty: Easy

Category: Problem Solving and Data Analysis/Rates, Ratios, Proportions, and Percents

Getting to the Answer: Don't make this question harder than it actually is. You don't need to find the new scale factor. Instead, use the length that the student drew the femur and the actual length to set up and solve a new proportion:

$$\frac{\text{drawing of sternum}}{\text{actual sternum}} = \frac{\text{drawing of femur}}{\text{actual femur}}$$
$$\frac{x}{6.7} = \frac{3.5}{19.9}$$
$$23.45 = 19.9x$$
$$1.1783 = x$$
$$x \approx 1.2$$

Choice **(C)** is correct.

16. B

Difficulty: Medium

Category: Heart of Algebra/Linear Equations

Getting to the Answer: Given two points (even when the coordinates are variables), the slope of the line between the points can be found using the formula $m = \frac{y_2 - y_1}{x_2 - x_1}$. You are given a numerical value for the slope and a pair of ordered pairs that have variables in them. To find the value of c, plug the points into the slope formula and then solve for c. Be careful of all the negative signs:

$$m = \frac{y_2 - y_1}{x_2 - x_1}$$
$$\frac{1}{2} = \frac{-8 - 2c}{-c - (4 - c)}$$
$$\frac{1}{2} = \frac{-8 - 2c}{-c - 4 + c}$$
$$\frac{1}{2} = \frac{-8 - 2c}{-4}$$
$$1(-4) = 2(-8 - 2c)$$
$$-4 = -16 - 4c$$
$$12 = -4c$$
$$-3 = c$$

Choice **(B)** is correct.

17. A

Difficulty: Medium

Category: Problem Solving and Data Analysis/Rates, Ratios, Proportions, and Percents

Getting to the Answer: Questions that involve distance, rate, and time can almost always be solved using the formula Distance = rate × time. Break the question into short steps (first part of trip, second part of trip). Start with the plane from DCA. Use the speed, or rate, of the plane, 338 miles per hour, and its distance from London, 3,718 miles, to determine when it arrived. You don't know the time, so call it t:

$$\text{Distance} = \text{rate} \times \text{time}$$
$$3{,}718 = 338t$$
$$11 = t$$

It took the DCA flight 11 hours. Now, determine how long it took the plane from MIA. You'll need to find the distance for each part of the trip—the question only tells you the total distance. Then, use the formula to find how long the plane flew at 596 miles per hour and how long it flew at 447 miles per hour.

First Part of Trip	Second Part of Trip
$\frac{2}{3} \times 4{,}470 = 2{,}980$ miles	$\frac{1}{3} \times 4{,}470 = 1{,}490$ miles
$2{,}980 = 596t$	$1{,}490 = 447t$
$5 = t$	$3.\overline{3} = t$

This means it took the MIA flight 5 hours + 3 hours, 20 minutes = 8 hours, 20 minutes. So, the plane from MIA arrived first. It arrived 11 hours − 8 hours, 20 minutes = 2 hours, 40 minutes before the plane from DCA, so **(A)** is correct.

18. D

Difficulty: Medium

Category: Passport to Advanced Math/Quadratics

Getting to the Answer: The graph of every quadratic equation is a parabola, which may or may not cross the x-axis, depending on where its vertex is and which way it opens. When an equation has no solution, its graph does not cross the x-axis, so try to envision the graph of each of the answer choices (or you could graph each one in your graphing calculator, but this will probably take longer). Don't forget—if the equation is written in vertex form, $y = a(x − h)^2 + k$, then the vertex is (h, k) and the value of a tells you which way the parabola opens. When a quadratic equation is written in factored form, the factors tell you the x-intercepts, which means (A) and (B) (which are factored) must cross the x-axis, so eliminate them. Now, imagine the graph of the equation in (C): the vertex is $(−1, 8)$ and a is negative, so the parabola opens downward and consequently must cross the x-axis. This means **(D)** must be correct. The vertex is also $(−1, 8)$, but a is positive, so the graph opens up and does not cross the x-axis.

19. D

Difficulty: Medium

Category: Problem Solving and Data Analysis/Statistics and Probability

Getting to the Answer: The two variables are certainly correlated—as one goes up, the other goes up. A linear regression model would fit the data fairly well, so you can eliminate (C). The spending is graphed on the x-axis, so it is the independent variable and therefore does not depend on the GDP, graphed on the y-axis, so you can eliminate (B) as well. The data does show that

as spending on students increases, so does the GDP, but this is simply correlation, not causation. Without additional data, no statements can be made about whether spending more on students is the reason for the increased GDP, so **(D)** is correct.

20. C

Difficulty: Easy

Category: Passport to Advanced Math/Rational Equations

Getting to the Answer: Focus on the question at the very end—it's just asking you to solve the equation for p_2. Multiply both sides by T_2 to get rid of the denominator on the right-hand side of the equation. Then divide by V_2 to isolate p_2:

$$\frac{p_1 V_1}{T_1} = \frac{p_2 V_2}{T_2}$$

$$\frac{p_1 V_1 T_2}{T_1} = p_2 V_2$$

$$\frac{p_1 V_1 T_2}{T_1 V_2} = p_2$$

Stop here! You cannot cancel the V's and T's because the subscripts indicate that they are not the same variable. In math, subscripts do not behave the same way superscripts (exponents) do. Choice **(C)** is correct.

21. C

Difficulty: Medium

Category: Problem Solving and Data Analysis/Rates, Ratios, Proportions, and Percents

Getting to the Answer: The factor-label method (canceling units) is a great strategy for this question. You're starting with tons, so work from that unit, arranging conversions so that units cancel. To keep units straight, use an E for Earth, an M for Mars, and a J for Jupiter:

$$1.5 \text{ T} \times \frac{2{,}000 \text{ lb (E)}}{1 \text{ T}} \times \frac{0.377 \text{ lb (M)}}{1 \text{ lb (E)}} = 1{,}131 \text{ lb (M)}$$

$$1.5 \text{ T} \times \frac{2{,}000 \text{ lb (E)}}{1 \text{ T}} \times \frac{2.364 \text{ lb (J)}}{1 \text{ lb (E)}} = 7{,}092 \text{ lb (J)}$$

The object weighs 1,131 pounds on Mars and 7,092 pounds on Jupiter, so it weighs $7{,}092 − 1{,}131 = 5{,}961$ more pounds on Jupiter. **(C)** is correct.

22. C

Difficulty: Medium

Category: Problem Solving and Data Analysis/Statistics and Probability

Getting to the Answer: Examine the shape of the data and familiarize yourself with the title and the axis labels on the graph. Data is *symmetric* if it is fairly evenly spread out, and it is *skewed* if it has a long tail on either side. Notice that the data is skewed to the right, so you can immediately eliminate (A). Choices (B), (C), and (D) all describe the data as skewed to the right, so you'll need to examine those statements more closely. For (B), "adverse reactions" include the last four bars, which represent $89 + 41 + 22 + 8 = 160$ participants total, which is not even close to 50% of 900, so eliminate (B). Note that you don't need to add all the bar heights to find that there were 900 participants—the title of the graph tells you that. Now look at (C)—"failed to have adverse reactions" means "None" or "Mild" (the first three bars), which represent $900 - 160 = 740$ of the 900 participants. Since, 75% of $900 = 675$, and 740 is more than 675, **(C)** is correct. For (D), the "None" column contains 320 participants, which does not equal approximately 50% of 900, so it too is incorrect.

23. C

Difficulty: Medium

Category: Heart of Algebra/Systems of Linear Equations

Getting to the Answer: Use the Kaplan Method for Translating English into Math. Write a system of equations with $p =$ the cost in dollars of the Pennsylvania bar exam and $d =$ the cost of the D.C. bar exam. The Pennsylvania bar exam (p) costs $25 less ($-25$) than 3 times as much ($3d$) as the D.C. bar exam, or $p = 3d - 25$. Together, both bar exams cost \$775, so $d + p = 775$. The system is:

$$\begin{cases} p = 3d - 25 \\ d + p = 775 \end{cases}$$

The top equation is already solved for p, so substitute $3d - 25$ into the second equation for p, and solve for d:

$$d + (3d - 25) = 775$$
$$4d = 800$$
$$d = 200$$

Be careful—that's not the answer. The D.C. bar exam costs \$200, which means the Pennsylvania bar exam costs $\$775 - \$200 = \$575$. This means the D.C. bar exam is $\$575 - \$200 = \$375$ less expensive than the Pennsylvania bar exam. Choice **(C)** is correct.

24. B

Difficulty: Medium

Category: Additional Topics in Math/Geometry

Getting to the Answer: The formula for finding the volume of a cylinder is $V = \pi r^2 h$. Leaving the top 5% of the silo empty is another way of saying that the silo should only be filled to 95% of its total height, so multiply the height (60 feet) by 0.95 to get 57 feet and then find the volume. Don't forget to divide the width of the silo (20 feet) by 2 to find the radius:

$$V = \pi r^2 h$$
$$V = \pi (10)^2 (57)$$
$$V = \pi (100)(57)$$
$$V = 5{,}700\pi$$

Choice **(B)** is correct.

25. B

Difficulty: Medium

Category: Problem Solving and Data Analysis/Statistics and Probability

Getting to the Answer: Always read the axis labels carefully when a question involves a chart or graph. *Frequency*, which is plotted along the vertical axis, tells you how many students missed the number of questions indicated under each bar. Evaluate each statement as quickly as you can.

(A): Add the bar heights (frequencies) that represent students that missed 5 or more questions: $7 + 3 + 3 + 2 = 15$. Then, find the total number of students represented, which is the number that missed less than 5 questions plus the 15 you just found: $2 + 3 + 4 + 6 = 15$, plus the 15 you already found, for a total of 30 students. The statement is not true because 15 is exactly half (not more than half) of 30. Eliminate.

(B): This calculation will take a bit of time so skip it for now.

(C): The tallest bar tells you which number of questions was missed most often, which was 5 questions, not 3 questions, so this statement is not true. Eliminate.

(D): The number of students from Mr. Juno's class who took the test that day is the sum of the heights of the bars, which you already know is 30, not 36. Eliminate.

This means **(B)** must be correct. Mark it and move on to the next question. In case you're curious, find the mean by multiplying each number of questions missed by the corresponding frequency, adding all the products, and dividing by the total number of students, which you already know is 30:

$$\text{mean} = \frac{2 + 6 + 12 + 24 + 35 + 18 + 21 + 16}{30}$$

$$= \frac{134}{30} = 4.4\overline{6}$$

The mean is indeed between 4 and 5.

26. C

Difficulty: Hard

Category: Passport to Advanced Math/Quadratics

Getting to the Answer: Writing quadratic equations can be tricky and time-consuming. If you know the roots, you can use factors to write the equation. If you don't know the roots, you need to create a system of equations to find the coefficients of the variable terms. You don't know the roots of this equation, so start with the point that has the nicest values $(0, 2)$ and substitute them into the equation, $y = ax^2 + bx + c$, to get $2 = a(0)^2 + b(0) + c$, or $2 = c$. Now your equation looks like $y = ax^2 + bx + 2$. Next, use the other two points to create a system of two equations in two variables:

$$(-6, -7) \rightarrow -7 = a(-6)^2 + b(-6) + 2 \rightarrow -9 = 36a - 6b$$
$$(8, -14) \rightarrow -14 = a(8)^2 + b(8) + 2 \rightarrow -16 = 64a + 8b$$

You now have a system of equations to solve. If you multiply the top equation by 4 and the bottom equation by 3, and then add the equations, the b terms will eliminate each other:

$$4[-9 = 36a - 6b] \quad \rightarrow \quad -36 = 144a - 24b$$
$$3[-16 = 64a + 8b] \quad \rightarrow \quad \underline{-48 = 192a + 24b}$$
$$-84 = 336a$$
$$-0.25 = a$$

Now, find b by substituting $a = -0.25$ into either of the original equations. Using the top equation, you get:

$$-9 = 36(-0.25) - 6b$$
$$-9 = -9 - 6b$$
$$0 = 6b$$
$$0 = b$$

The value of $a + b + c$ is $(-0.25) + 0 + 2 = 1.75$, so **(C)** is correct.

27. D

Difficulty: Hard

Category: Problem Solving and Data Analysis/Rates, Ratios, Proportions, and Percentages

Getting to the Answer: Read the question, organizing important information as you go. You need to find the ratio of mini muffins to jumbo muffins. You're given two ratios: mini to regular and regular to jumbo. Both of the given ratios contain regular muffin size units, but the regular amounts (2 and 5) are not identical. To directly compare them, find a common multiple (10). Multiply each ratio by the factor that will make the number of regular muffins equal to 10:

$$\text{Mini to regular: } (5:2) \times (5:5) = 25:10$$
$$\text{Regular to jumbo: } (5:4) \times (2:2) = 10:8$$

Now that the number of regular muffins is the same in both ratios (10), you can merge the two ratios to compare mini to jumbo directly: 25:10:8. So, the proper ratio of mini muffins to jumbo muffins is 25:8, which is **(D)**.

28. A

Difficulty: Medium

Category: Heart of Algebra/Systems of Linear Equations

Getting to the Answer: Graphically, a system of linear equations that has no solution indicates two parallel lines, or in other words, two lines that have the same slope. So, write each of the equations in slope-intercept form $(y = mx + b)$ and set their slopes (m) equal to each other to solve for k. Before finding the slopes, multiply the top equation by 6 to make it easier to manipulate:

$$6\left(\frac{1}{3}x + \frac{1}{2}y = 5\right) \rightarrow 2x + 3y = 30 \rightarrow y = -\frac{2}{3}x + 10$$

$$kx - 4y = 16 \rightarrow -4y = -kx + 16 \rightarrow y = \frac{k}{4}x - 4$$

The slope of the first line is $-\frac{2}{3}$ and the slope of the second line is $\frac{k}{4}$. Set them equal and solve for k:

$$-\frac{2}{3} = \frac{k}{4}$$
$$-8 = 3k$$
$$-\frac{8}{3} = k$$

Choice **(A)** is correct.

Practice Tests

29. D

Difficulty: Hard

Category: Passport to Advanced Math/Exponents

Getting to the Answer: The numbers in some questions are simply too large to use a calculator (you get an "overflow" error message). Instead, you'll have to rely on rules of exponents. Notice that all of the base numbers have 3 as a factor, so rewrite everything in terms of 3. This will allow you to use the rules of exponents. Because 27 is the cube of 3, you can rewrite 27^{90} as a power of 3:

$$27^{90} = \left(3^3\right)^{90}$$
$$= 3^{3 \times 90}$$
$$= 3^{270}$$

Now, the product should read: $3^{90} \times 3^{270}$, which is equal to $3^{90+270} = 3^{360}$. Repeat this process for the quantity that is being divided:

$$\left(\frac{1}{9}\right)^{30} = \left(\frac{1}{3^2}\right)^{30} = \left(3^{-2}\right)^{30} = 3^{-60}$$

Finally, use rules of exponents one more time to simplify the new expression:

$$\frac{3^{360}}{3^{-60}} = 3^{360+60} = 3^{420}$$

All the answer choices are given as powers of 9, so rewrite your answer as a power of 9:

$$3^{420} = 3^{2 \times 210} = \left(3^2\right)^{210} = 9^{210}$$

Choice **(D)** is correct.

30. D

Difficulty: Hard

Category: Additional Topics in Math/Geometry

Getting to the Answer: If needed, don't forget to check the formulas provided for you at the beginning of each Math section. The volume of a right cone is given by $V = \frac{1}{3}\pi r^2 h$. Here, you only know the value of one of the variables, V, so you'll need to use the information in the question to somehow write r and h in terms of just one variable. If the cone is three times as wide at the base as it is tall, then call the diameter $3x$ and the height of the cone one-third of that, or x. The volume formula calls for the radius, which is half the diameter, or $\frac{3x}{2}$. Substitute these values into the formula and solve for x:

$$V = \frac{1}{3}\pi r^2 h$$
$$384\pi = \frac{1}{3}\pi\left(\frac{3}{2}x\right)^2 x$$
$$384 = \left(\frac{1}{3}\right)\left(\frac{9}{4}x^2\right)x$$
$$384 = \frac{3}{4}x^3$$
$$512 = x^3$$
$$\sqrt[3]{512} = x$$
$$8 = x$$

The question asks for the diameter of the base, which is $3x = 3(8) = 24$, choice **(D)**.

31. 1/4 or .25

Difficulty: Medium

Category: Heart of Algebra/Inequalities

Getting to the Answer: The question is asking about $\frac{m}{n}$, so think about how fractions work. Large numerators result in larger values ($\frac{3}{2}$, for example, is larger than $\frac{1}{2}$), and smaller denominators result in larger values ($\frac{1}{2}$, for example, is greater than $\frac{1}{4}$). The largest possible value of $\frac{m}{n}$ is found by choosing the largest possible value of m and the smallest possible value for n: $\frac{0.4}{1.6} = \frac{1}{4} = \mathbf{0.25}$.

32. 6

Difficulty: Medium

Category: Passport to Advanced Math/Functions

Getting to the Answer: The notation $(f - g)(3)$ means $f(3) - g(3)$. You don't know the equations of the functions, so you'll need to read the values from the graph. Graphically, $f(3)$ means the y-value at $x = 3$ on the graph of f, which is 2. Likewise, $g(3)$ means the y-value at $x = 3$ on the graph of g, which is -4. The difference, $f - g$, is $2 - (-4) = \mathbf{6}$.

33. 85

Difficulty: Easy

Category: Problem Solving and Data Analysis/Scatterplots

Getting to the Answer: The *range* of a set of data points is the set of outputs, which correspond to the y-values of the data points on the graph. To find the maximum value

Practice Tests

in the range of the data, look for the highest point on the graph, which is (250, 85). The *y*-value is 85, so **85** is the maximum value in the range.

34. .06

Difficulty: Medium

Category: Problem Solving and Data Analysis/Statistics and Probability

Getting to the Answer: First, find the probability that the first employee chosen at random will be one who has been with the company for longer than 3 years. The total number of employees who participated in the study is $38 + 30 + 15 + 19 + 54 + 48 = 204$. The total number of individuals in both job categories who have been with the company longer (greater) than 3 years is $54 + 48 = 102$. Therefore, the probability of choosing one employee who has been with the company longer than 3 years is: $\frac{102}{204} = \frac{1}{2}$. Because the same employee cannot be randomly selected more than once, the chance that another selected employee will have been with the company more than 3 years is not simply equal to $\frac{1}{2}$. Instead, assuming the first employee chosen at random has been with the company more than 3 years, the chance that a second employee chosen at random will also be is $\frac{(102 - 1)}{(204 - 1)} = \frac{101}{203}$. For a third employee, the chance is $\frac{(102 - 2)}{(204 - 2)} = \frac{100}{202} = \frac{50}{101}$, and for a fourth, the chance is $\frac{(102 - 3)}{(204 - 3)} = \frac{99}{201}$. Thus, to determine the probability that all 4 have been with the company longer than 3 years, multiply all these probabilities together:

$\frac{1}{2} \times \frac{101}{203} \times \frac{50}{101} \times \frac{99}{201} \approx 0.06$.

35. 102

Difficulty: Medium

Category: Additional Topics in Math/Geometry

Getting to the Answer: The distance around part of a circle is the same as arc length, so use the relationship $\frac{\text{arc length}}{\text{circumference}} = \frac{\text{central angle}}{360°}$ to answer the question. The unknown in the relationship is the central angle, so call it *A*. Before you can fill in the rest of the equation, you need to find the circumference of the circle: $C = 2\pi r = 2\pi(840) = 1{,}680\pi$. Now, you're ready to solve for *A*:

$$\frac{\text{arc length}}{\text{circumference}} = \frac{\text{central angle}}{360°}$$

$$\frac{1{,}500}{1{,}680\pi} = \frac{A}{360}$$

$$\frac{1{,}500 \times 360}{1{,}680\pi} = A$$

$$102.314 \approx A$$

Be careful when you enter this expression into your calculator—you need to put $1{,}680\pi$ in parentheses so that the calculator doesn't divide by 1,680 and then multiply by π. If entered correctly, the result is about **102** degrees.

36. 7

Difficulty: Hard

Category: Heart of Algebra/Linear Equations

Getting to the Answer: To write the equation of a line, you need two things: the slope and the *y*-intercept. Start by finding these, substituting them into slope-intercept form of a line ($y = mx + b$), and then manipulate the equation so that it is written in standard form. Use the given points, $(-4, 1)$ and $(3, -2)$, and the slope formula to find *m*:

$$m = \frac{y_2 - y_1}{x_2 - x_1} = \frac{-2 - 1}{3 - (-4)} = -\frac{3}{7}$$

Next, find the *y*-intercept, *b*, using the slope and one of the points:

$$y = -\frac{3}{7}x + b$$

$$1 = -\frac{3}{7}(-4) + b$$

$$1 = \frac{12}{7} + b$$

$$-\frac{5}{7} = b$$

Write the equation in slope-intercept form:

$$y = -\frac{3}{7}x - \frac{5}{7}$$

Now, rewrite the equation in the form $Ax + By = C$, making sure that *A* is a positive integer (a whole number greater than 0):

$$y = -\frac{3}{7}x - \frac{5}{7}$$

$$\frac{3}{7}x + y = -\frac{5}{7}$$

$$7\left(\frac{3}{7}x + y = -\frac{5}{7}\right)7$$

$$3x + 7y = -5$$

The question asks for the value of *B* (the coefficient of *y*), so the correct answer is **7**.

37. 380

Difficulty: Medium

Category: Problem Solving and Data Analysis/Rates, Ratios, Proportions, and Percents

Getting to the Answer: You can use the formula Percent × whole = part to solve this question, but you will first need to think conceptually about what the question is asking. The question is asking for the Dow value *before* the 19.5% decrease to 306. This means that 306 represents $100 - 19.5 = 80.5\%$ of what the stock market was at its record high. Fill these amounts into the equation and solve for the original whole, the record high Dow value:

$$0.805 \times w = 306$$
$$w = \frac{306}{0.805}$$
$$w = 380.124$$

Rounded to the nearest whole point, the record high was approximately **380** points.

38. 25

Difficulty: Hard

Category: Problem Solving and Data Analysis/Rates, Ratios, Proportions, and Percents

Getting to the Answer: Percent change is given by the ratio $\frac{\text{amount of change}}{\text{original amount}}$. To find the total percent change, you'll need to work your way through each of the days, and then use the ratio. Jot down the Dow value at the end of each day as you go. Do not round until you reach your final answer. First, calculate the value of the Dow at closing on Black Thursday: it opened at 306 and decreased by 2%, which means the value at the end of the day was $100 - 2 = 98\%$ of the starting amount, or $306 \times 0.98 = 299.88$. Then, it decreased again on Monday by 13% to close at $100 - 13 = 87\%$ of the opening amount, or $299.88 \times 0.87 = 260.8956$. Finally, it decreased on Tuesday by another 12% to end at $100 - 12 = 88\%$ of the starting amount, or $260.8956 \times 0.88 = 229.588$. Now, use the percent change formula to calculate the percent decrease from opening on Black Thursday (306) to closing on Black Tuesday (229.588):

$$\text{Percent decrease} = \frac{306 - 229.588}{306} = \frac{76.412}{306} = 0.2497$$

The Dow had a total percent decrease of approximately **25%** between opening on Black Thursday and closing on Black Tuesday.

Essay Test Rubric

The Essay Demonstrates . . .

4—Advanced	• **(Reading)** A strong ability to comprehend the source text, including its central ideas and important details and how they interrelate, and effectively use evidence (quotations, paraphrases, or both) from the source text. • **(Analysis)** A strong ability to evaluate the author's use of evidence, reasoning, and/or stylistic and persuasive elements and/or other features of the student's own choosing; make good use of relevant, sufficient, and strategically chosen support for the claims or points made in the student's essay; and focus consistently on features of the source text that are most relevant to addressing the task. • **(Writing)** A strong ability to provide a precise central claim; create an effective organization that includes an introduction and conclusion, as well as a clear progression of ideas; successfully employ a variety of sentence structures; use precise word choice; maintain a formal style and objective tone; and show command of the conventions of standard written English so that the essay is free of errors.
3—Proficient	• **(Reading)** Satisfactory ability to comprehend the source text, including its central ideas and important details and how they interrelate, and use evidence (quotations, paraphrases, or both) from the source text. • **(Analysis)** Satisfactory ability to evaluate the author's use of evidence, reasoning, and/or stylistic and persuasive elements and/or other features of the student's own choosing; make use of relevant and sufficient support for the claims or points made in the student's essay; and focus primarily on features of the source text that are most relevant to addressing the task. • **(Writing)** Satisfactory ability to provide a central claim; create an organization that includes an introduction and conclusion, as well as a clear progression of ideas; employ a variety of sentence structures; use precise word choice; maintain an appropriate formal style and objective tone; and show control of the conventions of standard written English so that the essay is free of significant errors.
2—Partial	• **(Reading)** Limited ability to comprehend the source text, including its central ideas and important details and how they interrelate, and use evidence (quotations, paraphrases, or both) from the source text. • **(Analysis)** Limited ability to evaluate the author's use of evidence, reasoning, and/or stylistic and persuasive elements and/or other features of the student's own choosing; make use of support for the claims or points made in the student's essay; and focus on relevant features of the source text. • **(Writing)** Limited ability to provide a central claim, create an effective organization for ideas, employ a variety of sentence structures, use precise word choice, maintain an appropriate style and tone, or show command of the conventions of standard written English, resulting in certain errors that detract from the quality of the writing.

1—Inadequate	• **(Reading)** Little or no ability to comprehend the source text or use evidence from the source text.
	• **(Analysis)** Little or no ability to evaluate the author's use of evidence, reasoning, and/or stylistic and persuasive elements; choose support for claims or points; or focus on relevant features of the source text.
	• **(Writing)** Little or no ability to provide a central claim, organization, or progression of ideas; employ a variety of sentence structures; use precise word choice; maintain an appropriate style and tone; or show command of the conventions of standard written English, resulting in numerous errors that undermine the quality of the writing.

Essay Response #1 (Advanced Score)

In his speech to the National Union of South African Students in 1966, Robert F. Kennedy makes the claim that the guiding principle of Western societies must be the enhancement of liberty for all individuals. Through appeals to Western values, references to historical evidence, and calls to conscience, Kennedy constructs a powerful and effective argument.

Kennedy begins his speech by praising the core values of Western society—freedom and democracy, and the rights associated with them. In so doing, he both establishes common ground with his South African audience, who viewed themselves as part of Western society, and also highlights the ways in which the repressive government of South Africa in 1966 failed to uphold these values. To Kennedy, the freedom of speech is not merely the right to say whatever one chooses, rather, it allows us to speak up to our governments when they are derelict in their duties, and is a key part of what it means to be an active member of society. Kennedy also insists that the right of individuals to be heard by their government is essential to democracy, because it forces government officials to answer to the people who elected them. Frequently, Kennedy uses heightened language to describe these rights and values, which deepens the impact of his message. The freedom of speech separates us from the "dumb beasts of field and forest." The power to be heard allows people a voice in the decisions that "shape men's lives." Most powerfully, Kennedy states that these rights are "sacred." This kind of elevated language imparts a weight to Kennedy's argument that ordinary language could not.

Kennedy also makes references to historical and current events to bolster his claims. He asserts that the rights he describes are what separate democratic societies from Nazi Germany and Persia, countries known to be extremely repressive. This reference to brutal regimes strengthens his claim that these rights should be the guiding principle of any decent society. He also uses the United States as a model of a society that has been striving for the expansion of liberty and, while failing in some respects, is succeeding overall. Kennedy's father, he says, was barred from many jobs as a young man due to his Irish background, yet several decades later, his son John F. Kennedy became president, proving that conditions can change for the better. Robert Kennedy acknowledges that the United States still has far to go, just like South Africa, yet he cites examples of major progress, such as an African American astronaut and an African American chief justice, as well as Martin Luther King, Jr., who won the Nobel Peace Prize. Kennedy's implication is that the ideals of liberty and justice are worth upholding because they can make a society greater and more inclusive.

Another way Kennedy persuades his audience of the validity of his argument is by making calls to conscience. He states that the most important reason to grant freedom to all is because "it is the right thing to do." He reasons that feelings of compassion are common to all people, as are feelings of outrage when other human beings suffer; therefore, we should all join together in expanding human rights and lessening the suffering of people everywhere. By calling upon his audience's basic sense of right and wrong, Kennedy gives them a personal lens through which to examine his argument, thus making them more likely to embrace its validity.

Robert F. Kennedy passionately believed in the necessity for all Western societies to make the expansion of liberty their guiding principle. To build and support his argument, Kennedy exalts Western values of democracy and freedom, refers to historical examples in which the promotion of liberty made for a better society, and finally calls upon people's conscience to help them see that the expansion of freedom for all is the right thing to do.

Essay Response #2 (Proficient Score)

Robert F. Kennedy's central claim in his speech to the National Union of South African Students is that the guiding principle of Western societies should be the expansion of liberty for all individuals. Kennedy uses several techniques to build his argument, including heightened language, examples of countries that have been improved by the expansion of liberty, and appeals to his audience's sense of right and wrong.

Kennedy was not an ordinary man, nor was he an ordinary writer. His speech contains soaring language that makes his audience feel like they are listening to great literature. When he says that the freedom of speech is what seperates us from "dumb beasts," his vivid language makes that freedom seem even more important. He makes frequent references to God, even calling rights of Western society "sacred." And instead of merely saying that young people must stop racism and injustice, he says that it's there responsibility to "strip the last remnants of that ancient, cruel belief from the civilization of man." This type of language makes the audience feel that they are being called to a higher purpose.

Kennedy also provides examples of ways in which countries that promote liberty fare better than countries that don't. When he contrasts Western societies that value freedom with societies that don't—like Nazi Germany and Persia—he is suggesting that countries that deny people their basic rights eventually fail (in 1966, Nazi Germany and Persia no longer existed, but Western democracies still did). Kennedy then uses America as an example of a country that has been improved by expanding liberties for individuals. He tells a personal anecdote about the prejudice experienced by his Irish father, and acknowledges that the struggle to overcome discrimination can take many years. However he provides evidence that the struggle is worth it as shown by his brother's success in becoming president of the United States, and by the African Americans who at that point had risen to the highest ranks of American society—an astronaut, barristers, and a Nobel Prize winner, Martin Luther King, Jr. These examples support Kennedy's claim that enlarging the liberties of individuals is a worthy goal for Western societies.

Finally, Kennedy appeals to his audience's fundamental sense of right and wrong. He says that expanding liberty is "the right thing to do" and that God commands it. He lists multiple examples of evil in the world—"discrimination in New York, apartheid in South Africa . . ."—and tells his audience of students that they must answer the call to eliminate the suffering of others everywhere in the world. He states that evil is common, therefore it can only be cured by other qualities we all share in common, such as our conscence and determination to make the world a better place.

The argument Kennedy makes in this speech is strengthened by his use of the features mentioned above: heightened language, evidence, and appeals to his audience's sense of what is right and what is wrong.